Religion in America

ADVISORY EDITOR

Edwin S. Gaustad

LIFE AND CORRESPONDENCE

OF

THEODORE PARKER

John Weiss

TWO VOLUMES IN ONE

ARNO PRESS & THE NEW YORK TIMES

New York 1969

Reprint edition 1969 by Arno Press, Inc.

*

Library of Congress Catalog Card No. 70-83446

*

Reprinted from a copy in
The State Historical Society of Wisconsin Library

*

Manufactured in the United States of America

LIFE AND CORRESPONDENCE

THEODORE PARKER

THEODORE PARKER.

Eng.d by F. Halpin, from a Daguerreotype taken in 1853.

LIFE AND CORRESPONDENCE

THEODORE PARKER,

MINISTER OF THE
TWENTY-EIGHTH CONGREGATIONAL SOCIETY, BOSTON.

BY

JOHN WEISS.

IN TWO VOLUMES.
VOL. 1.

NEW・YORK:
D. APPLETON & COMPANY, 443 & 445 BROADWAY,
1864.

PREFACE.

Soon after this Memoir was commenced, in the spring of 1861, it became evident that the original plan of publishing a single small volume would serve to present hardly a sketch of Mr. Parker's varied and useful life. At the same time, the biographical material, principally in the form of letters, began to increase in such a way that the plan was insensibly enlarged, and the publication from time to time postponed. These delays fortunately coincided with a season of great dulness in the literary market, when the events of the War were absorbing every mind.

As the mass of letters which existed among Mr. Parker's papers became slowly reduced to a sequence of time and to alphabetical order, so that the subjects discussed and the names and qualities of the writers could be seen, it was plain how much important matter from his own hand remained yet uncollected from every part of the country and from the Old World. This index of correspondence registered, by the surest and most delicate of tests, his diffused and latent life. It was worth while to spend a good many months in obeying such directions —to bid the man rise from beneath these sumptuous epitaphs of love, reverence, and human dependence.

This has been done to the extent which these volumes will show. No friend of Mr. Parker will regret the laborious delay which has recalled so many expressions of his mind upon such varied themes.

The distribution of these letters conforms to the method of the memoir, which could not be a chronological one without greatly confusing the subjects covered by his life. To do justice to each subject, and develope his thought thereon, and to preserve distinctness of effect, the memoir remands into groups, as far as possible, the elements of his manifold career. The order of time is preserved in the narrative of his material and mental growth to full manhood and consciousness of the work he had in hand, and wherever else it can be done without running together too many themes.

The Journal is a collection of a dozen manuscript volumes, some of them bulky ledgers, which are thickly sown with extracts, analyses of books, notifications of thinking. They would be called commonplace-books were it not for the vein of his private life which occasionally appears at the surface, and for the fact that his book-reading and note-making are really personal; for they grow with his growth in a most simple and organic way. The diaristic matter makes a small portion of the whole contents of these volumes. I have given all of it that contributes to a knowledge of his life.

Besides the collection which I have called " The Journal," there are several little pocket note-books, out of which something has been gleaned, principally from those which he used during his last journeyings. But the few passages that are found in a condition to print appear as from " The Journal."

Wherever a citation occurs from his printed works, it is made from the only uniform American edition that has appeared. Many of the foot-notes would be trivial or superfluous except for the English and foreign reader, for whose benefit they were inserted. It is difficult to anticipate where a foreign reader might need a note or explanation ; sometimes I may have exceeded, sometimes fallen short of, the natural requisition.

His brother, Isaac Parker ; his nephew, Columbus Greene ; and other persons, have most kindly furnished recollections of different portions of his life, chiefly of his boyhood. And his friends have freely rendered up the precious letters which they had in keeping ; and distant and unknown, as well as famous, persons, in both hemispheres, whose names and habitat were discovered only by a sifting of the correspondence, have, with hardly an exception, responded to the call for the letters in their possession. Mrs. Parker would publicly return thanks to all these. It is hardly necessary for me to add how much the memoir is indebted to such contributions.

But it is indebted greatly to that devoted heart, that delicate disposition, and that good sense, which has been left ·to recall how loving a husband was this champion of oppressed thoughts and people, and to build, with most careful and assiduous hands, a memorial to the dear one, so illustrious to her by private sweetness as by public service. It is from her that I have derived all my authority and opportunity to undertake this work.

Only three years have passed since another ministry called the noble and variously gifted man, whom my pen, at a long interval and with many an imperfect movement, has been striving to recal, hoping, at least, not greatly to mar the character which is now perceived to have been bone of the bone and flesh of the flesh of America. But the consideration which is paid to him, in all quarters where it is worthy to be well remembered, through most diverse theological and political confessions, is a tribute which hastens very early to his grave. In England alone, the simultaneous publication of two distinct editions of his Works,* though both of them are quite unauthorized, and neither respects the duty and wishes which rule in his late home, sufficiently attests the importance of his writings to the popular mind, to develope therein free and manly thought.

The soil of no grave was ever more fertile. Men, who ex-

---

* One, edited by Miss F. P. Cobbe, and published by Trübner and Co., entitled "The Collected Works of Theodore Parker," &c. ; the other, published by Barker and Co., 4, Thanet Place, Strand, and called "The Works of Theodore Parker, Minister of the Twenty-Eighth Congregational Church, Boston, U.S." The latter edition, the price of which is but two shillings per volume, has the merit of cheapness, with good type and paper.

pected that his influence would become extinct, and that he had no gifts incisive enough to write his name upon the heart, acknowledge even now that he was a representative man, with conscience and humanity enough to feed a generation, to warn and to save, to build up with healthy tissue, to repair the degenerate waste of a noble people, and to pull down and trample on their crimes alone. He has been missed during these three years. The best men have asked for him, because they wanted New England granite to build with a breakwater, to have firm words to put in slippery places, that the country might be helped across into purpose and a definite policy of freedom. Men have said, at home and abroad, in various tongues, He grows upon us : he was healthy as immortality, he was as unconventional as a period of revolution always must be—a strong soil full of seeds : the more you till it, the better it nods with wheat, and corn, and all the substantial elements of human food. Foreign thinkers are very quick to perceive the drift of his mind, and very enthusiastic to recognize his capacity for entertaining righteousness They see from afar, what we are now beginning to see close at hand, that he was a pioneer of this America which has been sending her dreadful columns over roads of his surveying and which he helped to clear.

It would be surprising to see how readily everything which is now happening connects itself with his sincerity and indignation, if we did not know that God's hand holds nothing but things that are sincere, and that His earth must grow the things that are planted. It is the test of the symmetry of a great mind ; its anticipations Providence seems to have overheard, so readily do its thoughts, its just wrath, its salutary hatred, its heavenly hopes, become converted into history.

His Life appears at the very moment when the great struggle which he anticipated is going against the wickedness which he smote so valiantly. The sound of victorious cannon is a salvo of recognition over his distant grave—a thundering welcome paid, so soon after those mutterings of hatred and contempt, to the great sense of liberty which he represented. The Lexington blood is cold ; flowers cover that simple and manly presence, and divert our thoughts from its decay ; he is absent upon some ministry that requires a brave and unselfish heart. But look through the hearts of the common people who supply this redness and are blushing so frankly at Gettysburg and Charleston, — what American ever had so good a right as he to say, as for himself, " There is a day after to-day " ?

Through three-and-fifty years of his I have been wandering— for the last words of this Preface pass under my hand upon the anniversary of his birth—fifty, almost, of his faithful life, three of the proud tears and keen recognition of the noblest minds. As I must at length commit this imperfect memorial to the gentleness of all readers, can I help recollecting that my hand has been held by a stalwart nature, whose thought and affection have passed, to thrill and enrich me ? He has confirmed and guided me. He has befriended the conscience and the will ; he has been munificent with suggestion. He drops my hand, and leaves me for the host of friends and lovers to whom his presence has so long been due.

August 24, 1863.

CONTENTS OF VOL. I.

ILLUSTRATIONS TO VOL. I.

LIFE AND CORRESPONDENCE

OF

THEODORE PARKER.

CHAPTER I.

Ancestors and Family.—Thomas Parker, of Browsholme, 1609.—Emigrates, 1635.—Jonathan, 1680.—Hananiah, at Port Royal, 1710.—Benj. Stearns and Hannah Seger, 1754.—Capt. John Parker, April 19, 1775.—John Parker and Hannah Stearns.—Theodore Parker, Aug. 24, 1810.

It is surprising to find how many farmers of Eastern Massachusetts can still trace their lineage directly back to ship-board, whence their ancestors descended to possess the new soil. These sturdy men draw a straight furrow across two hundred years, but the waters of the bay obliterate it, and its course can be seldom resumed beyond. Of the English annals of the Parker family, only a few disconnected scraps exist. Names and places are confused, and many Parker families are scattered over the kingdom.* As nearly as can be now determined, our branch of the Parkers came from the parish of Browsholme, in the county of York, and this family appears respectable and flourishing early in the sixteenth century. A coat of arms, profusely blazoning leopards' heads, stars, and a stag pierced by an arrow for a crest,

---

* The name is as old as the word *Parcarius*, park-keeper or shepherd; *Parcus* meant a picketed enclosure for domestic animals, and also a preserve for game. *Parcarius* and *De Parco* are mentioned in Doomsday Book. They are found in "Liber Feudorum," and one Samuel Parker is noted in the reigns of Henry III. and Edward I. A James le Parker turns up in Norwich in 1261 ; the "Taxatio Ecclesiastica" yields the name, and we find the following in mediæval Latinity of 1205: "Johannes le Parker tenet dimid. hidam terrae, per servantiam custodiendi Parcum Domini Regis et Riesam forinsicum et valet hoc annum dimidiam marcam": John the Parker holds half a hide of land for the service (sergeantry) of keeping the King's park and pasture-ground, and receives this year half a mark. Fifty acres, and 6s. 8d. per annum for folding the royal sheep and driving them to pasture.

has the motto *Semper aude,* which many of the descendants did their best to vindicate. Our business begins with Thomas Parker, who brought over the spirit which earned a better blazon than the family arms which were afterwards discovered for his descendants. The nàme occurs so often among the enemies of the Church of England, that we may suppose Thomas had very good Puritan reasons for his emigration. Many Quakers and two non-conforming clergymen, bear the name. A Rev. Thomas Parker, of Newbury, brought over a company from Wiltshire, and settled Newbury and Newburyport.

Thomas Parker came over, in 1635, in a vessel fitted out by Sir Richard Saltonstall, who was then in London. There was some connection between the Parkers of Browsholme * and the Sir Richard Saltonstall who was Lord Mayor of London in 1597. Thomas Parker settled at Lynn, and he was made free-man in 1637. In the division of the town among its early settlers, forty acres of land were allotted to him. A lineal de-scendant occupied, not long ago, if a statement made by Alonzo Lewis be correct, the old homestead which has been in the family for seven generations. It is now, since a division of the town-ship, in Saugus, on the west bank of the river, about eighty rods below the Iron Works. Thomas removed to Reading in 1640, and was one of seven who founded the first church of Reading, of which he was a deacon in 1645. Here he died, August 12, 1683, having been the father of six sons and four daughters. In the course of a century and a half, many of the stones which marked the resting-places of these early settlers had crumbled away, and when a new place of burial was opened, the town let out the old place as a mowing lot. The lessor was bound not to swing his scythe beyond the line marked by a few grave-stones, already half-buried in the dust which they professed to celebrate. The scythe, however, slipped gradually over the whole ground, and the thrifty descendant illustrated scriptural views of

---

* Edward Parker, born 1602, married Mary, daughter of Richard Sunderland, of Yorkshire, whose wife was Mary, sixth daughter of Sir Richard Saltonstall. He had a coat of arms, displaying three bucks' heads and a buck for the crest, with the motto, *Non fluctu nec flatu movetur.* A seal engraved with this motto was sometimes used by Mr. Parker.

There is a Thomas Parker registered by Burke as belonging to this family, who was a son of John Parker of Little Norton and Jordenthorpe, and he was baptized March 31, 1609. The Thomas Parker who emigrated was 74 years old when he died at Reading in 1683. This age refers his birth to 1609. This is the only coincidence of date which can be discovered, and of its value we know nothing.

mortality through the grass which his ancestors were nourishing. *Hoc est veré monumentum patris colere.* Later still, in building a Town-house, where it was supposed no graves had ever existed, old ones were broken into accidentally ; the stones thus recovered were piled in a row against the wall, with Thomas Parker's at the head. So that the upright and sturdy old Puritan, who began life in America with forty acres in Lynn, ends with nothing this side the grave except the fame of his descendant.*

In the Massachusetts records we find the sumptuous prefix of *Mr.* to his name in the list of freemen : that was more charily pronounced in 1637 than to-day.† He and his posterity were flourishing and reliable. men : wherever they settled, we trace them by the offices they filled, the claims they adjudged, the boundaries they assisted in defining. They viewed land, reviewed the militia, and were lieutenants and captains of companies. The military spirit was very strong among them in days when fighting was often the final cause of training. The " dying words " of one Jonathan Parker, a discoloured sheet, with only the date 1680, and no other note by which his age or work in this life can be fixed, is a most tender and God-fearing document. He had passed through perils of the field in King Philip's war : perhaps he was one of the 150 volunteers under Turner, or one of Lathrop's picked company. This was in 1675-6 : but he was spared to die at home.

Then he was heard to say that he desiered, and that if it wear the will of God, that this cross might pass from him, but if not he did desier to submit, allso he desiered that God would soport his parents, and make them wiling to submit, if he must dey, that God would be pleased to make his pasing easy into glory, and if that he did dey he hopt to go to a heavenly Father.

He did entreat his father and mother to forgive him all his ofencis, telling of them that he would entreat them to submit to the will of

---

* From his grave-stone, as it stood in the yard of the Centre School-house, South Reading, this epitaph was transcribed:—

Memento Mori !
Fugit Hora !
Here lyeth within
This sacred place
The body of Deacon
Thomas Parker
who was won of
the foundation of
the church, who dyed
yᵉ 12 of August,
1683, aged about 74.

† Palfrey's New England, II. 67.

God. In parting with them, saying that he had cometted his case to God, and if it may make most for God's glory and youer comfort, I desier to live, if not I am willing to dey.

Being asked if he wars not afraid of deth, he sayed noe, for Christ had taken away the sting of deth, tho Sathcn had a thrust at him to make him fall, but he said he had no foothould, and had not yet prevailed, and he hopt that he never should, for he was a coward. Then his mother said that it was a great merci that God did coop him in the sins of the wars and brought him home to die by his parents—there was notice taken of him that he prayed, for had nothing els to do—he did desier to be remembred to his two sisters, and tell them that if they do see him no more, they should not see him sinn.

This Jonathan belonged to the family before its removal to Lexington, which was then called Cambridge Farms. John, a grandson of Thomas, left Reading in 1710, carrying with him all his children and grandchildren but Hananiah. This one, a son of John, junior, had already enlisted in the Massachusetts Regiment, which shared in the various operations against Port Royal from 1707 to 1710. A letter of his is preserved, dated March 8th, 1708, from *Annapolis Royal ;* for the soldiers in the camp before that place already called it by the name which it received after its capture, in honour of Queen Anne. Passages from this letter, showing his grave and virtuous bringing-up, are worth transcribing. Grahame * speaks of the great sickness and mortality among the troops. Hananiah's spelling is more than obsolete, but here it is as he penned it in the wet trenches, the Yankee spelling and disposition for 1708 :—

Honored Father and Mother,—After my Deuty Remembered to you and to my Grandfather and Grandmother, and my love to my brothers and all my friends. Hoping theas few lines of my Love Will find you in as Good health as I am at this present Writting, Blessed be god for it. And this is to let you understand that i Receaved youer Second letter, and that it is a werey sickly time with us, and we have Lost above Three scor men that belong to New England. Sr. Charles † has lost 11 men out of his Redgement. Coronal Whiting has lost 16 or 17 and he has 24 men sick. One man Dyed out of our Company : he belonged to Wobone, his name was Robert Peirce. But we hope to see you in a litle time, they that are living, but if we stay hear much Longer thair will but few of us se New England, but Sr. Charles saies he will cary us home as soon as yᵉ govenor coms : we hope to see you

---

* History of the United States, III., 39–43.

† Four regiments were raised in New England, two of which were commanded by Sir Charles Hobby and Colonel Tailer, of Massachusetts.

in a month or six weaks, if we live—for Sr. Charles is a wearey of this place and amost Discouraged, and wants to git home as much as we do.

Out of all New England men thair is but about 40 men fit for Deuty, and thair is hardly men enough to berrey ye dead and look after ye sick, for we berrey 2 or 3 men everey Night: for we berrey them in night becaus ye french Should not know how many men we loos, and we berrey them out of the buring place down by ye water side below ye fort and spread ye ground leavel over them that they might not be seen.

But i desire youer prayers for me that i may be kept from sin and sickness, beaing in a dangerous place for them both: for thair is nothing but wickedness carried on hear, cursing and swearing for every man's mouth.

We hear that thair is men a coming from New York to Releaive us. But No mor At Present, for i have No News to send you. So i

Remain your Deutyfull Son.

Hananiah was eighteen when he wrote this letter. We fancy him eager to return that he might share in the family removal to Lexington; and the father was longing to recover so much helpful muscle from the barren trenches, to plant the fresh acres, and bring in wood for that new hearth which blazed afterward so clear for freedom. But he was kept in garrison at Port Royal after the capitulation, and died there of the prevailing sickness, sometime during 1711.

The rest of the family (nine children), one or more of whom were married, went with the father to Lexington in 1710, leaving many of the name in Reading, whence they went to settle in various neighbouring towns. A Nathaniel had fourteen children; Bethiah, the mother of these, was ninety when she died. Each generation lost many children; but also reared many, who were strong and prolific, cleared many a good acre, and ploughed sinew into the soil of the coming commonwealth. They lived long and well, loved peace, and abated rural acrimonies; but always, from the time of landing, kept a musket for the frontier, against Pequod, King Philip, French, and Ojibways; they never shrunk from pain nor fainted at the inevitable blood-lettings of discomposed times, and always made a solemn business of militia drill, as old family almanacs and account books attest, in which the phrases of field manœuvres and words of command alternate with the price of hay and lumber and the settlement of a neighbour's bill. Take, for instance, this specimen, from "Josiah Parker's book, 1738," of the terms used in the manual by all the fighting men of Lexington :—

Joyne your right hand to your F.*
Present your F.
Rest your F.
Cock your F.
Present—fire.
Recover your F.
Half-cock your F.
Handel your primer.
Prime.
Shut your Pan.
Cast about to charge.
Handel your carthrige.
Open your carthrige.
Charge with carthrige.
Draw your rammers.
Shorten your rammers.
Put them in the barrels.
Ram down your carthrige.
With-draw your rammers.
Shorten your rammers.
Return your rammers.
Cast off your F.
Your right hand under the lock.
Poise your F.
Shoulder your F.
Rest your F.
Ground your F.
Take up your F.
Rest your F.
Club your F.
Rest your F.
Secure your F.
Shoulder your F.

May ye first, 1744.

Then setled y⁰ Dignity of Officers in Colonol Phip's Ridgement.

Captains.	Lieutenants.
1. Saml. Green.	John Tainter.
	Saml. Hendly.
2. Benj. Reed.	Josiah Parker.
3. Saml. Livermore.	John Baal.
4. Capt. Hayes.	Thom. Symms.
5. Capt. Codman.	Wm. Hide.
6. Capt. Fuller.	Jos. Bryant.
7. Capt. Kendrick.	Robert Mardock.
8. Capt. Brooks.	Benj. Blany.
9. Capt. Dana.	Stephen Hall.

* In the corner of the page is written, "N.B.—that F. stands for firelock."

And here is a note made by some painstaking captain, ambitious of perfecting his company drill :—

Reare half files, double the depth of your right flank. Left half files of left flank face to the left about. Front half files of left flank face to the left. Reare half files of right flank face to the right—march 10 paces—the whole face to the right—march 10 paces—face to the right.

Such matter as this lies confusedly mixed with charges made for mechanical labour and farm produce ; for the Parkers knew how to wield a good many kinds of tools :—

1752. To a harrow and exeltreeing your cart—to mending your Cyder-mill—to a chees mill—to making 3 keelers and a churn—to making a coffin—to 3 days and ½ work Stoning your Seller—to 3 Doz. of Compas boxes—6 pair of Bed Screws at £7 10s. a pair old tenor—to a beetel and how handel and sithe sneth—to my oxen to Cambridge and 3 Cartouch boxes—to whetting and setting your hand-saw—to my oxen to plough in your Rie—to shoeing your sled—to making your leading staff—to 23 pound of Veal at 15d. per lb.—to mending your Chimney back—to Cutting 19 lbs. of tobacco—to a tobacco tub and mending a brine tub lid.

But the pens which noted down rather laboriously the proceeds of meadow and garden land, and the number of planks which were rafted down the Mystic for ship-building, have left no trace of the early sufferings and sorrows. Hananiah's home-sickness was, I fancy, an achievement of garrulity uncommon in the family. Like all the pioneers of New England, they minded their business, and never hinted at their feelings. Their diary is their fair and lawful portion of the history of the plantation as it stands to be read in all authentic books.

Reminiscences of military life and border suffering came also into the family on the mother's side subsequent to 1754, when Hannah Seger was married to Benjamin Stearns, of Lexington. One of their daughters was the mother of Theodore Parker. His grandmother's ancestor, Thomas Seger, or Seager, came to Newbury before 1637. The descendants seem to have had a taste for frontier life. Nathaniel, of uncertain date, was one of the earliest settlers of Bethel, Maine ; the Indians carried him off into Canada, as they did many another man and woman, when they could surprise them in the fields, driving them thence through the desolate gaps in the White Mountains, to make a bloody trail where now the summer streams of fashion and invalidism so easily flow.

Nathaniel had a very hard time of it, which he must needs write about afterwards. Another member of this family enlisted during the Revolutionary war, was a sergeant in Capt. Bryant's company of artillery, and went through many an engagement. His captain lay mortally wounded after the battle of Brandywine, within the enemy's lines, whence he brought him away by night upon a litter, with two or three comrades helping, though he, too, had sustained a severe wound that day. Stories of the wilderness and of battle were told into greedy ears at the winter firesides of the Lexington families.

Toryism did not flourish among the descendants of Thomas Parker of Browsholme. "*Semper aude*" was the creed of five generations of them, who knew small Latin, but kept alive an instinct for supporting the weak against the strong, the wronged against the wronger. By-and-bye the doctrine was heard from the pulpit of Lexington Green, where Jonas Clark made sincere and earnest application of it, not to judges, tax-gatherers, and governors, who were groping in Sheol some time before the settlement of the Old Testament canon, but to flesh-and-blood Britishers waiting at Boston to carry Tory mandates up the country. Jonas believed in preaching directly to the point, in days when political sermons were not dictated by the nice distinction constructed for the benefit of the Fugitive Slave Bill, that the oppressing power, in '75, resided in England and not at Washington; they were inspired by the plain circumstance that there was oppression in America. Mayhew, Clark, and other brave pre-revolutionary preachers, did not withhold their word because Tory countrymen sat in the pews and helped support the minister. A divided opinion, a country tardy or irresolute, a prospect of irreconcileable divisions, were so many arguments for quickly reinforcing the spirit of liberty with words of protesting truth. This they did, seeing the green fields beyond the swelling flood.

The plain people hungered for these appeals, and their representatives knew how to use the great influence which a faithful pulpit then possessed. Here is a trace of it :—

In Provincial Congress. Watertown, May 22, 1775.

The Congress having requested the Rev. Dr. Langdon to deliver a sermon before the next Massachusetts Congress, at their meeting in this place, on the last Wednesday of this month, and he having signified that he will comply with such request,

Resolved, that it is the desire of the Congress, that the Reverend Ministers of the Gospel in this Colony would assemble at that time, agreeable to their ancient custom, and hold a convention, as usual (if they think proper); as, in the opinion of this Congress, the cause of religion *and the political interest* of this Colony may be served by such meeting.*

Old Dr. Byles, of Hollis Street Church, was singular in this respect, as in many others, and held out against the expressed desire of his own parish that he would consider the condition of the Colony in the pulpit, and against the enthusiasm of all of his Congregational brethren in Boston. The sermons of the time abounded, except in Western Massachusetts, with eager discussion of public affairs. Clergymen responded to invitations to preach by taking the popular side, not in veiled generalities, but with the plainest exposition of the doctrine for which Massachusetts rose in arms. "If it be," said one of them,† "in the nature and reason of things lawful for a people to enjoy their lives, liberty, and property, it must be also, in the same nature and reason of things, lawful to preserve them; for to suppose a right to them, and no right to preserve or defend them, is manifestly absurd."

Treason was levied in these terms in the house of God: the commonwealth sat wakeful in the high-backed pews of the old fireless meeting-houses, warmed by hearts that glowed in the pulpits, feeling Religion place the sword of the Lord and of Gideon into every hand. What wonder that the green before the church became wet with blood! What wonder that the drops sowed heart's love for liberty, fresh from praise and prayer, in the spring soil!

In the old meeting-house sat Capt. John Parker (born, 1729; died, 1775), Jonathan Harrington, his nephew, and fifer of his company, and Jonas Parker, who fell upon the Green. Captain Parker had been a sergeant in the French war, 1749–59, and was at the taking of Quebec. Jonas Clark, then forty-five years of age, had for some time discussed the successive points of the great controversy as it became developed. He drew up the instruc-

---

* Find the sermon itself reprinted in J. W. Thornton's "Pulpit of the American Revolution," and on page 255, the following note: "Governor Gage, in his proclamation of June 12, 1775, a few days after Dr. Langdon's sermon was preached, said 'To complete the horrid profanation of terms and of ideas, the name of God has been introduced in the pulpits to excite and justify devastation and massacre.'" It sounds like a modern Tory newspaper denouncing the introduction of "exciting topics" into the pulpit, and predicting that strife will be stirred up by the ministers of a Gospel of peace.

† Elisha Fish, minister of Upton, preaching at the invitation of the Committee of Correspondence for Worcester County, March 28, 1775

tions which his people desired to have presented to the Provincial Legislature by their delegate. This is a model paper, which simply and strongly sets forth the views often urged before in public and private by the revolutionary clergyman. He was more dangerous than all the military stores at Concord or in the Colony, and had so infected the whole district with his calm and deep indignation, that, when the regulars came marching up the old turnpike in the gray dawn of the 19th of April, after powder and flour, they found all the farmers converted to a doctrine of liberty which armed and provisioned a young nation for seven years of war. In the meeting-house and town-house, ringing with Clark's religious convictions, filled with his enlightened points and improvement, was the history of that glorious morning slowly prepared.

What a speech it gained at two o'clock, when the little belfry-tower opposite his meeting-house rang the inhabitants together for the action which had been foreshadowed in prayer and sermon ! One hundred and fifty men gathered to the call, and waited quietly for the reports brought in by riders who had been despatched a few miles down the road. The pastor was there, encouraging and reminding the flock that the opinions which they accepted in their pews must be advanced upon the Green. About one of the clock, their captain, John Parker, had been summoned, who was then ill with troubles which grew, by neglect and exposure, into the disease of which he died in September of the same year. He resided about three miles from the meeting-house. Being informed "that there were a number of regular officers riding up and down the road, taking and insulting people,"* he issued the orders which assembled his company, and hastened to his minister's side. He concluded "not to meddle or make with said regular troops, unless they should insult or molest us." At the approach of this body of regulars, which was 900 strong, he formed his own little troop of 70 men into the first line of the Revolution, and bade them charge their pieces with powder and ball. A scattering and ineffective fire was their response to the three volleys which the British delivered ; after this he told them to disperse and take care of themselves. Fifteen men had fallen ; seven of these were killed, including Jonas Parker, "the strongest wrestler in Lexington, pierced with both ball and bayonet." The men dispersed for a

* Affidavit of Capt. Parker, April 23, 1775. MS. copy.

time, to join in a few hours the great uprising of the country, which followed the regulars to Boston, with Jonas Clark's Sunday doctrine practically administered all along the road.

Captain Parker was not too ill to engage far and well in this pursuit. He was also at the battle of Bunker's Hill, in command of troops, but not engaged. The King's arm, which he took from a grenadier of the 43rd Regiment (the first weapon captured in the Revolution), and his own light fowling-piece which he had carried at Quebec, stood by the door of Theodore's study in Boston till the executors of his will consigned them to the keeping of the State. In the Senate Chamber they hang, and Massachusetts still yields children worthy to take them down who have not degenerated from those who first bore arms for her. The rusted pattern is still symbolical of the old spirit tried again in the same old cause, whose minute-men are again first in the field, and have drawn the first shot upon the same April date.* Jonas Clark and Theodore Parker are in array against a tyranny whose forms are various, but whose intention is evermore the same.

This letter, addressed to Mr. Bancroft, after the publication of the seventh volume of his History, contains some interesting notices :—

Boston, 10th September, 1858.

MY DEAR BANCROFT,—Last May came your beautiful volume on the Revolution. I was ill, and yet obliged to work. I read it with enthusiasm in the pauses of my toil. It ran into the night, and was soon in my head. I rejoice in it greatly. You confirm my suspicions that George III.—miserable old wooden-head!—was the real cause of the mischief. But you shed a deal of light I had no suspicion of on many matters; of course you do. It is thoroughly *democratic*, in the best sense of the word. This volume has more of the *Life of the People* in it than any of the last three. It seems to me history has been hitherto the life of kings, priests, nobles, soldiers, and the like—not the *Life of the Million*, as it should be. "*Les gens des salons partout se ressemblent*," but the people are every where different. I am glad to find a historian who cares for "the rest of mankind."

One fact or two let me give. At the battle of Lexington, when Capt. P. drew up his men as the British were nearing, he ordered "every man to load" his piece with powder and ball. "Don't fire unless fired upon; but if they mean to have a war, *let it begin here!*" I think these significant words ought to be preserved. They were kept as the family tradition of the day, and when the battle was re-enacted

* Written just after the Massachusetts three-months men had passed through Baltimore, April, 1861.

in 1820 (or thereabout), his orderly sergeant took the Captain's place, and repeated the words, adding, " For them is the *very words* Captain Parker said." Besides, some of the soldiers, when they saw the flash of the British guns, turned to run : he drew his sword, and said, " I will order the first man *shot* that offers to run !" Nobody ran till he told them, " Disperse, and take care of yourselves." Prince Estabrook, who was killed at the second fire, was a *negro*.*

Thankfully yours,

THEODORE PARKER.

Anu here is an extract from Mr. Parker's journal, written on occasion of a visit to Lexington to attend the ordination of Jason Whitman. The Jonathan Harrington herein mentioned was the grandfather of John W. Harrington, master's mate of the *Cumberland*, who was killed during the fight with the *Merrimac* in Hampton Roads :—

Jonathan Harrington was a fifer in my grandfather's company, and is the last survivor (1845), now 87 years old. He was then in his 17th year. I asked him how he felt as he marched on to the spot. He said he felt well enough then ; but when they saw the reg'lars march up, he felt kind o' queer. Some offered to run away, but Captain Parker drew his sword, and said he would run through the first man that offered to run away. He said Captain P. looked as if he could face anything, and so he could. He was a large-boned man ; his face longer than my father's, but in other respects built like mine (*i. e.*, stout, a stocky man.) His (Jonathan's) uncle, Wm. Munro, had been out in the French war. He showed me a pistol that belonged to him, and which he used there. Jonathan H. was in the American service at Prospect Hill, as one cf the guard of Burgoyne's troops, but never had a pension. His father (Uncle Harrington) dealt in ship timber. He often had trains of it that reached more than half a mile, and great quantities at his *bank* (depôt) in West Cambridge, whence he rafted it to Boston down the Mystic River. He was a patriot, but the Revolution ruined his business, and " kind o' broke it up." He lost great quantities of timber ; the British plundered his house at the battle—carried off his clock, leaving the weights and the case ; the pendulum was afterwards found dropped in the fields half a mile off, &c. Jonathan then went to school to Mr. Pitt Clark, " a pretty man." He taught on the Common. Jonathan studied Latin, but the soldiers took away his Latin books— all of them but the dictionary, which he still keeps (Young's Dictionary). He went to school no more. He would, perhaps, have gone

---

* This is a mistake, according to information kindly furnished by Hon. Charles Hudson, who is preparing a history of Lexington. He was wounded, but recovered and served in almost every campaign of the war. '' He is represented, by those who knew him, as a fine specimen of a man, tall, well-built, and muscular, having a carriage which fully justified the name of Prince." Estabrook was his master's name. He, with other negroes who served in the Revolution, obtained his freedom as a reward for military service ; but it was also secured to them by the Constitution of 1780, which entirely abolished slavery.

to college but for this. He remembers my grandfather as well as if he saw him now before his eyes.

John, Theodore's father, was born Feb. 14, 1761, and married Hannah Stearns, a daughter of Benjamin Stearns of Lexington and Hannah Seger. He was more of a mechanic than a farmer, and during his life the farm was mainly carried on by the boys, while he worked in the little shop just above the house, making and mending wheels, pumps, and farming-gear. He taught his children the use of tools, and Theodore became very handy with them. The cradle which he made (while he was preparing for college), for his sister-in-law's first child, is solid and shapely. He learned to hoop barrels and mend the plough. But his father was a great reader also, and thus many a book found its way into the house, borrowed of friends or hired from the little circulating library upon the Green, which Theodore would not have otherwise obtained ; they filled the long evenings, when all the children gathered around the table, in front of the fire, and the father read, sometimes aloud, when a passage pleased him, till eight o'clock struck, and with a wave of his hand he dismissed them to bed.

We gather from some rude notes which Mr. Parker made concerning his father, that he was a stout and able-bodied man, " uncommon strong," very ingenious and industrious. He had studied algebra and geometry, was particularly fond of mathematics, and was " great at figures." He was a good talker, and might have been an orator. If he ever got into an argument, which was seldom, as controversy did not suit him, he was very effective. He liked metaphysics, psychology, and all departments of intellectual and moral philosophy, and he had read all the English books upon philosophy. " He was a great reader, rising before day in the winter to study, sleeping but about five hours ; nice and acute in metaphysical analysis, jovial and funny," but not so exuberantly mirthful as Theodore was, nor so grotesque in his fun. He was well-mannered ; no clownishness, profanity, or indecency marred his humour. In religious matters he thought for himself, and hated Paley and Jonathan Edwards. " Paley left us no conscience," he used to say. He did not believe in eternal damnation, nor in the more extravagant of the miracles in the Old and New Testament, but he was a great reader of the Bible, and taught the younger children the ten commandments every Sabbath evening, and Sunday prayers and hymns.

"He did not like poetry, but read Pope, Dryden, Milton, Shakspeare, Trumbull, Peter Pindar, and Abraham Cowley. In the later years of his life he was fond of novels."

In theology he was a Unitarian, in politics one of the five Federalists in Lexington. "He was eminently just and magnanimous, fearless in the expression of opinion, often arbitrated in quarrels, was guardian of widows, orphans, &c., and administered estates, for there was no lawyer in town. He was not thrifty, and so, not rich. Devoted to education," he took great interest in the common schools, and was influential in bringing into them a better breed of teachers. He took great pains with the intellectual and moral culture of his children.

Mr. Parker described his mother as "a handsome woman, delicate and slightly built, industrious, thrifty, charitable to the poor." She was fond of hearing the father read aloud while she sewed. She loved ballads and popular tales, could repeat a great many of them, and had her favourites among the hymns. She knew the Old and New Testaments thoroughly, "was imaginative, delicate-minded, poetic, yet a very practical woman; far-sighted, and so nice in her perceptions and judgments that it used to startle me sometimes in the body, and does now as I think of it. She took great pains with the religious training of her children, but cared little for doctrines; no bigotry, no cant, no fear. Religion was love and good works. She had what I call piety, the ideal part of religion, love of God as well as morality." She had a critical eye to the religious reading of her household, and not much bigoted literature was allowed.

Her manners were grave and gentle, not hard, but touched, I surmise, with the old Puritan state, which made the frank blue eyes sometimes austere. She had a lofty soul; conscience and piety kept it both unbending and tender. The conscience beamed full, as the sun at eastern windows, and pervaded all the life of the house. Nothing could lay shadowy, yet a mellow warmth fell everywhere with its exacting light.

The phrases of religion had not tampered much with her heart: her spiritual sense knew to perceive the things appropriate to it, and it never occurred to her to question the soul's capacity for this immediate perception, or to be content with its mental and social simulations. Before her children she was not eager to explain or refute, and never tried to skim her religious life for their luncheon and nooning. The young minds breathed unconsciously her mountain air of trust and reverence. In this influence of a fine soul Theodore became filled with piety at a very early age ; he throve as much under her reticence as he did in her timely speech : for he learned few religious terms, and no formal habits. So buds seem aimlessly to unfold, while Nature really makes a point of soliciting each in her private and unannounced way.

When the children took their light and went to bed, the day had still one grace in store for them, as they listened till their mother came up to see that they were well tucked in, and to share the sweetness of their homely prayers.

Theodore learned many a nice moral distinction from this clear-judging mother. Her position in the world was wholesome ; her intelligence shared the fair country chance of everything that grew on the farm. Popular views of life and manners were within sight, but too far to become familiar. The father's thirst for knowledge and the mother's spiritual longing were satisfied in unconventional ways. And the children, in acquiring this independence, found faith and earnestness besides ; for to live in the country is not merely to riot in freedom from the constraints of the town, but to obey nature's simple regularity, which always surprises and stimulates. This was the health which Theodore brought at last to Boston from those inland acres. His tribute to the mother of a great New-Englander can now be paid also to his own. "When virtue leaps high in the public fountain, you seek for the lofty spring of nobleness, and find it far off in the dear breast of some mother, who melted the snows of winter, and condensed the summer's dew into fair, sweet humanity, which now gladdens the face of man in all the city streets." *

Theodore was the youngest of eleven children. He was born August 24, 1810, when his father was over 50 and his mother was 47 years old. Sweet and sound is the last apple, ripening high up in the tree, through the late golden days, discovered after the leaves begin to fall.

* Discourse on Daniel Webster.

[The Battle of Lexington was preceded by the famous midnight ride of Paul Revere, who escaped from Boston and warned the towns as far as Concord. While these sheets are passing through the press, the news comes that his grandson, Col. Paul Joseph Revere, of the 20th Massachusetts Regiment, died on July 4th (1863) of wounds received while leading his command at the Battle of Gettysburg, which was fought the day before.

The little Belfry, to which allusion is made later, in connection with the homestead of Mr. Parker, stands on the right of the Meeting-house.]

THE BATTLE OF LEXINGTON, APRIL 19TH, 1775.

CHAPTER II.

A FRAGMENT of an Autobiography, which was commenced at Rome, is printed here in its original condition, except that a few pages of botanical matter have been corrected and arranged by Rev. John L. Russell, of Salem, in conformity with a request transmitted by Mr. Parker to his old friend. When he found that he could write no more, he closed the manuscript with a *caveat* to the reader, which is here transferred to the commencement.

N.B. Caveat Lector.—This will require careful re-writing, and, as it stands, may contain many errors of detail,* for I write it when too ill to read, and with no memoranda to aid me. I should like to consult the deeds of the early settlers in my neighbourhood, to learn the original ownership of land, the date of the houses, and the names of places like "the great meadow." Few men, if any, now living will remember the name, but I have found it in old deeds.

I began this at Rome, March 16th, 1860. It is not likely I shall get far in it. I have waited more than a year for strength to begin it, and now commence at my weakest point.

The material and human circumstances about a man in his early life have a strong and abiding influence upon all, especially on those of a sensitive disposition, who are both easily affected by such externals and rather obstinate in retaining the impression made on them.

OF THE MATERIAL SURROUNDINGS.

About 1710, my grandfather's grandfather, John Parker, then somewhat advanced in life, with a part of his grown-up children, removed from Reading, where a family of Parkers had settled about 1640, to the Cambridge Farms, since called Lexington, where he had bought a considerable quantity of land, with one small house upon it, probably of logs. The next year he built him a large and commodious house, and furnished it with the usual out-buildings necessary for a farmer's business. The situation was pleasant; a considerable valley a mile or more in length and half a mile wide, with a fresh meadow at the

---

* Much may be omitted that he would have noted under favourable circumstances, but all blanks have been filled, and only one or two errors of commission needed attention. This Autobiography was commenced by Mr. Parker with the object of entrusting it, when finished, to his friend Mr. Lyman, to be used by him some day: the fragment, accordingly, was sent to him.

C

bottom, called in deeds of the time "the great meadow," wound among hills tall and steep on the western and northern side, while on the south and east the hills were of less height and more gradual in their slope. Indeed, it is the general character of the hills in that part of the country to be steep on their southern and eastern side, and of gradual ascent on the opposite side. A brook stole through the valley or percolated through the soft, spongy meadow; following a continuation of the valley, it falls into Charles River at length. The stream was then much larger than at present; for now the hills have nearly all been stripped of their trees and the meadows drained, and the brook is proportionally shrunk, except when a sudden melting of snow floods the meadow and restores it to more than its original size.

Near the upper end of this valley, in about the centre of his farm lot, the old settler built his house, in which children to the fourth generation were to be born to him. It stood about 80 or 100 feet above the present surface of the great meadow, on the south-east side of a high hill, which, gently sloping in front of the house, rose steep and abrupt behind. It faced as near the south as the rude science of the owner or builder could make it, and so was a perpetual sun-dial. It had but one chimney, that a huge one in the centre of the building. The large bricks, made half-a-mile off, were laid in clay as far as the ridge-pole, while the part of the chimney above the roof was *pointed* with mortar. Limestone was not found within many miles, and the want of it was a serious inconvenience in building. The house, like all the others in that neighbourhood, was two storeys high in front, and only one in the rear. The rooms were few, but large and airy; the windows not numerous, of various size, but all small: originally all the latches, except that of the "fore-door," were of wood, with wooden thumb-pieces, but these had nearly all passed away before my recollection. The house, as it stood in my day, had been built at different times, the eastern end being considerably younger than the western, and not furnished with the massive oak-beams which everywhere stuck out in the older part. A New England farmer of "comfortable estate" would hesitate a good deal before setting up his household in such a cheerless shelter; but three generations of stout and long-lived men were born and grew up there; and if the fourth be more puny and sink quicker to the grave, it is from no fault of the old house, but from the consumption which such spongy meadows in New England seldom fail to produce in the course of time; even children, who have removed to healthier situations, carry with them the fatal poison in their blood, and transmit it to their sons and daughters.

As the old man at sunrise stood at the front or south door of his new house on some fine October morning of 1710, he could see but a single house, and that half or three-quarters of a mile off, the other side of the valley: two other columns of pale blue smoke in that direction might tell him of other neighbours, while not far off in the same valley were two others, hid by wooded hills; in a different direction one more house had been built earlier than his own, but on the north side of the hill which sheltered him.*

* Childs: in the Snake Hill lot.

Agriculture was at a low stage; that part of the country was covered with thick woods, and when the farmer cut down or girdled the trees and run the ground over with fire, the land must have looked as we see it now in parts of New Hampshire and Vermont, like "the abomination of desolation." However, he planted many apple-trees, importing them from England; but they had not been grafted, and so many of them bore sorry specimens of fruit. Many of those which it is said he set out were standing in my boyhood. He, or his son Josiah, who succeeded to his lands at Lexington, planted also locust-trees, whose white blossoms used to fill the air with sweetness in June. He also brought lilac-bushes, a common ornament about the houses of New England in the last century, and planted a barberry-bush, which in my boyhood had grown to prodigious dimensions, besides having increased and multiplied and replenished that part of the earth with its descendants.

In the rear of the house was a monstrous elm which endangered the building and was removed as a nuisance; that was a full-grown tree in the days of my grandfather's grandfather: other huge oaks and elms once stood close by, but they had all perished before my birth, and only a white ash with a great round top stood at the north-west corner of the house. It was planted by my grandfather, and was the largest tree of the kind I remember ever to have seen in New England.

Huge boulders lay scattered about along the valley and its tributaries; some were of the hard blueish greenstone which forms the skeleton of all the hills in that neighbourhood, but others were of whitish granite, brought many miles from their original site to the north-west of that locality. Loose stones abounded; indeed, a more unattractive piece of land for a farmer to work could scarcely be found than that whole region for miles around in all directions. There were stones enough within a foot of the surface to fence all the land into acre lots, each surrounded with a strong "balance wall."

The most common trees were the numerous species of oak, the white pine, the pitch pine, and a variety of it called the yellow pine, the hemlock, and spruce; on the rocky hill-sides the juniper or red cedar; and in the swamps the cypress or white cedar; maples, the white or grey, black and yellow birches, the elm, white and black ashes, poplars, buttonwood, walnuts, chestnut, beech, sassafras, and wild hop or hop-hornbeam, willows; three species of sumach occurring on the homestead; indeed, most of the trees of New England grow within a few miles of my home.

The handsomest flowering shrubs and plants of New England could mostly be found in the immediate neighbourhood, the shadbush, the rhodora, the viscous or white azalea—the pink-flowered species was further off; the numerous cornels, though only a single instance of the large-flowering cornel; the several viburnums and the andromedas, the narrow-leaved kalmia, and even the broad-leaved kind, grew in a thicket in the vicinity; the choke-cherries, the spiræas, both pinkish-white flowered, and the other with steeple-shaped purple spikes; wild roses and sweet briars, the clethra, blossoming from July to October. In the meadows, spongy with soft mosses, were the arethusas and the cymbidium, and the rarer painted cup, successively disclosing their native beauties; while a little later the pitcher-plant offered its curious flower and leaf to the most careless eye. The cranberry bore in midsummer its rich pale red flowers and covered whole acres from whence the farmer hoped, often vainly, to win as fair a harvest in autumn to season his winter food. The beautiful water lily grew abundantly in a shallow pond not far off, and also in many brooks of sluggish water; nay, it did not refuse the benediction of its presence in some of the ill-formed ditches whence peat had been cut for fuel or for manure. Here the fringed gentian, not then to be seen, has happily since taken up its abode; the soap-wort gentian was uncommon, the trilliums rare; but along the brook-sides the cardinal flowers hung out their brilliant colours.

On the hard land saxifrages and columbines grew on the sunny sides of all the great rocks, blue violets and white were to be had every-where, the yellow species was rarer, and anemones nodded their hand-some heads on the south side of every wall where nature had her own way.

In the woods, the ladies' slipper hung out its mysterious beauty, the several pyrolas opened their blossoms; they, with the ground pine, the partridge-berry, and the boxberry, or Mitchella, kept a green life in the woods under the snow all winter through. What need to mention the humbler beauties of the New England flora, such as the meadow-pride and the sweet cicely, the craneflower and the buttercups? There were also red lilies and yellow, some of them stately and queen-like plants—on a single stalk I have seen forty-nine buds and blossoms; nor should the humbler-named dog-tooth violet be forgotten in the list of its liliaceous sisterhood.

My sisters cultivated the crimson peony, daffodils, white and yellow narcissus, white and red roses of the most delicious fragrance. Camo-mile, saffron, and the odorous balms were herbs for medicine, not flowers for sport.

In the thick, dark swamps, huge, corky fungi grew on the trunks of old maples, but more especially of the white birches; and curious puff-balls shot up in the hot, muggy nights of summer, and in two days became mysteriously as large as a quart bowl; while the usual variety of other fungi sprung up in their appropriate places, and the Indian pipe of seeming make and mould ; while lichens, some as large as a modern Kossuth hat, covered the north side of rocks and trees.

My ancestors had planted the white locust not far from the house, and a beautiful grove had grown up; some of the trees were very large, and sweetened the air for a week or two in June, and the grass all the summer through. When the autumn came—

> " Every bush did put its glory on,
> Like a gemmed bride."

How red the maples were, how yellow the birches and the walnuts, and what richly tinted leaves did the chestnut shake down !—last of New England trees to blossom, and bearing the richest, sweetest fruit the savage found in the austere land. Even the ivy and the poison dog-wood were clad in more glory than the Queen of Sheba, intent on wooing the King of Israel's son ; nay, Solomon himself, in all his glory, was not arrayed like one of these.

From the middle of May when the introduced trees, the plum, peach cherry, apple, and pear, began to bloom, till the middle or end of October, the eye need not seek a landscape of humble, quiet New England beauty more attractive than this, and all winter long the white pines, which seemed so cool and attractive in July and August, had a warm, motherly look, and told of life still sleeping in them, around them, everywhere.

OF THE HUMAN SURROUNDINGS.

At the age of 45, my grandfather, Captain John Parker, died on the 17th of September, 1775. He was sick on the day of the Battle of Lexington, but did his duty from 2 A.M. till 12 at night. On the 17th of June he was too ill to be allowed to enter the turmoil of the Battle of Bunker-hill, so he discontentedly commanded troops who did no fighting that day. He was never well afterwards, and an epidemic dysentery in September found him an easy prey; he died at an early age for his long-lived family, and left three sons and four daughters, with a widow, who died at the respectable age of 92, passing a portion of the last 47 years of her life in a second marriage, which both she and her children had bitter cause to repent. The respectable property of Captain Parker was wasted, the relict obliged to take her new husband and his children home, to be supported on "the widows' thirds." When my father married Hannah Stearns, the daughter of a neighbouring farmer, he went back to the original homestead to take care of his mother, while he should support his handsome young wife and such family as might happen. It was the day of small things—he wore home-made blue yarn stockings at his wedding, and brought his wife home over the rough winding roads, riding in the saddle his tall grey horse, with her upon a pillion. The outfit of furniture did not bespeak more sumptuous carriage—the common plates were of wood; the pitcher, mugs, tea-cups and saucers, were of coarse earthenware; while the great carving dishes were of thick well-kept pewter. The holiday service "for company" was of the same material. Yet, a few costly wine glasses were not wanting, with two long-necked decanters, a few china tea-cups and saucers, of the minutest pattern, and the pride of the buffet, a large china bowl. Besides, the young bride could show patch-work bed-quilts and counterpanes, and a pretty store of linen towels, and a tablecloth of the same, white as the snow, and spun, woven, and bleached by her own laborious hands; and her father raised the flax which her brother pulled, and rotted, and broke, and swingled, and hackled, and combed. Hannah made their work into linen.

In the course of many years, ten children had been born to John and Hannah (one had slipped out of life an infant), when their fourth son and eleventh child came into the world, on 24th of August, 1810, lagging a little more than five years after his youngest, and afterwards his favourite sister. I think I was the last child born in the old house, which then numbered just 100 years.

1. In my earliest childhood the family at home consisted (to begin in the order of age) of my father's mother, more than 80 at my birth. A tall, stately, proud-looking woman: she occupied an upper chamber,

but came down-stairs to dinner—other meals she took in her own room —and sat at the head of the table on the woman side thereof, opposite my father, who kept up the ancient Puritan respect for age—always granting it precedence. She busied herself chiefly in knitting and puttering about the room, but passed the Sundays in reading the large Oxford quarto Bible of her husband, bought for the price of more than one load of hay, delivered up at Boston. She had also the original edition of the Puritan Hymn Book, printed at Cambridge, which was much in her hands. She read the newspapers, the *Columbian Centinel*, which then appeared twice a week; but common mundane literature she seldom touched. It was a part of my childish business to carry the *drink* to my venerable grandmother—twice a day, at 11 A.M. and 4 P.M.; this was *flip* in cool weather, and in spring and summer was *toddy* or *punch*—the latter was, however, more commonly reserved for festive occasions.

2. Next were my father and mother : grave, thoughtful, serious, and industrious people. From an ancestry of five generations of his own name, who had died in New England, my father had inherited a strong and vigorous body ; in his youth, there was but one man in town who could surpass him in physical strength, and few who were his equals. He could endure cold and heat, abstinence from food and rest, to a degree that would be impossible to men brought up in the effeminate ways which so often are thought to be the curses of civilization. He was a skilful farmer; though, as he lived not on his own land, but on "the widows' thirds," which his mother had only a life-estate in, he was debarred from making costly improvements in the way of buildings, fences, and apple-trees, which are long in returning profit to him that plants. But he yet contrived to have, perhaps, the best peach orchard in the county of Middlesex, to graft valuable kinds of fruit upon the old trees, and to adopt nearly all of the improvements in farming, as they were tested and found valuable.

He was also an ingenious mechanic: his father and grandfather were mechanics as well as farmers, and did all kinds of work in wood, from building saw-mills, cider-mills, pumps, to making flax-spinning wheels, and turning wooden bread bowls out of maple stumps. He had religiously kept the tools of his father and grandfather, and like them continued to do all kinds of ordinary jobs; indeed, both he and they were such mechanics as men must be in a new country, and should not be in one where industry is more elaborate, and able-minded men are ready to turn their hand to anything. Mechanical talent was here-ditary in the family for several generations, and appeared in my remote relations, and even among women, on whose slender shoulders this mantle seldom falls. My father was a thoughtful man, turning his large and active brain and his industrious hand to the mechanical and agricultural work before him ; he was an originator of new and short ways of doing many things, and made his head save his hands. In this respect his father and grandfather resembled him.

His education—his schooling ended when the Revolution begun—was of course, much neglected, but he was an uncommonly good arithmetician, often puzzling the school-masters with his original problems. Works on political economy and the philosophy of legislation were favourites with him. He had learned algebra and geometry, and was familiar with the use of logarithms. He read much on Sundays, in the long winter evenings, sometimes in the winter mornings before it was light, and in the other intervals of toil. His favourite works were history—that of New England he was quite familiar with—biography and travels; but he delighted most of all in works of philosophy which give the *rationale* of the material or the human world; of course he read much of the theology of his times, and the literature of progressive minds found its way to the farmer's kitchen. He had no fondness for poetry. In his latter years, his reading was chiefly of novels, not to instruct, but only to amuse the old man, whose mortal life was all behind him. His fathers before him had been bookish men.

My mother, a woman of slight form, flaxen hair, blue eyes, and a singularly fresh and delicate complexion, more nervous than muscular, had less education than my father. Her reading was confined mainly to the Bible, the hymn-book, stories of New England captives among the Indians, of which there were many in the neighbourhood, some in manuscript, and perhaps never printed. Ballads and other humble forms of poetry gave her a great delight. Of course the newspapers passed through her busy hands. My father often read aloud to her and the rest of the family in the long winter evenings, while her fingers were occupied with sewing or knitting, making or mending. She was industrious, as indeed were all the women of the neighbourhood, but like them found opportunities, though too rare, for social enjoyment with them. Dinner was always at noon, and after that was over and its paraphernalia put in order, the household work was done, and a more comely dress took the place of the blue check of the morning.

She was eminently a religious woman. I have known few in whom the religious instincts were so active and so profound, and who seemed to me to enjoy so completely the life of God in the soul of man. To her the Deity was an Omnipresent Father, filling every point of space with His beautiful and loving presence. She saw him in the rainbow and in the drops of rain which helped compose it as they fell into the muddy ground to come up grass and trees, corn and flowers. She took a deep and still delight in silent prayer—of course it was chiefly the more spiritual part of the Old Testament and New Testament that formed her favourite reading, the dark theology of the times seems not to have blackened her soul at all. She took great pains with the moral culture of her children—at least with mine.

3. Come the brothers and sisters, nine in number, and one in infancy laid away in the grave. Some of these were much older than I, and had already gone to seek their fortunes in the various trades and callings of the time. There was still a houseful at home; all of them but three had a decided fondness for literature; they read all the good books they could lay their hands on, and copied the better parts. At school they were always among the best scholars.

4. The uncles and aunts come next. On my father's side there were two uncles and twice as many aunts; one of the former, a farmer not far off, a tall, grave man; the other, a more restless character, had served many years in the revolutionary war; he was in the battles of Saratoga and of Yorktown, had failed in business, gone to South

Carolina, and married a woman with some property at Charleston, where he then lived, the father of one son. Of the aunts one was a maiden, an uncommonly intellectual woman; another was a widow living in an adjoining town, while two were the wives of farmers, one living in Nova Scotia, the other in Watertown not far off. On the maternal side there was one aunt, a strange, eccentric woman, and ten uncles, rejoicing in the names of Asahel, Jepthah, Noah, Ammi, Ishmael, and Habbakuk, and the like, which, if not euphonious, are at least scriptural. They were farmers and labourers, some rich and some poor.

Besides, the brothers and sisters of my grandmother still continued to live, though aged people. Other relations from the Parker side of the family dwelt in more remote towns, who occasionally paid my father a visit, in special one very old and tall man, to whom he surrendered the head of the table and invited to say grace.

5. The neighbours about us were farmers; a shoemaker lived a mile off on one side, and a blacksmith within two miles on the other. These were generally, perhaps universally, honest, hard-working men; they went to meeting Sundays, morning and afternoon. " Their talk was of bullocks, and they were diligent to give the kine fodder." In their houses, generally neat as good housewifery could make them, you would find the children's school-books, commonly a " singing-book," Billing's Collection, or some other, perhaps a hymn-book, and always a good quarto Bible kept in the best room, sometimes another Bible inherited from some Puritanic ancestor; these, with an almanack hung in the corner of the kitchen chimney, made up the family library. Perhaps a weekly or semi-weekly newspaper was also taken and diligently read. Two families not far off were exceptions to this poverty of books. I now think of no more. Yet now and then the life of some great thief, like Stephen Burrow, or some pirate or highwayman, would show itself. In other parts of Lexington, " on the great road," in " the middle of the town," perhaps there was a better show of books. I only speak of my immediate neighbourhood.

From Birth till the Age of Eight.

On the 24th of August, 1810, early on a hot, sweltering morning, I came into this world of joys and sorrows. It seems one of my sisters thought an eleventh child improbable; for she had finished the " Family Tree " with the tenth—five years older than myself. However, a place was soon found for the new-comer both in the needle-work and the hearts of the household. As the youngest child, it may be supposed I was treated with uncommon indulgence, and probably received a good deal more than a tenth part of the affection distributed. I remember often to have heard neighbours say, " Why, Miss Parker, you're spilin' your boy! He never can take care of himself when he grows up." To which she replied " she hoped not," and kissed my flaxen curls anew.

Among the earliest things I remember is the longing I used to feel to have the winter gone, and to see the great snow-bank—sometimes, when new-fallen, as high as the top of the kitchen window—melt away in front of the house. I loved, though, to run in the snow barefoot, and with only my night-shirt on, for a few minutes at a time. When the snow was gone, the peculiar smell of the ground seemed to me delicious. The first warm days of spring, which brought the blue birds to their northern home, and tempted the bees to try short flights, in which they presently dropped on the straw my provident father had strewn for them over the snow about their hives, filled me with emotions of the deepest delight. In the winter I was limited to the kitchen, where I could build cob-houses, or form little bits of wood into fantastic shapes. Sometimes my father or one of my brothers would take me to the shop where he pursued his toilsome work, or to the barn, where the horse, the oxen, and the cows were a perpetual pleasure. But when the snow was gone, and the ground dry, I had free range. I used to sit or lie on the ground in a dry and sheltered spot, and watch the great yellow clouds of April, that rolled their huge masses far above my head, filling my eye with their strange, fantastic, beautiful, and ever-changing forms, and my mind with wonder at what they were, and how they came there.

But the winter itself was not without its in-door pleasure, even for a little fellow in brown home-spun petticoats. The uncles and aunts came in their sleighs full of cousins, some of whom were of my own age, to pass a long afternoon and evening, not without abundant good-cheer and a fire in "the other room," as the humble parlour was modestly named. They did not come without a great apple, or a little bag of shag-barks, or some other tid-bit for "Miss Parker's" baby; for so the youngest was called long after he ceased to merit the name. Nay, father and mother often returned these visits, and sometimes took the baby with them; because the mother did not like to leave the darling at home, or perhaps she wished to show how stout and strong her eleventh child had come into the world.

I must relate one example to show, as well as many more, the nice and delicate care she took of my moral culture. When a little boy in petticoats in my fourth year, one fine day in spring, my father led me by the hand to a distant part of the farm, but soon sent me home alone. On the way I had to pass a little "pond-hole" then spreading its waters wide; a rhodora in full bloom—a rare flower in my neighbourhood, and which grew only in that locality—attracted my attention and drew me to the spot. I saw a little spotted tortoise sunning himself in the shallow water at the root of the flaming shrub. I lifted the stick I had in my hand to strike the harmless reptile; for, though I had never killed any creature, yet I had seen other boys out of sport destroy birds, squirrels, and the like, and I felt a disposition to follow their wicked example. But all at once something checked my little arm, and a voice within me said, clear and loud, "It is wrong!" I held my uplifted stick in wonder at the new emotion—the consciousness of an involuntary but inward check upon my actions, till the tortoise and the rhodora both vanished from my sight. I hastened home and told the tale to my mother, and asked what was it that told me it was wrong? She wiped a tear from her eye with her apron, and taking me in her arms, said, "Some men call it conscience, but I prefer to call it the voice of God in the soul of man. If you listen and obey it, then it will speak clearer and clearer, and always guide you right; but if you turn a deaf ear or disobey, then it will fade out little by little, and leave you all in the dark and without a guide. Your life depends on heeding this little voice." She went her way, careful and troubled about many things, but doubtless pondered them in her motherly heart; while I went off to wonder and think it over in my poor, childish way. But I am sure no event in my life has made so deep and lasting an impression on me.

Thus it closes, but not abruptly, with the incident which marked the opening of his religious consciousness; for the life itself flows naturally on, drawing in both experience and education to make the whole of his career an amplification of the story, as he set free and vindicated in himself and others, the Life of God in the Soul of Man.

THE HOMESTEAD.

CHAPTER III.

OF the old homestead furniture Theodore possessed an oaken
table, which once belonged to John Parker, his grandfather's
grandfather. It was a substantial piece of work, and always
stood in the library. Two new legs were made for it out of the
oaken frame of the old rude farm-house, of which, excepting
these, scarcely a vestige remains. The old barn, however,
is still in existence. This farm-house faced towards the
south, and stood nearly in the centre of the farm which had
been in the family for 150 years. A cart-path led up to it
from the turnpike and went no farther. Now there is a road
passing in front of the new house, which faces to the east. The
old workshop still stands on the spot to which it was moved in
1794 from Lexington Green. A workshop indeed! What work
it did on that April morning, when it was the little belfry of
Lexington Church, and stood alone on the right hand of the
Boston Road; in the early light it gathered well-seasoned timber
from the country side, to make therefrom a cunning piece of
American joinery. When, in 1794, the new meeting-house put
forth a steeple of its own, and the bell was raised to its loft,
this old belfry was sold to Theodore's father, who moved it to
his farm, and made spokes and felloes, cider presses, and screws
in the space where the voice vibrated for the divine service of
liberty. But that reveille never got out of the rafters. It got
into Theodore, chipping and chiselling, planing and bevelling,
wasting a good deal, but learning at last not to spoil his work;
it was the old sound which afterwards rang in the sentences of
his manly indignation as he strove to rouse a new generation to
complete the father's labour.

Near the workshop stands a white ash tree which Theodore
planted thirty-six years ago from a seed, and which until the
year of his death always bore two crops of leaves, but has now

lost the singularity. Gentle critics of his theology are hereby furnished gratis with this fact that they may extol Nature's fine irony of his hatred for the exceptional and preternatural. The present garden was formerly a piece of scrub-oak which covered a rocky ledge as far as the top of the little hill behind the house, where he used to go for undisturbed study. The view from it is over a fine peat meadow, past a gently-rolling country, still liberally wooded ; and in a clear day the blue hills in Milton make the horizon. Stonybrook straggles southwardly through the meadows. Across the fields, in fair sight from the topmost rocks, where Theodore loved to read and dream, stand two great pine trees which his boyish regard had selected from the wood, one for himself and one for a favourite sister ; when the proprietor cleared the lot, his promise given to Theodore years before saved these trees from the axe.

Now their evergreen, more deep and balsamic with all the memories of the house, waves to the family across the changing fields. Just beyond them, on the turnpike, where a smart district school-house now stands, was the little old brown school-house, clinging like a lichen to the brown ground beneath the pines, whither Theodore went, three-quarters of a mile perhaps, across lots, in his first pursuit of letters. Around the farm-house was about half an acre of peach trees, now rather run out, which used to yield in fine fruit years 500 bushels of peaches. Very little produce was sold from the farm ; for the father was absorbed in his mechanical pursuits, and had turned the acres over to the boys. Theodore sometimes went to Boston to sell the peaches ; and people remember the bloom in the down of his young cheeks competing with the fruit, as he jogged down the road with it, unconscious of the ripeness he was one day to carry from the country into those streets. Elms stood like urns in the meadow. A great elm, which threatened the old house with its weight of years, has disappeared. A peach orchard is planted in front ; oaks and the ledge clothed with vines and columbines are in the rear. Half a mile farther west rises the hill called in those parts Mount Tabor ; what was once a cart-path is now a cross-road ; a simple one-storey house with door in the middle of its front, out-houses scattered about at random, a stone wall built by Theodore, near to the famous old belfry which keeps all its first oak framing unimpaired—such formed the landscape and surroundings of his youth.

DOUBLE-HEADED PINE TREE AT LEXINGTON.

The Parkers, for several generations, used to love to go to church; they were the best of hearers of the Word, and faithful doers too, but they had their own thoughts, and resolved as well as listened. Only one of these Parkers, so far as is discoverable now, ever joined the Church. He married the daughter of an orthodox deacon, and is suspected of a weakness for his wife's conventionalities. A strong digestive apparatus was hereditary in the family; but it was content with plain fare readily convertible into sinews and nerves. Theological side-dishes and hot sauces never seemed to agree with them. If the preaching on Lexington Green touched life at any point, it was welcomed; but the healthy appetite grew testy over mysteries. One can imagine the language of a sturdy countryman, disappointed of a righteous meal, and solemnly waved in to partake of the impossible. Tertullian's creed was instinctively rejected; the family was Unitarian long before the partizan phrase became known. It always wanted to stand upon the ground, though it would look beyond the stars; honest reverence, loyalty and trust, a scrupulous sense of duty, a love for neighbours, a hatred of all meanness and grossness, were never wanting. Hannah Stearns brought, with all a woman's tenderness and delicacy, a rare devoutness, itself unfettered, into this liberal family.

She belonged to the Church; and all her children had been christened, neighbours duly standing surety. Theodore, the last, and the mother's darling, must be christened in his turn. This ceremony was performed at home, when he was about two and half years old. Great was the gathering of friends and neighbours! As the water was sprinkled on his head, he entered his first protest against ceremonies, by lustily fighting off the clergyman, and ejaculating, "Oh, don't!" His curiosity about the whole affair did not speedily die out; and as he was always terrible for asking "Why?"—except when asked to do something for love—he "wanted to know" about being wetted, and what object the participators had in view. We have no doubt he received a sensible answer. But he did not struggle against the baptism of his mother's spirit, who led him through all his childish misgivings, though she did not discover the depth of all of them, into a tranquil recognition of the Divine Love.

Religion was the inheritance my mother gave—gave me in my birth—gave me in her teachings. Many sons have been better born than I, few have had so good a mother. I mention these things to show you how I came to have the views of religion that I have now. My head is not more natural to my body—has not more grown with it than my religion out of my soul and with it. With me religion was not carpentry, something built up of dry wood, from without; but it was growth—growth of a germ in my soul.*

There was an interval of five years between Theodore and the tenth child, so that he had no playmate for a time but his mother.

"Miss Parker, I reckon you're spilin' that boy." She used to smile, and hope not. We are not sure that his theological troubles would have begun so early if this gentle mother had mustered courage to chase him out among the boys; and, quick-witted as she was, he did not betray to her how a mob of notions hustled and bullied him.

"When a very small boy," he says, "there was no character in history that I knew so well as Jesus." For this he was in the mother's debt. But he "remembered with horror and a quivering of the flesh," the torment he underwent when he first found, in a copy of the Westminster Catechism, the doctrines of eternal damnation and a wrathful God. He was a little over six when he fell out with them.

I can scarcely think without a shudder of the terrible effect the doctrine of eternal damnation had on me. How many, many hours have I wept with terror as I laid on my bed and prayed, till between praying and weeping sleep gave me repose. But before I was nine years old this fear went away, and I saw clearer light in the goodness of God. But for years, say from seven to ten, I said my prayers with much devotion, I think, and then continued to repeat "Lord, forgive my sins," till sleep came on me.†

Either he kept the doctrine to himself as something horrible he had stumbled over in his play, the one black corner in the sunny house, or else father and mother had no idea of the way in which it haunted him. This experience was destined to be the first one of the many in which he had to feel his way alone. The child instinctively hugged the bitter moment of his opening consciousness, though it tore him. But his mother's influence was unimpaired; she never weaned him. He was not thinking of his own early life when he said, many years later, "Some parents have a strange way of educating their children; they

---

* MS. Sermon : on leaving West Roxbury.
† Journal, Jan., 1839. See also his story in "Sermons of Theism," p. 126.

take the breast from them spiritually as well as corporeally ; they do not train them up in love but in fear."

His early troubles on the subject of immortality are thus described in a letter to an Irish lady :—

When I was a large boy, and had felt more than I had reflected, I heard a minister preach on the immortal life. He told the arguments for it, said they were all of no value, guesses, but hardly *at* truth, only *after* it : the only sufficient proof was the resurrection of Jesus Christ. Boy as I was, I saw the folly of that as an argument to prove a universal proposition; but, boy as I was, I could not reason the matter out, and in default of understanding prove my immortality; so I felt constrained to doubt, almost to deny it. Some weeks passed over, weeks of torment ; at last spontaneous nature came to my help; and I settled the question, not intellectually and by philosophy, but sentimentally—in the child's way, not the man's. It was not till years after that I found a philosophy that satisfied the intellectual demands and helped me to prove it to myself.

I have no more doubt of my eternal life—eternally *conscious*, eternally *progressive*, than of my present and mortal condition. But I do not pretend to know anything about the *form* of that life or its conditions. Since I believe the entire *goodness of God*, which you so beautifully speak of, I have no fear—no desire to know more about the form of the next life, or rather of the next stage of this life. If I had only reason, which cares little about persons and deals more with ideas, I should not think, I suppose, or care about meeting my friends in the next stage of life; but as I have affections, more powerful, too, than reason, I cannot doubt that I shall see and know my friends in heaven. Once I did not think so; but at the grave's mouth, as it closed on a sister, I could not doubt where my logic had failed me. Nature came in and completed her work.*

Nature has a marvellous faculty of turning to account the " mumps and measles " of childhood. Her aim is to develope or to restore the spiritual health. Theodore was saved from drugs and quacking ; pure air, simple habits, and a loving home kept the catechism at bay ; while the sensitive soul, which had its crises almost before the body could dispose of its own, threw off the maladies which so seldom recur. He grew thus in power and sensibility ; and, succeeding these keen trials of his natural vigour, how simple and comely was his growth.

In the traces made by these trials awe and confidence sprung up, a profound conviction that a divine life pervaded all things, and an unassailable willingness to trust in it. No child was ever so loyal to its parents as his soul to this Father whom he

* May 5, 1848.

found caring for the country, for the farm and all its creatures, for himself among them. This was the ground of his future life. This positive spiritual enjoyment was so great in him, that his mind was active for a long time before it criticised and rejected the ordinary Unitarian theology. The religion of his boyhood grew more and more absorbing, the experience of successive years deepened it, gifts and acquisitions fell sparkling into its clearness and were seen through it, all the while theology touched him but lightly and did not trouble him. His views at that time of the Old and New Testaments, of miracles and inspiration, when pronounced at all, were not given with much emphasis, and were of the ordinary kind, as we shall shortly see.

No child ever had a purer piety. His soul was open night and day to heavenly influences. He and his visitant knew no frontier; and he lived so honestly, without tricks and lying, infested by no habits, untempted even by simple country dissipations, so homely and brotherly, yet so remote, that his soul never seemed to suspect that men could have other homes. Nothing stole in and slammed the door in his face. It was wide open, through all the strife and bitterness which beset his maturity; but the dust of the battle never rolled up to dispute the light on that threshold. In 1858, preaching to the Progressive Friends, he can say :—

I have swam in clear, sweet waters all my days; and if sometimes they were a little cold, and the stream ran adverse and something rough, it was never too strong to be breasted and swam through. From the days of earliest boyhood, when I went stumbling through the grass, "as merry as a May bee," up to the grey-bearded manhood of this time, there is none but has left me honey in the hive of memory that I now feed on for present delight. When I recall the years of boyhood, youth, early manhood, I am filled with a sense of sweetness and wonder that such little things can make a mortal so exceedingly rich! But I must confess that the chiefest of all my delights is still the religious. This is the lowest down, the inwardest of all—it is likewise highest up. What delight have I in my consciousness of God, the certainty of His protection, of His infinite love? God loves me as my natural mother never did, nor could, nor can, even now, with the added beatitudes of wellnigh two-score years in heaven. How the religious disposition inclines the little boy or girl to veneration and gratitude, virtues which in the child are what good-breeding is in the full-grown gentleman, giving a certain air of noble birth and well-bred superiority! There is a Jacob's ladder for our young pilgrim, whereon he goes up from his earthly mother, who manages the little room he sleeps in, to the dear Heavenly Mother, who never slumbers nor sleeps, who is never careful nor troubled about anything, but yet cares continually for the great housekeeping of all the world, giving likewise to her beloved even in their sleep. In the child it is only the faint twilight, the beginning, of religion which you take notice of, like the voice of the blue bird and the Phœbe, coming early in March, but only as a prelude to that whole summer of joyous song which, when the air is delicate, will ere long gladden and beautify the procreant nest.

This is a form of piety, springing up, like a form of polity suitable for a new world, with the wild flowers at Lexington. In its incense there is no smell of scented ambergris, but rather the smell of the fresh ground. No haggard and yellow-skinned mysticism, fed on parchment and the air of cells, loving God with passion, and Christ like a bridegroom, straining body and language to the point of tenuity to make out an artificial rapture : no doting on phrases and abnormal ecstatic conditions. The free west-wind on our hill-sides sweeps off this calenture— the east-wind, strong with iodine from the sea-weed, sweeps it out of the healthy boy while he is gathering New-England flowers.

It freshened what it swept through, and whirled nothing really tender away. When still quite young, he never went to a new place, or found himself in a wood or field or street striking to his sense, or not visited before, without indulging in quiet prayer ; " for the unknown was to me doubly holy." A natural ascription connected places and incidents with the great life over all. He said, " My Father in heaven," at every moment of awe, joy, or pain. Finding a scarce flower in the wet meadow, inhaling the piny odours, seeing first the spring blades in the garden, weeping at stories of Indian captivities, basking in the May sun at the top of the ledge, feeling the mother's heart in every room of the house,—no trick of consciousness shut up the word he had with God about it all, or hinted that a word would be highly proper.

We have seen that he tried at first, by asking the Lord to forgive his sins when he had none " to speak of," to pray himself into the conviction that his nature was depraved, and that damnation was a thing to be remembered in the days of his youth. This came from a catechism that was lying about the house. These old bundles of rags which emigration brings over will carry infection for a long while. Quarantine and a thorough smoking out is the only remedy. Few people were ever less depraved than he, or carried from birth a will and temperament more sympathetic for pure and noble things. A hasty temper, almost always the characteristic of sincere and morally indignant persons, but sometimes in the end mistaken for sincerity by them, was the only grave fault he had to struggle with. No kind of physical indulgence ever seemed to tempt him for a moment. He caught no habits from coarse boys, and his imagination was chaste as a girl's. Nothing crept into him through the loop-hole of an idle moment. When he was not at work in the field, or tinkering in the shop, he was deep in a book. In his day-dreams he looked down through a cool well : there was the blue sky at the bottom. He was very ambitious to perform all his tasks, to find out all that was learnable, to put the best foot foremost ; but the gifts of others only stimulated his immense energy. Later he has been accused of envying distinguished men ; but the root of envy was never in him. Not a trace of it can be found in the recollections of school-mates and kindred ; but, on the contrary, all the intimates of his boyhood testify how naïve and kind he was. Wrestling is a favourite rural fashion of testing back and wind : he wrestled with every mind, and openly emulated all his mates. " We love to measure ourselves," he said, afterwards, "that we may know our power, and approbation is welcome as assuring us of success ; but the true test of the purity of our feeling is whether we are also rejoiced to see another receive greater approbation for a better thing. A desire of future fame is only better than that of present applause as it is an appeal to mankind in its sanity and wisdom. To a great soul the presence of a superior is the greatest of blessings." * Men would call him envious because he did not worship their superiors as his own, and withheld his consent from the vicious estimate which made intelligence more loveable than righteousness.

But as a boy he was bashful, painfully conscious of a certain awkwardness ; and would underrate himself so far as to ask his teacher not to say that he wrote a composition, for fear that his name would reduce its appreciable value. He honestly felt it was good for something, and honestly doubted that he was esteemed. A burning flush and a suffused blue eye showed how sensitive he was to praise or blame. His simple delight in

---

* Saturday Afternoon Conversations, held with members of his parish. Feb. 24, 1849.

praise was as distant from ordinary egotism as sincere praise itself is. Here is something to the point, of his own record :—

I went to Boston—lectured before the men of colour upon the Signs of the Times. I have not been so much gratified with any applause received this long time as to-night. When Mr. Nell announced me, and that, too, as *a friend of mankind*, the negroes applauded. I was never so much gratified but once before ; that was years ago, when I was a little boy, at an examination of the district school. A spectator, one of the general committee of the town, asked my father, " Who was that fine boy who spoke up so smart ?". My father said, " Oh, that is one of *my* boys, the youngest." When my father told it at home that John Murray had asked so, I felt a deep joy, not so much for my own sake as for the satisfaction it seemed to give my father. I like this applause that comes up in the deep ground-tones of humanity; all other I care little for—" it plays round the head, but comes not to the heart." I don't think I could withstand a righteous condemnation —not I.*

This simple disposition, content with sympathy, and influenced only by the glory of knowing true things and of being true to them, never changed. The boy never told a lie or committed a meanness. He grew hot all over at hearing of wrongs, at witnessing slights ; so he did sometimes when contemptuously slighted. He was combative to defend, but never known to be aggressive. His courage was above suspicion, being the frankness of his moral sense in action. He was a rigid boy, but never took airs among freer companions ; no one was more tolerant of infirmities and angry with malice and chicane. His worst ambitions were proud motions which his mind made in the first self-consciousness of its great energies, as it were, like a young athlete, with short, scornful lip, superbly testing his symmetry and power. Then he thought he might become what he pleased, and visions of legal and political renown enchanted him for awhile. But such dreams could not for long beguile his manly and unselfish heart. He shrank from seeking any-thing for himself but a place to work in, though he was early conscious that he had a great capacity for work, and lofty aims that would chafe in any low or - dull routine. He sometimes said what he thought about this, as about everything else ; and there is no doubt that his strength often surged within him like a passion, and shook his temperate bounds till they trembled. In no respect did the man change from this, excepting that the controversies, which might be expected to unmask his testy

* Journal, Nov. 19, 1844.

humour, brought out instead his warlike disposition, and woke up an indignant sincerity ; but there was no place for mere touchiness in his formidable wrath.

He could not pray himself into the belief that he was a great sinner for a boy. The first hypocrisy which surprised him in the venerable garb of religion was the only one of his life, and in disposing of it his soul began its free, organic growth. If we know what a boy is, we can anticipate how he will talk about sin when he is a man; for whatever sin itself may be, the human statements of the fact will always betray a diversity in the mode of contemplating it. The practical contrast between a virtuous and a vicious life is plain enough : virtue seems normal and appropriate to man, and vice is constantly threatening the general health and order ; but what is the essential ground of vice, and what is its purpose? There must be some reason for the contradictory theories which try to answer those questions. The disputants mutually accuse each other of ignorance of spiritual laws : those who japan their systems with scriptural phrases, complain that their opponents will not accept the Bible theory of sin ; but the scripturalists themselves agree only in a liberal use of the japanning. Human nature is intrinsically bad, because the divine nature premeditated sin ; yet it is not inconsistent to declare that sin is enmity towards God, who predestined it—something devilish. Man has altogether gone astray ; his nature is a corrupt root, his will is not normally inclined to health ; there is no good in him, or, if there is, it is continually at the mercy of a lower law. This is scene-painting, and not definition. When compelled to weigh in nice scales these phrases, that their essential value may be tested and represented in spiritual equivalents, believers in depravity quarrel about their favourite word, because they really estimate moral evil by their own temperament and moral condition. The scriptural agreement is merely forced by the preconception of an infallible and supernaturally-inspired Book ; so that many a liberal disposition goes up and down yelling in war-paint, and flourishing tomahawks of texts. Especially if pantheists and naturalists are suspected to be settling in the neighbourhood, and threaten to encroach upon their hunting-grounds, every shade of orthodoxy rallies, and vermillion uniforms the league. If anybody is found who speculates a way of escape for the Infinite Goodness from complicity with moral evil, the dull texts rain upon his head. The effort is attributed to depravity itself, seeking for immunity. He has personal reasons for surmising that every bad act is only an inchoate good one; or, that evil is goodness underdone; or, that it is the schoolmaster bringing men to knowledge and self-consciousness; or, that the Divine Impartiality digests all actions into healthy history; or, that a developing God feels his way from stage to stage of matter, choosing thus gradually to eliminate its coarseness, clearly seeing the end of beauty; or, that all creating is but a coming to self-consciousness of the primæval mind through difficulties. But the feeling which invents such statements is a pure one; the conviction that human nature is intrinsically good because the divine nature is absolutely perfect, goes masquerading in them all.

In the meantime, both orthodox and liberal will show the colour of the leaf on which they feed. The black and passionate temperament will speak of moral evil in the Bible's most sombre language—the fair transparent disposition will borrow the most innocent and optimistic texts. Some natures grow with all the simplicity and fragrance of a flower, drawing only limpid sap from the black earth, conscious of passion by report alone. The pulse is even, the flesh is always cool, the eyes serene. Their faults have no malignity, the will is always disposed to deference, the imagination secretes no acrid and petulant images. The poisonous elements of life seem unconsciously rejected by this frank and florid organization. It never can recollect any crisis such as the theologians call a change of heart, and never desires it, except when infected sentimentally by a revival. Nothing may be very deep, but everything has been natural—a sense of dependence, a preference for cleanly and honest ways, a love of duty. There was nothing insurrectionary in the primitive motive.

But other natures have inherited the element of an internal conflict. They always have a great deal of trouble in learning to tell the truth, to keep the peace, to repress envious feelings; their fancy is precocious, and curiously anticipates the secrets of life, and is tormented with day-dreams of love or ambition. They fall into bad habits; have wretched seasons of remorse, which alternate with indulgence; they are secretive, and have a touch of the demoniacal. They are selfish, or hypocritical, or vindictive, or treacherous, or sensual, or proud, or all of these, according to the quantitive relations of their passions and affections. But their growth is more like the campaign of two armies than the silent ripening of summer nights and days. They have to fight for every inch of ground they occupy.

The first class speaks of sin blandly, except when horror-stricken at the sight of it, or conventionally taught to use the scripture terms. Clergymen of this kind are sometimes intellectually committed to human depravity and the concurrent doctrines; but their inmost feeling never preaches it. Both the pure and the passionate who live where the doctrine has its full traditional sweep, and is not vigorously criticised, will accept it.* Gentle young people will sometimes appear to suffer under conviction of sin. It is the sin of a traditional theology rioting in morbid conditions of the mind or body. If they become clergymen, and continue their bad health, they will continue to use bad language and defame human nature. But their sweet and blameless life totters under the ponderous phrases and shoots naïve glances at the listeners.

The people who have a great deal of trouble with their passions will remember their personal discomfort when they speak of moral evil. If they change their whole course of life, clean out their fancies, and banish their ambitions, they will estimate sin at the rate of effort and suffering they have endured. A clergyman who has lived a rather stormy youth will, if he has talent and dramatic power, astonish an audience with his knowledge of the demoniacal element, and convince them for a while that neither in himself nor in them is there one good thing. And how many good things he will say! Whatever faithfully repeats a personal experience is useful to men. But if a bad experience sets up to be a system of the universe, and to represent a divine intention that omits no soul, it is a hideous idol, and the pulpit its lumbering car in which it overrides all natural distinctions.

Now, between talking about moral evil, making one's personal

---

* After reading Miller's Life of Jonathan Edwards, Mr. Parker records his impression. "A most remarkable child, youth and man, mild, gentle and most lovely. How such a person must have revolted, naturally, from the stern, sour doctrines of Calvinism. How his heart must bleed before it could admit the dreadful doctrines—total depravity and eternal damnation, and the like. Oh! if they wrung his soul as they have wrung mine, it must have bled." Edwards's account of the developing of his spiritual life, which he calls his conversion, has hardly a trace of these doctrines, though there is a free use of the conventional phrases. With animal spirits and a robuster frame, his sense of his own wickedness would have considerably diminished.

Mr. Parker copied, for his own use, many of the resolutions which Jonathan Edwards wrote down before he was 20.

experience a subject of rhetoric, and defining the fact itself, there is a vast difference. The latter can only be approximately done by knowledge, as it subsidizes physical and moral science, and their analysis of human actions. The phenomena of moral evil are, like all other phenomena, subjects for a scientific investigation, that is, a complete observation of the inner and the outer man —including his locality, climate, culture, and circumstances. But anybody can talk about moral evil, from tradition and from feeling. The contradictory language which people equally sincere make use of in their attempts to speak of moral evil, is owing to their want of precise inductions from a sufficient number of facts ; in other words, to their want of knowledge. And believers of every shade of liberality think that they furnish a portable definition of sin, when in reality they are only expressing themselves ; their phrases are the net result of all their characteristics, or else a mere repetition of the tradition current in their circles. Allowing for disturbances, such as artificial teaching, and the truculent sentimentalism of conferences and revivals, it is true that the bias of a man's youth will decide his conception of the fact of sin.

Mr. Parker was healthily built, within and without, open to the air and sun, with no uncanny corners to catch dirt and vermin, and not a single rat-hole in the whole house. He shrank from vicious and slatternly habits, but knew perfectly well that he had neither. So that he could not pray against the whole sincerity of his nature in favour of any dogmatic statement of evil. At first he tried to force a conviction that in sin did his mother conceive him ; but the ingenuous boy learned, through much weeping, a holier feeling concerning himself and his mother. The unnatural attempt at last gave way to a sense of the Infinite Love, which kept his mind and heart bathed in health until maturer knowledge opened the question again, as we shall see, when the facts of evil challenged his youthful sentiment, and the understanding and the moral disposition came to terms. But a temperament undisturbed by the grosser impulses, full of warmth at feeling or perceiving wrong, neither secretive nor selfish, but magnanimous, indignant, plain-spoken, ruled by a very fastidious conscience, and penetrated by a tender piety,—this controlled his future treatment of evil and his views of sin.

But he was very early sensitive to the qualities of actions and feelings. It was almost a morbid delicacy, such as we find in weaker natures the cause of a precocious mysticism or ultra-Calvinistic views. Examples of this disease are sometimes paraded, in the interest of a preternatural theology, as evidences of early conversions from nature to grace. If this spiritual sensibility in the little Theodore had not been vigorously matched by a promising digestion, or if the family inheritance of consumption had developed earlier, the catechism might have done him some damage, and his clear strong soul might have had a harder conflict. Stalwart trappers will sometimes get debilitated by swamp mists, scurvy fare, and Indians. But Theodore came off embrowned, elastic, far-sighted, tenacious on the war-trail. The early trial taught him betimes the great secret of successful warfare, to reduce your baggage to its effective minimum. He was trained to dispense with the doctrinal impediments, and went into life carrying rations sufficient for the march.

Here he records an opportunity he had to attempt shouldering innate enmity and a perverse will. It is from a letter to a friend.

Did I ever tell you of the earliest fact of consciousness I ever felt pained at ? When in my 4th year my father had a neighbour, Deacon Stearns, come to kill a calf. My father would not do it himself, as other farmers did. I was not allowed to see the butchery; but after it was all over, the Deacon, who had lost all his children, asked me who I loved best? "Papa." "What! Better than yourself?" "Yes, sir." "But," said my father, "if one of us must take a whipping, which would you rather should have the blows?" I *said* nothing, but wondered and wondered why I should prefer that he should have the blows and not I. The fact was plain, and plainly selfish, and, it seemed to me, wicked. Yet I could not help the feeling. It tormented me for weeks in my long clothes.

Long clothes are certainly embarrassing, especially in the pursuit of truth. Many a seeker trips himself up and lies a mere heap of clothing by the way ; but Theodore soon got out of long clothes, and had a suit of lasting, for all work, comfortable to the sturdy limbs and delicate perceptions.

Here is a reminiscence which finds its place in this period of childhood. It is an extract from a letter written to a divinity classmate in 1839.

Death is no more to a man than the change from the infant's "long-clothes" to the "frock and trousers" of the boy. I understand, therefore, why Swedenborg found men in the other world who had forgotten all about their death; in a word, did not remember they had ever died. Perhaps most men do not remember anything about their change from baby-clothes to the boy's dress. I have not forgotten all about my change of dress. I remember that I cried, and struggled most lustily against the new dress; and when my legs were squeezed into their new envelopes, I was so ashamed that I went into the fields to hide myself. I doubt that I should complain half so much if death were to come with the new suit, and tell me to lay aside my rags.

Out of school there were various jobs for him about the house; he became a working member of the family as soon as he could steady himself upon two stout legs. All the chips must be picked up, to begin with; then he had wood to bring in, pretty soon to drive the cows to pasture, carry grain to the horse, and "*nubs* of corn to the oxen." His father was very fond of animals, a close observer of their habits; he had a respectful way of treating them, which taught his children to show kindness to every animated form. He always prevented them from witnessing any slaughtering operation. In the workshop Theodore learned to hold the chalk-line, to know the different tools and fetch them. He loved to make things, and became very expert; for he had a fitting and joining faculty not eventually to be limited by glue and scantling.

Across the meadow he went to that little brown district school-house; for he did not fancy following the cart-path into the turnpike, but saved time by putting stepping-stones across the brook. School was kept for the smallest children twelve or sixteen weeks in spring and summer; the winter term was twelve weeks long. For a year or two Theodore went to school both summer and winter, but after 1817–18 only in winter. He trudged off alone, or in bad weather was carried round, with a well-conned lesson, and a heart full of the new surmises of his conscience.

He was about six years of age when he begun to go to this public school. Oliver Locke was the male teacher, and "Aunt Pattie" (Mary Smith) the female. He was in Aunt Pattie's department. John Hastings succeeded in 1818. Theodore, then eight years old, dearly loved play, and was never left out of any game. Bat and ball, bows and arrows, and pop-guns, were successively rages. When pop-guns came in, he got his elder brother to construct one of the largest calibre, which he took to school. Till its range and effect were tested, he was very miserable; his young idea refused to shoot. Promptly, to solve the pain of a divided duty, he let it off. "Who fired that gun?"

Theodore's lips were spelling words with prodigious abandonment. Presently, however, his desire again overcame him—for such a sonorous pop-gun who would not brave the ferule—off it went, just as John Hastings happened to look up. Alas ! the reckless gunner, with his own hands, must consign his piece to the stove, where it crackled pitilessly to a reprimand.

His pop-gun was always of the biggest, for his mark was far and high.

He was never unpopular with his schoolmates, but they stood somewhat in awe of him, partly on account of his quantity ot character, and partly because he was so keen for the ridiculous, and had such overwhelming powers of mimicry ; the gait, gesture, tone of voice and pet phrases, even the habit of thinking, and the average opinions of a person, were all faithfully reproduced by him. This talent was afterwards the delight of intimates in the study at West Roxbury and in Exeter Palace, where politicians, professors, and clergymen slid, without extenuation or malice, through the dissolving views of his hilarious hours.

His weight of character was once well shown when he was hardly nine ; an old farmer came to the school-house to complain of some trick which the boys had played with his horse and waggon. His rage was not to be appeased without a victim. But the master, after asking one or two, came to Theodore, and said, " Theodore, do you know anything about this ? " Theodore got up and quietly remarked, " I don't know anything about it, sir." There was gravity enough in the reply for a complete outfit ; all the little fellows, culprits included, received their allowance, and the old man went away impressed with the collective innocence.

He was apt to be rough at play, and to tumble his comrades about in a shaggy fashion, as if with great, humorous paws ; but he never bullied or wilfully vexed them. All his strength was awkward then, but not unkind. And there was always in the school a wholesome sense that he could not bear to see anybody " put upon." Still we do not hear that he had lovers ; and if there were any who looked at him through devoted eyes, his glances repaid only protection and humanity. The little eyes did not meet his at a level, yet his never ceased to go hungering for their mates.

When Theodore was only eight, he was called one of the

greatest readers in the town. His father owned a share in the "Social Library," and was a devourer of books. Instead of visiting his neighbours when work was done, he sat down with his family around the dining table, where all quietly read. The women mended and darned the stockings at the same table, and the father read aloud what struck him. The old grandmother sat in the flickering fire-light—the past flickered in her mind. Much was learned in these winter evenings. Father and mother taught far beyond the school; they taught Theodore to be curious about human affairs, and the characters of famous men. He became such a glib expositor of the current politics, that older people liked to draw him out by pretended opposition; then his opinion grew ardent enough. But he also had books of his own to read, which his father brought him from the library.

When a little boy, an old man overtook me going to school, and walked a mile with me. He told me what it was possible for a bright boy to *do* and to *be*—what I might do and be; it had a great influence on me. I began to think I " might be somebody."

Homer and Plutarch I read before I was eight; Rollin's Ancient History about the same time; and lots of histories, with all the poetry I could find, before ten. I took to metaphysics about eleven or twelve.

We had in the family some MS. histories of the Segur family, and their captivity among the Indians; also Mrs. Rowlandson's adventures. Mother knew by heart many family histories of the old New-England times, and used to tell them to me. We had also a folio volume of travels in the Levant, which interested me much, as soon as I could read, and to this day; father and mother always read the books first, and examined me in every book I read. If I could not give a good account of it, I must not have another till I could satisfy the rigorous demands of father.

I began to write verses at eight, and could repeat at ten a poem of 500 or 1000 lines after a single reading, or a song from hearing it once. I used to commit the hymns which the minister was reading, and before the choir began to sing.

At ten I made a catalogue of all the vegetable productions, trees, and shrubs, which grew upon the farm; there were many of which I could not find the names, so I invented them—fanciful enough.

We had a copy of Morse's large Geography, which helped me a good deal, and a folio copy of Evelyn's celebrated Sylva. It was a great treasure to me; it contained bits of poetry too, which delighted me, passages from Tusser and Chaucer, which I had not seen before.

Mr. Lyman's garden, at Waltham, filled me with admiration at the rare trees, plants, and shrubs, which I did not know. I went there when twelve or thirteen. Then the foreign fruits which I saw at my first visit to Boston, the tropical husks and leaves which came wrapped around bales of merchandize, tea-chests, and other boxes, stimulated my love of nature still more.

I used to inquire after the conformation of the hills in other parts of the country, which I had never seen. In my neighbourhood they all had their steep sides towards the south and east. I always asked boys—and men when I dared—who came from a distance, if it were so in their country. I commonly got the answer, "*I den know.*" An Englishman told me about the peat mounds in Britain, which I could not account for. I got together all the odd stones, &c., I could find. A neighbour once brought me in my fourteenth year a bit of brown oxide of manganese, which abounded on the farm of his son in Vermont, and wanted to know what it was. It took me a day or two to find out, with the rude chemical apparatus I had made; but I did —and told him, to the amusement of the neighbours.

At ten I began to study Latin. This continued five winters, in which time I read the usual elementary books, with Virgil, Cicero's Select Orations and Sallust. I began Greek at eleven. Natural Philosophy, Astronomy, Chemistry and Rhetoric I studied by myself. Astronomy had always interested me much. When twelve years old I once saw the crescent form of Venus with my naked eye. It amazed me. Nobody else could see it; father was not at home. Nobody knew that the planets exhibit this form. So I hunted after a book on Astronomy, and got it from the schoolmaster, and found out the fact and its reason.

His first school composition was on "The Starry Heavens;" the teacher found fault with it—that it was too short.

In the summer "nooning," when the hands were lolling in the shade, Theodore took out his book, and kept tilling and sowing while others slept. He never shirked his chores of work, but the book came into all lawful intervals.

The father was too poor to buy many books. Theodore must find his own methods to appease this ravening for knowledge. He early began to help himself to what he wanted. Nothing was strong enough to dull for a moment this instinctive necessity of his mind—no amusement, no accomplishment. Dancing cost too much to learn, though it was thought highly of, and country balls were courtly occasions. But money must be saved for books. With the proceeds of a whortleberrying campaign in 1822, he bought his first book. He had to carry the berries to Boston for sale; so the city purchased the incunabulum of the noble library of 11,000 volumes, which he bequeathed to it at last.

In 1820, William H. White, afterwards a highly-esteemed Unitarian clergyman, took the South District school at Lexington, and taught there two winters. He saw the ambition and capacity of Theodore, and led him along with the tenderest sympathy. Nothing but English studies were pursued in the school ; but Mr. White volunteered to teach him Latin, and afterwards Greek.

The "Historia Sacra" was his first Latin book, with Smith's Latin Grammar and Young's Dictionary for help, all of them long out of print, and replaced by better books. He became very much attached to Mr. White, and years after used to write him tender and grateful letters.

I shall never cease to thank you for starting me in Latin,* and in Greek too, nor shall I ever forget how I hid my head in the bed-clothes and cried—for I was sick then, and could not rise—when they told me that you would not keep school next winter, but a stranger was coming.

The stranger was Mr. George Fiske, who kept it for three winters, and of whom it is told, that happening to misquote scripture one morning, Theodore rose in his seat and put him right, much to the edification of the school. The boy's memory already promised the vigour and capaciousness which afterwards brought home and warehoused such varied spoils. The teachers used to extol his memory first, and his rapid acquisition next.

Now let us see how much schooling he received. Eleven weeks each winter, from 1817 to 1827, and two summer terms, from 1817 to 1819. At 16 years of age, he had one quarter at the Lexington Academy. That was all. Algebra was added to Latin and Greek at the Academy. He mastered Colburn's Algebra in 20 days. In the winter of 1827, being then 17, he began to teach : the first winter, a district school in Quincy, the second in North Lexington, the third in Concord, and the fourth in Waltham, working on the farm and in the shop the rest of the year. The farmers used to reckon that the work their boys could do in the winter season was about equal to the cost of their board ; there was no objection, then, if they wanted to

---

* He was ready enough to learn Latin ; for a Catholic cradle-hymn, which he found in an old magazine when he was hardly seven, had tormented him a good deal. Nobody around him could unlock the mystery, only his brother told him it was Latin. The word "Jesu" filled him with an intense desire to know the meaning. Almost forty years after he fell in with it again, and thus translated it :—

Dormi Jesu—mater ridet	Slumber, Jesu—mother smileth
Quæ tam dulcem somnum videt ;	As sweet sleep her babe beguileth,
Dormi, Jesu, blandule !	Darling Jesu, go to sleep !
Si non dormis mater plorat,	If art waking mother mourneth,
Inter fila cantans orat,	Singing, as her spindle turneth,
Blande veni somnule.	"Gently, little slumber creep."

leave home. But if Theodore taught school during any other weeks of the year, or left home to make a visit, he hired a man to take his place and work on the farm. So he did when he left home finally, at the age of 19 : for two years, till he was 21, he furnished his father with a labourer.

At 17 he began to *train*, with what recollections of Lexington Green and Captain Parker we may imagine. He was very active and punctual in the discharge of his military duties, was clerk of the company, and rose even to the grandeur of a lieutenancy, or, as some say, he was ensign. If he ever did bear the colours at muster or May-training, it was with gravity, no doubt, and certain private thoughts of the value of the symbol. As clerk, he called the roll of the company ; the famous names were still upon it.*

So he trained, ploughed, built stone-walls, made spokes, bored pumps, mended farm tools, filled each crevice with a book, and lifted the varied toil with generous and aspiring thought. If from the school teaching he had any money left, after sumptuously paying his substitute, it went for books, long anticipated, dearly cherished as the blossoming of all his labour. He pushed his way to Greece and Rome, and far outread the average for his years. If he made an evening visit, he would study till two or three o'clock in the morning. At Waltham, he began to teach French, after taking a few lessons; a little later we find him mastering Spanish.

In the summer of 1830, the day before his birth-day, he went away from home, and was absent till near midnight. He had received permission from his father to be gone for a day, but was unwilling to say wherefore ; so nobody knew where he had gone. Returning, he went up to his father's bed-side, and said, "Father, I entered Harvard College to-day." He had spent the whole day in undergoing examination at Cambridge. The perplexity of the old man at his mysterious absence was not lessened when he heard the cause. " Why, Theodore ! you know I cannot support you there." " I know that, Father ; I mean to stay at home, and keep up with my class." He had quietly prepared to enter the freshman class. He remained at

---

* He did not like to see any popular indifference to the militia-system, and used to say that the time would come when we should depend upon it, and regret that it had not been vigorously sustained. He thought it one of the best things in Governor Banks, that he cherished the militia and strove to renew its effectiveness.

home another winter, doing all his work, carrying on his studies, and going down to Cambridge to participate in the examinations. He was not entitled to a degree, because he had been a non-resident, and had not paid tuition fees. But afterwards, at the kindly representation of his friend, Mr. Francis, of Watertown, the usual degree of A.B. was offered to him on payment of the usual fees of instruction for four years. But this amounted to a considerable sum, altogether beyond Theodore's ability; and he could not buy his degree. The degree of A.M. was afterwards bestowed upon him (*honoris causâ*) in 1840.

Here is an entry in his journal for August 23, 1850 :—

It is this day twenty years since I entered Harvard College! What misgiving I had at that time. Yet how joyfully I went home and told my father—a-bed, but not asleep—that I had entered Harvard College. How joyfully I went to work again the next day! But what changes since! Then I had a father and three sisters—a few friends whom now-a-days I never see. What sad times have I passed through since —not without the Star of Faith to guide me.

After making the above record, his prayer follows; for on all days set apart in any strong or tender way by memory his heart flowed forth in supplication :—

Father, who hast been my Help and my Reliance hitherto—in the dangerous period of passion, and my trial of poverty—be with me now in the more dangerous period of ambition. Help me to be one with Thee, obedient to Thy will in my heart, and faithful to all the monitions of thy guiding Spirit. If other twenty years pass by me, make me by so much a nobler, greater, better man.

The following extract is made from his journal for 1840 :—

I went a Sunday or two ago to preach in my native village. It was with no small emotion I ventured into the old pulpit, filled with so much holiness in my youth—a place so sacred that I scarcely dared place my unholy feet therein when a boy. But once, I remember, a Sunday noon, putting up a prayer in it, as a place peculiarly holy. How well has that prayer been answered! Great God, I thank Thee; for the recollection of that hour is warm within me. I prayed for wisdom; for the means of learning. Certainly, I have found the latter. I had the beginning of wisdom then—the fear and love of God.

The next spring, he left his father's house, never to return to it, save at long intervals and for hurried visits. Devout mother and downright simple-minded father had done their best for him. He had done the rest, finding help in every furrow of the farm, in the flowers of the meadow, the cool sincerity of midnight skies, the health of the wide country. His own hands had culled this harvest in the fields. Both mental method and religion had grown standing in an open lot. Self-denying, hardworking, homely boy, blooming with ambition and hope, refined by clean and pious thoughts—another wild-flower of New England's soil—with all the self-reliance and sturdiness of Franklin, and all the religion and moral delicacy which Franklin had not, he goes wandering after his work in life. He never changed. Meadow, wood, and sky went with him, everywhere looking after their dear child, lending fragrance and independence to the last. Not toned in a conventional atmosphere, having the politeness which is unstudied motion, and more sincerity than taste, grasping strongly things rather than phrases—a smooth spade-cutter, a liberal pruner, a broadcast-sower, and judicious with the harrow— the old farm sends him forth an Emancipator, and not an Amateur.

THE LEDGE.

CHAPTER IV.

Teaching in Boston—Hard Study—Dejection and its causes—Private School in Watertown, April, 1832—Theological Studies—Dr. Francis—Watertown people—Enters
the Theological School, 1834—Views and Studies—Contributions to the "Scriptural
Interpreter"—Visitation-Day.

THEODORE never forgot those winter evenings, nor the father
and mother who were not abashed in their homespun though all
the worthies came. It was a perpetual house-warming, with
Plutarch and Milton for guests, and Rollin, Shakespeare, Homer,
and New-England's Iliad in tradition. The gods repaid the
hospitable instinct by making the rude fare ambrosial and perennial. What culture is like an inartificial welcome to such a
company! The youngest child put fresh lips to this farm-bucket
dripping with wonder and delight.

Now he must leave the richly-endowed college which Nature
extemporized for him. The farm, with its cottage-house, and
the ledge, more liberally roofed, behind, and the parental love
overarching all, cannot shelter the young student more. But
Theodore took the Faculty along with him.

On the 23rd of March, 1831, he went to Boston, having
accepted an engagement to become assistant in a private school.
Eleven octavos, the *dii majores* of his little library, were not
difficult to transport. Among them were Virgil and Horace,
which he had read some twenty times each, and could repeat all
their finest pages. He was stimulated to pursue his mathematical labours by becoming acquainted with Mr. Francis Grund,
who had then hours for instruction in several of the Boston
schools: also, the *sight* of Newton's "Principia," which he could
neither borrow nor buy, increased his ardour. The whole of
Homer was read this year, a good deal of Xenophon and Demosthenes, Æschylus, and many books of metaphysics and physics.
The study of German was added to French and Spanish, and he
learned to write as well as read these languages.

He boarded at first in Blossom Street.   Of his life at this
time we have a trace in a letter written from Rome, March 23,
1860, to his friend Dr. Howe.

It is twenty-nine years to-day since I left my father's house and
home and sought a new in Boston.   A raw boy, with clothes made by
country tailors, coarse shoes, great hands, red lips, and blue eyes, I
went to serve in a private school, where, for fifteen dollars a month
and my board, I taught Latin, Greek, subsequently French (!), and
Spanish—both which I could read and write, though not speak—the
mathematics, and all sorts of philosophy.   I was not twenty-one, and
hired a man for eleven dollars a month to take my place for five months
at home and do the farm work.   My father refused to accept this, but
I insisted that it would be unjust to use me better than the other boys
before me.   I taught in the school six hours a day, and from May to
September seven ; but I always had from ten to twelve hours a day for
my own private studies out of school.   You may judge what sort of a
boy I was from the kind of man you have known since.   Life lay
before me then (it is all behind me now), and I had hope where now is
only remembrance.   Judge if I did not work : it makes my flesh creep to
think how I used to work, and how much I learned that year, and the
four next.   Had not I a constitution for a scholar ?   Oh, that I had
known the art of life, or found some book or some man to tell me how
to *live*, to *study*, to *take exercise*, &c.   But I found none, and so here I am.

No doubt in this way he planted deep in his organization the
weakness and dejection which subsequently appear from time to
time, long indeed before any definite illness took hold of him.
In consequence, it is not always easy to separate his physical from
his spiritual condition, to decide when his melancholy was the tax
which all powerful men pay while the soul is struggling to know
itself, to repose in God, to acquire pre-eminence of will, or when
it was the mood of an overworked brain, an eye that is just
turned from gazing at the sun.   Both causes marked themselves
together before he reached a full and conscious maturity.   After
that nothing but the invalidism can be traced.   Yet his friends
and followers who sunned themselves in his warmth, little knew
how often it had struggled through malign fogs of a neglected
body to fall upon them.   It could not have been suspected ; there
was never a trace of illness on the broad, fair countenance of his
thought—neither sadness nor indigestion ever went so deep.
The body often drooped in private, but every idea walked forth
erect, its bloom untouched by care or physical liabilities.

But another cause sometimes threw a shadow over his day.
Equal with his thirst for truth was his thirst for affection.   No
man ever lived so resolute as he, so competent to tell the truth

and to defend it, with such power of concentration, and such a sense of luxury in buffeting the great waves of knowledge, who was at the same time so insatiable for sympathy and friendship. " I want some one always in the arms of my heart, to caress and comfort ; unless I have this, I mourn and weep." While he was at home this craving was too sumptuously fed ; the youngest had the whole favour of the house. A dear sister, who had shared his tastes and was his heart's sworn companion, returned to the old farm a few years after Theodore had left it, and died there while he was living in Boston, in 1831. " Dear Sister Emily ! How I longed for her recovery—how gladly I could have lain down my life for her—how, in my boyish way, I asked the Father of All to spare her, though He took my life instead." How pitiless the streets of Boston seemed to this yearning heart —ten hours a day of glorious study could not hive up all he wanted ; on the contrary, there was a sting left in that spoil, pricking him in jaded moments with home and its artless delights. He sometimes threw himself almost with frenzy upon this breast of knowledge, that it should soothe him while it nourished. But companions, mentors, muses, all the stately train, swept by his secret door. Later still, after the great trials of his life commenced, when old friends grew very cool, and new ones were slow to take their place, many words—yes, and tears !—fell from this defeated sympathy. For he would be loved by men, as well as love and worship truth. He was never frigid enough to undertake the rôle of serene indifference. Great learning could not isolate him, great labours could not beat down his childish delight in human society : he longed to know men and women more intimately. He would pour out all his riches, and yet seem to forget that he knew anything, or had any great command, if a friend came near, so controlled was he by desire for sympathy, so instinctively did his passion to feel and lavish kindness break through and domineer at the touch of a faithful hand. Toss a flower into the bosom of this burly image-breaker, he caught and held it tenderly for your sake and its own. There never was a man of the heroic protesting sort more troubled with the anxieties of love. Those who stood before him, counting the grand, firm steps he took, could not see the ensanguined tracks from which the resolute foot was lifted. Nor need they now. Occasionally, surprise broke forth ; for he could not understand why a man who was seeking neither fame nor money, but truth alone, should be found so repellant. He desired love so much, that he did not readily accept the category of being hated so thoroughly; and when a little feeling mingled with the surprise, it betrayed his eagerness for human recognition. So earnest was he, and so absorbed in his high motive, that he always underrated the effect of his thorough speech and contempt. He was unconsciously performing his work before he saw that enmity as well as love must needs bear testimony to its vigour and sincerity. By-and-bye, he accepted the eminence of being the best-hated man in America; but it was with a great anguish that supplicated for more human sweetness in the cup of truth. Who would have thought it who listened to his unpitying delineations, or stood by when his mailed glove rattled on the pavement, in prompt challenge to the oppressor? It was man whose love he longed to share; but it was humanity which forbade him unduly to conciliate. It would be very wonderful if no effects of this noble incompatibility could be found in his private or public thought.

There was reason enough, then, for melancholy moods. His eighteen hours' daily work in Boston and elsewhere, pursued for half-a-dozen years, with very scanty resources either of friendship or of money to supply an hour of recreation, just impaired a little the perfect tone of a feeling which was in youth sprightly, gamesome, elastic with spirits and humorous perception. He had no mercy on his body; it always seemed to him capable of unlimited endurance. He threw himself upon the tree of knowledge, almost fierce to feed and to assimilate: he never knew when to leave off. He derived from his tough and simple paternal ancestors a great ambition of health: it tyrannized for a long time over the fatal legacy of his mother.

Here are excellent " canons of self-discipline," which were drawn up when he was in the Divinity School, after his ill-treated body grew revengeful.

 I. Avoid excess in meat and drink.
 II. Take exercise in the air at least three hours a-day.
 III. Always get six hours' sleep—more is better; seven hours' certainly; eight hours' very often, and always would be more suitable and proper.

Rule No. 3 shows plainly that his daily average of sleep was less than six hours, with daily virtuous intentions to increase the amount. The "intellectual canons" were more strictly obeyed; they show how ill the other canons must have fared in practice.

   I. Exhaust a subject when curiosity is awake. Sometimes this is impossible. Note the subject in a book, and examine as soon as possible in this manner:—

      1. By finding out what I really know upon the subject.
      2. Obtaining clear and distinct notions in some way.
      3. By stating in words the result of my study, and repeating till it has made a deep impression. Sometimes write them in this book.
      4. If historical, settle time; writers who relate it, their character.
      5. The cause.
      6. The effect.

   II. *Keep the mind obedient to the will,* so as to be independent of external affairs. This cannot be completely effected, but may be in a great measure, by the use of certain *intermedia, e. g,* "words of poets," &c.

In other words, he had a regular posse recruited from all ranks of letters, which he employed to break up his reveries and distractions. While he was engaged in long investigations these were mustered, in readiness to march in and carry off all rude or dissolute disturbers.

Here are the other canons, moral and affectionate.

   I. Preserve devoutness, by

      1. Contemplation of nature,
      2. Of the attributes of God,
      3. Of my own dependence;
      4. By prayer, at night and morn, and at all times when devout feelings come over me.

   II. Preserve gratitude by reflections upon God's mercies to me.

      1. In giving blessings unasked.
      2. In answering prayers.

   III. Restrain licentiousness of imagination, which comprehends many particulars that must not be committed to paper, lest the paper blush.

This is the old monastic foe which infests an ill-ventilated and over-studious solitude. The petulant body began to miss the old farm-ledge, "sun-blanched the live-long summer," and the expeditions of his guileless heart after things of its own kind in the woods and fields.

Here are words recorded later, but referrible to these earlier causes.

> I know not why, but heavy is my heart;
>   The sun all day may shine, the birds may sing,
>   And men and women blithely play their part;
> Yet still my heart is sad.   I cannot smile
> As I could smile all day in long past youth!
> There is no art my sorrows to beguile.
> Daily from utmost heaven descendeth truth,
> I look upon her with an unmoved face,
> And feel no leaping heart when fixed in her embrace.

It is plain that these accesses of sadness may be credited to a jaded spirit.

The other morning I arose and one side was numb; both hands were so, the left mainly. The right soon recovered, and I shaved, but the left kept mainly numb all the morning, with pricking pains from time to time.

These symptoms he had also when he was only 18.

I did not know how ill I was till I came here and find that all my *life* is *gone*.   I care for nothing save my duty, and that is not so desirable as once.   I feel like a heart-broken and ruined man, and think sometimes it was a mercy if Providence would take me back: not less a mercy to others than to me.   Still I will not murmur, but hopefully bear up.

Here is a health-gauge which he invented.

Scale of health.   When able to write the sermon Monday morning $= A$.   Evening $= \dfrac{A}{2}$.   Tuesday morning, B.   Evening, $\dfrac{B}{2}$; and so on, C, D, E, F.   If not all $= O$.

Have done little all the week.   Health $= \dfrac{F}{2}$.   This is too near an approach to O for this season of the year (September).   I have not begun this month so ill for some years.   If I had any of the usual humdrum parishes, I would leave it for a year and go off to Europe. But this is a parish which I cannot leave.   I feel as if I had squandered a fortune; for at the age of 39 I am ill, and lose more than half my time, while my father lived a hale man till 77.   For the next six months I will take especial care of my health, making all else bend to that, and that to nothing.

But he plunges straightway into researches for his work on the Development of Christianity, and with lecturing and preaching still carries the load of two or three men.

In 1842, he writes, during June, a little heart-touched as well as ill :—

I have done nothing for a month—am stupid beyond measure—was never in such a state before—never knew till now the sadness of that perpetual disappointment of hoping, hoping, and finding nothing come of that hope. But I submit. I think I should complete the Δραμα of my life well by dying next autumn, after the book is ended, but can't tell if it will then end. External sadness is in store for me, no doubt, but the light is all bright and beautiful within me.

Here is a glimpse of some experience whose root is obscurer than the body. It seems at first a shallow mood, but deepens rapidly to the whelming point.

This whole week I have had few thoughts and few sentiments. I am sorry to end and begin a year (1840-41) in this way, but I can't help it. Oh, how our life is streaked with sadness! I shall begin to believe, with some weeper, that all the birds sing in the key of grief, for the stars look melancholy now to me.

My thoughts have been low. I know not why; for I am well in body and temperate in meats and drinks. Vae mihi, quantus dolor in corde—dolor nunquam oculis humanis spectandus. Sed nunc, etiam nunc, Deus, speram in Te. Speram! dico? Non—Tibi meipsum committo, tuâ in manu recubans, molliter. Haud metuam quod mihi vir potest facere. De profundis clamavi.*

But a few months after, the old health blooms again :—

There is no end to the development of the soul. I feel the bird element is wakened in me anew. Wants of my nature never satisfied, but drugged to sleep by the will, open now their beaks, flutter their wings, and try the thin air. I feel a new development of youth. I thought once it would never return . . . there is a resurrection of myself. Last night, for the first time these many months, the lyric inspiration of joy came over me. My prayers ascend—home has a new charm. I start and tremble, and a new depth of Christian feeling opens to my eyes. Blessed be God for all!

Confinement and over-study, with deficiency of friendship, were causes which exaggerated a sentimental tendency of his mind. If he could have found his peer to live with in these early days, one earnest and strong, capable of invading his tired and dissatisfied moments with healthy confidence, he would have spoiled less paper with unquotable verses. Writing does not drain off these humours ; like tapping, it promotes secretion. A hearty slap on the back from a friend's hand would have shaken all the ink from his pen. A friend might have harmlessly received and dissipated these flamboyant moods, which grew to self-consciousness on paper. In default of a friend he

---

* Ah me ! what pain in my heart—pain never to be seen by mortal eyes. Yet now, even now, O God, let me hope in Thee. *Hope*, did I say ? No ; rather I commit myself to Thee, in Thy hand gently lying. Let me not fear what man can do. Out of the depths have I cried.

associated with the moods. I think he never quite recovered from this effect of his scholarly isolation ; a lively fancy and a great affectional instinct went sometimes wandering into vague places. The noblest objects had occasionally a wavering outline, as palms and temples seen through the trembling columns of tropical heat. But a true friendship always went through him, like a breeze blowing landward which dissipates the flickering scene. His friendships were of the manliest and simplest kind, honoured by duty and worship, and vitalized by all a woman's sensibility. Friendship, humanity, and truth always startled the brooding sentiment, and broke up its momentary rest. But it was sometimes built in high places, on the " coigns of vantage " of his finest thoughts.

For the sake of connecting these moods with their physical and moral causes we have travelled beyond our dates.

His early predilection for the profession of minister had never really been impaired by an occasional aspiration for some other career. Echoes of distinguished names stirred his imagination, a developing capacity offered success wherever he might choose to seek it. But the whole course of his thought had already consecrated him to the service of truth and humanity; nothing could overcome this original bias. It was in his simple disposition, in his exacting moral sense, in the joy of his piety. His powers asserted their capability for any work which he chose to cut out for them ; but the quality of his motives made him fastidious.

He writes in 1848 :—

Several persons of late—as well as formerly—have talked to me about going to Congress, as Representative or Senator. To which there are two objections :—I. *Nobody would send me.* I don t believe any town in Massachusetts would give me any post above that of *Hog-Reeve,* and I don't feel competent for that office—a man in spectacles would not run well after swine. II. Politics are not my vocation, nor yet my desire. I mean to labour for ideas—to set men a-thinking. I feel as if born for a pulpit, if for anything. If I could be *well,* well enough to *work,* and do a man's duty, I should be glad; yet that is not a thing I ever mention in my prayers. I am content, yes, content to pay the price of violating the laws of the body in struggling for an education, though I knew not what I did.

Father! help me to live better: more useful, more acceptable to Thee. As the years go by me, may I grow in manliness and all noble qualities. Teach me Truth, Justice, Love, and Trust. Let me not be idle, nor unfaithful. Give me a clean and holy life, and may each year bring me nearer to the measure of a man.

That was always the shaping prayer of his practical and ideal life. In Boston he commenced his first open preparation for this future work, in his studies which looked towards the Theological School. He must first get money enough to carry him there. But as he managed to save only three or four dollars out of each month's earning, the prospect was not bright. The Boston experiment only lasted till April, 1832 : then he would venture one of his own at Watertown. During the winter, he gave his first lecture, before the Lexington Lyceum ; the subject was the History of Poland, selected on account of the enthusiasm for the Poles which was then travelling through New England.

His life in Boston was desolate enough that winter. No friends—" nothing but thoughts, and books, books, books." But he records, in his letter from Santa Cruz [1859], one benefit which he derived from being in the city at that time.

For a year, though born and bred among Unitarians, I had attended the preachings of Dr. Lyman Beecher, the most powerful orthodox minister in New England, then in the full blaze of his talents and reputation, and stirred also with polemic zeal against " Unitarians, Universalists, Papists, and Infidels." I went through one of his " protracted meetings," listening to the fiery words of excited men, and hearing the most frightful doctrines set forth in sermon, song, and prayer. I greatly respected the talents, the zeal, and the enterprise of that able man, who certainly taught me much; but I came away with no confidence in his theology. The better I understood it, the more self-contradictory, unnatural, and hateful did it seem. A year of his preaching about finished all my respect for the Calvinistic scheme of theology.*

He took great pains, then, to understand the scheme which afterwards he attacked so unsparingly, and as its disciples aver, so ignorantly. Certainly it was an able advocate of Calvinism who indoctrinated him with disgust for it. He remembered also the great features of revival meetings ; and in his sermons " On False and True Theology," and " The Revival of Religion which we need," preached in 1858 during the great revival, he spoke from the confidence of personal experience.

The idea of going to Watertown to open a private school was probably suggested to him by relations, who were farmers living

---

* "March 31, 1852. Old Dr. Beecher came to see me, and spent an hour and a half. ' Tell me who you are,' he said, ' where you came from, and how you got so far from the common track.' I did so, and we had a quiet talk. He is genial, generous, active-minded, and expressed a strong sympathy for me, and a good deal of feeling of kindliness towards me."

in the north part of that town. Thither he went in April, 1832, without a pupil engaged, and without money enough to make the few needed preparations. He found a boarding-place at Mr. Nathaniel Broad's, who lived about half-way between the village and Newton-Corner, opposite the estate of Dr. Morse. Part of the inducement to lodge there lay in an old bakery, the second storey of which he leased of the proprietor. He assisted in flooring it, made a rude wainscot, constructed a dozen desks, and shortly opened school with a force of two pupils, one of whom he asked to come gratis. Collegiate and theological studies were going on all the while. Pupils came slowly, dropping in till he had enough to divide into an upper and a lower class. Members of the former paid each five dollars a quarter, and of the latter four dollars. If he found a boy or girl in the town too poor to pay him anything, he invited such to come in.* But he did not wait long for a full school, and the number rose, the first year to 35, afterwards to 54. Most all of them were paying scholars. He was a child with all of them, and dearly beloved, for he had sweet and gentle ways. But he felt great responsibility in undertaking to teach, and sometimes he doubted if he had the talent of imparting anything. It fairly oppressed him, and he took endless pains with the young minds; it touched him to see their confidence in him. But he was grave too, and looked after justice strictly; he had authority—only the children did not know it. He managed to govern with little demonstration.

They brought him flowers, and welcomed him to their out-of-school games; he loved to watch all their ways.

In one thing he had unlimited confidence—the ability of the children to learn any task he chose to set. This sometimes startled them, and it appeared as if he went too fast. Then he would draw them out, and restore courage by skilful questioning. In this way, too, he would make them answer their own questions, till he had an assistant in the awakened power of each one's reflection. He had a great aversion to the text-books of Natural Theology, declaring that they were attempts to prove what no child ever thought of doubting; and he would often bring the books to shame before the children, by drawing out their intuitions. He loved to teach by means of objects; and

---

* But after he had admitted a coloured girl who had been sent to him, he consented to dismiss her in deference to the objections of some of his patrons. This he always confessed with mortification.

when he took his class abroad, the fields seemed expressly provided with illustrations and representatives of some fair thought. All the flowers and plants of the country round were familiar to him, and the ways of birds and animals ; he tried to cultivate the observing faculty in the children. One of them remembers his lesson when the wind blew a trumpet-flower to his feet from the vine that overran her father's porch.

A letter from Rev. Charles Briggs, of Lexington, introduced him to Dr. Francis, who was then minister of the first parish in Watertown. In that red brick house, near the Charles River, were many books in many languages, a genial and liberal-minded host, a kind and cheerful wife. All these extended hospitality to the brave young student. Dr. Francis was among the earliest of New England scholars to read and appreciate a German book. His Latin, Greek, and Hebrew, were in admirable condition. Modern languages were not neglected, but among them German was especially cultivated. Here, then, were *Dogmatik, Metaphysik*, and *Hermenutik* for Theodore, with a competent guide to hold the clue for him. The two years spent with these advantages were always gratefully remembered by him. Theodore's questions accumulated frightfully when he found such a hospitable ear for them. He never forgot to say that he was in debt to the free and scholarly minister, who made a friend of the bashful student and favoured the generous unfolding of his mind,* and to the wife who soothed him with home-like associations.

The preaching of Dr. Francis must also be reckoned among the things which helped Theodore on his way. His sermons were the liberal efforts of a mind constantly studying and inquiring, welcoming light, and bold to speculate. They were free from dogmatism, perhaps disinclined to definite and final statements. The tendency stimulated Theodore to form his own opinions. But, above all, Dr. Francis was a humane preacher.

Theodore soon became superintendent of the Sunday school. Up the aisle of the old meeting-house he ventures on this new mission, very awkward and diffident, a little uncertain whether people would like him, in a suit constructed on the very frontiers of economy, which appeared so often and so long that a good many persons pretend to recollect it. But when he began to speak, in his gentle and pious way, everybody was glad.

* In his Journal of a later date he says : "Then I walked long days in the strength of the meat I ate."

He also undertook a Bible-class, in a Socratic style, making the pupils themselves discover what they had to learn. The doctrine of plenary inspiration was not held by Unitarians, but they had a vague opinion that everything of consequence in the Bible was suggested or preserved in no ordinary way. Theodore would read portions to his class, and invite them to exercise their common-sense upon them—" Must a man be supernaturally inspired to say or do this—did this require a special suggestion ? " But he did not yet carry this to the criticism of a supernatural element in the nature of Christ and the Apostles, or in the prevailing spirit of the New Testament.

Mr. Broad, his landlord, died ; and Theodore, very tender and helpful, was of great use at home. Several of his pupils lived in the same house, and he undertook the general charge of their manners and morals. He sat up very late—there was never a drop of oil in his lamp the next morning; "not that there was any scrimping in Mrs. Broad's house "—her lamps emulated her name—but Theodore could hold out to burn the longest. He was up at daylight, sawed and split the wood for the school and family, swept out and dusted the school-room, and took a walk of three or four miles.

His Cyclopean wall began each evening to the sound of music, for he had a chum, who was unhappily seized about the same moment after tea with a tendency to breathe his soul out through the flute. Theodore began with mild expostulations, when Amphion Sanger seized his melancholy reed, but the tenure of the chamber covered mutual privileges ; and the chum blew himself out by nine o'clock, but Theodore would sit up till the lamp went out at two. Between the strains, and while Amphion wetted the joints and called up the next melody, he could snatch moments of studious oblivion.*

This routine went on for two years. Twice a week he walked

---

* Theodore held to the Hellenistic interpretation of the word Music, which was a pursuit of all the liberal arts. The thoughts of great men built lofty harmonies in his mind. But he was heretical on the subject of Music. When Mr. Cranch, the painter, and Mr. J. S. Dwight, the musical journalist, were in the Divinity School, they sometimes met to meditate the muse upon a slender reed. Theodore bore it for a long time without flinching. "But on one occasion," says Mr. Cranch, "there was a movement in the entry just outside our door, executed upon a peculiar, and by no means musical instrument—a sort of *obligato ad libitum* bass thrown in as accompaniment to our strains. On opening the door to ascertain the nature of these strange sounds, there was Theodore, who had left his folios of the Latin Fathers, had rushed into the cellar, and brought up a wooden-horse, saw, and log of wood, on which he was exercising his vigorous sinews—see-saw, see-saw —to our utter discomfiture and amusement. As for Theodore, he barely smiled."

to Cambridge to take lessons in Hebrew of Mr. Thurston, then a member of the Theological School, and now settled at Belmont ; afterwards he walked as far as Charlestown to be instructed by Mr. Seixas, a Jew ; Greek and Latin literature, German metaphysics, as much political economy as he could find, mathematics and theology, missal reading, Hebrew, and a little Syriac, drained good Mrs. Broad's midnight lamp.

But a fairer light began to gild the old quartos, and red-letter the pages of dingy German paper. For Miss Lydia D. Cabot was not only a teacher in the Sunday-school, but she boarded at the same house with Theodore ; and this gradually became of great importance to the young student, who had hitherto resented interruption. Now the flowers discovered in the fields along the birch and alder-fringed bank of the Charles were not brought home for botanizing. The walks themselves were not companionless. There is a charming view from Wellington Hill, and some old oaks of famous girth not far off, which were great favourites. Beaver Creek runs from the oaks through meadow land, till in two miles or more it finds the Charles. The river has pleasant reaches near the Waltham factories. Smooth Helmet Hill lifts its crest from a wide sweep of apple orchards, and Prospect Hill is not too far, when for some reason every step is beguiled of weariness. Mrs. Broad's oil must eke the night out further, for by day the books were less admired.

Præposito florem prætulit officio.

TO MISS LYDIA D. CABOT IN BOSTON.

Watertown, Tuesday Eve, Oct. 30, 1833.

I walked to father's ; he soon returned from church, and I caught him in the garden, and informed him of the "fatal" affair, if you will call it so.

The tear actually started to his aged eye. "Indeed," said he. "Indeed," I replied, "and attempted to describe *some* of your good qualities." "It is a good while to wait," he observed. "Yes, but we are young, and I hope I have your approval." "Yes, yes! I should be pleased with anyone you would select ; but, Theodore," said he, and the words sank deep into my heart, "you must be a good *man* and a good *husband*, which is a great undertaking."

I promised all good fidelity ; and may Heaven see it kept !

Oct. 31.

I have attacked Mr. Herodotus with renewed vigour this week. I purchased a small volume which contains all his writings, and am not now compelled to wait for Mr. Francis to bring volumes from the

college; those are, however, to be consulted at leisure. I intended to
finish the work to-night, but fear I shall not be able. Now, I feel a
new pleasure in the discharge of all my duties. I love my books the
more, my school the more, mankind the more, and even, I believe, my
God the more, from loving *you*.

Nov. 21.

I have endeavoured to cheer your absence and enliven my spirits a
little by going this afternoon to Uncle Clark's, though I shall still find
ten hours for study, reading, and writing.

Dec. 5.

What shall I say to you for sitting until ten o'clock to write ? Why,
ten is as bad for *you* as one for *me*, and I would sometimes gladly extend my lucubrations nearer morning, but have kept my promise thus
far with all good fidelity.

Dec. 27.

It has been in other times than this my highest pleasure thus to pass
my time, thus to spend my nights, in "high concord with the god-like
past," to collect my own thoughts and search for new. But now I find
a *new* pleasure which, with a louder, sweeter voice, speaks to the heart
and tells *another* tale.

Thus was planted the tender root of a happiness which, in
after-years, helped him to tolerate contempt and bitterness, and
to temper the dejection which they brought. When disturbed
and repulsed abroad, he always hastened home to this reassuring
presence ; there his wounds were touched with gentleness.

This Watertown season must have been very delightful now.
The school was less oppressive, and he was led somewhat more
into society. There were many fine people among the farmers
in North Watertown. His cousins, the Clarks, were bright and
sympathetic, and old "Uncle Peter" was Theodore's firm friend,
a farmer, intelligent and fond of reading, but, better than all,
endowed with a sweetness and liberality, and a real courtesy,
which mere culture can never bring. These honest men and
women understood Theodore, and never forsook him when his
opinions were most divergent. Whoever was afterwards settled
over the First Parish in Watertown, found that it was no tax
upon his courage to exchange with him. The act was not
dangerous there, as elsewhere, and involved no loss of position
or influence. On the contrary, if the clergyman himself undertook to vindicate Mr. Parker, or to share his views, these
farmers were first to countenance and welcome it. Old Deacon
Stone never sat a formalist in that meeting-house; and his heart
was true to the young teacher, whose truth and innocence he

remembered. The Crafts, the Barnards, the Stones, the Clarkes —Theodore would gratefully repeat their names in this connection—were the first to know what he was, and the first among New England parishes, not his own, to rejoice when they saw him standing in their pulpit. In his earliest intercourse with these warm, unsophisticated people, he used to fill their hearts with his piety and gentleness, and inspire them with his great ambition to learn the truth. The opinions were of less consequence ; they knew their man. And so it might have been everywhere else, if his beautiful disposition could have been the harbinger of his doctrine. But there was neither *dilletanteism* nor dogmatism on those rich slopes where he passed his social hours, so that his pure motive was instantly discerned.

He was also recognized by some families of more wealth and cultivation, but who cherished, like the farmers, simplicity, independence and humanity—one or all of these high qualities. Among the Whites, and Thaxters, and Bigelows, and Shannons, he had always friends, and sometimes vigorous disciples. How delightful it is to inscribe all these names upon a page of his memorial ! and those, still living, who own the names, will tolerate the freedom from one who is not a stranger, for the sake of love and old companionship.

After teaching his school for two years, he reckoned he had money enough to venture with to the Theological School, where a frugal youth could live for less than 200 dollars a-year, all expenses included. He would still eke out his income with teaching, and perhaps with writing.

It was not a comfortable day for him when the leave-taking came. The scholars had devised to show their respect and love by a little presentation-scene, which was managed to surprise him. A neat speech was made by Master Briggs, and the silver cup being then revealed, Theodore seized it and vanished abruptly into the entry, being no longer fit to be seen. The scholars thought he had rushed into Mrs. Broad's, perhaps to execute one of the delotic * movements to which he was subject. He was not in condition, for some minutes, to return and dismiss the school.

* A word from the Greek is used, meaning gesture and motion demonstrative of internal feeling, to avoid applying the word dancing to Theodore's rather elephantine ballets.

He never had any trouble with his scholars, for he never stooped to coarse methods of maintaining influence. When he was afterwards Chairman of the School Committee of West Roxbury, he introduced a rule that no teacher should inflict chastisement upon a pupil without bringing in some ostensible reason for it. When asked what he intended by proposing that the reason should be "*ostensible*"—"Why don't you say *real ?*" he replied that the teacher could then say he punished for whispering, or for being out of place, while the *real* reason might be that he got up feeling very cross, or,—added he, in a whisper, "because the boy hadn't got a pretty sister." This also required explanation, and he told them that he had two pupils in Watertown, Frank and Harriett, brother and sister. Harriett was handsome, and a great favourite, with whom he used to read and take long walks. Frank was disobedient one day, and was threatened with chastisement after school, if the offence was repeated. Frank accordingly repeated it, and was told to stop after the rest were dismissed. "But upon approach-ing him with my ferule, he looked too much like Harriett. I had to kiss him and let him go."

During the school-keeping he read Tacitus, Cicero, Herodotus and Thucydides, and translated Pindar, Theocritus, Bion and Moschus, as well as Æschylus. He fell in with Cousin, and the new school of French philosophers, and became acquainted with Coleridge. He also pursued the literature of all the modern languages which he then knew, and made great strides in meta-physics and theology.

TO MISS CABOT.

Feb. 27, 1834.

Mr. Francis called here yesterday and lent me the necessary books, so I have commenced the great study, the criticism of the New Testa-ment.

I spoke again to Mr. Francis of the comparative advantages and dis-advantages of commencing study the first of April or next September, and he again expressed his preference for the former plan. He preached all day Sabbath, besides lecturing in the evening. How few ministers are so industrious ! but if any professional man can have an induce-ment to labour with all diligence, it is the clergyman.

I have been to examine a school this afternoon, and never have I seen a school better undergo an examination. This is the last of my services upon the School Committee, and glad am I.

Feb.

I consulted Mr. Francis about going to Cambridge soon, and joining the present junior class; he thought it a good plan, and gave me letters of introduction to Mr. Ware. I have walked to Cambridge this afternoon, and seen all the Faculty; have resolved to make the attempt; so I shall finish school-keeping on the first of April, and remove to Cambridge, take a room at the Hall, and commence study.

Nothing is too much for young ambition to hope, no eminence too lofty for a youth's vision, no obstacle too difficult for his exertions, and no excellence unattainable. Patience, perseverance, prayer have done something already; and when we consider that sincere desires are never neglected, and real endeavours never unassisted, we need not despair of making some *approaches* at least to the eminence Mr. Palfrey now occupies. Would not this be truly delightful? No situation can be more honourable, no task more pleasant, no prospect more celestial, than that of a virtuous, faithful clergyman.

He entered the Theological School during the last three months of the junior class, in 1834. The other members of this class were Samuel P. Andrews, Richard T. Austin, John S. Dwight, George E. Ellis, Oliver C. Everett, Abiel A. Livermore, and William Silsbee. The report of his scholarly acquisitions had preceded him, and the extent of his reading excited admiration. His talk was full of odd learning and scraps of curious information. He was crammed from books and observation, but everything lay about in undigested heaps. All the library privileges which he could find in the neighbourhood he laid hold of, and the students were frequently drafted to help him home with his bundle of folios. At one time he fancied that his memory was growing feeble: a friend found him posted before an enormous historical chart, covering one side of his room, which contained all the dates and incidents from Adam. He was committing this to memory. All real or imaginary deficiencies were attacked by him without loss of time. Everybody reproached him for taking no exercise, but he declared that it was planting-time with him, and relied upon his constitution to carry him through. He increased the bad effect of this fury for study by attempting to board himself, for a time, in his own room, a sad economy which brings expense upon later years. Classmates have said that he used to study fourteen hours a day.

He excelled in debate, but his first sermons were rather poor. Henry Ware, jun., would discuss them freely, and declare to Theodore that they were unworthy of him. This salutary candour cost the struggling student sleepless nights, broken by sobs. The next morning would find him in despair, believing that he had staked all—time, health, and hope, upon a profession, and had lost. His talk was superior to his sermonizing ; his prayers were already full of simplicity and pious feeling.

He was very affectionate, and relied upon two or three of his classmates ; he could not be happy without the privilege of frequent sallies from his books into their rooms, for a moment's gossip or a grotesque caper. Once he quarrelled with a friend who was reading "Philip Van Artevelde" with him, and who could not bear the execution of Occo and Gilbert Matthew at the close of the first part of that drama. "It is a great blemish," says the friend ; "Artevelde should have shown magnificent with mercy." "No," cries Theodore, "it is just : it is good, it is Christian." "It is downright murder," says the friend. "Then get out of my room," cried Theodore, in wrath because the measure meted to two villains was not recognised. He had to pay for that : whenever he referred to it, the tears stood in his eyes.

This letter shows that his critical tendency, which was wide enough awake upon most topics, still refused to notice the theology that he brought with him. His statement of belief is thoroughly conventional.

TO HIS NEPHEW COLUMBUS GREENE.

Cambridge, April 2, 1834.

I came last Saturday, or rather Sunday night, and of course have scarcely had time to see how I shall be pleased; but since I am resolved to be satisfied at all events, nothing is to be feared on that account. It is now vacation with the class, so I am alone in this great house. Term-time commences two weeks from to-day, when I shall join the class at recitations, though I shall not be considered a member till next commencement.

You enquire about my belief. I believe in the Bible. Does that satisfy you ? No, you will say : all Christians profess to the same, and how different they are.

To commence then : I believe there is one God, who has existed from all eternity, with whom the past, present, and future are alike present; that he is almighty, good, and merciful, will reward the good and punish the wicked, both in this life and the next. This punishment may be eternal; of course, I believe that neither the rewards nor punishments of a future state are corporal. Bodily pleasures soon satiate, and may God preserve us from a worse punishment than one's own conscience.

I believe the books of the Old and New Testament to have been written by men inspired by God, for certain purposes, but I do not think them inspired at all times. I believe that Christ was the Son of God, conceived and born in a miraculous manner, that he came to preach a better religion by which man may be saved.

This religion, as I think, allows men the very highest happiness in this life, and promises eternal felicity in another world. I do not think our sins will be forgiven because Christ died. I cannot conceive why they should be, although many good and great men have thought so. I believe God knows all that we shall do, but does not *cause* us to do anything.

The expenses at the school are 66 dollars annually; board in commons, 1 dollar, 90 cents a week; clothes, &c., will make in all about 200 dollars per annum. I shall have, when all affairs are settled at Watertown, about 150 dollars. This is too little, you will say. Well, I know it, but I have paid nearly 200 dollars for books within these two years; and clothes, you know, cost lots of money. I am now boarding myself upon dry bread; it will cost about half a dollar a week. I shall try it all vacation, and if I like it, all summer.

One scholar comes and recites once a day till commencement; the pay is 12 dollars a quarter.

I had almost forgot to mention, at the close of my school the scholars gave me a handsome silver cup, with an inscription testifying their respect, gratitude, &c. It was preceded by an address from one of the scholars. I never parted with scholars so sorrowfully in my life. I wept and so did they.

TO THE SAME.

April 28, 1834.

Let me advise you not to fear the opinion of the world. Satisfy your reason, and especially satisfy your own conscience, and all will then be well.

I hope I shall not want much money at all, and for this reason: I to-day made application to Prof. Palfrey, the Dean of the Faculty, for a benefice, and my application was successful. Of course nothing will be extended this season, but after next commencement about 110 dollars or 150 dollars will be afforded me annually. This will go a good way towards defraying my expenses; and since I have a little of my own, probably I shall not want to borrow any of you this year. This is an unexpected instance of good fortune for which I cannot be sufficiently grateful.

I tried cold bread for a fortnight, and at the commencement of the term went back again to commons; but I intend to try the old scheme again next autumn.

TO THE SAME.

July 11, 1834.

Should you be pleased to know something of our ordinary course of proceedings in this institution? We have about thirty scholars, divided into three classes; one of these graduates in about a week. Some one of the senior class preaches each Sabbath evening during the year; all the school and some few strangers attend. Prayers are performed at morning of every day by Prof. Palfrey, and at evening by one of the

F 2

senior class. The junior class, to which I belong, recites in Hebrew every Monday, Wednesday, and Friday afternoon; attends a lecture upon the criticism of the New Testament, Monday and Friday, when we translate the original, ask questions, and engage in discussion with the Professor. We recite and discuss the Evidences of Christianity with Dr. Ware every Wednesday. Tuesday afternoon we have an exercise in extemporaneous speaking with Prof. Ware, jun., one of the finest men I have ever known. Some subject is proposed to the class at one meeting and discussed at the next. Saturday morning Mr. Ware delivers a lecture upon composition of sermons, subjects to be treated, &c., to the whole school. Thursday we have no recitation. One-third of the school declaims every Tuesday evening. Friday evening the whole school meet for extemporaneous speaking. Thursday evening is spent in a religious meeting.

A society for the promotion of the interests of humanity, and called the "Philanthropic Society," meets once a fortnight on Wednesday evening. A report is always read upon some interesting subject, such as "Infidelity," "Temperance," "The License Laws," by a committee previously appointed to investigate the subject. Besides this, I have a fine lad who comes every morning to recite Greek and Latin, &c., and had a young gentleman who came twice a week to recite German, but I have not seen him this fortnight.

All my leisure is devoted to translating some papers of La Fayette, which I am doing for Mr. Sparks, who is going to publish them. This is his work, and not mine. I shall be constantly occupied upon this translation during the whole of vacation.

Sunday I visit the States' Prison, where I have an interesting class in the Sunday school.

TO THE SAME.

July 8, 1835.

I have two scholars now (young men), who intend to enter an advanced class in college. They come one hour a day. Besides, you know, I have two young misses, so my time is tolerably well occupied.

He was still the bashful and sensitive boy, filled with piety and pure feelings, yet very self-reliant and ambitious. He carried into the school all the energy and purpose which his peculiar education had served to develope. He attacked every subject with enthusiasm, and extemporized his own way of mastering it. He is represented as being very eager in the debates which were held once a week in the little chapel of Divinity Hall; there he judged everything in an independent fashion, was very reverent of truth, yet never calculated his phrases, offended the taste sometimes, but always stimulated inquiry and the deepest feelings. Dr. Ware would interrupt the ardent debater, suggesting, perhaps, that it was not quite handsome to say "old Paul," as the epithet no longer conveyed apostolic meanings. Theodore would subside, proceeding in humorous excess with allusions to the "gentleman from Tarsus." Rebuffs for want of taste, or for any disregard of conventionalisms, did not put him down, for it was in part his very eagerness which kept him so sensitive. On he went, finding his own way through everything, earnest to have a sight of genuine objects in all the fields of thought. It is singular that his colourless theology escaped so long. He still took a good many things on trust, for spiritual intuitions were very dear to him; but if a new doctrine rested upon evidence, he showed what the old doctrine might one day expect when he cross-questioned it to the extent of his critical ability. If it was developed metaphysically, each step of the process was tested by an instinctive health of all the faculties, which may be called his common-sense. It was his common-sense, and that of no other person : the most valuable result of his peculiar "bringing up." For common-sense depends upon the the personality, though in all persons it is a general soundness, or freedom from cachexy; not mere shrewdness, or ability to conduct material affairs, or perception of the best out of half-a-dozen ways, but the functional man in good condition, every part of the nature exhibiting an irreproachable digestion, and no part overnourished. A man shows his common-sense when he is seen not to be under the tyranny of any special knack or impulse; his shrewdness is not a talent, but an operative condition of his whole mind. He is too shrewd to exaggerate a single member; he promotes the fair development of all. Faith, conscience, and understanding receive their just amount of chyle; the pulse goes everywhere, touches at all the ports of entry and delivery, leaving and taking what is due. This is a sensible man, as distinguished from a commercial, metaphysical, mystical, sceptical, or sentimental man.

The common-sense which Mr. Parker began now to display had been carefully protected by his mode of life. The artifices of education injure ordinary people just where they need the greatest strengthening. Extraordinary people instinctively invent their own methods. The same drill, the same succession of text-books, the same set of theological opinions, the same clique, and neighbourhood, the same professional traditions, turn out vast numbers of conventional judgments, which for want of common-sense are considered sensible. It is said that the Flathead practice does not impair the natural capacity of the tribe ; nothing is said of the want of capacity which invented and pursues the practice. Fortunately, nobody caught Mr. Parker when his skull was soft, to lay heavy hands on the brain's gentle respiring beat. By-and-bye he possessed health and amplitude of organs fit for any work. And his instinct that he must relinquish to each function its appropriate freedom and opportunities had not been taught out of him. He, therefore, gradually and surely learned for himself how to bring all the functions to an understanding ; not thereby solving all spiritual problems, but preserving the inward health. The healthier he grew, the more he despised all doctrines which start from a presumption of human inability. The soul seemed to him well made for its work. It was this which made him ask for principles that are capable of promoting human welfare ; all opinions and beliefs which cannot effect this practical connection with humanity dropped gradually out of his favour. He wanted only available truths, yet his common-sense had a high and fastidious notion of availability. It was not a niggardly sharpness to discover the least amount that will keep alive a human being, to put men and women on famine rations of faith, thought, and feeling, but it was an instinct for the real interdependence of all these. There naturally belonged to this a shrewd and sarcastic vein, and no little impatience with all the mystical and ecstatical luxuries which have ever corrupted honest, manly blood. Sometimes he was disdainful, and sometimes merry, when he got into a field of these, and began to shake them out with his critical pitchfork.

After a thorough reading of the fathers, with careful notes and analyses, he breaks out one day thus :—

I am heart-weary and reason-weary of these same doting fathers. They have sense, but it is "a grain of wheat in a bushel of chaff." I shall soon be done with them, however, for the present at least. One of the greatest proofs of the darkness of the monastic ages is the folly-admiration bestowed upon these same nonsense writers.

I will say one word about "the resolute Hierome" as an ancient has it. He loved glory rather than truth, was superstitious, and an intro-ducer of important errors into the Church, both in doctrine and inter-pretation. Setting aside his extensive, perhaps immense, reading and faculty of sharp declamation, and, Leclerc says, nothing but moderate faculties remain. He was not a profound scholar in Hebrew, or even in Greek. He *tasted* of theology rather than exhausted it. He wrote his works in great haste.

St. Austin, we all know, introduced more error into the Church than any other man. Many of his doctrines fly in the face both of reason and virtue, to extinguish the eyes of one and to stifle the breath of the other. Everybody knows how he persecuted his opposers, Pelagius and Julian, to say nothing of others. Let him go. If anyone wishes to read an eulogy of undeserved elegance upon the Bishop of Hippo, he will find it in Maury, &c.

Tertullian I have always looked upon with considerable jealousy. He first introduced the notion that faith and reason contradict each other naturally—a doctrine so germane to the feelings of many in those un-reason days. He thought faith which contradicted reason was most acceptable to God. He has regular canons of criticism; some of them are indeed good, but his application of them is faulty. Everybody knows he thought the soul material, &c.; he thought it was *sky-blue*. A sister of those days had been elevated by contemplation so high, that she saw the souls all *sky-blue*.

These patristic studies were brought to a close in the winter of 1835. But they often reappear, and in 1845 Tertullian is noticed again :

Tertullian, it seemed always to me, was one of the worst curses to the human race that has occurred since the Flood. I don't know but Africa took its revenge on the European world in advance by sending Tertullian and Augustine into it. I think, at this day, it is easier to free the negroes from their white masters than it is to deliver the human race from this wretched yoke laid on us by those two shabby Africans. I remember, years ago, thinking most of the absurdities of Christian theology came in with Tertullian ; and reading a little since convinces me that he developed much iniquity that was only latent before, and brought in many wolves to the Christian flock, which have since been clothed in sheep-skins and have devoured the flock without mercy.

The Scriptures have been almost always interpreted in the interest of dogmatism, from Christ to this present; for instance, the *Regula Fidei* of Tertullian and the *Analogy of Faith* in our day. Chrysostom was better than most, but he was often absurd in his interpretations. Some of the old allegorizers equal Swedenborg—some of the Chiliasts. Irenæus, *inter alios*, was absurd as Charles Fourier.

JUSTIN MARTYR.—I admire the candour and beauty and sweetness of his *Oratio ad Græcos*, in which he shows the folly of their old mythi, if accepted as true. What is the value of his testimony to prove the fact of such acceptance ? A Greek philosopher becomes Christian, and reasons as if his nation believed the stories—how much does it prove ?) He urges them to accept the doctrines of one true God.

In his *Admonitio ad Græcos*, the same is done still better. Here he shows that Moses was older than the Greek teachers, and proves it from writers not Christian, after showing the folly of the Greek myths in Homer and the philosophers. Here he misunderstood both, I think, sometimes.

He says Orpheus and Homer taught some beautiful truths, and cites that fine piece of Orpheus to Musæus (which most unfortunately is spurious and of late date); the monotheistic passages from the Sybil (for he could say, " Teste David cum Sibyllâ "); and Sophocles. He speaks of the names of God, and says the name is holy for us—not for God ; so each and all names are indifferent to God. The whole piece is quite noble.

The list of languages which he studied in the school included Italian, Portuguese, Dutch, Icelandic, Chaldaic, Arabic, Persian, Coptic, and a smattering of Æthiopic. He attempted Russian, but there was no one to help him master the sounds of the alphabet, and he gave it up till he lived in Boston.

In November, 1835, he began to study Swedish. At the same time, translations of Eichhorn and Ammon were going on —reading Greek comedies and German commentaries, Vico's " Scienza Nuova," and parts of Plato. Before the month was out he was translating Swedish poetry, and in the last week of it he commenced Danish. In December he undertook the modern Greek. All languages, dead or living, were mastered with great rapidity. Everything he planted grew fast, but he always seemed to have a language under glass.*

He learned not merely the vocabulary of a new tongue, as so many American students do, to get at the general sense of a book in the most economical manner, and push over the ground with smart conjectures. But he loved philology ; the grammatical structure and derivation of a language attracted him first. The vocabulary came next ; in fact, his occasional mistakes in translating at a time when he was devoured by work were in the meanings of words oftener than in the idiom and structure. His knowledge of Hebrew and Syriac was so minute, that Professor Sidney Willard is said to have often applied to the young Divinity student for advices upon some nice point. And in 1843 he dropped into the middle of the course of the Arabic Professor in Paris, bringing, with entire comprehension of the subject, a capacity to criticise the lecturer's method.

To-day I made a new acquisition to my library, viz., Herder's Complete Works, in 45 volumes. I can never render sufficient thanks for God's goodness in giving me this opportunity of increasing my books, and of course my means of usefulness.

---

* "A kinsman of mine, one Thomas Parker, who lived a virgin, and 'went unto the apocalyptical virgins at death,' was such a master of the Oriental tongues that once, when some of his brother clergymen assembled to rebuke him for some heresy, he replied in Latin—they rejoined in Latin. He replied in Greek—they continued in that tongue. He answered in Hebrew—they questioned in Hebrew. He then retreated to the Arabic, where they could not follow him, when he bade them go home and study their primers before they undertook to school him."

He had in college a class of Hebrew students, which he met twice a week, and two private students ; and in 1836 he taught Hebrew to the junior class in the Divinity school, during the visit to New Orleans made by Dr. Palfrey.

Anglo-Saxon is added to the other languages before the New Year. Everything else is going on at the same time, and numerous odes and versicles are showered along the track. "A Bridal Hymn," for instance, "for the Wedding of Beauty and Truth," with choruses of earth-spirits and angels, which I forbear to disturb. He delivers a lecture in Concord during the vacation ; translates, dips into rabbinical matters, into books on Messianic prophecy, on which point he began to hold with De Wette, and asks himself some questions about the Miraculous Conception. He studies books about the Canon and the different versions of the Bible—Schrift-Erklärungs-Geschichte—translates the article " Rationalism " from the Conversations-Lexicon, and a good deal out of Eichhorn's "Ur-Geschichte." Paulus succeeds, and he writes a paper entitled " Hints upon German Theology," then goes through the "Wolfenbüttel Fragments" question, and begins to read Spinoza.

Under the head of "Horæ Platonicæ," he makes analyses and criticisms of the views in Plato's works. During the reading of the "Republic," his humanity gives significant and promising utterance.

Is a man bad, the good shall teach him *goodness*. And the teaching shall be good, not that which renders the vile doubly perverse, for that is unjust. When will this sentiment lie at the foundation of all codes of laws ? Penal legislature, now-a-days, has all the effect of the purest injustice, in driving the half-guilty to increased crime, and in making *doubly deep* the hatred of the revengeful. I doubt not the angel of humanity will beat, with her golden pinions, all prisons to small dust.

On Sundays he generally went to Charlestown, where he had a class in the State prison, which greatly interested him. But occasionally we find him in Watertown.

Sunday, 22 Feb., 1836.—I heard Mr. Francis preach two very good sermons, as may be supposed, since with him good sermons are the rule, and poor ones the exceptions, and rare ones too. I dined with him, and found as much pleasure and satisfaction as usual in his varied and instructive conversation.

Then follow notes of the table-talk about Coleridge, &c. It is needless to catalogue the books which marked his course of study during the next term. Wegschieder, Staudlin, Storr, Schmidt, and better yet, Cudworth, Henry More, Norris, Descartes, Lessing, Cousin, B. Constant, Leibnitz ; also books on Magic, about which he was always very curious. Descartes furnished him with rules for studying.

April 21.—It is now the commencement of a new term—of my last term of study in college. Where shall the end of it send me—what will become of me then ? What will eventually become my destiny ? What preacher shall I be ? And where shall I find a resting-place ? All these questions come up with mighty force—they weigh heavily at times upon my soul.

A part of the decision of these great questions rests with me, a part upon something exterior to myself—upon Providence. For *my own* part alone feel I any anxiety. God has ever protected me, and even in the times when there seemed no possible way of escape from present and impending disaster, His hand has shown a way. Shall I distrust it now ? Oh, no, I do not—I cannot. The Almighty will doubtless give me more than I deserve—why should I fear?

Wherever I am cast I can be happy. I will attempt to do my duty. But there are others dear to my heart. Shall I disappoint their cherished hopes ? Oh, no!

Much depends upon this little term. May I improve its blessings right.

TO MISS CABOT.

Tuesday Eve.

Brother Dwight just called at my door, requesting me "to bang him up in the morning," as he elegantly calls it, which you know means it is *something like* bed-time. But bed-time is not "the witching time of night," for you nullified all late watching long ago, by an imperial decree.

TO THE SAME.

June 10, 1835.

Were I to become an idolator I should worship the stars, since they are almost a personification of ideal beauty, so bright, so clear, apparently so frail, and yet outlasting human calculation—so uncertain and yet so constant. That folly could almost be forgiven which led men to imagine them animated with celestial souls, and endowed with superhuman, and only less than supreme power, and which made them no feeble actors in the fortunes of men and fall of mighty states. But since we are no idolators, but Christians, we can look beyond the stars up to the throne of the Invisible, which they surround and adorn with their shining.

What is more beautiful than a summer's night, when the hurry and bustle of day has gone by, and calm and stillness succeeds ? . . .

How happy is a mother's charge at night, when, with many a prayer, she folds up her little flowerets, and commits them to His care whose eye never slumbers nor sleeps! Perhaps you have not such associations as I have with this period; but now the days when I was a little, yes, a very little child, come up before me, when my mother taught me a prayer and a hymn, and, giving one farewell kiss, left me to repose. I cannot think of those times without a tear—a tear of regret for those days, and of sorrow that I am so little worthy of a fond parent's hopes and prayers and tears.

TO THE SAME.

June 17, 1835.

I suppose it is only by means of the imagination that we form any notion, at least any conception, of God, of the sublime, of the beautiful, the perfect. I do not mean mere fancy, which only presents us cold and lifeless pictures of things once seen, and combines them in unreal positions, but that power which acts *within, im-ago,* in-forms; which embodies our abstract notions, and gives them shapes, hues, and beauty, till they burn. . . .

When I was a boy I had always a world of my own, an ideal creation, where I could roam and luxuriate at random. Many a time have I strayed from the right path and gone far beyond my stopping-place, while I was brooding over some scheme not yet accomplished. How many times has my plough run upon a rock while I was expounding law, making speeches in the senate, or astonishing men with a display of intellectual power, fitly put forth, in my imaginary Utopia. . . .

It is delightful now to imagine myself a minister, to recount the duties of the station, and consider all the ways of performing them, and forefeel the glorious satisfaction of seeing God's work prosper in my hand. I turn to a home—to a home of beauty, of affection, of love! To a home where all noble feelings are cherished, and whence all jarring interests and strife are excluded. Calamities may fall upon that home; they come upon all men—each country has its own storms. But if it is built on the rock of holy affection, *it will stand:* the floods may pass over it—they can never shake its fixt foundation.

A great deal of his time in the school was spent upon contributions for the *Scriptural Interpreter.* This little magazine was commenced by Ezra Stiles Gannett in 1831. It had reached the middle of the fifth volume, in 1835, when ill-health compelled Mr. Gannett entirely to relinquish the supervision of it, and it fell into the hands of three divinity students, William Silsbee, George E. Ellis, and Mr. Parker. It was edited by them to the close of its publication in 1836, and the greater part of each number was also prepared by them. It was a little in advance of the average Unitarianism of the time on the questions of Messianic Prophecy, and of the Pentateuch, and gave the views of De Wette, Eichhorn, Astruc, and others. The subjects of miracles and inspiration were hardly yet deployed upon the field. It was only occasionally denied that the facts of miracles

lent any authority to the truths of Christianity. The controversy upon the Trinity and the Atonement had subsided, and
discussions upon the element of Divinity in Christ had not commenced. The Unitarians had now their position, and were
recognized in a sulky fashion. The acrimony of the contest with
Calvinism broke out less frequently in the religious newspapers
of the day. In carrying their point, the Unitarians had gradually absorbed a great deal of the wealth, talent and influence
in New England. Leading men professed the liberal faith. The
old protesting impulse grew languid with this achievement of
respectability. A good many generous and indignant things
which the flame of battle had nourished in their minds began to
fade out of the recollection. Instinctively they commenced to
fortify their position as the offensive warfare slackened, and both
parties stood narrowly watching each other. Decorum, regard
for opinion, the habits of an established sect began to set in. A
desire to be recognized as a truly Conservative and religious
body, with positive faith enough left to serve the soul in living
and dying, to serve education and the state, to refute practically the grave objection that they were upsetting the Bible
and society with their negative criticism, prevailed so strongly
that vigorous investigation nearly ceased. Tentative speculation
was undertaken by the young men with little positive encouragement. They had only the advantage of a negative good-nature,
which disappeared with the first serious alarm. "Whither is
this tending?" and, "What will the orthodox say?" are
questions which in plain language indicated the general mood.
It was not so expressed, and perhaps would not be so acknowledged, but it received during the next fifteen years a good
many instinctive confirmations. Thrift, housekeeping and civic
propriety succeeded to adventurous exploring. After getting
through swamps of Trinity and Vicarious Sacrifice in dashing
style, just as the clear outlook dawned at the end of the paths
cut through the matted undergrowth, and the blue lines beyond
piqued the mind to gain their height and freedom, the Unitarians
paused, dropped axe, rifle, and the ranging glass, and settled
the flat produce-growing prairie. They have tried to deter
their young men from pressing forward to penetrate the distant
bold ranges, entreating them not to compromise the settlement
and draw the attack of savages, and reminding them of the
perils of the vast drear interval. There was a kind of sense in

insisting upon content with the gently rolling fertility which they had discovered, and upon which they had stopped to plant, but this was not the highest kind of sense ; for the original squatters are sadly crowded now, and many of their young men are scattered, digging wells along a solitary trail, around which one day men and women shall gratefully cluster, and opening the green valleys where the mountain cedars stand.

The following anonymous contribution to the literature of Protestantism, shows how early the Unitarians betrayed this tendency for comfort :—

TO MESSRS. ELLIS, PARKER, AND SILSBEE, EDITORS " INTERPRETER."

April 20, 1836.

I read, in the last number of the *Scriptural Interpreter*, the article on the 52nd chapter of Isaiah, and with unmingled surprise and horror. What could possess you ? What is the object of the theologians at Cambridge ? Are they determined to break down the prophecies, and make our blessed Saviour and his Apostles impostors and liars ? Cannot our doctrines be sustained in any other way ? Must the pious Christian be compelled to give up one passage after another, one book after another, one prophecy after another, until he has nothing left to stand upon but what is in common with the Deist ? Where is it all to end ? Tell us, I beseech you, that we may quit, if necessary, the ship before it is too late ; before we have struck upon the last rock which the vessel of our faith will bear ?

This first-class passenger, so suddenly aroused, trotting up and down the quarter-deck in a minimum of clothes, with wringing hands and frantic glances, conjures the captain to alter his course, and then disappears down the companion-way for ever, thus :—

Pause then, I beseech you, before it is too late. I am a well-wisher to your work. I have always been a subscriber. I am one of the household of your faith. But another such a blow and I must quit all I value ; my religious faith above all things else. I cannot part with it. To escape, therefore, shipwreck, I must jump overboard before the last plank is taken away. And not I alone. Hundreds must do the same ; they will not bear to have the sacred records of their faith frittered all away, though it may be in a style a little more refined than that of Paine, but, nevertheless, resulting in consequences which are just the same. Mr. Noyes strikes a blow and alarms a sect. Mr. Peabody recovers the ground for a moment, by holding on to a few passages. The *Interpreter* follows to destroy one of the most essential of these few. The end cannot be far off. And then, the imposture of the New Testament and its authors will be the completion of the dreadful work.

A SUBSCRIBER.

Mr. Parker went forward, but with great deliberation; his papers in the *Interpreter* acquiesce in the average Unitarianism; they neither vigorously sustain nor oppose it. His understanding began to grow critical, and his intuitional beliefs looked through the accepted doctrines, but slowly at first, and not with one great gaze.

Here is a sentence from an article on the "Alleged Mistakes of the Apostles":—

It may be urged, that even admitting they were thus mistaken, no important conclusion follows from the fact; since supernatural instruction upon this subject was not necessary to the propagation of the Christian religion, and of course they had received no divine authority to speak on the subject. But it does appear important; for had Paul preached to the Thessalonians, for example, that the world would soon perish—as some maintain he did—and years passed away without any approach to a fulfilment of his prediction, they must have lost confidence in his teachings. And we ourselves could scarcely place the same unbounded trust in his other doctrines.

This is the ordinary opinion, which grew into great vehemence when Mr. Parker afterwards assailed it—that if the credibility of one portion of the Scriptures be invalidated, the authority of the whole is weakened, and that if you begin to doubt you know not when to stop. Better answers to his own original fallacy can be found nowhere than in the passages of his later writings, which maintain that a true thing has the only conservative authority, which it derives from its necessary intuitive character, and that truth only is worth preserving. This is a legitimate Unitarian doctrine, but the squatters were angry when the young men ran off with the dangerous element to blow up with it fresh obstacles in the wilderness. It was very useful in the Trinitarian morass, but should be kept shut up in magazines after the country is settled.

The best thing which he wrote for the *Interpreter* was an analysis of the Laws of Moses, extending through several numbers, all remarkable for their clear and exhaustive arrangement. His notes and authorities show, of course, a great range of reading in various languages; but it is already becoming organized by the awakening thought. Classics, commentators, travellers, Talmudic lore, lend learning and illustration; but without parade, and never without an object. It was a very handsome piece of work for a divinity student. A more compact manual of all the details of the Mosaic law cannot be found to-day.

But it is noticeable also as betraying occasionally the transition of his mind from the ordinary interpretation of the vindictive passages of the Old Testament to his later view. Here is a passage to show it :—

Some critics think it no grave heresy to deny that the laws which command the entire extirpation of the Canaanites were inspired. They think themselves safe in referring such statutes to the difficulty of the emergency and the hardness of men's hearts, rather than to the good sense of Moses; and still less do they attribute them to the counsels of a God of love. They think, too, that such interpreters as ascribe all these *sanguinary laws* to the inspiration of the Almighty "take more upon their shoulders than Atlas could bear." They admit the inspiration of Moses, but do not suppose *every word of the law* of divine origin. We know that many of the particular statutes had no such sanction expressed. They think, too, that the Oriental custom of ascribing all remarkable events, wonderful appearances, and striking thoughts to the immediate action of God, explains the *alleged* command of the Almighty. The religion of Moses, say they, was divine; but he was left to make use of such means as he saw fit to govern the chosen people, and to bring them to the Land of Promise. When ordinary resources failed, miraculous assistance was afforded. The *position* of Moses, and not his *religion*, is to be held accountable for those edicts apparently so sanguinary.

Here he cites authorities, and continues,—

How far the above remarks are worthy of notice others will judge; but it must be remembered, the nations to be extirpated were exceedingly vicious and corrupt, and if suffered to remain, would, doubtless, have led away the Jews from their better faith. If nations are by the Divine permission visited with earthquakes and pestilences, why may not the sword be employed for similar purposes ?

Both the confusion and the direction of thought in this passage are interesting. The good sense of Moses is quite sufficient to account for his policy towards the neighbouring tribes, and for the distinction which he made between dangerous and indifferent neighbours ; yet it was so important that the dangerous ones should be reduced, that the necessity might rank with those evils of the physical world which depend upon Providence itself, and might be therefore divinely decreed.

But his intuitive conviction that Infinite Love cannot send to man decrees subversive of itself, and that the Christian spirit outgrows the cruelty of the Old Testament, soon began to fill his mind with abhorrence for the very phrases which attribute an exterminating message to the Lord. What just contempt he had for the ordinary interpretation which made a spirit of love responsible for old Jewish vindictiveness, and what ridicule for the doctrine which tries to escape that imputation by supposing that God was hard because men's hearts were; that, at least, He had no alternative but to send them the revengeful messages they desired to hear. Would anybody accept such a plea made by any abomination in favour of itself? No pretext of piety in making it, sincere or fraudulent, would shelter any bad passion from the hatred of our unbiassed honesty; and yet no sooner does it seem to be sanctioned by the name of Moses, and the claim to inspiration of a book, than ingenuity is exhausted to defend it, and Mr. Parker credited with a motive hostile to religion.

He was, however, slow to clear his feeling of the Divine Perfection from these dishonourable imputations, that it might become for him a reliable test of theology and practice. It was very effective in his hands when he attacked the scriptural authority for slavery and slave-catching. Anti-slavery orthodox men were hampered by the necessity of supposing that in old times God inspired ignorance with ignorance, and inhumanity with inhumanity, the quality of the Divine Mind being unable to transcend the moral status of the race. A book places certain old and new iniquities under divine sanction : it would seem as if the alternative were to accept the iniquity or to deny the sanction. Not at all ; God was merely accommodating himself to geographical and historical exigencies ! Mr. Parker shows that neither morals nor religion were saved by such a subterfuge of criticism, that they were rather put in greater danger than before, because the slaveholder was left at liberty to appeal to the traditional sanction while pleading the exigencies of his position. Mr. Parker knocked the sanction away, with unsparing strokes ; what health and liberty they released to sit in judgment on the great sin, and what a priceless advantage he thus won in dealing with it ! When he redeemed the books of the Old Testament from their critical fetters, and raised them to the simple dignity of being treated for the sake of what truth they might contain, their truth of fact and of human nature, he redeemed also religion from her bondage to political and commercial wickedness. The facts of the past and the facts of the present were cited at the bar of morality and common-sense.

Who then, were he now living, could wield with greater effect the sublime prophetic denunciations of the wicked, the Psalms which call upon God to stand at the right hand of the lovers of justice, and to scatter its enemies? Who would have put the chapters of ancient indignation closer than he to the great conspiracy of iniquity against which he, too, prophesied with language as sombre, as vehement, as wrathfully righteous as any page of the Old Testament affords? Who could more consistently thunder the old texts against the modern villany, than he who had faithfully denied that any text could sanction, at any epoch of history, a single crime? He could all the more powerfully quote the justice of God against the injustice of man, because he had always scorned to make either God's love or justice seem to suggest to man one barbarous statute, or to inspire one crime of history. Would that he lived! to summon the old haters of iniquity to his side, that they might help him hurl the verdict of the past against the blasphemy of the present, which quotes a "Thus saith the Lord" against the Lord himself.

This he might have done, not, however, from any defection of his own. He was fully competent to upbraid and prophesy, and needed not to borrow a single Hebrew phrase to hold his new sense of the anguish which waits upon national iniquities.

The doctrine that the moral intuition is the critic of the morality of past and present history, in books and actions, is another genuine Unitarian doctrine. It was well applied to the moral aspects of the dogma of the Atonement, and our instinctive sense of justice and humanity was urged against its reputed scriptural authority. But it has been applied but feebly in other directions, in the interpretation of the Old and New Testaments. There has been instead, a tendency to take refuge in doctrines of accommodation and the second sense. The Universalists alone, as a sect, boldly put it beneath the texts which affirm eternal damnation, to dislodge them from their seats.

Mr. Parker began to write for the *Interpreter* in 1835, and wrote in all nearly forty articles. In translating "Astruc's Conjectures upon Genesis," he hopes that it will not create any *ausschreien* (outcry); for the editors remembered that they had been rather sharply rebuked by somebody who had squatted very early, for their latitudinarianism on the subject of Messianic Prophecy. Now, to-day, there is a retreating party, not content even to be settled, but who have one foot in the old evangelic bog, looking about for prophecies and types, and signs, or hoping that at least some liturgy may peep.

I am in a good deal of doubt upon the subject of the prophecies relating to the Messiah. Sometimes I doubt altogether that he was ever prophesied of distinctly, with sole reference to Jesus of Nazareth. Indeed, that any inspired prophecy was ever uttered concerning him.

I do not doubt that Jesus was a man "sent from God," and endowed with power from on high, that he taught the truth and worked miracles, but that he was the subject of inspired prophecy I very much doubt.

He then proceeds to give an explanation of the allusions to prophecy in the New Testament, and adds:

I know the above would appear like blasphemy to many divines, but I must stand by my own Master, not by another *man*. My confidence in the divinity of Christ's character, of the truth and sufficiency of his doctrine, depends not at all upon prophecies, or visions, or dreams.

The miracles have little interest for him, and little value. But he takes them for granted:

Mr. Dewey gave us the Dudleian lecture this year. It was the best, perhaps, I have ever heard, though upon the least interesting part of the Evidences of Revealed Religion, viz., Miracles. He removed the presumption against them. The objections were not only met, but overturned.

Ah, me! what an infinite distance between me and such men! But what of that? My little light may still burn on.

Mark, at the same time, the gathering boldness of his mind as revealed by these extracts:

Jonathan Mayhew's discourses show a profound and bold thinker, one who feared not the truth. Some call such men rash; but who dares say that the man who will adhere to God's truth is rash, and who will deny the presumption of one who dares depart from it?

And here is the result of a call upon one of the Professors:

He certainly is a very urbane man, and very mild and gentlemanlike in all his deportment; but a bigot in his opinions. All the Germans are "raw" in his opinion. German scholars are *not* accurate. They make good dictionaries and grammars, which are so large that but few can use them. They are "naturally unfitted for metaphysics, and their language still more so." Schleiermacher, he supposes, was a "Pantheist," who did not believe the immortality of the soul; at least, not any *personal* immortality, only a re-absorption of the finite into the infinite. "He gave up all that renders Christianity valuable and its promises precious." His doctrines were the same with Spinoza. He said I was happy in never having read the book. He acknowledged that Schleiermacher's contemporaries did not regard him in this light.

And the next day he calls upon an eminent Doctor of Divinity, who was settled in Boston:

He found fault with my article in the *Interpreter*, upon "Servant of God." Inconsistently, as I think. He said he was sorry to see it.

Thus he went on slowly, but in perfect freedom, and never biassed by the suspicious criticism of narrow men. It was not so easy then as now for a young divinity-student to keep at arm's length the traditional authority of Boston and its neighbourhood.

A good many books on Gnosticism were read this term, and some volumes of Kant, De Wette, Ammon's "Fortbildung,"* &c.; the passages which he quotes are characteristic of his developing condition. Verse-making does not slacken either— "To Sleep," "To the Logos," "Reflections at Midnight," "Spring," "To a little Flower," "To Lydia in Absence." Let the following suffice, entitled "Evening:"—

How sweetly from the western sky,
    Day's lingering colours fade:
How changing features softly vie—
    Shade deepening into shade!

How softly comes the grateful calm
    Which mellow evening brings;
The sweets of flowers, the breath of balm,
    Float on the Zephyr's wings!

How soft that wandering cloud appears,
    As the last tinge of day
Crimsons the peak it proudly rears,
    Then slowly dies away!

Now stars come forth, and one by one,
    In the broad field of night,
Who veiled their face before the sun,
    Now pour emboldened light.

Oh, night and stars! your voice I hear
    Swell round the listening pole:
Your hymns are praises, loud and clear,—
    Are music to my soul.

Sing on, sing on, celestial band,
    Till earth repeats your lays,
Till the wide sea, the sky, the land,
    Shall celebrate His praise!

* He translated the whole of Ammon's "Formation of Christianity," and found it serviceable in preparing De Wette's Introduction. But the book itself is of little value now. It was an attempt to make Reason and History account for orthodox doctrines, and was neither rational nor evangelical.

TO MISS CABOT.

Jan. 25, 1836.

Now, too, I fear,—yes, I *know*,—that you are quite too fearful of my *over*-studying. Now I tell you that I know best about these matters, and that my conscience would as little permit me to *study* too much as to *drink* too much. I am in no more danger of one of these vices than of the other: so I pray for the future you would rather urge me to study than dissuade me from it. I oftener *eat* too much than study too much. Reproach this sin as much as you please. . . . .

You have none of those stormy, violent passions that sweep, tornado-like, through my heart. . . . So I speak truth when I repeat my own unworthiness.

The month of April of this year was spent in a journey to the South, as far as Washington.

TO THE SAME.

April 13.

In the Senate, Mr. King spoke upon the bill "For Preventing the Circulation of Incendiary Papers," of course it applied only to the abolition papers. Mr. K. is a tall thin gentleman, with a long sharp Roman nose, a high but receding forehead, large black eyebrows, and a pair of keen, wicked, black eyes. Withal there is a sort of sly defiance written upon his face. I did not like his speaking much. He ranted, and has a bad voice. He implicated Mr. Calhoun, who replied to-day.

The bill alluded to was one introduced by a select committee, to whom so much of President Jackson's message as related to the transmission by mail of incendiary documents had been referred. It "subjected to penalties any postmaster who should knowingly receive and put into the mail any publication or picture touching the subject of slavery, to go into any state or territory in which the circulation of such publication or picture should be forbid by the State laws." The bill was eventually rejected.

Upon that committee was Mr. King, of Georgia, who dissented to certain portions of the bill and report after they had been brought in, and charged Mr. Calhoun with entertaining principles inconsistent with the preservation of the Union, and that he was, in fact, only striving to make a grave point of the incendiary documents in the hope to reach a dissolution of the Union. Mr. King, of Alabama, who opposed the motion to refer, was also sharply treated by Mr. Calhoun; but Mr. Parker alludes to the Georgian.

As it was expected Mr. Calhoun would reply to-day, all were anxious to get seats in the Senate gallery. I took mine half an hour before the session commenced, and found a gentleman who pointed out to me the men of distinction as they came in and strolled about, talking to one another, or writing at their desks. Mr. Calhoun came in early, and you could see from the thoughtful, restless expression of his fine face that he was meditating something. He kept aloof from almost all, and seemed lost in thought. About half-past one an opportunity offered for his reply. The whole chamber was hushed when he arose and announced his intention. There was an eager bending forward in the galleries to hear him. He began by lashing Mr. King, who had spoken of him the day before. He treated him with the most complete politeness, and yet with a severity of sarcasm which made Mr. King writhe in his seat and gnaw his lip. I could watch the changing expression of his countenance, now ashy, and now deadly pale.

I will tell you more of this when we see one another, and of many other speechifiers.

I saw the " little magician" too ; of course none can mistake his wily features. He glided about before the opening of the debate, clapping men upon the shoulders and shaking their hands. H ɔ looks very artful and naughty. I should fear that man.

Clay walks about in a dignified manner; he is tall and homely, as I think. I see no features of the great man upon him.

Plenty of negroes, of course, one sees here. I saw in the paper of to-day an advertisement offering cash for 700 negroes of both sexes. That sounds harsh to Northern ears. They are a queer set, these negroes; some of them are very merry, dancing and capering about on the sidewalk as if they had nought to do but dance. I saw two negro lovers walking arm-in-arm, cooing and billing, as if they could not restrain their joy in one another's presence. Why should *colour* prevent them ?

Before May he was at home again, and at work.

TO THE SAME.

Indeed I have felt *blue,* terribly blue, all the week. I never speculate on the causes of such chilling damps that come over the soul, like a frost in July, blasting all that the sunshine has beautified. It is enough to *bear* them without going about to analyse the nature of the complaint, and decide upon the exact quantity which was caused by an east wind, and tell how much is physical, and how much mental. . .

My muse has been kept upon " thin potations" and meagre diet so long that she refuses to soar to-night, otherwise she had led you such a long and lofty flight as would have quite worn down all your celestial vigour. . . .

My Aonian rill is only that very little trouting brook we have so often admired, and it is far prettier than the Helicon of old.

Here are some extracts from the journal :—

Sunday, May 8.—Preached for the last time in the chapel, once more, and all is over for school exercises ; then I hope to preach to real live men and women.

Monday, July 4.—Last night I preached *publicly* in Mr. Newell's church. This is the first time in my life that I have preached to a real *live* audience. I felt much embarrassed, though perhaps it did not show forth. Lydia, my own Lydia, and her aunt came over with me. I was less pleased with myself than they were with me. To say the truth, I did not feel the sermon so much as I usually do, for the hour usually spent in preparing for the service was consumed in " doing the agreeable," and so I did not get into the sermon so much as commonly.

May God in his mercy grant me power to improve in this holy duty. May I grow from strength to strength, increasing continually in godliness and wisdom, and thus show forth pure and holy Christianity in my life, no less than in my teachings. Oh, God, wilt thou help me to become more pure in heart, more holy and better able to restrain all impetuous desires and unholy passions; may I "put down every high thing" that would exalt itself against the perfect law of God. Help me in the intercourse of life to discharge my duties with a more Christianlike fidelity; to love Thee the more, and those with whom I am to deal!

He had been long preparing himself for the " History of Gnosticism," which was his subject for Visitation Day. " This was a ' day of trembling,' of sad uneasiness to most of us, a day of perplexity to all."

His first sermons after graduating were preached, July 24, in the meeting-house at Watertown ; in the morning, from Matt. vi. 33, and in the afternoon, xxii. 37.

This old meeting-house acquired its first distinction in the Revolution, when it was selected as a safe place for the sittings of the Provincial Congress. The second Congress met there on the 22nd of April, 1775. After John Hancock had been chosen delegate to the Continental Congress, Joseph Warren was the presiding officer. The third and last Provincial Congress assembled in Watertown on the 31st of May. Warren was President,* and Samuel Freeman, secretary. The General Court, which succeeded the Congress, also met in Watertown, on the 26th of July, and its sessions were prolonged till the 9th of November, 1776, when it adjourned to the State House in Boston. The Council of the General Court used to hold its sittings in the old house, nearly opposite, which is now occupied by Mr. W. Russell. Here, also, it is said that a printing-press was for some time concealed. I know not whether it was the

---

* The house where Warren boarded at this time is the one across the bridge now occupied by Mr. Robinson. Here he breakfasted on the morning of the 17th of June, and before setting out for the field urged the ladies to spend the forenoon in making lint. Mounting his horse he rode slowly down towards the bridge, paused, then, galloping back to the door, with kisses bade them all again farewell.

one with which Edes escaped from Boston to Watertown, and upon which he printed his *Boston Gazette and Country Journal*, from June 5th, 1775, to October 28th, 1776.

The meeting-house was built in 1755. It stood upon land at the corner of Common and Mount Auburn Streets, surrounded by a graveyard, which now usurps the site of the church ; and the old parishioners sleep where they only nodded before. It was one of the old-fashioned square structures, called lanterns, popularly, from the two rows of windows which went all round it. In a high wind, the house was filled with the chattering of the sashes which time had loosened ; so that the clergyman, preaching in the late autumn upon the mortality of man, was never quite sure whose voice turned the drowsy ears to seasonable thoughts. Against one side rose a tower, surmounted by an open belfry, which dwindled into a thin spire. The ancient cockerel, which promised fair to Warren as he last rode by, is newly gilded, and challenges the weather still on the steeple of the Methodist church. Within, the old house had a high white-pine pulpit in the centre of one side, with a pen in front to enclose the communion table. When a Sunday-school was formed, the library was deposited in a cupboard under the pulpit. Overhead was the sounding-board, which once gathered Langdon's sermons, and Hancock's and Warren's treasonable talk. Great deep galleries ran round three sides of the house, places of mystery and sombre imaginings to the little ones, who seldom even trooped into their shadows, much less alone. Very venturous boys, however, such as play truant at school or run away to sea, had been up to gaze upon the bell.

In the choir, Thomas Larned played the double bass, and William Harrington the violoncello, when Theodore gave out his first hymns ; there was also a a clarionet, and Deacon Bailey sang bass. The body of the church was filled with highbacked pews, whose seats were lifted during prayer, and clattered down with the amen. My informant says that it was a source of great grief to him that his father's pew-seats would'nt slam. All the other boys *amened* in concert.

The meeting-house was little changed from its revolutionary aspect, excepting that a one-storey addition had been made to it, to accommodate the growth of the parish, which was somewhat flippantly styled "The Kitchen." Here Theodore preached in the forenoon upon the "Necessity of a Heavenly Life," and in the afternoon upon " Religion, a Principle and Sentiment." He was not so flowery as his old friends anticipated, but more simple and direct.

These two sermons closed a fortnight of entire repose, spent in the society of the one he loved best. At the end of that time, however, he suddenly musters together, accuses himself of indolence, and almost depreciates the joy from which he must break away.

I am not so cold-hearted as to wander among the gardens of the graces with no sense that riots, and no soul that thrills. Nay, my heart has been warmed by the sweetest, I had almost said, the noblest impulses ; but it does not advance me in the journey of life as I would wish to move. It does not allow my soul to unfold its wings in this fledging-place and trial-ground, to prepare for the lofty and dangerous flight when it must "sail with uplift wing," against tempest and storm. I have sterner deeds to *do*. Greater dangers to *dare*. *I must be about my work*.

In this prophetic mood he went forth to preach.

HOUSE OF MRS. BROAD, AND SCHOOL-HOUSE.

VILLAGE MEETING-HOUSE, SPRING STREET, WEST ROXBURY.

CHAPTER V.

A Candidate—1836-37—Marriage—Settlement at West Roxbury—Neighbours and Studies—Choice Friends—Dr. Channing—Mr. Emerson's Discourse, 1838—Strauss—Come-Outers—Doubts about Physical and Moral Evil—Thoughts and Queries—1840.

But an itinerant vendor of the gospel, commonly called a candidate, is not a beautiful or heroic personage. Men hang his presageful heart on the hooks of their parochial steelyards, and narrowly scrutinize the figures. He pockets his presage, and it makes no difference in the weight.

In July Mr. Parker received an invitation to preach for four weeks at Barnstable. He started in the packet-schooner *Sappho*, and had his first marine experience.

Only one cabin, which was to serve as lodgment and lounging-room for the evening and night for more than twenty men and women. The ladies went down about half-past eight, for it was cold. Soon after, at nine, I descended, almost perpendicularly. They had gotten into their several berths, and were there lying with the curtains undrawn. I sat rather awkwardly, and chatted and laughed with them, who did not seem at all disturbed by the peculiarity of the scene. By-and-bye I, too, crept into a crib, one lady above me, another at my head, and a third at my feet.

All night long there was a noise; some getting up, and others getting down; roisterous fellows carousing, children crying, *vagitus et ingens*, and mothers attempting to quiet them. Sleep went up the hatchway, but did not find good quarters, and so came in with me, and staid till nearly five A.M.

On arriving he repaired to Mrs. Whitman's boarding-house.

TO MISS CABOT.

August 6, 1836.

We have three boarders besides myself, viz.: Mr. Drew, the school-master—*i. e.* he keeps a private academy; Mr. Brown, who keeps the store and post-office opposite; and " Squire Reed," cousin of the Hon. John Reed. He is Register of Probate, and several other things; besides, he is a good, pleasant companion, and keeps the table alive. He is about forty-five or fifty;—the others are young men. After each meal they retire to one of their rooms, and sit and smoke pipes in a right friendly and old-fashioned manner for about half an hour. This takes place regularly after each meal. It amuses me very much, for I usually join them in the conversation, though at the pipe I reluct. . . . . .

I trust you will not hang the leaden collar of " be careful and not do too much," about my neck.

At Barnstable he found out the most notable people, made their acquaintance, and drew them into conversation. This he never failed to do in every new place, to satisfy his thirst for facts of every description. And he afterwards used to keep lists of people worth knowing in the various towns where he lectured, and whose acquaintance he meant to cultivate. The persons thus selected were intelligent in some calling, or attractive by moral and spiritual characteristics. He was always particularly drawn towards persons of great amiability and high conscience. If they were shrewd and full of facts, so much the better ; but he seemed to love the artless man of a noble natural growth. For the society of such, he would relinquish that of scholars and cultivated men. In his list of favourites the greater number are the names of happy, unpretending, healthy people, with an unspoiled sense of right and wrong.

TO MISS CABOT.

August 10, 1836.

I felt somewhat awkward at first, as you may suppose, but I remembered the command, "Now *show what ye be*," and made an effort. I never felt in better spirits for speaking, and not only delivered the written Word, but added much that was better and more *reaching* extemporaneously. . . . .

I have been busy. I have read almost all my books—I had about a dozen—and have written two sermons. The air of the place braces one's whole soul. I could devour a whole library in a week. I think I should write three new sermons a week all the time I am here, but I have only enough of my favourite paper for two more.

TO THE SAME.

August 14, 1836.

It seems to me as if my mind had grown a-pace in some departments since I came here. I hoped it would. It seems to me I can feel a sort mental *crystallization* taking place within me, which brings order out of chaos. I hope I am not self-deceived in this regard.

TO THE SAME.

August 22, 1836.

Saturday is one of no little anxiety with me, and I am somewhat given to "jactations" on that night. This I hope to overcome, and finally to lie as stark and stiff in bed of a Saturday night as a Cape Cod fisherman . . . . .

The sermon was a new one: the greatness of Christ's character, its sources and its uses. I never felt one of *my* sermons more, nor was ever in a happier mood for delivery. Everything went right, and some of the least bad parts of the discourse were extemporaneous.

Nobody ever speaks to me about the sermons; they all have a proper delicacy about that, which is a little uncommon, too, among such people, perhaps. But to-day Mrs. Whitman said that Mr. Reed, our fellow-boarder, you know, said it was "the greatest sermon he ever heard."

This was a busy Sunday; with two funerals, a Sunday-school, two services, a visit to the sick, and calls in the evening.

This closed the labours of the day, being the seventh public prayer I had made. You may suppose I felt no little fatigue after such a variety of emotions in a single day. I went to bed quite early, but I " gat " as little sleep as King David did heat in his old age. But this morning I feel like a giant refreshed by the slumber of ages, and am gay as a lark.

TO THE SAME.

August 23, 1836.

You must tell your aunt that if I were to stay a thousand years I should not outlast that vile tremor; it is an infirmity that will cling to me. I can no more help it than a lady can keep from fainting in a crowd. Nor again do I wish entirely to avoid it, as it is a source of earnest feeling, and so of strength, for it never lets memory slip or the tongue falter.

Here is a difficulty which the style of his earlier culture helped him to overcome.

TO W. SILSBEE.

Barnstable, August 21, 1836.

How disqualified we are for contact with the real world I felt when first shown a real live man; and when brought to speak with him I was utterly at a stand, and scarcely knew what to say. Thus, indeed, we come away from our three years' studies at Divinity College, with some little knowledge of science, literature, philology; peradventure some small inklings of theology and metaphysics,—nay, even a little knowledge of the science of things in general (*allerlei - Wissenschaft*), and with beards on our chins, but with no other marks of manhood. Now, I maintain that, besides a great deal of knowledge, one needs as much skill to make it of any use to him. *Allerlei-Kunst*, then, we need to set off our *allerlei - Wissenschaft*.

This art of things in general I hope I have made some little advances in since I came to Barnstable. Indeed, it seems to me I have *grown* in this regard, so that I can really talk to men as if I were also a man, and not a student merely. A mere student is a sort of *homunculus*, an animal not treated by Pliny, except incidentally, when he speaketh of the war they once carried on against their arch-enemies, the cranes.

TO THE SAME.

I have been called to officiate at three funerals, and it was a solemn matter. I wept,—not so much, perhaps, as the mourners, but as heartily—from very sorrow. Who could see so many weep and not join them in such a time ? I could not help it. . . . .

I know not where I shall go after the next Sabbath. I can stay here, but—*haud ego.* Touching the place and the people, I like both very much, and hate to leave them, for I " would not willingly lose sight of a departing cloud;" but you know I have not seen *my Skyborn* these near three weeks, a separation which very ill comports with my desires.

TO MR. FRANCIS.

Barnstable, 12 Nov., 1836.

MY DEAR SIR,—I received a letter from Miss Cabot just now, stating that you mentioned that Mr. Burton would like to have me supply his pulpit for a time. I should be exceedingly happy to serve, if by so doing I do not debar myself the opportunity of preaching elsewhere with a view to a *permanent* settlement. If I supply his pulpit, and do not preach there *all* the time, I can get those to take my place who will doubtless do much better than I *can*. I shall be exceedingly happy to come upon these conditions, and if you will have the goodness to inform him of it, you will much oblige me. I would have written him, and not have troubled you, but I am but little acquainted with him, and I have other matters to speak of with you.

Sundry of my friends wish me to settle at Spring Street Church, in Roxbury. What do you think of it ? I suppose it is not regarded as a *desirable* parish by most men, but there are certain reasons which make me look towards it most favourably. I should like your opinion upon the matter, and I will come up to Watertown as soon as I leave B., and confer with you upon it. I am weary of " candidating ;" it is not only a " weariness unto the flesh," but unto the spirit. Men go to church when a youngster is to *hold forth*, not to hear something *good*, but something *new*, and talk of the services at home, rather that he may be criticised than that themselves may be edified. So one cannot comfort himself with the knowledge that he does any good. Besides, the frequent change of place is bad to "mind, body, and estate." One cannot pursue quiet studies ; he can scarcely grow in mind or in spirit when he is so frequently transplanted. I sometimes say, with the melancholy prophet, " Oh, that I had a lodging place of wayfaring men in the wilderness, that I might turn in thither and be refreshed !" When and where I shall find it I know not. If I am at R. I shall be near you and Mr. Stetson, and the College Library, to say nothing of other persons and things which will be within hail. I hope to give you that " labour of love " I have so long intended before the month is out, but I cannot determine with certainty. I am very much obliged to you for the present of your three sermons. I trust I shall read them with as much pleasure as I listened to them, and with still more profit, for they contain matter to be chewed upon. Please to give my respects to Mrs. F., and believe me, truly yours, THEO. PARKER.

1836, August 11.—Began to translate De Wette's " Einleitung " (Introduction to the Old Testament). I cannot tell what will be the result of this. I shall leave that for another time to determine. Meanwhile I will go quietly on translating it gradually as I wish, without interrupting important studies.

He read Schelling's lectures upon Academic Study, and pronounced them too ideal ; " an ideal within his own subjectivity, which is an impossible real, and contains the elements of its own destruction, since it involves a contradiction."

He went to a Barnstable tea-gathering, where among various goodly people, was a pompous old sea-captain from Boston, who had retired with a great deal of money : " *haud decet mihi facere notas, non mei peculium est. Mehercle !* "

These are notes made after attending a Methodist camp-meeting at Eastham :

The women I noticed were always the most noisy. But I was much struck with the cool indifference of one young woman, who sat very quietly munching gingerbread, while all the process of "bringing in" was taking place around her.

I always noticed, too, that the least learned were the most violent—had most of the "Spirit of the Lord," as they said. This accounts for the low opinion of learning among them, and for the great power of Whitefield, who was all *passion* and *feeling*.

The uninterested apologetic tone of one remark is amusing, when we recollect what thunder shook the Music-Hall in after years:—

There was occasionally a touch upon slavery. Who wonders at it?

He left Barnstable at the close of his engagement, trusting that they would find such a man as they needed, but doubting that he was that man. The parish in Northfield sent for him next. He spent there a part of October, and received an invitation to settle, but declined it. Then he returned to Barnstable for the month of November, and the good people proposed to give him a call, but he intercepted their intention,

Since it would involve an entire exclusion from books and literary society. Never do I expect to find so noble and generous and true-hearted a people. But others can labour there more effectually than I, to whom absence of books is no evil. There would be a general exclamation among my books if they are carried to the Cape, from the Reimkennar of Sweden to Saadi and Ferdousi. But still, did not I know that others are to be found who will be called upon to make no sacrifices in going thither, then would I hesitate not, but instantly plant myself among these noble men of the Cape, and live, and love, and labour there.

The death of his father occurred at this time.

TO MISS CABOT.

Nov. 10, 1836.

I received your letter, my dear Lydia, as I never fail to do, with unspeakable pleasure and satisfaction; but if the outside gave me pleasure, and the inside told me what I had long expected, yet I cannot deny that the intelligence found me unprepared. I had fondly put off the day of his departure, and when the event was told me, my sorrow was tenfold greater than I had anticipated.

After I read your letter, and sat silent and lonely by my own fire, I could almost see his fathers of other days, the wife of his youth, and his children and long-separated friends pressing gloriously around him to take him once more to their hearts. I lament not for him; he has no sigh to stifle, no tear to wipe away. But how *can* I, who have been cradled in his arms, led by his hands, blessed by his prayers, and moulded by his tender care, how can I forbear lamenting now he is gone?

But enough of this. He is gone. Let *us* say no more about it; and now I entreat you to say nothing upon that subject in your letters, nor when we meet. A thousand circumstances will bring it all up before me again and again; do not let us multiply them without need.

The valley of tears, if dwelt in, hath a poisonous influence upon the soul; but if only occasionally passed through, it is full of healing waters and fountains of strength.

A list of works, comprising 320 volumes, drawn up at the close of 1836, shows his reading for fourteen months. They are in various languages, and the best books on the subjects of which they treat.

In December he went to Salem to supply the pulpit of Dr. Flint, who was ill. He spent the time very pleasantly at the house of his classmate Silsbee ; some dialogues of Plato were his reading, with various books for a meditated lecture upon Etymology. The fine lines which have often been quoted were written this winter.

> Jesus, there is no dearer name than thine,
> Which Time has blazoned on his mighty scroll;
> No wreaths nor garlands ever did entwine
> So fair a temple of so vast a soul.
> There every virtue set his triumph-seal ;
> Wisdom, conjoined with strength and radiant grace,
> In a sweet copy Heaven to reveal,
> And stamp perfection on a mortal face ;
> Once on the earth wert Thou, before men's eyes,
> That did not half Thy beauteous brightness see ;
> E'en as the emmet does not read the skies,
> Nor our weak orbs look through immensity.

Among other books, the English State Trials were carefully studied.

Very soon the following questions are put down for consideration.

I. Sundry Questions in Theology.
　　1. What is the extent of known supernatural Revelation made to man ?
　　2. What is the foundation of the authority of Jesus Christ ?
　　3. What is the meaning of Faith in Old and New Testament.
　　4. How is Christ more a Saviour than Socrates ?
　　5. Why did the world need a Saviour ?
　　6. What has been his influence ?
　　7. Is Christianity to be a universal Religion ?
　　8. What is the foundation of Religion in Man—the Design of Miracles—the pretence of them in other Religions ?

II. Questions in Scriptural Criticism and Exegesis.
  1. The authenticity of the beginning of the Gospels of
     Matthew and Luke—The Miraculous Conception.
  2. The Resurrection—why was the body of Christ raised ?—
     why " carried up ? " How is the resurrection of matter
     proof of the Immortality of Spirit ? Is not the material
     Resurrection of the body of Jesus Christ unspiritualizing?

It is very evident that his conventional theology is about to
receive a thorough over-hauling. But these questions were not
disposed of in a day.

We find him preaching in Greenfield during February, 1837,
after another visit to Northfield in January.

TO MISS CABOT.

Feb. 10, 1837.

The very air of Greenfield inspires me, although you see no traces
thereof in the letter, and I feel more a man ; the cool wind from the
north braces the outer man, and the sight of mountains and great trees
and wide meadows refreshes the inner man not a little.

Besides all this I have seen little things which encourage me, make
me wiser if not better.

Walking the other day in the woods—i.e., in a road which goes
steeply through the woods—in the midst of the snow at the bottom of
the steep hill, there was a little spring of water, clear as the sky above,
and as unruffled, not frozen, though winter had set her seal stiffly upon
everything around. Over this beautiful spring there arose a great oak,
very old and " stern to look upon," one which had mocked at many
winters. Now, this great oak clasped a young hemlock tree with its
arms, and seemed to hold it in shelter from all the rude blasts of time.
The younger tree had evidently grown up under its protection, and
now repaid its defender by looking kindly upon him when his own
leaves had all fallen away. It was beauty in the arms of strength.

All this living scene was reflected in the little spring, which seemed
to smile at the tenderness of these giant plants. One would walk about
the streets of Boston a thousand years without meeting such a com-
forter as this. But in the country there is a tale in everything, and
every little object in nature hath its beauty to please by, and its moral
to instruct with. Indeed, the country is a great " system of divinity,"
while the city is but " a commercial dictionary," a " ready reckoner," or
a " cook-book."

TO THE SAME.

Feb. 13.

You know I lamented the missing of Mr. Emerson's lectures, but a
single walk along the banks of the Connecticut, or among the hills, or a
moment's listening to the pine's soft music, have taught me more than
Mr. Emerson and all the Boston Association of Ministers.

TO THE SAME.

Feb. 24.

You do not know how delighted I have been with my quiet stay in this beautiful place—apart from the absence of Miss Lydia. I have done more in the way of reading and writing and study than in the last two months before, to say nothing of the glorious walks and comfortable chattings I have had; for Mr. Davis kindly comes in almost every night, and sometimes stays till the witching time of twelve. Without him I should have died at least once a day. Paul says he did that, and the Apostle was not engaged and away from his lady. Mrs. D. is a sweet woman, and a sensible. I almost envy them their cup of connubial happiness, but *we* will have one soon, as generous and divinely tempered. I do not know anything in contemplation more delightful than this, that we may find some place where we may receive enough of this world's treasures; may labour in the most noble and divine of employments which man can conceive of, giving a loftier action to humanity; may exercise mutually the kindliest feelings of the heart, the intellect, and the soul, founding at the same time a family which shall bear up our name, know our virtues, reflect the sunshine of our hearts, and finish our work. Can you conceive anything more noble than this? I confess I cannot.

TO THE SAME.

Feb.

Only think that after a little bit of a courtship of some four years we are at length on the very brink of Matrimony! Within a span's length of the abyss! Without a parish too! Think of that! 520 dollars a year, may be—may be much less—to support a wife. Why, I intend to commence such a rigorous system of *sparing* that I shall never cross a *t* nor dot an *i*; for I'll save ink. I dreamed last night of being at a bookstore, and when the clerk showed me some book which I had long been seeking, and at a price most villainously cheap, " Oh, no," said I; " I shall *never* buy more books; at any rate, never so cheap. I *am a-going to be married!*" and down went the corners of my mouth till they touched my stock. But if soft words can win hard coin, if there is any money-getting virtue in a knowledge of some twenty tongues, any talent in my mind, or any magic in the most unshrinking labour, I will take care that a wife do not beggar the soul of the means of growth and nobleness. If I can find anything to do in the literary way which will get one coin, be it never so hard, so it conflict with no duty, I will put forth my might, be it little, be it much.

TO S. P. ANDREWS.

Greenfield, Feb. 15.

Sometimes, Samuel, I fear lest I have missed it capitally in becoming a minister; that as a lawyer, or in other departments of thought and action, I might have been more useful, and at the same time free from a certain restraining bond—invincible, but strong as fate—which convention has tied up every minister withal. I do not *even think* of deserting a ministry which would dignify angels, and has been honoured by the

Son of God himself. No: I never think of that; for I deem it writ down in my duty to preach the Gospel, come of it what will; and although some of my dearest expectations have already been disappointed, still I shall " bear up and steer, with upright wing, right onward, nor bate one jot of heart nor hope."

Yet sometimes the thought comes mightily upon me, " Thou hast mistaken thy calling !"

One sole thing encourages me, to wit, I know that one who keeps God's " Laws of the Spirit of Life," and puts forth his might manfully in obedience thereto, be his might never so little—be it less than mine even—he has for his friend and ally and co-worker the entire almightiness and perfect virtue of God. With such a co-adjutor it is nobler to be conquered, dragged at the wheels of the enemy, yea, trodden to dust by his followers, who shout aloud, " Great is Mammon of the Yankees !" than to engage in any other warfare.

Therefore shall I go on; consequences I have nothing to do with, they belong to God—to me belongs only duty. All that I have give I to the one cause.

He spent a great deal of time in Salem in the spring of 1837, occasionally preaching ; there are very meagre records of conversations with superior people, some of whom became friends for life.

On the 20th of April his marriage took place. And on the 20th of May he finished translating De Wette's " Introduction," which was the least part of the labour that preceded the publication of that work.

I now intend to revise the work diligently, to add notes from various writers, and to append divers essays and dissertations.

He had preached several times at West Roxbury, and at Waltham, and received a call from both parishes. He was also sought from Concord and Leominster, as well as Greenfield. He was awhile irresolute which to accept, but finally returned a favourable answer to the call from West Roxbury, which he received on the 23rd of May.

His ordination took place on the 21st of June. Dr. Henry Ware, sen., attended as a delegate from the college chapel, John Quincy Adams was the delegate from Quincy, Dr. Francis delivered the sermon, Henry Ware, jun., made the ordaining prayer, Caleb Stetson delivered the charge, and George Ripley gave the right hand of fellowship. His classmate, John S. Dwight, wrote for this occasion an original hymn. In 1849, recalling his ordination, he writes :—

These men had some hopes of me, that I might prove an ornament and a pillar of the Church! Now they look on me as a destroyer and a foe! Yet certainly I have been diligent and laborious. If I could have looked forward twelve years, I should have trembled, and said, "Oh, Lord, send by another hand, not mine!" Henry Ware, in his ordaining prayer, after Dr. Francis had recommended study, prayed that I might be a preacher of righteousness—"may no fondness for peculiar studies ever divert him from doing Thy work." I hope it has been as he would. Surely I have not sought *ease*, or *fame*, or *wealth*. On many things I have disappointed myself—in some things a little surpassed. I expected rather to be a scholar than a reformer—I mean, I looked to books as my means of reform. I did mean to be a reformer.

In this quiet little parish, of about sixty families, the parochial demands upon the clergyman were easily met. He interested himself in town matters, and as a committee-man regularly visited all the schools. Still there was a good deal of time for books and the garden. The pleasant white house, about a mile from the church, stood close to the straggling village street, but the study looked out through trees upon flowers, vines, and garden-beds. Two fine tulip-trees stood before the windows. The land adjoined the beautiful grounds of Mr. George R. Russell, his parishioner and friend, with whom and whose family he found such refreshment and delight. And next, going up the hill, came the grounds of another good and faithful friend, Mr. Francis G. Shaw. Mr. Parker had a right of way over the pleasantly settled hill-side. The hedges defined, but did not divide the respective places of his friends. When jaded with the old folios, he never failed to find some one at his garden limit, in whose attachment his heart recovered strength and joy. It was a gentle life, with pure friendship to lighten labour and to lift the heavy moods which sometimes came sweeping across the sky.

The Russells used to have famous visitors, those bright, fair girls, with literary and philosophic rages, who were just blooming into transcendentalism, but better yet, into womanhood. They used to hold "Olympicks," over which Theodore jovially presided. Sometimes the celestial council met in a barn, where the fresh, fragrant hay, which he had just helped toss and gather, served for the divan. Here Günderode, Bettini, and Göthe, the "Latest form of Infidelity," Fourier, Emerson's last lecture, and all kosmic questions, were discussed. The poetry in the *Dial** was somewhat lightly treated, and the Orphic sayings duly venerated. It is suspected that verses, which never

* The first number of the *Dial* appeared in July, 1840.

H 2

got so far as the "twi-light" *Dial* on the way to the light, were read to the blonde council, while the new hay contested for freshness and pabular availability.

He had many a "long chaffer with the fine ladies" in the next house.

TO W. SILSBEE.

July 13, 1837.

You will like to know a little of my matters, no doubt. Well, cleverly am I settled. Our neighbours are pleasant. About fifty to sixty families in the parish—a hundred to a hundred and fifty worshippers. Sunday-school teachers' meeting at the house of the pastor once a fortnight, wife's class at the Sunday-school, pastoral visits made, schools attended, calls received, baptisms, funerals. Such are my out-of-door matters. Within I have plenty of pleasant employment; De Wette done, almost; reading Jacobi and old Henry More. The life of Apollonius Tyaneus has afforded me no little pleasure of late. I have read Bulwer's "Athens;" a good book, but with mistakes, methinks. I am studying ethics, such as De Wette (a pretty good book), Fichte, Coleridge, and Descartes. Spinoza I shall take soon as I get my copy. I have a new work of Ancillon. All his *melanges* have been republished, and two more volumes added, making a fine work. I borrowed Gesenius' "Lectures on the Old Testament" of Cunningham; they are manuscripts, but will be a treasure, I doubt not. I have been reading Ovid, whom I have in a capital edition, ten volumes octavo. Seneca (and I own him in ten, octavo) I shall read with the other moral writers. The "Iliad" is a part of almost every day's reading. I have engaged to translate Ammon's "Fortbildung des Christenthums," four volumes, octavo, in the course of time. So you see I have enough to keep an idle man busy.

We have a very pleasant house, garden, "men servants and maidens," a cow, horse, and *pig!* I'm as practical as Stebbins; buy and sell, dig, lend and borrow. "To this complexion must we come at last."

TO THE SAME.

Sept. 22.

Touching things carnal, I assure you I am more disturbed than I had ever anticipated. This is between you and me. Men of the *actual*, and their name is legion, have a very cheap sort of logic, amounting to this—"My way is perfectly right:" this is the first axiom, an undisputed truth, self-evident. Then cometh the second, viz., "All important things are comprised in the actual, which alone should engross our attention." This is the theory of these worthies. Now for the practice. They see other men doing different from themselves, so they condemn them under the first axiom. They find them thinking of other matters than potatoes and turnips and railroads, specie-currency and the manners of their next neighbour, to wit, thinking of God, of duty, nature, destiny, cause, consequence, the right, the beautiful, the good, and so they condemn these under axiom the second.

Then yearn their bowels of tender mercy, and they attempt to reform
the thinkers, that is, to make their talk of turnips, &c., and, failing
herein, they beset me, till flesh and blood cry out, like that of Abel,
for vengeance. So goes it. I feel much of this harassing.

Yet, this apart, I am very pleasantly situated; the people good,
quiet, sober, church-going; capital listeners, none better; so much so,
that I tell my friends I think my parishioners are as much blessed in
preaching as those of even Dr. Channing; for what is wanted in
preaching they make up in listening, whereas the Doctor's people
depend altogether upon him. . . . .

I believe, brother William, that no good word is ever spoken in vain.
I may not see it grow, but what then? As Kepler said, if God could
wait four thousand years for some one to see his laws, I may wait
one hundred for men to understand my sayings. I preach abundant
heresies, and they all go down, for the listeners do not know how
heretical they are. I preach the worst of all things, Transcendentalism,
the grand heresy itself, none calling me to account therefor, but men's
faces looking like fires new stirred thereat.

Old studies go on, metaphysics, theology, criticism; all that used so
much to delight and instruct us flourishes and grows apace in my new
situation. Thoughts high as heaven, and profound as the centre of
the earth, sometimes visit me in my loneliness. Then, too, the smiles
of love cheer and encourage me.

You will come and stay a week with me, at the least. I have a
prophet's chamber all ready for you. You must come and stay at
least a week, and as much longer as you can make it agreeable; this I
shall depend upon. Remember how I stayed with you at Salem—how
much delighted I was. I shall never forget the day when we walked
over to Beverley; that day, as to the thoughts revealed there, was one
of the brightest of my life.

I have got lots of new books—upwards of one hundred Germans!
Come and see. Some of them are old friends, others new—all sorts of
creatures.

The polyglott library grew fast. So grew theologic misgivings,
and a dull sense that his great capacity of work and of humanity
must have more room.

During August he gets hold of Palæphatus, " περί Απιστῶν "
or " On Incredible Things." Palæphatus was probably an Alexandrine Rationalist, portions of whose book on the treatment of
the Greek myths survive, in various editions, of which Fischer's
is the best. He attempted historical interpretations of the stories of
Cadmus, Lynceus, Niobe, &c., saying, for instance, that Lynceus,
who saw through the ground, was a man who discovered beds
and veins of metals; that *Pegasus* was a clipper-privateer, and
Scylla also ; that the King of Lerna had a fortified town called
Hydra, which was defended by fifty bow-men : and so on. He
was a Greek Paulus, and equally jejune ; for he did not care to let

the myths bring allegorical honey to his hive, but only to extract
their sting of the incredible.   Mr. Parker's opinion after reading
this, betrays a mind fast becoming decided in its direction.

How the priests must have exclaimed against the "impious" book
in the day of its appearance.   Such books do good.   I wish some wise
man would now write a book περί Απιστων, or "On Vulgar Errors," and
show up the absurdity of certain things commonly believed, on the
authority of old Jews.   To be plain, I mean the Old Testament miracles, prophecies, dreams, miraculous births, &c.

Now there needs but the natural and quite logical generalization which extends the incredible element over the New Testament also.

He reads Gabler, Paulus and Bauer, and the question is first
presented in the form of application of the mythical system of
exposition to the New Testament : myths, not yet in the sense
of Strauss, but stories merely, as of the birth of Christ, the star,
the angels, &c., invented by people to give a supernatural origin
to a famous man.   The history of the Temptation is a myth of
this description.

About this time he wrote the two sermons upon the historical,
scientific and moral contradictions of the Bible, which he kept
in his desk more than a year before he dared to preach them,
taking advice of various lay and clerical friends, who seemed to
agree with his doctrine, but to dread having it proclaimed.   In
a sermon which he preached at West Roxbury, on going to
Europe, he describes the predicament.

You will have all the clergy about your ears.   An old friend, and a
clergyman of high reputation in the churches, asked me what peculiar
and specific thing I was aiming at.   I said : " To separate theology
from religion ; then to apply good sense to theology, to separate
mythology from that, and so get a theology which rested on facts of
necessity, facts of consciousness, facts of demonstration, &c." He said :
" Then you will not stay in your pulpit seven years ; no, nor three." I
answered : " Then, please God, I will stay somewhere else ; for this
thing I will do."

So, after considering the matter for more than thirteen months after
I had written, I preached the sermons.   I did not dare look you in the
face while I spoke.   I clutched the cushions of the pulpit, and read with
a trembling heart.   To my great surprise, I found you were able to bear
all that I had to say.

I did not wait thirteen months again before I ventured to preach a
truth not preached before, or expose a theological absurdity.

He thus describes, in the same sermon, his conversations with the two deacons of his society :—

You did not all accept my convictions. One of your number said, with the candour and fairness which marks his whole life, that, though he thought very differently about some things in the Old Testament, and New Testament, too, yet he should be very sorry to have me refuse to preach what I thought; for it would be almost as bad as to preach what I did not think, and would soon lead to that end.

Another said: All the difficulty lies in " rightly dividing the Word of Truth ;" there are things in the Bible, in the New Testament, that I am sorry to find there. But there are so many good things, that we all love it, spite of the bad. Now, if you can "rightly divide the Word," so as to leave all the truth on one side, and all the rest on the other, then you will do a great service to the Church and the World. But it is hard to do this. I don't believe it can be done without violence to the good parts. You know what Isaiah says—" As the new wine is found in the cluster, and one saith, Destroy it not, for a blessing is in it ;" so I say of the Bible, Destroy it not, for a blessing is in it. But still, if you can get the blessing out of the grape-skin, that is all we want.

It was afterwards charged that he was precipitate in framing and exposing his opinions. No opinions ever grew more deliberately, and never was there less of light audacity in the exhibition of opinions that had fallen out of harmony with the prevailing order.

At the beginning of 1838, he is spiritless, and filled with the vague dissatisfaction which creeps so often, like a sluggish earthworm, over the hopes of many a young clergyman, who has not the excess of power which tore up Mr. Parker's ease. No routine is so disheartening, because no other one involves such high thoughts and objects, to cope with which a man is not ready at set days and hours. The theory of parish-visiting is noble, the practice is sometimes exceedingly depressing. The act of prayer is tender and sublime. To pray tenderly at eleven o'clock precisely, every Sunday morning, is a preciseness which the spirit declines to accommodate.

I often ask myself what I am doing with my one talent, and can only reply that I deem myself well nigh wasting it. Preaching to an audience of 70 or 120 souls, going about and talking little with old women, giving good advice to hypocrites, and scattering here and there, I hope, a corn-grain that will one day germinate and bear fruit. Oh, could I be satisfied that I am doing even this last ! If I deemed it certain that any word of mine would ever waken the deep inner life of another's soul, I should bless God that I was alive and speaking. But I will trust. I am sometimes praised for my sermons. I wish men knew how cold those sleek speeches are. I would rather see one man practising one of my sermons than hear all men praise them. But of this I am satisfied—I am not doing what I ought to do.

And a few days after, the mood grows very heavy, but it is not easy to decompose it and declare its physical and moral elements, or the proportion in which they mingle.

I have lost many things. The greatest was Hope. Days there have been when I saw nought else to freshen my eye, weary with looking over the dull waste of my early life. Tired with labour, I have laid down, my books beside me, the lamp at summer midnight burning low, all else silent in sleep. Hope visited me; she sat beside me, trimmed my lamp. In her sublime presence I grew calm, and composed myself by her majestic features.

Here he plays good-humouredly with the tired mood :—

TO W. SILSBEE.

November 13, 1837.

Epistola tua, O Gulielme, omnium carissime mihi, gratissima venit, instar roris vespertinæ in flores sole perustos defluentis. (Hâc studium mei sanctissimum accedit conjux, in manu vilam *scopam* versans, nubes densissimas pulverûm jactura! Vae mihi!) Literas brevissimas, sic dicas, tibi scripseram! Culpam hanc gravem admitto. Pacem tuam atque indulgentiam, fortasse haud meritam, implore. Oppressus dolore, fatigatione, lassitudine corporis, multis cum malis quæ το σαρξ in vita hæreditatur in mediis hisce difficultatibus epistolam feci.

Tam sicca epistola ista, ut metui si longius protraheretur combustione spontaneâ incenderetur. Sic finem posui in metu.

Bona Dea te faveat, emens libros tam vilissimi pretii. Emens enim ab homine *Gruff* (Latinis cum literis animam suam nolo depingere), quum accedis Bostoniam, si apportabis têcum Krummacher, Twestenque, Tenneman et Wegscheider, deponens illos apud Munroe, multas gratias meritaris opus rusticum (Anglicè, yeoman-service) mihi perfungarentur.

Nunc pluma—penna stultissimæ anseris—defatigata, volitare Romano in cœlo abnegat.

But there were choice friends with whom he grew bright and happy. Mr. George Ripley, then settled over a Unitarian Society in Boston, was one of the oldest of these. Mr. Parker's debt to him was large, for counsel in all matters of the intellect, for a discriminating judgment in books, for liberal friendship of all kinds. There was strong sympathy, indeed it may be called love, between them ; a subsequent theological divergence did not impair it. If they discussed its points at all, it was done genially, and with the most perfect mutual understanding. For Mr. Ripley's convictions were held by a mind too scholarly, and a disposition too serene, to become intolerant. Mr. Parker was never tired of acknowledging the debt he owed to friends who were a few years his seniors ; and Mr. Ripley's name was among the highest on this roll of gratitude.

There was at that time in Boston, under the leadership of Dr. Channing, a Society of Friends of Progress. They met for a free and bold discussion of all current subjects of theology and social life. Here Mr. Parker found the charm of good companionship, for there came to those meetings, besides Dr. Channing, Jonathan Phillips, a dear parishioner of the Doctor's, and a man of acute and liberal mind,—occasionally Wendell Phillips, then a young lawyer, of the Suffolk bar ; Mr. Hedge, Mr. Ripley, Mr. Alcott and Dr. Follen.

To judge from some notes of these meetings which are preserved, Mr. Parker stood in little awe of the magnates. His mind willingly went down into the lists with them for a good-natured encounter. Mr. Emerson's views upon the personality of God were for discussion one evening, suggested by a late lecture of his (in the winter of 1837-38.). He was accused of maintaining that God was only an idea, formed in the mind of the individual, projected into ideas of Omnipresence, &c. Another charge was, that of Pantheism, which in those days was popularly understood to be the dread belief of a few suspected men, who were watched as jealously as Jews and witches ever were. In the last century they would have been accused of practising some diabolical ritual. Mr. Parker made a very sensible statement of what he considered the drift of Mr. Emerson's thought to be, and then nicely laid open the question of the Divine Personality.

What do we mean by the term ? Personality cannot exist without will. Suffer all my faculties to remain as they are, but annihilate the will ; I am no longer a person, an individual. I cannot say *I*—a faggot of powers has taken the place of *I*. There are attributes, but no substance to which they belong. How, then, can I conceive of God without personality ? But is will the only essential of personality ? The question is difficult. I conceive of God as a Being of infinite powers, directed by infinite love—as a Being easy of access, full of tenderness, whose character is summed up in one word—Father ! Now, the idea of God's *will* unites all these attributes into a being. Here, then, are the attributes of God united with a substance—the will. What is the essence of God ? I know not what is the essence of myself. I cannot tell. The idea of God is no more mysterious than that of self ; that of the Divine Personality is as clear as that of human personality. Men have always perplexed themselves in meditating upon this subject. And they have come to this conclusion, "He is past finding out." This is variously expressed by the thinkers of different ages and countries. "Search me after the essence of God and His laws," says the old Veda. God is "unrevealed light," "the ineffable," "incomprehensible," "the primal Being," say the Gnostics. "The most real of all beings," says Plato; "Himself without being." So the mystic can only say, "I am" —"He is."

Mr. A. talks of the *progress* of God: the Almighty going forward to His own infinity—progressively unfolding Himself! An idea to me revolting, &c.

Another friend, whom he met more seldom, but always with delight and profit, was William Henry Channing, the successor of Mr. Martineau in Liverpool, and now minister of the Unitarian Society at Washington, D.C.

July 13.

Went to Boston with Mr. Ellis, and at my return found Wm. Channing at home—to my great delight. The subjects of our conversation were sundry important questions on biblical theology, embracing most of the works of the recent German theologians; for there are no others at this day. We spoke of individuality (here follows a sketch of Mr. P.'s idea of two individualities, the phenomenal and the real; the first being a man's peculiarities, which separate him from other men; the second being the essential human truths and feelings, which bring all men together). I am exceedingly delighted with Mr. C. He seems true—a little diseased in the region of consciousness, but otherwise of most remarkable beauty of character; full of good tendencies, of noblest aspirations; an eye to see the evils of society, a heart to feel them; a soul to hope better things, a willingness to endure all self-denial to accomplish the end whereto he is sent; not covered by thickest wrappages, which rather obscure his worthy uncle, whom I venerate perhaps too much.

We spent all the time in conversation (to me) most profitable.

Conversations between ardent and truth-seeking friends were not confined to the theological points which agitated the denomination. The social problem attracted the same minds who sought a better authority for truth than miracles could give, in a spiritual perception of it which all mankind might share. A mutualism to secure culture and material welfare was consistently desired by those who believed in a community of the sources of moral and spiritual welfare. The social evils which result from the struggles of competitive labour seemed to outweigh all its benefits. Modern civilization was thought to be the culmination of isolated selfishness, madly struggling from bread to luxury and refined delights, which the strongest and least scrupulous only could acquire. Prisons and punishments were the defences of this artificial system, to repress instincts that were moral till they became illegal. Hospitals and benevolent institutions were also mere defences to absorb as much misery as possible ere it became malicious, to get the social gangrene reduced to limits. The providential impulses of the human being were forced to act in subversive ways and directions, when they might all be harmonized by their own inherent laws, and the blessing of mutualism succeed to the bane of antagonism. Each man ought to be the guarantee to all men against disorder ; the carefully adjusted elements of a selfishness which threatens continually to blow the social fabric to atoms, would become not only innoxious but salutary in its proper combination ; and a new civilization might arise in fair proportion from the serial development and movement of all possible human tendencies. Then all men and women might labour and be happy ; all might earn with a minimum of toil a competence of culture. Property would be the ally of the whole instead of the oppressor of the many ; and crimes would disappear, because the instincts would no longer have motives to be criminal.

These opinions, combined with sharp and legitimate criticism of the evils of civilization and the absurdities of modern society, were presented in a scientific form by Charles Fourier, and urged with great enthusiasm by his advocates in this country, who generally had the sense to let alone some of his conclusions respecting marriage and the intercourse of the sexes. Pure-minded men were fascinated by the idea that people could be shown and taught to work in harmony, to reduce drudgery and domestic annoyances by a skilful division of labour, to develope beauty as well as use, and to save precious time for the soul.

Mr. Ripley soon left a profession in which he seemed to be only recommending truths, to make the experiment of organizing the same truths into practical forms of use, into ideal forms of beauty. He would show the possibility of living in a system that should not hide its roots in misery and crime. The establishment at Brook Farm was not far from Mr. Parker's ; and Mr. Channing sometimes came there, the purest, most enthusiastic, most religious of all the speakers at those fine reunions, where the problem was discussed.

But Mr. Parker accepted the criticisms upon society, and waxed no less indignant than the rest, nor was he less warmed with the hope of a fairer future for mankind, without ever acceding to the schemes of Fourier, Considerant, or their American advocates. When afterwards the principle of association was tried at Brook Farm, he was occasionally rather sly over some of the details, and had a humorous eye for the little weaknesses of the recruits. The motive called forth his unbounded respect; but he never could be made to see the availability of any of the plans.

R. Dislikes the customs of property; a father transmitting it to his son. But I see no way of avoiding the evil. The sin lies deeper than the transmission of property from getter to enjoyer. It *lies* in the *love of low things,* and in the *idea that work degrades.* We must correct this notion, and then all is well. Let men see there are better things than gold can buy; that labour, *properly* pursued, gives a competence and leisure for cultivation of the man, and that labour elevates man, and the trouble is all over. How the world ever came into such a sad state it is difficult to conjecture.

Still a Phalanx seems no stranger to me than a city might have seemed to some old patriarch. Yet I suspect there has never been a time since the first settlement of this country, when morals or religion were really at a higher flood. I complain loud as others of the lowness of the common actual, and also of the common ideal; but I will not look back on any one age, and say we are worse than our fathers, but forward to an ideal, and say we are worse than that.

There are traces of his interviews with Dr. Channing, whom he began reverently to seek while teaching in Watertown; but no notes of this intercourse appear till later, when he had opinions of his own and felt encouraged to sustain them.

Went to see Dr. Channing last Thursday. I have not been this winter so often as usual (1838–39), though I delight to go as well as ever. We spoke of many things. The Doctor thinks the morality of Christianity as great an advance upon all previous systems as the religion itself. Praised my article in the *Examiner,** but thought I had not quite done justice to Christianity in that respect. I should be sorry if it were true.

Afterwards we were speaking of educating the conscience, a doctrine which I rather ridiculed. But the Doctor said it must be educated, like the understanding. But upon being asked if more was needed than this, that the understanding should be rendered capable of presenting the case distinctly to conscience, he seemed to favour the hypothesis. I asked him if conscience were not an *infallible* guide. He seems to doubt it, but is going to think of the question. To me it seems that conscience will always decide right, if the case is fairly put, and old habits have not obscured its vision. This he seemed inclined to believe, yet hesitated to assent. He said conscience was like the *eye,* which might be dim, or might see wrong. But in this case it is not the eye

* An article for January, 1839, reviewing Ackermann's "Das Christliche in Plato."

which sees, but the soul which looks out at the eye; now the organ may be defective, and so misrepresent. But conscience, when the facts are fairly before it, acts *directly* and not *mediately*, and therefore it is not liable to the same mistakes with the eye.

He seemed inclined to admit this, yet denied that we needed any infallible guide, and said the belief in such a want had led to the theory that the Scripture was inspired word for word. But Scripture was not an infallible guide, and if it were, it would do us no good, for we could not infallibly understand it.

He thought a man late in his life (in a case I put), who had not hitherto consulted his conscience, would, coming to that adviser, make great mistakes, and therefore be punished for his past sin of neglect. Upon the whole, he believed if a man should begin early to ask for the right, with sincere wish to find it, he never would get far out of the way. And even if he did, he was of course justifiable in the Court of Heaven.

Conscience is the last appeal. Never go beyond that ; even if it says wrong, the man is degraded who disobeys it. But if a man's conscience tells him something different from other men's, he is not to forego it, but to recast its plans, examine the subject anew, but at last adhere to conscience.

19 April.—Went to see Dr. Channing. Spoke about Strauss. He observed very archly he should not be *very* sorry if some of Kneeland's followers would do it into English. He would not advise me to do it.

He said Christianity could not be separated from Christ! Jesus had a miraculous character, different in *kind* from ours. To him was made a miraculous *revelation*, different in kind from that made to other men, excepting the old prophets and apostles.

Believes the Bible miracles, not those of other people. Thinks that Paul did appeal to the Christian miracles—δυναμεις is equivalent to "miracles."

May 2.—Saw Dr. Channing. Borrowed Origen of him. He is pleased with Luther's opinion on the Sabbath; says men ought to be told of these things. Why does he not tell them? He says Luther was a coarse man in the flesh. I compared him to Paul. Dr. Channing thinks the comparison favours the latter. So it does. Luther was melancholy in his latter years, because the Reformation had slipped out of his hands. He found the world ripe for his work : so it went easy.

July.—If Dr. Channing could be ground over again, and come out a young man of five-and-twenty, give all the results of his reading, experience, and life, all the insight, power, eloquence, Christianity he now possesses,—but let him hold the same religious, philosophical, political, and social opinions as now, and preach on them as he does, and let him, with such tracts as his "Letter on Slavery," &c., be all unknown to fame, he could not find a place for the sole of his foot in Boston, though half-a-dozen pulpits were vacant—not he."

TO W. SILSBEE.

August 10, 1838.

I must now say a few words of myself. I have never had a summer of more delightful study than the present, never found more satisfaction in theological and philosophical pursuits. I have solved many questions which have long perplexed and troubled me, and have grown in some small measure ₁calmer than of old time. Tranquillity, you know, is one of my *attainable*, but unattained virtues. Some of my inquiries have been historical, others critical, but philosophy has given me most delight this season. I do not say that the greatest questions are yet solved, or will ever be. They stand now like fire-breathing dragons in my path; I cannot drive them away. But though they often heat, they never bite me. Mr. H. says, in expressing his despair of philosophy, it is better to give it all up and study the facts of nature—with Kirby and Spence, and White of Selborne! Who can do it if he would? The Sphinx will have an answer or you die. You must read the riddle. Love of philosophy may be "the last infirmity of noble minds," but I will cling to it still.

You ask me what effect my speculations have on my practice. You will acquit me of boasting when I say, the most delightful—better than I could hope. My preaching is weak enough, you know, but it is made ten times the more spiritual and strong by my views of nature, God, Christ, man and the Sacred Scriptures. In my religious conversation I tell men religion is as necessary as bread to the body, light to the eye, thought to the mind. I ask them to look into their hearts and see if it is not so. They say I tell them the doctrines of common sense, and it is true. Questions are often asked on the heretical points. I tell men that Moses and the writers of the Old Testament had *low* views of God, but the best that men could have in those times. They understand it and believe the New Testament account of God. In regard to Christ, they see a beauty in his character when they look upon him as a man, who had wants like theirs, trial, temptation, joys and sorrows like their own, yet stood higher than the tempter, overcome in every trial. They see the same elements in themselves.

I dwell mainly on a few great points, viz., the nobleness of man's nature, the lofty ideal he should set before him, the degradation of men at this time, their low aims and worthless pleasures; on the necessity of being true to their convictions, whatever they may be, with the certainty that if they do this, they have the whole omnipotence of God working for them, as the artist brings the whole power of the river to turn his wheel.

Also I dwell on the character and providence of God, and the exactness and beauty of his laws, natural, moral, and religious. My confidence in the Bible is increased. It is not a sealed book, but an open one. I consider there are three witnesses of God in creation. 1. Works of nature: these do not perfectly reveal Him, for we cannot now understand all its contradictions. 2. The words of our fellowmen: this confirms all the wisdom of all the past; it includes the Sacred Scriptures. Parts of it differ vastly in degree from other writings, but not in kind. 3. The infinite sentiments of each individual soul. Now, I lay stress on the first, but more on the second, and still more on the third; for a man may have just as bright revelations in his own heart as Moses, or David, or Paul; I might say, as Jesus, but I do not think any man ever has had such a perfect God-consciousness as he.

Men no more understand his words than they can do his miracles. "Be perfect as God," do they know what this means? No, no. My confidence in the Gospel is immeasurably increased. I see it has meaning in its plainest figures. "He that is greatest among you shall be your servant"—what meaning! It will be understood a thousand years hence, not before. But I see the Gospel is human, but almost infinitely above present humanity.

I feel bound to communicate my views just so fast and so far as men can understand them,—no farther. If they do not understand them when I propound them, the fault, I think, is mine and not theirs. I often find it difficult to make myself understood.

We will have a long *talk* upon these points, for you know the pen is dull and cold, while the tongue is nearer the heart. My heart and my hand go together like two turtle-doves, who perch on the same bough, and eat of the same food, and drop water in one another's beaks. My religion warms my philosophy, and my philosophy gives strength to my religion. You know I do not boast in all this.

TO W. SILSBEE.

Dec. 9, 1837.

1 am reading the Phædrus. It was the first of Plato's *own* I ever read. Several years since strolling (idly perhaps) about the library, I took down the volume which contained the Phædrus. I read it in a night. I was appalled by the grandeur of the thought, the beauty of the style. The noon of night passed before I could lay it down, and then sleep came not, for the procession of the gods, and the ideal flight of the soul, upborne on celestial wings not yet defiled by earthly stain, gazing upon the lofty countenance of Truth,— all this floated in my mind and kept off the drowsy god. I shall never forget that event in my life. How I read, and re-read, and read again, the more delighted at each perusal. Subsequently I forgot the name of the book, and have sought everywhere else in the mighty master for the passage so exciting to me, but all in vain till now. I commence with this, and all the old ideas re-awake in my soul.

Some notes of reading and conversation belong to this period.

BOPP'S VERGLEICHENDE GRAMMATIK.—I can read almost any book that promises instruction. This doubtless contains stores of facts relating to comparative philology; but I can't read the book. It is awfully written; none but a German could write such a book, none but a German could read it; yet it is doubtless valuable.

The Germans, as Mr. Norton says, are "too raw to write books." Certainly they have had but few good models of writing in Germany; but they have not much improved those they have. The book belongs to the same class with Lobeck's "Aglaophamus." It is not a book, but a collection of valuable materials which might be put into a book. It seems necessary to have a board of attorneys in Germany to write the books which learned men are full of. Then a scholar like Bopp should hie to his glib attorney, with all his facts and philosophy in his satchel; should state its case to him, and let Mr. Attorney lay the matter before the public in the most perspicuous and forcible manner possible. Authors might then express themselves; the public could understand them.

KARCHER's ANALECTA.—Eichhorn's " Præfamen," as he calls it, contains a clever defence of the Masoretic text, as he calls it. The book contains the results of an immense reading of books that are not valuable, at least, not valuable to me. Karcher read all the books mentioned in Wolf's " Bibliotheca Hebraica," and added what was omitted by Wolf, if it seemed important. Of course he tells you that Rabbi Mier Hallodami Ben Job Ben . . Adam, besides the 998 ascribed to him by Wolf, wrote another called " The Fool's Way Wiser," and that one of the 998 cited by Wolf is mentioned as the " Book of Fools," and it is " The Book of Stupid Men," and the like. Doubtless the work is very valuable to those whom it concerns, but not to me.

LIFE OF SWEDENBORG.*—It seems written with the most honest intentions, but is not satisfactory to me, farther than this, it shows he was a very remarkable man. As to his wonderful deeds, I have no antecedent objection to them, though the evidence is not always sufficient to establish their actuality. If actual they are of no value to my mind as proof of spiritual inspiration. I cannot believe in his interpretations of the Scriptures, if he were to move mountains. There is a little unfairness in giving part of the testimony of Kant, without giving the part against the credibility of Swedenborg.

CONVERSATION WITH PROF. STUART.—He says it is Emerson's doctrine, that man has in him all he attributes to the Godhead; that he has elements of religion in him; all he has to do is *to find it.* This is certainly giving up the Bible. Why ? *Ecce argumentum :* God gave man the Bible. Now this gift supposes it was God's opinion man needed it, and could not get religion or knowledge of God without it. Acting on this supposition, he made revelations of Himself, &c.

The above is beautiful reasoning, and sounds much like the following:—God gives oxen grass; therefore He supposes they need it; therefore He thinks they would never have been hungry had He not given them grass. To say an ox would be hungry if there were no grass, is as bad as to say man would have religious wants if there were no Bible or miraculous revelation of God. Truly Jonathan Edwards was wiser than this. See his sermon on " Spiritual Light Everywhere."

But I am surprised at the general liberality of Moses Stuart. He detests littleness, and would rather give up revelation than reason. He has no notion of going back to the dark ages, as the English theologues have, with whom he has no patience, and says they belong to the fourteenth century.

CONVERSATION WITH PROF. NORTON.—Returned to Cambridge and called on Mr. Norton; left with him Mr. Stuart's note. I found Mr. Norton in the midst of books, all neatly arranged about him. His MSS. looked as neat as a lady's album; three pretty portfolios con-

---

* No name of author. Perhaps it was the Life prepared by Nathaniel Hobart. That contains the letter of Kant upon the alleged intercourse of Swedenborg with the spiritual world.

tained various papers. He proceeded to speak about a work lent to me when at Cambridge—Matter's work on the Gnostics. He pronounced it a romance founded on Gnosticism, and *not* a "critical history." He says M. Matter is wrong in his facts, inferences, and conclusions; is a man of considerable talent, but is hasty, and therefore inaccurate and loose in his statements. He gave me some instances.

I inquired if he had ever seen Bauer on the Gnostics—he had not; but he expressed some little dislike of the plan when told that Bauer found Gnosticism in Schleiermacher, Schelling, and Hegel. I told him Bauer found no *essence of Gnosticism,* and did not tell what was the one doctrine which showed itself in all sects, and affirmed that there was no such common doctrine. Mr. Norton differed on that head; he said the essence of Gnosticism consisted in two things:—I. A denial that Jehovah of the Old Testament was the Supreme God. II. An affirmation that the world was made by an inferior being (Demiurgos). To these he added a third tenet, scarcely distinctive, that Matter has an evil influence on Mind.

In these, he says, all the Gnostics agreed; he does not count the *Carpocratians* members of this sect. This is original with him, so he requests me to make no use of it, as he designs to use it for himself.

I am delighted to see so profound and accurate a scholar; it does one good; it sharpens attention, and is a stimulus. I wanted to ask him about the authenticity of the Pentateuch, but could not bear to trespass on his time.

During this year, 1838, he composed a treatise upon the Origin of Writing among the Greeks, Hebrews, and Egyptians, in the course of his preparation for publishing the translation of De Wette. On this, and the Homeric question, he anticipated Mr. Grote.

May 13.—To be done this week. Plant the other side the brook. Sow the garden vegetables. Plough the new land, and plant the old alleys. See about the Sunday-school. Get the benches for the vestry; and ask Mr. Ellis to be superintendent."

Following this are pages of Greek inscriptions, from tables found at Herculaneum, the two tables at Amyclæ, the Sigean Marble, &c., &c. From ploughing to Boustrophedon is not an abrupt transition.

Sunday, July 15, 1838.—Proceeded to Cambridge, to hear the valedictory sermon by Mr. Emerson. In this he surpassed himself as much as he surpasses others in the general way. I shall give no abstract. So beautiful, so just, so true, and terribly sublime was his picture of the faults of the Church in its present position. My soul is roused, and this week I shall write the long-meditated sermons on the state of the Church and the duties of these times.

How many generous youths were fired by the same famous sermon, which Mr. Emerson preached at the invitation of the graduating Divinity Class ; and how many, unfortunately, became infected only with certain idiomatic peculiarities : it was sometime before the neighbourhood recovered from " Ever the sun shines," &c., and all the apothecary shops were mobbed, to discover what else beside "myrrh and rosemary" Religion was. The critics used to toss and trample these phrases with great zeal, thinking they had the man in them and were punishing him well. The man was a long way off in safety, serenely viewing this taurine fury. Not critics alone, but a good many promising young men who learned better, began their career with popular satire of the idiom which clothed this pure and independent spirit. It was a mark too palpable, and the fingers could not hold the string. Some of these satirical Sauls who set out on that keen Damascus journey, were converted by the way. A noble, genial mind, in the very act of discharging its spark into such a peculiarity, is disarmed, and the man beneath the idiom holds him prisoner. How many he held fast, not by spreading the snare of a system whose definiteness chokes a little, like a noose, while it retains, but by enveloping their minds in a tranquil and poetic freedom, through which the objects of nature might be sought and into which an exacting theology could not pursue. The liberal gesture itself was worth a whole body of divinity.

Reverend doctors collected over this discourse in great alarm, declared that "what was not folly was impiety," and hoped, perhaps, to pick it to death by force of numbers. To Mr. Parker and others it imparted the lesson much needed at that moment, how salutary is the boldness of a pure and constant mind.

But with his usual good sense he set aside certain phrases which subjected the generous thought to misconstruction.

Mr. E. says, "if a man is at heart just, so far he is God." Now, it seems that he mistakes likeness for identity. My spirit is like God, but is it necessarily God ? There are ten peas in a pod, exactly alike in all things : are there not ten peas, and not one alone ? Now, if a man's spirit could become exactly like God's, would his be the same as God's ? &c.

This is very prosaic, for a mystical word does not like to be accounted for ; but it is characteristic of his love of order. Love of freedom never overcame that humane as well as scholarly instinct.

I begin to fear my own sermons are too speculative. Is it so? I wish to stand on the earth, though I would look beyond the stars. I would live *with men*, but think with philosophers.

The autumn of this year ripened his surmises about Inspiration. And here is the first formal reduction to words of his future doctrine.

We say a *good* man is inspired to do good deeds. Here we only mean he has *moral goodness*, which all men may have if they will. We say a *wise* man is inspired to teach wisdom, without supposing his will is interfered with, or that an unnatural (query, preternatural?) communication is made to him. We say the writers of the Scriptures were inspired, but this means the same as was meant in the other case. The inspiration of Jesus Christ could not differ *in kind* from that of Socrates, only *in degree*. He had much inspiration; Socrates little. All truth comes from God, for it is God's thought; all morality, for it is God's will (query, moral wishes?); all religion, for it is His feeling (this is afterwards changed). So far, then, as a man is *true*, virtuous, religious, so far he is *inspired*—no farther. This inspiration comes by the use of the proper faculties. Be true to your conviction, be patient, and wait for it. The inspiration will come.

In the July number of the *Boston Quarterly Review*, which commenced its career in 1838, under Mr. Brownson, there is a long article by Mr. Parker upon Dr. Palfrey's "Lectures on the Jewish Scriptures and Antiquities," which marks very clearly the progress of his mind. It is also a model of simplicity and analytic ability; the reader sees at once that the critic has a thorough knowledge of the field to be examined, the languages, the learned helps, the opinions of scholars, as well as principles of his own that are independent of theology. Upon Miracles, the immoralities of the Pentateuch, upon Revelation, the views were so decidedly liberal, that epithets not over-choice were applied to the writer. His religious motive was said to be blasphemous. The best-informed people were quite certain it was written by an atheist.

Here is a sentence upon Dr. Palfrey's treatment of the miracles of the Pentateuch, p. 269.

While he admits the abstract credibility of miracles, he seems desirous of restricting the miraculous agency to the smallest sphere possible. But when the *deus ex machinâ* is once fairly introduced, neither the frequency nor the marvellousness of his operations can

I 2

produce any embarrassment. It is no relief to explain away ninety-and-nine miracles, while the hundredth is permitted to remain. If one camel may go through the needle's eye, all may.

But at this time he believed, with some exceptions, the miracles of the New Testament.

He wrote to his friend, " My hair stands up when I think of what I have written." His friend, after reading the article, gives it considerable criticism, to which the following is a reply :—

TO WM. SILSBEE.

27 November, 1838.

You think there is sarcasm. I do not think that is too strong a word, though I never intended anything like it. I hate sarcasm, yet am, perhaps, sarcastic. I wished to indulge in a little harmless pleasantry, but I fear the Dean would not share in the mirth he excited. You think I indulge the ludicrous vein too much. Such is my propensity, no doubt ; but how ought things to be treated ? Light things lightly, grave things gravely, ridiculous things ridiculously. I must think ridicule has its place even in criticism. For instance, suppose M. Poyer should write a book on the miracles of the Saviour, attempting to explain them as the results of animal magnetism, a critic might show, 1, that the attempt was not successful ; and 2, how ridiculous it was to make the attempt, and represent the Saviour as filling the 5000 with a fancy they had eaten, and letting them go off with that impression.

Mr. Parker alludes to the following sentence in his review " He considers the religious principle as the most important element in human nature ; but at the same time so weak, that, unlike all the other principles, it cannot be trusted to shift for itself, to discover the truth and adhere to it." The letter then proceeds :—

To my mind, William, there is something strange and startling in the assertion, that man has been so constituted that he can, by the use of his faculties, on condition of obedience to their laws, achieve all the wonders of science and art, tell the dimensions of the planets and their whereabouts, and yet never be able by the use of his highest faculties—I mean the spontaneous religious sentiments—and by obedience to their laws, become able to learn religious truth, and to be certain it *was* truth he learned and not error. Is it not most of all important for man to settle the questions of duty, to possess religious truth and religious life ? Has God, so bountiful in bestowing other powers, given him none to discover those truths, the most important, the most necessary ? If I was told, by an angel from Ouranus, that the inhabitants of that planet differed much from us, that they had 70 senses for communing with the outer world, I should say with confidence, with my present views of God, then must they have 700 internal

senses for communing with God, and I should expect him to add, 7000.
Is it not the case, William, that, while the Almighty takes such
bounteous care of all little things, that no animal can be found in
utmost height or utmost deep, all of whose wants are not perfectly
satisfied—none found wandering up and down, seeking rest and finding
none—He lays most stress on the most important of his works? . . . .
Truth flashes on the man. You have felt such visitations; we labour
upon a thought, trying to grasp the truth. We almost have the butterfly in our hands, but cannot get it. Again we try; it will not come:
we walk, sit, pray, it will not come. At last in some moment it flashes
on us, the crystals form, the work is all done. Whence came it? I do
not know. It is in these burning moments that *life* is lived; the rest
is all drudgery, beating the bush, ploughing, and weeding, and watering.
This is the harvest hour.

These hours are few to any man, perhaps not more than two in a
week; but yet all the real thought of the man is compressed into these
burning moments.

Now, I believe God is the fountain of all Truth, which overflows
from Him into all minds that lie low in his power, wishing to feed these
minds of theirs in a wise passiveness; but how this influence comes, I
do not know. I know nothing about the manner in which my soul is
connected with God: I only know the fact. It is a matter of experience.

FROM THE JOURNAL.

Jan. 15, 1839.

The things that are around us,
    What wondrous truths they tell!
Though flesh to earth has bound us,
    The gaol's our oracle.
The sunshine in its splendour,
    The meeker moon by night,
The stars that do attend her,
    And people the broad light,
In us an open ear address,
    And tranquilly they whisper
Their Word of Holiness.

So I composed, walking along in the beautiful night from Boston,
where I had attended a meeting of ministers. The stars were unusually bright and large. The pale northern lights came out, and
speared up with rare and exquisite beauty. The air was clear, cool.
The Great Bear looked like a constellation of suns that kept watch over
the earth. I had become somewhat excited by silent meditation, when
I stopped to look at the heavens more attentively. A little brook, not
bound by the frost, ran beside the road, and emitted that clear tinkle
so remarkable when white ice covers part of the water. As Henry
More said, "My sallies towards Nature were almost ravishing!"

1839. Visited Dr. Channing, but had only a short time to converse
with him. He is in fear lest the same state of things should at length
be produced in this country which now exists in England, among the
manufacturing population. The cheapness and quickness of the pas-

sage to Europe will produce competition: their dense population renders wages lower there, so they will become lower here. Then they will work fourteen or sixteen hours a-day; the same will be done here, and then—farewell, all culture, all progress, and come debauchery and ruin. " Oh," says the Doctor, " oh, that we might be a poor people for the sake of the highest." He thought manufactures would not be a blessing to the nation.

We talked about great men. He said, "Truth shines first upon great men, who slowly or suddenly communicate it to the mass. But to produce the proper effect, the mass itself must be in a fit state. Thus for a reform is needed not only *talents*, but an *opportunity* to use them. Had Luther been born a century before, he would only have shared the fate of Huss and Savonarola. He was a less man than Wickliffe. There are two errors touching the influence of great men. One makes them simply the mouth-piece and consciousness of the people; the other calls them the makers of the people, not allowing enough for reciprocal action. But the greatest man stands farthest in advance of his time, and so makes his thought dominant for ever.

Some enterprises are carried through without any great men. Such was the American Revolution. No man shot above the rest. Dr. C. thinks Sam. Adams the greatest of those heroes. I pitted Jefferson against Adams, and he (Jefferson) stood it best. I have been surprised in reading his letters to notice how he foresaw the troubles that would grow out of the States-Rights question, and from difficulty in apprehending the precise meaning of the Constitution, both of which he proposed to remedy by a Bill of Rights prefixed to the Constitution.

1839. Plato—A study. Write an article on Plato, setting forth— 1. his Method and System; 2. the Sources of both; 3. his Influence.

Consider the relation of Platonism to Christianity. See Ackermann, Bauer, and the reviews of these works in the *Studien und Kritiken*, and *Rohr's Bibliothek*.

Ritter's article on New Platonism in *Stud. u. Krit.*, 1838, p. 247. On the Formation of the World-Soul. *Daub and Creutzer*, III., 7–89.

Consider Plato's own Idea. How far did he come up to it? His opinions on those greatest subjects — 1. God; 2. Man; 3. Their relation.

Consider his influence till Christianity. And after Christianity, running parallel with it—sometimes streams falling from Platonism into Christianity. Note Platonism producing mysticism in Dionysius, Scotus Erigena, the Victors, &c. (See the various mystical articles.)

Consider Plato as one pole of thought, and Aristotle the other.

TO G. W. ELLIS, IN PARIS.

January 3, 1839.

I have often told you of the noise that Emerson's Address made. The other day they discussed the question in the Association, whether he was a Christian! —— said he was not, and defended his position rather poorly, you may suppose. —— maintained that he was an atheist—a downright atheist. But nobody doubted he was a virtuous and most devout man, one who would enter heaven when they were shut out. Of course they were in a queer predicament; either they must acknowledge a man may be virtuous and yet no Christian (which most of them thought it a great heresy to suppose), and *religious*, yet an *atheist* (which is a contradiction—to be *without God*, and yet *united to God*), or else to affirm that Emerson was neither virtuous nor religious, which they could not prove. Walker and Frothingham thought he should be called a Christian, if he desired the name.

Some of the ministers think we need to have certain "*fundamentals*" fixed for us all to swear by, lest the new school among the Unitarians should carry the whole body up to the height of Transcendentalism. Now, it is notorious that the old Unitarians, in the days when there was fighting for the faith, had no such fundamentals; so Mr. Ripley showed Dr. —— that he (the Doctor) belonged to the new school, and the movement party were the lineal descendants of the old school of Unitarians.

It is quite evident there are now two parties among the Unitarians: one is for progress, the other says, "Our strength is to stand still." Dr. Channing is the real head of the first party; the other has no head. . . . .

Some day or another there will be a rent in the body; not soon, I trust, however.

TO DR. FRANCIS.

Feb., 1839.

Is Revelation at an end? Is the Bible better than the soul? The Hindoo says that of his Veda, the Mohammedan of his Koran. But if the Christian says so he *dies;* for Christianity is the religion of freedom. So the fact that we always take texts from the Bible, read its *good* passages, and pass over its objectionable clauses and allegories, or hit upon a higher sense to passages, tends to mislead men as to the true nature of the book.

Do not suppose I have any disposition to undervalue the Bible. I only want the people to understand it as it is. I remember talking with old Mr. John Richardson once about the Bible. He said he had recently read the first part of the Old Testament again, and *he was sorry he had read it,* because he could not believe it, and before he thought he believed all.

TO THE SAME.

March.

You don't know how much I rejoice at your discovery of More's Poems. I saw the announcement in your letter, and leaped up and shouted for joy; so that some men at work in the garden were boisterously mirthful, thinking I had "gone daft." I am coming to see you the last Saturday in March, if nothing prevents, to talk over 1001 things, among others about Elohim and Jehovah.

1839.—MEINER'S HISTORY OF RELIGIONS is a much better book than I expected to find it, though the author sets out with wrong notions. He does not deem religion connatural with man, nor regard it as the development of an innate principle. It is quite wonderful that he does not do this, for he comes very near it, and admits the universality of religion among all the tribes of earth, and seems to be religious himself. He thinks with Lucretius (though not acknowledging the origin) that ignorance of the true causes of things is the cause of religion. Foolish man! the ox is more ignorant thereof than Abraham; but he is not more religious. Besides, as men come to understand the causes of things, they become more religious, as a thousand examples show, with their Lockes and Newtons. It is only your Diderots and Fredericks of Prussia that see no God at the end of their telescopes.

He takes the same view in regard to Polytheism, as in his " Historia doctrinæ de vero Deo," and he is mistaken, I fancy. But I admire the man's fairness. He thinks there is no little paganism in Christianity. He sets out with two fine principles, viz., that all religions agree more than they differ, and that all popular religions are false in some points ; but the scholar did not look deeper and see that there can be but one religion, as there is but one kind of love, or time, or space, though various degrees, and perhaps modes thereof ; nor did he see that every form of religion must at one time contain more of good than evil, of truth than falsehood—relative to the state of development in the mass of men —or it could never stand as long, or find acceptance with the mass. He does not regard religion as the standard of the development of man, nor regard it as the consciousness of man coming to himself. He would make the superficial classification of religion into Polytheistic and Monotheistic, which does not reach below the skin. It is only a cutaneous classification. The man did not know that all men saw the same religious truths at the same height of development.

I like the largeness of the man, his wide reading, his English common-sense, his cool way of stating things ; but I protest against his superficial view. Poor fellow! what did you see in the great Book of Nature ? Little worth seeing. But he lived in a bad time.

1839. RIMANNI, HIST. ATHEISMI, &c.—This is a very weak book ; of little value, save as a guide to the other literature relating to the subject. He seems to have read few of the writers whose works are examined, but takes the opinions of Buddeus or some other writer. He often says such or such an author is accused of Atheism by this or that man, but he concludes nothing, having never seen his works. In general he seems to mean to be fair, and perhaps is not very hasty in pronouncing upon the case of scholars—certainly not so hasty as M. Leclerc in Bib. Ch., Vol. I. But the book is weak—it leaves no mark on your mind. The man wrote this mechanically, as he might have written any other book, or have made a pair of shoes. You would not look there for principles or first truths. I expected to find some curious learning, but there is none such. It is, however, curious to see how foolishly he trusts to statements of travellers alleging poor barbarians to be atheists, and how queerly he sometimes concludes a man was an atheist; for he thinks, holding this or that paradox, the man must, if consistent, be an atheist, forgetting that not two philosophers in ten centuries are consistent, logical consistency of thought being a rarer gift than genius itself. Still further, it is instructive to see how the best of men have been called atheists—Locke, Leibnitz, Socrates, Leclerc, Simon (Richard), Henry More, and Norris.

I would commend that book to the illiberal, that they may see how easy it has been for others to call names—even the worst names—and take heed to their ways. You and I may tell what is Atheism (perhaps); but God only can tell who is an atheist. There are atheists in speculation, but they are very rare—somebody says there never was one—but in heart there are many.

CONSERVATISM.—To hear men talk of the danger attending new things, one would fancy the world was in the best possible state, governments perfect, churches full of God's Spirit, all men contented, and the whole nation in the highest degree happy and joyful. The conservatist in Religion tells you all the world will come to an end if his old creed is left behind. He never fancies God's Spirit always takes new forms, each suited to the age, climate, &c.

To hear others, you would suppose all so bad that no man could find justice in any court, piety in any church, freedom or truth in any man, or bread in the market—that of old things all were over-old; of new things none were new enough.

Now light comes in a great tide from God down to man, it comes from him through the future, and is only reflected to us from the past. But new light is ever on the way from the primal light of all our being. Far before us, in the celestial spaces, are the stars; millions there are not yet seen, their light still loitering on the way, all the space between us and them is filled with their light not yet reaching us. So all the space between the finite and the Infinite Soul is full of truth; why not open the heart and welcome the light of truth? Each man is connected with the past; our ancestors were the first man and woman; all the vicissitudes of the universe—its eclipses of the sun and occultations of the stars, the earthquakes and famines, the jubilees of the world—all these have our parents shared in, joyfully or with sadness. So the light of experience comes to us from them. But we are connected also with the future. Why turn our backs upon it? its life is not yet lived. We also may one day be patriarchs—certainly we are all links in the great chain which winds round the two axles of the Past and the Future. They seem immeasurably distant, yet are infinitely near—the little moment called *now* being all that is between them—and that is all we are.

1839. QUESTIONS TO BE PONDERED.—MORALITY.—Is there any valid distinction between subjective and objective morality? In what does it consist? What is the value of each, separately taken? What is the result of their identity in a man's mind?

I. It is commonly supposed there is an objective standard and criterion of morality, (1), and it is shown or said to exist in the Bible; but this is not true in any practical sense; and, if it were, still it is to be found out from an examination of many passages, and the power of doing this pre-supposes an internal and subjective criterion, which renders the external useless. Besides: the Bible, taken as a whole, is progressive, and adapts itself to the rudeness of the Jew, as well as to the absolute ideal of the Christian. It is vain, therefore, to look for this criterion there. (2) We are remanded to the laws of the land, and (3) to the customs of men. But these are, many of them, arbitrary and conventional: the work of men no wiser nor better than ourselves. Here, then, is no objective standard. Nor is such an one in the lives and maxims of wise men collectively taken; for, none being perfectly wise, the aggregate of their wisdom can only be gathered by a wise eclecticism, which is only possible on the supposition that the standard is already in our bosom.

II. There can, therefore, be no objective criterion; as there is no perfect circle objective and actual in nature, and no perfectly beautiful woman objective and actual in human life. There are perfect circles *undrawn* in the air; so there are perfect men, physically and morally in life, only not actual. Yet there is an absolute circle—beauty and morality—though they exist ideally and not actually. All attempts hitherto to produce them are, in part, failures. Euclid and Newton could not draw a perfect circle, nor Phidias make a perfect beauty, though five hundred Spartan criteria stood naked before him; and Jesus of Nazareth says, " Why callest thou me good ? " for the objective result was still so far below the subjective idea.

Thoughts and queries respecting Biblical matters multiply very fast. They involve all the points which were soon so vigorously made against the current theology. He wonders at the silence of Paul and Justin Martyr respecting miracles as evidence of the divinity of Christ's mission ; the Book of Acts appears to be mythological, and the immoralities of the Pentateuch are observed farther.

Notice the plea set up of the wickedness of the Canaanites, and compare the similar pleas of the Romans respecting the wickedness of the Carthaginians, of the Spaniards respecting the savages in the New World, who were murdered because they were not Christians.

The Rev. Henry Walker, of Charlestown, Massachusetts, who died at Santa Cruz, in 1838, brought home the first copy of Strauss's " Life of Jesus " which was seen in this vicinity. He studied in Germany, and, procuring there the first edition, which was published in 1835, lent it to Mr. Parker on his return in 1836 or 1837. This he studied, and it helped to mature his growing suspicions that the New Testament had a mythology, as well as the Old, and as well as all transmitted history or religion, and that the evidence upon which miracles rested was in all cases insufficient to establish clearly their claim to be facts. But the book of Strauss had no further direct influence. He saw that it was impossible to apply Strauss's definition of a myth to the New Testament. For Strauss says that a myth is the product of the average state of mind of a people, and embodies their prevailing temper and anticipations. To create a myth, nothing historical or personal is requisite. The people will take any lay-figure that happens to attract them, and drape it with their preconceptions. The Jews took Jesus in this way, and dressed him up with the Messianic and spiritual costume of their own ideas and hopes. The religion thus presented may be genuine, but was never displayed by a person, simply because it is the possession of humanity, and continent of ideas that are beyond the capacity of any one person to display. Mr. Parker shows, in his capital article * upon Strauss's book, that " if there was an historical Christ to idealize, there could be no ideal Christ to seek in history," that the effect cannot precede the cause, and that Christ is historical in the sense of actually incarnating the religious ideas attributed to him. Otherwise there would be no mythology in the New Testament, no miraculous conception, no temptation, no ascension. The person must be large enough to carry the mythology ; but according to Strauss, the myth itself is the only real thing—the essential just outgrowth of a people, which pretends a person, or catches one for ground-tackle to hold the myth in its place. Mr. Parker shows, in two or three pages of excellent raillery, how any historical event whatsoever might be dissolved, in the Straussian fashion, in a mythical solution, as preliminary to a precipitation of its " seminal ideas " in their primitive form. And he exposes the pantheistic features of the theory : and justly, too, for it is one thing to say that impersonal ideas create and exhibit themselves in history, and another and an erroneous thing to say that impersonal ideas are the only history. The boundless generality of Pantheism could never stay in Mr. Parker's field-bred and muscular mind ; but he did not sit panic-stricken in his study, and shriek to see the nebulæ blotting here and there the sky.

Perhaps Strauss's book also confirmed his growing idea of the simply human nature of Jesus, "a carpenter's son ; " but into that presentation of Jesus there flowed awe and love for the divine character, a glad recognition of every spiritual and beneficent trait of a son of God's holy soul, of a son of Man's fraternal heart. He still accepted some of the miracles, with entire indifference, however, not caring whether the evidence sufficed or not to establish them as facts.† A genuine, holy person, Jesus, containing the highest known religion and morality, was always held by him with emphasis, and prized as a guarantee, with

* *Christian Examiner*, April, 1840. Review of the second edition, 1837, brought home to him by Rev. George Ellis.

† His tendency at this time may be found in an article in the *Western Messenger*, Dec. 1840, and Jan. 1841, "The Relation of the Bible to the Soul."

other saintly men and women, of that which is possible to mankind.

By-and-bye he said that, although Jesus still overtopped the race, the time might arrive when a new manifestation of the Infinite Truth and Love would be made ; for it was absurd to insist that the past had exhausted in any direction the divine capability. This was, in the first place, only an injunction to restrain men from bigoted trespassing upon the Omnipotent and Infinite God: as when he said he would not declare that a miracle was an impossibility, but would wait for the evidence of its reality. But it was, in the second place, very characteristic of his hope. That was wonderfully strong. It was an intuitive expectation of more goodness, more truth, more happiness, a hunger in behalf of men, that they should be recipient for ever of an ever-amplifying love and joy. He would cast himself with ardent and generous predictions upon a future when even the pirate, the kidnapper and the adulterer should equal the manly beauty of a Christ. He would throw himself against the brazen door of a fateful theology, to hold it open for the vilest man and woman, for all men, to keep it ajar for the free communications of spirit, to let into the world era surpassing era, savior after savior, to preserve salvation for all eternity. There never was a more tender and fraternal hope ; in the interest of the miserable and profligate, and in the interest of truth, it stood in the way to forbid theology drawing finite lines against the Infinite perfection. The very bluntness of his language, when he imagined new Christs, or bade the harlot equal the old one, was honourable and worthy of respect, as when a hardy fist fights a fainting woman through a brutal crowd into air and safety. All his characteristics helped this humane hopefulness forth into the service of mankind.*

His depressing moods were no bar to it. Cheerfulness was only in favour with it, and indigestion could not thwart it. The resentment of an overworked brain did no harm to this beautiful disposition of his whole interior life.

It prompted him to seek the society of people who were in earnest to discover what was true, humane, and pure. It made no difference whether they knew much or little. John Augustus†

---

* Compare "Sermons of Theism," pp. 29, 364.

† The famous shoemaker of Boston, who devoted his time, love, and substance to youthful unfortunates of either sex, through instruction, charity, and active intervention in the Courts.

was more to him than any magnate of rhetoric or science. And where two or three came together, drawn by their hopeful seeking, he, too, was drawn to observe and sympathise. One expedition of this kind took place in the summer of 1840, when he set out, with one or two friends, to walk to Groton, attracted by the call for a Convention issued by Come-Outers and Second-Adventists. Sympathy and liberal feeling sent him that road, but good sense and knowledge of man appears also to have gone with him.

Aug .10.—At Newton we fell in with Cranch, and haled him into our brotherhood of pedestrians. We walked on to Concord, stopping ever and anon at farm-houses by the way-side. The route is beautiful, and talk of various kinds beguiled its length. At Concord, we saw old Dr. Ripley, in his 90th year, who charged us to keep the true faith, and admonished us of the evils of becoming *Egomites*, as he called certain men who claimed a divine mission for themselves (*ego, mitto.*) We all assembled and took tea with R. W. E. He and Ripley had all the talk, which turned entirely upon the *Dial*,* its merits and defects, its uses and abuses. Really it was quite too bad. The only good thing he said was, " Come and look at this print of ' Endymion,' which is very beautiful; so likewise is its rival, the ' Coming of Morning,' drawn by two dappled steeds, and attended by seven virgins, daughters of the sun." Carlyle sent it to Mrs. E. In our walk, E. expressed to me his admiration of —— and his foolish article in the *Dial*. He said it was full of life. But, alas! the life is Emerson's, and not ——'s, and so it had been lived before.

At Groton we went to reconnoitre, and find Mr. ——, the person who called the Convention which we went to attend. Our host directed us to a certain house, which we could not find, so we accosted a man in the street,—

" Can you tell us where Mr. —— lives ? "

" He boards with Brother Hall, about a mile and a half off; but his wife is up there in that house."

Ripley replied, " It is ——, sir, and not his wife we want to see."

" Oh, you will find him down at Brother Ruggs's, just behind the meetin'-house."

Thither we went, and found a body of men gathered about the door

---

* " *The Dial* : a Magazine for Literature, Philosophy, and Religion," was commenced this year. Margaret Fuller was the leading editor, Mr. Ripley the acting editor, and Mr. Emerson a contributor much relied on. It was designed to encourage a free speculation, to report the good things in Philosophy and Religion which the other journals considered bad, and to concentrate the genial thinking of the neighbourhood. Many crude notions crept, through its courageous invitation, into print. Some of Mr. Parker's best articles were contributed to the *Dial* : " German Literature," Jan., 1842 ; " The Pharisees," July, 1841 ; " Thoughts on Theology," a careful review of Dorner's Christology, April, 1842 ; " Hollis Street Council," a very plain-spoken review of the proceedings of a Unitarian Council called in the case of Rev. John Pierpont, who had preached against vice in his parish, Oct., 1842. Of these, the article on " German Literature" is full of learning and humour.

of the Brother. We were introduced to —— and found that dignified personage a youngster about four-and-twenty, about the middle size, with a countenance pleasant rather than otherwise. He had a cunning look, appeared designing and ambitious. His natural language was not prepossessing. It said to me, " Take care—take care !" After further introductions, we inquired as to the work to be done, and were told by the dignitary himself, that there were two questions not to be discussed —to wit, *What constitutes a Christian?* and *What constitutes a Christian Church?* Here we saw for the first time the mark of the Beast and the print of his foot. That night we were told the discourse would be very interesting. Brother Jones was to hold forth on the Millennium and the Second Coming of Christ in 1843. But thinking if Christ could not come till 1843, we could not wait so long, but would say with Sisera, " Why tarry the wheels of his chariot ? " we adjourned, and had a good talk.

THE COME-OUTERS.—These are a body of men on Cape Cod, amounting to some hundreds in the several towns there, who are called by this name. They take no distinctive appellation themselves, but receive this name from the other sects, because they have come out from the churches. We had seen some of them in various places during the meeting, and asked them to come up to our room in the tavern, when they and others assembled to the number of twenty or thirty, and we had a talk.

1. NICKERSON AND DAVIS, OF BREWSTER.—These are called the "ministers" of the Come-Outers. They were two as rough-looking men as you would meet in a summer's day—rough, I mean, in their exterior, for their countenance was full of the divine. Their hands, their dress, their general air, showed they belonged to the humblest class in society. Mr. N. was asked to state his views of progress in the Christian course, which he did most beautifully. There are three stages of growth. 1. The man sees the truth and resolves to embrace it. Here he finds no great satisfaction; the longing is not appeased. He sees light, however, and goes towards it. 2. The man is in righteousness, but is not made perfect. He struggles, is *virtuous*, but not yet good; life is a battle in which he is beginning to conquer, but has not yet won the victory. 3. He gains the complete victory. He fears nothing in this life or the next; distress does not trouble him, nor success elate. He lies low in God's hand. God dwells in him, and he in God. All his thoughts are brought into subjection to Christ. He has become one with God, just as Christ was one with Him.

THEIR VIEW OF THE ORDINANCES.—The Christian ordinances, say they, we esteem most highly : they are *our daily work.* As to the Lord's Supper, they think little of that. It is rarely administered, and never except some one is moved to it by a spontaneous action of the divine feelings. They told how it was administered the last time. Several had met at Sister Nancy's house for worship one evening, and Brother Some-one said the Spirit moved him to eat the Lord's Supper; so Sister Nancy went to the pantry, and brought forth bread and wine, and set it on the table, and the Brother sat down and ate and drank. " All our meals," said they, " are the Lord's Supper, if we eat with a right heart."

CHURCH DISCIPLINE.—When one wants to become one of their number, he comes and associates with them. No questions are asked about his creed. We asked, "Then suppose some one should come who did not believe in Christ, or the Bible, or in God, what would you do?" "Take him by the hand," said they, "and bid him welcome, and God-speed in the good course." "But would you suffer such an one to speak in your meetings like any other Brother?" "Most certainly," said they; "do you think we fear that error is stronger than truth?"

PREACHING.—These ministers said they were *ministers of silence no less than of speech*, and only spoke when moved thereto; and each who was moved spoke without restraint, *for it took the whole Church to preach the whole Gospel.*

THEIR MINISTERS.—One of them was well educated at a theological seminary before he came among them, but he cast off his doctrinal views, and became useful with them. If he wants anything, they give it him. If they want, he gives them, which is oftener the case—for the fathers ought to lay up for the children, not the children for the fathers. Mr. L. is their strongest man. He is called on to visit infidels and the like on their death-bed, and in other extreme cases. He works out for his daily bread, yet contrived last year to expend in charity 100 dollars. We asked, "Do you count your calling sacred?" "Oh, yes, but no more so than that of the humblest Sister among us, if she be but six years old." This Brother Joshua never sleeps more than four hours in the night; rises at four o'clock the year round. Often before daylight, the family hear him at his devotions, sending up his pious ejaculations; and when very fervent, so that he may not disturb others, he goes out to the barn, and lets fly the torrent of his prayer.

Mr. B——, of Centreville, Barnstable, is a plain Cape-Cod fisherman, a skipper, it may be. His bright, cheerful countenance charmed me. He made a short speech, with many gestures, which troubled Brother H—— not a little. The speech was to this effect: "I see about in the land many little Babels of sectarian churches, as you call them—now I see you wish to pull down these little Babels, to take the combustible materials of which they are made, and erect one great Babel into which you may enter. You are in a fair way, and if this is not confusion of tongues already prevailing, I don't know what confusion is." Brother H—— was not a little horrified at the statement.

A good while after, Mrs. B——, or "Sister Olive," as they called her, arose and spoke, her husband cheering her on as she faltered a little, and another calling out from the distance, "Go on, Sister, Jesus is with you." She stated meekly and beautifully—that Cape-Cod saint —her religious history, her connection with an orthodox church, then with a Free-will Baptist, and her persecution in both. "Now," she said, "the Lord has set me in a large place." Her remarks showed plainly that she spoke from the divine life.

I afterwards talked with her, and saw how divine her heart appeared, and her countenance also; for she has one of the fairest faces I have seen for many moons.

THE BIBLE.—They use the Bible, but do not worship it, nor call it master. Said B—— to me, "Men worship it now, just as the old Pagans worshipped their idols. Now the Bible is a scripture of the

Word, not the Word itself; for the Word is never written save in the living heart."

They admit that a man is inspired so far as he is obedient, and that he gets the Truth by obedience.

There was a young man of twenty-five, perhaps, who interested us much. His exterior was that of a plain working-man. Indeed, he is still a farmer, but he is a minister also, and so preaches. He has little education in the way of books, but has thought much and deep. Alcott asked him about Christ, and he said to him, "Truth was Christ, and Christ Truth." He expects salvation from the inward and living Christ, by becoming the Christ. In short, he had the same notions of Christ that Cudworth sets forth in that remarkable sermon. His idea of life and death was peculiar; if we possessed the entire truth, this body would never die, but would be caught up and spiritualized. I don't know that I understand this notion completely, but if I do it is rather weak.

Mr. Mantalini.—This illustrious person has another name. I have given him this merely as a *nom de resemblance*, on account of his striking likeness to that distinguished worthy. His air and address are the same; even his dress, his watch-chain, and all the cockney equipments are the same. His whiskers would have been the admiration of his prototype. He spoke several times, and with the most dandiacal air conceivable. Among other things, he likened the Christian Church to Samson going down to Timnath, and slaying a lion. I thought to give our friend a touch, so I replied, and said, that our brother, in a manner no less significant than touching, had compared the Christian Church. There was a resemblance, for Samson was a Nazarite from his birth. The locks of his strength were not to be shown, nor the wine of pride to pass his lips. So long he was invincible, and bore off the gates of his enemies, and slew a thousand men with the jaw-bone of an ass. So was the Church, so long as it remained as God designed, invincible. But when it relied on that Dalilah of visible organizations, she shore off the locks of its strength, delivered it into the hands of the Philistines, who put out its eyes, and made it grind in the mill of its enemies. Well for the Church if it can pull down the temple of its foes, and crush them in its own death, &c. After the meeting was over, my distinguished friend came up to me with an air of most intolerable patronage, and told how glad he was to hear me speak, and that he assented to nearly all I had said.

This man has a history. . . . Now the Christians * are fishing for the amphibious gentleman, but the draught will not be miraculous if they capture him. I should think the question would be who shall *not* have him.

Results and Impressions in my own Mind.—1. I am surprised to find so much illiberality amongst the men who called the Convention; they were not emancipated from the letter of the Bible nor the formality of a Church. They simply wish to pull down other sects to make room for their own, which will probably be worse than its predecessors. 2. I

* Pronounced Christ-ians; the name of a sect in the United States, which, with unimportant differences, sympathizes chiefly with Methodists and Baptists. The more cultivated members approach the Unitarians.

am surprised and enchanted to find these plain Cape-Cod men with numerous others who have made actual my own highest idea of a Church. I feel strengthened by their example. Only let it be united with the highest intellectual culture. 3. I am surprised to find many others who have emancipated themselves from the shams of the Christian Church, and now can worship God at first hand and pray largely and like men. I don't know that I have got any new ideas; but certainly my confidence in my old ideas has been deepened, for I see they may be made actual.

CHAPTER VI.

Groton Convention—Letters—Speculations upon Physical and Moral Evil—Sin.

AFTER the private record of impressions, given in the last chapter, it will be interesting to have the speech which Mr. Parker delivered before the Convention. It is taken from a newspaper which existed at that time to advocate reforms in theological and ecclesiastical matters.

We have had already several definitions of sectarianism; but it is useless to attempt to define *sectarianism* until we know what Christianity is, as useless as to define a crooked line before knowing what a straight line is. To find out what Christianity is, if we go to the usages and opinions of Christ himself, the work is plain and easy. The way of Christianity, which is identical with the way of salvation, is *so* plain and easy, that none can mistake it. A young man asks of Christ, " What shall I do to have eternal life ?" The answer is very short : " Keep the commandments." And when the young man asked " Which ?" the chief moral precepts were pointed out, and the *practical duties* of love to neighbours enforced. The same question was put to him in a little different form. A scribe asked, " Which is the great commandment of the law ?" He answered, " Love God with all thy heart ;" " love thy neighbour as thyself; on these two commandments hang all the law and the prophets." This is the Christian scheme ; here is its righteousness, its religion ; all are here. Christianity is a divine life : a life of outward goodness—a life of inward holiness. Try this by reason—reason enlightened by holiness ; there is nothing which jars with reason—nothing that conflicts with human nature. Try it by conscience—God's most intimate presence in the soul ; and when this light shines most fully into the heart, you shall find nothing wrong— nothing harsh—nothing arbitrary in this scheme of the whole duty of man. Here, among things essential to morality and religion, to Christianity and eternal life, not a word is said about belief in any dogmas ; not a word about the Atonement—the Old Testament or the New Testament—not a word about Baptism, or anything ritual. Christianity was a *divine life*, not a belief.

Now, I take it, sectarianism is a departure from this simple method of Christ. We find departures even in the New Testament, as I will show, though not in historical order. 1. At dead of night, the jailer, alarmed by an earthquake, asked Paul, " What shall I do to be saved ?" The answer was, " Believe on the Lord Jesus Christ," &c.; *i. e., believe in Christianity;* for the concrete is often used for the abstract in the New

Testament. " The " word of the Lord " was soon " spoken to him," and he was baptized " the same hour of the night." Here, the only departure from the method of Christ, previously laid down, consisted in the ordinance of baptism being insisted on. Christ had caused some to be baptized, in compliance with the spirit of the times, and as a symbol of the divine life. But Paul seems to consider it as something of importance—an *essential matter*. He was not satisfied without the *sign*, though he had the *thing signified*. Perhaps, however, the great apostle did not deem it essential; and the fact that he baptized but few would favour this supposition. Here, then, is Paul's scheme. He says not a word about the Old Testament—for he cast it behind him as a law of sin and death ; not a word about the New Testament—for it was not written save in faithful hearts; and never, in his epistles or elsewhere, does he insist on belief in those things deemed most essential by the modern Church. He knows nothing of the miraculous birth, and proclaims no miracle but the Resurrection. Examine Paul's scheme, as that of Christ, and we can object only to the ritual observances ; and perhaps even that is, with him, but a symbol, and so is legitimate and Christian.

2. Now, Peter and the first Christians departed more widely from the simplicity of Christ. Peter, who had once denied his master during his life, misunderstanding the Old Testament, declares, " Every soul that will not hear that prophet " (meaning Christ) " shall be destroyed from among the people ;" and, with right Jewish narrowness, adds that " there is no other name given under heaven whereby men can be saved," words which seem to have a different meaning from those of Christ,—" I am the way, and the truth, and the life." It is not very easy to determine exactly what method Peter did propose; for he taught one thing at Jerusalem and another at Antioch. This seems clear that he did not, like Christ, count a divine life as the all-in-all of Christianity ; but, while he himself lived as the Gentiles, compelled the Gentiles to accept the whole Mosaic law, for which cause Paul " *withstood him to the face.*" Peter, it seems, was inclined to go all lengths with the other Jewish Christians, and insisted that the old law,—wrathful, foolish, and absurd as it was in its form,—should be bound like a millstone on the disciples' necks. The most revolting rite of the law was selected as the point not to be given up ; for without this rite there was no salvation. Such was Christianity, according to the Jewish Christians at Antioch.

The controversy between Paul and Peter (who seem to represent the two poles of the new religion) became important, and the whole matter was brought before the council at Jerusalem. That body, like similar bodies at all times, compromised the matter, and added to Paul's list of essentials certain others of their own, viz., abstinence from blood, from things strangled, and from all food offered to idols, of which Christ said not a word. Paul did not acquiesce in this decision, except as a matter of occasional convenience, and in cases where he feared to hurt the conscience of the weak. Wonderful to tell, at this council we find inconstant Simon has shifted again, and takes sides with Paul; or if we take a different view of the chronology, and suppose that Peter " feared them that were of the circumcision " *after* this council, then his conduct was still more inconsistent; at any rate "he walked not uprightly according to the truth of the gospel." There was *sectarianism* in the New Testament; sectarianism among the

K 2

very apostles, whom my friends appeal to as infallible. The followers of Christ did not catch the whole of his spirit, and some of the apostles became exclusive, prudish, and mechanical.

But yet they all insisted on the *divine life* as the one thing needful, though they added what suited their own caprice.

3. But in our day the departure from Christ is still more wide. Were some penitent scribe, not far from the kingdom of heaven, or some jailer in distress, to ask some of our teachers of salvation " What shall I do to be saved ?" the answer would not be so short as that of Jesus or Paul. He would be told there was no hope for him unless he believed certain doctrines ; he must accept the Scriptures as a " rule of faith and practice;" must believe the world was made in six days; that man was created pure, yet fell from that pureness; that Moses out-juggled the magicians of Egypt; that prophets predicted the Messiah, who was at last born miraculously, wrought miracles, and ascended to the right hand of God. Now, even admitting in argument that all these things insisted on were true, neither Christ nor Paul, nor even Peter ever demanded assent to them.

You go into the Catholic Church, and are told that the Church, the Scriptures, and unscriptural tradition comprise the whole sum of moral and religious truth. You go into the Protestant Church, and the magic circle, within which all truth is supposed to be contained, is drawn still narrower. You are told it is all in the Scriptures. Now Christ said " Search the Scriptures." Paul recommends them as profitable reading. But that either tells you to believe the Scriptures against reason, I have yet to learn. The Bible was made for man, not man for the Bible ; but men's minds have been forced into bondage to its letter.

Our teachers of commandments will give you a scheme of theology, when you ask the way to be saved. In one church it is larger, in another less ; still all the churches trust in their creeds, and not in the divine life. To such a pass have matters come, in this respect, that were Paul to come to us now, in New England, it is quite doubtful whether he could be admitted to our churches. Her ministers would say to him, " Paul, what thinkest thou of the Old Testament ?" He would reply " It is a law of sin and death ; only a schoolmaster's assistant to lead us to Christ. I settled that matter 2000 years ago." The astounded priest might proceed, " What thinkest thou of the miraculous birth of Christ, his miracles, his bodily ascension to heaven; of the authority of the church ?" The apostle would say, " I know them not ; I never taught them to the churches ; only the divine life and the resurrection, these were my doctrines. Wise are you in your generation! Festus thought much learning had made *me* mad ; but I never heard the tithe of those things whereof you are so certain, though I had visions and revelations of the Lord." The sum of the whole matter would be that the great apostle of the Gentiles, who found the Christians an obscure Jewish sect, and left them a mighty band in all great cities, *was not up to the level of the times, and he must not sit down at the Lord's table.* But this is not the worst ; to such a pitch has the sectarianism of the church arrived, that should Christ himself return to the earth, not stating that he was Jesus, should he live as before, and apply the truths to the time, he would be abused in our newspapers, called infidel and atheist, and only not stoned in our streets because we have another way to treat such men.

Jesus of Nazareth was the greatest soul ever swathed in the flesh; to redeem man, he took his stand on righteousness and religion; on no form, no tradition, no creed. He demanded not a belief, but a life,—a life of love to God, and love to man. We must come back to this; the sooner the better.

The Americans are marked for their good sense; they apply this to moral things, and so far are successful; they apply it to navigation, and outsail other nations on every sea; to their manufactures, and weave and spin for the antipodes; to their legislation, and have a code that comes nearer than any other to the natural laws which God has writ on man. It yet remains for us to apply good sense to religion; when this is done, it will be of very little importance what a man thinks of the Old Testament or the New Testament, so long as he loves man as himself, and God above all. Then the difference between the creed of Hopkins and Edwards, the dogmas about the Miracles, the Ascension, the Resurrection, even, and the inspiration of the apostles, will be subjects of speculation for the curious, but which have as little to do with our *religion*, as a farthing candle has with the shining of the noonday sun.

If we thus apply our good sense, Mr. President, we have but two things to fear, the flesh and the devil; but so long as we have the flesh in the world, and the devil in the Church, there is much to fear. (Expressions of agreement.)

At a subsequent stage of the discussion Mr. Parker continued his remarks. The reported interruptions and remarks of other members are here omitted.

We were invited to establish the largest Christian liberty; but this resolution* gives permission to any individual to infringe that liberty by imposing a test.

* * * * *

There is a distance heaven-wide between Christ and the apostles. If they are presented as being equally high authority, what shall we do when we recognize the difference in their teachings? Then again we find a difference between the apostles themselves: one was a thousand miles from the other. (True—amen.)

* * * * *

A gentleman who has just spoken, considers it a heinous offence for a minister of the gospel to support himself otherwise than by preaching. He will no doubt permit me also to quote "the apostle," who held a different opinion on this point. "I have coveted no man's silver, or gold, or apparel, yea, ye yourselves know that *these hands have ministered* unto my necessities," &c.

Another speaker thinks it not altogether safe or sufficient, to rely on Jesus for authority in ecclesiastical matters, but prefers the authority of the disciples to that of the master,—if I do not misapprehend

---

* Resolved—That for an individual Christian, or a church, to require more of a person, as a condition of his or her fellowship, than what they deem necessary to salvation, is an assumption unwarrantable in its nature, and schismatical in its tendency.

him. He thinks the apostles were the "foundation of the Church."
Now Paul thought otherwise, for he says, "Who then is Paul, and who
is Apollos, but ministers, (i. e. *servants*), by whom ye believed? I have
planted, Apollos watered, but God gave the increase ; so then neither
is he that planteth any thing, nor he that watereth. *Other foundation can
no man lay, than that is laid, which is Jesus Christ.*" "Therefore let no
man glory in man, for all things are yours, and you are Christ's, and
Christ is God's."

Again : my worthy brother assumed that the apostles were *inspired;*
this will be granted on all hands. But he assumed they possessed a
perfect and *infallible* inspiration, which cannot be granted. It must
be denied that they had the inspiration requisite to make them masters
of conscience, reason, and faith, in all coming time. I deny that
they had this inspiration, or even claimed to have it. If they
had this inspiration, it may be proved from the New Testament,
or from some other source. But the authority of tradition, oral or
written, does *not* establish the fact. If we look at the New Testament, we find nowhere any claim set up by the apostles to such
inspiration. But supposing they were too modest to claim an honour
they really desired. Let us look at the facts. It can be shown
very clearly that they were not thus inspired perfectly, so as to be
incapable of mistake. If thus inspired, they must have agreed in
doctrine. Now it is quite plain they did not agree. If they
were thus inspired, why was the first council at Jerusalem called to
deliberate and decide what should be done? One man *perfectly*
inspired needs no council, but is wise as a whole synod of inspired
men. I deny not that the apostles were inspired, like other good and
wise men, in various degrees. But I do deny that they were so
inspired as never to commit a fault. I do deny that Peter was inspired
by God to dissemble, or Paul to curse Alexander the copper-smith.

A worthy brother, some time ago, in a manner no less significant
than touching, compared the Christian Church to Samson going down
to Timnath, and slaying a lion. I wish he had carried out the comparison, it is quite felicitous and suggestive. Samson was a Nazarite
from his birth, as the story reads ; his locks were not to be shorn, nor
was strong drink to pass his lips; so long as he obeyed God he was
invincible. So is it with the Church; so long as it was true to the
law of God, so long was it invincible; but when it yielded to that
Delilah of a Jewish organization, with a lust for power over men's
freedom, and drank deeply the wine of pride, and forgot there was a
God, it was shorn of the locks of its strength, its eyes were put out,
itself bound to toil at the mill of its enemies, and happy will it be if
it destroys at last the temple of its foes.

I believe most fully in inspiration. There have always been inspired
men; in all times, in every land. The line of apostles reaches down
through all the ages. The tide of inspiration sets through the world,
and such souls as Numa and Solon, Moses and Solomon, Paul and
John, have drank largely in the Holy Spirit; and each, as he appeared,
was seen in conflict with the age on which he shone,—and each was
scorned and rejected of those whose selfishness obscured their vision :
yet each, in the after-age, came to be thought a demigod or an apostle
by those to whom his teachings were found to be a blessing, and then

his merest words became injunctions, from which it was heresy to dissent, and his most careless modes of life became the statute-laws for the lives of mankind. Men organized upon them; and then the spirit of a true life began to die out,—and men looked to these dead forms from the depths of human suffering for comfort, and found it not. But, still in their distress they hovered around the lifeless image as we have seen orphan girls cling to the garments of their dead mother, as if these poor relics could still give shelter and consolation. Then came Jesus; and his was a larger soul. He saw all through the conditions of humanity. He saw the poor suffering, man fallen, and the yoke of olden time pressing heavily upon him, so that he might not rise. And Jesus said to him, " Why do you not look to God ? Why will you go back to Moses ? Here is something greater than Moses. Why will you talk of Solomon ? A greater than Solomon is here. Why cling to dead forms ? Why not trust to the living spirit ? Why not take religion at first-hand ? " And then they cried out against him, for destroying their religion. " Why do you not fast, they said, and why do you not preach Moses ? " And he replied, " Why don't you put new wine into old bottles ? because the bottles will burst." He had not come to destroy but to fulfil. He had nothing to do with their organizations. He let those who would not come out of their shadows, sit there. He came not to tear down their cherished temples, but he knew that they *must* fall at the voice of teachings like his. And ever, when the true man appears, the false ones disappear before him; and when Jesus came, the dwellers in the old order of things, shrieked and fled, like owls and bats at the coming in of morning.

At only thirty years of age, they scourged him and put him to death. But his *truth* lived, and dwelt in the hearts of those poor, plain, humble fishermen, till, through their blood and sacrifice, Christianity came to be accounted a religion,—and its votaries went on spending and being spent. Men gathered themselves everywhere together in its name, at Ephesus, at Antioch, at Corinth, and at Rome; till from thence it ascended the throne of the world, and cities and broad realms bent beneath it. Then the love of power quenched its first true spirit, and now we hear men talk about its *doors!* and quote the 18th chapter of Matthew! A church! why, what does *church* mean there? Simply a gathering of men; nor can you find any mention of a church in the sense in which the word is now understood, in the whole range of Christian literature, from St. James to Hildebrand.

What is the church now? Paul says, "Where the Spirit of the Lord is, there is liberty." But where the spirit of the church is, there is slavery! The Holy Spirit says, Be a true soul! live a divine life! The church demands a *belief*, and *not* a divine life! The best men come to her, and find no life—no power; only——

The President announced that Mr. Parker's time had expired.

To go and confer with these men and women, and fraternally consider their views, required a good deal of modest humanity in those days. It was quite enough that some of them wore their hair long; such a symbol of radical infidelity was more damaging to their reputation than a disregard for the Sabbath and all scriptural ordinances. The newspapers ridiculed those singularities which always appear among people with little culture who undertake a new theology. Books and free intercourse would be fatal to these little pomposities, which are signs of isolation oftener than of egotism. But few people credited that a tender and devout spirit urged many of these Come-Outers to separate from the Church.

Mr. Parker had a native love for man. It was not an abstract recognition of new phrases of Equality and Fraternity. His nature was not of the cool and serene kind which prefers truths to people, and would never invite the latter except under compulsion. Every scholarly attainment, only seemed to widen the channels for his human pulse: it mantled in every gift, it beat to shatter all doctrines which degraded or depreciated man. He had all Dr. Channing's reverence for human nature, with a prompt, practical friendliness, gentle to visit the humble, terrible to defend them. Whenever he found a truth, he placed it in the glittering row which sits upon the rugged forehead of humankind: there it looked handsomer to him than in æsthetic and transcendental cabinets. For all things look best where they belong.

What, indeed, was the whole movement of his mind at this time, but that act of highest and most Christ-like humanity, a liberating of the Human from the Conventional! As fast as his own strong intentions struggled through scriptural views and theological finalities, he recognized them, not as his own but as Man's. He possessed them in virtue of his membership in the great society of men and women, whose hearts the Infinite Father directly nourishes with truth and love. No distant and fastidious conceptions were for him. He could not belong to a clique any more than to a sect. His very distinction as a radical thinker was his conformity to absolute and universal truths. His unsparing criticisms were efforts to rejoin his comrades, to level the pale-work and text-hedges, and let out the poor huddled creatures into the common where the untaxed food grows for all.

So he instinctively drew near whenever he saw people gather. No pride of books, or luxury of fine thinking, held him back from seeing what his brethren were about. There must be something going on, he surmised, else there would not be a crowd. Mere stupidity, folly and impiety cannot convene; some natural want makes folly cohere long enough to be marked and exposed. Yet he did not confuse movements in favor of a new theology with those in the interest of the old : it was for the sake of the human nature that is found both in a liberal convention and in a Calvinistic revival that he preferred the former. He loved to be in the company of hope, and was more tolerant of ignorance and error where he saw the work of reconstruction going on. But he had a very quick and humorous eye for the knavish little parasites who infest a growing truth; he did not relish new hypocrisy any better than the old.

This was the human temper which he afterwards brought to the consideration of Spiritualism and Mormonism. They were new movements of sufficient magnitude to challenge the attention. He undertook a deliberate examination, to weigh their good against their evil, and especially to understand their original determining impulse. Camp meetings and revivals he and all the world knew enough about, the good and the evil which they did to the soul. The new thing deserved to be know as well, to become the object of a human observation. And when, as in the case of Spiritualism, he found a theology thoroughly anti-Calvinistic in every respect, a reassertion of the universal instinct for a life after death, and a vehement impulse to emancipate souls from degrading notions of a vindictive God, who, if He prepares immortality at all, prepares it as an opportunity for the damnation of the greater number of His own children, he bestowed his hearty sympathy upon the men and women, while he told them frankly, that their supernaturalism was no better than the old kind, and that though the evidence in favor of their miracles was as good as that in favor of any, their liberal thought and feeling would be impaired by their inclination for the marvellous.

EXTRACT FROM A LETTER.

All the world and " the rest of mankind " is talking about "spiritualism," "rappers," "tippers," "writers," "talkers," &c. There are many strange things testified to by some of the soundest and shrewdest of men; things which I cannot explain as yet. But I do not accept the hypothesis that they are the work of " SPIRITS," either the souls of dead men, or " angels " good or bad. I know nothing to justify the "spiritual" hypothesis. I am not successful in my investigations; I drive off the "spirits" by looking at the table. I once—and once only—got a *response* from a "spirit;" that was of a man whom I knew to be safe and sound on *terra firma* here below. (I have seen him since.) I got any answer that I wanted to get. If I had time I should like to look into the matter a little further. But scientific men give it the go-by—which seems scarcely right. It does not now appear in *Catholic* districts I am told. Is it so? They have enough to excite their marvellousness without tipping tables!

EXTRACTS FROM THE JOURNAL.

THE EARLY CHRISTIANS.—All I read of them convinces me more of their noble character, aim and life. But I see their limitations. They were superstitious, formal (at least after the middle of the second century, and perhaps also in the apostles' times,) the *letter* burthened them. But they were full of the noble manly spirit. Their ascetic doctrines of marriage, dress, amusement, education, I dislike, vastly. They laid too much stress on baptism, the eucharist—giving the latter to men to keep at home, carry in their pocket, &c., gave it to little children just after baptism, put it in the mouth of dead people, and the like.

But how they died—how they prayed—how they lived! We cannot yet afford to criticise these men. Certainly they were not gentlemen, but they were *men*. The wonder is that *being* so much, they *saw* no more. One thinks if Seneca could have been Christian, he would have seen truth as Schleiermacher and De Wette saw it. But who knows!

The early Christians were not literary men—none of them. They spoke because they had something they could not help saying. So the spirit found very vehement but very imperfect utterance. Culture did nothing for them (this with exceptions—Justin Martyr, Clemens, Alexandrinus, Origen, &c.) Inspiration did all, so there was no grace.

HERETICS.—They began very early. Indeed we find them in the times of the apostles. In Jesus you are in the *Pleroma* of light; step into the apostles, it is already evening, and the light is behind you. Take another step, and you are in fathomless darkness. Heretics have always been treated as the worst of men. Imaginary doctrines have been ascribed to them, immoral ceremonies; they have been charged with sins of the blackest dye. This treatment the Jews received of the Gentiles, the Christians of the Heathen, the Heretics from the Catholic Church; the Protestants—in a word, the *Come-Outers* of all ages have been abused. Jerome says the heretics, even if they lead blameless and beautiful lives, have only the image and shadow of virtue. Tertullian chides Marcion, after the fashion of Dr. South, with his God who is not to be feared; and asks him why, if he does not fear God, he does not go to the theatre, and bawdy-houses, and game and drink? Philastor and Augustine censure some heretics who would think the planets, sun, moon and stars were worlds, because they denied the resurrection of the flesh. Christ was put to death as a heretic. The treatment which the Come-Outers, and some others, Mr. Dyer, &c., have lately received, shows me how the heretics were treated in all times, and how much truth I am to expect in Irenæus, Tertullian, Epiphanius, Philastor and Jerome, when they treat of heretics.

1. A bad name is given them.
2. Some one is discovered or invented who has the same name and very dangerous doctrines and a wicked life. This is blazoned to the world, and then,
3. The heretic is charged with the same doctrines and life ; and so it goes.

Truth is unchangeable, but orthodoxy and heresy vary with each country and every age. The world seems to defend doctrines in the inverse ratio of their value, as mothers love best their weak and sickly children.

Nothing will ever save us but a wide, generous toleration. I must tolerate and comfort my brother, though I think him in error, though I know him to be in error. I must tolerate his ignorance, even his sin— yes, his intolerance. Here the only safe rule is, if some one has done you a wrong, to resolve on the spot never to do that wrong to him or any one else. It is easy to tolerate a man if you know he is a fool and quite in the wrong. But we must tolerate him when we know he is not a fool, and not altogether in the wrong.

Mr. Parker's speculative freedom brought him into suspicion as early as 1838 :—

Nov. 13.—A rare thing has happened to me to-day; simply this— a certain Mrs. —— pronounces me an *infidel* in good set speech. The reason is, that I do not think as she does of the authority of Jesus. She thinks he has a different authority from that of the truths he taught ; therefore, that we are bound to obey him, even if the doctrine in question does not seem true to us. I think Jesus Christ is to be reverenced and obeyed solely for the *intellectual, moral,* and *religious* truth which he brought to light by his doctrines and life. If sentences of his did not seem true to me, I should reject them ; for I can accept no opinion which annuls my own reason.

I honour and revere Christ more, perhaps, than she, though not in the same way. Afterwards, she retracted the offensive term, " infidel ; " but this does not mend the matter. I something doubt that my sermons breathe the spirit of infidelity.

But all this shows me—what needed no proof before—how much easier it is to censure another, and damn him with harsh names, than to amend one's own life, or even to apprehend the difference between his creed and your own.

May, 1839.—I am often struck with the great freedom and boldness of Christ's remarks. The Jews venerated manna. He told them it did not come down from heaven. They superstitiously honoured the sabbath. He said it was made for man, not man for it. He said that one greater than all the old prophets was inferior to the least of his disciples.

Consider the surpassing boldness with which he rebuked men and taught doctrines.

Here is a boldly chalked study, to serve in the composition of his mind :—

June.—How much do we idealize Christ ?   Very much, I suspect ; I look on the Christ of tradition as a very different being from the ideal Christ.   The latter is the highest form of man we can conceive of—a perfect incarnation of the Word.   The former, a man, perhaps, of passions not always under command, who had little faults and weaknesses that would offend us.   His thoughts came like mine ; and he was sometimes in doubt, perhaps contradicted himself, and taught things not perfectly consistent with reason, or, at best, gave utterance to crude notions.   From the nature of the case, he could not do otherwise.   Thought is life generalized ; it arrives, therefore, only as we live—so, from year to year and day to day, Christ must have generalized better as he lived more.   His plans were evidently not perfectly formed at first.   He fluctuates ; does not know whether he shall renounce Moses or not.   He evidently went on without any plan of action ; and, like Luther at the Reformation, effected more than he designed.   At first, perhaps, he meditated simply a reform of Mosaism, but finally casts off all tradition, and starts a fresh soul.

His power of miracle-working is an element of the soul.   It is a vein running through all history, coming near the surface of life only in the most elevated characters, and in their most rapt states of mind.   So the central rocks only crop out in mountains.   We all feel this miracle-power *ideally* (A—— says *actually* likewise, and perhaps he is right ; I can feel something of it, supposing it is what E—— calls demoniacal influence).   Jesus, a greater man than ever lived before or since, lived it actually ; his miracles, therefore, were natural acts, not contrary to outward nature, but above it.

His inspiration I can understand still better.   There can be but one *kind* of inspiration ; it is the intuition of truth.   And but one *mode* of inspiration ; it is the conscious presence of the highest, either as beauty, justice, usefulness, holiness, or truth—the felt and perceived presence of absolute being infusing itself into me.   But there may be infinite degrees of inspiration.   The degree depends on the being of the man to be inspired ; a noble being is capable of more, a smaller soul of less.   It depends also on the faithfulness of the finite soul.   It may perfectly obey the conditions on which it is obtainable, then it will have all the inspiration it is capable of at that stage of its growth ; or it may do this imperfectly, when it will have less.   It depends, then, on the finite soul itself, whether or not, and to what degree it will be inspired.   Hence, in all times we see instances of souls, humble by nature, obtaining a higher degree of inspiration than others, their superiors in innate capabilities, and so becoming the superior beings.   Such were many prophets of the Old Testament ; such was Bunyan.   Now Christ, I fancy, was one of the greatest souls born into the world of time ; and did also more perfectly than any other man fulfil the conditions of inspiration ; so the spirit dwelt in him bodily.   His was the highest inspiration—his the divinest revelation.   But this must be said of *actualities*, not of *possibilities*.   It is folly, even impiety, to say that God cannot create a greater soul than that of Jesus of Nazareth.

Who shall attempt to foreshorten God, and close the gates of time against him, declaring that no more of his spirit can be by any possibility incarnated? Jesus was cut off at an early age—the period of blossom, not fruitage. What are thirty years? How much could he have lived? All the great works of reflective genius have appeared after five-and-forty. It is only by long practice and much life that the soul's instruments—thought and language—are matured. The *reflective* had scarcely began to dawn in him; the *spontaneous* alone was active. He, then, is not a model for us in the reflective powers, only in the spontaneous. Why may we not see a soul uniting them all, and so revealing manhood in a higher form—I will not say the highest, *that* I know not of—by a revelation nobler and more perfect than his?

The Christ of tradition I shall preach down, one of these days, to the extent of my ability. I will not believe the driving beasts out of the temple with a whip;* the command to Peter to catch a fish; still less the cursing the fig-tree, and the old wives' fables about the Ascension. His predictions of his death I have reason to doubt; but I know not but they are real. He, doubtless, was mistaken in his predictions of the end of the world, or rather his disciples were; for the prediction is manifest and its failure obvious. The ideal Christ is what we are to preach; and, perhaps, we shall not need the Gospels much in delineating him. Yet I should be sorry to lose even the little they afford us, were it not for the lamentable matter they connect therewith. Christianity is much indebted to Paul. He freed it from its narrowness. Was it limited in Christ, or did its limits come from his disciples? Christ seems himself to fluctuate—once he refuses to heal a stranger-woman's child, as not being part of his mission. But he is afterwards surprised to find a greater faith than in his own nation. I doubt that he designed it to be universal; yet many passages towards the end of his life favour it.

Nov. 1839.—Saw Bancroft at his house. He spoke with delight of the intense desire of the "commonality" for spiritual truths. They will not rest their Christianity on something outside. He agreed with me that the old mode of presenting religion has ceased to have any effect, and that the Church needs to be more *democratic*, but sees not the "*how*," an important category in this connection.

He showed me a passage in Spinoza which shocked me, where he goes farther than Machiavelli, and denies the obligatoriness of a promise farther than it can allay fear or stimulate the hope of the promisee, and adds, the promiser is a great fool to think otherwise.

Bancroft thinks Jonathan Edwards was the great man of New England. The centre with Edwards, I said, was the *Bible*, and with Spinoza the *soul*. B. says no, the centre with both is *God*; the Bible does not hamper Edwards, nor does any human authority. He looks through these.

TO MISS ELIZABETH P. PEABODY.

August 30, 1839.

I should make an apology, my dear Elizabeth, for not writing before, were it not contrary to my theory, and practice, also, to make apologies at any time. It has not been lack of inclination, but of leisure, you

---

* This sentimental touch disappeared in the exigencies of his own protesting, and the scourge of small cords seemed less mythological.

will do me the kindness to suppose. Both L. and myself were highly edified by your letter. I am highly grateful for the advice you offer, and doubt not it will bear fruit. I think you have formed a very just estimate of L.; indeed, you had done so *before*, but she will not admit the fact. Thinks you make her too *good*, and the like. Touching my becoming a martyr, as you and Miss Burley conjecture, I think I shall have no occasion for the requisite spirit, even if I had that article in as great abundance as John Knox or John Rogers. I have precious little of the spirit of a martyr; but inasmuch as I fear no persecution, I fancy I can " say my say," and go on *smoothly ;* but if not, why—well, I can go *roughly.* I trust I have enough of the Spirit always to speak the truth, be the consequence what it may. It seems to me men often trouble themselves about the consequences of an opinion, or action, much more than is necessary. Having settled the question that an opinion is *true* and an action perfectly *right*, what have you and I to do with consequences? They belong to God, not to man. He has as little to do with these as with the rising of the sun or the flow of the tide. Doubtless men said to Galileo, " Your system may be true,—but only think of the consequences that follow! What will you do with them?" The sage probably replied, "I will let them alone. To do duty and speak truth is my office ; God takes care of consequences." I am sorry you and that wise woman, Miss B., should form so high an opinion of me, for all my subsequent life will do nothing but cancel it, and show on what an airy base your kind feelings have erected an imaginary character.

Dec. 4.—Mr. O. C. Everett came to see me to-day. He said some good things—to wit, about speaking ill of others. He thinks one ought never to say of another what he would be ashamed to say in his presence. But this is wrong. I should be ashamed to praise as well as to censure. A better rule would be—1. Say nothing ill of any one unless certain it is true ; 2. Say nothing ill, unless certain that no evil or selfish motive animates you.

He thinks also that I confound the attributes with the *personality* of God. But how can it be? where is the difference between the two? Is God separate or separable from his wisdom, justice, or love? Surely not.

Jan. 2, 1840.—Preached the Thursday lecture on Inspiration. After it was over, Dr. —— came up to me, while conversing with Dr. Francis and Mr. Cunningham, and said, "When you write about Ralph Cudworth,* I read ye and like ye ; but when you talk about future Christs, I can't bear ye." There was a great deal more of the same kind. He called me " impious," whereat I was so grieved, that I left him, not in anger, but in sorrow, and went weeping through the street ; but, at length bethought me of Ellis, and went to see him, and so dried my tears.

This is not the temper of an over-conscious man, who deliberately hatches new opinions, and hastens to annoy the general convictions. His mind worked in an impersonal manner, and

* Article in the January number, 1840, of the *Christian Examiner*, upon Cudworth's Intellectual System.

he never calculated the effect of his opinions, or of the plain speech into which they flowed. He was often very much astonished at the effect of passages which slipped from his pen with no design beyond that of putting his thought into clear and strong expression. So he was surprised, and sometimes a little hurt, when his friends told him that his satire occasionally degenerated into sarcasm. It never entered his mind to be sarcastic or sneering. He vindicated the use of all legitimate intellectual weapons to defend truth and attack error. He employed the whole of his mind to enforce all his convictions, backed by health and homely vigour. He grew in a way to be plain and muscular in the performance of his function as teacher and liberator of men's minds. And he put forth his strength in such instinctive fashion, under the dominion of such an earnest motive and such absorbed convictions, that he could neither stop to think of his style nor to dilute his eagerness. There is sometimes a want of taste, but no malice, in the speech which his fiery honesty had mastered. His whole language, with its glories and its faults, is himself, in unflawed integrity, untampered with by second thoughts, the characteristic product of such education and native power as fell to him, *idiomatic*, in all the possible senses of that word. It is " a nipping and an eager air," and as little charged with malice.

His dear friend, Rev. S. J. May, of Syracuse, once urged him to abate the sarcasm ; to this he replies :—

April 1, 1845.—What you say about the sarcasm, and all that, I by no means plead guilty unto. I wonder that *you* should bring the charge. I fully sympathise with Burns in his compassion for " auld Nickie Ben," and don't like to think of hell for his sake. I wish he would " tak' a thought an' men'." But, my dear friend, I never wrote a line with any ill-will, or *sarcastic* humour, towards maid or man. I should not dare write with such a feeling, least of all in such a cause. I wonder that you can read " Pilgrim's Progress," finding nothing of the kind therein, and then discover it in my poor writings. What if I had called men a " generation of vipers," " snakes," " children of the devil," and the like ? But enough of this.

The following letter explains itself :—

West Roxbury, 22 January, 1840.

MY DEAR BROTHER,—I have just received your letter and hasten to reply, though not without deliberation. I am much obliged to the good people of Lexington for their favourable opinion, and wish I deserved it better. It is doubly delightful to learn that any one in my *native village* should be pleased with anything that I could do. But in respect to coming to Lexington as a minister I have several things to say. I think you know that I came here *against* my own consent. My friends advised this measure of settling at Spring Street, and I consented with a good deal of unwillingness, for *I neither liked the salary of* 600 *dollars, nor the small audience of* 80 *or* 150 *souls.* But I gave up my scruples, was settled—*not for life;* but can at any time leave the place, on condition of giving notice of my intention six months beforehand. The parish also can discharge me, by a majority of votes, on the same condition. Thus stands the matter between us, as settled by the contract. The parish could have no legal or common claim upon me if I wished to leave to-morrow.

But there are other considerations that have and ought to have a strong influence. This parish is small, and the people poor; their only chance of getting and keeping a minister depends on the advantages arising from their position in the neighbourhood of Boston, Cambridge, &c. Now, if I were to leave them *at this time* I fear they could not secure the services of a minister of respectable talents, who would be *really* of use to them. It is, therefore, my *duty* to stay. I could wish with all my heart for a larger sphere, a greater number of hearers, and those more intelligent and cultivated than the majority at Spring Street; but I think *they* would lose more than *I* should gain by my leaving them. Again, I intend, in the course of my life, to do more through the *Press* than the *Pulpit.* Here I can find *ten hours* a day for *five days* in the week to devote to works not directly connected with the exercises of the pulpit, and yet neglect no duty I owe to any man, or to the whole parish. I could not thus control my time in Lexington, where the people are both more numerous and more scattered. Still further, I doubt that I could long *suit* the people at Lexington. My theological opinions differ very widely from those of the Unitarians in general, and, perhaps, would not be acceptable at Lexington ; though I fear very little on that ground, since I never knew men *really religious* to find any fault with them. . . . . You know my attachment to Lexington, and how much it would delight me to be near your family, and all the *good old people of the good old town,* but taking all these things into consideration, and weighing the matter fairly, I think, my dear Isaac, that you would decide as I do.

I am glad to hear you are all well. I hope the children study as well as you and I used to do at school, and wish they might profit by the *same* instruction at home, for which I shall never cease to thank you all my life. If you can do for your children what you did for your little rebellious brother, it will be better than to give them all the houses and farms in the county of Middlesex.

Your affectionate brother,
THEODORE.

His journal, in commenting upon this call to Lexington, has the following :—

Now, it is very pleasant to me to be thus kindly received by my old friends ; the men who patted me on the head when I was a boy, and are now surprised that I am grown up. God be with you, old parish; may you receive more men like the Clarkes and Hancocks and Easterbrooks, to freshen your souls once more.

1840.—Dr. Channing says the Universalists have the idea of Good. It is a powerful idea; men have been governed too much by *fear*. He wishes the idea of good to be held up—not material, sensuous good—not pleasure, but spiritual good. The Universalists have only the idea of material good. Let the celestial good be held up to man. Unitarians have, perhaps, preached too much the law—morality. They make man depend on himself. Let it be shown how God, the All Good, the Altogether Beautiful, labours to diffuse Himself and spread goodness, celestial good, through all the world. This will be effective. Man does little through fear. It is negative, and leads only to defence, or offence for the sake of defence. But good is positive, the love of it creative, and not barely critical and defensive. Consider that all creation comes from love, not fear. Notice the action of the good upon men in the arts and sciences. See how fear belittles and love magnifies.

At various periods during 1839 and 1840, the phenomena of moral and physical evil disturbed his mind, which was now so fully awakened to difficulties both in nature and theology; and of course his intuitive beliefs had a sharper struggle to become adjusted with nature's mysteries than with man's.

He began to notice more anxiously the habits of animals, and to ponder the secrets of physical laws. Doubts of the infinite goodness besieged his mind at the spectacle of the play of brutal instincts. He still remembered, and had not recovered from, the shock at first witnessing a certain cruel trick which male squirrels practise. Nature seemed no longer innocent, an abyss of deformity opened before his guileless feet. What is the meaning of all these things? Suspicion filled with dreadful counts an indictment against his earliest instinctive faith. The alligator devours its young till they become too large for the parental jaws. The permitted barbarity of the cat to the mouse—the eagle's injustice in robbing the fish-hawk—the destruction of young by the large black wasps in the beginning of October—the buccaneering of some birds, who steal the nests of other birds, and throw out their eggs—the reputed enslaving of the black by the red ant—the sin against nature of dogs—the vile habits of apes and of frogs—who can explain these things? They look devilish. Is there a dark ground in the creative mind, or does matter possess properties which are not under the Deity's control? No!—such Gnostic notions are inconsistent with common-sense. Is the world, then, after all, the reflex and product of human nature, so that the vices of men ordain the instincts of animals? Even if it were possible to make the evil in man accountable for the evil among animals, that would not preserve a conception of the infinite beauty and goodness. But it is not possible; for though man creates his environment, for better or worse, he cannot obtrude animal tendencies upon the Divine mind, which is the sole creative source. Whence comes the power of deformity originating deformities? Has God delegated to man the peopling of the woods, fields, and waters, by occult moral agency? Besides, it remains to account for the existence of the animal tendencies in man himself. Thus he wrestled with the problem.

He soon observed the tentative efforts of Nature on her road to man, arrested members and faculties, "the toes in a horse's hoof, the fingers beneath the skin in the manati, the singular mannishness of some monkeys, the resemblance to human limbs noticed in some plants, as the orchis and lady's slipper—the marriage and adultery of plants." Then he frankly acknowledged the great capacity for ugliness in Nature, the strange forms by land and sea, the congenital abortions—"calves with three heads—fruits, half peach and half plum; apples, one side early and sweet, the other winter fruit and acid." Thus he gradually made his way to the speculation that there are certain "immoralities of nature, which are distinct, definite predictions and prototypes of kindred sins in man." If at this point his understanding had been enlisted in the service of a supernatural theology, which provides a supernatural atonement for the fact of sin, he might have used these marks of divine premeditation to invent the theory of "anticipative consequences."* For such a theology makes perennial demands upon human ingenuity, as any tremendous assumption must when it is persistently credited. Human reason will never put up with merely crediting an assumption, it must contrive some way of making it seem reasonable. As fast as knowledge drives it out of one statement, it hastily throws up another, which serves only to cover its retreat. What adroitness we have seen since the developments of geology threatened Genesis and all the sacrificial schemes! Reynard, in the mediæval poem, never saved his brush so often. Death, sin, the federal head, the "primal, eldest curse," all the precious objects are snatched away before the

* Nature and the Supernatural. By Dr. Bushnell. See Chapter VII.

trained, impassive advances of science, and placed in new positions. The fetiches of the tribe must not fall into the hands of the enemy. May the day of utter rout and disenchantment end not too soon : a kind of melancholy metaphysic interest we find in the shifty spectacle !

But the shiftiest thing to do is to sally forth, seize some of the hostile facts, and convert them to evangelic service. This is the theory of "anticipative consequences." Its distinction is that God foreknew that men would have to sin. His whole being was so penetrated with anticipations of this sombre exigency, that His creative skill turned itself to the preparation of abhorrent symbols, which grew gradually worse through a long course of geologic epochs, till at last the degradation was *ripe for man*. It is very possible that if a God had been in the habit of indulging such imaginations, he might originate at length a good deal of misery. Geologic epochs framed in this Dantesque conception might circle down, through subversive instinct and deepening deterioration, to man himself, "the bright, consummate" wretch of all. And he would be associated with snakes, wry-mouthed flounders, with the rage and cunning of wild beasts, with all deformed antagonistic types, that he might not forget that he was conceived in sin and disappoint parental expectations. He would be obliged to fall to sinning, because a special effort to save him, which could not take effect unless he first does his best to be lost, has also been preordained. So his rudiments are insinuated by a set of ominous pictorials ; venomous reptiles, carnivorous animals, repulsive forms of life by sea and land, the bloated spider, the chattering ape, all ruthless and stealthy creatures, are mnemonics for man's life-long lesson in the business of developing the tendencies which they prefigure, that the tendencies may be overcome by grace !

What could more strikingly display the horrible necessities of that supernatural theology, which Mr. Parker so justly hated, than this representation of an infinite Creator, seeing clearly that He must accept evil if He would go on to organize His thought ; that He is confronted at the first step which he takes out of potentiality by this infamous companion, without whom He must not make the worlds. He accepts this *sine quâ non*, but at the same time there occurs to Him the idea of a great supernatural remedy, into which cunning trap the cloven foot will set itself at last. He is powerless to shake off the bad condition, but is sagacious enough to make it serve a purpose. What a God is that who consoles Himself through ages of a sin-haunted imagination which deliberately invents symbols of its dreadful surmises, with anticipating that He can at last interpose Himself in person to save a ruined mankind from the consequences of his own enforced complicity with evil ! How humiliating is the thought that a few words in the Bible subject men's minds to the drudgery of rearing these elaborate fantasies to imprison the stubborn facts of Nature ! The facts escape, and are again at large.

Mr. Parker did not possess, and did not need, this kind of subtlety to adjust his mind to the problem which disturbed it. No adjustment, made in the interest of any theology, can answer all the questions which the intellect is capable of raising. But one mode of treatment is less fantastic than another. And every mind must make its own terms with the problem. His own broad health and common-sense, his unconquerable hope, his great humanity, and the intuitive conviction of a perfect love which ruled all his thoughts, saved him from an elaborate and tyrannizing scheme. It was a great advantage to him in exposing particular sins and sinners that he had no theory of sin to defend. He went to his reforming work uncrippled, full of faith and hope in man, full of indignation for bad men, full of pity for those who struggle in degraded conditions or in partial growth.

Now, were I to draw conclusions solely from organic nature, what attributes should I ascribe to the cause of the world ? Certainly not just the same I now give Him. But, looking into my consciousness, I find there a different idea of a God ; so the first witness is insufficient —the last perfectly competent.

I do not understand how all the evil which man inflicts upon another animal, or one animal upon its fellow, can consist with the ultimate happiness of that animal. But if God is infinitely just, it must be so. I know how all things may work together for the good of the extremest suffering among men, but not among brutes.

Now, in estimating the phenomena of evil, my own faith says there is a perfect system of optimism in the world ; that each man's life is to him an infinite good. Of course all his physical evils must be means of progress, all his errors likewise unavoidable steps in his course to happiness. But to legitimate this in the court of the understanding, where all other truths are legitimated, I find difficult. Faith has nothing to do there. I will imagine a person who denies that all things work together for good, and suppose myself to reply to the arguments I should bring in such a case.

Here the notes end abruptly, and the mental controversy re-appears only in the statement of a few results.

The virtues of a baby are easily learned while fondling in the nurse's arms, but the virtues of a man require the stern cradling of affliction. I think no sin can make an indelible mark on the primitive Monad—so to say—what I call the soul. I take it the atoms of matter never change, though they take the forms of gas, fluid, and solid, though they are in the form of a crystal, vegetable, or animal. So I think sin makes little mark on the soul; for, 1, much of it is to be referred to causes exterior even to the physical man; and 2, much to the man's organization. I think $\frac{9\,9}{100}$ of sin are thus explicable—the result of the man's limitation—A, the result of his circumstances; B, of his organization. Now, I am sure that sin, the result of A or B, can make no permanent mark on the soul. God will not damn a man because his father *had bad neighbours,* nor because the man was born with a bad head, more than with a lame leg. Now, I think many struggle with both A and B, and apparently make no progress, who will yet rise in the next life far above most of us. They may make a great *inward progress,* but from defective organization or circumstances it shall not appear.

Men complain of wild beasts in the forests, of monsters in the sea, of toads and snakes, vipers, and many a loathsome thing, hideous to our imperfect eye. How little do we know! a world without an alligator or a rattlesnake, a hyæna or a shark, would doubtless be a very imperfect world.

Theologians often talk mythologically about sin, as if there was something mysterious in its origin, its course, its process, its result, and final end. They tell us that as it is a transgression against the infinite God, so it is an infinite evil, meaning an absolute evil, demanding an eternal punishment. To this scholastic folly it is enough to reply, that if sin be for this reason an absolute evil, then the smallest suffering coming from an infinite God is an infinite suffering, and cancels the sin.

That is, what the finite can do, and what it can suffer, must be of the same magnitude. You must rate both as infinite, or neither.

I am pained by every evil thing I do. In the next life I hope to suffer till I learn the mastery of myself, and keep the conditions of my higher life. Through the Red Sea of pain I will march to the Promised Land, the divine ideal guiding from before, the Egyptian actual urging from behind.*

This letter to Hon. James G. Birney gives a clear and compact statement of his belief concerning punishment :—

Boston, 3rd Oct., 1852.

DEAR SIR,—I have been so busy in removing from summer to winter quarters that I have had no time to reply to your note until this

* Sermons of Theism, pp. 361–62. See the sermons on the "Economy of Pain," and the "Economy of Moral Error," for his completed views on the subject of Sin.

moment. It seems to me that we should not use the word *punish* at all in reference to the action of God. The only punishment that we know is this—*the arbitrary infliction of pain from without.* Usually it is accompanied with ill-will and a desire of vengeance, but sometimes with kindly feelings and a desire to hurt for the sake of healing. Now, theological books commonly represent God as punishing men in this or the future life with ill-will and a desire for vengeance. "Hell" is for God's sake; damnation is of no advantage to the *damned*, only to the *damner.* Well, all of that language is unphilosophical, and ought to be blotted out of all decent speech, it seems to me. The trouble I believe is this—men do not believe that God is infinite, but finite and imperfect, and therefore they attribute such motives and such actions to Him. If you start with the idea of God as infinite, possessing all the attributes of a perfect and complete being, perfectly powerful, wise, just, loving, and holy (*i. e.*, self-faithful), then the difficulty is all over; for God must have created men from a perfect motive, for a perfect end, as a perfect means for the attainment of that end, and so the attainment of the ultimate end of God's design cannot fail.

Now, the infinite God must desire the ultimate welfare of each of His creatures, must have means for bringing it about—means that are adequate to the purpose. I know very little what these means are; but this is plain, that all which a man suffers by the providence of God must be for the *good of the sufferer.* It is absurd to suppose that the infinite God will allow anyone to be miserable forever in consequence of the grossest and the worst of "sins" here; for the sins are often as much involuntary as the stumbling of the child in learning to go alone. It seems to me that all the suffering of men—and in such a town as this I see enough of it—is in the end to work out a good result, not only for the race, but for the individual sufferer. Indeed, it must be so if God be infinite, and his work perfect for His purpose. I never speak of future punishment, but of *future progress*, by the justice and the mercy and the love of God.

Respectfully and truly yours, &c.

When I see the suffering of animals, the father-alligator eating up his sons and daughters, and the mother-alligator seeking to keep them from his jaws; when I see the sparrow falling at a dandy's shot, I know that these things have been provided for by the God of the alligator and the sparrow, and that the universe is lodged as collateral security to insure bliss to every sparrow that falls.*

Thus, instead of fashioning with great labour a theory that shall seem to account for all the facts, while in reality it shall fail to account for the origin of evil whence all the facts have flowed, he overcame doubt with this happy temper of his whole mind, a humane and tender optimism, which strove to embrace all the facts with something like the Divine impartiality.

The subject of the following letter gives it a place here, though it is of a later date by twenty years. It was addressed

---

* Speculative Theism, p. 176.

to Rev. James F. Clarke, who had preached a sermon about him while he was sick at Rome, 1859-60, in which he made the criticism upon Mr. Parker's preaching, that it did not sufficiently magnify the fact of sin. Whoever has a great deal of natural piety for sin, is advised to pass this communication by :—

Many thanks for standing in my pulpit and preaching about me and mine; all the more thanks for the criticisms. Of course I don't *agree* with your criticisms—if I had I should not have given you occasion to make them.

* * * * *

Now a word about *sin*. It is a theological word, and is commonly pronounced *ngsin-n-n-n!* But I think the thing which ministers mean by *ngsin-n-n-n* has no more existence than *phlogiston*, which was once adopted to explain combustion. I find *sins*, i.e., *conscious violations of natural right*, but no *sin*, i.e. no conscious and intentional preference of wrong (as such) to right (as such); no condition of " enmity against God." I seldom use the word sin—it is damaged phraseology, tainted by contact with infamous notions of man and God. I have some sermons *of sin* and of *sins*, which I may live long enough to prepare for printing, but also may not.

Deacon Wryface, of the Hellfire Church, says, " Oh, I am a great sinner; I am one mass of sin all over; the whole head is sick, and the whole heart faint. In me there dwelleth no good thing. There is no health in me." " Well," *you* say to him, " for once, Deacon, I think you pretty near right; but you are not yet quite so bad as you talk."

" Why—what have *you* got against me—what do *you* know against my character ? " says the Hellfire Church deacon.

" If you want a bill of particulars, here goes," say you; "just answer as I call them off.

" 1. You will lie!" " '*Tain't true*."

" 2. You cheat in your trade, and lately wronged Widow Crosby out of her house and land ? " " That's a lie—I never cheat! "

" 3. You get drunk—on other men's wine—and were boosy only day before yesterday, and had to be helped up-stairs." " That's a slander."

" 4. You are inhuman, and have got ships in the Coolie trade, and I think in the African slave-trade besides ?" " Well—there's no wrong in that—the niggers are the descendants of Ham, of whom God said, ' Cursed be Canaan.' I do this to bring the benighted heathen under Christian influences."

" 5. You are avaricious, and dodge all the charities. You put your name at the head of subscriptions to decoy others, and then never pay up." " That's a lie ! "

" 6. You are a consummate hypocrite, pretending to all the virtues of humanity, while you practise only the vices." " It is all a lie."

" Well then," say you, " what *are* the special sins you do commit ? "

" Oh, *there ain't any*. I hain't got a bad habit in the world—no, not one ! "

"Then what did you mean by saying just now that you were such a sinner?"

"Oh, I referred to my *natur'* : it is all *ngsin-n-n-n.*" That is the short of it—all men are created equal in *ngsin-n-n-n.* Dr. Channing was as great a sinner—in the theological sense—as ———— : it is his *fallen nature*—his will can never clean him from that o-d-i-o-u-s gall.

Oh, James, I think the Christian (!) doctrine of sin is the Devil's own, and I hate it—hate it utterly. Orthodox scholars say, "in the heathen classics you find no consciousness of sin." It is very true—God be thanked for it! They were conscious of wrath, of cruelty, avarice, drunkenness, lust, sloth, cowardice, and other actual vices, and struggled, and got rid of the deformities, but they were not conscious of "enmity against God," and did not sit down and whine and groan about non-existent evil. I have done wrong things enough in my life, and do them now; I miss the mark (ἁμαϱτανῶ), draw bow and try again. But I am not conscious of hating God, or man, or right, or love, and I know there is much "health in me;" and in "my body," even now, when it is really not worth much, there dwelleth many a "good thing," spite of consumption and St. Paul.

Here at Rome you see the odds between the old classic conception of man, and the modern Christian (!) conception. The heathen men and their gods, &c., are represented as stout able-bodied fellows, who did their work manfully, ate their dinners, married their wives, and begat sons and daughters with thankfulness of heart. But the statues and paintings of the Christian heroes hang their heads, and wring their hands, and draw down the corners of their mouth, and go without their breakfast; they don't sleep well o' nights, they make "a covenant with their eyes not to look upon a maid," and are always making a fuss about their s-o-u-l. I would rather have a good, plump, hearty heathen, like Aristotle, or Demosthenes, or Fabius Maximus than all the saints from Peter, James, and John (δοκοῦωτες στυλοι εἶναι) down to the last one manufactured by the Roman Church—I mean as those creatures are represented in art; for the actual men I have a reasonable respect—they had some spunk in them, while the statues even of Paul represent him "as mean as a *yaller* dog." But let *ngsin-n-n-n* go—I will turn to something else.

This letter indicates how a portion of the autumn of 1839 was spent.

TO WM. SILSBEE.

Westfield, October 15.

Here we are; I say we, meaning George Ripley, Henry Lee, jun., and myself, on a pedestrian expedition of great extent and most uncertain duration, but *here* at all events, and obliged, since we have perishable bodies, to lay by, on account of a violent rain which has continued all night and all day, and threatens to be perpetual. Doleful it is, with the scent of the bar-room on the one hand, and on the other the pattering of rain, the jingling of crockery, the neighing of horses, and the cackling and crowing of little hens and cocks. Yet withal it is not dismal, for we have right fair weather within ourselves, and I have just now, this blessed rainy day, read through Sterne's "Sentimental Journey" and "Peter's Letters to his Kinsfolk," not to mention the fibs we have told one another this morning.

I wish to know if you have read Ripley on the "Latest Form of Infidelity," and what you think thereof. To me it seems excellent, both in design and execution—equally fine in manner, matter, and spirit. The Professor may well thank Heaven that he has fallen into the hands of a Christian man and not the clutches of a Philistine. Some men would have treated him as the giant charitably designed to treat Jack—would have broken every bone in his body. But, after all, the Professor is not to be despised nor abused. He has done a good work, so let him be honoured for that; for there are few scholars who have done *one* good work.

Our party, hoping for a pleasant expedition, design to spend this and the next week in roaming about among the hills of Berkshire county; we should have much pleasure if you were with us. It grieves me to think how much we are separated, when we of old time were so strictly conjoined. Pray write me of your plans, and tell where you may expect to be the next few months. Give my best and most affectionate regards to Charlotte, and the little unshod Carmelite who blesses your arms the greatest part of the time I fear.

TO THE SAME.

September 15, 1840.

Dr. Walker's discourse before the Alumni was exceedingly good, and so far from "prohibiting the banns between Religion and Philosophy," he said matters had gone so far between the two parties already, that the affair could not be winked out of sight (by the old folks); it could not be hushed up in the family, nor was it safe at this stage of the progress to call Philosophy by a bad name and then let him go. He recommended immediate union, as soon as the priest could be got ready.

Now I suppose the parties, for both Religion and Philosophy were in the church, took the hint, and went off to Providence or New York, and were made man and wife with all convenient despatch; for not a word has been heard from either of them since. I suppose they are now making a nuptial tour through the States; for I hear of "ferments" and "excitements" in other parts, which make me suspect the couple are still active. If they do not return to New England for some years I trust they will come back with their arms full of giant babies, who shall build up the shaken walls of the church, and the school, and so revise the work of both parents.

TO MISS E. P. PEABODY.

December 18, 1840

I love to lie a bright day in June, under a tree, while the growing leaves produce new modifications of beauty in shadows on the grass each moment, to look up to the rich clouds and half think, half dream about the manner in which the Infinite created the Finite. But when I get upon my feet, it all becomes a dream again. The idea of something created out of nothing is an absurdity. God created the world—*out of Himself*, so He is still in it, creating every day—not only worketh *hitherto* but *now* likewise. Creation in its essence may not be a profitable subject of contemplation, but some of the aspects of it are infinitely touching I think. At different stages of life I have been amazed at the power and the wisdom that are involved in the creative act. But of later years, as I look more through the surfaces of things, or at least try to do so, it is the beauty and *loving-kindness* of God that strikes me most. I think with you that we can apprehend the creative moment through love, and through that alone. It is this that solves all the mystery ; it cares little for the details of the work, but tells us at once—" Out of the depths of infinite love God drew forth the world. Oh, mortal, whoever thou art, thank God that thou art born; and take courage, for thou also art a child of infinite love, and all of thy past is working on thy behalf. So fear not ; what though you weep a little while you scatter the seed, and the cold rain of spring drenches and chills you, from this very field you shall fill your bosom with sheaves of satisfaction."

To me this thought, this feeling is enough to wipe the tear from my eye at any time. It is infinite counsel, and infinite comfort. It has been adequate for all the trials I have yet found, and I trust it "will keep me" till the world ends. I often wish I could impart this same feeling to others. But the attempts always remind me of the truth in Plato, "It of all things is the most difficult to find out God, and impossible to communicate Him to others." Yet it has come to me with little *conscious* difficulty. I sometimes try—yes, it is the object of my preaching—to lead all to this same " watch-tower in the skies;" but they tell me, " Look at the evil, the wretchedness, the sin of the world — the wrongs that patient merit of the unworthy takes," as if I could not not see them all, and feel some of them. I wish you would tell me, my dear Elizabeth, some better method of doing this. You are the all-sympathizer, and must know how to do *this* kindly office also.

TO THE SAME.

Saturday Night.

My VERY DEAR ELIZ.—I deplored more than you could the sad interruption to our talk—I am glad always to see Mr. ——. I respect him much, though he bored me a little then. I got some hints from him which will be useful, I think. The evil was he came when I wanted two things, repose and Elizabeth. He disturbed both. I should have come into your house, Monday, but I did not get into town till four o'clock, had many errands in all parts of the town, came under your window with Alcott, and saw the back of your head at the window, and was besides obliged to go home at eight, for then the carry-all and Aunt Lucy came in. Do not fear that I shall leave or forsake you. I should not commit the unusual sin of writing a sermon Saturday night. But Monday morning I went in quest of a cow ; so there was no sermon. It would not come into shape on Saturday morning, but now it is fortunately all done, but is shockingly poor. It lacks unity, strength, and height and depth, and all dimensions.

Your journal pleases me amazingly. It is *parsemè* with beautiful thoughts, though I had rather tell this to some other than to you. But you criticise yourself with dreadful sharpness. If I had only my own merit, and all your self-condemning modesty, I should expire at once in universal bankruptcy. Nobody would trust me for a shoe-tie. But it is fortunate that such supercelestial self-distrust should be balanced as it is. I need not tell you *how*.

I don't agree with you on the question of the Resurrection. The Berkeleyan hypothesis solves it quite as little as the *Hartleian*, I think. That God should suspend, violate and contradict the laws He has made for no purpose at all, or in such a way as to prove nothing, I find it difficult to conceive; the contradictory accounts puzzle me. Christ comes *through the door that is shut, vanishes* like a ghost, walks with the disciples to Emmaus; and in spite of the wounds in his hands and feet, they do not know him, until he breaks the bread. All these and many more are puzzling circumstances to me.

But the matter itself is of small moment. I am certain of my own immortality. That is enough. I have no doubt that Jesus Christ wrought miracles—though I find it difficult to believe he turned water into wine or fed five thousand with a few loaves. But these things never trouble me. The purple clouds that gather round the setting sun are but the proper accompaniments of the all of light. Still I do not look upon them as the sun, and when I think of him at mid-day the clouds with all their purple are but an insulting thought. I regard the stories of impossible miracles as the refractions of his light in the gross atmosphere of Jewish and Pagan minds.

FROM THE JOURNAL.

BERRY STREET CONFERENCE, 1840.—Last week in May attended the annual meetings of the Unitarians. The following proposition was discussed: "Ought differences of opinion on the value and authority of miracles to exclude men from Christian fellowship and sympathy with one another?" This is the substance. L—— says it smacks of the 12th century to debate such a question. I was not a little horrified to think a doubt could be raised; but men went so far as to ask if it were proper to exchange with one another, if they differed on this question. This is the 19th century! This is Boston! This among the Unitarians! Some good speeches were made by Ripley, Stetson, and Hedge, quite to the advantage of the New School, but the fundamental questions were not touched. I wished to disenchant men of their delusions, but could not. I said nothing. However, they all parted in peace, and with this conclusion, that though there were differences of opinion, there was yet no cause for withholding Christian sympathy—a result they might as well have brought with them as gathered from such a discussion. For my own part, I intend, in the coming year, to let out all the force of Transcendentalism that is in me. Come what will come, I will let off the Truth fast as it comes.

June.—I look upon my office as giving me an opportunity twice a week of addressing men on their dearest interests. The creed of the Church I have nothing to do with. I wish to make men more moral and more religious. If they think as I do, very well; if they do not, very well also. The rites of the Church do not disturb me much. Baptism I like—it means something. The Lord's Supper I don't like, as it is now administered. It is a heathenish rite, and means very little, I think. Cast away the elements. Let all who will come into a parlour and have a social religious meeting; eat bread and wine, if you like, or curds and cream and baked apples, if you will; and have a conversation, free and cheerful, on moral questions, or simply personal good feelings and prayers. Only let all be rational and real.

I do not believe in the Old Testament or the New, as my Christian fellows do. I know there are not ten churches in New England where I could be admitted, if moral as James and pious as Christ.

About this time Mr. Parker appeared in the discussion which was opened, in 1839, by Professor Norton, in his discourse entitled "The Latest Form of Infidelity." Mr. Ripley undertook a reply, in which he ably controverted Mr. Norton's view of the value of miracles as the exclusive evidences of Christianity, and corrected the Professor's bad translations from De Wette. It was a just vindication of German theologians, and of liberal thinking, from official imputations of infidelity. Professor Norton reiterated his statements in a rejoinder. Then Mr. Ripley, in two letters—the first, an admirable development of Spinoza's metaphysics, the second a full defence of Schleiermacher and De Wette, betrayed his own philosophical culture and thorough knowledge of the subject, and in thus closing his share in the controversy, gave it dignity and value. An anonymous pamphlet appeared about the same time. Mr. Parker's contribution immediately followed, being a pamphlet entitled "The Previous Question between Mr. Andrews Norton and his Alumni moved and handled, in a Letter to all those Gentlemen. By Levi Blodgett." It is an excellent statement of his own belief at the time; and it argues the necessity of putting the evidence for Christianity upon an immutable spiritual foundation.

June 21.—S—— had some good things to say in comparing Plato with Jesus, though I think she assigned him too high a place relative to Jesus Christ—a fault very few Christians commit. We should always remember the different culture of the two, the differing atmospheres they breathed; and still more, that one lived eighty, the other less than thirty-five years. One realised his idea, the other was "soon cut off." Take those three great ideas of each, Man, God, and their relation, and, though Plato were godlike, Jesus is divine.

May, 1840.—Had a long talk with ——. She doubts the infallibility of conscience, under any circumstances—seems phrenologically inclined—denies the will of man. I could shed no light upon the subject at all. She took the ground of *Owen*, that everything is forecast in the mental or physical structure of the man. She will have a *motive* for all things, and makes action the result of the balance of forces inclining this way or that. She will outgrow this. It can only be lived down. I have passed through the same stage, and regard it as I do the chicken-pox—something that must come, and which we are glad is well over, but which confines few persons for any length of time.

May, 1840.—How my own thought troubles me! I have a work to do, and how am I straightened till it be accomplished? I must write an Introduction to the New Testament—must show what Christianity is, its universal and its distinctive part. I must write a Philosophy of Man, and show the foundation of religion in him. In my days of leisure, when I am not hard at work—on a beautiful Sabbath, for instance, or in a moony night, or one filled with stars, when I walk out, this burthen presses me heavily. I must do or die. I sit down to hard work, and then only do I feel free from this tormenting spirit ; at other times I am consumed by self-reproach for the nothings I have accomplished, for the nothing I have undertaken. My heart beats audibly, so that my hand quivers. Hard work only relieves me for the time it lasts. But I must do much hard work before I can approach the *Introduction*. This I am now preparing for. Still harder work must be done before the *Philosophy* can come forth, and much more before the crown of *Theology* can be put on the work. Here is work for digging, for flying, and for resting, still yielding to the currents of universal being that set through a soul that is pure.

June 22.—Saw ———, who, though sick, is strong at his clear heart. I suppose his day and work are over, so that his death would be simply a domestic affair. Oh, that I may live like Dr. Channing and Göthe in this respect, and work on to the end, with spirits only mounting higher.

Heard of a sermon on the New Idolatry, which, if I understand the extracts rightly, is excessive trust in the soul. Now, if this is the most dangerous idolatry in New England, I am glad. I fancy there are very few led away by a false philosophy. But all the clergy are out upon some half-dozen transcendentalists as if they were to set the world on fire. Have not the clergy *always*, from the time of Constantine, preferred the chivalrous office of fighting a few persons who break the trammels of the Church, to attacking robust sins that lead off many men and women? And is not the present position of the conservative clergy *a case in point?*

Write a sermon on Idolatry. Show that there is as much now as ever. Idols change names. No worship now of Pluto, Neptune, Venus, &c. But show the essence of idolatry, viz., the love of something, *not God*—more than *God*.

The common forms of it—love of money, of show, &c. These are among the wicked. But among the pious, two things usurp the place of God: 1. The Bible; 2. Jesus Christ. Show how, by showing the common notions. And talk with Dr. Francis about it.

Sept. 23.—Went to Boston to attend the Non-Resistant Convention. Don't agree with them entirely, but like their spirit and upward tendency. Like not their formula of " No Human Government." Think circumstances render it needful sometimes to take life. If a man attack me, it is optional on my part to suffer or resist ; but should he attack my wife, with the worst of purposes, why should I suffer the wicked to destroy the righteous, when I could save her by letting out his life ?

I should deprecate the issue being tendered, but if it were tendered, I have little doubt which course would be revealed to me as the true one.

CHARDON ST. CONVENTION. L— doubts the Convention, fears bad use will be made of truth. *Nous verrons.* Thinks Quincy sincere, disinterested, good. L—— is a beautiful soul.

Dr. C. also doubts the propriety thereof, since it looks like seeking agitation, and fears the opinion of Garrison, Quincy, and Maria W. Chapman. Here again we shall see. I have my own *doctrines*, and shall support them, think the *Convention* as it may. I look on the Church as a body of men and women getting together for moral and religious instruction, on the minister as a moral and religious teacher, and on Sunday as a day set apart from work and common secular vocations. All of them are human institutions. But each valuable—I would almost say invaluable.

Nov. 17, 1840.—Attended the "Sabbath Ministry and Church Convention," of which I shall say nothing, for an account thereof will be published in due time. I will only say that all my friends after the flesh, and some of my friends after the spirit, regretted that I had any agency in calling the Convention.

Dec. 5, 1840.—Work for next week.

1. Write a Sermon on Evil—its power in the world and use.
2. Finish Æschylus.
3. Finish all the "little reading" on hand—to wit, Ozanam on Dante—the Journals, &c.
4. Read all I can find *about* Æschylus.
5. Go to Boston once and see Dr. Channing.

I have solicited an exchange repeatedly with ——, could not get it; with ——, and ——. To ask either of these men again would be a dereliction from Christian self-respect. So let them pass. I feel no ill-will towards any of them. I will try —— soon, for the experiment's sake, and so with others. Their answer decides my course for the future. Let us see! I should laugh outright to catch myself weeping, because the Boston clergy would not exchange with me!

These are brave words, but a soft heart penned them, and infected the page with its own self-distrust.

Last Leaf.—It is the last day of 1840, and I finish this book. To-day I finish Sophocles, with the Trachiniæ, which is scarcely worthy of its author, though the passage on the power of love is "haughty, beautiful, and high." I love and honour this poet. What a portrait of a heroine he gives you in Antigone! But she is hard as marble, she is all over a heroine. She will not mention her lover's name when she dies—not flinch the tithing of a hair from circumstances, and seems to say to them, bind the actual tight as you will, the ideal is winged with freedom.

Oh, Thou Spirit whom no name can measure and no thought contain; Thou to whom years are as nothing, and who art from everlasting to everlasting—I thank Thee that my life still lasts from year to year. I thank Thee that my cup is full of blessings. But I would bless Thee still, if Thou didst fill my cup with grief, and turn my day into night. Yea, O God, my Father, I will bless Thee for whatever Thou shalt send. I know it is all very good. I bless Thee that Thou art still very nigh me, that Thou speakest to my heart from year to year. Thou kindlest my faith; Thou quickenest my love; Thou castest down my fear. When my father and mother forsake me, Thou wilt take me up. Oh, my God, bless me still this coming year. Be not afar off. May I never become false to thy gift. Let my eye be open, my heart true and warm, my faith pure and heavenly. May religion dwell in the inmost sanctuary of my heart. Let it be my daily life, and wherever the years shall find me, may I do my duty, without fear, and so live on—lying low in thy hand and blessed by thy goodness. Amen.

THE PARSONAGE.

CHAPTER VII.

The "New School"—"The South-Boston Sermon, May 19, 1841—Discourse of Matters pertaining to Religion"—De Wette's "Introduction to the Old Testament."

THE decade commencing with 1830 was a memorable period in the spiritual history of the liberal men of Cambridge and Boston. That was the neighbourhood where everything on "tiptoe for the American strand" first planted its foot; it still is early to welcome the remotest thought from many provinces of human culture. Here, of all American regions, the German language was first received gratefully and with eagerness for the sake of its new literary and philosophic forms. Ingenuous youth were told that it was the natural language of infidelity and spiritual despair, but few of their seniors knew enough of it to misrepresent it, and their mental tendency was distasteful to the new thought which was learning to wield those portentous adjectives, "empirical" and "transcendental." It is not easy to trace to any special cause this new impulse to reconsider the old grounds of faith. A few Unitarian scholars, tired of the English commentators and divines, invited into their study the best thought of other countries; but there was something else besides liberal scholarship at the bottom of this instinctive combining of many ardent youth, bent upon "New Views," and a "New Church." Mr. Emerson had just begun to draw from the living well of his American genius, which owed as little to France or Germany as Concord River owes to famous transatlantic waters. But he proclaimed the new tendency, and generously nourished and vindicated, but did not originate it. Neither did Dr. Channing, though his preaching implied much, and the moral fervour of his protests against degrading views of God and human nature kindled many a mind. But his lack of wide scholarship indisposed him to encourage the new criticism, and his timidity and fastidious dread of crudeness kept him back from novel speculations. The " Old School " complained that a parcel of fools were rushing in where angels feared to tread. A little Hebrew, with Kueinoel and Rosenmüller, with Yates and Wardlaw, and the sound old Unitarian apologists, with Locke, and Reid, and Stewart, with Butler, Paley, and Watson, no longer appeased these young Hyperions, who meant to travel on the "high *a priori* road."

That was, indeed, an epoch which brought sensitive and aspiring minds at once so close to the great names, which, if mentioned, would present a series of Europe's choicest moments for a hundred years. Imagine a troop of New-England boys, fresh from " up-country " scenes, as they plod along some widening valley, and come suddenly upon a line of beach, where for the first time their feet, that bring down meadow scents to the new mysterious flavour of the sea, touch the edge of that great bosom which heaves with sport and earnest and conceals a myriad unsuspected thoughts. No subsequent deliberate classification of those depths can make them forget the first exaltation of the mind as it struggled to occupy the new horizon.

No doubt it produced some confusion when Leibnitz, Spinoza, Kant, Göthe, Herder, Schleiermacher, Jean Paul, Jacobi, and the rest, sailed all at once into Boston Harbour, and discharged their freight. Here were crops which we had not grown ; they might come in rotation, but as yet the old woods covered their germs. The wharves were littered in a day with the spoils of a century. Distracted critics stumbled up and down, and received a great many tibial bruises in trying to invoice the lot. It was altogether beyond any process of registering. There was no patent thought-distributor to move with untiring facility through this wealth of many-zoned Germany, and sort it for delivery. We all rushed in and helped ourselves.

The somewhat incompetent inspectors withdrew from the scene, condemning the whole importation as impracticable. A few boys, operating with straws and gimlets, were not unseasonsonably whipped by these critical officials. But very soon, and ever since, the persons to whom the freight had been consigned came to claim and to store it. The great intercourse of thought is self-adjusting, and the producing finds the consuming mind.

As if the confusion were not already sufficient, Mr. Carlyle must needs make his first venture westward, about this time, in "Sartor Resartus." His ship was at once pronounced, if a Dutchman at all, a phantom Dutchman, which you might run down to, and hail, and get nothing for an answer. Such was, doubtless, the ill-luck of our admonishers, but other ears gathered with little difficulty a manly and stimulating speech. Mr. Carlyle's Essays were soon republished ; they lent courage and independent direction to many minds, to others nothing but a grotesque idiom. But the youthful hours when thought began to grow are never forgotten : he made us feel glad that we were desiring to know the truth rather than the form, and his electric temperament of spiritual freedom passed helpfully over the expanding mind.

The French also assisted to increase this embarrassment of riches. For, besides Fourier, Leroux, and the writers of the Social- istic school, there came, first, Damiron, then Benjamin Constant, with his theories of the development of religion, Jouffroy, and Victor Cousin, that brilliant expositor of German philosophers, who contributed his famous phrase of the " Impersonal Reason " to the problem of inspiration. And, in America, Mr. Brownson, in the early liberal phases of his preaching and writing, was in- strumental in letting loose among us a great many of the Gallic terms and views.

At first the Unitarians offered hospitality to this great migra- tion of new literary and philosophical forms. Before their pro- testing movement became in turn conservative and sectarian, there was a liberal condition of the body which unconsciously served the purpose of admitting here the speculations whose method and terminology were foreign, but whose substance was really native to men proclaiming the dignity of human nature, and who had repelled vilifying doctrines. The new thoughts should have been, in some form or other, the legitimate deduc- tions of a belief in man's original capacity and freedom. Mr. Emerson began to tread this pre-established path with unbor- rowed power, before the neighbourhood had become much in- fected with the foreign technicalities. But his generous claims in the soul's behalf seemed exorbitant, and they served, with his bold depreciation of historical religion, to set critics and guar- dians on the watch. His influence, though it did not invite, yet helped to welcome the transatlantic speculations to which his own views were persistently attributed.

But this was not entirely just. For it was in the nature of Unitarianism to develope a spiritual philosophy that should claim for the soul primitive notions of God, right, and immortality. Cudworth, the preacher of immutable morality, was the English representative of this tendency. It belongs not only to those who would show the harmony of Scripture with absolute truth, but to those who deny that some doctrines are scriptural, on the ground that they are repugnant to reason. The right of judgment is derived from ideas in the Reason which precede scriptures and doctrines, and subject them to review. The right of judging if a doctrine be scriptural depends upon the capacity to discern if Scripture itself be reasonable. So that the Bible itself is subject to the ideas which the Bible is supposed to embody. It is of no consequence how far criticism may go in this direction after Reason has assumed her right. She herself alone can regulate the extent of her applicability. This is legitimate Unitarianism. And it is also Transcendentalism, properly defined.

Thus there arose a new school of Unitarianism, that sought to found a philosophy, giving to truth her own authority, to the Bible the authority of a record harmonizing with reason, to Christ the authority of displaying what the soul can recognize on its own evidence. And a voice or two was heard to add, "and to reason the right of rejecting everything everywhere that is irrational." This school did not yet deny that the miracles were wrought, but only that they added no authority to things morally and religiously true, because with such things they had no essential connection. Nor did this new school deny generally that some special divine quality supernaturally interpenetrated the Son of Man.

On the other hand, the representatives of the old Unitarianism, which had fought the Trinity and the Atonement on virtually transcendental grounds, now refused to be implicated farther with an independent reason, partly because they were sincerely opposed to its anti-supernatural tendency, and partly because the vagueness and misuse of the new terms disgusted them. They said, very properly, that whoever denies that a miracle is the authority for Christianity, might as well, and soon would, deny that any miracle was ever worked. The semi-supernaturalists vehemently repelled this insinuation; but it was well-founded. For either reason or external authority must rule.

M 2

Whoever accepts a premise of either binds himself to all the consequences.

It is certain that the new phrases were very loosely used. The more liberal thought borrowed them instead of growing its own. Such terms, when adopted, should be subjected to a strict survey, for an old ship cannot sail in all waters. The words "transcendental," "intuitive," "immanent," "innate" come down to us from scholastic times, and every epoch of thinking has modified their meaning ; any theology can use them if it has the liberty of adjusting what they connote. But a new school cannot assimilate an old term without getting itself thereby misrepresented. When a critic in the interest of Locke, who believes that all ideas are derived from the various sensations of experience, hears the proclamation that perception of truth is "intuitive," that ideas are "innate," that the Word which lighteth every man is "Impersonal," he has all the advantage of *vis inertiæ* in his question, "What do you mean by those words?" To define them is a delicate operation, and the longing for a spiritual philosophy preceded the careful framing of a code of signals that should, without the possibility of misleading, be current everywhere in the great commerce of thought. What is an "innate idea," for instance? The phrase can bear three interpretations :—1st. An original divine mark fully made on the soul, to appear in the sympathetic heat of experience. 2nd. A divine germ, predestined to unfold by gradual stages if the climate be favourable. 3rd. A mere capacity to deduce from the inward and the outward life some absolute conceptions of God and right. But men are not safer in an empirical philosophy because accidents result from the illegitimate and careless handling of abstract words.

Some of the Unitarians, however, thought so ; for no possible definition of such phrases as "cognition of absolute ideas," "impersonal reason," "à priori evidence of truth," could pacify their sincere supernaturalism. A few who had good-naturedly assisted at letting in the foreigners, were now aghast at their brogue and uncouthness. The shew-bread began to disappear, and the sacred utensils were handled in a playful manner that boded no good to little sentiments and proprieties, if the new importation were left to run at large. The orthodox began to ask unpleasant questions ; and if a Unitarian undertook to pilot "over-soul," or "immanence," or "spontaneity," through Cambridge and Boston, get for them New-England home-spun, and attempt their introduction in respectable quarters, the watchful Calvinistic shoulder went up to the ear. To such ominous shrugs a man is very sensitive when he is just on the point of being admitted into recognised circles. If he is only an amateur at singularity, he promptly drops his notion and becomes fanatically conventional.

There were some of these amateurs, who for a time used the phrases of progress and spiritual freedom with a grand, ingenuous air, which seemed to extend the patronage of Christianity to Transcendentalism. They lamented over the formalism of the Church and the decay of interior religion. Sometimes they magnificently asked the brethren if their hearts were not large and tolerant enough to hold Mr. Emerson and all of that ilk. They were young then, and had a sentimental feeling for liberty, to which the new phrases lent dignity and picturesqueness. They were just baring their breasts with *abandon* to the universe, and calling to the "over-soul" to come on, when Mr. Parker's sermon of "The Transient and Permanent," struck their bellying sails with a sudden dismay, and they were never hoisted more.

That revolutionary sermon also converted a good deal of lively, bantering criticism of historical religion into the most inflexible conservatism. Unitarian scholars had indulged a light way in private of talking about the miracles, although they really accepted the greater part of them as facts, and nominally held them as a basis of authority. But criticism had broken just far enough with the old reverence to render a jest on Balaam's ass, the possessed swine, the money in the fish's mouth, not inadmissible on week-days. And men spoke freely to each other of the Orientalisms of the New Testament, among which they would sometimes class, not only the Conception and the Star in the East, but also the Transfiguration and the Ascension. Mr. Parker did not understand this raillery. If he shared the smile, it was from a strong and ever-deepening conviction that Sunday was as good a day as Monday on which to expose these unhistorical elements.* Fancy his astonishment at the stern and sudden orthodoxy which seized the liberal circle where he used to hear this half-considered talk. This must be remembered when

---

* The specimens which have been collected by Mr. Parker point to private interviews with the friends whose names are also given, and not to any discussions held at the meetings of Associations or other clerical gatherings.

he is found afterwards hinting at a scepticism which uttered in the study what it was unwilling to utter in the pulpit. It was not really that, but it seemed so to him; for he soon saw how untenable was the assumption of selecting miracles to suit your taste, and preserving one set for banter and another for belief. When the mythological element is once admitted the right of choice expires.

He and his friends were really afloat upon this principle: they without knowing it. What was their perturbation when this island on which they bivouacked and built their crackling, merry fires, began to move off to sea! He might go voyaging in that fashion, but they scrambled for the deck again, and were glad to feel the old ballast underneath.

TO WM. SILSBEE.

April 23, 1841.

I am no Pantheist, nor ever was. My friend —— says "he burns between two fires, Anthropomorphism" (which is the theistical side of Calvinism), "and Pantheism" (which is the religious side of nature, as Coleridge would say if he were here.) Now, for my part, I find a *tertium quid*, and am no more troubled by Pantheism or Anthropomorphism than, at noonday, the evening and morning twilight trouble me. The whole difficulty comes of attempting to get a logical and definite notion of God. The sentiment of religion in a man would naturally come at first to Anthropomorphism, for the human is the highest form known to us; just as an ox, had he religion, would think of God in the form of an ox, counting that the highest. Hence the stories in the Old Testament among the Greeks, Hindoos, &c. Then reason looks at the stars, and says, God is not like a man. It feels God is *infinite*, so it attempts to separate from the idea all that is finite,—1, the human form; 2, passion; 3, memory, &c., and so on with each attribute of the *finite*, till it comes at last to make God nothing but an abstraction, of which even being cannot be predicated. Plato got up so high one day, and Hegel says, "Seyn und Nicht-seyn" are the same thing—no difference between God's *being* and being *not*.

But neither the head nor the heart will subsist on abstractions; so they say the infinite concretizes itself in nature, has no consciousness except through the consciousness of individuals. "God first comes to consciousness in (Adam) man; to *self*-consciousness in Christ, who is the sum total of mankind," says a Hegelian. So God never could say "I," nor distinguish between the divine "me" and "not me," till the birth of Jesus Christ. But with all reverence for philosophy, I would ask, "Who told him this?" I think the instinctive feeling and reason also lead direct to God—God all-wise, all-powerful, all-good—who is the good, the beautiful, the true. But they do not *define* him, except so far as to distinguish the idea of God from all other ideas, either actual or possible. Love, wisdom, &c., in Him who made the stars, must be very different from what I feel and know. Now I bow to this Being and live in him, but I cannot " by searching find out God unto perfection," *i.e.*, perfectly. We see that there is *nothing but the Creator and the Creation.* I feel no desire, as some do, to attempt to simplify the matter still more, and find only a Creator. Creation is to me the glass through which I see God. I can know much about the manifestations of the Creator in the Creation; but can only know of God that He is perfect.

FROM THE JOURNAL.

GOD.—God is in the soul of man, and gives us all the life we live. Reason is not personal, but is a great plane, which cuts the centre of all souls—the larger the soul, the greater portion of the one and indivisible God is intercepted thereby. The life of God is in my soul: it is vain that you tell me of God out of me. The *senses* wish for such a God; they find him, for all they perceive is but the varied deity. Light and beautiful forms are God to the eye, perfumes to the smell, and so of the rest. But the one God, I find and hear of in my soul, all nature is his dress, stars spangle his robe and light is but his garment. Oh, Thou ever-present, I feel Thee evermore! There is nothing where Thou art not. Oh, all in all! I adore Thee, and melt with blissful tears into the deep of Thee!

The following extracts mark the tendency of his thought at this time; how earnest it is, and palpably in the interest of religion:

Christianity is a field on which may be raised the strangest crops— wood, hay and stubble, wheat and beans. The soil remains, the crop varies.

The Christianity which many men embrace is a very poor thing; a belief in the stories of the New Testament. These stories corrupt the truth. None of them rest on evidence. Jesus lived, taught, was crucified. His life was higher, I presume, than any one has ever described it. A great soul lay at the bottom of the Christian movement; men do not tell such stories save of great men. But the miracles—that contradict the natural law—such as the transubstantiation of bread, water, &c., the sending the devil into the swine, the resurrection of dead men, the resurrection of Jesus himself—all these have nothing to do with Christianity. I do not know what to make of them.

But this I feel, that the time is coming when men will wonder quite as much at the Christianity of the nineteenth century as we wonder at that of the ninth century after Christ, or that of the nineteenth century before Christ. The attempt of the times is now twofold, 1, to rationalize Christianity; 2, to Christianize reason. The scholastics began this in the eleventh century. The fathers took Christianity in its *enveloped* state, and *developed* it; so they were *Patres*, as Hegel says. Hence the Church, controversies, synods, and persecution. The scholastics took the speculative Christianity they found in the fathers, the councils, &c., and *methodized* it, and attempted to reconcile it with reason. Scholasticism is the attempt to marry philosophy and religion, to find a principle in man answering to each doctrine of Christianity. They did not first ask, What is Christianity? nor second, What is man? So they did not marry Christianity to philosophy, but only a saucy kitchen wench to fancy. Now is the question, What is Christianity? We are to hunt up the bride, and then, if they will, to marry them. The scholastics were not *Patres* but *Doctores.* We have neither. We are *Scrutatores.* We need, 1. An anthropology. 2. A critical history of religion.

Christianity is progressive, because it is not *positive,* but natural. We may say its main idea is the incarnation, reconciliation, the God-man, union of the absolute and the finite, or a perfect character for all; these mean but the same thing, as I understand it. Christianity, therefore, is the hope of the world, the desire of all nations.

1. Christianity may be considered as *objective* in the whole, and so as a process in God's development of Himself. The supernaturalist is obliged, if logically consistent, so to view it. This was the view which prevailed in the Catholic Church from the Council of Nice to the Reformation, and still prevails. The idea is this—God created the universe, the angels were a part of it—all was perfect; the angels fell, they must be replaced. It was tacitly supposed that God could not create *de novo* angels, so men were made. But they also fell; still the angel's place, and man's place also, was not filled. An instinct of perfection lay in the Divine mind, which led to the restoration of man (and of the angels also, thinks Origen.) He must restore man, so Mosaism as the preparatory step, and Christianity as the completion of the work, *i.e.,* both were phases which God must assume in the process of his self-development. To me it savours of arrogance to decide in matters that are too high for me. " Hardly do we guess aright," &c.

2. Christianity may be regarded as *subjective* as a whole, that is, a phase of human nature in its development. I think this the true notion, if we do not separate the divine too much from the human. If we allow that God still creates as ever, still "worketh hitherto," perhaps this the true view. It is mortifying to human pride to look back and see the crop of errors which have grown on the field of Christian speculation. It serves, however, to quicken one's humility; for each of the *Fathers* in the first age, each of the *Doctors* in the middle age, each of the *Scrutators* in this age, each heretic in all ages, has been certain that he was right. Where they failed, what modest man shall lift up a presumptuous thought? The history of thought teaches us all to be *modest.* The great truths of morality and religion are read us daily in New England or New Zealand by consciousness and faith—we need make no mistake; but when the meddling intellect comes in to do its work, what theologies we form! The Fathers milked the ram, the Doctors held the pail, the Scrutatores are divided on the question to whom the milk belongs.

Anselm, no doubt, thought he had solved all the mysteries of Christianity in his " Cur Deus homo?" Kant, Hegel, and Conradi have thought the same of their systems. But who, alas! shall mould for us the cup in which a single age can drink the water of life?

With most men there is a little of religion, with some there is much; this is only saying that there is more or less of it among men. But thought about religion is quite another thing.

He translates with astonishment a few choice paragraphs of a German book which presents Hegelian-Evangelical views :—

The first point which comes to be considered in this connection is that pure logical or metaphysical one contained in the proposition which stands at the head of Hegel's religious philosophy, viz., that God, as Absolute Spirit, is Triune. In so far as God is spirit, it belongs to His nature to reveal and objectivate Himself ; but it is likewise equally essential that, in this separation, He should remain identical with Himself. There must, therefore, take place a separation in God, without which there would be no process, and therefore no life in God ; but this separation is immediately neutralized in the Divine idea. Here is no serious, deep, penetrating differentiation, but that first attains its rights in the Son, who has proceeded from God, and stands beside Him, as the world, or the finite God, in free subsistency ; but from this separation and divulsion He comes again to unity with God, and returns to the Absolute Spirit which is identical with itself.

Upon this verbal juggling Mr. Parker remarks :—

Here is a subject which has occupied the attention of the greatest minds of the world, from Hierocles down to Hegel. Yet to me the whole question seems to rest on a false position, viz., that Jesus of Nazareth was the Supreme Being. Admit that he was a man—the noblest, best man who ever lived ; admit that if I do my duty as faithfully, I shall be equally accepted by God—the mystery is all over. I am perpetually astonished that men should reason so—on such premises. Still more, that, starting from such premises, they will plunge into the sea of Deity, and tell us the metaphysics, and the physics, too, of God. The history of man's *body* is a series of abuse and war, wrong and suffering. The history of man's *mind*, a story of delusions—brilliant thinking on false assumptions. It is a game that serves to pass the time and sharpen the faculties, but it is played for straws. The victor gains—nothing. It seems, in the history of Theology, as if there was a *tertium quid* between a lie and the truth ; as if the opposite of a lie was also a lie, and not truth ; as if truth and falsehood were the two extremes of a *tertium quid*, and the real way was deemed to be between them both.

There was nothing in his mind or education that could sympathize with the fruitless subtleness of some metaphysical schools. His theology did not need to be shored up by them ; they were alike distasteful to his plain, strong understanding, and to his humanity, It is evident that his late studies were preparing him for the " Discourse of the Transient and Permanent in Christianity," in which a simple intuitive feeling speaks through a well-instructed mind.

That sermon, which conjured bigotry, liberality and amateurship into their proper shapes, was preached at the ordination of Mr. Shackford at South Boston, on the 19th of May, 1841. The occasion passed off without any preliminary stir. The venerable clergyman who offered the ordaining prayer, recognised the heresy, and petitioned that the young incumbent might have a living faith in a Son of God of Divine works and nature. But beyond this the pulpit and the pews made no sign. One person rose during the discourse and retired, whether on account of a badly ventilated building, or a heresy ventilated but too well, remains unknown to this day. After the services a good many clergymen expressed admiration for the discourse, with the qualifications that might have been expected. And to all appearance it was about to be consigned to that limbo of imperfect sympathies whither so many of Mr. Parker's productions had gone before.

He had often preached and written things that were quite as radically defective when tested by any theology that admits the supernatural element. It was not one of his most energetic sermons, by any means, for he had written it during a week of langour and illness. It was diffuse, and too rhetorical. It neither accepted nor rejected the miracles, and the language held towards the person Christ was vague. Its positive merit was a warm and enthusiastic preference for permanent spiritual life to transient theological forms. But Dr. Channing, at least, had enforced the same vital distinction. He, too, would have set free the growing soul from the doctrines of an outworn past, so that intelligence might always preserve its chartered right to build the house for the inner life to occupy. And everybody heartily accepted that tendency which Mr. Parker strove to embody in his sermon.

Still, it was a revolutionary sermon, for its negative portion left some logical inferences to be made from its positive statements, which were not clearly seen at first. If Christ is inspired by means of a law which makes the same inspiration possible to all men, the supernatural distinction of his nature is no longer credible. The denial of miracles and of every exclusive element of divinity, is only a question of time and boldness. Were the Unitarians ready to accept all that lay latent in the discourse, as well as all which was patent for the world to read? And how was their qualified sympathy to be interpreted? When these questions were asked by some orthodox gentlemen, who did not care for a reply, as they intended only to embarrass the Unitarians, and force them to accept or repel Mr. Parker, it became necessary to issue vigorous manifestoes of belief. Sympathy with one por tion of the discourse was then more firmly expressed by a few, while the majority vigorously denounced its anti-supernatural tendency. Clergymen began to define their theological positions. Necessity drove them into a sudden consciousness of the paramount importance of a Christianity supernaturally revealed and attested. No doubt this had been sincerely deemed important before, but the sermon compelled them to see that there had been too much amiable concession to the excellence of spiritual views. That sermon really created an opportunity to see precisely the reverse, that these spiritual views might become the positive life of a sect which had hitherto only protested against bad doctrines, and that religion, rescued from all kinds of empiricism, might win a sound philosophy, a more ardent piety, a bold and warm philanthropy, at the hands of these men, fresh from their good fight, and eager to reap its glorious advantages. What liberal subjects were languishing then to be organized and led! What causes of justice and pure morals, and the dear country's vital hope, Anti-Slavery, yearning to be welcomed by the intelligence and spirit of a great religious party! Instead of occupying this great future, the Unitarians sent a few exiles forth to the whitening fields.

But it is better to attempt a narrative of history than to pick a quarrel with it. Mr. Parker's sermon and its amplification, the "Discourse of Religion," which soon followed, was a peremptory summons to the Unitarians to evacuate their thin didactic lines and come over to him. They fell back in alarm, to select their own position more carefully, and to remain there entrenched. He did not issue an invitation for fraternal co-operation in a reform of theology and a renewal of piety. A tea-party or a picnic may be inaugurated upon those terms, but not Protestantism. He stated the problems of religion, of the Church, and of society in sonorous and uncompromising phrases, and was so possessed by his subjects that he disregarded some points of taste and of religious observance about which people are sensitive. His intuitive beliefs stepped forth fully armed, in revolutionary mien, from the theology which hitherto he had only tolerated. In breaking with it, he displayed all his faults and virtues with a child's sincerity, impetuously rushing forward to claim recognition for his dear convictions; with strong hand pushing to the right and left what barred his way. Were the Unitarians ready to recognise this new revolution fresh risen, with lustihood and menace, from Lexington Common? They were not. They did not yield to the more silvery summons of Mr. Emerson. It was a historical necessity that the personality of the appeal should should enforce a personality of opposition.

Thus commenced that controversy, the details of which it would be no longer fruitful to recall. It is plain to see why Mr. Parker suffered so much at the sudden loss of scholarly and genial friends, and why he exaggerated the enmity of the genuine Conservatives. It is not wonderful that he should have despised the timidity which could preserve its spurious liberality only during the term of amiable neutrality which his own clear voice broke up for ever. He suffered when old friends refused to exchange with him; he jealously counted the precious names of those who yet remained. His heart was too tender to pass all these things by. He bore it out of the conflict into comparative quiet and the solace of new friendships, but the broken names still hung in it and kept their festering hold. He remembered too vividly, and the old griefs came often straying into his beautiful speech. Charmed hearers felt that the call to pity was an interruption to the inspiring thought. But these passion-flowers never drew malignant sap from the past, of which they were the emblems.

The Unitarians forgot a great many indignant words which their leaders had uttered when the orthodox refused to continue the fellowship of exchange and ministerial intercourse. And their plea was that the old controversy arose from a difference *within the limits* of Christianity, but that the new one was between Christianity and something else. Was not this assuming the very point at issue? And the orthodox never allowed their distinction; but had previously declared that men who denied the Trinity, the Atonement, and Original Depravity were outside of Christianity. If a man is permitted to decide that he is inside anything, he can put his head through his own assumption, and others will appear to him outside.

But this inconsistency was sincerely held, because the Unitarians venerated Christ as a teacher, having discarded him as a person of the Trinity and a sacrificial agent. They struggled to oppose a great authoritative teacher, the Son of Man and of God, to the mysterious doctrines of Calvinism. To construct an adequate idea of such a person, through whom men are to be saved by the more rational process of believing his remedial truth, it was necessary to secure the conditions of infallibility and authority for the truth which is to save. The infallibility was provided in special inspiration, the authority was claimed under miraculous attesting acts. It was objected to Mr. Parker, that without this supernatural basis the idea of a divine teacher could not be maintained. In this respect, then, Unitarianism was quite as consistent as its doctrine.

The newspapers swarmed with notices of the South Boston sermon, written generally in ignorance of the philosophical points which these great religious themes involve. The theological papers exercised their ancient privileges. Editors penned misleading articles, and correspondents sent in contributions of laical piety. A few conservative Unitarians defended Mr. Parker's liberty of prophesying, and in attacking his doctrines did not misrepresent them. Others were not so fortunate.

Divinity students must also splinter their brittle quills against the shaggy breast of this " Orson of Parsons." Some of them lived to know better, and were drawn near enough to feel the beating of that generous heart. Thus, for instance, did one, in discharging his callow petulance, disarm himself and fall a speedy prey to a friendship that led to a better appreciation of the truths involved :—

What, then, has Mr. Parker done for us ? He has with justice annihilated the Transient, but where is the Permanent? The path he pointed out does not conduct to the goal. We miss the substance for a shadow ; Revelation itself and Holy Writ shrink away at the presence of an Impersonal Reason. Is love to God and love to man, intuition, instinct, the only Permanent ? Can Revelation afford us nothing else ? Where are all our hopes of repentance, regeneration—our assurances of immortality ? And where, too, all this time, is Christ ? Our moorings are all cast loose ! We had already caught a glimpse of the Holy Land—we felt its celestial breath upon our souls—swiftly and sure each little bark was making for its destined haven, when, with one mighty upheaving from some Tartarean depth, we are cast back into the infinite void—into primeval chaos—no Christ, no religion ; only some grim-smiling, sinister Impersonal Reason, brooding over the vast abyss.

It is the divine privilege of youth and a good constitution to get well rid of such perilous stuff as that.

TO DR. FRANCIS.

Away-down East, Aug. 26, 1841.

My most excellent Friend, most sagacious, and wise, and Christian,—I wish you were here to enliven the solitude of the wilderness with your talk and your laugh. But here I am alone among the "salvages." I have been travelling on foot and alone "in these diggins" for several days. Yesterday I walked 35 miles; to-day 22 and rode 18; and from these remote quarters of the world I send you a word.

In the history of religions, which do you take to be the true notion: was this the order in which the human race "evolved" itself, viz.—1, Fetichism; 2, Polytheism; 3, Monotheism; or was a part of mankind monotheistic from the beginning? This involves the question of civilization. Was mankind (or a part of the race) *created* in the civilized state, and have the others *fallen*, or was man created savage, and has he gradually emerged from this state? The Germans, Eichhorn, Herder, and others, think man had no language at first (following Monboddo in this), but gradually developed the faculty of speech. They, therefore, ought consistently to say man began savage; his religious progress was 1, Fetichism; 2, Polytheism; 3, Monotheism.

Now there is much in history to confirm this latter opinion; such as the state of theology in the oldest nations at the time of the earliest historical notices. On the other hand, there is much to confound and overthrow this notion, which presents itself very obviously. Besides, all the metaphysical arguments tend the other way, viz., to the notion that *part* of the race at Creation was in a civilized state. What do you think of this idea: that different races were created in different degrees of civilization—some in Fetichism, even in the inferior degrees of it, as it is *now* found in Australia; others in Polytheism; and even some in Monotheism? I feel somewhat interested in this question, but suppose it cannot be solved even *ideally*, much less factically (as the Germans say).

I am writing this in the midst of a great crowd in a tavern reading-room, and there is no little buzzing all around me. It is queer to hear men at the far end of this state talk of going east, and of down east, as if they lived on the Missouri. I asked one of them what he meant by *going* down east. He said, "I once went down among the Blue-noses (*i. e.* into New Brunswick), and there they talked also of going east; so I went down to the point of Nova Scotia (the very jumping-off place), and even there they talked of going east!"

The blunt and distasteful way in which he sometimes uttered his criticism, furnished the persons who would not be touched by his real spirit with a convenient reason for avoiding him. Doubtless many who could sympathise with the pure, enthusiastic thought, were disturbed by some of his uncalculating rhetoric. And among his old friends were to be found a few, who, becoming suddenly enveloped in the startling publicity of his views, declared that it was not the light which hurt their eyes, but the rudeness with which he threw the shutters open. They complained of his spirit. That was an unfortunate word to use, for his spirit was the most unexceptionable part of him; his phrases sometimes misinterpreted it. How common are all the faults of style, how rare is the spirit which counts all the fashions of this world, and of its speech, a little thing compared with seeking truth.

People will speculate upon the possible results of a decided fact, as if it had been in some respects a different fact. Thus, it is said by his friends, he would have done more good, and by his enemies, more harm, if his temper had been somewhat more diplomatic, and his revolutionary matter couched in cautious phrases. They would tinker the fact, like Alphonso of Castile. Such speculating mends all the world's strong men out of sight. It is the old story of complaining that Luther gets into a great heat with taking the Pope's Bull by the horns, and that Latimer shocks people's sensibilities at Charing Cross. You can have your Luther who fights a good fight, or some other individual good for something else, at whom the Pope and his monks will snap their fingers, if they deem it worth the while. After you have boned your Reformer you might as well boil him, for he is of no other earthly use.

TO MISS C. W. HEALEY.

December 3, 1841.

What you say about touching men's prejudices more gently is true and just. I can only say that while I feel great tenderness towards the preconceived notions of *individuals*, when I am to speak of a mass of doctrines that come between man and God, I think the blow must be strong enough to cut clean through, and let the light stream through the rent. Besides, the sentiments in the South Boston sermon had so long been familiar to me, I had preached them so often with no rebuke, that I was not aware of saying anything that was severe. I thought the sermon would be reckoned tame and spiritless, for it so poorly and and coldly expressed what burned in my heart like a volcano. . . . . . .

Your sympathy is exceedingly precious to me. I never feared the reproaches nor coveted the praise of the hostile or the friendly, but the sympathy of the true-hearted is blessed to me: it is the dew to the herb.

TO HIS BROTHER-IN-LAW, CHARLES MILLER.

12 July, 1841.

You seem to think it *possible* that my *motives* were not good in writing and preaching the sermon which men make such a noise about. Now, I never in my life wrote a sermon with a deeper conviction of its truth or of the good it would do in the world. I wrote what I felt to the ends of my fingers, If you can find anything bad, pernicious, or likely to injure morality and religion, I am very sorry ; but I am certain it contains nothing of that character. The noise which men make, the bad names they call me, the threats they utter, move me as little as they move Monadnock . . . . . Do *you* think I could have any but the *best* of *motives* for this work? What could I gain but a bad reputation? Nothing else. No : I felt the difficulties of the common opinions. I wished to show that religion was independent of the foolish doctrines men have piled upon it. I wanted to break the yoke of bondage bound on men's necks, and have done what I could to make men better here and hereafter. The opinions in the discourse are nothing new to me ; not the random thoughts of a young man, but the sober, deliberate convictions, the result of thought and study. The end will be good, no doubt of that ; but the end *is not yet.*

The following alludes to a letter which about this time he addressed to the clergymen of the Boston Association :—

TO MISS E. PEABODY.

June 26, 1841.

Thank you a thousand times for your letters ; your criticisms are also encouraging ; nobody knows better than I how numerous my faults are, and certainly none feels them so strongly as I do daily. I know I am quick—sudden and quick in quarrel it may be—particularly after a good deal of intellectual excitement ; but in the case you instance you are mistaken entirely. I meant in sober earnest that those people were *wiser* as well as older, and *mean it now ;* not that all are older or wiser, but the leading persons I know to be both older and wiser, so I beg you not to misunderstand me here. It did not occur to me that anyone could misconceive the matter so entirely as to think I would insult a respectable body of people by a sneer after that fashion. Again, the letter was not written quickly, nor until after a good deal of reflection ; and then the original draught was shown to a cool, cautious, delicate-minded man, who said it was good, but *too weak.* He objected to nothing therein. Then Lydia read it, and thought there was nothing amiss in it. Now, my usual hastiness had nothing to do with this letter. But if others' eyes have the mote of suspicion, as yours and Sarah's have *not,* why they will see an innuendo in my wish that they may found a more *liberal* church, and even in my subscription as their "friend in the Christian faith." But, believe me, I should not interweave *innuendoes* or sarcasm in a letter to a Church, though I think sarcasm a legitimate weapon to use in certain cases of argument and fun.

This letter indicates the commencement of that popular sympathy, which was preparing to secure for him a more magnificent hearing than any man ever had in America :—

TO MESSRS. WM. LARNED, S. E. BRACKETT, CHARLES L. THAYER, AND CHARLES ELLIS.

West Roxbury, 26 June, 1841.

MY DEAR FRIENDS,—Your kind and very flattering note came safely to hand, and I have given it the best consideration in my power to bestow. I am thankful for the interest you express in my views of the Christian life. I know of no finite happiness so great as that which attends a successful attempt to set forth the great truths of religion, on which our welfare depends. It is with great reluctance that I conclude it is wisest and best to decline the invitation you have so generously made me. My reasons are chiefly a distrust of my own ability to effect the object you contemplate. Besides, I can still utter my word in the pulpit, and occasionally through the press, and, perhaps, can do what is given me to do better in this than any other way. The subjects you suggest offer a most noble and beautiful theme ; and would to Heaven I were able to discuss them as I feel they *now* require to be treated. The lectures of Dr. Walker, however, will more than supply anything I could attempt with any hope of success.

Believe me, gentlemen,
Very affectionately,
Your friend and brother in the Christian faith,
THEO. PARKER.

This invitation of a few friends who desired to maintain his privilege to speak and to define his own position had important results, notwithstanding his first refusal. He was persuaded to deliver a course of lectures in Boston during the winter of 1841-42. The old Masonic Temple was filled to hear him. The young men walked in from Cambridge, and back again over the long bridge in the darkness, with hearts aflame. All the earnest thinkers came to hear what he had to say, and many a girl who is now a noble mother, and many strong women whose names have since stood for some humanity of letters or of life.

These lectures appeared in the spring of 1842, somewhat more elaborated, in the volume entitled, " A Discourse of Matters Pertaining to Religion."

When this volume appeared, people were puzzled to reconcile the popular warmth and simplicity of the text with the remote and varied learning piled up in the foot-notes. They observed the anomaly " as a curious traveller counts Stonehenge." It led them to suspect an illusion. Had all these leading books, in all languages, been faithfully read and assimilated ? Then, where is the trace of it in the composition ? The terminology is neither German, French, nor Latin. There are no terms : every sentence is a lucid drop. When he states that, in the last analysis, the root of religion is a sense of dependence, you expect a popular re-hash of Schleiermacher. But his speech merely borrows the phrase as a temporary convenience. The word Fetichism, with references to Constant, whose extravagant love of system he really blames, put the critics on the scent of a French theory of development. So also did the sight of Comte's name, to whom he generally refers to note his disagreement with the Positive Method. The names of Strauss, Hennell, Baur, Bayle, and Hegel were presumptive evidence against the genuineness of the volume. The religious newspapers scorned an infidel dish which caught the drippings of all foreign kitchens. They supposed that an American could not associate with the thought of other nations upon terms of equality and dignified reserve. He would infallibly be sent home in a suit of foreign livery, of fantastic cut. Though they could not undertake to read Mr. Parker's authorities in order to trace the audacious plagiarisms, the fact was assumed by every subservient mind which felt that one volume of Kant would be quite enough to swamp its own style and carry down its cherished sentiments. All the pocket-tapes broke in measuring up against the poor boy from Lexington.

There were errors in this book, no doubt; inaccuracies and marks of haste. They were duly noticed in the reviews of the day.

This was a genuine American, who had loves and tastes which were cosmopolitan, Massachusetts' independent hardihood without the Know-nothing prejudice. His mind was like the republican idea itself; it could afford to be hospitable, but could not afford to be exclusive. Vigour, simplicity, a sensitive heart, a kindling enthusiasm, greatness to welcome great things and to remain still greater, breadth, homeliness, use, and the plastic power of natural elements,—these are the New World's character. He represented it. His mind, in its prime, was the first thorough democrat. He never Platonized, Judaized, nor Germanized. The hordes of emigrants found they were no match for the country. Their obtrusive characteristics were seized by the climate and made over; they gained protection, but no exclusive immunities, from his self-relying mind.

He had read all the books which assumed to lead thought in their respective provinces. He knew perfectly well what had been said upon all great points. His references indicated honest study, for careful analyses and estimates crowd the pages of his common-place books. What a proof of absence of confusion and surfeit is his simple American style, in which his home-bred piety and ethical sincerity flow and sparkle! Some of the pages of this volume are like broad, sweet waters, heated by the summer sun. The foot-notes show below; sharp Kant and stony Hegel, and uncertain Schelling, thin, sinuous grass, and all the waifs of time. In the still shadowy reaches the lily of religion floats.

His style is wonderful for its absence of all taint from scholastic and metaphysical terms. It has other faults, precisely such as the self-grown vigour might be expected to betray; but it steals, begs, and borrows nothing. It has the cant of no school, transcendental or parti-evangelical; no bristling words of Teuton or of Gallic origin. He finds the country language capable of telling his most spiritual thought.

That was the danger, men considered; it would be better if his sentences were subtly involved, and his ideas only half conscious of themselves. And it was alarming that a man of such undoubted piety should be furnished with such an aggressive common-sense. What shall be done for the Church, when a single man can show so clearly how religious he can be without the expense of miracles and mystical formulas? Men of all creeds instinctively saw in him those elements of a revolution, the primitive human right, the possession of weapons, and the defiance of authority.

Aside from private griefs, he enjoyed the struggle which bade him put forth all his powers. Now he stood in a wider horizon, and felt the excitement for which, without knowing it, he had languished. Without it he never would have vindicated his own ability, nor acquired that unrivalled expression and trained courage which made him so formidable in the great questions of the day. The contest came just in time to give humane love for man and for man's ideas, the advantage over scholarship and seclusion.

Duty, freedom, truth, a divine life, what are they? Trifles, no doubt, to Monk Tetzel, to the Leos and the Bembos, and to other sleek persons, new and old. But to a heart that swells with religion, like the Atlantic pressed by the wings of the wind, they are the real things of God, for which all poor temporalities of fame, ease, and life are to be cast to the winds.

He that feareth the Lord, when was he not a prey? He must take his life in his hand, and become as a stranger to men. But if he fall and perish, it is his gain. Is it not the world's? It is the burning wood that warms men.*

* Discourse of Religion: Am. Ed. 1842, pp. 110, 443.

N 2

TO DR. FRANCIS.

Feb. 14, 1842.

It is not often I have an hour for a letter, since to write two sermons a week, and spend five days of the week in other matters, and get no Sabbath on Sunday, though it may do well with stronger heads, yet goes hard with mine. I never cared much for the sympathy of other men, and never less than now; but once in a great while I feel it is not altogether pleasant to stand alone, to be viewed with suspicion and hatred. Blessed are the men who can take things as they find them, and believe as the mob believes, and sail in the wake of public opinion. I remember you told me a year ago, he that defies public opinion is like the man who spits in the wind; he spits in his own face. It is so. But what then? Let it be so. Better men have found less sympathy than I. I do not care a rush for what men who differ from me do say; but it has grieved me a little, I confess it, to see men who think *as I do* of the historical and mythical matter connected with Christianity, and who yet take the stand some of them take. It is like opening a drawer, when you expect to find money, and discover that the gold is gone and only the copper is left. This has been my fate very often. I put my finger on a *minister*, and " he ain't there."

TO THE SAME.   March 8, 1842.

You must have thought me a great fool to write so lugubrious a letter the other day. I ask as little for sympathy as any man, and when I mourn it is not on my own account; but I have seen some manifestations in certain persons that, I confess, made me feel sad, not for *my* sake, but *their* sake. I will tell you of this some time, but not write, for *scripta manent*.

But then there are times when I am sick, worn out and shattered, and I have nobody to fall back upon. " Wo unto him that is alone when he *falleth*." Paul could *stand* alone. I often think of those lines of Coleridge, which I trust are not so frequently on your tongue, nor so deeply graven in your memory, as in mine:—

> " There was a time when, though my path was rough,
> This joy within me *dallied with distress*,
> And all misfortunes were but as the stuff
> Whence fancy wove me dreams of happiness:
> For hope grew round me, like the twining vine,
> And fruits and foliage not my own seem'd mine.
> But now afflictions bow me down to earth:
> Nor heed I that they rob me of my mirth.
> But oh, each visitation
> *Suspends*, what nature gave me at my birth,
> *My shaping spirit of imagination.*
> For not to think of what I needs must feel,
> And to be still and patient, all I can,
> And, haply by *abstruse research* to steal
> *From my own nature all the natural man*—
> This was (is) my sole resource, my only plan:
> Till that which suits a part infects the whole,
> *And now is almost grown the habit of my soul.*"

But I will trouble you with no more threnodies, and I know you will forgive me this once.

TO THE SAME.

May 5, 1842.

I should have answered your last long ago, but the book I have in the press (" Discourse," &c.) has demanded from fifty to eighty hours a week of me, for the last six weeks, and I have had sermons to write, and neighbours to visit, and a thousand little "notions" to attend to, so that really I could not gratify my wish to see you or write to you. But this morning I sent the last sheet to the printer, and am now at leisure for a little while; so you may not only hear from me, but peradventure I shall waylay the tome-devourer, like Cacus, in his den, and that before long.

The other day I found a little bit of "literary history matter," which perhaps you have not seen; and as it concerns a favourite book of yours, I will copy it for you. Luther's "Table-talk" " did so promote the Protestant religion in Germany that each church had one of them (a copy of the 'Table-talk') chained in it, on which the Pope and the Emperor caused them all to be burned. Only one of them was afterwards found wrapt up in an old wall, by a German gentleman that pulled down his old house, who, not daring to keep it, for fear of the law against it, sent it to his friend, Captain Henry Bell, in London, desiring him to turn it out of German into the English tongue. The said captain, through business or otherwise, deferring to translate it, one night, between twelve and one o'clock, there appeared to him, then awake, an ancient man standing at his bed-side all in white, with a broad white beard down to his girdle, taking him by the right ear, saying, 'Sirrah, wilt thou not take time to translate this book which is sent thee out of Germany? I will shortly provide thee both time and place to do it in,' then vanished. His fright and sweating astonished his wife; yet, not heeding visions, the book again slipped out of his mind, till warrants from Charles I.'s council-board laid him up in the gate-house in Westminster for ten years, without showing him any cause, five of which were spent in composing the said translation, which was published by the Assembly of Divines."

This is from the "Surry Demoniack; or An Account of Satan's Strange and Dreadful Actings in and about the Body of Richard Dugdale, of Surry, near Whalley, in Lancashire," &c., &c.; London, 1697. Of course, you who own the book of Captain Bell must believe the story, for the translation must have divine authority, such as no translation pretends to except the LXX. Since you are a logician and casuist I will propound a *practical* question growing out of this case; *An liber fallibilis sit ne infallibilis si translator infallibiliter atque miraculose, &c.?* The "Tisch-reden" of honest Martin may be a human book, fallible, to be judged of like other books, and censured when it talks nonsense or contradicts itself. But the " Table-talk " as it comes from the hands of the aforesaid captain, is a divine and infallible production, and as such is not to be tried by " carnal reason." Then a question rises, whether the miraculous character is vested in the letters and points (the single parts) or in the book (the universal), and whether all subsequent editions would therefore be infallible, or only the *Codex Bell* which came from the hand of the captain. My book will appear about May 20. After that I suppose you will never speak to me except to say, *Apage Sathanas!* So I shall come to see you before.

TO MRS. DALL.

Faithful are the wounds of a friend. I do not love to be admired. I like much better one who sees my faults also, than one who only sees what little excellence I may chance to have. Yesterday I had a note from a stranger, calling me a *wolf in sheep's clothing*, and other gentle titles. To-day comes your note with its womanly tenderness, and its manly rebuke.

But while I thank you for your frankness, I by no means admit the justice of what you say. I am by no means conscious of giving utterance to "an unchristlike sneer or an unkind accusation" in any of my writings, preachings, or prayings. I do not admit the justice of your remarks about *sneering tones*. I never spoke of such as have faith in the Gospel record in terms of sarcasm and abuse, say Mr. —— what he will. If you will read over the passage where I quote the lines of Pope,* I think you will see little to censure. If I sneered at such as still believe in the ordinances, do you think I should still administer these ordinances? I? And invite others to participate in what I publicly administered—that I publicly mocked at! When I quoted these lines, I rejoiced that at God's table there was milk for the maidens, meat for the men. In short, that there was something for all—that man can take such things, water, bread and wine, and by means of association therewith connected, can find them helps in their spiritual progress. I think that in comparison with the great work of forming a Christian character and living a Christian life, all will confess that the " ordinances " are but straws, rattles and childish playthings. I never *mocked* at anything. I am not aware of uttering contumely and reproach. I pray thee, where or when? I have spoken strongly, and I have strongly felt. I feel willing to stand up before men or God, and declare that I am not conscious of having written one line with any unchristian feeling. I knew I should be misunderstood, misrepresented and abused. Once I said, " We whine and whimper in our brother's name," &c.; for that I have been called mocker, yet I wrote that sentence in tears of anguish, in great burnings of heart. I say to you, what I never said before—not even to my wife—that after writing some of those sentences for which I am most commonly abused, I have been obliged to pause, then throw myself on a couch and get relief in tears. I don't know why I tell *you* this, for I do not like to talk of myself. So I beg you never to repeat or show it to any one. But it is in such mood that I have written such pas-

---

* Discourse of Religion, Ed. 1842, p. 261. The lines were applied to the ordinance of the Lord's Supper : —

"Behold the child, by Nature's kindly law,
Pleased with a rattle, tickled with a straw ;
Some livelier plaything gives his youth delight—
A little louder, but as empty quite."

sages as some men read in coldness or in passion, and then call me an infidel, a heartless man for writing!

He that reads my books twenty years hence—if I am not quite forgotten before that time—will not find in them the abuse, the sarcasm, the contumely, and all that, which so grieves you. At Salem they said I painted the Salem ministers, at Marblehead the clergy of that place, and at Boston it was the " Brethren " that I " abused," and on whom I " poured scorn and contempt." I think some of the brethren ought to fall down on their knees and thank me for my forbearance, that I have not told what I most assuredly have known and still remember.

FROM THE JOURNAL.

May 6, 1842.—To-day I received the last proof-sheet of my "Discourse on Matters," &c. It fills me with sadness to end what has been so dear to me. Well: the result lies with God. May it do a good work! I fear not, but hope. There may be a *noise* about it; it will not surprise me. But I think it will do a good work for the world. God bless the good in it, and destroy the bad! This is my prayer.

May 11.—The life of Dr. Follen is written by his wife. It interests me exceedingly. The character of the man was deep, sensitive, and beautiful. He had a *religious genius:* most of the New Englanders have *moral talent*, but very few have, or understand, what I call religious genius. Henry Ware has much of it, Dr. Channing less.

Oct. 5.—I have to-day heard of the death of Dr. Channing. He has fallen in the midst of his usefulness. His faculties grew brighter as age came on him. No man in America has left a sphere of such wide usefulness; no man since Washington has done so much to elevate his country. His life has been spent in the greatest and best of works. A great man—and a good man—has gone home from the earth. Why, oh! my God, are so many left, when such are taken? Why could not I have died in his stead?

Here is a downright famous letter, which Luther, journeying to Worms, would not have been ashamed of:—

TO DR. FRANCIS.

June 24, 1842.

I trust you have long before this made up your mind to go to Cambridge.* I can't help thinking that the welfare of the denomination depends upon it. It seems to me to be the bloom and fruitage of your life, your going thither and pouring out the learning you have hived up in diligent summers, and drawing from the wells of thought and emotion which you have so long frequented. I rejoice at it most continually. The young men at the school, I learn, are much gratified with the arrangement. I know the intellectual and the liberal party of the clergy—I am sorry it is a small number—will also rejoice at it.

---

* Dr. Francis had just received an invitation to occupy the Parkman Professorship at the Divinity School.

But there is one thing of some consequence to me, though of little to you, of which I want to say a word or two (I am not complaining of any one, nor writing a Jeremiad to grieve you). The experience of the last twelve months shows me what I am to expect for the next twelve years. I have no fellowship from the other clergy. No one that helped in my ordination will now exchange ministerial courtesies with me; only one or two of the Boston Association, and perhaps one or two out of it, will have any ministerial intercourse with me. "They that are younger than I have me in derision;" they turn the cold shoulder. Well: *Quorsum hæc spectant?* If I stay at Spring Street, I must write 104 sermons a year for about 104 people. This will consume most of my energies, and I shall be in substance *put down*—a bull whose roaring can't be stopped, but who is tied up in the corner of the barn-cellar, so that *nobody hears him;* and it is the same as if he did not roar, or as if he were muzzled. *Now this I will not do.* I should not answer the purposes of life; but only execute the plans of my enemies—of the enemies of freedom of mankind.

I must confess that I am disappointed in the ministers—the Unitarian ministers. I once thought them noble; that they would be true to an ideal principle of right.

* * * * * * * *

Now this I shall do when obliged to desert the pulpit; because a free voice and a free heart cannot be in "that bad eminence." I mean to live at Spring Street, perhaps with Ripley. I will study seven or eight months of the year, and four or five months I will go about, and preach and lecture in city and glen, by the road-side and field-side, and wherever men and women can be found. I will go eastward and westward, and southward and northward, and make the land *ring;* and if this New England theology, that cramps the intellect and palsies the soul of us, does not come to the ground, then it shall be because it has more truth in it than I have ever found. I am perfectly free of two things—fear and ambition. What I have seen to be false I will proclaim a lie on the housetop; and, just as God reveals truth, I will declare His word, come what may come.

It grieves me to the very soul of my heart's life to think of leaving the ministry (which I *love* as few *ministers* love it) and this little parish. But, if duty commands, who am I to resist? If you have any word of advice to give me I shall be glad; and, in the meantime, rejoice in the new field of usefulness opening its harvest to you. I hope you will teach the young men to be valiant and fear not.

TO THE SAME.

July 25, 1842.

You give me ground to hope you will come over and see me soon; the sooner the better, you know. I see very few persons, especially scholarly folk; and, though I have little claim to the society of such, yet enjoy their visit, perhaps, all the more. But, after all, books, nature, and God afford the only society you can *always* have, and on reasonable terms.

I rejoice in the motto you mention, *Sursum corda.* Many men live on the motto, *Sursum et deorsum,* and so go see-sawing through life.

Here and there one takes sadly the motto, *Omne ferendum*, and lives on.

You will go to Cambridge soon; and I rejoice in your prospect of long usefulness, and the society of men that will appreciate your worth and sympathize with your aspirations. I look forward to a brighter period than you have ever rejoiced in before, when the wine of your life, hoarded and ripened in fruitful years, shall show itself worthy of its *mark*, and quicken the blood of youth, making their pulsations more generous than before. Well: God speed you, and keep and bless you! Farewell!

TO THE SAME.

St. John's, August 9, Down East, 1842.

I am here for the sake of health, strange as it may seem; I do all physical work, but none metaphysical. This is a queer place, an odd, amorphous, undescribable city, in which there is absolutely nothing attractive to any but a native or a speculator. . . . . . .

Don't you know that the charge brought against you by certain of the "brethren" is, not that you have done, written, or said or thought anything specially naughty, but that you are *notoriously the companion of suspected and abandoned persons?* It *is* so. Now I will speak plainly. I do not wish to stand in your way; I will not, knowingly, bring on you the censure (or suspicion) of your brethren. Therefore, after you go to Cambridge, I don't see how I can visit you as heretofore. Certainly Mr. ——, and Br. ——, will say, "It won't do, Francis holds intercourse with Parker! we be all dead men." Now I hope you will consider these things. I might, like Nicodemus, come by night, privately, but it is not my way. I hope neither you nor Mrs. F. will suspect anything unkind in this, for I only write sincerely. To come to other things . . .

May young divinity students heed the sound advice in the letter which follows :—

TO THE SAME.

September 25, 1842.

Mr. Withington of the Divinity School has passed an hour or two with me, and told me what I knew must take place, namely, that the school already wears a new aspect, as it has a new soul; that you stimulate the dull, and correct the erratic, and set right such as have prejudices inclining to narrowness, if not bigotry. I knew that this was *the* place for you; but besides awakening the soul of piety in the youth who are to teach it, there is one work which (you will pardon me for suggesting it) the *wiser* part of the public look to you to perform.

There was a time when *sound scholarship* was deemed essential to a Unitarian minister. I think the denomination has more *first-rate scholars* from the age of Frothingham down to that of Upham than any other denomination, in proportion to our numbers. But among the younger men there is a most woful neglect of sound study of all kinds. A man's library is, in some measure, the index of his mind; and the library of a young minister presents a deplorable picture of our theology; a few reviews, popular histories, Hülfsmittel for New Testament exegesis in *English,* perhaps an unused copy of Kuinoel, works of fiction, show books, and the scum of the press make up the whole, saving a few volumes of sermons. This neglect of sound study has been *excused* by the example of some pious men, and *justified* by the demands of the time, that a man should lecture on intemperance, slavery, &c., visit all the old women in his parish once a week, and retail gossip from house to house.

Now it seems to me that the denomination has a *right* to expect the first *scholar* that has been Professor of Theology since Norton to reform this evil, not only by his example but by his precept, and by the discipline he gives the young men under his charge. The orthodox and even the Baptists are doing much more than we to encourage good scholarship. One of two things I fancy must be done, either, 1, all study of theology must be abandoned; or, 2, it must be studied in a method and with a thoroughness and to an extent which bears some resemblance to the state of other sciences. Theology is contemptible at present in comparison with astronomy, geology, or even the pretended science of phrenology. Even this last pretends to verify its facts and legitimate its principles. Does theology do either? Is not a minister to do both of two things, viz., 1, to teach truth about man and God, and the relation between them; and, 2, to promote goodness? Is the present method adequate to the first object? It seems to me that the whole matter of theology requires to be taken back to the shop and cast over anew. Is not theology in about the same state with us that natural philosophy was in before Bacon? Shall we leave the reformation of it to the orthodox, or do our part?

I hope you will excuse me for what may seem very impertinent, and the intrusion of a boy's advice.

In the winter of 1842-43 he delivered a course of " Six Plain Sermons for the Times," which he prepared at the invitation of friends who desired to hear from him again. They were repeated in seven different places in the vicinity of Boston.

Everywhere I have found a much better reception than I had reason to anticipate. It has been to me a season of no little trial. I have no doubt that good will come out of the great evils of the present day.

April 13, 1843.—Went to Cambridge. Saw W——, who expresses a great horror at the unfairness with which some men have treated me, " who believe just the same thing." I don't understand good ——.

Went afterwards to Medford. Saw Schoolmaster Thos. Starr King— capital fellow, only 19. Taught school three years—supports his mother. He went into Walker's three courses of lectures, and took good notes. Reads French, Spanish, Latin, Italian, a little Greek, and begins German. (He is a good listener.)

Now, he was much sought after, but he was not always found.

FROM HORACE SEAVER.

Boston, January 11, 1843.

REV. AND DEAR SIR,—As chairman of the committee of arrangements for the celebration of Thomas Paine's birthday in this city, on the 30th instant, I am instructed to perform the highly pleasing duty of soliciting the honour of your company at the dinner ; and to say to you, in addition, that it would give the committee great pleasure, as well as many others of your personal friends, if your health and time will allow you to comply with this invitation.

I am, very respectfully,
Your obedient servant,
HORACE SEAVER.

REPLY.

West Roxbury, 14th January, 1843.

DEAR SIR,—Your favour of the 11th instant came in my absence from home, and I now hasten to reply to the invitation you offer me. With the views I entertain of Mr. Paine's character in his later years, I could not, consistently with my own sense of duty, join with you in celebrating his birth-day. I feel grateful, truly so, for the service rendered by his *political* writings, and his practical efforts in the cause of freedom ; though with what I understand to be the spirit of his writings on theology and religion, I have not the smallest sympathy.

I am, respectfully,
Your obedient servant,
THEO. PARKER.

Horace Seaver, Esq.

April 17.—Read " Rousseau's Confessions " and the article upon him in *Biographie Universelle*. Rousseau—a liar ! a thief ! a great knave !— I abhor him. He seems sadly ill-born—one of the creatures that are the sport of destiny. I shall never read his works with much interest after the developments of the " Confessions."

18.—Read Gliddon's " Ancient Egypt." It is a confused mass of valuable matter gathered from the recent works on Egypt. Mr. G. wishes " to run with the hare and hold with the hounds ;" so he professes, apparently, his respect for the Scriptures, and really despises them, it seems to me. His notions about the LXX. and Mas. Heb. text, which he calls the " Masorite Hebrew Version," are highly erroneous.

JOHN WOOLMAN'S JOURNAL.—This is one of the most encouraging books I ever read. What depth of insight into divine things, and not less into human things ! How lowly and meek ! How lofty, too, his aspirations ! What gentle courage—what faith ! He reminds me of Isaac Hopper.

TO REV. INCREASE S. SMITH.

October 10, 1842.

You asked some time ago about De Wette, and the "Introduction to the Old Testament." It is in the press, and about 300 pp. of the first volume are stereotyped. But it goes on slowly. All summer I have been ill, and able to do almost nothing. Had I been well, the book would have been out of the press before now. But I find I can improve it. What has often been hammered, I take back to the anvil again, to file over the filed, and linger on the manuscript with a superstitious regard for the accuracy of quotations, references, &c. About the first of April, 1843, I think it may see the light.

I am glad you mentioned the mistake in my poor book ("Discourse," &c.) There are several errors—some of them in the notes—in the book, which are lapses of memory, or slips of the pen, or errors of the press. After the last sheets of manuscript went to the press, the excitement that sustained me in the work failed. I was not well enough to look over the book and make a *complete* list of errata, for a few weeks. But a list of six or eight errors was printed in about a fortnight; and some *weeks* later, as friends pointed out a few mistakes, or as my own eye detected them, I printed a more complete list of them. I gave Mr. Stevens two copies of the printed errata, and requested him to give one to you; but I supposed he forgot it, so I send you one.

Brownson's review, I hear, is not vindictive. I have not read it yet, nor looked at it, though it has been in my hands for more than a week. I have lent it to my friends, and when I have a convenient season I *shall* read it.

ECCLESIASTICAL RELATIONS.

January 23rd, 1843.—I attended a meeting of the Association by particular request. It seems that, so early as last September, at a meeting at Putnam's, the Association thought proper to discuss the affairs of myself and my book ("Discourse," &c.) The discussion was continued from time to time. But once, in December, I think, or the latter part of November, some felt a delicacy in discussing such a matter in my absence. Therefore they considered it meet to request me to come and talk the matter over with them in a friendly way. So I came. The Association met at R. C. Waterston's in Temple Street, and what follows is a faithful history of the events that took place.

After tea, which was got through a little after six, ——— * called the meeting to order, and with a considerable degree of embarrassment, stated the business of the meeting. ——— followed him, and also stated the occasion, the circumstances that gave rise to the meeting, viz., that the Association felt a delicacy in discussing me and mine in my absence. He said he, however, and the Association had felt a difficulty in asking me to come; for, first, it was my place without invitation, and second, the invitation might look like a summons. Here the record of the last meeting was produced by Mr. Robbins, and the resolution inviting me was read; it was stated

* The blanks are the same throughout this relation, but they cover the names of half-a-dozen speakers, who, however, never cared to conceal any opinions that referred to Mr. Parker.

that the resolution was worded with great care, and debated on some time before adoption.

These preliminaries settled, ———— opened the business by going *in medias res*, stating, however, beforehand that, first, I was not to catechise them, nor second, were they to catechise me. Then he said that he could have no ministerial intercourse with me—though still he hoped to have a friendly and social intercourse. The reason was, the character of the book I had written. That he charged me with two offences. 1. It was vehemently deistical, using the word in the worst sense; and 2. It was not only not Christian, but subversive of Christianity, as a particular religion, for it aimed to dissolve Christianity in the great ocean of absolute truth.

Then ———— took up the word, and spoke of ministerial exchanges again, and said also that the book was not the only offence, but the article on the Hollis Street Council,* was also bad, for it reflected on the members of the Association. He confirmed what ———— had said relative to the book, but added that the doctrines of the book were not a matter of discussion, and that it had been so agreed at a former meeting.

Then I stated that it seemed there were two sets of offences I was charged withal, to wit, 1. in the book, and 2, in the article on the Hollis Street Council. To each I would say a word, but first of all, I. On the matter of ministerial fellowship. I begged them to consider that I had never complained on that account; never felt an ill-natured emotion—nor uttered an ill-natured word respecting them, or any of them, on that ground. I would, however, tell the result of their refusing fellowship, viz., (1.) Soon after the South Boston sermon, men refused to exchange with me. I had some very curious letters in my hands relative to that affair, which might be printed after my death or before it. Some from clergymen refusing to exchange with me—they agreed to do so before. The result was this—some members of churches in the city asked me to come and deliver five lectures on five subjects. I pleaded youth,—inability,—and refused. They would not be satisfied with the plea. They said, "you are excluded from the pulpits of the Unitarians for no sufficient reason. We want to hear what you have got to say : we can't hear you in the old way, let us try a new one." I consulted two ministers, they said "Go," and I went; delivered the lectures in Boston, and five other places, before some thousands of people, and printed them in a book.

2. In 1842, some young men repeated the same arguments, and called me to come and preach, continually, old sermons every Sunday evening. I thought it better to preach six sermons, such as were needed for the times. I did so in Boston; they saw the result. Others in other places made the same request. I went there also. That was the effect on the public of their treatment of me—on myself it had no effect.

3. I spoke of the article on the Hollis Street Council, and said that it was no wonder different men took different views of that affair. I could not expect them to take the same views as myself.

* Published in the *Dial*, exposing the clerical servility to the prominent interest in Mr. Pierpont's parish.

II. I turned to the book and said: It was curious that a theological book was to be discussed, and we were not allowed to speak on the subjects of the book, and discuss the doctrines on which we differed, or were alleged to differ. (I ought to have said before, that I showed at the beginning that I took the spirit of the resolution, but did not see any good that could result from that meeting.) However, I would avoid touching doctrines so far as it was possible. Then again, as it was said, I was not to be catechised, I would avoid catechising others. Then I proceeded to the 1st charge (under "the book") made by ———— that it was "deistical," and said that I knew but little of the Deists, but so far as I knew anything, there were four classes of them, which were named by Dr. Sam. Clarke, in a book familiar to all of them; but all Deists denied the possibility of direct inspiration from God. Therefore, as inspiration was a cardinal point in my system, and I maintained that all men were inspired just in proportion to their quantity of being, and their quantity of obedience, that I did not come under the caption; or if I am a Deist, I must be put in a class by myself alone—and then it was arbitrary to call me by a name that did not describe my belief. Then I proceeded to the second charge of ————, viz., that the book was subversive of Christianity, &c., and said that though an author's opinion of his own work was of no value to others, yet I sincerely thought it was a most Christian book. Christianity was one of three things: either (1) less than absolute religion, or (2) equal to absolute religion, or (3) absolute religion, and something more. No one, I would assume for argument's sake, would admit the 1st proposition. I affirmed the 2nd, they the 3rd. Therefore, if they would point out the precise quiddity that made absolute religion, Christianity, they would do a great service. That other sects defined the shibboleths of Christianity to their mind, but the Unitarians had no symbolical books, and therefore a young man like myself, and not learned, found a difficulty. I ended by asking ———— to tell just what it was in which Christianity differed from absolute religion. He replied, "But I will remind Mr. Parker, that he is not to catechise me."

Then ———— took up the article on the Hollis Street Council. ———— said that in that article I held up the Council to the scorn and derision of mankind, representing them as a set of hypocrites, and double-dealing knaves: that I called the "result in council" a "Jesuitical document," and as he was one of the Council, and one that drew up the "result," he contended that I had traduced him, representing him as a double-dealing and base man; that I had undertaken to weaken his influence and ruin his character with the world and his own congregation, and so far as my influence went, that I had done so. This kind of charge he continued at length—in language and manner which are peculiar to him.

I then replied that I was not answerable for the inference which other men drew, only for the fact of what I had written. One man said I slandered the brethren in the sermon of "Pharisees;" another in the conclusion of South Boston sermon; and ———— that I held him up to scorn in the article of the Hollis Street Council. I was not accountable for their inferences.

———— then said, that he did consider that I meant the Association in the "Pharisees" and in the South Boston sermon; an orthodox gentleman in the country said to him, " You have madded Parker, and in this way he shows his spite. He is in your confidence, and knows what you talk about in the Association, and tells your secrets." To which I observed that as it regards the "spite," and the being " mad," the facts spoke — the "madding" began in May, 1841 : the sermon was written December, 1840.

The " Pharisees" spoke of six classes of Pharisees; nobody complained but the ministers. I should be ashamed to say that I meant no personalities in either the " Pharisees," or the South Boston sermon. Then says ————, " since Mr. Parker will not say he did not mean us—I will take it for granted that he does," &c., &c. He then enlarged more on the article on the Hollis Street Council. I replied that if need were, I would condescend to say that I meant no particular and definite persons or body of men, in either case, but aimed to expose sin and Phariseeism wherever they were—if in the Association, then there. But had no individuals before my mind. The letter on the Hollis Street Council stood on different ground, and there it was plain who was meant. I had nothing to alter or add to that. Some said, You called the result in council a " Jesuitical document;" another, you brought together a great deal of matter about ecclesiastical councils, and about cowards, and knaves, and hypocrites. It meant somebody— I suppose it meant us. I did not read it very carefully, for I disliked it so much. To be sure, you treated the writers of the New Testament in about the same way, and said the apostle St. James "roars like a fanatic radical." Then some one said "You quoted the words of somebody—' Expect no justice of the Council,' as if you endorsed them." I told them I did not endorse them; since, as the words of a great and wise man, they required no endorsement of mine. " But you applied them as if you expected no justice." I did so then, and do now. I expected no justice from the Council at the time. When I wrote I thought the " result," &c., a most Jesuitical document—I think so still. I then added that I didn't wish to write the article; asked others to do so; they refused. I consulted several persons, telling them the view I should express (three of them were present— but I did not say so). They said, " Go on." I wrote carefully, deliberately, conscientiously. I told one clergyman—who had no affinity with me—a man older than most of them, distinguished for good sense and piety—what I had said, before I published; he said, " You are right, say it in God's name." I read it to another, who had little theological affinity with me—he said, " Well, it ain't much after all for you to write, and I have but this criticism to make, that you have been too severe on Mr. Pierpont, and not half severe enough on the Council." Then said ————, " Well, Mr. P. can't disown what he has said; if he is conscientious, as no doubt he is, we can't ask him to do so. I will say that I freely and from my heart forgive him, as I hope God Almighty will forgive me; but I can never grasp him by the hand again cordially."

Let us leave this subject and proceed to the book. He then said that as I asked what was to be added to absolute religion and morality to make them Christianity, he would add, the miracles, the authority of Christ, which I did not acknowledge. To this I replied, that I made

Christianity to be love to man and God; and, admitting miracles were performed (for argument's sake), I did not see how they affected the case—making that true and a duty which was not so before, or of authorizing what was in fact true and a duty. But further than that, I did not believe the fact of his working miracles as a general thing. I was by no means certain that the four Gospels came from the men to whom they are ascribed; and, if they did, I could not take their word in the circumstances of the case. I had no philosophical objection to a miracle—in my definition of it—but only demanded more evidence than for a common event. Then some one said, that was enough; it was plain I was no Christian: for Christianity was a supernatural and a miraculous revelation. To which I said, that it might be, but it had not been shown to be such. It seemed preposterous to make miracles the shibboleth of Christianity. Each sect had its own shibboleth. The Trinitarians the Thirty-nine Articles—the Catholics the Church, &c. Nobody accused me of preaching less than absolute morality and religion. If they could exist without Christianity, what was the use of Christianity? So I thought it a mistake to make absolute religion one thing and Christianity something different.

Then some one said, "It is plain we can't have ministerial intercourse with Mr. Parker: he denies the miracles."—Then I said that I didn't think it depended on that, it was only a theological matter at best. The difference began before the article on the Hollis Street Council, before the "Discourse of Religion"—the theological lines were drawn immediately after the South Boston sermon. I had a collection of curious letters on that theme, which I might publish one day. I was at first surprised at the effect that sermon had on the Unitarian ministers. I thought the sermon a poor one—I was sick when I wrote it—read it to a friend before preaching, who said it was the weakest thing I had written for a long time. I looked round to see who would stand by me in the pulpit, and I had not been disappointed in general. I knew the ministers pretty well. But in two —Here somebody interrupted me, and —— brought me back to the point. Mr. P. says there are two things; I want to hear that. I replied that I had not been disappointed in general; but in two persons I had been disappointed—grievously disappointed. ——'s face fell, for I looked full upon him as I said it. However he soon recovered, or I should have told him that he was not one of the two. Then said ——, "Since Mr. Parker finds the feeling in respect to him is so general, I think it is his duty to withdraw from the Association." Others spoke to the same purpose—I hurt their usefulness, compromised their position, &c. I told them that if my personal feelings alone were concerned I would gladly do so, but as the right of free inquiry was concerned, while the world standeth I will never do so. The matter was then discussed at length. —— said, if it were a meeting of free inquirers he should very soon withdraw. I showed that theological agreement in all things was not necessary to our union, and quoted the case of Dr. Freeman, for many years a member of the Association, who never exchanged with him. To this —— replied the case was not in point, for many others of the Association were not Unitarians. "Indeed," said I, "did they say so?" Then —— said, "But the difference between Trinitarians and Unitarians is a difference in Christianity, the difference between Mr. Parker and the Association, is a difference between no Christianity and Christianity." Then ———— said, they did not deny that I was a Christian man, but only that the book was a Christian book, affirming it, as it was on account of the miracles being rejected. Then it was argued that I should not now be admitted to the Association, when my opinions were known; and therefore that I either had changed my opinions since I came, or came with the opinions not known to the Association : in either case that I ought to withdraw. I replied that I was not examined as to my opinions on admission, and was not asked to promise never to change. If I did them an injury they had the remedy in their hands, and could pass a vote of expulsion at any time; but it was a new thing that the shibboleth of Christianity among the Unitarians was miracles. A few years ago, it was said in the Association, that formerly Christianity was thought to rest on two great pillars,—Jachin and Boaz—prophecy and miracles. Dr. Noyes knocked down Jachin, and George Ripley, Boaz, yet Christianity stood. If I remember right it was ———— who said so. "True," said the Doctor, "I do remember something about Jachin and Boaz; but I did not say that I was one of them who said Christianity did not rest on the two, still less did I say that George Ripley had knocked the miracles down."

So they talked much more to the same effect. At last, a little before nine, Bartol spoke in praise of my sincerity, which some had called in question—spoke many words of moral approbation; so likewise did Gannett, at length, and with his usual earnestness. Then Chandler Robbins opened his mouth to the same purpose. I burst into tears, shook hands with Waterston, and left the room. Going below in the entry, I met ————, who had gone out a little before. He shook hands with me with apparent cordiality—hoped I would come and see him, &c. So the matter ended, and the bells struck nine as I left the house. I ought to mention one thing more, namely, that ————, in course of the discussion, said that I dipped my pen in gall when I wrote, and my razor in oil.

GENERAL NOTE ON THE ABOVE.—I may have mistaken the order in which things were said, and have put in one sentence what was uttered at several times. But I am confident that I have preserved the opinions of each that spoke, and often the language ; and also that I have omitted nothing which would alter the character of the discussion.

Soon after this (three or four days) I received a letter from Chandler Robbins.

To which the following is a reply :—

TO REV. CHANDLER ROBBINS, BOSTON.

Plymouth, Sunday Morn., January 27, 1843.

MY DEAR FRIEND,—I thank you truly for your kind note of Thursday last ; thank you for your sympathy ; thank you, too, for the caution you give me. I can live with no sympathy but that of the Infinite, and His still, small voice saying, " Well done !" but when sympathy—human sympathy, comes, it is truly welcome. You mistake a little the cause of my tears the other night. It was not a hard thing said by yourself or others. All might have said such as long as they

liked ; I would not have winked at that. It was the kind things said
by Bartol and Gannett, and what I knew by your face you were about
to say; it was this that made me weep. I could meet argument with
argument (in a place where it is in order to discuss " the subjects " of
a theological book which is talked of), blow with blow, ill-nature with
good-nature, all night long; but the moment a man takes my part, and
says a word of sympathy, that moment I should become a woman and
no man. If Pierpont had been present, I should have asked him, at
the beginning, to say no word in defence of me, but as many of offence
as he liked. I felt afraid, at first, that a kind thing might be said
earlier in the evening, and am grateful to the " brethren " that they
said none such till late.

But to leave this painful theme. I knew always the risks that I run
in saying what was hostile to the popular theology. I have not forgotten
George Fox, nor Priestley ; no, nor yet Abelard nor St. Paul. Don't
think I compare myself with these noble men, except in this, that each
of them was called on to stand alone, and so am I. I know what Paul
meant when he said, " At my first answer no man stood with me ;" but
I know also what is meant when a greater than Paul said, " Yet I am
not alone ; for the Father is with me."

If my life ends to-morrow, I can say,—

" I have the richest, best of consolations,
The thought that I have given,
To serve the cause of Heaven,
The freshness of my early inspirations."

I care not what the result is to me personally. I am equal to either
fate, and ask only a chance to do my duty. No doubt my life is to be
outwardly a life of gloom and separation from old associates (I will not
say friends). I know men will view me with suspicion, and ministers
with hatred ; that is not my concern. Inwardly, my life is, and must
be, one of profound peace—of satisfaction and comfort that all words of
mine are powerless to present. There is no mortal trouble that disturbs
me more than a moment—no disappointment that makes me gloomy, or
sad, or distrustful. All outward evil falls off me as snow from my cloak.
I never thought of being so happy in this life as I have been these two
years. The destructive part of the work I feel called on to do is painful, but is slight compared with the main work of building up. Don't
think I am flattered, as some say, by seeing many come to listen.
Nothing makes a real man so humble as to stand and speak to many
men. The thought that I am doing what I know to be my duty is rich
reward to me ; I know of none so great. Besides that, however, I have
the satisfaction of knowing that I have awakened the spirit of religion,
of faith in God, in some twenty or twenty-five men, who before that
had no faith, no hope, no religion. This alone, and the expression of their
gratitude (made by word of mouth, or made by letters, or by a friend),
would compensate me for all that all the ministers in all the world could
say against me or do against me. But why do I speak of this ? Only
to show you that I am not likely to be cast down. Some of my relations, 200 or 300 years ago, lost their heads for their religion. I am
called to no such trial, and can well bear my lighter cross.

Perhaps I ought to say that, if the Association think I compromise them, and injure them and hurt their usefulness, they have the remedy in their own hands, and in one minute can vote me out of their ranks. At that I will never complain; but so long as the world standeth I will not withdraw voluntarily while I consider rights of conscience at issue. I think, too, that, when I shall have more leisure (as I shall in a few weeks), I shall attend the meetings more frequently than heretofore. To withdraw voluntarily would be to abandon what I think a post of duty.

Excuse this long letter, and believe me,

Truly your friend,

THEO. PARKER,

In the summer of 1843, his translation of De Wette's " Introduction to the Old Testament" appeared. He had so modified the arrangement of its text, by throwing all the bibliography into notes, and introducing illustrative matter from the German sources, that his edition became more convenient than the original. He also judiciously interpolated matter of his own, as in the chapter on the Latin versions of the Bible, the 'excellent description of the Venetian version, and a continuation of the author's account of the Samaritan Pentateuch. In the books of Samuel and of the Kings, he has several pages to bring out more fully their characteristics. His pen assists materially in clearing up Leviticus. His contribution to Daniel is now acknowledged by most theologians. He finds a historical occasion for the prophecy which Isaiah uttered against Tyre. Occasionally he gives a reason for not agreeing with De Wette, as in Vol. 2, 188, and he boldly shows the mythological elements where the author's pen is disposed to falter.

This was a labour of great service, which was frequently recognized in various quarters by intelligent persons who never before could acquire clear ideas of the composition of the Old Testament, the canon, the Jehovistic and Elohistic documents, and the intention of the various books. A book in English, based upon the latest learning, and carefully treating the Old Testament from the point of historical criticism, and in the interest of no theological party, was a want which this translation met. Later labourers in this field, of more narrow and orthodox tendency, acknowledge still a healthy direction in De Wette's work, and that he opened the way. De Wette afterwards modified a few statements in his "Supplement to An Introduction ; " but his original judgment was more sound. A vast amount of valuable information is brought together in these

two volumes, in an orderly and scientific way, subservient to the
only kind of criticism which can save the Old Testament from
the marauding of superstition, and leave it cultivable by simple,
reverent human sympathy.

Nothing shows so well the value of De Wette's method of
treating the Old Testament, as the attempts of later critics to clear
up in a historical way the historical difficulties he finds. Thus
the very point in dispute between bibliolatry and reason is
surrendered. The Bible must be treated like any other ancient
collection of documents. The appeal is made to uninspired
sources to defend the authenticity of the so-called inspired
books. Nineveh bricks and sculptures, excavators, explorers,
Egyptologers, comparative philologers, a more careful investigation of the whole written and monumental past, will doubtless
yield many historical confirmations to whatever history the Old
Testament contains. It may occasionally discover an actual occurrence embedded in supernatural and legendary stuff. That will
be clear gain, for it substitutes a fact for a fancy. Let the smallest
relic be carefully hammered out of its conglomerate. The scholars
of all creeds ought to countenance this rational tendency. It is
not difficult to prophesy the end of it—an extrication, namely,
of the historical from the mythological. Ahasuerus, for instance,
may turn out to be Xerxes, and the Feast of Purim the commemoration of a real event. So much the better ; we have a
historical fact. There may be fewer incongruities in the book of
Daniel, but that does not reinforce its mythological element. The
horns of its visions will not the less toss and worry the prophecy-
mongers of every description, till scholarship rescues the whole
book from ignorance. The historical may be everywhere proved
and vindicated, so much the worse for the mythological ; its
incompatibility will only the more appear.

What an astonishing infatuation is that of some English
scholars, who think that the more historical they find the Old
Testament to be, the less incredible its supernaturalism becomes !

In the autumn of 1843, Mr. Parker found himself fairly exhausted with the unusual labours and experiences of the two
previous years. He chafed as he recorded the days and weeks
which had been lost in consequence of illness and depression.
Following the advice of friends he left his parish, to prosecute a
long dreamed of tour in Europe. Here are extracts from the
sermon which he preached just before he started, from the text,

"I have not shunned to declare unto you all the counsel of God." After describing the duties of a minister of religion, he says :—

Such being a minister's function, it is plain there are two several dangers which await him : one, that he becomes over-confident, opinionated, and teaches mere whimsies and spectres of his own brain instead of everlasting truths—in short, that he err through excessive confidence in himself—aspiring to lead where he is only competent to follow. The other danger is, that he succumb to things as they are about him ; take the opinions of his sect, or the public, for truth, and the practice of his neighbourhood, or the public, for religion, and sit down contented to repeat the echoes of his time and place. Then the man becomes a mere thing—with no independence, no self-respect, no power, a mockery set up in a place designed for a man. If a minister consents to hold this place, he may have the greatest original power of thought, fortified with the finest culture and the widest learning;—what does it all avail him ? Nothing! He becomes a Prophet of Lies, a blind leader of blind men, fit only to dangle about the tables of rich men. His genius goes from him, his learning becomes of no value, his culture ridiculous. Though born a giant, and armed in the panoply of clerical mail, and master of the most crafty skill to boot, a single shepherd boy with a true heart can bring this boastful champion to the ground and smite off his giant head. The fate of such a man shall be that which is recorded of one who disobeyed God and ate the bread of a liar—he fell by the wayside, and the men that passed by saw there a dead prophet and a living ass.

I have attempted to show that sentiments, ideas, and actions, belonged to religion—that what was at first a feeling got next an intellectual expression and became an idea, then a functional expression and became a deed. Taking Christianity as the absolute religion, I have insisted on Christian sentiments as the foundation of all, on Christian ideas, on Christian works. I have endeavoured to legitimate the sentiments and ideas, and then to apply the ideas to life, in part to criticise existing institutions, and in part to create new institutions thereby. Tried by Christian sentiments and ideas, you know how the popular sentiments, the popular opinions, and the common life must appear. I have shown that these ideas must at length prevail, for they are the ideas of God; in this connection I have dwelt often on what I call the immanency of God in matter and in spirit, His perpetual presence and activity in the world of matter and the world of spirit, the laws whereof are but modes of His activity, and the results forms of His manifestation. I have shown that there was fate nowhere, Providence everywhere and always. Hence it followed that the material world is inspired by God according to its measure of reception ; that mankind as a whole, and each man in severalty, is also inspired just in proportion to the man's natural ability and his faithful use thereof. From all this it follows, that the providence of our Father in heaven has created a perfect system of optimism, of which we comprehend but little by the understanding, though we have a fore-feeling thereof by the affections and religious sentiment ; that this life was but a small part of the whole, and the evils incident to the present conditions would at last lead to higher good.

I have not taught these results on the authority of any church, any book, any man ; I have appealed only to facts, facts of necessity, facts of consciousness, facts of demonstration, and facts of observation. I have tried to teach absolute religion on its own authority.

I found less than ten Unitarian clergymen who were willing to exchange with me. I often said with the melancholy prophet, " Woe is me, my mother, that thou hast borne me to be a man of strife and a man of contention to the whole earth ; I have neither lent on usury, nor men have lent to me on usury, yet every one of them doth curse me." Fear in the churches, like fire in the woods, runs fast and far, leaving few spots not burned. I did not know what you would do; I thought you would do as others did ; there are times which try men, there are men who must not be tried ; I feared that this church might be of that metal; others had promised more but fled at the first fire. I made up my mind that you might ask a dissolution of our union ; I calculated ts value ; I did not think of begging, I knew I could dig,—

> " For since these arms of mine had seven years' pith,
>   Till now, some ten *years* wasted, they have used
>   Their dearest action in the *furrowed* field."

I knew my hands could win my bread, for they could toil at numerous crafts, and were perhaps better educated than my head; I never thought of being silenced. The fact that a truth was unpopular was the reason why it should be spoken with a thousand tongues. In case you had refused to hear my voice, this was my plan, to betake myself for six or eight months of the year to any work which might offer, and the rest of the year to go forth and proclaim the word which was so unpopular in all parts of the land. If I could not find a place in a church, then I meant to take it in a hall, in a school-house, or a barn, under the open sky wherever a word could be spoken and heard.

But I must bring all this to a close ; what shall I say ? Has my ministry thus far been a faithful one ? I cannot judge myself. In some things it has surpassed my expectations : in others fallen far short of it. You shall say whether or not I have done good to your hearts, and thereby made your lives better. If I have deepened your love of truth, if I have helped you to a clearer knowledge of duty, if I have enabled you to bear better the burthens of life, to love man and God, to obey His laws, meekly and reverently to trust therein with a calmness which the world cannot disturb ; if I have persuaded or helped any of you to aspire after a manly character and a divine life, then I feel that I have not laboured in vain.

We have discoursed on the loftiest themes ; for six years our prayers have been mingled together. Here we have assembled for a closer remembrance of one so dear to our heart and the world's heart. The recollection of these modest walls, of these familiar faces, while they bring tears to my eyes, will bring not less joy to my heart. May God bless you and keep you, and lift the light of His countenance upon you; may reason guide you; may religion be your daily life, your hope and your portion for ever and ever. Farewell!

FROM THE JOURNAL.

September 5.—To-day I leave home for a year; it had long been a day-dream with me to visit Europe, it now approaches fulfilment. A friend kindly furnishes me the means.

G. W. RUSSELL'S HOUSE.

CHAPTER VIII.

To Europe—France, Italy, Germany—Extracts from Journal.

WHILE Mr. Parker was waiting in New York for the ship to sail in which he had taken passage, he made a visit to the city prison called the "Tombs."

The taste which would expend all that architecture on a building so loathsome as a jail is most wretched. Shame that the disgrace of society should be thus arrayed in costly dress, and made to flaunt before the public eye. In New England we hide our jails; for we are ashamed of them, and very justly. You shall go through our shire-towns again and again and never see the jail. I went into the court-house to see justice administered. A negro was on trial in the Court of Sessions for abusing his wife. It seemed to me the place was well called "Egyptian," for the darkness that covered over justice in that place; and "Tombs," for it appeared the sepulchre of equity. This poor negro at trial for a crime showed me in miniature the whole of our social institutions. 1. He was the victim of Christian cupidity, and had been a slave. 2. From this he had probably escaped, by what was counted a crime by his master. 3. He was cast loose in a society where his colour debarred him the rights of a man, and forced him to count himself a beast, with nothing to excite relf-respect either in his condition, his history, or his prospects. Poor, wretched man, what is life to him! He is more degraded than the savage, has lost much in leaving Sahara, and gained infamy, cold, hunger, and the white man's mercy—a prison of marble. Oh, what wrongs does man heap on man!

Here was a man who had got drunk, and was clapped into the "Tombs." His wife and two children were left with no protector. He had waited five days for his trial. This was a hard case, truly. I might have got drunk at the Astor House and have gone to bed every day; the police would take no notice of that. This poor fellow must smart.

He sailed on the 9th in the *Ashburton*. After five or six days of sea-sickness he attacks books again, and makes observations of a practical nature.

There is one thing that disturbs me much at sea; that is, the awful difference between the cabin and the steerage, or the forecastle. If I were in the forecastle, perhaps it would not appear so bad; I might think the men in the cabin deserved their pre-eminence of ease and comfort. Now, I *know* it is not so. Here are 160 poor wretches in the steerage, with almost no comforts, while the 30 in the cabin live in luxury. As the lion in the wilderness eateth up the wild ass, so the rich eat up the poor. Alas! this truth is told us often enough; in great cities it is thundered in our ears each moment, but in that little despotism, a ship, you see the whole thing more clearly, because more compendiously. There must be a cure for this terrible evil. What is it?

Here comes a list of various patent medicines for social ills. But he proceeds :—

The evil lies deeper. I look for relief only gradually, by applying good sense to religion, and religion to life. This is the field in which I design to labour.

I am now to spend a year in foreign travel. In this year I shall earn nothing; neither my food, nor my clothes, nor even the paper I write on. Of course I shall increase my debt to the world by every potato I eat, and each mile I travel. How shall I repay the debt? Only by extraordinary efforts after I return. I hope to continue my present plans in this way.

A. Practical.

  1. To work in behalf of temperance, education, a change in the social fabric, so that the weak shall not be the slaves of the strong.

  2. To show that religion belongs to man's nature, that it demands piety and morality (the inward sentiment, the outward action), and theology (the mediator between the two.

B. Speculative.

  1. To write an introduction to the New Testament.

  2. To write a historical development of religion in the history of man.*

  3. Such other works as may become necessary, *e. g.*, a popular introduction to the Old Testament, in 12mo.

In this way I hope to work out my debt.

Finding that the sea life did not favour reading, he began to gather hints for sermons. There are 37 subjects in all ; one of which is designated by the Italian proverb, " *La farina del diavolo va tutta in crusca* " (The devil's wheat grinds all to bran).

As soon as he lands at Liverpool he begins to visit and observe everything—nothing escapes. All is characterized with

* This is the projected work for which he gathered a great amount of material, under appropriate heads—enough for one or two volumes.

a touch; the warehouses, enormous docks, monuments, beggars in the streets, the markets, with the prices of all the meats and vegetables, clean servants "looking like Methodist ministers," rich churches; "but I have thought there were two ways of honouring God, one in marble and mortar, the other in benevolence and daily duty. I love the beautiful like a poet; but potatoes first and paintings afterwards is my rule;" factories at Manchester, machines, men, colleges, and curiosities everywhere. He draws the plans of public buildings, occasionally gets in a Puseyistic profile, unscrupulously strips an evangelical sermon; seeing Scotus Erigena, "De Divisione Naturæ" on a library shelf, he forgets everything and sits down to read. In the libraries he is particular to examine as many manuscripts as he can find time for. He took dinner with Mr. John James Tayler, a Unitarian clergyman, and met Professor Newman.

We talked about various matters of scholarship. He thought Xenophon gave the truer account of Socrates—so thought Tayler. I stood out for Plato's account—of course somewhat idealized, else we could not explain the hostility of the Athenians (excited by the orators, who were all sophists), nor for the influence he exerted on the world, then and since then. Professor Newman did not like Plato; he thought he never did the sophists justice; that Protagoras was not so bad as Plato made him. This led to a long discussion of the *functions* of the sophists, and the cause of their origin at that period. Newman thought they were a sort of private tutor, and not so black as they were often painted. I added that the state of theology naturally helped form this race of men. Then we came upon the "Republic." Mr. N. thought it foolish to attempt such a work, which must necessarily be vain. I defended the scheme as a method of putting forth great thoughts. This led to a talk about the truths which lay at the bottom of the treatise. Then we spoke about Aristotle; his better method of giving an account of the actual.

Professor Newman surprises me. I know many that I think have more native power than he; but few of our scholars show such accurate and varied learning—such accomplished scholarship."

Few indeed; but here is one who meets the scholars of the old world, in England and on the Continent; knows what they know; has read as fully, if not as minutely; and can hold dignified intercourse upon their varied themes—and they, too, bred in the costly force-houses of universities. It is singular to follow this poor boy, who carries learning back to its seats in Europe.

In the Bodleian, he applies himself to reading some scholastic books not to be found in America.

At Paris, he carries on the same minute investigation, noticing the men and women, the habits of the street and house, as much as the monuments of art. He begins to attend lectures on Arabic, Corneille, Cicero, philosophy of Gassendi and Descartes, law of nature and nations, ancient history, mysticism of the Alexandrine school, unity of the human race, and Italian literature. There is an analysis of every lecture which he hears. He even goes to the Jardin des Plantes, to hear Geoffry St. Hilaire lecture on vultures ; and carries classification, habits, and anecdotes—the whole spoil, home with him. But all these scholar's notes are not in a condition to be published. Pretty soon the journal begins to be written in French, by way of exercise.

In the Spanish Gallery of the Louvre :—

I would that I had a copy of the " Saviour " to hang in my house, to cheer me in my hours of sadness, and inspire me in my moments of happiness. But I am rejoiced to see it here, where all see it.

I saw a Frenchman kiss his horse in the street to-day ; a fine, noble horse it was, too. I also came up and paid my respects, though not with my lips.

He carries off a list of the curious names of streets, to be enquired into at leisure :—*Gît-le-cœur, Pic-pus, Tait-bout, Tire-chappe, Brise-miche, Tire-boudin, Chat-qui-pèche, Cloche-perche,* and all the rest.

To AVIGNON.—Sunday, Dec. 31.—In the morning I strolled out to enjoy the Sabbath awhile, on the *pons ingens et sublicius* which crosses the Rhone, and had myself to myself. At 4 P.M. we started in a diligence for Avignon, and passed the Rhone.

We rode, and rode, and rode on the left bank of the Rhone ; and, at 12, wished one another a happy new year, which awoke separate trains of thought in our heads, and sent us far from the Rhone.

Jan. 1.—We rode all night, and in the morning took a hasty break-fast at a little inn. This is the first day of January, 1844. It is mild as an April day with us. The Rhone is on one hand, the mountain chains come down on the other, bold, naked, and picturesque. Here the plains are covered with mulberry-trees, kept from attaining more than eighteen to twenty-five feet in height, and reared to feed the silk-worms ; underneath, crops of wheat are raised, or else, where the trees are far asunder, the whole is covered with vines. Some of them have been pruned already. Some of the towns are beautifully situated. Here the rocks rise up 200 feet almost perpendicularly, and just at their foot the village is built. On the top of the rock are the remains of a wall and towers, which still look imposing at that height. All round in the fields there grows a shrub resembling the box, it is called *buis.* Here, too, the olive grows in perfection; all the soil seems wretchedly thin and poor, yet on the poorest knolls the clumps of olive-trees offer their perpetual green. In the summer, I fancy, they do not look beautiful, for they have a dusty aspect, and are not *bright* green; but now they give a very cheerful appearance to the fields.

To-day we have passed the place where Hannibal crossed the Rhone, and pushed on towards the Little St. Bernard, where he crossed the Alps. The whole country is to me one of great historical interest, rich with incidents from the times of Cæsar to the Crusades. I regret that all my life I have been so poorly supplied with maps, that much of my historical reading has not half its value, because I could not designate the special place where events happened. I feel the want now particularly.

FROM AVIGNON TO ARLES.—We went to the diligence-office to go to Arles. We had taken our places the day before, and found that we had before us a *chapter of accidents* as follows:—1. The diligence had no *intérieur* (where we had taken the four first places), but only a *coupé* and a *rotond.* 2. There was a large woman, hideously dirty, and *puante* to the last degree, with a squalling *enfant* in her arms, which she ever and anon regaled with the breast, or an apple, for he alternated between the two. 3. After riding about half-an hour, we came to the Durance, which had lost its bridge, in 1840, perhaps, and had not found the whole of it yet; so we had to dismount and be ferried over the blue stream, this took us a good while; we thought it durance vile. 4. I left my *parapluie* in the diligence, at the suggestion of the *conducteur,* and when I went back to take my place, found the great woman, whom we named *Mdme. Fumeau,* had *se mit sur la,* and it was *cassée*; therefore, *voila ma parapluie cassée.* 5. We reached Tarascon, and passed over its long bridge, and got safe into Beaucaire at 5 o'clock ; where we had to sit down in a coach-office, with a stone floor and heaps of luggage, and in an atmosphere which would generate onions, to wait till 7 for the coach to Arles. 6. At last it came, and we got in and went to Arles, when, behold! there was nothing at Arles to see, and we were further from Marseilles than before. However, one finds the Scottish lady and gentleman are with us still.

Went to the Cathedral. It contains a curious bas-relief, representing the Passage of the Red Sea. Here the Lord is riding on a horse, and *troubling* the Egyptians; for He rides over them, while Moses and his friends reach *toute de suite* the dry land. The front of the church, about the door, is quite rich in carved stone ; a huge figure over the door represents the Almighty, as Ezekiel dreamed of Him, looking like the Devil. Even the Scotchman said, " *It is blasphemy."* There is a profusion of carving—lions, toads, devils, and angels, not to mention men. It betokens the exuberance of childhood, and belongs to the time when the church was built.

FROM ARLES TO MARSEILLES.—Soon after leaving Salon, we came upon the most beautiful sight we have yet seen in France. The sea was far off in the distance, but before it, and as far as the eye could reach, were plantations of olive and almond trees. The almonds look like large old peach trees. The air was soft, and the sun looked out upon the lovely scene as if to bless the whole. On one side of the road was a rock, extending for miles, with only here and there a trace of vegetation ; on the other, this garden of perpetual verdure.

GENOA.—I have seen some handsome women here. In general, there is something quite pleasing in their appearance. I like their covering for the head—a sort of scarf, sometimes of white muslin, elaborately worked; but oftener of gay calico—white ground and violet figures. They hold the ends of this—the hands often crossed on the breast—in a very graceful manner. To-day, as I went early into the Chiesa San Matteo, I saw a most beautiful woman kneeling in the church; her face was much like some of the Magdalens. She might have sat for one. She is the handsomest creature I have seen in Europe.

PISA—DUOMO.—But it is painful to see such a building surrounded by a fringe of beggars. At Genoa—yes, and at London—we see the same thing. The first time I heard the Italian language spoken, it was by blackguards and beggars. Here, at Pisa, the one are more obtrusive—the others more tenacious. As I stepped into the street, I know not how many offered their services—or their caps; one begged for a *crazia*—one said, " *Vuolate un cicerone, por videre il Duomo, Campanile,*" &c. (You can't look at a building, but out comes a knave *to show it.*)

The Duomo and its neighbours seem not to belong to Pisa. Not only do they stand apart from the town, but they have a foreign aspect, and seem, indeed, to have no affinity with the rest of it. However, the *Campanile* has one descendant—illegitimate, but not natural: another tower, which resembles the great one only in its *leaning*. This is like all imitators; they get the prophet's halting step, not his inspiration.

DUOMO.—The effect of the whole building is wonderful. The enormous columns, their great number, the lofty arches, the prodigious dome, the altars, the varied marbles, the curious mosaic beneath the dome, rich with its many hues—all fill one with wonder, though not with the same reverence that steals over you at Notre Dame or Westminster Abbey.

I am surprised at the fewness and smallness of the windows; but the brightness of the Italian sky compensates for this. The stained glass is very rich. The effect of the enormous cross, with John and Mary, in the roof, just over the choir, is marvellous—a mosaic, with a gold ground. I think there are twelve altars in the nave and transepts—all beautiful, all different, and all harmonious. The black and white marbles alternating produce a curious effect.

The best painting, I think, is a Madonna by Allori.

In Florence, he went into the convent attached to the chapel of St. Antonin, called sometimes Del Salviata, " and saw the cell in which Savonarola used to live. It is like all the rest, small—ten feet square, perhaps, and ten feet high. There is a fresco of Beato Angelico, representing the coronation of the Virgin. Here lived that dauntless soul who feared nothing *but wrong and fear ;* a soul of fire was in him."

He takes at once the thought of Michael Angelo :—

But the Day and Night, oh, how they strike your soul! The day is dawning—a man huge and brawny, full of lusty life. He is just awakening, " as a bridegroom coming out of his chamber, and rejoicing as a strong man to run his race." Here you do not find ideal beauty—

you never meet it in Michael Angelo, but boldness of thought, and wantonness of unconscious strength. He is the Middle Age all over, as it seems to me, yet he has the profound wisdom that comes of long studying the best models, the profounder wisdom which comes of that inspiration " which rounded Peter's dome." I never see one of his works, from the Young Apollo unfinished in the gallery, to the Fates at the Pitti Palace, without feeling his awful depth and strength. His Aurora is fresh, strong, and full of *rhythm*—you feel this in all his works with the chisel; I can't think his Day was quite finished, but Night bends her head in slumber, and seems, like the Night of the old mythology, to be the mother of all things, who, of her own consent yields to Fate and resigns the field to Day. I do not see the connection these figures have with a tomb or a chapel, but I feel their force.

SANTA CROCE.—This is the great burial-place of the illustrious departed of Florence; here sleep in peace the men that were persecuted when living, and driven from their native land.

He copies the epitaphs, and in some cases the shapes of the monuments.

The first time I visited this beautiful church it was a very sad day, and not knowing what to do, I turned into the home of the departed. While I copied the inscriptions the priests chanted their service, and ever and anon the organ poured out such music as might have fallen from the sky; it was sad, sweet, and soothing to the soul.

It is a little curious that Galileo should be buried in *this* church and have such a monument *here*, for the tribunal that persecuted him had its residence in this very cloister. So the world goes. The conventuals of St. Francis, to whom Urban IV. entrusted the inquisitorial power in Tuscany, meet in the cloister of Santa Croce. Now the Grand Duke of Tuscany is curious to preserve every relic of Galileo, even his finger, kept in the Laurentian Library.

FLORENCE.—I have now visited most of the wonders of this charming place. Let me say that the great paintings of Raphael— the Madonna Della Seggiola, the Julius II., the Leo X., the Fornarina, affect me more than I had ever dreamed of. The first time I went to the Pitti Palace, I did not know what I was to see; all at once my eye fell on the Madonna. What a painting! God in heaven, what a painting! What a genius! I must say the same of the great work of Titian—the Magdalen, and both the Venuses; but the Laocoon, the Venus de Medici, and the Apollo did not fill my mind as I had expected. The statues in general have fallen a little below my imagination, the paintings (I mean the great ones which I knew well by engravings before) have risen above it far; so have the public buildings.

I have visited one or other of the galleries almost daily, and devoted almost all my time to the study of art. I have, however, lost a good deal of time by illness. I have had a bad cold ever since I left Paris ; it became at last a violent pain in the region of the right side of the frontal sinus. It came on regularly from 3 to 4 p.m., slight at first, but increasing in violence, till at last it was like the tooth-ache, condensed agony ; then it gradually abated and disappeared about 9 or 10. It lasted me about ten days.

We have had a fine lofty situation, No. 1189, Lung d'Arno, with a beautiful prospect far off to the snowy hills.

Feb. 1.—We left Florence with sorrow, and at night reached Livorno, on the way to Naples.

PUTEOLI AND BAIÆ. Mem. The girl near the Cento Camarelle, who *filéd à la mode antique*, the pretty girl whose teeth Mr. Freeman looked at, and the beauty to whom I gave half a carline, and who knelt down that we might look at her necklace.

All day long we have been on classic ground, and a fine day it has been; but what a difference between the ancient tenants of this place and these their successors! Here those old Romans revelled in their Titanic lust, here they poisoned one another, here they framed plans or conspiracies which affected the welfare of a world, and here, too, a scholar wrote immortal words, and a poet said—

"Exegi monumentum aere perennius."

What a mutability in the affairs of men! Mæcenas is forgotten, or remembered mainly as the poet's friend; Baiæ, Puteoli, have perished; the monuments of brass are lost for ever; but the poet lives and will live for many a year (See Carm. iii., Od. xxiv., and the "Beatus ille," which he never wrote in the country, except the four last stanzas.)

Italy is the land of artistic elegance and social deformity. She has taught refinement to all Europe and kept treachery for herself. Oh, when is the great Phidias to come, and carve out of the expectant marble the perfect form of society, and realise in fact the ideal often dimly seen in dreams?

In vintage time, when you throw grapes into the press, by their ow weight they exude their juice, and there runs out a girlish liquor which is sweet, frothy, and will keep two or three days. At the first pressure there comes forth a liquor deeper in colour and more potent in character, which will last half the season, and it is fit for boys' potations and weak men. But it is only the strong pressure that forces out of the grape's reluctant heart that rich and generous wine which keeps good for centuries, bettering by age—the invigorating spirit which fires the heart of hardiest men. So is it with the works of human thought.

At length he approaches Rome, "the widow of two antiquities."

Had no chance to taste the wine of Albano, yet a "*plenus Albani cadus*" might be forgiven. I had Horace in my hand all the way, and read, not without new pleasure, the Satire II. viii. 13.

Then we came in sight of Rome. Oh, what thoughts it awoke in my heart when first I saw its domes, and rode down the Via Appia!

ROME.—There is no city, except Athens and Jerusalem, so full of recollections to me as Rome. Twice it has been the capital of the world—once, of the Pagan, by physical violence; once, of the Christian, by spiritual violence. She has made a desert about her twice. The memorials of the arts, however, came from the times of the Emperors, scarce any from that of the republic.

Then they only *produced great men*. Compare the two eras in this respect. What great Romans came up after the empire was fixed in Augustus? How many before.

Wherever the English go they carry with them their pride, their prejudice, their port, their porter, and their pickles. Here they have their national amusements—fox-hunting and horse-racing. When the Americans also become numerous, I suppose we shall have our national amusements—elections and banking.

I love to walk about the streets, or sit in the Forum, and think of the armies that marched out of this little city—the influences that went forth to conquer the world. What traces of these stern giants are written all over the earth. One might, in travelling in the land of giants, come all at once on the footprints of one in the sand ten feet long—and from that judge of the race. So it is with the Romans, but you meet their footsteps everywhere. Yet they *invented* nothing, not even the arch. They borrowed their literature, their art, their religion, but their *arms* they made. But, alas, what a contrast, as one sits in the Forum, and looks on the crowd of beggars and of blackguards. Oh, city of crime from the days of Romulus till these days! Thou that stonest the prophets! The blood of martyrs is upon thee from thy earliest to thy latest days.

We went to Sta. Maria Maggiore, which is exceedingly rich, but not imposing. It is not a religious architecture. It seems to me the modern Unitarians would like this style; it is clear, actual, and the work of logical and demonstrative heads, wholly free from mysticism. It has a continuous architrave over the pillars, which I think is universal in Christian churches.

Mem. The fragments of Christ's *cradle* that are preserved here. In St. John of Lateran is the table on which the Twelve took the Last Supper—the heads of St. Paul and St. Peter—the actual Well of Samaria, between two pillars from Pilate's house at Jerusalem—the stone on which the soldiers casts lots for Christ's vesture—the pillars between which Pilate stood when he told the people to take Christ and crucify him—the column that split asunder at his Crucifixion (very neatly done)—and four columns supporting a slab which shows the exact height of Jesus—*just six feet!*

Here too I saw a hole in an altar—through the marble slab—made in this way; a priest did not believe in Transubstantiation, so, one day when he was celebrating mass, the wafer whipped through the slab of marble, and left a great spot of blood on the column beneath which supported it. The red spot is still faintly visible. The hole is an inch and a half in diameter!

Really, I think I shall turn Catholic, and be baptised on Easter-day in the baptistery of Constantine, where Rienzi bathed, and where all converted Jews and infidels are baptized.

St. Clement.—This is to me one of the most interesting churches of Rome. It is in the early style of churches, with three naves, a separate place for the presbytery, two pulpits, one for the gospel, one for the epistle. Here too is the seat for the *Episcopus.* All this was constructed by John VIII. Here, says tradition, are the remains of Clemens and Ignatius under the altar in the presbytery. I did not *want* to doubt it; but what thoughts it brings up to stand over the bodies of Clemens Rom., and Ignatius of Antioch! Here, they say, was Clement's house—here lived the "true yoke-fellow" of Paul! How it brings home the words of the New Testament to visit these places.

After strolling about all day, to the Baths of Caracalla, the Pyramid of Cestius, the Columbarium of the Freedman of Augustus, &c.,

We went to the prison—the Mamertine Prison, where Jugurtha died, and the conspirators that were with Catiline. Yes, here was Paul a prisoner! The custode shows a spring that spouted up for St. Peter (who was here nine months with Paul), in which he baptized forty-nine soldiers, all of whom became martyrs. There is a stone which records the same event. I drank some of the water. But all nonsense apart, it is something to sit down in the dungeon where Paul was a prisoner!

ARCH OF TITUS.—It wakens deep thoughts to see the sevenfold candlestick of the temple at Jerusalem on the arch of a Roman Emperor. Amongst other things I really thought of Dr. Palfrey's Academical Lectures, with *their* sevenfold golden candlestick. One Pope took great pains to preserve and restore this "*monumentum insigne religionis et artis.*" I don't see how it is a monument of religion; but, as the Pope says so, it must be true.

But I fancy the Romans who took Jerusalem differed a little from the wretches we saw at work to-day in the neighbourhood of the arch. It is a curious spectacle to see the Romans work! However, they begin early, for they rise as the old Romans did.

Sunday, 25th February.—I was ill all night with a headache and feverishness, and all day in a slighter degree. Indeed, my old evils return upon my head. However, in the afternoon we went to the Villa Borghese, a few steps from the gate. It was delightful to hear the wild-birds sing, and gather the wild violet, so modest and fragrant, in a spot where the water trickles all day long. I found, too, some forget-me-nots of a species that I never saw before.

AT THE CAPITOL.—A bas-relief on a sarcophagus attracted me much, but more from the singularity of the conception than the beauty of the work. The story is the Creation of Man by Prometheus, Man's Fate and Death. On the left of the spectator are the four elements out of which man is made: 1. *Fire*, typified by Vulcan with fire beside him. He and a servant are at work hammering iron on an anvil. 2. *Water*, typified by Oceanus with an oar, &c. 3. *Air*, by Æolus blowing a trumpet. 4. *Earth*, by a woman with cornucopia and other emblems of abundance.

Cupid and Psyche embracing, denote the union of soul and body. Aurora, the newness of the world's life. In the centre sits Prometheus, with a clayey-looking, lumpy fellow he has just made, on a block before him, and another in his hand. Minerva puts a butterfly on the head of this latter, to denote the soul's entry into the body. The three fell sisters are there—one writes his destiny on a globe—one looks hard at him and spins her thread—another folds her arms in her robe and regards him. Then you see him lying on the ground—dead; a Love stands over him—I know not for what purpose. The Dawn is flying away in a chariot, to denote the separation of soul and body,

and Mercury waits to conduct the soul to its own place. Apuleius*
would have been delighted with it, and Henry More, I fancy, would
have written another ψυχωξοια if he had seen it—to be read as often
as the first.

Mem. The busts of the Emperors and of the illustrious men. It
makes one feel humble to stand in the presence of such marbles as
are collected in the Hall of Illustrious Men. If one were arrogant, I
would put him there to become humble. Yet the Romans had a very
coarse and materialistic organization. I never find in them (excepting
Virgil) that keen sensitiveness to the beautiful, which belongs to noble
men. Their faces in general have very little that is spiritual, little
that is elevated.

Sunday, March 3.—We were presented to the Pope, with some
other Americans. He stood, in the simple dress of a monk, with his
back against a sort of table, and talked with Mr. Greene, who had
introduced us. He blessed some rosaries which the Americans had
brought. We stayed about twenty minutes. He has a benevolent
face and looked kindly upon us. Talked about the state of Rome—
about the English language in America—about the famous polyglott
Cardinal at the Propaganda—made a sign, and we withdrew.

Catacombs.—I know no place that fills one with deeper emotions
in Rome than the catacombs. Here the persecuted when alive found
refuge—when dead found repose for their ashes and bones long tortured.
Here the relatives of a martyr laid down his lacerated body—and in
the *ampullæ* deposited the blood they had piously collected with sponges.
Well: the master died the martyr's death—the servants need not fear
to do the same!

I am confirmed in my opinion that, long before Constantine, the
Church had departed from the ideal simplicity of the primitive state,
so often contended for by Protestants. Indeed, I am now more than
ever persuaded that as Christ gave no form, the first one used by the
apostolic churches was much less simple than we fancy. I shall never
forget the impression left on my mind by this visit. I should like to
come and sit here all night and read the Fathers, Origen's cohortation
to his young converts, urging them to be martyrs,—or something of
Cyprian or Tertullian, or the lives of the martyrs themselves. No
wonder the Catholic Church has such a hold on the hearts of the
world, while she keeps in her bosom the relics of the sainted dead!
Yet, as I walked about here, I could not but think how easy it must
have seemed, and have been, too, to bear the cross of martyrdom,—the
recollection of Christ, of the apostles, the certainty of the prayers and
best wishes of men of earth, the expectations of heavenly satisfaction—
all would conspire to sustain the spirit, and make the man court and
not shun the martyr's death.

St. Paul in the Corso.—Perhaps Paul actually lived here and
died here! It is something to stand on the spot where Paul once
stood. I should like to sit here and read his Epistles. Oh, the soul-
stirring man! It is easy to build churches to his memory.

---

* This sarcophagus belongs to the time of Apuleius, who was born in the early part
of the second century. It shows the passage by Neo-Platonism into Christianity; and
Apuleius himself has a touch of the same in his beautiful story of "Cupid and Psyche,"
which belonged not to him, but came down to him, gradually improving, from older times,
and only owes its Neo-Platonic form to him.

Saw Father Glover, of course a Jesuit, in his room at the Roman College, *i. e.* the College of the Jesuits. He is a good-looking, benevolent old gentleman of sixty to seventy, with a frank English way with him. He is an Englishman. St. Ives introduced me. It was in his room, with a brick floor, a bed, a rough writing-table, a few books, a single window, no fire-place—a cheap place, a divinity student would sicken at the thought of such a place at Cambridge. Yet he is a man famous for his talents and learning, and more and better than famous for his charity and practical Christianity.

I asked him about some doctrines of the Catholic Church, but he would have a controversy; so he had it for a moment or so, but it was all on his side. He thought there could be no religion without believing all that God taught. Of course I assented. God taught the Divinity of Christ; that I did not see proved—so he attacked me for denying that Divinity, and talked as men usually do on that point. However, he desisted at length. Then I asked him,—

1. About Inspiration, or the Catholic doctrine thereof. Inspiration was the Spirit of God acting on the soul of man, and preserving it from all error in regard to the matter in hand. It does not direct the words, but superintends the thought, or substance of what is to be written, so that no error intervenes. No error is in the New Testament when truly expounded. The Holy Scriptures do not require merely an inspired expounder, but an infallible expounder—there is but one such, *i. e.* the Catholic Church. He does not know that anybody has been inspired since the days of the Apostles; may be so, and may be not. Aid is always given by God in proportion to the necessity. Some of the saints have been inspired always. (Dr. Grant said, when the Catholic Church canonized a man, it pronounced his works to be truth with no error by this act. Still, I think there must be limitations to that statement.) Father Glover said the Old Testament was inspired; but it was only a figure of the New Testament, that is, in the main. The Apocalypse was as true and authentic as the other parts of the Old Testament. The Church told him so. (Here I think he was a little mistaken. See Jahn, but, on the contrary, Mühler.) The Apocryphal Gospels might be inspired, but he did not know it, for the Church had not declared concerning them yea or nay. (Here I think him mistaken a little.) The Apocryphal Epistle of Paul was quite like Paul's writings—its doctrines true, but whether inspired or not he could not say.

2. Of Miracles. The Catholic Church works them certainly when there is need. Now there is not the same occasion for this work as in the time of Christ, for then Christianity was preached to the heathens. Now when this is done, miracles always follow, *e. g.* Xavier raised three or four dead to life in the East. Miracles were wrought continually by saints, &c., &c. The liquefaction of St. Januarius' blood at Naples on the 1st of May is a real miracle continually performed. He mentioned the miraculous cure of a young lady in consumption on Conception-day; she lay in a dying state. All at once she said the blessed Virgin had appeared, and told her that she should not die that day, but recover! So she rose and walked about, well as ever! He cited the cure effected by Prince Hohenlohe of a lady in Wash-

ington, U.S.A.   He had the printed documents before him.   (I knew the case before.) He mentioned a miraculous conversion—a Jew, Ratisbonne by name.   One night he knew nothing of Christianity; at 12, raved and blasphemed both God and his Church.   At 12¼ he was converted and found to understand Christianity so well that he needed scarcely any instruction! This conversion was quite as miraculous as St. Paul's.   Now God only wrought these miracles to attest the truth, *i. e.* the truth of the doctrines of the Catholic Church.

Went afterwards to see Bishop Baggs.   Had a long interview with him.   He is very courteous, and as free from all cant as one can be conceived to be.   Indeed, I have not seen a Catholic who spoke through his nose, or had a hypocritical whine.   I never saw one roll up the whites of his eyes.   This, though but negative, is no small merit.

1. He said—for I turned the conversation that way—that the Catholic Church was making great exertions in all directions in the way of missionary enterprise, and with great success.   Proof, or, rather, sign of it—the young men of all nations in the Propaganda.

2. He said the Catholic Church had never determined whether the infallibility rested in the Pope, or in the General Councils, as the matter of faith.   In other words, whether the declarations of the Pope, touching matters of faith, were infallible before they received the assent of a Council, or a Church in general, and independent of that assent or not.   Some thought one way, some another; but a man was not a heretic for thinking either way.   I mentioned the opinion of Baron von Wessenberg,* which he did not concur in, but said, still, that others shared the opinion, though to him the case was quite clear: (1.) It was not a practical question, or the Catholic Church would have decided it; for during the 1,800 years of the Catholic Church's existence, no one bull of the Pope touching any matter of faith had been without the assent (open or tacit, I suppose,) being granted.   Therefore the question is merely speculative.   (2.) He thinks that the Pope in other matters, of his private opinion, may err, as any other doctor; yet, in matters of faith, God will infallibly preserve him from mistake.   The Gallican clergy were once hostile to the Pope's infallibility, but are now coming round to the Roman side of the question.   The question does not concern Philosophy, which the Catholic Church leaves untouched, as far as possible.

3. He said that Galileo was not brought into trouble on account of maintaining that the earth went round the sun, but because he taught that such was the doctrine of the Holy Scriptures, and in this point conflicted with the doctrines already proved by the Church to be true. (Doubt all this, very much.) In matters of philosophy, the Church did not meddle, except they come directly in contravention of the doctrines of the Church.

4. He said, too, that the Church taught that out of the Catholic Church was no salvation.   Here he went into a quite able and very clear statement of the scriptural argument for the power of the Catholic Church to bind and loose, enjoin duties, and give absolution for sin.   That what the Catholic Church bound on earth should be bound in heaven.   Still more; Christ made a distinction—some men

* Geschichte der grossen Kirchenversammlungen.   Band I.

to be teachers, some not teachers; "Go preach the Gospel," &c.; "they that believe and are baptised shall be saved;" "he that believeth not," &c. Here belief in what they (the teachers) are commanded to preach (that is, of course, the doctrines of the Church), and the reception of baptism (the rite and sacrament of the Church), are made essential to salvation. Strictly speaking, therefore, such as do not come under this rubric are to be damned by the very letter of Scripture. But this letter of Scripture is to be explained by reference to the attributes of God, e. g., justice. Therefore, we are not to suppose that God will damn any one, except for what is his own fault. If he is out of the Church, not by his own fault, he is not to be damned for that. Nevertheless, a man may deceive himself, thinking he is not to blame for his unbelief, while he really is. Still, in special cases, it is not for man to say who is wilfully out of the Church, and therefore to be damned. God only can search the hearts of men and decide this.

He said, very truly, that the Protestants abused the Catholics; that very few persons knew what were their real doctrines—they would not inquire: all of it is very true. Yet, for myself, I have endeavoured always to learn their doctrine from their own writers, and have never wilfully erred in regard to them.

He is in time for the Carnival :—

Notice the beggars in the midst of this festivity, and their hideous deformity. They are sad enough objects at all times—on a festal day what shall we think of them? Men throw flour at each other, and the rich spoil the coats of the rich with what would have gladdened the heart of the beggars! "Whatsoever ye would that men should do to you—." Ah, this is the city where Paul was crucified. God bless men!—they can't crucify Christianity.

We went to St. Peter's, and heard the sweet music at vespers, and smelt the incense. The music is really very fine—the perfection of music; it would stir the heart of a statue to hear it. The children were gathered together (i. e. a few children) to be instructed. Half a loaf is better than no bread, and I make no doubt the essentials of Christianity are inculcated.

VENICE.—I see the secret of the Venetian colouring here in the actual sky, ocean, houses, and men and women. I rose each morning an hour or more before the sun, and watched that beautiful purple spread itself out in all directions from the point where the sun would rise, and then disappear in the dimmer light of day. The solemn stillness of the horseless city was broken only by the fishermen going out to sea, their white sails against the purple. The numerous bells only announce the general silence.

Venice is a dream of the sea. Occidental science and Oriental fantasy seem to have united to produce it. A Pagan Greek might say that Neptune, drunk with nectar and Amphitzite, slept in the caves of the sea, and dreamed as he slept. Venice is the petrification of his dream. The sun colours curiously the walls of the palaces and churches. It seems as if their wealth had run over and stained the walls.

VIENNA.—The Strauss music is rich, rhythmic, and graceful. It reminds me continually of Paul Veronese's pictures, examples of a joyous festivity of well-bredness. There is the same colouring in both. But there is music that affects me like Michael Angelo's works, with its grandeur and terrific strength; a great thought strongly carved out in the air, as his in stone.

PRAGUE.—After many inquiries for the *Judenstadt* (Jews' quarter), which I visit in all the towns, an old woman offered to be my *guide de place*; but she spoke a dialect so corrupt, that I could not understand one word in ten. However, she led me to the place. The Jews are as busy as those in Rome—eight or nine thousand of them in all. Some of them are rich. They do business in all parts of the city, but lodge here. There are no gates to shut them in, no soldier to watch them. Alas! for them—they that once dwelt in the fat of the land of Egypt, and went out to a land flowing with milk and honey! Well, they are better off here than anywhere else in Europe.

The old woman put me in the hands of a lad of nineteen, perhaps, who conducted me to the *Alte Friedhof* (Old Cemetery), a small enclosure of half or three-quarters of an acre, surrounded with old houses and old walls, full of dead men's graves. Stone touched stone. There were long inscriptions in Hebrew: the earth was full of Israelitish bones. Old trees, *elders*, grew there to an enormous size. They were the patriarchs of the place. Some of them were a foot thick. The guide said they were more than 600 years old, and I can believe it. Here are the graves of famous Rabbis, of good Levites; of nobles, also, for in this land the Jews sit down with princes. I never saw a Jewish grave-yard before, and this spot made me feel as never before. I have an inborn affection for this mysterious people, for ages oppressed, yet green and living still. I thought of the service they had done mankind—and the reward they got! Abraham, Isaac, and Jacob, Moses and the Prophets, came up to my mind, and He who was the culmination of Hebrewdom, the blossom of the nation. I shall never forget my feelings as I also laid a stone piously on the tomb of a Patriarch who died 1000 years ago, and plucked an elder leaf from the tree that rooted among his mouldered ashes.

The boy showed me a tombstone 1200 years old—so he said; it looked amazingly fresh. I saw the humble shed, with its elliptical block, on which, in a rude coffin, all the sons of Jacob who die in Prague are placed—rich and poor, the Rabbis full of honoured years, and the virgin daughters of Israel—before they are gathered to their fathers. They bury here no more; but they scorn to mingle their dust with that of Christians. No spot this side of Rome or Venice has interested me so much as this.

Went to the famous bridge over the Moldau, from which John of Nepomuck was thrown. Saw the cross, in brass, on the parapet of the bridge, to mark the spot where he was thrown over, and to commemorate the miraculous flames that issued from his body, after his death, while it lay in the water. Numerous statues of John, in various attitudes and actions, are on the sides of the bridge; here and there are bas-reliefs, telling how he converted eight thousand Jews and twenty-five thousand infidels to Christianity. Of course, he was greater than Paul, who could hardly convert *one Jew*. Here was a crucifix of gilt bronze, erected out of the fines paid by the Jews for blaspheming the Christian religion! It stands there to insult them every time they pass the stream! What would Jesus say of them who take his name in vain, could he come back.

Went to the Black Tower and the White Tower, from which there is a beautiful view of Prague. I love to take the *profile* of a town: that of Boston is exquisitely beautiful. But the Middle Age towns are by far the most picturesque. How degenerate and prosy our towns are getting!

I went into a Jewish book-store, and bought a few Hebrew books as memorials of the place and the nation; Hebrew prayers and Hebrew stories—no nation excels them for both—and a little modern Hebrew poetry. The little old man was attentive, and seem pleased that a stranger took interest in Hebrew literature. He had a fine copy of the Talmud, twelve volumes, large paper, for forty gulden!

In Berlin he attended many lectures :—

Heard Werder on Logic. He made a great fuss about *Bestimmtheit*, and was, as I thought, in a remarkable fix himself. When he wanted to touch upon anything very deep, he laid his fore-finger with its tip between his eyes on the organ of individuality, and then gradually drew it down the length of his nose. He goes down so deep, far below the nature of things, that one must take off not only his clothes, but his *Sinnlichkeit*—his memory, his common-sense, imagination, affections, and then he becomes a *blosse Geist*, and is prepared to go down to the deep, deep sea of Philosophy.

Mem. The pudding-faced youth who tried to comprehend the distinction between *Daseyn* and *Realité*, and could not.

This youth is sketched—

Heard Schelling on Offenbarungs-Philosophie. He found a good deal of fault with Kant, but praised Fichte, and said he had done great service to philosophy; thought his " Naturrecht " his best thing; praised the " Way towards a Blessed Life " for its *dialectic* skill, compared it with Hegel's works, which he said were merely mechanical, though he only alluded to Hegel and did not name him; some hissed at the allusion. Then he added that in his (Hegel's) case the work was mere mechanism, the grinding in a mill, and men paid much more attention to the noise of the *clapper* than to the meal which was alleged to be ground. Upon this all laughed.*

Schelling is about seventy, short, 5 ft. 6 in. or less, looks mild, his nose is short and slightly turned up, hair white as snow, an ample forehead, large mouth and pale face, his eyes blue, and have once been very bright, his voice is feeble—he has lost some teeth, so the articulation is

---

* Schelling did not recant, in set terms, his early philosophy of Transcendental Idealism, but was trying to make Evangelical Religion appear to be the same thing. The old philosopher, with his cosmetics and hair-dyes, deceived nobody. His long silence was interrupted by this call to Berlin, with the well-understood object of lecturing down Hegelianism, which was then in its prime. It was a curious piece of legerdemain, during which the Divine Personages and the Church itself, which men had seen Schelling actually swallow in 1800, turned up again quite briskly, saying, " Here we are ! "

not very distinct. Audience 150 to 200—the largest by far that I have
seen; when one came in after the lecture began, the rest hissed at him.
It seems to me a pity he should lecture; the greater part, I am told,
come to hear him from curiosity—to see a famous man, and smile at his
doctrines. Others come solely to mock at the senilities of a man who
is going to "squash the head of the great serpent of scepticism as if it
were a Göttingen sausage." He has few that follow his notions here
at present, though of course all respect a man who has done so much
for philosophy. The Hegelians regard him as the foe of freedom,
brought here to keep up the existing order of things.

He also heard Vatke on Psalms iv. v. : Michelet on Logic ;
Twesten on the Relation between Faith and Knowledge ; Böckh
on the Antigone ; Steffens on Anthropology.

After some delay he obtained permission to visit the public
schools of the City of Berlin, which he did in company with
Mr. Fay, the American Chargè des Affaires. He heard various
recitations, extracted from the teachers all the details of their
method, and observed the habits of the boys and girls. The
notes are too disjointed for publication.

WITTENBERG AND LUTHER.—We entered the church by the door
where Luther put up the 95 theses. I bought a copy of them in the
church; here they are (a pamphlet of 16 pages) ; what a change from
then till now ! When shall the work end? At night I walked in front
of the door to meditate. The evening star looked down. A few persons went and came. The soft air fell upon my head. I felt the spirit
of the great Reformer. Three centuries and a quarter, and what a
change ! Three centuries and a quarter more, and it will be said, the
Protestant religion did little in comparison with what has since been
done; well, if *this* work be of God ! *
Went to Luther's house. Here it is (an engraving). I saw the
very room in which he used to write, and think, and work; the stove
which he devised himself, with its reliefs representing the four evangelists and other scriptural characters. There was the seat at the
window where he sat with Catherine de Bore, and looked at the
evening sky; there the table at which he sat with Melancthon and the
rest. The books are gone, (he never had many), the papers, the man.
I went into another room which served for family purposes, and yet
another where he lectured. Here are still curious things of his; his
beer-jug ; a glass cup given him by the Elector, and broken to pieces
by Peter the Great. Here are some embroideries from the hand of

---

* There is a bronze statue of Luther in the market-place, on which is the inscription :—

" Ist's Gotteswerk, so wird's bestehen,
Ist's Menschenwerk, wird's untergehen."

" Is it God's work, 'twill always stay,
Is it man's work, 'twill pass away."

Catherine, a face of Luther worked perhaps by her. Here were the impressions of his seal. I bought one, and here is the explanation of it (a printed sheet in German hand-writing, entitled Dr. Martin Luther's Petschafts-Erklärung). I saw the genealogical tree of his family. Six of his descendants still live, at Berlin, Erfurt, Potsdam, and Leipsic, all in humble circumstances. I plucked a few leaves from a linden and a rose-bush that grew in the garden. The guide had great reverence for the reformer *der heilige Dr. Luther*, as he called him. I had heard "stout old Martin" often enough, but here I felt nearer to the man than before. God be praised that he has lived!

We went out of the walls to the spot where he burned the Pope's Bull. It is railed round, planted with shrubs, &c. A young oak grows now in the midst of it; the old oak under which the thing was done was hewn down in the Seven Years' War.

We went to his monument; the pedestal is of polished granite; I only regretted the polish. Beneath the canopy is a fine brown figure of Luther in his preacher's robes, with his Bible in his arms—a grand figure—large, manly, with that peasant's expression, but full of nobleness and commanding faith.

NEAR FRANKFORT.—Went into a little Catholic church, very poor, and very dirty. It had an old brass skillet at the door to hold the sacred water. Some daubs hung up here and there, wretched crucifixes, &c. The stone floor could not have been swept for a year at least; it was like the street itself. There were great cracks in the main door, which was closed, and I could put my hand through in many places. Yet comfortless and unæsthetic as it was, it was affecting. Here some poor man labours on all his life, in celibacy and silence, perhaps a man of genius, no doubt of learning; a little band call him their father. He baptizes, marries, buries them; tells them of heaven, and perhaps goes there to see the Pope.

FRANKFORT. — Went into the *Jüdengasse*, which is the greatest curiosity in the place to me. It looks like the middle ages. The Jews of Frankfort, I am told, have split into two parties:—1. The old Biblico-Talmudistic Jews, who expect the Messiah; and, 2. Those who reject the notion of a Messiah yet to come. Strange to say, the Government, which of course has no belief in a Jewish Messiah yet to come, takes the side of the old party and wars against the new school of Jews. What a curious phenomenon this, of the Jews living in the civilization of the 19th century, and sharing so few of its ideas.

In Halle he met Tholuck, and heard him lecture. In Heidelberg, he visited all the notable professors, who received him kindly, and talked at great length with him, and he had very pleasant interviews with the veteran historian Schlosser, and with Gervinus, who was then about thirty-four or thirty-five years of age, and had just been called to that university. He learned to prize highly Mr. Parker's subsequent works, and expressed his warm acknowledgments in 1856, with a hope that a friendship might be cultivated.

Gervinus thinks that the influence of Strauss has passed away; so says Ullmann. I think them mistaken. The *first* influence, that of making a noise, is over, no doubt; but the truth which he has brought to light will sink into the German theology, and mould it anew. Just as the doubts so haughtily expressed in the Wolfenbüttel fragments have done. *Men mistake a cessation of the means for a cessation of the end.* Strauss organizes no party, so there is no obvious action; but his thoughts are not dead—not even inactive, I fancy. They will yet do some work. By-and-bye his falsehood will get separated from his truth, and be forgot. The truth of his book will appear.

He travelled to Tübingen with a very talkative young man, who booked himself as a *Bekleidungs-Kunst Assessor* (a euphuism for journeyman tailor) who was travelling for the *æsthetische Angelegenheiten seines Herzens* (to give his heart æsthetic advantages.)

Went to see Professor Ewald. We sent up our names, stating that we were Americans. He came out and very kindly brought us into his study. He is about fifty, with long hair that hangs about his shoulders. He wore a sort of blouse of calico, with no vest or neckerchief. Has a fine spiritual countenance. He expressed surprise that I in America should know his works; still more that his works upon the Prophets should have fallen into my hands. He complains that the Bible is not studied with freedom; says that the more you study it, and the more freely, the more excellent it appears. He laughed about men fearing for religion lest it failed. I was glad to hear him say that the irreligious tendency of philosophy had received an entire check, and mainly from the higher philosophy itself.

He was glad to hear that I had translated De Wette, for, he said, in ten years it would produce a great change in theological affairs. De Wette was a noble man, but a little too sceptical. Thus in Job he is too sceptical.

Here he heard lectures from Schmidt, Ewald, and Baur. On reaching Bâle, he made the acquaintance of De Wette, who took him to visit various people and places.

Heard De Wette again on the Introduction to Dogmatik. In this lecture he stated that there were no ideas ready made in the human soul, but a tendency to such—laws that necessarily produce them. So the idea of God did not originate in feeling, but in an undetermined tendency which consciousness determines from time to time.

He took us to the library to see some curious MSS.; *e. g.*, the Codex which Erasmus printed the New Testament from—the Codex A of Griesbach—one of Gregory the Great, with a commentary, not yet printed. Some beautiful Hebrew MSS., some of them full of miniatures, remarkably well done, many of them quite like the Old Florentine School. I saw a curious copy of Erasmus's " Laus Stultitiæ," with marginal illustrations from the hand of Holbein, which give me a higher opinion of his genius than all the Eves, Adams and Venuses which he has painted in such numbers. There is one cut representing the Immaculate Conception; the *homunculus* or *corpusculum*, in the shape of a griffin, was entering the mouth of the Virgin. This was quite in the taste of the times. All these were marvellously well done—the ink strong and black as if new.

And here is a very fine portrait of Erasmus. He sits with that peculiar cap and writes. There is a remarkable unity in the whole piece. Erasmus was an *elegant* man in all respects—genteel; all the fineness of his character is pourtrayed here, the cunning mouth, compassed with sharp lips—the nose, slender, delicate—the eyes bright, but cast down, sly, witty.

Here I saw a curious piece of MS. in the handwriting of Erasmus. It was a satire in Latin iambics on Pope Julius II., keen and terrible. It has never been printed.

Took dinner with Dr. De Wette. He was very pleasant. I sat by him at dinner; we talked a good deal about German theology.

De Wette, I learn, has of late years become much more Conservative. Indeed, I think there is not a sound and settled philosophy out of which his opinions have grown. Hence the wavering uncertainty of the man. In youth he was the leader of the enthusiastic young men, the champion of freedom. Now, a life of misfortune has in some sense soured him. Last year, at Jena, all the students came out to receive him; he made a speech, advised them to go home and study their books, and be silent!

He received me quite warmly, and our parting was rather tender—certainly quite affectionate. I do not think my interviews have either raised or diminished the esteem I had for the man.

At Zurich he heard Hitzig lecture on certain points of Hebrew Syntax, and Oken on the Amphibia. After visiting all the famous places of Switzerland, he returned to Bâle, to pass down the Rhine. At Bonn, he stopped to deliver letters, and saw one or two professors. Thence he went to Cologne, through Belgium to Antwerp, where he took the boat for London. Here he made the acquaintance of Hennell, took tea with Carlyle, and met Sterling, who was then " near the skies—a consumption shortening his life." After a brief trip to several places in England, he went to Liverpool, where he was fortunate enough to find Mr. Martineau, and preached for him.

Somewhere in England he met an Episcopal clergyman whose liberal sentiments enticed him into conversation.

I asked him if it were not possible for all classes of Christians to agree to differ about their theological symbols, ceremonies, disciplines, modes and the like, while they fell back on the great principles of religion and morality; in a word, on religion and morality themselves; and I told him that I had aimed in my humble way to bring this about.

He said he liked the plan much, and did not see why all could not unite on these principles as they were expressed in the Thirty-nine Articles!

There is hardly ever an attempt at a fine description in the journal in this tour: but all which he saw and heard is briefly characterized in notes and phrases, well equipped with the necessary statistics. He observed the soil, the rocks, the method of culture, and the crops; collected newspaper scraps, and little engravings of places and edifices; made with his pen sketches of professors, soldiers, plans of buildings, monuments; curtly described every man he spoke with. Nothing escaped his cool and simple observation. He found himself at home with each learned man in his own province, and thus saved the talk from evaporating in generalities. No American ever travelled with a better passport.

Sept. 1, 1844, Sunday.—After a most prosperous and felicitous voyage of twelve days, completing the quickest passage ever made, I reached *home*—saw the household, and the blessed Russells, all the four little and live plants in bed. Who shall tell my joy at returning, who the rapture with which I saw old friends!

GARDEN BRIDGE.

CHAPTER IX.

Letters written in Europe— To Isaac Parker—Dr. Francis—Dr. Lamson, 1844.

TO HIS BROTHER, ISAAC PARKER, LEXINGTON.

Naples, Feb. 12, 1844.

MY DEAR BROTHER,—I suppose you have been to meeting to-day, with wife and children in the sleigh, and now sit in your room, with a great fire to keep out the north-westers. To-morrow you will sled wood out of the forest, or the swamps, perhaps. But here we have the verdure of spring. Flowers are in blossom everywhere, roses in the gardens, and oranges hang ripe and golden on the trees. It is a fine sight, too—a tree full of oranges. An apple-tree full of Baldwins, or a peach-tree loaded with yellow *Rare-ripes*, is beautiful; but an orange-tree, with its green leaves and its gold fruit, far surpasses it. Here you see in the fields what we cultivate in hot-houses. The fig ripens its fruit in the open air, the prickly pear grows on the side of all the mountains, and dirty boys sell the delicious hill-side figs in the streets. Every inch of ground is cultivated, not as we cultivate it, but with the nicety of a garden. I have not seen a plough in Italy. Almost all the cultivation is with the hoe and the spade, even where grain is sowed. But their farming tools are a century behind ours. They bring hay to market on the backs of asses, each ass carrying three bundles, or about 300 pounds. In the same way they carry wood, wine, and even *manure*. The harnesses are rudely made, and gall the cattle unmercifully. They put one single ox into the shafts of a cart, and a horse, a mule, an ass, or a *cow* on each side of him : then the driver mounts the cart, and takes the reins, fastened to a ring in the ox's nose, and drives off. It is a queer country in its customs. In all the public-houses men do the *chamber-work* (for the women get into other kinds of work, and so can't be trusted), while you find *women* driving oxen, and even sweeping the streets ! Some of the customs are very strange. The Carnival is a sort of holy time : it begins the 6th of January, and lasts till the 22nd of February (this year). During the last week of Carnival, on Sunday afternoon, men dress themselves up in masks—in all sorts of foolish disguises, and walk or ride about the Strada di Toledo, one of the principal streets of the city. To-day we went to see it. The street is about a mile and a-half long, and quite wide. It was full of people, and the windows and balconies of the tall houses were crowded with men, women, and children. In the centre of the street was room left for the procession of carriages to pass, one end of the procession going up while the other end came down. First came private carriages, hackney-coaches, &c., some of them containing maskers, others not ; then came an enormous carriage, drawn by four horses, in the shape of a dragon, with head, wings, and tail, as you see in the picture books : it was full of people covered with masques ; then came the Prince of Salerno—brother to the king ; then a carriage full of men dressed up in the shape of horses, asses, bears, rabbits, &c. Private carriages followed : then came the carriage of the king, with the king himself also in a "fancy dress;" then others of the royal family, nobles, gentlemen, &c. Well, they all threw sugar-plums at one another, and at the people in the streets and at the windows. The king, and some others, threw real sugar-plums, but most of them prefer such as are made of lime or chalk, which hurt a little where they hit. Some one in the king's carriage, when it passed ours, threw a handful and broke the glass of my spectacles. A wagon followed close behind the king to supply him and his companions with sugar-plums when the stock failed, and a barrel would not last ten minutes.

You will think this very absurd conduct, and so it is. It seemed worse than the sports of boys—they are well for boys ; but here the whole population of the city spent the afternoon, with the KING at their head, in this foolish frolic. What would they say if the Yankees were half so foolish ! Let me give you some idea of the state of the population. There are no *free* schools, and few schools not free. Of course the people are ignorant. Beggars swarm in the streets, yet a most abundant provision has been made for their support, which is *eaten up by the overseers of the funds,* one man, a *nobleman,* making about 18,000 dollars a year out of one establishment, in which he half starves the poor wretches. The taxes are enormous, never less than 20 per cent. of the income, and often 50 per cent. The king, however (they say), is a wise man, and wishes well for the people. I hope he does. Provisions of all kinds are abundant and cheap. Salt is a monopoly of the Government, and could be sold for 18 cents the bushel, but is sold for about 300 dollars. The profit of this necessary of life goes into the *royal* chest. For four cents I can buy ten enormous oranges, or in Sicily I can get forty for the same money.

I have been up to the top of Vesuvius to-day. There is no better way of passing the Sunday here, or, rather, there is no Sunday in Europe, and no day of rest. It (Vesuvius) is just as the books describe it, but it is a most magnificent spectacle, after all. I went so near the centre of the crater that it was necessary to run and escape the large masses of melted stone which fell continually. Some of the little fragments fell on my shoulders, but did no harm. The whole mountain, and, indeed, all the surrounding country is volcanic. Yesterday we went to the ruins of Baiæ, and visited the spot where Cicero had his villa, where Horace wrote his poems, and where Pollio fattened the lampreys with his refractory slaves. But my letter must end. It will be a good while before I shall see you again, so pray remember me to yours. Tell Uncle P., if you see him, that I shall write him by the *next* opportunity. So, believe me, your affectionate brother, not at all changed, T. P.

TO DR. FRANCIS.

Oxford, October 18, 1843.

Puseyism is getting forward rapidly; it has already embraced the greater part of the piety, and the learning, too, of the Church; and men look forward confidently to the time when the Puseyites will all secede in a body as not far distant. Really the rise of this party in the English Church is one of the most encouraging signs of the times. The Old Church is not so dead as men fancied; some are found who say to the fat bishops and easy deans, " Go to the devil with your livings and your rents—your tithes and your distrainings; let us put life into these old forms which you are humbugging the people withal. We want a revival of Christianity—primitive Christianity, and will *believe* anything and sacrifice all things, but we will have it." Here is Dr. Newman— gives up a rich living out of conscientious scruples! Dr. Pusey, born of one of the oldest families in the kingdom, who at Pusey Hall keep a horn of gold given them by Canute—a man bred in all tenderness, rides on the outside of coaches, and submits to all manner of hard fare, to save money to give to the poor and promote education, Christianity, and the like of that! He says a man in good circumstances ought to give up a fourth part of his income for benevolent purposes!—and does it!

*   *   *   *   *   *

When we were at Manchester we went into a very old church, the newest part of it built in 1422. It was very beautiful. We saw where Cromwell's soldiers—for they made barracks of the church—" broke down the carved work." I felt the natural emotions of reverence at treading such ancient aisles, consecrated by the prayers and remembrances of 400 years; and felt, too, a sort of hatred towards Old Noll, who did such things. But the next day I went to worship in the old church. The organ gave out its beautiful tones; the sexton, arrayed in a surplice, showed *us* into a handsome pew, but sent an old, tottering, venerable man into a little dirty box. Presently the dean and canons came in, in their robes, preceded by an usher. The dean has a salary of about 25,000 dollars per annum. A fat chough, with a face like George III., got into the reading desk, and " galloped like a hunter over his prayers;" and another preached a most stupid and arrogant sermon. I could not but think Cromwell did only half his work, and when I was at Oxford I wondered why he never went there with his breaching cannon.

*   *   *   *   *   *

I have been to Kenilworth, to Warwick Castle; have been in the room where Shakspeare was born, and have stood over his grave—you may judge with what feelings.

*   *   *   *   *   *

I have seen Carlyle twice, taken tea with him on Sunday night; and taken breakfast with Babbage, and had a fine visit; saw his wonders and heard his wonders. I shall have much to tell you some day.

He wrote thus to Dr. Lamson, after slightly describing the buildings and pictures at Oxford :—

October 18, 1843.

I heard a great bell tolling. I went into the church (St. Mary's), surrounded by colleges, and was told that Mr. Monkhouse, a Fellow of Queen's College, was to preach before the Vice-Chancellor and Fellows. Aha! though I; I am lucky indeed. I shall hear an Oxford sermon—profound, beautiful, eloquent. Here is something to make a plain Yankee preacher blush for himself and his friends. I walked about over the dust of Wallis and Hoadley, and around the monuments of Sir William Jones and other great clerks, till the Vice-Chancellor came, and sundry ushers, with silver wands and golden, and a great flourish.

Mr. Monkhouse read a little prayer, for the University of Oxford, for Queen's College in special, and, in particular, for Queen Victoria and the Duke of Wellington. Then came the sermon, from 2 Timothy, iv., 7, 8. He stated that he should inquire "if Paul were certain of salvation at the time of writing," and on what grounds his hope of salvation rested. 1. Paul "was no common man, he was infallibly inspired," therefore his notion of salvation must of necessity be the true one. Paul did not rely on his own works. No: he knew that God never relied on human means. He gave the apostles this power to raise the dead, &c., but never relied on the apostles to spread Christianity. So Paul did not rely for salvation on his works. 2. There is a twofold doctrine in the text:—1, Hope, 2, Encouragement or Joy. I. Joy. Didn't look as if there was anything to rejoice for ; but "*opera Dei sunt in media contraria*," as Luther said : still Paul was joyful, because he was righteous. A Pagan said "*nisi justus non felix* (or *fortunatus*)." Here he proved from the Old Testament, the Pagans, and the Fathers, that "good men, in general, are happy." Then he showed that "wicked men are not happy," from the case of Haman, and also by citations. II. Hope. Paul had hope of heaven. Here he proved from the New Testament, especially from James and Peter, that Hope was a good thing, and they that had none of it were badly off. He quoted the ancients to the same effect, "*Spes hominum consolatio sola.*" After all that has been said of Hope, the half hasn't been told. Hope never fails ; for "whom God hath justified," &c. Paul hoped for a "crown of righteousness." Paul sure of enjoyment now—just as sure of heaven hereafter. No wonder he rejoiced. Before Christ, pain was a bad thing ; now it is a good thing—"count it all joy," &c. Trouble is a greater teacher than Reason and Revelation, too. Our great business is to be saved. Salvation depends on justification. Here he fell upon the Antinomians and smote them "hip and thigh." Paul's prize was not for himself alone. So we must not be proud if we are saved, since it don't depend on our worthiness ; it is the gift of God. Besides, we may fall from grace, and then, Paul says to the Hebrews, "it is impossible to save such an one."

Application 1. Have faith. David had faith that he could conquer Goliah ; so we. Great religious movement now-a-days. But God never began a work without Satan trying to subvert it. God wrought miracles in Egypt: the Devil tried. God incarnated Himself in Jesus; the Devil possessed many bodies. God inspired the Apostles; the Devil raised up false prophets. God raised up the Reformers; the Devil Anti-reformers. 2. Avoid all lukewarmness. That is a fair analysis of the sermon.

TO THE SAME.

Lyons, Dec. 31, 1843 ; Jan. 4, 1844.

It is now the last day of the year, and while you are getting ready to preach, I will sit down and write you a letter from this famous old city—the City of Massacres, it might be called—for Antoninus, the illustrious and philosophical, butchered 9000 Christians here at once, as the legend says ; and the wretched Terrorists of the Revolution guillotined, and noyaded, and mitrailled, I know not how many. I have seen the bones of the Christian martyrs piled up in a large vault. I have been into the cellar where Polycarp preached the Gospel of Christianity, when it *cost* something to be a Christian (and *meant* something, too), and have stood on the very grave of Irenæus.

I wish you were here, you would enjoy all this even more than I do. Here is a church—that of St. Irenæus, built over the very spot where many of the Christians were massacred; over the very vaults where the early heroes of the faith preached, and where, too, they died. Really, one forgets the Christianity of the Boston Association, the heroes of the Thursday Lecture, and the trials, dangers, and sufferings of Brothers —— and —— (the last things one *ought* to forget, no doubt), and comes back to the time when the world said, " Thou shalt not be a Christian," and the modest man said, " Please God, you lie in your teeth, for I shall be a Christian ! " When you stand on the spot where such men perished, with their bones under your feet, you begin to feel the difference between those days and ours.

I began this letter at Lyons ; I shall finish it at Arles.

*   *   *   *   *

Here is a curious Cathedral, built at a time when Christianity filled the mind of the artist, but before it had taken a peculiar architectural form. Of course there is a struggle between the old form (the Roman architecture, with its round arches and heavy, solid columns), and the new sentiment, which at length shot up into those wonderful buildings, the Gothic churches. Oh, how they fill the heart, those old piles ! You feel that they grew up just as the great forests grow ; that each age altered them, and took away and added, just as it does in nature. Here, however, the old form prevails, but on the portal the artist has lavished his genius in wanton luxuriance ! He has carved out the Almighty over the door, and the angels on the slopes of the sides, and the Last Judgment, with apostles, and saints, and devils *à discrétion*. The whole looks odd enough. It might excite devotion in the Middle Ages ; now it only makes one laugh and think of the boys that creep before they walk.

We came here from Avignon, and from Lyons to Avignon, through a very interesting country. Here " Cæsar swam the Rhone, but kept his Commentaries dry" (every school-boy knows they are dry still), and here Hannibal passed the same stream. A whole host of recollections comes up in my mind as I ride along the banks of the Rhone and read Cæsar's own words, and think of what has taken place since he came here, and had a "talk" with the Helvetii in this neighbourhood.

*   *   *   *   *   *

Here everything differs so much from home, and I depart so much from my common way of life, that I sometimes doubt if I am the same Theodore Parker that used to live at West Roxbury. I am half inclined to believe that he is a mythological person, and has no real historical existence. But when I come to a college, a book-store, or a Roman temple, and above all to the *Palais des Papes* at Avignon, I believe that I am my old self, not a whit changed.

I hope you preach at Spring Street, in my absence; and if the brethren do not freely exchange with Francis and Ripley, really I shall think it shameful. I care not for myself a *sous*.

TO DR. FRANCIS.

November, 1843.

I heard several lecturers at the Sorbonne—Damiron, amongst others. He lectured about Gassendi. He looks a little like Dr. Lamson, and is about as old. He comes into the *salle*, pours his *eau* upon his *sucre*, and stirs it up; lays an ill-written MS. before him, looks up and says "*Messieurs*," then looks down upon his paper and never raises his nose from his notes once during the *leçon*. He flourishes his left hand continually, while he holds on the text with his right. He has not written out his discourse in full, so he begins, goes back, and begins again, in almost every sentence. His talk is as ragged as that of ——, but not half so rich.

Jules Simon is not twenty-six years old. I went to his *salle* half an hour before the time; it was half full then. By-and-bye, I heard a step at the private door, and the audience clapped their hands. Then entered a finely formed young man, elegantly dressed, with one of the finest countenances I ever saw—pale, with deep, dark eyes; he looks religious, mystic, and philosophic. He lectured on Proclus and his school, on the mysticism of Proclus, its origin and effects. He had no notes, but leaned back in his chair, looked up towards the ceiling, then at the audience, then began. His words were musical, his manner perfect; it was the *beau ideal* of lecturing. He did not quite do justice to Plato, for he went back to Plato to trace the mystical element in Proclus. I never heard or read a *neater* exposition of doctrines than his of Plato's notions of God, though I think them a little erroneous.

Once I heard De Portet lecture on the Law of Nature to four listeners, which was four more than the lecture deserved. I went many times to hear some of the theological faculty, but the knaves did not lecture when they promised.

I heard Lenormant several times. He is the successor, or substitute, of Guizot, and is an able fellow, witty and wise. In one lecture he undertook to prove the "unity of humanity" by demonstrating that all the race descended from one pair. He said he could not prove the fact in one *leçon*, but it was a fact as much to be taken for granted now-a-days as any of the admitted truths of astronomy. Then he pointed out the means of proof, and flourished away with great brilliancy. Again, he lectured on the influence of Christianity upon the institutions of Europe. I heard him discuss quite ably the rise and progress of asceticism in the Church. It was wise and witty, too, what he said. Christianity looked in the face the great problems of the nineteenth century, the problem of *Egalité*, of *Travail*, of *Fraternité*. Cœnobitism, Asceticism, and Monachism were various solutions, not the *real* solution. Christianity is yet to give that in the form of a new society, for which the St. Simonians are in the right to strive. He carried us off to the Thebaid, and gave pictures of the life there, quoting from a translation of Jerome made and printed in the age of Louis XIV.: so he made a contrast between the Christianity of the Thebaid and that of Versailles.

TO THE SAME.

November 20.

Yet, after all, there is a certain unity of character in the French that has its merit. They are always gay; gay in their business, gay in their religion; their churches even have a style that is peculiarly French—at least since the time of Delorme all their architecture has been gay. The Frenchman would "dance before the Lord." Now, John Bull all the week long is spinning cotton, raising potatoes, fatting oxen, and sending ships to the end of the world, He has managed matters so that the income of his Church is £44,000 more than the income of all the other Churches of Europe put together, and so that six per cent. of his whole population receives support from the public purse. All the week long he never thinks of God, nor cares for truth and righteousness; but Sunday comes, and then John is mighty religious all at once. He transports to Botany Bay a man who danced round a maypole, and shuts up an old woman in jail because she sold apples during the hours of service Sunday morning. Here is no *unity*, at the least.

TO THE SAME.

Florence, January 28, 1844.

The effect of the church within—dark, vast, and solemn as it is—must be felt—fancied it cannot be. The rich music of more than a hundred voices (men's and no-men's), joined with the sweet notes of an organ placed high up in the wall, rises and falls upon the ear in tides of harmony that fill the soul with reverence, with zeal, with faith, and waken love of God, just as the south wind of summer when it comes tossing gently the tops of the pines. I love the music and the architecture of Catholicism; its doctrines, its rites, and its general effect, I must say, I *hate* all the more in Europe than I hated at home.

In one church I saw a great crowd of people about a certain door, so I drew near and found the *avviso* setting forth that all persons who on that day visited a particular shrine of the Virgin should have plenary indulgence for forty days. I went with the multitude, so I need not fear for the next six weeks. Indeed, the Pope offers plenary indulgence for all sins—past, present, and to come—to all such as attend five sermons that are to be preached in Holy Week at Rome this very year. I shall hear not only five but fifty, if possible, and so shall be able to "*indulge*" you and eight others when I get home, and save them by vicarious atonement; it will be the height of mercy to do so.

*　　*　　*　　*　　*　　*

Here, amongst the mummeries, they serve God by ringing bells. I wonder no one ever thought of doing the thing by firing cannon. It seems to me to be peculiarly proper for a military people, and they might find warrant for it in Scripture (as for all other things), only by adopting a slight emendation of the common text, " Praise Him with psaltery," reading (by conjecture) " with saltpetre." Pray suggest it to Dr. Noyes.

*　　*　　*　　*　　*　　*

There is one thing which I always admired in the *idea* of the Catholic Church, to wit, its democracy. It (ideally speaking) honours *personal qualities* alone, the real virtues of real men, the apostles, the saints (who are not honoured for accidental qualities, as wealth and fame, but for what are reckoned sterling merits of their own), the prophets (of past times), and Christ himself. The lives of these men are immortalized in stone and brass, and great men and kings are told to kneel down before their relics, or their images, for nothing is so great as goodness. You feel this idea becoming a sentiment in a Catholic church, and it buds out towards an action, and you say, " Fools and blind! damned fools and stone-blind! Why not go and do likewise, honouring virtue by *action*, not with brass and talk ?" If a real man were to come and stand in these old churches, over the graves of the noble, with these images of the holy and inspired before the eyes of all his hearers, it seems to me he might make every stone in Santa Croce ring again with eloquence, and every heart burn with love towards man, and faith towards God. Yet, perhaps, he would feel that a marble temple, profuse with silver and gold and precious stones, and cunning handiwork more precious than either, was not the place in which to preach humility, the greatness of the soul, the nothingness of life's poor distinctions. No: the marble devils would grin at him from the arches, and he would fare forth into the free air and predict the destruction of that temple.

Oh, is the time ever to come when men shall be content to honour God by keeping His laws, being good and doing good, when they shall know and feel that the life of heaven is the real service ? The longer I live the more my reverence for the real God and the real religion—yes, and the real preacher of it—continues to deepen, widen, and make my heart throb; but at the same time my abhorrence of all false gods and false religions, and false preachers, too, waxes stronger and stronger. I know while men are as now, there must be such things; but I know also that if men are ever to be made better, such things must be warred on, not with earthly weapons, as cunning and spite (the Devil will beat all the saints with them), but with swords of celestial temper, and celestial keenness, too.

I have now had five months' leisure to consider my own position. I feel all its melancholiness, the severity of the task laid on me; but I feel, too, that I must *on, on;* that the time of rest will never come in my day, and for me; but, so long as I live, that I must war against the false gods and their priests as false. I have done little hitherto; if health continues I may, perhaps, do somewhat. I am grateful for this opportunity to pause in the middle of my course and see where I am going. I have done wrong things, no doubt; but, the more I think of it, the more the general tendency of my path seems to me the true one, and the less do I feel an inclination to turn away or to stand still.

Let me leave this theme. I thank you most heartily for remembering me in absence, and not the less for the good words that you are speaking to the few at Spring Street. Do tell me if "the brethren" exchange with you, and who; what Ripley is doing, and what the *Examiner* does with that good, sound, modest man, Lamson, at its head. Do you know all his worth? He is a noble fellow.

I am sorry you should say what you do about yourself. It is not given to many men to taste or even see the fruits of their labour. You *ought* to have the consciousness of having done more than any clergyman of your age, in planting principles that will bear fruit for mankind. If you continue at Cambridge a few years, I know the result will be to impress on the Unitarian sect the spirit of thoughtful and serious inquiry, of the greatest individuality conjoined with the widest toleration.

You speak about your sister's * book. I read some of the " Letters " as they appeared from time to time, and on the passage I read the book anew, and with increased delight. She has spoken nobly a noble word, and may God bless her more and more! It is a great thing to speak words that sink into the nation's heart. It is not every passing cloud that rains drops into the sea which shall become pearls; it is only the dews of Heaven which can do that.

TO THE SAME.

Rome, March 18, 1844.

My dear Friend,—I owe you many thanks for all your kindness in writing to me when I am a stranger in a strange land. You tell me good tidings also. I am rejoiced to know of the doings of Ripley, Channing, and Brownson. But I hear that the latter has done what he advised the Unitarians to do, " re-establish the *Boston Quarterly.*" I suppose he will devote it to the overturn of the principles established in the first series. I rejoice very much in the *Fourier* movement, not that I accept the statements of F., but because I think our present form of society is irrational and unchristian; that society makes criminals, and then hangs them; that trade (in the main) is robbery, and "justice" catches only at petty rogues—never forgiving their offences, gradually makes them worse, and at last hangs them. Men are born in Boston into a condition far worse than that of the Esquimaux. Strong men build their castles by the hands of the weak and out of the property of the weak. The feudalism of money is not so bad as the feudalism of

* Mrs. Lydia Maria Child, who had just published the first volume of her brilliantly written " Letters from New York," which was followed by another of like excellence.

birth, nor that so bad as the feudalism of the sword, but too bad to be borne in a Christian land, it seems to me. I do not believe the Socialists see very clearly what they would be at, yet they will help open men's eyes, it seems to me. Three things are needed to make a complete revolution—the sentiment, the idea, the action. I fancy their sentiment is not far from right, but if their idea be wrong, so must their action be. I see no cure for the evil but this, to give each individual clear views of the right, and then leave it to him to do what he thinks best. A complex evil has a simple cure, it seems to me. England is the richest country in the world, perhaps, but that in which there is the most misery. It is the paradise of the rich, the purgatory of the wise, and the hell of the poor. In Italy there is much begging, but less starving. One million of the English are fine men ; what are the nineteen millions ?

Now, we, the Yankee nation, are going in just the same way as the English, and, unless we change our whole system, radically, in regard to the pursuit of wealth and the pursuit of power, we shall come to just the same result, and have the Christian feudalism of gold in Boston as in London. But of this when we meet face to face.

I think I shall become a Catholic, that I may be *Cardinal*, and will come to Boston, in my red coach, with three footmen on behind—that is the way they ride here—and will preach a sermon on humility and contempt of this world, and assure the people at the end that there is no salvation out of the Church. Here I have seen not a few relics of the saints, and other worthies, enough to convert a heathen. Let me name them : the chains of St. Peter; those of Paul; the column Christ leaned on when twelve years old ; the veil which burst asunder when he gave up the ghost; the actual well of Samaria (the woman of Samaria, I suppose, is lost—but, enough could be found here to which the words of the Fourth Gospel would apply just as well) ; the twenty-eight steps of Pilate's house, down which Christ was led to be crucified; and a piece of the true Cross. Besides these, they have the heads of Peter and Paul. I wish they were on some of their shoulders. I wonder that they have not the original " tables of the law " written by the finger of Jehovah, which Moses broke, or the garments which Elohim made for Adam and Eve.

They tell a pleasant story about St. Peter. A persecution once broke out while that Apostle was at Rome. He did as at Jerusalem— cut and run. But, as he was getting towards Ostia with might and main, down comes the Lord Jesus from heaven, and alights on the ground before him. The people can still show the dent where his feet lighted on the flint. The footprints are actually to be seen at this very day, marks of the toes and all! Then, too, I have been into the prison where Paul was confined—the famous *Tullianum.* They tell you that Peter was there also; and point out a spring that started up miraculously on a certain occasion, and Peter baptized forty-nine Roman soldiers in it, all of whom became martyrs. Apart from the murmurs of tradition, it makes a man's heart beat a little to stand in the prison where there is little room to doubt that Paul was once held as a felon. It carries you back over 1800 years—to the time when Christian was a name of contempt, and cost a man his life. I went to the place " where Paul dwelt in his own hill-house," &c. You forget the Church, the

Pope, the Cardinals, and think of that man who found Christianity the faith of a few poor fishermen, and left it flourishing in all the great cities of the world. I never felt so near the Apostle as at Rome. I have been to the Catacombs, which interest me more than almost anything at Rome. You know their history, of course. Here I saw proofs enough that some of the alleged "corruptions of Christianity" date back to 107 A.D. The worship of the Virgin can be traced nearly as far; that of the invocation of saints for the dead quite to that very year, I think. Indeed, if I were an Episcopalian, I must needs become a Catholic. You find the ceremony of saying mass, as at present, pretty distinctly traced back to the beginning of the second century; and the Catholics mention a symbol of transubstantiation which shows that it was well known in the second century, and pretty early too. In the Catacombs there are chapels, of course; in the chapels are frescoes painted in the second century (at the latest, in the early part of it), representing the miracle at Cana, in such conjunction with the saying Mass, that it shows a distinct allusion to the transformation of the bread and wine into the body and blood of Christ; at least, they say so. Of course, *I* should laugh at any argument built on such premises, even if I admitted the premises; but many would be overwhelmed by it. In the tombs you find the bottle of blood, which marks a martyr who died a bloody death; and often the instrument of his martyrdom, still sticking in his bones, or laid beside him. Some of the Catacombs have not yet been explored, as they have been filled with earth ever since the time of Constantine (I think), which an inundation of the Tiber deposited there. Therefore, here is no chance for saying, "The monks of the Middle Ages did it!" as some have often said. I should like to sit in this city of graves, and read the Fathers. Here, in Rome, is one Father Marchi, a priest, who has devoted his life to the study of the Catacombs. He went with us, and explained everything; besides that, he took me through a fine collection of Christian antiquities in the Roman College (the great priest establishment), and showed me curiosities without stint, relating to the early Christians, bottles of dried blood of the martyrs, instruments of torture, images of Christ, of the Virgin, &c., &c.

Mr. Shaw sent me a letter of introduction to a young American Catholic here. He introduced me to several Catholics, eminent men and capital scholars, to a D.D., a Bishop, and a Cardinal. I have talked a good deal with them about their *faith*, though I have not disputed, but only questioned. I feared that I might have sometimes done them injustice, but I think I have not. I have found them universally kind, perfectly free from cant; they don't draw down the corners of their mouth, nor talk through their nose, nor roll up the whites of their eyes, and say "O-ô-ô-ô!" There is much about the Catholic Church that I always liked—its music, architecture, paintings, statues. Besides, there is a long list of saints, whom I truly reverence, enrolled on its calendar. The Church is democratic (in the good sense) in appointing its saints. None are made saints except for *personal* qualities; not for wealth, or birth, or power, but goodness. What if they do pray to the saints, as the Protestants say, or through them, as *they* say? The true God, I take it, would as lief be called St. Cecilia as Jehovah; and a true prayer must be acceptable to the true God. I told a Jesuit Father so, the other day; but he said that was an *odious doctrine*—it justified idolatry.

I love to hear Bishop Baggs talk about the Catholic doctrine. He is one of the most learned men in Rome, and one of the gentlest and kindest of men. I love him much. The Catholic Church practically, I think, cultivates the feelings of reverence, of faith, of gentleness, better than the Protestant Churches; but I can't think it affects the conscience so powerfully, and I know that at present it does not appeal to the reason or practical good sense. How true it is that it takes the whole Church to preach the whole Gospel!—but few men will see it is so. One can't see beyond Unitarianism; another will not budge beyond the Westminster Catechism, and here a whole Church refuses to go an inch beyond the decrees of the Council of Trent. However, while Bishop B. says, " *Out of the Catholic Church* is no salvation," he adds, " *but none is damned except for his own fault, and many may be in the Soul of the Catholic Church who are not in its Body.*" God only knows who! I wish I could think better of the priests here. A " divinity student," an American neophyte, said he had known hundreds of priests, and never one who had defiled himself with woman!—that they were far purer in all respects than the Protestant clergy! But a Roman, also a Catholic, said that about one-tenth were pure, conscientious men; the rest—here he shrugged his shoulders, and said, " The walls have ears!" About a year ago, in a conventual school for young ladies, seven of them were unexpectedly found in the same state with Rhea Sylvia, but in this case the *deus ex machinâ* was a priest. I asked a *guide de place* one day about the priesthood. He looked over his shoulder, and in bad French, gave me an awful account of them.

Here each person is obliged to take the Communion once a year, and before the Communion to confess and perform any penance that is enjoined: if they refuse they are excommunicated! This, of course, is adapted to make hypocrites of bad men, and martyrs of good ones. Then, besides, here is an inquisition; if a Catholic be found uttering heresies he is clapped into the inquisition, when " Heaven help him!" as Uncle Toby said. He is not tortured, but only confined. I am told there are about 400 or 500 in it now. It is close to St. Peter's. They don't prevent freedom of *thought* : a man may think what he pleases, but as Dr. —— said, " *What is the use of talkin' on't?* " A rigid political censorship is exercised over the press. Austria has a voice in that and a theological censorship. English newspapers are often stopped at the Post-office because they contain *incendiary matter*. If our friend the Heaven-stormer, were to come here, he would find his *Quarterly* in the " Prohibitorum" directly, and himself—anywhere but at ease, I am thinking. If I wanted to convert a fop to Christianity, I think I would send him to Rome; but if I wanted to put a philosopher in the Catholic Church, I would send him anywhere but to Rome. Nowhere is there more to disgust a thinking man with its doctrines or its practical effects. However, here are also the bright ornaments of the Church, such men as Cardinal Odescalchi, such women as the late Princess Borghese, both of whom spent enormous sums of money and their whole lives in works of mercy. I really believe, that in no place and no Church are such persons more honored than here, in the Church at Rome. When the Princess was to be buried, 500 young men of Rome took off the horses from the hearse, and themselves drew the body to the grave. One day they will make both her and the Cardinal saints. Their doctrine ofthe Communion of Saints is beautiful to the feelings, not like the cold wordy rubric of the Protestants. Here, at Rome, all is in the hands of the priests. Over a lying-in hospital I saw "R.C.A."* The irony of nature is a little sharp sometimes! Here, lottery tickets are sold by authority; the R.C.A. manages that affair also, and once a fortnight there is a drawing, and the apostolical functionary appears in a balcony, and the list of numbers is read off in his presence to the people. You go to the Colosseum; in the centre of it is a cross, and a little tablet states that everybody who kisses that shall receive plenary indulgence for 200 days; another at the entrance states that indulgence for a year and forty days shall be given to all who kiss that! In a beautiful church, that of Sta. Maria Maggiore, is preserved the portrait of the Blessed Virgin by St. Luke. It is in a beautiful chapel, built by the Borghese family, and a Bull of the Pope, in marble, on the wall, tells, that if mass be said in that chapel for any of the faithful who are dead, and have died penitent, they shall be forthwith delivered from purgatory *quibus-cunque non obstantibus.*

It is difficult to say what is the present condition of the Catholic Church; they are certainly making great exertions to extend their faith in all parts of the world; the present Pope is a pious and excellent man, I should judge, one that fears God and loves mankind, believing himself fallible as a man, but infallible as Head of the Church, and his character has had an influence on the Church. I should be sorry to see the Catholic Church fall now, for which of the Protestant sects could take its place? Perhaps it will outlive them all, for there is a terrible unity in its system, and it holds to its first principles with remorseless fidelity, while the Protestants feel that their principle of sole reliance on the Holy Scriptures as the only and sufficient word of God and rule of faith, is felt by many to be false, and known to be so by some, and yet they will not admit it, and fall back on absolute religion, taking all tradition (scriptural or non-scriptural) for what it is worth.

But I will not annoy you any more with such talk. Let me go to other things. And, before I forget it, Father Marchi is publishing a work describing the Catacombs—not merely the old but those hitherto inedited; the work will correct the errors of former writers on that subject, and will be a valuable contribution to the history of art, and still more to that of Christianity in a period for which we possess unfortunately but few documents. Cannot it be got for the College Library? When finished it will cost about 60 dollars.

Shall I describe to you the wonders of Rome? No, not I; you must come to know them. I went up to the top of the Capitol soon as I got to Rome. I saw one mountain in the distance, standing by itself, and said to a friend, " *Videsne ut alta stet*," &c., for then it was covered with snow. Below me were the Seven Hills, not prominent, but made out with a little difficulty; the Forum, a dirty irregular oblong space where the countrymen leave their carts and oxen to bait. The Colosseum is close at hand; the ruins of the Palace of the Cæsars cover the Palatine, and an Englishman has a house on the very top.

* *Romanum Collegium Apostolicum.*

The greater part of old Rome, the Rome of the Republic, is covered with vineyards and gardens!—cabbages and artichokes grow where the pride of the Cæsars once held its dwelling-place! Alas for Rome! She is the queen dowager of the nations. Her power has passed away; but a shadowy respect is still paid to her name, and the recollection of her greatness yet awes the world. I have studied the relics of Pagan Rome, but I cannot tell where it ends and Christian Rome begins. When they baptized the people, they baptized their institutions; alas, I feel that I am in old Pagan Rome still! I was presented to His Holiness the other day. He looks mild and benevolent, has written some books, and is thought a clever man by nature, apart from his infallibility.

Norton's book is as I fancied, but does not he attack the authenticity of the books of Moses? How is the *Examiner* in the hands of L. and G.? Remember me to Sears when you see him and Stetson. Ever yours, good bye,   T. P.

All your books shall be diligently sought for and duly forwarded. I have made arrangements with a house at Florence for the purchasing Italian books. Write again soon, tell me all the personal gossip and literary and theological news.

TO THE SAME.

Berlin, May 26, 1844.

My dear Friend,—Men, in respect to their mobility, or passive faculty of being moved, may be divided into three classes, viz.: 1, the ductile, who may be led by the hand; 2, the tractile, who can be drawn by the nose; and, 3, the *projectile*, who can be *kicked by the part* which is wanting in cherubs, but fully developed in school-boys—in short, by what the "Secretary of the Commonwealth of Massachusetts," commenting upon Moses, called a *retiring glory.** Well, in Italy, the Pope thinks the people consist only of the *tractile* and *projectile* classes, so he sets on the tractors (the priests) and the projectors (the soldiers) to conduct affairs. In Austria, the Government proceeds on the supposition that *all* are projectile, and, therefore, has soldiers everywhere, and gives its faithful subjects a sight of its cannons in every little village. At home there are a few who think that mankind are ductile, but the political partisans suppose all the nation to be merely tractile. Nobody, but General Jackson and George III. ever thought we were projectile.

And here I am, in the heart of Germany, in the very spot where the " Geist des Deutschlands " culminates. I have wished you were with me a thousand times here in Europe, but never more than now, for none *deserves* so much to come, and none would enjoy it more, for you have the many-sidedness that receives, the magnanimity that welcomes, and the soul that appreciates all that is good.

Excuse me for saying this *to* you, for I forgot myself and the limits

---

* "One day," said Dr. ——, " I went out to Cambridge as a delegate for the Society for promoting Theological *Knowledge*, to see what Dr. Palfrey was doing. I had my doubts of his fitness for the station, but I went into the lecture-room. He was expounding Moses (at first I felt like Apostle Philip when he saw *one* reading Esaias). He took that *very difficult* passage, ' Thou shalt not look upon my *face*,' &c., and went on translating, ' But a retiring glory shalt thou see.' I confess I felt ashamed of my doubts, and was myself instructed."

of epistolography for a moment. How you would riot in the *Bibliothek* and smile at the philosophical casuistry one hears lectured forth, and look with wonder on *Hengstenberg* discovering the Trinity in the plural form of *Elohim* (and also in *Behemoth* I suppose). Berlin is so full of great men that nobody looks at one more than the Parisians look at the giraffe. I believe it is rather a *disguise* here to be a great man. You will say, in your wicked way, that is so everywhere, and in your "Unitarian way" will cite the case of Jesus and Socrates (nobody but the Unitarians ever mention them in the same week you know) as examples; that is true, but here the great men are so common that if —— ever were to come here, he would be thought a very common-place sort of man, fit only to eat beef and cream-cakes. But *revenons à nos moutons*, to the great men again. There are 180 of them connected with the University, not counting the Grimms, who would make a score; then there are Crown Princes, and *Fürsten*, and *Erz-herzogen*, and that sort of vermin, in any quantity. I always thought the German philosophers were lean, pale sort of men who "on the barren heath," as Göthe has it, did nothing but think, in short did nothing but think of thinking. It is not so; they look sleek, well-fed, and cosy as other men. Drs. Twesten and Marheineke are plump as partridges. Indeed, I have not seen but one lean man in Berlin, and he was a Yankee. I heard a professor the other day (a sleek man of forty, with a great forehead, and great white teeth, and great black whiskers tied under his chin) lecture an hour or less on *Dagesh forte*, making a slight digression upon *Dagesh lene*, and an episode upon *Chappik*. I thought of your philosophical colleague and wished he had my seat. He would have gone up in raptures, and have been (what has happened to Job and the Prophets) *translated!* But here I am telling you about German affairs and not saying a word about how I got here. Well: then we rode four days and four nights in a diligence to Bologna, from Rome, and then went to Venice—which, by the way, is such a city as Neptune might have dreamed of when a little drunk with ambrosia (and Amphitrite)—thence to Verona, stopping at classical Padua; thence two hundred miles up the valley of the Adige, through the Tyrol to Innspruck. It was delightful to get away from the dark wily character of the Italians to the open faces and blue eyes of the Germans. You feel that you are in *Deutschland* very soon. The horses are well fed, the asses disappear and the priests; the women are seen in abundance. In France and Italy the *femme de chambre* was almost always a *garçon*; there is a certain safety in employing these. But soon as we came to Germany, we found some nice girls to make your bed, move the table, &c., girls with great open blue eyes, rosy cheeks, and well-developed forms. But, alas! I am afraid that the virtue of the Germans is not just what old Roman Tacitus says it was in his day. However, some of the Germans say it was *peu de chose* even then, and he painted an ideal and no actual people solely to shame the shabby Romans and their women.

We went from Innspruck to Munich, saw many festivities—for the King of Bavaria had just given a daughter to the son of the *Erzherzog* Carl of Austria, who in his day is to be *Erzherzog*. Not only that; a wretched son of the said King of Bavaria was just married to the pretty daughter of the Grand Duke of Tuscany; the poor girl was given away in her cradle, and when she grew up had the audacity to love the Duc D'Aumale, but married the stupid Bavarian none the less, for princes no more want love in their wedlock than water in their wine.

This same Bavarian and his Tuscan wife came from Italy at the same time with ourselves, so we also rode through their triumphal arches, and heard the music intended for them. From Munich we went to Ratisbon, saw its lions, Kepler's monument amongst others, the famous Valhalla —you know all about it, I have no doubt, and that Luther has no bust among the heroes of Germany, though the Stolbergs have a place in the national temple. Then we went down the Danube in a steamer to Vienna. Two beautiful days we passed there on that majestic river. The spring was just calling out the individualities of the trees: we had all the varieties of scenery conceivable, from bustling towns to lonely *castles* (so-called by men, by God *robber's dens*), and mountains still covered with primeval forests. I expected to meet old Armenius or Attila at the very least. The Archduke Charles was in the same boat with my humble self, and a small boat it was, too, to contain two such great men, and *we* had, of course, all sorts of honours paid to *us*, as we went along. At Vienna we saw the lions, Von Hammer Purgstall amongst them, and then went to Prague. I saw John Huss's house. A *Schneidermeister* (Boss-tailor), lives in it now, and sundry mantua-makers, wine-dealers, &c.; the famous university, the grave of Tycho Brahe; and the place where John of Nepomuck was thrown off the bridge into the river. It is a sacred place now, and John is the patron of bridges —a pretty piece of irony that. We saw the famous *Judenstadt* and the old burial-ground of the Jews. I don't know that Abraham, Isaac, and Jacob are not buried here—perhaps Noah and Adam (Dr. Noyes can tell), were the place old enough. The Hebrew boy, who shows the place and reads the Rabbinical inscriptions into most uncouth Bohemian German showed me a gravestone for the year 600 A.D.! I believe all that the Jews tell me, and they have not lost their national peculiarity. In old times, if a Hebrew were asked for a truth, *he told a story* (at Venice, now, "*parola Ebrea*" means a *lie*). I never see a Jew but I think of Moses, and Noah, and Baal, and Balaam. (By the way, Balaam is the only saint the Romans have taken out of the Old Testament.) I don't feel at all anxious to convert them to the popular form of Christianity, for I think the *nonsense* of the Rabbis is nearly as good as the *nonsense* of the Fathers, schoolmen, and doctors of divinity. To real Christianity, God send that all the world may be converted, though it is just what I think the above-mentioned three classes know little about.

From Prague we went to Dresden down the Elbe; a beautiful river it is, too, with Bohemian villages and robber's dens (vulgarly castles) on its banks, and nice Saxon towns, with *no cannon* in them; for the King of Saxony is not an Austrian, so he has faith in something beside cannon. From Dresden we came here, passing through Wittemberg, and at a distance doing reverence to the church where Luther posted up the 95 theses, and where the grave covers his hardy body. I ought to add that in one of the towns we passed by on the Danube, there is a street called "*Dort Hinab*" from this circumstance: once when Luther was there, some enemies wished to seize him, and as he turned to escape, the

Devil (who loved Martin like a brother, in spite of the inkstand) shouted out " Down there! " pointing to a little lane. There is a *fresco* representing the event. Of course, the miracle is a fact, if there is any truth in *Douglas's Criterion* and Leslie's *Short Method.*

Here I am at Berlin, in the third story of the British Hotel. Do you know what sort of a place Berlin is ? No ? Imagine a sandy plain forty miles square, with one or two nasty rivers trying to get through it, but doubtful all the time that they had taken the right way. In the centre of this plain, and on the banks of the most doubtful of the rivers, imagine a great number of brick houses covered with stucco, and a few churches, &c., of the same material. Then imagine one street sixty or seventy feet wide, and two miles long, with another street two hundred feet wide and one mile long, having four rows of lime-trees in it, a foot walk in the centre, and two carriage ways, one on each side ; then add some hundreds of other streets, all straight, and you have a *conception* of Berlin. For the moving part of it, imagine 1000 hackney coaches, the drivers with cows'-tails on top of their caps, 100 private carriages, 400 drags for beer, 150 carts, and wagons for other business, 30,000 soldiers, 1650 students, 180 professors (it will take a day to imagine them all), a King, Baron Von Humboldt, and 270,000 others, Imagine the King with a belly like Uncle Tom Clarke, the students with mustachios, the professors lecturing on *Dagesh lene,* the King " counting out his money," Baron Von Humboldt sleeping on his laurels, and the 270,000 smoking, walking, weaving, making pipes, and getting dinner, and you have an idea of the *personale* of Berlin. I have heard lots of professors since I have been here—Schelling, amongst others. He lectures on the Offenbarungs-Philosophie. I heard him twice. He looks old and feeble, is seventy, his articulation is feeble ; he has an audience of 150 or 200 : most of them come only from curiosity, or to amuse themselves at the senilities of this *philosophe.* He hates Hegel. In one lecture he took up a certain notion that Hegel had wrapped up in many words, and after disengaging it, said, "Accordingly, when Hegel's doctrine is understood—which seldom happens with many of his followers—it is an absurdity!" He is not professor, but member of the Academy of Sciences, so has a right to lecture, and avails himself of it. The right in a Mem. Soc. Scientiæ is inalienable! His coming here, I should judge, was a failure ; Hegelism flourishes like a green bay-tree, full of leaves, and *threatening* fruit. The King don't like it. Bruno Bauer has lost his *Lehrfreiheit* (liberty to teach), so he abandons theology and takes to writing history. I never thought Bruno Bauer was a great man, though he made a great noise ; the other Baur, whom Mr. Norton holds in such disesteem, is really a man of *Tiefsinnigkeit* (profundity) and genius too. The other day I heard Werder, a young Hegelian, lecturing on "*Logik.*" The point at issue was "*Bestimmtheit.*"* He got into a great passion and a desperate fix with his *Bestimmtheit,* trying, as I dimly gathered, to discover the *Ur-Bestimmung.* He said, in *Bestimmung* there was *Daseyn* (being) *and Realité.* Hereupon a fat, chubby student, with cheeks like one of your class-

---

* Literally meaning Definiteness ; but, in this connection, connoting the essential ground (in reason) of all necessary conceptions.

mates, evidently his Ma's darling, tried hard to conceive the difference; but after numerous ineffectual attempts gave up in despair. Then said the professor, " In *Daseyn* there is *Etwas real und Anders*" (something real and something else); now, " *Etwas ist durch und durch Etwas und nicht Anders; Anders ist durch und durch Anders und nicht Etwas.*"*

He got into quite a dithyrambic mood upon this, put his finger on the organ of individuality, then laid it alongside of his nose, then flourished it in the air. It is no easy thing to go down to the profound of Hegelism. You must take off your *Sinnlichkeit* (corporeity), which is all of many men; then lay aside your *Vorstellungen* (notions), which is, with most men, like plucking Æsop's jay; then take off your *Begriff* (conception). Then you are "far too naked to be ashamed;" in short, you are an *Urmensch* (primitive man), a *blosse Geist* (pure spirit); you have then the proper "alacrity in sinking;" you go down, down, down, and learn that *Seyn* is equal to *Nicht-seyn*. Yet, after all my *persiflage*, the hope of the world lies in Hegelism, *so they say*, and the King hates it. So do the ministers. Rosencrantz and Marheineke were going to start a journal, Hegelian, of course; the King forbade it; the minister called Marheineke before him and read his instructions, but would not let Marheineke have a copy. Thereupon the "faculty" had a meeting, and decided that this violated their " *Lehrfreiheit.*"

I don't know what will come of it. I get this from a Bremen paper, not a Prussian. Men at Berlin know nothing about it. Bettina published a book; it was *verboten* (forbidden) and *confiscirt* (confiscated) years ago. Then she wrote another, drove up to the King and asked, "May it be published?" "Yes," said the King. So it appeared with the title " Dies Buch gehört dem König." (This book belongs to the King.) It was worse than the first; the ministers "kicked," it would not do. Now she prints another, " Clemens Brentanos Laubenkrantz," Charlottenburg, 1844, (Clemens Brentano's Wreath), and will carry it to the King for his *privilege*. She is writing another on the sufferings in Silesia; a terrible book it is, too, to judge from the pages of the manuscript she read me. She showed me a letter from your sister, and sends thanks. Paulus's " Schelling" † sells here. Schelling tried to have it suppressed, but could not.

I have received accounts of your noble sermons at Spring Street, and thank you with all my might. I am somewhat in doubt that my poor head will be well when I return, for it is certainly in a dubious state now; but don't tell *this* to any one. You will soon have the Anniversary Week," ‡ and the Unitarian dinner. I send my good wishes to the " Brethren," but learn they are getting rapidly behind-hand in liberality and freedom. Of course, this does not surprise me; but what will they do with *you* and *Noyes* at the *School?* Really they are in a pretty " *Bestimmung* " (fix) with a real philosopher in one chair, and a scholar in the other, who denies the inspiration of the Old Testament and the authenticity of many parts of it, declaring too that myths run through the whole of the Gospels! Really it was a mistake to

* Something is out and out something, and not other; other is out and out other, and not something.

† Written by the famous Rationalist of Heidelberg—since dead.

‡ The last week in May; devoted to various clerical and philanthropic gatherings in Boston, and to a Unitarian banquet.

appoint both Noyes and you! Better have —— for the Bib. Lit. (he has a *fac-simile* of the first edition of "James' Version," as old Horner would say), and a P.P. for the other chair! Do resign, or become converted. Give my love to the faithful-hearted, and believe me just as really yours as of old, when no ocean "rolled between."

T. P.

I learn that the brethren don't exchange with you! I can hardly forgive it in ——, for he is a wise and good man. I fear that I may get you into trouble by your supplying so excellently (as all say) the pulpit at West Roxbury. God forbid it should be so. Will you, when you meet Brown, beg him to make some arrangements with an English house, if he can; and if he does, let me know before the middle of August, for I shall sail the 19th of August. Tell me all the news of Ripley, Brownson, R. W. E., Stetson, Lamson, Walker, and, above all, Francis. I have bought some books for you that you did not order, because you did not know of them, but to no amount. Adieu.

TO THE SAME.

Auerbach's Keller, 12 June, 1844.

DEAR DOCTOR FRANCIS,—I wonder if a Doctor of Divinity and Professor of Sacred Theology ever received a letter written in Auerbach's Keller, under the influence of the Unmentionable, who guided and directed the outgoings and incomings of Herr Dr. Faust, and was with him when he lay down and when he rose up? I am sure that *you* never did—therefore, in due course of time, if the mails fail not, you shall have that felicity! No doubt you will say I chose the place as one whose inspiration was congenial to my devout notions and theological whimsies! Well, men say Dr. F. (not Dr. Francis, but Dr. Faustus), was inspired by the Devil, but I have sometimes thought that he did nearly as much good as some men, who, it is said, were inspired quite differently. I won't pretend to judge, but I wish some D.D.'s, here and elsewhere, might be inspired by the same *Geist*,—whether it were a blue spirit or a black! Here are pictures of the great scenes of Dr. F.'s life painted, not so very badly either, just over my head. Here is the door out of which he rode on a tun (I take it he signed the pledge here before he went out!) You know the inscription, and I hope it will be a warning to you and to all others, who are willing to eat the Devil's bread. The rhyme states he got for his pains the Devil's reward! so don't you enter into a compact and covenant with that prolific master—pray advise all the students of Sacred Theology never to meddle with such things!

Well; one Martin Luther preached here in Leipsic, though not in Auerbach's Keller—as I now do. He held forth from a high balcony in the street. It stands there still.

Here the relentless hours overtook me, and notwithstanding my sacred occupation, drew me out of the famous Keller, and sent me off to Frankfort A.M. It is now the 20th of June, and I am near, not the tun of Dr. Faustus, but the great tun of Heidelberg. You must know that this tun is not that out of which Dr. Paulus drinks wine and beer, but one quite other and different. But let me not travel away from

Leipsic so fast. I wandered all about it, and a nice place it is too, with its 143 booksellers, its Brockhauses, its Tauchnitzes, its Schneiders, and Fleischers. But there is not a street called after them—not even a steamboat! By the way, a pious American said, "You see by the very names of things how wicked these Germans are. They call a steamboat a *damdship*. So you see that their 'Atheism' extends even to small affairs." At Leipsic I thought often of old Homer *—not the poet, but the preacher. I walked in the library of the University, and saw busts of many of his favourites; grim enough they looked too, as if they were made to write books for old Homer to read, or as if he were made to read books which they should write. Here were *Cocceius* and *Buchenhagen*, and fifty others, whose names I never heard pronounced except by the redactor of Bibles. At last I fell upon "Martinus Geier." He was H.'s particular friend: "Rich, very rich," said H., as he took down once for me a copy of" Geier." Here he was on the canvas, looking a Commentary on the Psalms, and threatening one on the Lamentations.

I have often thought I met Homer in old corners of old libraries—like the 20 Alcove in the former College Library. Here I have had him pursuing the shades of "various readings," and hunting through this and the other unreal "codex." Then I have fancied him in Purgatory, allowed to have a sight of "Tindal's Edition of 1536," yet not allowed to touch it. Then, too, going up to the ghost of great printers—Aldus, Froben, Elzevir, and Stephens—with the shadow of *his* Bible under his arm, trying to find a publisher, seeking rest but finding none. Still further, I have fancied him released from limbo and put in the only heaven he had prepared himself to enjoy, surrounded with forgotten tomes, his favourite "versions" among the rest, and conversing with the kindred spirits, from the eleventh century, who split hairs all their lives, were always labouring, and never came to the truth. Especially would he revel in the company of that great army—"part of the host have crossed the flood, and part are crossing now"—of grave theologians who have expounded the Song of Songs, explained the nature and extent of the sins of Solomon, and given curious conjectures about the Virgin Mary. But let H. go to his own place.

I saw old Hermann here. He looks like Deacon Arnold, who sits at your left-hand on Sundays, and looks up devoutly to catch the words of wisdom that fall from your lips; only the Deacon has the more intellectual face, and the best tempered. Hermann is about seventy-two years old, with little fiery, spiteful eyes that are never still. He is small and thin, has lost his teeth, and therefore does not speak distinctly. It was Sunday when I went to see him with Dr. Flügel. He had not been to church; indeed, I doubt that the *Deutsche Gelehrte* ever go, except to be baptized when they are babes. He had spurs on his feet, for he rides an hour every day in the riding-school. In consequence of this experience in riding, the illustrious man thinks he is peculiarly qualified to write on the equestrian terms in the Greek language. I remember to have seen him praised in some of the journals for his great knowledge of equestrian affairs, "gained," said the *laudator*, "by his daily and praiseworthy habit of riding on horseback." Now,

---

* Allusion is made to Dr. Homer, of Newton, a clergyman of the old school, whose Calvinism was tempered by a love of book-collecting. For the most part, however, his books were like his doctrines, very venerable and very futile.

if he bathes in a pan every day, he will be particularly able to write on the natatory terms in Greek, and on the naval tactics of the ancients in general. Pray suggest this to Felton, and you will no longer be a "speckled bird," and no jay will ever peck at you!

Hermann talked about America like a book (printed before 1492) ; about Felton and Woolsey. He thinks Lobeck is a *great* man, though not quite five feet high—that the Aglaophamus is a master-piece. I glory in the honour, which is hitherto peculiar to myself, of having *read it*. I heard Hermann lecture one day on the Trachiniæ, Vs. 1075. He lectured an hour in Latin ; sometimes he followed his notes —sometimes spoke with no reference to them. He got into a great heat on a small particle, and destroyed I do not know how many reputations without stint. You would have thought he looked over the author's shoulder, and knew, not only just what he wrote, but just what he meant by what he wrote. How much wiser critics are than authors! I have no doubt that Coleridge said something, for no prophecy is of any private interpretation, whereof he knew not the meaning. Now there will, no doubt, arise critics who will tell future generations just what Samuel Taylor Coleridge meant by his thesis, metathesis, and synthesis.

But let me come to sadder things. I went to Wheeler's grave.* It was a beautiful Sunday afternoon. The roses were all in blossom, and a sweet fragrance filled the whole spot where the dead lay sleeping. In a pleasant little enclosure was the grave of Wheeler—grassy, green. A pan of forget-me-nots was on the head of the grave, all fresh and blooming, bright-eyed and beautiful. The birds sung out a cheerful song. I almost envied him the repose which his body has here. A spirit, pure as his, is, I doubt not, tranquil and blest.

I got your letter—kind, welcome, hearty, as they always are. I need not say how much I thank you for having the courage to go and preach to the good folk at Spring Street. I fear that it may make you more of a *speckled bird*, as I hear the brethren don't exchange with you. Really, I have no patience with them. I do not care for myself, but to refuse to exchange with you at Spring Street is past endurance.

I have seen Ullman and Umbreit, having many talks with both ; also Creutzer and Paulus—a noble old fellow is Paulus, eighty-three years old, and hale and flourishing yet, hating nothing but Schelling. He talked an hour to me about German theology.

TO THE SAME.

Zurich, 12 July, 1844.

MY DEAR FRIEND,—If it were not for the horrible postage of letters I would write you at least once a week, for I see a thousand things, and think of ten thousand which I would gladly tell you of. To-morrow you will send forth your body of youths commissioned to bind and to loose,† and of course with the express understanding that

---

* Charles Stearns Wheeler, graduate of the class of 1837, son of a Lincoln farmer, self-educated, industrious, and filled with scholarly enthusiasm. He was a tutor of Greek at Cambridge, and edited Herodotus with taste and ability. He died at Leipsic some time previous to Mr. Parker's visit.

† Referring to the Annual Visitation Day at the Cambridge Divinity School, when the members of the Senior Class read their Essays before graduating and commencing to preach.

whatsoever and whomsoever they bind shall be bound in heaven, and the rest. Only imagine the youths fagotting for eternity both opinions and passions! By the way, do you believe Jesus Christ ever told his disciples, or anyone else, that *that which they bound on earth should be bound in heaven*? I don't believe a word of it, and think it one of the greatest heresies of the Church (the great parent of heresies) to have told such a story. But of this some other time, or no other time, as the case may be.

Here I am in the great theatre of the actions of Zwingle, with "Zurich's fair waters" spread out before me. I wish you were here to visit the famous places with me, and to talk of famous men, and to speak of our fathers that begat us. Since I saw you (or a letter) I have seen many famous men. At Heidelberg *I saw one Paulus*, who assures me that a third, at least, of the educated men of Germany are Anti-Trinitarian; but they dare not say a word against the Trinity, only to weaken certain modes of proving it. Rationalism, he says, is still the real faith of the nation, *i. e.*, of the educated. Schlosser* says the same, only adding that "my friend Paulus goes too far. To me the Bible is full of *poetry;* it is not truth but poetry: as such I like it. But if I tell the people so, they won't take it as poetry, but to their great loss will reject it altogether; so I call it *Offenbarung* (Revelation), and hurt nobody's feelings." Now, this is worthy of the ——. Pray instruct the hopeful youth in the art of mystification; it will save controversy, and hurt "nobody's feelings." I wish I could have learnt it, and certainly it was not for lack of precept and example that I did not, but from an actual stupidity in myself. But suppose you know your brother is in bondage to a lie, why not let him alone to find it out for himself? Let the blind lead the blind till they fall into the ditch. So far as I can learn, there is precious little faith among the Germans, in the old wives' fables of theology—much less than appears; only the knaves know how to mystify, to save appearances, and so forth. Of course I except such men as Hengstenberg, and in some measure Tholuck, who proves the Trinity *à priori*, and with no help from Revelation. I saw Ullman several times at Heidelberg; he is a pacificator, a *medium-iter* man. One party says $1 + 1 = 2$; another $1 + 1 = 4$. "No," says Ullman, "my dear friends, you are both mistaken, why quarrel? Truth takes the *medium iter,* $1 + 1 = 3$." There may be three parties in theology, viz.—1. That of *midnight;* and 2. That of *mid-day;* and 3. That of *twilight.* I think Ullman belongs the latter class, and stands on the *indifference-point* between day and darkness; yet he is a good man, and I like him much. He is a little *petit maître-ish*, dignified in littleness. Yet he is kind, amiable, fearing a split in *the party* (the *denomination*, as we say), more critical than courageous; in short, a very careful *Geheime-rath*, a *Consistorial-rath.* He tolerates both Strauss and Hengstenberg, and writes treatises on the "Sinlessness of Christ," and the "Reformers before the Reformation," letting alone his pacificatory articles in the *Studien und Kritiken.*

Umbreit is a dapper little man, that expounds the Old Testament, and, wearing fine linen, walks out with the young princes that study (?) at Heidelberg, and fearing to offend them, walks sidewise, with

* Professor of History—since dead.

his face towards the object of reverence—their sublime transparencies! I hope *you* will follow a practice so commendable, and recommend it also to the youths. Saw old Creutzer also, and had a long talk with him. He wondering that nobody had translated his *Symbolik* into English. I like the old toothless and skull-capped man very much, though he did not impress me as the thin, eagle-eyed old Paulus did. Paulus is a man of genius; Creutzer of talent, learning, industry only. I saw the Reuchlin-Meldeg, whom they call professor of philosophy here. He looks a good deal like —— or as —— will when he has gone to seed. In short, he is an exaggeration of ——, and keeps his skin so full of beer, that when he opens his mouth, as he often does for self-protection, it goes off like a beer-barrel, pop, fiz, pop! He has written a funny piece of *persiflage*, the *New Reineke Fuchs*; Göthe is the nightingale, Kant the lion, Fichte the eagle, Hegel the bear, and Schelling is Reineke. When the lion died, Reineke got his mane; when the eagle demised, he took his wings, and thus appearing as lion-eagle, taught that the Absolute was the Real and Ideal, adding that the Absolute was in *his* burrow. So then comes a quarrel between him and the bear, and the bear digs him out of his hole, and shows the admirers of Reineke that the Absolute was nothing but an old cloak hung over a white spot on a rock. So off goes Reineke, and digs another hole, and remains in it till the bear is dead. Then he comes out at open day, smelling to see if bear is really no more ; goes into bear's den and teaches his old nonsense. But an old eagle (Paulus) sees him, and comes like lightning from his eyrie, screams over him in the sky, soars down, tears off the lion's mane, the eagle's wings he had stolen, and leaves the fox naked, ashamed, and silent! It is a quite pleasant piece of nonsense.

Schlosser is a fine old gentleman, who wrote history for amusement, so he says, equally scorning money and renown. I saw Gervinus, who, they say, has read more books than any man in Germany, except Schlosser. He is about five-and-thirty, has a nice pretty little wife, plump as a partridge, and full of *Geist*. Then he lives in a pretty little cottage, on the banks of the Rhine, in the midst of a vineyard: don't suppose from the proximity that he ever drinks wine; no American would ever read his books if he did; of course he slakes his thirst at the Rhine. Well: Gervinus is just appointed Professor of History in Schlosser's place, for Schlosser would rather run away from his *publikum*, than have it run away from him. Of course, you know that Gervinus is one of the seven famous professors driven away from Göttingen. Ewald and the Grimms are of the same clique. They had the impudence to think, and to speak too, upon the powers that be, which of course are " of God," saith Paul, who never interfere with freedom of thought; they however lay a slight embargo on the spoken word, still more on the printed. At Heidelberg, they let a man not only speak after he has thought twice—but before he thinks once, as with us at home.

At Tübingen I saw Ewald, one of the hardest heads in Germany, at least, in the theological camp. But like other hard heads, his is a little wrong, and he quarrels with everybody, inclusive of his bread and butter, which latter proves his wrong-headedness. What is the use of great abilities, if they don't give you bread to your butter? I saw a good deal of Ewald, walked with him, took tea with, &c. I had no letter of introduction, but went boldly up and said, "Sir, I am an American, have read your works, and want to see you." No man that I have seen in Germany strikes me more as a man of genius than Ewald. Yet he is often wrong, I think. He has just published the first part of a History of the Hebrews. I have got it for you. He fears the Catholics; so do all the men that I have talked with, especially do they fear the Jesuits. I think they are right. Ewald represents the condition of things as alarming in Germany—the people have no freedom; no confidence in the Government, which they cordially detest.

Baur is a great hard man—big as Sam Ripley, and looks burly and savage. He is Hegelian all over. I have his History of the Trinity and other books, but he only looks through Hegelian glasses. He is a friend of Strauss, says Strauss is a Christian, that his writings have a deep and radical influence, all the stronger because not much talked of. Tholuck, and others, have told me about the "atheism" of the Hegelians, and that Strauss was no Christian. The talk about atheism is not limited to the circle about Boston. Somebody told me that Strauss was ho Christian. "Well," I said, "do you know anything evil of his life?" "Nothing. It is manly, noble, above reproach." "He has had his child baptized, besides. Eh?" "Yes." "Can you say as much in the defence of the Christianity of most cultivated men dignified with that name of Christian?" "No, certainly not. *I did not mean to say anything against the man!*"

I doubt that there is in Germany a university where there is a more able theological faculty. Here is Zeller, a young *Repetent* (such an office exists only at Tübingen—is like that of tutor at Oxford), is thought to be full of promise. You have seen his work on Plato. Here they concoct one of the best journals in Germany. It is Hegelian and new-schoolish of course. But I must not delay too long at Tübingen: we went through the Black Forest, Simmons with us, to Freiburg; saw the famous Munster, but old Professor Hug we did not see. Had it not been so late, I would have gone and told him, as I have a good many Germans, theologians and philosophers, "I have read your book." But the old gentleman had, perhaps, gone to bed, and in the morning I went off before it was decorous to call on the worthy Catholic. At Bâle, of course I saw De Wette, a compact little man, with a rather dry face, a little irritable, I fancy, perhaps something soured by his long disasters. He had not received the copy of my translation which Mr. Brown was to send him. This grieved me much. He is preparing a new edition still, but with no considerable alteration from the last. It will soon appear. During the time I stayed at Bâle, I saw a good deal of him, first and last, heard him lecture, &c., spent an evening with him at a friend's—his wife is away—dined with him at his son's. His functions are not great; he has from twelve to twenty students of theology, and the whole University of Bâle numbers but about sixty pupils! You may fancy that De Wette spends his time more agreeably in the study than elsewhere. But then he has leisure enough to write, and think, and speculate, and print, too. He knew but little of ecclesiastical affairs or theological matters with us. He only knew Norton as one that polemized against him. The light of the seven gold candlesticks, on the back of the academical lectures, had never gladdened his eye. Even Grey's Key was known only by name. Wouldn't it be a good plan for the "body," as Father Briggs says, to send out —— with a lot of Grey s Keys to enlighten the Germans withal? Some of "our excellent tracts" might also be circulated to advantage. Pray suggest it. Who knows but it may stay the flood of Rationalism which threatens to leave sundry dogmas where Grotius says the Ark may still be seen?

I heard De Wette lecture on the Harmony of the New Testament. He cut right and left and made no bones of saying that such a passage was probably *unächt* (spurious), that John knew nothing of it, &c. "Carpenter's Harmony" would set the Professor right on this point.

I cannot tell you all the thousand things we talked about in Bâle, theological and philosophical. Of these at home. Last year or earlier he went to Halle and Jena, and was received with great enthusiasm by the professors and students at Jena, he made a speech to them, and advised them to *study their books*, get their lessons, and keep silent. So some one told me, which advice they will keep as well as George Fox the similar advice which some one gave him; but it takes a great deal of soul to bear up well under exile and long misfortune. Yet De Wette has never retracted ungenerously anything he has said. The good men, says Ewald, justified him in all his course at the time of his exile, but the journals never dared to say one word in his defence. I think he is a great and noble man. Perhaps no theologian in Germany has more influence at this moment than he. He is both critical and mystical, so seems sometimes to waver, and does lean as one or the other element gets the upper hand. At Bâle I saw some curious paintings by Holbein, amongst others a schoolmaster's sign-board of the year 1516. It was not a Massacre of the Innocents, as you might suppose, but the process of instruction, not without the birch, an adjunct which has been sacred to pedagogues from the days of Solomon. Here, too, was one of the most curious and felicitous pictures of Erasmus I ever saw, and I have seen a hundred, I think. He sat writing; all about him is exquisitely genteel, yet with no foppishness. There is a good deal in Erasmus to admire, his exquisite taste, his consummate skill, the singular refinement and delicacy of his taste is curiously apparent in the midst of his smutty talk. His handwriting is elegant; the letters not bold like Melancthon's, nor so feminine as Luther's (strange contrast with the battles they thunder forth), but graceful and most elegantly cut. Here are many manuscript letters of Erasmus never printed, one curious little Latin poem in iambics upon Pope Julius II. Pray why have not all his letters been published, and why has no really satisfactory life of the man appeared? But, alas! there is none of Luther, nor even of John Calvin. Here is, in the library of Bâle, a copy of Erasmus' Praise of Folly in quarto, with wide margins, and on each page is a "scrap" by Holbein, beautifully done with a pen, and just as if made but yesterday, illustrating the text. I remember one illustrating the miraculous conception of the Blessed Virgin; the *Homunculus* was entering her mouth, the angels applauding in the meantime. Indeed, I have seen the same thing in churches on a large scale, shamefully disgusting, and bad almost as the doctrine they represent. Nothing shows more fully Holbein's genius than these little sportive touches in the manuscript. They have been engraved, but poorly. Stähelin has published his work on Genesis ; De Wette thinks it excellent. I will bring it home, knowing the interest you feel on this special matter. Indeed the poor Books of Moses are fought over with as much violence as Patroclus' body, but the divine Achilles has not come yet to end the strife and rescue the *corpus delicti*, giving it honourable burial.

From Bâle to Bonn. Here I saw Professor Vogt, who married Dr. Follen's sister, Professors Schultz and Schnell, revolutionary men and exiles, all of them. The latter is a terrible fellow ; he has been banished nearly a dozen times from as many different States, and got up perhaps twenty revolutions. He looks like a giant, and keeps always full of beer, now and then running over.

At Geneva I learned all about the Swiss Unitarians. They are going down rapidly, they gain nothing, but lose continually. However, the church in Switzerland has its outer form fixed, but its inner spirit perpetually progressive. Nobody believes the "five points" out of Germany in all Switzerland ; the greater part of the clergy here at Zurich in Bâle and elsewhere, are as much in advance of our Unitarians at home as they are before Dr. Codman. I am rather startled myself at their radicalism in theology. But the influence of Zwingle is one thing and Calvin's another. I have seen Hitzig and Oken—famous men both. Hitzig was surprised than an American had seen all his works at home ; but it was so. Here are letters of Zwingle, and his "Battle-axe" and his Greek Bible.

But I must end ; I hope you will have a little frolic during the vacation and keep strong, rejoicing in your good works.

TO THE SAME.

Brussels, July 29.

MY DEAR FRIEND,—I have remembered that you are probably not in Cambridge, and therefore that my letter will probably reach you as soon by my hands as by "Her Majesty's mails;" so I shall keep the epistle, and make additions thereto from time to time. Were it not that letters cost dollars, I should have piled up your study-table with them till the stout wood cracked and the legs gave out. All that I see I want to tell *you* of, from the rosy hues of Mont Blanc at sunset and morning to the gossip of German professors. Then, too, such suggestions are made to one's mind by the little angels who people these old places, that I want to talk of a thousand things that never come to me at home. "Home-keeping youths have ever homely wits," says somebody. But it is no more true than its converse, "that home-shunning youths," &c. Yet one does forget old prejudice when he sees new customs ; and though he loves his little village all the more after seeing many other little villages, and great ones too, yet he ceases to think that "Waltham is the finest parish in the world." I have learned that reading books is one thing, and seeing the objects therein treated of quite another—yes, sometimes the opposite. To come to some particulars. I think rather worse of the Catholic Church since I have seen its works and its men, and rather worse also of the Protestants too. The Protestant dungeon is wider, neater, and a good deal newer than the Catholic; then, too, the air is better; the thumb-screws of better workmanship; and the whole apparatus of torture has a more wieldy and scientific appearance—but still there is a dungeon, still there are thumb-screws, and an apparatus for torture.

Bay of Fundy, Sept. 1.

Alas! I have had time to write no more; but I shall soon *see* you again, so God bless you! Ever yours,   T. P.

CHAPTER X.

Return—Odium Theologicum—Letters—Leaves West Roxbury—Melodeon—Massachusetts Quarterly Review.

THE dear friends in his parish joyfully welcomed him back to his work, which he reassumed with equal joy, and a longing for an undisturbed pursuit of his favourite objects.

I thank you heartily for the cordial greeting with which you welcome me back to my home; for your expressions respecting my past labours, and your generous hopes for my future works. The pen you are so good as to send me is almost too beautiful to be used. I shall always prize it highly for the associations connected with it, and as a token of your esteem and friendship. I trust I shall never use it badly, nor in a bad cause. Gratefully and respectfully yours, T. P.

He immediately began to discharge the obligations which he felt had been incurred by this year of enjoyment and repose. Three lectures were prepared for delivery during the winter. Of these, one upon the "Signs of the Times," filled with warm anticipations and a too honest criticism, excited afresh the public interest in him. It also aroused, of course, the old opposition, which had gone to sleep, thinking that his influence ended with his departure for Europe.

FROM THE JOURNAL.

I have, now-a-days, some few struggles with myself to repress indignation at insults, real or fanciful. I must outgrow this.

My real troubles are, that I am short of my own ideals of goodness and usefulness. I feel that I ought to do more for what I receive; but I feel, too, that my head is clay, and requires to be treated as any other earthenware—with carefulness and discretion. I rejoice to write a few lectures; would that I could do more!

In October he received a letter from Mr. Martineau, acknowledging the "Discourse of Religion" and some other publications which he had sent.   Mr. Martineau remarks, with creditable perception,—

I am almost angry with you for supposing that I need any answer to the scoffing accusation brought against you. Who that has any insight into an author's spiritual physiognomy, and can apprehend its expressiveness in the smallest degree, could ever attribute a sneer to you?

Mr. Martineau does not deny that the manner in the "Discourse of Religion" is occasionally a little too slashing among the convictions of other people.

But every great writer must put forth what is in him in his own way; and the excess of manly strength is healthier than the scruples of effeminate forbearance.

Mr. Parker preached the Thursday lecture in his turn once more and for the last time in December, from the text, "Have any of the rulers, or of the Pharisees, believed on him?" This sermon sets forth in clear and enthusiastic terms the human nature of Christ, and the relation of simple truth and goodness which he held to his age and to the ages. He had never been so clear before upon the person of Christ. Such clearness involved obnoxious statements, which startled afresh all his brethren who were beginning now to take great care of their conservative theology. And yet when they are repeated, they seem ridiculously out of proportion to the clamour which they raised.

Jesus looked to God for his truth, his great doctrines, not his own private, personal ones, depending on his idiosyncracies, and therefore only subjectively true, but God's, universal, everlasting, the absolute religion. I do not know that he did not teach some errors also, along with it. I care not if he did. It is by his truths that I know him.

No wonder, then, that men soon learned to honour Jesus as a God, and then as God himself. Apostolical and other legends, &c., believe men of these things as they will. To me they are not truth and fact, but mythic symbols and poetry; the psalm of praise with which the world's rude heart extols and magnifies its King.

That God has yet greater men in store, I doubt not; to say this is not to detract from the majestic character of Christ, but to affirm the omnipotence of God. When they come, the old contest will be renewed, the living prophet stoned—the dead one worshipped.

But henceforth Mr. Parker never preached without offending every conventionalism more fatally by his moral tone than by his technical denials. His indignation at the vices of society and the Phariseeism of the Church was too positive, too thoroughly reconstructive. Men will sooner tolerate what they call an infidel theology; for mere negative criticism of Scripture and of doctrine does not put men's livelihood in peril, nor disturb their ease. But when a sensitive conscience cries out with pain, "Woe unto you, Scribes and Pharisees, hypocrites," the sound penetrates and shatters farther than the most persistent depreciation of Moses and the Prophets. The more sublimely the moral sense of an anti-supernaturalist emulates the dreadful indignation of Jesus, the more likely will he be to share his fate. As of old, the theology becomes the pretext for the hatred.

Mr. Parker would not give up his right to preach the Thursday lecture, nor his membership of the Association, because he would thereby ignominiously recede from the principle which liberal thought had hitherto represented. He did not think he had a right to do what nobody had a right to demand. If, therefore, at this juncture a new principle was to obtain control, it must be without his connivance. His right of rotation to preach the Thursday lecture was adroitly cancelled, and non-intercourse would do the rest.

TO REV. CHANDLER ROBBINS, BOSTON.

West Roxbury, 29 Jan., 1845.

MY DEAR FRIEND.—Your note, which I did not see till five minutes ago, for I have been absent since Monday noon, was as kind as it was characteristic of yourself. I thank you for it, and for the spirit which suggested the motion you made at the meeting. I wonder any one should doubt that I should meet in kindness any kind proposition from the Association : I have no unkind feelings towards any one of them. I had feelings that I thought a little unchristian towards one of them a few months ago; I will tell you how I got rid of them. I never said anything against him ; I said all the good things I knew of him ; I defended him several times, and palliated the severe judgment others pronounced on him. He went on abusing me (so I think it). I avoided, so far as possible, all that he said or printed. At last he did what I think was really a shameful thing, and most unchristian towards me, and now I feel not the faintest sparkle of unkindliness towards him. I met him, not long ago, and shook hands with him, and feel that I have triumphed.

I will meet the committee any time that it is possible for me to see them, and will most cheerfully entertain any proposition they shall make. I think you could not have made a better selection of persons for the work; for (excuse me for saying it) there are no members of the Unitarian ministry that I prize more highly than these three. Still I don't see what we can do. I don't suppose I shall convert you to my belief; I think you will not in a few hours alter my convictions, deliberately formed, examined and re-examined again and again before they were given to the world. What I wish is, that the Boston Association would fall back on the large principles which I once thought they all entertained—remembering that theology came from the head, and religion from the heart; that while there is only one religion, there may be a great many and quite diverse theologies, each imperfect, yet each helping towards the truth, and that a man may have the Christian religion in his heart and live it, too, who has neither your theology nor mine. I wish they would allow each man the Christian name who claims it and lives a Christian life, leaving the defence of that name and its definition to himself. Then, too, I wish they would treat matters of science (and such I reckon both theological doubts and theological affirmations) as matters of science and not as proofs of a good heart or a bad one. I may have many astronomical errors; they come from my Heart and Will quite as much as any theological heresies; yet no man would refer the first to a wicked heart, nor think to make me orthodox in my astronomy by calling me hard names. I know some of the brethren are offended at that poor sermon of mine at the Thursday lecture. But yet, at the very last meeting of the Association which I attended, a year and a half ago, it was stated to be advisable that the preachers should treat such matters as would disclose their views. I have heard sermons there from some of the brothers that are quite distasteful to me. But I did not feel implicated in a sermon of Mr. Young's or Dr. Pierce's, only in my own. I will not trouble you with more of my hasty scrawls, but will thank you again for all your kindness, and assure you that I shall not tread such a pearl as you offer under my feet.—Believe me, yours truly,

THEO. PARKER.

TO THE SAME.

West Roxbury, 28th Feb., 1845.

DEAR SIR,—I understand that at the last meeting of the Association, the management of the "great and Thursday Lecture" was transferred to the hands of the minister of the First Church, to whom it originally belonged. I do not know what was the design of this movement, but I know well that its effect will be to exclude me from preaching that lecture. I find no fault now with this, though for the honour of the Unitarians I could wish, if that were the design, that it had been effected in a manner not so circuitous: I like directness. I write to ask you—formerly, if not now, the scribe of the Association—to inform me of the facts of the case. Please tell me what was the design of the movement, and "all about it." Don't think I am offended, for I am not, and have no personal feelings in the matter at all. Does the Association make any public statement of the movement they have made?—Believe me, as ever,

Yours faithfully,

THEO. PARKER.

TO THE SAME.

West Roxbury, 18th Oct., 1845.

DEAR SIR,—Mr. Pierpont told me that you informed him that you once prepared some resolutions, intending to offer them at a meeting

of the Boston Association, which resolutions had reference to Mr. Pierpont's leaving the city. I have thought for a good while that his departure from Boston was a sign of the times that ought to be noticed in
some way. I meant to ask you to do the very thing you intended yourself to do. I now ask you to do it, *i. e.* to prepare certain resolutions
expressing the fact of Mr. Pierpont's faithful and self-denying labours
in this city, the troubles which his fidelity and zeal have brought upon
him, and also the fact that the Association feels a strong sympathy with
him, and an earnest desire for his welfare and usefulness. It seems to
me the Association owes this to a man who, for more than twenty
years, has been among the foremost in all the great Christian enterprises of the day, and who now withdraws from the city and the state.
I beg you to tell me soon if you feel disposed to do this, and also to
inform me where the Association will meet the next time, for I wish to
be present also. If you decline offering any such resolutions, please
send this letter to James Clarke, who, I think, will do it, though I had
rather it should come from you. If no one else will do it, I shall feel
compelled to undertake it myself.

Very truly yours,
THEO. PARKER.

TO MRS. DALL.

West Roxbury, 30th May, 1845.

MY DEAR CAROLINE,—It is near the end of Anniversary Week, and
I wish to write you a word or two. You need not fear that I shall
take pains to withdraw from the Unitarians, who are separating from
me. I actually attended a meeting of the Boston Association a few
weeks ago, to demonstrate to them my existence as a member thereof.
I was received as you may imagine. I have attended their conferences
and the like, and my opinion is confirmed that, as a sect, they are
irretriveably sold to bigotry. The race of scholars is getting extinct
among them. I know only four—Francis, Lamson, Frothingham,
Noyes. You know what their influence is; the majority can settle
questions without the aid of philosophy or learning. I shall expect
to see them become more and more narrow for years to come. It
seems to be written on the iron leaf of fate, that our progress in
theology shall be only by revolutions, not gradual and regular, but
spasmodic. I can honour a man who differs from me, who abuses me;
but, at the same time that I admit the worth of many of the Unitarians, I must deplore the false and unphilosophical way they go to
work in. They confound theology with religion; they then think that
theology must be studied, not as a science, in the spirit of freedom,
but with fear. So I think they are weaving cobweb, and calling it
cloth; and if a man tears asunder their cobweb-trousers in putting
them on, they call out "Infidel!" and if he complains that he is cold
and naked when he wears them whole, they cry, "Away with him!"
It may be this business is always to continue; but to-morrow may
bring new things; other and former to-morrows have done so. I trust
in the future. In the meantime, I learn to wait, as I have before

learned to labour. I beg you to accept my kind salutations, and to be assured that I shall welcome you back to Boston with great pleasure. Remember me tenderly to Mr. Dall, and believe me,

Faithfully yours,
THEO. PARKER.

It was now not a pleasant thing to exchange with him. The Rev. J. T. Sargent, who was a minister at large, and preached to the poor gathered in Suffolk Street Chapel, continued to exchange with him, though dissenting from his views. But the congregation at the chapel liked to hear him. The executive committee of the Fraternity of Churches had the technical right of asking Mr. Sargent not to admit so dangerous a man into that pulpit. It was feared that the poor would be corrupted and misled. They dreaded his influence. What an influence it soon became in Boston, and the region round about, to expose the causes of pauperism and crime, to lift up the hearts of sorrowful men and women, to bring the strong moral help of everlasting truths to a languishing society! He could not preach in the chapel, and Mr. Sargent resigned sooner than take a pledge that he would not exchange with him. Mr. Parker became a minister at large, with seven thousand names upon his private list of men and women who depended upon him for comfort and guidance, to whom he was bound to minister by word of mouth or epistles from his own hand, and with a parish settled in almost every town from East to West, centres of influence and sympathy whither his spirit swiftly ran to bless. How shallow is every technical advantage!

Jan. 17, 1845.—Two members of J. F. Clarke's Society came here this afternoon to state to me that in the Church of the Disciples there was a strong feeling about my exchanging with their minister. They came with the kindest intentions to notify me of the fact—to state, furthermore, that some of the society would abandon the Church if I came. But I think the principle in virtue of which Clarke asked an exchange is true. I feel inclined to live out this principle. *Frisch auf, mein Herz! Frisch auf!* I am shut in, but shut in by God. Shut in for my good. What I can't rejoice in for itself I will welcome as a quickener of humanity and faith.

His next controversial publication was "A Letter to the Boston Association of Congregational Ministers, touching certain matters of their Theology." In a sermon preached to his parish at West Roxbury, he thus explains his object:—

To relieve the brethren from the embarrassment of being held answerable for my opinions while they had no opportunity of showing men how much they differed from me, I address them a public letter. Now, only two possible courses can be conceived: 1. To reply to all the questions. This, I know, they could not do, for there was the greatest diversity of opinions amongst themselves. They could not agree. 2. Such being the case, they could state to me and the public that they could not answer my letter point for point, *because* they were not agreed.

This they ought to have done, and it would have relieved the Association from every appearance of complicity with his opinions, excepting that it might be inferred that where there was so much disagreement with each other, there must be some virtual agreement with him.

What parishes were divided—what sentences were written— what feelings were displayed! But it will not be profitable to revive the details of the controversy. Several liberal men said from their pulpits that the right of free preaching must be maintained, undisturbed by the application of any doctrinal test. Some valuable discourses were thus preached in favour of righteousness before doctrine. An article in the *Examiner*, by Dr. Gannett, was distinguished for its impartiality and kindliness. He has always sent forth his generous indignation at the first symptom of oppression. There are letters from some of the brethren, testifying to the manly and equable demeanor of Mr. Parker in one or two conferences, which were held in the hope of discovering some adjustment, but which, of course, came to nothing.

TO MRS. DALL.

West Roxbury, 14th December, 1844.

MY DEAR CAROLINE,—I thank you for remembering me in the midst of so much happiness. Yet perhaps it does not seem so meritorious in you; for your " heart, when filled with love for one, grows bountiful to all." I have no doubt it is so. Most of our common theories about love are foolish; for they teach that, if you love one, you must forget all the rest. In short, that you can't follow God (or your husband) without hating your father and mother. I subscribe to no such heresy. If I love one dearly, I am all the more likely to love another, or several others, strongly. I thought the wedding service in the church a little too solemn. Serious must all weddings be where the parties are thoughtful; but I don't like a dirge in a flower-garden. Dr. Lowell's remarks were beautiful. I don't know whether young women on such occasions *hear* all the excellent things said by the minister; but I know, at my marriage, I thought very little of the fine sentences which Brother Young ejaculated with pontifical gravity.

I don't believe you will do much harm, though you write strong articles in favour of the ministry to the poor. I think you are in the most living portion of the ministry. In Boston, I always thought that the chapels for the poor were the most aristocratic institutions of that blessed city, though they were founded with the noblest intentions and have done no little good. I believe in a *ministry* to the poor; not at all in *chapels* for the poor. Let us have a common temple—" The rich and the poor meet together." The newspapers tell you about Mr. Sargent and the shabby conduct of the committee of the Fraternity of Churches ; at least you will see it in the *Register*. It proves the love of freedom which these "liberal Christians" have at heart.

I was sorry to read what you said about Torrey ;* for I took him to be a noble man. I once met him—I think at the Chardon Street Convention ; he called me an infidel. But I wrote him a letter, since his imprisonment, telling him to play the man, that his position was noble as that of the Christian martyrs. His answer was good, though his mind now and then wandered : for he was sick. I hope you are mistaken.

What can you do to christianize the heart of the slave-holder ? I think there is a great deal of injustice here at the North in the treatment which the strong bestow upon the weak, and am not well pleased with the condition of domestic service in Massachusetts. I was going to say something a little stronger. Still I hate slavery, and can't find the faintest toleration for it. Will your ministrations reach the black directly ? I suppose you must christianize men before you can make them take measures to liberate their slaves. To do that must be very hard work.

I am not doing much externally this winter. I go about and deliver Lyceum lectures, here a little and there a little, and am preparing something for the next winter. I am also getting ready a volume of "Six Lectures on Morality, Theology, and Religion," which will see the light in due time.

Your friend and brother,
THEO. PARKER.

TO THE SAME.

West Roxbury, Sept. 21, 1846.

MY DEAR CAROLINE,—I thank you for your kind letter of the other day, for I am always glad to get a letter from you, though you sometimes ask questions that I cannot easily answer about anti-slavery matters. I can't give you just the information you want ; perhaps I have been obliged to keep such a bright look-out in theological and philosophical matters for several years that I have fallen behind-hand in the literature of the reformers, though I hope not in the spirit of the reforms, or in zeal for their advancement. I suppose you have Jay's books ; they are good reading, as good as anything. Then the articles now publishing in the *Liberator* by W. I. Bowditch are of great value. I believe four numbers have already appeared. Equally good are the articles by Dean Palfrey in the *Boston Whig*, on the slave-holding power. I think you will hardly find more profitable anti-slavery reading for the Society than these afford ; I think some one in

* A clergyman, at that time imprisoned in Baltimore for violation of the Slave Laws of Maryland.

Portsmouth must take the *Liberator* and the *Whig*, and if so, you have the matter at hand. I own few such books, though I have now just borrowed over a bushel of anti-slavery documents, and soon as I am well enough, I mean to read up on the subject The *Liberty Bell* [*] is a good thing, and I am thankful you mean to write for it. I mean to write something if I can do so.

The Misses Osgood have always been friends of me and mine: noble women are they, and full of intelligence and piety. I fear it will always be the fashion for the Boston Association to speak ill of me until the dust returns to the earth as it was. For myself I care not. It never made me feel the smallest unkindness towards them. It has sometimes saved them from more severe strictures, for I do not like to speak hard against men that try and injure me, lest a little of the old Adam should appear in my own heart. However, in due time, the errors and follies which are personal with me will pass off with me, and the real truth that is in my doctrines will stand free of my follies, and do its work. If I live ten years, and work as now, I hope to do something. But who knows? I have no lack of faith—not belief in the Thirty-nine Articles, in the Creed, or the Catechism, but trust in God. I am content to walk by that. I often find I can *feel* further than I can *see*, and accordingly I rest the great doctrines of Christianity not on reasoning, but reason on intuition.

The Resurrection in its common sense I don't believe. But the soul's immortality I cannot for a moment doubt.

TO REV. JOHN PIERPONT.

West Roxbury, 15th October, 1845.

DEAR SIR,—I called to see you yesterday, but unluckily missed you, and as I shall not, it is probable, have another opportunity to take you by the hand, I will now say a word to you before you leave Boston. None can regret your departure more than I ; we have not been much together ; you have been busy, so have I, therefore I have not seen you so often as I could always have wished. But I have always felt encouraged and strengthened by your example, and that long before I had any "troubles" with my theological "brethren." If you had done as the other ministers, you had been as they are—you would not now be leaving Boston. If you had flattered the follies and winked at the sins of the rich, you would have had, not *your* reward—that you have now—but *their* reward, I mean the reward of the ministers you leave behind. But you have chosen another part, and have your reward, a little different from theirs. You must go in triumph, for you have fought a good fight and a great one. For nearly thirty years you have been foremost in all the great reforms of the day which had the welfare of men for their object ; you have been fearless before force. If others did not help you, you thought that was a reason why *you* should work the more. When your valour was called for, you did

* For a number of years published, by gratuitous contribution of articles from prominent Anti-Slavery persons, for sale at the Annual Fair of the Massachusetts Anti-Slavery Society.

not turn round to remember your discretion. None of the great moral enterprises of the day would have stood where now they stand if you had not raised your manly voice in their behalf. Where would Temperance have been if John Pierpont had been silent? Where many other good and noble causes? It is your zeal for the great cause which Jesus died to serve that now has brought you to your present position. Your reward is with you. The confidence that you worked faithfully and wrought a great work will go with you and bless you to the end of your days. Nothing has happened for years so reflecting disgrace on the Boston clergy as your departure from the city under the present circumstances; but what is their disgrace is your glory. Go, and may God be with you! For *my* sake, for the sake of *many*, I could wish you were to stay; but it is better you should go. I know you will find work enough to be done, and warm hearts to welcome you in doing it. You leave behind not a few to bless you for your toils, and to pray for your future success and welfare. Your memory will live ever in their affections, and their good wishes will follow you wherever you go. I beg you to accept my thanks for all that you have done, and to believe me ever your friend and brother.

TO DR. FRANCIS.

February, 1845.

What do you think of Newman's opinions on the "Parmenides?" He thinks it was written in mockery of Plato, but has become foisted in with his works. To me it seems a most ingenious piece of *persiflage* of Plato's, to show the absurdity of Parmenides' logic. He shows that you can prove anything by it, for the last paragraph concludes that neither the *one* nor the *many* has any existence. The conclusion is not extant, if Plato ever finished it. Do look over the "Parmenides" and tell me what you think of N.'s opinion, for it is six or seven years since I read it.

I wonder if he never thought that much of our popular theology rests on no better foundation than Hartley's vibratiuncles. It seems to me this is one of our sins, that we rest on *facts of fancy*, and so build a mythology instead of a theology. On an imaginary hook only an imaginary garment will hang. We have woven a good many cobwebs and but little cloth; the cobwebs look imposing at sunrise, glittering with dew, but the *boy* walks through them, and at noon no man can find one of them.

FROM THE JOURNAL.

May 28, 1845.—Attended the anti-capital punishment meeting; nothing remarkable, but as a sign of the times. Soon this sin of judicial murder will be over. Notice the remarkable variety of persons: all conditions were represented there. Saw Mr. Porter, my critical foe, or friend.[*] I told him that I actually wore a hat and no turban. Saw, too, Mr. Bushnell. Had a very pleasant talk with them about the

---

[*] Professor Porter, of New Haven, who wrote a kindly and discriminating article in the *New Englander*, July, 1845.

miracles. They do not think miracles a violation of law, or anything like it. They take the ground that God has imparted, or continually imparts, to nature a certain power, so that only certain circumstances take place; new things also follow. Well: here was a remarkable condition of the human race, and so a child is miraculously born, and capable of working miracles all his life. Should the same condition of the human race return, like results are to be expected.

May 30.—What is to come of my position, I know not. Am I to stand always alone, and when I go down shall all this movement end? I cannot believe it. And yet it seems that no man is like to rise up and take my place and help forward my work. Let the truth prevail.

TO DR. LAMSON.

July 19, 1845.

I thank you heartily for your noble address * yesterday. It was just the thing that is wanting. I regard it as laying the corner-stone of a grand and noble edifice of theology. I hope you will not allow it to be spoiled in printing. Do, for Heaven's sake, print strong, very strong, and not let it be spoiled. I liked it more than I can tell you, and think great good will come of it.

Yours in haste.

TO REV. INCREASE S. SMITH.

November 10, 1845.

It would give me great joy to come over to your meeting next Thursday, if it were possible; but consider, all summer long I could not work. I stuck in the ground like a turnip, only I could not perceive that I grew. Now I begin to work again. I can think a little, read and write. I must make hay while the sun shines, for my mind-weather is not to be depended on to last long, certainly not all the year. Then, besides, I am obliged, conscience compelling, to lecture all over the land; on Friday night at Fall River. Further still, I am writing a work on the Reformation, which demands all my spare hours; therefore you see why I hold myself excused. I should be amazingly glad to come and share your hospitality, and enjoy the society of yourself and yours; but when a whole *Garrison* is to take the field, and there is such a stalwart *Smith* there ready to lay on iron strokes, I think it needless that a *Parker* should be called on to beat the bush when the others will capture the game. For me, I prefer to go and labour in places where there is not a *Smith* in the land.

TO DE WETTE.

West Roxbury, 28th September, 1845.

HONORED AND DEAR SIR,—I received from you some time since the sixth edition of your *Einleitung ins A. T.*, which you had the politeness to send me. I am much obliged to you for your kindness. My

---

* "Plea for Theology"—delivered before the Association of the Alumni of the Cambridge Theological School, July 18, 1845. Printed in the *Christian Examiner* for November, 1845.

translation of your work has not produced the effect here which it is yet destined to do. The Liberal party, in fact, are weak; the *so-called* Liberal party, the Unitarians, are partly afraid and partly hypocritical. None of the stout critics had touched it, until recently Moses Stuart, Professor in the Theological Seminary at Andover—a learned man of the *Hengstenberg-Richtung* (tendency)—published a work called "A Critical History and Defence of the Old Testament Canon." In this he refers continually to your views, and of course attacks them; but he always treats them with respect, and entertains a high esteem for yourself as a critic and a scholar. He attacks also Mr. Norton, and treats him with less respect than yourself. Mr. S.'s book will have a wide circulation here, but in Germany it would be considered *ganz unbedeutend* (quite unimportant). Here is a small party who think that Christianity is the Word of God; but the documents connected therewith, like the institutions connected with it also, are to be treated like other documents, criticized, studied, and believed only when they are *probable*. None of our conspicuous theologians belong to this class; a traditionary theology is the curse of the Church in America. But I have strong hopes that to-morrow will be brighter than to-day. In a country where the mind is in general so free as it is here, theology cannot always be kept from becoming a science. I hope much from the introduction of German thought into America, especially from your own writings. I am at present preaching each Sunday to a large congregation of Liberal Christians in Boston.* But I am called a heretic by my Unitarian brothers, who are themselves called heretics and infidels by all the rest. I am also preparing a work on the Protestant Reformation, its causes and its consequences. When that is done, I mean to write a history of the progress of thought in matters of theology and religion from the Reformation to this day. I intend also to prepare, with *your* help, a critical and historical introduction to the New Testament. . . . . If you prepare a new edition of your *Einleitung in das N. T.*, and will send it me, it will be a favour. My translation is printed with stereotype plates, and therefore it is costly to make alterations from one edition to another; but of course I shall in the next edition notice the points in which you have differed from your earlier opinions. When you print a seventh edition I will thank you to send it me.

With sincere desires for your long life and continued happiness, I remain your friend and obedient servant.

FROM THE JOURNAL.

Feb. 7, 1845.—I have just conferred with part of a committee for procuring a place in Boston for me to preach in. I consent for two Sundays, commencing on the 16th, and, if it is possible, to continue to preach for them every Sunday morning for a year. I know not what will come of it. I don't wish ever to leave my Patmos at Spring Street. If the parish will consent, I will continue here and preach half the time, and furnish a substitute the rest of the time.

* See the next extract from the Journal.

The parish consented.

I know not what will come of it, but think only good. God grant it shall be so! There is much to conserve, there is somewhat also to destroy.

16th.—To-day I have preached at the Melodeon, for the first time. The weather was highly unfavourable—rainy, and the snow deep—the streets passable only with difficulty. Still, there was a large audience, mostly of men, unlike most of my audiences. I felt the greatness of the occasion, but I felt it too much to do justice, perhaps, to myself. I felt not at ease in my service. I felt as one that is with some friends, with some foes, with many strangers. It has been a day of struggles. A long, long warfare opens before me! Shall I prove worthy? How much can I do? How much can I bear? I know not. I look only to the soul of my soul, not with over-confidence in myself, but with an adamantine faith in God.

The greeting of some friends did me much good. I love to take a *friend* by the hand. Mrs. —— came into the little room, and took me by the hand. I am a child in some things, I hope I shall always be.

March 3.—I have but one resource, and that is to overcome evil with good—much evil with more good; old evil with new good. Sometimes when I receive a fresh insult it makes my blood rise for a moment; then it is over, and I seek, if possible, to do some good, secretly, to the person. *It takes away the grief of a wound amazingly.* To be true to God, and "that one talent which 'tis death to hide"—this depends on me. To know that I am thus true depends on others, and if they know it not, why that is not my affair, but theirs! Sometimes I wish that death would come and fan me to sleep with his wings: but faith soon stops that murmur, and a "Thy will be done!" is prayer enough for me.

During this winter of 1844–45 he lectured forty times.

At New Bedford I saw some interesting persons. Andrew Robeson I admire, and love as I love few men. I look at him with rapture. He is my ideal almost of a rich man, a Christian man. I speak not of his kindness to me, but of his character, his life. I know not why, but I love better the society of such than the companionship of the most cultivated men. They meet you, and don't dodge.

Sometimes I feel a little satisfied with myself. Then I always know that some mortification is preparing for me; all my swans prove geese soon as they begin to sing.

The old trouble in his head recurred, and he lost a great many days. He called them lost, but they were filled with respectable labour. Still, the physicians reduced him to the smallest amount that was compatible with his peace of mind. He often left his sermon unfinished, and wandered listlessly into the fields. Sometimes he went to see the brave people at Brook Farm.

His preaching in Boston attained a popularity which astonished him. The Melodeon was crowded with a keen, sturdy, and inquisitive audience, many of whom had never before been submitted to the influence of positive religion. His manly piety and powerful assaults upon the conscience, his humor and good sense, above all, the manifestation of his love for man, won them from curiosity into reverence and exalted feelings. He did not believe that he should be able to sustain himself long before such a congregation. He had always been told that he was a mere book-worm, and he loved meditation and seclusion. He was surprised and delighted when he found his words taking a genuine hold upon the people.

Occasionally there was a chance, by exchange with some liberal brother, to preach in another pulpit. He never failed to impress people if they did not know him, or know that he was coming. If they did, the opinion would be divided. An excellent person lingered in Mr. Clarke's vestibule, after one of these sermons, loud in her grateful praises. "Oh, I wish that infidel Theodore Parker could have heard that!" Yes, indeed, such love to God and man, flowing forth strongly in such lucid speech, found the great want in every unguarded heart.

November 27.—To-day my friends met in Boston to organize more fully, with a view to my settling with them. I would gladly for my own quiet remain always here, but I shall go to Boston and work, if they need me, and wish me. I pray for this only, that I may be greatly good and pious, and thereby greatly useful unto man. If I pass ten years in Boston, labouring at that church, I may do something, it seems to me. If not, why I have done my best, and will not complain.

My chosen walk will be with the humble. I will be the minister of the humble, and, with what of culture and love I have, will I toil for them. I rejoice to see that most of my hearers are from the humbler class of men. If it had been *only* the cultivated and the rich, I should feel that I was wrong somewhere ; but when the voice *comes up from the ground*, I can't refuse to listen to it.

Those aspirations preserved their warmth and purity ; every gift and acquisition was subservient to feed them alone. Did any man, of so strong a mould and of such ardent sensibilities, ever have more innocent ambitions ?

TO DR. JOHN WARE.

West Roxbury, 2nd January, 1846.

DEAR SIR,—I hope you will excuse a stranger for venturing to address you a letter. At any rate, I shall take the liberty. Your memoir of your brother has affected me so deeply, that I cannot forbear expressing my gratitude that you have prepared so noble a memorial of so noble a man. Sir, I knew your brother well. It was my good fortune to be in the Theological School two or three years, while it most fully enjoyed his services. I loved him as I have seldom loved a man heretofore, and perhaps shall never love another. He was not always equal—sometimes was absent, and *seemed* cold. But he drew my heart after him by the very tones of his voice, by his look and his kind way of speaking to a young man. He never flattered. He told truth, and did not wound, even though it was a painful truth. I can't believe any student ever slighted any hint he gave. I treasured up his words as oracles—not Delphic, but Christian. His presence at our religious meetings was the presence of a saint; it was the fragrance of violets in a library; and we felt it. He tuned the most discordant strings.

His lectures, I mean those delivered before the whole school, were not professedly religious; but they brought a man step by step to the throne of God, and before he knew it he knelt and prayed. His influence was wholly through his holiness. But that affected all he said and did. His opinions on books we received as from no other man who knew much more of books. I used often to hear Dr. Channing preach in the morning, and in the afternoon your brother, at the chapel. I have heard Dr. Channing, perhaps, preach some of his best sermons; but I could not tell which I liked best, Dr. C. or Henry Ware. One had the magnificence of religious thought, the other had the heavenliness of piety.

Your brother began moderately, with no promise of a great soul-stirring sermon; but gradually he gained greatness of thought, and lovely images, and a sweetness and poetry of devotion and trust in God which charmed your heart away. And then his prayers! I have heard none such. I know nothing to compare them with, public or private, unless it be the music I have heard sometimes in a cathedral, when one little voice begins—like our own thrush in the mornings of May—and softly, gently sings out strains exquisitely tender; then comes another, different but accordant; and then another, and so on till every column, arch, altar-stone seems vibrating with the psalm. His arrow kindled as it rose, and disappeared a flame.

When I left the school I always went to him for advice, criticism, help, and I always found it—found more than I asked. At my ordination *he* laid his hand on my head—and I believe in the imposition of *such* a hand—and prayed words that not only *I* shall never forget, but the people of this church still lovingly remember.

Your memoir brings him back to me just as I knew him. He tells often his own story, and lives again before me. I carried to England and Geneva the tidings of his end, and you know what hearts they were that loved him, and may judge of their grief. He has gone, and your father, too! They were not long separated, now again are together with the Father of us all. They both prophesy after their death, and both will be ever remembered by one who gratefully received instruction and counsel from each.

I am, sir,
Your obliged servant,
T. P.

In the year 1845, he opened a friendship with Charles Sumner, which became valuable to both of them, and was ennobled by a mutual sense of fidelity to truth and of suffering in her service. Mr. Parker made a characteristic advance, in an acknowledgment of Mr. Sumner's oration on the "True Grandeur of Nations;" its principles were dear to his heart, and with his customary unselfishness he proffered welcome and admiration.

I hope you will excuse one so nearly a stranger to you as myself, for addressing you this note. But I cannot forbear writing. I have just read your oration on the "True Grandeur of Nations" for the second time, and write to express to you my sense of the great value of that work, and my gratitude to you for delivering it on such an occasion. Boston is a queer little city, the public is a desperate tyrant there, and it is seldom that one dares disobey the commands of public opinion. I know the reproaches you have already received from your friends, who will now, perhaps, become your foes. I have heard all sorts of ill motives attributed to you, and know that you must suffer attack from men of low morals, who can only swear by their party, and who live only in public opinion.

I hope you will find a rich reward in the certainty that you have done a duty and a service to mankind."

A society had been organized at the Melodeon, and he accepted its call in December. His parish made mournful preparations for his departure :—

FROM THE JOURNAL.

The Parish Committee have been here to consult about my leaving the church. It seems worse than assisting at my own funeral—the only *real* calamity that has befallen me in the ecclesiastical way; all the other troubles have been blessings in a mask—this is a sorrow. How can I bear to stand in the dear old familiar pulpit for the last time, and look in the dear old faces for the last time out of that pulpit? But it must be, and soon will be. I cling tenaciously to all I ever loved. I even hate to lose sight of a departing cloud. Well, perhaps this also will be a good—to those dear old friends, to me, to all.

TO THE SECOND PARISH IN ROXBURY.

West Roxbury, 3rd Jan., 1846.

DEAR FRIENDS,—It is with great grief that I write you this note, fixing the second Sunday in February next as the day of resigning my connection with you. Circumstances which I could neither prevent nor foresee constrain me to leave a place which has become dearer to me each year I have filled it—a place in which I had fondly hoped to live long and usefully, and die as I had lived amongst you. I need not say now how painful the separation will be to me, for I think you all know that; I need not say that no personal ambition leads me to this step, for I think you all know the circumstances of this case too well, and know me too well to believe for a moment it is so. If my brethren of the Christian ministry had stood by me, nay, if they had not themselves refused the usual ministerial fellowship with me, then I should have been spared this painful separation, and my life might have flowed on in the channel we have both wished for it. But I bear no ill-will to my brethren. I trust you will bear none ; I hope you may again hear their voices in your own church, and be again instructed by their words. I shall soon cease to be your minister ; I shall never cease to be your friend. I hope long to be your neighbour and fellow-citizen. But wherever I am, I shall always feel grateful for the uniform kindness and forbearance you have shown towards me. There is nothing in all your dealings with me which I could wish otherwise. You have borne patiently with my infirmities, and if I have ever had a new truth to offer, though scholars and clergymen treated it with scorn, you welcomed the word to your hearts, and heard it gladly. When my personal friends forsook me and fell off, you stood by me. Your hearty sympathy has been of more value to me than words can tell. Think not I shall ever forget that. And now I am obliged to leave you. But my heart never shall leave you. My *desire* is to remain still with you; my *duty* commands me elsewhere. If I am ever able to serve you in any way, I beg you to consider me still your servant, and always your friend. It will always give me pleasure to be of use to you.

With the best wishes for your success, I remain affectionately, your friend and Christian brother.

On January 4, 1846, he was installed over the Twenty-eighth Congregational Society, in Boston, preaching his own sermons—tender, brave, unsparing, and humane—on the True Idea of a Christian Church. That was the first of a long series of discourses, rich with the application of religion to life, through facts, criticisms, and ideas, which made the designation of the "Twenty-eighth Congregational" famous at home and abroad.

Mr. Parker had several times been to Andover for books and conversation with the professors. He knew Professor Stuart, who, acknowledging some publications in the autumn of 1845, addresses Mr. Parker in terms which show a scholarly and magnanimous recognition :—

Accept the accompanying little volume as a small return for your kindness.

As to the liberty which I have taken to controvert some of your opinions, you are the last man to call this in question. You will see, that in drawing the comparison between you and your *non-committal* opponents, I have given you the preference. No half-way measures are consistent in such a case. The Bible is either the word of God, or else it is only a part of the book of nature, standing on the same level with Plato, Plutarch, Cicero, Seneca, and others of the like class. I understand you as taking the latter position, with the modification that the New Testament, in particular, contains a more thorough and explicit morality and religiosity. Mr. Norton will not relish the preference I have given to your views, in comparison with his. I cannot help it; I have only spoken my deep convictions.

I have more hope that you will yet be won over to orthodoxy, than that he will. Not because you are less sincere and ardent in your present views, but because you let Reason have full play, and carry you wherever you think she leads. A thousand things may yet change your views of the nature and necessity of Christianity—things not in your hands, nor mine, but in the hands of Him who has life, comfort, prospects, hopes, convictions even, entirely at His disposal.

What I have said to Mr. Norton, I can truly say to you—*Utinam nostrúm esset!*

In speaking plainly my convictions, which I have felt obliged to do, I hope and trust that I have not transgressed the laws of courtesy. I am, with kind regards, however we may differ in opinion, your friend and obedient servant, M. STUART.

In the summer of this year (1846) he spent the month of July in a journey through Western New York, the White Mountains, and Canada; but of this there is only an itinerary. Rough drafts abound, notes and statistics, hints, anecdotes, for the sermon of merchants, of war, of pauperism, on the state of the nation, material to serve the discussion of slavery, mixed with a great variety of theological and philosophical suggestions. His activity was very manifold for the next five years. The business of lecturing had greatly increased, and his reading had not diminished, as the regular lists of books for every year show plainly enough; and yet his time in Boston was torn to pieces with interruptions. He met them blandly, and his business was more successfully achieved, for obstacles piqued him into great wariness, economy, and system. He used to say that time stretched like india-rubber. Here is an attempt to write a sermon :—

I had been to the Post-Office, had sewed the sheets of my Easter sermon together, and sat down to make a brief of the matter, when— 1, in comes Mrs. K——, to talk over her *connubial* affairs. She stayed till about eleven, when—2, in comes Mr. McKay, and as we talked of various things it was announced that—3. Dr. Papin was downstairs. I went to see him, and—4. R. W. Emerson was coming up the stairs. I left him in the study, and saw the Doctor, who came seeking relief for a poor woman; then returned, and we talked of the *new journal:* saw Carlyle's letter about Margaret. Nos. 3, 4, and 2 successively went away. I was descending the stairs, when, lo!—5 appears, George Ripley, and we talked of the condition of civilization, the prospects of humanity. Dinner came, one hour. Went to see Mr. ——: not at home; visited other people in the afternoon: tea. At half-past seven sat down to the sermon: in a minute came—6, Mr. F. C., wanting to borrow twelve dollars, which I lent him gladly. Then sat down to write: at a quarter past eight came—7, Mr. M——. All chance of work was now at an end, so I gave up, and went down to the parlour. A little before nine came a ring, and then—8 appeared, Mr. ——, who was interested to kill a man that had done a wrong to one of his friends, and brought a letter of defiance. I burned the letter after a long talk, but could not wholly overcome the man's feelings of revenge. At ten he retired, and at a quarter before eleven, I also, to rest—not to sleep for a long time.

The new journal referred to became the *Massachusetts Quarterly Review*, of which he reluctantly undertook the co-editorship with Mr. Emerson and J. E. Cabot. The first number appeared in December, 1847. It proposed to discuss the questions of American society and politics, which were just beginning to assume their great and threatening proportions, of science, and of theology. Mr. Emerson prepared the editorial address, from which this is an extract:—

What will easily seem to many a far higher question than any other is that which respects the embodying of the conscience of the period. Is the age we live in unfriendly to the highest powers; to that blending of the affections with the poetic faculty which has distinguished the Religious Ages? We have a better opinion of the economy of nature than to fear that those varying phases which humanity presents ever leave out any of the grand springs of human action.

In the rapid decay of what was called religion, timid and unthinking people fancy a decay of the hope of man. But the moral and religious sentiments meet us everywhere, alike in markets as in churches. A God starts up behind cotton bales also. The conscience of man is regenerated as is the atmosphere, so that society cannot be debauched. That health which we call virtue is an equipoise which easily redresses itself, and resembles those rocking-stones which a child's finger can move, and a weight of many hundred tons cannot overthrow.

TO A FRIEND.

DEAR FRIEND,—When you come to see me again, don't ask if I am busy, but come in, whether or not. I am not likely to be too busy to see you. If I am, I will tell you frankly.

I want to see you very much. We need a new periodical, for philosophy, literature, theology, religion, and practical morality. Are not you the man to undertake it? If not you, who is? Not ——, who has not the culture, the patience, the stability (in place or idea); not ——, who is too ultramontane for the nineteenth century.

We want a tremendous journal, with ability in its arms and piety in its heart. Cannot you do something for it?

Yours heartily,
T. P.

TO THE SAME.

DEAR FRIEND,—The more I think of it, the more certain I am that —— will not do for our newly-talked-of periodical. He has not the *entireness*, not the firm courage which we want. I admit he has much courage, but not quite enough. Then, too, he is a member of the Boston Association. They would whine round him and choke the life out of him if he undertook, not to say a manly thing, but to let others say it. He is a good man; I honour him, love him, expect much of him: but I don't expect *that which we want*.

We don't want a man of the Middle Ages, but of the nineteenth century, for our work. I have written a letter to Emerson, asking him to undertake the matter. If he will, it will succeed. He is the better man, if he will take hold. He is a downright *man;* we never had such a jewel in America before. I think him worth two or three of Dr. Channing.

How many young men do you know that could write in such a work? It should be literary, philosophical, poetical, theological, and, above all, human—human even to divinity. I think we may find help in unexpected quarters.

Come, and let us talk over the matter one of these days.

TO CHARLES SUMNER.

I think we want a new journal, devoted to letters, poetry, art, philosophy, theology, politics (in the best sense of that word), and humanity in general. You know better than I the *North-American Review*, the *Christian Examiner*,* &c. They are not *jusqu'au niveau de l'humanité*. They will not be, cannot be. The better minds of the age cannot express their best thoughts therein. If there were such a journal, ably conducted, it would have two good influences: 1. It would strike a salutary terror into all the Ultramontanists, and make them see that they did not live in the Middle Ages—that they are not to be let alone dreaming of the garden of Eden, but are to buckle up and work; 2. It would spread abroad the ideas which now wait to be organized, some in letters, some in art, some in institutions and practical life. I know you love letters not less than law, and man before both, and so I write to ask you what you think of the matter—how far you would aid in such a work? Don't suppose I want to be one of the head and front of this movement; I want no such thing, but not to appear at all. I wrote to R. W. E. to ask him to take charge of such a work. If he fails, what say you to that?

---

* In a diary which Mr. Parker kept during his last illness in Rome, is this entry:—
"Received, to-day, the *Unitarian Quarterly*, with a notice of my Letter (the Letter from Santa Cruz). What a change in the tone of Unitarian periodicals in a few years!" And he recognized the more liberal character of the *Christian Examiner* under its new management in 1859-60, and was accustomed to say that it was then the best religious periodical in America. He sent a number of it, containing his own article upon Massachusetts, to Moleschott, the distinguished chemist of Zurich, with a note, in which he says:—
"There is an admirable article on Asiatic Civilization in the *Christian Examiner* for July, 1859, written by that very able and enlightened man who wrote those on India and China in 1857-8."

TO THE SAME.

DEAR SIR,—It has been decided in the council of the gods that you must undertake the business of conducting a new review. Remember, now, that you are a mortal, while the gods live on Olympus, and rule the world after the divine sentence of the Fates. Therefore, O mortal, there is nothing for you to do but to set about the appointed work.

I saw Emerson yesterday; he came to my house, and we talked the matter over; thought as I did about it, but "more so;" offered to do his possible in the way of writing, &c., but thought that *you* were the man for editor. He thought we had better talk the matter over at the *Consessus Divorum* presently to be held at Concord, where we could mature the matter.

This review was mainly fed by the voluntary contributions of a few writers in the neighbourhood who were most interested in its principles; * but almost all the labour, and a large share of the writing, fell to Mr. Parker, who was ever ready where he was most wanted, and supplied all deficiencies. Some of his finest compositions appeared in its pages; the biographies of J. Q. Adams and of Dr. Channing, his elaborate criticisms of Mr. Emerson and of Mr. Prescott, and an article on the "Political Destination of America." For three years he kept it from falling to the ground. But there did not exist a sufficient corps of trained and ready writers, who had no interest beyond that of independent criticism, nor a sufficient public, to establish it as an organ of the Liberal School. Such a journal must happen some day; it cannot be deliberately plotted. Mr. Parker went to work in his systematic way and drew up, carefully classified, a list of the subjects which cover the province of such a journal. Some of these he wrote upon, others he offered to friends. Then he prepared a list of contributors under three heads: " A. Certain and valuable; B. Valuable, but not certain ; C. Certain, but not valuable." And not more than one or two names there recorded contradict his estimate.

His enemies used to say that he had a wonderful instinct for depreciation. It was because his common-sense seldom found more in a person than he contained. He deemed it a sacred power, worth developing and protecting from every ignoble disturbance, to judge men with absolute sincerity. He could even bid some of his controversial prejudices stand aside, if any

---

* Extract from a letter to Rev. S. J. May, Aug. 14, 1847. "Dr. Howe keeps still his interest in the work, but *I* thought his name had better not appear among the 'wise master-builders,' lest some should suspect that he was abandoning his duty to the blind who have no eyes, to attend to the blind who have eyes but see not."

matter came to a public judgment. This is different from the
prevalent American habits of wholesale eulogy or complete
defamation ; and it is the secret of the hatred which he incurred
when, to lift pure models and to correct an indiscriminate taste,
to rescue the young men from their abject homage to power and
talent, he drew his matchless portraits of distinguished names.
There are traces of his preparations for these biographical estimates extending for years, careful hoarding of facts, traits,
elusive circumstances, distinct references to each characteristic
act or speech, correspondence with distinguished contemporaries
who could either confirm or contradict a rumor, a most painstaking testing and collecting, ruled by a sad prescience that some
day would bring to him the disagreeable duty of clothing these
pure facts in speech. He was a self-elected arbiter by character
and genius ; courage, jealous conscience, intuitive observation,
health, clean hands and a pure heart, were the judicial robes in
which he sat. These are certainly essential, though they cannot
always be infallible, qualities. They justify one who is ordained
to lead and purify the people when he undertakes to exhibit its
great men.

He took a pleasure in calculating the forces which result in
the direction taken by a public man, the original character, the
nature of his education, the associates of his profession, the
passions within and the passions without, the worthy acts as
well as the doubtful ones, the first great mistake or the first
decided sacrifice. Many notes of this description were slowly
gathering, under the heads of various distinguished names, from
his earliest preaching days ; they were continuing when that
and every labour besides was interrupted by the voice which bade
a tablet be prepared for him.

TO A FRIEND IN GERMANY.

Boston, June 5, 1847.

My dear Friend,—Your kind and welcome letter of April 10th
came to me two days ago, and I write with a very joyful heart to thank
you for the kindly estimate which you have formed of my labours, and
the hearty words you address to me. It gives me great joy to find a
man in Germany who welcomes my books. I feel so much indebted to
your country for the efforts so often made for the freedom of mankind,
that I rejoice at the thought of paying back to any one a small part of
the debt which I owe to the great souls which have risen up in Germany. German literature is well known in this country, and is sowing
the land with fruitful seed. When my book was first published in

1842, I sent a copy to the *Wissenschaftliche Kritik*, but I never heard of its reception. A year ago I sent a copy to Wislicenus, and a letter therewith, but never heard from him afterwards, and do not know that he has ever received book or letter. I know your colleague very well by his writings, and therefore can appreciate your position beside him.

I cannot tell you how it warms my heart to find such a friend at such a distance. I wish I could do something to show my sense of your great kindness towards me, but I must beg you to believe that I am very grateful for your kind opinion of my book, and for your desire to translate it. It will give me great pleasure to introduce my work to the German nation in the German tongue; but though I read German easily enough, it is quite difficult to write, for I think in English. I will send you from London a copy of the third edition of my work, which contains some additional notes not found in the edition of last year. If it arrives in season, you can make use of it; but if not, why it is of no great importance. It has slowly found its way into notice here, but all the periodicals, especially the Unitarian, raised the *Zeter-geschrei* (cry of heretic), which is not entirely ended. I am called infidel, atheist, and other pleasant names of that sort. But if they call the master of the house Beelzebub, it matters little if they treat the household no better.

I had formerly a small parish in Roxbury, but abandoned that a couple of years ago and came to Boston, where I have a large audience of intelligent and noble men and women. I send you a little tract published by the Unitarians themselves, which gives some account of them. What I must add is not much in their favour. They started originally with a protest against the doctrine of the Trinity. They denied the divinity of Christ, but they did not declare the humanity of Christ. So they only affirmed a negative; their history was but the development of a negation, and little more; the protest began amongst a class of cultivated men in the most cultivated part of America; with men who had not the religious element developed in proportion to the intellectual or the æsthetic element. Therefore, they had not the element of piety in their preaching to the same extent as their opponents. Unitarianism always had a worldly character; gradually the opposition of the Trinitarians grew less and less, though the name of Christian is still wickedly denied to the Unitarians by their opponents. The Unitarians formed themselves into a sect, with the regular machinery of a theological party, *i. e.*, officers and missionaries, money and tracts. Then it was necessary for them to publish their symbolical books. But they have not ideas enough to form a theological party; the development of their negations is all that is left for them distinctively as a party. If they would affirm the humanity of Christ, they might become a great sect; but they do not see far enough for that. They declare the paternal character of God, but yet do not (as the Universalists) declare the eternal salvation of all men. They are not now making any advances towards a liberal theology; they stand still, and become more and more narrow and bigoted from year to year.

Yet, among them there are some very noble men who are entirely free, and desirous of further progress. From them as individuals much is to be hoped, but from the sect, as a sect, nothing must be looked for. It is curious to see the distinguished men who have once been Unitarian preachers, but who now preach no longer. Andrews Norton, the best scholar of the party, who, however, devotes himself exclusively to theological pursuits, is narrow, bigoted, and sectarian, but an able man. His chief work is "A Defence of the Genuineness of the Gospels," 4 vols. 8vo. Jared Sparks, eminent as an historian and editor of American State Papers; Edward Everett, formerly Governor of Massachusetts, and American Ambassador to England, now President of Harvard University; George Bancroft, now Ambassador to England, the historian of the United States, a man of great ability and genius as an historical writer; R. W. Emerson, the most original author we have produced in America, a man of wonderful gifts, and the author of some volumes of Essays, which I wish might be translated into German; John G. Palfrey, now a member of Congress, and Secretary of the State of Massachusetts; George Ripley, a sound and philosophical man, who is devoting himself to the doctrines of Fourier. All these men have left the pulpits of the Unitarians. The most prominent scholars in the denomination are Dr. James Walker, Professor of Intellectual Philosophy at Harvard University; Dr. Convers Francis, Professor of Theology at the Unitarian Theological Seminary; Dr. George R. Noyes, also Professor of Theology at the same place; Dr. Lamson; Dr. Gannett; Dr. Dewey, a showy but superficial writer; Dr. Putnam, an eloquent preacher, but nothing more. There is little scholarship and less philosophical thinking among the Unitarians. Some of their members engage in the great moral movements of the day, such as the Temperance Reform, and the Anti-Slavery movement. But the sect as such is opposed to all reforms. However, it has already done a great work in liberalizing the minds of men; the misfortune is that it is not disposed to go on further. However, "*non omnia possumus omnes,*" and others are rising up with nobler ideas than the Unitarians, who go more profoundly to work, and preach absolute religion, not controlled by the traditional authority of men, but resting in the instincts of man, and the primeval revelation which God makes to mankind. The triumph of this liberal movement, I think,i s certain; for every year the people become more and more emancipated from authority, and disposed to think freely, and to allow all others to do the same. Some of the most liberal theologians in the country are not in the Unitarian ranks, but are men of enlarged minds and generous culture. I think the destiny of the sect is to liberalize the mind of the nation in some measure, and then gradually to decay and perish. There is now a powerful movement going on in favour of the most *entire freedom of thought.* This will sweep away all the absurdities of tradition. Some valuable things of tradition will likewise be dropped, and then we must wait till some one goes back and gathers them up. Hitherto our *political* and *industrial* progress has been greater than our advance in literature and philosophy. That was unavoidable. But now intellectual things are getting attended to.

I hail with enthusiasm every great movement in Germany, and feel that the English, the French, the Germans, and the Americans are working together for the common good of the human race. It will be as in the old story of the building of Solomon's Temple; one man hewed a stone at Carmel, one a cedar at Lebanon, each working after the pattern which the great architect had put before him, not one of them having an idea of the work he was building up. At last, on men's shoulders, and upon the backs of beasts, marbles and cedars were brought together, and, 'midst a noise of harmony, the well-hewn material grew into a temple, where the people could worship, and find that God dwelt.

I hope, as opportunity allows, you will oblige me with a letter, which I shall hold very dear. I think I recognize your hand in some articles in the *Halle Allgemeine Zeitung.* Is it not so? Believe me, with the heartiest wishes for your welfare and usefulness.

Most truly, your friend,
THEODORE PARKER.

P.S.—Your *Oster Predigt* gave me great pleasure. I recognize there a noble soul, whose words cannot fall in vain upon the ears of men. I send you also Dr. Baird's book on the various denominations of America. It is an accurate book, and will help your friend, Dr. Fork, also in his work.

The next letter shows the date of his removal to Boston for permanent residence. He was obliged very unwillingly to take this step, which involved a separation from the country scenes that were so dear to him, in consequence of the distance of Spring Street from his new parish, and from the various new duties which beset him in Boston.

TO MRS. DALL.

Boston, 17 Jan., 1847.

MY DEAR CAROLINE,—Here I am in Boston; it is Sunday night, the first Sunday night I have passed in Boston these ten years. But for the trouble of removing the household and my books, I should have answered your letter before now.

What are you driving at? What have I done? *How* is the writer in the *Examiner* generous? How is truth all at once a lie because it gets into my mouth? You talk riddles. I know not what they mean, unless it be that you think I say hard things out of spite. If you will think that, why, you must, and I can't help it; only I protest and say, *such is not the fact.* Why should I forbear to tell the truth when it presses on me to be told? I must speak. Do you think I feel spite against the poor Boston Association? Not the faintest, nor never did I. Nay, nor need I ever. If they, aided by New England rum, drove John Pierpont out of Boston, and thereby disturbed the Temperance movement, why should not I tell the truth, painful though it be to me? I think it is quite Christlike to do so. I know men need to be taught reverence, not fear of men, but reverence for right, truth, justice, reverence for the laws of God, and for God who made these laws. If I lose friends, I can't help it—I must be true to *my truth,* not to *theirs.* I cannot help it, if I lose all my friends. Perhaps I am to have that trial—perhaps to sink under it; who knows?

I will send you my "Sermon of Merchants," soon as I get a little "fixed up." Perhaps that will grieve you yet more. If so, tell me. I prize your friendship all the more for its sincere statement of dissent. I like not to meet a mock concession, but a wall which sends back my words with vigorous rebound. Tell me always my faults; I will thank you for it. Still, it seems queer to me that nobody finds fault when I speak of the fraud of politicians. Nobody finds fault when bigots revile even the sectarians. But when I say a word, never so true and *notoriously* true, about the clergy, straightway a cry is raised! Even you say I use my opponents' weapons. Not so, kind Caroline; I use but my own lawful weapons—Christian weapons.

Believe me, faithfully, your friend and brother,

THEODORE.

TO THE SAME.

Boston, 28th Jan., 1847.

MY DEAR CAROLINE,—Your letter does not make the matter any clearer than before. Either what I say *is true* or *not true;* either I say it *in a good spirit,* or *not in a good spirit.* I affirm it is true what I say, I affirm that I say it in a good spirit; of the last I am sure. I know I speak only in a good spirit, in a spirit *wholly good.* The other I believe; I am confident that what I say is true. As to taking pleasure in saying what you call sarcastic things, I never felt the least pleasure—nothing but pain: if Horace or Juvenal did, it was their affair, not mine. You seem to think when I speak of the clergy, I mean the Boston Association. Far enough from it; when I mean the Boston Association, I shall say so. Many things I say of the clergy, which belong no more to the Boston Association than to the London Association, but to the clergy.

I should like to know when I ever came out with a flat untruth in regard to men like ——— and others. I never thought of ——— in a sermon. As to the "*good of the clergy,*" I have spoken time and again, till I have been told all round that I exaggerated the matter, and subsequent events have taught me to fear it was true. If I had been writing to a *Sophist,* I should not have made the allusion you speak of as to the abuse which bigots pour upon sectarians. I saw the construction which might be put upon it. I did not think *you* would put that construction on my words. As to sarcasm, I know not what you mean by it. I know of no sarcasm in the sermons under consideration. Censure is not sarcasm. I call sarcasm *malicious irony—a stripping-off the flesh* in wantonness. I plead "not guilty" to the charge. I seldom use *irony* at all; sometimes I have done it.

I have often cautioned my friends against defending me. The bitterness of my own sufferings has been to see others suffer for me. I am strong and old—older than ever before, at least; I am broad-shouldered for suffering, and have borne that all my life; *not to suffer* would be a new thing. But to have others suffer for me, I have not yet got wonted to. I have considered my course again and again in all lights, and I can't see the error you speak of. If it gave me pleasure to say hard things, I would shut up for ever. But the TRUTH, which costs me bitter tears to say, I must speak, though it cost others tears hotter than fire. I cannot forbear. I thank you for your kindly rebukes, not less because I follow not your counsel.

I hope soon to see you, and am truly, your brother,

THEODORE.

TO THE SAME.

Boston, June 2, 1847.

MY DEAR CAROLINE,—I like very much the little book of Munch. It is clear, manly, and popular. The author makes no concealment. He speaks right out. He seems to be a sincere and pious man. I do not like his views on war, and I think he is mistaken sometimes in his exegesis of Scripture; but still I hope the little book will do much good. I suppose he likes the name of Rationalist. I wonder it should be a reproach in New England; but so it is, and poor Mr. —— really seemed afraid the Unitarians might be suspected of the thing, though I think there is not the least danger of that. By the way, do you see how sectarian the denomination is becoming? I find no such sectarianism among the orthodox on Anniversary Week, as among the Unitarians. Our doctrines are so much better than the bulk of theirs, that our sectarianism seems a good deal worse.

The attempt to put down YOUR-*ism* by MY-*ism* is always bad, but in a Unitarian it is ridiculous. The Unitarians have not a sufficient dogmatic basis for a sect, and they do not develope their humanities enough to make their way as a body of working men; so I do not know what will become of them.

I hope they will protect with their ashes the ember truths of time, which the world needs alike for light and heat. We must have a good deal of charity for all men, both conservative and radical.

" Be to their faults a little blind,
Be to their virtues very kind "
is no bad rule for the active or passive part of the world.

Truly yours,

THEO. PARKER.

FROM THE JOURNAL.

Christmas, 1847.—To-day I received from Archdeacon Wolff, at Kiel, the translation of my Discourses, &c. The work awakened such heart-beatings as I have not often had for a cause seemingly so slight. I read the lines of his preface, in which he speaks so tenderly of me, not without many tears. Is it possible that I am to be henceforth a power in the world to move men, a name which shall kindle men to goodness and piety, a name of power? I think little enough of fame. But to be a man who can lead mankind a little onward, that thought would charm me.

Well, at reading that, remembering, too, how I have been treated here, I must confess I wept; and since have felt the better for my tears. God grant I may be more and better as the years go by!

February, 1848.—On Tuesday I attended a funeral of a child, five or six years old; but the parents do not believe in the continuous and conscious life of the soul. It was terribly sad. The friends that I talked with were superficial and conceited. I have seldom attended a sadder funeral. They wanted no form of prayer, but for decency's sake, wanted a minister and an address. I suppose they sent for me as the *minimum* of a minister. I tried to give them the *maximum of humanity* while their hearts were pliant, and they excited by grief. The man seemed a worthy man, humane, but with an unlucky method of philosophy. I see not how any one can live without a continual sense of immortality. I am sure I should be wretched without a *certainty* of that.

In February he went to New Haven and spent two days, very profitably, in the company of the distinguished Professors there, Taylor, and Salisbury the Orientalist, Woolsey, Gibbs, Thacher, and Goodrich.

I stayed with my good friend Noah Porter. Him and his wife I long ago learned to like and since to love. I have seldom enjoyed two days so much as these. I have found these professors kindly and gentlemanly.

He contrasts their treatment with that of more liberal thinkers, and proceeds :—

They all seem to have *liberal methods* and lofty aims. If they have not arrived at conclusions so liberal as the Unitarians, their method is decidedly better. Dr. Taylor loves philosophy and looks for advance in theology. Yet in him I thought I saw the ill-effects of Calvinism. His conception of God was a poor one.

He says most distinctly that in any contest between Reason and Scripture, Reason must be followed : " What in the name of Reason must be followed if not Reason itself ? "

TO REV. INCREASE S. SMITH.

Feb. 4, 1848.

The *Anti-Sabbath Convention* is not to be an *Anti-Sunday Convention :* not a bit of it. I think we can make the Sunday ten times more valuable than it is now, only by abating the nonsense connected with it.

I have all along been a little afraid of a reaction from the sour, stiff, Jewish way of keeping the Sunday, into a low, coarse, material, voluptuous, or mere money-making abuse of it. But if we take it in time, we can cast out the Devil without calling in the aid of Beelzebub. The Past is always pregnant with the Future. The problem of the Present is the *maieutic,* to deliver the Past. If the case is treated scientifically, the labour is easy, the throes natural, and the babe is born. The dear old lady, the Past, who is mother of us all, is soon " as well as could be expected," and receives the congratulations of her friends, and is told how well the little sonny looks—exactly like his " ma." So she cossets him up, nurses him, and gives him a Christian name. But if the case is *not* treated scientifically, the labour is long and difficult, the throes unnatural, and the sufferings atrocious ; the poor old matron must smart under the forceps, perhaps submit to the Cæsarean operation, perhaps die ; and the little monster who thus comes into the world by a matricide, is himself in a sad condition, and will have a sad remembrance all his life of the fact that he killed his mother.

Now, I think that we can deliver the Jewish Sabbath of a fine healthy Sunday, who will remember that he comes of a Hebrew stock on one side, but that mankind is his father, and while he labors for the human race, will never make mouths at the mother who bore him. But if the matter be delayed a few years, I think there is danger for the health of both child and mother.

I hope you will come to the Convention, and will speak, too. I mean to do so, but as I am not a bit of a Reactionist, and share none of the excesses of either party, I suppose I shall be too radical for the Conservatives, and too conservative for the Radicals, and so be between two fires, *cross*-fires, too.

An Anti-Sabbath Convention was held in Boston during the last week of March, 1848. The call for this meeting, written by Mr. Garrison, proposed the creation of a public opinion adverse to the penal laws requiring the religious observance of the Sabbath. This Convention sought to effect their repeal by the State Legislature, so that all persons might observe the day or not, in strict accordance with their conscience. There had been no particular enforcement of the Sunday Law to stimulate this meeting; it was only another demonstration of the criticizing and protesting spirit which ruled at that period, before all reformatory interests became swallowed up in the magnitude of Anti-Slavery. Prison reform, anti-capital punishment, peace, non-resistance, temperance, and some more transitory subjects, struggled with anti-slavery to possess the public ear. These various meetings for reform were the most vigorous and attractive of all the May Meetings; they had the best speakers, for they were countenanced by all the earnest and independent men. There was a passion for witnessing the powerful agitation of these great questions, which was not equalled by a passionate practical devotion to them. The causes themselves moved languidly, but so long as they were eloquently advocated there was no lack of audience. In this temper, any call, which involved a point that was debateable, might win a respectable hearing upon its abstract merits alone.

Mr. Parker signed this call, in company with all the prominent reformers of Boston and the State, and there was a two days' discussion of the origin, authority, and use of Sunday. Mr. Parker's speech, prefacing some resolutions, was filled with information : he objected to penal laws to enforce the formal observance of Sunday, but contended that many happy effects flowed from the custom of devoting one day to rest and to purposes of spiritual culture. His resolutions did not pass : they were not quite radical enough for the temper of the meeting. But his speech is remarkable for its common-sense.

Men commonly think they are never clear of one wrong till they have got the opposite wrong. So the Puritans, disgusted with the frivolity which they saw in the Romish Church—disappointed at finding in the Catholic Sunday, in its freedom and its frolic, so little for the direct nurture of religion—went over to the other extreme. That was a time of fanatical reaction against old abuses. There is no great danger of resisting a wrong too powerfully, but there is great danger of going over to the opposite wrong, and contending that that wrong is the right. I would not commit the same fault that the Puritans did, and go to the opposite extreme. If men are fanatical in their notion of keeping the Sunday, I would not be a fanatic and destroy it ; for, if men now are driven by the spirit of reaction against the Puritanic idea of the Sunday, and go to the opposite extreme, why, all the work must be done over again till it is well done.

I heard a man say, that if he had the whole of God Almighty's truth shut up in his left hand, he would not allow a man to unlock even his little finger. That is not my creed at all. I do not believe mankind is in the least danger of being ruined by an *excess of truth.* I have that confidence in truth, that I fear it not under any circumstances ; but I do fear error, whether coming from Churches, States, or majorities, or minorities, in the world.

When, at a later date, the community was vehemently agitated by the penal enactments against the selling of liquor, which passed the legislature notwithstanding a vigorous opposition, he preached a sermon upon the good and bad elements in the Maine * Law. That law prohibited the traffic in all kinds of drinks that intoxicate, affixed a penalty to each case of violation of the law, confiscated the property when it was found on sale, and authorized the destruction of the liquor. All previous laws upon this subject of the sale of liquors were merely regulative. This one was intended to destroy the traffic altogether, though it could not interfere with the use of liquor in private houses. Under its authority, State agents were appointed, who were empowered to keep stores for the sale of liquor for medicinal and mechanical purposes to all responsible persons, that is, to all those persons who were known by the agent not to be habitual drunkards. The name of every buyer, and the kind and quantity of liquor

* So called, because the first law of that kind was passed, and partially enforced, in the State of Maine.

he called for, was entered in a book. The mechanic arts never required so much spirit for employment in their various processes as now, and the calls for medicinal purposes showed a sudden and alarming deterioration of the public health.

This law went into operation in the State of Maine in the spring of 1851, and was enforced with great vigour. Steamboats were watched, and occasionally overhauled ; railroad stations were searched, all the dram-shops were closed, hotel barrooms hid their diminished splendour in back-rooms, and the whole traffic was driven out of sight, not without occasional disturbances of the peace. Common carriers contested the right of the State to invade their parcels and vehicles, and the constitutionality of the law was doubted by many who were not interested in the making or selling of intoxicating drinks. Practically, little was gained, because the liquor degenerated in quality as it ran out of sight, and rum-drinkers were poisoning themselves on the sly more rapidly than they did in gilded saloons. The police occasionally laid a trap to procure evidence against notorious dealers, and a race of informers began to spring up. This odious feature, inseparable from the strict enforcement of all sumptuary laws, increased the clamour of the disaffected, and provided them with a good deal of magnanimous declamation. Still, there can hardly be a doubt that a State possesses the right to abate all nuisances, and seize or remove whatever is destructive to the general health. Tainted meat and young veal are seized ; gambling and counterfeiting apparatus are looked for by the police. Bad rum and whiskey are more debasing than counterfeiters' tools. And if the State must support the hospitals, asylums, prisons, and almshouses which are so liberally peopled from the frequenters of the drinking-shops, it might rationally protect itself in some way against a traffic which directly increased its burdens. The whole difficulty lay in the practical enforcement of a principle that seems abstractly just ; so difficult, indeed, that it never became organized by permanent effective operations. Severity soon relaxed ; the police was, in general, as unwilling to unearth rum-sellers, as it was in general willing to help kidnappers, and the law fell into decay.

Mr. Parker had studied well the statistics of intemperance, and understood and powerfully depicted its immoral effects. See his " Sermon of the Perishing Classes in Boston," and " A Sermon of the Moral Condition of Boston." He never made use of wine or ardent spirits, except by medical advice, after his original vigor had become seriously impaired. He saw that the great movement for total abstinence was saving many souls and bodies; but he also saw that the question was wider even than these wide and striking facts, and he treated it in his own way.

FROM THE JOURNAL.

The law seems an invasion of private right. It is an invasion, but for the sake of preserving the rights of all. Wine is a good thing; so is beer, rum, brandy, and the like, when rightly used. I think the tee-totallers are right in their practice for these times, but wrong in their principles. I believe it will be found on examination that, other things being equal, men in social life who use stimulants moderately live longer and have a sounder old age than teetotallers. I don't know this, but believe it. I fancy that wine is the best of stimulants. But now I think that nine-tenths of the alcoholic stimulant that is used is abused; the evils are so monstrous, so patent, so universal, that it becomes the duty of the State to take care of its citizens—the Whole of its parts. If my house gets on fire, the bells are rung, the neighbourhood called together, the engine brought out, and water put on it till my garret is a swamp. But as I am fully insured I don't care for the fire, and I contend that my rights are invaded by the engine-men and their water. They say, " Sir, you would burn down the town!"

FROM A SERMON.

They burnt up a man the other day at the distillery, in Merrimack Street. You read the story in the daily papers; and remember how the bystanders looked on with horror to see the wounded man attempting with his hands to fend off the flames from his naked head! Great Heaven! It was not the first man that distillery has burned up! No: not by thousands. You see men about your streets all a-fire; some half-burnt down; some with all the soul burned out, only the cinders left of the man—the shell and wall, and that tumbling and tottering, ready to fall. Who of you who has not lost a relative, at least a friend, in that withering flame?

During the winter of 1847–8, he commenced a series of Saturday afternoon conversations, which was attended chiefly by the ladies of his parish, for theological and spiritual discussion. He also organized a society, with the object of giving the people to whom he preached an opportunity to practise philanthropy in the streets and lanes of Boston, whence many a friendless and tempted girl was rescued by their efforts, and provided with honest work.

The Melodeon was left in August, 1851, for three or four months, that some repairs might be made; and the Parish Committee applied for the Masonic Temple to hold their meetings in for a few Sundays; but this was refused, " on the ground that it would injure the reputation of the house." This result was not unexpected by Mr. Parker, who only said, " All things have their penalty. The jug of Boston is broken in more than one place."

He spent the time of this enforced vacation in thinking out new sermons :—

The germs, or thought-cells, have long been floating in my mind. I hope, for the next five or six years, to have less to do with social, civil, and political duties, and attend to my function as scholar, philosopher, theologian, and writer. There is much that I want to do.

He occupied his leisure Sundays with a visitation of the churches through all the denominations in Boston. This he did to understand, by personal observation, what the various clergymen were thinking about, and to note their tendency. He heard, perhaps, twenty sermons by prominent men :—

Heard Starr King preach on the late Celebration * in Boston. It was the best service, on the whole, that I have heard in the seventeen services that I have attended lately in and about Boston.

Many Sundays of his successive summer vacations were thus spent in hearing the different styles of preaching in the neighbourhood. His criticisms were in no case weakened by too great partiality for the doctrine which the preachers represented. Here is a specimen from the journal :—

Last day of my vacation (1856). Heard Rev. Mr. ——, of ——, preach at the Old South, touching the " brazen serpent "— a silly, worthless sermon, which, with that of —— last Sunday, makes me think even worse of the ministry than before, which was needless. The sermon had nothing of piety or morality ; the prayer scarce any touch of either. What an admirable opportunity the. minister has ! An audience which comes of its own accord to listen to the best words of a free man on the greatest of themes ! What use the minister makes of it ! I sat in the pew of a man who is engaged in the Chinese (coolie) slave trade ! The minister of the Old South Church is one of the " No Higher Law " men—an advocate of slavery. The building is historical ; and preached to me of the times that tried men's souls.

Aug. 23, 1852.—Two-and-forty years ago, my father, a hale man, in his one-and-fiftieth year, was looking for the birth of another child before morning,—the eleventh child. How strange it is, this life of ours, this birth of ours, and this death—the second birth. How little does the mother know of the babe she bears under her bosom—aye, of the babe she nurses at her breast ! Poor dear father, poor dear mother ! You little know how many a man would curse the son you painfully brought into life, and painfully and religiously trained up. Well, I will

* Visit of the President of the United States, and visit of the Canadians, to Boston, Sept. 17–19, 1851, to celebrate the Opening of the Grand Trunk Railroad into Canada.

bless you—true father and most holy mother were you to me: the earliest thing you taught me was *duty*—duty to God, duty to man; that life was not a pleasure, not a pain, but a *duty*. Your words taught me this, and your industrious lives. What would I give that I could have added some more of gladness to your life on earth—earnest, toilsome, not without sorrow!

As you look down from heaven, if, indeed, you can see your youngest born, there will be much to chide. I hope there is something to approve. Dear, merciful Father—Father God, I would serve Thee, and bless mankind!

Aug. 12, 1852.—One of the greatest advantages of a clergyman's life is this:—He has all his time devoted to the development and use of his noblest faculties. Men of science all come under this same obligation to a great degree; but they generally are devoted to matters of a purely intellectual discipline, not moral, not affectional, not religious. Doctors of medicine are an exception, and hence their superior *affectional* character; but, then, the sight of death tends, as Dr. B—— says, to make them think man is nothing but a "demnition body," and hence they are prone to materialism and lack *elevation* of intellect; but they have great tenderness of feeling.

They usually associate chiefly with well-cultivated and highly intellectual men. This is of great value to their *intellectual* development, but unfortunate for their *totality of manhood*. There would be no Kants, Leibnitzes (*Lieb-nichts*, a love-nothing, the Hamburghers called him), Voltaires, and Humes, and Hobbeses, with such as live in daily contact with the mass of men, women, and children. The good and ill of these men is apparent, and much comes of their position.

A clergyman must be a rare man to be intellectually great, or accomplish any great intellectual work. Schleiermacher, Luther, &c., had an *exceptional position*, which accounts for their exceptional character. But clergymen have a noble chance for a most manly development, if they will, and do not *herd too much with one another*. Even cabbages and lettuces do not *head* well if they touch. I am deeply grateful for the opportunity I possess, and know how much it increases my debt to mankind, and how it must be paid back.

Oct. 31.—Preached sermon on Mr. Webster—a sad and dreadful day to me: it was so painful to criticize him as I needs must. The preaching of the sermon occupied two and a half hours; it would have required three-quarters of an hour more to preach all that was written. At eleven o'clock, Wednesday, not a line of it was written; at two P.M. Saturday not a line unwritten.

In this short space of time, deducting some interruptions which he mentions, did he give shape and informing power to the materials and suggestions which he had been gathering concerning Daniel Webster for many years.

Nov. 14, 1852.—Preached the last sermon in the Melodeon. It has been a good place to us, and I feel sad at leaving it, though all the elements were hostile. I shall not forget the dark rainy Sundays when I first came, nor the many sad and joyous emotions I have felt there. Still, it was never quite so dear to me as the little church at Roxbury—my earliest one.

APPLE-TREE AND BENCH.

CHAPTER XI.

Exeter Place—The Country—Friendship—Pleasant Traits—Some Letters.

EXETER Place, into which the family moved, is terminated by a huge trellis, substantially built against the end wall of a house. This is covered by creeping plants, which take their rise in a diminutive railed space in the shape of a triangle, with a waterless fountain like an *epergne* in the centre. The end of the lane looks like a theatre-flat which has performed the garden-scene during several highly melodramatic seasons. A Flora stands there, as if for a label, to prevent misconception in the civic mind and to enforce rurality, which she does in melancholy fashion. It was a poor substitute for the woods and fields of West Roxbury. Mr. Parker languished for the natural scenes to which he had been from birth accustomed : next to books, they were essential to his comfort and happiness. He used to anticipate his summer vacations, when for several years the family would return to the house at Spring Street, with childlike delight ; every spring he began to time the blossoming of the shrubs and trees, and to tell over what he should be too late for and what he should find. It was a sore disappointment if he did not get out of town in season for the apple-blossoms, but his favourite walks and secluded spots for prayer and meditation remained to welcome the worshipper, and after he ceased to spend the summers in his old home, his occasional visits there were pilgrimages to a shrine.

Went over to West Roxbury to see the old familiar places—the dear old places! The seat under the willow was there just as I made it; the *Rudbeckia* was in blossom just as I planted it—the *hibiscus* where I set it. But the new proprietor has torn up the *sumachs* that I used to nourish with such care. I got some apples from the tree that I grafted —it was full of porter-apples, rather small, but fair.

Then there were the two favourite spots in the woods—the little *cosy place* under the cedars, where I have spent so many delightful hours; the favourite walk in the woods, with the *houseleek*, the *golden moss*, and the *peppermint* all there; all the rest had died; the rose-bush was gone, even the old pine was dead. I planted two peach-stones side by side, touching one another, and they, too, will come to nothing.

I went and gathered my favourite flowers in the old favourite locations, the *Houstonia recurvata*, &c. The trees have grown abundantly, all else looked natural, save the new division of some land; but a devil of sadness comes into the heart on visiting alone the places which are endeared by association with others, such as the rocks in the woods.

These were two large rocks in the precincts of Newton, upon land of the Brackett family. By dint of much heaving with a

THE ROCKS.

crowbar, and by propping, Mr. Parker had succeeded in converting them into a pair of rude seats; above them the summer trees whispered to his thoughts.

The dear old pines looked green as ever, and grew finely, heedless of the heads they shade; the tulip-trees have grown very big, and their leaves tinkle as sweetly as ever. The dear old church looked welcome and friendly. How I have loved it, and still love it!—but I hope I shall never preach there again, and get such a touch of the heart-break as the last time.

Here is a spring day during his residence in the old parish :—

May 3.—To-day has been one of those beautiful spring days when mere existence is a pleasure. The sun has been lovely, and a light wind from the south-west played among the pines, like the noise of the sea. As I sat beneath some cedar trees, the birds sang, the winds murmured, the bees hummed, and to show that the scene was human, a symbolical snake, more than six feet long, glided forth in the sun close to me. I felt my skin roughen up into little waves. I love to lie on the ground in such days, and dream under the clouds, and sleep. Beautiful dreams, native to the scene, start up in my slumbers, and when I awake are gone like the spring itself. It is a churlishness towards nature to sit indoors in such weather.

Spring in Boston.—May 19.—It has been one of the beautiful days we sometimes have in May: it is summer come in without singing at the door. The thermometer says 90° in the shade, yet all the morning the weather was perfect. Oh, how bright the sky was, and so deep the blue ! Then the grass on the common was so green, the children so happy, and the dogs so delighted with their swim in the frog-pond. It did me good to see such a day; I feel in love with all creatures, and such as I love most I feel quite tender to—I long for their presence ; for when I have anything so good as existence to-day I want to share it with one I love.

What a place the city is for outward action ! But it is no place for thought, least of all for *poetic, creative* thought. This summer I hope to fill up my little cistern by intercourse with nature. How I long to sit down in the woods on my favourite rock, to gather the *lady's slippers* and *polygalla*—to get a *forget-me-not*, and to swim. Oh, the apple-trees, they are in blossom now ! How grateful I feel for them ! I hardly dare think how happy I am with them. But there is one thing which affects me more, a blossoming soul, especially a young woman, a girl. I thank God that one dear friend has children, and I can play with the little rogues. I love to have them call me Mr. Parkie—a tender diminutive, which does my dry heart good.

He cannot get out to West Roxbury for a week.

Again have I been cheated out of the apple-blossoms. I never lost them but once before, and that was last year, and I felt as if I lost the whole spring in consequence. But now they are gone again, and I have but had a glimpse of them, so the sweetest of blossoms *I have missed.*

His knowledge of the flowers and trees was extensive : he knew where to find all the lowly beauties of the New England woods and meadows, and could go to fetch them on the very day of their blossoming. "Leave some," he would say, however; "do not take all." In travelling, the aspects of nature challenged observation with his regards for men. He notices the grasses, and the weeds flowering by the hard causeway, the *lapis lazuli* of the lakes, the moraines, the ice-billows of the Mer de Glace, and the veined appearance of the ice itself, the rhododendrons, bluebells, and harebells which contest a patch of soil with the snow. He has an eye for the *Aiguilles*, huge monoliths of nature, and the Alpine church, mimicing them far below with its slender spire. He makes drawings of the roofs, cart-wheels, and women's caps; but his notices of nature never expanded into wilful description; for the commonest objects, which rhetoric makes ridiculous, gave him that sort of pleasure which a child enjoys when he runs to fetch the thing that delights him, or runs to bring somebody else to look. The sublime aspects of mountain scenery escape, in his hands, with a few abrupt word-tracings, mere mnemonics for renewed enjoyment after his return.

But he also went after things which escape through ordinary dredges.

> The quiet farmer tills his field,
> Joying in grass and wheat;
> Not knowing what his meadows yield
> Before my wandering feet.

All his compositions betray this deep and discriminating sympathy with nature. They frequently breathe the freshness of the open country, where shadows, like moods, sweep across the light and are chased by light in turn. You will stumble over little reminiscences of woody brooks, over which he used to hang in the June weather, letting the sinuous ripple fascinate his gaze. Only a boy born in and of the country could run with such clovery feet through the wastes of theology.

My father, a hale man of threescore, laid in the ground his own mother, fourscore and twelve years old. She went thither gladly, with no anguish, no fear, with little pain—went as a tall pine-tree in the woods comes to the ground at the touch of a winter wind, its branches heavy with snow, its trunk feeble, its root sapless, worn out, and old. . . . .
But if he lost a child, it was a sad day, a dark year; for the child perished immature. Sadly in June or July the gardener sees his unripe apples scattered on the ground, disappointing his hopes of harvest.*

* Sermons of Theism : "Economy of Pain," p. 309. And see, in "Providence," his minute description of that "great woodland caravansary," the oak-tree, p. 255.

Look up at the stars, study the mathematics of the heavens, writ in those gorgeous diagrams of fire, where all is law, order, harmony, beauty without end; look down on the ant-hill in the fields some morning in early summer, and study the ethics of the emmets, all law, order, harmony, beauty without end; look round on the cattle, on the birds, on the cold fishes in the stream, the reptiles, insects, and see the mathematics of their structure and the ethics of their lives; do you find any sign that the First Person of the Godhead is malignant and capricious, and the Fourth Person thereof is a devil—that hate preponderates in the world? *

No doubt the Bible contained the imperfection of the men and ages concerned in writing it.   The hay tastes of the meadow where it grew, of the weather when it was made, and smells of the barn wherein it has been kept; nay, even the breath of the oxen housed underneath comes down to the market in every load.

Hark! the Bible rustles, as that southern wind, heavy with slavery, turns over its leaves rich in benedictions; and I hear the old breath come up again—" Thou shalt love thy neighbour as thyself."

How much a great man of the highest kind can do for us, and how easy!   It is not harder for a cloud to thunder than for a chestnut in a farmer's fire to snap.

Little boys in the country, working against time, with stints to do, long for the passing-by of some tall brother, who, in a few minutes, shall achieve what the smaller boy took hours to do.   And we are all of us but little boys, looking for some great brother to come and help us end our tasks.

This at my side is the willow; it is the symbol of weeping, but its leaves are deciduous; the autumn wind will strew them on the ground. And beneath here is a perennial plant; it is green all the year through. When this willow branch is leafless, the other is green with hope, and its buds are in its bosom.   Its buds will blossom.   So it is with America.

In a sermon upon speculative atheism is this mark of a nice observation :—

Convince me that there is no God—then I should be sadder than Egyptian night.   My life would be only the shadow of a dimple on the bottom of a little brook, whirling and passing away.

In his journal for 1857 occurs the following :

The night spreads her broad soft wings over me and all nature, and I feel inspiration in her presence.   What thoughts of other times come thronging upon me when I have lain, such nights as this, with the soft south-western wind sheeting gently through my half-opened

* "The Popular Theology," p. 107.

window, now listening to the hum of some far-off walker's voice, now letting my feelings take wing to the loftiest, till, lest I forget the body, my charm is pleasantly broken by the sound of an apple dropping softly to the ground.

He took pleasure in animals of every description, and was never tired of watching them. Bears were his especial delight : he said they were great humorous children, with a wary Scotch vein in them. His house was full of bears, in plaster and ivory, and wood, from Berne, and in seal-metal. It was a short and economical way to his heart to fetch him home an odder bear than usual. He once collected materials for an article on bears, and at that time he made the acquaintance of every brute bear between this and the White Mountains.

A French caricature from the Revolution of 1847—48, representing the different characters in the shape of bears, was given to him by Wendell Phillips, and straightway raised conspicuously above his bureau.

TO MISS CATHERINE JOHNSON.

Anti-Slavery Office, New York, 28 May, 1858.

My dear Cousin Kathie,—The new bear came the other day—the famous new bear. I assembled all the other bears of the family, introduced them to each other, and left them in their mutual admiration society. You don't know how the little bears rejoiced to welcome this new one ! When the great original bear* came home, and went into the parlor, and saw all the household of bears assembled together and the new bear among them, great was her amazement thereat.

Many thanks for this bear, which, it is thought surpasses all the rest.

For the bears, faithfully,

Cousin Theodore.

When he passed through Berne upon his last journey, he spent a great portion of the time in leaning over the pit where the symbolical animals are kept, nor could he be got home to breakfast till he had duly fed them, and exhausted upon them his choicest ursine epithets.

Here is an allusion to another present : —

But the bear,—the *bear*. Why, it is a most admirable specimen of that genus—he stands now, hat in hand—that old slouch hat, such as none but a bear ought to have (I left *mine* at Desor's—I suppose he will wear it when he goes to meeting), and is looking at the brown bear which my wife always carries as one of the Penates of the family.

---

* "Bearsie" was a pet name for his wife.

Why, it is a perfect beauty; I shall be tempted to seal all my letters, but this to you will have the first stamp, to consecrate the seal.

Here is something upon hens :

FROM THE JOURNAL.

The hen has four notes. 1. She has a *common note*, and in it she speaks all day long to her little charge. She never tires; cluck, cluck, by sunshine and in rain. Is her brood large, she does not despair. Is it small, she is still faithful in little as in much. So Providence ever watches over all men, great and little, and never wearies.

2. She has also a *special call.* This she uses when she discovers any corn of wheat, an insect, or a worm. The chicks come thronging in to share the bounty. So Providence sends us unusual favours.

3. She has a note of *alarm.* When the hawk or the weasel is at hand she utters a piercing scream; the young ones betake themselves to the nearest shelter.

4. She has a *brooding note.* At night and at noon, and often in the rain or the fierce heat, she calls her little ones under her broad motherly wings. With delicate beak she urges them beneath their shelter, and tucks them in. Then with a low, parental, purring note she lulls them to repose. It has a composing sound. At first they interrupt its tranquillizing monotony with sharp "zip," as one crowds upon the other, but soon all is still and they sleep.

So God broods over all His creatures. The voice of nature speaks softly in its brooding note.

HABITS OF BIRDS.—Wild geese will eat frogs. I saw a couple of tame ones attempt to catch a poor inoffensive frog in the brook to-day. I heard their voracious jaws snap together as they struck at the defenceless croaker, but he skipped away, laughing in his sleeve.

Saw two little birds on a pear-tree eating the little insects that prey on the blossoms. Thus both they and the insects aforesaid aid in consummating the mysterious marriage of the blossoms. I never knew whose matrimony the birds celebrated in their songs before.

He was never able to maintain any respectable sentiment for cathedrals, for the abject rows of the poor and ignorant upon the pavement were so many figures of the total waste in stone of their bread and education, and he believed that the only effect of magnitude and solemnity was to keep stupefied their poverty-stricken natures.

Here is an extract from a letter :—

I should like to look at the cathedrals once more. What grand things they are to look at, and to think of! But they always struck me as great *tombs.* The men who built them are dead, and the soul which wrought in the builders now works at quite different things; while the mob of people, and the mob of priests, seem quite unworthy to live in such a huge shell,—a caterpillar in the magnificence of a sea-conch. Pœstum is not deader to Europe, and further behind the civilization of this age, than the mediæval cathedral is behind the life of the more progressive people of New England.

The music has a soul in it; but that now-a-days is often operatic. Yet I love the simple grandeur of some of the great pieces I used to hear in the Italian Churches. There is one—I heard it many times—which seemed to represent the life of man: the top of it light, trifling, foamy, frothy, changeable; but underneath it all, a great ground-swell of music went on as regular as the psalm of the ocean. It always reminded me of the hymn—

> " Our lives through various scenes are drawn,
>   And vex'd with trifling cares ;
>   *While thine Eternal Thought moves on*
>   *Its undisturb'd affairs."*

But his sympathy for men and women soared far above his feeling for nature, animate and inanimate, and for all the expressiveness of art.

This is the last day of my vacation—for though my preaching is put off another month, my study begins in earnest to-morrow. I miss much that belonged to me at West Roxbury, not to speak of the Human Face. I miss the sweet little spots which were to me my *oratoires* in the fields. There, too, I know every spot where the flowers grow, but here none at all.

This Human Face belonged to a very dear friend, but the phrase becomes impersonal when put on record, expressive of that broad world of kindred people whose horizons enclosed for him the brightening weather of friendship and spiritual delights. "Daylight and Champian" could not show him God's grace so clearly. It seemed to him wonderful what friends could do for a troubled and buffeted spirit.

How soon the memory is clear of disagreeable recollections, of pain, of suffering, of ugly things, and how perpetually do beautiful fancies and dear affections dwell with us! It is only by effort that I recall the painful things of my life, and when they come back, it is "trailing clouds of glory" that they come. And there is one face in my past life which comes with all the beauty of a new moon, the few hours of her brief sun on a June evening after a shower,—as the moon with the evening star beside her.

1.

Oh, blessèd days were those,
  When thou and I together,
Sought through the fields the wild red rose,
  In the golden summer weather !

The lilies bloom'd at morning's glow
  On the breast of the winding river :
I brought to thee their purest snow,
  Less welcome than the giver.

2.

There's beauty in the morning flowers,
    And in the noon-day sun;
Time measures out these golden hours
    With the fairest sands that run.

I know not what it signifies,
    But a single look from thee
Comes fresher than the morning skies
    Or noonday light to me.

Oh, people thou my thoughts by day,
    Adorn my dreams by night;
So cheer my sadden'd heart alway,
    By faith when not by sight.

His susceptibility in the society of women to that influence of mind and presence which they have in the society of men whom they attract, was a very decided characteristic. That subjective quality of sex, which the poet calls *Das ewige weibliche* (the everlasting womanly), and which sustains the everlasting difference between woman and man, that draws and piques them both, drew him along, a most willing captive, held and led by all the pure and gentle elements of his own nature.

My companions of choice, and not necessity, are almost all women. I wonder at this; I never willed it so. I have always been intimate with eminent women,—that is, for nearly twenty years; and I number but few eminent men among my acquaintance. Yet in literature, I am no great admirer of the efforts of women. Mrs. Hemans and Margaret Fuller are the only learned women that adorn my book-shelves; among my correspondents, ladies fill a large place. Is it their affection or the beauty of their mind that attracts me to them? The beauty of the person was once a dear attraction, and has lost none of its charms even now. I love to look at a handsome woman. Her beauty has a subtle fascination for me which my weak intellect does not quite understand. I love the subtlety of woman's mind, in striking contrast to my own direct and blunt modes of mental operation. Thus, I love the nimble adroitness of Mrs. H—— and Mrs. A—— much better than the Macedonian-phalanx march of good Miss ——. I like not this dazzling subtlety in men.

Strong is the effect of this diversity of sex; I like the presence of woman, as such. I love to feel the presence of incarnated womanliness.

The other day I met a young woman in the street, and our *eyes met*. I felt a sensation of unspeakable delight which lasted all the morning. I cannot tell why it was, but so it was. It was involuntary delight.

This has been one of my unfortunate days. I went out to Roxbury, but saw not the chief object of my visit. She had gone to visit a sick friend. It makes me better to see her; it is like visiting a shrine which has the gift of miracles, and heals men of sadness, lowness and despair. So I visit my *Madonna Miraculosa* from time to time, and come home a better man, I hope, certainly with each faculty brightened and enlarged. I barely missed her on the return, for the wagon was in sight just as I got into the 'bus to come away. But, well, I shall take as penance and mortification what I receive with sorrow; and if angels' visits be few and far between, will make much of the angel that I missed.

He made the following confession to George Ripley :—

There was a pond a mile off (in Lexington), whither I used to go a-fishing, but only caught the landscape. I never fished much, but looked down into the water and saw the shadows on the other side creep over it, and listened to the sounds from the distant farms. When I was from six to seven years old, there came a perfectly beautiful young girl to our little District School; she was seven to eight. She fascinated my eyes from my book, and I was chid for not getting my lessons. It never happened before—never after the little witch went away. She only stayed a week, and I cried bitterly when she went off. She was so handsome, I did not dare speak to her, but loved to keep near her, as a butterfly to a thistle-blossom. Her name was Narcissa. She fell over into the flood of time, and vanished before I was seven years old.

TO MISS HUNT.

24th August, 1853.

DEAR SARAH,—It is very kind in you to wish me all the sweet and beautiful things which came in your note. I wish I was worthy of half the affection you feel for me, and have so often shown.

But I will try to be nobler, and deserve it better.

I believe no man ever was more blessed with the affectionate friendship of men and women than I am. I often wonder at it. For to my theological and political foes, I appear as one of the most hard and unfeeling of this world's wretches. But perhaps, there is some " silver lining " to this ragged cloud, and the dear eyes of some kind women turn to it, and make sunlight there.

I thank you many times for all the kindly sympathy you have shown me, and the strength you have given.

So every blessing on you, and good bye. T. P.

You forgot to send the customary kisses, but I will call to-morrow, and take them.

Birth-days and anniversaries seemed as impressive to him as they do to a child. Every year underscored them afresh with tender thoughts and holier wishes : the date of his leaving home, of his sister's death, of his ordination, of his South Boston sermon, of his settlement in Boston—all the days whose date hope or trial had deepened, moved his heart with grateful awe at the mystery of life, as when the great bodies of the sky roll, faithful to a moment, out of absence into our expecting gaze. So he used to ask his friends to tell him their birth-days, and some of these he had set apart for simple observance in his house. In the same feeling he received the gifts and mementoes of his parish or of friends.

Gifts which he received from members of his parish always drew from him some half-surprised recognition.

Dec. 24, 1853.—Had a family gathering of sixteen persons—all ages, from eighty-five to four. Isaac and I, the last of eleven children.

In the morning, to my great surprise, came a piano. Not one of the company could play on it. But it speaks to me continually of the old sad times, when men who aspired to teach mankind, paid for it with their lives. I will try to be a nobler man, to deserve all the kindness which shows itself more tenderly than in gifts.

What a comfort it is to have about you the mementoes of dear ones when they are absent! I am surrounded by the gifts of tender friends I wipe my pen on the gift of one; the pen itself a remembrance of another; a third gave me the lamp which shines on my writing to-night. The spectacles beside me are the gift of a fourth person; the little delicate glass-wiper came from a dear old lady; the portfolio is from one hand now still in the grave; the *presse-papier* is also a gift; the knife in my pocket, and the pencil, the basket which holds my letters, the seal I stamp them with, are from a most welcome and dear soul; even the chair I sit in, and the ornament beside me, is from that fountain of friendship; the little porcelain vase which holds remembrancers, the sweetest and daintiest flowers in their season, is from the same friendship; and tender mementoes of affection, there are, too dear almost to name. But what are all these things to the living person? They are steps in the ladder of love. Affection mounts up, and if the throne be vacant—what emptiness!

I found the wild rose in blossom to-day for the first time this season, and the white azalea, and sent them off to a friend to whom I love to consecrate the first flower of each pretty kind that I gather, and have done so for many a year.

These things are picked up on the field that shook with his polemic tread, across which liberating truths bore their sparkling scorn against oppression. The gentle tokens strew it far and wide.

> " The bravest are the tenderest,
> The loving are the daring."

Here are lines amid notes of an excursion to the White Mountains :—

> When sunder'd far from one so near
>   My fancy fetches thee;
>   And to my soul's society
> I welcome thee most dear.
>
> And often as I walk along,
>   The sweetest sense of thee,
>   Comes trickling down my memory,
> And I run o'er with song.
>
> More keen am I for God in prayer,
>   To find myself with thee;
>   For in that high society,
> Thy spirit seems to share.

No friends ever received such a generous measure of appreciation as his ; yet it was not, as might be suspected, because they were not his enemies, but because the same sincerity which loved them knew also their faults. He spoke of these things to them, like a frank child, and if they proffered the same courtesy in return, in a clear spirit, free from reproach, he was always gratefully surprised.

One day, in quoting the following lines, he adds a commentary which expresses his method of dealing with his friends :—

> " Man muss um gut zu seyn,
> Um jede Pflicht der Menschheit zu erfüllen,
> Nur eine Kunst, die schöne Kunst verstehen,
> In jede Menschenbrust *das Gute nur zu sehen.*"*

Now, this is partly true; but let us know the whole that is in man, and then honour him *spite of his faults.* No doubt it is a hard thing to love John and Peter with all their faults. But it must be so.

REQUISITES OF FRIENDSHIP.—I am not exactly perfect myself, but I should be glad to have perfect friends—men without conceivable fault or blemish. Yet, as such are not given on earth, perhaps not in heaven, I am glad to take men as I find them. I don't find it necessary to conceal my friends' imperfections; I like them in spite of their faults, not because they are faultless. I should be sorry if my friends found it necessary to render me perfect before they could love me. I am willing to acknowledge their errors, and still to love what remains unsullied.

In 1859 he writes to a friend :—

Nothing surprises me so much as to find how many persons *love* me, not only in New England, but in Old England, and also in Germany. Rejoice with me.

Though he longed to be on good terms with all people, and had a tender vein which would have betrayed a smaller person into transient, destructive partialities, yet justice meted out all his dealings, and he wanted nothing but conscience to rule between him and his friend.

Oct. 12, 1839. C——'s visit was an April shower to me. It has made me flowery and young again. I cast off my years as if upon a summer's ·day in the green meadows gathering flowers. He has awakened the slumbering love of song in me. Oh, I love C——! he is so good, so rich, so full of spontaneous fellowship with all that is noble. Yet he is not a man whom the world will use well. So let it be. He that hath the joy of his genius, let the world wag as it will for him.

* Would you be good, and fill each human duty ?
One art's enough for that—the finest art—
See but the good in every human heart.

Miss P—— came to spend the Sabbath with us. Her magnanimity almost surpasses conception, or, rather, she has no magnanimity; it is all great-heartedness, and she never dreams that she exercises the virtue of magnanimity.

Her kindness is inexpressible. How much love the divine woman has! It is her life. How disinterested, too! Oh, the perfection of woman's heart—and sometimes the depravity of woman's heart!

What shall I say of ——? I grieve to say what I *must* say. I did not think that religion had softened a spirit naturally so austere, nor that charity had tempered a character so selfish and tyrannical by birth. I did not dream those silken cords had joined her so softly to the sky. But I did dream that considerations of prudence, suggestions of the understanding, not a little experience of the world, and a very subtle mind with considerable insight into first principles, had done the work as well as such agents could effect it. Now I see my mistake. Nor that alone, but my old rule, to which, in her case, I was making a conjectural exception—that religion alone can regenerate a spirit at first ill-born—holds good. After wandering some thirty years in the Saharas and Siberias, the Englands and Egypts of life, finding a sad mingling of earth and heaven, to see one of vast gifts of intellect, great and diversified culture in elegant letters and the arts, of deep experience in the detail of life, one tried by suffering, mind and body —to see such a one giving way to petty jealousies, contemptible lust of power, and falling into freaks of passion, it is ludicrous first, and then it is melancholy.

. It is not for me to forgive anything. Thank God, I have no occasion; but it is for me to pity and to mourn. It is for me to show others the only salvation for themselves.

About 1840, Miss Burley told me of the fine genius and finer moral endowments of Mr. Cheney. He made some crayons for her family then, which I admired much. In 1841-2, Mr. G. Russell sat in another artist's room, and heard a conversation in the next apartment relative to the sermon of the " Transient and Permanent in Christianity." One was attacking it and its author; Mr. R., learned that the defender was Mr. Cheney, an artist with fine genius. I was surprised to find an artist who thought enough about religion to venture from the beaten path of theology, and still more to find he was from the heart of Connecticut. In 1842 or 1843, I went and introduced myself, and asked him to make a portrait of Lydia, but he was just going to Europe. I met him in Rome, and we had many good times together. In 1851, I thought that he was to marry E. L., but said nothing until the engagement took place; then I told him of it. It pleased him much that my feeling had indicated what his had told him before. I helped marry them, May 19, 1853. He painted Lydia's and my portrait the following autumn.* Now he is dead. I went to Manchester, Conn., to attend his funeral, to-day (Sept. 12, 1856), my wife's birthday. He was not quite forty-six. A dear, noble man of genius.

Mr. Cheney owed the awakening of his religious life to Mr.

* This was a labor of love which Mr. Cheney would insist upon performing.

Parker's influence, which cleared away a good deal of inherited rubbish, and set his pure and lofty soul open to the light. We shall never know all whom he thus liberated, to whom he gave righteousness for doctrine.

When Mr. Desor, the accomplished naturalist, was in America, he was a welcome guest at the house in Exeter Place, for he brought what Mr. Parker always craved, facts, fruitful suggestions, systematic views, a great familiarity with many provinces of science. Seldom has a man better equipped with knowledge, or with a finer capacity for sure and careful synthesis, come from the Old World to lend his talent to the New. But he brought also a pure heart, simple habits, great personal integrity. These qualities were more welcome to the preacher and doer of righteousness than all his scientific attainments, and they became most intimate and dear to each other. It was a dark day to Mr. Parker when Desor felt obliged to return to Europe.

It is pleasant to remember that we, at least, have always appreciated him, have always been friendly to him ; and nothing has ever occurred, in nearly five years' acquaintance and almost four years of intimate friendship, to cause the least regret. He has always been on the humane side, always on the just side. His love of truth, and sober industry, his intuitive perception of the relations of things, his quick sight for comprehensive generalizations, have made me respect him a good deal. His character has made me love him very much. There is no man that I should miss so much of all my acquaintance. I count it a privilege to have known him, and it will be a joy to remember him.

Travellers and exiles from all lands reported themselves early at the house of the man of whose humanity and love for liberty they had heard. Exiles especially, who were generally cultivated and enlightened men, with patriotic reasons for expatriation, received a fraternal welcome. He obtained employment for many, was ready with pecuniary assistance to the extent of his means, and only levied a toll upon the knowledge of the applicants. But they could never smuggle anything intelligible past his scrutiny into the country. Of one he learned the latest speculations of comparative philology ; of another, the state of religion ; of another, curious facts of physiology ; of another, popular statistics; of another, information concerning professors and public men. He knew how to find, across the disabilities of various languages, the precise *forte* and vocation of all these talented men. Notes of conversations are recorded which were carried on in five or six different languages in the same evening company. But he did not speak any foreign language with fluency.

TO REV. S. J. MAY.

June 17, 1851.—I have just had a letter from Dr. Otto Fock, Professor of Philosophy at Kiel, in Denmark, who wants to come to America. He is about forty years old, learned and able, but, alas! a republican. He cannot live in Germany : the police look after him too sharp. Can we do anything for him here? He is learned and industrious; will *work*. Can we find a place worthy of him? He has written a valuable book—History of " Socinianismus." Perhaps he might write an " excellent t-r-a-c-t " for Father B—, or prove that the Apostle Thomas was a Unitarian, or if not Thomas, then, at least, Jude or Judas.

Besides Dr. F., another German Doctor of Philosophy has written for the same purpose, to find a home in America. He is a philologian, Dr. Lobeck, from Königsberg, a learned man, librarian of the University at that place. He has written some books, and has been an editor of a *Volksbote* (" People's Messenger,") and is a democrat. Do tell me if we can do anything for these noble-hearted men.

TO HON. GEORGE BANCROFT.

Boston, March 1, 1852.

DEAR SIR,—I am waiting impatiently for your new book; if it is not the finest piece of historical composition in the English language, I shall never quite forgive you ; for then it will not fulfil the prophecy I have often made. But I write now about other matters. There is a noble German *Gelehrte*, Dr. Günther, from Leipsic, about to establish a school for boys, at Newport, and I wish you to send him your little folks. Dr. G. is a very accomplished man—a great *Historiker* and *Philolog*, and a true gentleman. He was one of the Frankfurt Parliament men ; is now in exile, and has been teaching Danish, Swedish, Icelandic, and old Gothic, in Boston this winter. Please remember him, and not forget   Truly yours, THEO. PARKER.

When one or two intimates, who were good listeners, and knew what to expect, came into his study, he would turn towards them from his desk, dropping instantly the care of the moment, to set forth in racy flow, as if the business of the week were to anticipate and enjoy this visit in particular. No matter what lay upon the desk—Welsh Laws—History of Canon Law —a volume of Littrè's Hippocrates—a heap of authorities for an article—or sheets where a sermon was just on the turn of a wave, with whose break the Music Hall should echo,—he would start with the matter which he had in hand, as if you came to see him about it, and thence find his way into a most delightful monologue, which lasted, with occasional runlets from the listeners, as long as they had the hardihood to remain. It was neither metaphysical nor theological, had no didactic malice, and was not oppressively bent upon convincing. You would say it was a reverie, speaking aloud before he knew it, if it were not for the pleased recognition of your presence. As it went on, he would make such compact and portable statements of whatever subject happened to be caught up, that you felt for your pencil and note-book. It seldom failed to draw in his humor, which was an inexorable common-sense at play, engaged mischievously in steal-ing the clothes away from some skeleton doctrine, or the rouge and false teeth from some mediæval spinster of the popular churches. And it was none the worse for a touch or two of mimicry, just enough to let a person here and there appear to color the bigotry or the foolishness,—not to make you despise whomever you recognized, it was too genial for that, and imper-sonal, like an improvisatore. If a phantom of some "fee grief" swept across the surface, and chilled it for a moment, it was soon gone; you had hardly begun to feel uneasy. It was let out by his absolute sincerity, which was the only patrol he had around his wealth and beauty: as ineffective as the broad bright mea-dows of Conway to repress the mountain streams. And how you rejoiced that he was incapable of secrecy when some feeling of Religion, that almost prayed in the deepening voice, some personal conviction of his own immortality, or of the universal love which his faith seemed to draw and condense for you in that book-lined study itself, as if to dim its titled wisdom, took advan-tage of his life's obedience to endow your morning call.

It was also a good thing to find him in the cars, going to or returning from his lectures in the East or West. He was never so deep in his carpet-bag of books as to miss the opportunity for some gentle and courteous word. He often would approach women who appeared to be plunged in sorrow, to befriend them with good words and offices. At the end of one of these jour-neys he said:—

"Now, I have given up my seat to several women, fed babies with candy, and made myself agreeable, and nobody but an old squaw with a load of baskets has recognized it. And she only touched her hat."

He liked to draw bright-looking young men into conversation, and sometimes in this way has given determining courses to vague and restless lives. He was very sharp to see who might be helped in this way. In his carpet-bag he always carried a little silk bag of comfits for the restless children, and thought it no loss of time from his book to leave his seat and win them back to quiet.

It was one of the greatest and most real sorrows of his life that he had no children. He was capable, as few men are, of guiding children towards the Blessed Life. He had all which a child needs—love, simplicity, contempt for doctrinal views, wonder and awe for natural marvels, and none for ecclesiastical, an intense sympathy with the "joys of mere living," a genius for truthfulness. He could never conceal that he languished for the society of children.

At one time in our life we need objects of instinctive passion, then objects of instinctive affection. Neither can take the place of the other, and both are needed for the welfare of man. But how many are destitute of both, in the present state of society! I suffer continually from lacking an object of instinctive affection. I want a little *Mites o' Teants*, or *Bits o' Blossoms*.* I nursed my affections for Mr. Russell's little ones, till the affections grew to a great growth. Now there are no objects for them to cling to. So my vine trails on the ground, and earth-worms devour the promise of the grape.

Oct., 1856.—But my immediate help I find in industry—literary and philanthropic work. Yet even with that help, in the pauses of my toil, the sense of loneliness comes over me and fills me with pain. How much worse must it be with women, and especially *the unmarried!* With women the love of children is stronger than with men, and they have fewer external duties to divert their thoughts from their own sadness.

A neighbour, and member of his parish, sends in joy to tell him of the birth of a child. He thus replies, addressing the father and mother :—

I thank you for so kindly remembering me in such an access of new gladness to your hearth and hearts—nay, heart, for there is but *one*, especially at such a time, in man and wife. I have sons and daughters, sympathetically, in the good fortune of my friends. I was expecting to hear of this advent in your family. God bless the little immortal, who comes a new Messiah to cheer and bless the world of home.

Here is another reply, made on a similar occasion :—

It is my lot to have no little darlings to call my own. Yet all the more I rejoice in the heavenly blessings of my friends. The thing that I miss most deeply in coming from Roxbury to Boston is the society of my neighbours' little children, whom I saw several times a day, and fondled, and carried, and trotted, and dandled, in all sorts of ways, as if they had been mine own.

Well, God bless the life that is given, and the life that is spared, and the life which rejoices in them both! I thank the new mother for remembering an old friend in *such* an hour. So give her my most affectionate greetings, and believe me, happily, yours.

These letters to the Rev. Wm. H. White, his old teacher, now deceased, come from a warm and faithful heart. It need not be

* Pet names for the children of his dear neighbours.

told here in what way, more substantial than by letter-writing, he befriended his teacher's family, and for years supplied a generous culture to his daughter. And that is only one instance of Mr. Parker's beneficence, out of which pure pleasures flowed for him every year :—

West Roxbury, 26th March, 1846.

DEAR FRIEND,—I found your letter in the Boston Post-Office yesterday, and thank you most heartily for remembering an old scholar who has never thought of you but with gratitude and affection. I supposed you had forgotten me, or I should have sent you my little publications before. I did not know that you would take an interest in one whom you so much befriended twenty-five years ago. But, trust me, I have inquired all about you with the greatest interest. If the *boy* Theodore was affectionate, I think you will find the man is the same old sixpence. I may be "*proud*" and very "*wicked*," for aught I know; I will not say I am not—you shall come and see—but at least I do not forget my old teacher. I passed through your town once, on a rainy day, with three ladies in a coach. I did not pass within a mile of your house, to my great disappointment; but I learned of your welfare from one of your parishioners whom I found in the way. Once since I passed, in the Rail Road I think, through Littleton. Otherwise I was never in your town. You inquire after my doings, &c. I have been married almost nine years, but have no children. This is the only affliction of my life almost. But I never complain of that, for I am a singularly happy man. You shall ask my wife if I *love* her—or shall see her, and then guess. I think my neighbours love me—I know their children do. I have been nearly nine years in this place, and think I have but one *enemy* in it—that is a dog whom I never treated ill, but give a bone to now and then. Still, he growls at me, and *bit* me the other day : since that time I have given him over as not to be overcome by me. I think he is the only thing living that owes me a *personal* spite. I had rather have the affection of good plain folks, like my neighbours, than all the fame of Luther and the power of Napoleon. As for my *theology*, it has grown out of *me* as unavoidably as my arm has grown with my body. I think it a Christian theology, and a true one. Doubtless there are errors connected with it : I will gladly cast them away, soon as I find them *errors*. Yet I think there are truths also which will not perish; still, I am but a very humble seeker after truth. That you may judge for yourself, I will leave for you, at Munroe's book-store, a copy of all my works, which I beg you to accept as a humble token of esteem from an old pupil, though it may be an unworthy one. I remember how it grieved me once to get a spot on *your* Latin Grammar (Smith's N. H. Lat. Gram.), on the pronoun *ille, illa, illud*, which you kindly lent me. I hope you will take my gift as a return for the damage I did your book. I wanted to send you the first thing I ever published, and all since, but I feared you would not care for it, and so, through sheer modesty, have been thought *proud*. You ask for my sister—she has passed on where she belonged; so have all my sisters. Out of eleven children, three only are left—my brother Isaac, at Lexington, whom you never knew; my brother Hiram, at Lowell, whom you remember; and *myself*. The reddish haired girl you mention was only a friend; she became *almost* a sister, but not quite, and has gone I know not where. I have not seen your face since you were at a school-examination in Lincoln. Then you sat down beside me, and did not know me! I cried all night at the thought of it, and weep a little now in sympathetic recollection. If you ever come this way, it will gladden my heart to see you. Next winter I shall live in Boston, and will entertain you hospitably, if you will visit your "dear old pupil,"   T. P.

TO THE SAME.

Boston, 14th March, 1848.

DEAR FRIEND,—It was not I that sent you the sermon on J. Q. Adams, so you have one friend that you did not think of. I sent none of those copies of the sermon. One of these days I think I shall print the sermon myself, in a more full and complete form, and shall then be happy to send it to you. You object to the "Cohasset Rocks;" the words were not in the MS., but I selected the figure at the moment, and for this reason: I once went a-fishing with Mr. Adams (and others) on the Cohasset Rocks. They are large, and extend a long way on the coast, and are much assailed with storms. Everybody at Boston knows the Rocks, and Mr. A. often went down there, and so they were in my mind *connected* with him. I prefer the "Cohasset Rocks" in such a connection to "Gibraltar," because they are an object well known, and the other not well known by the sight. If I were to speak of birds in a sermon, I should not mention the nightingale and the skylark, but the brown thrasher and the blackbird, for the same reason. I am glad you like the sermon: it is the only production of my pen that I have heard *praised* more than *blamed*. It has been *popular*, if you will believe it. I know not why, and do not know whether it is to my credit or otherwise, that it is so. You were kind enough to say it had not *my usual faults of style*, or *of thought*. I thank you for the frankness of the statement. I have always been most grateful to persons who made me ashamed and not satisfied. If you will tell me what are my usual faults of style and of thought, you will do me a great service. I never sought praise so much as perfection, and shall be very grateful to you if you will do me that kindness. *Fas est et ab hoste doceri*, but my *hostes*, though numerous enough, have done me little good by their criticisms: you were an early friend, and did me a great service once. Why won't you do me a greater one now? Once, when I was a little bit of a boy, in the *old* school-house on the *north* side of the road in Lexington, the first winter that you taught a school there, one of your acquaintance told my sister that you had spoken of me to her at a party the night before. "Well," said I to my sister, "what did he say?" She returned, "He said that he was disappointed in Theodore; they told him he was 'a smart boy,' and he found him a *good* one, and put him upon Latin, but he would not study; he did not get along well, was lazy, and loved play better than his book. He was sorry he had put him into Latin," &c., and I was eight years old, turning to nine. I went off and cried awhile—that I had disappointed *you*, whom I loved with all my might;

but the next day you had to take it, the lesson was the verb *sum*, and its compounds, in " The N. H. Latin Grammar." I recited six times that forenoon. It was Saturday, and you heard *me* when I had anything to say, and asked me repeatedly *what had got into me.* I didn't tell you, but thought *you knew.* The next day my sister, who had seen what took place, told me that you had never said so of me, but quite differently. Well, the impulse lasted, and I remember well that I repeated all the rules in the Syntax (I think they were eighty-four) without prompting or without a question being asked me. So much for your criticism *then.* Now, I think it might do me *more* good, for certainly I am quite as humble as then. So let me have the criticism. I sent you a sermon this morning before receiving your letter, and am truly your old pupil and present friend,

THEO. PARKER.

TO THE SAME.

Boston, 13th May, 1851.

MY DEAR OLD MASTER,—It was very kind of you to write me such a nice, good, generous letter the other day. Trust me, your words of sympathy and of esteem are very dear to me, and your words of rebuke, of caution, of warning are as dear and as much valued. I love most those that are so sincere as to tell me of my faults, and shall always value your admonitions as much as when you gave them to me over a little Latin Grammar, in the little black school-house at Lexington. You have forgotten that you once rebuked me for asking to have the same thing explained twice. I met, in " Historia Sacra," the word *avulsum*, and asked you what it came from. You showed me *avello* in the dictionary; but the next day, or the next week, I met the same *avulsum* again, and asked the same question a second time. You told me " I showed you that the other day." " I know it, sir, but I have forgotten it." " You must not forget it again," said you, and showed me *avello* for the second time. Well, I will try and profit by a rebuke now as much as then. So if you will always point out my *faults*, while you commend any excellence you may discover or imagine, I shall rejoice, and will try and mend.

I had hoped to see you at your own house long before this, but much work forbids; still I hope to see you at mine on Anniversary Week. With best regards to you and yours, believe me your old pupil and hearty friend,

THEO. PARKER.

TO THE DAUGHTER.

Newton Corner, 21 Sept., 1853.

MY DEAR MISS WHITE,—I thank you for the tender letter you wrote me about your late lamented and beloved father. I have been living out of town all summer long, and seldom see a minister, and never a theological newspaper; and still more, at the time of your father's departure I was absent on a little journey. After I wrote the letter, as I went in to Mr. Crosby's to leave the book for your father, Mr. C. asked me if I did not know that Mr. White was dead. It came upon me with entire surprise. I knew from his last letter to me that he was ill, but I heard afterwards that he was better, that he preached as usual, and supposed the sickness was all over. Judge, then, of my surprise when informed of his departure to a fairer world. But my letter was in the post-office, and perhaps already on its way. I could only wait till some one should reply to it.

How much I lament now that I have never been to Littleton to see him! But, in a life a good deal too busy for the delights of friend-ship, even when friends are within "ten minutes' walk," I never found just the right time when I could go as well as not, but continually put off the pleasure against a more "convenient season." Several days this summer I fixed for visiting him, but something always prevented. Now, the good man has outgrown my friendship. I have always felt a great veneration for him, such as I felt for but few men. He was a most excellent teacher, taking a school at Lexington (my father was the school committee-man who engaged him) when it was in a sad condi-tion, and improving it quite surprisingly. He filled his pupils with a love of study. I know not why, but in a little country school he set me to study Latin. I went through the Latin Grammar, and began to construe "Historia Sacra" the first winter, and finished it the next, and began the Greek Grammar. The school lasted only twelve or thirteen weeks. I shall never cease to be grateful to him for all the kindness he showed me, and the gratuitous interest he took in my studies, for it was no part of his duty to teach a boy Latin.

He lent me his Latin Dictionary, a copy of Young's Latin Dic-tionary, a book which I look up to with great respect. This is the only copy of that dictionary that I ever saw; it has long been out of print, replaced by better works, but the old well-worn copy he lent me lives in my memory as a sacred *memorial* connected with the remem-brance of one I hold so dear. He taught school for us at Lexington two winters, then he found a better place for the next winter, at Lin-coln. I was sick in the autumn after his second winter, and one day, as I was better, and out of danger, one of the neighbours told me that "Master White ain't a-going to keep the school this winter." I turned my face to the wall and wept aloud, and would not be com-forted.

He endeared himself to the hearts of all his scholars, and of their parents too. Two years ago, I went up to Lexington to dedicate a new and handsome school-house on the very spot where he first taught, and it did my heart good to recount the valuable services of your father and his successor, Mr. Fiske, also from Lincoln, in the little, mean, and uncomfortable house which was there thirty years before. Some of his scholars were present, and approved the statements; but most of them have already passed on in the road which he has now traversed. I only lament that I never visited him in his own house. From Mr. Emerson and Mrs. Ripley I have often heard accounts of his excel-lence as a minister, as a husband, and a father, Mr. Pearson also has been abundant in his praise: others that I have seen confirmed to me what I suppose the "daily beauty of his life" sufficiently attested to you. I thank you for writing me the account of his last moments, full of a tender interest and melancholy to me. Yet there is a triumph in the death of such a man. I wish he could have been spared longer, but it is well to die in " God's time," and he rests from his labours. I dedicated the little volume of sermons,* which I wrote about, to him and Mr. Fiske. I am sorry he could not have known it. The dedication was printed before he ceased to be mortal.

Present my kindest consolations to your mother, and believe me, with respect and affection, truly yours,

THEODORE PARKER.

Here is part of a letter to Miss Margaret Fuller, written in 1841 :—

Touching the article (for the *Dial*,) I think I shall finish it before Wednesday, for there are two working days, and still more, two working nights, 'twixt us and that time. My design was to have finished it on Saturday, and then come to perpetrate a long-contemplated visit upon you, Monday evening. But thought would not flow smooth, and I made small progress last week, for my brain was dull (I never write well when Mrs. Russell or Lydia are out of the neighbourhood), and it would not go forward.

Herewith I send you a couple of little bits of verse, which I confess to you, *sub rosâ rosissimâ*, are mine. Now, I don't think myself made for a poet, least of all for an *amatory poet*. So, if you throw the " lines " under the grate in your critical wisdom, I shall not be grieved, vexed, or ruffled; for though I have enough of the *irritabile* in my composition, I have none of the *irritabile vatis*.

FROM THE JOURNAL.

Went to New York to see the Hunts and Apthorps embark for Europe in the *Arago*. It is sad to think of it, but they mean to stay three years (365 × 3 = 1095. 52 × 3 = 156)! It is appalling to think of. Objects of affection I miss more than all others, and they are also objects of intellectual and other excitement and delight.

A week or two after this he went out to West Roxbury to look up the favourite spots and solicit their refreshment. But another very dear friend was absent from her home for the season, and the visit was a failure :—

> Unheeded grow the precious flowers,
>   No eye woos now their beauty :
> I only came in plaintive hours
>   To strengthen for sore duty ;
>
> But the new sadness of the place
>   Upon my heart is stealing :
> Nature without that July face
>   Will paralyse my feeling.

The departure of his friend has done an injury to all the associations of his old home. The altar remains, but he cannot

---

* Sermons of Theism, Atheism, and the Popular Theology.

muster heart enough to perform the simple rites of friendship :—

> There grows a pale but precious flower
>   In a consecrated spot:
> How oft I've gathered it for thee,
>   And said, " Forget me not!"
>
> But now the gem ungather'd blooms.
>   I pass the symbol by ;
> Why should I take it from the earth ?
>   It will not meet thine eye.
>
> Still grow, O pale and precious flower,
>   In consecrated spot;
> And often as I pass thee by,
>   I'll say, " Forget me not!"

The first letter which follows was written in the railroad
car. He complains of the fatigues of travelling and lecturing,
but these were aggravated by his custom of studying and
writing in the cars. His most formidable article of baggage
was a carpet-bag stuffed with the books which at any time were
occupying his attention. When he was not conversing with
some acquaintance, or a stranger resolved upon a confidential
interview with the victim whose head and face he recognized,
he was drawing knowledge out of his portable library. All
the traction during the journey was performed by himself and
the locomotive.

TO MISS HUNT.

March 12, 1857, Northern New-York Railroad Cars.

DEAR, GOOD SARAH,—If I don't write you now, I shall have no time
for next mail, so this little mite of a pencil scrawl. It won't be worth
much, for I am tired and worn out with over much work and exposure.
Some weeks since, I went to Western New York; travelled from Monday morning till Saturday night, and expected to have a reasonable
dinner each day, and to sleep quiet in my bed at night, and so come
home sounder and stronger than when I went away. " Man proposes
and God disposes." I had *two* tolerable dinners, and one night in a
bed, four nights in railroad cars. I have not recovered from it
since, but have been slipping behindhand more and more each week.

This will be the last winter of my lecturing so extensively (perhaps).
Hereafter, I will limit my services to forty lectures in a winter, and
put my terms, as Chapin does, at F.A.M.E., *i. e.*, Fifty (dollars) And
My Expenses.

This business of lecturing is an original American contrivance for
educating the people. The world has nothing like it. In it are combined the best things of the Church, *i.e.*, the preaching, and of the
College, *i.e.*, the *informing thought*, with some of the fun of the Theatre.

Besides, it gives the "rural districts" a chance to see the men they read about—to see the lions, for the lecture is also a show to the eyes. Now, I think this is one of the most admirable means of educating the people. For ten years past, six or eight of the most progressive and powerful minds in America have been lecturing fifty or a hundred times in the year. Surely, some must dance after so much piping, and that of so moving a sort! I can see what a change has taken place through the toil of these missionaries. But none know the hardships of the lecturer's life. Curtis has a most funny article thereon.

[A long extract.]

This is extravagant for a description of the *instantial* of lecturing; but, alas! it is below the exceptional cases.

Thus: in one of the awful nights in winter, I went to lecture at——. It was half charity. I gave up the Anti-Slavery Festival for the lecture, rode fifty-six miles in the cars, leaving Boston at half-past four o'clock, and reaching the end of the railroad at half-past six—drove seven miles in a sleigh, and reached the house of ——, who had engaged me to come. It was time to begin; I lectured one hour and three quarters, and returned to the house. Was offered no supper before the lecture, and none after, till the chaise came to the door to take me back again to the railroad station, seven miles off, where I was to pass the night and take the cars at half-past six next morning.

Luckily, I always carry a few little creature-comforts in my wallet. I ate a seed-cake or two, and a fig with lumps of sugar. We reached the tavern at eleven, could get nothing to eat at that hour, and, as it was a temperance house, not a glass of ale, which is a good night-cap. It took three quarters of an hour to thaw out:—went to bed at twelve, in a cold room, was called up at five, had, what is universal, a tough steak, sour bread, and potatoes swimming in fat. —— wanted me to deduct from my poor fifteen dollars the expenses of my nocturnal ride, and would have succeeded, but I "could not make the change." Afterwards —— wrote to apologise for the omission of supper. " Forsan hæc olim meminisse juvabit," says the hearty young man; but to graybeards and baldheads a little of *protinus* is worth a deal of *olim*.

Monday last at seven, George and I walked down to the Lowell Depôt, and at eight started for Rouse's Point, two hundred and eighty-seven miles off, sick and only fit to lie on a sofa, and have day-dreams of you, sweet absent ones! and think over again the friendly endearments that are past, but may yet return. A dreadful hard ride ends at nine P.M., and I find myself in the worst tavern (pretending to decency) in the Northern States. Bread which defies eating, crockery which sticks to your hands, fried fish as cold as when drawn from the lake. Rise at half-past four, breakfast (?) at five, off in the cars at half-past five, lecture at Malone that night, lie all day on the sofa, ditto at Potsdam next day. The third day, leave Potsdam at nine, and reach Champlain (if I get there) at half-past eight, spending ten and a half hours in travelling by railroad ninety-three miles! Thence, after lecture, to Rouse's Point, and at half-past five to-morrow morning return to the cars which are to take me home.

Next week, three days in the " East Counties,' and the next four days in Central New York. That, I hope, ends the business, bating nine or ten more in April and May.

I have been mending all the time since I left home, but have not taken up all the stitches let down in the last New York expedition.

What a stupid letter—all about myself! Now of better things.

You have said nothing about the *Schatz-Kammer* at Dresden. It is one of the finest collections of jewels in the world, and is worth more than all the railroads and school-houses in the kingdom of Saxony. I should take great delight in studying it anew, with more knowledge of such things now than before.

Do look often at the Christ in the " Tribute Money" by Titian. Did you ever see such an ear as the questioner has? That is a portrait, I take it. Write me always your impressions of all you see and hear.

Much that you say about the aspect of the people—gentle and simple—instructs me a good deal.

What a shame, dear Sarah, you don't read and speak German! Commonly, it is the lone sister who attends to literature. Here her chief delight is in the family baby, who " is nothing but a boy," as Mr. R. says of Bobbie, and so of no great moment. I fear lest the perpetual stimulus offered to this *Bobschen* (small Bob) should not be the thing for him. It is green wood which needs continued puffing at with the bellows—not such kindling stuff as Willie. I wish he was in some good farmer's family for a year or two, to get bottom—material basis. But it can't be. What you write about him is full of interest to us all.

*   *   *   *   *   *

If Eliza wants to read a good philosophical book, she will find it in Kuno Fischer's " Franz Baco," and when you go to Heidelberg, she will see the man, whom I know. She read one of his books at Newton; but he does not know *me*, so I can give you no letter. Oh, how I do wish Bear and I could step over to Germany and pass the summer with you! But it can't be. I trust you will be with the Becks this summer, and next year will drop down into Italy. Well, here is the end of the second sheet. Love to Potamousie ;* love to grandmother of one grandchild ; love to Lizzie and Robert ; love to Sallie—love and something beside. Never fear that my love for you abates, or will or can. Good bye!

THEODORE.

TO MRS. APTHORP.

Boston, Monday Night, 21st September, 1857.

MY DEAR ELIZA,—There is a new moon looking in at my window, or was when I pulled the curtain down ; and for you, I suppose it looks down on Pisa, or Genoa, or Florence. How grand the dark, heavy architecture of these old narrow-streeted Italian towns looks in the light of the full moon ! I could never tire of Rome or Florence by moonlight, and shall not soon forget how Venice looked in the full moon, in the end of April, 1844. The illumination of a great festival came also at the same time, and the canals swarmed with people in festal dresses. Balloons of light, parti-coloured material hung on all the steeples,

* Pet name for the Willie.

whose bells spoke to the ear the same rhythm of sound the lanterns intimated to the eye. I was in Trent once at midnight, and saw the Great Bear hang over the Cathedral, where a famous council once sat so long and with such world-wide significance. Once, too, at full moon, I went to the Colosseum, and stayed till midnight, and heard the owl hoot over the ruins of that terrible amphitheatre of blood, where, oftener than once, 80,000 men and women were brought together to see gladiators butcher one another. Once, too, the last night I was in Rome, I went at full moon to see the arches of the aqueduct which used to water a city of 1,500,000 men—the London of the old fighting world, as London is the Rome of the modern industrial world; now it is a huge ruin, full of beauty to all lookers on; also full of wisdom to whoso stops to think of the Whence and Whither of mighty states.

What a dear child you are to take all that pains (for me, too) to hunt up an old book! These, I take it, are the facts.

It is Ramusio that occupies the corner I spoke of; in 1844 I had been up to the rooms above the library, and thinking of Sebastian Cabot, looked at books of voyages (I have a weakness for folios), and opened that, and found at the head of the page, or the chapter, the "Navigazioni di Sebastiani Gabotti." Before I could make further explorations, my companions hurried me off to some other place, so I put up the book, and "cast one longing lingering look behind," and saw "Viaggi" on the back, and supposed it was "Viaggi di Giovanni ed Sebastiani Gabotti," or something like that; the book has haunted me ever since. I have looked in all libraries for it, in bibliographies, asked men well-read in such things, but found no satisfaction. Now it is all cleared up. Keep the book given to you, unless you find an opportunity to send it home by private hand. I have ordered all the Italian books you mention—the new edition of "Marco Polo" I had ordered before in vain. But my friend, Mr. Christern, a German bookseller, was here last night, and I sent again direct to Venice, where he has a friend; they will go viâ Leipsic, and before the first of January, I shall have them in handsome parchment on this desk, perhaps. Sorry to put you to so much trouble; but I think it paid for itself by making you acquainted with persons you would not else have met.

Many thanks for it all, and the forty-seven grapes which commemorated the years that have made me *glatz-köpfig* (smooth-headed). It was *glass köpfig*—at least *I* read it so—in my copy, and boggled over it a long time, and looked in dictionaries, and wondered and wondered, but was so stupid as not to think of *glatz-köpfig*. It is a queer piece, with a deal of truth in its *Verfehlte Liebe verfehltes Leben*.*

But it is not the deepest truth. No—no—no! Whoso does his possible best, never fails in *Leben*, but straight out of the deeps of misery and worldly ruin rises in his proper motion up to heaven. Even to the wickedest I think life is no absolute failure. But it is an experiment he could not do without; one in which he learns what else he had missed. Heine has a deal of the Devil in him, mixed with a deal of genius. Nobody could write so well as he—surely none since Göthe; that Hebrew nature has a world of sensuous and devotional emotion in it, and immense power of language also. But this genius is lyric, not

* Love that fails in life a failure : the allusion is to a piece written by Henry Heine.

dramatic, not epic; no Muse rises so high as the Hebrew, but it cannot keep long on the wing. The Psalms and Prophets of the Old Testament teach us this; Oriental sensuousness attained their finest expression in the Song of Solomon, and in Heine's *Lieder*. In the latter the idol is veiled in thin gauze; in the former it is without the veil. Much in Heine I hate—much, likewise, I admire and love. The " *Romanzero.*"* I never like enough to read. Heine was malignant and blasphemous.

I don't want you to take less pains than you do with anything, only don't get the nettle-rash and the neuralgia, that is a dear child. The old churches, with their cold stone floors, which no sun ever sweeps with his light, the damp, chill air never renewed by a fresh breeze from an open window, are dangerous to American women, with soles of letter-paper on their tiny feet, and oyster-shell bonnets behind the organ of self-esteem on their heads. Let you and S. beware. Your mother has the prudence which needs no caution. I would see all that is worth seeing, and see it thoroughly too, and understand it also. Of course you will learn Italian, and I shall hear your " speech ringing like silver coin falling on marble," as you so poetically describe that at Venice. But Venetian is sweeter than any other Italian. Florentine has more majesty, but less tenderness and grace. The Americans pronounce the vowels better than the English, marking all the delicate variations of their softer sounds, while the British dwell more on the consonants, the *hard peaks* of the language. The Briton says, " The clim-met's rrigrus; " the American, " The climate is rigōrous." The Venetians drop the consonants, and make a language almost wholly of vowels— thus : " *Bo gioro, Sioe,*" for " *Buon giorno, Signore.*" There is a little hardness in the Tuscan consonatization (to make a word), but there is dignity and strength. It is the language of man. But, after all, I like the old Latin, so direct, masculine, and concise in its strength, better than even the " *Lingua Toscana in bocca Romana.*" For one who knows Latin and French, it is easy to know enough Italian to read and talk it with plainness; but it requires a deal of toil and time to master its subtle beauties. It is the most circumlocutory of all modern tongues : the language of subtlety and finesse.

I long to know what you and S. will think of the *people.* I found them the handsomest of men : I never saw such fine heads, faces, mouths, hands, and feet, as in Central Italy. A good assortment of nationalities was mixed together centuries ago, and now the elements, once conflicting and making homely—as at this day in New England —are blended into one homogeneous mass, which combines various qualities not known before. In Northern Italy you find German faces, German eyes, hair, hands, and feet; this is partly due to the old Lombard stock, partly to the " *damnate Tedeschi* "—the Austrian soldiers of to-day; for the military river leaves the stain of its waters on every bank. Doubtless, your and S.'s sharp eyes detected the German face in many a Hebrew mother's baby at Prague, and found *black* eyes

---

* A book of poems in the form of ballads, but not so simple in idea and sentiment. It contains also a prose postscript, half mocking, half serious, in which Heine proclaims his conversion to a belief in a personal deity and personal immortality. His sentiments hardly succeed in escaping from his prevailing irony and *persiflage.*

common in Catholic villages of Saxony or Bavaria, and wondered till you saw the Italian priest. In South Italy you find much of the old Greek beauty in the people. At Rome, look at the *Trasteverini*, and you will be surprised at the odds between them and the other Romans.

I have been prosing away here as if I were preaching; I think you are right in your desire to pay in thought for the delight you get in travel. It is a great bounty that is given you. I felt how much I was adding to the debt I owed mankind, and did not often lay my head on the pillow without counting the cost to the human race of my enjoyment on that day when I had received only, but given out nothing in return. Now, I could learn twice as much as then, as carrying a head "steadier on its shoulders," as you say. Alas, me! my head was always *steady* enough; I wish I had other qualities in proportion to sobriety.

Of course, you won't read much in Italy; but you will go to the theatre, and learn the language with such help as you can get. We went to the theatre at Florence, but only once.

What exquisite culture of the *ground* you find in Italy, but what a *Church*—what monks, and *preti*, and *cardinali*—what a *Pape!* I always like to call the old fellow by the French or the German name, *Pape*, or *Papst*. Rome is a Commentary on Revelations. I fear you missed the Papal visit to Florence; the old fellow will go back to his humble shed of the Vatican, "*nostro humile tapino Vaticano*," with a million dollars in presents. In reading the correspondence of Mabillon, I was struck with the fact that, while the great ecclesiastics do not appear to have any brothers or sisters, they are blest with many nephews who required places in the Holy alone-saving Church of Rome.

Tell me if you hear of any literature that is new or worth notice. Florence is the head-quarters of Italian letters, now. I think no country has such a reserved power of educated gentlemen, fond of literature, art, science, who never print anything; many works are written in the country-houses of these persons which never see the light. How is it possible for a Government to curse a people! You saw something of that in Germany; more is before you. Tell me what you think of man's relation to the animals in Italy. Tell little Potamousie how much I thank him for his letter in German, every word correct. "He is a precious," as his auntie says, and I think you had better send him home to me; he is only a bother in travelling.

T.

TO MISS HUNT.

Boston, Saturday Night, Oct. 31, 1857.

MY DEAR LITTLE MITE O' SARAH, AWAY OFF AT FLORENCE,—It is All Saint's Eve to-night, and my sermon has been long since ended, the last-word added at the end, and I have had a little time to gather up my soul for the coming Sunday. I don't like to rush from a week of hard work into the prayers and the hymns of the Sunday without a little breathing time of devotion, so I walk about the study, and hum over bits of hymns, or recall various little tender emotions, and feel the beating of that great Heart of the Universe which warms us all with the life that never dies. I don't know that these are not the richest hours of my life; certainly, they have always been the happiest.

At Roxbury I had a better time for this—more uninterrupted opportunity, I mean. Nature is a continuous oratory, and the pine-trees near, or then not far off, always came to me with their sweet voice full of religious emotion. They did not feel it; I did, for man is the consciousness of nature. In him its facts are ideas, its deeds and habits are laws, and its sounds become the music of a prayer. Here, in the city, one must fall back on his own soul, or, as most men, on some social help of companionship. Mankind makes a world of art in the city to take the place of absent nature. Hence, there are Milan cathedrals, and Duomos of Florence, and St. Stephen's of Vienna. In the Tyrol, or even the White Mountains, you need no such things. When our friend's face is before us, as a grace before and after meat, we need no picture, but when he is afar off, we look on his daguerreotype as a benediction to our daily bread. Hence, the world of religious art, which is only a toy in the fields, a gilt bauble compared to the clover, and the blue-eyed grass, and the dandelion, in the town becomes quite friendly and dear to us.

*   *   *   *   *   *

Well: it is All Saints' Day to-morrow, and as it is the three-hundred-and-fortieth anniversary of the public beginning of the Protestant Reformation, I shall preach of the Catholic and Protestant Churches, the chief theological ideas in which they differ. Last Sunday I spoke of the power of false theological ideas to hinder the welfare and the progress of the individual and the race. Next Sunday I mean to say something of the power of true theological ideas to develope man's possibilities of good. I shall speak historically of what has been done by the best ideas of the Catholic and Protestant Churches, and prophetically of what will be the future of some great truths I now try to set forth.

I take great delight in writing, great also in preaching, sermons on such high themes. The audience seems pleased and looks interested. It is a grand audience to preach to, and it inspires me only to look upon the faces of two or three thousand persons so met together.

But my eyes grow a little dim, dear Sarah, and I see blue suns flitting about the paper, and then green ones; so, for this moment, good night, with a little mite of a kiss to lay under your pillow.

Sunday is gone. Monday has folded her wings, also, and now night broods over the tired city, and the children of toil are beginning to cuddle themselves down under that warm, motherly influence, and sleep off all their cares, at least, for a few hours. What a strange thing sleep is! I think I don't quite understand it, spite of some considerable experience; but I won't inflict a philosopheme upon you.

We got your letters of October 5th, and I have mailed six to Florence. Some of them were directed " Al Illustrissime Signore Robert E. Apthorp." Perhaps the modest man did not inquire for the letters of so distinguished a person. Henceforth the letters shall be to " R. E. Apthorp, Esq." I think they will all come to hand.

What a good soul you are to hunt up the book of " Populari Toscani!" It will have a manifold value—not only its intrinsic, as a book not known before, but its extrinsic, as the gift of good, kind Sallie. The bigger work you mention I also took a note of. It is too bulky for your trunks, and, besides, would have to pay duties, here and there and everywhere, and be a world of trouble. Moreover, now I know the title, I can make a long arm, and reach down to Venice or Florence, and pick it up some day.

Please find the title of such books as *Conti populari*, not so much the *conti villereschi*, or *fantastichi*, but rather such as come out of the mouth of the people in their serious moods.

But I doubt that the Italians have much of this literature in which the Germans are so exceeding rich. With the Germans, imagination is diffused among all the people, just as the inventive, organizing, and administrative talent, which we call thrift, is among New Englanders. I doubt that it is so with the Italians; they have been a cultivated people too long, and when the ground has been ploughed, and harrowed, and raked over so many times, no sweet little violets and wind-flowers come up of their own accord, but marigolds, pinks, and passion-flowers grow in the artificial garden-beds, offensively enriched; while in the lands where the seed of art is sown, the ground spawns forth its litter of weeds, ugly and poisonous, too.

You kindly ask for commissions—something to do. Well, this in general, dear Sarah: drink in just as much health and happiness as you can all the time, and let it come out in your soul when you return; that is the general commission. . . . . But there is one thing more: I should like to be made a cardinal, and have a red hat, and a red cloak, and a red coach, with six horses, and five great servants to wait on me to the Music Hall. Now, couldn't you wheedle his Holiness into making me a cardinal? You know how to get round the Pope. Tell him what a dear little Pope he is, and that I will be the best cardinal that ever was in all Boston, from the North End to the Neck. Then I should so like to go into the anti-slavery meeting in the Melodeon next January, and sit on the platform between Henry C. Wright and Eliza J. K., with my red clothes on. Why, I should overawe Abby Folsom. Then it would be so delightful to read the paragraphs in the *Liberator*, and the *Standard*, and the *Boston Post*, and to have all the boys and girls in " South Sthrate " running after me; and to see the whole " County Corrrkkk " take off his hat to my red one! Now, do tell the Pope how I should like it, and, if he will give it to me, he will be a dear little love of a Pope, and I will not call him the naughty names which (the Protestant Christians say) the Bible has got ready for him.

I saw old Josiah Quincy in the street to-day. He has a backbone which, old as he is, sticks out through his great-coat.

I am applying electricity to my side, and, after thundering so long against various enormities, I now strike my own sides with lightning. It does me good, and I am mending like a family seamstress.

I sent one fringed gentian to you long ago. Here is another, the last of the season; it was on the pulpit Sunday.

So I shall expect my cardinal's hat by the very next steamer after you receive this letter.

FROM THE JOURNAL.

March 3, 1851.—Seven years ago to-day I plucked violets in Rome, and some of them are still in being to-day with me. Some others are with the one for whom they were plucked.

What an eventful seven years it has been! How little could I, or any one, foresee the course of the next seven years, nor how little that of the forthcoming year, if indeed it be forthcoming! But the good God rules all.

How much of our life depends on *accident*, as it seems—*Providence*, as it is! How much of my life has been shaped and ennobled by one or two persons that I have known! The knowing them was not of my will, but it has changed me much, for good and ill. Men would not see it; God knows it all. So the difference between character and reputation—what men think you, what God sees you! Here is a man who bears a scarlet letter in his heart, that burns and scorches all the day. Here another who bears a crown of glory round his brow within. No man sees it, or either; but God both.

March 22.—It is now just 20 years since I packed up my trunk at Lexington to leave my father's house for ever. It was never *my home* after that. Half of my life has now passed, at home 20 years, and 20 years away from home. All of it has been a *struggle*, all that I have sought for has been sought under difficulties.

23rd, Sunday.—Yet it seems to me that if I live 20 years more I may do something. As yet I have done nothing to justify the hopes my mother formed of me, or I of myself. I might as well have stayed at home, and minded the farm, and been one of the select men of Lexington, surveyor of the highways for one-twentieth part of the town, now and then. What fools we are to think so much of the slate and pencil we cypher with, and so little of the sum we are to cypher out. I might have had just as much to carry to heaven from the farm as from the different *field* I have chosen.

Much weary with the services to-day; for I have been ill many days, not so much from any bodily cause as from one more difficult to cure or to come at. Ah, me! my life is a pursuit of its object under difficulties. Took tea with Howe, and retired much wearied, and sad, and sick.

There are those who are a continual joy and delight to us. I know one whose presence is to me continual sunshine.

> Te spectem, suprema mihi cum venerit hora :
> Te teneam moriens, deficiente manu.

Kind Gussie Curtis has just sent me some fringed gentians, the first of the year that I have seen. They have always been consecrated with me, and the dearest flowers that I know, save two or three. But now they will not perform their usual service. I shall carry some to a sick girl.

Feb. 1, 1851, Saturday Night.—All the household are now a-bed, and most are asleep, for it is near midnight. I love to compose my soul a little before I go to rest, and especially at the end of the week look back a little on it. This has not been a happy or a successful week; the fault is my own, which makes it all the worse to bear. How little do men who look on our faces know what they cover! The good God knows all. I have no fear of Thee, great Father, for Thou art infinite. But Thy children—I fear their erring eyes. I can trust the justice of my God, not that of men.

May, 1851.—At West Roxbury in the afternoon. The *Polygalla pauciflora* just opening; laid some at the foot of my favourite tree in memory of old times—the great oak.

THE WHITE OAK.

CHAPTER XII.

Familiar Letters, to Hon. Charles Sumner, Rev. S. J. May, E. Desor, Peter Lesley, Professor H. D. Rogers, to his Niece, and others.

THESE letters, of a lighter and less formal kind than those in which Mr. Parker deliberately weighed his favourite subjects, follow here more naturally. They are, however, veined with all his qualities of sense and conscience. The pen is still chartered to transmit them. Such letters of mixed play and earnest show a very characteristic mood of his, better than a mere description.

To begin with some specimens of his impromptu notes. A young clergyman writes to him complaining of the number of Sundays, especially of the months which contain five, which he considered an imposition. To this Mr. Parker replies :—

There is *no* peace for the wicked. There is only one place where there is no Sunday. In this world, on *earth*, it is a weekly visitation. *Heaven* is a continual Sabbath. So you see the lot of the ministers who *follow their calling* thither. Only in one place is there no Sunday. I do not like to name it : they say, a great many Unitarian divines have gone thither. *There* is no Sunday, but—a continual Monday, a perpetual *Black Monday*, a great washing-day of souls that will not come clean, scrub you never so tightly !

Will you stay on the earth, there is the Sunday. Will you go to heaven, the inexorable Sunday is still there, and of course, "nulla Dominica sine sermone." If you go to——alas, me ! I dare not hurt your feelings with the *name*, you have not a preach-day, but a wash-day. You are not the *washer* but the *washee*. Here you are not the preachee. Comfort yourself with that. The agony of writing sermons is doubtless great, but oh, think of the tenfold agony of *hearing* the sermons, of sitting *puncto singulo*, in the worst of situations, to listen, "seized and tied down," not to *judge*, but only *hear*. Rejoice, O —— ! in the strength of your cloth, but know that not yet are you a hearer of sermons.

A contributor to the Massachusetts "Quarterly," had promised
an article upon Coleridge, which never got written. His delays
are thus vigorously followed up :—

No. 1. MOST EXCELLENT ——. It is known to thee that thee is to
write for us a paper on one Samuel Coleridge, and this is to tell thee
that we expect that paper from thy pen about the first of July.

No. 2. Thee will not forget thy article on Samuel Taylor Coleridge,
which is to be in readiness by the tenth of seventh month. Thy friends
will look for it with large eyes.

No. 3. Oh, promising ——, hast thou seen the new little book of
thy friend Coleridge? He also was a promising man, and has come
upon his resolutions before this time, unless John Calvin lies—which
may he!

No. 4 was written just after the procrastinating critic was
burnt out of his dwelling.

That's the way they treat the wicked—burn 'em up—burn 'em up!
Books and all, babies and all, wife and all! O Lot, that hast fled
out of thy Sodom and Gomorrah ; I am sorry for thee, and hope there
is no *smell of fire* on thy wife and the babies! I sympathize heartily
with you, and if you lost your books, will give you some of mine;
especially Coleridge. Did you keep your sermons *dry*—as Cæsar *his*
Commentaries ?

He exchanges with a young friend.

I will come and lecture you out of the year, if you will. The subject shall be what you choose. The Progress of Mankind. I will take
tea, and if it storms, pass, perhaps, the night. Somebody said it was
cruel of me to let you exchange with me the other day, because it
would get you into hot water! If so, I hope you will get out—or the
water get cool before spring.

Not long after John Ronge in Germany had exposed the fraud
of the Holy Coat at Treves, and had organized a free German
Catholic Communion, a similar movement was commenced among
the Protestants by Julius Rupp, of Magdeburg, who wanted free
parishes and no political church of one recognized confession.
His first offence was a letter to the Consistory, in 1844, opposing the preamble of the Athanasian Creed, which pronounces
damnation on all who differ from its articles. He attacked in
sermons the dogmatism of the Church, and denied several points
of doctrine that are deemed essential. Whereupon, the Königsberg Consistory excommunicated him, and he thereby lost his
privilege of membership of the great Protestant Association of
Germany called the Gustavus-Adolphus Union. A furious war
of pamphlets and sermons broke out, and the Pietists demanded

the intervention of Government. Mr. Parker thus tells the story of Ruppism to a friend with whom his pen was never very staid.

Rupp was a member of the Boston Association of Ministers in Germany (*they* call it the Gustav-Adolph. Verein); he had some notions that were called heretical—*e g.* he thought a *man* had a right to do his own thinking, and in case he wanted help, might hire a hand on his own account. Then he said, in thinking, a *man* must rest only *in the truth.* Now said the Boston Association, " Brother Rupp, it hurts our feelings to hear you talk so—'taint Christian. It is heathen—it is infidel." So ——, whose German name is Hengstenberg, and ——, who is called Guerike, when he lives at Halle, both of them nice men at hunting heretics and disembowelling them when found, they stirred up the said Boston Association, and got them to *expel* brother Rupp. Still more, they asked the Government to kick Rupp out of his pulpit off there in Magdeburg. But says Rupp, says he, " I won't go, nor stir one step out of my pulpit." So he stayed there : and the King says to Rupp, says he, " What do you want ? " Rupp : " To do just as I'm a mind to." "Well," says the King, " go ahead." So Rupp goes ahead ; his church is a *Landeskirche,* and not a mere *Privat Gemeinde,** and so Rupp may come into the *Verein* if he will, and much good may it do him when there!

TO HON. CHARLES SUMNER.

September, 1846.—I thank you most heartily for your noble and beautiful Phi Beta Kappa Address. It did me good to read it. I like it, like it all—all over and all through. I like especially what you say of Allston and Channing. That sounds like the Christianity of the nineteenth century, the application of religion to life. You have said a strong word, and a beautiful ; planted a seed " out of which many and tall branches shall arise," I hope. *The people are always true to a good man who truly trusts them.* You have had opportunity to see, hear, and feel the truth of that oftener than once. I think you will have enough more opportunities yet : men will look for deeds noble as the words *a man speaks.* I take these words as an earnest of a life full of deeds of that heroic sort.

You refer to a passage in the Greek Epigrams about the picture of Philoctetes. By whom is the line ? * I remember it, but cannot turn to it, and as you don't name the author, and my Anthology, though it has eleven volumes, has no *index verborum,* I don't find it.

Many little notes passed between Mr. Parker and Mr. Sumner, upon the subject of books upon law and jurisprudence, for these things were an important element in Mr. Parker's studies. He wanted, principally, the sources of knowledge in

---

* One is a State parish, recognized by Government ; the other is a conventicle, only tolerated.

† From an epigram of six lines, attributed to Glaucus, an Athenian poet.

this province, all codices, and books of historical investigation of the subject, State trials, and the journals in various languages devoted to jurisprudence, and the report of cases. He began these investigations while keeping school at Watertown, and never allowed them to subside. When he came to framing his "Defence," his knowledge of State trials, of the jury, &c., saved him uncounted time and labour. How thoroughly trained he was for all the exigencies of his career!

TO HON. CHARLES SUMNER.

Sept. 20, 1852.

My dear Sumner,—Some day or other I shall publish—if I live, and nothing hinders—a book on the progressive development of religion in the leading (Caucasian) races of mankind. Amongst other topics, treated in one of the later volumes, will be the development of religion in its politico-ethical form, that is, the form of law. Now, I can ascertain the points I need, in the historical development of law, among the classic nations, Greeks and Romans, with their descendants, Italians, French, Spanish, &c., the Slavic nations, and most of the Teutonic, viz., in all the semi-barbarous tribes of that family, and of most of them in their present condition. I am in the way of ascertaining all I wish of the Scandinavians, but I lack the requisite information on the development of law in England. I make it out very well up to the time of the Conqueror. After that I want a little help from you. I wish to understand the complete history of the whole matter, so I beg you to give me a list of authors to be studied. You may go on the supposition that I know nothing of the matter, as the Professor was to do with M. Jourdain; and if you set down works that I knew well twenty years ago, no matter. "Surplusage does not vitiate" in the matter of counsel.

March 21, 1846.—I thank you for the kindly note you wrote me the other day, and which I would have answered before now, but have been so ill that I only have done what was unavoidable. I do not think the sermon * you spoke of worthy of much praise, but yet I have heard so much commendation of it, that I am inclined to alter my opinion. I sympathize most heartily with what you say about the *Nebelwind*. † I know well how *unerquicklich* it is, and among what *dürren Blätter* it *säuselt*.

There are few of the clergy that I respect or esteem. Few of them are intellectually competent to their task, fewer still morally capable of doing any good thing for mankind. Among the more respectable portion of society, religion—using that word in its widest and best sense —is not the leading influence. Of course, therefore, religion is a

* The True Idea of a Christian Church.
† Faust: Scene I. The ordinary preached words
      " Sind unerquicklich wie der Nebelwind,
      Der herbstlich durch die dürren Blätter säuselt !"

Refresh as little as the drizzly wind
Which rustles through the wither'd leaves of Autumn.

secondary thing in their church—in their minister, &c. Of course they get a minister, and have a church, in which religion is to have little to to. Christianity, therefore, is the last thing they will ask of him, the last thing they will *take* of him, or *tolerate* in him. " Give us," say they, "give us anything but religion—and if you must give us that, give us any religion but the Christianity of Jesus Christ: that we can't bear, nor won't." I don't say this takes place consciously. I have translated the *latency* of such men into *patency*. I don't wonder there is a *Nebel-wind* : the *Säuseln* thereof is, however, applauded, and lulls men to sleep. The fact that no minister of any *famous* church signed the Anti-Slavery Protest,* is to me proof of their deep degradation—the crowning act of their infamy.

Mephistopheles gives some capital advice to a theologian :—

> " Am besten ist's auch hier, *wenn ihr nur Einen hört,*
> *Und auf des Meisters Worte schwört.*
> Im Ganzen—*haltet euch an Worte !*
> Danu geht ihr durch die sichre Pforte
> Zum Tempel der Gewissheit ein! " †

TO REV. S. J. MAY.

April 24, 1846.—I trust you will attend our annual convention at Berry Street. Alas! that it should so often be a convention to *bury ;* a convention of the *dead,* though unburied. I wish some of the wiser men would do somewhat to make our meetings more profitable, more alive. I don't think it of much consequence to know that Dr. —— has baptized sixteen children, and Dr. —— added to his church twenty-six children of a little larger growth. Even the detail of " our excellent tracts," and the "great extension of our views " in the "West " or the "North," seems to me no great matter. Cannot something be done and said to stir men's hearts, heads, hands, so that even the drowsy shall go home with hearts beating in their bosoms ? Cannot we set men on and make them take hold of war, slavery, drunkenness, crime, and pauperism, and popular ignorance ? I love theology and philosophy, love them as ways to truth and therefore avenues to human welfare, to goodness and piety. But it seems to me affairs are so managed that the powers of a good many in the denomination are crippled. The best minds are told not to think, or if they do, not to think on theology, still less on reform, but to follow the counsel of Dr. Byends or Mr. Facing-both-ways. We do nothing; nothing in theology, nothing in civilization, *i. e.* in the reforms. If there is an

---

* A protest against American Slavery, in 1845, to give emphatic expression to the feeling of Unitarian ministers. A great many signed it—one hundred and seventy—but *no leading metropolitan minister.*

† Faust : Scene III. Mephistopheles, advising the student who asks about the study of theology :—

> " Here, too, 'tis best, for some one man declare,
> And by your master's dicta swear.
> Upon the whole—the form of words hold fast ;
> Then through the temple-gates you're pass'd
> Securely into certitude.

old woman in the denomination, a *born granny*, we make him, (her, or it,) our oracle, and then at his command drive out of the State such men as John Pierpont—drive them out because they are righteous.

I ask you if this is always to be so, if men like *you* are willing it shall be so, and younger men continue to be disheartened, muzzled, and untimely slain? I speak to a wise man; judge *you* what I say.

Niagara Falls, July 15, 1846.—I actually slipped through Syracuse without seeing Archimedes; I know it seemed unfriendly to do so; it was quite against my will. When I purposed to make this journey, I said to your uncle Sam, "I shall see S. J. M." "And you will preach for him, too," was the answer. So I intended to stand in your place all of last Sunday, but was hindered. Yes, "I have been let hitherto." We got delayed by one accident after another, and having *three women* (!!!) with me I was constrained to pass through Syracuse, stopping only to take a "hasty plate of tea." What made it worse is, that I did all that on the *Lord's* day, or rather, the Lord's *night*, for it was after sunset before we left the town where they make good salt and rejoice in a bishop who hath not lost his savour.

I have not been idle, but I have long been so ill at *head* that I have shunned all intellectual action which I possibly could avoid. I am now travelling wholly for health; I have a most excellent appetite and digestion, but all else is poor enough. I will write you soon after I get home, when I hope to be a deal better.

I wanted to talk over many things with you, this amongst others (which please not name). I have long been intending to write an anonymous "Letter to the American People touching the Matter of Slavery, by One of the Million." I wanted to ask you about the utility of such a thing, and for any hints that you could give me touching the matter or the mode of treating it. I wished to write *anonymously*, because I have a *bad* name; for though I am baptized Θεου Δωρον (God's gift) I believe most men think me a Devil's child.

I am amazed at the way good men and politicians look at the matter, amazed at their silence. Of course I shall not *condemn* the Church or the State; for though bad enough, they are the best *institutions* we have.

Nov. 13, 1846.—I am weekly astonished at myself, that I can do so well as I do. Dr. Jackson has *caulked* my head with quinine till it is air-tight. I was never better off in my head; I can write a sermon that takes an hour to preach, at one sitting and not leave my chair. Isn't that brave? I don't do so often. It is riding the horse a little too hard, and I am careful now, very careful, for I dread the old fire that threatened to burn my head off. I would lend you sermons, but you could not read them. I have about 1001 contractions, and make a dart into a sentence, and then it goes; I can make it out, but I alone.

TO THE SAME.

I am glad that you preach to the young men; do tell them not to become sectarian; but human as they will, and divine as they can. The Unitarians are getting shockingly bigoted and little; their late meetings were windy, and they meet to ventilate their narrowness;

yet how contemptible must be a sect who only *deny the divinity of Christ*, affirming a denial, their life the *development of a negation!* Anniversary Week had painfully little of the Channing, much of the ——, bating his scholarship, more of the ——, cunning, specious, superficial, and worldly. The Universalists are more human than they; they declare the *fatherhood of God*, and do not stick at the consequences, everlasting happiness to all men. I think they are the most *human* sect in the land. They had an address on temperance, one on slavery, one on war, delivered before their ministers on Anniversary Week!

TO THE SAME.

June 14, 1847.—Would teach me " chirography"! As if my hand-writing was not the best in the world! I am offended. They say that S. J. is a good man; I do not believe it. He offers to teach me chirography! That is an insult, a downright insult; no frequency of repetition makes it less. You must have told other persons of your intention, for several others have intimated similar things; certainly the thought could not be original in so many. I forgive everybody but you. I shall hate *you* for ever.

Alas, me! I am so *well* this year that I shan't take any vacation; so *busy* that I mean to work all summer; so *poor* that I can't afford to travel. So my health, my business, and my poverty make a trinity of reasons against my doing what would be so very agreeable to do. But don't tell anybody of the latter reason, for while there is this world of misery about me in Boston, and some of my own kin leaning a little on my shoulders, and the anti-slavery men wanting money for their work, I grudge every dollar which I pay to the butcher and the baker for myself.

TO THE SAME.

Feb. 16, 1852.—"The Rev. Miss Brown" was to have preached for me yesterday afternoon, but there was a blunder made by "Miss Dr. Hunt" touching the time, and so between the two Doctors we fell to the ground. She was to take up Paul's text, "I suffer not a woman to teach," and pitch into the poor apostle, adding a peril that he never dreamed of, the peril of woman! The apostle escaped, but only for a week. Miss Brown is on his track. Really we must have an "Association of Ministers" that will license maidens as well as men to preach. You must be the *head* of it, must organize it (and write its letters-missive), call it together, &c. There are Sargent, Weiss, perhaps Stetson and Stone, and others. We might make a nice association, with the apostolic power to bind or to loose; we might vote that we alone had the apostolical suggestion, "None genuine unless signed 'S. J. May';" that we are infallible, &c. Then we might license, and do all matters and things pertaining to the function of associated congregational ministers. Do think seriously of this.

Then, about the Indians. I saw ——, and I informed him of your doings. "I was afraid," said the Rev. Divine, "that in the f-ô-ô-ô-ô-lish course he hâs pursued, that he had furgê-otten the Ind-yan! I find he has lawst â-âul of his în-flooence as a minister of the Gê-âwspel."

Still, I told him of all that you had done—the meeting-house that you had built, the school-house, and the double dwelling-house. I told him how you mortified the flesh with a buffalo-robe, making yourself "all things to all men," that you might by all means save a squaw: and he was delighted. So I told him of the dogmatic difference between the Pagan Indians and the Christian Indians; the one called the Great Spirit Ka-ka-gee-ga-wah, and the others Ka-ka-gee-ha-wah. But the practical difference was, that the Pagans made the women do all the work, and the Christians did it themselves. He was yet more delighted, and began to think you were not so bad as he at first thought. Still, "He put himself in opposition to the Govern-ment," said this Christian father. Just as I was coming away, I told him that there was not a young man in your society that habitually drank—even wine: and then I fled.

TO THE SAME.

Thanksgiving Night, 1851.—I expect to be a grandfather one of these days, and then shall be reading Dutch or writing to you (as now) on Thanksgiving Night. But as I am not a grandfather now, and have no children to gather under my roof, I keep this day after rather a dull and mouldy sort, as monks do in their cells, reading Dutch books, or some other light nonsense of that sort—say, Ulphilas' version of the New Testament into the Gothic language, or regaling myself with the pleasing fancies of St. Chrysostom, or the Venerable Bede. Nay, Thomas Aquinas comes sometimes and comforts me on Thanksgiving Day after the sermon. Well: that is enough about myself.

Now a word about S. J. M. When we received his letter here,* *we* did not believe it; we knew him better. We had intelligence by the underground telegraph that Mr. May was the head and front of the mob at Syracuse; that he mounted the horse called in heaven *Steadfast*, and on earth *Immoveable*, took the sword which his venerable father, the colonel, formerly wielded so terribly on election days, and shouted, "The sword of the Lord and of S. J. M.!" "*A bas* Millard Fillmore!" "Down with the kidnappers!" "Give 'em ——! —— 'em!" and rode through the town on the same gallant beast, whose vigour Mr. Bradford and I know very well. Yes, sir, we know who it was that broke the marshal's arm. But we never trumpeted the story around. After the Rescue Trials are all over, and you are acquitted of the crime of treason, we shall publish the true account of your exploits in the *Christian Register*. Then see what they will say of you at the Berry Street Conference. You will never preach the Great and Thursday Lecture again. No, sir. It is doubtful, even, if you ever hear it again!

March 7, 1852.—It grieved us all very much to hear of your misfortune, the downfall of the spire. It was undoubtedly the work of the "Divil," who, as Cotton Mather says, has a particular spite against meeting-houses, and in his capacity of Prince of the Power of the Air,

---

*Concerning the Jerry rescue in Syracuse, on which occasion Mr. May, who was with the slave and the marshal's posse, acted his customary pacific part. But it is suspected that his noble and touching appeals so far influenced the guard as to make the rescue more practicable.

smites them with lightning. As Dr. Franklin has taken the lightning out of his hand, he, poor Divil! has nothing but the wind left to strike with.

Good Friday, 1853.— "If you have tears, prepare to shed them now," for a most melancholy event has "turned up." It is terrible for "The Denomination," and all "interested in *our views*." I mean —*horresco referens*—the

DISSOLUTION OF THE GREAT AND THURSDAY LECTURE!

Oct. 24, 1853.—I was over at Cambridge the other day, and looked in at the Divinity School, and saw several of the *bodies* which were waiting their turn. The operators were not in at the time, so I saw nothing of the *modus operandi*. The Egyptian embalmers took only seventy days, I think, to make a mummy out of a dead man. Unitarian embalmers use three years in making a mummy out of live men. I think at Meadville they do it in less.

Do you know Mr. ——, of —— Seminary? He does the mummyizing for the Baptists. I saw him last July, when he exhibited the result of his work. Pitch, gum, asphaltum had never done their work better. There stood the mummies, dead and dry as Shishak or Shoophoo, ready to be ordained and set up in a pulpit.

I hope you read the *Register* of last week, and an account of the "Annual Convention." What subjects for discussion! "Have we a Litany among us?" Shall we have one? Again: "On what Terms shall Persons be admitted to the Communion?" *i. e.* "on what terms" shall a person be allowed once a month, in a meeting-house, on Sunday, to eat a crumb of baker's bread and drink a sip of grocer's wine, which the deacon has bought at a shop the day before!

What if *nobody* at all is allowed to come to the Communion, will not Christendom be in just as good case at the year's end? Dear me, what a world it is! Drunkenness all round us; covetousness eating the hearts out of society; ministers, with kidnappers, members of their churches, discussing a litany and the terms of admission to the Lord's Supper! Bless me! if the Nazarene were there, at the Worcester Convention, I think he would have made a scourge of *large* cords, and let loose upon the assembly till they had such a stampede among the brethren as one does not often see among the reverend clergy!

Well: the age is leaving these old boys to their litanies, and their communions, and their miracles. What politician, what philanthropist, what merchant (of any head at all), what man of science, cares a pin for all this humbug? Religion rises early every morning, and works all day.

The next letter, of the date March 27, 1854, addresses Mr. May in Hebrew, Greek, Latin, and Russian, and then proceeds, with a grotesque fabrication :—

So much for spelling me in Greek, and calling me learned. You say that you are not so odious as I am. You ——! I never got at the cause of your offence till a few days ago, when it was "*communicated*" by the late—no, the prompt—Dr. Pierce. This is it. You preached a sermon at the "Great and Thursday Lecture," taking Dr. Parkman's place, I think, before a very select audience, such as usually convenes at that place and time. You were in a little bad odour, and wished to show that you had some grace; and so showed what Mr. Somebody, in "Pilgrim's Progress," says is the first sign of it, viz. a disposition to pick holes in the saints' coats. So you let in upon the faults of the brethren; and, after enumerating a host of them, thus concluded:—

"Dear brethren, it pains me to say it, but it is true—most of you are so far behind the age, and all ages, past not less than present, that you will hear nothing new till the last trumpet; then you will not *rise* in time to take part in the first resurrection, and will be up in season only to catch your second death! And now the Lord be with you! Amen!"

After that, the brethren thought you made "havoc of the churches," and doubted that you were a peace-man. They decided that a man who entertained such an opinion of Unitarian ministers could not be a Unitarian himself, and voted "not to ask Mr. May to our pulpits." How many men have extended the hand of the churches to you of late?

TO THE SAME.

Feb. 11, 1856.

My new edition of the "Discourse on Matters pertaining to Religion" is out, and I will send you twenty-five. I have made some alterations of considerable importance, as I do not now believe that John wrote the Fourth Gospel.

I cannot comprehend the spirit in which that book has been treated by the Unitarians and other liberal Christians. I can now look at it as if you had written it, and not I. I have not looked into it since 1846, till last autumn, when I revised it for the new edition; and the criticisms made fourteen years ago quite amaze me. How can a man be so stupid and so wicked as to mistake the *drift* and *purpose* of the book; but they did. Orthodox Professor Porter, in the *New Englander*, did admit and appreciate the religious aim and spirit of the book in a most kind and generous manner. But how the brethren mocked at it!

Well, it did not break my heart; though I had to go to Europe for a year, and take breath.

TO CORNELIUS COWING, ESQ., WEST ROXBURY.

Paris, Nov. 19, 1843.

My dear Friend, Squire Cowing,—You will say I have not forgotten my own joke, and you will say truly. Here we are in Paris, enjoying French "comfort." We are now in private lodgings, which we entered yesterday for the first time, and we have an idea of French comfort, such as we never had before. The furniture is elegant, a handsome timepiece on the marble mantle, and very dashy urns on each side thereof, full of very dashy artificial flowers; there is a wardrobe of elegant mahogany, with a great mirror for its door, and everything in the room to match, but, withal, we find it utterly impossible to be warm in our superb *apartement*, so they call it, and the winds keep up such a whistling on all sides of us, that you might think you were in a steam saw-mill.

The good landlady promises to remedy all these inconveniences. To-morrow we are to have a grate and some good soft coal in the fire-place; the doors and windows are to be caulked, and *superb* red curtains are to be hung up in the windows. So, you see, we are to be as comfortable as a fly in a barrel in mid-winter. I know you will be specially interested in what concerns the *drinking* in this good city. Let me tell you that we have dined in half-a-dozen different *restaurants*, and have seen all the visitors take wine with their dinner, each half a bottle. The wine commonly drunk is very red, and about as strong as good lemonade, perhaps as strong as your root beer. Here is a market for wines, the *Halle aux Vins* they call it, on the banks of the Seine, which covers, I know not how much ground, certainly many acres. Here are great "magazines" of wine, and counting-rooms of the dealers in that article. You can't walk for two minutes in any street, without coming upon a "magazine of wines." Yet I have not yet seen a man intoxicated, not in the smallest degree. In England you see drinking—coarse, hard, vulgar drinking, and men drunk. I have no doubt that men do get drunk in Paris as elsewhere, but they keep it close from the eyes of the curious. I wish some of those who, in Boston, would like to have Sunday made a day of amusement, might look in upon Paris some Sunday, and see the state of things that goes on there. The shops are open for the most part, all sorts of work are going on as on other days; the churches are open, but there are few persons in them, women for the greater part; in the evening, the theatres, all 26 of them, are open, and crowded too, for the best pieces are then performed. There seems no rest for man or beast; carts, coaches, omnibuses, and all sorts of vehicles are flying about. Now, I have no doubt at all, that the popular way of keeping Sunday in Massachusetts is strict beyond all reasonable strictness. Still, it is better by far than the popular method in Paris. I have no doubt that many in Paris go to the theatre Sunday night for just the same reason that many go to church Sunday night, because they do not know what to do with themselves, and must do something. In America, put a man of a great deal of energy, a restless spirit, in some country town, large or small; his business will not occupy all his energy, perhaps. If it does, then he becomes an intense money-getter, nothing else. He thinks money, he works money, he dreams money. Suppose his business does not occupy all his attention, and this may happen from various causes, then he must do one of three things, either become a flaming politician, or else a sectarian enthusiast, who gets up four-days meetings, and "hopes to merit heaven by making earth a hell," or else he will be a drunkard—one of the three he must be. Now, however, the temperance and anti-slavery movements are offering new fields for such men, which they will enter, and where they will go to extremes, I fear, and sometimes I think I see. Now, if we had more of innocent amusement, it seems to me we should have less of several things; viz., less intensity of money-making, less political violence, less sectarian bigotry, and less drinking one's self drunk. I don't wonder that some good men were afraid of amusement, when amusement meant getting drunk; but now the Washingtonians have done their work so nobly, it seems to me we might venture to play a little, "with none to molest or to make us afraid."

Here the Government gives 400,000 dollars a year to support the theatres in Paris, a wise measure no doubt, for if the "surplus revenue" of spirit in the effervescent population of France is not expended in frolic, there will be revolutions and mobs and all sorts of trouble, so the Government find it more politic to pay dancers and musicians and mountebanks, who make the people laugh by their fun, than to pay soldiers who make them sour with powder and cannon shot. Do not you think it would be a pleasant joke for some one to present a resolution in the House of Representatives of Massachusetts that the State pay 40,000 dollars to support the theatre in Boston? I cannot tell you of all that I have seen or heard in Paris. I shall do that in the long evenings that we shall spend together, I trust.

TO PROF. EDWARD DESOR, NEUCHATEL.

Newton Corner, August 24, 1853.

I have lately been to the White Mountains, where I got this original kind of paper, the bark of the Canoe Birch (*Betula Papyracea*), which I write on as a memorial to such a naturalist as you are. Four of us went together: we walked up on the east side, and down on the west, and spent several days in wandering about the mountain valleys. I found some fine plants, *Eupatorium Album, Arenaria Greenlandica*, &c. This latter I have found on the sea-shore at Gloucester, in the decaying granite, but in a temperature quite different from that at the mountains. How I wished you had been there to explain to us the structure of the mountains as you did one Sunday at Pottsville! I went up Kearsarge Mountain also; it is to the east and south of Mount Washington, 3300 feet high and of conglomerate to the top. Of course, not like the conglomerate which we saw in Pennsylvania. From that you get a fine view of all the principal White Mountains. You see them *en famille* as it were.

I have no news to tell you. Hillard has a book in the press, "Six Months in Italy." We are to have an opera-house in Boston which costs 250,000 dollars. It is next door to the Natural History Building. I found the everlasting "Coast Survey" upon Mount Washington—measuring the height—I expected to meet also the "Nautical Almanac," and the "Smithsonian Institute," but found only Dr. Harris with a *Peranychia Argyrocorna* in his hand, and a box full of bugs which he had caught and impaled on German pins—the cruel entomologist! I fear you will miss the Coast Survey. So I send you a report of their doings that you may read and rejoice.

You will be glad to know that my ten sermons are reprinted in England, and in process of translation at Leipsic, when they will be published as a *Festgeschenk*. I shall send you in a few days another little volume, viz., "Sermons of Theism, Atheism, and the Popular Theology," and along with it the Report on the Geology of Iowa; a nice book is the latter, which I begged for you. If you want any of the things published by Congress, I will try and get them for you.

TO THE SAME.

May 24, 1854.—I will send you a sermon and a speech before long. I should like to see you looking at a lithograph in my parlour; when shall I? We take our sacrament of *Schabzieger* * on Natural History nights; but there is no Desor. So I imitate you, call the *Katz*, tell some imaginary discovery in science, and recall the good old times when I saw you. All send our love; no doubt ———— would if she were here.

TO THE SAME.

July 19, 1854.—We have not much scientific matter of interest. I hope you have seen Dr. Whewell's "Plurality of Worlds." He admits no habitable spot in *Rerum Naturâ* but this little dirty globe—all else is *chips;* no intelligent creature but man, none else possible. Jupiter is all water; Saturn a Scotch mist; and Mercury all smoke. But the book is amazingly well written. Whewell is able and diligent, learned and earnest. I never read a book of his I thought so able, nor one I disagreed with so much. Murchison has an able book—so says Professor Rogers—which I have not seen. So you want a copy of the Census. I have one for you.

Dr. Füster is quite happy just now. He teaches *Franzözisch* at Newton, the *Lateinisch und Italienisch,* drinks some *dutzend* glasses of *Baierisches Bier* in a day, and thinks the Germans are the *Schlechteste Leute.* The good old soul wishes me to send his *love* to you every time I write. Dr. Günther is going to Nebraska, for one does many "thincks" in a new country, as he says. Arthur, his son, has gone already, and Clara, I hope, will go and get a husband. ———— sends her compliments and her thanks, and has read your pamphlets with great pleasure. She is a dear nice creature, brilliant as a star.

Wife sends all sorts of kind messages, and now, dear good Desor, good-bye.

                                            T. P.

TO THE SAME.

                                   Boston, 24th August, 1854.

We are all well—have just returned from a three weeks' expedition to Vermont. We have been the length of the State, up one side of the Green Mountains and down on the other, travelling chiefly by horses. I am surprised to find no more variety in the *botany* of the State. I find many things at Mt. Washington I seek in vain on the Green Mountains. I made the acquaintance of two half-domesticated bears. They were about three years old, and so tame that I fed them out of my hand with nuts, berries, bits of bread, lumps of sugar. In a

---

* Chap-Sager—Sap-sago, goats'-milk cheese.

week they became much attached to me. I put my hand in their mouths and played with them a good deal every day. They were fastened by a chain twenty feet long to the opposite ends of a beam, which revolved on a pivot: so they could walk about as much as they pleased. Now, this surprised me: they always walked their round from the west to the east by the south—*i. e.*, against the sun's course; this was so when the two walked round turning the beam, or when a single one walked round his own special centre. Do they always do so—and if so, why? Who has written a good treatise on bears? Tell me, do bears pair for life, or, like so many other animals, only for the season?

TO THE SAME.

Indianapolis (Indiana), Oct. 18th, 1854.

DEAR DESOR,—Here I am, a thousand miles from dear old sedate Boston. I come on a lecturing expedition. I am to lecture eleven times, and preach once in Indiana, Michigan, Ohio, and Pennsylvania. I have many things to say about the country and the people. I wish I had you to help me observe and to generalize after the facts are known.

The West, which I have now visited three times, impresses me much with the width of all things; there is a certain largeness to everything —streams, plains, trees, pumpkins, apples, swine (a hog in Ohio, 1854, weighed, alive, 1980 pounds, another 2150), and men. But there is a certain *coarseness of fibre* also noticeable in all things; the wood is coarse-grained, the nuts are big and fat, not nice and sweet, the apples have a coarse texture—all the vegetables and all the fruit.

Did you ever see the fishes of the Ohio? They are the most un-couth-looking monsters I ever saw, save the Roman fishes in the market at Rome. The cat-fish, an ugly-looking devil, with a face like an owl; the spoon-billed cat-fish, looking yet worse; the buffalo, an over-grown sculpin; the reed-horse, and the sucker. One must be hard-pushed to eat one of these wretches. The men look sickly, yellow, and flabby. In Indiana I saw but one rosy-cheeked girl, about eighteen or nineteen. "Were you born here?" "No, sir; in New Hampshire." "I thought so!" I saw 300 or 400 children in the schools at Indianapolis—not a rosy cheek! The women are tall and bony, their hair lank, their faces thin and flabby-cheeked.

What effect is this western climate to have on the human race? It must check the intensity of the Anglo-Saxon character: the fertility of the soil, the dulness of the air, the general enervating influence of the physical circumstances, must deteriorate the human being for a long time to come. Health is poor, activity small in comparison with New England. You are right in your estimate of the American climate on Europeans.

But I fear the West deteriorates Americans quite as much. It is too early to undertake to determine the full character of the Westerners; but this is pretty plain, they will no more have the same energy as the New-Englanders than the Britons have the same as the Norsemen and Danes who went from Scandinavia to England.

There has been a great Baby Show in Ohio; 127 babies were offered for prizes. One received 300, one 200, one 100 dollars, and besides several gratuities were given to others; the prize, of course, was given to the mother. I think Jonathan is the first to offer prizes for the *best baby.* An agricultural society in England, a few years ago, gave £25 for the prize ox and five shillings for the model peasant; but you will see an account of the baby show in the *New York Tribune.*

TO THE SAME.

Nov. 14, 1854.

Dr. Füster is well, but *schlimmer*—poor old soul!—he has only one scholar who pays, and that is myself, studying Polish. I learned Russian, Illyrian, and Bohemian a little, with him, long ago. A young Mr. Krebs studies Latin, &c., but is poor, and pays nothing. The old Pachyderm is in a sad condition. He wants to go back, but fears the priests, and their *Pax vobiscum* (*Nicht den Kaiser nur die Priester !*). He is a good soul, and I love him. He is preparing a course of lectures on German *Philosophie* (!) and *Literatur.* Your beautiful prints adorn my parlor, and remind me of dear old Desor, who is duly remembered also in the Swiss sacrament of cheese. I send you Lyell's "Travels in America," two volumes in one, the two numbers of the *Christian Examiner*, with Agassiz's articles, and another book ("Types of Mankind"), which contains things from him. I am always glad to get such things for you—the Humboldt's "Schriften" delighted my heart. Tell me of any new scientific books : what is a good monograph on bears ? Remember me to those at Berne. What has Vogt done lately ? Tell me about Johannes Ronge, now in London. He has written a friendly letter to our society. I shall publish a volume of sermons, speeches, &c., next month. Did you ever get the "Sermons of Atheism," &c. ? Let me know about the atheists of Germany. Let me see all that you write ; if it be about the *Metaphysik* of Echinoderms it will interest me. Mrs. Follen and Aunt Susan keep house in Brookline, all happy. I have attended only one meeting of the Natural History Society, for six months. Poor old Dr. —— is breaking to pieces, but is more and more interested in science. Alas! old age is beautiful in Alex. Von Humboldt, but sad and ugly in —— and most men. I wish I could talk to you about it. A natural old age is a fair evening, but an unnatural —bah! let me never see it! I will send you an engraving of myself before long in the parcel. I don't know how it will look. Dr. Füster sends love, so would —— but calls it "regards." Hannah sympathizes with your gout, but says "he must always call it rheumatism, never gout." Wife sends all sorts of kindliest remembrances, whereto George, now a "young man" of twenty, adds his.
Good-bye.   T. P.

TO THE SAME.

August, 1856.

I have lately been reading the works of your friend Vogt, viz., "Zoologische Briefe," "Physiologische Briefe," "Thierleben," &c. He has great ability—writes uncommonly well, *for a German.* But his books are to me quite sad, so utterly material and atheistic. There is *Natur*, but no *Geist*. He does not merely deny *a God*, such as יהוה, ZEUS, Odin, Thor, but all God—God *an sich*: there is no *Bewusstsein* to the world, no *Grund* to this *Immerwerden*. So all is *planlos* and *wüst*. Nature looks bad enough from the stand-point of the *altglaubige Lutheraner;* but with them there was a *Gott*, a great capricious force, with a blundering mind. A *Dummkopf* is their *Gott*, but a vast will; so He gave a certain order and unity to the world: it was a *Kosmos*, though the kosmifying principle was only a will, not a mind, still less a conscience and a heart. But to me, Vogt's view of the universe is more unsatisfactory, for he admits no ordering mind or will in the universe; there is no *plan*, no planning. I admire his genius, his knowledge, his power, and his love of freedom. I like the man, but his view of the universe seems to me utterly unscientific. I know he would say that I am only a *Pfaff* (priest), and scoff at any judgment I could offer; but *you* know better. His view of man is also sad. Life so short here, old age so gloomy, so hopeless, *steif*, and *starr* (see Physiol., 1854, pp. 671–680), and no pursuits, no immortality!

While I read his books, I am enjoying a few weeks' vacation in the country. I live in the house of ——, an old lady, seventy-one or seventy-three years of age, a tall, stately, handsome-looking woman,

    *   *   *   *   *

    *   *   *   *   *

    *   *   *   *   *

    *   *   *   *   *

    *   *   *   *   *

    *   *   *   *   *

    *   *   *   *   As I think

of Vogt's view of the world, it seems utterly absurd and unscientific. You know that I am as far from all *Pfaffenthum* as Vogt himself; but, with his convictions, I think I would not live at all. I should be worse off than his *Gregara*, or *Diplozoon*, who have no self-consciousness, no general ideas. I should like to know how far his views are shared by the *Gebildete* (learned men) of Germany and France. (Look at his Physiol., 1853, pp. 632–634, 648.)

There are many things in his books which I want to talk with you about, relating to affairs of science. I shall now read all of his works. I own all but the "Mittelländische See" and "Kohlerglaube." But to-day it is a leisure Sunday, and I do not preach. I have been looking at a brand new work, "La Vie Future; par Henri Martin, Membre de l'Institut, Doyen de la Faculté des Lettres de Rennes," and am thoroughly disgusted with it. It is "*approuvé par Monseigneur l'Evêque de Rennes, et Monseigneur l'Evêque de Coutances et d'Avanches,*" and is a piece of humbug. I thought well of the man from his "Philosophie Spiritualiste de la Nature," &c., but now have *no confidence* in him. Tell me about him; does he *lie,* or is he so *borné* as he seems?

What a long letter I am writing you! and yet there shall be another on my birth-day, three weeks hence. But do you remember that you and I are to visit Sweden together? No doubt you want to see Lilli; but I, the midnight sun, Upsala, &c. Besides, we must go to the tropics together; neither you nor I have been there. Now, in a few years we shall have settled our political quarrel. You must come over to Boston, and you and I, Howe, Cabot, and others, will go down to Trinidad, and pass the months of December and January in those parts! What do you say to that? Let us see the tropics first. Tell me what books to read on the vegetation of the tropics. I will freshen up my Spanish a little, so as to talk with the natives. Perhaps we could go to the Amazon: to Trinidad we *must*—perhaps in 1858 or 1859.

Now, do you know that you have not yet sent me your book on Echinoderms? Don't say, "It is a *specialité*, and so Parker will take no interest in it;" for if you will write on the religion of the man in the moon, I will study *Selenistic* to be able to follow your researches. Tell me all that you do; how you pass your week-days and your Sundays. What sort of preaching goes on about you? Tell me, also, if there are any good works in any department of human activity. What is Vogt's position (*Stellung*) now-a-days? Is he also professor? How is he treated in Germany? Tell me of any books you want from America, and I will get them for you. And now, good bye, and God bless you!

Yours ever,
THEODORE PARKER.

TO THE SAME.

Staten Island, New York, 24th Aug., 1856.

MY VERY DEAR DESOR,—I am forty-six years old this day, and no wiser, no better, have done no more! But I have a fondness for dear old Desor, who is yet not so old as I, but an old friend. So I must gratify my inclination, and begin a letter here and to-day, but which will not get finished for some time to come. First, let me tell you about myself. I fear you would hardly know me, I am grown so old in look. My head is bald, and my beard is gray. I have a full beard, excepting the moustache. (Beards are common now in Boston as in Berne or in Wien.) I have grown very old within the last three years; too much work and too many cares have done this for me. But I shall mend one day when I take a little leisure, and you and I run down to the tropics and see the Orinoco; I shall recruit straightway, and become young once more. Here and now my life has not enough of sociality, of conversation, and joy in it. What you Germans call *Heiterkeit*, I have too little of. I mix with men chiefly as a teacher, to preach, lecture, or harangue. If I had at twenty-five joined some club of good fellows, and met with them to talk, laugh, dance, bowl, or play billiards once a fortnight ever since, I should be a wiser and a happier man. But let me mend for the future.

I look back with great pleasure on the happy times I have had with you when you used to come to our house. I was a little afraid of you at first, thinking it would not do for me to visit such a *savant* and *Gelehrte* as "M. Desor." But Cabot took me over to East Boston and I saw the crabs and the Echinoderms, and got acquainted with you right well. Few men ever stimulated my mind so much as you, for you not only had the knowledge of details in your sciences, but also the comprehensive generalizations which I value much more, and which so many naturalists lack. From my earliest recollections I have always had a tendency to make general rules and find out universal laws. I remember one example, when I was not quite seven years old. I looked over the lichens on a rock, and the reindeer-moss which grew close by it, and the huckleberry bushes, and then at the nut-trees, which were not far off, and said, "Here, now, is a regular ascent, the rock, the lichen, the moss, the grass, the bush, the tree; and it is so everywhere." I went in and told my mother of my discovery of the scale of things, from the rock to the tree. Gradation seems a general law, *nihil per saltum*, though I had no Latin and hardly English to say it in. Dear me, I *am* growing old, talking so much about myself; but as it is a birthday letter you will forgive its *egotism*.

Well: you had a grand talent for generalization—and helped me much in many things. Now, I miss you greatly, not only affectionately, *as dear, good Desor*, but scientifically, as " Wise Mr. Desor, who looks so deep into things, and so wide too." Well: do you never mean to come back ? To live with us, I suppose, never; but surely to visit us ?

September 11.—Well: the *Scientific Association* has met at Albany. I could not go, for I must attend to my friends the Hunts. But they had a regular quarrel, and the Cambridge clique say that " My Brother," William B. Rogers, you know, "made all the mischief." But Lesley says the boot was on the other leg. I enclose a slip from the *New York Tribune* which gives a general account of the meeting. Of course you will receive the report by-and-bye, and will smile at the little vanities of great men. I wish you would tell me who has written a good book about *bears*. I know of none. Tell me also about the distribution of sensation in animals. What is the primitive sense— Ur-sense ? Is there any animal which has the sense of hearing subject to the will, as we that of sight ? I think sight is not volitional with spiders and some other insects. What do you think of Moleschott ? Have you heard of Silgeström lately ? Tell me what books of mine you have, and I will add what you lack. Is there never to be a *Madame Desor*, a *Frau-professorin* ?

Yours, ever,   T. P.

TO THE SAME.

Newton Corner, near Boston, Aug. 8, 1857.

You want to know about your scientific friends, what they are doing. Well, then, here are a few particulars. Agassiz, Pierce, and Horsford, have been attacking " Spiritualism," not without a good deal of bitterness and violence, and some unfairness in the method of treatment, though they may be right in their conclusions. Somebody offered 500 dollars to any spiritualist, who would do what they all profess they can do, in the presence of a committee of unprejudiced and competent witnesses accustomed to investigation. The attempt was made before Agassiz, Pierce, Horsford, and others, and failed utterly. The *savans* publish the result to the world in insolent and boastful language. But the spiritualists claim that they were unjustly dealt with, were prejudged before the examinations, and insulted in its process, all of which

I think is true. Felton has been writing in the *Boston Courier*, the wickedest paper in New England now, conducted by a club of inveterate Hunkers, who love slavery, and all manner of injustice, against "Spiritualism," in the style of the sixteenth century. His opponents reply in the same style. Of course *you* will not suppose I believe the *spiritual* character of the few phenomena which have made so much noise. I don't think Dr. Franklin and Dr. Channing have become fools since they left the flesh. Two-thirds of the *mediums*, I think, are skilful jugglers. Mr. Hume, you see is humbugging the Parisians. I don't know whether Napoleon the Little believes in him, or merely *uses* him as the priests the "Virgin of La Salette;" but it is not uncommon for tyrants to be superstitious. Atheists, I mean *practical atheists*, often believe in magic. Spiritualism is doing two good things. 1. It knocks the nonsense of the popular theology to pieces, and so does us a negative service. 2. It leads cold, hard, materialistic men to a recognition of what is really spiritual in their nature, and so does a positive good. But there is a world of humbug, nonsense, and fraud mixed up with it.

I was down at Plymouth a few weeks ago, and while walking on the borders of a large mill-pond, noticed some curious facts. The shores are of fine, delicate sand, and slope down quite gradually. In the night the mill does not run, and the pond becomes full; but in the day, while the mill is at work, the water falls five or six inches, or more, causing the shore line to recede, and leaving a wet belt all round the pond. Of course, this happens with all mill-ponds. But during the night, the wind blew moderately, and produced a quantity of foam on one side of the pond, which lay there in spots when I visited it. But when the foam had disappeared, the sand was covered with those peculiar marks which you find on the old sandstones, and which are attributed to rain-drops. I know your theory as to their origin, if I recollect it aright; and thought this fact might interest you. I am a poor draughtsman, or I should send you a drawing of the indentations which these bubbles make as they perish in the sand. But you can see the same thing for yourself, no doubt. Do you know, you never sent me your remarks on *Old Age?* I am quite anxious to have the work, for I am almost forty-seven (!), and my head is bald and my beard gray.

TO THE SAME.

Boston, 26th September, 1857.

I made a little voyage in a yacht, with a dozen other persons, in August, and had a good time. We went to Nantucket, and thence to New York, and up the Hudson. At Powder Hole, south of Cape Cod, we found the fresh water fill the holes we scooped out of the sand, though they were made within a foot of the salt water. You remember this fact, on the little sand-spits at Chatham, on Cape Cod. I never found it so on other beaches. Do you know of other examples of the same thing? What explanation do you give of the fact?

TO THE SAME.

Williston, Connecticut, August 24, 1858

—— The dear, good old Dr.Wesselhöft died September 7, at 4 A.M. It was his 65th birthday. He has been overworked continually for the last seven or eight years. In the spring he was ill, and went to Newburyport, then to the White Mountains for the summer. He returned to Boston, in the end of July, a little better. But he became worse again. Dropsy of the chest set in ; carbuncles came, one on his leg, one on his neck, and though they yielded kindly to medical treatment, it was too much for him. The morning of September 1st, at 4, he was sitting in his great chair beside his bed, and said to his wife, " Are you getting ready also ? " She asked him what he meant, and he said, " Why, you know you are likewise invited." He then laid his face on the side of the bed, and was immortal.

Neither he nor his friends thought he was likely to die. He was the recognized head of the Germans in Boston, very kind to many who forgot his kindness ; for gratitude is the latest-born of all manly virtues, the youngest and fairest. I fear W. leaves little property. His two sons will continue the business, I suppose. . . . . I attended the funeral. Dr. Douai also spoke a *Leichenrede* (funeral address). But an atheist had not much that was *tröstend* (consoling) to offer at a funeral. Dr. W. was a brave, good man.

I hear that you have discovered the remains of an ancient people, squatting on the Swiss Lakes. They must have been Dutchmen—Hollanders, I mean, to build on piles in Switzerland, as at Java. Do tell me about it. It seems strange that in Switzerland every antiquity has not been sucked dry many years ago, with so many antiquarian mouths pulling at it all the time.

TO PROFESSOR HENRY D. ROGERS, EDINBURGH.

Boston, 29th December, 1857.

MY DEAR MR. ROGERS,—It did me much good to take your excellent brother by the hand a few days ago, and to see that he had not suffered so much as we all feared from that boulder which came upon him *in transitu* in England. He bears no marks of it now. Perhaps he will have a new theory of the motion of erratic bodies ; but I hope will witness no more such experiments. He told us how pleasantly you were all settled in Auld Reekie, and what a nice time you had both for work and play. I am glad to hear that your book gets on so famously, and will see the light so soon.

What is one man's joy is another's grief ; the English make a Professor of you in Glasgow—alas me ! they also, at the same time, make you a Scotchman, and what Glasgow and Edinburgh gains Boston loses. No part of it will feel the loss more than the little house in Exeter Place, and the few persons therein, whom you so often gladdened and instructed of a Sunday night. But, notwithstanding, we all rejoice in your new honours, and pleasant position, and certainty of useful work.

No doubt you can tell me who Henry Thomas Buckle is ? He has just printed a great book on " The History of Civilization in England ; "

Vol. I., a thick 8vo, of near 900 pages. This is only Vol. I. of the Introduction to the work. I think it a great book, and know none so important since the "Novum Organum" of Bacon. I mean none in English. Of course I except the "Principia" of Newton. This is a "Novum Organum" in the department of history—the study of man; it is a *restauratio maxima.* Nobody here ever heard the name of Henry Thomas Buckle before. If you can tell me, I wish you would; and also what is thought of the book in that Northern Athens where you dwell. In many particulars it reminds of the "Vestiges of the Natural History of Creation." I don't always agree with the author, even in matters of "great pith and moment;" but always think him a great man. His learning also is admirable.

Have you seen Agassiz's book?   : . . . . . I wish you would tell me what you think of it. There are two things I wish in special to hear of, namely—1. About his idea of God in the world of matter. Do any thoughtful naturalists, who of course doubt, and must needs doubt, the ecclesiastical idea of God, find any satisfaction in his God who thus intervenes to create new *genera,* while individuals and species get created without that mode of help?

2. About his ideas of the distinction on which branch, order, genus, &c., are to be based. How original is he there—how correct? I thought that part of his work the most valuable of it all, but defer to the judges in such a court. My wife and Miss S. send warm greetings to Professor Rogers, Mrs. Rogers, and to Babie Rogers. Need I also to send mine?

Yours faithfully,
THEODORE PARKER.

TO REV. DAVID A. WASSON.

Boston, 30th June, 1856.

MY DEAR MR. WASSON,—I don't know what to advise you, but yet will try and give my opinions about the matter.

1. If you remain in Groveland, you will satisfy your feelings of affectionate regard for the people who have been with you in times of trial, and stood by you. But you will be tormented with the conviction that it is not the place for you, not large enough to occupy your powers, and will die at last, rather early too, with the bitter thought that you have not done what your talents alike demanded and promised.

2. If you go to Medford, you will try to graft an apple scion into a scrub oak. You will keep grafting, and the more you try the more it won't live. Nobody can do any good to that class of men: they would crucify Jesus if he were to come; your merits will be a perpetual torment to them. You have only two things which they will appreciate—1, intellectual power; 2, diligent industry: they will feel one and see the other. But the deep religious feeling which warms you all through, the fair humanity which comes out like a green summer all over your features, *that* they will only make mouths at. I know the Hunker genus right well, and take it the Stand-bys of the parish are unmitigated specimens of that genus.

But there are a few men of a different stamp, and a few young persons also; of them there is great hope. But, alas! for the minister who attempts to settle in such a place. I know few persons in Medford: the Misses Osgood, who are noble women, as extraordinary in their moral excellence as in their deep and wide intellectual culture, and Mr. and Mrs. Stearns, earnest and progressive people; I hear of others of that stamp; one young man I partly know. If the controlling Hunkers would be "translated to a brighter sphere," or would enter the Episcopal Church, where they are cakes of the right leaven, all would go on well.

At Medford you will have these advantages—1, a material competence, regular and certain; 2, time for study; 3, opportunity to obtain books. Harvard College is three miles off, and you could now and then buy a volume; besides 4, occasional communion with literary men, the opportunity for lecturing. All these are admirable things.

3. At Columbus I suppose you will find things much in the rough; earnest, hearty, vigorous men and women, progressive also, but a little coarse, irregular, not cultivated. Columbus is the capital of Ohio, and is not without books; half the year it is filled with the political talent of the State. You will have a permanent circle of able men and women whom you will mould and influence, and ennoble them and their children.

Then flouting men will come and hear you from time to time, attracted by your power, and forced to think by what you say and do. You will be one centre of religious power in that great State, where now is not one. You will work hard, fare hard, and grow to great stature. You will not have the nice culture so easily acquired at Medford, so graceful, so beautiful, so desirable. But strength of manhood, nobleness of life, you will have, it seems to me.

I know you better than you think I do, and let me say there is no minister in New England from whom I expect so much. If you go to Ohio I shall not see you a great deal; if you come to Medford we shall meet often and help each other.

Now, pardon me for writing this long letter, and don't let it influence you; do nothing hastily, be sure of the actual state of things at Medford and Columbus, for I may be misinformed of both. The fact that the Medfordians invited you may be taken as qualifying their Hunkerism, showing that the weather is more moderate.

I must preach for you sometimes, and you for me. God bless you!

THEO. PARKER.

TO PETER LESLEY, PHILADELPHIA.

Boston, Nov. 15, 1857.

MY DEAR MR. LESLEY,—It did me good to see your handwriting again; but I fear there is little to be done this year in the way of lecturing, even on iron. The lecturers hereabouts complain of no work. Some societies have sent out their circulars and cancelled the engagements already made. Others have "suspended" for this season. The way to make yourself known in that line is to send a line to the *New*

York Tribune, and ask it to put your name in its list of lecturers. But I fear little will be done this winter. Labour stops, and all stops.

I wish you lived where I could see you often, and talk over matters of science. Since Desor has gone, and now Professor H. D. Rogers, I am in great want of scientific company.

* * * * * *

I wish you would tell me what you think of Agassiz's essay. I wish you would tell me if Agassiz, in Chapter I., removes the difficulty which philosophers find in their way, and which makes atheists of them —so the ministers say. I find more real atheism amongst theologians than amongst philosophers. The former deny the substance of God in the world of things and men, and send us off to some phantom which lives (or stays) at a distance, and now then "intervenes" by a miracle —this *deus ex machinâ;* they are ready to deny his laws. But the latter deny the existence of that God, and yet admit the immanent reality of a power of thought, will, and execution which fills all space and all time, is ever active, and never needs to "intervene" where He for ever dwells.

* * * * * *

TO MISS EMMELINE PARKER, HINGHAM, MASS.

West Roxbury, Aug. 2, 1843.

MY DEAR EMMELINE,—I thank you for your pleasant letter, but beg you not to suppose that I should ever criticize your letters. No, no ; write just as you think, just as you feel. A person of real elevation is never an unkind judge or critic. Your letter pleases me very much. I understand the feeling of bashfulness that troubles you, but you must overcome that. Try to forget yourself; don't think that anybody is looking at you, or thinking about you. I have suffered a great deal from the same feeling. I have been to see a person, and got to the door, and found it impossible to ring the bell, and walked away till I got the necessary courage. But I overcame it ; so will you. Don't keep thinking about what you are going to say ; say it as well as you can. You had better take pains to see other persons, as many as you can, and to talk with them, only don't talk when you have nothing to say, but have something. I know you have enough in you, by-and-bye it will come out ; what you want is confidence. Habit will give you this. Mr. Smith will be glad to talk with you ; he is a little precise in his ways, but no man has a kinder heart, or a better soul, towards all persons that wish to learn. I hope you take care of your health— that you use air, water, and exercise, not forgetting to sit up straight.

Very truly your friend,

THEO. PARKER.

TO THE SAME.

West Roxbury, Aug. 22, 1843.

MY DEAR EMMELINE,—I thank you for your letter. I like the spirit with which you write. Always write as you think and feel. I knew what the cost would be at Hingham before you went. Mr. Smith has only charged what we agreed upon beforehand. The scruple you have about going to Lexington is nothing. I wish you to go, and shall feel myself the party obliged if you accept of my offer. You will help your mother most effectually in this very way. I think everybody ought to work in some mode or another. You will make the experiment; if you find the mode that Providence designed for you is to work with your hands as before, why you will go back to that, a position, in my eyes, just as honourable as any in the world; if you find it is to work with your head, and keep a school, why, you will continue in that. I have no doubt of your abilities; try, try, and we shall see. I know you will succeed. At Lexington the expense will be less, about two dollars a week, and no charge for tuition. I do not think you can do anything to lessen that cost.

I shall want John, perhaps, to go with you to Lexington on the Tuesday before the second Wednesday in September. I will give you a letter of introduction to Mr. May, the teacher of the school. I will have the bills sent to West Roxbury, and will leave directions about returning the money to Mr. May.

Believe me, very truly, your friend,

THEO. PARKER.

TO THE SAME, WEST NEWTON.

West Roxbury, Oct. 4, 1844.

MY DEAR EMMELINE,—Don't be discouraged about yourself. All will come in its time; I have no doubt you get the lessons well. In a short time you will learn to recite them well likewise. Try to keep composed. Don't think of yourself. I don't mean, don't be selfish, for I know you are not that, but try not to think about yourself more than of another person. Little children are always easy and natural, because they are not self-conscious; they don't think how this will appear, so they always appear free. I expect much of you. I knew you would find Mr. Pierce a little harder, and apparently colder, than Mr. May. But he is quite as good a man, I fancy, and certainly as good a teacher. By-and-bye this appearance will wear away, and you will find the man—the man with a large warm heart—not without imperfections, truly, but with real merits and kind sympathies. I know you did not find any fault with him, but I saw how you felt, as well as if you had written a volume. Take good care of your health, sit up straight, don't go out in the damp evenings without a cloak or a shawl; when you study, be careful not to take a constrained position. Then I would try to be free and sociable with others. I know you used to complain that you did not talk; you will overcome that by-and-bye; not all at once, but naturally and slowly. Of course you must continue at the school, and become a teacher. I doubt not you will be a successful one, valuable to the shy and timid as well as to the forward and bold. I was sorry that I could not get over to Brookline to see you before you went away, but so many persons come to see me that I have no time to go abroad. I have not been to Lexington yet. Well, I know you will always be a good girl, and come out right at the last.

Believe me, always truly, your friend and uncle,

THEO. PARKER.

TO ⸺⸺.

Boston, 23rd March, 1849.

MY DEAR ⸺⸺,—I should be very sorry to have you suppose I would advise you or any one to marry for anything but the most pure and holy affection. I think that marriage is the great sacrament of life, and I hate to see one profane what God meant to be so holy and beautiful. What I said to John, I said as much in joke as in earnest. Do not suppose I meant you should say, " Well, now this year I will look me up a man, and be married ! " It is no such thing. Still, I think a good deal of happiness depends upon marriage ; a good deal of a man's happiness, and a good deal of woman's : there may be one or two persons in a hundred to whom marriage would not be a good thing or natural thing, but to the great majority of mankind and womankind it is a desirable thing. But it is very bad to marry one not fit for you ; one for whom you are not fit. There are whole marriages, and there are fractional marriages, where only a part of each is married, and the rest remains as single as before. I like not the fractional wedlocks. I have thought that you lived too much by yourself, that you saw few persons, and most of them of not a very elevating character ; that you were shutting yourself up in a very narrow circle, where there were few liberal ideas, few liberal sentiments, and that the effect on yourself would be a bad one. At one end of your business is the school-room, at the other end an orthodox meeting-house, with an illiberal man in it, setting forth rather degrading ideas of man, of God, and of the relation between man and God. Now, I don't want to make you discontented with your business. I think any condition is high enough to rear the loftiest virtues in. I think your calling is a noble one ; the school-room a beautiful place to develope the mind in ; the meeting-house I am not a-going to quarrel with. I only want to introduce a little more variety into your life, to get some new influences to work there. I thought a new scene, new duties, new faces, would effect that, and therefore I felt a little sorry that you did not go to St. Louis ; but you know best. I think good books would help you a good deal ; I don't mean " Josephus," nor " Baxter's Saints' Rest," nor the " last words and dying confessions of "—anybody, but the real sterling literature of the English nation. If you will read good authors, I never will joke you any more about a husband, for I don't think a husband is one of the things which you *must* have, only *might*. I will help you to any books that you may want ; a husband you won't ask me to look up for you.

With best regards to you and all, yours affectionately,

THEODORE.

TO MISS E. M. WHITE.

Boston, 6th May, 1858.

MY DEAR ETTA,—I shan't let the mail go back to-day without taking my thanks for your kind and most welcome note. I am very glad to hear you are well and pleased with your school, teacher, study, &c. I think you could not do better than attend Mr. Briggs's meeting. He is a warm, affectionate man. I hope you will become acquainted with his wife also—a noble woman, of a quite superior character. I hoped to see you at the lecture in Salem, and supposed you were gone from town. You must not be afraid of me; I am not at all formidable, and "won't bite." Perhaps I shall see you at Salem before the term ends, and show you how little reason you have to be timid before me. But I was once quite as diffident as you are now; we all get over such things.

I hope you take exercise in the open air, and so will keep your health firm; many of our young women break down in their studies because they don't know how to live. It is difficult to learn without living first; then the knowledge often comes too late.

When you write to your mother, please remember me kindly to them, and believe me affectionately, your friend,

THEODORE PARKER.

TO MISS E. P. PEABODY.

Friday Morning, 1841.

* * * * * *

But you remember that as Christian tranquillity is the fairest and the costliest fruit on the Christian stem, so it is the last that matures. Even Paul, great-minded and deep-hearted as he was, could not find it till old age. Paul the *aged* alone could say, "I *have fought* the good fight. I have finished my course. I know whom I have served, and am *thereby persuaded* that God is able to keep what I have committed unto him. God hath not given me the spirit of fear, but of love and of a sound mind." Even if you are not yet *triumphant*, I know that you will be. The human will is strong and excellent; but not the strongest nor most excellent; when perfectly coincident with the will of God, I suppose, we are not conscious of any *personal* will. Then the Infinite flows through us and we are blessed. Why should not you be egotistical in your letters? It would grieve me if you were not. Do not fear, in the name of all that is good, to tell me your sorrows. I know by very bitter experience that the full heart finds comfort in communing with others, in telling its sorrows even to one who can only mingle kindred tears, but cannot stay them except with compassion and deeper love. I cannot "wonder" at your sorrow, I only wonder that you bear it; that you do not faint beneath the cross. This disappointment is truly the greatest. Love is its own reward, but when changed to a different feeling,—to one almost *opposite*, there is nothing but Christian faith that can bear it. Oh, the depth of the human heart that can suffer, and suffer, and still live on! Your case is well imaged by Milnes:—

> "They who have sat at heaven's own gate,
>   And felt the light within,
> Come down to our poor mortal state,
>   Indifference, care, and sin;
> And their dim spirits hardly bear
> A trace to show what once they were."

TO THE SAME.

Jan. 7, 1841.

MOST EXCELLENT ELIZABETH,—I have often wished for your criticisms on my sermons, and now I will ask you in all friendliness to send me such strictures as you can make from recollection on the "Sermon of Pharisees." If you will do so, you will really confer a great favour. I write swiftly, though I think slowly, and so many of the literary defects of all my sermons are no doubt the result of haste. But still more, perhaps, arise from the principle of saying the best things I have in the plainest way I can. The good folks of Spring Street are not men of dictionaries, and so I never use a word of Latin origin when I can find one of native birth. Besides, I design to take illustrations from the commonest objects. Hence come words, and things, and illustrations, and allusions, which are not in good taste when viewed from any point except the pulpit at Spring Street. Still farther, in all my sermons there is an excess of metaphors, similes, and all sorts of figures of speech. But this is my nature—I could not help it if I would.

> " My mouth I do but ope,
> And out there flies—a trope."

This will not always be natural, but so long as it is, why, I suppose I must dwell in the tropics. Now if you, my good and dear Elizabeth, will be good enough to point out my redundancies and defects, my sins against good taste, and any others you think of, in my sermons in general, and that on Pharisees in particular, you will do me a great kindness, for I will try to mend. I think I can bear any severity which you would be apt to display.

Yours, as ever,

T. P.

TO MRS. DALL, PORTSMOUTH, N.H.

West Roxbury, 4th August, 1846.

MY DEAR CAROLINE,—Many thanks for your kind letter of the 13th instant. It came when I was far off, else I should have indulged myself with an answer immediately. I had a great mind to write you from Niagara, but my good resolution went where many before it have also gone. I know how busy you must be, even if you have all the " help " in the world; for you are in a new place, and a woman like you will find quite work enough in an old one. I rejoice in your active head and noble heart, believing they will find much to do anywhere.

The work you are engaged in is curious as a sign of the times—a reproach to us, and an honor; a reproach, that there should be a class of the poor, that they should find no place in our steepled churches—for the rich and poor do not meet together now-a-days; an honor, that some should devote their lives to the work of enlightening the ignorant and comforting the afflicted, that others should give their money for this work. Still, I must count it a dreadful disgrace to a

town of 12,000 people that such a ministry is needed. I don't believe
in chapels for the poor, or preachings for the poor; but a minister for
the poor I do believe in with all my might, and think it the noblest
ministry that we know of in these times. The place and duty of
woman it is quite impossible for a *man* to define. I suppose each
woman must consult her own nature and her own circumstances, and
then do the best she can. The present arrangement of society I think
a very imperfect one, and I hope it is soon to pass away; a few live in
leisure, with a town-house, a country-house, and a house by the sea-
side. They have nothing to do, and do it; but, in doing nothing, they
multiply the burdens of others, and keep some in perpetual toil, with
no chance to cultivate their nature.

What you say of Mr. —— rather surprises me. I had thought him
a very good man, and quite remarkable for his skill in turning wood,
ivory, and the like. I have heard him spoken of as quite as dry and
hard as the wood and ivory he turned in his lathe. But what we see
depends as much on ourselves as on what is before our eyes.

I don't believe a woman will arrive at the "Science of Universals"
in frying fish; if so, she is the most fortunate *friar* the world ever saw.
I must confess, however, that I have found all the real problems of life
most happily solved by labouring men and women; not, however, by
such as did nothing but fry fish.

I doubt not, a great genius would arrive at much wisdom if shut up
in a jail all his life. But most men depend on their circumstances
more than on their souls. Set ten women to cooking fish all their
lives, and nine of them will know nothing but how to fry, stew, boil,
broil, and bake. I query if Mr. —— would have learned more in that
way. I think the next time your "help" goes away, you had better
send for Mr. ——, and give the baby to me. Perhaps I could learn as
much from the baby as he from the mackerel. I think a man who has
no children is deprived not only of a solace and a joy, but of a quite
important element of his education. I have always noticed this fact
in others, and *feel* it in my own case. I wish you all manner of joy in
your home and your work. Give my regards to Mr. Dall, and believe
me heartily and truly yours, THEO. PARKER.

TO THE SAME.

Oct. 23, 1846.

I don't believe it needful for you and Mr. Dall to think alike; true,
it is pleasant, but we can't all think alike, however much we feel alike.
I don't believe a tenth part of the folks at the Melodeon agree with me
in theology; they agree with me in religion, and in the application of
that to life. So we agree! I think I have been true to my own first
principles.

Harwood* is a quiet, noble man; I admire him, love him very much.
But we differ a good deal in our philosophy, I think. He took in
Strauss whole. I have been so long familiar with theological thoughts,
that Strauss did not much surprise me, except with his terrible ability.

I should teach the little one positive religion; I mean absolute
religion—Christianity. I should use the mythical stories in the Old

* Philip Harwood, a noted English writer, of the Liberal school.

Testament, New Testament, and from other sources, as helps. I should present Christ as the model; other good men as helps also, but inferior. I would not teach him what he will wish to *unlearn when he becomes a man.* Write to me always when you will and can, and I will answer as I can. Don't fear with wearying or troubling me. I am not very well; but better than before for a year.

About letters, I am caution itself; I am sometimes afraid of myself, I am *so* cautious. I suppose men take me for rash, but so they *mis*-take me.

Give my regards to your husband, my kiss to your baby, and believe me truly your friend,   THEO. PARKER.

TO MISS ELLEN GROVER, LAWRENCE, MASS.

Boston, Nov. 1, 1853.

DEAR FRIEND,—I fear you underrate the actual value of the Bible, and the literary culture of some of its writers, as well as the deep nobleness of their best productions. But I have no time to speak of that subject at length. I can only refer to the books you wish to hear of, and read.

It strikes me that a history of the Christian Church would be of great service to you. The "Church History" of Neander is a master-piece in its way. In that you will find a good history of the opinions of the Christian Church in various ages, and will see the gradual rise of the Institutions which have done so much both good and ill. But Neander does not complete the work—there are four volumes of his book. The history of the Reformation you will find in Mosheim's "Church History." There is no good work in English that I know on the doctrines, but Hagenbach's is the best ("History of Doctrines," &c.) The Ecclesiastical Histories will give you some account of Mohammed and his doctrines. But you had better read the Koran itself.

There is an excellent translation by Sale, with a "Preliminary Dissertation" of much value. Mr. Merrick's "Life and Religion of Mohammed" (Boston, 1850), will help you much in understanding the opinions and whimsies of the Mohammedans.

I do not know any good book in English on the doctrines of the Catholics. In the "Family Library," there is a nice little book on the History of Philosophy, in two volumes. They are Nos. 143 and 144 in that set. Mosheim's book, on the "History of Christianity in the First Three Centuries," is a valuable work.

Mr. Greg's work on the "Creed of Christendom," is also a work of great merit.

Believe me, your friend and servant,
                                    THEO. PARKER.

TO THE SAME.

. . . . I never take texts out of Shakespeare. I once took a text from the Governor's proclamation, "God save the Commonwealth of Massachusetts!" once from the Declaration of Independence, "All men are created equal." . . . . . .

Religion is the most important of all human concerns, as it seems to me, and requires both the heart and the head. But there is only one *kind* of religion—though there may be very many degrees of it. Religion, I take it, is piety (the love of God) and goodness (the love of man.) one man has much of it, and another little. . . . . . .

TO THE SAME.

Boston, 15th Nov., 1858.

My DEAR FRIEND,—I have mainly recovered from the troubles which have afflicted me a long time, and had a rather alarming look for awhile. It will give me great pleasure to do what you suggest on the first day of the new year. The rings and the flowers shall each have their place in the services of the occasion. This is the way I proceed: —I shall first make a little address of a few words. This part will apply to the special character of the persons, and here the flowers may show their fragrant beauty. Then will come the words of the marriage union—and the rings will appear. Finally, I shall make a brief prayer, I hope suited to the feelings of the parties.

If you will let me know at just what hour you will present yourself with the bridegroom, it will be a great convenience, for January 1st is a pretty busy day with me, and I may have other services of the same nature to attend to.

It gives me great pleasure to learn that you have found you a fitting mate. Long may the highest earthly happiness be yours, and in due time the super-earthly !

Yours faithfully,

THEODORE PARKER.

TO MISS CARRIE H. PRATT, CONCORD, MASS.

Boston, 3rd Sept., 1855.

My DEAR LITTLE CHICKIE,—I was very glad to receive so joyous and hearty a letter from you. Soon as I knew who "Agnes Atherton" was, and saw her cheery face, I knew there was nothing to fear. I rejoice with you in your new-found joy. Love—pure, noble, refined love, brings a new consciousness to us. I know of no delight that is merely mortal, so high, so ennobling, so divine. It transforms all the world to us, when another gives us his heart, and we give him our heart.

I say merely mortal, but this is also *immortal*, a foretaste of heaven. I hope you will find a husband worthy of you, and that you will be worthy of anybody. But you have not told me his name.

I am sorry to have missed you, and hope to see you before long; so when you are in town, let me *see* how this joy has writ itself in your eye. I have just returned from the country, and have no more time for a word, so good bye.—Affectionately,

THEO. PARKER.

TO THE SAME.

Boston, Dec. 14, 1855.

My dear little Maiden,—" The course of true love never did run smooth." So it is writ in many a history. This particular affair may turn out quite different from what it now appears. There are many ups and downs in a courtship. If there were not a true congeniality between you, it is fortunate *he* made the discovery so early : by-and-bye it would be more painful to break off. But be the future what it may, of this you are sure—*the love which filled up the four months with its handsome flowers,* that leaves a mark like the traces in the rocks of New England, which will never be effaced from the character.

I know it is very painful for a young maiden to bear such disappointments, especially for deep-hearted maidens; but there is a source of strength and comfort in the religious faculties within you, which will never refuse supply in the time of sorest need. Burnt spots in the woods bear the earliest plants, and the most luxuriant and most delicate flowers. So can it be with you. So I trust it will be.

It will always give me pleasure to see you, and hear from you. Truly yours,

THEO. PARKER.

TO THE SAME.

Sept. 12th, 1857.

My dear Carrie,—I have in young days been often in just such a mood of mind as that you now suffer from, and found none even to tell it to. But do the duty which lies next your hand, and you will find the way plainer to another duty, and also that it is not so difficult to bear any special cross that is laid upon you. There are two kinds of sorrows; 1st, such as have a real outward cause, and 2nd, such as have only an unreal and imaginary cause. Yours are chiefly of the latter, and perhaps for that very reason the more difficult to endure.

There lies on my desk at this moment a note—it came a half-hour ago—from a European exile. He has been Court Preacher, and a Professor at the University of Vienna, has had large sums of money at his disposal, and lived in elegance and wide charity.

Many persons thronged his doors, so that it was difficult for his servant to arrange the visitors in his ante-chamber. Now he lives in a little, miserable, dirty room in a German boarding-house, with a rum-shop in the cellar, and gives lessons in English to German immigrants at 25 cents the hour. Nobody visits him, and though a good scholar, speaking eight or nine languages, he has no society except the low Germans who frequent the groggery downstairs! But he does not complain—only looks forward to his departure out of this world, to him so sad. I wonder if you would not bear that sorrow better than the imaginary griefs which now disturb your fancy. Do the day's duty, and thank the good God when it is done: bear the cross and be content that it is no worse.

What is not delightful is disciplinary; I don't know a bitter drop that I should dare say I could have done without in my cup.

Cheer up your little brother. Give my best regards to your father and mother, and believe me,

Affectionately yours,

Theo. Parker.

TO THE SAME.

Boston, 9th March, 1858.

My dear Carrie,—I was sorry to see you no more in Boston this winter. You must not make yourself so much of a stranger for the future, when you are here. But I am glad to hear of your present employment. Trust me, actual duties faithfully done are the best ally against ideal woes. There are sorrows which can't be thought down, nor dreamed down, nor wept down, but which may be *worked down*. The common duties of life are the best training for mankind and womankind. They furnish us just the discipline we need. Education by things is the better part of our schooling; at least it has been so to,

Affectionately yours,

Theodore Parker.

TO THE SAME.

North River, Aug. 18, 1858.

My dear Carrie,—When your letter came to me I was too tired to do anything, but yet obliged to do much; and since I have had no time to write any answer. Now I have a moment of leisure while steaming down the Hudson, and write with a pencil (as you see), and not a pen, for the convenience of the thing.

I shan't *scold* you, having small belief in the good effect of that method of procedure; but I think you quite unreasonable in your unhappiness. Why, really it is wicked for a fine, healthy, rosy-cheeked young maiden, with bright eyes and a good appetite, to be unhappy or sad in circumstances like yours. Think a moment how well you are situated. Father and mother rather over-fond of their only daughter; brothers whom you love, while they return the feeling; a congenial and useful occupation, wherein you learn while you teach; and a world of life before you, where you may shape your course as you like, at least very much as you like.

I would disdain to be unhappy, but would chase off and put to utter rout all thoughts of melancholy. You have read too many works of a romantic and foolish character, and the mind, like the hand, gets "subdued to what it works in," or even *plays* with, continually. I think it is not grateful to allow such dreary feelings as you seem to cherish, if not cultivate.

Your school will soon begin once more, and I trust you will cast all these complainings to the wind. By-and-bye you will find some worthy young man of good principles, good habits, and with a hearty love for you, and then you will wonder you could ever have constructed so great winter out of a cloud which hung only in your own fancy. But if this should not happen (and I make no doubt it will, and *hope* it will), yet you have resources enough within yourself to make you happy. I would not be a piece of last-night hanging in the house, but rather a great piece of a bright to-day, spreading warmth and light all round.

I would devote a considerable part of my leisure to the domestic duties of home, would be skilful in all housework, and famous for making *good bread;* the actual plain duties of life are the best outward medicine for the unreal romantic woes of our day-dreams.

Yours truly,

THEODORE PARKER.

TO THE SAME.

Boston, 10th Sept., 1858.

MY DEAR CARRIE,—Your lot is harder than I fancied, for I thought your occupation was a fixed fact, which would continue, and that Theodore's health was mending, and would finally be restored. It is, indeed, very sad to see a *boy* thus fade away. It is natural the old should die; it is against nature that the young pass off so premature. Still, I see no reason for the foolish melancholy you indulge in, and seem to cherish. I know not how much of it is constitutional, and so beyond your control; still, I fear much of it is wilful and within your own power; this latter you should check at once, and finally make way with and end. It cannot, perhaps, be done by a direct act of the will, but indirectly by the performance of daily duties. The common events of life afford the best opportunities for happiness and noble character. House-keeping, school-keeping, and the like, is the best thing for the majority of women—it is as good as grass for the cattle.

By-and-bye you will find a school somewhere—a common school will not be an unfit place for you to work in: I would seek the highest I was fit for, and put up with the best I could find. But, for the time, you must, no doubt, stay at home, and do what you can for your little brother. I trust you will find comfort and satisfaction, *but it must come out of your own soul.*

Remember me with kind sympathies to your father and mother, and Theodore, too.

Affectionately yours,

THEODORE PARKER.

TO THE SAME.

Brot Dessus, Canton de Neuchâtel, Suisse, August 14, 1859.

MY DEAR CARRIE,—I learned your brother's death at St. Croix, about a month after his release took place. I always felt a strong interest in him, both because he was the first child born at Brook Farm, and because he was the first ever named after me. But of late years I have been so overborne with all sorts of work, that I have had no time to visit him or his parents, whom I learned to honour and esteem long before he was born or Brook Farm thought of.

The fortitude he showed in his long and terribly painful illness is very extraordinary; still more remarkable is the intellectual activity and application he carried on in the winter. I am glad the poor fellow got his release at length, and in a manner so gentle and painless. The emancipated soul has passed on to another sphere of existence, of which we know not the details, nor cannot know till we enter there, I take it. But resting in the infinite perfection of God, we have nothing to fear, but every good thing to hope for and confide in. No misfortune happens to him who dies; he is but born again. He has taken one step more in the endless progress of the individual, to be joined ere long by his earthly dear ones, who with him will pursue the journey of immortal life. "From glory to glory" is a good word for this perpetual march of the human soul.

I know what consolation the religious heart of your father and mother finds in this, as in other sorrows; for great religious truths have fallen into that deep soil, and bear fruit after their kind. But I wish you would tell them of my tenderest sympathy for them.

I am glad you are busy with the work of the house and the dairy, that you can make good bread (I think it one of the fine arts), and also good butter. We lived (or stayed) ten weeks at St. Croix, and had never a morsel of tolerable bread. There are few American women who can make a decent article; many of them commit the (female) sin against the Holy Ghost continually, by transfiguring good meal into bad bread.

By famous, I meant *eminent,* which is in your power; not *renowned,* which is both undesirable and out of your control. I should rather be eminent for bread and butter, than famous for straddling about on platforms, and making a noise in public meetings, and getting into the newspapers, as many women do.

If you can find a school that you suit, and which suits you, I would take it; but if not, I would make the most of the duty which lies about me at home. By-and-bye you will have that opportunity to be *loved* which you wish for so much, and perhaps in the most attractive of all forms. But I should not lightly esteem the purely affectional love of father and mother for an only daughter, nor cherish romantic nonsense in my head. The river of life is not all foam; indeed, the froth is a very small part of it—one, too, which neither waters the meadows, nor turns the mill, nor adds much to the beauty of the stream.

Books will enliven the else dull hours of winter, and both strengthen and enrich your mind, if you choose them well. There must be a plenty of intelligent people in Concord of your own age to afford you the company you need. I see not why you should not be as happy at home as a young maiden need be. The prose of life is quite as indispensable as the poetry, and about twenty times greater in quantity. The apple-tree is in flower a *week,* in bearing some *twenty weeks,* and besides is still and silent long months, but active all the time.

Remember me kindly and tenderly to your father and mother, and also to your uncle and aunt, the Adams, at Boston, whom I both honour and esteem.

Yours faithfully,
THEODORE PARKER.

TO MR. AND MRS. CROOKER, TISKILNA, ILLINOIS.

Boston, October 26, 1857.

My dear Friends,—Your kind letter came to me last Friday. I thank you for remembering me when so far away, and often think of you, especially when I pass the house you once lived in at South Boston. I did not know that you intended to leave New Hampshire till your letter surprised me with the fact that you were already settled in a place I never heard of before. I am glad to learn that you have escaped the financial troubles which now disturb all the industry of New England. We had never such *hard times*, at least not for thirty or forty years: great factories stop their wheels, little industries cease, and thousands of men are out of employment. Where their bread is to come from I know not! But the nation has brought this trouble on itself by various causes, chiefly, I think, by relying on *bank bills*, which will not do for money in America, any better than potatoes will do for bread in Ireland; but we shall grow wiser by our suffering.

I know how much you must, both of you, miss the intellectual and religious advantages which you could find in New England, but am rejoiced to learn you find so many in Tiskilna, more than I expected. They will grow up about you, and your own demand for such things and effort to create them, will "help the cause along." Last October at Waukegan, Illinois, I found a congregation of "spiritualists" who had the same hymn-book we use at the Music Hall, and preached to them on Monday. Some time, perhaps, I shall drop down among you and find somebody to listen. Many thanks for the kind words you say about my services at Boston. It is exceedingly pleasant to me to find out that my words in sermon or in *prayer* waken so deep an echo in your hearts; I am particularly glad to hear of the *school*. The manuscript did *you* good to write, and so is not lost even if it never gladden other eyes. Believe me always,

Yours sincerely,

Theodore Parker.

Many thanks for the *flowers:* they will blossom anew with me for a long time. Let me hear from you again.

TO THE SAME.

Boston, June 7, 1858.

My dear Friends,—Many thanks for the kind letter from each of you. I attended the meeting of "Progressive Friends" (May 30–31), at Chester county, Penns., and when I came home I found the two welcome letters from you both. I know how many material difficulties attend the settlers in a new country. Money is worth twice as much there as here with us, and landsharks prey upon the people. In ruder days the strong oppressed the weak by *brute violence;* now the crafty do it by *brutal cunning.* But the present is an improvement on the old form, and a yet better time is coming. The nature of man shows clearly that he was made to find his perfect development only in the co-operative industry of a large community. One man is naturally a farmer, another a blacksmith, wheelwright, schoolmaster, captain, sailor, trader, tailor, &c., a poet, a botanist, a preacher.   Each one is helpless alone, but all united together become immensely strong.   You can't make a carriage wholly of wood, or wholly of iron, leather, or cloth; but if you put all these materials skilfully together, how light, strong, convenient, and handsome you can make it.   Now, what we want is, to frame the various human elements together into communities, so that each shall do just what he is fit for; then all will be helped by each— each, likewise, by all.   Mankind will come to it at length.   But, alas! we have suffered much from the violence of old time, and now suffer a great deal from the cunning of these times, and shall suffer in days to come.   But, as you and I learn by trial to use our individual powers, to walk on our feet, not also on our hands, so will mankind, one day, learn to organize men better.   The suffering by landsharks, who ask 60 per cent. and take 20 or 40, is like the pain little children feel when they fall in their early stumblings before they can walk erect and well.

I was pained to hear of Dr. Otis's death.   I don't believe it is natural for man to die at forty, but I doubt that doctor or wheelwright would wish to come back, even if he could.   Death is but a new birth—no baby would wish to go back, no man!   I am glad you liked the sermons, and put them to so good a use.   I will send you more by-and-bye, if published.   I thank you for the handsome flowers.   The yellow lady's-slipper grows in New England, but not common; the others I never found here at all.   I know how you miss the pine-trees of New England, the streams, the hills, and the rocks, but I hope you find some compensation in the fairer and more abundant flowers, and in the deep, rich, black soil, which yields such wheat and Indian corn.   In the Sunday prayers we always remember " the dear ones who are near us, though yet afar off," and the words bring back the special tender memories to each one of us.   With hearty regards—which Mrs. P. joins in—

Believe me, yours faithfully and truly,

THEODORE PARKER.

TO THE SAME.

Boston, Nov. 15, 1858.

MY GOOD FRIENDS,—Many thanks for your kind letters, which came some days ago.   I have been confined to my chamber for several weeks—most of the time to my bed.   Now I ride, or walk out a little in fine weather—of which November does not offer much.   I preached yesterday, and am better for it.

I am glad to find you are settled so comfortably; that the school thrives and you find delight in it.   I think I told you that I began to keep school when I was *seventeen*, and continued the business, more or less, till I was twenty-three.   I also loved the little ones the best— they were only objects of affection, and could properly be fondled, and kissed, and hugged.   But the large boys and girls, with good minds, were yet the most interesting.   I like the business now, and never was without a young girl or two, who could not pay for education, till I came to Boston. Indeed, I have had pupils for a whole year in Boston itself.

I think you must miss the green pines of New England. In the Western States I always feel the absence of rocks and evergreens, to which we get so tenderly attached at home. I shall prize the little bits of cypress you sent me, and keep them always.

I don't wonder you miss the Sunday services of New England. In such a state as Illinois, where all is new and rough,—the people more rude, with fewer opportunities for education or enlightenment, there must be a little home-sickness now and then. But it wears off; for there is an admirable power in man of accommodating himself to the circumstances that he must live with. I am glad you don't forget me, and hope I shall never do what will make me wish you could. I send you some little sermons, which I should have despatched before, had not illness, all summer long, turned off my mind from others to myself.

Believe me, always and truly, your friend,

THEODORE PARKER.

CHAPTER XIII.

TO MISS HEALEY.

West Roxbury, November 29, 1842.

Press of business has delayed my writing before, my dear sister, in
answer to your kind and most welcome note. I have been delivering
" Six Plain Sermons for the Times " in the Marlborough Chapel, Boston,
during the last successive Monday evenings ; and as each sermon occupied nearly two hours in the delivery, and only a part was preached,
you may suppose the preparation of the said sermons required time
and labour. To speak in the style of the Old Testament, they have
been a " work of sweat and watching."

Last night completed the course, so to-day I have had little to do
but hear a few scholars recite who come to me to be helped in their
studies, and to read Mr. Brownson's review of my poor book, which I
have not had leisure to study or look at till now. Now I have the
evening to answer letters of long date, and yours, my good Caroline, is
the first to be answered.

Don't think I shall ever be hurt by persecution or neglect. I think
I can stand in a *minority of one*, if need is, and feel no danger, except
from an access of pride. I have lived long enough to know that a
serious man is not to look to men for his reward. He that sows to the
flesh " shall of the flesh reap corruption."

However, I have had the sweetest sympathy expressed from some
very true and noble hearts, as you know very well. I am sorry for
your position in the midst of what you must needs despise, if you had
not a Christian heart still. I think it will be advantageous to you.
It will call you away from leaning on external things, and teach you to
rely still more on yourself and the invisible supporter of man. Ten
years hence, I doubt not, you will rejoice in a depth unfolded by these
very circumstances, now so disagreeable. Still more, you will help
even the bitter evils about you : a good word, I fancy, never falls idle
to the ground. You or I may not live to see it bear fruit, but others

will, and rejoice in it. It seems to me that you will yourself be a lesson and a beacon-light of blessings to those very persons whose touch would be pollution. The sound man goes among the sick to heal the sick. It is not agreeable, but useful. If you can't speak all you think, the wisdom which you do speak will supply, I hope, for what you keep in silence. The worst evil, next to separation from your friends, perhaps, I should think would be the presence of *Slavery*. Can you bear it? My soul has been moved with the deepest indignation at the very sight of it for a few days. But if you teach the universal benevolence, the absolute justice of Christianity, you will be an angel of mercy to the oppressed slave. Do write me your experience on this subject of slavery.

I told the affair of the descent of our nations from Adam to some friends the other day, who laughed heartily at the ignorance and bigotry of the good folks, though they thought it must be no laughing matter to you.

What do you do for society? Tell me about your friends, I mean your acquaintance: about "the church," and the "minister," and all that. I wish I could step in daily and cheer you when dejected, my dear girl; but as that cannot be, I hope when your heart is heavy you will remember that you have the sympathy of at least one heart who thinks of you when you know it not. The sympathy of men *whom I knew not*, has often cheered me when I was sad, though I rarely suffer for lack of the communion of kind hearts. I hope you will find better men than the wealthy planters, and will find goodness in men and women, as I know you must in the children.

Excuse my bad writing; I have endeavoured to make it a little more plain than before.

My wife is now at home, and sends her best wishes to you. I saw your mother last night at the "chapel"; she spoke of having favourable news from you lately. I will send you a sermon of mine on the death of Dr. Channing, if you will accept it. Believe that distance does not lessen my sympathy for you, though it forces me to express it on cold paper,

Yours most really,

T. P.

TO THE SAME, AT GEORGETOWN.

West Roxbury, April 4, 1843.

MY DEAR CAROLINE,—It is a very long time since I received your welcome and interesting letter, so long indeed that I fear you have forgotten me, or what is almost as bad—think that I have forgotten you; but I told you I was a bad correspondent at best; and all winter long I have been journeying and lecturing up and down the land in my capacity of heretic, so that I have scarce had time to write a decent letter to any one. But now I can hold in no longer and must write to you, if to none beside.

We used to hear much of the *gentilesse* of Virginia. I hope you will find some of it in fact as well as fiction. That horrible mildew of slavery!—I hope you do not learn to like it any better than at first.

No doubt God will bring good out of *this* evil as of all others, but that excuses no man for his sin. In time, and I hope in no distant future, we shall be crushed with it no more. Then how men will wonder that it was ever possible! how they will praise all who lifted up a word against it!

I suppose your friends tell you of all the talk and gossip of Boston; but have they spoken of two "Apostles of the Newness," Messrs. Lane and Wright, two transcendentalists of the first water, that Mr. Alcott brought with him? They came to set the world right, and heal its diseases, and supply its wants. One is at Lynn, expounding the doctrine of no property; the other (Mr. L.) with Alcott at Concord, helping that gentleman build worlds; all these are men of a singular elevation of character, not without a little greenness. Their heads swarm with new notions, from some of which good will come: at present they do nothing but abstain from eating flesh.

This winter the Bostonians have had their usual treat of lectures and concerts. Dr. W. at the Odeon was not so interesting as usual, they say. He seems in a strange position between the old and new, holding on to opinions which his philosophy long ago declared *could not be held on to.* Then Mr. Gliddon "confirmed all the stories in the Old Testament" (but does not believe a word of them in private), in his lectures on Egypt. Animal magnetism is fashionable just now, and Dr. B. astonishes everybody with neurology but the "philosophers," who wonder only at his effrontery and the "gullibility" of the public. The Millerites think the great quantity of snow in Boston and the comet together will burn the world up in April. The excellent clergy of Boston are about their old work in their old way, and make more noise in beating the bush than in catching the game; a most manifest hydrophobia of ideas possesses sundry members thereof. I know not what shall cure them except the end of the world. Mr. Brownson has made numerous overturns in the last year, exhibiting curious specimens of "ground and lofty tumbling"; where he stands now I know not, as I have not heard from him for eight days, when he defined his position in public. He seems tending towards the Catholic Church. God bless him, wherever he is! He has a hard head.

But I must close my random letter, with a hope that you will not let my long silence deprive me of a speedy answer. Tell me of all your pursuits, what sorrows you suffer, and what consolation you receive, and all that troubles or comforts you, and believe me, ever

Your friend and brother,

THEO. PARKER.

TO MR. AND MRS. JOSEPH H. BILLINGS, WEST ROXBURY.

Leipsic, 12th June, 1844.

MY DEAR FRIENDS,—It grieves me much to hear of your affliction—so sudden, so unexpected! I little thought the last time I was in your house that it would again so soon become the house of mourning.

But the ways of the All-wise Father you and I cannot scrutinize. We are only to submit; we feel they are right, we know they are good, and lead to a higher and nobler end than we had dared propose for ourselves. I have often thought that they who died in early childhood were to be envied more than lamented. "Of such is the kingdom of heaven," said the great Teacher. You could not wish to call the little one back. He has only gone, as the birds in autumn, to skies more genial and serener days. But the birds come back to our land, where the storm mingles with the serene weather, and must encounter the darkness and the cold. But the spirit that wings its way in innocence from the earth encounters its trials no more. It dwells for ever in the serenity that God appoints for such as die pure as they were born. You and I cannot know just what that untried state of being is into which we enter when we shake off the body. I would not wish to know what God has put out of my reach. But this we all feel, that the Infinite Father who loves each man He has made in his image, will so order the circumstances of the next world, that what is best for each one shall take place.

Do you know what is best for you? No, nor I for me; but the Father for us all. There is a great mystery in death. It will always be serious; but yet, after all the tears we pour upon the cold clay, there is yet a satisfaction in the death of the good—in that of a child. The pure has gone back to the pure: perhaps, at some future period, you will meet that child again; no longer a child, but grown in spirit to a stature of goodness and piety which we think is not possible for human beings in either world. I beg you, my friends, for your sake, for my sake, not merely to dry your tears—for time and the business of the world will gradually dry the eyes that weep—but to look to that everlasting source of consolation and strength; and then, though each bright link that binds you to the earth be broken asunder, you will yet live happy the life of the children of God, who lie low in the hand of the Father, and are always safe and always blest.

I don't know but all this will seem cold to you, while your hearts are yet fresh from suffering; but I could not help writing as I have done. I know your disappointment. I know your heaviness of heart. I need not tell you how much I sympathize with you in your sadness. I cannot avoid telling you of the comfort—the relief which comes also upon the sorrow-stricken heart. It will not be long before you cease to think of your little one as cold and laid in the earth, but you will think of him as a superior being—an angel of the other world.

When I have lost those dear to my heart, they have gradually come to take their place in my affections as beings no longer mortal, but purified above the power of death, and in many a dark and gloomy hour the thought of them has come back, a most welcome guest, to give me strength and peace—to banish the darkness and the gloom. Perhaps our most useful guides are those long deceased from the earth, whom we think of, not as men, but angels. When we think of them, we cannot bear to do a mean thing, lest it grieve them, while it cheats us. I know that worldly families are sometimes led to religion by the fact that they have a relative in the ministry, and they would not wish him to have the reproach of ungodly relatives, though they would have had no disdain of ungodliness themselves : I have seen cases often of this sort. But I have seen cases, too, when the recollection that he had a child in heaven has blessed the man more deeply than he thought for. With a child in heaven he felt ashamed of anything not heavenly ; and so the young lamb, which the shepherd took with gentle violence, and in his arms carried up the mountain to purer air and fresh pasture, gradually brought up all the rest of the flock, which the shepherd could not carry.

I beg you to remember me to your mother and sisters, and all the family. Tell good Mr. Keith that I rejoice as much at his last step as at all the news I have heard this many a day.

Give my regards to all, and believe me truly your friend,

THEO. PARKER.

TO REV. S. J. MAY.

Nov., 1846.

I think Jesus was a perfect man—perfect in morality and religion. A religious genius, as Homer a poetical genius. I can't say there never will be a *greater* man in morality and religion, though I can conceive of none now. Who knows what is possible for man ? If Jesus had lived now, I think he would have been greater; yes, if he had lived to be forty, fifty, sixty, or seventy years old—why not ? I think him human, not superhuman—the manliest of men. I think him inspired directly, but not miraculously ; not unnaturally, but naturally—inspired in proportion to his genius and his use thereof. I think God is immanent in man; yes, in *men*—most in the greatest, truest, best men. How much of the excellence of Jesus came from organization, I don't know. Artists are true to nature, it seems to me, and give him an organization exquisitely human—noble, intellectual, and heavenly. But I have seen no full embodiment of the Christ in art—none of *my* Christ, though enough of the Church's Christ. I doubt not, that as men follow the laws of nature, we shall have nobler forms, features, heads, and so nobler men. We have loved force hitherto, and bred *draught cattle* —men for war. May we not one day have a man with the philanthropic genius of a Socrates, the poetic of a Homer, the practical of a Napoleon, and the religious of a Christ ? Even Dr. P. knows not that *it cannot be !*

How did Jesus become so great? Who can tell ? Why do you turn to peace, to reform, to Christianity, and —— to eating and drinking, and —— to money-making ? What made Homer the poet, Bacon the philosopher ? Much is due to *birth ;* much to *breeding ;* how much to SELF ? Who made us to differ ? I doubt not many men go out of brothels, and jails, and from the gallows, with more merit than I have, and will take a higher place at last in heaven ; for they have better worn *their* birth and breeding than I mine. I think God alone has absolute freewill ; we only relative and partial—a conditional freedom—one foot booted, the other chained—that as we live truly, we get more freedom, and so on. I can't think there was a special opening of the heavens to Christ. Each man's measure of ability is special, and for him ; but the use

A A 2

thereof subject to general laws. Inspiration, I think, comes by universal laws. Just as we obey the laws of our being, *we get inspiration*, it seems to me ; a little being *less*, the larger being *more*. I look on Jesus as the *celestial blossoming of man*, the highest fact in our story.

It seems to me there is a progress of man's capabilities here on earth. I don't mean that man changes in his essence, but practically in his potency. We don't find Waldo Emersons among the Choctaws, but among the Yankees. Let the world have peace for 500 years, the aristocracy of blood will have gone, the aristocracy of gold has come and gone, that of talent will have also come and gone, and the aristocracy of goodness, which is the democracy of man, the government *of* all, *for* all, *by* all, will be the power that is. Then what may we not look for ? Hitherto our hero has been of force, his symbol the sword or the sceptre of command. It will not always be so. We are now developing the hand, and shall one day the head, and then the heart. All this is conformable to Christianity.

I think Jesus saw the great law of man's nature and taught absolute religion, *i.e.*, religion with no limitations ; free goodness, free piety, free thought, and free development of man's consciousness. By the reception of that are we to be " *saved*," and the world saved, and by that process alone.

What men and women shall we not raise up ? In prospect of that how little seem all the " sects," from the " Catholic " to the " Unitarian," and how melancholy all the swelling insolence of some hero of a coterie—a saint in long-clothes—a demi-god, who at best can fill a surplice ! But how encouraging is it to work ! Men tell me of the littleness of men—I see it, feel it ; of their folly, stupidity, sin—I feel that, and know it well enough. But I say, Well, we have had a Jesus, and see what comes of that Jesus ! I am full of hope ; I see each day more good in man than I knew of before, and trust *men* more than ever, and am less often deceived. God is in history, slowly getting incarnated.

TO ALBERT SANFORD, ESQ., BOSTON, MASS.

Newton Corner, Aug. 24, 1853.

DEAR SIR,—The article in the *Massachusetts Quarterly*, on Swedenborg, was written by Henry James, of New York. Emerson, in his " Representative Men," has given the best criticism which I have ever seen of Swedenborg. But that is not adequate to the purpose you refer to. Swedenborg has had the fate to be worshipped as a half-god, on the one side ; and on the other, to be despised and laughed at. It seems to me that he was a man of genius, of wide learning, of deep and genuine piety. But he had an abnormal, queer sort of mind, dreamy, dozy, clairvoyant, Andrew-Jackson-Davisy ; and besides, he loved opium and strong coffee, and wrote under the influence of those drugs. A wise man may get many nice bits out of him, and be the healthier for such eating ; but if he swallows Swedenborg whole, as the fashion is with his followers—why it lays hard in the stomach, and the man has a nightmare on him all his natural life, and

talks about "the Word," and "the Spirit;" "correspondences," "re-
ceivers." Yet the Swedenborgians have a calm and religious beauty in
their lives which is much to be admired.

I shall always be glad to see you and *hear* from you, and am yours
truly,

THEO. PARKER.

TO MISS E. PEABODY.

I am glad to be the receiver of your sorrows even, as well as the
hearer of your bright and kindling thoughts; though I suppose I can
only sympathize with them, not remove them. Still sympathy is not
always to be despised, nay, is of itself often a relief; so I pray you
send the letter, if you have it still. I lament that your visit to us was
so much abridged, in particular as I wanted your opinion on so many
matters, and had so much to say that was left unsaid, and to *hear* that
is yet unheard. But I trust this is but the beginning of your kindness to us, and that I shall have yet many of those "conversations that
make the soul." I am sorry for the disappointment you met with in
Boston, but hope you will be more successful some other time.

Miss Fuller's scheme will supply a defect in the system of education
most erroneously pursued, which gives no instruction in the art of conversation. It does something to instruct the mind, and fill it with ideas,
perhaps occasionally help it to make ideas; but certainly does little to
teach the art of correct and felicitous expression. How dull it is to
visit most of the ladies of the best circle even in Boston! Their conversation turns on subjects of no consequence, and they are discussed
in a spirit and manner fully equal to the subject. It seems to be
thought unworthy of a lady to do more, or understand more, than
"to suckle fools and chronicle small beer," or perhaps read a magazine
or novel that will never excite a thought. Now, Miss F. can do away
the foolish notion that this is the chief staple of conversation. She
will awaken minds to think, examine, doubt, and at last conclude, and
will set them an example of conversation, for she smites and kindles,
with all the force, irregularity and matchless beauty of lightning.
"Teaching should be inspiration," you say, with deep truth. Hers
certainly will be in this respect. But to leave Miss F., have you seen
Mr. Norton's address? Is it not weaker than you ever fancied?
What a cumbrous matter he makes a belief in Christianity to be! you
must believe it is authenticated by miracles, nor that only, but this is
the *only* mode in which it could be attested. I doubt that Jesus himself could be a Christian on these terms. No wonder Christianity
finds little favour with the learned—who, by the way, he says, alone are
able to "ascertain the true character of it, if it rests on the same
foundation with the Egyptian and older forms of religion." Did you
notice the remarkable mistranslations of the German passages, p. 40,
sqq.? They are such as no tyro could make, I should fancy. Mr.
N. professes a great knowledge of the German theology; if so, he
must have got it as Heine says Cousin obtained his acquaintance with
German philosophy, being ignorant of the language,—that is, by abso-

lute intuition. I have seen some that thought the book profound, not at all one-sided, just, and, to use the phrase, "just the thing." It will do one good work, will present the subject to the public mind, and now we may have a fair discussion. "Come," said the old Hebrew warrior to his foe, " come, let us look one another in the face !"

I feel, my dear Elizabeth, that I have made you a very inadequate return for your fine and comforting letter, but trust you will not be discouraged, but try us again, and perhaps we shall do better. L. sends her thanks and best love, to which Aunt Lucy adds hers ; mine you may be sure of always having. I hope in future you will not fear to "trouble" me with your sorrows, as you did before, but will write freely as you speak. I will send you books and other matters as you desire.

Yours in truth,
Theo. Parker.

TO DR. FRANCIS.

Boston, May 18, 1847.

My dear Friend,—Catch Dr. Francis a-nappin'—know something that he don't know! But it is not so. He only asks the question about the "Evangelium Æternum," as he would pretend to a little child that he (the Professor) can't spell *wall-nut*, just to encourage the little fellow, so I will be the little boy, and will tell Pa that I can spell such easy words as are found in "Mosheim"! Know, then, most erudite Professor, that you will find an account of this book in "Mosheim," Eccl. Hist., Book III., Pt. II., Ch. ii., Secs. 28, 33, and 34.

In the notes to Murdock's Version (note 2, pp. 6–9) you will find references to the literature. Fleury also gives an account of the book : H. E. Tom. XII., Liv. lxxxiii., sec. 54, and Liv. lxxxiv., sec. 35, *et al.* Some attribute it to John of Parma (*sed male*) ; Mosheim thinks it was falsely ascribed to Joachim (*sed pessime*) ; while Grätze (" Lehrbuch Allg. Literargeschichte aller bekannter Völker der Welt, von der ältesten bis auf die neueste Zeit. II. Band. 2 Abthlg. 1te Hälfte," p. 25) thinks it certain that nobody wrote the book but Joachim himself. However, the *Introductorius* has the wickedest part of the matter —sin lying before the door—and that was written by I don't know whom; but I suppose Engelhardt has settled this matter in his " Kirchengeschichtliche Abhandlungen," for he has a tract, " Der Abt Joachim und das Ewige Evangelium," in which you will find all about it—and everything else. Besides this, Fabricius has something about Joachim in his Bib. Med., &c., Lat., and that very *rare* author Gieseler (Ch. Hist. II., p. 301) has two notes about the book.

The "Everlasting Gospel" I never saw—perhaps no transatlantic eye ever rested on its pages ; but it was published in the year of grace 1554, without the author's name. Cave will tell you something ; and Schroeck, and then one Schmid, which is a proper common name in Germany, wrote a treatise about this terrible Gospel. All these things have been printed, but the "Eternal Gospel" got burnt up by the Pope, and so, as it went to the stake, I suppose it will never come to the press.

I hope you will come and see us to-morrow, though I doubt that you can be allowed a seat among scholars, when you are convicted of such ignorance! How did you get your degree of D.D. and not know all about the "Eternal Gospel"? Why. I thought they held an examination and made the candidates repeat all of the Bollandist Lives of the Saints before they gave them the title! What would Dr. G—— say of a *Doctor Divinitatis* who did not know all about the MSS. which the Popes burnt? I don't see the use of having Doctors of Divinity if they don't know everything which is of no use to the world.

Why don't you come and see me? I won't infect you with the plague of heresy, nor examine you in the "Bibliotheca Max. Vet. Pat.," nor in the "Vitæ Sanctorum," but will be always, and as ever, your old and faithful friend,

THEO. PARKER.

TO THE SAME.

12th March, 1852.

DEAR, GOOD DR. FRANCIS,—I have been down to the cold State of Maine or I should have answered your agreeable and instructive letter before. I thank you for the information about the dragon's yoke. Some of the old fellows thought that Miss Cynthia now and then slipped her little neck out of the yoke she commonly wore; in short, that she was not ἀεὶ παρθένος. Old Burrman, after his civil fashion, has collected the learning on this matter in a note upon Claudian, which, as old Dr. Homer used to say, is "very rich." Milton's dragon's yoke is quite modern mythology, I fancy. I like still to connect it with the quaint old palaces at Florence or Pisa, where I think he saw the picture.

* * * * * * *

Really, my good friend, it seems to me you ought to be happy. Think of me, hated, shunned, hooted at—not half a dozen ministers in the land but they abhor me, call me "infidel." I have no child, and the worst reputation of any minister in all America. Yet I think I am not ill-used, take it altogether. I am a happy man. None of these things disturb me. I have my own duty to do, and joys to delight in. Think of these poor German scholars in Boston—poor, companionless exiles, set down in vulgar, Tory Boston, shivering with cold, yet thanking God that it is not an Austrian dungeon. Why, you and I might have "glorified God in the grass-market" if we had lived 200 years ago, or 3000 miles east of New England. I have had quite as good a time in the world as I ever merited, and daily bless God for favours undeserved.

TO THE SAME.

Boston, Nov. 21, 1853.

DEAR DR. FRANCIS,—I thank you heartily for your Servetian contributions; some of them were quite unknown to me. I had a duplicate of Mosheim's "Ketzergeschichte," but I thought you owned it, or I should have sent it Francisward; as it was, the book went to a *young* minister. I fear it is rather rare. I saw lately two copies of Servetus' " Restitutio " advertised in the catalogues, and sent for them post-haste (ed. ·1790), but expect neither. Baur's books I had not heard of, but will order forthwith. What a learned thunderbolt of Hegelianism the brave man is! But how do they write *so many* books? Oh, *dura messorum ilia!* Buchat I do not know, but must borrow of your library. Do you know the Wertheimer Bible? What a fool I am!—of course you do. Good-bye.

T. P.

P.S. — Baur has a nice analysis of Servetus ("Dreieinigkeits-geschichte," B. III., p. 46), the best I have seen. Saisset is not so good as one might expect after all that has been written. Why can't you get some of your young men on their graduation day to write a paper on Servetus? At the Unitarian Convention at Worcester some man proposed that a monument be erected to S. One gentleman would give 100 dollars, others objected : " It would *offend* the ortho-dox!" I am afraid it will hurt the feelings of the Jews to have Paul commended.

TO THE SAME.

5th January, 1855.

All you say of S. T. Coleridge is abundantly true. He was a great collection of fragments of precious stone, and had such an influence as no Englishman has used for many a day. His followers will write his books.

" Schuchardt " I must borrow of you by-and-by. Cranach was a noble fellow. I have seen many letters of his in MS. in Germany—some charming correspondence between him and " Dr. Martin " ; for Luther, who wrote everything else, wrote letters also. How fine they are sometimes, though at others coarse as Dean Swift and B—— united! I have a new " Life of Lessing," by Danzel, about 1200 pp. 8vo. It looks rich.

That little book, " Meeting of Bayle and Spinoza," I never saw—only references to it; and I do not know who wrote it. On the " Satyre Menippe " you will find something in *Revue des Deux Mondes*, xxxii. p. 266 sq. 280 sq. It is a queer subject.

I have a little volume, " Literæ Pseudo-Senatûs Anglicani Cromwellii, Reliquorumque Perduellium nomine ac jussu Conscriptæ, a Joanne Miltono. Impressæ anno 1676 " (no place). The editor says he doubted, when the MSS. first came to hand, whether " *illas præbo potius aut flammis committerem.*" But he spares them on account of their style. " *Est enim forsam dignissimus qui ab omnibus legeretur Miltonus, nisi styli sui facundiam et puritatem turpissimis moribus inquinasset.*" Then follow the well-known Latin letters. I never saw the book before, but doubtless your eye had bored into it long ago.

Do you know Caspar Barthius? I have had his " Adversarium Commentariorum, Libri LX.," &c. (1624), this good while (mine was Sharon Turner's copy); and Saturday there came his " Juvenilia "

(1605), and "Amabilium" (1612), which seem of the Johannes Secundus school. There is a deal of learning in the "Adversaria."

I hope to see you one of these days, when you have no scholars to teach, and I nothing to do. When shall we have one of those *brood-days* which we have enjoyed so much at Spring Street, or at Watertown ?

TO THE SAME.

10th May, 1855.

I have just been reading " Lambruschini, Sul'Immacolato Concepimento de Maria (Roma, 1843, 1 vol. 8vo)," which came yesterday. It is funny to see such a piece of nonsense. You must read it to help your *exegesis.* In Gen. iii. 15, the *Mulier* is *Beata Virgo*, of course ; but Cantic. iv. 7 refers to her. *Macula non est in te* declares the Immaculate Conception. The Κεχαριτωμένη in Origen. VI. Hom. in Luc. means *formata in grazia* (*i. e.*, without original sin). Here is one interpretation from St. Epiphanius, Ps. LXXVII. in Vulgate (LXXVIII. in ours), v. 14 : " *Et deduxit eos in Nube diei ;*" the *Nubis levis* is *sancta Maria nullo semine humano prægravata!* In 1830, at Paris, it was revealed to an old maid, *ad una Semplice Virginella*, that Mary was conceived without original sin.

I wish you would read the last page of *Huntington's Religious (!) Magazine* for May, and see what an admirable " professor of the heart " you are to have in Cambridge. I think he might as well be made professor of the liver, or the gall, as of that tough muscle.

Did you ever read Sulp. Severus his Epistles ? I have just got Le Clerc's edition of " Sulpicius " (1709), and read in them for the first time. There is one to St. Paulinus (Bp., you know), to introduce a cook. It seems the saint's cooks had renounced his kitchen, because they would not provide such mean dinners as he required of them. I wonder if the Bishop of London's cook ever repudiated his service for that reason. And Sulp. sends him a *puerulum ex nostra officinâ*, who knows enough to bake beans, to pickle beets, and make gruel for the monks. He has one fault: he is a *flibustier*, and appropriates the contents of his neighbour's gardens, wood-piles, old houses, and fences. But as there are failings which " lean to virtue's side," he sends him *non servum sed pro servo filium.*

There is a letter to Sister Claudia on the Day of Judgment, and another on being an old maid, " De Virginitate," which he thinks the most glorious condition in the world, "*grande est et immortale . . . . . vivereque contra humani generis legem !*" How much such an old fellow has got to answer for, filling the world with old maids in the name of God ! The poor *devotæ* were worse off then than now ; they must wear no ornaments. One day, I hope, somebody will write the *true* history of what is called Christianity. What a story it will be !

I have got Wolff, " Lectionum Memorabilium Centenarii XVI." (2 Fol. 1600), one of the greatest books in the world—full of *cuts.* It is equal to the Know-nothings in hostility to the Catholics.

In Pater Balbinus, his account of the miracles of the Mother of God at Wart, in Silesia, he speaks of Copernicus as an author of no reputation or authority: " *Stare cœlum, et volvi terram credidit Coperni-cus, falsus sine dubio et nullius exempli auctor.*" The reason why the astute Jesuit thinks the earth does not move is exquisite—"*nam nihil ad motum pigrius centro !*"

TO THE SAME.

Dublin, N.H., 8th August, 1855.

DEAR DR. FRANCIS,—Here I am rusticating in one of the nicest little towns in New Hampshire or New England. Good Dr. Leonard has written his natural piety all over the town, and in all the people. How much a noble minister may do for mankind in such a town as this! There are 23 copies of the *New York Tribune*, and nearly as many of the *National Era*, taken here. No rum in the town, excellent schools, not 1100 inhabitants, and 1200 dollars devoted every year to schools. I often mention Lincoln, old Dr. Stearns's parish for so many years, to show what a minister may do. Concord is also a good example; but Dublin, I think, will bear the palm from all the rest. But why is it that such cases are so rare ? There is not a town in New England but would rejoice to have such a minister as Dr. L. Why is it that we don't *raise* that sort of minister ?

I got from a foreign catalogue a copy of a rare book ; *you* doubtless know it well, but *I* never saw it before, though I have been hunting for it some years : " Epigrammata Clarissimi Dissertissimique viri Thomæ Mori Brittani pleraque ex Græcis versa (Basileæ, apud Joannem Frobenium, Mense Martio, An. MDXVIII.)." I think it was reprinted in the collective edition of " Op. Mori," and again in 1635 ; but I never saw all of the poems before. One thing pleases me in his iambics, " Ad Candidum, qualis uxor deliquenda." You know what interest he took in the education of women. It appears in this little poem :—

" Sit illa vel modo
Instructa literis,
Vel talis ut modo
Sit apta literis.
Felix, quibus bene
Priscis ab optimis
Possit libellulis
Haurire dogmata.
Armata cum quibus
Nec illa prosperis
Superba turgeat,
Nec illa turbidis
Misella lugeat
Prostrata casibus.
Jucunda sic erit
Semper," &c.

Next time you are in the library, will you be good enough to ask Dr. Harris to lay aside for me the " Op. Mori," and all the " Lives of More ?" I will take them soon as I return. Of course you have read " Campanella, De Monarchia Hispanica." It was written about

1600. My copy is an Elzevir (Amst. 1653, 16mo) ; it is a nice book, wholly heartless, though he rebukes Macchiavelli for his want of principle. His view of the state of Europe is curious and instructive. He is the first author that I remember who recommends crossing the breed of nations. I ought to mention that the edition of " Mori Epig." was printed from a MS. which Erasmus gave to Beatus Rhenanus, who dedicates it to Bilibald Percheimer. It seems from the preface that Beatus had the gout while it was in the press. I have got Danzel's " Leben Lessing " (3 vols. 8vo !). Have you seen it ? It is dreadfully minute, and I do not like L. quite so well as before. But he was a great man : the book could be written nowhere but in Germany.

TO THE SAME.

Boston, December 16, 1855.

DEAR DR. FRANCIS,—I do not remember to have seen Hallam's works in your library, and it strikes me that they would fill up the place you were speaking of a few days ago. You were one of the lucky men who bought the "Retrospective Review," before it became so dear. I am destitute of it still, but will not pay the fancy price now demanded. Do you know Walter's " Life of Sir Thomas More " (Phil. 1839) ? It is curious, written from the American-Catholic point of view. I doubt that I shall get an edition of Thomas before the public—few would buy him; but I wish it might be done. He was one of the noblest that stood out against the progress of religion in England. How he loved good letters, and the education of women !

Yours, ever,

T. P.

TO THE SAME.

Boston, April 21, 1856.

DEAR, GOOD DR. FRANCIS,—Your last letter came on the 23rd February, and since then, I have not had a moment to write a letter, save unavoidable notes, and have not seen a streak of you even. In Leibnitz, I find reference to a set of men, whom I find nowhere else—nor ever hear from out of his pages. I had quite a list of those old fellows marked down once—the last time I read his chief things—to confer with you about. But some of the powers of darkness blew them off to *limbo* or some other purgatory.

I remember the Ἀποκατάστασις πάντων, but never knew who its author was. That *savant médecin de Hollande*, Dr Beverwyk, is a famous old fellow. He was born in 1594, at (the same place as the Synod of) Dort : but he ought to have been born at Beverwyk, a little Dutch town, which seems named on purpose for his birthplace. But he would not consent, and so made Dordrecht immortal. His book is *intitule* " Epistolica Quæstio de Vitæ Termino Fatali an Mobili " *Dordr.* 1634, 4to et sup. He discussed the question, as I understand it, whether the day of death is a fatal day, or whether the doctors can stave it off—or perhaps bring it on! He collected the "Opiniones Eruditorum," and his book made a deal of noise in Dort, and (I fear) some of the D.D.'s let fly at him. Three editions of his "Quæstio" got published at *Lug. Bat.*, only one at Dort. Perhaps the bookseller got scared, and did not dare reprint. He wrote also on *Women* ("De Excellentiâ Fœminei Sexûs." Dord. 1636, 12mo). But they say he did not write so much for the race of womankind, as for the *kind woman*, viz., *Anna Maria Schurman!* That last third of her sounds too Dutch—write it Annie Maria Sherman, and suppose he found her so sweet, and so pretty, and so tender, and so dear, that he fell down—his heart full of love to one growing beautiful to all—and wrote "De Excellentiâ Fœminei Sexûs;" and what a pretty piece of medical gallantry it is! Besides, he wrote in Dutch, "Schat de Geezondheyd," or, "The Treasure of Health," a book said to be translated into many tongues, and of great value.

I have a copy of "Tyndale's Exposition," which I have laid aside for you the next time I shall get out to Cambridge, whither I much wish to go. Do you know that we are to have Hedge back again in the midst of us—as of old? Let us renew the old meetings which were so pleasant from 1837 to 1842, and then broke down and vanished, only not "everlastingly."

Hoping to see you soon, believe me, ever yours,

T. P.

TO THE SAME.

Feb. 22, 1858.

It does me good always to see even your handwriting on the outside of a letter before I open it. How much instruction I have to thank you for, it is only *I* that know! When I lived at West Roxbury and you at Watertown, both of us had more leisure than we are likely to find again, and many and many a good time did I have with you. I have walked in the strength thereof for many a forty days since. So if I don't often see you, don't think I am likely to forget the help I once had from your learning—which none that I know equals—and from the liberal direction of your thought.

I don't remember any rationalistic explanations of the absurdities in the Indian Vedas. It would be contrary to the genius of the people. It seems to me that fancy predominated over all else with them. They revelled in the improbable; the grotesque took the place which the beautiful takes with us. The scientific-true, it seems to me, they cared little about. I seldom open their works without disgust. Their historians lacked both geography and chronology, "the two eyes of history"; and their philosophers were *grannies*, I think. Emerson has come upon them *late*, and both exaggerates their merits, and misleads himself by their *bizarréries*. Their conception of God in general was gross enough and unsatisfactory, but they had nothing which, for horror, came up to the Calvinistic God. No heathen, with his "light of nature," could come up to the *Rex tremendæ majestatis* of "Revelation." *Deus Damnator* should be his title : *deus damnator hominum infantumque.*

Grotefend's Θεῖος μέν ὁ Πλάτων, &c., I have seen before, but I can't think where. I have tried to remember while courting sleep, but the old passage does not come. Yet I incline to Cyril of Alexandria. I have hardly looked at him these twenty years, but have a dim remembrance of it in his book against Julian. Yet it may be in Chrysostom, whom it seems like—though he snubs Plato. You remember he says, "*Platonem quippe ejecit [Deus], non per alium sapientorem philosophum, sed per ignarum piscatorem : ita enim et major clades fuit et splendidior victoria.*" I quote the Latin translation, for I have no Greek Chrysostom. This is from his Fourth Homily on 1 Cor., near the beginning.

*　　*　　*　　*　　*　　*

That other passage, *delirant homines plectitur ipse Deus*, I don't remember ever to have seen before.* It is funny. What ideas men have of the *Deus !* No faculty of man has made such blunders in its development as the religious. No wonder : it is the greatest of all.

I have many questions to ask you, and shall get more satisfactory answers than I can give. I shall come and take tea with you before long, and we will talk over many things.

*　　*　　*　　*　　*　　*

TO REV. MR. SENKLER, CANADA.

Boston, 6th March, 1858.

My dear Friend,—What a sweet and beautiful letter you wrote me not long ago! I have waited for an opportunity to answer its loving words. It comes now. It is Saturday night. I have finished my sermon. I commonly write it at the beginning of the week and leave a page or two for Saturday night; then, when it is all done, and the last tear shed over it—for I seldom get through without moistening my ink a little in that way—I put all the signs of my week's toil aside, and gird up my soul for the other duties of Sunday, which are also great joys. How can I do it better than by thanking you for the letter you sent me? So kind, so tender—it need not be said so welcome. I read it with great emotion, with devout gratitude. I have just ended a sermon "Of the Soul's Normal Delight in the Infinite God," and wish I could read it to you before I preach it, or send it afterwards; but I can do neither, so only a letter will get forward.

First of all, let me thank you heartily for pointing out some errors in my books. In the Discourse of Religion, p. 65–66, I did take ἱστίη for ἱστία, the Ionic (though perhaps rare) plural of ἱστίον, and thought the sails were taken by metaphor for the ship. I was misled by the authority of a friend whom I once heard quote the familiar passage and translate it "ship." I think too that I have found the thing in some *scholion* where νηῦς was put for ἱστίη, but I can't recall the passage. I have no doubt you are right in making it mean "house" or "family." I shall alter the stereotype plate. The other blunder of putting Cithæron for Taÿgetus I corrected in the stereotyped edition. It furnished an Englishman with a paragraph to this effect :—" Mr. Parker is no classical scholar," &c. It was Cranmer and not Ridley (Ten Sermons, p. 233) and I have been burnt in an orthodox fire for making the slip, and that long after it was corrected in an *erratum.*

---

* Horace has "Delirant reges, plectuntur Achivi."

It is all right in the last edition, stereotyped. I made the best reparation I could to the Archbishop by preaching his funeral sermon on the 300th anniversary of his last trial on earth. The other error, p. 67, stands uncorrected in the new edition; how I made it I know not. But a few days ago, or a few nights, when I could not sleep, I was busy with some mathematical matters, and recalled the well-known formula of falling bodies, and then remembered that I had in a sermon *once* stated it wrong, and meant on the first leisure moment to find the passage and see if it was still left as at first. You are right in both the corrections in De Wette, Vol. I. The δεσπισθέντα for Θεσπισθέντα is so in three editions of De Wette. I have not Philo's " Vitæ Contemplat " to see if it be so there. In Vol. II., p. 32, fourth line from bottom, there is a greater mistake than you think it; the whole sentence should read, " the name of God in these cases is often a superfluous expletive, and no sign that God has ever interrupted the course of things." The reference should be to Eichhorn, § 422.

I thank you heartily for calling my attention to these things. The translation of De Wette cost me a deal of labor. I began it when a student of theology at Cambridge, 1836, and published it in 1843. Nobody knows how much toil it cost me. I lived in a little country village, and had a plenty of time, health, and vigor. It must contain many errors, and I am sometimes astonished that I did the work so well as it is. It cost me 2000 dollars to stereotype it; I have received about 775 dollars back again ! So adding my interest to my principal—and that to my outlay for books on that speciality—it makes a pretty little sum, not to speak of my toil. But if I were to live my life over again I would do the same. I meant it for a labor of love. It has had no recognition nor welcome in America—it served the purpose of no sect. But I must now bid you Good night.

It is Tuesday morning now (March 9th) and the newly-fallen snow lies six or eight inches deep all around—at least it looks so from my window. Let me write you a word or two more touching your letter, so full of kindness. I take great delight in the Greek Classics, which you are probably yet more familiar with—as your nice criticisms seem to show. I read Homer, in Pope, before I was eight, and the greater part of Plutarch's Lives at the same time. Latin and Greek I learned early, and for many years lived in the noble classic authors (of course the Bible was made familiar to me in my earliest youth). Of late years my political duties, contending against slavery, have kept me away from many favorite pursuits; but I still keep my love of the classics fresh, and all the best new literature relating to them finds its way to my table.

It gives me great pleasure to find some of my works meet with your approbation, and touch and soothe your feeling when so tenderly tried. Your *mourning* card, which I found at my house the day after you left it there, told me of some bereavement; weeks later a friend from Canada related the special form of the affliction. I wish I could have seen you. But I was ill *all* the spring *and* summer, and fled into the country to nurse myself up to vigorous health again. Last winter, 1856-7, I had two parishes, one at Watertown, where I preached in the afternoon, and lectured eighty times in thirteen northern States ! Just a year ago this week I broke down, and I am not quite well repaired yet. So I do little this winter. I send you by my friend Mr. Phillips a little parcel, containing a sermon "Of Old Age," which I think you never saw. It is the last copy I had. The little pamphlet on "False and True Theology" is only a newspaper report of a long sermon I preached —I have not read it, and don't know how well it is done. The newspaper printed it without asking me. But it seems to have provoked the wrath (or zeal) of some of my ecclesiastical brothers, who held a prayer-meeting last Saturday afternoon; about 40 *men* were present. Here is one of the prayers:—" O Lord, if this *man* is a *subject* of *grace, convert him,* and bring him into the kingdom of thy dear Son: but if he is beyond the reach of the saving influence of the Gospel, *remove* him out of the way, and let his influence *die with him,*" &c., &c. The prayer-meeting was called on purpose to labor with the Lord " for the conversion of that notorious infidel, Theodore Parker." So you see the tyranny of the old theology is about as strong in New England as in Old . . . . . (I was "the boy who sobbed himself to sleep" that is mentioned where you refer.)

I never saw the book of Varenus you speak of. I only know his work on Geography, as Dugdale has translated it. (London: 1724, 2 vols. 4to.) The extracts you so kindly made, are very significant, and wholly new to me. I have several books on Japan, but had only known this one by repute. How easy it would be to teach the Japanese and similar nations both natural piety and natural morality! How absurd to attempt to impose such unnatural and hideous theology upon the poor creatures who had nonsense enough of their own, before we sent them either Catholic or Protestant Jesuits! Mr. Browning, in his instructive book on Siam, says the people there think God can't be so wicked as to damn men for ever! I was glad to learn that our American missionaries made almost no converts to their *theology* (the Siamese had quite as much *religion* as the missionaries we sent them to save their souls). Did you ever read Mr. Halkett's " Historical Notes respecting the Indians of North America," &c. (London: 1825, 1 vol. 8vo)? He treats of the attempts to convert the savages of your and my neighbourhood; you can't read the story without tears. I am amazed that men think they serve God by such evil treatment of his creatures. Many of his anecdotes resemble those which you copied out from Varenus. I am now studying the Indians of this Continent, intending to write on their religion, &c., part of a larger work on the Development of Religion in Mankind. Have you seen a remarkable book by Mr. Buckle, " History of Civilization in England " (London: 1857)? I have hardly space to say how much I am

Your obliged and hearty friend,

THEODORE PARKER.

P.S.—Some ministers refused to ordain a young man because he did not believe in the eternal damnation of babies. The fact led to discussion and *clerical lying* in the newspapers. One of the sermons relates to the pleasing doctrine—Infant Damnation.

TO THE SAME.

Boston, May 6, 1858.

MY VERY DEAR SIR,—Your kind letter came quite welcome and instructive. The account of your training in Cambridge, [England]

makes many things clear to me in the character of educated Englishmen. I love the Greek and Roman classics, especially the first, and in early life read the most admired authors pretty liberally. I wish I could have had the careful training in the languages which you both had and conferred on others. But I learned them almost wholly alone—without help; and though I began Latin at nine, and Greek at ten, I think I never had in both so much help from a teacher as you would bestow on a boy in a quarter, perhaps in a month. Still, I learned to read and master them. Teaching these tongues forced me to a more careful study of them. They have always been a great delight to me, and I try to keep up in the recent literature relating to them, but of late years have fallen a little behind. I see Mr. Gladstone has got out a large work on "Homer and his Times" (3 vols. 8vo). What nice classic culture some of your men have! Had I been born in England or Germany, my predilections for literature and science would have made more difficulties for me to overcome than I have *yet* found in the rude culture of America. By the way, have you seen Rawlinson's translation of Herodotus, with huge annotations? There are to be 4 vols. large 8vo, very thick. He omits *indelicate* passages! I suppose he would in a translation of Hippocrates or Galen. The work seems to me highly valuable. But Baker's edition I have found of great service. The new reprint of it (1856, 1858), Vols. I. and II. (III. and IV. are to follow), contains the latest literature and discoveries. You ask, also, of Cudworth. We Americans printed 1500 copies in 1836 or 1837, and sold them all in five or six years! The American edition is difficult to find, and not worth buying now. The mistakes were not rare. Mr. Harrison has made an edition which leaves nothing to be desired. This is in 3 vols. 8vo, published in London, 1845. I think it costs 45s., but I got my copy in Boston for 4 dollars 50 cents. I think it may be had at Burnham's, in Boston, for that price now. Mr. C. published the original in one volume. It abounds with extracts from Greek and Latin authors; but he did not tell where the passages might be found in his author. Dr. Mosheim, that most laborious man of the most laborious nation, read through all the authors C. had quoted, and made reference to *every passage* in Cudworth's book. He translated the original into Latin; added notes, dissertations, prolegomena, indices, &c., and published it in 2 vols. 4to. Le Clerc introduced Cudworth to the Continent in his courtly and generous way; and then Mosheim taught him the manner and language of the learned, and he acquired a distinction in Germany, Holland and France which he did not have in England itself. The next English edition had Mosheim's references. When I was a youth at college, I wanted to get out an American edition of C., with all of his apparatus: a bookseller had it under favorable consideration, when lo! the other publishers announced theirs as in press. My scheme fell to the ground. But Harrison has done like a man what I fear I might have done like a boy. You ask about Strauss on the New Testament. I think you will admire his masterly scholarship. He handles his text with the acute learning and admirable tact you admire in the English classicists, but I think has *more soul* than they. Strauss's idea of God is quite unsatisfactory to me; so is his notion of a future state. He is a destructive critic, but quite fair, and exceedingly able. He has left theology for literature.

What you say of your ecclesiastical position in England is painfully interesting. We are bred very much so in the United States, in all our theological seminaries. The rawest professor is taken for "learned" by the rawer laymen who appoint him, and by the youth (not less raw) who sit and listen, and say "*Ipse dixit, qui contra dixerit anathema sit!*" I remember, with horror, that I used to sit, and see and hear the professor at Cambridge turn his mill for grinding the toughest or the mouldiest Hebrew or Hellenistic grain into homogeneous Unitarian meal, which we were to knead, leaven, bake, and distribute as the Bread of Life to all who came for food! He was very conscientious ; we also. He thought he was teaching ; we that we were learning. It was neither one nor the other. He milked the wether and we held a sieve, to use an old figure of Ramus. The first three months of trial showed me the folly of all this method ; and that, if I wished to find the bottom of the sea, I must sound with a plummet and a strong line, not with a cork and a hair. I took Eichhorn's "Introduction to the New Testament," and prayed (kneeling) that I might not "be led astray by one whom some called an infidel, while I sought after truth." I think most ministers begin honest ; but I fear few of them continue so in a long life. Surely they are not more so than lawyers, innkeepers, pedlers, and shoemakers.

I studied Butler once with much care. But his "Analogy" puzzled me with the same inconsistency you name ; yet he still means honestly. His stout affirmation of the rule of right in human nature itself was a great step at that time ; yet the admission vitiates the purpose of his "Analogy." If man, by the light of nature, can find out justice and all the rules of conduct necessary for the noblest life, it certainly is rather a low function which is left for Revelation, to come and teach us *circumcision, baptism,* &c.

But I have purposely abstained from writing on the main subject of your letter. Let us *talk* it over when we meet. But "*qui enim tam sim vanus ut eruditum erudire, ipse minime eruditus, præsumam?*" . . . You will find good accommodation at No. 34, Chauncey Street, with the Rev. David Read, formerly a Unitarian minister, now keeper of a genteel boarding-house. The best hotels are Revere House and Tremont House. Please let me know when you will come, and I will secure the rooms for you. With gratitude and esteem, yours,

THEO. PARKER.

I sent you a sermon, with the "prayers" of my brethren on its back. Rev. Mr. Burnham, one of the pray-ers last Sunday P.M., in his sermon, said, "Hell never vomited forth a more blasphemous monster than Theodore Parker, and it is only the mercies of Jesus Christ which now preserve him from eternal damnation."

The common additions of the LXX. have Theodotion's translation of Daniel, which, in III. 1, reads as you find and quote. But, in the true LXX., of which the Cod. Chisianus is the witness, the reading is as I say in pp. 510, but I have it not at hand. See Vol. I., pp. 148, 157 ; and II., p. 508. I have no copy of the genuine LXX. version of Daniel, but will look at it the first opportunity, and see if I represent it fairly.

That word *Rahab* occurs several times in the Hebrew text of the Bible, where neither the English version nor the LXX. show any direct trace of it. The word itself has given rise to no little discussion among the learned. Some think it an Ægyptian word imported into Hebrew. But I think nobody has yet found it in the Ægyptian monuments. There is a verb, *rau-hab*, which means to be fierce, to rage, to make fierce, &c. Then the noun adjective, *rau-haub*, means insolent or proud, perhaps fierce. The noun *ra-hab* is a little difficult to make out. Sometimes it means only violence, fierceness, &c., then it is the mythological name for Ægypt, then the name of a sea-monster, we don't know exactly what. It occurs in Isaiah xxx. where our translation reads "their *strength* is to sit still," where *ra-hab* is rendered "strength." The literal translation is "insolence—they sit still." I fancy it was a proverb—but as th⸍ writer was speaking of Egypt, which bore the same name mytʰᵘₒₗₒ lly (*ra-hab*), I take it he made a pun, which is now buried up, and nᵣ ⸍ₑₑₙ often. The LXX. don't try to preserve it, but read ματαία ἡ παράκλησις ὑμῶν αὕτη. The Vulgate misses the sense : *superbiæ tantum est, quiesce*. In Isaiah ii. 9, *Rahab* appears in the English version, which represents the Hebrew text reasonably well. But the Vulgate translated, *numquid non tu percussisti superbum, vulnerasti draconem?* while the LXX., like a naughty boy who has not got the difficult lesson, passes over it as Moses went through the Red Sea, dryshod, *siccissimis pedibus*, and skips it altogether. It is clear *Rahab* is Ægypt in this place, the *dragon* is only a synonym in the Hebrew parallelism. In Psalm lxxxvii. 4, we have *Rahab* again in English translation, where it clearly means Ægypt. But the LXX. give the word Ραάβ, and attempt no version. In lxxxix. 10, we have *Rahab* in the English, which seems to mean Ægypt. But the LXX. has Σὺ ἐταπείνωσας ὡς τραυματίον ὑπερήφανον. In Job, *Rahab* appears in ix. 13. Our translation calls it the *proud helpers*, the Vulgate renders it *qui portant orbem*, the LXX. has κήτη τὰ ὑπ' οὐρανόν. This variety of meanings shows how uncertain the tradition was which guided the authors of the Greek and the Latin version. Ewald, one of the profoundest Hebrew scholars in the world, says, on this passage, in which he renders *Rahab* "helpers," that as *Rahab* is the mythological name for a sea-monster even when it means Egypt, so this verse alludes to a legend, which relates that once in a great battle God conquered a monster, and for an example of punishment nailed him up as a constellation in the heavens, where it should always give light to the world, and tell how vain it was to resist God. If this be so, then the LXX. are not far out of the way with their κήτη ὑπ' οὐρανὸν, for (as he quotes Lach's dissertations on the Oriental names of the constellations to show) κῆτος, πρίστις, *Balena, Bellua,* and *Pistrix,* are al so constellations. I don't know how far this use of the word would justify the remark you refer to in the *Westminster Review*, for I fear we are not well-informed as to the date of these names. I have long been satisfied that Job was one of the most recent books of the Old Testament. Bating the spurious parts—Introduction, &c., it is wholly un-Hebrew. God is not called Jehovah in the genuine parts, I think, and there is nothing narrow or *Jewish* in it. The character of Job is one of the finest pictures of a "gentleman" in the whole compass of ancient literature: certainly few moderns come up to him.

How the harlot Rahab came by her name I do not know. By the way, she was not a very respectable character to put into the ancestry of Jesus, though she is so abundantly commended by biblical and other writers.

I think you will wish you had not touched on this unlucky subject. But I promise I will never worry you with the matter again; but I do not think she was *justified* by the general or *special* works she is related to have done.

TO THE SAME.

Boston, December 9, 1858.

MY DEAR, KIND FRIEND,—Your warm-hearted letter came a little while ago full of indications of a tender regard and esteem which touch me deeply. I think no man has more generous friends: I wish I deserved them. But I will try. I have not perhaps been so sick as the newspapers represented, and am now a good deal better. I *did* preach the 14th November, and on the text named. It was against the advice of all my friends, and the doctors also; but it did me good and not harm. I treated of Needless Sickness, of Premature Death, and their Causes. I meant it for myself as much as others. Since then I have preached twice, once on the Progress of the Anglo-Saxon People in 300 Years — it was close to the 300th anniversary of Elizabeth's coming to the throne—and once on the Elements of Progress in the American People, and the Duty they have to Do.

This is the short story of my health. I have been singularly able-bodied all my life, and free from sickness. But in February, 1857, after excessive labors, I was exposed in a terrible manner all night, and found myself with a pleuritic fever in the morning. I fought against it for a month, bustling as before. But in March, I was obliged to yield and give up all work. The case was not understood by the doctor, nor treated well. An effusion of water in the chest followed, which it took nearly eight months to subdue, though it did not much interfere with my work. In the meantime a *fistula in ano* developed itself, and last summer produced painful and alarming consequences. I lost twenty pounds of flesh—had a cough, night-sweats, &c. It looked like the conclusion of all things here below. I bought no books, and did not look over catalogues. But I had a surgical operation performed in the beginning of October last, and am now gradually recovering from all the evils which tormented me before. But I had a sad relapse a fortnight ago. I attended a funeral of a little boy drowned by accident, and in getting into the railroad cars, strained and wrenched both my leg—which is lame from the fistula—and the abdomen. This now keeps me from walking, and will trouble me for some weeks perhaps; but if an abscess does not follow, there is nothing serious in it all. I think I shall live to be seventy or eighty, but I shall be more moderate for the future. Pray excuse all this talk about myself. I was much grieved that your visit was so short last summer, and it only tantalized me to see you but a minute.

It was Miss Stevenson who saw your son. She is one of the noblest and most intellectual women I have ever known. She lives with me, and has for ten years.

I am glad you found Tindal. He was a great man, shooting so far before his age. Over one hundred replies were made to his book! I read many of them when a student at college, but they amounted to nothing. Abuse was lavished on him by men not worthy to unloose the latchet of his shoes. I thank you for calling my attention to it again. I have not read him for twenty years or more. Toland wrote "Christianity not Mysterious," which drew a storm about his ears, and made him flee his country (Ireland)!

I have Mosheim's Cudworth (2 vols. 4to.), and will gladly lend it to you. Did you ever read Daillé on the Right Use of the Fathers?—that is at your service too. "Middleton's Inquiry into the Miraculous Powers of the Early Christians," is another book of great note, once making an epoch in ecclesiastical doctrine. Both D. and M. are a little unfair now and then, but right in the main. Mr. Blount, of Oxford, I think, wrote against them both in 1856 or 1857, a great, thick, learned, but uncritical book on the Fathers, which would amuse you; it contains really some good things. . . . . There is a curious passage in Photius' Bibliotheca (No. 232, Hoeshel's edition,) in which he gives an extract from Hegesippus, the earliest Church historian. He was a Jewish-Christian, and hated Paul. He speaks of Paul's, 1 Cor. ii. 9, "Eye hath not seen," &c. Then says, Ἡγήσιππος μέντοι ἀρχαῖός τε ἀνὴρ καὶ ἀποστολικὸς, ... οὐκ οἶδα ὅτι καὶ παθὼν, μάτην μὲν εἰρῆσθαι ταῦτα λέγει, καὶ καταψεύδεσθαι τοὺς ταῦτα φαμένους "τῶν τε θείων γραφῶν καὶ τοῦ Κυρίου λέγοντος "μακάριοι οἱ ὀφθαλμοὶ ὑμῶν οἱ βλέποντες," &c. This shows what some of the early Christians thought of Paul! It would astonish the ministers a little, if they could understand what the apostles thought (and said) of one another. I hope sometime to have an opportunity to talk some matters over with you at length. I know you will be pleased with dear old Ralph Cudworth, with his wide comprehensive learning (though he had no *criticism*, and often was wrong in his exegesis, as all men then were), and with his deep fervent religiousness and genial freedom. His sermon before the House of Commons I used to think one of the best in the language. Certainly it would astonish the Commons now! I wonder who wrote the article on Newman in the *Westminster*. It seemed to me cold, but open and manly.

With kindest regards to you and yours, faithfully,

THEODORE PARKER.

TO THE SAME.

Roma, Jan. 22, 1860.

MY DEAR SIR,—I have long intended to write you, and shall perhaps find no fitter place than this to address a scholar from, and, it may be, no easier time to write in—for a consumptive man's days are too uncertain to count on. To a man who looks for the progress of mankind, Rome is one of the most hopeless places in the world, for it is the head-quarters of sloth and reaction; its religion is despotism; the subordination of man to an authority outside of his nature, and even alien to its noblest instincts and reflections; nobody knows how bad the principle of the Roman religion is, and how fatal to humanity are its logical measures, until he comes here and studies, and sees how it works the ruin of the people. But to a scholar who loves letters and a generous culture of the arts, and a philosopher who seeks to learn the great laws that control the welfare of the nation and the individual, perhaps there is not a more interesting spot on earth. The general aspect of all things is sad, the face of the people (thoughtless as they look) is more melancholy than I have elsewhere met with. All seems to respond to the popular chant,—

> "Roma! Roma! Roma!
> Roma non è più come era prima!"

I have four pretty, spacious, and comfortable rooms at No. 16, Via delle Quattro Fontane, on the Quirinal Hill, 140 or 150 feet above the river, which is about 20 feet more above the sea. I live 120 steps from the ground-floor, and yet I am not one of those poor poets that Juvenal speaks of—

> ———"Quem tegula sola tuatur
> Apluvia, molles ubi reddunt ova columbæ."

There is an English family 150 steps up, directly over my head, where he has the advantage enjoyed by that poet,—

> ———"Nam si gradibus trepidatur ab imis,
> *Ultimus ardebit!*"

But I have the sun all day from rise to set, and the whole city lies spread out before me, and the Ciminian Hills over on the Etruscan side of the Tiber, and I sleep secure in my lofty perch.

> "Vivendum est *et hic* ubi nulla incendia, nulli
> Nocte metus."

This part of the city used to belong to the 6th Regio, Alta Semita, and indeed it is the *highest* part of the town: the Pope's Palace of the Quirinal is close beside me, with its unprolific gardens, which look as celibate as the Pope himself has vowed to be. The Temple of Semosanctus (Dius Fidius) seems to have been in this neigbourhood. The Campus Sceleratus was not far off, where they buried the vestals who had more fealty to nature than respect for a conventional vow. The τις ἐντὸς τῆς πόλεως ὀφρὺς γεώδης παρατείνουσα πόῤῥω must have been the brow of this hill that I live on. Ἐνταῦθα κατασκευάζεται κατάγειος οἶκος οὐ μέγας ἔχων ἄνωθεν κατάβασιν, &c.; but pleasanter memories cluster about it. There was a temple to Salus, and I have come here to obtain the blessing if haply I may find it. The temple of Venus Erycina was near by. *Extra Portam Collinam*, Livy says, but within the present walls I fancy, not far from the Via della Porta Pia, the favourite walk of the priests, perhaps not unmindful of the old votaries of Venus, who did not wear cocked hats, and black stockings, and buckles in their shoes when they visited the same place. It seems readers of poetry lived here in old time, for Martial tells his book—

> "Vicini pete porticum Quirini:
> Turbam non habet otiosiorem
> Pompeius, vel Agenoris puella," &c.

That *vicini* I suppose refers to the fact that he lived not far off (on the Esquiline, as my landlord says). I have forgotten the passage that proves it, and have not the author at hand just now, and I never liked him much, the dirty fellow! But enough of this; I don't spend much time in identifying the old localities, which is indeed a most difficult and uncertain work so soon as you come to small details, and I think that a "live dog is better than a dead lion." It is curious to see how polytheism clings to this old heathen place. There is not a church in Rome dedicated to God, only one to Jesus of Nazareth, all the rest are consecrated to the Mother of God, the Virgin (conceived without original sin!), or to some of the saints, whose name is legion. The new Christian mythology drove out the heathen one, but the heathen is much the most interesting. The deities of the Roman heathen and the Roman Christian mythology, I take it, are alike mythological, representative of beings who are purely non-existent, or at least never had the qualities assigned them. Surely Jupiter is a more interesting character than the Deus Pater of the actual Roman mythology of to-day! Jupiter had vices of passion, and acted like the Evil One sometimes; but the Deus Pater is going to damn the greater part of mankind, and shows a disposition that would have made even the old Titan giants shrink with horror only to hear of. Besides, he does little, in these times nothing at all: he created the world, and intends one of these days to knock it all to pieces, but in the pictures he is represented as looking down on the *conception*, or the *birth*, or the *circumcision*, or the *crucifixion* of his only-begotten son, or as cockering him in heaven. So the Son, Deus Filius, is a most uninteresting person, adoring the Father, or blessing his Mother, or (in his human character) hanging his head, whining, and canting. The actual Jesus of Nazareth was none of your *dilettanti* men, but one who took hold of things with a man's grip. But the mythological Christ is a Miss-Nancyish sort of a nobody that I hate to meet, in marble, or mosaic, or oil colours. The Holy Ghost does but two things: he broods over the immaculately conceived Virgin at the conception, and over the only-begotten Son at his baptism; else he is commonly as idle as the crowd that Martial found round Pompey's house.

"Vel primæ dominus levis carinæ,"

to follow his verse. The Roman Christian mythology (and theology) discourages the vice of licentiousness, and so this is better than the heathen, but it encourages bigotry, hypocrisy, cant, and many another vice which the older Mother of Abominations kept clear from. Yet, on the whole, I don't deny that the banished gods of Old Rome were worse, in many particulars, than the new adventurers who have taken their place. But God send us the good time when Pope and Pagan, in fact, as in Bunyan's grand fabling, shall sit down in the same cage, and only make mouths at the pilgrims who pass by on the great highway of mankind! Oh, for a religion which suits the conscious needs of men, and a theology which explains the phenomena of the world, with a God that is adequate to the needs of science and of instinct too! In due time it will all come; but, How long, O Lord? we all say continually. If you could but see the *mere externals* of this city, you would feel like Paul at Athens, when he saw the whole city given to idolatry. He that comes to fulfil must also destroy; and there is no considerable

human development possible for Italy but by the destruction of the
Papacy. 1, The *temporal power*—the ability to cut men's throats and
scourge women's backs—must cease; and, 2, The *spiritual power*—the
ability to shut up the truths of nature and science from the eyes of
men, and to tie a millstone on the neck of the child, and drown him in
the depths of the Dead Sea of theology. To this complexion the
Pontifex *Christianus* must come, and then be whelmed in the same
stream which righteously drowned the Pontifex *Paganus*. Then what
a relief will this be for the more advanced Catholic nations! Even
Austria and Spain would warm with new life! And the Protestant
nations also would draw a longer breath, and begin to cast *their* idols to
the moles and the bats, and to worship the actual God of nature, instead of that hideous spectre which now *glowers* out of the Athanasian
and other creeds, intending to damn them and their babies not wet
by the fingers of a priest. I said just now that I lived near the Esquiline. On that hill of old time was a place for throwing down the dead
bodies of slaves and poor people—which I take it were neither burned
nor yet even buried; but, as Horace says (Epod. V. *ad fin.*),—

> " Post insepulta membra different lupi,
> Et Esquilinæ alites."

(See, too, 1 Sat. viii. 8–12). It was something better in Horace's own
time, for he says,—

> " *Nunc* licet Esquiliis habitare salubribus atque
> Aggere* in Aprico spatiari, *quo modo tristes*
> Albis informem spectabant ossibus agrum."

The old scholiasts on Horace (Cruquius and Acron) give the true
geographical explanation. Well, now, just out of the gate in this
neighbourhood is a modern *Campo Santo*, which has 500 pits. One of
them is opened every day, and the dead—the *poor* dead, I mean—are
pitched into the hole at the top, and tumbled to the bottom " without a grave, unknelled, *uncoffined*, and unknown!" Dead bodies are
carried to certain churches and left there; at night the dead-cart takes
them to this place, when they are thrown in *naked;* lime is next
thrown on them, and, at night, the pit is closed till the time comes to
open it anew. In the great Church of Santa Maria Maggiore, not far
off, are two tombs, which, with the chapels that are but their adjuncts,
must have cost three-quarters of a million dollars!—there is an epitome
of *Christian* Rome! You once wrote me about the account of Nebu-
chadnezzar's statue in the *Greek* Bible! Here is the passage, Daniel
iii., from the actual LXX., as contained in the Chigi MS., in the
Vatican:—Ἔτους ὀκτωκαιδεκάτου Ναβουχοδονόσορ βάσιλευς διοικῶν πόλεις καὶ
χώρας, καὶ πάντας τοὺς κατοικοῦντας ἐπὶ τῆς γῆς ἀπὸ Ἰνδικῆς ἕως Αἰθιοπίας,
ἐποίησεν εἰκόνα χρυσῆν τὸ ὕψος αὐτῆς πηχῶν ἑξ, καὶ ἔςησεν κ. τ. λ. You see
how much this differs from the *Hebrew* text, as represented by our version, and Theodotion's Greek. I believe I am really getting better
here at Rome, where the mercury has not fallen below 25°. I hope
this will find you in good health and spirits, and that you will believe
me   Yours faithfully,
                                        THEODORE PARKER.

---

* A part of the Agger of Tul. Hostilius is still extant.

TO DR. JOHN RONGE, LONDON.

Boston, May 19, 1854.

DEAR AND RESPECTED SIR,—It was with great pleasure that I received and read your letter of the 27th of April. I was in Europe at the time of your early demonstrations against the Holy Coat, at Treves, and since then have looked on your course with interest and admiration : but for the last two years have heard little of you except that you were at London. I am quite glad to learn that you are so successfully at work. England is a promising field to work in ; for freedom is indigenous in the British mind, notwithstanding a certain insularity which often limits her development. It is a glorious time to labor in ; there is so much activity of mind and body, and so much intelligence in the people.

I am glad to find that you do not follow the lead of Feuerbach or of his coadjutors. He does a service, but it is purely the destruction of the old, and then he roots up the wheat along with the tares. There are some Germans who accept him as their Coryphæus—atheistic men whose creed is—" There is no God, Feuerbach is his prophet ; a body but no soul ; a here but no hereafter ; a world and no God." They are much to be pitied—for the superstition of the Church, with despotism of the State, has forced their noble natures into this sad conclusion.

It is natural for the bud of new life to crowd off the old leaf, but not good to tear the leaves away before the time.

Here in America the work of liberalizing the minds of men goes on rapidly. Science destroys men's belief in miracles ; history shows the human origin of the Churches and of the Bible, and while the old rubbish gets removed, there is no firm ground-work on which to build up the great temple of true, natural human religion. In all the religious sects of America, there are earnest young men looking for better things—longing for truth and religion. The Germans will do something to correct our superstition. But alas ! most of the young Germans here are *Feuerbachianer* ; yet they are more *materialistich* in their theology than in their lives.

Here is a noble man whom you know well, Dr. J. G. Günther ; I think he first published your earliest communication respecting the Holy Coat. He speaks of you with enthusiasm. I shall always be glad to work with you on all the good things you contemplate, on both sides of the water ; and wish to make a long arm and take you by the hand with affectionate esteem. I look with eagerness for the books you speak of. The letter you speak of from your society to ours here in Boston will be warmly welcomed by us all.

It is now thirteen years this day since I first drew upon me the wrath of the Churches by a sermon " Of the Transient and Permanent in Christianity." It led nearly all of my personal friends among the clergy to abuse me. But there were noble and independent men who said, " No ; let us look at the matter with our own eyes, and see what we may see ! " It is to such men that we must both look for the advancement of the true and humane religion.—Faithfully yours.

TO REV. E. J. YOUNG.

Boston, May 4, 1854.

DEAR MR. YOUNG,—I thank you for your kind and welcome letter, which came last night. I reply immediately that you may get the letters of introduction in season. Do not dream that my estimation of a man depends at all upon coincidence of conclusions, theological or political. One thing I prize above all others, fidelity to a man's own sense of the true and just, the lovely and the holy ; then it is of small consequence to me whether the man be a Jew or a Christian, a Catholic or a Tübingen Rationalist. Of course I must love a rich, noble nature more than a poor and ignoble one ; but self-fidelity I put first of virtues. I trust you will study impartially, and decide after your best ability, not unduly influenced by the "Progressionists" or the "Reactionists."

I was sorry that I advised you to go to Berlin, when I looked round and inquired who was there to teach. I think you mention all the men worth much notice, for Twesten, I fear, is too *eng* (narrow) to help you much, and Hengstenberg is a man not likely to have a good influence, intellectually more than morally. I thought Tübingen would be a little too strong meat for a Yankee, though there is the ablest theological faculty in Europe. I look with amazement at the learning and *Fleiss* (industry) of Dr. Baur. I was glad to see what Guerike said in his last book. I will look for Rudelbach's account, which I have never seen. I saw no men in Germany who gave such decided indications of intellectual power, as Baur and Ewald. Ewald was then at Tübingen—the quarrelsome fellow ! I hope you will tell me a good deal about him when you return.

Your father's death took me as much by surprise as it did you. I had a letter from him but a couple of weeks before his decease ; he was ill, but no one thought him dangerously ill. I used to attend your father's meeting ; had once a class in his Sunday-school ; he married me. I had been in his meeting-house but once after the wedding. There was much in your father that I always honored and esteemed. He had no nonsense about him ; was " a scholar, a ripe and a good one," with wide scholarly sympathies, and I cannot bear to think that he is dead. I miss him at the book-stores, at the Athenæum. But the immortal man has gone to his better world !

I am glad to see how you feel about America ; our conduct is more infamous than that of Russia. You will soon hear that we have seized Cuba, I think. There will be work enough for you to do when you return, whether you come back *réactionnaire* or the opposite. Only be faithful to yourself—then you are faithful to your God.

TO H. C. BOSTON.

West Newton, 31st Aug., 1852.

The Law has these disadvantages :—1. That it exercises and develops the intellectual to the detriment of the other and higher faculties ; 2. That it does not allow a very complete and generous development of the intellect itself, especially of the higher departments thereof,—say the reason and imagination,—but only of the understanding. Most of the lawyers that I have known are examples of this defective and vicious development. Indeed, most of the lawyers that I know make a mere money getting trade of their profession, and no science at all; so that with them law is not a *liberal* pursuit, only a head-craft, and they are only *Mechanics at Law*, with little more elevation, and sometimes less than is law to a handicraft.

* * * * * * * The same onesidedness which keeps lawyers from the study of·the permanent-abstract of metaphysics deters them from the permanent-concrete of natural science. So they look on the arbitrary statutes of man, which are only a temporary accident of development, as if they were absolute and fixed, as much as the permanent-abstract or the permanent-concrete mentioned above. A statute is a temporary rule of conduct devised to suit the passing emergency. The metaphysician and the naturalist deal with natural laws, which are the constant modes of operation of the forces of the universe; the lawyer deals with those statutes which are the variables of man, while the philosopher deals with these laws which are the constants of God. But the misfortune of the lawyer is that he looks on his human variables as if they were as permanent and as absolutely imperative as the divine constant, the laws of matter or of mind. Hence he loses his natural conscience and gets a fictitious and artificial conscience; loses the conscience of Nature and gets the conscience of Doctors' Commons or of the Old Bailey or of the Supreme Court. The study of science helps to correct this. Yet I fear few lawyers care much for science. Judge Parsons was a man of large scientific attainments. John Pickering also—a quite uncommon man in many respects—was familiar with the highest results of science. Both of these were better lawyers, as well as more complete men, for this scientific development. I know a young lawyer who had to manage a case of damages for injury done to cows by water artificially contaminated, who in preparing for the case set himself to study the entire physiology of the cow, and so understand the effect of poisons upon her. That was the true way for a scientific lawyer to go to work; the rule applies everywhere.

I would not waste my time on mean authors. I would study the masters of poetry before I played with their apprentices, and still more before I played with the lackeys of the apprentices. You see uneducated persons waste a whole evening in silly talk about silly men or women. It is yet worse for an "educated man" to waste his time on silly books; they are always bad company. The books of great men will be good companions.

You need not fear that you shall suffer as a lawyer for what you gain as a man. Reputation for strict veracity, integrity, and honesty would be most eminently valuable to you as a lawyer. It would give you the best kind of business of the best men. I am glad you are to study with Mr. Charles G. Loring,—for I take it his moral character is loftier than that of any lawyer, of his age, in Boston. His personal influence will be good and greatly good. I need not say to you that I think there is no real nobleness of manly character without manly religion—the love of God and the love of man.

TO REV. JOSEPH H. ALLEN.

Boston, Oct. 29, 1849.

MY DEAR ALLEN,—Your very kind and welcome letter came to me some days ago, and I have had no time till this minute to reply to it. You may judge of my business when I tell you that during the first five days after I came in town, fifty persons came to see me : then I have other things to do besides the entertaining of visitors. But it is very kind in you to write me nice letters, and long ones, too, when I am so rare a correspondent, though I would gladly be a frequent one. I liked your book on orthodoxy much. It has a good deal of originality in it. I wrote a little paper on it which you crowded out : I do not like to write on the books of one I hold so dear as yourself, because I always fear that private friendliness may mar my critical justice, or else my justice would seem unkind. I saw S. J. May a little while ago, and he delighted in your book. I asked him to write and tell you what he thought of it, and, still more, to write a little notice of it for the *Quarterly*, which he promised. I saw nothing inaccurate in the book, and admired very much the catholic spirit in which it was written. I understand the course you propose—your lectures, I mean. It seems to me a good one. You omit one man in the early age, the greatest name in the Church for many a day; I mean old brass-bowelled Origen. He comprehended the liberality of Christianity better than any one for a long time. You cannot fail to make the lectures interesting and valuable, it seems to me; but they will demand a deal of work. The practical affairs you speak of must take up much of the attention of a minister, for a part of his function is to concretize religion, and *make* the "kingdom come" which he prays for. Getting employment for the needy is a great charity, one of the best at the present time.

There is another that you do not mention—public education : can't you do a little for that also ? Much depends on the minister, and in a few years he can do a great deal, with a good will for the work and some practical good sense. I take it, sentimentalism is the degeneracy of religion. Thought and feeling, idea and sentiment, seem to be the male and female elements in religion, both of them needful to beget actions. What comes of mere thought or mere feeling is poor, and does not grow up or perpetuate itself. I long to see a more real union of various minds in religion. We live now in a state of heathenish isolation, and lose half our strength from want of concert. I see not why there might not be an association of theologians for the advancement of theological science, as well as one of "geologists and other naturalists" for the advancement of natural science. They would quarrel a little at first, as the Neptunists and the Vulcanists were wont to do, but soon the quarrelling would end, and Neptunists and Vulcanists would both by-and-bye cease to exist. They need not call one another Christians if they did not like, only theologians. At present the Unitarians, we think, are the most liberal sect in New England, or, the least illiberal; but they do not contain all the liberality in the land, or exclude all the illiberality. Dr. —— is more illiberal than Dr. Taylor, of New Haven. I do not attend their conventions, nor would it be desirable in me to do so, even if inclined. They often take pains to have me away from their assemblies, and certainly I would not intrude upon them; and, indeed, I do not like to appear to make them responsible for doctrines of mine which they do not share.

Good will come out of this all. Men are getting to trust reason more, conscience more, affections more, and the natural religious element more. Of course, they rely less on authority, less on the Bible; upon the Churches less, and less on the ministry; but more on man and on God. Reverence for the letter declines, for the spirit thrives and grows strong. I shall always be glad to hear from you, and will be a better correspondent for the future.

I am, yours sincerely,

THEO. PARKER.

TO THE SAME.

Boston, January 29, 1851.

DEAR ALLEN,—I thank you for your kindness in remembering me in your new position. I am so bad a correspondent that I am not at all surprised if my friends forget me, though I do not forget when I do not reply. I have heard good things of you through Mr. Appleton, whom I saw not long ago, and hope you will find a more congenial field to labor in than at Washington, though you must miss many things which you had there. The library of 8000 vols. must come up to you as the "leeks which we did eat in Egypt freely," to the migrators out of that land of "cucumbers," &c.

I should be glad to be rid of the sight of slavery, though the imagination would still haunt me. I know well how much is a mere matter of *latitude;* it is so in all things. How many of the good folks of Boston would have become Protestants if born at Rome, or Christians if born at Constantinople? Why, it is not a great stretch of fancy to conceive of —— born at Constantinople and a Turk, with all the accompaniments of charity, hospitality, and fatalism. So of us all; I feel great sympathy with slave-holders; still, my abhorrence of the thing is not in the least diminished by the remembrance that I have relations of my own name, in the city of Charleston too, that are slave-holders. I hate the thing, while I love the men.

I am glad you ask me if I ever said that my present opinions or convictions *did not give me support in sorrow.* The great points on which I differ from most Christians is this. I believe in the infinite God, who is perfectly powerful, perfectly wise, perfectly just, perfectly loving, and perfectly holy. Of course He must have a *purpose* in creation, a *plan of creation,* both perfect and consistent with his infinite wisdom, justice, love, and holiness. This plan must be adapted to secure the ultimate welfare of each creature He has made, must be perfect in detail as well as in the sum. How, then, can I fail to find comfort in every sorrow, even in the worst of sorrows, consciousness of sin? I cannot: I have unspeakably more delight in religion, more consolation in any private grief, personal or domestic, more satisfaction in looking on the present or for the future than ever before, when I trembled at an imperfect God. I never said, never thought, never felt the sentiment imputed to me; quite the contrary.

Now, a word about the philosophical books. I think Ritter is a dull old plodder. I have his books, all of them, one on the "Erkentniss Gottes," not much known in America, nor much worth knowing. Still, let us eat his meat with thankfulness of heart; who else would give us an analysis of Albertus Magnus, of heaps of schoolmen, and write for us *ten volumes* of "Geschichte der Philosophie." I felt the want you complain of, and know not how to make up for it: the best way, perhaps, is to read "Colebrooke" or "Windischman," and "Schlegel on the Indian Philosophy." But you don't get much that is satisfactory. We are a little too early to learn the Hindoo philosophy. Ten years hence it will be easier. Bernouf is at work on something (Hist. Buddhism), that will help a good deal.

But Greece, after all, is the country where spiritual individuality got on its legs for the first time, and though Socrates believed *Helios* was a God, and not a "mass of iron red-hot," yet his contemporaries did common service for us in daring to think: Pythagoras, Anaxagoras, Hippocrates, even Theodorus, did us great service. I am glad you are studying this matter thoroughly, taking notes. The study of the Greek philosophers was a great help to me when in the Theological School; but I was too much of a blunderer to do the work well at that time, and the road was not so well turnpiked as it is now. I honor your spirit, and love your brave, good heart. If I can ever help you by lending a book, you know it will give me pleasure. Why not read Grote's Vol. I. and VIII. in connection with Ritter? Both are of much value in this matter. I shall read your article on "Comte" with pleasure. I could not give you any hints about him, only can say that he is able, dull, materialistic, and ill-natured, and has made a book of sterling merit. But what a pity he can't get out of his more material phrenology!

Remember me kindly to any friends I may have in Bangor.

Yours truly,
T. P.

TO THE SAME.

Boston, May 5, 1851.

DEAR ALLEN,—I have not time to write you a long letter, but will say that I am satisfied from your letter, that I was misinformed about you and your doings and sayings at Bangor. I never named my suspicions to anyone; but all I ask of a man is to be true to his own conscience, and take all pains to develope that conscience. He is to be faithful to *himself,* not to *another man's* self. Still, I admit the possibility of a man's being false to himself, of his violating his own conscience; and I think this is a common occurrence—a very common one with ministers, and, I fear, more common with Unitarian ministers than others. For, as a general thing, the Unitarian ministers have ideas in advance of the Orthodox ministers, while they have, generally, congregations more mammonish, hunkerish, and worldly, than the Orthodox congregations.

Then, I think the ministers take counsel, not of God, but of the congregation, and turn out such men as —— and ——, *et id genus omne.* Now, these men may be faithful to their conscience: it is not for me to say they are not. I never said that of any man.

I have been told that I stabbed everything I ever touched. Once I "stabbed" religion, then Christianity, then Unitarianism, then education, temperance, peace, prison discipline.

Still they all live after their "deadly wound."

Yours truly,   T. P.

TO THE SAME.

Brookline, Aug. 1, 1851.

MY DEAR ALLEN,—I read your paper before I read your letter. It is a grand paper, the best thing you have done as yet. I see in the critical part of it the influence of Comte and Gfrörer, two able helps. I have no criticism to make on that part,—the two first books of your discourse,—only to say that I think there is no man in the Unitarian denomination who would not be honored by writing it. The third part seemed to me not quite equal to the preceding, not conceived with so much vigor, nor expressed with so much scientific sharpness. I don't think it goes quite down to the deeps of the matter. The short of the matter, I think, is this: the old theology, all previous theology, has been bottomed on the idea of an imperfect God, not always imperfect in power, but in wisdom, in justice, in love, or in holiness—commonly in all four. There is a Devil as the Fourth Person of the Godhead in the common theology. In some schemes he is the *First* Person. Hence, there is a personal Devil who is a creation of God. Of course, God must have created the Devil out of his (God's) own substance, so there must have been a devilish element in God at the beginning. Others say there is no personal Devil, but yet must admit the *devilish in God;* for they believe there is absolute evil in the world. Hence, they have a hell, not as a *hospital* built by the Divine as house of care, but as a rack chamber, or torture cellar, built by the devilish as a place of torment and vengeance. Now, I take it that philosophy (physics and metaphysics) is at war with the Devil-god, but not also with the God-god. Philosophy believes in no Devil, neither in God nor out of Him. Hugh Miller finds "footprints of the Devil in the old red sandstone;" they will turn out very different tracks. The time has come for affirming the infinity of God by his attributes as well as by his essence. Men have said God is infinite in nature (*Seyn*), but denied it when they came to treat of his *function* and *modes of being* (*Daseyn*). The future theology must rest on the idea that God is perfect in power, wisdom, justice, love, and holiness (self-fidelity), then it may be a scientific theology. Sometimes the expression in your writing is vague, and so the thought difficult to grasp. A German writer would not make this objection to you, for he loves the vague clouds he breathes from his own tobacco-pipe. Perhaps Comte is not likely to have a good influence on your style. With these exceptions I like your paper very much, and wish the *Massachusetts Quarterly* were alive to publish it to the world.

I like your scheme of Hebrew lectures. The patriarchs, I think we know very little about. I don't know whether you consider them historical or mythical. I have only one book which you need, that is

Ewald's " Geschichte des Volkes Israel," 4 vols. 8vo. If you like that, it is at your service. Knobel would help you on the Prophets. I have most of the books Mackay refers to in his " Progress of the Intellect." The misinformation was that you preached " an old Hunker sermon denying the higher law."

Truly yours,

THEO. PARKER.

TO ROBERT WHITE, NEW YORK.

Boston, Feb. 11, 1848.

DEAR FRIEND,—Your letter of the 25th ult. came to me a few days ago, accompanied by J. Dunlary's manifesto. I feel glad that you can approve something which I have written about religion, and also I rejoice to hear of another man who loves the freedom of the truth. I think I understand the doctrines of the Shakers. I am not wholly ignorant of the books they have issued, which set forth their history and their opinions. I have always admired the order, the neatness, the economy, the plenty, and the peace which are so noticeable in their establishments. I rejoice to confess that they have solved the problem of association, at least so far as to show that men can live harmoniously in a community, and thereby make a great saving of time, labor, and all the material things which help to make up the comforts of life. But you will excuse me for my frankness when I say that I think they have made a capital mistake in attempting to nullify the distinction of sex : that is not a distinction of man's making, but of man's finding as God made it. From that distinction there comes the union of one man and one woman, united by the most sacred and most beautiful and endearing ties. Each is a complement to the other. Out of their union grows up the family—each new-born child to them a new Messiah, a new revelation from God. I admire the wondrous ways of God. I reverence his wisdom, I love his love, as I find this everywhere. But I see nowhere more lovely instances thereof than in the very distinction of sex, and the effects which grow out of that cause ; yet I think I see the causes which led the founders of the Shakers to renounce all this. I know, too, the history of similar parties in other days, and the doctrine which led them also to renounce marriage.

One thing more let me mention, and that is, the neglect of education in the establishments of your friends. You are a man of cultivation : it is evident the men who transact the business of the societies, and come in contact with the world likewise get some culture. But I have looked with great pain on the countenances of the young men and women that I have seen in Shaker settlements ; they look so ignorant, so undeveloped, so clownish, and sometimes stupid and almost animal. Excuse me, my friend, for mentioning these things ; think not that I do not honor the much of good that is in your friends, because I point out what seem to me the evils. God gave us many faculties, all good in their place ; certainly all good when acting in harmony, and each in its proportion. The problem of life is to tune all these strings to harmony.

Now I think the Shakers found one or two strings a little difficult to tune, and so they broke them off; then they tuned the rest quite well. Still the cords broken off were wanted. So the Shaker music is not yet *the whole human hymn.* Excuse me for writing this long letter, and believe me, truly your friend,   THEO. PARKER.

TO THE SAME.

West Roxbury, July 31, 1848.

DEAR FRIEND,—I received the other day a copy of the *Knickerbocker,* which reminded me that I have long been remiss in not replying to your kind letter, received a great while ago. They who are good at excuses are commonly good at nothing else, so I will not try and excuse my silence,—only will break it now, and thank you for that letter as well as other favors, and also for the magazine, and the interesting notice of a visit to New Lebanon. What you said in your last note about the superiority of the domestic economy of the Shakers, I am not only ready but happy to admit. Certainly, you have no menial service—none of your community think work is degrading; while, in society at large, many men are ashamed of work, and, of course, ashamed of men (and women) who work, and make them ashamed of themselves. Now, the Shakers have completely done away with that evil, as it seems to me; that is one of their great merits, and it is a very great one. At the same time, they secure comfort, and even wealth; the only charge that I can bring against them is that of the neglect of marriage. In an argument you would very likely say a great many things against marriage, and all connection between the sexes; but still, the fact remains that God created men and women, and left the perpetuation of the race to the union of the two, doubtless intending that marriage—of one man with one woman—should continue so long as the race should endure.

It seems to me, also, that some of the best qualities of human nature are developed by the connection. I look on it as much a spiritual as a carnal want. It seems to me that the omission of this is the great defect of the Shakers. If they could still preserve the family tie and then have all the other good things, they would have all that the Associationists are contending for. I feel grateful to the Shakers for all they have done, and to you for bringing me better acquainted with them and their opinions. So, believe me, truly, your friend,
                              THEO. PARKER.

TO THE SAME.

West Roxbury, Aug. 11, 1848.

DEAR FRIEND,—Your kind letter came to me a day or two ago with the communication in the newspaper. I will forward that to the author of the article in the *Quarterly.* I will presently write you about the matter which you refer to—that is, as soon as the hot weather is over, and I have written two pieces which are now on my hands, but only laid away till the Dog-days are past. I have not done it before for this reason, I dislike controversy. You may think it strange that I, who have been mixed up in so much of it, should have no natural appetite therefor, but I have not even an *acquired* taste for it: I always fear that I shall not do my opponent justice. I like to make my statement, to have him make his, and then let the two stand for what they are worth. One thing I am sure of in *this* matter, viz. the entire fairness, candour, and love, of the person who will confront me. If I can be as fair as I know you will be, I shall be glad. I will write it all out as plain as I can. But I suppose the end will be that each of us will be thoroughly confirmed in his own opinions. Differences of temperament, education, &c., make a deal of difference in the conclusions men arrive at. I shall not be able to attend to this, I fear, before October; but then I will do so, only I shall write with no thought of publication. I think it takes all mankind to represent all of the truth that is known as yet, and each particular sect, or party, or class, has some function thereof which no other possesses. I aim to find out all the new truth I can, not yet known by anybody, then to take all I can get from each sect, party, or class of men, and put all together, the new and the old, and set it before men. If men do not then accept it, I proceed to point out the particular truth of each party, and also its particular error; and when that is done, I do not suppose that I am free from errors, nor do I expect that all will come over to my way of thinking. I shall be very glad to write the papers I speak of to you, knowing very well that it can only increase my esteem for you.

So good bye.

Truly your friend,

THEO. PARKER.

TO THE SAME.

Boston, Oct. 7, 1849.

MY DEAR FRIEND,—If I did not know that you are a true man, I should suppose you would think me a very false one for not writing to you on the subject I long ago promised to write on, and which you have been kind enough often to remind me of. But when I am well, I am a busy man, and when ill, a silent one. Now I have a little time at command, and thus proceed to write.

I find that Mr. Dunlary admits that marriage, or the sexual union of men and women, belongs to the order of nature; but if I understand him, he thinks this order of nature has been superseded by a new dispensation, and of course, all the accidents of the order of nature are likewise superseded, and marriage among the rest.

Now, to make out his case, he must (first) show that there has been such a dispensation which thus supersedes the order of nature; or else (second), show that there was a new order which expressly forbids marriage to the persons who accept the new. I do not find that Mr. Dunlary has done either of those two things.

Marriage seems to me as plainly demanded by the constitution of the human body, as copulation amongst animals is demanded by the constitution of their bodies. So long as the human race continues in the body, the body itself is an argument for marriage. Now, it seems to me that if the duties of the body are not fulfilled, the body suffers and deteriorates, becomes a poorer instrument of the spirit (I use this word to mean all that is not body), and so the spirit cannot fully perform its functions.

I think this is the case with many who have never married; I think I know some unmarried women who are examples of this.

With men, cases of involuntary chastity seem to be more rare; men finding a satisfaction for the appetite without marriage. Some men there are, and some women, who do not need marriage, to whom it would be irksome.

Perhaps there is one such in 100, imperfect men and women. Now, if this were all, I should very much distrust any mode of religion, or any school of philosophy, which should teach that marriage was to be superseded. I should say, Here is the body, with its organs and its appetites; this is an argument against you, and one straightway from God.

But I go further, and think that marriage is a spiritual affair as well as a merely physical—it is love as well as lust, and a great deal more love than lust. When man is a savage and subordinate to his instincts, the appetite commands him, and the connection of man and woman is chiefly sensual.

But when he is cultivated and refined, the sentiment is more than the appetite; the animal appetite remains, but it does not bear so large a ratio to the whole consciousness of the man as before, while the sentiment of love bears one much greater. It seems to me that love between man and woman resulting in marriage, leads to the development of all the spiritual powers of man, or helps in their development. Out of that comes the society of man and wife, then of parent and child, and so on. So, it seems to me that marriage is more spiritual than carnal.

Now, if it could be shown to me that Jesus of Nazareth taught that marriage and all communication of man and woman ought to cease with religious persons, it would not weaken my regard for marriage in the smallest degree. I should say, "Here is my body and my soul (I mean my affections), the external and the internal evidences of the naturalness of marriage. I cannot resist their testimony." In short, I should not set aside the old dispensation until the body and the affections of man were themselves set aside.

But then, the question comes, *Did* Jesus teach such a doctrine? It is quite difficult to determine with accuracy what was the opinion of Jesus on some points. But, notwithstanding my reverence for Jesus and my love for him, I cannot attach much importance to that inquiry, for if I think that the work (and so the will) of God is against him, I cannot follow him against God.

I know this is no answer to Mr. Dunlary, and I say it only by way of introduction, hoping to hear from you soon. I am, as heretofore, faithfully, your friend,

THEO. PARKER.

TO THE SAME.

Boston, Dec. 31, 1849.

MY DEAR FRIEND,—Soon as I received your last letter, I set myself seriously to work to write an answer in detail, but continued interruption for the sake of other duties renders it impossible that I should be able to do this; therefore I will limit myself to considerations of a more general character, which require less time and space, and will leave the other matter to be talked over when we may meet, as I trust we shall; for a little conversation will do more than a good deal of writing.

I shall take it for granted that, in making man male and female, providing them with instinctive desires for union, and providing no other way for the perpetuation of the race except by such union, God established marriage in the very nature of man's body. I think the spirit of one sex is as incomplete without the other as the body is, and that there is as much a spiritual desire for the spirit of the other sex in men and women, as a bodily desire for the bodies of the opposite sex. Only in most persons it is not so strong.

On these two points I think we do not differ.

Now, the question comes, Did Jesus Christ intend to forbid marriage to his followers? or, allowing it, Did he think celibacy the better state? Before answering that question, it is necessary to look a little at the state of opinion in the world about him on this matter:—

1. The Jews considered marriage necessary and sacred. Celibacy in a man was thought impious, in a woman disgraceful. But afterwards marriage got into worse repute among the Jews, and moralists found it necessary to commend marriage (*See, e. g.* Ecclesiasticus xxxvi. 24 and 26; xxvi. 1, 3, 13, 16, 20, 21; xl. 23; and other passages). At length there grew up a sect which abandoned marriage—the Essenes. They had some excellent ideas, it seems, and had a good deal of influence on the early Christians in many matters.

2. Amongst the heathens, marriage was generally held in esteem, or, at any rate, celibacy was not much allowed or practised. Still, it was sometimes practised as a religious duty, by a caste of men or women: the vestal virgins are examples.

In the offering of sacrifices, it seems early to be thought that what was most valuable to men or most dear, was also the most acceptable offering to God. Hence, the fruits of pastoral life (oxen, &c.), or of agricultural life (wheat, fruit, &c.), and not the spontaneous productions of the earth, were the sacrifice. As the organs of generation were of value in keeping the race in existence and in satisfying the instinct of man, in a fit of religious excitement men mutilated themselves in the name of God (the priests of Cybele are examples of this), and others made a vow of temporary or continual chastity.

3. The Hebrews never had a high idea of woman. Man is created for his own sake, woman to be a helpmeet for him (Gen. ii. 18 and 24). Man is of God, woman only of man and for man. This, also, is Paul's notion (1 Cor. xi. 7, &c.). The common notions of woman in the Old Testament is, that she is a wanton, or a drudge, or a shrew. She lost us Paradise; her heart is "snares and nets": "Any wickedness but that of a woman" was a proverb. Among the heathens there was great wantonness; there was, also, among the Jews, to judge from complaints in the Old Testament, and the numerous words the Hebrew language has for the crime of sensuality.

4. These things being so, it is not at all surprising that some of the Christians thought it was best to cut off that passion altogether which

they found it difficult to regulate; not surprising that they thought they ought to sacrifice their powers of generation, as the vestals or priests of Cybele had done. Especially would this be so among the rigid Christians; and the persecutions tended to make them all rigid. Still more, if men came from the Essenes to Christianity, would they bring their own notions of marriage with them?

This being the case, I am not at all surprised to find St. Paul speak of marriage as he does. But, yet further, the early Christians thought the world was soon to end in their lifetime, so marriage was not needful to perpetuate the race. So Paul suffers it for such as cannot do without it; but to him it was a mere physical necessity, not at all a spiritual affection, which led to wedlock. I am not surprised to see such language attributed to Jesus as occurs in Matthew, Mark, and Luke, but I do not find reason to believe that Jesus was at all desirous of disturbing the natural order of things in relation to this affair. Still, I think such opinions were attributed to him before the Fourth Gospel was written, for in that Christ is said to work his first miracle at a marriage. It seems to me the author meant to show that Christ sanctioned marriage, and the use of wine, of which Christ makes taree or four barrels for the occasion.

Now, if Christ intended to overthrow and supersede the union of the sexes, I think he would not have left it at all ambiguous, but would have said so with great plainness, speaking as distinctly as he did of the Sabbath and of the Jewish institutions, fasts, and the like. Many of the interpretations of Mr. Dunlary seem to me mistaken; e. g. his account of the "abomination of desolation" seems to me wholly a mistake; yet, in other passages he shows a great degree of ingenuity as well as fairness, and I feel much respect for the man. But you see how much time it would take for me to go over the whole matter, text for text; it would require me to write a great book, which I have not time or health to undertake.

I hope you will forgive me for my long delay and neglect; I know you would, if you knew the amount of matter I must attend to.

Allow me to wish you a happy new year, and believe me,

Your friend,
THEODORE PARKER.

TO THE SAME.

Boston, October 20, 1850.

MY DEAR FRIEND,—I was very glad to receive your kind letter of the 13th, and thank you for the kindly interest you take in me and mine. The *Massachusetts Quarterly Review* came to an end directly through the failure of the publishers, though they always found the *Review* profitable to them. It still owes me a little sum of money. But I was never a suitable person to conduct a *Review*. I am the most unpopular man in Massachusetts, and probably am more hated than any person in the State who is not connected with politics.

I shall not write in any periodical; for there is none in America which would accept my articles if I should write, and I am just now too busy with other matters to write in a journal, even if there were one for me.

If I wrote at all, I should prefer the *Westminster Review*, which you so justly praise. I thank you for calling my attention to the article on "Buddhism." I have been studying the subject, but had not seen the paper before. Buddha came in a period of general decline of religion, and recommended great austerity in morals. His followers, for a time, refrained from all sexual action, but they also refused to dwell in houses, to sit on a chair or bench; but they gradually returned to the common practices of mankind. I had not seen the article on "Prostitution" till you called my attention to it; for I have been out of town all summer, and out of the way of the journals. It is able and awful. I know not what is to be done. The industrial feudalism of the 19th century leads to some terrible results. As I look about Boston, I see the ghastly misery of social life, and know not what to do. Last Sunday afternoon I preached at Deer Island, to a congregation of drunkards (men and women), and street-walking harlots, in a sort of hospital. There I saw some 40 to 60 broken-down women of the town, in bed with the venereal disease ! I see daily sights in Boston of awful sin and misery, not the product of lust alone, but of intemperance, ignorance, poverty, and manifold crime, which make me shudder. All that I can do seems like putting a straw into the ocean to stop the tide. But I do not despair of mankind. No, never ! It is better than ever before, and the good God has a remedy for it all.

A history of the gradual development of the sexual element in mankind would be a noble theme. I wish I had either the talent or the time for the work. The passages you quoted from Mill interested me much ; I read his work soon as it appeared. He is one of the few writers on political economy who have a due respect for woman. He at least does not think she is merely to serve as a receptacle for the lust of man.

I hope you will excuse me for not sending you my little speech on Mr. Webster, but I did not know that it would interest you at all; so I beg you to accept a copy, which I send you now. I will send you a little sermon in a few days, and am,

Truly your friend,

THEO. PARKER.

TO THE SAME.

Boston, November 29, 1850.

MY DEAR FRIEND,—The kindness of your letters surprises me as much as their beauty. I thank you for all the generosity of affection which you have always shown for me, and extended even to my writings. At the same time, you have made a deep impression on my heart, and though I have never seen your face, yet your character has made an image of your person in my breast which will not depart from me. I wish it were possible for me to write the book you speak of ; but I live in a noisy city, in " a world where want and suffering are." I have a large parish, and many daily duties which call me early from my bed, which keep me late from it, and give me little time for the studies I most affectionately cherish. I have been at work on a book about Christianity a long time, and it does not approach completion ; so I must despair of doing what you speak of. But it will give me great pleasure to visit the " Shakers " you mention; only, such are my engagements in the winter, that I shall not be able to do so before May. I think then I shall be glad to meet you there.

Believe me as ever,
Faithfully yours,
THEO. PARKER.

TO THE SAME.

Boston, July 15, 1851.

MY DEAR FRIEND,—Your book came in due time, and a very friendly note a few days later—both welcome, as all that comes from that source always is. I happened, accidentally, to be at leisure that day, and so I read your book through directly. Your informant seems to me a little mistaken in the character of the work.

I think it was written by a very licentious person, for the most obscene purpose. He seems destitute of all true reverence for man or God. He is smutty, and vulgar, and low. Sexual passion is always in his thoughts, and so he rifles the Bible, and the classics, and Christian writers, to find matter to his taste. He teaches that the tree of knowledge, which Adam and Eve were forbidden to touch, was the sexual union of man and woman. He does not seem to believe what he teaches. Some of the Christian fathers were of this opinion. It is contrary to the genius of the Hebrew nation, and to their interpretations of their own literature. I know a clergyman who adopts the above-named opinion. He is a queer man, with the most intense passion for women, and the most erratic notions of forbearance. He seems continually desiring what he never dares to do, and is one of the most unhappy of men—lascivious as a goat, abstemious as a hermit, capricious as a monkey, and (now) as irritable as a hornet. He is the only minister I ever met who publicly maintained this opinion.

I hope you have a nice and quiet time this summer. I am now at Brookline, three or four miles from Boston, and in a place where all is green about me; there is no noise, and the quiet, the silence, the freedom from interruption is delightful. I can do twice as much here as I can in the city. In August I shall go off to the mountains of Pennsylvania, and spend a few weeks there in examining the natural history of the place—studying the coal, the rocks, and the plants. I have some friends engaged in the geological survey of the State, and I hope much rest from the change of scene and the change of thought.

Yours faithfully,
THEO. PARKER.

TO THE SAME.

Boston, Sept. 21, 1851.

MY DEAR, GOOD FRIEND,—I had a good time in Pennsylvania, saw the coal country, went about there with my scientific friends, and learned a good deal that was new to me. I am amazed when I think of the material riches which God has stored up in this world, as school-furniture for the human race. For, I take it, these great forces which science slowly brings to light, out of the ground, are, at last, to serve the great moral purpose of human life; to make the mass of men better off, wiser, juster, more affectionate, and more holy in all their life, without and within. But, hitherto, the great results of human science have been for the few, not the many. The steam-ships that weave the two Continents together are palaces for the wealthy man who takes passage in them. But the poor sailor on board them is hardly better off than the Norse seaman, who sailed to Labrador, dressed in bear-skins, 1000 years ago, and they have not so much self-respect.

You might step from the Crystal Palace to St. Giles's parish in London, and what a contrast you would see between the "London labour and the London poor!" The magnificence of luxury is achieved at immense cost!

The men who make the finery of Birmingham and Brussels, of Lyons and Geneva, never wear it. The ass used to carry papyrus to the Roman bath, but himself was never washed! So it is now with the workers and their work. You, the Shakers, I think, have solved the problem of industry with remarkable success. The labour of each blesses all: none is cursed with drudgery, none with idleness, none with poverty, none with the wantonnesss of unearned riches. Now, I think that, some time or another, the human race will solve this dreadful problem, and do without poverty as easily as without war. Then these great forces,—steam, electricity, and a hundred more which no man dreams of yet, will do their higher work of civilizing, moralizing, refining, and blessing mankind. We must work and wait.

I wish I had the time for the book you speak of, but I have already laid out more work than I shall be able to do in my lifetime, I fear. I have made the preliminary studies for them, so that if I should turn off now to other pursuits I should lose too much that has cost me too dear. I am now engaged on a book which ought to have been done long ago, and would have been, but for the Fugitive Slave Law, which kept me contending with the officers of law all last winter. Now I am at work on that, and hope to have it done by next spring, if I am well all the winter.

I have not yet found out the name of the author of the little book you sent me. Still, it seems very obvious to me that the man had no object in view but an obscene one. Of course I may be mistaken. He enters into such wanton details of wantonness as none but a licentious man would do, as I should think. But I should hate to judge any man too severely.

I will yet ascertain the author, if possible. I write on a slip of paper the name of the clergyman I spoke of. I should prefer that no one knew his name but you. He is one of the most self-denying men that I have ever known. His conscience has grown out like a sickly tumor on him, it seems to me. But I respect and honor him. If you took him out of the ministry in ——, I know not what would become of them.

We have just returned to Boston, or I should have answered your kind letter before.—Truly yours, THEO. PARKER.

TO THE SAME.

West Newton, June 8, 1852.

MY DEAR FRIEND,—Your kind letter came to me yesterday, and I was glad to find your handwriting on the envelope, and marks of your kindly soul in the letter itself. I ought to apologize to you for not visiting you at New Lebanon, as I have repeatedly promised; but two reasons prevented—one was the incessant labor to which I have been compelled all the season: no sooner is one thing over but another comes in its place. The next was this: whenever I laid aside the money for the enterprise, some poor person came who needed my help, and I could not say, "No, sir, I can't help you; I want to spend for pleasure the trifle you need for support," so I have been debarred of the pleasure of seeing you and your friends. I hope you will not mention this to anybody, for it is not a fact that concerns the public, and I only mention it that you may see it was no lack of will on my part. Yet, do not think that I am poor—I am rather rich than otherwise—but can always spend my means more profitably than on my personal enjoyments. This season, several scholarly men of this country and other countries have looked to me for a little help, and I could not say nay.

I saw the article in the *Tribune* which you refer to, and liked the extracts from the book. In my lecture, in quoting the Highlander's remark, " *Wherever McDonald sits, there is the head of the table,*" I meant to say, the head of the table was where the greatest worth was, and, if the mutton was better than the man, then the platter was the head of the table, not the owner of the mutton. I fully accord with all you say about gentleness—the native kindliness of heart which seeks to comfort and delight others, and which you so well exemplify in your own house. It is before all natural or acquired gracefulness of manner, which, indeed, is nothing without this inner light of good manners. We should agree perfectly on that matter.

In respect to repelling force by force, I should differ from you widely. I respect the conduct of the Friends in this matter very much, and their motives also, but I do not share their opinions. I follow what seems to me the light of nature. It appears to me the opinion of Jesus is made too much of in this particular.

He supposed the "world" was soon to end, and the "kingdom of heaven" was presently to be established. He therefore commands his followers to "*resist not evil*"—not only not to resist with violence, but not at all. In like manner he tells them to "take no thought for the morrow." These counsels I take it were given in the absolute sense of the words, and would do well enough for a world with no future; the day was "at hand" when the Son of Man should come with power and great glory, and give fourfold for all given in charity, and eternal life besides. But the Son of Man (or God) is to use violence of the most terrible character (Matt. xxv. 31–46). Men were not to take vengeance, or even to resist wrong; not to meditate the defence they were to make when brought before a court—all was to be done for them by supernatural power. These things being so, with all my veneration for the character of Jesus, and my reverence for his general principles of morality and religion, I cannot accept his rule of conduct in such matters.

Yet, I think, violence is resorted to nine times when it is needless, to every one instance when it is needed. I have never preached against the doctrine of the non-resistants, but often against the excess of violence in the State, the Church, the community, and the family. I think cases may occur in which it would be my duty to repel violence, even with taking life. Better men than I am think quite differently, and I respect their conscientiousness, but must be ruled by my own conscience; and, till otherwise enlightened, should use violence, if need be, to help a fugitive.

I went up to Vermont last week, to conduct Miss Stevenson to her residence for the summer (at a tavern in Sudbury, Vermont). She would send her greetings to you, if at home.

My wife sends her most kindly greetings to you and yours. I get on slowly with my book; but have a little volume of sermons which will see the light, I hope, in the autumn. I think nobody has written on the subject you speak of. If I can find such a book, I will inform you.

Remember me kindly to all of your family, not forgetting the visitor from New Jersey.

Truly,

T. P.

TO THE SAME.

Boston, March 15, 1853.

MY DEAR, GOOD FRIEND,—I should have written you long ago; but when I came home from New York I had another of the comforts of Job, which seated itself on my right hand, so that I could not write with it. Some indispensable letters I wrote with the left. You would laugh to see them, but give up the attempt to read. Now that is gone, and all its companions, I hope. I was never better than now.

Your old and intimate relative has taken that step in his life which we commonly call death. I doubt not it was a pleasant step for him to take, though painful always it must be for us, the living, to separate from such as go to a higher life. But there are so many beautiful associations which cling to those we love, and come out with all the more beauty when they cease to be mortal, that the departure of a friend is always attended with an exaltation of our spirits if we have faith in the infinite goodness of the great Father.

There are some men whom I pity exceedingly,—

1. Such as have no belief in the soul, eternal life, and look on death as an ultimate fact.

2. Such as only fear a God, but do not know the infinite Father (and infinite Mother) of all souls, and so have nothing on which they can perfectly rely.

I meet both classes of men (the latter oftenest), and I pity them most exceedingly. To one, the grave is only a deep, dark hole in the ground; to the other, it is a hole which leads down to hell.

The popular religion makes death a most formidable enemy—a thing to be shuddered at.

I am amazed at the feebleness of men's faith in God. Death is one step in our progress; birth was a step once. But birth was a death to one form of being, and death is a birth into another form of being. To die in infancy, youth, or manhood does not seem after the true course of nature; but to die in old age,—

"Life's blessings all enjoyed, life's duties done,"—

that is no misfortune, but a blessing also. My father, when an old man—seventy-and-seven years old—laid down his weary, mortal bones, and was glad to die We wept over his toil-worn hands and venerable head, which we had kissed so many a thousand times; but we were glad that the dear old man rested from his labors, and went home to his God and our God—the earthly father to the Infinite Father and Mother. So shall we all one day be glad to go, and knock with our feeble hand at our Mother's door. "Undo the gate, and let me in," shall we all say, as we go willing and welcome to meet her. I hope you and yours are all well. We send our kindest salutations to you all. My wife and Miss Stevenson admired your daguerreotype, and thought it quite faithful.

Sincerely yours,   THEO. PARKER.

TO THE SAME.*

Boston, January 15, 1855.

MY DEAR, GOOD FRIEND,—It is long since I have seen your kindly venerable face, or even had a line from your hand. I was never so busy as now; all things conspire to make me *solitary* (in my study) one-half the time; and *public* (in some great assembly) the other half. Just now I have scarce time for anything but public duties, and the arrest and "trial" will only aggravate the evil for a little time to come; but by-and-bye it shall be otherwise and better.

I passed through New York in October, reaching at 9 P.M. and leaving at 8 A.M., and again last week, arriving at 3 A.M. and departing at 8 P.M., but had no time to see even you and yours. Mr. and Mrs. Brace were at our house a few days ago, and I promised them to pass the night of my lecture at their house, and I must keep the promise, else I should have the pleasure of stopping with one so very dear to me as yourself, but I shall come and see you and yours.

I thank you most heartily for the 50 dollars, which shall be put in the treasury for the "Friendless Girls," in the manner you suggest. We will send any girls to the Shakers who wish to go; they are usually sent to families in the country, but doubtless we shall find some who will desire the quiet seclusion of the Shakers. I love to see a man who makes his money serve as a ladder towards heaven, whereon he and his fellow-creatures may climb up to higher heights of humanity: the strong man lifting up the weak! What a ghastly vice this of prostitution is! It comes from the false idea that woman is to be the tool of man, not his equal, but slave; but gradually we should outgrow this folly and wickedness, as we have many others.

I am sorry that I do not see more of your son. I am so busy that I seldom go to Cambridge, not twice in six months, and he does not visit us so often as I could wish. By-and-bye he will get better acquainted.

Remember me most kindly to all, and believe me,

Heartily yours,   THEO. PARKER.

* See in the Appendix VI., Vol. II., a letter from Mr. White's son, in acknowledgment of the benefit which the father derived from his correspondence with Mr. Parker.

TO REV. DAVID WASSON.

Boston, December 12, 1857.

My dear Wasson,—Many thanks for your kind and welcome letter. I know how much it cost you to write it, and that dims my joy in reading it. You must not write much; you learned to labor long ago, now "learn to wait." I ate my lunch in the railroad station, and thought over all Higginson said in defence of the Irish. I like good *plump* criticism, and need it oftener than I get it; but I think he was mainly wrong, and still adhere to my opinion of the Celtic Irish. In other lectures I have showed at length the good they will do our country; when I give this again I will do so, and name the good qualities of the "gentlemen from Corrrkk," and the poor wretches from Africa.

I take Blumenbach's five races only as provisional—five baskets which will hold mankind and help us handle them. In respect to power of civilization, the African is at the bottom, the American Indian next. The history of the world, I think, shows this, and its prehistoric movements. I don't say it will be always so; I don't know.

You and I do not differ, save in words, about the Greeks. In the emotional element of religion, I think the Shemites surpass the Indo-Germans, and the Jews were at the head of the Shemites. The Phœnicians took to trade, and cared no more about religion than a Connecticut tin-pedlar, who joins any Church for a dollar. Somebody found one of the scoundrels, a mummy now in an Ægyptian tomb, who was circumcised. He took the religion of the place just as the current coin. Religious emotion, religious will, I think, never went further than with the Jews. But their intellect was sadly pinched in those narrow foreheads. They were cruel also, always cruel. I doubt not they did sometimes kill a Christian baby at the Passover or the anniversary of Haman's famous day! If it had been a Christian *man*, we should not blame them much, considering how they got treated by men who worshipped a Jew for God. They were also lecherous. No language on earth, I think, is so rich in terms for sexual mixing. All the Shemites are given to flesh. What mouths they have, full of voluptuousnesss! only the negro beats them there.

The Jews, like all the Shemites, incline to despotism; they know no other government. The Old Testament knows no king, but one absolute; the New Testament is no wiser, if perhaps you bate a line or two which Jesus spoke—and they indicate a feeling more than a thought. The New Jerusalem is a despotism with a lamb for the autocrat; a pretty lamb too, by the way, who gathers an army of 200,000,000 horse, and routs his enemies by the Euphrates, and then comes to Italy and kills men, till he makes a puddle of blood 200 miles wide and three feet deep. (See Rev. ix. 16, and xiv. 20.) In the Old Testament, Jehovah is King, a terrible King too. He is not a constitutional King, but arbitrary. His word is law. There is no proof of anything, no appeal to individual consciousness. With the Greeks, all this was different—Indo-Germanic, not Shemitic. I love the Greeks, especially the authors you name; but for moral helps and religico-emotional helps, I go to that dear Old Testament, for all Æschylus and Sophocles. Do you remember any example of remorse in the Greek literature? The Hebrews had a pretty savage conception of God; but He is earnest, there is no frivolity attributed to Jehovah. He is the most efficient Deity of old times: none of your *dilettante* gods. Beside, He is wholly superior to the material world, while none of the Greeks or Romans got above the idea that, in some particulars, it was more than any deity or all deities.

Get well as fast as you can.   Yours,   T. P.

TO F. E. PARKER.

Boston, April 15, 1858.

MY DEAR SIR,—I send you herewith some rambling thoughts about the Provident Association, and they will gain nothing by *my* name, so I put them on another sheet with no signature. Show them to whom you like—this to none, nor let the writer be known.

I think 70 per cent. of our out-door charity has only a reflex good action: 30 per cent. helps the receiver, 70 *only* the giver. Now we might reverse the proportions: all would bless the giver, but 70 per cent. would also elevate the receiver.

When I first came to Boston, I meant to go into that work of looking after the perishing class. But three things hindered:—

1. Men had a great horror of me.

2. They had no correct ideas as a basis of action, in general or in special, and

3. The slavery question assumed such an alarming shape, proportions, and position that we must turn head and put it down, or turn tail and die—conquer as *men*, or die *niggers*.

So, for twelve years, I have been laboring to diffuse the true idea of man, God, and the relation between the two—of life for the individual, the family, community, nation, church, world; and also fighting slavery in all its forms. I shall never do for the perishing and dangerous classes what I primarily intended. But I will bore you no longer with this sheet, for I am,

Yours truly,

T. P

SOME THOUGHTS ON THE CHARITIES OF BOSTON.

1. The effect of our in-door municipal charity is excellent, not without some evil, of course, but in the main it works well. I am thereby insured against starvation. It is quite a step in civilization when a nation guarantees its citizens against death by hunger and cold.

A little shame attaches to the recipients of this charity: it ought to be so as a rule; and a little more to their children: that ought not to be so.

The State almshouses, I think, are an improvement on the old mode of treating foreign paupers.

I have altered my opinion after a little observation, and by the results of trial.

2. The effect of our out-door charity—municipal, social, individual, is mainly bad. The *secondary* (or reflex and subjective) action is admir-

able; it blesses the giver. I think of few persons who make an investment for their own sakes which gives so good dividends as what they spend for the poor; what they lay out for others comes to more than what they lay up for themselves.

But the primary (or direct and objective) action is quite bad. I sometimes think it does more harm than good; but this is a little extravagant.

1. This charity is badly distributed, without discretion, conscientiousness, or industry. Most of your visitors lack those three virtues. The want of the least of them is a great fault. No business in Boston requires a more liberal measure of all three. S—— is a capital good fellow, highly useful in his place, truly benevolent, conscientious—most religiously so—and devoted to this work. He is tender and tenacious both—rare metallic qualities to unite in one person. You will not do better than to keep him. But, spite of him, things are as I say.

2. You have to deal with exceeding bad material. The ethnology of pauperism is worth more than a hasty thought, which is all I can give it *now*. (1.) Anglo-Saxon pauperism, American, English, Scotch, is easily disposed of. (2.) German pauperism will give us little trouble. (3.) Jewish pauperism will take care of itself—it is quite inconsiderable, and will be taken charge of by Jewish almsgiving, which is the distributive virtue of that people, as thrift is their cumulative virtue (and an *evil odor* their cumulative and distributive vice, chronic and progressive with the children of Israel). (4.) African pauperism is easily dealt with. The negro is the least acquisitive of all men; his nature is tropical. He is an equatorial grasshopper—not a bee of the Temperate Zone. Still, he is so pliant that we can do with him as we will, if we will justice and charity. (5.) Celtic pauperism is our stone of stumbling. The Irishman has three bad things—bad habits, bad religion, and, worst of all, a bad nature. In dealing with Irish poor, I lay down three maxims:—

(1.) The Irishman will always lie, if it is for his momentary interest. (2.) He will not work while he can exist by begging. (3.) He will steal when he can get a chance, and preferentially from his benefactor. I can recall but *one* instance of a grateful "gintleman from Cork." These vices—lying, begging, stealing, are *instantial* of the genus "Paddy from Corrrck". The opposite is exceptional—of Bridget and John, eccentric individuals. I might add a fourth: Paddy will get drunk if he can find liquor.

Now, the bulk of our pauperism is *Irish*. Suffolk County is "County Cork"; Boston is a young Dublin. What shall we do with this wild Irishism which is yelping around us? I'll tell you a wrong thing we *have* done: we have put the head-quarters of charity near the centre of the Boston Paddy-land! What is the consequence? Ward VII. *squats* in the anteroom of the Provident Aid Society; it passes its mornings there, that by its continual coming it may weary the wisdom of charity into a foolish gift. I would not have the room too near; as the tap draws the idlers, so the till of charity draws Paddies. If it were half a mile off it were better. Bridget and Michael will feel the "swate influence" from the North End to the Neck; but from Franklin Street to Fort Hill, why, it draws all the virtue out of them. We want a new suite of rooms, for which I would give two limits :—1. They should not be in such fatal proximity to the Irish. 2. They should be ventilated well. The Irish are poisoning our agents with their contaminating nastiness.

Last autumn the benevolent men of Boston said, "There will be much suffering, and then much crime. Let our charity prevent both!" It was religiously meant; it was well done. I think there has seldom been *less suffering* in a winter in Boston, especially in the class of people who seek our relief. But where you sow alms beggary springs up ; as the tare amid *this* wheat there came theft, the exceptional but regular weed amid the instantial crop. Next autumn and next winter we shall see such demand on our charity as we never knew before. If charity be organized, dependence becomes also an "institution," and beggary is organized beside it. Ours is a society for the *preventing* pauperism. Why, we are making it a society for the promotion, diffusion, and organization of pauperism!

Now, we want a good, able-bodied, able-minded man as the out-door organizer and supervisor of this work. He should be a *religious* man, having *piety* without narrowness, *morality* without cant or asceticism ; one upright before God and downright before men ; and with a theology he believes in, but does not wish to strangle other men withal. I think Rev. Mr. Ritchie, of Roxbury, is just such a man ; Capt. Goodwin is perhaps still better.

TO A FRIEND.

Boston, Feb. 6, 1852.

DEAR SIR,—I take the first leisure hour to reply to your note of last Sunday. Regarding Jesus of Nazareth as a man, there is no reason why we should suppose that he could never be mistaken. You make a distinction in this matter, and admit that he might come short of the truth through lack of ability to see it, but seem to hesitate to admit that he could be mistaken or wrong in any of his positive teachings. Yet I think a careful study of the Gospels will force us to the conclusion that he was sometimes mistaken.

There is a little—nay, a very great—difficulty in ascertaining the opinion of Jesus on some quite important matters; for (1) it is not certain that any of the writers reported his exact words ; and (2) the writers disagree so much among themselves. Thus, there is an immense difference between the first three Gospels and the fourth—a difference in the history and the doctrines. In the first three there are remarkable diversities of doctrine. Thus, Matthew represents Jesus as saying (x. 5), "Into any city of the Samaritans enter ye not;" and, again (xv. 24), "I am not sent but unto the lost sheep of the house of Israel ;" and Luke puts no such words in the mouth of Jesus, but represents him as sending messengers "into a village of the Samaritans." Of the ten lepers he heals, only one returns thanks, and he a Samaritan (xvii. 16) ; and the model of practical piety that he speaks of (x. 30-37) is also a Samaritan. Luke had Matthew's Gospel before him when he wrote. Mark had both Luke and Matthew, yet Mark omits all that Matthew and Luke report about Jesus in relation to the Samaritans. This could not have been by accident. Matthew seems still to have clung to Judaism, hence he gives such passages as that in xxiii. 1-3. Luke was more liberal, and broke away from Judaism, and so never gives such a command as that in Matthew. Notice also the account in Matthew of the sending out the Twelve (x. 1) and that in Luke (vi. 13), and Luke's account of the sending out of the seventy (x. 1-16, and 17-18). Luke is not favorable to the exclusive claims of the Twelve Apostles. Since this is so, I find it difficult to be certain how far opinions have been ascribed to him which he never held, and how far he changed his opinions, and so taught differently at different times. He did the latter it is plain, for in Matthew (v. 17-19) he says he was not come to destroy the law (*i. e.* the law in the Books of Exodus, Levit., Numb., and Deut.), but to fulfil—*i. e.* to keep. He affirms the doctrine of the orthodox Jews, that not a jot or tittle of the law should be altered or repealed till the end of the world (v. 18), and would not have one of the least of the Commandments (of that law in these books) set aside or neglected. Yet, by-and-bye, how differently he speaks of the Sabbath and of fasting, *e. g.* in the same Gospel! How very different are his own doctrines in the Fourth Gospel (*e. g.* John iv. 21-23), and in the Epistle of Paul, who rejects the law which Matthew would have us keep.

If the First Gospel is correct, Jesus believed the end of the world was presently to take place (Matthew xxiv. 3-27, 29-34). Unitarian and other interpreters refer this to the destruction of Jerusalem, I think very unjustly. It is plain from the Epistles that the Christians thought the world would soon end; Paul, John, and James seem to agree in this. In Peter there is a remarkable passage (2 Peter iii. 3-4, 7-10). All this is enough to show that Jesus was greatly mistaken if Matthew reports him correctly.

Now, I think that Jesus was a greater man than the Gospels represent him. I look on him as a man of vast genius, a great mind, a great conscience, a great heart, and a great soul. I mean that he was a man of great genius—intellectual, moral, affectional, and religious genius; and of course lived a great life of piety. But when he was a boy I suppose he stumbled in learning to walk; miscalled the letters in learning to read; got wrong conclusions in his thoughts. From his very nature as a finite person this must be possible and actual too. When he reached the age of thirty he must have made mistakes in his intellectual processes, and in his moral and religious processes. We always stumble in new things: the greatest men must do so. Kepler, the great astronomer, first discovered the great law in astronomy which governs the planets in the solar system; but he had made many a wrong hypothesis before he hit the right. From the nature of the case this must be so with any mind except the Infinite God.

Now, I should be much amazed to find a man, with even the vast endowments of Jesus Christ, at that period teaching the idea of the infinite perfections of God, and never saying anything inconsistent with that idea.

But look at the facts, and see what the others teach about God which implies a limitation in his idea of God. He tells men to "*fear* him (God), which is able to destroy soul and body in hell" (Matthew

x. 28). This (with its parallels) is the only place in which Jesus commands men to fear God. And this alone might easily enough be explained away, but in other places the character of God is represented as worthy of fear more than love, *e.g.* Matthew xviii. 23–35; xxi. 44; xxii. 11–14; xxiv. 48–51; and xxv. 30. I think in the New Testament there is no indication of the idea that the suffering of the wicked in the next life is for the good of the wicked themselves: it is vengeance, and not medicine, that they smart under. I think the Evangelists believed that Christ taught the eternity of torment in hell, otherwise I cannot explain such passages as Mark ix. 43–48; xxv. 41–46; Luke xvi. 25–26. Good and holy men try to explain away such passages, and so violate the language they ought to interpret, because the idea of eternal damnation, or of any torment which is not for the welfare of the man who suffers it, is too atrocious for us to accept. This alone shows that Jesus did not conceive of God as infinitely perfect, as it seems to me.

Then: the fact that Jesus believed in a Devil, an actual personal Devil, seems to me abundantly plain, if we can trust his biographers. The account of the Temptation presupposes this existence, and that in the most literal kind. But I pass over that. In that beautiful prayer which is so deep that the world prays it, the petition, " Deliver us from evil," means from *an evil one* (*i. e.* the Devil). The same word is used in the same sense in Matthew xiii. 19. It is he, the Devil, that sows tares in the field, and so is the rival of God (xiii. 38–39). Nay, as " many are called, and but few chosen," so it would appear that he was the successful rival of God, and got more souls than the Father Himself at the end of the world. But it is needless to cite passages to show that Christ believed the actual existence of a Devil and devils (*i. e.* demons) that " possessed" men; the whole thing is so plain and obvious that it needs no argument.

Now, if there be a Devil, absolutely evil, and so eternally evil, then, so far as he has any power at all, he checks the power of God and hinders Him from accomplishing his purpose. So God is not infinite in power. But if there be such a Devil, then God must have made that Devil; and if God made such a Devil absolutely evil, it could only have been out of evil in God Himself. Then, God could not be infinite in wisdom, or in justice, or in love and holiness; for a Being perfectly wise, just, loving, and holy, could not make a being perfectly unwise, unjust, unloving, and unholy. If God be infinitely perfect, then there can be no absolute evil in the world, no evil that does not come to serve a good purpose at the last. You and I stumbled when learning to use our legs in childhood, and got hurt in the fall; we stumble in learning to use our higher powers, and get hurt by the error or the sin. But the stumble of the child and the sin of the man must alike have been foreseen by God, and are alike accidents of development, requiring no Devil as author of the child's stumble or the man's sin. You and I have outgrown the first form of mistake, and walk erect; the little hurts we got in our fall made us take better heed. So we shall outgrow the moral stumbling ; and the pain of our error, the smart of our sin, will make us take better heed, and so the suffering be medicine.

I think Jesus had a feeling of the infinity of God, and hence the grand and beautiful words of comfort that he speaks, which are the things that you doubtless value most in the New Testament. Such passages as these, Matthew v. 3–12, 23–24, 43–44; vii. 7–12; ix. 13; xi. 28–30; xviii. 11–14, 21–22; xx. 25–27; xxii. 37–39, &c. &c. The marvellous story of the Prodigal Son, in Luke xv. 11, is a most touching example of the same thing.

I have the greatest reverence for Jesus, the greatest gratitude and love, and feel the vast obligations we all owe to him, perhaps no man more so; but I love and reverence him for what he *is*, not for what he is *not*. I know how these opinions will shock men, but must take up that cross also, and bear it as I can.

TO A FRIEND.

Oct. 5, 1858.

Many thanks for your interesting letter, with the reminders of numerous friends you met. Gurowski is a man of great talents, of truly wide and deep historic learning. I know few men that are his equals in respect to these things. He and I have often picked that crow—the diversity of races. He does not satisfy me, nor I him. Perhaps both of us are a little wrong, only I see his error and not mine.

Buckle *did* read many poor books, but it was unavoidable. To cross the Continent, we must go through much poor land, which yields nothing to the artist or the man of science. The charm of Buckle is—his poor books don't hurt him.

Since I saw you, I, too, have had a little journey in an open wagon, with Mr. Lyman. We drove about 700 miles in New England and New York State—the Hudson River Valley. We were in the open air about ten or twelve hours a-day, and saw the farmers and mechanics of the small towns. I saw but one *American* drunk in all the journey; not a ragged *native*, or his windows stuffed with old clothes. The evidences of industry, thrift, temperance, intelligence, and comfort, were a happy surprise, even to me, though I am pretty familiar with New England. We kept in the small towns, and slept only once in a "first-class hotel" at Albany.

If I were Governor of Massachusetts, I would visit all the gaols, all the asylums, State almshouses, and other public institutions. I would set my mortal bodily eye on them all, and *see*, and *know* how the State's hired men did their work. All the normal schools, likewise, all the teachers' conventions would I visit. Of course I would not neglect the farmers' show, the mechanics' show, or the soldier show. I liked Banks's speech much. We have too much neglected the militia; we may need the armed men when we little think of it. I hate the armies of Europe—putting the destroyer or the defender before the great creative classes who manage the thought and toil which give us all desirable things.

TO GEORGE RIPLEY.

Boston, Nov. 19, 1858.

My DEAR GEORGE,—What a troublesome correspondent I prove to you! With this note you will receive the third edition (stereotype) of my translation of De Wette's "Introduction to the Old Testament."

It has never received any reasonable notice in America, for it favors the truth and not the prejudice of any sect. It has never had a friendly word said for it in any American journal.

   *   *   *   *   *   *

Let me say a word about the work.

I. Of the Original.

It is the most learned, the most exact, and the most critical introduction to the Old Testament ever made in any tongue. It contains the result of all the critical investigation of the human race on that subject, up to the date of his last edition. Since then no important additions have been made to the science of biblical introduction, except as f ' lows :—

1. The learned researches of Mr. Movers, a German Catholic priest, at Breslau, on the Phœnicians, have shed new light on the Books of Chronicles, Jeremiah, and some other passages in the Old Testament. But what he has adduced belongs more to commentaries than to an introduction.

2. The labors of Mr. Ewald, a man of genius and enormous learning, clear up some dark things in Hebrew history. He gives his conjectures on the composition of the Pentateuch, but he is so subjective and capricious that his works are vitiated by uncertainty. Still, he saw some things which De Wette saw not.

3. Recent researches in Egypt (Lepsius', &c., I mean), may hereafter give some help in biblical introductions, but *not yet*.

4. Light may come out of the Assyrian darkness at Nineveh, and shine on obscure things in the Bible. But it has not reached us yet.

With these exceptions, the original of De Wette bears the same relation to the actual learning of the age as in 1842 and 1843.

II. Of the Translation.

1. I read the original carefully, studied it (beginning in 1836), and the new editions, as they successively appeared till 1843.

2. I translated the work word for word.

3. I read up on the subject thus :—

    (1.) All the previous introductions of the Old Testament, from Simon down to Hengstenberg. That was a labor.

    (2.) All the early Christian writers (Fa 'ers, &c.) who treated of such matters down to Jerome and Augustine; that also took *some* time.

    (3.) I read all the modern works relating thereto—often a weariness.

    (4.) I added from those what I found necessary, to make the matter as clear to the popular audience I hoped to address, as the original was to the learned reader of De Wette himself.

I popularized the original thus :—

    (1.) I translated in the text all the Latin, Greek, and Hebrew (Rabbinical) passages which De Wette put in without translating, and I put the original extracts into the margin. It was a pretty piece of work, you may guess

to do into English the awful Latin and Greek of the
old choughs who wrote so barbarously!

(2.) I looked over the references to the Bible. Where he
said, "comp. Isa. ix. 1, with Jer. xlv. 16," I printed
the passages side by side, sometimes in the common
translation, sometimes in Noyes's, and sometimes in my
own. Thus I made easy and obvious what else were
difficult and obscure.

Now, if you will give some little notice of the book, I will consider
that you renew the right hand of fellowship once extended me.

Good bye.

T.

TO DR. R. L. HOWARD, COLUMBUS, OHIO.

Boston, April 30, 1849.

DEAR SIR,—Your letter reached me to-day. I cannot suffer any
business or any weariness to prevent me from answering it before I
sleep. I thank you for the candor with which you write. I confess
my work seems to me somewhat fearful; it did so when I began it, and
I was often tempted to be silent, for I saw what a revolution would
take place, suddenly or slowly, in the popular theology. If my principles were true, I saw that a mountain of rubbish must be swept
away; that many reputations, many hopes, many institutions, likewise,
were based on that mountain of rubbish, and of course must perish
with their foundation. I saw that many men would look on me as the
enemy of religion, and so as the enemy of mankind; that some would
think that, while I opposed the folly of so much which men had believed in as religion, there was no reality at all for religion. But, at
the same time, I had a strong confidence that what was true was also
safe; that falsehood was not safe. I thought I could show men that
the popular theology had no natural, at least no indissoluble, connection with true religion; that underneath the shifting sands of sectarian
theology there lay the eternal rock of religion. I have never been
sorry that I undertook the work; indeed, I could not have forborne
if I would. I have felt the loneliness which you speak of; that
comes from breaking away from early associations and tender ties.
But that has long since passed away; still, I do not like to be hated,
as I sometimes have been.

I have been compelled to pull down; but I have no delight in that
work. It has always been painful. I did it only that something better
might be built up in place of what but cumbered the ground before.
I saw that religion was natural to man; the infinite goodness of God
I could never doubt; the connection between God and man seemed to
me so obvious, so essential to the nature of each, that I wondered any
man could doubt of these facts. The more I live, the greater religion
appears, the more attractive, the more satisfying, the more beautiful.
But it seems plainer and plainer that religion is one thing, and the
books written about it quite a different thing. At one time the Bible
rested on me like a nightmare; I could not bear it nor get rid of it;
now that I take a different view of it, the imperfections which I find

D D 2

in both the Testaments no longer disturb me, and the truths I find in both are the more welcome, because I feel free to come and to go, free to examine and satisfy my own mind and conscience, before I accept the conclusions of men who lived in another age and wrote from a different point of view.

I think I understand the circumstances in which you are placed. It requires not a little heroism to do as you seem disposed to do. But who can be contented with a divided heart? You do not lose your sympathy with the religion of your old associates, only with their theology. In all that is real piety, love of God, or real goodness, love of man, you will sympathise with them the more. Still, I suppose men not much enlightened will think ill of you, and speak harshly of your name. Sometimes it requires a little charity to be just to men who, from their ignorance, are unjust to us, but such charity is twice blessed. I hope my poor book will do no harm, but some little good to mankind. It would be a comfort to think that I had helped men in the way to religion, and all it brings; even to have helped a little. I have no doubt committed many errors, which, of course, must do harm. I hope they will be exposed, and left to perish. Now and then, some one writes me a letter like yours, which shows me that I have not spoken in vain; altogether, we may all be grateful for the liberal spirit of this age, which allows men to keep their heads on their shoulders, while these heads are full of thoughts which must work a revolution in the world. But let me not weary a busy man with a letter over-long. I will send the *Review*, as you suggest, and such of my sermons as are still on hand, though I lament that some which I value most are out of print. If I can ever be of any service to you I shall be glad, and am,

Truly your friend,

THEO. PARKER.

TO P. D. MOORE.

It seems to me that the Christian world has honestly made two great mistakes, in common with the rest of mankind: namely,—

I. They consider that God is finite. In our time they do not say so in so many words, yet, when they come to speak of his works and motives, it continually leaks out that they think so. Hence comes the notion of the wrath of God, of vindictive punishment, of eternal hell, of God changing his plans, either directly, as related in the Bible, or indirectly, by miracles, such as are spoken of in the Bible and the religious books of most of the nations. The belief in miracles rests on two things. 1. A Deity who can control the material world; but, 2, a world previously shaped by this Deity in so poor a way that it does not answer his intentions, and he, therefore, must alter it to suit the particular purpose in hand. The alteration is not according to the nature of the thing, as the blossom of the bud, and the fruit of the flower; but against the nature of the thing, as a man born with no human father, an ass speaking Hebrew, and the like. The notion of a miraculous revelation made to man rests on this previous thought, namely, that God had made man so poorly at the first, that he would not ascertain the religious truths needful for the safe conduct of his life, and so God must by miracles supply the defect of nature, that is, He must alter and mend what He made badly at first. The Bible represents the world as not turning out as God expected. The common notion of the Christian pulpit is, that mankind is a disappointment to God; the world is not what He meant it to be. All this comes from the imperfect idea men have of God,—of God as finite.

II. They conceive of religion as something unnatural to man. In human nature there is either too much, something to be cut off, members of the body to be mutilated, as in the Hebrew Church; then of the spirit to be mutilated, as in the Christian Church, where the reason is thought a dangerous thing, and all good Catholics or Protestants are to circumcise that, and cast it from them; or else too little; so something must be added in opposition to human nature. This is a second birth, or a gift of the spirit, which does not mean a development of the original faculties we are born with, but the acquisition of qualities from some foreign source—from God or Christ. Then the deeds demanded in the name of religion are not such as are the flower and beauty of human nature; they are not natural perfections, but things often against nature. The conventional sacraments, which are thought to make a man a "good Mahometan," or a "good Catholic," or a "good Jew," or a "good Calvinist," are things not needful to make him a good man. The man is put down; the sectarian is put up. The consequences of this mistake as to the nature of religion are seen all about us. There are noble men in every sect; but the sects themselves seem to me working with poor tools, and not trying to do the thing most needful to have done. We want men, not Mahometans, Catholics, and Protestants.

I take it, the remedy for these two evils is simply the true idea of God, the true idea of religion, and a life in accordance therewith.

I. God is not finite, but infinite—a Being of perfect power, wisdom, justice, love, and holiness. Doubtless, God possesses other perfections of which we have no idea. We, having no corresponding power of conceptions but these, make up our idea of a perfect being—the infinite Being. Then He must be perfect cause and perfect providence. He must make and administer the universe—including matter and spirit and each creature therein—from a perfect motive, for a perfect purpose, and use a perfect means thereto. Of course, the work would not require alteration and amendment, in whole or in parts. It would require only development. Then all notions of the wrath of God, of the jealousy of God, of his changing his plans, of his hating men, of eternal damnation, and the like, must end at once. Everything is insured against ultimate shipwreck at the office of the infinite God. His hand is endorsed on all that is.

II. Religion is natural to man; I make it to consist of two things, namely, 1st, piety, our consciousness of God and of our relation to Him in its perfect form, this absolute love of God, absolute faith in God, and absolute delight in God; and, 2nd, morality, the keeping of all the natural laws of the human constitution in all the relations of life. Thus, then, religion taken as a whole in the service of the infinite God by the normal action of every faculty of the spirit, intellectual, moral, affectional, and religious; every limb of the body, every power we possess over matter or over men; this religion will appear in all forms of singular or associated action, in the life of the individual, the family, the community, the State, the Church, and the world of nations.

To awaken this idea of God in the souls of men, and to induce them to live out such an idea of religion, that, my dear sir, is a great and noble work; but it will be done by the prayers, the tears, and the toil of earnest and noble men. I wish you much joy in this manly undertaking.

Yours sincerely,
THEODORE PARKER.

TO MASTER WASSERBOHR, AT THE LATIN SCHOOL, BOSTON.

Montreux, Canton de Vaud, Suisse, September 2, 1859.

DEAR MASTER WASSERBOHR,—I was quite glad to hear of your progress at school, and of the welfare of your father and mother and all the family. I often think of your fighting your way along at the Latin School, and overcoming both the difficulties of the Roman and the English languages at the same time. When Mr. Gardner, at your request, put you into a higher class, I hope the additional studies were not too much for you, and that you went on with fresh heart and strong hope. Nothing can be done without regular persistent industry,—

"Labor improbus omnia vincit."

The talent of work is one of the greatest of all; without it no other brings much to pass. At your time of life, two things require to be specially attended to; one is attention, the power of fixing the mind on what concerns it, as steadily as an auger bores into a log; the other is memory, the power of keeping what you get, and reproducing it when needed. These are the two great things you must cultivate now; if you do it faithfully, you will find by-and-bye, that you can master a book by reading it once, and remember all the good things that are in it. Other intellectual powers will come into play later. Of course, the imagination always has work to do. It is a good plan for you before you go to sleep at night, to think over all you have seen, and heard, and done, and thought in the day; that will help to fix the attention, and confirm the memory, and, besides, it has inestimable moral advantages, for you can't fail to ask of all, "Is it right, or is it wrong?" Indeed, education must be of the moral and religious powers, as well as of the intellect: a good scholar, who is also a bad boy, is a shameful monster. Of course, you don't forget your play; few boys do that. But you must take great care to keep good firm health; a sick scholar is a good-for-nothing—about as worthless as a horse with but three legs, who needs propping up at one corner in order that he may stand still.

Remember me to your father and mother, and believe me always,

Your friend,
THEODORE PARKER.

We have some Holsteiners boarding here at the same house with us, intelligent people.

THE MUSIC HALL.

CHAPTER XIV.

Twenty-Eighth Congregational Society—The Music Hall—Preaching—The Fraternity.

THE engraving represents the interior of the Music Hall during the lifetime of Mr. Parker. It is at present (1863) in the hands of mechanics and decorators, who are refitting it for the reception of the great organ which has been built in Germany for the Music-Hall Association, at a cost, as finished in Germany, of 25,000 dollars (£5000). The Twenty-eighth Society is worshipping elsewhere, and will not probably return to the Hall after its re-opening.

The project of erecting a hall in Boston for musical entertainments was the subject of frequent discussion, which had no result, until a committee of the Harvard Musical Association took the matter in hand, and secured the amount required, 100,000 dollars, for the purchase of land and the erection of a building. A vacant lot of ground, known as the Bumstead Estate, and a small adjoining lot, comprising in all 16,642 square feet, with an entrance from Bumstead Place and one from Winter Street, were purchased. The passage way from Winter Street is 15 feet wide and 110 feet long.

The greatest care was taken in elaborating the plans for this noble building. Mr. Snell, the architect, submitted his designs to competent judges, such as J. Scott Russell and Dr. Faraday in England, the former a distinguished architect, the latter a man well versed in all that was then knowable on the difficult point of acoustics. The result was the finest building in America for its special purpose, and stately and convenient for all the objects of a popular assembly.

The main hall is 130 feet long, 78 feet wide, and 65 feet high. In the day-time it is lighted by semi-circular windows on either side, above a cornice that is 50 feet from the floor; by night the cornice of the four walls springs into jets of flame. There is a passage-way in the wall large enough for a man to move along in lighting.

The ceiling is deeply moulded into diamond-shaped spaces, which are flat, and of a blue color. Arches spring to it from the pilasters of Corinthian capitals; and between them are the windows. Two rows of balconies with latticed fronts extend around three sides; there are fourteen doors to each. The floor, covered with oval-backed chairs of stuffed damask, each with its porcelain number-plate, will seat 1500 people: fourteen doors empty the audience into ample corridors. A faint rose-color prevails over the whole interior of the building.

The stage is five feet from the floor, with a level foreground, whence it rises in seven steps, the whole width of the hall, to a gilded screen of wood-work in the centre of one end. At first a small organ that was used in the Melodeon was concealed behind this screen. The stage-steps might accommodate 500 people, and the whole building would comfortably seat 2700.

When the audience was perfectly still, the ordinary voice of a speaker could be heard with ease; but every little sound in the body of the house accumulated so readily as to blur the sentences coming from the stage. The clapping of the two-and-forty doors was sometimes a great annoyance, but generally there reigned a silence so eager and deferential when Mr. Parker preached, that his level, conversational style could be heard with ease ; and it was only towards the close of his services that his speech was sometimes marred by belated or impatient listeners.

On one of the stage-steps stands Crawford's bronze statue of Beethoven, presented to the Association by Charles C. Perkins, of Boston. It was cast at Munich, on the 26th of March, 1855, the anniversary of Beethoven's death, and placed in its present position, with appropriate ceremonies, chief of which was a poem of great vigour and beauty by Wm. W. Story,* on the evening of March 1, 1856. It is seven feet high, of yellow, almost golden, bronze. The head is erect, and the face has a firm, earnest, and inward look. The neck is open, and a large cloak is thrown over the right shoulder. The hands are crossed, lightly dropped before him ; the left holds the score of the Choral Symphony, and the right holds over it a pen. On the score are the first notes of the strain

" Freude, schöne Gotterfunken,"

the opening line of Schiller's Song to Joy, and the first of the Chorus in the Ninth Symphony.

The seal of the Music-Hall Association is a figure of St. Cecilia, with a motto that was furnished by Mr. Parker :—

Cœlo venit aurea dextro,†

which he translated,—

She comes, resplendent, from auspicious skies.

Here is Mr. Parker's prayer on Sunday, March 2, the day after the unveiling of the statue, privately reported :—

O Thou infinite Spirit who fillest the air that is about us, and the ground underneath our feet, and the heavens above our head ; and who Thyself art the Spirit whereby, wherein, we live and move and have our being ; we would draw near unto Thee, who art never withdrawn from us, and feeling Thine infinite presence in our heart and soul, would worship with our morning prayer, that we may serve Thee in our daily, nightly, long-continued flight.

O Thou, who art the life of all things that live, and the being of

* Son of Chief Justice Story, of Massachusetts, and sculptor of Cleopatra, The Sybil, and other noble works, including the bust of Mr. Parker, which is given in this Memoir.

† From Manilius : Astronom. Liber N., p. 539.

whatsoever are, we pray Thee that Thine infinite soul may stir us in our poor prayer, and quickened by Thine infinite life, may re-ascend in our aspiring flight to higher and higher nobleness and human growth.

O Lord, we bless Thee for Thy providence, which broods over the world, and blesses it with Thy fourfold year. We bless Thee for the summers and autumns that have gone by ; for the winter, whose brilliant garment of resplendent snow has been so broadly spread across the shoulders of the Continent. Yea, Lord, for all the providence whereby in winter Thou preparest for spring, and makest summer to be the porch and entrance for harvests, autumns full of beauty and abounding in fruit.

O Lord, Father and Mother of the ground, the heavens, and all things that are, we bless Thee for Thy loving-kindness and Thy tender mercy. We thank Thee that Thou art kind and large in Thy providence to every created thing; that from Thy hand we take our daily bread, and from Thy cup Thou pourest out to us all things whereby we live and are blessed. We thank Thee that Thou watchest over us in our prosperity, in our distress, and followest the exile from his native land to every home, giving the wanderer Thy blessing, that when despair comes to Thy children's heart, Thou, who knowest their weakness, takest them home to Thyself, and blessest every wanderer with Thine infinite peace, whence no soul shall ever be exiled long.

O Lord, we thank Thee for noble men Thou raisest up in the world ; for those great souls who proclaim truth to mankind ; for those who reveal justice to the earth, enacting it into laws and institutions, building up Thy righteousness, Thine ever-living truth.

We thank Thee for those great souls to whom Thou confidest the precious charge of genius, blessing them with lofty gifts. We thank Thee for the sons of song, who make sweet music in the hearts of men, and when their own body crumbles to the poor ground, their breath still surrounds the world with an ever-new morning of melody, giving to highest and lowest, and blending all into one magnificent family of souls who are lifted up by the sweet strains of art.

O Lord, we thank Thee also for those sons of genius who, with kindred power, stretch out their plastic hand over the hard elements of earth, which become pliant at their touch. Father, we thank Thee for the creative genius of the sculptor, which folds a kindred genius in brazen swaddling-bands, and so hands down form and lineament, all glorified by art, from age to age.

O Lord, we bless Thee for another power, which is music and sculpture to other faculties ; for the poet's kindling eye, whose wide embracing heart is vision and faculty divine, whereby, to listening crowds, he anticipates the spontaneous feelings of our hearts, and makes perpetual in speech the transient feeling of an hour.

O Lord, while we thank Thee for those whom Thou hast blessed with creative genius in the intellectual sphere and moral, still more do we bless Thee for those whom Thou hast gifted with genius for loving-kindness and tender mercy, whose art is the art to love, and who embalm in affection such as are near and dear, and put great, all-embracing arms about the universe of men, lifting up the fallen, refining the low, raising those that are dropped down, and encouraging the sons of men.

O Father, while we bless Thee for the sons of poetry, the children of song, and those great geniuses born for creative art, still more do we bless Thee for the dear fathers and loving mothers, the great philanthropists of the world, who have blessed us with more than music; they make perpetual Thy thought which shall endure when the marble shall perish, and brass exhale as the vapor, unseen and forgotten to the sky.

O Thou, who possessest manifold gifts, we would ask of Thee a double portion of the spirit of love, that while we serve Thee with our hands, while we honor Thee with our mind, while we serve Thee with our conscience, we may serve Thee more nobly still with sweet sacrificing love. May we so love Thee, O Lord, that we may feel Thy perfections in us, Thy truth making us free, Thy law a lamp to our feet, a staff to our hands, and the love which Thou bearest to every mute and every living thing, a great moral inspiration in our souls, bringing down every vain thing which unduly exalts itself, making us of cleaner eyes than to behold with favor iniquity, and setting our affections on things divine.

O Lord, help us to love our brethren everywhere; not those alone who love us with answering touch of joy, but those who evil entreat, and persecute, and defame us. So we may be like Thyself, causing Thy sun to shine on the evil and on the good, and raining Thy rain on the just and on the unjust.

O Father, we ask Thee for that gift all divine which is righteousness, and mercy, and love, in our hearts. May we chastise ourselves for every mean and wicked thing, set our soul in tune to the music of Thine own spheres, and so, hand in hand accordant, journey round the world, blessing without with toilsome hands, and inwardly blessed by the spirit Thou puttest in our souls. Amen.

And here are extracts, privately reported also, from the sermon which he preached on the same day, called " Of the Culture of the Affections :"—

I honour great power of thought, few perhaps more so. I reverence with great esteem a man of genius for art, poetry, science, practical life, with executive power to plan and build, to organize matter or men into forms of use and beauty. When I meet with such an one, spite of me, down go the stiff knees of my veneration. And most spontaneously do I bow to a man of great justice, one of the pillars of righteousness. I know several such, whom the good God has set up here and there in great towns and little, and I take off my hat thereto, with an inward relish of the homage that I pay them, as I shudder a little with delight, as a poetic-minded New-Englander needs must when he first sees a great antique temple of Grecian or Roman art, or when he stands for the first time before the statue of Apollo, which enchants the world, or Olympian Jove,—

" —— which young Phidias wrought,
    Not from a vain and shallow thought,"

or when he stands before this majestic figure, in which one great American artist, cradled in poverty, has incarnated the lofty lineaments of another great artist, also cradled in poverty, who beforehand had builded for himself a monument more lasting than brass, for he had carved out of the unseen air a figure of himself, which will endure when this brass shall have dissolved itself into gases, and escaped into the sky.

I say, when I meet one of these great pillars of justice, I take off my hat, not without a shudder of that awe, wherewith all men must contemplate the great of life, or the great of art. But if I could have one, and only one, of these three gifts, intellectual, moral, or affectional, I would take the latter.

What delights of affection there are! Love is the great idealizer of man's life. There are many such. Beauty is one, in nature and art. There is music, a common and sweet idealizer; and " the magic harp of David soothes the haunted heart of Saul." There is also the plastic art; and these two are great idealizers, fellow-workers with men in the cause of humanity.

There, my friends, stands a new colleague, whom I welcome to the work of philanthrophy and piety. He is ordained as colleague, pastor with myself. It is a great honour, that I, prosy man as I am, stand at the feet of that incarnation alike of music and poetry; and when I am silent, that majestic brow will speak to you; those eyes, turned upward and inward, will disclose to you the vision through his faculty divine; and when my hand writes not, that still will be to you emblematic of higher thoughts than I can set to music in poetry or speech. That, I say, is one great idealizer; there is a dearer, and that is the *love* which his song represents, and which the sculptor's art would fail to portray.

Francis,* deeply loving his kith and kin, and his immediate friends, like-minded men and women, has yet a great, robust, broad-footed heart which travels out beyond individual persons, leaps over the Atlantic Ocean even, and loves men of diverse tongue, other colour, varying religion, distinctive race—loves even the wicked men who persecute him, and casts the garment of self-denying charity on the shoulders of men who hate him the more abundantly that he loves them.

The New Music Hall was opened for the religious services of his parish for the first time on November 21, 1852.

FROM THE JOURNAL.

What shall befall us, I know not, the next eight years; what will befall the country, what the society, what me? Dear God, Thou only knowest!

---

* Here, as often, some living friend is the hint on which he speaks,—Francis Jackson, now departed into the company of his beloved pastor

There was a great audience, which made me feel littler than ever. That is the sad part of looking such a crowd in the face. Whence shall I have bread to feed so many? I am but the lad with five barley loaves and two small fishes. Yet I have confidence in my own preaching.

He immediately drew up a "provisional scheme" of subjects to be treated in sermons, to occupy the time till the end of 1856. That is, he anticipated his subjects for four years, and adhered to the scheme in almost every particular. At the same time he began to collect information under the heads of some subjects which required a basis of facts, as for the "Duties and Dangers of Woman," the "Characteristics of America," the "Physical Condition of Nations," some of which were not preached for three years. Among other sermons, he premeditated one for the first Sunday in March, 1855, the 85th anniversary of the Boston Massacre, "On the Ultimate Triumph of the True and Right," which was delivered according to the programme.

FROM THE JOURNAL.

Aug. 24, 1853.—I am this day forty-three years old. I used to think I should live as long as my fathers; but certain admonitions of late warn me that I am not to be an old man. The last three years have made great alterations in my health and vigor. I write and work more with a will than by the spontaneous impulse which once required the will to check it. I neither grieve nor rejoice at the thought of departure. But I will try to keep my affairs in such a condition, that I can at any time go over the other side when summoned, and leave no perplexity.

Work for the year.
I. Ministerial.
  a. Parish.
  b. The Perishing and Dangerous Classes of Boston.
II. Non-Ministerial.
  a. Lectures.
  b. Article on Seward. Books upon Slavery. Historical Development of Religion; finish Vol. II. by Sept., 1854, if possible, and have it in print.
Work for September.
  I. Letter to the Unitarian Association.
  II. Lectures.
  III. Paper on Seward.

In the great audience, sometimes of 3000 people, which repaired to the Music Hall every Sunday forenoon, there was a small nucleus of devoted friends who constituted a parish, and from whose ranks came all the reliable workers and representatives of the Twenty-eighth Congregational Society. But their parochial action had nothing formal or conventional : they had recourse to none of the usual methods of preserving an ecclesiastical organization. Rites, conference-meetings, prayer-meetings and lectures gave place to practical attempts at applying the human doctrines of their great preacher. The Sunday service was perfectly simple. The desk raised upon one step, with a vase of flowers at the right hand of Mr. Parker, where his fingers might touch and caress them ; the chair in which he sat, just in front of the choir ; — these, and an assembly of beating hearts, such as Boston never saw before, and will hardly soon see again, furnished forth his occasion. No finical upholstery of liturgies, and chantings, and invocations, and responses ; no fine singing, no prim and well-dressed silence; the costliest things were the flowers and the speech : next to the living souls who yearned for truth, the most imposing thing in the house was a Bible, read with natural joy and reverence. The most impressive thing in all Boston on those famous Sundays was the moral sincerity of the preacher's voice, as it deepened from common-sense to religious emotion, or sparkled into indignation that was not for sale, or softened into sympathy and human pleasure at the Beautiful and the Good.

He read the hymn quietly and evenly ; then went forth the breathing of those prayers, still, natural, and simple, but laden with awe, and falling irresistibly into every heart with all the glad weight of his own joyful feeling.

Some words from a very dear friend and parishioner will be found effective to restore those Sundays. They also help us to appreciate his personal and pastoral relation to those families in the great congregation whom he might call his own :—

Those nearest to him feel that the central heart of his life, his dearest and highest function, has been most inadequately appreciated. Others thought of him as the great theologian, the bold reformer, the accomplished scholar ; he thought of himself as the minister of the Twenty-eighth Congregational Society, the shepherd of a flock of earnest souls who looked to him for help, and consolation, and guidance in all their private griefs and difficulties as eagerly as they listened to his deep and bold lessons on all great public questions. Why he has not appeared in this light to the literary world is plain ; his society was not composed of learned and scientific men, but of simple, practical people, whose life is occupied more with action than expression. I hope to be pardoned if I cannot give utterance to my views of the great value and importance of his pastoral relation without personality ; it is this very close personal relation which I wish to prove and illustrate. Even a friend can speak of his Sunday *Lyceum*, where he harangued a promiscuous audience on all themes of thought, science, or politics, but to Mr. Parker it was far otherwise. He knew that every Sunday a crowd of unknown persons were there to hear him, but to him there was always a central group of well-beloved faces, in whose eyes he read all the trials and struggles of the week. There was his "glorious phalanx of old maids, on whose aid he could confidently rely for every work of charity or mercy." There was his St. M——, her face a constant benediction; his beloved John, "who idealized his life after a day of hard toil by providing for the wants of every poor child in his neighbourhood;" there was the faithful clerk, who was, he said, more important to the society than himself; there were the grey heads, so precious in his sight; the young men, in whom he saw the hope of the country and the world; and the young maidens, in whose culture and well-being he ever felt the most paternal care.

Who can forget how he would come into church, and sit there, partially screened from sight by the desk, and look around on the faces of his congregation? Then he gathered up from the multitude all the joys and sorrows of the week—the tear-dimmed eye of the mourner; the earnest struggling of a soul wrestling with temptation; the new joy of happy lovers, or a mother rejoicing in her firstborn child—all sent up their incense to him, and he gathered their fragrance into his heart, and bore it up to God in his prayer. Nor did he fail to bring his own life into the same holy presence. Who has not at times felt some deep sorrow or penitent tenderness of his own private heart veiled in the universal language of his prayer? Those early days of his ministry at the Melodeon can never be forgotten by those favoured to share them. The dark, dingy building, with its dirty walls and close atmosphere, became a holy temple, for it enshrined a living soul. The cold, rainy Sundays which succeeded one another so constantly could not keep us away. "How could we bear the burden of the week," said many a listener, "without the inspiration of that hour of prayer, of that lesson of wisdom and truth?" The constant offering of flowers on the desk was a beautiful emblem of the faith in and love of nature which so characterized his teachings. As spring advanced, we often first saw the dear remembered friends in field and grove on the desk; the violets and barberry-blossoms, the purple rhodora, the sweet wild-rose, the lilies of the valley (now sacred to us from his last look on them), the fragrant magnolia, the stately laurel, the blue gentian, in its autumn loveliness, all came as offerings from one or another friend. Nothing was too precious or too lowly to be laid at that shrine; and as the great teacher gathered lessons of divine wisdom and truth from the lilies of the fields and the grass of the plain, so did he never fail to point some moral or enforce some lesson of love and truth by reference to these beautiful emblems of God's presence and power. How sacred was his feeling in regard to them, a little circumstance will show. Being called to the country to pay the last tribute of love and reverence to a dear friend, he gathered some blue gentians from the little brook which ran before his old home, and the next Sunday he placed them on the desk, and wrote to his absent parishioner how she, too, was not forgotten by pastor or people in their Sabbath prayer.

But we were speaking of those old days at the Melodeon, dear to us as the first little humble home of boyhood, or the first dwelling of a married pair. We could never have quite the same feeling in the ampler space and more elegant arrangements of the Music Hall, but it made no change in the constant ministry of our friend. How many incidents might be told of those early days, when his words were so strange and new to many! "Well, I never heard before that toads were prophets and grass was revelations," an old lady was heard to mutter angrily as she went out of meeting one day. But to him all beings did preach, and all nature did reveal the truths of the religion he believed and taught.

One of Mr. Parker's noblest efforts was his sermon on John Quincy Adams. The house was densely crowded, and all were held in rapt attention by the tribute, full of glowing heat, and yet of manly truth, which he paid to the great departed. As he spoke of the only blots on the fair fame of his hero, the snow, which covered and darkened the roof, fell with a tremendous crash, which sent a thrill through the audience and preacher. Mr. Parker recovered himself instantly and added, " So may the infamy slide off from his character, and leave it fair as open daylight!" As he closed, the wind, from some unknown cause, sounded through the organ pipes a wild, sweet strain, which seemed, to our excited minds, like an amen from the spirit of the brave old man, who accepted the bold and true words which had been spoken of him.

One tribute of honor we can never bring to Mr. Parker—that which a distinguished lawyer paid to his reverenced pastor.* We could never fail to be reminded of the whole week on Sunday; our errors, our shortcomings, our dangers, our blessings, our hopes, trials, and fears, all came up in review before us, and the words which were spoken for all seemed most special to each one. Once, when preaching on the forgiveness of sin, and showing how the infinite love of God had provided means of recovery for the most guilty soul, a man in the gallery suddenly cried out, " Yes, I know it to be so! I feel it to be so!" Mr. Parker paused in his sermon and addressed him in words of strong faith and assurance. "Yes, my friend, it is so; and you cannot wander so far but God can call you back."

The special event of the day of which his congregation were thinking seemed to him the appropriate subject on which to give them words of religious advice, comfort, or warning. Sometimes he waited a week or two for the excitement to subside, that he might speak from and to a calmer mood, but he never left such occasions unimproved. In this he resembled the early Puritans, to whom he had, indeed, much likeness. Who does not remember the strength and wisdom of his words on occasions like those of the trial of Professor Webster, the fugitive slave cases, important elections, and the commercial crisis? He never rested till he had withdrawn these startling facts from the list of exceptional accidents, and shown how they resulted from sufficient causes, and were co-ordinate with the whole providence of the Divine government. He did not suffer us to believe that a man, good

* To the effect, namely, that the pastor in question never made allusions to professional or political iniquity, but only to the glittering generality of sin.

and pure in heart, became suddenly a murderer from the force of an untoward circumstance, but showed us how the yielding to minor temptations had weakened the power of resistance to this fatal one. And yet how tender was his pleading and his trust in God for the poor sufferers! Many of us then, for the first time, realized that God had consolation in store, even for such misery.

When the slave Shadrach was arrested, but released by a spontaneous movement of our citizens, the event occurred on Saturday. We were still anxious on Sunday in regard to his final escape. Mr. Parker preached that day an anniversary sermon—the fifth of his settlement in Boston. At its close he said, "When I came among you I expected to have to do and to bear some hard things, but I never expected to have to protect one of my parishioners from slave-hunters, nor to be asked to read such a note as this:—' Shadrach, a fugitive slave, in peril of his life and liberty, asks your prayers that God will aid him to escape out of bondage.' But," he said, "he does not need our prayers. Thank God! we have heard of him safe, far on his way to freedom." I cannot describe the intense excitement of the audience. For a moment there was perfect silence, and it seemed as if our hearts would burst with the pressure of feeling. Then one spontaneous shout of applause re-echoed through the building, and gave us the relief so much needed.

Here let me say that, while Mr. Parker felt the genuineness of such expression when inevitable and fit, he yet very much disliked the habit of applause in church, and kept it in check by remonstrance whenever a disposition to indulge in it appeared. He was a great lover of decorum and order. He always wore at church the plain dark dress which he thought befitting the service. The Bible and hymn-book were laid in their places—everything was in order before he began to speak. But he loved freedom and individuality also, and he would not suffer them to be sacrificed to his own comfort. How gentle was his remonstrance against the noisy slamming of the forty-four doors of the Music Hall towards the close of the sermon! how patiently he took it for granted that only important engagements led people to such a violation of good manners towards those who held their doors invitingly open to them! He said to us once, "I do not like to see people reading books and newspapers before the services commence. It troubles me very much, and I have often been tempted to ask people to abstain from it; but I remember how precious a half-hour's reading was to me often when I was a young man, and I feel that I ought not to ask anybody to give it up for the sake of my comfort when it is not wrong in itself."

So thoroughly conscientious was Mr. Parker in the performance of the duties of his parish, that he never seemed quite reconciled to having Sunday afternoon for his own use, and not devoting it to some special service in their behalf. In vain they assured him that they neither required nor wished it—that one such sermon as his was quite sufficient for a week's digestion, and that they preferred to spend the afternoon hours with their families or in other ways. He tried various plans—occasionally he would hold meetings for free discussion, but, when held in a public place and open to all, some of the troublesome fleas of conventions were sure to intrude and destroy all quiet and peace. The subject of a Sunday-school often occupied his thoughts, and he made two different attempts to form one. The first effort was to gather in poor and ignorant children from the streets, and teach them reading and the general principles of morality and religion. But the preponderating influence of the Catholic priests over our foreign population, the only class needing this charity, rendered all efforts to keep the children together fruitless. He also attempted a school for the children of the parish. The young men and women professed themselves perfectly ready to assist him in his plans, but generally incredulous of its value or necessity. He took the superintendence of the school himself, always either making some original remarks or reading a story to the children. But a few months' experiment convinced him that the teachers were right, and that this class of children had sufficient direct instruction from other sources. A pleasant incident connected with this school illustrates his considerate thought for others in the most trifling matters. One stormy Sunday, one of the most constant attendants at church and Sunday-school was absent in the morning. The storm was so severe that he announced there would be no school in the afternoon; but feeling that the teacher might come out from a sense of duty to others, though not for her own pleasure, he sent her the following pleasant note: —" The little birdies will be all safely folded under their mothers' wings this afternoon, so you need not wet yours by coming out in the storm."

Another plan for Sunday afternoon was a series of lectures explanatory of the text of the New Testament. In these he gave, in condensed form, the results of all the latest criticism of English and German theologians, as well as his own private interpretation of the text. The information thus given was exceedingly valuable, but the dry and methodical form of a critical analysis did not enchain the attention of a large number of hearers. The attendance was always small, but constant on the part of those most interested; and he did not complete the course proposed, but continued the lectures only a few years. He thus reviewed the Four Gospels, the Acts, and Epistles, but we believe neither Revelations nor the Old Testament.

On Saturday afternoons, for several years, soon after his settlement in the winter of 1847–48, he invited the ladies of his parish to meet at his house for conversation on themes of moral and religious interest. He always considered the culture of women to be of the highest importance, and often said that a body of highly educated women could do more to elevate a community than any other influence. Nothing can exceed the skill and courtesy with which he conducted these meetings. So thoroughly did he put himself in relation with his pupils, for such they might well be considered, that he often seemed to understand the action of their own minds better than they did themselves. He listened with patient attention to the stammering, diffident expression of thought from any earnest mind, and, placing it in the light of his own vast intelligence, reflected it to her and others in grander proportions and clearer beauty than she had imagined. The subject proposed one winter was the formation of a perfect character, and all the helps to it. Another time it was the gradual development of the religious nature in communities and individuals. Another time it was education in its broader sense. Although he allowed free play to fancy and wit in the illustration of all these themes, he never suffered the conversation to be aimless or profitless and without result; but at its close he gathered up the scattered thoughts of the company, and wove them into a concise and full expression. This wonderful power was still more strikingly displayed at Mr. Alcott's. For two or three hours the stream of thought would seem to flow at its own wayward will, without direction or aim. No other member of the company, perhaps, could have reported more than sparkling fancies or pithy, orphic sayings; but Mr. Parker would surprise all by briefly reviewing the whole course of the conversation, placing the remarks of each speaker in their proper relation to those of all the rest, and giving them the pleasing consciousness of having said far wiser and profounder things than they had dreamed of. Little record of these genial and profitable occasions can be made. Surrounded by loving friends and disciples, he could here forget something of the stern battle in which he was forced to mingle, and the whole sweetness and warmth of his nature had free play. We remember once, in speaking of the life of Jesus, the stress which he laid on the mental isolation in which he was forced to live. Although the multitude followed him, not one seems even to have attained to a full understanding of the grandeur and loftiness of his idea. We cannot estimate, he said, what he would have accomplished surrounded by those who could fully receive his mission and work with him. Once he said, "It is the greatest of all blessings to a man to meet his superior."

Speaking of sex in souls, a lady quoted Coleridge's famous remark, that "the man who does not recognise sex in souls has never known what it is truly to love a mother, a wife, or even a sister." "Yes; I remember that passage well," said Mr. Parker. "I had a profound reverence for Mr. Coleridge, and felt very badly to fall under his anathema, but I never could recognise any sex in souls." The class were often pleased to see the strain of thought which was called forth at conversation reappear in the service on Sunday. Nothing was ever buried in his mind; all was planted seed, and sure to come up in fresh life and beauty.

His valuable library, now so wisely placed at the service of the citizens of Boston, was always freely open to the use of his parish, as of all other friends; and the book was always selected for the young borrower with discriminating care, and with words of criticism, or recommendation, which added wonderful interest to the perusal. Yet, I think, he lost much fewer books than most who lend them; for they were evidently so dear to him, yet so freely loaned, that the most careless did not like to neglect the trust. It did annoy him to have a book kept a long time, and returned *unread*; but while it was faithfully used he was quite willing to spare it.

While he thus cared for the spiritual and intellectual wants of his parish, he did not forget their claims in suffering and trial; no, not even when the greatest public excitement demanded his strength and energy. I chanced to be seriously though not dangerously ill at the very time when the slave-hunters were in Boston, in pursuit of William and Ellen Crafts, whom he sheltered and protected in his own home. Although obliged to arm his household, and to watch the door

E E 2

narrowly against a cunning enemy, and taking part in all the exciting discussions, and active exertions of that period, he yet came in person, almost daily, to inquire after his sick parishioner; and soon as he saw the hunted fugitives safely afloat on the free Atlantic, he turned his steps to my sick room, where for the first time I was able to see him. What an atmosphere of health, and strength, and life he brought thither! So was it with all who needed him; he never forgot individual claims, any more than public duties. His power of consolation was great, and never-failing. It is not time, nor occupation, nor forgetfulness, which can console us for a real sorrow. It is only that time and a healthy re-action puts the grief in its right place, enables us to see the great eternal truths which a passing cloud obscured, shows the wise Providence ordering all things well, when all seemed ill to us. Of this, which we must often slowly and painfully learn, his ever-living, ever-acting faith, helped us to consciousness at once. Tender and sympathetic as a mother, he was yet wise and strong, and demanded life and right action from others. Did life seem valueless, because the one who blessed it was gone, he made us feel that all life is one; that this life and eternity are close together, and that we work with those who have passed beyond the veil as truly as if they are here. Trusting wholly in a perfect God, how could he doubt his perfect providence? "No man ever dies when it is a misfortune to him," he often said. His scheme of the universe admitted of no accident; an immanent God must order all things well. He usually prefaced his remarks at a funeral by a statement of the cardinal doctrines of his faith, the two great truths of religion dear to every human heart, and sufficient to sustain it in all trials—the loving fatherhood of the perfect God, and the immortality of the human soul. Often, when some peculiar circumstances in the life or death of the departed one seemed to render all attempt at consolation but mockery, his clear and full enunciation of these truths, and the beautiful application of them to special circumstances, which he never failed to make, seemed to take the sting from death and the victory from the grave.

Not less impressive and beautiful was his performance of the marriage service; always a solemn and touching sight to him. His appreciation of the mysterious holiness and blessedness of the conjugal union and of the joys of the family relation, was so great that his parishioners sometimes complained that he never gave thanks for anything else; and his single friends petitioned that their joys, however inferior, might sometimes be remembered. Yet, perhaps, no one has ever done higher justice to the maiden aunt. Speaking of the struggles of earnest young men to gain education and a wider sphere of life, "it is the maiden aunt often," he says, "who, when father and mother forsake him, like the Lord, has taken him up."

Oh, how little can we tell of what he was to us in his fifteen years' ministry; of what a pillar was taken from us when he was gone! His place standeth desolate, and none cometh to fill it. Days of peril seem before us; where is the warning voice which ever prophesied the storm afar off, but ever spoke words of courage and hope when it was nigh? All the changes and chances of life are yet ours; where is the steady arm on which to lean, the heart to cheer us?

It remains for us, his disciples, his parishioners, to take up his work and carry it on ; not as he could, with the wonderful genius and power which were his alone, but with the same devotion, the same independence, the same unselfish labor for others. When one of his parishioners thanked him for all he had been to him in years past, " I will be more to you hereafter," he said, " than ever before." Few months were given him to redeem that promise by deeds of earthly love and kindness, but will it not surely be fulfilled in the influence of his life and teachings, on, not one, but all who sat at his feet? How little it seemed to him that he had reaped of the vast field of labour, which had opened before him! Let not those who must follow him with slow and patient gleaning, faint because they are few and feeble. Fewer and seemingly more feeble were the hands to which the dying Galilean trusted his truths, but Paul planted, and Apollos watered, and God gave the increase.

In looking back over the fifteen years of Mr. Parker's pastoral life in Boston, we are astonished at its richness and importance, when we remember also his great labors in other connections and other spheres. Great as he was in the pulpit, many a one felt he was more to them in private. We can see no failure, no want in the relation. He was the friend when a friend was needed ; he spoke rebuke, or encouragement, or consolation, or counsel as it was needed ; and, alas ! he did not remit his labors, even when continued at a risk of his precious life. " How can I refuse to go ?" he said, when sent for to attend a funeral while very unwell ; and he went, in spite of all entreaty. The last precious hours of strength were all exhausted on Sunday ; when too feeble even to take his meals with the family, he went out to the desk, and spoke with all his whole fervor, though the husky voice betrayed the fearful cost at which we bought the hour. And yet we can hardly mourn or complain at this excessive labour, although its penalty was early death. What generous heart can remember to be always prudent, when the claims are so pressing, and no other hand is ready to work ? He is the faithful shepherd who giveth his life for the sheep.

Here are fragments of sermons, not hitherto printed, which were gathered up from Sunday to Sunday. They are not his best, but still characteristic of him, both by subject and treatment :—

Of the Education of the Religious Faculties. *Preached March 9, 1856.*—How great is the power of education in the soul of man, and how strongly is he influenced by the circumstances in which he is placed ! The cradle is the place whereon we stand to move the world, and education is the Archimedes for that universal lift. Take a single example. Look at the history of the Warren Street Chapel in this town, for the last five-and-twenty years. A quarter of a century ago, perhaps less, some wise men made a sacrifice, and by sweet self-denial they built up a little conservatory, wherein they might take and shelter the precious plants which they found in the mire of the streets. How many hundreds, how many thousands, are now honorable, noble, heavenly-minded men and women, simply because they were transferred from the cold, bleak atmosphere of the street, where temptation lay in wait to destroy them, and were set in this green-house of souls, and blossomed into fragrant flowers !

OF THE DANGERS AND DUTIES OF YOUNG WOMEN. *Preached Jan.* 18, 1857.—Oh, young woman, cultivate your mind, shun frivolous reading, poor, weak, silly books, sentimental books.   Read for knowledge some hard book which demands attention, memory, thought; master one good book, no matter what—geography, arithmetic, astronomy, history, what you will; but study it, and know it well, understand one thing certainly.   Read, also, for beauty, what feeds the imagination, fills it with handsome shapes, and wakens noble thoughts.   There are poets, our own or those abroad, who can do this ; some of the present generation, some long passed by.   Read, also, for the reason—something that gives you general laws, universal views.   Read for inspiration ; you may be poor, and have little time, or rich, and have much, still, there is one humanity and one womanhood in the idle and the active, in the rich and the poor, and the same noble book will speak to each and to all ; and so is America favoured and blessed that the poorest, the activest, can find the book and the time also to read it, if she will.

Next, reverence your own moral instincts ; ask your conscience, *Is it right ?* as well as your heart, *Is it kind ?*   Man is more likely to go astray through self-love, you through the opposite path.   Keep your individuality sacred ; surrender that not to priest, nor husband, nor father, nor mother, nor lover, nor child.   Look to your own moral sense for approbation, not to man nor to woman ; but,—

> " As that pronounces lastly on each deed,
> Of so much praise in heaven expect your meed."

Be faithful to yourself !   Are you single ? " Come into port greatly, or sail the seas alone with God."   Are you wedded ? it will be a part of woman's domestic function to " soothe, and heal, and bless "—aye, she will often be called upon to soothe where she cannot heal, and where she is not suffered to bless ; and the self-denial for the sake of soothing will heal others and bless you, when neither you nor they asked for such result.

Cultivate the religious faculty ; develope the instinctive religious feelings; have reverence for God, not the God of Calvinism—I cannot ask any one to reverence that—but the dear God who made the heavens and the earth, who speaks in your heart, uttering parable, prophecy, and beatitude.   Develope a great piety in yourself, and let this be the central fire to warm, still further, your human affection, spreading it from mother, father, husband, child, clear round to neighbourhood, kinsfolk, all the world.   Let it light your conscience, and give you a general moral rule whereby to find your path.   Let it beautify your intellect, and stimulate your understanding, imagination, reason.   Let it correct that poor temptation to frivolity, peevishness, vanity, discontent.

Remember that all the little every-day duties of woman's life are just as much means to help you as the rougher discipline of man is to aid him in his course.   The little cares, sorrows, and joys, the vexations of the household lot, the perplexities of those careful and troubled about many things, these are the elements to help form the noble woman; only she must have a noble ideal, a noble will. So the artist takes the little chips of many-coloured stone and constructs his grand mosaic of creative skill, a queen, a Madonna, an angel, and the dead stone becomes a living oracle, a moral prophecy of nobleness to come. Grandeur of character is not easy to young women or men; God be thanked, it is possible to both! and one noble woman, she is parent of many more; in her spiritual image and likeness she shall create women and men to the end of time; aye, people eternity with noble souls, beautiful in their life, and welcome unto God!

OF GRATITUDE AND INGRATITUDE. *Preached March* 8, 1857.— There is to be a *future* of the benevolent emotions, when what is prophecy to-day, instinct in your heart and mine, shall become fact and institutions through all the land. Now, in the walled garden a single handful of snowdrops comes out of the ground and looks up and welcomes the sweet sunshine of March. Everywhere else the ground is dry and frozen, and the trees are leafless and bare. These are a prophecy as well as a beauty, and ere long the snow has run off from all the hills, the frost has come out of the ground, the trees shake down their odorous flowers, the spring is everywhere, summer is coming, and the harvest is not far away.

OF THE ULTIMATE PURPOSE OF HUMAN LIFE FOR THE INDIVIDUAL AND THE RACE. *Preached Sept.* 13, 1857.—Now, the power of moral good in the world is destined to overcome the power of evil. I mean, the constant tendency towards the right, the just, and the true on the part of man, will overcome all the general evil attendant on the experience of human life. God has so created the nature of men that instinctively they long for the triumph of good, pray for it, and presently will, with reflection, devise means, and put their shoulders to the wheel, and so work in conformity with their internal desire, and bring that result to pass. This triumph of good is just as certain as the infinite perfection of God's character. Sure of Him, you are sure that everywhere good will triumph over evil, truth over falsehood, justice over wrong, love over hate, and holiness over all uncleanness, for God's nature is endorsed as security, and lodged as collateral, for the fulfilment of every holy desire that enters into the heart of man.

This triumph of good is for the individual, and for each individual. It comes partly here, for the individual's course begins here; it comes partly hereafter, for that course ends unseen above. There is no man to whom existence on the whole will not be ultimately a blessing, a triumph of those faculties which lead to good, over such as contingently tend to evil. There is no earthly life that can be altogether a failure, wholly a misfortune. You shall take the worst woman in Boston, foul and loathsome with long-continued wickedness, yet, before her there is a future development in all the grand virtues of humanity. You and I in our weakness cannot but loathe her; we treat her as the world's vermin. Not so the infinite God, who will never shirk His responsibility. In this poor wretch, likewise, lies the power of good, for she, too, is human; and though they sleep, they are not dead, and the Father and Mother of the universe has so arranged the world of here and hereafter, that some event or some person shall come to her as a saviour, take her by the hand, and say to her, " I say unto thee, arise; take up thy bed and walk !" and the humanity of the wretch shall cast off its filthy garments, and stand on its feet clean and erect. I feel sure that her life here, howsoever mean and abominable it may be, is no complete failure; it is a step towards triumph, a step which she might not have done without.

Look at this fact: in the world of matter no atom is lost, in all the busy changes thereof, of growth and dissolution. No straw, no particle of dust ever flies off from the world's swift wheels. In all that world of starry motion yonder, there is not a movement in vain ; all is planned before-hand, and made subject to the scheme of the universe, in the vast designs of God, which hover over it, and penetrate it through. This being so — so much care taken of man's material house—do you believe that God, who made it for man's abode, will take less care of you and me, will save the cradle and spill the baby out ? When that material universe is so wisely planned, do you think He will allow a whole human life to be a failure, even that of the wickedest of wicked women ?

There are men whose early lives have been spent in the meanest, humblest, and most loathsome toil, who yet rise to great eminence of wealth and station, and, though they crept into social life through the lowest hole, yet go proudly out through its golden gate. So, I doubt not that from the gaol, the brothel, the gallows—from the murderer's den, from the kidnapper's office, from the hypocrite's pulpit, by many a long and winding slope, the soul shall go up into God's highest heaven; for though human charity fail, there is One whose love knows no beginning and no end. Oh, infinite Father and Mother, it is Thou !

Suffering is a merciful angel here, which scourges us to virtue. You and I are thankful for many a stripe in kindness laid on us. Our Father provides the best teachers, and is sure to give us the best education. In what men call hell, Swedenborg tells us, the murderer writhes in his dream of murder, and the covetous in his dream of covetousness. Be sure that the suffering which is before us is only the sinner's porch into heaven—a means to an end.

This triumph is for the race, and of course a great part of it must take place here. The life of individuals is short, that of humanity knows no end. There are fluctuations of people and nations—Ægypt, Judæa, Chaldæa, Syria, were and are not; but though the populous waves rise and fall, the ocean of humanity continues steadfast, and on that great deep the spirit of God moves continually, bringing light out of darkness, changing chaos into creation. As you look on the sum of human history, and on the present condition of men, and see the amount of wickedness in the world, you cannot fail to ask if mankind could not have been created on a little higher plane, with less animal grossness and ferocity, and so human history be not so writ in blood. But presently you remember it is the work of the infinite Creator and Providence, who from His very nature could only do the best of possible things, and you recall the thought, and you content yourself with human nature as He gave it, looking with joy at the signs of past growth and future prosperity, justice, and humanity, and you toil for the progress of mankind, with earnest efforts which you know shall not fail. This triumph of the individual and the race is part of the divine plan and divine providence of God, which underlies all human affairs, which directs Columbus, Franklin, Moses, Jesus, Paul, you and me, to ends we know not of. But it will be brought about also partly by human consciousness, looking before and after, and working for a definite purpose of good. It is the destination of mankind on earth to develope the higher powers, and in such sort that the moral and religious faculties shall control and guide all the rest; then shall the power of evil prove only an instrument of good. You and I, in our short life, are here to achieve this triumph, and mankind collectively in its immense duration; you and I with conscious individualism. This is our work.

My life is valuable to me just as I use my talents and opportunities for the development of my highest faculties, and no more. Simply to have large talents shall avail me nothing; to have small shall be no hindrance. As growth in the highest human qualities is the purpose of life, and all lines providentially converge to this central point, so the question to be asked of each man's life is, " How faithfully have you used your talents and opportunities?" not " How great was your gift?" Money is the pecuniary end of business, office of ambition, knowledge and power the aim of study, and the delight of self or the tickling of others' eyes is the aim of many a beautiful dress or other ornament; but while these are ends to individuals, as traders, office-seekers, scholars, and fops, to them as men and women they are only means and helps to manhood and womanhood—no more. If she will, the young woman's showy dress may be worth as much to her as John Rogers' garment of faggots was to him; if she will not, it is worth to her less than the leafy girdle of a savage woman at Nootka Sound.

I deny not the local, temporary value of ornament, of knowledge, power, and fame, but, after all, their chief value is moral. That is not the best business which gives the most money, nor the best policy which affords the highest office, nor the best school which teaches you the most knowledge; but that which affords the highest development for your highest faculty is the best business, policy, or school. He is the most fortunate who hives up the most character of the noblest kind. If he does it in the sunshine of honor or riches, well; if in the dark, nocturnal storm of disgrace and ruin, still well; it is the hive of sweet character that is the end, not the toil by day or night. By this test we must try fortune and misfortune, forms of government and religion, and ask what men and women they bring forth and rear up. That is not the best farm which gives us the best cotton and sugar, not the best manufactory which best weaves the one into muslin, or changes the other best and cheapest into candy; but that is the best farm or manufactory that raises us the noblest men and women. In the vast variety of human occupations, from that of the naked hunter of New Holland to the astronomer of Cambridge, in the vast variety of human fortunes, God has provided the best circumstances He knew how to provide for the training up of His children. If we use them ill, there comes smart, and harm, and loss, and inward woe, which scourge the nation or the man. If we use them well, then eye hath not seen, nor ear heard, nor the heart of man conceived the magnificent welfare and the grand progress which there is before the individual, the nation, the race ; and that infinite Father and Mother who broods over the world, who breathed it from his love, and warms it with that same breath, has so tempered human nature and human circumstances, that at last this result shall be brought about for the whole of mankind, for each nation, for each individual, howsoever wicked.   Smarting in that wickedness, there is heaven over us, and God leading us !

OF THE PRACTICAL CONSEQUENCE OF THE IDEA OF GOD AS INFINITE PERFECTION. *Preached June* 13, 1858.—A thousand years ago, your and my Saxon fathers, living in mean hovels, for their favorite sport had mimic battles, wherein with quarter-staves, or spears, or swords, men laid at each other in their savage joy, and were often hurt and sometimes slain.   Looking on that howling wilderness of amusement, who could have foreseen the time when, in another land, peopled by other Saxons, in Boston, two thousand Christian men and women should come together in a theatre, paying large prices, to see a great scene of ambitious human life, done into magnificent language by an old English Saxon poet, the chiefest of his tribe, and that grand poetry enacted into a great drama by a New England Saxon woman,* who transfigured his thought to life, teaching how the justice of God comes and torments the murderer, and her who excited the murder, walking in such ghastly sleep ?   Who, a thousand years ago, in the rough sports of our Saxon fathers, could have imagined a Boston audience, thrilled with æsthetic and religious delight at seeing " Macbeth " fitly enacted by fitting men and women ?

OF THE POWER OF HUMAN WILL OVER OR UNDER ADVERSE CIRCUMSTANCES. *Preached October* 8, 1854.—Here is a woman who sits spell-bound in her chair. Her feet are fettered by disease, which long ago froze every joint and limb : her arms are bound by the malady, and *embrace* and *caress* are figures of speech, no facts, to her. A foreign hand must feed her mouth, or wipe a tear away. But how large a soul is perched upon that spray, and in that sickly nest finds room to rear a family of virtues large enough to people a whole kingdom with innocence, faith, and wisdom, and love !†

OF THE IMMEDIATE AND ULTIMATE CONSEQUENCES, TO THE INDIVIDUAL AND TO MANKIND, OF THE PERFORMANCE OF DUTY AND THE CLAIM OF RIGHT. *Preached December* 23, 1855. — Here is a woman in Massachusetts who has travelled all over the North, labouring for woman's cause. She bore the burden in the heat of the day ; she was an outcast from society ; other women hated, and men insulted her, when defended only by her own nobleness and virtue. Every vulgar editor threw a stone at her, picked out of the mud. Many a minister laid sore stripes on her with the epistolary whip of Hebrew Paul. The noble woman bore it with no complaint, only now and then in private

* This was Miss Cushman.

† This is another picture drawn from the life, and recognizable by all who need to know it.

the great heart of Abby Kelly filled her eyes with tears; but she never allowed tears to blind her eyes, nor quench the light shedding its radiance along a steep and barricaded path. But when the cause of woman had won something of respectability, and a great convention of women and their friends was summoned in the heart of this common-wealth, they who controlled the matter thought it would not do for their stoutest champion to sit on the platform; she must sit beneath the platform, lest it hurt the cause and peril the rights of woman, to have woman's champion sit in woman's honored place.

His method, already mentioned, of blocking out his time was habitual. Generally whatever was projected was duly performed within the assigned limits. But soon after his coming to Boston, the calls upon him for public and social service of every descrip-tion accumulated in a way that seriously disturbed all his favorite plans of study and composition.

FROM THE JOURNAL.

Sept. 1, 1853.—My vacation is now at an end. I had some knots I wanted to untie, so I went to Nahant to get the sea to help me, not without profit, I hope.

Notice the profusion of life in the sea. Homer calls it barren and boundless, ἀτρυγέτοια καὶ ἀπεῖρα. But how full it is of life! It is lined with green and purple plants, which cover snails, muscles, barnacles, and certain *echini*, and insects innumerable; then there are the fish of countless number, of immense variety. This strikes me more and more, the more I get acquainted with the sea.

Notice the little pools of water in the rocks, the sides and bottom lined with little shell-fish, who live secure in the clear tranquillity, and know nothing of the tide which scours the coasts. But when the ocean is chafed by the storms, and licks out its tongue against the rocks, how all these vanish, and the insects fail!

Sept. 4, 1853, Sunday.—How delightful it is to begin preaching again! It was so pleasant to see the dear old familiar faces, and to read again to those persons the hymns and psalms which I have read them so often, to pray with them also, and feel that many a soul prayed with me. I preached of the nobleness of man's nature.

Sept. 6.—This day my new book appeared, "Sermons of Theism, Atheism, and the Popular Theology." It seems to me so poor and dull now I look it over, to find the printer's mistakes, that I hate to touch it. I was too ill to work well when it went through the press, hence, doubtless, many an error. Well, I meant well, if I have not done so. I wish there was no *fighting* to be done, but, alas! *non veni pacem mittere sed gladium* must be said by every man who would make the world better.

In a few weeks is the following, without a date :—

I have been very dull all this week past, all this, and the last month. The journey did me little good, the old difficulty in my head (or stomach) troubles me ; I know not why, I feel ashamed to be ill, as if I had wrecked an estate. As I lie awake in the night, I feel as if I had done nothing. My idea shames me. I must *be more* and so do more. I have never had either a friend who continually stirred me to nobler activity by *words,* nor a rival who did it by his own *action.* I wish I had both.

Here are some rough notes upon spiritualism, meant for use in sermons :—

SPIRITUALISM.—In 1856, it seems more likely that spiritualism would would become the religion of America than in 156 that Christianity would be the religion of the Roman Empire, or in 756 that Mohammedanism would be that of the Arabian populations.

1. It has more *evidence for its wonders* than any historic form of religion, hitherto.

2. It is *thoroughly democratic,* with no hierarchy ; but inspiration is open to all.

3. It is no *fixed fact,* has no *punctum stans,* but is a *punctum fluens;* not a finality, but opens a great vista for the future. Its present condition is no finality.

4. It admits all the truths of religion and morality in all the world-sects.

SPIRITS.—1. Man's spirit more interesting than his body to him. Thence, stories of miracles are more interesting than science, for they presume an effect of mind over matter by direct action ; and ghost-stories are more interesting than history.

2. Scholars in America neglect spiritual and turn to material nature. Metaphysics have gone to physics, ethics to political economy, theology to politics.

3. Ministers keep up the old metaphysics and superstitions of spirit, but it is restricted in Protestant countries to the old Bible times, their ghosts, miracles, inspiration, speaking with tongues, &c., but not to our new ones.

4. Life is intensely practical—all work, little account of imagination and fancy, little sport; money-making and dress—no games, no *Volks-lieder* (people's songs), &c. So,

5. The mass of the people take up a popular spiritual metaphysics ; it feeds spiritually, and pacifies the hunger for the marvellous.

But the dangers are,—

1. Those which befall the sincere believers; moral and bodily derangement.

2. Of insincerity itself. .

3. Of a reaction from all this; libertinism, &c.

And the good is,—

1. Appeals to the immaterial against the material.

2. Destroys the prestige of old things.
3. Removes doubts of spiritual life in some men.

May 18, 1855.—Lectured on slavery, at Wilmington, Del., the first time in a slave state. My theme was, "The Relation of Slavery to the Democratic Institutions of America." Received with much applause, and a vote of thanks at the close.

May 19.—Preached a sermon at the opening of the Meeting House of Progressive Friends, Longwood, Chester County, Pennsylvania, "Relation between the Ecclesiastical Institutions and the Religious Consciousness of the American People." It is fourteen years, to-day, since I preached at the ordination of Mr. Shackford, at South Boston. Since that I have taken no part in church festivals, having no invitation.

20.—Preached again, "Of the Blessedness of True Piety."

And he gave three lectures on the three succeeding days.

In 1858 he again attended the meeting of the Progressive Friends, and delivered four sermons : "The Biblical Conception of God ; " "The Ecclesiastical Conception of God ;" "The Philosophical Idea of God ; " "The Soul's Normal Delight in the Infinite God." These are strong and lofty discourses ; they contain his most unsparing criticism of the popular ideas of God, expressed occasionally in phrases that do not shrink from the plain odiousness of ecclesiastical doctrines, as he saw them all bare and mischievous. For his object was not to show how human nature often proves too much for its beliefs, clothes them in its sentiments, and mitigates their influence with instinctive tenderness, but to show, for human nature's sake, the more important fact, how the beliefs devastate it and continually make war upon its excellence. Sturdy language and an unwincing pen are needed for that operation. Any rhetorician can perform the other useless task.

In no sermons can the essentially *constructive* nature of Mr. Parker's work be more distinctly seen. The criticisms of doctrine are burly workmen clearing the field of its rubbish, that Piety may serenely raise her dwelling there. All the work tends to growth ; it is undertaken in the dearest interests of the soul, and with a motive which the soul's highest faculties alone can worthily represent, to make the law of the spirit supreme in man and in society, to compel the imperfect conception to yield to the perfecting idea, that man may be saved from the license of igno. rance by the freedom of purity and health. Did he undermine venerable doctrines and sentiments ? Of course he did ; and as they sink into a little heap, which just marks the circuit of their former proudness, the glad soul steps over it into the great labors and glories of a world. It is plain that God has this work done for His children as often as it is needed, and when the time comes He does not send a boy upon a man's errand.

The four sermons glow with positive ideas and feelings—with definite religious faith. That makes them so tenacious and intolerant. If he did not see the beauty of holiness so clearly, he could not be so indignant with the sin of ugliness in low conceptions of the infinite God. The fault with Mr. Parker always was that he saw too much, and undertook to tell it. Only two other ways are possible—to see nothing, or to say nothing: and neither of these was his misfortune.

FROM THE JOURNAL.

March 23, 1856.—I find I need more time for my own daily religious meditation, for contemplative internal life. Once I had much, now little. The intense busyness of my late years is not favorable to certain religious joys I once had time for, and still have inclination towards and longing after. So a little more time shall be daily given thereunto.

Aug. 16. Saturday Night.—It is now the third week of my annual vacation. I have been rejoicing in quiet, in idleness, and doing just as I have a mind to. I have read a good deal in Vogt's works, also in works of art, and translated divers little gems, which are in the leaves before this.

But when Saturday night comes, I feel a little uneasiness; solemn emotions of awe, and reverence, and delight, spring to consciousness. I don't feel quiet, but wish I was to preach to-morrow; and on Sunday night I feel a little dissatisfied that I have not preached.

Sept. 9.—To-day, I received from Messrs. Voigt and Günther, booksellers, of Leipsic, B. II., of Parker's *Sämmtliche Werke*, which makes four in all, accompanied with a collection of notices of me and mine, which are mostly quite friendly—more so, indeed, than the books entirely deserve. One, quite pleasing, was a hearty appreciation of the earnest religiousness of the writer. Faults I must have committed, and that in no small number, but I am glad to find that the motive is set down as human and religious.

His activity was very great just after he began to preach in the Music Hall. To the year 1852 belong the "Ten Sermons of Religion," the "Discourse on Daniel Webster," a sermon on leaving the Melodeon, and one, "The Function of a Minister," on entering the Music Hall. He also preached consecutively the six sermons, perhaps his most elaborate ones, upon atheism, the popular theology, and theism.   These, with four more, make the volume entitled " Sermons of Theism:" to this he prefixed an historical introduction, which is a good popular exposition of the development of Christian Churches and nations, and of the religious needs of mankind.   Nothing can be better than all the statements in these sermons, of the different kinds of atheism, the errors of the popular theology, and its past services, of providence, of evil, of the economy of pain.   They are simple and racy, marred by no difficult terms, full of proverbial sentences.

Everything is addressed with warmth and sincerity to the simplest comprehension.   Broad facts are displayed without subtlety ; all the essential points and movements of religious history are given without any compromises to rhetoric or popular predilections.   There never was a more thorough, yet more religious, attempt to emancipate the common mind from the vices of traditional belief.   No wonder such unadorned consciousness of theological absurdities became odious to the strong believers of every creed, who accused him of loose statements and immoral misrepresentation ; of a vague spite against doctrines which he feared to examine, but which in reality he saw uncolored and unclad.   A different estimate must some day be made of these great popular utterances of a pious and sensible spirit.   The sermons silently do their work among the people, flowing into the minds that are the most accessible by birth or culture to their approaches, and thence making their fertilizing way.   Bigots will resist in vain an influence which they style insidious, but which shares the silence and the breadth of every elementary force. The Music Hall is empty!   Men will look in vain for his parish ; it waits in Europe and America upon his printed speech, which addresses, with a rare comprehension of the general intelligence, and in a style born to emancipate the longing of all men for simple religion, and charity, and good works.   Delegations of this great parish of mankind sits even in churches the most traditional, listening through the open windows to the sweet voices of the natural world, while the preacher, perhaps himself also listening, vaguely, with half an ear, hums the prescriptive texts, and spins with the old assiduity his doctrinal snares.

It is not easy at once to gauge the precise nature and limits of a man's influence, who has sounded the world's popular systems with the plummet of learning, held by a humane and vigorous hand, and whose primitive sentiments look from above through a broad, pellucid understanding, in which, as in a dry light, things appear to him as they are. He has not the beneficence of a great organizer of thought, or of imagination ; he displays no special knacks of metaphysics, and does not make progress by mining and boring ; the long roll of the orator does not call men together for a day's muster. His excellence was not merely in the exposition of some preliminary processes of mind. No processes appear, but instead of them, light and warmth, broad elements of hope, and humanity, and faith.

FROM THE JOURNAL.

Oct. 5, 1858.—The Music Hall opened three weeks ago, and has been filled with quite large congregations. Our course of lectures begins to-morrow. Mr. Sanborn gives the introductory poem.

The course of lectures was that known as the Fraternity Course, which was put forth by a parochial organization of the Twenty-Eighth Congregational Society, established for charitable and philanthropic purposes. It was very active, and did a great deal of good in a quiet way. The character of the lectures reflected the free, progressive character of the Society. Men and women were invited to speak who had something to say upon all the great humane subjects of the day, to which the ordinary lyceums in cities seldom tolerate any direct allusion. In the country and the small towns, the real questions of society fare better, and the stock subjects of lecturers are heard with indifference. It is plain that Mr. Parker could not lecture before any of the associations in Boston which annually blossom into a course. His words were welcomed by great audiences, from the Penobscot to the Mississippi. But the east wind blew in Boston at the mention of his name.

After the establishment of the Fraternity Course, he had an opportunity to lecture, which he occasionally improved. We owe to it the admirable Biography of Franklin, which he first preached in a fragmentary form as a sermon, and then presented as a lecture. It was a favorite subject ; he loved to trace the lives of strong men who grew in an American fashion. This lecture he elaborated with great care, and wrote it three times over ; once, however, in consequence of losing the manuscript on his return from delivering it in South Boston.

There was not a religious society in Boston at the time of Mr.

Parker's last illness that wielded so great a practical and charitable power as the Fraternity of the Music Hall. Its earnest young men and women took the life of Mr. Parker's great heart as he poured it into them, and carried it out through Boston streets, to put it to the lips of the fugitive and the miserable. Is not that a sacrament for a Church to blossom into, better than a conventional communion? The bread and wine, and the Christian fraternity, went out for those who needed them. These true disciples did two things—they showed their faith by their works, and they showed how faith could flourish without rites and observances.

The bronze statue of the man whose greatest symphony broke forth into a song of joy for earth's millions, looked over the preacher, steadfast as bronze himself, while the warm heart beat and flowed. An earth must be rugged and solid to contain its own broad tides. The preacher and the composer were kindred in sorrows and in moral quality, in love and in scorn; they built faith upon the essential harmonies of the great world of nature and of man, and bade the tumultuous passages of life resolve themselves, with all their low, presageful thunder, into the triumphant security which only the man who has kept himself like a little child can feel.

In this world there is no end of fine coincidences where things themselves are fine. The great German stands mutely in the hall of the great American, while he preaches a universal doctrine.

" In the mighty realm of music there is but a single speech," and that is the speech of all hearts who yearn for the harmonies of God; deep religious awe, tender dependence, flashing, sarcastic sincerity, fiery indignation, pure humanity, love that melts all races, like kindred drops, into one heart, even that heart which the Father, through all diversities, is striving to create.

Some people say they are not indebted to Mr. Parker for a single thought. The word "thought" is so loosely used, that a definition of terms must precede our estimate of Mr. Parker's suggestiveness and originality. Men who are kept by a commonplace-book go about raking everywhere for glittering scraps, which they carry home to be sorted in their æsthetic junk-shop. Any portable bit that strikes the fancy is a thought. There are literary rag-pickers of every degree of ability; and a great deal of judgment can be shown in finding the scrap or nail you want in a heap of rubbish. Quotable matter is generally considered to be strongly veined with thought. Some people estimate a writer according to the number of apt sentences embedded in his work. But who is judge of aptness itself? What is apt for an epigram is not apt for a revolution: the shock of a witty antithesis is related to the healthy stimulus of creative thinking, as a small electrical battery is to the terrestrial currents. Well-built rhetorical climaxes, sharp and sudden contrasts, Poor Richard's common-sense, a page boiled down to a sentence, a fresh simile from nature, a subtle mood projected upon nature, a swift controversial retort, all these things are called thoughts; the pleasure in them is so great, that one fancies they leave him in their debt. That depends upon one's standard of indebtedness. Now a penny-a-liner is indebted to a single phrase which furnishes his column; a clergyman near Saturday night seizes with rapture the clue of a fine simile which spins into a "beautiful sermon;" for the material of his verses a rhymester is "indebted" to an anecdote or incident. In a higher degree all kinds of literary work are indebted to that commerce of ideas between the minds of all nations, which fit up interiors more comfortably, and upholster them better than before. And everything that gets into circulation is called a thought, be it a discovery in science, a mechanical invention, the statement of a natural law, comparative statistics, rules of economy, diplomatic circulars, and fine magazine writing. It is the manœuvring of the different arms in the great service of humanity, solid or dashing, on a field already gained. But the thought which organizes the fresh advance goes with the pioneer train that bridges streams, that mines the hill, that feeds the country. The controlling plan puts itself forth with that swarthy set of leather-aproned men, shouldering picks and axes. How brilliantly the uniforms defile afterward, with flashing points and rythmic swing, over the fresh causeway, to hold and maintain a position whose value was ideally conceived. So that the brightest facings do not cover the boldest thought.

We are only really indebted to that thought which premeditates and selects the great points for a moving world, and that is always a combination of insight, temperament, and will. The whole man is the thought to which we are indebted. His sentences are not smart traps into which he steps to be held while you look at him. You cannot bag your game in that way, and stock your larder. Probably your whole house would not hold him. In that case, his is not the thought to which you care to be indebted. You will go hunting for other marsh birds, who live by suction, plunging their bills, sensitive to fare, in every pool.

Certainly the exigencies of a commonplace-book are not the measure of originality. And as no single thought in any form can be pronounced new, so all thinking which is full of the blood of old thoughts, and beating with nature's primitive pulse, is original. It may be quotable besides; but its originality is movement, direction, sincerity, and power. It is a bold, deep-breathing man who plants the whole of himself forward with each step, sowing all the furrows, not with a gift, nor a view, nor any knacks of mind or fingers, but with the health of his personality, as he lets conscience, intellect, and heart forth in one untrammelled jubilation over nature's beautiful spring day. His audacious looks reflect the climate and the sun. It is his genius to stifle in a close room, and to be well enough to rough it in the open air. We sit inside cramming note-books, putting bugs in spirits, labelling drawers full of fossils and tenantless shells, enriching our cabinet. His cheery voice comes in like the warm, meadow-scented wind, recommending the living and thriving nature outside to us who are cataloguing nature within. If we cannot stand a draught we slam down the window, pitying people in the weather and predicting various ills.

This kind of originality will not respect our preconceptions. It has no time for that. Persons who join exploring expeditions find at first that Nature disdains their city ways; she is very rude, and occasionally there is a touch of contempt in the way she handles them. They bear all this for the sake of getting eventually upon the sky-bounded prairies; there they discover something better than buffaloes and Indians; better, even, than clear-water valleys with distant blue gentian-fringed mountains. They discover a capacity to be on friendly terms with the sincerity of the air and the earth. The disdain is found to be nothing but the unconscious freedom of the weather. So we fare with men whose thoughts emancipate. Not dreaming that our chamber needed ventilation, we set forth some day, and at first find it cheerless sleeping with the ceiling fled off to the stars, while vague perils assail us. It is very shocking to be without our usual conveniences. When the exigencies of the scene dispense with the little delicacies and contrivances of our genteel housekeeping, it is like trifling with sacred subjects. We suspect that something malignant, under pretence of enlarging our estate, has robbed us of all that is dear and precious.   If we have made an attempt to bring with us a cherished utensil, to serve whatsoever turn—crockery and tinware, to maintain some culinary traditions—one by one they are sacrificed to freedom of movement, and our course is marked by household relics. When the pack is well cleared out how lightsome is the march !   We smile at our old horror, and enjoy Nature's satire upon impediments.   Nature never means to hurt our feelings ; she shines and grows ; the brightening weather laughs at the retreating thunder ; the grass has no bad motive in drenching our feet ; the lightning but emphasizes the element which the bud and wheat-ear gratefully confirm.

CHAPTER XV.

THE wide influence which the sermons preached in the Music Hall attained, as they were scattered in volumes or the phonographic reports of newspapers, is shown in a remarkable way by the letters received by him from all quarters of the world, from persons of both sexes, and of every estate in life. If they could be published, they would create the most emphatic endorsement and guarantee of the fitness of his nature to reach the heart of mankind, and to feed its inmost longings. He was sought by young and ardent minds, during the period of transition in New England, and later in the West, when parties were changing, and old modes of thought were breaking up. They came to him as to a master : there was no reservation in the eagerness and positive abandonment of their hearts to his brotherly society. People who desired to know what were the facts about theology and religion, troubled by creeds, just cast adrift from them, and uncertain where next to go,—soldiers, students, laborers, shop-keepers, Catholics, Methodists, and members of all sects,—people with special questions about retribution, God, non-resistance, miracles, free-will, many who were in distress or uncongenial circumstances, suffering from intemperance, pining for want of remunerative labor, and all people who longed to be of service to their kind; young converts who had become suspicious of the machinery which turned them out Church members ; old men, filled suddenly with profound dissatisfaction at dogmas which they fancied they believed ; and whole neighborhoods speaking through their ready writer, who had been put forward to ask some news of him ; it was as if a great crowd hurried towards a clear and steadfast voice that hailed them to come over where it spoke, by the only safe and speedy way. What a testimony to the horrors of Calvinism sleeps in these still letters, that were once wet with tears before they came to him—and often afterwards ! It was in this way, that his dread of the logical effects of that violent and narrow creed became confirmed. He had documents enough, sealed with the heart's blood of the writers, to bear him out in the strongest things he ever said.

He prized above all other communications of this kind, the awkward and ill-spelled letters of laboring men, through whose grotesque sentences divine desires struggled to reach him, as if with gnarled and calloused hand, to grasp his own large and manly one.

In December, 1857, he writes to a friend :—

I send you a letter, which I count as precious. Here it is—from Minnesota—a curious specimen of our civilization, and the proof of the relation which a thinking scholar may stand in to the great mass of the people. Please return it by-and-bye, or keep it safe against our meeting—which is the better way.

Here it is, a little helped in spelling, perhaps, but not otherwise meddled with :—

Aug. 30, 1857.

Mr. Parker—Dear Sir,—I take the liberty to make you acquainted with a request that has been made to me a number of times, and that is this—to ask what way we may obtain your sermons regular, or such ones as would be adapted to our situation. I came to this place one year ago. I had a town laid out, &c., and commenced operations. We have a flour-mill, two saw-mills, blacksmith-shops. My hotel is most done. I am now living in a log-house, which answers for hotel, church, town-house, school-house, and last spring was used for a fort to keep secure from the Indians. But we are fast completing other buildings for the same purposes mentioned above.

I left Boston last June with my family, and among our library we have two volumes of your sermons, Nos. 1 and 2, and in the absence of our minister, I have taken the liberty to try and satisfy the audience by giving them something from your works, which has had the effect to cause them to ask for more, and to-day I have been requested to give them one more of your sermons, as our Close-communion Baptist is not present, " A Sermon of Old Age."

It is now requested that a part of each Sabbath be occupied in listening to one of your sermons. Now, sir, if you will send to me such of your sermons as in your judgment will suit a frontierman's mind best, I will settle the bill whenever it is presented. You think strange of this way of proceeding, but that may be explained hereafter. There are a number of your hearers in this place. You will not know the signature of this. I have attended your meeting at the

Music Hall but little, from the fact that soon after I heard you preach I moved from Boston to Melrose, which made it inconvenient for me to attend your meeting in the city.

Among the numerous examples of Mr. Parker's influence, let one suffice. It is the story of the beautiful development of a soul, out of poor and ordinary circumstances, and notwithstanding all the discouragements which friends, the Churches, and society so well know how to deploy against the independent seeker. This poor boy tells his life in letters from the Far West. The first two or three are illiterate, without punctuation, and of uncertain spelling, but they improve rapidly, and blossom with all the refinement and fragrance of a religious heart. It is almost like the miles of waving western corn, the miracle of a single season.

"Four years ago," commences the first letter or call of this lad to the strong and famous preacher, "I had the misfortune to lose my left hand by an accident. Since that time, until the winter before last, I went to school where I live. The winter before last, my brothers and friends raised sufficient money amongst them to send me to a school in Wisconsin. While there (1854–5), I saw one of your works, with the title, ' Discourse on Matters pertaining to Religion.' "

The next winter he made a little money by teaching a district school. Part of it he sent to Little and Brown for more volumes of Mr. Parker.

I had several disputes with prominent Church-members, and soon the hue and cry ran through the village that I was a confirmed infidel, and when I would give them arguments that they could not answer, they would ask with a sneer, whether a boy like me—being only twenty-one years old—should attempt to teach ministers. Last week I made a public lecture against Slavery and for Fremont, during which I quoted a passage from the Bible. Since that, the whole town nearly have risen against me, and with pious horror they ejaculate, " An infidel to quote Bible as argument! " Even my brother and friends have turned against me, and I expect in a few days to have no home. I am poor. Last summer I worked out as a day-labourer on a farm, but even that has failed—nobody will receive the infidel —— in their family. If I had the means I would stay here, and alone I would face and tear down their dreadful theology.

He wants to get some employment in Boston, where " I may clasp you by the hand, listen to your noble words, and take example from your manly life." We can imagine what answer the farm-bred preacher sent to this day-labourer with the divine thoughts waking in his soul.

TO MR. H. A. W., MENDON, ILLINOIS.

Boston, Oct. 10. 1856.

DEAR SIR,—You case is a very hard one, but I do not know what advice to give you. It would be in vain to venture to Boston or any of the eastern towns—where the avenues to all kinds of business are more crowded than with you at the West. I feel the warmest sympathy with you, and trust that patient efforts will secure you the victory in the end. There are several modes which men try to overcome an enemy withal; one is to knock him down, another to talk him down, but, I think, the manly way is to live him down. After a little while, farmers will sow the wheat which gives the largest crop of the best kind of grain, and will not care much by what name it is called. If Hebrew wheat only yields ten bushels to the acre, and heathen wheat yields thirty of a better quality, the bad name won't keep the wheat from the fields.

It is always pleasant to try and live down the evil name which good deeds bring on a man. You are always sure of the peaceful victory at last.

Believe me, yours truly,

THEO. PARKER.

THE ANSWER.

DEAR FRIEND,—Allow me to call you so. I received your letter, but words cannot express the delight with which I read it, and the strength that I received from your advice and expressions of sympathy —sympathy on a subject that of all subjects is the dearest to me, but which for many years I have had no one to sympathize with.

Then follows a little sketch of his personal history. The father and mother were English, of the Episcopal Church ; he was the youngest of a large family, which emigrated when he was eleven years old. Three weeks after they reached the West the mother died. "She only knew my wishes and desires, and sympathized with me. My memory still goes back to the time when I sat at her feet and heard of a loving God." The family was decent and moral, but absorbed in the day's work. No one spoke to him to ask if the soul also hungered. But when the "Discourse" fell in his way,—

I had at last found a key to that something. I knew not what it was, lying dormant within me. My relations and friends are pained and angry with me. They ask me why I do not go too, and make money ; they tell me that I have talents and eloquence which, if I will throw away my suicidal notions, will place me in a high position and fill my lap with gold. But you can sympathize with me. I feel like one that has just awoke from a horrid dream. I have found there is something to live for, and that instead of my pocket I have a mind to cultivate. It is as you say, a person with natural talents can live without much effort here in this magnificent country. But consider my situation; I can live here easier than any place that I know of, but I want some one to sympathize with me, not that I am afraid, or have no faith in the truths that I have read, but there is something within me that longs for that twin sister of love. I am a child in feelings if not in body. Ofttimes as I have been reading your manly words, my heart has gone out towards you, and I have longed with an irresistible longing to be near you. And since I have been writing, I have wished that I could be in the place of this letter, and that you could look into my eyes and read me as you can this letter. But if that cannot be now, let me hear from you often. Write brave words to me. And I will endeavour to live down all opposition.

He has caught the Western frankness and intuitive apprecia-tion, which created for Mr. Parker one of his chief consolations. It hailed him unsolicited, from every social rank, as pioneers shout to each other across the prairies, for guidance and good-cheer.

TO THE SAME.

Boston, Nov. 3, 1856.

MY DEAR SIR,—I thank you for your kind letter which I find on returning from your State. I confess I know of nothing which calms, cheers, and strengthens a man so much as a fixed and abiding con-fidence in God. If I am sure of the cause and providence of the universe, I am sure that all things at last will turn out well. If I am not certain of Him, I am sure of nothing else. The great vice of all the religious systems in the world is this—they do not know the per-fect and infinite God, so they have only a poor and imperfect trust in God, and, instead of love, nothing but fear. To my apprehension, reli-gion is natural piety—the love of God—and natural morality, the keeping of the laws He has written on matter and man.

It is not easy to find any wide sympathy with opinions dear to you, for they are yet too new in the world. But the noble man gradually makes a little circle of friends about him who sympathize with his best emotions, and soon the circle grows wider. The history of mankind seems dark as you look back, so much stumbling for so short a walk, but when you look forward you see the signs of triumph for the indi-vidual and the race. It is sure to come, and every earnest, good man, put him where you may, will do something to help the victory to draw nigh.

Let me hear from you from time to time, and believe me, truly your friend,

T. P.

The next letter describes his success at inoculating the chief minister and enemy with the " Discourse on Religion." " He has now your sermons on Theism, Atheism, and the Popular Theology, which he has taken without any of his former reluct-ance, and which, in fact, he seemed anxious to take."

Dear friend, you know not with what joy I read and re-read your last letter, and treasured up your expressions of friendship ; and when I think of the terrible opposition that you have braved and are still braving, it gives me a confidence and hope that nothing can subdue.

Now a change has come over the hand-writing, and the arrangement of the sentences. There is a rhythm in the feeling and the style.

When the cold shoulder of contempt is turned towards me, when the finger of scorn is levelled at me, when there is no one to whom I can look for sympathy and instruction in the great truths of religion, I turn to thee with all the confidence of a child to a parent—confident of thy sympathy, confident of thy love. Oh, how I wish, now, while my mind is forming, that I could be near you, and mould my mind after the manliness, the beauty, and all-embracing love of thine! But, with the assurance of God's aid and thy sympathy, I will go forward a seeker after truth, let it come in whatever form it may.

There has come a change over my mind, a calmness, a contentedness, a peace, that I never knew before. I can compare my life up to the present time to a vine without support, crawling along the ground, clasping and clinging to all kinds of dirt and rubbish, but which has at last reached a support, and begun to climb ; it looks back on the time and strength it has expended in reaching that support ; it looks up though the path seems steep and rugged, and the winds of adversity for the moment arrest its progress. Yet it will only cling the closer, and go on climbing till it dies.

Following this are some questions addressed to Mr. Parker upon immortality, and the future growth of the soul out of its present habits and restrictions.

The next letter is dated two months later, in 1857.

I wish I could express to you on paper my feelings, the joy, the peace, the satisfaction I feel in contemplating the thoughts of the good God in His works. It is not a great while since the thought of God was the most terrible that ever crossed my mind. What hopeless agony I have suffered, as in the dead of night I have thought of the endless hell to which in all probability I was hastening ! and yet the grim and ghastly hell of the Christian theology was preferable to its idea of God. But, thank God, it is past, though it is hard to have " Infidel !" hissed in my ears, to have those whom I once considered my bosom friends turn away. Yet I gladly bear it ; yes, ten times more, than turn back to my former belief.

I have new thoughts, new objects, new aspirations ; everything is new, new heavens, new earth, with no dark future beyond. But I look forward to a future bright, glorious, grand ; and I look forward with a peaceful calmness that is surprising to me. There is no fear, for I cannot fear what is good.

My mind is settled as to my future object in life. It is my wish to follow in your footsteps, and preach to others the truths you have awakened in my mind, and, God help me! I will do it faithfully and fearlessly.

This is the emancipation which the broad and humane thought proclaimed, as it won thousands of souls from the slavery of indifference or fear.

The next letter was written in the spring of 1858.

Last summer I worked on a farm, though it may appear somewhat strange to you that a person with one hand could work to advantage as a farmer. Yet, I find that knowledge is power. Last winter I devoted three months to study, but as soon as spring came, the warm sun called me to the open fields. I know not why, but I love to turn the generous soil, to scatter wide the seed, to watch the peering blades as they come forth, and to meditate on the laws of growth and reproduction. The little birds, mate with mate, seem to be full and running over with joyous notes, as they flutter hither, choosing a place to build their nest and raise their young. I love the noble, generous steeds that draw my plough, fleet as the deer, graceful in proportion as nature made them, their spirits unbroken by the whip or spur; but they will come at my call, and look at me with such expression in their large eloquent eyes, that I have often wished they could talk and tell me their feelings. I know they love me, and their love is returned with compound interest.

* * * * * *

I hope I have done something. I have circulated your works to some extent here, and, with one or two exceptions, they have not failed to convince all who have read with them with care.

* * * * * *

For three weeks past there has been here what is called a revival of religion; meetings have been held every day, and the whole town is stirred up in such a manner as I have never seen it before. The farmer has left his plough, and the mechanic his shop, and all joined in the general commotion. I respect any effort that a man makes to approach his Maker, yet I do not see that this way makes their minds any freer, or their ideas of God purer. Last Friday, two ministers came to see me: we had a long talk, which only resulted in making me still stronger in my opinions, and to wonder still more that educated men should cling to doctrines without foundation.

In the summer of 1858 he reported as follows :—

I can see a gradual and steadily advancing inquiry after truth. Much has been done since spring. The books of yours, which I own have been going steadily from house to house, and the desire to read them has been growing stronger every day. I have been thinking lately that we ought to form ourselves into a society, as by that means the bond of union would be closer, and more could be done in the way of distributing books and papers to others. I would like your opinion on the subject.

He had seventeen acres of noble corn planted, during a dry season, part of which he got into the ground on Sunday, because it promised rain on the morrow.

Oh, what a hubbub it caused! Old ladies threw up their hands and eyes in horror. Old gentlemen handled their canes with threatening motives. It furnished a text for four preachers. The young gazed on me with eyes at least a third larger than ordinary. The middle-aged, to a man, have been waiting impatiently for some special interposition of Providence. But, no—I am not stricken with incurable disease, nor is my corn blasted, contrary to their expectations and wishes, and, I suspect, prayers. There is no change in nature, no special providence in their behalf, unless they consider it was the cause of the long-continued and soaking rains.

But the next letter is from another hand :—

SIR, —— has bin sick, is now beter; if i should not recover, I should always think your doctrine right; he wishes a sermon on immortal life.

The explanation follows, in Nov. 1858, from his own hand :—

I was very sorry to hear of your sickness, and sincerely hope that, when you receive this, you will be convalescent. Should you die, it would be a severe trial to me, for thou art near and dear to me. When I stood alone with no one to encourage and advise, I wrote to you. Your answer nerved me for the battle. At the present time, instead of standing alone, I have powerful and influential friends, and the number is slowly but surely increasing. It has been the influence of your letters that has encouraged me to go forward, and should they fail the loss to me would be great. . . . . . .
Frequently while discussing religious subjects with others, they have said that my belief would do to *live* by, but it would not do to die by. The day of trial came. On the evening of the 26th of September, I felt that I could not live till morning. My stand being close to the bedside, while my friends were absent for a few minutes, I with great effort wrote these words on a piece of paper : " I die in the belief in which I live," dated and signed it, and placed it with my other papers. When my friends returned, I told them I thought I was going to die ; and I settled up my worldly affairs. The physician and my friends conversed with me, and tried to shake my belief, but in vain : my reliance on the infinite perfection of God grew stronger ; there was no doubt, no fear, but a peaceful happiness came over me. Gradually I lost all consciousness, my body lost its feeling, my pulse was gone. I lay in that state for several hours, when, contrary to expectation, I rallied ; for a week life hung in the balance. No one could say which way the balance would turn. Part of the time I was conscious, and conversed freely with those that came to see me ; my bed was besieged daily by church members and ministers ; daily I was urged to renounce my belief, but daily that belief grew stronger, and the contrast between natural and ecclesiastical religion grew wider and more distinct. At the end of a week, my youth and excellent constitution triumphed.

TO THE SAME.

Boston, Dec. 2, 1858.

MY DEAR SIR,—I thank you for the letter you so kindly sent me Nov. 6th, which I have not been able to answer till now, and at this moment but briefly.

I am glad to find that you seem to be permanently convalescent; so likewise am I; but, though a great walker, I cannot yet accomplish more than two miles a day, and use another's hand to save my own when possible. I trust we shall both be entirely well, and that soon.

I am glad you held fast to your faith amid the weakness of disease and the assaults of well-meaning but bigoted men. It required some courage to do that. It gives me great pleasure to find that I have helped any one to learn the road of true religion. Bigotry and fear are the great enemies of the human race. If I can destroy them, and bring up in their stead piety, which is the love of God, and morality, which is the keeping of His natural laws, then I shall feel that I have not lived in vain.

Believe me, yours truly,

THEODORE PARKER.

Mr. Parker highly prized this letter from John Brown, a blacksmith of Rhinebeck :—

TO THE REV. THEODORE PARKER.

Rhinebeck, Dutchess Co., New York, Feb. 4, 1859.

REV. SIR,—It's with sincere heartfelt regret I've being made acquainted, through the public press from time to time, of your severe sickness. Although we differ somewhat materially in our theological views, I have long been an enthusiastical admirer of your talents and virtues as a man, a scholar, and a gentleman. I take this method of conveying to you my heartfelt sympathy and condolence in your affliction; permit me to express a hope it may be of short duration, and that you may be speedily restored to your former good health and usefulness. And in doing so I believe (in fact I know it to be so) I'm expressing the sentiments of hundreds, if not thousands, in the circle of my acquaintance, which is pretty extensive through the State, and particulary in Dutchess Co., where I've resided for the last 25 years.

You'll perceive I've made several mistakes, which you will please pardon, as I am nothing but a poor blacksmith, with a wife and family depending upon my labor for support. In conclusion, accept of my best wishes for your present and eternal welfare, and believe me your sincere friend and well-wisher, now and for ever,

JOHN BROWN.

TO MISS PATIENCE FORD, DORCHESTER, MASS.

West Roxbury, April 18, 1841.

MY DEAR FRIEND,—I have just received your letter and have read it both with pleasure and with pain; it gives me great *pleasure* to find that a thought which has burnt in my own bosom, finds a warm resting-place in a pious heart. There is no sweeter joy on earth than the thought that you have comforted or strengthened one single human soul; have made truth brighter and heaven more high. But it gives me *pain* to find you look *to me* for light, when I am so ill-qualified to give it. Out of the depth of your own spirit it will spring up. "A man's mind is sometime wont to tell him more than seven watchmen that sit above in a high tower," said the old wise man. The infinite Parent of truth sheds light, without let or hindrance, down into all souls that look reverently and obediently up to HIM. It seems to me, that if we *always* obeyed the law God has written on our hearts, the decisions of reason, of conscience, and of faith, would be as infallible in their action as the instinct of the bee and the law of gravitation now are. But no man is in this state; so as the penalty of our disobedience, "we grope for the wall like blind men," and "feel after God if haply we may find Him." We are not *one with God* as Christ was; so we are in doubt and fear. The best and wisest men feel this the most deeply. *Jesus alone felt none* of it. His obedience was perfect, and so God's truth passed through him as light through the celestial spaces where there is no atmosphere, and was not bent to either side. You ask an explanation of one passage in the sermon. After I preached it, I felt it might be understood to mean something I never assented to. It belonged originally to a course of several sermons, and the others would perhaps explain what was obscure in this. I meant simply that Jesus was not *all that human nature is capable of becoming,* that is, He was not a poet, astronomer, architect, or musician. He did not come to be a Milton, a Leibnitz, a Michael Angelo, or a Mozart. This does not diminish his greatness. I meant to imply that *each* blackbird is all that *any* blackbird or all blackbirds *can be.* But no one man has ever developed on earth *the whole of the capabilities involved and folded up in his nature.*

This was doubtless the case with Jesus. If you wish to learn astronomy or music you do not go to the Gospels, for Christ did not come to teach these arts. I take it, this statement would harm no man's feelings. But, on the other hand, in his own department of morality, religion, a divine life, perfect goodness, I think he was true, perfect, and complete. We can see no limitation to his perfection in this respect. He was all that man can be of goodness and religion. He was all of God there can be in a perfectly good and religious man. So he could say, "I am the way, the light, and the truth." "I and the Father are one," for he thought God's thoughts, felt God's feelings, lived God's will. I never said that man would outgrow Christianity—never thought it possible. To me Christianity is perfect love to man and God. Can mankind outgrow this? Not even when they become angels. I think St. Paul had this in mind when he says, "we shall judge angels," viz. that Christianity is perfect truth by which even the higher beings are judged. If future revelations of truth are made, they can never supersede the Christian doctrine, for one truth is congenial to all truth. Therefore, if God should create a man wiser, better, holier than Jesus, the revelation this new messenger brought would not destroy the old.

Whether such a being ever will be created, no one can tell but He who possesses the riddle of the world. The counsels of God—no one knows them. I think it becomes Christians to leave the future to Him whose it is. For my own part, I cannot conceive of a being more good, and beautiful, and holy, and true than Jesus of Nazareth. His words judge the world. The higher we think, the holier we live, the more we find in them, the more we admire and love in him. I do not worship Christ, but I love him, and would kiss the hem of his garment. As you say, he is still "the Star of Promise." He has not come, oh, no! It is not the Christianity of Jesus, that most of even pious men assent to. It is still in the world, but not known by the world. The wisest and best have at most only after*thought* what he fore*knew*. In love, and religion, and truth, I think no one has come up to him, and man cannot go beyond the truth, as you so well say. I think we are yet to have a period of real Christianity on the earth; so we all pray, "Thy kingdom come," and often say, "How long, O Lord?" What you say of your experience of one of Christ's sayings is true of all of them. To-day a man says this is Christianity, to-morrow he lives it out, but then he finds Christianity is still above him, for he sees a new meaning with the new eyes his life has given him. "Inasmuch as you have done it unto the least of these, you have done it unto me." What a world of meaning it has! It condemns us all. I thank you, my dear lady, for the confidence you have placed in me, and rest assured that if I can be of service to you in any way, it will give me the greatest pleasure to do so.

I remain yours, in the bonds of Christian love.

TO THE SAME.

West Roxbury, June 15, 1841.

MY DEAR SISTER PATIENCE,—I thank you most heartily for your kind letter. You felt moved, as you said, to help me; and your letter did help me, and that not a little. There are times when the strongest men need help, and if it is so with the strong, how much more is it the case with me, who am only strong when I am weak! Your letters have given me encouragement and new vigor. It is delightful to find one who sympathizes in what is deepest and highest in your own mind, who is true to what is truest in your own heart. In this world, where sinners are so much more common than saints, it is very refreshing to find one who is pursuing an upward path, and asking God, reverently, for more light and higher truth.

I sent you "Fénélon," because I thought it would not have fallen in your way, and I know it must speak to your heart of hearts. A religious book is always understood by the religious heart, and by that alone.

The common people counted John as a prophet, and seem to have heard Jesus gladly; while the *wise men of earth* slew both the prophet and the Savior; so it always is. In "Fénélon" you will find something that you will not like, perhaps. He would *destroy* self, not merely *bring all into subjection* to the law of the Spirit of Life. Did you ever read Dr. Channing's remarks on Fénélon? If you never did, Mr. Hall will be glad to lend them to you; and you will find many good words that came out of a good man's heart, and have already reached other good hearts and made them better.

You must take great delight, I think, in Mr. Hall's pulpit services, and his conversation also. If there are any pious ministers—and *I* think there are many—he is one, and one of the most excellently pious. He does not make the kingdom of heaven consist in meats and drinks, but in righteousness, and peace, and joy in believing. He has an unction from the Holy One, if any have it now-a-days. I rejoice, my dear sister, in the strength of your convictions and the brightness of your inward life.

TO THE SAME.

West Roxbury, July 5, 1841.

My dear Sister Patience,—Your last letter gratified me much. That alone was worth all the hard things men say in the newspapers. But, as you say, they *cannot hurt* any one. I thank you most heartily for your kind sympathy. It makes me feel strong. It is delightful to get the fellow-feeling of one good religious heart that is full of faith, and tries doctrines by *feeling* of them. I do not care much whether a person agrees with me in opinions or not; that is a very small affair, but if we *feel* alike about the highest things, we can walk together; for we *are agreed.* But now I have time only for a few words. I shall *not* be at home next Sunday; but I shall the *Sunday after that,* when both my wife and I shall be very glad indeed *to give you the right hand of welcome,* if you will come, as you propose.

Very affectionately,

Your brother,

THEO. PARKER.

TO THE SAME.

West Roxbury, September 11, 1844.

My dear Sister Patience,—I have not time as yet for a long letter, but yet for a few words. I was quite sorry to see you so sad as I thought you on Sunday. I had not then opportunity to speak of it, but you seemed less happy than I was wont to see you. Pray tell me the cause. Is there any occasion in the state of the body? any reason in the state of the mind? or has any trouble you do not outwardly speak of befallen you? I know that you used to welcome angels, whether they were dressed in wedding robes or mourning garments. Then, too, you say in your note—which, like all yours, came in the right time, and was most heartily welcomed—that a dispensation of silence is upon you. Surely not, if you have anything to say. A misfortune, I think it would be to be silent when you were certain you had somewhat to speak of, and felt certain you had something good and true. Be not faithless, but believing. I know God waiteth to be revealed to all such as lie low in His power and reverently look to Him. But He expects them also to reveal what is granted them, not hiding their wisdom in its own beauty, but letting their light shine. Life is one way, speech is another form of our revealing to men what the Great Father reveals to us; such as can speak the truth are in duty bound so to do, as well as live it. After I have got over the hurry of business, and the no less urgent hurry of friendships, I hope you will come up and pass some days with us, and in the meantime will send me more letters.

Yours faithfully,

THEO. PARKER.

TO THE SAME.

West Roxbury, Feb. 7, 1845.

MY DEAR PATIENCE,—I thank you for your kind and seasonable letter. It came, as your letters always came, at the right time. I have delayed a little while my reply, because I have been too much occupied to find time to write any letters but the most urgent: so you will excuse my delay with the same charity you have always extended to me.

What you say of the love of God is true and beautiful. I understand your feelings and your experience—at least I think so. No one can dwell too deeply in the love of God, for it is the noblest sentiment we are capable of feeling, and it leads out to a love of truth, goodness, usefulness, loveliness—for these are among the modes in which we conceive of God. It leads, therefore—in a sound and healthy state of mind—to a life full of truth, goodness, usefulness, and loveliness. But there is always a danger that such as dwell in this sentiment should lose themselves in contemplation, become dreamers, not doers, and so should be abundant in the blossoms of piety and yet bring no fruit to perfection, so that when the Lord comes, seeking fruit, he shall find leaves only. Now there is always a strong temptation for a mystical man—and I think still more strongly to a mystical woman—to dwell amid the sentimental flowers of religion, charmed with their loveliness, and half-bewildered with their perfume, so to say,—a danger lest common sins of the times should not be thought so sinful and injurious as they really are; and lest the man should sit down patient and contented, not heeding his brother's condition, nor helping him out of the ditch into which he has fallen. At a certain stage of religious progress, we lose sight of the human element; we look perpetually at the Divine; we think God does all; we resign ourselves unconsciously to His will, our own will ceases to be. Many stop there, and stop in outward inaction; then they become one-sided, and at length dwindle. But, if a man goes on, he catches sight of the human again, and does not lose the Divine. He serves God consciously, and knowingly lives in obedience to the Great One. He ceases to be one-sided, but loves God with all his understanding and reason, as well as with all his heart. Then, too, though he loves contemplation none the less, he loves action all the more. One lives like a worm in the heart of an apple, fattens and grows, and then flies off; the other not only grows and fattens, but comes out not a moth, but a bee, and visits all the flowers of the garden, culling from all its sweets, carries off honey for other bees, and builds up the comb—the residence of future bees that are to rejoice in his labours. We must not only fly, but, as we mount up, we must take others on our wings, for God gave one more strength than the rest only that he may therewith help the weak! I hope you will one of these days come and see us, and let us talk with you. I had a very pleasant conference with Mr. Hall, the other day. I wish there were more such men in pulpits.

Remember me to your parents and sisters, and believe me, as always,
Truly your friend and brother,
THEO. PARKER.

TO THE SAME.

West Roxbury, 27 Aug., 1845.

MY DEAR PATIENCE,—I did not hear of your affliction until Saturday, or I should have come up to see you instantly. Now I am obliged to go off for some few days, so I fear I shall not see you till next week. I hope you not only sustain yourself with a Christian fortitude, but are able also to comfort your father, whose afflictions are greater than your own; and your sisters, who naturally will look to you for consolation in this hour of sorrow. I know you will be calm, resigned, lying low in the hand of God. I know you will know that all is for the greatest good of her that is gone and those she has left behind. I hope you will be able to cheer hearts which are sadder than your own. They will see more than patience in you, I doubt not, even resignation, cheerful acquiescence in the will of the Great One who always is doing us good, not less when he causes us to weep than when he makes us smile. I beg you to assure your father of my sincere sympathy for him in this loss, and my hope that he will find comfort and peace. Let your sisters see and feel that you are superior to affliction, and you will gradually take away the grief of this sudden wound, and at last heal it. I have time to say no more, for I go presently; so good-bye.
Sincerely,
THEO. PARKER.

TO THE SAME.

West Roxbury, July 10, 1847.

MY DEAR PATIENCE,—I have not had a convenient opportunity to write you before. In your note you do not give me very distinctly to understand why you expect to lose the love and affection of your friend. It seems to me that you may "study the laws of the spirit," and live the life of the spirit, without losing the affection or even the sympathy of your friends. The laws of the spirit may be as well studied in one place or one sphere of life as another. Living itself affords the material of that study, and the study consists in reflecting on the material thus given. But perhaps you are looking for some new form of activity in which to work—I am no judge of that. You must determine that for yourself; but I hope you will not mistake any transient impulse which has its origin in some physical derangement for a serious monition of a lasting duty. I know you will be faithful to your own convictions of duty—my only fear is that you should decide without due deliberation, and without a complete understanding of your own case. Then, of course, the decision will be incorrect, and the result vanity and vexation of spirit. Would not it be well to state distinctly to yourself what it is that you wish to do, and how you wish to do it; then you will know exactly what you are about, and not "fight as one that beateth the air." I know you will be true to yourself, but only fear lest you should not always consult your permanent self, but only a fleeting emotion of the day or the night. If I can ever be of any help to you, you know it will give me great pleasure to be so; so, dear Patience, farewell.

T. P.

FROM MISS PATIENCE FORD.*

Dover, October 14, 1851.

MY DEAR FRIEND,—Moved by an inward impulse I do not resist, I take my pen to address you. It is very long since there has been any communication between us, yet the associations of the past come thronging upon my memory and filling my soul with grateful love. Perhaps we may now meet again upon paper, as there seems an insuperable barrier interposed to our meeting elsewhere. I must speak to you from the inner temple of my being, because it is only from thence I can speak, and it is only of that which you would care to hear. It is a temple of truth and purity, erected for the abode of our Father. God himself superintended the construction, and polished and fitted each stone before it was brought hither, so that " there was no noise of hammer, or axe, or any tool of iron, heard in this house while it was in building." But, oh! the rubbish that had to be removed ere the foundation of this temple could be laid strong and enduring! How much which I thought was pure gold had to be cast aside as base and useless metal, so much so that it seemed at times there would be nothing left upon which to base a superstructure. But the wise Master-builder knew better than I did; and as I earnestly besought Him to permit nothing but genuine material to remain, nought but would bear any test of time or change, He kindly bore away that which I had previously erected with much pains and care, and showed me it was of a crumbling nature, and liable to be swept away by the floods of time and decay. But what is more than all, He has promised to take up his abode in this temple He helped me to rear for his worship, so that now I have nothing more to ask of Him. I have but to put forth every faculty and power he has bestowed upon me, with the full assurance that I am going forward in harmony with the great creative spirit; and, oh! He brought me, when He came to take possession of this inner temple, the key to the outward universe, by

---

* This beautiful spirit passed away in the summer of 1863.

means of which I can penetrate into the very centre and essence of things, and discern of what they are composed. And He also brought other rich and costly gifts, the nature of which it were not possible for human language to describe.

*　　　*　　　*　　　*　　　*　　　*

TO PETER ROBERTSON, STONEHAVEN, NEAR ABERDEEN, SCOTLAND.

Boston, April 16, 1849.

My DEAR SIR,—I thank you for the very kind and affectionate note you sent me on the 10th of the last month. It reached me by the last mail-boat from England, and is very welcome. Such a letter shows me that my words have not fallen idle, nor been spoken wholly in vain. I have lamented from my childhood that such a subject as religion should be involved in such a cloud of superstition. But I thank God that we live in an age when many men, in all parts of the world, are ceasing to fear God, and learning to *love* him. The old theologies are fast going to pieces; new systems are taking their place, which rest on a truer idea of God, and a juster appreciation of the nature of man. It is a great and glorious age we live in. I trust that Christianity has great triumphs in store for mankind; for Christianity is the just and complete action of human nature. We shall do a little towards this good work in America. You in England are contributing to the same end; so is all the world. To me it is delightful to think that every truth is eternal, and each error is local and temporary. The Christian nations are gradually learning that there is but one religion—that is, in its *internal* form, piety, the love of God; in its practical development and manifestation, goodness, the love of man. Christianity is free goodness, free piety, connected with free thought. When nations believe this, as now a few individuals believe it, what a beautiful world we shall have—what societies of men and of nations! I love to look on the great temples which once were built in the name of religion, on the priesthoods and ecclesiastical institutions it has founded. In them I see signs of the power of religion; and I look forward to the time when religion will be a yet greater power, and will build up, not theocracies, but democracies—when the government is of all, for all, and by all; when we shall build up institutions to educate all men, so that we shall have a Church without bigotry, a State without despotism of the few over the many or the many over the few, and a society with no want, no ignorance, no crime. It seems to me that our human nature demands this; that God designs it—and that it must come, not in our day, but far hence. We can do something to help it forward. Wealth is power, wisdom is power, religion is power; and when mankind have all these three, what great results shall we not accomplish ? It is pleasant to think that each one of us may do a little towards a work so glorious.

I will send you a few sermons which I have published as soon as an opportunity offers. I have long been intending to print a volume of sermons relating to subjects like that which you name, and hope to do

so in the coming season. Hitherto I have had so many things to
attend to that it has been impossible. It will give me pleasure to hear
from you at all times, and to be useful to you in any way.

Believe me faithfully your friend,

THEO. PARKER.

Rakhal Das Haldar, an intelligent Brahmin, now a Unitarian missionary in India, after expressing private gratitude for
the awakening of his religious feeling, writes,—

It could not be otherwise than pleasing to you to know that the
better portion of the community of this country take an unusual
interest in perusing your theological works.

I ought to mention here a fact, that whenever there happens a conversation among my educated countrymen about religious compositions,
they unanimously point out those of yours as models. Dr. Channing's
sermons are undoubtedly excellent; but they want that energy, that
manly boldness, that brilliancy of thought which characterize your
sermons.

TO GEORGE ADAMS.

West Roxbury, June 24, 1842.

I cannot tell you how much your letter interested and *encouraged* me.
I know there are many whom the Church and the ministers drive into
infidelity, by their bigotry and contempt for reason. If I can ever do
anything to remove the cloud of darkness which men have collected
about the temple of truth I shall rejoice; still more if I can help any
one to see the real beauty of true religion. I feel it is a great work
which I have undertaken. I know that, so far as the ministers are concerned, I am alone, all alone. But I have no ambition to gratify, and
so neither fear the disgrace nor count the applause which they can give
me. If I can speak the truth plainly to honest and earnest men, it is
all I ask; the result is with the God of all, and you and I have no
cause to fear. I have received the ready sympathy of intelligent and
religious laymen, and confess that it makes me feel strong, for most
men have moments of depression, when a kind word is like rain to the
parched grass.

FROM JAMES T. DICKINSON.

Middlefield, Conn., May 21, 1854.

DEAR SIR,—I give below an extract from the private journal of a
congregational minister, which, as it relates to one of your books, may
interest you. The writer is in "good and regular standing" among
the orthodox; was formerly for several years a missionary to the Chinese, is now an invalid, but preaches and lectures occasionally. He is
thought, I believe, to be rather peculiar in his notions—somewhat rash
and radical, yet, on some points, conservative enough. Some have
called him a Swedenborgian, and one man was known to whisper it

about that he was a "kind of Atheist." A few weeks since he preached a sermon which contained a number of startling sentences, one of which, as a specimen, I quote :—" Deliver us from that religion which claims to have the love of God, whom it hath *not* seen, while withholding love from the brother, however dark in color or weak in faith, whom it hath seen; which communes with the orthodox slaveholder, but casts out as unholy Dr. Channing and Theodore Parker, heterodox in creed, but so beautifully, bravely orthodox in life."

Now for the extract:—

" May 21st, 1854.—During the past week I have read Theodore Parker's ' Discourse of Matters Pertaining to Religion.' A great and good book, notwithstanding its want of orthodoxy. It is a strong help to me to find a man standing on the extreme verge of liberal theology, holding so firmly, so *tenaciously*, the one true religion, *love to God and man*. No doubt this is the absolute religion, and Mr. P. deserves the thanks of the world for setting it forth so clearly and beautifully. When *will* men learn that Christianity consists not in saying, ' Lord, Lord,' but in ' doing the Father's will '; not in believing a creed, but in living a true life; not in opinion, but in character; not in dogma, but in duty; not in understanding the ontology of Christ, but in possessing his spirit ? When will men see the broad distinction between theology and religion, between formula and righteousness ? Though I dare not adopt a theology so extreme, so different from that so long and generally received, yet I rejoice that others can do so without peril to our holy religion. I still adhere to the idea that Christ is God, ' God in Christ, reconciling the world unto himself ' ; but it gives me great joy to find that a man can be an earnest and noble Christian, while believing Christ was only a man. But remembering Mr. P.'s excellent philosophy, that God is always present and helping in all our goodness, does it not follow that there is in Christ *so much* of God that, *practically*, we come to nearly the same point ? If T. P. were but the Pantheist he is said to be, could he help asserting the divinity of Christ ? Pantheist ! Who, then, is a theist ? who a believer in individual responsibility in sin, if not the man whose energy of conscience and will and word can send forth living, burning thoughts that pervade the continents, making Everett and Cass and Douglass turn pale, Pierce tremble on his four years' throne, breathing into the nation heart and hope ? Noble is the spiritual philosophy of T. P., which brings God back into the worlds of matter and mind, from which materialism and a half-atheistic theology had almost banished him, making him ' immanent,' living, loving, in all nature and all spirit. Baptism, the Lord's Supper, the Church, the Bible, the possible inspiration of all men, creeds, theologies, hold their proper place in this remarkable book, though I should sometimes prefer language less severe and impatient. But we must pardon much to the spirit of liberty. The Luthers are not mealy-mouthed. Against creeds, not even T. P. can invent words too severe. Though wrong, it is natural enough in the orthodox to excommunicate such a man from Christianity, but in the Unitarians it is weak and wicked."

Sincerely and respectfully yours,
JAMES T. DICKINSON.

TO JAMES T. DICKINSON.

Boston, 25th May, 1854.

I am much obliged to you for your kindness in sending me the opinion of your friend, so highly commendatory as it is. I wish I was worthy of half the praise he bestows upon me. But it is a strange state of things which now prevails. Mr. Webster denied that there was any law higher than an Act of Congress. When he stood and looked at the magnificent mountains of Virginia, he scoffed at the thought of a higher law than their tops. And when he came to die, more than a hundred and fifty clergymen preached and printed sermons eulogizing him as a great Christian. The evidence was:—he went to meeting, knew Watts' hymns, and in the Girard will case declaimed in behalf of the Christian religion. But on the other side, all the philanthropists of the age in America are denounced as heretical, unchristian, often as irreligious, and atheistic. *Not to love your brother* whom you have seen seems to be a sign of love of God whom you have not seen.

The great difficulty is, we have not an *idea of God* at all adequate to the wants of mankind; the popular theology does not know the God of infinite perfection. It is a partial and exceedingly imperfect God that all the churches worship. Hence they have a form of religion which is not adequate for the purposes of science, of politics, of philanthropy, or of piety. So the philosophers, the politicians, the philanthropists, and the men of solid piety turn off from the popular forms of religion. The *politicians comply* with it—it is a part of their policy, and means as much as their praise of democratic institutions, which they subvert while they profess to honor ; but this is not to last long.

TO J. P. HAZARD.

I hope good will come from these spiritual manifestations. Indeed, I see two special good things which are getting accomplished by them, viz.; 1. some men who had little satisfaction in any form of religion, who were disgusted with the foolishness taught as " divine wisdom," have found in these phenomena something higher than the mere *material* elements connected with them ; and they rise up thence to nobler forms of internal life, to satisfactory modes of religion. Such as did not believe in the immortality of the soul find a " proof" of it here. 2. These phenomena lead men to think about the miracles of the Bible, to disbelieve and reject them. Thus the old theology of the dark ages is rapidly melting to pieces.

No doubt other good results will follow. But I must confess that as yet I have seen nothing which leads me to believe in the *spiritual* origin of these strange things. I see nothing but the action of faculties not much studied hitherto, and but little understood. Much deceit also I find—deceit and fraud. But the real genuine cases only report to me the action of human faculties not as yet well understood.

TO WM. L. AND WENDELL P. GARRISON.

If you have a vehement desire for a good literary culture, and if a college were the only place which could afford it, I should say, by

1

all means go there and get the coveted pearl in spite of the age of twenty-two. But the case is not exactly such ; a college is by no means the only place to furnish this culture, nor is it at all the best place to help a man of your years and experience of life. The discipline of a college is designed for boys, not for grown men ; so the studies are adapted to the boyish mind, not the manly. What you want, I take it, is (1) a vigorous development of all your intellectual faculties, and (2) competent literary and scientific *information*. Both of these you may obtain without going to college, and without even quitting the regular methodical business at the bank. Here is what I would suggest for your consideration ; to find some good, well educated man to guide you a little in these particulars, in studying such works of science, physical and metaphysical, as you and he may think advisable, in studying such foreign languages as you may need—perhaps French will be sufficient, —and in studying the history of mankind in various countries and in all ages. Some well educated friend would be needed simply to give you the list of books, to tell you the order you shall follow in reading them, and to point out the right method of study. Should you pursue this method, I think in four years, by using only your spare time, you would secure more development and more information than you would in the six years necessary to fit you for college and take you through.

Now a word to the other brother. I am glad to hear of your Students' Temperance Society. It was more needed than in any other part of N. E. Your class seems fortunate in having a little company of noble minded young men in it. I put *you* among their leaders. It is a great thing for any class to have even but a few such in it. * * * *Litera- ture* is a good staff, but a poor crutch, and reform makes but a poor *profession* for any one. The public is naturally jealous of a *professed* reformer, and looks upon him much as it does on a common scold ; no profession probably has more and more terrible temptations. * * * I regret that so much of our best talent is of necessity forced to occupy itself with this matter of slavery, and to take up the time of the peo- ple with discussion of what our grandfathers thought they had settled forever, while the great work of organizing society, so that there shall be no idleness and no want, no involuntary celibacy and no prostitution, no drunkenness nor crime, remains almost untouched. * * * *

I hope your friend Hallowell justifies the high hopes formed of him, both in talent and character. Russell and Shaw, in the class before you, I hope will do no discredit to their fathers and mothers—old friends of mine. Spalding I am sure of. * * * *

I should like to step into the A. S. Rooms and see Mr. Wallcut and his green bag, Sam May writing letters, and H. C. Wright covering the desk with one of his hands.

TO THOMAS G. BARNARD, NORWAY, MAINE.

Boston, March 30, 1853.

DEAR SIR,—I thank you for your interesting and welcome letter, which I have just read. It gives me great pleasure to know of such men as yourself, bred by deeply religious parents in the old forms of religion, yet coming out of bigotry into freedom with a continual increase of piety and faith in God. I know some men who cast off the old forms of theology and of church service for the sake of getting rid of the restraints of religion. I always love to find one who grows in morality as he advances also in intellectual freedom.

I know many persons whose history is the same as yours. The Methodist Church does a great deal of good; the Methodist minister,— poor, badly educated, often quite ignorant,—goes amongst men more ignorant than he, and rouses up the religious spirit in their souls, and quickens them with new life. How many thousands of men there are who owe their earthly salvation to the labors of some modest minister of that persuasion? I have great respect for them; but, alas! they find men in fetters; they make men fear; they drive by terror while they ought to draw by love; they make too much of a separation between life and religion. Their idea of God is dark and sad, so are their notions of the next life. But when one comes to the conviction that God is infinite,—I mean perfectly powerful, perfectly wise, just, loving and faithful to himself,—then the great difficulty is over: you do not fear God, you love him; you will not seek to shun his laws, but to keep them, and if you fall away sometimes through the strength of temptation and the weakness of your character, you feel mortified, ashamed, and penitent, and come back full of vigor and resolution anew, and go on your way rejoicing.

I am sorry I did not know you while you were here in Boston, and hope you will continue to grow in all religious and manly excellence.

Truly yours,

THEO. PARKER.

TO A FRIEND, A PHYSICIAN IN UTICA, NEW YORK.

October 2, 1848.

I thank you for the kind things which you say of my writings. I sincerely hope they may do a little to direct the attention of men to the great realities of religion, and help make the earth the paradise which God designed. I see most hopeful signs. Here in Boston and its vicinity there has been a great change for the better in half a dozen years. Men do not insist so much as formerly on what is reckoned miraculous in Christianity. The more I study the nature of man and the history of his progress, the more I am filled with admiration at the genius of Jesus of Nazareth, and with love for his beautiful character and life. He is the greatest achievement of the human races, and Christianity the greatest idea which mankind has thought out as yet; for, take the results of Christianity into account, it is the greatest fact in human history.

But I look on all that has gone before as only the spring-time of religion, the few warm days in March which melt the snow off the most southern slopes of the hills, and only promise violets and roses. The real summer and autumn of Christianity, I think, are a good way off. But they are certain, and every good man, every good deed, every good thought or feeling, helps forward the time.

I am glad you like what I said of Mr. Adams. I certainly studied the matter carefully, and read every line he ever published which

I could find, and looked at every vote he cast. Then I had several times met the old man, and conversed with him.

As you say, he had more justice than kindness, and kindness is the more popular virtue. But justice is far the more excellent. Some men here rate him higher than I do. But my article on him has met with more favour than anything else I ever wrote. It has been circulated very widely, and I hope will do some good work.

When a public man dies, we ought to take warning from his faults and be guided by his merits. It seems an ungrateful work to hunt the one dead fly out of the whole pot of ointment; but if all else be fragrant, it is profitable to detect the cause of the offence which arises from the one ill thing.

TO MISS COBBE, ENGLAND.

May 5, 1848.

My dear Friend,—Your letter of April 2nd gave me great delight. I rejoice exceedingly at being able to smoothe the difficulties away which have been thrown in the way of religion, and so your kind letter warmed my heart anew with the thought that I had actually helped one fellow-mortal—one, too, whom perhaps I shall never see. Your history lends additional interest to it all. I know how you must have suffered under that bewildering orthodox theology which you were taught to accept instead of religion, and which you could not receive, still less be satisfied with. We have the same orthodoxy here in America, only, as we think, a little more—as everything is a little more—intense on our side of the water.

I confess to a strong love of that good and true man, Blanco White. His " Memoirs " have brought much comfort to many a man's and woman's heart in America. What I love most is the entire truthfulness of the man, and his entire trustfulness. He felt and he knew the goodness of God, and, loving Him, forgot all fear.

You ask me if Jesus believed in eternal punishments, &c., or why I call myself a Christian if he did. I don't believe he did; I see not how he could. I doubt that even Paul believed it. Why, Jesus is teaching that God loves all men, the sinner as well as the saint. I know there are many passages, some parables, which plainly teach this odious doctrine. Still, I don't believe Jesus taught it, though it was easy for a Jew to misunderstand his words, and long after his death relate such things of him. I cannot ascribe a very high historical value to the Gospels; they rather indicate its facts than tell it. I call myself a Christian because I believe Jesus taught absolute religion, goodness, and piety; free goodness, free piety, free thought. He was, in some things, fettered by the follies of his nation and age, but did men such a service by setting before them the true *method of religion*, that I love to call myself a Christian out of gratitude, but I would not think ill of another who disliked the name; nay, I doubt if Jesus himself would recommend it. I have written you a longer letter than I thought I should at first. If I can be of service to you in any way, it will give me pleasure to do so, and I shall always be glad to hear from you when it is agreeable to you to write. Allow me to subscribe myself,

Sincerely your friend,

THE⸳. PARKER.

TO THE SAME.

Boston, June 5, 1855.

My dear Miss Cobbe,—Your kind letter came to hand in due time, and the book followed it, reaching me a few weeks ago. I did not go to bed till I saw through its whole.* The next day I gave it a more careful study. Let me say I admire the work throughout; the plan, the execution, and all the details. It is a noble work, in many points reminding me of some of the best things in Leibnitz, in others coming close upon Milton in its tone and language. Your learning also surprises me. I am making efforts to have it reprinted here, for it is much needed to counteract the sensationalism of the Locke school, who still occupy most of the chairs of philosophy in New England. It will do good service among our young men and women. If I succeed, you shall have a copy as soon as possible, only the depressed state of the money market makes my success doubtful. In your note you seem to think you and I might differ as to the use of *experiment* in morals. This is my notion: moral experiment furnishes *new facts of moral consciousness*, which else we should not acquire so soon—perhaps never. Still the ultimate appeal is to the *moral element* within us. By experiment alone we can never learn what is (scientifically) just —only what is (empirically) convenient in a special case. I hope soon to have the other part, the "practice of morals."

Be pleased to accept a copy of a new book of mine, though made up of old matter, and believe me respectfully and sincerely yours,

THEO. PARKER.

TO THE SAME.

Boston, December 20th, 1855.

My dear Miss Cobbe,—When your book first reached me I submitted it to my friends, Messrs. Little and Brown, who said they would take it up at once on my recommendation, were it not for the deranged condition of the country at that time, they having much capital at risk, and getting but slow sales. I tried another house, and was determined it should be published if I took the risk myself and gave away the edition, for I thought it so valuable. The other house, Messrs. Phillips and Samson, delayed a long time, their reader not liking to take the responsibility of deciding on a book which lay outside of his lines of knowledge. So he delegated the matter to a minister of the Unitarian denomination, a man of nice scholarship and fine character, though quite conservative. In the meantime I was busy making ready for publication the "Defence," which I send you with this letter. But a few days since the reader sent me the note from Mr. Hale, which I enclose, so the book will appear 'ere long. To make it as perfect as possible, I will beg you to send me another copy, with such corrections, emendations and additions, as you see fit to make. The mistake of those writers who copied the strange errors of Mosheim, were first pointed out to me by an acute Catholic lawyer of this city, who wrote a lecture on "Robertson's View of the Middle Ages," detecting that

* The volume written by Miss Cobbe, entitled "Theory of Intuitive Morals."

and other errors; as I looked into the matter I found the whole passage of St. Eligius was given in Schröckh, Kirchengesch, b. xix. p.
438, and in Gieseler K. G. b. i. 123. You refer to Sharrolu's book
ὑπόθεσις ἠθική. I had never read a word of the man, but in a few days
received his De Officiis secundum Jus Naturaê, (Gothæ, 1667, 1 vol.
18mo.) bound up with Puffendorf's de Officio. Is it the same book as
the ὑπόθεσις?

I send you two or three little sermons which you have not yet seen,
and my defence, which will tell its own tale. I shall print another
volume of miscellanies, and one more of sermons and speeches, as soon
as I find time for the work.

With many thanks for your noble book, believe me, affectionately
yours,

THEODORE PARKER.

TO THE SAME.

Boston, Aug. 11, 1857.

MY VERY DEAR MISS COBBE,—It is more than a year since I wrote
you a line, and my last letter, I think, you never received, for I gave it
as an introduction to one of my friends, who took an Irish wife, and
went to show her parents the new baby. It was Mr. Brace, who has
written some clever books, and is one of the best young men that I
know. He married a Miss Neile, of Belfast, and lives at New York,
busied in picking forlorn children out of the streets of that Gomorrah
of the new world, and placing them in worthy families. So he saves
" such as be ready to perish."

I had no right to expect a letter from you when the last one came,
but as the telegraph announced the arrival of the steamer, I said:
" Now there is a letter from dear Miss Cobbe," and when the letters were
brought up—behold there were many, some from Germany, one from
England, but *none from her*. I felt sure there was some mistake, and
the next morning yours actually came; it had been overlooked the day
before, but I did not think of the heaviness of heart with which you
had been writing. I suppose the sad event—sad to the survivors—has
taken place before this, and the venerable head is laid peacefully to rest,
while the soul has gone home to its Father and Mother. I am the
youngest of eleven children, and of course my parents were old when
I was born; my mother was forty-nine, my father more than fifty. My
father's mother lived with us, and passed on at the age of ninety-two.
She was more than eighty when I was born. My father died at seventy-
seven. So you see old age is familiar to me. I love the venerable
hairs of old persons, not less than the brown locks which curl so handsomely about youthful brows. But we don't sorrow for the old as for
the young. It is right and natural that the ripe apple should fall in
Time's autumn night. My grandmother, my father, grown old but
with faculties still bright, were glad to pass further on, taking the next
step in the continuous process whereof birth is the first. We shed
natural tears, and the place felt cold when the shadow of an empty
chair fell on the household fire. But we recognised the fitness of it all.
There are two points of certainty: the infinite perfection of God, the
immortality of man; those are fixed, and the consciousness of them is

not merely a matter of reflective demonstration for the philosophic few, but rather of spontaneous instinct for the sympathetic many. Between these two points hangs the great world of human consciousness, with its hopes, fears, doubts, uncertainties, disappointments, errors, follies, joys, sins, terrors, and unbounded aspirations. But all are supported on these two points of certainty, and I think it is the end of wisdom to *know* this, as it is the beginning to feel it. Sure of my continuance, and sure of God, I fear nothng. There is compensation for all sorrow, and recovery for all sickness of the soul.

Your book came most welcome; it is every way worthy of its predecessor. I read it with joy—not always without tears. I meant to have it republished here a year ago, and took it to my bookselling friends. Two wealthy and excellent houses—Little and Brown, and Ticknor and Co.,—thought well of the work, but said such a book on such a theme would have but a slow sale, and they should make no money by it. Now I am very anxious to have it brought out here, and but for a little trouble in my own finances during one or two years (I have been stereotyping some of my own books, which took all my spare money), I should have taken the risk myself, and spread the work before the American public. I think if I am financially prosperous, that when the work is finished I will stand as godfather, and secure the publisher from any loss, and so honor the Continent with so valuable a birth. A Rev. Mr. Buckingham, a Unitarian minister in Hartford, Connecticut, found a copy by accident in a book-store, and was much delighted with it. He wrote to me to enquire for the author, and has now written a review of it for the *Christian Examiner*, the Unitarian periodical, one of the best journals in America. It will appear about January; I fear not earlier. He says, "she is a fine fellow, though a little old-fashioned." He envied your wide and deep learning, as well he might.

Now let me say a word or two about myself. I have been ill for nearly six months, a thing quite unusual with me, who have not before passed a day in bed since I was twelve years old, which is now thirty-four years. I had a fever, with typhoidal and pleuritic symptoms. For a long time I could not preach, Mr. Phillips, R. W. Emerson, and similar men taking my place. Even now I am ill; feebler than usual, but likely to recover. My wife and I are passing the summer in a charming little country place, seven miles from Boston, where I do nothing but gather wild flowers, swim in the fresh water, sit under trees, and read what takes my fancy. To-day I start with a few friends in a yacht, for a sail along our coasts, to be absent a fortnight. I hope to preach again the 6th September, and be as well as ever. You will receive this about August 24, I fancy, which is my forty-seventh birthday. I wish you would tell me when you were born, that I may keep the day as a festival. So I do with other dear ones. Please grant me this favor, and I shall mark with a white stone one more day in my friendly year.

TO THE SAME.

Boston, Dec. 4, 1857.

MY DEAR MISS COBBE,—I meant to write this letter so that you should receive it on your birthday; but the relation with the day is still the same, though the time be different. I send you the last number of the *Examiner*, the chief Unitarian periodical, and one of the best, if not the best, in America. It is edited by the Rev. Dr. Hedge, Professor of Ecclesiastical History in the School at Cambridge, and Rev. Mr. Hale, whose note touching your book you received some time since. The article on your "Intuitive Morals," p. 370–84, is written by the Rev. Mr. Buckingham, a man about forty years old, not settled now, but a pleasant preacher and serious, earnest man, with a touch of genius about him it is said. You will see the earnest, progressive spirit that is in him. I hope you will be pleased with the article. Mr. B. saw a copy of your book on a friend's table, was much interested in it, borrowed it, read it, and then wrote me, asking what man (!) had written so noble a book? I put him in the way of the other volume, and he then wrote the article. The last paragraph is by Mr. Hale.

One of these days I will send you the photograph you speak of, if I can ever get a good one. There is a crayon portrait by my friend, Mr. Cheney, now dead, which my intimates like, and a great lithograph which they do not like. I judge neither. The London *Times* says of Lord Brougham, "Nature certainly did not make him a handsome man." I fear the oracle would not be more complimentary to me; but when I get a photograph which is decent, I will certainly send it.

We have been married nearly twenty-one years, and have never a child. We have a moderate little property, partly my wife's inheritance, partly my earnings; a good house, a large collection of books. Her name was Cabot. The family *claim* descent from the famous Giovanni Cabotti, who discovered these parts of the continent. Her domestic name is Bear, or Bearsie; and various symbols of " Beauty and the Beast " appear in the house. As usual, she is nearly the opposite of her husband, except in the matter of *philanthropy*. A young man by the name of Cabot, one-and-twenty years old, lives with us. We have brought him up from infancy; his mother died when he was five or six; he is now in the store of a large West India goods dealer. An unmarried lady, a little more than fifty years old—Miss Stevenson—a woman of fine talents and culture, interested in all the literatures and humanities, is with us. These are the permanent family, to which visitors make frequent and welcome additions.

You are very dear to us all. I ought to say that my wife was born September 12, 1813; and so is three years younger than I. She is tall, with blue eyes and brown hair, a little white beginning to steal in insidiously. My eyes are also blue, my head is bald, and my beard grey. I am five feet eight inches high, and weigh about one hundred and fifty pounds .All my forebears were great, tall, stout men, six feet without their shoes, weighing two hundred pounds and more. My mother was a slight delicate woman, with a fine organization. . . . . So much about ourselves. As my letter is dated *your* birthday, and your last note was on *mine*, and you asked for some particulars about us all, it is not so egotistic as it looks. Now to other things: No. VII. in the *Examiner* is by Dr. Hedge; you will be surprised at the freedom with which it criticises parts of the "New Test."; it has already wakened the wrath of some of the bigots, who have attacked Dr. H. in the *Christian Register*, the Unitarian newspaper of Boston.

Have you seen a quite remarkable book by H. T. Buckle? It is a "History of Civilization in England," vol. i. (pp. xxiv. and 854, London, J. W. Parker). It is one of the most remarkable and instructive books I have seen from the English press in this century. I do not always agree with him, but he is a great man—learned too in many departments of thought. I have read only the first part of his book. Can you tell me who he is, what his antecedents were, and his surroundings. The work is not less significant in its department than the "Vestiges of the Natural History of Creation" in another sphere.

What a terrible time dear old England has in India. Both parties are in the wrong; England has treated India harshly, exploited her. No doubt her native rulers did the same, perhaps in a worse manner, and to a greater extent; but it is more inexcusable in Father Bull to do such an evil thing, for he knows better. But I suppose he will conquer, kill ten men and violate twenty women where the Indians did but one or two, and then celebrate thanksgivings in all his churches. I look with great pride on this Anglo-Saxon people. It has many faults, but I think it is the best specimen of mankind which has ever attained great power in the world. One day I fancy Asia will be divided beween the Russians and the English, and the English people will have the whole of America, South as well as North. I think it *can* be done by no violence or cruelty, but it *will* not be. I wonder what the moral effect of your two recent wars will be in England. Will it make you a nobler people, as trouble did in the sixteenth and seventeenth centuries?

In America we are to have much trouble from the question of slavery. You in England, I think, do not see how slavery corrupts everything. Politics, theology, literature, trade, it is the *bête noire* which threatens to devour all the flock. Every national administration pets and cossets it. The democratic party thinks it is the only American institution worth spreading. Every Irishman in the United States is in favour of slavery, so are all the Jews. The Germans go the other way. So strong is national disposition! No property here is held so sacred as property in *men*. No laws so important as the laws of slavery. There is trouble before us! I care little how soon it comes.

Of course, you know what a sad commercial panic we are passing through in America, as in England. I hope both nations will come out of it wiser than before. I hope your honoured father continues comfortable, and your own health and spirits are as good as your heart. We all send you our love.

FROM D. H. TWEEDY.

Stamfordville, New York, Feb. 10, 1856.

DEAR SIR,—"The world does move." It was very gratifying to me, on the receipt of your pamphlets at the Post-office in our country store, to see the physician, the merchant, and some of my most bitter opponents, each with book in hand, lost to everything else, and to hear them exclaim, "good," "here's a good idea," "just hear this," &c. One said, "these are my sentiments, but I did not know how to express them," &c.

When I gave a home to Stephen and Abby Foster, Parker Pillsbury, &c., those same persons could hardly find language bitter enough wherewith to denounce them and me. But this was not my worst offence: universalists and heretics of all sorts, when travelling, have found a resting-place with us, and occasionally I have dared to question the doctrine advanced by their minister; but now I could not get away without leaving some of those anti-slavery and heretical works with them, and promising to loan the rest at some future time.

The Baptists in our vicinity are holding a protracted meeting; it has continued near a month, only letting off the steam now and then, long enough to establish or confirm their new converts by immersing them in ice-water.

A more interesting and progressive society has been organized in the same village, who meet regularly to read and discuss the merits of your discourses; sometimes they elicit so many comments that but a few pages will occupy a long evening, and we do not consider it lost time, as it induces people to think for themselves, the first progressive movement, and calls forth their ideas another step.

Those meetings are composed of such as have very little sympathy with the churches called orthodox; we have two volumes of your Discourses on Religion, and those you sent me come in play.

So you see we have a counter revival, and the prospect is that we shall make the most converts; and that ours will be of that class who possess the most intelligence.

My wife joins me in wishing you success in your labours for the cause of humanity.

Yours, &c.,   D. H. TWEEDY.

FROM E. H. BOWMAN.

Edgington, Illinois, December 25, 1857.

MY DEAR SIR,—Somewhere in the neighbourhood of a year ago, I took the liberty of addressing you. Although an entire stranger, and destitute of all claims of a personal character on your time and attention, still your kindness did not deceive or rather fail me.

I received the volumes you sent me, and have perused them, not only once, but again. I feel truly grateful; I was like a chick just pipping the shell, so to speak; you kindly assisted me, and very materially expedited the process. You requested me to let you hear from me again. If I have delayed near a twelvemonth, it has not been without reason. In the first place I know "new converts" to any views, party, or sect, are apt to be carried away by enthusiastic feeling and excitement. The novelty wears off by time and the attrition of circumstances. Not claiming any unusual exemption from the frailties of humanity, I deemed it prudent to try myself, and give time for sober second thoughts.

A year is probably a reasonable probation, and on careful retrospect I find myself more and more strongly confirmed in the radical change which has taken place in my views of God and Man, and the relation between the two.

When I wrote to you last, I was quite sanguine as to the possibility of extending such views in my neighbourhood. The observation and reflection of a year have materially moderated that sanguine expectation. I find many good men seem to look on me with a suspicious eye. I cannot get access to their ear. One of my intimate friends, an old-school Presbyterian preacher, who has known me familiarly for thirteen years, and been more conversant with my mental habits than any other man, gives me no chance to broach any controverted subjects. I can scarcely indulge the vanity that he fears an encounter. Being a man of good reasoning powers, close observation, and a *most excellent heart*, he possibly misgives as to the strength of his fortress. Yet he does preach the hardest sermons and doctrines extant. He seems to me sometimes almost desperate, as if his own mind was not satisfied with its meagre fare, yet determined not to acknowledge it, even in his inmost soul. I heard him preach a sermon not long since on the miraculous and divinely-inspired character of the Bible. I could not help pitying him. With solemn earnestness he took the ground that if a single word were untrue then the whole must be false. It looked to me like the desperation of the gambler who risks his pile on a single throw, and that made wildly, with shut eyes. Just as if a single truth of God could be corrupted or negatived by mountains of error. I found men hard to approach. Touch any of their favorite views and they turn fiercely, somewhat like Micah of old—" Would ye take away my gods, and what would we have left?"

It seems hard to make entrance for a new idea. It took me a good while to progress to where your writings found me, and I believe I am more than ordinarily inclined to think for myself, and assert man's right to personal individuality. I am inclined to doubt the success, to any great extent, of diffusing a correct knowledge of religious truth by efforts directed to *adult minds*. They have generally received their impressions, and become hardened into such shape as the operating forces may give. You cannot change them; the capacity is not there. The advocates of the " popular theology " have imitated the wisdom of the Jesuits, and much of their labor is expended in special efforts upon the mind of childhood and youth. Now, the friends of absolute truth, it seems to me, must imitate the wise example, and spend their efforts in the same field. In adults, far more labor is requisite to pull down error already established, than would be needful to instil truth into the unoccupied minds of children. Teachers of common schools could do more than preachers among adults. The system of Sabbath schools could be advantageously imitated, and made to contribute as actively to the moral and affectional growth of the human soul, as now they do to fetter and confine. I am busy everywhere I go, trying to do good. In my capacity as physician I have access to many. I can help to introduce some knowledge of truth; and the connection between obedience to physical and moral law is so close, that it is impossible to separate the two. I believe the vocation of physician and preacher should be combined, and will be, ultimately. In my address as one of the officers of our county medical society, I took for my theme the relations of our profession to the moral and intellectual progress of mankind. The views which I then presented to my brethren seemed to strike them as novel, and yet, at the same time, to be true. I claimed for our profession that, with all the rubbish of centuries, it still had in it the master-key of human progress. Theology is finished. Law looks to no new truth; it is all learned already, and is now stored up in the musty records of the past. Medical science has man for its subject, and extends to the investigation of every cause that can or does operate favourably or unfavourably on the human organization. We are already on your platform, a simple but sublime one. We investigate fearlessly after truth. We acknowledge practically "no master but God," and accept "no creed but truth."

I feel now more than any other single thing the want of intercourse with those of similar views; "iron sharpeneth iron, so doth the countenance of a man his friend." I can in a small degree begin to comprehend the firmness needed to not only "go alone," but in addition to stem the current of opposition which has its source in ignorance, fanaticism, and intolerance.

On the subject of slavery I do not entirely harmonize with you; I spent several years in the midst of slavery in its mildest form, that is, in Kentucky. Having had my birth and what little education I possessed in a free state, I was disposed to observe closely, and the sum of my observations led me to the conclusion that the dominant race was more legitimately the proper object of pity than the servile. The servile is gradually improving by contact and *amalgamation* with the white race; on the contrary the white race is visibly retrograding.

God's eternal law of right is setting its seal there, in characters so plain that it seems to me, " He that runs may read it ;" just in proportion to the wrong inflicted by the powerful and knowing on the weak and ignorant, is the rebound on the wrongdoer of righteous retribution.

That retribution is, it seems to me, intensified in proportion to the difference in the moral and intellectual development of the races. With this view, I cannot help feeling that the wrongdoers are in need of more pity and commiseration than the enslaved and oppressed Africans. The steady result is the gradual elevation of one race, and the depression of the other until an equilibrium is attained. " God's balances are even."

One of the sources of vitality in slavery is the infusion of new material from the North. Commerce, theology, teaching, and adventure take every year many young men from the free states. A limited view of their own interest converts them to supporters of the "peculiar institution," and in time they " out-Herod Herod."

But I fear I have been trespassing on your time in rather garrulous style, so will stop.

Very respectfully and truly yours,
E. H. BOWMAN.

I should like to hear from you, if not incompatible with your duties and inclinations, when you may have leisure.

FROM HENRY THOMAS BUCKLE.

59, Oxford Terrace, London, March 27, 1858.

DEAR SIR,—I have delayed several days answering your very obliging letter, in the expectation of receiving the review of my history which you mention having sent to me.

Several numbers of the *Massachusetts Quarterly Review* have been forwarded to me, but not the *Christian Examiner*. However, I will defer no longer thanking you for a mark of attention which I value highly as proceeding from one with whose writings I am so familiar.

That men simply urged by a love of truth should know and communicate to each other without personal acquaintance is a cheering consideration, and thus it has always been in the history of literature, and thus I trust always will be.. I will not reply to your objections, partly because I dislike controversy, and partly because it would be impossible to state in the limits of a letter my view of the most important point, namely, the moral and intellectual laws.

I have requested the publisher to send you a copy of *Fraser* as soon as it is issued, which will be on the 1st of April. It will contain a report of a lecture which I delivered a few days since, at the Royal Institution here, and which has made some little talk.

Possibly you may be interested in my view of the too empirical character of English science.

Believe me, dear Sir, with great regard, very sincerely yours,

HENRY THOMAS BUCKLE.

FROM THE SAME.

59, Oxford Terrace, London, April 4, 1858.

MY DEAR SIR,—I have just received another parcel, containing not only the *Christian Examiner*, but (what I value even more) a collection of your own works. By sending these last you have really placed me under a very considerable obligation, as, apart from the interest I feel in whatever you write, such productions are among the best materials I could have for estimating the highest points of American speculation and American knowledge.

My next volume will contain a history of the civilization of the United States, and I shall, perhaps, some day encroach upon your kindness by troubling you with some questions on the subject. The importance of the investigation is only equalled by its difficulty. Before publishing my next volume I shall, if possible, pay a visit to the United States, and the prospect of making your acquaintance will be no small inducement to do so.

You will no doubt have received a letter which I wrote to you towards the end of March.

Believe me, my dear Sir, yours very sincerely,

HENRY THOMAS BUCKLE.

I hope you have received *Fraser* for 1st April, containing my lecture on the " Influence of Women."

H H 2

FROM THE SAME.

59, Oxford Terrace, London, July 9, 1858.

MY DEAR SIR,—Absence from town prevented me from receiving till yesterday your very kind and friendly letter. I certainly shall not venture to write upon the civilization of your noble country until I have visited it, and satisfied myself in regard to many matters respecting which books (as you truly say) supply no adequate information. Indeed in the national character of every really great people there is a certain shape and colour which cannot be recognized at a distance. But, at present, I am exclusively occupied with an analysis of the civilization of Spain and Scotland, which I hope to publish early next year ; and should I fulfil that expectation, I shall hope to visit America in the summer of 1859.

In regard to Scotland, the leading facts are its religious intolerance and the absence of the municipal spirit during the middle ages. The causes of these phenomena I have attempted to generalize.

Spain I have almost finished, but I find a difficulty in collecting evidence respecting the rapid decline of that country during the reigns of Philip III., Philip IV., and Charles II. In investigating the *causes* of the decline (both remote and proximate), I trust that I have not been wholly unsuccessful. In Mr. Ticknor's singularly valuable " History of Spanish Literature " there is more real information than can be found in any of the many Spanish histories which I have had occasion to read.

You mention a book on America by a Pole as being important, but I cannot quite decipher his name. I should be very glad to buy it, and if you would take the trouble to send its title either to me or to your London bookseller, with a request that he should forward it to me, you would render me a service.

I do not like reading at public libraries, and I purchase nearly all the books which I use. I have at present about 20,000 volumes.

I believe you correspond with Mr. Chapman; if so, would you kindly beg him to send me any criticisms which appear in America on my book. You ought to know of some which he would not be aware of.

Sometime ago I received from an American publisher a request that I would write my life; at that time I was very unwell, worn from over-work, and harassed by domestic anxiety. I also thought the form of the request rather blunt ; and from all these causes I was induced to return a somewhat curt answer, and one very foreign to my usual habits. But you and I are no longer strangers to each other, and I willingly send you the particulars which you desire for your friend.

I was born at Lee, in Kent, on the 24th of November, 1822. My father was a merchant. His name was Thomas Henry Buckle, and he was descended from a family, one of whom was well-known as Lord Mayor of London in the reign of Queen Elizabeth. He died in 1840. My mother, who still lives, was a Miss Middleton, of the Yorkshire Middletons.

As a boy, my health was extremely delicate, and my parents were fortunately guided by the advice of that good and wise man, Dr. Birkbeck (whose name I believe is not unknown in America), who forbade my receiving any education that would tax the brain.

This prevented me from being, in the common sense of the word, educated, and also prevented my going to college. When I was in my eighteenth year my father died (January, 1840), and left me in independent circumstances, in a pecuniary point of view.

My health steadily improved, and to this moment I had read little except "Shakespeare," the "Arabian Nights," and "Bunyan's Pilgrim's Progress," three books on which I literally feasted.

Between the ages of eighteen and nineteen I conceived the plan of my book—dimly indeed—but still the plan was there, and I set about its execution. From the age of nineteen I have worked on an average nine to ten hours daily. My method was this. In the morning I usually studied physical science, in the forenoon languages (of which, till the age of nineteen, I was deplorably ignorant), and the rest of the day history and jurisprudence. In the evening general literature. I have always steadily refused to write in reviews, being determined to give up my life to a larger purpose.

I have, therefore, produced nothing except the first volume of my "History," and the "Lecture on the Influence of Women."

This, I think, is all you requested me to communicate. Any further information which your friend may require will be much at his service. I should always feel it a pleasure and a privilege to hear from you, and am, my dear sir, yours very sincerely,

HENRY THOMAS BUCKLE.

FROM THE SAME.

Eltham Place, Eltham Road, near Blackheath, July 5, 1859.

MY DEAR SIR,—I have been in town for a few days on business, and found your card on my table in Oxford Terrace. I cannot tell you how much I regret that we should not have met. The great respect which I feel for you as the most advanced leader of opinion in one of the two first nations of the world, would of itself suffice to make me eager for the pleasure of your personal acquaintance.

And when I add to this, the memory of your obliging and friendly letters to me, you will easily believe me when I say how much I have been disappointed at being unable to call upon you, and make arrangements to see you.

But the severest of all calamities has befallen me, and has so prostrated my nervous system that I am now enjoined the strictest quiet.

Your conversation would arouse in me so many associations, and excite me to so many inquiries respecting your noble country, that I feel myself, alas, unequal to meeting you; and, as you might possibly hear from some of my friends in London, I have been compelled to give up all society. In such cases, the more I am interested the more I am hurt. I do not know how long you are likely to stay in England;

but it would give me great pleasure to hear from you, and to be assured that you understand the cause of my apparent inattention. I shall probably remain here until the end of August.

Believe me to be, most truly yours,

HENRY THOMAS BUCKLE.

TO REV. M. A. H. NILES, NORTHAMPTON, MASS.

West Roxbury, March 4, 1845.

MY DEAR SIR,—I thank you for the kind and affectionate letter which you wrote me the other day. I have just received it, and as I shall be absent for a few days I will reply now. I felt a strong interest in you from the much that I heard and the little that I saw of you at Marblehead. You have certainly left a strong impression of yourself on some who were not your parishioners in that place. Mr. F. told me of the peculiar circumstances of your case in that town. I confess I thought you were too far before them for their appreciation; and this is a very peculiar circumstance for a minister now-a-days. The questions that you mention have been to me one of the greatest interest for many years. The relation between man and God, and the inspiration that man can receive through that relation, was a subject of deep interest to me when a child. As a boy, I had reached in sentiment the same results that I now hold as ideas translated out of the unconscious into consciousness. The canonical nature of a book is still of a good deal of importance to me (though not the same as to you, I fancy) for I like to know how near a man stood to that mighty soul of religion which so aroused the world. Still I do not always find the canonical books, such as came from the disciples of Christ, so much better than those of men a little more remote. Thus the Epistle of James is worth more to me than the 1st of Peter, though there is little doubt of the genuineness of the latter, and little evidence for the genuineness of the former.

I think the matter of the Apocryphal Christian writings of the first and second centuries has never been duly inquired into. Mr. Norton has written something which I think is quite shallow, on this matter in his late work. I can't find evidence, internal or external, that the writers of the Bible had a mode of inspiration, or kind of inspiration differing from that of other men. Some of them certainly had a very high degree of it—Jesus the highest—so I think, that was ever attained by man. I don't wonder you do not accept my conclusions, I wonder much more at the kindness with which you speak of them. I must of course have committed errors in reasoning and in conclusion. I hoped once that philosophical men would point out both; then I would confess my mistake and start anew. But they have only raised a storm about my head; and in a general way a man wraps his cloak about him in a storm and holds on the tighter. It would be very surprising if I had not gone to an extreme, and yet I do not think I have (pardon my apparent want of modesty) in this matter; for after looking again and again, reading and talking, I find a flaw in the process. God is infinite; therefore he is immanent in nature, yet transcending it; immanent in spirit, yet transcending that. He must fill each point of spirit as of space; matter must unconsciously obey; man, conscious and free, has power to a certain extent to disobey, but obeying, the immanent God acts in man as much as in nature, only in a higher mode. Hence inspiration. If the conditions are fulfilled, it seems that inspiration comes in proportion to the quantity of a man's gifts and his use of these gifts. I feel in me a something that leads me to reverence, worship, trust, &c. I reckon this a distinct faculty (as much as judgment, reason, imagination, &c.), or, it is the man acting in a special direction; of the existence of this I am sure. I can't analyze it further than this, into a sense of infinite dependence; here the subject and the predicate seem identical, and the analytic process ends with me; others may be more skilful. I think Brownson sometimes merely splits hairs, with no very certain desire to get at the truth. Now I think that as the man developes, he finds as facts given in his consciousness, an idea of God; where this idea is fully unfolded, that it is the idea of a Being of infinite power, wisdom, and goodness; but we are not content with that, but add various human appendages thereto, and thus generate what I call a conception of God (I tried to find better terms to express this difference, but could not). The idea represents an objective Being corresponding to it exactly, viz.:—The God who is of course not only all our idea represents, but much more; while the conception of God, added to the idea, has no objective reality corresponding to it. Jesus, Jupiter, Mars, &c., denote conceptions of God purely subjective, with various limitations; there is no objective reality that corresponds thereto. But when I speak of the infinite God, I speak of an objective reality, in whom I live, and move, and have my being. In short, we create our conceptions of God in our own image.

About miracles, I agree with you that it is a question of fact, to be settled by historical evidence only. I believe in something extraordinary in the case of Jesus; his healing of diseases is special, but not miraculous. I think miracles are entirely possible. I think God can manifest himself in a thousand ways that he never did reveal himself in, and I can't say that he won't to-morrow. But I see God much more in what I understand than in what I am ignorant of. *Omne ignotum pro miraculo habetur* is an old proverb, but *Optime notum optime adoratum* suits me better. The deeper I look into nature and man, the more do I see a certain orderliness, a lawfulness; not the action of fate, but of the immanent God. And the further I look the deeper is my admiration, and the more absolute is my trust. I say with Thomas, "My Lord and my God!" I beg you to write me often; but do not speak to me with so much deference, as if I were some great man; for I know that I am a very humble one; and if ever you can make it agreeable to come to West Roxbury, you shall find a prophet's chamber and hospitable hearts to give you a welcome.

Believe me, truly, your friend and brother,

THEO. PARKER.

TO THE SAME.

West Roxbury, April 16th, 1845.

MY DEAR FRIEND,—I thank you for your kind letter of the 9th, and having now a little leisure, I will reply to some of the points you refer to. I hope, however, we shall sometime have an opportunity to confer together with the living voice, for in that way we shall the more readily come to an understanding. I am, like yourself, an humble seeker after truth. I learn a little one year and a little the next; but the vast ocean of truth spreads out before me, immense and unvisited. I feel often a sense of imperfection; yes, always, and sometimes the sad consciousness of positive sin. My ideal hovers far over my head, while the melancholy fact of my life foots it humbly through the dust. I suppose it must always be so; for with progressive beings the ideal of to-day must be far above the attainment of to-day. It is indeed the prophecy that to-morrow is to fulfil, or some to-morrow. I can say also with Paul, "The good that I would," &c. It is one thing to see the right, another to will the right. It is not easy to account for this abnormal state, in which a man introduces a contradiction into his consciousness, and voluntarily keeps it there. To explain it I think we must look far away into the future destinies of the man, just as to explain the caprices of a little child—its preference of the showy before the substantial—you look forward to the maturity of that child, and find that the feelings of infancy are but a trifle compared with the rational moral action of a full-grown man, living in his normal state. Can't we in this way get at some nearer solution of the problem of sin? I confess it seems so to me. Many men, I think a great many theologians, make mistakes in this matter; quite as absurd as it would be in a physician who should suppose that the child of four years was always to remain a child of four years. Of course there is then no explanation of its conduct, its tendencies, or its instincts.

About the matter of intercourse with God, I think this doctrine of His immanency in spirit, or in space, follows from the very idea of God as infinite. Of course he transcends creation (spirit as well as matter), so that his existence and action are not limited either to this, or by it. I suppose that all the action of the creatures who have no freedom is, in a word, the action of God; for they are tools of God, not self-moving artists. But I think he has given man a certain degree of freedom—not absolute freedom, which he alone can have, but relative freedom—so that, compared to God, we are bound, but compared to nature we are free; in virtue whereof we may, up to a certain point, do wrong, abuse the powers that are given us. In that case we act by the strength God has given, but not in the direction he commands. If we do this ignorantly, it is an error, a mistake; if consciously, wilfully, it is a sin, and we have brought a contradiction into our consciousness. In each case we suffer; in the first negatively, by the loss of the satisfaction that would come from conscious obedience; in the second, positively also, from the remorse that we have brought into our soul.

Now I think that God has placed in the world checks to disobedience, such as (1) negative—the loss, or at least the absence, of the satisfaction that comes of obedience—a state of uneasiness and discontent; —positive remorse, grief, and also the outward obstacles which come from the world of nature or the world of man, and resist what is not in harmony with God; which hurl a despot from his throne, which arrest the thief, the glutton, the miser in his course of sin. If you conclude that man ends with the body, these checks are inadequate; but I regard death as another check also; and, if that is not enough, I doubt not the same love that guides us here has other means yet in store, and will at last reclaim us all; and incentives to rectitude, such as the satisfaction one feels from simple virtue, the sense of wholeness, of unity of consciousness, the being one with God, all of which come directly from the various degrees of our obedience. Then, too, I think that death also must be a still further help in the way of perfection; for, as God orders the material world with perfect wisdom and infinite goodness, so must it be with the spiritual world. His world is one great system of optimism; of this I feel sure as that $1+1=2$.

My notion of forgiveness is this,—that by a perfect law each conscious departure from the right (for that only is sin) is followed by painful consequences that we call God's justice; that these painful consequences will gradually lead to repentance, change of life, obedience; that then we feel a unity of consciousness, once more a sense of restoration to God. This also is effected by the action of the same laws working jointly with ourselves, and this we call God's mercy; yet it is the same thing in different parts of the progress. All this, I think, we can learn with no miraculous or abnormal action of God.

It seems to me that our notions of interposition, mediations, and the like, come from the notion that God is purely extra-mundane, and not also intra-mundane (using mundane as the sum total of creation, material and spiritual both). But if God be immanent, and be the mover of all, then the interposition is not occasional and rare, but continual. I think the notion that there is only an *omnipotentia operatica* (in virtue of which God is in my garden only as the watchmaker is present in my watch) and not an *omnipræsentia essentialis*, has been productive of much evil, very much. It leads to all those notions of God's interfering, sending messengers, &c., which fill so large a place in popular theologies, and make the whole spiritual world a piece of mechanism, cold as clockwork, and dead as brass, in which God has nothing to do, but now and then sends some one to wind up the weights or alter the pendulum—a mechanism which all the rest of the time gets along very well without God! This to me is awful!

Now, about inspiration of the Bible. I believe all truth is divine, and from God, *in ratione originis* (for he is the author of it, he is the body of the truth if you will) but none peculiarly divine *in ratione acquisitionis*. Antecedent to all experience, it would have been as probable that God should make his communications in one way as another, but with the experience that in all matters, excepting such as pertain to religion, He communicates with men in a regular manner, through the normal exercise of their faculties, it becomes probable that the same rule holds good in religion also. At least the opposite is not to be assumed outright. I look at such things historically, and cannot settle matters of fact *à priori;* and looking in this way, I don't find evidence which makes it probable to me that God, even in his communication with men, departed from this normal method. I doubt not that He can do so, I don't know but He will to-morrow, but I don't find that He has hitherto.

To meet great emergencies I don't find that God makes use of new means, or new modes of means, but only more of what is regular and normal. Thus, there was a time when there were not more than 1000 men on the earth, and possibly some of them found it hard to get enough to eat, &c. They would have said, "When the earth contains 10,000 men we shall all starve." That is what the Malthuses would have said. "No!" said some pious man, "God will rain down bread from Heaven." But when there are 10,000, 10,000,000, or 10,000,000,000, neither prophecy comes true; the nations do not starve, and the regular mode of production continues still sufficient. So I find in great emergencies of philosophy, &c., there is no departure from the common mode. I doubt not that God is no less the Providence of the world in all affairs of politics, science, &c., as in affairs of religion; yet, to produce great results, I find that Solon and Washington, that Aristotle and Newton, that Homer and Shakespeare come regularly into the world, receive aid through their faculties, and produce the results we see. I don't find that they had anything differing in kind from what belongs to you and me; but only a greater quantity of the same powers. I take it this rule holds good in the religious history of men. I think God raises up men with a great religious genius, so to say, who differ from you and me as Homer or Newton differ from us; not in kind of faculties, not in the mode of receiving truth, but in degree only. Men have pretended that Homer had miraculous aid from the muses and Phœbus Apollo; that Numa held communications with Egeria. It was thought that Wallenstein could be shot only with a silver bullet; and the Indian who "had seventeen fair fires" at Washington with his rifle, concluded "he was not born to be killed with a bullet!" Yet I think there was nothing miraculous in these cases.

Now, these great religious geniuses, I think, come in the plan of Providence, take men by the hand, and lead us on in civilization upwards towards God. They help us to see for ourselves. But for Christ, what would you and I have been? Surely vastly less than we are now. All the providential men before Jesus helped the race on towards him. They are παιδαγωγοι (child-leaders) to conduct us to the Διδάσκαλος! You may call these men mediators, it matters not to me. Jesus is certainly the medium through which millions of men have gladly come to God, only I don't think He stands between us and God, so that we must go through Jesus to come to God.

Now, about the Miracles and the Resurrection, I don't reject these things à priori, but simply because I find so little historical evidence in their support. I must have more evidence to support a statement at variance with all my experience than I demand to support what agrees with my experience. In the case of the New Testament Miracles, I don't find adequate evidence; but this circumstance does not make me think any writer of the New Testament designed to deceive, still less that Christ was a deceiver. Among such a people, under such circumstances, it would be quite surprising to me if such a religious teacher had arisen and had not been popularly believed to work miracles! About the immortality of the soul, I think, as Justin Martyr says, in that remarkable fragment of his work, πέρι αναστασεῶς, that the Resurrection was no proof of that doctrine, for it did not need a proof, as it had been taught before by Plato and Pythagoras. I find abundant proofs of the soul's immortality. I have no more doubt of it than of the fact of my present existence. But long before I abandoned the resurrection of Jesus I saw that it had nothing to do with this doctrine. I don't believe in any outward criterion of spiritual truths.

It seems to me the conscience of you and me is the Lydian stone, with which we are to try the gold of truth. I doubt not that God will make at last this existence of ours a blessing to each one of us, even to the worst of sinners, for I can't think of Him otherwise than as a kind father, who leads the human race by the hand, and will lead us all home at the last, losing none of his little ones, neither you nor me. To believe the eternal damnation of any one of the human race is to me worse than to believe the utter annihilation of all; for I take it the infinite damnation of one soul would make immortality a curse to the race; and the fact that immortality has seldom been taught so that it would be a blessing to mankind to have the doctrine true, is the main cause why some reject the beautiful doctrine of Christ on this point at this day. I know but a little ways, but when my knowledge ends my trust in God does not end. My knowledge is finite, and very little, but my faith in God is absolute; and just as I distrust the traditions of men, does my faith in the truths of God, in His goodness and love, become deeper and more strong. I fear you will find this long letter wearisome and unsatisfactory, my dear brother, but I hope we shall some day have a chance to confer face to face, and more fully.

Truly your Brother,   T. P.

TO MR. JAMES B. PATTERSON, DAYTON, OHIO.

Boston, Feb. 28, 1855.

Dear young Friend,—I am the person whom you met in the cars, and parted from at Albany. I sought you in the cars, but in the dim light I failed to find you. I took a good deal of interest in the bright young face, looking so pure and hopeful, and thinking that some five-and-twenty years ago I was on the same road that you are now. I am sorry that you have met with the " misfortune " you refer to. It certainly casts a shade over a young man's prospects for the moment, not for the day. You have a good start thus far, and seem to have laid the foundation well. It will be no misfortune in the end that you must get your own education. It will bring out the deep manly elements at an earlier period; will make you more thoughtful when you would else have been more gamesome and playful. If you are a teacher you can find much time to study by yourself. I began to teach when seventeen years old, and continued it for four winters, working at home on my father's farm in the other parts of the year. I always found from eight to ten hours a day for study, beside the work hours in school; then I taught a high school for three years more, and kept far ahead of the class in college of which I was a (nominal) member. You can do all that, and perhaps more.

Perhaps it will be well to pursue the same studies you would have taken at college; with the addition of such as belong to your calling as teacher, or you may perhaps teach till you accumulate money enough to go through the college at a later date. No good thing is impossible to a serious and earnest young man with good abilities and good moral principles.

But above all things be careful of your health; your success depends on a sound body. Do not violate the laws which God writes in these tables of flesh.

Let me know where you go and what you find to do, and I will write you again when more at leisure.

Truly your friend,
THEO. PARKER.

TO THE SAME.

Boston, Jan. 7, 1856.

MY DEAR SIR,—Your note came a day or two since, and I take the earliest opportunity to answer it. I replied at once to your former letter, but it miscarried, I suppose. I have often wondered why I did not hear from you. Please send me any newspaper that contains communications from you, with a mark on the article to draw the eye thither. I hope you are well paid for your fifteen hours work in a post-office, otherwise it is waste of time. I thought you would be a lawyer. You may easily be a distinguished one, and, with a little more effort, a noble man in the calling of a lawyer, which is a quite different thing. I hope you will try for that also.

The love of surpassing others is a common but dangerous quality. Love of absolute excellence (ideal perfection) is one thing, love of excelling others is quite another; not a noble quality at all, but only an expansion of selfishness: it is vulgar and low. I trust you will avoid that utterly. Set a high mark of intellectual and moral and religious character that you will reach, the other things will take care of themselves. If I were amongst low men, I would try not to be low; if among high ones, to be as high as possible. Always be yourself, not another man's self.

But I have not time to write you a sermon, so I send one or two that are printed. Let me hear from you as you have inclination, and believe me,

One of your friends,
THEO. PARKER.

One more letter must suffice to close a chapter which, after all, can only vaguely reproduce the extent and method of Mr. Parker's influence:—

FROM PROF. GERVINUS.

Heidelberg, Dec. 29, 1856.

HONORED SIR,—Mr. Apthorp has sent me from Dresden your letter of the 18th August of this year, as he tarries there longer than he thought. The lines from your own hand are so precious to me, that I hasten thankfully to reply. The announcement in your letter that we already have the pleasure of *personally* knowing you—in fact, without being aware of it—took me not disagreeably by surprise. When we saw you at our house in 1844, it was, in fact, before we knew *who Parker was*, for it is only since the German translation of your writings that we have become acquainted with you, American books are so seldom sent to us. And, unfortunately, so many people pass through this little gathering-point of the great routes, that the interesting visitors rejoice us less in the mass of indifferent ones; but that *you* should have been lost to us in this manner, disturbs us greatly. It must, however, humiliating as it is, be confessed. My wife, who is an enthusiastic admirer of yours, was in a sort of despair.

We rejoice every day at the happy idea of Herr Ziethen to translate your works. I hope that, gradually, this will have wide and deep results. We possess your liberal stand-point in theory, in learning, in the schools; we have it in the broad circle of the world, among all people of common sense, but we repel it from the place whence it ought to be taught and planted, so that morality and religion might not disappear *with* obscurantism. Everybody among us knows how it stands with the religious convictions of the majority, only the pulpit does not dare to say it; that is the domain of official hypocrisy. Consequently the calling of the clergyman has been altogether corrupted; let sermons sound ever so high, the whole profession is one of the most despised in Germany. I hope that the impression of your discourses will be favourable to a practical theology among us. I can remark how much they have improved the orthodox themselves. I do what I can to circulate them, in order to make propaganda of the theologians.

To this end, the communications which you have twice sent me are invaluable. I read them with joy and edification. It is a pity that all efforts towards a more rational theory of divine things among us must have only a preparatory significance. We shall have no rational Church until we have a rational State. In this respect, a great apathy now reigns since the failure of 1848; but there is a deep and powerful fermentation, and I venture to predict that the next attempt, which may come late, but certainly will come, will not pass so fruitlessly away. Political storms must free us from a good deal of literary choke-damp, before anything can come out of us. The blessing of our literary revolution of the last century has become a curse, just as Luther's theology did one hundred years after him. I strive with my own scribblings to demonstrate this to my good countrymen, and I shall frequently recur to this theme in the "History of the Nineteenth Century."

You say generous things about this book, which make me feel very proud. But the humanitarian tendency which you discover therein is rather a German one than peculiar to myself. An exclusively partizan history-writing will not be possible here for a long time. I confess that I hold deliberately to the old-fashioned faith that history should be free from all partizanship, except for the universal facts of reason and progress. Whether such a principle can be steadily maintained, after a stable government has been founded, in which parties will strive to rule, is very doubtful to me. It is one advantage of the political disability in which we find ourselves, that the historian can sustain himself upon a height of humanity which he will be obliged to relinquish as soon as earnest talk begins among us concerning a nation, parties, and a state.

Pardon my pen for rambling so. But may I hope that you will embrace future opportunities to communicate with me? You may be assured that you will thus lend a great pleasure to our home. My wife joins her sincere regards to mine.

Faithfully, your obliged
GERVINUS.

END OF VOL. I.

LIFE AND CORRESPONDENCE

OF

THEODORE PARKER,

ΘΕΟΔΩΡΟΣ

Engraved by H.Adlard from a Marble Bust by W.W.Story

LIFE AND CORRESPONDENCE

OF

THEODORE PARKER,

MINISTER OF THE
TWENTY-EIGHTH CONGREGATIONAL SOCIETY, BOSTON.

BY

JOHN WEISS.

IN TWO VOLUMES.
VOL. II

NEW·YORK:
D. APPLETON & COMPANY, 443 & 445 BROADWAY,
1864.

CONTENTS OF VOL. II.

APPENDIX.

ILLUSTRATIONS TO VOL. II.

LIFE AND CORRESPONDENCE

OF

THEODORE PARKER.

THE LIBRARY.

CHAPTER XVI.

The Library—Habits of Composition and Study—Articles—Greek Classics—Goethe—
Sentences—Verses—Translations from Heine and others—Some original lines.

WHEN Mr. Parker went to Boston, he fitted up the fourth story
of his house for a study, by lining the walls with shelves of

the simplest description, without mouldings or ornaments, so as to save every inch of space for books. These shelves gradually crept over the door, the windows, and the chimney-pieces, thence into little adjoining rooms, and finally stepped boldly down the stairs, one flight at a time, for three flights, colonizing every room by the way, including the large parlor in the second story, and finally paused only at the dining-room close to the front door. The bathing-room, the closets, the attic apartments, were inundated with books. Unbound magazines and pamphlets lay in chests of drawers above-stairs; miscellaneous matter was sorted in properly labelled boxes; cupboards and recesses were stuffed full. He had evoked this inundating demon, but did not know the laying spell. In the centre of the study floor rose two or three edifices of shelves to receive the surplus which could find no other bestowment. No house was ever so adorned from basement to attic. To his eye, who knew so well the contents of each volume of the twelve thousand, the walls were frescoed with the ages of human thought, and the solemn tragedies of all the great souls, who counted life a little thing to exchange for the liberties of truth. He traced, too, many a mediæval grotesque, while he recalled from those old chronicles of German cities, bishoprics, and monasteries, the slow emancipation of the power of thinking from the constraints of superstition, marked as it was with burlesque, satire, blood, and terror. In these ponderous folios some of that incongruous literature is collected,—license, that grins like the sly sculptures among saints and apostles in the old cathedrals; thoughts, like truncated spires arrested by the exigencies of the times; human aspiration, mounting and buttressed far above the blackened pediments, above the leaning shops, above the gargoyles of apes' heads and monks with lolling tongues, above the last thin curl of the incense and the mutter of the mass, above even the silvery accents of the chimes, where a purer zone begins, whence the last touches of man's chisel melt into the sky. What sights and voices of old history swept through his well-instructed mind, as he sat at his task amid this unrivalled collection of the sources of knowledge! In his despondent hours what shapes, that drained the hemlock, that blushed with the fagot's blaze, that were white with loss of blood, bent upon him, their eyes burning with triumph in peaceful faces, authoritative looks to bid him revert to a true demeanour! The wonderful companionship which intellect solicits from past intellect, as it entreats each great book to become again a great man, to rise from his lettered tomb into the very room where a dear disciple sits, was his by night and by day. He toiled among these volumes with a will as long-breathed and persistent as any old scholar of them had ; but in the dusk and quiet he could dream too, and fling on the walls of his dwelling the glorious colors of this great Past on which he fed.

He had a good deal of literary appreciation, but it was no-thing to the living sympathy he had. He *knew* Socrates, and had been about with him to the braziers' and the leather-dressers' shops, to learn how to frame those fatal questions, which, whether answered by a yes or a no, took all the conceit out of the answerers.* He had been with him to the plane-tree on the banks of the Ilyssus, considering as he went that restraining Daimon, that voice of God in the soul of man. On such a walk he might have taught the great Athenian, who was as bad a cockney as Charles Lamb, and sneered at nature, to love the fields, and even to try his hand at botanizing.† But he loved men too, and better than Socrates, who only set their minds revolving in order to keep a finer edge upon his blade. Their distrust of mythologies and contempt of the tribe who strive to be both orthodox and rational, the accommodating tribe, was mutual : but Mr. Parker would destroy, in the interest of man-kind, what Socrates was disposed to tolerate. Both loved truth better than Athens and Boston, and the glories of the fields and skies.

He knew Savonarola and peasant Luther ; and the obscure men, whose names scholars seek for curiosity, he *knew*, and had suffered with them in their unblazoned martyrdoms. He sought through all his books the footsteps of men and women, and the drops of blood which betray wherever conscience stood, and the traces of long-forgotten tears upon the pages. He put every withered flower that he found between the leaves into the fresh

---

* See in particular "A Friendly Letter to the Executive Committee of the American Unitarian Association, touching their new Unitarian creed, or General Proclamation of Unitarian Views." 1853.

† Socrates would have mockingly put such a passage as the following into the mouth of some speech-maker like Lysias :—

"In cities there is less to help us communicate with God than in the fields. These walls of brick and stone, this artificial ground we stand on, all remind us of man ; even the city horse is a machine. But in the country it is God's ground beneath our feet—God's hills on every side—His heaven, broad, blue, and boundless, overhead. . . . .

"These continually affect the soul, and cause us all to feel the Infinite Presence, and draw near to that ; and earth seems less to rest in space than in the love of God."

full cup of his heart, and it bloomed like one he gathered yesterday   His library was loved because it was a developing mankind ; he had few books in it that could not illustrate human
thoughts and passions, or the Divine premeditations ; and to this
living assemblage all races sent their representatives, for God
hath made of one blood all nations to dwell on all the face of the
earth.

It will be seen that, even in the indulgence of a taste for
curious books and rare editions, he sought principally those
which were once vitally connected with some human thought,
with the ignorance, vice, and passion of an epoch, with the growth
of law, or religion, or knowledge of the world.   Whoever will
look over this list, which includes some of the rarities of his
library, will hardly find one book that gratifies merely a
dilettante taste, or the mania for having what is difficult to
procure.   There is genuine intellectual or human interest in all
of them.

There are nearly a hundred editions of the Bible, including
" Biblia Germanica, Nuremberg, 1483 ; " another of the same,
with coloured plates ; " Biblia Hebraica Lucensis, Antwerp,
1584 ; " " Biblia Sacrosancta Test. Vet. et Novi, 1550 ; " " B.
Pentapla, Hamburg, 1711 ;" and a Dutch Bible with Hooge's
engravings, 1702.

There is a beautiful folio Plutarch, Paris, 1624 ; a very rare
Virgil, with engravings, Venice, 1544 ; another beautiful Virgil,
printed at Paris in 1500 ; a Homer, Basel, 1558 ; a fine copy
of Herodotus, London, 1679 ; a fine Horace, Venice, 1559 ;
a folio Aristotle, Paris, 1629 ; and Athenæus, London, 1657.

Old geographies and books of travel attracted him ; such as
" Umständliche und Eigentliche Beschreibung von Africa," with
engravings, Amsterdam, 1670 ; two Dutch folios about Tartary,
Amsterdam, 1705 ; " Claudii Ptolemæi Alexandrini Geographicæ
Enarrationis, Libri Octo, Lugduni, 1535," with the imprint of
Melchior and Gaspar Trechsel.   In a note to this volume, Mr.
Parker says : " I received this long-sought volume on the seventy-
ninth anniversary of the Battle of Lexington. It is the edition
of Michael Servetus, whereon see Mosheim, Gesch. MS., s. xviii.
p. 60, *et seq.* " Rauwolf's " Aigentliche Beschreibung der Raisz,"
Journey through the East, 1588, with the notes of old readers.

He bought the very curious book entitled " Chronicon Nurem-
bergense," Hartmann Schedel, Nuremberg, 1493, printed by

Koberger, for 3 dollars 43 cents. It is a history of the Seven Day's Creation, six ages reaching down to the date of the book, with a seventh of Antichrist, and a last of Judgment. The woodcuts in this volume are by Wohlgemuth, the master of A. Dürer; the child-vignettes are as old as Wohlgemuth, and have a great deal of grace.

In mediæval history the library can show some books that are seldom to be met: here are J. D. Schoepflin's "Historia Zaringo-Badensis, Carolsruhæ, 1763–66," his "Vindiciæ Celticæ," and the rare "Alsatia illustrata Celtica Romana Franca; Colmar, 1751 ;" "Schannat's Annals of Fulda," "Thuringia Sacra; " "Antiquitates et Annales Trevirensium, 1670."

Here also are "Leonici de Varia Historia, libri tres, Venice, 1531, 16mo ; " "Leti G. L'Italia regnante, Geneva, 1675 ; " 4 vols, 16mo, a rare book; "Jobi Ludolfi, alias Leut-holf dicti, Hist. Æthiopica," printed at Frankfort-on-the-Maine, 1681, being an account of Prester John's Kingdom; "Historia Generale de los Hechos de los Castellanos en las Islas i Tierra Firma, Herrera, 1601 ;" "Helvetiorum Respublica, 1627," by different authors.

To a copy of Alexander Murray's "History of the European Languages," Mr. Parker has the following note :—"I had long been looking for a copy of this curious book, which I borrowed years ago and studied, when I found it advertised in a newspaper published in Charlestown, S.C., and sent to me that I might profit by a violent and abusive article against me. *Fas est et ab hoste doceri.* I sent and bought the book. It came on my forty-fourth birthday."

He procured all the editions of Thomas More that he could find, of London, 1557; Basel, 1580 (the Epigrams) ; "The Life and Death, 1630," no place ; the "Utopia, Cologne, 1629," and another, London, 1634 ; and the whole works, Frankfort, by Zeiss, 1689.

Here is the rare and costly "Monumenta Germanica Historica, Hanover, 1826" (continued) ; Cardinal Maï's "Classicorum Auctorum e Vaticanis Codicibus editorum ;" the beautiful Bible of 1857, and ten volumes of "Script. Vet., nova collectio."

Here are ten volumes of Jerome Cardan, London, 1663 ; the Works of John Damascene, Basel, 1575 ; the "Historia Salisburgensis—hoc est Vita Episcoporum et Archiepiscoporum S. Salzburg, 1692 ;" old editions of Picus Mirandula, Campanella, and Galen; the rare book of J. Grynæus, "Monumenta S. Patrum Orthodoxographica, Basel, 1569;" a rare volume, "Exercitationes Paradoxicæ adversus Aristoteleos, &c.; Auctore Petro Gassendo," Canon of the Cathedral of Dinia (Dijon), an Elzevir, Amsterdam; the very rare book, "Gasparis Scioppi Franci, De Arte Criticâ et Priapeia, sive diversorum Poetarum in Priapum lusus;" the first part printed at Amsterdam, "*apud Judocum Pluymer, Bibliopolam, sub signo Senecæ,* 1662;" *the* second part, "*Patavii, apud Gerhardum Nicolaum V. sub signo angeli aurati; comment. in rubro xantho et nigro.*"

In a copy of Jacobus de Voragine, "Lombardica Historia, de Sanctis" (lived at the end of 13th century), is this note : "*homo ut verè quidam judicabat, ferrei oris et plumbei cordis, alioqui vix dignus qui inter Scriptores locum inveniat.*"

Of books excessively rare there are nine various works, illustrated by De Bry, as for instance : "Boissardi Theatrum Vitæ humanæ—Vita Davidis;" "Boissardi Emblemata, Vita Mahumetis; crudelitas Hispanorum in Indis;" "De Membris humani Corporis petrifactis;" "Historia Monstrorum"—320 plates by Theodore De Bry, Francfort, 1596 to 1609. This includes "Lithogenesia, sive de microcosmi membris petrefactis; et de calculis eidem microcosmo per varias matrices innatas;" "Pathologia historica, per Theoriam et Autopsiam demonstrata. Accessit Analogicum Argumentum ex Macrocosmo de calculis brutorum corporibus innatis. Auctori Ioanne Georgio Schlenkio, à Grafenberg."

Another book of great rarity is, "Vincentius Bellovacencis, of Beauvais, or de Burgundia;" "Speculum quadruplex, naturale, doctrinale, morale et historiale, Argentorati, Johannes Mentelin, 1473–76;" this is a large folio, in seven volumes, when complete. The chain and staple by which the old books were fast anchored to the reading-desk are still affixed.

Mr. Parker's copy includes volumes of the original edition, which is very rare.* His copy is not complete, and not all of that edition; but out of all the volumes, there may be made a complete copy of the *Speculum Quadruplex*, except the third part of the *Morale* and a leaf or two at the beginning of Vol. III. of the *Historiale.*

* For information concerning this book of Vincent of Beauvais I am indebted to Mr. Jewett, the polite librarian of the Boston Free Public Library, whither the books of Mr. Parker were transported in the summer of 1862. Mr. Auerbach was also very kind while I was looking up the above-mentioned specimens of the library.

While Mr. Parker was carrying on his Saturday afternoon conversations with members of his parish, he drew from his copy of old Vincent specimens of well-attested miracles to offset those equally well (or badly) attested in the New Testament. There was not a book in the whole great collection which did not at some time or other serve his practical turn, to teach withal plain truths to the people.

He found very valuable such a book as "Io. Henr. Feust-kingii, Gynacæum Hæretico Fanaticum," or history and description of false prophetesses, Quakeresses, enthusiasts, and other sectarian and inspired female persons, by whom the Church of God has been disturbed. This was printed at Frankfort, in 1704; and Mr. Parker's copy came from the library of Christian Frederic Eberhard. Also, "De suspectis de hæresi opus. Romæ, 1703."

So, too, all books concerning demoniacal possession and agency, in which he was very curious, such as "Johannis Nideri, de vision-ibus ac revelationibus," 1517: reprinted in 1692, an *opus raris-simum;* "Bodin, de la Demonomanie des Sorciers, 1580," and the "Dictionnaire Infernale," became valuable in his hands; and books like "Geschichte der Deutschen Geistlichkeit im Mittelalter;" "Die fliegenden Blätter des XVI. and XVII. Jahrhunderts;" "Das Kloster;" "Das Schaltjahr;" "Directorium Inquisitorum;" * "Die komische und humoristiche Literatur der deutschen Pro-saisten des 16ten. Jahrhunderts. Auswahl aus den Quellen und seltenen Ausgaben, von Ignaz Hub;" "Historia de la Vida y Excelencias de la Sacratissima Virgen M. Madrid, 1657;" a rare edition of "H. C. Agrippæ Operum, pars posterior;" and "Jacob Gretzer, de jure et more prohibendi, expurgandi et abolendi libros hæreticos et noxios," a book levelled at Francis Junius, the Calvinist, and John Pappus, and other Lutheran preachers, 1603, became endowed with life and immediate value in his hands.

There are many books of civil and canon law—codes of different countries: "Joachimi Potgiesseri," commentaries on the German law *de statu Servorum* (Lemgoviæ, 1736). Staats-Archiv., 1796; "Corpus Juris Germanici Publici ac Privati. Francofurti ad Mœnum, 1766;" the "Sachsenspiegel" (Leipzig, 1569); "Savigny's Zeitschrift;" "Rheinisches Museum," which includes Jurisprudence; Heineccius, Puffendorf, Mohl, Miruss,

---

* A rare and extraordinary book.

Spangenberg, Ahrens, books on *Jus Parochiale* of various places, Gesterding, Gagern, Pütter.

He had well cradled all such books, and melted down their gold.

If you were looking for didactic books, or writings which manipulate the ordinary religious proprieties, and vigorously enforce, with rhetoric more or less inflamed, a feeble sentiment, his shelves would at once disappoint you and instruct you what to seek. For they had selected from each province only the essential thoughts and characters.

But poetry and literature sent also their highest representatives. All the great names of Greece and Rome, Italy and Germany, France and England stood there, Burns as well as Dante, and Chaucer quite as well thumbed as Shakespeare, and many a Servian, Russian, Bohemian volume of provincial character, hardly known yet beyond their own firesides, but full of the ethnic peculiarities which he loved to trace. And the best hymns of all nations met their best songs upon these cosmopolitan shelves, which were tolerant of all the forms that strength, beauty, and religion can put on. But they had a pitiless discrimination against the mere fabricators of religious and literary cant which sneak well-dressed into a library's great society.

Some book always lay upon the desk, to fill up the pauses of writing or vacant moments in the day. There was generally more than one, as many as he had trains of thought or research collateral with the business of the week. The desk, the chair, the gas-light above, which could be adjusted at any height to suit the caprice of the moment, the slides for books,—all this environment was the perfection of a student's corner : its convenience betrayed him into the deep hours, and it would have been better for his head if one of Mrs. Broad's lamps had crustily offered the alternative of darkness or repose. He always waited for those starlit hours, after the great city has roared and vexed itself to sleep, and the quiet breathing of all things in the Father's house, like a slow pendulum, tells the soul in conspiracy with truth that its time has come.

His method of labour may be gathered from the traces of the composition of articles and sermons. Nothing was commenced until a brief or scheme of it lay complete upon his desk. When reading and meditation, taking copious notes meanwhile, had furnished him with a view of the whole subject, so that he saw not only the end from the beginning, but the details and sub-divisions of each head, he began to write. Or, if he intended, in the case of speeches and sermons, to address his audience extemporaneously, if the subject was not already, by frequent speaking and arranging, made familiar, every point was premeditated, and occasionally one or two leading sentences put down, just where he felt instinctively that he might need a stepping-stone. He was not obliged to recur to his brief during speaking, because he had assigned to each thing, the facts, the statistics, the allusions, the helping phrases, its post in the memory. The same system and comprehensiveness which insisted upon a perfect brief made it non-essential at the moment of speaking. But he never undertook to lay his track until he had made a most careful and methodical survey of the route which he must travel. He was all the time making statements and organizing thought. How many clergymen use their brains for bait, and wait in resignation for the nibble of a text!

In reviewing a book his conscientiousness would have been a matter of affright to Sidney Smith, who did not like to be prejudiced by reading the book. He not only actually read the book in question, but all the books he could command which furnish information upon the subject that was involved.

FROM THE JOURNAL.

Sept. 20, 1839.—Finished Villemain. He has a strong, almost passionate love for the English orators of Burke's time, and gives long extracts from their speeches. He admires the thorough education of the younger Pitt, his skill in classic literature, and those austere studies so little known to the French wits of the 18th century, but which are the only foundation of real excellence.

If I had the requisite knowledge, I would criticize the work in the *North American* or *Christian Examiner;* but the habit, so common in America, of getting all your knowledge from the author you review, and then censuring him, is villainous and unworthy. Cattle drink, and then foul the water: so these critics. Mr. Somebody reviewed Cox's "Life of Melancthon," getting all his information from Cox, who had little himself!

We need and must have a new kind of criticism. It must be like the German in its depth, philosophy, all-sidedness, and geniality. It must have the life, wit, and sparkle of the French. What need it borrow from the English? Most of our critics are somewhat shallow men at the best, and they write often of what they understand but feebly and superficially, and so the result is as it is.

He did a great deal in obeying his own high standard, to excite a desire for a more thorough critical ability among us. His papers on German Literature, Strauss, Prescott's Histories, are among the best furnished with knowledge upon the subjects which are discussed of any yet published in our reviews.

FROM THE JOURNAL.

Sept. 1839.—Write a critique of Menzel's "History of German Literature,"* when it appears, and treat, 1, of the whole subject of German literature, its *sources*—classic, romantic, and nature now living —its *influence* at home and abroad—compared with the French of the 18th century. Speak of the proper histories of German literature. [Here follows a list of names]. 2, of the book itself, its merits and faults. One-sided, smart. Its author's position and character: The aspects of German literature. 1. Literary, moral, philosophical, religious. 2. What we have to hope, to fear.

Let us see how he prepared himself for reviewing Strauss. First, of course, he read the original text of 1600 pages : then all the *Streitschriften,* or books and pamphlets defending or attacking Strauss, which had appeared up to the time of his article, by Tholuck, Ullmann, and others ; then the notices in the foreign reviews. This, with his previous knowledge of the German theological field, made him competent to apply his own judgment to the book.

Before he undertook to review Mr. Prescott's popular histories, he spent all the leisure time which he could command during seven months, in reading the authorities. He read everything excepting some MSS. in the possession of Mr. Prescott himself, and thus he verified nearly every citation made in the eight volumes which were under review. The first article, published in the *Massachusetts Quarterly,* March, 1849, contains an admirable statement of the office and duty of an historian. This is derived from his own humane and philosophical spirit, criticizing in the interest of the future of the people all the best histories yet written of the past.

He had collected a great many notes for an article which was to be entitled "The Supernatural in Literature." Under this title he meant to treat, first, of violations of ordinary laws in composition, common-sense, common honesty, and recognition of a common intelligence ; second, of theological and religious hypocrisies ; third, cases of bombast in ancient and modern literature (his classical references here are curious) ; fourth, the

* Translated by President Felton for Mr. Ripley's "Specimens of Foreign Literature." 1840.

mistakes in newspapers, pamphlets, sermons, &c., which unconsciously assert a ridiculous impossibility, *e. g.* " both the obelisks
are in a state of perfect preservation ; the larger is about 82
English feet high, and the other about 336 feet shorter ;"
fifth, cases of American exaggeration, from reports of southern
and western grandiloquence and congressional appeals. Under
this head, probably, he would have cited American humor,
which delights to " play at bowls with the sun and moon," and
belittles the great and magnifies the small with irresistible
audacity.

I have made these various heads from the illustrations
which he had confusedly gathered ; for, apparently, he had no
time to subject them to his usual formal treatment. But such an
article in his hands would have excited mirth and hatred without limits. How would religious sentimentalists have recoiled
from their own offspring, stripped and turned loose in inclement
prose ! The Hollis Street Council would have sat again upon
his translations of their diplomatic sentences into the vernacular, *e. g.* :—

" Circumstances that call for a liberal measure of that wisdom which
cometh from above." This is the supernatural in form, and the plain
English is, " Cunning enough to soften the doctrines of Christianity
down to suit a rumseller's case."

The indiscriminate allusions to a Providence, which Americans
indulge to profanity, and the popular conceit which interpolates
the divine agency in all the chores of the house, form a tempting
branch of his subject. But he made the following distinction
to apply to all his illustrations :—

1. The supernatural in *substance.* 2. In *form.* Find no fault with
what is *really* supernatural. Some things are written for the *subterranean* men : of these the terrestrial will not complain, but only neglect them. Others are written for the *terrestrial,* and of these the
celestial will not find fault. And still others for the *celestial:* of these
neither the subterranean nor the terrestrial have any right to complain.
Many things *are* above our comprehension : we need not fash our
heads about that matter. But the *formally* supernatural is fair game.
" *Quid vetat dicere ridiculum verum ?* "
            " Hail, honest weapon, left for truth's defence,
            Sole dread of folly, vice, and insolence !"
Use it against all the things which are—
            " Safe from the bar, the pulpit, and the throne."

Part of the article was intended to be purely literary, as he
has noted the false antitheses in Junius, the tragic degradations

in Seneca's plays, and the vices of Heine, Coleridge, Richter, Ariosto, Dryden, Cowley, and Carlyle. He was driven from such subjects which involve a careful literary treatment by greater claims.

There is also a curious collection of the miracles of all ages and nations, cases of resurrections, healings, miraculous conceptions, &c., each with its reference, so that the time, place, and amount of evidence could be found. He meant, of course, to use these to show the universal tendency towards the marvellous in men of all races and religions, and the ease with which extraordinary individuals gather a concrete of the supernatural. A portion of his book upon religious development would probably have included this catalogue, to prove that where there is so much (apparently) good evidence for so many alleged occurrences, they are either *all* genuine or *none*. On the basis of such a collection he might have composed an interesting chapter on the imperfection of all human testimony, save that of the trained and scientific observer. For to observe, and thus to create evidence, is as much a speciality as to invent, to compose, to discourse, to labor with the hands.

In like manner, he collected remarkable prophecies made by sagacious and far-seeing men, which received historical verification, in ancient and modern times. These would serve to show the true nature of the prophetical spirit, and what immutable laws control it.

All these researches were undertaken in the interest of mankind, to contribute something to that accumulation of exact knowledge which alone can pay real honors to religion, by driving ignorance and superstition out of the mind. The humane and courageous thinker swings such material with both arms, and meditates his blow; the timid shrink from the sparkling indignation of his eye, as it notes where the fetter clasps the flesh—for they, too, think they are serving man by maintaining his confinement—down comes the blow, the flesh is not mangled, only the fetter is hopelessly broken, and the man stands fast in liberty. There is no such nice calculator as knowledge.

In general, he saw it was necessary to be acquainted with the subject which he intended to use. This simple precaution is ludicrously neglected among us, and quite as often in the pulpit as elsewhere. He did not believe that excellent intentions, or even the most generous impulses, sufficiently furnished forth the preacher for his work ; and he sighed to see the hasty preparations, the neglect of the classics, the contempt for laborious investigations, with which, and with youth, we step into the service of our brethren, under the conceit which all the habits of a new country foster and forgive—that good raw material just *extemporized* into a person, can take the pulpit, the chair of science, and the bar by storm. The very man, of all men born in America, who could have done this most successfully, preferred to set a better American fashion. One self-made man thus taught modesty and discipline to all the men self and conventionally made.

He had his own way of deliberately making the acquaintance of all subjects — the Homeric Question, Æschylus, the Greek Drama, Aristophanes, Goethe, Heine, Marriage, Woman, Socialism, &c. Many of these are yet unwritten upon ; the blocks are drawn to the site, and lie in various stages of preparation. So far as the necessary reading is concerned, let it suffice to say, that he read and carefully spread out in analyses, with his private estimate, every attainable book.

Here, it is perceived, are literary as well as philanthropic questions. How did he promise to discuss them ? A few of the preparatory notes will show what ability he had in this direction, and what tastes he sacrificed to the claims of humanity and the pressure of the hour. Such notes have little novelty or intrinsic value, but they help to betray all his thought..

This, looking to an article upon Socialism, will introduce more scholarly themes :—

"Murphy's Science of Consciousness." This is a queer book, written by a Materialist, Socialist, Owenite. He says, "Life is a vortex or whirlpool of material motions." He denies any immaterial spirit, and makes all depend on organization : there is neither free-will nor moral responsibility ; our character is made for us, not by us. God is the *collectivum* of the universe, all-knowing and ever-present. Of course, there can be no immortality. Such is the man's philosophy— or want of it.

What is his aim? To make the world a more comfortable place. How is it to be done? By giving up property, *i. e.*, individual property. He wants to try the experiment of living in a great establishment, feeding at a common table, &c. In short, he wishes for a *family* like the Shakers, but with the prevalence of marriage. He seems to doubt whether man would be always faithful to one wife, or would move from one to another. He says that in countries where subsistence is very easy, divorce takes place without difficulty, for the state feels no anxiety about the children coming to want, and being a burden upon the community. There is no eloquence, perhaps, in the book, but some passages of no little power.

This book is but a straw in the stream, but it shows which way the current sets, and God knows what will be the end of this awful movement. For my single self, I fear the result will be, as often before; the "rich" and "noble," becoming alarmed, will shed blood, and then the mob, getting scent thereof, will wash their hands in the hearts of the "rich" and "noble," and we shall have a worse tragedy in the end of the 19th century than in the end of the 18th. Heaven save us from an English Reign of Terror!

The same question must be passed on in America. Property must show why it shall not be abated. Labor must show why it should exempt so many from its burdens, and crush others therewith. It is, no doubt, a good thing that I should read the Greek Anthology, and cultivate myself in my leisure, as a musk-melon ripens in the sun; but why should I be the only one of the thousand who has this chance? True, I have won it dearly, laboriously, but others of better ability with less hardihood fail in the attempt, and serve me with the body. It makes me groan to look into the evils of society; when will there be an end? I thank God I am not born to set the matter right. I scarce dare attempt a reform of theology, but I shall be in for the whole, and must condemn the State and Society no less than the Church.

These property notions agree not with my own. Yet, certainly the present property scheme invokes awful evils upon society, rich no less than poor. The question, first, of inherited property, and next, of all private property, is to be handled in this century.

Can one man serve another for wages without being degraded? Yes, but not in *all relations*. I have no moral right to use the service of another, provided it degrades him in my sight, in that of his fellows, or himself.

In the meantime, let us see what some of his Greek studies were. They began very early, and did him great service. His constant recurrence to favorite Greek books amid his various reading tranquillized his mind, and helped to save his style from becoming barbarized with metaphysical terms and idioms. He was more indebted than he knew to the "tender, grave Hellenic speech."

Juno.--I take her for a type of the average woman. 1. She has no general ideas. 2. No conception of truth and justice—still less any love for them. 3. She is capricious to the last degree. 4. She has great preponderance of will—not over her passions, but over her better affections. 5. She thinks all must yield to her whim. 6. She is restless, rather than active. 7. She perpetually scolds at what is lofty and noble. 8. She teazes her husband beyond measure. 9. She is jealous of all rivals, and watches them with the most curious eye. 10. Judgment precedes knowlege, I. 518-523. She thinks Troy must be destroyed, because she chanced to sweat, as well as her horses, in getting up the war. She has no regard for justice, and asks Jove to send Minerva to make the Trojans violate the truce.

1840. *Batrachomyomachy.**—This poem cannot be Homer's. I wonder any one can fancy he wrote it, unless there is *strong* external evidence to that effect. It has very little merit, as I think. However, it teaches one thing, viz. how ridiculous human affairs would seem to a superior being, unless that being were perfect. The war of the mice and frogs, conducted with much valor on both sides, and attended with no little suffering, moves only *our* ridicule: what right had the Greek to conclude Jupiter did not laugh at the wars of Greeks and Trojans? Again: this is a picture in little of human affairs. The frog leaves his hazardous friend in danger, and because one had been slain by accident, many must be slaughtered by design. Again: the one who counsels war, does it because the cat and the trap have deprived him of two sons, and the mouse has taken the last.

Hymns attributed to Homer.—Some of these hymns are beautiful. I like especially the hymn to Venus: the affair with Anchises is most beautifully told. One to Bacchus also is pleasant. Taken together they disappoint me. I see no reason to refer them to Homer, or perhaps even to his age.

Some of the *Epigrams* (Hermann's ed.), please me much. Here is one " On the Senate House ":—

Children are the crown of men ; of cities, towers ;
Horses are ornaments in the field, and ships at sea;
Wealth builds the house, but precedent builds kings—
In council sitting, ornaments to be admired before all others—
And yet a house lit by a blazing fire is nobler still to see,
On a winter's day, when Saturn's son sheds down the snow."

After a long course of Homeric studies, he writes in 1840 :—

Here close my present studies of Homer, and with this conclusion on the whole :—1. That the greater part of the *Iliad* was the work of one man, whom we may call Homer. 2. That he did not *write*, but only *sung.* 3. That he sung in detached pieces, which were repeated by others. 4. That they all became more or less corrupt. 5. That other pieces were reckoned as Homeric which are not so. 6. That the men who reduced the Iliad to writing did it gradually—now this, now that part, ballad, or story. 7. That when all were collected, the genuine and spurious were not separated sharply. 8. That interpolations were made by these men also to make the whole work fit together. 9. That the theology and morality, considering the age, are very high, though not so high as the theology and morality of the Old Testament.

Again: that the *Odyssey* belongs to another age, and is also the work of various hands, and that it is quite possible to separate the *Odyssey* into its constituent ballads at this day.

During his Greek studies he notices the variations of different editions, and discusses the merits of their text, entering into the minutiæ of such criticism, showing why he supposes, for in-

* Battle of the Frogs and Mice.

stance, that some lines have slipped out of an elegy of Tyrtæus found in Stobæus, &c., &c., dwells with pleasure upon epithets and compounds, translates, though not in a finished way, bu merely to mark in his memory, elegies and lyrics which he likes. These studies were not preliminary to any composition, but to gratify his scholarly inclinations.

SIMONIDES OF CEOS.—I cannot sum up the whole of Simonides, and all that marks him as a poet; for here are doubtless the works of numerous poets, carelessly thrown together; and one finds that the editor has no critical tact, I think. Certainly an air of sadness penetrates all of them. Many are religious. Leave all to the gods, is the perpetual lesson. Simonides and Mimnermus represent the sad side of life. They are the shades in the dazzling picture of young and flashing life among the Greeks. What a contrast between Simonides and the hymns of Homer or Orpheus! What exquisite sweetness and power of rhythm!

But I must consult Schneidewin's edition. He is the same who edited Ibycus some years before: that was censured, and he submits to the censure very quietly, and tells his critics he had learned " mea non admirari," and hopes to do better than before.

Simonides, it seems, was a miser, as well as a biting satirist. He quarrelled with the Corinthians, imitated the old wise men in their "sayings," had always a smart thing ready to say. Sweetness and subtlety are his characteristics, and he has a simple way of exciting the feelings, e. g., Danae, Dysoris, Timarchus, and Gorgo. It was with him "tot verba quot res," so they called his poetry ξωγραφία λαλοῦσα, talking pictures.

PINDAR.—The ethical tendency of Pindar is beautiful and striking. He takes always a lofty tone. The unity of his pieces consists in the ethical virtue he has set forth—bravery, good fortune (which is always the meed of virtue), strength, and the like.

I should be glad to know the history of his love. One thinks at first it must have been sweeter and more celestial than is wont among the sons of men. But the fact always limps after the fancy. Perhaps his wife was prosy and cross; at best she was but the creature of his will, or the toy of his flesh, it may be.

ÆSCHYLUS—"Prometheus Bound." If I were fool enough to turn matters into allegories, and facts into fictions, I would get an improvement of this masterly drama as follows :—

Zeus represents a Conservative aristocrat who has lately got into power. He turns round and abuses his friends who helped him to the office, and wishes to govern the people ad arbitrium, caring nothing at all for their welfare. Nay, on one occasion (232), he would destroy them all. Then comes up one ancient as himself, and equally immortal, who rebukes the wickedness of the aristocratic parvenu, and seeks to make all things better. In a word, Prometheus is a gentleman of "property and standing," of a "very ancient descent," who is a thorough democratic reformer. He is a philanthropist in all senses ; discovers fire and letters, metals and navigation, agriculture, astronomy, medicine, and the like, and, besides this, gives Father Jove some clever advice.

He recommends mild measures. He is the son of *Themis*, which shows that *right* is on the popular side. The aristocrat would disturb and destroy the people, and because Prometheus opposed, he is angry. Now the established powers, Strength, and Force, and Skill (symbolized in Vulcan), serve him. But Vulcan serves unwillingly; for he knows his kinship with the people, and remembers his familiarity. Both are immortal; so there will always be a quarrel between these two principles—the selfish-conservative and the disinterested-progressive. But the latter has Truth on its side—for Themis is its parent—and so will ultimately prevail, and knows the fact. Therefore it tells the other, "Thunder as loud as you may!" and mocks the heralds of the aristocrat to scorn. "You cannot kill me, and the day will come when you shall fall." The ruin of conservatism is to come from itself. Zeus is to ally with a descendant of Io (Thetis), and she will produce one greater than its father, &c. Prometheus knows this, and whence the danger is to come; but Zeus cannot keep continent and cool, and so must know who the person is. Prometheus will not be specific until all his fetters are taken off. Then he helps Zeus out of his troubles. If I were a German Radical, I should call this the moral of the story.

It is evident that Zeus here is not the Supreme. There is no allusion to such an one here. So heaven is headless. Zeus is but a *parvenu*, &c. Still further, the timid friends of Prometheus, the Chorus and Oceanus, advise him to hush up the affair, and be a little more courteous to the one in power. They tell him, "You are mistaken, ἥμαρτες; you are saucy, too, but it avails nothing."

Strength would have him leave off his benevolence, and asks, very properly, "Why don't you hate whom the gods (the upper classes) hate?"

There are many good hits in the piece, *e. g.* 221, where Prometheus says it is the curse of tyranny to distrust friends.

Is not the episode of Io a violation of the unity of the piece? She might appear, and the story of her descendants might have been told without bringing in the whole history of that maiden.

In this way he goes through all the plays of Æschylus, and hopes at some proper time to write an article on him; "but he cannot be understood without studying all of his contemporaries, especially the other tragedians and Aristophanes."

Then he translates fragments of Æschylus.

On the whole, my estimation of him is very much raised by this new study. But a good edition of Æschylus is still to be sought. It would embrace, 1, an improved text, with copious various readings and critical notes. 2. Copious notes, historical, archæological, and æsthetic. 3. A good interpretation, philological notes, &c. 4. Dissertations after the manner of Heyne on the Iliad. Hermann, I think, could not do this work, but he might help to it. The religious significance of Æschylus I have never yet seen adequately treated.

June, 1840.—Read the "Hero and Leander" of Musæus. I can never sufficiently admire this beautiful poem. I read it four years ago, and ever since it has dwelt in my mind like remembered music, which comes up from time to time. This poem has the naked freshness of olden time, and the delicate sensibility of later days.* Homer (or Orpheus, or Hesiod), would have despatched the matter of love in three words, and then would have told us how he fought during the day before he swam over the Hellespont. He would tell us nothing of Leander's feeling as he swam—only of the constellations over his head. He would describe to us the carving on Hero's lamp, never telling us how she felt or what she thought. His love is always stark naked, without a single fig-leaf to cover its shame. What would Homer make of lines 75–85, or of 101 *seq.*? Could Homer fancy Achilles swimming the Hellespont, or even the Scamander, for a lovely woman? Not so; he was too catholic in his taste, while Briseïs was in his tent, or one of his father's maids in the kitchen chamber. Those *old* Greeks were brutes in their lust; for it was not always love. Yet there was something quite æsthetic and graceful in their love-adventures. Why cannot old Greek freedom and real, unconventional love be united with Christian morality, and woman stand in her true position? A—— S—— was right in saying she disliked my figure comparing woman to a *vine*, and man to an oak, she climbing his tough branches, giving verdant gracefulness to his trunk, and hanging his boughs with the purple clusters of love. She would have them two trees, which grow side by side, and intertwine their arms. How right that is! If woman were not deemed a *vine*, and so inferior to man, these present abominable abuses could not take place, nor could they have taken place in Greece. We should have had no Trojan war and no rape of the Sabine women.

He reads everything—Gnomic poets, Skolia, Hymns, Orphic fragments, pursues every trace of a philosopher, as well as the great footsteps of tragedy and comedy. All the prayers of the ancients are carefully examined, to discover their precise religiosity underneath the mythical names. His volumes of the classics have a good many notes on the margins and loose leaves.

After reading Meineke's " Fragments of Greek Comic Writers," Vol. I. :—

Feb. 1841.—Comedy has turned on the same points in all ages. The lower nature of man, it seems, loves to burst the bonds which confine it in general, and assume the sway. But there are passages of the most beautiful morality and poetry in the Greek comic writers. They charm me exceedingly. They indicate, as I think, a higher state of morals and decency than has been found in any comic writers since their time. It seems melancholy to say this, but it is true. However, the condition of woman seems the shady side of the picture. These fragments, it is likely, are the best pieces in all the plays, selected for their excellence. Of course, they are not to be taken as fair samples of the average morality of the times. I doubt not a larger collection might be made out of the comic writings of Shakspeare alone.

---

* It was written in the 5th century of the Christian era, and was the first attempt at making love the exclusive motive of a poem. It was translated by Marlowe.

ARISTOPHANES—"*The Acharnians.*"—It is a most wonderful play. Such versatility of language, thought, and imagery is surprising. He tells truth boldly—witness the account of the war and its causes, 498–510. The scene with Euripides is masterly, 370; so is the return of the ambassadors. The mockery at *Theognis, cold as snow,* is exquisite.

He makes brief notes through the play, as above, and concludes :—

"I hate the obscenity of many passages. But vice is ridiculed—put down, it may be. A dreadful state of licentiousness is disclosed; but the play itself would not encourage it. In this respect it is better than Wycherley, Farquhar, and others, and the Parisian drama.

"*The Knights.*"—It seems to me there is less poetry, and more good sense, in this than "*The Acharnians.*" For boldness of satire nothing could surpass it. Here not only three of the most powerful men of the state, Nicias, Demosthenes, and Cleon, are satirized with unsparing severity; but the people of Athens, the Demus itself, is done to the life. It is one of the boldest pieces of political satire I have ever seen.

"*The Clouds.*"—The philosophers are treated very much as the Transcendentalists are now. There is a devilish satire in the plot of making Justice and Injustice contend, and the latter conquer; and then throwing the blame upon Socrates. To the vulgar this must have been sufficient proof of the falseness of the philosoper, but to one who looks deeper there is a different moral, viz. if you follow virtue solely for the loaves and fishes, you ought to be cheated out of them; for it is loaves and fishes you seek. Then, again, Strepsiades is justly punished by the folly and sin of his son. He represents the vulgar fathers who do not ask a generous education for their children, but simply the skill that will get them a living out of a wicked world, by any means. The play is a sermon on that head.

Xenophon's "Memorabilia" is the answer to Aristophanes. This play shows that ridicule is no test of truth, as the foolish think ; for the blame as often rests with the laugher as with the laughee.

"*The Birds.*"—I like this piece amazingly. It shows us human relations in such a new point of view. It revolutionizes the gods. It was a capital idea to wall up heaven and shut out the smoke of sacrifice ! So the question of inheritance raised between Hercules and Neptune, in the case of Jupiter's death, and the felicitous manner in which the Bird-Archon makes use of it to gain the vote of Hercules, is a fine hit. Then, see in how human a way the case of Bird-Archon is decided. The two real gods, Hercules and Neptune, are neck-and-neck ; so the matter falls to the barbarian *Triballos.* Then see also the characters that come up to *Cloud-Cuckoo-Ville,* and their talk ! The new fashion among men who took to imitating the birds. He proves very prettily that the birds are older than the gods, and so have a right to all, as waifs and strays belong to the lord of the manor. The beauty of language I think unrivalled. The choruses are sugar steeped in honey.

THE CLASSICS AND MODERNS.—The works of Æschylus were slowly formed. They grew piece by piece, till they became clear, large, massy, beautiful, perfect ! Those of Voltaire, for example, are made at a few dashes, and are done. One is a huge crystal, without flaw, the work of ages; it will be admired, and never perish. The other is an ice-cream, made at an hour's warning, to serve one night. One grew slowly and silently, by the laws of nature, in a grave cavern which men never enter. The other is a little dirty shop, in a bye-lane, noisy, frequented, filled with chattering gossips.

Voltaire, with his erudition, wide though not deep, with style so clear and bright that it never wearies, with imagination ever on the wing, and flying in most strange, capricious circles—is a mocker, after all. The highest faculty of the soul he never conceives of; religion, he knows nothing of it.

His reading of Goethe was no ordinary enjoyment. It was a deliberate exploration of his life and character. First he read through the whole edition, excepting the Grand-Cophta, on which "the reading faculty broke down;" then the supplementary volumes; then collections of letters, Jacobi, Nicolai, and others; then lives of Goethe, by Döring, Schäfer, &c. His observation of Goethe is made with great equanimity, and his opinions do not reflect the conventional tone. They have, on the contrary, the air of being the first opinions ever formed on Goethe's life and works. He always held himself in this way superior to the books he read, and kept them off at a proper distance to be seen with clearness and convenience. Even in his earliest studies he had no rages for one author at a time, and never fell into fits of imitating favorite styles or tendencies of thought. He had great reserve in this respect; in other words, he was strong and healthy, and felt competent to extend an impartial invitation to all the great names in letters and in thought. There was no want of susceptibility here. It was fortunate that a disposition so simple and enthusiastic as his could hold out a hand for so much unimpeachable good sense to seize.

A disciple of Goethe would not go far with a critic who should announce himself in this way :—

Thus far in reading Goethe (Autobiography and half a dozen plays), I find no indications of greatness, nothing, in short, but commonplace morality and an exceedingly graceful use of language. To him it is perfectly fluid. The richness, clearness, and beauty, are above all praise.

But here is something more promising :—

There must be a period in the life of a great and thoughtful man, when he passes from the fiery madness of youth, from the deep enthusiasm for particular good things, and a determination towards one special object, to a more passive state, when the enthusiasm has become reverence for the good, and true, and lovely, and will has given place to resignation. We see this change well marked in most great characters, in Coleridge and Goethe. It is less marked in Schiller, because his was so eminently an ethical genius. Jean Paul never passed through the change, so he gains with the million, but loses with the cool admirers of real greatness. Emerson and Channing have passed this period.

Goethe is a beautiful instance of a man reaching this state. To many who themselves scarce dream there is such a condition, he seems indifferent, fish-blooded, feeding the world on snow-broth; but not so to the wise. The self-renunciation and intense diligence of Goethe are the secret of his success, of his long life, and permanent creativeness. Such were some of the great men of antiquity, Æschylus, Sophocles, and Cicero, and all the sages, Plato, Socrates, Aristotle, Anaxagoras, Pythagoras. One cause of the longevity of philosophers is doubtless to be found in the nature of their studies, which leads them to renounce the individual will, to forbear shrieking, and to acquiesce in God.

But that abstract consideration for the mood in which Goethe carried on his creations, does not restrain a very free criticism of the works themselves :—

Went on bravely in Hebrew, and likewise read much in Goethe. My admiration of the man rises more and more; but he was a selfish rogue.

After finishing the Autobiography :—

He was a great Pagan. His aim was to educate Herr Goethe. He leads one to labor, but not for the highest, not by any means for others. His theory was selfish, and the Christian was not in him. He would have been nobler had he struggled for education, or even for bread, like Herder, Schiller, Jean Paul, Heyne. Excess of good-fortune was his undoing.

The "Confessions of a Fair Saint" charm me much. What richness of piety, what faith, what a fine view of life ! Now, could a man write this out of his own heart, and yet live a licentious life, without God in the world ? The example of David, to look no nearer home, shows how easy it is for a wide space to exist between the pen and the heart. Goethe stood at arm's length from religion. But this he did not write out of his own heart. He confesses he drew from the conversations and letters of Frau von Klettenberg—and how much, he knew not. · Probably his own youthful experience of religion gave him power to appropriate skilfully the divine ejaculations of that religious woman.

His untiring industry strikes me as the most remarkable feature of his character. Goethe was not born a great man. His indefatigable assiduity did the work. Nothing was beneath his notice, and no labor too great for him to undertake. He was curious in particulars, and, besides, went over things at large. Wherever he went, he studied all that could be seen and studied. He sought the principle that showed itself in the result.

EGMONT.—Clärchen is a complete woman. Certainly Goethe understood women, *i. e.* clever, loving women, exceedingly well. Clärchen is all over woman, from first to last. So is the mother. Like women universally, when cool, she judges of counsels by their consequences, not by their causes. Clärchen, excited by love, trusting to that beautiful instinct, cares nothing for the consequences.

Clärchen's end is precipitated, but this also is woman-like. A man would have reasoned himself into the belief that Alva would only humble him on the scaffold ; but woman, by her natural divination, sees through it all, and is resolved to unite with him at last in death.

WILHELM MEISTER.—The women are well drawn. Goethe understood the psychological anatomy of woman to perfection. But what women! Philina has not a fig-leaf of modesty. Mignon is the creature of passion—all passion from crown to heel.

I don't like it. The effect is not moral, not pleasing upon me. The actors in the scenes are low, selfish, for the most part mean and lewd. Now and then an angel looks in upon the scene, like a small patch of clear sky and a moment's sunshine in a March storm ; rather like a single star seen through a rent cloud in a night of storms. Now and then one of the Muses enters, but goes quickly away, shuddering as she runs. Wisdom, from time to time, is seen in the distance ; nay, sometimes she comes near, but tarries not long.

Yet there are some fine pictures of life.

The multiplicity of Goethe's love-adventures is not a little remarkable. His life seems unworthy of such a genius. But his biographer smoothes it all over. Poor Friedrike! hers was the saddest fate, for she had a noble heart ; and the cold-blooded " genius" plucked her as a flower from the garden, wore her on his bosom, then threw her away. Noble heart! Solicited by others, as Lenz, for example, she said, " Whoever has been loved by Goethe can belong to no other man."

To me Goethe was less of a man than Voltaire, on the whole. He was not such a scoffer as Voltaire, for he did not propose to himself such a work—to remove a dreadful obstruction from the path of mankind. But he was less earnest, less humane, less intellectual by far, and with less large influence on man. His range of subjects was narrower, his productiveness less. I think Voltaire had a larger influence for good on his own age, and will reach farther into posterity. Goethe has produced better poetry—and worse. Neither affords much help to lofty men in their lofty works; both are destitute of a religious poise of character, so essential to real greatness in literature.

He goes to bed on a surfeit of Hebrew and Goethe :—

Last night I had a queer dream. I thought I read Hebrew with Dr. Robinson for a long time in Michaelis' Halle Bible, and with great ease and pleasure. We talked familiarly about the language and its literature. Then Prof. Stuart came in, and Prof. Hackett, and we renewed the theme. Mr. Stuart examined Prof. Hackett in the Vulgate, making him translate it into English. Robinson laughed at H.'s being Professor of Hebrew, and said he used to be a very dull scholar. Then Robinson showed a collection of Hebrew antiquities, ancient alphabets, machines, clocks, and the like, all of which he seemed to understand perfectly.

I asked him about Goethe, and repeated the long passage in the Wisdom of Solomon, chap. ii., " Go to, now," &c., and dwelt with emphasis on this, " Let us leave tokens of our joyfulness in every place," asking if Goethe did not leave many such, to which he assented, with good-will and humor. But, alas! as in all dreams, he related no new facts, and spoke only in the most general way of his dissoluteness.

Then Stuart and I took a walk, and discoursed of the state of theology, which he thought was *mittelalterisch* (middle-aged)—as it is. He lamented the darkness that prevails. Next we came upon geology, for we found a strange ledge of basaltic rock, with queer paths winding up and down its sides. I scrambled up the steep rocks, and left him to plod along in the dusty and crooked road that wound at the foot of the rocks, and led to a shoemaker's shop and a tavern.

CORRESPONDENCE OF SCHILLER AND GOETHE, VOL. I.*—It is a pleasant volume, but does not make me impatient for the next. I think the impression it leaves does not elevate the character of either poet. Goethe is wide, wise, full of practical sagacity, always the man of generous views, with little heart, except for his artistic creations. He has a wide range rather than a lofty flight. I admire his activity, his cheerfulness, and his elegant self-reliance. Now and then he has a deep insight. But it seems to me he is over-conscious of the processes of his work ; and so is Schiller.

I dislike Schiller heartily, and always did. He is proud, inflated, stiff, diseasedly self-conscious. He is little like the great, gushing genius of Goethe. Even in his letters there is the same oratorical pedantry which disgusts me in his poetry. In all this correspondence there is talk about little matters with pedantic solemnity. I like neither Goethe nor Schiller so well as before. There are some remarks on Goethe's appreciation of religion in Letters 57, 58, that confirm my own convictions of Goethe's character and his method of treating religious subjects.

In the background there stands always the German public. Envy, hate, and malice sometimes appear in the ranks of the public, but sometimes come within the Arcadian circle of Goethe and Schiller. The remarks made about Nicolai are neither manly nor temperate.

It is certainly a valuable book. But it will make silly maidens of both sexes all the sillier. They will fall in love with this solemn trifling, this use of vague, indefinite expressions, which look as if the men were always learning, but never coming to the truth.

SCHILLER'S ÆSTHETIC PROSE.—Hardly worth the oil, it seems to me. I have, when a boy, sometimes climbed up a high fence, and looked over, expecting tulips and violets at the least, and found—toadstools. So in books; after climbing over a palisade of tall words, I have found a great space covered with—nothing!

The following meditations belong to subjects which he never had opportunity fully to discuss :—

OF MARRIAGES.—A *whole* marriage is when each portion of each person finds its satisfaction in the other ; a *partial* or functional marriage

* Correspondence between Schiller and Goethe, from 1794 to 1805. Translated by George H. Calvert, Vol. I., 1845.

when but a part is thus met. Hence there are whole marriages, half marriages, one-third marriages, and so on, *ad infinitum*. Sometimes the unmarried portion is infinitesimal, and neither party knows of the loss. Sometimes the married portion is infinitesimal, and none knows of the marriage.

Sometimes, by society, friends, good-breeding, &c., the parties are so welded together that they cannot easily be sundered, but are yet only *welded*, not *wedded*. Solitude is the trial of marriages ; for, if the shoe does not fit, and you wear it but in going upstairs to bed, you think little of the pinch ; but when it must be worn all day, for travel and for rest, with never a change, if it be not completely accommodated to the foot, it will in the end gall you sore.

Marriages are best of dissimilar material, as iron runs not so well upon iron as upon brass ; only the dissimilarity must not be too great, else it is all wear and tear.

All marriages that I have ever known, or almost all, are fragmentary. If I read aright, a perfect and entire marriage can only take place between equals, or, at least, equivalents. I know a man whose wife has no *passion*—sentiment enough, but the passional part of marriage is hateful to her. In this point, then, the man is not married. I know many where in soul there is no equivalent, and in *soul* the man is not married. So with intellect, affection, benevolence, &c. A man not mated, or a woman not mated, seeks sorrowing the other half, and wanders up and down without rest. Most men are married only in their philoprogenitiveness or their acquisitiveness—perhaps in their amativeness. Marriage is mainly a discipline to most men, to few is it mainly an enjoyment. A man's courtship often begins after his marriage, and he tries to piece out a wife, a little here and a little there. With women the case is worse still. To a sluggish nature this is a slight thing. He wants to sleep, and sleeps. But to a great active soul it must be a terrible curse.

A man marries a wife far superior to himself. He cannot carry her. She wants sympathy in the unsupported part, and she must have it. Suppose she does not have it—that part of her nature perishes and corrupts the rest. If she does have it, then in that point her legal husband is not the true one. So it goes—the world is polygamous from necessity.

You can only marry your equal. A man may be tied to your soul, but it droops and hangs down awhile. Then it must have some one else to hold it up, or it will die. I have seen a foolish man so silly because he was to be wedded to a fine woman. Poor fellow ! so he was ; but he *married* only a fool. All the rest of his wife hangs down, and will die !

MARRIAGE AND DIVORCE.—From psychological considerations I should think that monogamy was the natural law of human nature. I find the same thing shown in the numerical equality of the sexes ; and the same conclusion is confirmed by history. For example, among the negro slaves there is no *marriage-form*, the whole is voluntary, but separations almost never take place. The same is true of the North-American Indians ; *e. g.* the Osages know nothing of divorce, though there is no law or custom to prevent it. If intercourse were more free in social life, I doubt not that marriage would be happier and divorces more rare. What a deal of prudery is there about the matter here in New England!

Under this head come the following reflections after returning from a lecturing trip to Nantucket :—

A nice place that Nantucket. It contains the finest-looking set of girls that is to be met with in New England. The older women are not so good-looking, as the wind, and glare of the water and sun in a town without trees, spoil their complexion. But alas! they will always be girls—the greater part of them. There are 1600 men now absent from the island! Three-fourths of the audience at lecture were women. I think there is no town in New England where the whole body of women is so well educated. There are no balls, no theatres, no public amusements—even *courting* is the rarest of luxuries. I should have said *being courted;* so *they fall upon their heads,* the poor women, when they drop out of that other Eden, and make for the Tree of Knowledge when debarred from the Tree of Life. Literature thrives well in Nantucket. There is a deal of reading. But much as I prize intellectual culture in woman, it made me sad to think of the condition of the majority of these young girls, with generous affections which could never find the natural objects to cling to. There is something wrong in any state of society which compels so many women to celibacy. I do not speak of such as *choose,* only of those whose fate it is. . . . . .

Yet, out of eight emigrants to America, five are of the *superior sex!* Hence I fear it is worse the other side of the sea. In this age, as in all preceding, woman is treated as the old men are with savages—left to perish when not needed for the purposes of the tribe. So shall it not always be.

Some other unappropriated sentences are worth preserving :—

WAYLAND'S LIFE OF JUDSON.—It contains less information about the Buddhists than one might look for, but the noble memoir of Mr. J. and Mrs. J. is beyond all praise. Yet they carried absurd dogmas to the Burman, who had a plentiful supply of their own. Had the same pains been taken *at home,* to remove poverty, ignorance of natural laws, to abolish slavery, drunkenness, prostitution, and teach piety and morality in general, what a good result would have come from it!

Bigotry must be expected in a missionary. He says to one he tried to convert, "A true disciple inquires not whether a fact is agreeable to his own reason, but whether *it is in the Book.*"

This is rather queer :—"We finally concluded that as such an order (a passport from the Government) would cost several hundred ticuls, we would prefer trusting in the Lord to keep us and our poor disciples."

The "creed for his Burman Church" is a dreadful document.

Judson's character is truly noble. If the only result of missions were to raise up such men, it were enough. For one such man is worth more to mankind than a temple like the Parthenon.

COLERIDGE'S CONFESSIONS OF AN INQUIRING SPIRIT.—Seven poor letters on the inspiration of the Bible. The book is vitiated by the absence of a definition of inspiration, It seems to me unworthy of its great author, and indicative of the low state of theology in England.

Perhaps this is one of the best theological works of England (1840) in the present century! But what a disgrace to the island to say it! It seems to me their scholars are at dinner, and their divines gone a-hunting. What would the stout old fellows, with manly piety in their bosoms, and no lack of good sense in their heads, say if they could rise up—what would Taylor, and Chillingworth, and Hooker, and Law, and Butler say to these champions of modern times? Shame on the English—they do nothing, they say nothing, except on the commonest subjects!

There has been an age of *fine thinking*, which began with Henry VIII. and ended with the 17th century. Then an age of *fine writing*, which of course takes in the wits of Queen Anne's time, and is not quite ended yet. And now we have the age of *fine printing*, and can see the tombs of the prophets built up by Basil Montague, and the editors of new editions of all the old.

STUDY ON MAN.—One day the history of man will be written, as that of a single man—Dr. Franklin, for instance; as we say that Dr. F. learned Latin at seven, and began philosophy at twelve, and in such a year learned such and such a truth in science and religion. So will the progress of mankind be treated of; and it will be seen that we learned this from Plato, this from another, &c. So only shall we know what we gained by Christianity, the Reformation, &c.

SUSPICION AND OVER-TRUST.—Give a man an old dollar, which some boy has worn round his neck, and drabbled in the mud, and played with a half-score of years—he will take it, though it is dim, dingy, and light of weight. Give him a new dollar, fresh from the mint, every leaf sharply defined in the olive branch—ten to one but he will ring it before he takes it. I remember one Wheeler was once found to have some bank bills in his straw bed. They were counterfeit—the president of the bank said so. They were all new. But one man took one of them, rubbed it over his head, then on the floor, then with thumb and finger till it looked worn, and the president said *it was good*.

There is a worm, the *arenicola piscatorum*, which is found with its stomach full of sand, but the sand is full of little microscopic characters, foraminifera, diatomeæ, &c., and which in reality are the food of the arenicola; the sand is the vehicle, not the passenger.

So there are a good many Christians found with their stomachs full of awful doctrines, about eternal damnation, reprobation, the wrath of God, &c., and men think they live (spiritually) on this food, but you find some little goodness and piety behind these doctrines, and the doctrines serve only as a vehicle for the food

I had rather die a sinner than live one.

On condition a great thought be true and revolutionary, it is hard to get it made a thing. Ideas go into a nunnery, not a family.

Let a party wrestle never so hard, it cannot throw the dollar.

How ridiculous the allegorical interpretation is of such books as Solomon's Song, Daniel, the Apocalypse, &c. Here is an example from a common nursery tale: "This is the house that Jack built." This bears a double meaning. "The house that Jack built" is the Christian Church, Jack is the Savior; Jack is the vulgar for John, which is the English for *Johannes*, the Latin of Ιωαννες, the Greek of

יוֹחָכָן: the etymology indicates this. יוֹחָכָן is θεοδῶρος; Gottesgabe, God's gift. The "Malt" is the Doctrines of the Christian Church, as containing the spirit of Christianity, The "Rat who ate the malt" is the Catholic clergy, symbolized by the Pope. The "Cat who caught the rat" is Master Luther, symbol of the Reformation. The "Dog that worried the cat" is the opponents of the Reformation, especially the priests, of whom Loyola is the symbol. The "Cow with the crumpled horn, that tossed the dog," is the French Government, which drove out the priests, and the crumpled horn denotes the Gallic cock, and thereby seems more clearly to denote the French Government than any other, for the crumpled horn is much like the crest of a cock. The "Maiden all forlorn" is Liberty. "The man all tattered and torn" is the French people, enamoured of liberty, and courting it (in a most *feline* fashion) in the Revolution. The "Priest all shaven and shorn" is Lafayette; *shaven* because divested of his dignity and wealth by the Revolution itself; *shorn* as despoiled of *his liberties* and shut up in an Austrian dungeon, &c.

GLIDDON'S MUMMY.—You take one of the popular saints, a man who has the vulgar piety in the vulgar form. You are told he is a great saint; that when you come to analyze him you will find proofs of his vocation. But you make the analysis and you find no such thing. So have I seen a huge sarcophagus of wood, containing a mummy. It was storied all over with great care, and bore an inscription setting forth that it was the relic of a priestess, herself the daughter of the great high priest of Thebes. Jewels, it was said, would be found on her, and a roll of papyrus; probably one jewel of great value—the roll of great extent. So the exhibitor removes the wooden case, and discloses the other, the case of linen. That also is sawn asunder and carefully removed. Then the bandages are unrolled, and after long looking you find, no jewels, but a scarabæus of common clay, a scrap of papyrus, no priest and priestess—not even the daughter of the priest of Thebes, but a common man of the vulgarest pattern, reduced to nothing but a mass of *pitch*, the eyes gone out, the features marred.

The author of the treatise, De Mirab. Sac. Scrip. says :—"*Tota enim justitia hæc est, Virginitas, Sacerdotium, et Martyrium.*" How Christianity had degenerated, when all righteousness—the Law and the Prophets— was summed up in being an *old maid, a priest,* and *a martyr !*

1851.—For several days I have been studying the new edition of Hippocrates. (Paris, 1831-1851. E. Littré.) I was a little surprised to find how much he knew. This seems clear : he believed there was a law everywhere ; a law of nature. All has a cause ; so the *sacred disease* has a natural cause. He has no faith in *divine diseases* or divine remedies. He abhors quackery, and bears the same relation to the charlatans of medicine that Socrates bore to the charlatans of metaphysics. In some things he is a wider man than Socrates ; more emancipated from the popular theology. He would not have believed that Helios and Selene were gods, and I think did not sacrifice a " cock to Æsculapius" when he died.

What a pretty piece of confusion it would lead to if the doctors thought Hippocrates was "inspired," and treated the Hippocratic works as doctors of the soul treat the Bible! Nay, they once did worship *Aristotle* in the same way.

CRITICISMS ON ART.—I am astonished at the boldness of Americans in passing judgment on works of the fine arts. I once rode in a hack with an American, aged 21, through the *Via Condotti*; we passed a shop whose windows were full of cameos. My companion put his glass up to his eye, squinted at them, and said, "Poor things, by Jove!" Since then it has not astonished me to hear the most sweeping judgments from Americans—especially women—on painting, sculpture, &c. It is not at all necessary for the critic to know anything about art, or to have any feeling for nature, only to have insolence and a tongue.

Who has not seen some man of unbalanced mind, intellectual always, but spiritual never; heady but not hearty; roving from Church to Church; now Trinitarian, then unbeliever, then Universalist, Unitarian, Catholic—everything by turns but nothing long; seeking rest by turning perpetually over, and becoming at last a man having experienced many theologies, but never religion; not a Christian, but only a verbal index of Christianity—a commonplace-book of theology? Such a man runs from Church to Church; from Cambridge to Oxford, and from Oxford to Rome, in his belief, only as a stone runs down-hill, and for the same reason, because its centre of gravity is not supported. How different the progress of his life who leaves behind that which is outgrown, and never turns back, but with all his progress is never an apostate!*

Numerous verses of no great value are mixed with these scraps and sentences, for his pen ran readily to rhyme. It is a vice of his prose that it tends occasionally to hexameters, and the ground tilts beneath the reader. Sometimes there is almost half a page of consecutive sentences in his earlier compositions, which could be rendered metrical by knocking out a word or two. Prose parts with its dignity and gains no recompense when it leans upon this eunuch's arm.

But sometimes, when these verses alight on the paper, fresh from some personal association, or a moment of friendship gentler than usual, they are sweet and hearty. How quickly he would vibrate to a sound of home!

A GOLDEN WEDDING.†

1.

Should youthful courtship be forgot,
  And never brought to min';
Should youthful courtship be forgot,
  And the days lang syne?

---

* From a Sermon on Religious Rest, preached April 2, 1848.
† Of his friend, Deacon Samuel May, 1859.

2.

Those days of love we ne'er forget:
  How sweet your lips to mine!
Your mother did not heed the theft
  In the days lang syne.

3.

A half a hundred years ago
  We stood at wedlock's shrine:
We're fifty years the better for
  The days lang syne.

4.

Brown ringlets round your snowy brow,
  That seemed like light to shine ;
Now, changed to gray, they're still more fair
  Than in auld lang syne.

5.

How fond we pray'd our lovers' prayer
  I' the moon's romantic shine !
'Tis deeper now, and tranquiller
  Than in auld lang syne.

6.

We've tasted many a bitter cup
  Of mingled myrrh and wine;
But the draught has made us stronger far
  Than in auld lang syne.

7.

How vain they talk that age can mar
  The feelings most divine !
Our hearts now beat with warmer love
  Than in days lang syne.

8.

A willing bride and eager swain
  We stood at wedlock's shrine ;
But other hearts are with us now,
  Than of auld lang syne.

9.

Let youthful love be ne'er forgot
  Though a hundred years decline;
A household now rejoices in
  That day of auld lang syne.

10.

These labor on the blessed earth,
  Those heavenly flowers entwine ;
And we are nearer heaven to-night
  Than of auld lang syne.

11

And when beyond the grave we rest,
    Where saints in glory shine,
We'll still look back and God will bless
    For the days lang syne.

Some of his translations of German poetry are well done,
but many are left in an imperfect condition.   There are specimens
from "Hymns of the Mystics," of Paul Gerhardt, from the poetry
of the "Boy's Wonder-horn," from Schwab, Simon Dach, "Popular Collections," Rückert, Körner, Geibel, and Heine.   Here are
two : the first from Rückert.

LANGUAGE OF THE EYES.

Oh, not in many languages
    My youthful love rejoices ;
But with her eyes she better speaks
    Than others with their voices !

Oh, what a copious stock of words
    In this open letter treasured !
A single glance, a paragraph
    Of meaning all unmeasured.

Artists have painted Love as blind ;
    Dumb were he better painted,
The pains of silence done away
    By speech the eyes invented.

That is the only speech among
    The blessèd stars in heaven ;
And flowers discourse it in the spring
    From morning until even.

That is the speech whose character,
    With rays of stars eternal,
Is written by the pen of love,
    And shines through space supernal.

This language not by mind is known,
    But better by emotion ;
Therefore, Love only speaks in this
    On every land and ocean.

MOHNIKE, IN WILHELMI'S LYRIK.   No. 567.

A light skiff swam on Danube's tide,
Where sat a young man and his bride :
    He this side, she that side.

Quoth she, " Heart's dearest, tell to me
What wedding gift I'll give to thee ?"

Upward her little sleeve she strips,
And in the water briskly dips.

The bridegroom did the same straightway,
And played with her and laugh'd so gay.

" Oh, give to me, Dame Danube fair,
Some pretty toy for my bride to wear."

She drew therefrom a handsome blade,
For which the young man long had pray'd

The groom, what holds he in his hand?
Of milk-white pearls a costly band.

He turns it round her raven hair;
She looked like any princess there.

" Dame Danube fair, to me impart
Some pretty toy for my sweetheart."

A second time her arm dips in,
A glittering helm of steel to win.

The youth, o'er-joy'd the prize to view,
Brings her a golden comb thereto.

A third time she in the water dipp'd;
Ah, woe! from out the skiff she slipp'd.

He springs and grasps, alas, the day!
Dame Danube tears them both away.

The Dame to use her toys began,
Therefore, must perish maid and man.

The empty skiff floats down alone:
Behind the hills soon sinks the sun.

And when the moon stood overhead,
To land the two lovers floated, dead:
    He this side, and she that side.

Some translations from Heine, which he made while he was meditating an article upon that poet, are well done. Here is a specimen :—

This is the old poetic wood;
    The linden's breath comes stealing;
And glancing wondrously, the moon
    Enchanteth every feeling.

I walked therein, and as I went
    Above I heard a quiring;
It was the nightingale; she sang
    Of love and love's desiring.

She sang of love and of love's woe,
    Of laughter and of weeping;
She joy'd so sadly, plain'd so gay,
    That dreams came back from sleeping.

I walked therein, and as I went,
    Before me saw, extending
In ample space, a castle huge,
    Its gables high ascending,

Windows were closed, and everywhere
    A silence and a mourning,
As if in those deserted walls
    Was quiet death sojourning.

Before the door a sphinx there lay,
    Part joy, part fear, half human;
Body and claws a lion's were,
    The breast and head, a woman,—

A woman fair ; her pallid face
    Spoke of most wild desiring;
The silent lips were arched with smiles,
    A tranquil trust inspiring.

The nightingale, too, sweetly sang.
    Could I resist her ?   Never!
But as I kiss'd the handsome face,
    My peace was gone for ever !

Living became the marble form,
    The stone began to shiver,
She drank my kisses' fiery glow
    With thirsty lips that quiver.

She almost drank away my breath,
    And then, with passion bending,
She coil'd me round, my mortal flesh
    With lion-talons rending.

Extatic torture, woeful bliss !
    Joy, anguish, without measure!
And while the talons grimly tear,
    Her kisses give such pleasure !

The nightingale sang, " Handsome sphinx !
    O Love, what is intended—
That all thy bless'd beatitudes
    With death-throes thou hast blended ?

Oh, handsome sphinx, come, solve for me
    The riddle, tell the wonder !
For many a thousand years thereon
    Thought I, and still I ponder."

And here is an impromptu translation from memory of Heine's
" Lörelei ":—

> I know not what's the meaning
> That I'm so sad inclined;
> But from ancient times a story
> Will not away from my mind.
>
> The air is cool and it darkens;
> The Rhine flows tranquil on :
> The top of the mountain sparkles
> In the rays of the evening sun.
>
> A snow-white maiden sitteth
> Above there, wondrous fair;
> Her golden garment glitters,
> She combs her golden hair.
>
> With a golden comb she combs it,
> And sings a song thereby,
> A song that has a wondrous
> And graceful melody.
>
> In his small bark the sailor
> It takes with longing sigh ;
> He looks not on the ripples,
> He only looks on high.
>
> At length the billows swallow
> The sailor and his canoe ;
> And this with only singing,
> The Lörelei can do.

This, also, is musically rendered :—

> Oh, knew but the blossoms, the wee things,
> How deep I'm wounded at heart,
> They'd mingle their tear with my weeping,
> And blandish away my smart.
>
> And did but the nightingales know, that
> I'm gloomy and sick so long,
> They would joyfully come and sing me
> A life-awakening song.
>
> If they, too, could know all my sorrows,
> The dear gold starlets we see,
> They would all come away from their glory,
> And empty their love into me.
>
> But all of them lack understanding,
> One only, she knows of my smart,
> For herself 'twas who rent asunder,
> She rent asunder my heart.

FROM THE RUSSIAN.

Moaning, moaning, through the oak wood,
Clouds the field all overhanging,
Her only son drives forth the mother :
" Hence, thou son, out of my cottage,
Thee may cruel Moslems capture !"
    " Oh, well remember me the Moslems,
    Offer me the dearest horses."

Moaning, moaning, through the oak wood,
Clouds the field all overhanging,
Her only son drives forth the mother;
"Hence, my son, out of my cottage,
Thee may cruel Tartars capture ;"
    " Oh, well remember me the Tartars,
    Offer me most precious garments."

Moaning, moaning, through the oak wood,
Clouds the field all overhanging,
Soft her darling clasps the mother.
"Come, my son, come to my cottage,
Thy fair hairs let me comb over !"
    " Mother, oh, the rain will wash me,
    And the thickest thorn-bush comb me;
    The sharp winds know how to dry me."

Brings his steed the oldest sister,
And the second brings the weapons ;
Of her brother asks the youngest,
" When return'st thou from the battle ?"
    " Take thou up of sand a handful,
    Strew it then upon the ledges,
    And bedew it still with weeping,
    By the morning star just shining ;
    When the sand shall blossom, sister,
    Then shall I return from battle."

Some more from Heine follow :—

Thou hast diamonds and jewels,
    Hast all that mortals adore,
And eyes thou hast most handsome ;
    My darling, what would'st thou more ?

Upon thine eyes so handsome
    I've written many a score
Of poems, all immortal;
    My darling, what would'st thou more ?

And with thine eyes so handsome
    Thou hast tortured me full sore,
And hast me ruined utterly ;
    My darling, what would'st thou more ?

The lindens were blooming, the nightingale sung,
    The sun smiled on us with friendliest fire,
You kissed me so, then, and your arms round me flung,
    And clasp'd to your bosom that throbbed with desire.

The raven croak'd dull, the leaves they all fell,
    The sunlight salutes us gloomily now,
We frostily said to each other, Farewell,
    And courtly you bow'd me the courtliest bow.

    Many a form of days forgotten
      Arose from out its grave,
    Again to show me clearly
      What life thy presence gave.

    By day I wander'd dreaming—
      Through all the streets I'd range ;
    Men looked astonish'd on me,
      I was so sad and strange.

    At night it all went better,
      For then the streets were clear ;
    I and my ghost, together,
      We wander'd silent there.

    On the bridge, with echoed footsteps,
      My rambling way I took ;
    The moon broke through the night-clouds,
      Greeting with serious look.

    I stood before thy dwelling,
      And gazed upon the sky,
    And gazed upon thy window :
      My heart beat wild and high.

    I know that oft the window
      Thou'st open'd with thy hand,
    And seen me in the moonlight,
      Like a marble statue stand.

    Thou art a little flower,
      So pure, and fair, and gay,
    I look on thee, and sadness
      Steals to my heart straightway.

    My hands I feel directed
      Upon thy head to lay,
    Praying that God may keep thee,
      So pure, and fair, and gay.

My child, when we were children,
 Two children small and gay,
We crept into the hen-house,
 And hid us under the hay.

We crow'd, as do the cockerels,
 When people pass'd the wood,
" Ki-ker-ki!" and they fancied
 It was the cock that crow'd.

The chests which lay in the court-yard,
 We paper'd them so fair,
Making a house right famous,
 And dwelt together there.

The old cat of our neighbor
 Oft came to make a call;
We made her bow and courtesy,
 And compliment us all.

We ask'd, with friendly question,
 How she was getting on;
To many an ancient pussy
 The same we since have done.

In sensible discoursing
 We sat like aged men,
And told how, in our young days,
 All things had better been.

That faith, love, and religion
 From earth are vanish'd quite;
And told how dear is coffee,
 And money is so tight.

But gone are childish gambols,
 And all things fleeting prove;
Money, the world, our young days,
 Religion, truth, and love.

Here is a fragment of Geibel's "Tannhäuser ":—

Now is the night so joyous,
 Now blooms so rich the wold,
And on all hill-tops whisper
 Such voices manifold!
The streamlets twinkle and glisten,
 The flowers give fragrance and light;
The marble statues listen
 In the dark-green of the night.

The nightingale singeth, " Beware, beware !"
The boy looks forth, and forth will fare;
Wild beats his heart—he heedeth not:
What once he loved is all forgot.

A castle in the garden :
    With light the windows glance,
At the door are pages waiting,
    Above resounds the dance.
Up the stairway he is leaping,
    He enters in the hall ;
There are silken garments sweeping,
    There gleams the gold pokal.

The nightingale singeth, " Beware, beware !"
The boy looks forth, and forth will fare ;
Wild beats his heart—he heedeth not :
What once he loved is all forgot.

The fairest of the women
    Holds out to him the glass,
While cool, delicious shudders
    Through soul and body pass.
He drains the magic measure,
    The door-dwarf answers shrill,
" Now, boy, thou art our pleasure :
    This is Dame Venus' hill."

The nightingale singeth, but from afar ;
The boy is drawn by his evil star ;
Wild beats his heart—he heedeth not :
What once he loved is all forgot.

FROM MARTIN OPITZ.

Come, dearest, let us hasten
    While time is ours ;
Delay is fast consuming
    All of our powers.

The noblest gifts of beauty
    Fly wing and wing ;
And all that one possesses
    Is vanishing.

The rosy cheek is paling,
    The hair turns gray ;
The eyes' bright fire is failing ;
    The breast is clay.

That dainty mouth of coral
    Will soon be cold,
Those hands, like snow, hang heavy,
    And thou'lt be old.

Then, let us seize, in rapture,
    Youth's fruit of gold,
Before we're called to follow
    Years that are told.

As thou thine own self lovest,
　　Love me as true;
Give me—what else thou givest,
　　That love I, too.

Here is Hymn No. 1400 in Chevalier Bunsen's Collection:—

The gloomy night is gathering in,
　　The day's sweet light is dead;
Oh, then, my soul, sleep not in sin,
　　Commune with God instead!

O God, the world's eternal Lord,
　　Whom no one can perceive,
Thou seest me daily in Thy tent;
　　Wilt Thou my prayer receive?

The daylight, which is ended now,
　　In chief belongs to Thee,
And so ought I, from morn till night,
　　Thy holy servant be.

Perhaps my duty is not done,
　　For I am flesh and blood;
And trespass ere the day is gone,
　　Although the will be good.

Swedish, Servian, and Russian verses appear occasionally, just well enough translated to convey their popular and domestic feeling, but not metrically finished. He loved best the songs and hymns of the people, which are full of simple sentiments, and frankly wear the costume of their race and locality.

These are original lines :—

She never came to visit me
　　When sickness laid me low,
Nor ask'd, when pallid was my brow,
　　"Dear child, what ails you so?

And when 'mid whelming tides I strove,
　　Struggling for mortal breath,
She never reach'd me out her hand
　　To save my soul from death!

Ah, once I fancied otherwise!
　　"When waters gird me round
She'll come, an angel through the storm,
　　And I shall not be drown'd."

Then wither'd be the flowers she gave,
　　And perish every thought
Wherewith she peopled once my heart,
　　And be herself forgot!

Ah, no! forgot she cannot be—
That hand will still remain;
For ever I shall dread that hand
Whose touch empoisons pain.

The following lines he introduced in a sermon, entitled "The Practical Effect of the Ecclesiastical Conception of God."

In darker days and nights of storm,
Men knew Thee but to fear Thy form;
And in the reddest lightnings saw
Thine arm avenge insulted law.

In brighter days, we read Thy love
In flowers beneath, in stars above;
And in the track of every storm
Behold Thy beauty's rainbow form.

And in the reddest lightnings' path
We see no vestiges of wrath,
But always wisdom—perfect love,
From flowers beneath to stars above.

See, from on high sweet influence rains
On palace, cottage, mountains, plains!
No hour of wrath shall mortals fear,
For their Almighty Love is here.

With this prayer let the chapter close :—

O Thou eternal One, may I commune
With Thee, and for a moment bathe my soul
In Thy infinity, Mother and Sire
Of all that are? In all that is art Thou;
Being is but by Thee, of Thee, in Thee;
Yet, far Thou reachest forth beyond the scope
Of space and time, or verge of human thought.
Transcendant God! Yet, ever immanent
In all that is, I flee to Thee, and seek
Repose and soothing in my Mother's breast.
O God, I cannot fear, for Thou art love,
And wheresoe'er I grope I feel Thy breath!
Yea, in the storm which wrecks an argosy,
Or in the surges of the sea of men
When empires perish, I behold Thy face,
I hear Thy voice, which gives the law to all
The furies of the storm, and Law proclaims,
"Peace, troubled waves, serve ye the right—be still!"
From all this dusty world Thou wilt not lose
A molecule of earth, nor spark of light.
I cannot fear a single flash of soul
Shall ever fail, outcast from Thee, forgot.

Father and Mother of all things that are,
I flee to Thee, and in Thy arms find rest.
My God! how shall I thank Thee for Thy love!
Tears must defile my sacramental words,
And daily prayer be daily penitence
For actions, feelings, thoughts which are amiss:
Yet will I not say, " God, forgive !" for Thou
Hast made the effect to follow cause, and bless
The erring, sinning man.   Then, let my sin
Continual find me out, and make me clean
From all transgression, purified and bless'd!

CHAPTER XVII.

Correspondence—Knowledge of the People—Hand-writing –Projected Work on the Development of Christianity.

WHEN books and thoughts released him to the family below, straightway gentleness, humor, and all natural ways flowed forth. He never disdained a bit of fun, indeed his motions were sometimes demonstrative of a boy's bubbling heart, to the threatening of his cloth. Nor was a prized domestic ever left to feel that she was not a member of the family but a mere convenience ; he was free, and kind, not without his quip, if it suited him ; but he knew his place. Does not one faithful and cherished member of that loving household still recall those courtesies, which warmed the heart like a Christmas fire ?

Sometimes he could snatch a pleasant hour in the evening, between nine and ten, when he descended to the parlor, and cut the leaves of a fresh book while pleasant talk went round the table. But he generally contrived to get the family off to bed by ten o'clock, that he might remount the stairs to those walls well lined with a great horizon.

After the morning Scripture had been gratefully read, he was eager to reach his books. But how tolerant he was of interruptions ; especially if the children of his dear friends climbed the long flights to have a chat with Mr. Parkie ! Then he would open the top of a secretary, in which he always kept a store of carts and jumping-jacks, and the floor became a playground. He was on the carpet with them, and the biggest child of all.

How he would pull his books about to show them to a friend, explain their uses, and glory in their strength ! Pretty soon your chair was entrenched with folios, and you sat within an enforced excuse not to escape too soon.

Sometimes people did not understand that fine art of rising to go. Then his fingers went tracking for his pen. Once, they were prepared to make a heave-offering of an eminent member of the old Whig party, who called for the purpose of chastising him in his study, for some violation of the creed of Hunkerism. A firm and sensible demeanor disarmed this man, and he went downstairs with new thoughts in his heart.

The hours of the day which calls and claims of every description did not embarrass, were apt to be laid waste by correspondents. Letters and visitors were continually making onsets upon those marshalled books. Few public men ever sustained such a wide and varied correspondence as he. It seemed as if his powerful mind set loose in every direction doubts, speculations, hopes which were never before betrayed, for want of some sympathetic listener. All the passions, too, posted to his study ; bigotry, hatred, envy, gratitude, sleep now in those heaps of many-colored paper which are sorted on the shelves where the books lately stood. In that pile of sheets of all sizes, from long, thick, and dingy foolscap to bad commercial post, a parcel of anonymous attacks lie dead in their skulking paper, slaveholders threatening him with castigation and the bowie-knife, in sentences, or rather agglutinated masses, of extraordinary rhetoric and syntax ; northern critics, liberal only in their epithets ; feeble creatures, panic-stricken at his speech and afraid to subscribe their panic ; pious and proper laymen, begging him not to use the words "dry-nurse" in the pulpit, and complaining that the audience laughed when he said that "in most churches people came for nothing, and got what they came for ; " bitter atheists, charging him with being religious, and with suppressing in print things which he said in the pulpit ; all kinds of malignity, startled into their proper shapes by the touch of his sincerity, coiled for one spring at him, but missed, and sunk away. He kept the sheets, as a naturalist puts abnormal specimens in spirits, to show the amount of divergence.

But thankful and cheering words also reached him ; these have been already hinted at. They came "not single spies but in battalions,"—confessions of grateful hearts who had been saved from horrible distress, brought on by old theologies ; noble souls born in a narrow place, and emancipated by his faith ; tender and mystic communications from women, alone in this world, but finding near approach to God through him, and clinging for guidance to his strong, kindly · hand; confessions of critical moments of spiritual history, when his word came, like the belated column which turns the day; manly thanks from persons in England, Scotland, Germany, and the Far West of his own country, who learned from him to worship without superstition. Apparently, his words came always just in time. The punctuality was in the quality of the word.

It also went wherever it was wanted. Such a cosmopolitan collection of post-marks is seldom made. They have a conventional range, from Buckingham Palace and Osborne, through university towns, scholars' libraries, remote parishes in Scotland, the seats of power in British India, to places Down East, and towns at the West not yet gazetteered; posted by Brahmen becoming Unitarian, Germans admiring his scholarship and freedom, scholars in confidential talk, Orthodox and Presbyterian clergymen acknowledging his worth, and sometimes, too, his doctrine; plain New-England farmers, Western "roughs," Kansas emigrants, Quakers, both mild and militant, maids of honor, politicians, divinity students, and all people inquisitive about their souls. Anthony Burns is taught writing, and sends his first specimen of bad grammar, but irreproachable gratitude, to the great scholar who never felt so accomplished as when standing in the dock with him. Charles Torrey sends him thanks from Baltimore Gaol. What exquisite revenge to lay such letters over the other impudent and cruel sheets! In reply, he must acknowledge, advise, encourage, defend, explain, thank, and make innumerable statements of his opinions and hopes in politics, his position in theology, his views of books, his estimates of public men. What wearisome and endless repetition! But, doubtless, each person was contented with his ration.

His publications greatly stimulated those people, so numerous in America, who are without cultivation, but robust and sensible, given to independent investigation of all possible problems, which are sometimes maltreated at their hands—people like that gray-headed Hoosier, who presented himself one day at the Patent Office with a model of the Archimedean screw, of which he had never heard. Their minds refuse to take anything for granted, prefer to rough it and to grow old in toil to making a hospital of a meeting-house. These persons would sometimes astonish, and

sometimes afflict, Mr. Parker with their lucubrations. They
would dare everything, even to imparting to him instruction upon
the Old Testament Canon, the dispersion of the Ten Tribes, and
the epoch of Buddha. They had theories about the Miraculous
Conception, and the Crucifixion, Pre-existence, and Immortality.
Their views were very curiously and adroitly put. But he
patiently replied, and humanely welcomed every word of an
earnest inquirer.

How many there are in this country ! They do not sit in the
pews of any of the churches. It is very doubtful if the "free"
seats sanctified to the use of the colored brethren would hold all
these white recusants and nonconformists. Mr: Parker's correspondence gave him the inestimable advantage of an introduction to the mind of the people. He learned their wants and
difficulties, and gloried to know what hardihood and religiosity
waited outside of all the creeds for some word of life, a
recognition of the human heart itself, and a popular defence of
it against superfluous doctrine. His works will always feed and
comfort this unincorporated and invisible communion.

Thus, by means of a correspondence of astonishing extent,
and by lecturing campaigns, which brought him face to face with
the people through the East and West, he gradually established
a relation with a great lay constituency, like that which prominent politicians achieve in their perpetual canvass, but more
intimate and serene. For ten years his lectures would average
more than forty during each winter ; their number varied from
forty to eighty. Wherever he went he surrendered himself to
popular intercourse ; it was his passion to know men, and the
luxury of his laborious life to find human nature everywhere
nobly justifying the confidence he placed in it. He felt, in the
process of lecturing, that the people, though cautioned against
his heresies, and taught by newspapers and sermons to suspect
his disposition, were gradually overcoming this monstrous misrepresentation, which the political prejudices of the majority
helped for some time to foster. That prejudice was the first to
give way, as men saw more clearly that his words upon
the state of the country and the horrible disease which
was destroying it were just. Then the popular heart began
to be with him ; a great parish was his before, it waited
each winter for his steps as he bore his brave American
heart, in neglect of physical weakness, through the chief

towns of the North, with a dispensation of humanity. The number of those who loved the freedom of his doctrine was beginning to increase by a large conversion from the parties which once detested his anti-slavery principles, and shrunk from his unsparing delineations. The more right he was found to be, the larger his constituency grew; the people were fast rallying to the call of their own instincts from his lips. Of all the things which he ever said, none was truer than his conviction penned to Mr. Sumner, "*The people are always true to a good man who truly trusts them.*" The day will come when Americans will remember him regretfully as the representative and prophet of the purer future which they shall live to enjoy.

FROM R. W. EMERSON.

Concord, Mass., March 19, 1853.

My dear Parker.—Before that book* came to me, though not until several weeks after it was sent, I read the inscription, if with more pride than was becoming, yet not without some terror. Lately I took the book in hand, and read the largest part of it with good heed. I find in it all the traits which are making your discourses material to the history of Massachusetts; the realism, the power of local and homely illustration, the courage and vigor of treatment, and the masterly sarcasm—now naked, now veiled—and I think with a marked growth in power and *coacervation*—shall I say?—of statement. To be sure, I am in this moment thinking also of speeches out of this book as well as those in it. Well, you will give the times to come the means of knowing how the lamp was fed, which they are to thank you that they find burning. And though I see you are too good-natured by half in your praise of your contemporaries, you will neither deceive us nor posterity, nor—forgive me—yourself, any more, in this graceful air of laying on others your own untransferable laurels.

We shall all thank the right soldier whom God gave strength and will to fight for Him the battle of the day.

Ever new strength and victory be to you!

R. W. Emerson.

He received a good many letters from his friends devoted mainly to anathemas upon his handwriting. Sometimes after his manuscript had in turn baffled all the compositors in an office, it was returned to the editor of the magazine with an abject confession of ignorance of the language. It is indeed an extraordinary hand. In 1835 it was large, round, and deliberate, all the words were furnished with their lawful contingent of letters, and there were no cabalistic marks to make the reader suspect occasional quotations from the Sinaitic, or other

* Dedicated to Mr. Emerson by Mr. Parker.

absence of language. As his work increased, this honest hand became depraved. In the epoch of gradual deposition all the characters are distinctly preserved, but when disturbances commenced, and cataclysms interrupted his creative day, the marks became huddled and confused. The letters gave up their individuality, and suffered a kind of pantheistic absorption into the sense of the word, which was then to be intuitionally conceived. The abbreviations and symbols become more intelligible than the actual failures to depict a whole sound word. A facsimile, if such a thing were possible, of a page from the manuscript of the "Historical Development of Religion," would afflict the learned world like Dighton Rock. His enemies would generously demand the publication of the book.

His friend, Rev. J. F. Clarke, wrote to him that it was a great popular delusion that he was not afraid of saying what he believed, since he wrote it so that he could declare at any time that he had not said it. Mr. Parker had no feeling for his friends on this point; he probably thought, and with justice, that his handwriting was the only thing he could not reform.

DEAR FRIEND,—Find fault with my handwriting! Mine! Me Hercle! Was ever such fastidiousness dreamed of? Why, I write nearly as well as Dr. Parr. I will lay a wager that in three cases out of ten I can decipher (pretty accurately) my own handwriting, even a month after it has been laid aside. Shame on such fault-finding; study the Babylonian, the Cufic, the Chinese, the Bengalee, and then you will—

It was a terrible man who taught me to write, or made the attempt. He set me near fourscore copies before he suffered me to join any two letters. All that I had created before were natural *celibates*, unfit for wedlock.

It had become rather bad as early as 1841, if the following did not exaggerate :—"Your good letter gave me so much pleasure, that despite the hard work I had, assisted by my wife, in spelling out some parts of it, I felt truly grateful for it. I reflected that the gods give us no good thing without labor, and if, after digging through the hieroglyphics, I found a treasure, I had no right to complain." And here, too, is an amiable expostulation:—"Do you know," writes a friend, "that I am sometimes puzzled with your handwriting? Not but that I am willing to break any shell to get at such meat." But this note from an editorial chair is not so willing :—"Metcalf absolutely refuses to print from your handwriting ; it must be copied, or he must be paid double." In this last case, however, there is reason to suppose that the matter written was only too intelligible.

In giving the names of these books will you please to exert all your energies to make them legible, and do not hold it " a baseness to write fair." In this respect I think you sometimes abuse your privileges. A man so ready to avow his opinions in speech, ought not to conceal them so cunningly when he writes.

The facsimile of a letter which is inserted in a later part of this volume for the sake of its opinions, shows a specimen of his handwriting better than usual. But what would a reader make of this, for instance, which is faithfully copied from a manuscript sermon, save the disintegrated letters.

I wuld. hae. Rel. Inst. & fr. tht. I would not take a min. with a Book-Rel., bt. a P. of Ht. & Life, nt. a Pt. who thinks man a little weak Dl. by Nt. & God a gt. sg. one by will, bt. a Man who kn. th. Inf. Gd. by Ht.

Which may be thus translated :—

I would have religious instruction, and for that I would not take a minister with a book-religion, but a preacher of heart and life, not a priest who thinks man is a little weak devil by nature, and God a great strong one by will, but a man who knows the infinite God by heart.

Hh., *Hps.*, *Fids.*, stand for health, happiness, friends ; *Dts.* is daughters ; *Hty.* is history ; 12 H. T. is 1,200,000 ; ⟨ ⟩ is a symbol meaning *more or less than ;* =ly is equally.

Occasionally in his love of realism his pen played with the text, and became pictorial.

Why, the road which reaches from the last △ of Æ. to the newest log ⌂ in Oregon is called after רו one-half the way, the other after J.

The travelling in ill-ventilated railroad-cars, with the sudden transition from them to all the chances of winter weather, and an hour's lecturing in large halls closely packed with people, exhausted him more than he was willing to confess. When he returned he was hardly fit for study ; yet the preparations for his elaborate work on the Development of Religion went on. The composition of lectures, sermons, and articles, the care of his correspondence, and the other taxes to his fame and notoriety which he had to pay in loss of time, interfered sadly with his labor upon the book; but, though thus constantly suspended, it was never abandoned or given up.

His purpose in setting about the composition of this book was to establish a historical and philosophical ground for pure theism, by marking the different epochs of religious development in the races of mankind, so that the divine premeditation might be discovered, following a definite plan and purpose parallel to that which appears in the history of the material world. He would trace the logical sequence which binds together, in the continuous creative act of God, all the successive types of the religious consciousness. These are to be studied in the ethnic strata of mankind, exhibiting the general conformity to a great plan amid specific differences, as the later forms absorb, correct, and amplify the earlier ones. Such a method would show the old roots of notions which still linger in the human conscious-ness, the gradual development of opinions still in their maturity or about to decline, and the striving to approach new and purer forms of belief, in strict obedience to the overruling thought. This would account for past phenomena, by laying open their laws. Nothing is found to be arbitrary or capricious, and the human investigation must tranquilly accept the divine method, just as it does, in the highest and most reverential manner, when scientific and historical facts are determined. There is nothing to exempt the growth of man's spiritual consciousness from an application of the great method which preserves its unity amid all varieties. Nothing stands in the way but the old superstitious methods themselves, which, like similar abortive methods in science, having failed to account for the facts, are to be quietly set aside, for the sake of truth and in the highest interests of mankind. If some points in the growth of the religious consciousness can be fixed beyond dispute, so much is contributed towards the true method and the deduction of a law of development; and such a law, once clearly established, will lead men, between materialism and superstition on the one side and idealism on the other, towards a ground of certitude. The points which are essential for framing such a deduction are to be gathered from an examina-tion of the leading races of the past, what they thought, did, and believed; and also, from an examination of the races of the present day, what are the invariable facts of their mental and spiritual organization.

What purpose could be more religious than this, or pervaded with a truer deference for the welfare of man ? Though his work remains unfinished, and might have been imperfectly prosecuted, it was beneficent, both religiously conceived and laboriously carried on, with all the instincts of a scholar and of a lover of men. The idea remains, bone of the bone and flesh of the flesh of the great theory of scientific development to which this epoch has obtained a clue. Many books and tentative speculations, much painstaking gathering of facts and cautious classification, must yet precede the deduction of a law that shall safely express in human language the invisible thought to which the golden links of life are hung. But the end is sure : knowledge will slowly set aside tradition, ignorance, and bigotry. The intellect and piety of man will engage in a continuous act of worship, learning to recognize everywhere the laws of God.

Astronomy destroys the doctrine of a local heaven, and restores the doctrine of the divine omnipresence to its proper place, and pronounces judgment on the *Jenseitigkeit* * of the angels.

Geology destroys the whim of a six-days' creation and of a local hell.

Biology makes death natural, not penal.

Anthropology denies the descent of mankind from a single pair, or, at least, makes it doubtful, as well as the absolute perfection of the primitive state.

Biblical criticism shows that inspiration is not limited to the Old Testament and New Testament, and not infallible there.

Psychology explains visions, ecstacies, &c., as not miraculous.

Comparative religion shows that Christianity is one among many forms; that inspiration, revelation, holy scriptures are not confined to any one religion. All reach their highest form in Christianity; and they are not, as some fancy, caricatures of religion.

The manuscript of Mr. Parker's work, so far as completed, is contained in about 270 pages of a blank book. Elsewhere, notes and lists of books, meant for use in different chapters, are scattered ; but there is no formal treatment of the subject except in those pages. And it is plain that they have not assumed the final form which he intended should precede publication. A few selections are given here, just in their present condition ; and, first, a careful premeditation of the whole ground of the work, which he calls a " provisional scheme." It is strictly followed by him as far as the composition extends : —

* *Yon*-sidedness ; existence in a place distinct from and beyond the visible universe.

Book I.—Of Religion and the Evidence.
  Chap. I. Nature of Religion and the Form of the Evidence thereof.
      1. Of Religion.
      2. Of Theology.
      3. Of Mythology.
      4. Institutions.
      5. Nature of the Evidence of Religion.
  Chap. II. Of Assent and the various Forms thereof.
      1. Of Possibility.
      2. Of Credibility.
      3. Of Probability.
      4. Of Certainty.
  Chap. III. Of Degrees of Assent demanded in different Departments of Thought.
  Chap. IV. Of Ideas as distinguished according to their Modes of Acquisition.
      1. Ideas of Perception.
      2. Ideas of Intuition.
      3. Ideas of Demonstration.
      4. Of Testimony.
  Chap. V. Of Ideas distinguished as Necessary or Contingent.
      1. Of Ideas of Necessity.
      2. Of Ideas of Contingency.
  Chap. VI. Of some important Facts of the Religious Consciousness.
      1. Modes of Studying Religious Consciousness.
      2. Periods of the Development thereof.
        (1). Period of Vague Feeling, anterior to Fetichism.
        (2). Period of Definite Feeling, anterior to Fetichism.
        (3). Period of Distinct Idea of God as Influent.
        (4). Period of Distinct Idea of God as God.
  Chap. VII. Of the Things to be Considered in the Evidence of Religion.
      1. Of the Three Things to be Demonstrated.
      2. Nature and Form of Proof.
        (1). Of the Religious Consciousness in Man.
        (2). Of the Existence and Character of God, and of His Relation to Mankind.
        (3). Of the Religious Duties of Man.
  Chap. VIII. Of the Function of Religion in Human Development.

Book II.—Of the Development of Religion in the Caucasian Race into various National Forms, to the Time of Christ.
  Chap. I. Introductory Statement of the Question.
  Chap. II. Development of Religion in Ægypt, or Ægyptian National Form of Religion.
  Chap. III. National Form of Religion in India.
  Chap. IV. National Form of Religion in Persia.
  Chap. V. Of the Shemites in general.
  Chap. VI. Heathen, or Non-Jacobic Semitic Nations.
  Chap. VII. Heathen, or Non-Jacobic Hebrews.
  Chap. VIII. Heathen or Non-Jacobic Greeks (Hellenes.)

Chap. IX. Heathen or Non-Jacobic Romans.
Chap. X. The Union of Oriental and Greek Philosophy.
Chap. XI. Teutons and Kelts.

Book III.—The Moral and Religious Condition of Mankind at the Birth of Jesus Christ.
Chap. I. Effect of Rome in Gathering into a Unity the Diverse Nationalities.
Chap. II. Popular Consciousness of the Educated in Religion, and its Ideal Effect on Morals and the Public Life.
Chap. III. Relation of Woman to Man.
    1. Hebrew; 2. Classic; 3. Barbarous, German, &c. (*Domestic*.)
Chap. IV. Relation of Rich and Poor, Slaves, &c. (*Social*.)
Chap. V. Relation of Government and People (*Political*).
Chap. VI. Relation of State and Mankind (*Kosmic*).

Book IV.—Chap. I. Generic Agreement of Christianity and other Forms of Religion. Christianity of Jesus Christ in the Gospel of Matthew. (Other New Testament Developments in Book V.)
Chap. II. Specific Difference between Christianity and other Forms of Religion.
    1. Anthropological :—1. Internality (Sentiment)
        2. Free Spirit (Individuality).
        3. Ethical Character.
    2. Theological—Character of God.
        1. Relation to Nature.
        2. Relation to Man (Devil, Hell).
    3. Critical—Judgment applied to Ideas of Christianity.

Book V.—Historical Development of Christianity.
    1. As a Religion, Speculative and Philosophical.
    2. In Practice, Ethical, &c.
Part I. As a Religion. Four Periods : 1. Preponderance of the Hebrew Element : Ebionites, Matthew, Mark, and Apocalypse, Jewish Christians in general.
    2. Preponderance of the Greek Elemen: Philosophy, Paul, the Subtleties, show the Value of the Dogmatic Disputes.
    3. Preponderance of the Roman Element : Practice, Results in the Catholic Church.
    4. Preponderance of the Germanic Element : Individualism, Protestantism.
    Notice the two forces : one tending to *Unity of Action* (Orthodoxy), Monarchy, &c. The other to *Variety of Action* (Heresy), Episcopacy, which is Aristocratic; Presbyterian, which is Republican; Congregational, which is Democratic.
    Notice also : 1. Piety, Personal Religion.
    2. Theology.
    3. Literature (Theologico-Religious).
Part II. As a Practice.
    1. Individual Life and Character (the Individual).
    2. Domestic Life and Character (the Family).

3. Civil Life and Character (the State).
    (Effect on Law, Civil Law, Law of Nations.)
4. Mundane Life and Character (the World).

Book VI. Problems yet to be Solved in the Religion of Mankind.
Part I. Philosophical Desiderata.
Part II. Practical Desiderata.
    1. In the Individual ; 2. Family ; 3. Society ; 4. State;
    5. Race. A Criticism : 1. Of the History of Mankind hitherto ;
    2. Of its Condition now ; 3 Of its Ideas; 4. Desiderata, under
    heads from 1 to 5.

After laying open the four kinds of proof or argument by
which the existence of God is commonly shown—the cosmolo-
gical, teleological, ontological, and psychological—he proceeds,
assuming some conclusions previously made out :—

All these various arguments are attempts of mankind to legitimate
by the intellect what is given as a fact of consciousness, and what
seems to me is not attainable by any of the modes enumerated.
Reasoning, I think, will never furnish us with the idea of God, which
is a datum of spontaneous consciousness, any more than with the idea
of cause in itself.   But starting with the notion of God, distinguishing
it from other notions, developing it by the *à priori* law of intuition,
analysing the facts of intellectual, æsthetic, moral, affectional, and
religious consciousness, till we separate the infinite element from all
the finite, uniting all this together by an act of synthesis with the One
Whole Being who is given spontaneously by our nature, we then find
that philosophy and nature agree: we have an idea of God which fulfils
the conditions of the mind, conscience, heart, soul, taken in their
separate activity, and also the conditions of human nature taken in its
whole action.   Thus we have an idea of God clear and consistent,
adequate to represent the first spiritual emotions of God with which
we set out.   But all that this process of thought, of analysis, of consciousness, and synthesis of ultimate facts thereof has done, is to legitimate before the mind the consciousness of God, which comes spontaneously, and is a part of nature.   All this process of demonstration
makes me no more certain of the existence of God than at first, as all
the demonstration of my own existence, or of the existence of the
world, would make me no more certain of either than I was at first.
It only legitimates, by analysis and synthesis, what I knew before
either.   It only brings to a distinct consciousness what I held in
solution therein.
    Starting thus with the notion of God as a fact of consciousness in-
tuitively known, examining it, and developing it to its proper conclusion, I then see that the existence of God is a fact of necessity, not
merely actual, but uncontingent and necessary, as the *à priori* cause of
all things, and the reason thereof not less.   If any finite thing exists,
say myself, then by the laws of my own nature I am forced to the
infinite existence implied therein, and as certain of that as of my own
existence.   The only thing I take for granted in the matter is the
validity of my own faculties.

Let us examine the nature of God, thus authenticated, more carefully. I lay off all that is limited and conditioned, and separate the idea of God from the conceptions added to it. Thus, I eliminate all that is idiosyncratic or peculiar to myself, all that is sectarian and of my own party, all that is national of my tribe, secular of my age. Thus removing the idols of my own den, of my family den, of the tribe, the age, there is left the idea of God the Infinite. It is not Jehovah, who is Hebrew; nor Baal, who is Tyrian; nor Odin, Zeus, or Jove, who have the generic peculiarities of the Caucasian race, the form of the successive ages which gave birth to such conceptions, and the national form and colouring of the Jew or the Canaanite, of Scandinavia, Greece, or Rome. It is not the Allah of the Mahomedan, nor the Triune Deity of the Christians, that I seek, but God Himself—God, blank and bare, unclothed by human conditions—the idea of God, a primitive fact of nature, separated from the dust of human consciousness. This is the *Infinite*, the *Absolute*, not conceived as a manifold, but a unit; and I call it *a* Being, the Absolute Being. Then I examine it in the light of all my several faculties, and I find God is the perfection of existence, self, being, the cause uncaused; the perfection of power, all-mightiness, of will, self-determining; the condition of all things, but conditioned by none; autonomic, with absolute freedom; with the perfection of mind, all-knowingness, not reasoning, inducing, deducing, imagining, remembering, &c., but knowing without process, regardless of our categories and modes of conception; but knowing in forms to me unknown; the perfection of conscience, all-righteousness, all-goodness, goodness unconditioned by motive, as hope, or fear, or self-love; the perfection of affection, infinite love, not limited by the character of the object, or with limited affection, which needs reciprocal influence, and is raised or let down by the character of the object of love, but loving, irrespective thereof, maid and man, saint and sinner; the perfection of soul, perfect holiness, fidelity to self; therefore as wise as powerful, as good as wise, as just as good, as lovely as just, as holy as beautiful. I call this the Supreme Being. Looked at from various points of view, and named from specialities of representation, it is now infinite power, now infinite mind, reason, and understanding, now infinite beauty, then infinite good, then infinite love, then infinite holiness. I unite all—being and the modes thereof—and name it God.

While I attribute these qualities, I of course conceive of God as immanent in all of the modes into which I divided existence—matter and spirit, but as infinite. I do not put a limit there. God is transcendant; and as there are qualities in a rose, which the slug who eats it knows not, but I know; so doubtless there are other qualities in God which far transcend all I can know thereof as yet. The dog that runs at my side, the fly that buzzes about my temples, know very little of me, of my nature, purposes, aims in life, notions and consciousness in general, but yet I doubt not comes nearer to an exhaustive knowledge of me than I of God. Suppose that fly to plan about me, as most men about God, then He must conceive of me with the enlarged attributes of a fly, and put His muscous limitations upon me; He may say there is a certain *musculity* in man—a *flyiness*. I dare not attribute personality to God, lest I invest the Deity with the limitations of my own, ending in anthropomorphism; nor impersonality, lest I thus affix the limitations of mere matter, and abut in Hylism or in Pantheism. Yet infinite self-consciousness must belong to God, only I can have no adequate conception of any consciousness but my own; so I know thus that I cannot know the mode of the consciousness of God. The consciousness that I ascribe to God must be as alien and as unlike as the bear of the strolling bear-tamers is to the constellation called the Bear in heaven.*

In use, as symbol of the reverence of men, all nations speak of God in their highest forms of speech, and, considering the bi-sexual animals above the unisexual, and then the masculine as more dignified than the feminine, call God He, not It, nor She. It is not worth while to depart from common language while we know its use, though some of the attributes of God find a better symbol in woman than in man.

Follow out the idea of God this gives, and, thus distinguished and declared, let us see the relation He must sustain to the world. As the Infinite, He corresponds to infinite perfection in each of the forms we can understand. He is the infinite cause and reason, the infinite designer, making all things with his own aim and purpose; the infinite law-giver, cause, reason, and designer of the modes of action in the universe, of matter and of spirit; the infinite befriender, that loves all—the infinite father. He must be the infinite providence—a providence that is universal, so special and general both. He must be infinitely present everywhere, immanent in space; every Now also pervading, and eternal in time. Space and time—nay, immensity and eternity, may then poetically be called the temporal and local extension of God—the ultimate cause of all things, the ultimate condition of all, the law of all, the befriender and the provider of all.

In Book II. " Of the Ante-Christian Modes of Religion," let us take the introductory chapter, " Statement of the Question :"—

As religion has its ground in the imperishable nature of man, and its support in the continual activity of God, both directly in the Holy Spirit and mediately through nature, so religion is a fact of human consciousness, inseparable from human nature, and appearing at all periods of man's history. It is a constant force, with a variable quantity, in human history. But the phenomena of its development must depend on the general development of mankind. The actual manifestation of religion, therefore, is the result of all the culture of the people, and its index and test. Nothing is done per saltum in human history more than in material nature. Mount Washington does not rise sheer up from the sea, with perpendicular sides seven thousand feet high; there is an upward slope all the way, though irregular, from the sea to the mountain, else the ascent were impossible, except to the eagle. Poets like Milton and Goethe, men of science like Achard and Newton, do not spring up among the Mandans or the Lestrygonians. If we bring together two extremes of religion, the religion of the Bushmen and of a rational Christian or philosophical Deist, at this day, the two seem unlike and irreconcilable. All the difference of civilization appears in the religions thus wide asunder. But supply all the intermediate links, and the transition is not abrupt. The history slips all the way from the

* This illustration is Spinoza's.

rude natural representations of the Bushmen to the free spiritual religion of the Christian. The difference between the Bushmen and the Christian is not of nature, but of development. This will appear in the modes of religion.

From the beginning of human history there has been a gradual development of man's spirit, of his soul as well as mind; and, as the result, a gradual development of religion. This appears theoretically in his idea of God, of man, of their relations; and practically in the literature, ritual, art, manners, laws, institutions, government, ethics, and daily life. These are the moments which frame the religious history of mankind; all modes of religion agree in this, that they are religious; they differ *substantially* on account of the different degrees of culture of the nation, and so represent degrees of religion; and they differ *formally* in this that the peculiar genius of the nation, or of its great men, appears therein. To understand the religious history of mankind, we must study these various forms of religion, as to know the religion of a man we must know the phases which religion has assumed in his consciousness. No one must be neglected. To understand any one phase thereof, we must see it in its relation to the whole. Especially is this so with the later modes of religion, *e.g.* with Christianity. That cannot be understood except in its relation with other forms of religion before Christ. We must understand the religious history of mankind before that time, and the religious condition thereof at that time, the highest, as the result of all the natural thinking of the human race. Plato and Aristotle helped Kant and Hegel, and Thales of Miletus was the forerunner of Schelling of Berlin.

As the present inquiry must needs be brief, I shall neglect the nations which had little or no perceptible influence on the nations then ruling the world. Thus, the nations then savage or barbarous may be left out of the account.

> Humana ante oculos pede quum vita jaceret
> In terris, obpressa gravi sub religione ;
> Quæ caput a cœli regionibus obtendebat
> Horribili super adspectu mortalibus instans.*

Mankind was separated into various nations, divided by geographical obstructions from one another, and developing their idiosyncracies, separated also by governments, names, languages, &c. They thus developed their own peculiar national character in all directions. Each had its own peculiar mode of religion, which often purposely separated it from other nations. All of these religions had something general— of mankind (souls of religion), as well as special, of their nationality (forms thereof), and this was its contribution to the sum of the religion of the world. When the separation was removed by a transient war, or a lasting peace, and a form was found free enough, the several nationalities might all be moulded into one. There is no more that is arbitrary in the religious development of mankind, than in the scientific or political development thereof.

Each nation has a form of religion which accords with its genius and progress, and represents the sum-total of its actual ideas of right,

* Lucretius, I. 63.

good, the beautiful, &c. So all the forms of religion, like the classes with their lessons in a school, are to be taken as *momenta* in the religious progress of mankind. Idolatry is one form of religion, and as much belonging to the need of human history when it came, as rude attempts of a child to walk are indispensable. Each form of religion is to be tried by its relation to the nation at the time ; and every form once grew out of the actual life of some one, even such doctrines as that of the depravity of man, and, of course, of God, and the form of human sacrifice ; and also by its relation to the absolute religion. Each is an attempt to get towards it and to it. All these lines of human religion do tend to that central point, as the stumblings of the child to walking, as the abortive theories of Ptolemy and Copernicus to the true astronomy : a mistake in religion (doctrinal or practical) is not therefore capricious.

In science and religion much is done by a few great men, who give their names to discoveries or to systems, but they do little in comparison with what is done by the race of ordinary men, though the ordinary men are forgot in the *éclat* of the great men. Great originators of ideas in politics, like Jefferson, or great executive men like Cromwell and Napoleon, do much, yet very little compared to the work of the nation. So in science, how little did Newton and Leibnitz, compared with the work before them ! The mere man of genius tells the work of his older and his younger brothers. Religious progress did not begin with Moses, and end with Jesus of Nazareth. There had been much done in religion before ever Moses was possible ; and since Jesus of Nazareth, the development has gone on intrinsically and extrinsically with more rapidity than before. The advance since Jesus is greater than what he himself made. But now as the scientific achievements of mankind do not represent all the facts of the universe, no more does the religious thought of mankind represent all the religion which mankind has *in posse*. The beginnings of religion were small ; we creep before we walk, we put out our hands and feet before we could crawl, and spread wide our fingers, and stared at the world with great eyes, not knowing what to make of it. In religion there was a good deal of creeping before there was any walking at all, and the creeping was as natural at first as the walking afterwards. What is once gained by mankind is gained forever ; for there is this noticeable, —that man loves truth and the right, in all forms thereof—will be satisfied permanently with nothing else, but will discard all things for this, and, getting it once, will never let it go. Therefore, if any form of religion contain good and evil—as all do—it will not disappear and perish before any new form, until all the good of the old is taken up by the new.

Christianity is one form of religion amongst many. It was dependent on the Jewish forms of religion in many ways—much of the good and much of the evil now current under that name were mixed with forms of religion before Christ. It can only be understood when taken as one step in the religious history of mankind. But in a brief sketch like this I shall neglect the forms of religion which had little influence on the people of the world since become Christian, and which had no great influence in the development of Christianity itself. Thus, the religion of the savage may be left out of the account, also the religion of the Chinese.

All the nations of the earth at the time of Christ had their formal religion—they all agreed in several things: in a belief in the existence of a God, of a religious nature in man that had need of religion, and has communication with God. These are two great facts on which religion rests—deny either, and religion is not possible. They agreed in a third thing: the immortality of the human spirit. These are the three greatest facts in religious consciousness at this day. Individuals doubt or deny all these, but nations never. Such as deny the existence of the material world, are more numerous than these exceptional deniers. But these three are a part of the primal revelation made by the nature of man, and therefore *to* every man in the world; a spontaneous revelation, made of God and by God, but in the nature of man, and in conformity with the laws thereof.

These three things are taken for granted in all formal religion then, and are three points of agreement among all men. But they differed in the character they ascribed to God, and therefore in the idea of his relation to man, and accordingly in the doctrines which religion demanded, the hopes which it allowed. They differed as to the nature of God and of man, and the form of immortal life. The degree of their revelation, and so of religion, and the forms thereof, differed with the cultivated and with the natural genius of different people. Nations differed also in the prominence they gave to the religious nature of man, some making it of great account, and others of little, as they had much or little organic tendency to religion.

Let me look at the forms of religion, taking them in their chronological order, limiting myself to the Caucasian race.

THE FORM OF RELIGION IN ÆGYPT.—In the present state of inquiry relative to Ægypt, it is not easy, or possible, for one who has no access to the monuments, to make out or detail the religious facts of consciousness of the Ægyptians, from the time of Menes to that of the Ptolemies. It must take the labor of some centuries, perhaps, before this can be done. Still, the *chief* facts of religious consciousness in that time may be gleaned from what is known (from the monuments) to the learned world. Beyond that, all must be considered as provisional, and respecting what is *now* known, the works of Lepsius and Bunsen will furnish much information not now accessible to the public.

In regard to antiquity, Ægypt surpasses all known nations. Her civilization goes back beyond the rudest traditions of the nations of Europe and Western Asia. (Von Bohlen, in his "Alte Indien, mit Rücksicht auf Ægypten, 1830-31," thought Egyptian civilization derived from India, but retracted the opinion—Lepsius, "Die Chronologie der Ægyptier. Einleit. u. erster Theil. Kritik der Quellen," Berlin, 1849, 4to, p. 3.) Greek and Roman history furnishes us no facts before the seventh or eighth century B.C., while Ægyptian history furnishes us with rigorously historical facts, and Ægyptian chronology with accurate dates, years, months, and days—from the third and fourth thousand years B.C. (Lepsius, l. c. p. 1.) In the time of Menes, the first king of the whole of Ægypt (say 3500-4000 B.C., though Manetho's system would place him 5702 B.C., *apud* Müller, II. 600), hieroglyphic writings had been long devised, were established, and in extensive use. There was a library, fourteenth century B.C., established in a temple by

Osymandias (Ramses Miamun) ; we have still papyri from the thirteenth and fourteenth centuries B.C. (Lepsius, p. 36–39.) The Ægyptians had a calendar of 365 days, established 3282 B.C., and reformed it in 2782 B.C. (Lepsius, p. 211 *sq.*, p. 220; 216 *sqq.*) Note: It is curious that the Asiatic and European nations agree so nearly in their early historic facts; the Chinese place their *Jao (yau)* about 2300 B.C.; the Chronicles of Cashmir, their first king, Govada, 2448 ; the Babylonians, the termination of their great cyclic period about 2400, and their Flood about 2500 ; and the Hebrews their Deluge at the same time ; while Manetho, following authentic documents, places Menes about 1500 years earlier (4000 B.C.), and then makes him found a new kingdom by a division of an *older* one (Lepsius, p. 24). The Ægyptian claims to antiquity are supported by monumental evidence, while those of Asiatic and European nations are not. (Lepsius, p. 28.)

Ægypt seems to have been in a state of high civilization 1000 or 2000 years before the time of the Hebrew Flood. (Ægypt, "the young lion of the nations." See the chronological systems about Ægypt, viz. Manetho in Syncellus; also in Müllerus, "Fragmenta. Histor. Græcor., Parisiis, 1848," Tom. II., p. 510; Müller's "Frag. Chron," appended to Herodotus, Didot's ed., Paris, 1844. Eusebius, "Aucher." I. p. 199, 8vo. ; see, too, the older edition, Opp. Lat. (Fol.) Julius Afric. Chronicon, in Routh, Reliquiæ," Tom. II., pp. 124–192. His "Epistolæ," *ibid.* III. *sqq.* See, too, the remarks of Lepsius on all these and other subjects, pp. 405–547 ; and Bunsen, "Ægyptens Stelle in der Weltgeschichte" (Hamb. 1845), Buch I. pp. 25, 304; Pritchard, "Analysis of the Ægyptian Mythology ;" Ideler, "Handbuch der Chronologie.")

Bunsen thinks the Ægyptian mythology old as Menes (4000 B.C.), and yet thinks "the religion of the Ægyptians, like the language, has its seat in Asia, in the Armenian Caucasian fatherland, and that the Ægyptians brought the civilization of their age with them in some migration, as the Norwegians carried that of Norway to Iceland "!

The chapter proceeds in this way, with a great accumulation of authorities, and a canvass of the merits of some to whom he thinks too much deference has been paid, *e. g.*—

Such writers as *Apuleius, Iamblichus, Porphyry, Philostratus,* are of scarcely any value here. See how they deceive Cudworth and Wilkinson. The Greeks were often mistaken on the Ægyptian religion. See, for instance, Sallustius de Diis Mundi (*apud* Gale) ch. iv.; Wilkinson's second series of the "Manners and Customs of the East" (London, 1841), Vol. I. pp. 205, 229, 290, 302, 369 ; 55, 236, 465, *et al.* Iamblichus was a philosophical gentleman of leisure, who derived his facts from his theories, and his theories from his lively fancies.

*   *   *   *   *   *

It may seem a bold generalization to assume that the Egyptians did not believe in the freedom of their gods, though in their caprice; but absolute freedom could not be ascribed to any of the ˌgods in that period. The figures of several of the gods indicate this in their maimed forms. (See what Eudoxus relates in Plutarch : Isis, § 62. Bunsen, I. 490.) Note how the restless life of animals and their certain instinct attracts men, and so they worship. Some of the deities were represented with human forms, but the heads of animals. This indicates an advance upon Fetichism, for the human form is taken as the highest *type* of visible life; and to emphasize that, the special function of some animal is added, and symbolized by the appropriate animal. Still it is a rude step of religious development when an aggregate of animal functions, added to the human, is the mode of approximating man to the Divine. (See the plates in Wilkinson, or Montfaucon, Rosellini.) This is lower than the Indian mode, whereby this augmentation of powers is represented by multiplying human limbs—hands, heads, feet, &c.—for here is a unity in the quality of consciousness.

Still, the deities are artistically symbolized by the human form; the distinction between men and gods is completely preserved; and it was taught that no god had ever been a man, and no man a god. This is still below the Greek development.

All nations believe in some mode of revelation, by which the gods make themselves known to mortals; here it was by living on the earth with men, in the period before Menes, before the strictly historical age. The manner of this manifestation of the deities (of Osiris, *e.g.*) in a human form, without partaking of human nature, was probably not explained in a very philosophical style. (Wilkinson, I. 317, 338. Plut. Isis, § xi. 20.) It seems that the revelation had not entirely ceased; for though there was no need of the old revelation in the literature and the deities of the country, the *Oracles* supplied men with the new and living revelation—the gospel for the day.[*]

But if the deities were not connected with any inanimate thing, as in Fetichism, they were not a mere abstraction, as is the deity of Pantheism. They partook of human attributes, if not of human nature—had parents, passions, and marriages, and children. So difficult is it to rise above the form of human life after men escape from those of mere matter, the deities were confounded with time in its succession of events; the year, the month, and each day was consecrated to some deity. Perhaps the Ægyptians were not the first who thus brought their gods into connection with time.

   *   *   *   *   *   *

Someone relates that Ægypt is so full of creative vigor, that animals may be found in the process of becoming—half-lion, and the rest dirt, not yet formed. The fable (see how Cowley handles it) typifies the spiritual condition of the people: the spirit seemed half-born, and struggling to be free from the gross matter which still environed man. Man is not before *nature*—the individual not before his *kind*. Men can be divided into castes, and so their lot determined before they are born; for no man was allowed to follow any calling but that of his

---

[*] Notwithstanding these partial revelations, it appears the Ægyptians considered the nature of God still a mystery, hidden from men. This appears from the name of a deity who must be placed at the head of their gods—*Ammon.* His name signifies *hidden.* (Bunsen, i. 437.) This deity seems originally to have been the sun (Rè), and a fetich-god, and at length to have developed into the Unknown God, and to have been put before all forms of the known. (But see how dangerous it is to reason on names, in Schwenk, p. 50.) Plutarch was aware of this, and says they called their first God, who was *obscure*, and *the hidden*, Amun, and entreated him to become clear and manifest to them. Isis and Osiris. Christians do the same now.

father's. (Diod. lib. I. ch. 6. Herod. III.) The government was a despotism, in which the people were little cared for.

Man was not free *before his God* (Noack seems mistaken in Cyclop. p. 322. See, too, the phantasies of Hegel, " Phil. der Religion, Werke," Vol. XI. Berlin, 1840, pp. 435, 456) ; all was fixed for him before-hand, and compliance seems all that was allowed him. Thus to the social fate, represented by caste, was added a divine fate, indicated by the fixed and immovable character of religious rites. The priests were the controlling class—rich, powerful, and free from taxation. Even the king seems subject to their iron rule, but fought against it. (Hegel, XI. 447.)

    *   *   *   *   *   *

Religion appears as *ritual.* But it had some moral power, for there was taught a future retribution, which it is difficult to understand. The Egyptians believed the immortality of the soul. Osiris was the judge of the dead; all mortals appear before him. The forty-two assessors make examination of their actions; they are registered in the volume, and rewarded or punished. (For the reason of embalming, see Baur and Zeller, VIII. 285.) But still the human spirit is subordinate to matter, and must pass into the bodies of animals. (Herod. II. 23, says *all*, but this may be doubtful, see Pritchard, p. 195 *sqq.* Bunsen, I. 467, 501.) The importance they attached to the immortality of the soul may be measured by the magnificence of their tombs. (Hegel, XI. 436–7, 444.) Polygamy existed in all classes but the priests. (" Comptes Rendus," Jan. 1851, p. 79 ; Diod. Sic. I. 80, and references.)

In this form of religion there is a dim feeling of the immanence of the *Divine in nature*—not in all parts indifferently, as in Fetichism, nor as a whole in nature as a whole, as in material Pantheism—but without the sense of the transcendance of deity. Hence, there was no separation of *God from man,* and gods not wholly from the beasts : above mere Fetichism, but not attaining the point of deification of men, though approaching it. Hence, while Amun seems a mere *nature-god* (? Re=Sun), Osiris is much like one of the man-gods of Greece, subject to the accidents of human life—birth, marriage, death, &c. No *avatar,* or *descent of God* into the human form ; no apotheosis, or ascent of man to the divine form. The deity is still mysterious—the sphinx a good symbol. (See thereon Hegel, XI. 455.) The power of religion was great. This is attested by the tombs and pyramids. Yet its aspect must have been that of awe and of fear more than of love. (Aspects severe and ugly, " so high that they were dreadful,"—a great activity—see all the architecture—an attempt to write out this consciousness.) The priesthood tended to make all immovable in religion, the castes in society, the government (despotism) in politics. (Yet a a great life in this compared with India.) Mummy the type of man, so swathed about, his hands and feet still pinioned.

This is the way the Ægyptian chapter closes. The Chaldæan, Arabian, Phœnician, Shemite chapters show the great extent of his Oriental reading and scholarship, but they are hardly more than a series of annotations. The Hebrew chapter is more finished, so is that upon the Greeks. He traces the development

of their conception of God through the poets—the subordination
of deity to the universe—what was borrowed from other
nations—gives the representative principle of each philosophical
school from Thales to Plato; has sections upon the Epicureans,
Stoics, &c.; he covers, in short, completely the whole ground.
The Greek chapter is the longest of all, but it is in an unequal
condition of preparation.

PLATO'S CONCEPTION OF GOD.—In Plato we have a distincter statement of God, still it is difficult to reconstruct his notions. But God
is one, though he uses the popular form " gods." (Brandes. II. 349,
and the *Timæus*, where he thinks the world is "a blessed God.") He
is spirit, and the universe depends on him and originates with him.
God is self-existent and absolute, unconditioned, all-powerful, all-wise,
all-just. He cannot alter or be changed for the better or the worse.
Prayers move him not, he is incapable of wrong (Θεὸς οὐδαμῇ οὐδαμῶς
ἄδικος, κ.τ.λ.). He is absolutely happy, and seeks to make the world like
himself, the effective ultimate cause of all things. Accordingly he is
perfect providence of the little and the great. (See his ingenious
answers to the doubter, Laws. X. 903, B. and D. Ast. VIII. 282.) So
justice will be done to each, here or hereafter. (Note his Metem-
psychosis, VII. 383–4.)

This is Plato's scheme of things.

I. There is matter—the elements—the raw material of which things
are (subsequently) composed. This is eternal, necessary, with properties of its own, but inert and not susceptible of thought (intelligence,
νους). Tim. p. 30–6, 52–3, 68. E. 69.

II. A certain motive power, eternal, necessary, extended, divisible,
incorporeal, not sensible, and only known by its effects, but susceptible
of thought, intelligence. (Laws. X. 895. Tim. 37 C. 46, D.E. Phædrus, 245 C.D.)

III. God, eternal, necessary, &c. (as above). To organize bodies
He makes intelligence penetrate the moving power, which becomes the
soul of the world. This intelligence is also the good, and is the
supreme God—the soul of the world participating in intelligence par-
ticipates in God, and is a created God; but not wholly so, for the motive
power is co-eternal with God, the first of created things. By it God
forms the world, other gods inferior are also formed, their number no
man can tell; among them are the souls of the stars. (Tim. 38–40.
Laws. VII. p. 821, 822; X. p. 848, of the planets. See Martin, "Etudes
sur le Timée," note, 24, 27, 31, 38, and his "Mémoire sur l'Opinion
de Platon sur les Dieux," in "Mémoires de l'Académie Royale des
Sciences Morales et Politiques," Tom. II. "Savans Etrangères," Paris,
1847.) These inferior gods are the cause of the irregularities of the
world, God intervenes sometimes to set things right. Then there
are demons (genii), of which each soul has one.

Plato is a monotheist; for he makes the chief god creator and
monarch of the rest. Thus he makes a kosmos of gods out of the
former chaos thereof. The subaltern gods no more interfere with the
unity of the divine operations than the angels and saints of the more

modern mythology. The limitation of God comes chiefly from the co-eternal matter and motion.

This power of matter and of motion seems a dim remnant of that Fetichism which made all nature divine. We may trace a yet later form of it in the "plastic nature" of a later day. The dynamic property which modern science finds in matter is of a different origin in the mind of men.

About the punishments, &c., see the queer remarks of Nathanael Chumnius in Creutzer's Ed. Plotinus (Oxon., 1835), II., 1428, *et al.* See, too, the remarks on the natural immortality of the soul, in the "Dialogus de Animâ" of Joannes Chumnius, *ibid.*, II., 1442, 399.

Still, God is not the Infinite in his conception. His consciousness is a disturbed one; He is not the absolute Creator. There is evil in the world; not annual evil—an accident of development, and no more a flaw in the world than the milk-teeth and tottering step of the child—but absolute evil, a constant for ever, though in variable quantity. "It is not possible that all evil should be abolished" (Theæt. 176, A.). God, in forming the world, "desired that, as far as possible, all things should be good, and nothing bad" (Tim. E. and 30, A.). But matter is eternal as God, and is not absolute good. It has certain evil properties which are constant, and God cannot overcome them. Therefore, if not limited in himself, God is *ab extra.* This duality of the universe affects all things; the flaw extends to God. The world is indeed a "blessed God," but it does not correspond to the perfect God. It is the prison of God; he cannot transcend it (hence hatred of matter).

Hostile to all sensualism, Plato demands a high and free ethics. Not the desire of the senses but soul is the Norm; not pleasure but virtue is the aim. The dualism appears here—the body is evil, and must be spurned as much as possible. The chief virtues of his ethics are wisdom, bravery, temperance, justice (?). The highest object is the absolute God—that is, likeness of God—*i.e.* to our highest idea. Justice (subjectively) is a harmonious disposition of the faculties—the balance of all; (objectively) is doing your work and giving each his own. He is the happiest man who most attains this—the wretchedest who least.

The result of right and wrong does not end with this life. The soul is immortal, even moral evil cannot destroy it. Conduct here determines condition hereafter; the bad are punished—some, it seems, eternally—the good rewarded and exalted. But there is a purgatory in the other life; from it some go up to higher states of bliss, and others down to lower of misery. He admits absolute evil in the primal matter of the world; this flaw affects the conduct if not the character of God, the character of man (the evil coming from the body), and his condition.

His moral ideas are not perfect. Intellectual qualities are before all others, hence they in whom these predominate are the masters of mankind. His idea of the good is thus metaphysical not moral—the good of the intellect, not of conscience (Rep. VII. 517, B. and C.).

Woman is only the handmaid of man—subordinate to him as a medium for posterity; her marriage is subordinate to the state. Not monogamy, but partigamy is the law in his ideal state. Man is subordinate to the state—for it, not co-ordinate with it—the weak to the strong. There is no equality, no brotherhood. Slavery is eternal in his ideal state. The weak (slave) is an organ of the strong; woman of man; the individual of the state.

The same dualism appears in his ontology, psychology, theology, ethics, and politics. No sense of personal obligation to right. His morals are a medium between the Hedonism of the Cyrenaic school and the Cynism of the others. There is no complete subjective freedom—God is hampered by matter, the soul by the body, the individual by the state, woman by man, the weak by the strong; the part is sacrificed to the whole.

The Platonic theology and ethics were a great improvement over all that had preceded him. A great future was before them. We shall see great evils and much good from this school.

Next comes Aristotle, Pyrrhonism, Epicurus, the Stoics:—

THE STOICS.—The same causes which developed the Hebrew prophets —political downfall, moral corruption—produced also the Stoics. They were earnest persons, with a zeal for philosophy and for morals; but with the excessive subjectivity which makes so much of the Greek philosophy after Aristotle. Their philosophy is marked and individual. In a time that demanded the heroism of a Jeremiah, they were disgusted with the vice and sensuality which found its philosophy in Epicurus. They were tired of the dogmatism and empty generalities of the Platonic philosophy, which, beginning with an idea snatched out of the blue of subjectivity, ended in nothing but disappointment. They applied common sense more than inspiration to solve the problems of philosophy and ethics—not acutely analytic; not desperately subtle; less rash in generalizing than Plato and his school.

I shall treat Stoicism as a whole, neglecting the differentia from Zeno to Seneca; and shall take its truest or highest doctrines as the development of the whole school—in general describe the tree, gather the fruit, but not paint each crooked limb.

In regard to physical things, the mind of man is a *tabula rasa*—all knowledge thereof derived from sensation—so Zeno taught, and thus every cause is corporeal. But in other matters, it seems, they appealed to an innate sense as a ground of knowledge. (Cic. Nat. D. ii. 5, p. 49). The universe (ὅλον) consists of two principles (ἀρχαί, query, plural?)—one passive, which is matter; one active, which is God; both unborn and indestructible. The two are eternally and inseparably united. Matter has no properties which manifest themselves alone. God puts reason (λόγος) into it; forms it into the elements (στοιχεῖα), them (i. e., the elements) into worlds (the differentiæ of the universe), and retakes them to himself, to reform them anew (Diog. Laert. VII., c. 134, 137). There is a solidarity of matter and God; they are one, as the body and soul are one. Looked at from the passive side, the universe is matter; from the active, God. He is the permanent constant of reason in the transient variable of matter. Thus formally they escape the dreadful dualism of Greek philosophy. Matter and God are declared one, but the twofoldness still remains: matter is distinct from God, who has a functional, not essential (?), union with it: is coeval, co-extensive, co-equal, co-eternal with God; its properties, denied in form, but held in fact, continue still immutable and indestructible. (Ritter, 582 *et al.*, is mistaken in referring the organization of matter to God; and it is a *transitive act* in the history of God, not a *continual doing.* He is not the author of its Genesis, only of its Exodus and Deuteronomy—a *demiurgus*, not a *creator.*) The universe is not infinite, but only indefinite, and so is God. But in two great matters the Stoics improve the old idea of God; they teach—1. That there is now a unity of causal force in the universe; 2. That that cause is rational, self-conscious, good. (See the authorities in Ritter, 574.) He is the moving-power of the universe, the universal nature, without which not the smallest thing could be, the fatal force and necessity of future things, fate and foreknowledge both—alike the spermatic seed and the animating soul of things; the plastic fire that walks its way in the production of the world; the intellectual fire, like soul, that has no form but changes into all it will. God is immortal, rational, perfect; free from all evil of every sort, blessed; the providence of the whole and of the parts, not limited to the form of man; the Former of all things, and, as it were, the common Father of all—the universe his body, and he its soul. The variety of matter finds its unity in him.

The limitation of God comes from the dualism, the Greek philosophical stone of stumbling. The universe is not infinite, it is perfect as a whole, but of imperfect parts. Much of this seems evil that is not; they are perfect if taken in reference to the whole, not to themselves. *Magna Dii curant parva negligunt.* (Cic. Nat. D. II. 66.) Still there is a residual of real evil in the universe, to the individual sufferer an unmitigated and unmeasured (evil), but it is indispensable, necessary for the whole; so in well-ordered houses some chaff and even corn is lost. But whence comes this much and necessary evil that is mingled with the universe? From matter which the divine mechanic of the world could not change. God himself is subordinate to the law of matter (Plut. Stoic. 37; Seneca, De Prov. ch. v.) something he dislikes and neglects from his own imperfection; and instead of God, evil demons or wicked men have a sorry care over the good! God will destroy the world by fire, the self-moving element which most partakes of his nature. He is the plastic and destructive fire, and will draw back the universe to himself—to destroy it for ever? No, he had not the power; but to form it anew (Plut. Adv. Stoic. c. 17; Ritter, 586; Cic. Nat. D. II. 46, whereto Creuzer's Note, 2 Pet. Epist. iii. 7–10, and Wetstein), but the material necessary evil still remains. There is a dark back-ground of evil in the universe, which even God cannot overcome : immanent in matter, and not transcendent, he is subordinate to that.

The ethics of the Stoics were closely connected with their theology and physics. All things are subject to universal and unchanging laws, including man; God, the active part of the material world, gives it his reason for its law. In man there is the same distinction of the active and the passive. The law of nature demands the subjection of the passive to the active, the low to the high. Those who have the moral rule follow nature, live conformably to human nature, in its relation to the nature of the universe, conformably to right. There is an absolute right of nature and not of man's appointment. Happiness consists not in repose, not in pleasure of the senses, but in activity of the reason, the flow of life. There is a dim sight of what is morally just, but the clearest (Preller, § 400; the good, bad, indifferent) yet sees the function of τὸ ἀγαθὸν, τὸ ὠφελειν (Diog. VII. § 103) ; but the moral element is not distinctly seen as separate from the intellectual. This defect in psychology comes out in morals, yet the sense of duty is severely felt, more than in any philosophy before. The consciousness of sin faintly appears; virtue is a permanent disposition of the soul harmonious with itself through its whole life. Stob. Eccl. II. 104 (note the distinction, Aristotle calls virtue ἕξις: Zeno, διαθέσις. Simplic. in Aristot. Cat. 61, B. and Scholia.) The Stoic must stand up firmly against an evil world ; he must know the right, and separate it from the desirable, have moderation, fortitude, and justice ; but there is no such thing as justice to himself; justice is for others. Himself must be of no value in his own eyes. In the theological notion of Providence, the part is sacrificed to the whole, men not seeing that thus the whole is no more whole; so in ethics the individual is sacrificed to the universal, and it is not the harmony of all the natural appetites of sense and soul which Stoicism aims to produce, but it annihilates passion after passion, and proclaims peace when it makes solitude. It is thought that nature aims at genera, not individuals; so the individual desire, appetite, and welfare are of small value. The object of an action is of no value, only its moral use. Virtue is its own reward, but rewards theoretically are indifferent; a man must not desire money, honors, and agreeable things in general for himself, but for his friends, not for satisfaction at all, but their moral use alone. All must depend upon the will of the individual man ; he must not lean on circumstances, or the world, but stand erect, and out of his own subjectivity create his virtue.

There is no medium between vice and virtue. Plato and Aristotle exaggerated this ; the Stoics, yet more, magnify this crisis. There is no holding-ground between the wise man and the fool (as in Christendom none between a saint and a sinner). Virtue is a certain round in the ladder of life, and all below it is vice. A sharp and narrow line is drawn below the true, and at a certain period of life the young Stoic "experienced" reason or virtue. But virtue was capable of no increase or diminution. He that broke the law in one point was guilty of all ; a doctrine which has since had a great fortune. The ideal wise man is independent of circumstances, free from desire and ambition; he has no fear, follows his reason, and is truly free; but is proud also of his noble life,—for God needs the good man as much as he needs God. He is raised above every law. The Stoic Antinomian may violate all the common laws of human life, and lie, and cheat, and kill. (Ritter, p. 647).

With undeniable merits it yet lacks a sufficient and definite moral principle. There is no inborn rule of right. The Greek philosophy knew none without the law of the land. Stoicism knew none within. Its notion of the just is wholly from experience. They had nothing which transcends history. They had no conception of the moral sense of man. All is too intellectual ; the good is of the mind, not the conscience. There is no spontaneity of moral consciousness. Justice is not done to the spontaneity of the flesh; the body is under-valued. This is not wonderful—while so many placed the chief good solely in the sense, and Athens, Corinth, Rome, ran over with excess of riot. It takes all the philosophy of the time to represent the consciousness thereof. The Stoic tended to virtue's side. But virtue was obedient to the Categorical Imperative, and not spontaneous. The ideal Stoic would have been as unlovely as loveless, heroic, and hateful.

Yet, for the first time in human history, all limits of nations fall away; we must, says Zeno, be not of one state or people, but we must reckon all men for clansmen and countrymen, for there is one life for all mankind, and the universe is the common pasture of the common herd of men. (Plut. De Alex. Mag. Virtute, I. c. vi.) Plutarch calls it a *dream or phantasy of the benevolent philosophers.* It was the first time the ideal appeared in human history. Under this philosophy Cicero sees the one law for all, the same at Corinth as at Rome. [Note in its place how Christianity differed, and came to its conclusion from *love*].

But the Stoics despair of mankind. Homer looked on his contem-poraries as degenerate men, Hesiod called his own age iron, Aristotle looked back for models, and Plato made all good the reminiscence of the soul now fallen from a higher state. The Stoics yet more looked back; they had an historical reason for it in the evil times they fell upon in Greece and Rome. But their philosophy makes virtue hard to be found and difficult to win, acceptable only to the few; the primal virtues, which shine aloft as stars, could only be seen by the telescope of the understanding, and what experience of being reveals Infinite Love, the absolute law, was not in the nature of man and of it, but from without.

The soul of man was part of the soul of the world, and shared the federal immortality thereof. But is this all? Here the Stoics differed, and developed no peculiar view of Eschatology. Some thought at the incremation of the world all would be dissolved into the Indefinite; others that all souls would live forever, the bad for punishment; others that only the wise would survive death. The character of God gave them no certain ground of future bliss, at least none for the wicked. The doctrine on the whole was fitted for strong men in a rude time—fit to make martyrs, and it made them. It was much more manly than philosophical.

After the Stoics the Greek mind produced nothing more out of its own stock. It went eastward and came in contact with a *mystical* people, westward, and found a *practical* race from which it received new additions to its consciousness. Euripides and Aristotle show that the cultivated people of Athens had lost respect for the popular mythology and cultus; they indicate the decline of the national religion. Pyrrho and Epicurus show the decay of philosophy. In Pythagoras and in Plato the influence of a foreign spirit is visible, something of the dogmatic mysticism of the East. Aristotle and Zeno seem purely Greek. But Stoicism is the last production of Greek philosophy out of its own materials and on its own soil.

The manuscript comes to an end in the chapter upon the Keltic tribes, with the following paragraph:—

All this previous matter must be recast and put into three sections: 1. Of the Goths; 2. Of the Germans; 3. Of the Skandinavians (study Strinnholm again in Section Three; note the story of the Rigsmal, in Strin. II. p. 123; Use of Letters, II. p. 200; Favorable Condition of Women, II. p. 271).

Mr. Parker thought, in the early stages of this work, that he could complete it in ten years, by using all the time which he ordinarily had at his command for serious study. But that time diminished rapidly, and all literary and scientific pursuits were rudely thrust aside by the domination of slavery in the thoughts and affairs of the nation. A violated Conscience found her champion in that upper room, and called him from his books and favorite schemes. Her disfigured aspect filled him with pity and indignation, and as he turned his back upon the great companions of his peaceful thought, to resist the successive encroachments of statutes framed for wickedness, and laws passed to extend and perpetuate the wrongs of man, is it strange that a vision of Lexington, and hands of fathers and relatives reaching for the old muskets, received him at the door?

THE OLD MUSKETS.

CHAPTER XVIII.

Anti-slavery—His Position and Tendency—Early Speeches—Letters from Slaveholders—
Mexican War.

To trace the life of Mr. Parker through the great agitation for
anti-slavery principles, which commenced nearly thirty years ago,
would be almost equivalent to writing the history of the anti-
slavery movement since 1845, when he first became connected
with it. From the annexation of Texas to the last day of his
intellectual and moral activity, he was identified with every
critical movement in the national politics, and in the local
troubles which they occasioned. His life is written in his
speeches, lectures, and sermons ; they form a body of anti-
slavery literature of great value for clear statements, abundance
of facts, and supremacy of conscience. The same industry to
gather material, and skill in organizing it, which gave him such
practical efficiency in handling other subjects, made him pre-
eminent in this. Whether you desire a simple and perfectly
intelligible narrative of the development of the Southern policy,
from its original acquiescence in the evil of slavery to its present attitude, or a noble statement of the American idea which
gives to the Constitution and the Union their value and glory,
or a stern impeachment of the men who were betraying that idea,
and with it their country's safety and prosperity ; whether you
seek the facts, the history, the patriotism, the religion, the bold
invective, or the personal indignation, which are the body and
soul of anti-slavery—say rather, the thought, passion, and
threatening youth of Americanism, suddenly awake, righteously
angry, and with the light of a glorious future upon its countenance—you will find what you seek in those speeches and dis-

courses ; and that vigorous "Defence," into which Mr. Parker emptied the whole of his true New England nature. There is his memoir and the history of his time.

The care which he took in preparing for each of those grand popular indictments and prophecies, which perpetuate the disgrace and the hope of the last fifteen years, is evident enough. Documents, biographies, state papers, and newspapers of the South and North, correspondence with slaveholders and public men, conversations with men of information from every quarter of the country, contributed the pragmatic material. His power attracted the sources of information; people volunteered letters and sent him papers; public functionaries were accessible to his requests. Southern men who hated him would send him, in spite, just what he desired to see. If a man called upon him out of curiosity, he paid toll for the gratification, if he was solvent. Whoever came near him, complimented his sincerity with all the facts and prejudices which they had.

His acquaintance with so many of the prominent men engaged in politics was of great service. No thoroughly anti-slavery man had quite all his advantages. His wide knowledge and culture held men to him by various ties, and he knew how to sustain a genial intercourse which prevented any one idea from becoming oppressive or being suspected as an adventurer. Men admired his honesty, as well as his gifts ; if they did not wish to be as honest themselves, they liked to contribute to him ; perhaps they felt a secret pleasure, a kind of penumbra of open honesty in recognizing his mighty zeal and feeding it. A man who is so thoroughly hated by the ignorant always has the sympathy of the intelligent, even if they are not of his own party, provided his nature is not narrow and sectarian.

He represented no technical phase of the great anti-slavery sentiment. He believed in voting and in the Union as means for thwarting and eventually overcoming slavery. But he hastened to stand by the side of every sincere opposer of that iniquity. He was in intimate relations with some of the chiefs of the Republican party, and knew them all ; it was his hope that at last a Northern sentiment would secure a Republican victory, as the first preliminary of emancipation, but he always said that his office was to preach, to enlighten, to help to frame the sentiment. So he would be identified with no man to the extent of every party exigency. He preferred the isolated position which he had the power and conscience to occupy ; and he was sagacious enough to see that he thus preserved a chance of influencing friends and associates whom various motives drew and held around him.

I am responsible to nobody, and nobody to me. But it is not easy for Mr. Sumner, Mr. Seward, and Mr. Chase to say all of their thought, because they have a position to maintain, and they must keep in that position. The political reformer is hired to manage a mill owned by the people, turned by the popular stream; to grind into anti-slavery meal such corn as the people bring him for that purpose, and other grain also into different meal. He is not principal and owner, only attorney and hired man. He must do his work so as to suit his employers, else they say, " Thou mayest be no longer miller." The non-political reformer owns his own mill, which is turned by the stream drawn from his own private pond ; he put up the dam, and may do what he will with his own ; run it all night, on Sunday, and the Fourth of July; may grind just as he likes, for it is his own corn.

The anti-slavery non-political reformer is to excite the sentiment and give the idea ; he may tell his whole scheme all at once, if he will. But the political reformer, who, for immediate action, is to organize the sentiment and idea he finds ready for him, cannot do or propose all things at once; he must do one thing at a time. He is to cleave slavery off from the Government, and so must put the thin part of his wedge in first, and that where it will go the easiest. If he takes a glut as thick as an anti-slavery platform, and puts it in anywhere, head foremost, let him strike never so hard, he will not rend off a splinter from the tough log ; nay, will only waste his strength, and split the head of his own beetle.

The business of political reformers is to haul in the slack, and see that what the windlass has raised up is held on to, and that the anchor does not drop back again to the bottom. The men at the windlass need not call out to the men at the capstan, " Haul in more slack !" when there is no more to haul in. This is the misfortune of the position of the men at the capstan ; they cannot turn any faster than the windlass gives them slack rope to wind up.*

How well men fought when they heard his undaunted voice far in the front ! It rolled with the very shock of the encounter ; but they comprehended that it was leading them to no impossible position. He wanted organization and a definite plan of a campaign. His object was to throw a million votes. The Constitution and the Union was the bridge to resound with the feet hastening over to deposit this great ballot of freedom. But his opposition to the Fugitive Slave Bill was personal and humane. He did not care what political issues it might have ; it did not deter him that the Bill nominally became a law, nor did he

---

* The Great Battle between Slavery and Freedom, considered in two speeches delivered before the American Anti-Slavery Society, at New York, May 7, 1856 ; pp. 31 32, B. pamphlet.

trouble himself much about its constitutionality. He hastened in a moment of peril and dire distress to save such as were ready to perish—to plant his person and his intellect in the way of the kidnapper, to be sudden, instant, imperious, for the supreme necessity of liberty and the things dearest to the soul.

Mr. Parker had occasionally preached against slavery at West Roxbury, but he did not become prominently active in this field till 1845, the year of the annexation of Texas. A sermon "Of Slavery" was preached January 31, 1841, repeated by request January 4, 1843, and then published. In 1845, he was very busy preparing material for a History of Slavery among the Romans, its causes, its effects, and its extinction. This was never written, but the material did not lie unused.

The speeches which are not yet published in any edition of his works are quite numerous. Here is a brief account of the most important of them. He delivered one at Fanueil Hall, December 28, 1847, for which he had framed comparative tables, showing the growth of Northern and Southern States, in railroads, their length, their known and estimated cost, the valuation of the principal States, and their gain for a series of years, the free whites, &c. Another was delivered at Worcester, August 4, 1849, on occasion of a special fast for the cholera, the point of which is that repentance from the sin of slavery is a practical observance, to which the country must be called. Before the Anti-Slavery Convention, May 28, 1851, he discussed the action of the Government in the matter of slavery, weighed the threats of secession uttered by South Carolina, followed the political track of Mr. Webster, and quoted generously from anti-slavery sermons. This is a grand speech, lucidly arranged, and full of meat. At Framingham, on the anniversary of West-Indian Emancipation, 1852, he analyzed the two great forces of slavery and anti-slavery. In Boston, at the annual meeting of the Massachusetts Anti-Slavery Society, January 28, 1853, he made a fine speech, full of life and humor. He criticized the tone of the Northern pulpit on occasion of the death of Daniel Webster, and that of the press on the Duchess of Sutherland's letter respecting American Slavery. He noted the hopeful signs which the Church gave, and spoke some generous praise of Mr. Beecher. He examined the criticisms of the abolitionists upon Mr. Sumner. Another considerable speech was made before the New England Convention, May 26, 1853.

This speech repeats his vindication of the Duchess, and then proceeds to state the American idea—1. That men were created free. 2. That they have natural rights. 3. That these are inalienable. 4. That all men are equal in respect to the first three. 5. That the function of government is to organize these. Then he states the despotic idea in the same country, and here he describes the "irrepressible conflict" clearly. A criticism of parties follows, and the influence of slavery on courts, on trade, on the clergy ; but he gives the clerical exceptions. Then he makes a point of the fact that Thomas Sims reached Savannah on *the* 19*th of April*. He shows the advantages of the North in being based on free labor. The peroration of this speech is fine ; it is a description of the right kind of rebuke to administer to the Duchess and all foreign critics by inaugurating antislavery policy.

In Fanueil Hall, at an Anti-Nebraska meeting, which was held February 16, 1854, he made a speech, which was extensively noticed by the Southern papers. It traced the consecutive steps of the slave power. The *Charleston* (S.C.) *Courier* for May 2 says of it :—" There are frequent passages in this strange exhibition of the mad parson which, in the main, truthfully as well as strongly detail and depict the various occasions on which Southern interests have obtained the mastery in Congress, or, at least, important advantages, which are well worthy the consideration of all who erroneously suppose that the action of the general Government has been, on the whole, adverse to slavery." A passage from the *New York Times* for February 23, commenting upon a speech delivered in that city six days after the Fanueil Hall Meeting, upon the "Aggressions of Slavery," shows the condition of public opinion at that time, when the people still hated his prophesying, and were loth to find it true :—" But patriotic, Union-loving, faith-keeping Southerners ought to be apprised of the fact, that people of all classes and of all parties at the North, are beginning to say to one another that, after all, there is a great deal of truth in what Theodore Parker says."

Against an article from the *Charleston Courier*, which ridiculed him and the anti-slavery idea, Mr. Parker placed no other comment than advertisements, extracted from the same number of the paper, of sales at auction, "sound and healthy, likely and smart negroes," "valuable negroes," "children, nine years, four years, *six months*, old," and an "intelligent brown woman."

The satire is sufficient. In the same sheet are advertisements of " oxen and stallions ;" underneath "a buggy and harness for sale " is a " good man cook, in the prime of life."

He made another speech at New York, on the 12th of May of the same year, which is crammed with information to exhibit the actual condition of the country relative to slavery. On the 9th of May, 1855, he delivered a very racy speech before the American Anti-Slavery Society, describing the different political parties and the way they ignored the only political fact which the country then could furnish.

A speech at New York, on the 7th of May, 1856, " The Great Battle between Slavery and Freedom," is valuable. It gave a history of the Kansas troubles, very full comparative statistics of North and South, and described a true democracy.

But many of the lectures which he delivered before lyceums were filled with the same sentiments in a less technical form. The spirit of the American idea pervaded them all ; and at length his audience were disappointed if, in the course of the evening, he did not encourage and instruct the awakening conscience. His subjects were always so related to the culture and elevation of man, that the one great theme stepped with ease into them, and proved their strongest illustration. With this ceaseless reiteration he went everywhere, moulding the public opinion and insinuating the morals of politics into the minds of men of various parties.

Whoever would understand the deep complicity of his life with the great Northern movement for freedom, must look for it in his best moments, in those discourses inspired by all the critical events and measures of his time. Through him the anti-slavery idea seemed to be passing over from the earliest periods of its awakening into the popular consciousness, to assume a practical republican form. He represents this second phase of the great agitation. The first, commenced by Mr. Garrison, and supported by the men who are distinctively called Abolitionists, had performed the greater part of its glorious work. Patiently bearing obloquy and persecution for many years, and fighting with a mere handful and on an extreme position purely moral campaigns, it had effected a lodgment in reflecting minds. They were converted by the faith and suffering of these noble men. Thus the idea entered upon its second stage with increased numbers, but removed from its first ground, and seeking, through various inconsistencies, to gain a working political position. Then the original Abolitionists became the critics of their own idea as it strove to organize a great party of the North. Many were the fallacies of men who undertook, through all the forms of an immoral Government, to conduct a moral idea to a constitutional triumph. The Abolitionists preserved the consistency which had arrested popular attention ; the people, in turn, undertook to write the history of the last ten years, with a divided North and a united South. Mr. Parker's conscience was as thoroughly anti-slavery as his understanding was thoroughly practical. He detested the Government, which was then a Southern domination, but he believed in using the forms of the Government against the spirit which was then pervading it. His conscience prevented him from being a politician, but his common-sense was on the side of the people in their efforts to reconstruct the Republic. He was one of the first to see that such an effort was but the final stage of the first American Revolution, and that it might be driven by Southern opposition and Northern subservience into blood. The facts and the history were with him, as all men can now plainly see.

His letters and private meditations will help to show the position which he held, and the manifold influence that was exerted by him upon the political developments of the time. We thus also get some idea of his personal activity in the excitements which followed the passage of the Fugitive Slave Bill.

TO G. ADAMS.

West Roxbury, Dec. 5, 1842.

But to come to the Latimer petition.* Perhaps you feel a stronger interest than I do in the welfare of Latimer, and of the slaves in general. It must be a very strong one if it is so ; but I will not boast of my zeal. When Mr. Cabot, a noble young man of our village, asked me to read the petition, I said " Yes, I will." As I thought more upon it, I doubted that I should serve the special purpose by reading it, at that time, so well as by omitting to read it, and by leaving the sermon to produce what effect it might in that special direction. I sat down and read the last dozen pages of the sermon, to see if reading any petition would accord with my own spirit then. I thought it would not. I revolved the matter in my mind many times, and asked myself, " Shall I do the slaves a service by presenting the petition at this time? I thought I should not. I think so now. I con-

* Concerning the case of a fugitive slave, who afterwards escaped while his examination was pending.

sulted a friend, an Abolitionist, a thorough-going one, who is often called fanatical on account of his abolition; he thought it would do more harm than good to read the petition then. Monday afternoon I went to the chapel twice to see if I could find any of the Abolitionists there, to tell them I could not read it conscientiously at that time. I could find no one. When in the chapel Mr. Cabot brought me the petition. I don't know what I told him. I was in a state of great anxiety, as I always am for half an hour before I begin to preach on such an occasion. I do remember this, that, as he looked surprised, I said, " Do not think my zeal for the slave is cooling off," or words to that effect. After preaching the sermon I could not, in the state of feeling it left me, have read the petition at that moment, even if I had promised to do so. Now, my dear sir, you may condemn me if you please; but my own conscience acquits me of anything but the best motives. I may have erred in judgment, certainly not in motive. I thought I should offend some of the Abolitionists by refusing; but fear of man never stopped me yet when conscience said " Go." Perhaps it will in time to come. Then I beg you to rebuke me severely as you will. Do you think I was afraid to read the petition, and thought I should hurt my popularity? Then either you know me very little, or I know myself very little. Perhaps I am not zealous enough in the cause of humanity. No man can be over-zealous therein. Let my life speak; if that tells one tale and my tongue another, you shall be welcome to call me " Talker" forever and ever. I don't come up to my own ideal, of course; but I trust I do not shrink from performing what I consider my duty. If I had read the petition with the feelings I then entertained, I should have been false to myself, though all the men in the Hall had said " Amen," and signed it at once. But I have said already more than I meant to say on this theme, and will only add, that I think God is to be served by loving man, and that I think the only " ordinances of religion" that are of real value, and intrinsic value, are being good and doing good.

May 12, 1845.—I went to the meeting of the Unitarian Association; a stupid meeting it was, too. The brethren looked on me much as the *Beni Elohim* looked on Satan, as he came last of all. However, they shook hands all the more tenderly, because the heart was not in it, and then turned the cold shoulder. It was a queer meeting. I went as a demonstration of my existence as a member of the Association.

Anniversary Week, May 26.—Went in the afternoon to the meeting of the Clerical Anti-Slavery Convention. Found the brethren organized. The hall was full of laymen and women also. Stetson spoke well. Then an attempt was made to vote the lay-folk out of the room; but this would not go, so they continued to listen. Then —— spoke. He thought that anti-slavery was in its last stage, when it seeks to destroy existing institutions. The leaders of anti-slavery wanted to pull down Church and State, to build up an institution and put themselves therein. They cared less for the advancement of the slave than for their own advancement. The clergy had done more than any other class—all that could be expected.

John L. Russell replied, speaking of the evils of slavery, the great efforts made by the Anti-slavery Society, the dilatoriness of the Churches, the beauty of Christianity, and its power to heal all these woes. Then G. W. Briggs spoke, and beautifully; begging men to let the anti-slavery party alone, and apply themselves to the work before them. The clergy had done little, the Churches little: witness the character of the Southern Churches, colleges, &c. Stetson spoke with great beauty, and Pierpont with force I never shall forget. The audience cheered him with tremendous applause. He turned John the Baptist round upon the first speaker (who had said that John the Baptist represented the first stage of reform—that of simple exhortation). After that I came away, and wended my course homeward.

27.—Meeting of the Unitarian Association at Berry Street, to alter some arrangements. They discussed trivial matters involving no principle, with such technical skill, that I came away, leaving one party milking the ram and the other holding the sieve.

Went to the Anti-Slavery Convention—nothing great. McClure, of Scotland, spoke, in a bad spirit and with a bad face. I liked not the spirit of the man. Heard others, but nothing great. I intended myself to have spoken, and defined the position of the Churches in relation to reform, but could not.

28.—The Berry Street Conference met this year in Phillip's Chapel. The "*concio ad clerum*" . . . . . . told well on the audience; but I felt, as I listened to it, that the Unitarian sect was gone—gone past redemption. . . . . . .

I know not where they will go nor what will become of them. I fear that I shall feel myself obliged to leave the ministry, but not the calling to preach Christianity. I see so much of the falseness of the clergy, that I have little respect for them or their calling.

William H. Channing spoke well in favour of freedom; so did Bulfinch. I said my say, but it met no response. I looked down, but into indignant eyes.

The settlement of Texas, by exciting the internal slave-trade of the United States, which was sufficiently great before, stimulated slave prices and slave-breeding in Virginia, and destroyed the small party for emancipation which had existed there. The idea of Southern domination and unlimited slave territory began then to make slavery the corner-stone of our Republic. Both branches of the Texan Congress passed the laws of annexation to the United States, and the measure, which had been long maturing, was consummated in 1845 by the enactment of similar and corresponding laws in the American Congress. Mr. Parker had frequently lectured against it.

July 26.—I wonder if some good result will not follow the constant preaching of truth! It must tell at length; not in my day, but it will tell at last. At this early age of the country, a few good men of great ideas can do a great work, that will make a mark on the nation forever. It needs not *many* to do this, but *much*. I am resolved to spend what little strength I have in this way. What happens to me I care little for; but the welfare of men I think may be advanced by my humble efforts.

In 1846, the *Ottoman*, a vessel owned in Boston, and manned by New England men, arrived in the harbor. A slave was found secreted in the hold, lying naked upon the cargo, almost suffocated and half dead with fear. The owner of the vessel had him carried back to New Orleans, to preserve the integrity of his connection with a Southern market. Men in Boston were indignant at this who have long since forgotten that their hearts once throbbed. It was the occasion of a great meeting at Fanueil Hall, over which John Quincey Adams presided. Mr. Parker was very active in getting up this popular protest, and he made his first speech in Fanueil Hall.

TORREY'S FUNERAL.—May 17th, 1846.—I went to Boston in the afternoon, though I was ill and the weather raining, to attend the funeral of the Rev. Charles T. Torrey, who has just fallen a martyr to the State of Maryland and its infamous "patriarchal institution." However, he set free over 200 slaves before he fell, the first martyr of Maryland.* I honor the man, and place him high in my list of martyrs. When I first came home I wrote him a letter, and have his reply now.

The funeral was advertised to be in Park Street Church, but it was not allowed, so it took place in the Tremont Temple. Colver made the prayer; a most manly and able one it was too—a real old Puritan prayer—calm, deep, forgiving, full of charity and nobleness, but full of religion too. Then came a hymn read by Mr. Coolidge. I honor him for it.

Lovejoy delivered the sermon. It was not equal to the occasion. But the occasion spoke for itself, and the most meditative needed not any words to stir their hearts. But nothing will come of it; we are too dead—so sold to money that it takes a terrible blow to cut through the golden skin that covers the sins of our age. Where are the Churches who honor the martyr? Did the Church of the Pharisees at Jerusalem honor the first Christian martyr, just as this Church at Boston honors this?

His first sermon on the war with Mexico, which resulted from the annexation of Texas, was preached June 7, 1846. This is published. Afterward, when President Polk was raising volunteers by proclamation, he attended an anti-war meeting in Fanueil Hall, at which a good many soldiers were present, who

---

* Imprisoned after conviction under a State law against enticing slaves from their masters; and died in prison of consumption.

undertook to interrupt his speech. But he had all the courage and good-humor which pilots an obnoxious speaker safely through the most threatening demonstrations of a mob.

If God please, we will die a thousand times, but never draw blade in this wicked war. (Cries of "Throw him over!" &c.) What would you do next, after you have thrown him over? ("Drag you out of the Hall!") What good would that do? It would not wipe off the infamy of this war—would not make it less wicked!

He proceeded leisurely to review the facts connected with the war, and said a good many things to make the volunteers ashamed of themselves.

Did not Mr. Webster, in the streets of Philadelphia, bid the volunteers — misguided young men—go and uphold the stars of their country? (Voice, "He did right!") No, he should have said the *stripes* of his country; for every volunteer to this wicked war is a stripe on the nation's back! Did not he declare this war unconstitutional, and threaten to impeach the President who made it, and afterward go and invest a son in it? Has it not been said here, "Our country, howsoever bounded!"—bounded by robbery, or bounded by right lines? Has it not been said, all round, "Our country, right or wrong"? I say I blame not so much the volunteers as the famous men who deceive the nation. (Cries of "Throw him over! Kill him, kill him!" and a flourish of bayonets.) Throw him over! You will not throw him over. Kill him! I shall walk home unarmed and unattended, and not a man of you will hurt one hair of my head.

And he finished his speech. Did any of those volunteers for slavery belong to a Webster regiment? We have lately sent a Webster regiment *against* slavery, and the men marched down Broadway, in New York City, on their way to the war, singing the refrain of "John Brown"! How the revision of history corrects the bad logic of men!

His next undertaking is a letter to the American people touching the matter of slavery, which at first he intended to publish anonymously, because, he said, he had a bad name. But it appeared in 1847, over his proper signature.

"I am amazed," he wrote to Mr. May, while meditating this letter, "at the way good men and politicians look at the matter ; amazed at their silence."

It fell into the hands of a Southern slave-holder, who commenced a correspondence with Mr. Parker, which, for the sake of his replies, and also for some characteristic marks of Southern cultivation which it bears, is worthy to be published. From it the reader may infer the nature of many of the communications received by Mr. Parker from the South, in which there is a fine, chivalric disdain of the syntax submitted to by the North, and even the spelling is patriarchal, the letters being separated and sold off, while a few have *drapetomania,* and entirely disappear.

TO MR. PARKER.

Wellington, near Athens, Ga., January, 1848.

T. PARKER,—SIR,—A lengthy and measureably incoherent and bombastic letter from you in a book form has been sent me from Boston, purporting to be for the People of the United States.

You Negrophilists may write and publish for ever in your style and with your matter, without striking the Southern heart or enlisting its sympathies. *Until* and *only until* you prove by the Bible collectively —for it is a collection of theologic truths in its own stability, unchismatic—that God *did not* allow slaves through Moses' prophetic writings to the Israelites, and that Jesus Christ, instead of being *silent,* and St. Paul *coherent,* had been of your own conclusion, that "it was a sin without an excuse." This is the great point you have evaded. In all your work on slavery, not a syllable is remarked from the Scriptures on the proof directly in favor of or against the slavery of the children of Ham, who are veritably the negro race, and until this be treated on in full, and the conviction sent the slaveholders, that God never once countenanced slavery, it is utterly futile for you and your brother Abolitionists to attempt successfully to gain the Southern ear!!!

We cannot think the God of Moses less the true, pure Deity than Jesus Christ; nor that He in one age *permitted* and *regulated* a domestic servitude only to be found to have altered his *fixed Providence* in another! God (you infidel!) is always stable in his purposes. The Old and New Testaments are one, and Jehovah never gave laws of such weight as that forbidding to "covet a neighbour's manservant," &c., only to revoke them under a newer name and a new dispensation! Prove first from the Bible alone, and not by your egregious statistics and inuendoes, that slavery is wrong, without also making God wrong or inconsistent, and then the whole structure of bondage would fall to the ground. Otherwise for ever hold your peace!

The Old Testament forbade you to covet my property. The New, as see Paul's letter to Titus or Timothy, discountenanced your "manstealing" of my servants from me! The Bible is either inconsistent— the Almighty a changeling—or you are a horrid monster of infidelity or blasphemy in your execrable spirit of Yankee conceitedness against the South.

No, *Sir,* till you inform us better than I have ever been yet by your long printed letter, and by J. P. Blanchard's letters, that in God's and Christ's eye we are doing wrong—we cannot free the slaves without looking on Moses as an old fool, and Jehovah with no better reverence than you and he.

Against all your rhapsodies the thing still remains this : that either Ham's progeny's slavery is wrong, or it is right. If wrong, as God has not informed us this in His oracles of light and life, we can only be so informed by such infinatessimal atoms of vanity and mental rascality as you Negrophilists.

Indeed, the whole controversy between slave-holders and anti-slavites hinge on the proofs from God's book—God's will—for either side! Till then, Heaven forbid we should arrogate to condemn Moses, and to sneeze, as you, at the Creator!

To tell you plainly—representative of Beelzebub's heart!—my own private opinion, the negroes ought to be colonized back into Africa, whence came their ancestry, and we shall thus return measureably civilized men for the savages that left their native "country for that country's good," and ultimately, if they would be of any service to God, Christianize that benighted continent.

While they remain here, it would have been better had your abolition heart been pregnant with ways and means for their domestic ameliora-tion, education, and marriage rights, without attempting only their freedom. Can you do nothing for the blacks and swarths but give them liberty? Can you never find food for your philanthropy in bet-tering their condition in slavery, instead of forever harping on the liberty of those Noah, with plenitude of authority from on high, *irre-vocably* doomed to servitude, and for the best of reasons. It was not intrinsically Noah, but *God*, who made Ham's progeny in the mysteries of a Providence, punishing his faults that deserved death, death, death! with a life of deserved slavery and inferiority to the rest of man-kind, having to do with such a family! Ham's fault at a naked sire, saved from such a destruction, was intense, and proved himself and family unworthy constitutionally. Jehovah, without executing a miracle to cleanse a voluntary pollution, sanctioned Noah's curse, and you are but censuring the Eternal Word at every progress of a nefarious attempt to assimilate negroes to white men.

Again and again, I say that your reaching the conscience of the Southern people must come by the *Bible alone*. All else is in our eyes detestable blasphemy and treasonable evocations of fetid abomination. Take my warning. Never again open your mouth southwardly, unless you can come backed by the Bible; and, at the same time, never also prove the Father of Jesus Christ inconsistent. If men were to pre-sume to overjudge Moses and the prophets, and to twist the New Testament to hallow a race of constitutionally unworthy Africans, and cast a stigma on your brethren, the injury done to religion, aye, to Christianity itself, by thus indirectly disproving the authority of Scrip-ture, would synonimise with the effects of the infernal Jacobinism of the French Reign of Terror. Pause, or else speak to us by reading the Bible only. *Negro Slavery is just!* The only alternative is coloni-zation.

The bottom, perhaps, of all your errors is the ignorant persuasion that Ham's progeny are not negroes. In this, perhaps, you agree, at least, those from whom you take your *cue* do, with Faber and some other antiquarians, that the white races of Europe are the children of Cush—of Ham. But Bryant and other archiologists of deeper note have proved that the Africans are the literal descendants of Cush—of Ham. And the Bible itself sustains Bryant. Faber's researches are superfluous, and mostly Hindostanic; Bryant's the profound and laborious investigation of accumulated years, and more precise, since dating from Assyria, Phœnicia, Egypt, the Caucasus, and Greece. The fact, then, is that Africa is Ham's lot.

Have you seen Este's work on slavery? I wish he could review yours and you his; or else, that you and himself could controvert by writing, and print your respective letters in one volume. In this way we may have the reasoning of both sides.

Yours for peace.

Mr. Parker replies to the above :—

Boston, Feb. 2, 1848.

SIR,—Your letter of January last has just come to hand, and I hasten to reply. I thank you for your frankness, and will reply as plainly and openly as you write to me. You need not suppose that I have any spite against the slaveholders; I wish them well not less than their slaves. I think they are doing a great wrong to themselves, to their slaves, and to mankind. I think slave-holding is a wrong in itself, and, therefore, a sin; but I cannot say that this or that particular slave-holder is a sinner because he holds slaves. I know what sin is—God only knows who is a sinner. I hope I have not said anything harsh in my letter, or anything not true. I certainly wrote with no ill-feeling towards any one.

You seem to think that the Old Testament and New Testament are just alike, that Christianity and Judaism are, therefore, the same. So, as a Christian, you appeal to the Old Testament for your authority to hold slaves. Now, look a little at the matter, and see the difference between the Old Testament and New Testament. The Old Testament *demands* circumcision, a peculiar priesthood, the sacrifice of certain animals, the observance of certain fast-days, full-moon days, new-moon days, the seventh day, and the like. It demands them all in the *name of a Lord.* Yet you do not observe any of them. Now, you say, I suppose, that the ritual laws of the Old Testament came from God, but were repealed by Christ, who also spoke by the command of God. If that were so, then it would appear that God had repealed His own commands. You say, God could not change. So I say. I do not think God ever makes laws and then changes them; but if the Bible, as a whole, as you say, is the Word of God, then it is plain that in the New Testament He takes back what He commanded in the Old Testament. In the Old Testament a man is allowed to put away his wife for any cause, or none at all; but you know that Christ said *Moses* gave that command on account of the hardness of men's hearts. In Exodus xxxv. 2, 3, it is forbidden to kindle a fire on Saturday—Sabbath—on pain of death. In Numbers xv. 32–36, it is said, the Lord commanded a man to be *stoned to death* because he picked up sticks on Saturday; yet, I suppose you have a fire in your house Saturday and Sunday, too, and, perhaps would not think it wicked to bring in an armful of wood to make a fire on either of those days. Now, I do not think God changes; therefore, I don't believe He ever uttered those dreadful commands in the Old Testament. I believe that God has the attributes of universal justice and universal love. Doubtless, you will call me an

" Infidel," but that makes no odds; I try to be a Christian, but do not begin by discarding conscience, reason, and common-sense. I think Saint Paul was a Christian, and you know what he says about the law, that is, the *Law of Moses*, as recorded in the Old Testament.

Now, let us look at the case of the negroes. You think the children of Ham are under a perpetual curse, and that the negroes are the children of Ham. The tenth chapter of Genesis treats of the descendants of Ham, but it does not mention among them a single tribe of negroes. I don't think the writer of that account knew even of the existence of the peculiar race of men that we call negroes. He mentions the *Egyptians*, it is true, and other *North African people*, but it is well known that they were not negroes. But even if some of the descendants of Ham were negroes, though it is plain from Genesis x. they were not, still, that does not bring them under the curse of Noah, for Noah does not curse *Ham and all his children*, but only *Canaan*. Now, the descendants of Canaan are mentioned in Gen. x. 15–19; not one of them was ever an *African people;* they all dwelt in the *western part of Asia*, and are the nations with whom the Hebrews were often at war. The Hebrews conquered many of these tribes, seized their country, and often their persons. Many of them fled, and I think, settled in *North Africa;* the Berbers, and, in part, the Moors are of that race, *perhaps*, but none of them are negroes.

But even if the negroes were the children of Canaan, as it is plain they were not, what title could you make out to hold them by? It would be this:—4000 years ago Noah cursed Canaan, and, therefore, you hold one of Canaan's children as a slave. Now, do you think a *man* has power to curse so far off as that? But you will say, God gave the curse; well, the Bible does not say so. You say, Canaan and his posterity were " constitutionally unworthy," but you don't know that. On the contrary, the Sidonians, who were the descendants of Canaan, were a very illustrious people of antiquity — a good deal like the English and Americans at this day—and actually held great quantities of the Jews in slavery. Before you can hold a single negro under that clause in Gen. ix. 25, you must make out—1. That the negro is descended from Canaan; 2. That the curse was actually uttered as related; 3. That it announces personal slavery for more than 4000 years; 4. That the curse was authorized by God Himself. Now, there is not one of these four propositions which ever has been made out or ever can be. My dear sir, I am really surprised that an intelligent man, in the nineteenth century, a *Christian man—a Republican of Georgia*—could seriously rely a moment on such an argument as that. Fie on such solemn trifling about matters so important as the life of two or three millions of men! For my own part, I don't believe the story of Noah cursing his grandson for his father's fault. I think it all a foolish story got up to satisfy the hatred which the Jews felt against the Canaanites. I know Bryant's book and Faber's, but never use either now-a-days. B. had more fancy than philosophy, it always seemed to me. I may be as " confident " as you think me, but don't call myself a learned man, though I have read about all the valuable works ever written on that matter of Noah's curse.

You ask if I could not propose some good to be done to the slaves now. Certainly; their marriage and family rights might be made secure, their work easier, their food and clothing better, they might not be beaten. Pains might be taken to educate them. But all that is very little, so long as you keep the man from his natural liberty. You would not be happy if a slave, would not think it right for a Christian man to hold you in bondage, even if one of your ancestors but fifty years ago, had cursed you, still less if 4000 years ago. If I were a slave-holder I would do this—I would say, " Come, now, you are free, go to work and I will pay you what you can earn." I think, in ten years' time, you would be a richer man, and in two hours' time, a far happier one, a more Christian one.

Dear sir, Christianity does not consist in believing stories in the Old Testament, about Noah's curse and all that, but in loving your brother as yourself, and God with your whole heart. Do not think that I *covet* your slaves. No consideration would induce me to become a slave-holder. *I* should be a *sinner*, though God grant that you are not one for that act! Let me ask you, *while you take from a man his liberty, his person, do you not violate that command*, " Thou shalt not covet anything that is thy neighbour's " ? *Do you not break that golden rule*, " Whatsoever you would that men should do unto you, do ye even so unto them " ?

I do not think you feel easy about this matter. What you say about colonization convinces me that you do not believe slavery is a Christian institution; that you are not very angry with me, after all. Do not think that I assume any airs of superiority over you because I am not a slave-holder. I have never had that temptation ; perhaps if born in Georgia, I should not have seen the evil and the sin of slavery. I may be blind to a thousand evils and sins at home which I commit myself. If so, I will thank you to point them out. I hope you will write me again as frankly as before. I wish I could see Este's book. I will look for it, and study it, for I am working for the truth and the right. I have nothing to gain personally by the abolition of slavery, and have, by opposing that institution, got nothing but a bad name. I shall not count you my enemy, but am

Truly your friend.

In reply to this, Mr. Parker received a very lengthy epistle, making points out of almost every line he wrote. But space cannot be afforded to quote it entire. Here is a specimen :—

February 25, 1848.

You Abolitionists are children—you utter strings of nonsense for wisdom, and have the audacity to elevate your heads, as if your reasonings were admired at the North or favoured at the South !

To ameliorate the slave would be to go to expense for him, and to render the profits of his slavery, as now existing, narrower. Thus,—1. 'Tis to school him, and endure the probable tricks of his intelligence, if he be *innately* a scoundrel. 2. To secure his marriage inseparable from his wife and children, and thus to render him less valuable by not being able to sell him alone, and wife and children separately, at so high a price as they altogether would bring in a family. For many *cannot* buy a whole family, and can a single slave at a high price. 3. To ameliorate his condition by giving him better food, clothes, and less work, and hence find less profit from his labor or keeping! Ameliorate slavery—render it valuable! Surely a cabbage has a head, and so has William L. Garrison or Theodore Parker!

In conclusion, friend Theodore Parker, let me admonish you not to be for serving God's Holy Prophet of Prophets, Moses, as the Abolitionists, in their infernal conceits, are "after doing," as you see other prophets which I hinted at also spoke like him, or " *worse.*" And if you could fling away Moses, you must the prophecies also; and if you can these, by diminishing the credit or authority of *anything they say*, you would knock the butments of Christianity also away, and reduce Jesus' Gospel to a skeleton, or rather to so much flesh without bones. This I have tried, almost in agony, to show to Mr. Blanchard's mind, for he said, " There may have been a black Adam as well as a white," thus insinuating the want of fulness in Moses, or supposing his Genesis subject to speculations; and as I could not, my horror and distrust of Abolitionists has become so greatly increased, that I now pronounce them American infidels and Jacobins, and Boston as the Paris of this phrenzied sect. The scenes of its Revolution only is wanted to finish the revolting picture.

Farewell, sir! write back, if you can, and if I see any solid reason in your reply deserving another from me, I will not withhold my pen. I think it much better to let off a deaf man like me, and to attend to Matthew Este, whose book on slavery I will send, if one be in Athens. Este, like yourself, and Blanchard, and Drew, I feel to be inferior as writers to myself. I feel among you as a Samson among a certain host, or a Titan, even, among your giants To attempt to prolong the contest with me would only sink you in the Serbonian bog. Deaf though I be, yet I am mighty in spirit. As Abner said to a young man pursuing him, "I say to thee, turn thou aside upon ' Este,' and take thou his armour," for why should I use thee up?

Mr. Parker rejoins :—

Boston, March 4, 1848.

SIR,—Your favour of February 12th was received in due time and carefully read; but I have hitherto been unable to reply to it, on account of absence from the city and various duties while in it. I see it is altogether useless for me to undertake to dispute with you on the matter of slavery. I should prefer, certainly, a different antagonist. Your first letter led me to think you were a very extraordinary man; your last more than confirmed the opinion. I confess my inability to reason with you. I see it is of no use for one with weapons like *mine* to prolong the contest. I will take your advice and select an opponent more suitable.

Allow me, however, in parting, to thank you for your long letter—such as I have seldom read.

Learned sir, I remain,
Your obedient servant.

These letters also, though of a later date, find their natural connection here; unfortunately I am not able to furnish the replies. But the letters are characteristic of an epoch that is passing away. These and the preceding ones have been made to correspond somewhat to the vulgar exigencies of printing.

FROM ——, NEAR CHARLOTTE, N. CAROLINA.

February 11, 1855.

DEAR SIR,—It has been on my mind for some time to address you; to urge that more mild methods and phrases should be employed in judging and discussing the differences which prevail North and South, in manners or opinions.

In order to show the necessity for care and caution, I will detail for your consideration two scenes in Eastern States which fell under my notice, and I think are entitled to reproof and amendment.

Being in Boston on a Sunday, I was astonished to find that respectable-looking housemaids were required to take, *that* morning, very early, to scour and wash the extensive necessary houses of one of the most prominent hotels in your city.

I felt so much dissatisfied at this discovery, I could not avoid asking an intelligent, decent-looking white woman if it was the custom of the house. She assured me it was so regularly! The women were all Irish Catholics. They seemed gratefully surprised at my notice and intervention, but vexed and indignant at the selection of time for such service.

One of them calmly and modestly observed, "It was the time she had been allowed to go to mass elsewhere." I could but regret some other day was not substituted for such employment. The women looked inquiringly, as if they supposed I had some authority.

I told them, "I was a stranger from the South, who owned slaves, and would certainly not allow my servants to be thus employed on a day which *demanded* general rest, specially for servants."

The next morning an Irish waiter ran a long distance after me to the cars, expressly to bring me a lunch, as he had observed I usually ate no breakfast.

Going on board a steamer at Burlington, in Vermont, I found a number of Irish emigrants on their way from Canada, taking the route by Lake Champlain from Quebec, to seek their friends, or employment in the United States.

The noise of the escape steam, and the tumult in the trans-shipment of passengers, baggage, and goods, induced me to take a stand on the upper deck.

Women and children formed a principal portion of the crowd.

With the abstracted devotion which appears peculiar to Catholic instruction or habits, several were on their knees upon deck, their lips and hearts uttering prayers as they passed beads of rosaries through their fingers.

It seemed impossible to avoid a feeling of pity for the poor creatures, however we might differ about forms.

There were a number of horses in the bow of the boat, to be landed at Burlington. Those who had charge led them with the greatest indifference and brutality among and over the kneeling women and children.

In the foreground, an aged widow, with seven children surrounding her, never moved amidst all the disorder. The noises, the tumult, the dangers, the rude countenances of boisterous strangers, did not distract her attention from her prayers, although she was evidently sensible of the hazard to her infants.

Her faith was strong, and though expressed with manners and devotion differing from those I have been taught to confide in, I trust were as acceptable before God as mine own.

A number of gentlemen on the upper deck looked at this scene, and also said that the clerk of the boat, aided by a negro steward, made exchanges of foreign monies with the male emigrants, much to the disadvantage of some of the poorest and most ignorant of the strangers.

I felt excessively angry, and turning round, said to those about me, "Gentlemen, I am a slave-owner from the South, but, by God! no one should treat my negroes as you stand here and see these poor Irish treated."

I was immediately followed to the lower deck, and we requested an officer to have the transfers made with more regard to the kneeling women and children.

The kindly look I received from the patient widow's eye was grateful to me. It is difficult to know the secret hearts of men, yet, from what judgment I could exercise, the formal mode employed by these poor people, *to aid remembrance,* by their beads, while asking the protection of the General Parent, seemed offensive to the rude and reckless men who did not comprehend it.

I could not avoid an impression that if the sympathies of Northern hearts were sincere and honest for the improvement of our slaves, they would be shown in a prompt manner towards these poor "strangers."

Believe me, very respectfully,

Your obedient servant.

FROM THE SAME.

Near Charlotte, N. Carolina, March 5, 1855.

To the Rev. Theodore Parker, — I have read with satisfaction your appeal on account of the perishing classes in Boston, August, 1846. But that sermon, entitled by you, "The New Crime against Humanity," I cannot conceive to be in the right spirit to effect any moral good. As you do not show objection to honest frankness, I wil be very plain to be better understood.

By what you term "higher law," I presume you mean "moral law," as we read it in the Scriptures. By looking back to *its principles,* we who reclaim stolen or secreted property, are *not* man-stealers. The moral law permits servitude; some of the earliest precepts teach how servants should be treated by their masters, and while it places them under the great law of mercy, recognizes them distinctly as *property*. In the same manner, your fathers, while engaged in the slave trade, did not believe they did an unlawful act unless *they stole* the negroes from the coast.

They purchased from those who did steal or capture them, and sold them to our fathers in the South, who paid an honest equivalent for them. By secreting, detaining, or coveting our slave property, *you* show a disregard for the higher law you claim to be ruled by, which was given to an ancient people as their constitution of government. Our constitution was formed upon similar principles, and we are as much bound in faith to it as the Hebrews to theirs. In my opinion, by resisting the constitution, you disregard *both* moral and civil obligations. Abraham had " servants bought with his money, at home in his house." We call *such* servants, " slaves." The Egyptians and Assyrians knew such property. At the time of the Exodus, why was not slavery denounced like idolatry, hypocrisy, deceit, violence, and false witness? Instead of being denounced, it was modified in accordance with other similar improvements, in a very special manner. The Hebrew was not allowed to enslave one of his own people. He was permitted to purchase servants from neighbouring savage people, who would otherwise have tortured and put them to death, as savages now do. The Hebrew was not allowed to steal men *for himself*, but was told not to covet his neighbour's servants. If a Hebrew master maimed his own servant in hasty passion, or revenge, he was obliged to compensate the slave with his liberty. All such facts prove the lawfulness of slavery under the higher law system among the Hebrews. But your people say that law directs that the runaway slave should not be returned to his master. This injunction could not have had reference to a runaway from one tribe or state of the Hebrews to another; but must have been intended to protect the runaway from neighbouring wandering tribes, not under the same constitution of government as the Hebrews, whose common law gave special directions for humane treatment and forbearance, abundant supplies of food, clothing, and instruction. If we in the South have not accepted all the laws of the moral code, as binding upon our slave property, encourage us to put them in force, in order to benefit that property and the common welfare of our country, North and South.

The higher law gives *no* sanction to the master to retain, or delay, or conceal, or to covet our slaves. Give them up, and let us be induced to review our enactments and modify our customs in correspondence with the principles of faith, justice, and mercy those moral laws are founded upon, and which clearly maintain our right to such property, under modifications of humanity your conduct at the North prevents or deranges. Those who have known this system to the South, understand it differently from you; with you, slavery is an abstraction, and your imaginations are too actively employed upon it, to your own injury and ours.

I once asked a sensible preacher of the Society of Friends, in Penn., who was about to visit a business meeting in the South for the first time, to tell me on his return which were most slaves, the servants or their masters.

His inquiries and examinations showed him difficulties and defences he knew not of before. I have seen your Northern senators struck with surprise at the demeanor of our slaves in the South, who, from savage barbarians, as they were when your friends brought them here, now exhibit as gentle, courteous, and honorable demeanor as servants anywhere.

Your powers of reproof are very great, and your independence of expression corresponds; but do not lose sight of the original truth, that the institution of slavery in higher law stands side by side with laws which object to covetousness, false witness and false devotion, violence, enmity, and every injustice.   No such condition exists South as you explain in Boston.   All the crimes, and weaknesses, and faults, and enormities, which now exist in society, *also* prevailed *before* the days of Moses.   The great deliverer of high law was a reformer: with the sanction usually conceded to him we may claim, at the South, to regard that law as closely as you at the North, and in a spirit quite as much in accordance with the liberality of that honorable code.

I wish the condition of the negro to be improved by his servitude among us. Your violent expressions interfere with his advancement as with ours. I write before day, and in haste.

Sincerely and respectfully.

No doubt he wrote before day ; but the day now breaketh. Let one more of such letters suffice to indicate the nature of Mr. Parker's correspondence with slave-holders.   It also reveals the nature of his replies :—

FROM THE SAME.

March 7, 1855.

The ancient moral law appears to yield to the ordinary prejudice of our nature in its first gloom, and to *confine* attention to "our neighbours."   Yet, afterwards we are cautioned to regard the interests "of the stranger" as well.   The honorable liberality of moral law directs the true *principles* of justice and mercy to be exercised towards all colors, classes, and conditions; but, in my opinion, plainly indicates *varieties* in the races of man. We distinguish occasionally apparent contradictions in those Scriptures which solely arise *from extreme simplicity* in the language employed by the Hebrew writers.   The original Hebrew designs to denominate a *different* race of people *consistent* with the family of Adam, among whom Cain obtained "a wife," had "a son," and "built a city."

Adam is described as a civilized man at the beginning, stationary and industrious in his habits, employed in agriculture, or gardening, according to our literal translation.

I am instructed by a Hebrew scholar that the word "Nod "left untranslated in our English Bibles, as a noun-substantive, exists a Hebrew *adjective*, signifying "The wandering."   Quite an important interpretation !

" The mark set upon Cain lest any finding him should kill him " alludes to these wanderers, others than his own father's family, and to some law or custom then existing to punish murder with death, as men, both wild and civilized, have continued to do. We cannot discover the absolute *origin* of slavery among men, for the most remote records indicate such an institution as prevailing. Biblical history informs us it existed in the days of Abraham without apparent objection. It most probably commenced among the civilized nations of antiquity from a desire to save human life from the relentless vengeance and retaliations in kind of savage and wandering wild men.

The subsequent improvements in moral law which regulate the conduct of masters and mistresses to their own servants or slaves, among the earliest precepts of the Hebrews, have been strangely misconstrued. In order to prompt and enforce humane treatment to that condition of persons known long anterior to the promulgation of the Hebrew Decalogue, and to check hasty impulses of passion or revenge in masters, a compensation for the slightest personal injuries to servants was ordered in a style of language we cannot believe intended to authorize vindictive retaliation *in kind*.

The expressions, " eye for eye," " tooth for tooth," " hand for hand," " foot for foot," had reference to previous customs and manner of speech among bordering savages who credited advantages from acts of unequivocal retaliation. This appears in the decided command which follows the inventory of damages, " If a man smite the eye of his man-servant, or the eye of his maid-servant, that it perish, he shall let him or her go free, for the eye's sake."

Liberty was thus conceded as the appropriate compensation or payment for violence to any of these members of a purchased servant or slave, and was surely designed to repress cruelty and inhumanity towards this description of legalized property, as it is plainly called and treated of in Hebrew moral law, in correspondence with preceding usages, yet obviously to modify and humanize them by generous restraints. The more I study it, the more I am persuaded this ancient code of practice is based upon a permanent foundation of exact science not to be overruled by alterations in customs or instructions. If those of our country who do not own slaves, but largely aided to introduce them among us in the South, would more carefully examine the discreet provisions of the moral code on this subject, they would do more to benefit " their neighbours " in the South, and " the strangers," our slaves, than by general denunciation of an abstract principle in which they do oppose the plainest wording of these writings, and the feelings of truth, justice, and mercy offered by the Scripture as the measures or exact rule of proportion, by which we should regulate our own conduct, opinions, and actions towards each other for the advancement and progress of society, and the benefit of every diversity of the human family, both bond and free.

None are disregarded in the honorable system of the Hebrew Reformer, who includes cattle, slaves, children, strangers, neighbours, and enemies! This noble moral code is the base of every modern improvement in humanity. It forms the principles of our constitution of civil government, probably somewhat distorted by false or feeble interpretations. It ruled the minds and the characters of the men of our Revolution, and its precepts were intended to influence our common law. Let not differences of opinion lead us to any violence in argument or in action, for as surely as the principles of this code are comprehended, so surely will our peace, security, and happiness increase!

Believe me, sincerely and respectfully, &c.

P.S.—I think I noticed, in a letter sent you a few days ago, an objection to the ordinary construction of language with regard to "a runaway servant." I cannot credit, from the general and generous tenor of moral law, that the order designed to interfere with the rights or title of property so unequivocally countenanced among the Hebrew tribes, but had reference *solely* to fugitives *from without*; the servants of wild, barbarous masters on the borders of Syria, whose servants were ordered to be treated with humanity, and not given up to savages. The common law of the Hebrew made it obligatory upon all masters and mistresses to be kind and attentive to the feelings and wants of servants; such a law with regard to runaways, as you understand from the English text, would not be required if the moral precepts of the Hebrews were obeyed. Aid us to have them attended to everywhere.

His second sermon upon the Mexican War was preached June 25, 1848, after the announcement of its conclusion by the treaty of peace, negotiated by Mr. Trist.

Well: we have got a new territory, enough to make one hundred States of the size of Massachusetts. That is not all. We have beaten the armies of Mexico, destroyed the little strength she had left, the little self-respect, else she would not so have yielded and given up half her soil for a few miserable dollars. Soon we shall take the rest of her possessions. How can Mexico hold them now—weakened, humiliated, divided worse than ever within herself? Before many years, all of this Northern Continent will doubtless be in the hands of the Anglo-Saxon race. That of itself is not a thing to mourn at. Could we have extended our empire there by trade, by the Christian arts of peace, it would be a blessing to us and to Mexico; a blessing to the world. But we have done it in the worst way, by fraud and blood; for the worst purpose, to steal and convert the cities of men into the shambles for human flesh; have done it at the bidding of men whose counsels long have been a scourge and a curse—at the bidding of slave-holders. They it is that rule the land, fill the offices, buy up the North with the crumbs that fall from their political table, make the laws, declare hostilities, and leave the North to pay the bill. Shall we ever waken out of our sleep? Shall we ever remember the duties we owe to the world and to God, who put us here on this new continent? Let us not despair.

CHAPTER XIX.

The Fugitive Slave Bill—Vigilance Committees—William and Ellen Craft.

Mr. Webster made his speech in Congress in favor of the Fugitive Slave Bill, on March 7, 1850, and another speech in Boston the next month, in which, countenanced by the political sympathy of the city merchants, he attempted to instruct the State to surrender its anti-slavery convictions. But the country population of the State could not recover from its astonishment at the abjectness of his speech so quickly as Boston did ; the conscience of the city is kept sinuous by the crooked streets where interest walks ; the conscience of the State has all the open fields to move in, and sees the shortest line between two points. Mr. Parker spoke for the country and the people.

The Fugitive Slave Bill was enacted on September 18, 1850. There was a faint hope that it might be vetoed upon the ground of the unconstitutionality of some of its provisions ; but, as soon as the Attorney-General Crittenden, a citizen of a slave-holding state, informed President Fillmore that the Bill was constitutional, it received his signature. He signed the warrant of misery of thousands of innocent and unfortunate beings, for it was not unconstitutional to do so. They have been the black pawns in the great Southern games of politics, capable only to tempt or to restrain a move, and to be sacrificed with equanimity.

Who can describe the distress and anguish of this persecuted class in Boston, Worcester, New Bedford, and the other principal towns, where large numbers of them were gathered for the sake of employment ! They were afraid to remain even in places where a formidable anti-slavery sentiment existed, for no man could guarantee to them protection against the well-framed wickedness of the law. They might stay, and take their chance of a popular manifestation which, in case of arrest, might paralyze the arm that held them, or they might sacrifice every· thing, and fly, dreading the unreliable temper of the people. Some of the boldest chose to remain, and armed themselves to defend their freedom, instinctively calculating that the sight of such an exigency would ·make the Northern heart beat too rapidly for prudence. Sometimes it did so : but it was nothing for this race of men who had hitherto been uniformly betrayed to depend upon. More than forty fled from Boston alone, within three days from the signing of the Bill from the President. The anti-slavery men of the State had to sustain the double afflic- tion of the Bill itself, and the misery of its victims ; but it brought upon the negroes expatriation, the sacrifice of little properties, the loss of employment, the sudden disruption of family ties, and an uncertain and melancholy future. The humble annals of these sufferers from that base political expedient, would compose the vital history of Massachusetts for many long and gloomy days. For as these hunted men fled they drew the secret tenderness of the people along with them, and left behind only slave-commissioners and marshals, men in Southern trade, and their political sympathizers.

But were not the officers created by the law, or clothed in new disgraceful functions by it, sworn to support it against humanity itself? Yes: and they did not hasten to resign the godless position, so that by letting it drop to the natural level of men, without gentleness, scholarship, culture, and various merit, its naked brutality might terribly shock indifferent specta- tors, and work a peremptory cure. For, when evil is driven out of respectability into the herd of its own, it rushes down a steep place, and disappears. Society is protected by careful pro- fessional services, and is betrayed when professional excellence lends its *prestige* to inhumanity.

The people held indignant meetings, and organized Committees of Vigilance, whose duty was to prevent a fugitive from being arrested, if possible, or to furnish legal aid and raise every obstacle to his rendition. The constant activity of these com- mittees in the principal towns was a serious check to the activity of pursuing committees sent on by slave-holding masters. It became a rather difficult thing to run a fugitive to earth, and get him before the commissioners. The Vigilance members made it everywhere appear such a troublesome and expensive, as well as uncertain operation, to slave-holders, that the attempts were very few ; but spies were often commissioned to the North with the errand of discovering the chances of success. And, if success had been more probable and less costly, many a slave-hunt would have been undertaken by Southern disunionists for political effect. But policy could afford little till the time came when the plundered nation itself furnished the means by which its life is threatened.

With all the difficulties, however, more than two hundred arrests of persons claimed as fugitives were made from the time of the passage of the Bill to the middle of 1856. About a dozen of these were free persons, who succeeded in establishing the claim that they never had been slaves ; other persons, equally free, were carried off. Half a dozen rescues were made, and the rest of these cases were delivered to their owners. These arrests took place more frequently in Pennsylvania than in any other Northern State. Many fugitives were caught and carried back, of whom we have no accounts, save that they were seen on the deck of some river steamboat, in the custody of their owners, without even passing through the formality of appearing before a commissioner. About two-thirds of the persons arrested as above, had trials. When arrests to the number of two hundred, at least, can be traced, and their dates fixed, during six years, we may suppose that the Bill was not, as some politicians averred, practically of little consequence.

The Vigilance Committees were also the *employés* of the " *Underground Railroad*," and effectively disposed of many a *casus belli* by transferring the disputed chattel to Canada Money, time, wariness, devotedness for months and years, that cannot be computed and will never be recorded, except, perhaps, in connection with cases whose details had peculiar interest, was nobly rendered by the true anti-slavery men. Their recollections now rejoice in every such practical defeat of the inhuman law. The judges, commissioners, and marshals are in debt to the anti-slavery men, who so many times interposed thus to save them from the disgrace which would have attended each new discharge of their unchristian function. Shall we not hear of their presenting some testimonial to the Vigilance Committees ?

In those dreadful days Mr. Parker hastened from his study,

and forgot all calm delights, that he might rescue the noblest of the humanities from the barbarism and ignorance of men. Of all his knowledge he remembered best the golden rule.

Here are the resolutions drawn up by Mr. Parker, upon which the future action of the anti-slavery men were rested : —

RESOLUTIONS.

1. That we disapprove of the new Fugitive Slave Law, considering it UNCONSTITUTIONAL—in general, because it does not tend to form a more perfect union, establish justice, ensure domestic tranquillity, provide for the common defence, promote the general welfare, or secure the blessings of liberty to the people ; and in special, because it takes away from men the privilege of the writ of *Habeas Corpus*, and the right of trial by jury, because it violates the right of the people to be secure in their persons against unreasonable seizures, and takes away their liberty without due form of law; and also UNJUST—in general, because it violates the golden rule of doing to others as we would have them do unto us; and in special, because it offers a bribe to the magistrate to decide against liberty, and leaves men with no protection for their freedom but the opinion of the people.

2. That we will not entertain the opinion that any man can be found in this city or its vicinity, so destitute of love for his country, and so lost to a sense of justice as to endeavour to return a fugitive slave under this law.

3. That we advise the fugitive slaves and colored inhabitants of Boston and the neighborhood to remain with us, for we have not the smallest fear that any one of them will be taken from us and carried off to bondage; and we trust that such as have fled in fear will return to their business and homes.

4. That we will appoint persons from each ward in this city, as a Committee of Safety and Vigilance, with power to add to their number such as they shall see fit, and it shall be their duty to endeavor by all just means to seeure the fugitives and colored inhabitants of Boston and vicinity from any invasion of their rights by persons acting under this law.

FROM THE JOURNAL.

Oct. 23, 1850.—At work on book; continually interrupted by company; continual stream of people till night.

At night second meeting of Vigilance Committee, this time at No. 46, Washington Street. This is the same number where the Anti-Slavery Society met, when the mob broke them up in 1835. That is a good sign.

Filled up our numbers to about eighty. Chose all the lawyers for a Legal Committee. The function of the committee is this:—To be on the watch, and warn when an attempt is making to procure a warrant to arrest a fugitive; to see that he has knowledge of it; if brought before an officer, that he has counsel, and that all legal delays are made use of, and if he be adjudged a slave, then to alarm the town.

Francis Jackson proposes that an agent shall be appointed to look after the fugitives, help find them places, help them to flee. The first business of the anti-slavery men is to help the fugitives; we, like Christ, are to seek and save that which is lost.

The Boston Vigilance Committee soon numbered 250 members. Out of that number there was raised, besides the Legal Committee, an Executive Committee of eight or ten members, who could be relied upon for any probable emergency. Mr. Parker was its chairman.

Returning home from Plymouth late in the afternoon of the 25th, found Howe * had been at our house, to warn me of slave-hunters in town; found the Legal Committee had been in attendance most of the day. A slave-hunter is here in Boston, named Hughes, and warrants are out for the arrest of Ellen Craft and her husband !

Saw J. B. Smith, who says that writs are out also for the arrest of two other men working at Parker's *restaurant*, in Court Square ; that five or six fellows came there at dinner-time, stood on the steps, looked in, but didn't enter. After dinner they went in and inquired for their fugitives. No such persons there—looked round and went off.

Smith says Craft is armed, and Ellen secreted. Informal meeting of Vigilance Committee at the office of *New Englander*. Craft has consented to be hid to-night, at the south end of Boston. Mr. —— took him up in a coach. Ellen is to-night at ——, in —— Street. So all is safe for this night.

The blank spaces for names of places and persons are left blank in the manuscript. This precaution is taken on many pages, in the interest of the fugitive ; for there were times when devoted anti-slavery men felt that the future could not be trusted. Warrants and indictments let loose upon their traces with blood-hound scent, might yet, and how soon none could know, run down both the slave and his protectors.

26th.—It seems a miserable fellow by the name of Knight came here to Boston from Macon, Georgia, sent out by the former owner of the Crafts. He used to work in the cabinet-shop with William, but was dull and imbecile ; so that his chief function was to wait upon the rest. There came with him a Mr. Hughes, who is the gaoler at Macon.

Last Tuesday, Knight called on Craft at his shop, expressed pleasure to see him, &c. ; Craft asked him if he came on alone ? " Yes, there was nobody with him." But he wanted William to go round with him, to show him the streets and the curiosities of Boston. No! William

* Dr. S. G. Howe, of Boston, always the champion of oppressed people, the good physician, true leader of the blind.

was on his guard, was "busy," "had work to attend to," and could not go."

The next day he came again, wanted William to go round the Common with him! No, he could not go. Then he told William, "Perhaps you would like to come to the United States Hotel, and see me; your wife would like to come also and talk about her mother. If you will write, I will take the letter home."

Finding that Craft rejoiced in a very appropriate name, and was even too much for one who had drawn his vital nourishment of stealth and treachery from slavery's breast, he returned to his hotel and laid the following little lucid trap. Spelling is of small consequence, when the heart swells with generous intentions :—

WILLIAM CRAFT—SIR,—I have to leave so eirley in the moring, that I cold not call according to promis, so if you want me to carry a letter home with me, you must bring it to the united states Hotel tomorrow, and leave it in box 44, or come yourself to morro eavening after tea and bring it. Let me no if you come yourself by sending a note to box 44 U.S. hotel, so that I may no whether to wate after tea or not by the bearer. If your wif wants to see me you cold bring her with you if you come yourself.

JOHN KNIGHT.

PS.—I shall leave for home eirley a Thursday moring.   J. K.

The journal proceeds :—

The man who brought the letter informed Craft of the other person (the fraternal gaoler) who came with him, told his name, &c.

Finding this failed, Hughes applied to the Court and got a warrant. I have not yet ascertained who granted it.

I saw William this morning. He seemed cool and resolute. I told him I thought it was no use to put the matter off and cut off the dog's tail by inches. If he were to take the bull by the horns, he had better do it to-day, rather than to-morrow. So he thought. I inspected his arms—a good revolver, with six caps on, a large pistol, and small ones, a large dirk and a short one. All was right.

The next day the Legal Sub-committee of the Vigilance Committee had Knight and Hughes arrested for slander against Craft, they having called him a thief, for leaving Georgia with his clothes on when he left with himself. But they were immediately bailed out. Hughes declared his determination to have William and Ellen at all hazards. "It isn't the niggers I care about, *but it's the principle of the thing.*"

Monday, 28th.— ——, a broker and treasurer of U.S. Hotel, told Francis Jackson, "he would carry out the law if it was to apply to his own daughter!" No doubt; but suppose it came to his dividends?

There was by this time a good deal of excitement in Boston, and the committee decided to run off the slave-hunters themselves.

30.—I was at the U.S. Hotel. None of the committee there. Inquired of the landlord if Hughes and Knight were in. "I don't know, sir. No, sir: they are out, Mr. Parker."

I walked about awhile, then asked one of the clerks for Hughes and Knight. "If you will send up your name, you can see." Sent up a card; the servant came back with a little bit of paper, and this on it:— "Mr. Hughes is inguage." The others had assembled by this time, ten or twenty of them. Dr. Kraitser inquired if he was in the breakfast room. "No, not there." Fearing that they might escape us again, I went up to the room, No. 44, and walked back and forth in front of it. By-and-bye Knight came in. Channing guarded one of the stairways, Brown another: Ellis came to me. About three-quarters of an hour thus spent. The landlord came and requested me, not very politely, to walk downstairs, promising to meet me very soon. I went, and soon Mr. Silsbee came and politely informed me that Spooner would introduce me to the slave-hunters. I went up and was introduced.

I told them I came to keep them safe from harm; that I was a minister, and came as a friend to them. Some were disposed to violence, I not. Hughes said he knew I had called before, that I was a minister, and he had understood that I was "a great moralist"—meaning philanthropist—"but this don't look much like it." "What does not look like it?" "Mobs and violence." "But I came to prevent that." "But we came here to execute the law." "Yes: but you must be satisfied that you cannot arrest William and Ellen Craft, and if you do that, you cannot carry them out of the city." Hughes said he was satisfied of that.

They both complained that they were ill-treated; that they could not step into the street but that they were surrounded and followed by men who called out, "Slave-hunters, slave-hunters! there goes the slave-hunters!" Knight said it was too bad; he was not a slave-hunter, he had nothing to do with it, but was treated as badly as the other. Hughes said he had the assurance of sufficient help in Boston; that he did not fear violence—was prepared for it, &c. I told him they were not safe in Boston another night. They said they had determined to go in the train at half-past seven (and indeed they had put their names in the call-book to be called at six), but they saw a crowd at the door, "and," said Knight, "there would have been forty or fifty fellows hurrahing, and swinging their caps, and calling out, 'Slave-hunters! there goes the slave-hunters!'" I told them we (the committee) came to give them a safe conduct, and allow no one to hurt them. Said Hughes, "We don't want a safe conduct; we can take care of ourselves."

I told them that I had stood between them and violence once—I would not promise to do it again: that I should not have been successful had it not been thought that they had promised to depart that morning at half-past seven. He said they had never made any promise, nor should they make any. I told them that I could not guarantee their safety another night. We bid one another good morning, and I came away. They were considerably frightened.

At half-past 2 P.M. they took the New York train at Newton Corner.

Nov. 1.—Reading the diary of John Adams. How much the old times were like the present times! Most of the men of property were on the side of tyranny. Adams was made of good stuff, but vain, irritable, and intensely ambitious; still, he could not be driven from the right by violence, by intimidation, by fear of poverty and disgrace. Nobody could buy him, or flatter him into a continuous course of wrong.

It is amusing to see how trifles affect a man. He was much elated at his election as select-man of Braintree, when he was thirty years old. Nay, his election to be one of the select-men seemed a great affair.

As representative of Boston he contended manfully for the right. It is curious to find how defective collegiate education was then. He had to study "Horace" and "Cicero in Catalinam" after he was a practising lawyer! But it is pleasant to see his literary taste, which struggled against poverty, sleepiness, and want of books.

It is painful to find that the "men of property and standing" who at first inclined to freedom almost all fluctuated, and how many of them went over to the other side. Note the character of the clergy, and how the greater part of them sided with Power.*

Many interruptions all this week, and little done; almost nothing on the book. I make no doubt I shall have to go to gaol this winter, and then I shall be as well off as Carlyle's "Notability No. 2," free from taxes and botheration, when I clutch my MSS. as if in a conflagration! Well: I am ready.

The allusion is to "Model Prisons"—visit to a prison of the exemplary or model kind. Mr. Carlyle says :—" Next neighbor to him was Notability Second, a philosophic or literary chartist ; walking rapidly to and fro in his private court, a clean high-walled place ; the world and its cares quite excluded, for some months to come ; master of his own time and spiritual resources to, as I supposed, a really enviable extent. What 'literary man' to an equal extent ? I fancied I, for my own part, so left with paper and ink, and all taxes and botheration shut out from me, could have written such a book as no reader will here ever get of me. Never, O reader, never here in a mere house with taxes and botherations. Here, alas! one has to snatch one's poor book bit by bit, as from a conflagration," &c.

---

* Where John Adams alludes to "Reverend Tories," he means to designate chiefly the Episcopal clergy of his time, who sneered at the Calvinistic "preachers of politics," and made it a point of boasting and special laudation that *they* never touched on politics in the pulpit, except of course to decry from it the republican politics which they detested.

The Journal proceeds :—

Ellen Craft has been here all the week since Monday; went off at a quarter past six to-night. That is a pretty state of things, that I am liable to be find 1000 dollars and gaoled for six months for sheltering one of my own parishioners, who has violated no law of God, and only took possession of herself!

Talk in the newspapers about the President sending on 600 or 700 soldiers to dragoon us into keeping the Fugitive Slave Law! The Bostonians remember how that business of quartering soldiers on us in time of peace worked in the last century! It is worth while to read Hutchinson and Adams.

Dr. Osgood* came to see about the Crafts. All must be secretly done, so nothing here at present. Nell came to say they wish to be married, I advise to-morrow, so it is agreed, to-morrow at eleven, at No. —— Street. I never married such a couple and under such circumstances.

Nov. 7.—Married William and Ellen Craft. They have long been married, but their marriage lacks the solemnity of law, so yesterday they got a certificate, and this day I married them.

A note from an old parishioner named Webster, asking if the account in the newspapers of this marriage was to be depended on, brought out a reply which contains Mr. Parker's own description of that ceremony :—

I have known them ever since their flight from slavery. After the two slave-hunters had gone, they wished to go to England, and requested me to marry them after the legal and usual form. I told them how to get the certificate of publication according to the new law of Massachusetts. It was done, and at the time appointed I went to the place appointed, a boarding-house for colored people. Before the marriage ceremony I always advise the young couple of the duties of matrimony, making such remarks as suit the peculiar circumstances and character of the parties. I told them what I usually tell all bridegrooms and brides. Then I told Mr. Craft that their position demanded peculiar duties of him. He was an outlaw; there was no law which protected his liberty in the United States; for that, he must depend on the public opinion of Boston, and on himself. If a man attacked him, intending to return him to slavery, he had a right, a natural right, to resist the man unto death; but he might refuse to exercise that right for *himself*, if he saw fit, and suffer himself to be reduced to slavery rather than kill or even hurt the slave-hunter who should attack him. But his *wife* was dependent on him for protection; it was his duty to protect her, a duty which it seemed to me he could not decline. So I charged him, if the worst came to the worst, to defend the life and the liberty of his wife against any slave-hunter at all hazards, though in doing so he dug his own grave and the grave of a thousand men.

Then came the marriage ceremony; then a prayer such as the occasion inspired. Then I noticed a *Bible* lying on one table and a sword

---

* A Boston physician.

H 2

on the other; I saw them when I first came into the house, and determined what use to make of them. I took the Bible, put it into William's right hand, and told him the use of it. It contained the noblest truths in the possession of the human race, &c., it was an instrument he was to use to help save his own soul, and his wife's soul, and charged him to use it for its purpose, &c. I then took the *sword* (it was a "Californian knife;" I never saw such an one before, and am not well skilled in such things); I put that in his right hand, and told him if the worst came to the worst to use that to save his wife's liberty, or her life, if he could effect it in no other way. I told him that I hated violence, that I reverenced the sacredness of human life, and thought there was seldom a case in which it was justifiable to take it; that if he could save his wife's liberty in no other way, then this would be one of the cases, and as a *minister of religion* I put into his hands these two dissimilar instruments, one for the body, if need were—one for his soul at all events. Then I charged him not to use it except at the last extremity, to bear no harsh and revengeful feelings against those who once held him in bondage, or such as sought to make him and his wife slaves even now. "Nay," I said, "if you cannot use the sword in defence of your wife's liberty without hating the man you strike, then your action will not be without sin."

I gave the same advice I should have given to white men under the like circumstances—as, escaping from slavery in Algiers.

The following letter to Millard Fillmore, then President of the United States, shows how deep his feeling was at this time, and what a resolution ruled his heart to resist to the utmost the hateful statute. Yet it has all the calmness and dignity of a man who disobeys the law because he worships God.

TO PRESIDENT FILLMORE.

Nov. 21.

HONORED SIR, — This letter is one which requires only time to read. I cannot expect you to reply to it. I am myself a clergyman in this city; not one of those, unfortunately, who are much respected, but, on the contrary, I have an ill name and am one of the most odious men in this State. No man out of the political arena is so much hated in Massachusetts as myself. *I* think this hatred is chargeable only to certain opinions which I entertain relative to theology and to morals. Still, I think I have never been accused of wanting reverence for God, or love for man, of disregard to truth and to justice. I say all this by way of preface, for I need not suppose you know anything of me.

I have a large religious society in this town, composed of "all sorts and conditions of men," fugitive slaves who do not legally own the nails on their fingers and cannot read the Lord's Prayer, and also men and women of wealth and fine cultivation. I wish to inform you of the difficulty in which we (the church and myself) are placed by the new Fugitive Slave Law. There are several fugitive slaves in the society; they have committed no wrong; they have the same "unalienable right to life, liberty, and the pursuit of happiness" that you have; they naturally look to me for advice in their affliction. They are strangers, and ask me to take them in; hungry, and beg me to feed them; thirsty, and would have me give them drink; they are naked, and look to me for clothing; sick, and wish me to visit them. Yes: they are ready to perish, and ask their life at my hands. Even the letter of the most Jewish of the Gospels makes Christ say, " Inasmuch as ye have not done it unto one of the least of these, ye have not done it unto me !" They come to me as to their Christian minister, and ask me to do to them only what Christianity evidently requires.

But *your* law will punish me with fine of 1000 dollars and imprisonment for six months if I take in one of these strangers, feed and clothe these naked and hungry children of want; nay, if I visit them when they are sick, come unto them when they are in prison, or help them, " directly or indirectly," when they are ready to perish! Suppose I should refuse to do for them what Christianity demands. I will not say what I should think of myself, but what you would say. You would say I was a *scoundrel*, that I was *really* an infidel (my theological brethren call me so), that I deserved a gaol for six years ! You would say right. But if I do as you must know that I ought, then your law strips me of my property, tears me from my wife, and shuts me in a gaol. Perhaps I do not value the obligations of religion so much as my opponents, of another faith; but I must say I would rather lie all my life in a gaol, and starve there, than refuse to protect one of these parishioners of mine. Do not call me a fanatic; I am a cool and sober man, *but I must reverence the laws of God, come of that what will come. I must be true to my religion.*

I send you a little sermon of mine; you will find the story of a fugitive slave whom I have known. He is now in Quebec, in the service of one of the most eminent citizens of that city. He is a descendant of one of our revolutionary generals, and members of my society aided him in his flight; others concealed him, helped him to freedom. Can *you* think they did wrong? Can you think of the Declaration of Independence—of its self-evident truths; can you think of Christianity, and then blame these men? The Hungarians found much natural sympathy all over the United States, though some men in Boston took sides with Austria; the nation is ready to receive Kossuth; but what is Austrian tyranny to slavery in America? The Sultan of Turkey has the thanks of all the liberal governments of Europe for hiding the outcasts of Hungary, and can you blame us for starting " Joseph " and helping him to Canada? I know it is not possible.

William Craft and Ellen were parishioners of mine: they have been at my house. I married them a fortnight ago this day; after the ceremony I put a Bible and then a sword into William's hands, and told him the use of each. When the slave-hunters were here, suppose I had helped the man to escape out of their hands: suppose I had taken the woman to my own house, and sheltered her there till the storm had passed by; should *you* think I did a thing worthy of fine and imprisonment? If I took all *peaceful* measures to thwart the kidnappers (legal kidnappers) of their prey, would that be a thing for punishment? You cannot think that I am to stand by and see my own church carried off to slavery and do nothing to hinder such a wrong.

There hangs beside me in my library, as I write, the gun my grandfather fought with at the battle of Lexington—he was a captain on that occasion—and also the musket he captured from a British soldier on that day, the first taken in the war for Independence. If I would not peril my property, my liberty, nay, my life, to keep my own parishioners out of slavery, then I would throw away those trophies, and should think I was the son of some coward, and not a brave man's child. There are many who think as I do : many that say it—most of the men I preach to are of this way of thinking. (Yet one of these bailed Hughes, the slave-hunter from Georgia, out of prison !)

There is a minister who preaches to the richest church in Boston. He is a New Hampshire man, and writes as any New Hampshire politician; but even he says "he would conceal a fugitive, of course." Not five of the eighty Protestant ministers of Boston would refuse. I only write to you to remind you of the difficulties in our way; if need is, we will suffer any penalties you may put upon us, BUT WE MUST KEEP THE LAW OF GOD.

This extract also shows the temper of his mind :—·

I am not a man who loves violence ; I respect the sacredness of human life, but this I say, solemnly, that I will do all in my power to rescue any fugitive slave from the hands of any officer who attempts to return him to bondage. I will resist him as gently as I know how, but with such strength as I can command ; I will ring the bells and alarm the town ; I will serve as head, as foot, or as hand to any body of serious and earnest men, who will go with me, with no weapons but their hands, in this work. I will do it as readily as I would lift a man out of the water, or pluck him from the teeth of a wolf, or snatch him from the hands of a murderer. What is a fine of a thousand dollars, and gaoling for six months, to the liberty of a man ? My money perish with me if it stand between me and the eternal law of God !

FROM THE JOURNAL.

Nov. 18, 1850.—It is plain now there will soon be two great parties; 1, a slavery-protection party ; 2, an anti-slavery party. Protective tariff parties and free-trade parties will soon be swallowed up in the vortex of these two. Then the fate of slavery is sealed.

Feb., 1851.—To-night a meeting was held at the Tremont Temple, to consider the case of General Chaplin. I opened the meeting with prayer, and introduced Mr. Chaplin to the audience. Mr. Sewall was in the chair. I think it a disgrace to Boston that there were no more present. I saw *no minister*. It is not to be supposed that many such would attend, for the meeting was called for a purpose wholly Christian, *to seek and to save that which was lost.*

If General Chaplin had done in Algiers what he did in Washington, all the snobs in Boston would have turned out to welcome him ! But Wisdom is justified by her own children !

Feb. 28.—To-night a meeting of a few members of the Twenty-eighth Congregational Society was held at our house, to see what we could do for General Chaplin. It was thought by some that 1000 dollars might be got. I thought 500 dollars would be more than we ought to expect. A little more than 200 dollars was paid down by those present.

I have had within three months at my house a fugitive slave, whom I had to conceal from the Marshal of this district, a woman and a wife—I mean Ellen Craft. I have been to visit a slave-hunter, who came here to catch her. I have had a man here—General Chaplin—under bonds of 25,000 dollars, for helping two slaves of members of Congress escape from the capital of the United States! I believe this will seem a little strange one of these years.

" Oh, how ridiculous
Appears the Senate's brainless diligence,
Who think they can, with present power, extinguish
The memory of all succeeding times!
They purchase to themselves rebuke and shame."

THE CASE OF SHADRACH.

Shadrach was arrested on Feb. 15, 1851, and confined in the United States Court-room. The case was adjourned by the commissioner soon after it was opened ; and while the crowd was retiring a body of colored men boldly entered the room, told Shadrach to follow, which he did, and was outside before the officers in waiting clearly saw it was a rescue.

FROM THE JOURNAL.

Feb. 16, 1851.—The fugitive slave, Shadrach, put up a "note," asking the prayers of this church and of all Christian people for aid in seeking his liberty ! But this Shadrach is delivered out of his burning, fiery furnace without the smell of fire on his garments. Of course I refer to the rescue of the man yesterday. I think it the most noble deed done in Boston since the destruction of the tea in 1773. I thank God for it. I went down to Court Square as soon as I heard of the arrest, understanding that the slave was still in the Court-house, in the custody of the Marshal, intending to make a rescue, if possible. But it was better done before I heard of the arrest.

The next day, after taking leave of some friends who embarked for Europe, he adds,—

I know not what may take place in times like these, and in such a city as this. But I doubt that they ever see me again; for I must not let a fugitive slave be taken from Boston, cost what it may justly cost. I will not (so I think now) use weapons to rescue a man with. But I will go unarmed, when there is a reasonable chance of success, and make the rescue.

This placard, issued about this time by the Vigilance Committee, and posted at all corners, must be preserved as a characteristic of the period :—

PROCLAMATION!!

TO ALL

THE GOOD PEOPLE OF MASSACHUSETTS!

Be it known that there are now

THREE SLAVE-HUNTERS OR KIDNAPPERS

IN BOSTON

Looking for their prey.   One of them is called

"DAVIS."

He is an unusually ill-looking fellow, about five feet eight inches high, wide-shouldered.   He has a big mouth, black hair, and a good deal of dirty bushy hair on the lower part of his face.   He has a Roman nose; one of his eyes has been knocked out.   He looks like a Pirate, and knows how to be a Stealer of Men.

The next is called

EDWARD BARRETT.

He is about five feet six inches high, thin and lank, is apparently about thirty years old.   His nose turns up a little.   He has a long mouth, long thin ears, and dark eyes.   His hair is dark, and he has a bunch of fur on his chin.   He had on a blue frock-coat, with a velvet collar, mixed pants, and a figured vest.   He wears his shirt collar turned down, and has a black string—not of hemp—about his neck.

The third ruffian is named

ROBERT M. BACON, *alias* JOHN D. BACON.

He is about fifty years old, five feet and a half high.   He has a red, intemperate-looking face, and a retreating forehead.   His hair is dark, and a little gray.   He wears a black coat, mixed pants, and a purplish vest.   He looks sleepy, and yet malicious.

Given at Boston, this 4th day of April, in the year of our Lord, 1851, and of the Independence of the United States the fifty-fourth.

God save the Commonwealth of Massachusetts!

When, after repeated attempts to convict the Shadrach rescuers, a jury acquitted the principal one in November, 1851, we find the following entry :—

Hon. John P. Hale came in, all radiant and flushed with delight, to say that the jury had acquitted Morris.* "Lord, now lettest thou thy servant depart in peace; for mine eyes have seen thy salvation." This is more than I expected. All that Boston influence and the money of the United States could do—all that shameless impudence could do—has been done, and the jury acquit! Well, the jury is not yet to be despaired of, spite of the judicial tyranny which seeks to unman them!

Feb. 21.—These are sad times to live in, but I should be sorry not to have lived in them. It will seem a little strange one or two hundred years hence, that a plain, humble scholar of Boston was continually interrupted in his studies, and could not write his book for stopping to look after fugitive slaves—his own parishioners!

Feb. 22.—Washington's birthday! Very busy with fugitive slave matters.

Feb. 24.—Not well. Writing report on fugitive slave petitions, &c.

Feb. 25.—At home—about anti-slavery business. P.M. at the State-house with Anti-Slavery Committee. Phillips, Sewall, and Ellis spoke. Vigilance Committee sat at night.

Feb. 26.—Much time in fugitive slave matters.

And on a later page, undated,—

I am getting sad now-a-days; for the one great earthly joy, which for years has idealized and beautified my internal life, is with me no more. I suppose I must bear it with what philosophy I can. The great joy of my life cannot be *intellectual action*, neither *practical work*. Though I joy in both, it is the affections which open the spring of mortal delight. But the object of my affections, dearest of all, is not at hand. How strange that I should have no children, and only get a little sad sort of happiness, not of the affectional quality. I am only an *old maid in life*, after all my bettying about in literature and philanthropy.

These thoughts come to me in some hours, and I am deeply sad. But anon there comes the thought of the infinite goodness of God ; and I cheer up and soon regain my habitual cheerfulness. But the sight of all the suffering of these poor fugitives is with me continually, and I cannot be very happy now-a-days.

Feb. 28.—Mem.: The story of James Martin, this day delivered out of the jaws of the merciless. I will leave this page blank to write the story on when it shall be safe.

* Robert Morris, Elizur Wright, Lewis Hayden, Charles G. Davis, and others, were arrested, and all but Mr. Davis bound over for trial. But the juries refused to convict, though, there is little doubt that they were constructed with reference to pliability. Hon. John P. Hale and R. H. Dana, Jun., defended Robert Morris, a coloured student who had been admitted to practice at the Suffolk Bar.

James Martin's story is not written.

Continual alarms about the poor fugitive slaves. A reported arrest of a new one ; but this turned out to be a false alarm.

Mem. : The case of ——, who concealed —— in his cellar until night. Also ——, who came and gave information about an attempt to be made upon —— ; and he escaped.

Mem. : The confession which —— made to —— about the intentions of the ——, and the provisions he made.

The strategy of Mr. —— in getting information, and how he does it.

The entry of ill and sad feelings continues through the week. On Wednesday he re-writes his will, which he drew up when the fugitive slave troubles commenced, and has it executed. In the evening he attends a meeting of the Vigilance Committee. His meditations reflect the sorrow which he had to witness; and the mood lasts a long while.

FROM THE JOURNAL.

I am sad in the midst of great religious delight. Ah, me ! one thing cannot take the place of a different thing. The eye cannot listen for the ear, nor the ear look for the eye. Even religion will not fill the void left by the absence of certain other things which I have not. Alas! it helps me to *still* the aching part, not to fill its void. The poor St. Theresas and St. Brigittas felt Jesus, as they thought, come to their sole and joyless couch. But with all their pious joy it was not the particular satisfaction they wanted that the phantom brought! Religion cannot supply the demand of the finite affections, more than a plough can take the place of a flute. It can assure us of a *recompense*—that it is all right !

28.—Ill all day. Mrs. Russell came and cheered me greatly with a daguerreotype of *Miles o' Teants*.

The next fugitive slave case in Boston was that of Thomas Sims. He was seized in the night of the 3rd of April, 1851, in the street. The bystanders interfered ; the police officers pretended that they were arresting him for disturbing the peace, for he drew a knife upon them. He was illegally arrested, and the " great writ of right " was denied to him. An observance took place before the commissioner,* which was called a trial, and the decision, remanding him to slavery, was applauded by the crowd in the Court-room ! He was put on board a vessel by night, and reached Savannah on the 19th of April.

* George Ticknor Curtis.

FROM HON. CHARLES SUMNER.

Court Street, Boston, April 19, 1851.

May you live a thousand years, always preaching the truth of Fast Day! That sermon is a noble effort. It stirred me to the bottom of my heart, at times softening me almost to tears, and then again filling me with rage. I wish it could be read everywhere throughout the land.

You have placed the commissioner in an immortal pillory, to receive the hootings and rotten eggs of the advancing generations.

I have had no confidence from the beginning, as I believe you know, in our courts. I was persuaded that with solemn form they would sanction the great enormity, therefore I am not disappointed. My appeal is to the people, and my hope is to create in Massachusetts such a public opinion as will render the law. a dead letter. It is in vain to expect its repeal by Congress till the slave-power is overthrown.

It is, however, with a rare *dementia* that this power has staked itself on a position which is so offensive, and which cannot for any length of time be tenable. In enacting that law, it has given to the Free States a sphere of discussion which they would otherwise have missed. No other form of the slavery question, not even the Wilmot Proviso, would have afforded equal advantages.

Very truly yours,
CHARLES SUMNER.

TO HON. CHARLES SUMNER.

April 19, 1851.

DEAR SUMNER,—I wish it was the 19th of April, 1775, on which I was writing, and the times would not so bad for Boston. What a disgrace has the city brought on herself! Oh, Boston, Boston, thou that kidnappest men!—might one say now.

I never had any confidence in the Supreme Court of Massachusetts, in case the Fugitive Slave Law came before it But think of old stiffnecked Lemuel visibly going under the chains!* That was a spectacle. But it all works well.

Thank you for your kind words, and kind judgments of,
Truly your friend,
T. P.

No slave had been sent back by Massachusetts since the Revolution. This first case of Boston kidnapping was duly commemorated the next year by the Committee of Vigilance. Mr. Parker preached the discourse, and also furnished at the last moment, in the failure of various men of poetic fame, who had

---

* Chief Justice Lemuel Shaw, who was holding court in the same building ; it was surrounded by a chain, behind which a strong police force were patrolling.

been desired to write, an ode, which he composed in the railroad-cars, on one of his lecturing excursions. The discourse is published, and is known by all.

This is a copy of the poster which announced the commemoraration of this first case of rendition:—

FIRST ANNIVERSARY

OF THE

KIDNAPPING OF THOMAS SIMS,

BY THE

CITY OF BOSTON!

Our Fathers commemorated the Massacre of the Fifth of March, 1770, till that dark hour was lost in the blaze of the Fourth Day of July, 1776, and the events which followed it. It is for us, likewise, to keep before the people of the Commonwealth the late infamous deed of the City Government, until it be atoned for and forgotten in the joy of a

GENERAL EMANCIPATION!

All the lovers of justice and liberty are therefore invited to assemble,

ON MONDAY NEXT, THE 12TH DAY OF APRIL,

at the

MELODEON,

At 10 o'Clock, A.M.,

To commemorate the First Anniversary of the Surrender of Thomas Sims, arrested on false pretences, by a lying and disguised Police; subjected to the farce of a seeming trial before a Commissioner sitting behind bayonets and chains; carried off, at night, by armed men; all under the direction of a City Government confessing that they knew they were violating the Laws of the State, and intended to do so—such was their "Alacrity" in the discharge of this infamous "Duty." The Morning Session of the Convention will be devoted to an Address by

REV THEODORE PARKER,

with appropriate religious exercises; the Afternoon and Evening Sessions to Addresses from many of the most Eloquent Friends of the Slave.

Boston, April 9, 1852.

And here is Mr. Parker's ode:—

> Sons of men who dared be free
> For truth and right, who cross'd the sea,
> Hide the trembling poor that flee
> From the land of slaves!
>
> Men that love your fathers' name,
> Ye who prize your country's fame,
> Wipe away the public shame
> From your native land!
>
> Men that know the mightiest Might,
> Ye who serve the eternal Right,
> Change the darkness into light—
> Let it shine for all!
>
> Now's the day, and now's the hour;
> See the front of thraldom lower,
> See advance the Southern power,
> Chains and slavery!
>
> See! the kidnappers have come!
> Southern chains surround your home;
> Will you wait for harsher doom?
> Will you wear the chain?
>
> By yon sea that freely waves,
> By your fathers' honored graves,
> Swear you never will be slaves,
> Nor steal your fellow-man!
>
> By the heaven whose breath you draw,
> By the God whose higher law
> Fills the heaven of heavens with awe;
> Swear for freedom now!
>
> Men whose hearts with pity move,
> Men that trust in God above,
> Who stoutly follow Christ in love,
> Save your brother men!

FROM THE JOURNAL.

April 24.—To-day Charles Sumner was chosen to the United States Senate for six years. This is the great triumph of the season. Dear old Massachusetts! Money has not quite eaten the heart out of thee, only out of Boston and its vassal towns!

But it is a little curious to see the odd things which happen. Within a week Sumner has been sent to the Senate for six years for obeying the higher law, and Simmons * has been sent out of his parish for ever for the same thing.

TO DR. FRANCIS.

1851.

Now tell me about various matters: have you ever seen Jo. Luzac's "Lectures Atticæ?" I should like much to see them. Jacobs often quotes them, so do the other writers on Greek philosophy. It ought to be in the College Library. I have got some nice books (old ones) coming across the water. But, alas me! such is the state of the poor fugitive slaves, that I must attend to living men, and not to dead books, and all this winter my time has been occupied with these poor souls. The Vigilance Committee appointed me "spiritual counsellor of all fugitive slaves in Massachusetts while in peril." So, you see, I am to save that which is lost. The Fugitive Slave Law has cost me some months of time already. I have refused about sixty invitations to lecture, and delayed the printing of my book—for that! Truly, the land of the pilgrims is in great disgrace!

Yours truly.

TO REV. J. H. ALLEN.

Boston, April 23, 1851.

DEAR ALLEN,—I have not time for a letter, or you should have one "as long as the moral law," but now only a word; I did not reply to your last but one, for I had not time, fugitive slave matters pressing, and the books you wanted are otherwise occupied.

Let me answer what you ask about. I think if the slave power continue to press their demand as they have for a few years past, that there will be a civil war, which will either decide the "Union," or else extirpate slavery ; that is what I refer to. The time is not come for fighting. How soon it will come nobody knows; it may not come at all. God grant it do not. But this is αρχη ωδίνων και ούπω έστιν το τέλος.

It is rather a queer state of things. Some of Gannett's parishioners attempt to kidnap some of my parishioners. I hide them in my house, and guard the doors night and day, to keep them safe. Gannett preaches sermons which justify his church members in kidnapping. But Gannett is a "Christian," and calls me an "Infidel." His doctrine is "Christianity," and mine "Infidelity." I have heard some things of you "in this connection," which I hope are not true. God bless you!

Yours heartily but hastily,   T. P.

---

* Rev. Geo. F. Simmons, a Unitarian clergyman, gentle, pious, and devoted, who lives no longer. He alone, among Unitarian clergymen settled at the South, dared to utter his testimony against slavery. This was in Mobile, where of course his stay was short. He was turned out of his parish in Springfield, Mass., for rebuking, in a manly and not extravagant sermon, the spirit which had just mobbed Geo. Thompson, the English Abolitionist, in that town. Parishioners of property and standing, sympathizing with the mob, and secretly rejoicing at a blow given to free speech on that topic, could not sit under the rebuke.

TO HON. CHARLES SUMNER.

Boston, April 26, 1851.

DEAR SUMNER,—I have not been able to come and offer you my congratulations on your election. I was almost at your office this morning, when I met some one who told me you were not there, so you will accept my written congratulations instead of the spoken, and let me read you a little bit of a sermon. Perhaps you had better lay this away till Sunday, for I am going to preach. You told me once that you were in morals, not in politics. Now I hope you will show that you are still in morals although in politics. I hope you will be the senator *with a conscience.* The capital error of all our politicians is this : with understanding and practical sagacity, with cunning and power to manage men in the heroic degree, in moral power, in desire of the true and the right, "first good, first perfect, and first fair," they are behind the carpenters and blacksmiths. Look at Cass, Woodbury, Webster, Clay, Calhoun—nay, even at J. Q. Adams. The majority of the shoemakers in Norfolk County had a love of justice which bore a greater proportion to their whole being than Adams's to his. He never *led* in any moral movement.

Now, I look to you to be a leader in this matter; to represent justice, "*quæ semper et ubique eadem est.*" If you do not do this, you will woefully disappoint the expectations of the people in the country. It is a strange sight to find men as much inferior in moral power as they are superior in intellectual power; as much inferior in willingness to make a sacrifice for their country, as they are superior in station! I expect you to make mistakes, blunders; I hope they will be intellectual and not moral; that you will never miss the Right, however you may miss the Expedient.

Then, you told me once that you should never find it more difficult to make a personal sacrifice for the True or the Right than in 1845. It seems to me that just as you take a high office in the State, you are bound more and more to perfect yourself for the sake of the State; to deny yourself for the sake of the State. I consider that Massachusetts has put you where you have no right to consult for the ease or the reputation of yourself, but for the eternal Right. All of our statesmen build, on the opinion of to-day, a house that is to be admired to-morrow, and the next day to be torn down with hootings. I hope you will build on the Rock of Ages, and look to eternity for your justification.

You see, my dear Sumner, that I expect much of you, that I expect heroism of the most heroic kind. The moral and manly excellence of all our prominent men is greatly over-rated by the mass of men. I hope you will never be over-rated by the people, but will overshoot their estimate of you. Yours is a place of great honor, of great trust, but of prodigious peril, and of that there will be few to warn you, as I do now; few to encourage you as I gladly would. You see I try you by a difficult standard, and that I am not easily pleased. I hope some years hence to say, " You have done better than I advised! " I hope you will believe me what I am, sincerely your friend.

FROM MR. SUMNER.

Court Street, July 9, 1851.

Your last speech in the *Liberator* I have read with the interest and instruction with which I read all that you say; but pardon me if I criticize one point.

You speak of me as having "an early reward for good deeds." This language reminds me of the *Atlas*,* which did not see what I had done "to be thus *rewarded*."

Now, I am not conscious of doing anything to deserve "reward," nor am I conscious of receiving any "reward." The office recently conferred upon me, and to which you probably refer, I regard as anything but a reward. In my view it is an imposition of new duties and labors, in a field which I never selected, and to which I do not, in the least, incline. But enough of this. It seems to me that you accidentally fall into the language of the world.

Let me again express a hope that you will collect your speeches and sermons into volumes with hard covers. In that form they will be permanently accessible, and will be a source of power to you.

Ever yours,

CHARLES SUMNER.

TO HON. CHARLES SUMNER, BOSTON.

Brookline, July 11, 1851.

DEAR SUMNER,—I spoke of your receiving a reward in no invidious sense. I think your election as senator came in consequence of your honest, powerful, and noble efforts in the cause of humanity. I agree with you that it imposes great and very difficult duties upon you. I know you never sought the office. Still, I think it both an honor and a reward—an honor, because it puts you in the highest office which the people of Massachusetts have at command, and so is the highest mark of appreciation they can bestow; a reward, for it is (1) given you in consequence of your actual deservings, and (2) while it brings difficult duties, it yet gives you a higher and wider field for the same activity you have previously displayed. I don't think money a mere name; an opportunity for ease is an honorable reward for honorable toil; an opportunity for greater usefulness is the appropriate return, though it bring with it greater trials and harder duties.

I am glad of the kind estimation in which you hold my speech in the *Liberator*, and, indeed, all that I have ever done. As to collecting my occasional publications into volumes, I will think of it, and see. But you must remember that I am probably the most unpopular man in the land, certainly the most hated of any one in it. There are enough to buy a pamphlet that I print for a shilling, but few would care to buy a costly volume. It is not with me as with you. There is no party in the

---

* A paper representing Massachusetts Whiggery of that date : that is, the country, right or wrong, and "however bounded" by the extensions of the area of slavery : in general terms, the constitutionality and nationality of slavery.

State, no sect in the Church, that has any respect for me or mine. I don't complain of this, nor ever did. I only say it, and the fact, of course, enters into all my calculations of printing or preaching.

Truly and faithfully yours,

T. P.

A subject of debate in the Berry Street Unitarian Conference for May, 1851, was the duty of ministers under the Fugitive Slave Law. The occasion exposed the bias of some prominent clergymen, and drew a speech from Mr. Parker. The subject was introduced by Mr. May, of Syracuse, on Tuesday, but did not reach debate till Thursday forenoon, a great deal of the interim being wasted judiciously on trifles, which, like a parcel of fussy beadles, succeeded in keeping the "colored brother" standing on the steps. A report of the doings preliminary to Mr. Parker's speech may be found in the volume of his works entitled "Additional Speeches," Vol. I.

When Mr. May's resolution finally reached debate, a good deal of excited talk ensued, and members, as usual, misunderstood each other, and made desperate efforts to set each other right. But as the majority were wrong, the attempt might have been abandoned. In those days peculiar difficulties beset the discussion of slavery by religious bodies. Never was a plain question of right and wrong approached under such disadvantages by men of ethical cultivation. Climatic influences have, doubtless, much to do with this occasional debility of men who are understood to be ordained upon the basis of the golden rule, and of that rule even miraculously attested; having thus, were it not for climate, an advantage over men who take it plain. But no advantages, unless, indeed, it be that of simple-mindedness, which Mr. Parker possessed (though he was badly off for miracles), can overcome the influence of locality and causes which are endemic. Clergymen from abroad were seized as soon as they came into strong Union-saving regions. They instantly began to "save the Union," which never otherwise would have been endangered, and lost in that business some inestimable things.

Religious bodies made the duty of obeying the Fugitive Slave Law to rest upon two points. First, the disobedience of one law would lead to the disobedience of all law. "There were two things : law without liberty, and liberty without law. Law without liberty was only despotism, liberty without law only license. Law without liberty was the better of the two. If we begin by disobeying *any* law, we shall come to violating all laws." The second point which was strongly urged then, and always, as a reason for overcoming our disgust and yielding support to that infamous law, was "that our obedience would preserve the Union!" What critics events are upon both these favorite arguments of politicians and clergymen! The Union has just almost gone, in consequence of *too much* Northern obedience! If, at the time when politicians were prescribing subservience, and clergymen were showing the people how to swallow the poisonous draught, the pulpit and the parties had prescribed resistance, while it was yet in season, and before the conspiracy which fed upon our obedience had grown to its opportunity, it would not now be necessary for clergymen to bless the Stars and Stripes, spread it over their pulpits, and rhetorically bid it take the field. The present could not then have been foreseen, but obedience to righteousness secures the only safe future, and does the best man can to anticipate the sword. What good theology and what undefiled religion Mr. Parker uttered when he lifted up his generous voice in that Conference, and said :—

Oh, my brothers, I am not afraid of men. I can offend them. I care nothing for their hate or their esteem. I am not very careful of my reputation. But I should not dare to violate the eternal law of God. You have called me "Infidel." Surely I differ widely enough from you in my theology. But there is one thing I cannot fail to trust: that is the Infinite God, Father of the white man, Father also of the white man's slave. I should not dare violate His laws, come what may come. Should you? Nay, I can love nothing so well as I love my God."

That might have saved the country; but clergymen and politicians were doing all they could to save it by disobeying God. They called it " being constitutional." Politicians, at least, have made a merit of it in the midst of a war which is partly due to their subservience. "Yes," they say, " it has come to this, *notwithstanding* our alacrity!"—the men who deserted the patriot minister of Boston when he offered his body, and his mind, and his estate, to his country every time he denounced the wicked measures and lifted up the fugitive! A voice from that distant grave penetrates the battle-cloud that covers the country, to correct the false interpretation : " It is *in consequence* of your alacrity."

For though the weakness of men is the opportunity of history, it is no less a disgrace to the men ; and we cannot wipe it out by thanking God for His ability to make the weakness serve His turn.

August 24, 1851.—Here is something to be done:—1. Finish and publish my book before August 24, 1852 ; 2. Lecture some forty or fifty times (1851-2) ; 3. Do better at preaching than ever before ; 4. Work with more industry.

But who knows that I shall be able to do this ? Last year I laid out much, and how little of it I did ! The wicked Fugitive Slave Law came and hindered all my work. It may be so again.

I intend, for the future, to devote myself more exclusively to the great work of my life, to theology (speculatively) and religion (practically) ; less to politics. Indeed, I would never preach on a political matter again, if it were consistent with duty to avoid it. If I am to live twenty years more, and devote my life to religion and the science thereof, with health and no outward impediment, I may do something to serve my God by blessing mankind. Surely I will try. But I have not so much confidence in my own judgment as to slight the demands of the day and the hour. Suppose I could have given all the attention to theology, &c., that I have been forced to pay to politics, slavery, &c., how much I might have done! I was meant for a philosopher, and the times call for a *stump orator*.

When, in 1851, a member of a publishing firm, to whom he had offered two volumes of speeches, asked him if they would contain any discourses and speeches relative to slavery, he replied, " By all means ; they are the principal things. I wish to go down to posterity, as far as I shall go at all, with the anti-slavery sermons and speeches in my right hand."

This was the publisher who had among his Southern customers a bookseller from Charleston. One day, while this patron of a literature that, knowing no North and no South, could not be suspected of any latitude, was ordering a quantity of Northern books, the publisher said to him, " You don't find us so bad as we are represented." " I have looked over your list of publications," was the reply, " and so long as you *conduct properly* I will trade with you."

Mr. Parker's volumes were not added to that list. After preaching a fast-day sermon, " The Chief Sins of the People," he wrote to a friend :—

Men in the street look *long-favored* at me as I go by. Nevertheless, the good God lets the skies rain on me, and the sun shine (I saw my shadow to-day), and I am allowed to ride in the cars and walk on the side-walk.

And he finished his letter with telling about the Boston clergyman who, when requested to put up a petition for Thomas Sims, then under arrest, replied, " I never pray for anybody but my own parishioners."

Sept. 14, 1851.—Sunday, went to hear James F. Clarke preach. He is here only for a few days. In the beginning of the sermon, Mr. Emery B. Fay came and touched me on the shoulder, and I went out. More anti-slavery matter. So the rest of the Vigilance Committee came out and went to the *Liberator* office, consulted, and acted according to our consultation.

Dec. 31.—Soon the year will be at an end, and what a year it has been to Boston, what a year to me! How little could I have foretold the public or the private events. The next year—how uncertain it is! But the same Father—yes, Mother! that has blessed me hitherto, and all mankind, will yet bless all.

Father in earth and heaven! Father and Mother, too! help me to know thy truth, to will thy justice, to feel and share thy love, to trust thine infinite holiness, and to live blameless and beautiful from year to year. I know not the mysteries of time; help me to learn the lessons of eternity, live full of truth and justice, full of holiness, and love and faith in Thee!

When the slave Jerry was arrested in Syracuse, New York, the bells of the churches were tolled, and a great crowd gathered. While the commissioner adjourned for dinner, Jerry was seized and carried off. The officers recovered him, the military was ordered out to assist in holding him, under the pretext of preserving the peace. But though a few companies armed, they refused to act. At seven in the evening, when the commissioner adjourned again, the officers were obliged to entrench themselves in the police-office, and to fire upon the crowd; but the place was carried by assault, and no one was seriously hurt except the Deputy-marshal, who broke his arm in jumping from a window.*
Jerry was forwarded to Canada.

Mr. Parker rejoiced in every rescue of a fugitive, and in every successful resistance to slave-holders or their Northern officials. He would not bear arms, nor would he premeditate violence. Yet he was never a non-resistant, and there is no doubt that, if at the call of humanity he had ever personally engaged in a rescue, he would not have shrunk from its contingencies. The people of Syracuse celebrated the first anniversary of the rescue

---

* See, in Chapter XII., Mr. Parker's letter to Rev. S. J. May, upon his reputed share in this transaction. Vol. I. p. 321.

of Jerry, on which occasion Mr. Parker sent a letter to be read, containing sentiments like this :—

I say, well done ; do it again, if need be. Do it continually, till the American Government understands that, though they make wicked statutes in the name of " Union," and though the clergy in the name of religion call on all men to obey them, yet the people, in the name of man and the name of God, will violate any such wicked device and bring it to nought. Then the Church will pipe a different tune, and the State dance after a quite other fashion.

His letter, upon the second anniversary of the same rescue, which reached Syracuse too late to be read, and has not yet been published, here follows :—

TO REV. S. J. MAY.

DEAR SIR,—I am sorry that other duties render it impossible for me to attend the meeting at Syracuse, to celebrate the second anniversary of the rescue of Jerry from the hands of the official kidnappers, on the 1st of October, 1851. Since the battle of Lexington and the Declaration of Independence, few events have taken place in America which better deserve commemoration. There are certain outward acts which represent a great principle of eternal right. It is well to pause on each anniversary thereof, and use the historical occasion to deepen in our minds respect for justice, and the disposition to be faithful thereunto, even in the midst of peril. I rejoice in these sacramental days of America—thinly dotting the calendar of this young nation. If I were with you, doubtless I should make a long speech ; as it is, I will say but a few words, which you can read to the audience.

We call our Government a Democracy, and profess to found it on the essential and unalienable rights of human nature, which are equal in all men at birth. We declare that the only function of Government is to preserve these natural, essential, unalienable, and equal rights for each and all the persons under its jurisdiction. We go on to specify some of these rights, and mention the right to life, the right to liberty, the right to the pursuit of happiness, as things of the uttermost importance for the Government to preserve and secure to each person in the country, until he has alienated the right by some positive action which has in a formal and solemn manner been by the people declared unlawful. What just indignation is felt all over America when a tyrant of Europe. deprives his subjects, or any one of them, of their rights ! Not only America, but all Protestant Europe was indignant at the outrage committed by the despotic Government of Tuscany upon the Madiai family. The honorable interposition of the British authorities found gratitude in the generous democracy of the United States. When an Austrian officer, with the crew of a man-of-war's boat, arrests a Hungarian claiming the protection of our flag, and the American naval officer clears ship for action, and runs out his guns, to protect the alleged rights of the victim of tyranny—what applause do the people bestow on the officer who uses his power on the side of justice ! But yet, in defiance of our first principles of government, so often affirmed, so perpetually boasted, the nation deprives one-seventh part of its population of the dearest of all natural rights. Despotic Tuscany and Austria have never a slave. Republican America has three millions and three hundred thousand!

We admit no hereditary claim to political or ecclesiastical honor: we will not tolerate the idea that a man can be born a *noble*, or a king, and in virtue of the accident of birth be entitled to rank and power irrespective of his merits and the consent of the people.

If a new State should be formed, with an order of hereditary nobility, an immovable aristocracy bottomed on birth, that State would be hustled out of the Continent when she applied for admission into the Union. "The Constitution," Congress would say, "requires a republican form of government." In this particular we stand alone in all Christendom. It is a most honorable solitude. But alone of all Christendom do we admit the idea that one man may be born a slave, and other men may have irresponsible power over his time, his limbs, and his life. "No king," says America, "has any right to rule against the citizens' consent; but a white man may steal at birth the black man's children, and hold them as his absolute property all their life; may scourge, and maim, and mutilate, and sell them when he will." A noble would destroy the Republic—a slave is the necessary trial-ground of democracy. To heathen and aristocratic Seneca in Rome, eighteen hundred years ago, slavery seemed monstrous. To "democratic Christians" in America, to-day, it is a "most beneficent institution," "established by God Himself," "approved of by the Savior," and "supported by the chief Apostle"!

Just now, slavery is the favorite institution of the American Government; it yields to nothing; all gives way to that. The Constitution gives Congress no authority to establish slavery, more than to establish Buddhism, or an empire; yet by the authority of Congress it exists in the capital of the Republic, in its territorial districts, and has been spread over nine new States. It thus lives, and thus spreads, in defiance of the Constitution. Laws of the "Sovereign States" are no protection to their soil. Federal slavery, horsed on a statute, rides over all the constitutions, all the laws, all the customs of the Northern freeman. "Legally" the kidnapper sets his hoof on the very spots of Boston earth which were made classic and sacred by the noble deeds and the outpoured blood of our fathers. The American Pulpit is the sworn ally of slavery, the negro's deadliest foe. I know there are exceptional pulpits. I congratulate you that one of them is in Syracuse; one which I trust no winds will ever silence, howsoever often they may blow it down. But how few they are!—little lamps hung out from windows, here and there, on a country road at night, they only show how deep the darkness is, and what long miles of space are all unlit. The character of the American Church is one of the saddest signs of the times. What is preached as "religion," and called "Christianity," demands slavery as one of its institutions. If a man publicly doubts that God commanded Abraham to commit human sacrifice, he is set down as a "dangerous man;" even Unitarians and Universalists denounce him as an "infidel." But a man may preach in favor of kidnapping men, in Philadelphia, New York, and Boston; he may offer to send his own mother into slavery to "save the Union," and it shall not damage a hair of his ecclesiastical reputation. The American Pulpit dares not rebuke the public sin. Nay, it is thought indecorous in a New England minister to hide his own parishioners from the official stealers of men. *Bewray him that wandereth* is the clerical text.

In consequence of the existence of slavery, some strange phenomena occur in the commercial morals of our land. If a ruffian, at the instigation of another, should steal a water-melon from the shop of a certain colored citizen of Boston, he would be properly punished by fine or gaoling; but if, at the instigation of another ruffian, he should steal the body of that colored citizen, tear him from his wife and children, and doom him to slavery for ever, he would be paid ten dollars for that work by the Government of the United States, and have the praise of the commercial newspapers, and the blessings of the metropolitan churches. I cannot forget that I live in a city where a wealthy merchant stole a man, where Boston mechanics publicly boasted that they assisted in the theft, and showed the money, the price of blood, in their hands. I shall not forget that the authorities of this city trampled on the laws of Massachusetts and the rights of man, to kidnap a miserable boy; that they hung the Court-house in chains, and the judges of this commonwealth crouched down and crawled under them: nor that the clergy publicly thanked God for their success in stealing a man; and that one of the most prominent ministers of Boston declared that if a slave asked of him shelter, "*I would drive him away from my own door.*" Yet if an Irishman steals a yellow pumpkin, he is locked up in gaol!

Well: are you and I to stand still and see these things done? Am I as a minister to witness the public denial of all the great principles of practical religion, and hold my peace? To see my parishioners stolen by the vilest of men, and never stir? We must make continual aggressions against slavery; resent its attacks; nay, invade slavery on any suitable occasion, and with any weapons that it is just, manly, and effectual to use. All human enactments are amenable to the justice of God.

Injustice mounted on a statute is not the less unjust; only the more formidable. There are some statutes so wicked, that it is every man's duty to violate them. In the days of the Bloody Mary, the Government made laws forbidding our fathers to worship God: our fathers broke the laws. The fire which burned their bodies, lit a pathway across the sea; faggots and the gallows did not make such laws dear or welcome. The atrocious laws of the Jameses and Charleses, you know what obedience they got from Puritans and Covenanters. We are the children of those Puritans and Covenanters. Have we forgotten the blood in our veins? The American Republic is the child of "Rebellion;" the national lullaby was "Treason." Hancock and Adams slept with a price on their heads. Now it is an heirloom of glory for all their kinsfolk. Is not America proud of her rejection of the Stamp Act, and her treatment of the "Stamp Commissioners"?

The Fugitive Slave Bill is one of the most iniquitous statutes enacted in our time; it is only fit to be broken. In the name of justice, I call upon all men who love law, to violate and break this Fugitive Slave Bill; to do it "peaceably if they can; forcibly if they must." We can make it like the Stamp Act of the last century, which all Britain could not enforce against disobedient Americans. I do not suppose this can, in all cases, be done without individual suffering; loss of money, imprisonment, that must be expected. Freedom is not bought with dust. I think Christianity cost something once. I mean the Christianity of Christ; there is another sort of " Christianity " which costs nothing—and is dear even at that price.

I congratulate the men and women of Syracuse on having resisted this Bill, successfully, openly, at noonday. In her youth the city of Syracuse has done a noble deed which your children's children will be proud of; and, when this anniversary comes round, they will, each of them, say, " *My father was one of those who, in* 1851, *rescued a man from the purchased stealers of men.*" That is an honor to be coveted. In the towns round Boston, we have monuments which tell us of men who dared be faithful, and obey a law higher than the mere caprice of governments—they stand at Lexington, and Concord, and West Cambridge, and Danvers, and Charlestown, to tell of famous deeds of old. None of them records a nobler act than what you are about to celebrate. But great virtue gets many a rub in the straight and narrow path, and cannot go through the world with a whole skin. We build monuments of dead men's bones. We must expect to suffer—"inconvenience" at least.

The Government for the time being is the servant of the slave power; the past administration was no more so; the present is of the same stripe. I suppose, that whatever uniform the future President may put on his flunkeys and footmen, he himself will be striped all over with its livery of slavery for some years to come. He must not forget "the hand that feeds him." It is to be expected that the Federal Government will do its utmost to delight and fatten the slave power; will seek to make slavery national and freedom non-existent. The higher North the President comes from, the lower South must he go to. General Taylor could afford to be more anti-slavery than Mr. Fillmore or Mr. Pierce. Of course, we are to expect that the President will allow South Carolina—the Old-Fogy State—to violate the Constitution, and imprison all free colored citizens of the North, who venture into her dominion; and that he will endeavor to enforce the Fugitive Slave Bill at the North, and to punish all who violate it. How can the South let him off with less. Is he not bound to perform that function? Do the two Baltimore platforms* mean nothing?

The Federal courts, with the " commissions " which they create, are the tool wherewith this work is to be done; a tool more suitable could not easily be devised. The value of a good and noble judge can hardly be overrated—a man who uses law and the judicial modes of procedure as an instrument for promoting justice and preventing wrong; who now resists the prejudice and fury of the people ; then the prejudice, the crafty ambition, and relentless hate of the Government; who always stands up for the eternal right; whom no statute, nor constitution, nor ruler, nor people can ever force to do official wrong. Such a man

* Declarations of democratic want of principle in two successive Presidential campaigns. The American who called himself a Democrat has, until this war, always protected Slavery.

deserves high admiration while living, and the hearts of the public when dead.

But it is difficult to estimate the amount of iniquity which a base judge may do; a man with no love of right, no conception thereof; now following the rage of the public clamoring for injustice, now shaken by the tyrant, thirsty for innocent blood; a man who abuses law as a tool for doing wickedness, himself appointed to his post because he is mean and base—he can debauch the higher morals of the nation beyond what most men conceive possible.

You know how the Federal judges are appointed in America; for what qualities possessed; for what services rendered already, or yet to be performed. You know what bias they commonly have. A short memory is enough to furnish us a long lesson; yes, to create perpetual distrust of the United States courts in all matters where the freedom of a colored man is brought in peril. I believe no judge of any United States court has been found at all averse to execute the Fugitive Slave Bill "with alacrity," and "to the fullest extent." This need surprise no one. Does the whipping-master in the public flogging-house at Charleston or New Orleans, refuse to lay the lash on any bondman or bondwoman, whom their masters send to be tormented under his hand? Does he ask any questions about the justice of the torture? He is paid to strike, not to listen to humanity. Injustice, in these matters, is his vocation. He is to retail cruelty. This is one of the functions of the Federal courts—to peddle injustice, with the Fugitive Slave Bill as their measuring pot. From these courts and their officers we are to expect the most strenuous efforts to enforce the most odious provisions of this Bill. I shall honor fairness in these cases when I see it, but it is what I do not hope for; we are to expect injustice, and only injustice, and injustice continually. I hope nothing from the court, only from the jury.

But here there are two difficulties in our way. One is the traditional respect for the courts of America. This is founded partly on the excellent character of some great men who have honored the Federal Bench. I speak with pride and gratitude of the really noble men who have administered justice in these courts. But they have given that institution a respectability and venerableness which it is now fast losing. Still, the mass of men, who long overrate the worst of rulers, look with confidence to these courts, and allow their own conscience to be overridden by men whom venality has raised to a high place.

The other is the claim of the court to determine for the jury what is law. Here is an evil which assumes two forms:—I. The judge charges the grand jury whom to indict; he assumes to be the norm of law for the grand jury; they must indict all persons who have done the deeds which *he* chooses to denominate a crime.

II. The judge charges the trial-jury whom to convict; he assumes to be the norm of law for the trial-jury; they must convict all persons who have done the deeds which *he* chooses to denominate a crime. Thus, the jury is only a two-edged sword with which the judge lays at any man whom the Government wishes to ruin. If he is the norm of law, then he may instruct both these juries that it is a violation of the Fugitive Slave Bill to read aloud these words out of the Old Testament:—"Take counsel, execute judgment, make thy shadow as the night in the midst of the noonday; hide the outcasts; bewray not him that wandereth. Let mine outcasts dwell with thee; be thou a covert to them from the face of the spoiler" (Isa. xvi. 3, 4); or this, out of the New Testament:—"Inasmuch as ye did it not unto one of the least of these, ye did it not unto me" (Matt. xxv. 45), and tell them they are bound by their oath to indict and convict any man who has read these words aloud. Nay, he may try and swear the jurors to accept his private and purchased opinion for national law and against the universal and unbought justice of the Eternal God. If the jurors cannot so accept and take the opinion of a judicial mind of the slave power for national law and against universal justice, then what safety is there for any man whom the Government wishes to destroy?

This is not theory alone: the evil is actual, is imminent, it hangs over many heads this day, and over some of the best heads in America. In the purlieus of the Court-house there are always men like Empson and Dudley in the time of Henry VII. We found some of that family in Boston in 1851, greedy for notoriety (which they certainly got), and lusting for the price of blood. When a cabinet of successful politicians elevates such an one to office, and we have Empsons and Dudleys holding a "court," with the Fugitive Slave Bill as weapon, and obedient jurors as servants, what safety is there for any man whom the cabinet, or its court, wishes to strike? In Charles II.'s time, a "lawyer of profligate habits and inferior acquirements," "the sordid tool" of other men, was made a criminal judge. He once instructed the grand jury "that a petition from the Lord Mayor and citizens of London to the King, for calling a Parliament, was *high treason*." Chief Justice Scroggs defiled the soil of Britain: it is just as easy to make Scroggs a judge in America—the material is always at hand. George Jefferies was not only Chief Justice but Lord Chancellor. Who knows how soon the noxious heat of slavery may swell some appropriate *fungi* of the American Bar into such judges as Jefferies and Scroggs, those poison toad-stools of the British bench! All that is lacking is a submissive jury; and, thank God! we have not yet found that even in Boston. No judicial "packing" has hitherto crowded twelve jurors of that sort into one jury-box. How soon it may, I know not. "Threats are powerful and money seductive!"

I take it in criminal trials the function of the jury comprises these three things; they are to ask—1. Did the man complained of do the deed he is charged with? 2. If so, is this deed, thus done, a crime according to the formal and constitutional law? 3. If so, then shall this man, who has done the deed, be punished? If they answer yes to all these questions, then the grand jury is to indict and the trial-jury to convict him; if not, not. It seems to me that if the jury allow the judge to determine for them what is the law, that they betray their trust, and throw down the great safeguard of our civil liberty, the breakwater which fends us from the sea of despotism, whose waters cannot rest, but cast up mire and dirt. All true democrats have a righteous horror of what is called *judge* law, *i. e.* law manufactured by the judge to suit his whim, or the caprice of Government. It is as bad as *king* law, or *mob* law, and in this country yet more dangerous.

I take it, it belongs to the function of the judge to tell the jury what *he thinks* the law is and the constitution is, then the jury are to take his opinion for what *they think* it worth. His opinion is one element, often a very important element, which they are to consider. Still, the jury are not a *subordinate* but a *co-ordinate* branch of the court, and are not to shift the responsibility of this function to the shoulders of one who is probably only a creature of the party in power, put in office as a reward for his venality, and as an instrument to execute the unjust and unconstitutional purposes of the Government. They are to answer the three questions just named on their responsibility, not on that of a judge. If he rules wrong and unfitly, they are to decide right, for they are not a tool to do what the Government bids, but men to do justice before God.

Surely, it does not stand to reason that the opinion of a drunken judge is to pass for law with sober jurors ; that the opinion of a partial, prejudiced, unjust, and purchased judge is to outweigh the reason, the conscience, the heart, and the soul of twelve impartial, unprejudiced, just, and free men. Shall a Scroggs and Jeffries overawe twelve honest men, contrary to their own convictions and justice, and so punish a man for keeping the golden rule, and obeying the holiest commands of the Christian religion ? They could hardly do it when England was ruled by a despotic king. Can it be done now in America—in New York ? Then let us go and learn justice of the Oneidas and Onondagas ; for the welfare of future generations is in our hands.

Faithfully yours.

Here is a specimen of numerous letters which Mr. Parker received about this time, asking counsel or giving information :—

Manchester, N.H.

FRIEND PARKER,—At 2 o'clock Sunday morning, two colored men arrived here from Lowell, informing us that the kidnappers would be here on Monday morning to steal from us and God a colored MAN who escaped from slavery in Norfolk, Virginia, some eleven years since, by name Edwin Moore.

They stated a letter was received by yourself from a Mr. Simmons, of Virginia, stating that five Virginians were about to start, or had started, for Boston and vicinity in search of fugitives.

They say that you ascertained that these men were at the Revere House in Boston on Saturday, and that they were to visit Lowell in search of prey.

They state that you wrote to friend Grant, who ascertained that they were coming to Manchester, after Moore, on Monday morning, with the United States Marshal from Portsmouth.

We, of course, sent Moore, on his earnest request, to Canada, although we should much have preferred to have had him remained, and tested the strength of the Fugitive Slave Bill (accursed Bill !) in Manchester.

There is great excitement with us this morning. Will you state to me by the return mail this evening, if the statements made by the colored gentlemen are, so far as you are concerned, true. Will you state any other facts which you may know regarding the case, which you may deem proper to communicate ?

Yours, for God and humanity,

A. T. Foss.

TO MR. ELLIS.

Boston, Feb. 12, 1854.

I have long been trying to write you a letter, but am either so busy, or else so weary with the business, that I have found no time since those two little grandchildren went to the kingdom of heaven. It was a very sad thing for them to lose the little ones—both their " pretty ones at one fell swoop." But "it is well with the child." By-and-bye it will also be well with the father and mother, with you also, and with me. I do not know how they will comport in their first great sorrow. I have not been able to see them since the burial of the last, but hope to be there to-morrow. They try to be calm, but

" 'Tis the most difficult of tasks to keep
    Heights which the mind is competent to gain."

I wish you and Mrs. E. could have been with them, for your sakes and theirs. But it could not be. So all alone they had to look the great sorrow in the face. It is not a fortunate thing when affliction does not come till we are old and grey-headed. I can't speak for others, but I am afraid I have not learned so much from success as from defeat. One day I trust man will outgrow both this kind of sorrow and the need for it. Now, it is a necessity—we can't avoid it —and also a part of our education. But the parents will not always bury their children, and with such bitter weeping.

I will send you a sermon before long. I have three getting ready for print. One, " Of Old Age," goes to press to-morrow ; one, " The Jesus of Fact and the Christ of Fancy," will be soon ready ; the third I have just preached: "Some Thoughts on the General Condition of the Country, and the New Attack on the Freedom of Mankind in America." I meant to preach only one hour, so put under the desk about half of what I had written, and skipped a third of the rest, and held on an hour and a half. Now, as I write, my words are ringing in my own ears. What a wicked business is the Nebraska-Kansas matter! But here there is no enthusiasm. Men "hate it, but know it will pass ;" the prominent men do nothing, not even call a convention ; the Free-Soil State Central Committee have called a meeting of Free-Soilers at Fanueil Hall next Thursday. I passed Thursday night at Governor Davis's, in Worcester. He is indignant enough—bold enough ; headed a petition to Congress ; Lincoln a similar one ; Knowlton a third. But that is all in Massachusetts! Not a Whig stirs. The *Advertiser* is against the Bill, but opposes it feebly and respectably. Evil times! Evil times!

CHAPTER XX.

Anthony Burns—Fanueil Hall—The Placards—The Rendition—The Indictment—The Defence.

Soon after the passage of the Kansas-Nebraska Bill, to be mentioned hereafter more particularly, another attempt was made to test the devotion of the North to constitutional freedom.

Anthony Burns was arrested on the 24th of May, 1854, upon a false charge of robbery, and taken to a room in the Court-house, where he was kept under guard and heavily ironed. His master, Col. Suttle, belonged to Alexandria, Virginia. On the morning of the 25th he was brought before the commissioner, still in irons, though he was guilty of nothing, and not even yet adjudged to have been a slave. The Marshal was determined that this time the preservation of the Union should be substantial and complete ; if Anthony Burns escaped for want of handcuffs, distinguished men would be mortified. But the officers knew that their tyranny had commenced before the commissioner had time to countenance it ; and the fact of the irons was afterwards denied. It is a small matter now, except that it brings Mr. Parker near to the unfortunate man. He says, at a later date, when the ironing was denied :—

The first day of the " trial " he *was* in irons, for I was with him, and saw the irons with my mortal bodily eyes. The next day of " trial " I was not allowed to speak with him ; but came near enough to see that he held his hands as if handcuffed. (I was rudely thrust away by one of the officials). I brought the fact of his being in irons to the knowledge of his counsel, who made complaint to the court. The slave-hunter's counsel made some remarks. Commissioner Loring asked Mr. Burns to stand up. He did so, and had no irons on ; but the officers had taken the irons off while the discussion was going on. This I knew at the time, or was satisfied of, for one whispered to the two who sat with Burns between them, and I saw them busy with his hands ; and after his subsequent return to Boston, Mr. Burns told a gentleman of this city that such was the fact. Mr. B. also stated that on every day of the "trial" he was brought into the court-room in irons, which were kept on till the court came in, and were replaced when the court adjourned.

No risk must be run this time of missing the dark link which was to bind the North and South in new fraternal bonds. Notwithstanding these precautions, the dreaded catastrophe almost occurred.

The best account which I can find of these transactions is contained in the Annual Report of the American Anti-Slavery Society, for 1855 :—

He was arrested on the usual lying pretext of a charge of robbery, by the United States Deputy Marshal, who held a warrant against him as a slave, in order to avoid the danger of a desperate self-defence on the part of his prey. At the Court-house he was suddenly introduced into the presence of the man who claimed him as his property. Ignorant of his rights, cowed by the presence of a slave-holder, surrounded only by the infamous tools of his natural enemy, with no friend near him, he was betrayed, as they alleged, into admissions which his judge afterwards seized upon as the pretext of consigning him again to slavery.

It was probably the expectation of the claimant of Burns, and of the creatures he hired to help him, Seth J. Thomas and Edward G. Parker, that the business could be despatched in a truly summary manner, and without any general knowledge of the villainy in hand until it was done, and its object beyond the reach of pity or succor. If such were their wish, they had selected their tool well in Commissioner Loring, who, before hearing the case, on the mere *ex parte* statements of the master and his counsel, advised Mr. Phillips to attempt no defence, as the case was so clear that the man must go back. Fortunately for the cause, if not for the individual, Mr. Phillips and Mr. Theodore Parker, accidentally hearing of the case, procured admittance, though with no little difficulty, to the slave-pen in the Court-house. Messrs. R. H. Dana, Junr., and Charles M. Ellis, volunteered their services as counsel of the alleged slave. Encouraged by friendly voices, poor Burns expressed his wish to have a hearing, which the commissioner had regard enough, to appearances at least, not to deny. The hearing was adjourned over, at the request of his counsel, though strongly opposed by those of his master, until Monday from Friday.

Time having thus been gained, no pains were spared to put it to the best use. A public meeting was demanded, to be held in Fanueil Hall, to consider what the crisis required. The request was acceded to by the mayor and aldermen with cheerful readiness. The rules were suspended, and the necessary permission granted unanimously. The mayor even expressed his regret that another engagement for the evening should prevent him from presiding at the meeting. But he assured the gentleman who waited on him that no police officer or public servant of the city should take any part in the reduction of the wretch claimed to slavery again.

The meeting in Fanueil Hall was truly an immense one. It filled the entire room, the staircases, and stretched out into the street. George R. Russell, Esq.,* a gentleman of eminent character and high social position, but not "a technical Abolitionist," presided. Speeches were made by the President, Messrs. Wendell Phillips, Theodore Parker, John L. Swift, Francis W. Bird, and others. The meeting seemed perfectly unanimous in its sense of the character of the crime impending, and desirous of knowing what was best to be done. The speeches were of a high and stirring order of eloquence; but any attack upon the Court-house or the kidnappers was strongly deprecated as unwise, and likely to be of mischievous consequences. The Court-house was known to be garrisoned by armed men, who had control of the gas and every opportunity of defending themselves, or of smuggling away their prisoner to safer quarters, in case of a serious alarm. The meeting seemed to acquiesce in the opinions of the platform, and it adjourned, to meet the next morning at the Court-house, to watch, if they could not guide, the event.

But the zeal of a portion of those who had a keen sense of the wrong and indignity of which the city was at once the scene and the object, could not be restrained. A small body of men, about nine o'clock, made an attack upon the Court-house. By means of a piece of timber they succeeded in bursting in the outer door. The garrison made a stand in the breach. One of the Marshal's assistants, James Batchelder, was killed, but whether by the assault of those without, or the awkwardness of those within, has never been clearly ascertained. The time which it took to break in the door, and the noise which necessarily attended the operation, drew the police of the city to the scene. The attacking party were not strong enough to follow up their first success, or at least, had good reason to think so. And the accident of a volunteer company marching into the square, on their return from target practice in the country, helped to discourage the attempt, through the belief that it was a company of marines, detailed to strengthen the force inside. So the rescue had to be abandoned. It was a gallant and generous attempt, but ill-advised and injudicious, under the circumstances. It should not have been made without a larger co-operation, and a more general understanding. Its failure complicated very materially the possibilities of subsequent operations, and gave the slave-catcher's minions the occasion they desired, of calling in the aid of the military.

That very night the Marshal despatched a request for aid to the Navy Yard, at Charlestown, and a force of marines were marched over before morning. The next morning a demand was made, and answered, for the help of the regular United States troops at Fort Independence. The mayor, also, was eager to signalise his loyalty to the slave-catcher, and to make amends for the incautious weaknesses of the day before; on pretence of

---

* Friend and neighbor of Mr. Parker when he lived at West Roxbury.

danger to the public property, a danger which the regular police of the city were amply sufficient to guard against, he called for the aid of the volunteer companies, which was joyfully granted. An opportunity for a holiday ; a chance of showing their uniforms ; a share of the good cheer and good liquor provided for them at the public expense,—any one of these inducements was enough, but all together they were irresistible. The Independent Cadets, or Governor's Guard, were proud to add the title of the Slave-catcher's Guard to their other honorary distinctions.* For nearly an entire week the city was, virtually, under martial law, in order that Suttle might make a slave of a man who had had the address and courage to make himself a freeman.

For the distinctions which were attempted to be made between keeping the peace and keeping the man were too transparently absurd to deceive any one of sense and reflection, had they not soon afterwards stopped their own mouths by greedily taking the blood-money proffered by the President. There was no apprehension or possibility of a breach of the peace except for the purpose of the rescue of the slave. To prevent such a breach of the peace, the United States soldiers held the Court-house, and for the same purpose the militia held the streets. Their purpose was one and the same, and they accomplished it in common, the only difference being that the United States troops, composed chiefly of Irishmen, and officered, probably, by slave-holders, were in the discharge of their regular business, and, it is said, had the grace to be ashamed of it, while the service of the militia was strictly voluntary, any pretence of military necessity being a transparent show.

The President of the United States was eager in the interest with which he looked on, and prompt in the services he could afford, at this critical moment. The despatches which passed between him and his minions in Boston are worthy of preservation, as showing the natural relation of the Chief Magistrate of the nation to the lesser kidnappers under him.

Boston, May 27, 1854.

To the President of the United States,—In consequence of an attack upon the Court-house last night, for the purpose of rescuing a fugitive slave, under arrest, and in which one of my own guards was killed, I have availed myself of the resources of the United States, placed under my control by letter from the War and Navy Departments, in 1851, and now have two companies of troops from Fort Independence stationed in the Court-house. Everything is now quiet. The attack was repulsed by my own guard.

Watson Freeman,
United States Marshal, Boston, Mass.

Washington, May 27, 1854.

To Watson Freeman, United States Marshal, Boston, Mass.,—Your conduct is approved. The law must be executed.

Franklin Pierce.

* Since then, what veins have been nobly emptied to obliterate these distinctions of the past together with Slavery, their cause !

On Tuesday last the following despatch was sent to Boston by direction of the President :—

Washington, May 30, 1854.

To Hon. B. F. Hallett, Boston, Mass.,—What is the state of the case of Burns?

SIDNEY WEBSTER.

Boston, May 30, 1854.

To Sidney Webster,—The case is progressing, and not likely to close till Thursday. Then armed resistance is indicated. But two city companies on duty. The Marshal has all the armed force he can muster. More will be needed to execute the extradition, if ordered. Can the necessary expenses of the city military be paid, if called out by the Mayor, at the Marshal's request? This alone will prevent a case arising, under second section of Act of 1795, when it will be too late to act.

B. F. Hallett.

Washington, May 31, 1854.

To B. F. Hallett, United States Attorney, Boston, Mass.,— Incur any expense deemed necessary by the Marshal and yourself for city, military, or otherwise, to insure the execution of the law.

Franklin Pierce.

On the same day the President ordered Colonel Cooper, Adjutant-General of the Army, to repair to Boston, empowered to order to the assistance of the United States Marshal, as part of the *posse comitatus*, in case the Marshal deemed it necessary, the two companies of United States troops stationed at New York, and which had been under arms for the forty-eight preceding hours, ready to proceed at any moment.

Boston, May 31, 1854.

To Sidney Webster,—Despatch received. The Mayor will preserve the peace with all the military and police of the city. The force will be sufficient. Decision will be made day after to-morrow of the case. Court adjourned.

B. F. Hallett.

Yesterday morning the following despatch was received :—

Boston, June 2, 1854.

To Sidney Webster,—The Commissioner has granted the certificate. Fugitive will be removed to-day. Ample military and police force to protect it peacefully. All quiet. Law reigns. Col. Cooper's arrival opportune.

B. F. Hallett.

In the meantime the examination proceeded. The defence was conducted with great zeal and ability by Messrs. Dana and Ellis. A much stronger case than had been supposed possible was made out on the side of the prisoner. It was incontestably proved that Burns had been in Boston before the time at which it was sworn by Suttle and his witness that he was in Alexandria. The case of the claimant was broken down to all intents and purposes on the facts. For two or three days earnest hopes were entertained that the decision would be favorable to the prisoner. During this time attempts had been made to purchase Burns of the man that claimed him. More than once he had agreed to do so, and the papers were actually drawn by the very Commissioner who sat on the trial, who thus made but too manifest the foregone conclusion at which he had arrived. But the slave-holder was too good a representative of his class to regard himself bound by any promises to a slave or to his friends. It is believed that instructions came on from Washington to the District Attorney, Hallett, to prevent any such termination of so promising a case. There is no doubt, we believe, that Suttle was threatened with chastisement, if not with death, by his fellow slave-holders of Alexandria, if he dared to let this opportunity of triumph and vengeance escape him. . At any rate, he showed that he was a liar, and the truth was not in him, for he paid no regard to his engagements, and finally refused to part with his claim, even when it was hoped that it was most desperate. But he, doubtless, had a well-founded belief that he would not be sent empty away.

It was a great meeting at Fanueil Hall on the evening of May 26. A thoroughly aroused and indignant crowd was there, not needing the eloquent speeches which were made, to be convinced that Massachusetts was about to be disgraced again in the name of law, and that the people were expected to be silent, if not sympathizing, witnesses of the destruction of a man's liberty. The feeling ran very high through the whole of Mr. Parker's speech, which was continually interrupted by fiery assent or disclaimer as he played upon the passion of the hour. Judge whether he was not in earnest :—

"There is no North," said Mr. Webster. There is none. The South goes clear up to the Canada line. No, gentlemen : there is no Boston, to-day. There *was* a Boston, once. Now, there is a North suburb to the city of Alexandria,—that is what Boston is. And you and I, fellow subjects of the State of Virginia,——(Cries of "No, no ! " "Take that back again !") I will take it back when you show me the fact is not so. Men and brothers, I am not a young man ; I have heard hurrahs and cheers for liberty many times ; I have not seen a great many deeds done for liberty. I ask you, are we to have deeds as well as words ?

Then he told them that the sympathies of the police and the Mayor were with the slave, and could not be depended on to support the Federal officers, who, however, depended on themselves :—

I say, so confident are the slave-agents now that they can carry off their slave in the day-time, that they do not put chains round the

Court-house; they have got no soldiers billeted in Fanueil Hall, as in 1851. They think they can carry this man off to-morrow morning in a cab. (Voices: " They can't do it !" " Let's see them try !")

Then he recalled the pre-revolutionary opinion of Boston, when its citizens resisted the Stamp Act, and threw overboard the tea.

Well, gentlemen: I say there is one law—slave law; it is everywhere. There is another law, which also is a finality; and that law, it is in your hands and your arms, and you can put it in execution just when you see fit.

Gentlemen: I am a clergyman and a man of peace. I love peace. But there is a means, and there is an end; liberty is the end, and sometimes peace is not the means towards it. Now, I want to ask you what you are going to do? (A voice: " Shoot, shoot !") There are ways of managing this matter without shooting anybody. Be sure that these men who have kidnapped a man in Boston are cowards—every mother's son of them ; and if we stand up there resolutely, and declare that this man shall not go out of the City of Boston, *without shooting a gun*—(Cries of " That's it!" and great applause)—then he won't go back. Now, I am going to propose that when you adjourn, it be to meet at *Court Square, to-morrow morning, at nine o'clock.* (A large number of hands were raised, but many voices cried out, " Let's go to-night !" " Let's pay a visit to the slave-catchers at the Revere House ; put that question.") Do you propose to go to the Revere House to-night? then show your hands ! (Some hands were held up.) It is not a vote. We shall meet at Court Square, at nine o'clock to-morrow morning.

This was certainly a direct appeal to the people to attempt a rescue, but Mr. Parker's idea was that a demonstration could be made so formidable, in point of numbers and cool purpose, as to overawe the armed guard and sweep the slave away. The democratic papers preferred to represent the speech as advocating violence under thin disclaimers.

> " ' Freemen, keep cool !" he said, with reason ;
> ' To rip the bowels of State were treason.
> I warn ye not to rescue Burns
> Before the morning sun returns ;
> For then a band of bloodhound troops
> May sharp defend the Court-house loops.
> Let no friend seize a goodly timber
> For battering ram—the door stands limber ;
> Nor think to mob the negro's master.'
> This said he to restrain them faster.
> Doth he not lodge in tavern yonder ?
> Yet ere ye go your pistols ponder,
> Arm not yourselves with stones of paving,
> Nor otherwise be misbehaving ;

But now adjourn like citizens good,
Don't rescue Burns—oh, no! who would ?'
As when a roguish boy sees high
A nest of hornets, passes by,
Yet hurls a missile 'mong the pack,
And draws them on his comrade's back;
So the soft spokesman of this crew
Drew on the war, and then—*withdrew!*"

The people did not wait till the next morning. While Mr. Parker was finishing his speech, news was brought that an attack was meditated that evening—was even then begun. The confusion was great, and many persons left the hall while he was putting the question to the vote. He declared it to be negatived ; for he anticipated failure, unless with daylight and an imposing front of the people from the suburbs and the country. The attack was precipitated by a small body, not well organized. The door was broken in, and in the melée one of the Marshal's guard was shot. The guard was frightened, and fired in the dark at random ; and the attacking party was also seized with a panic when it was known that a man had been killed, and withdrew. If they had pressed on with determination, the rescue might have been effected. But Mr. Parker's plan was better, though it did not preclude the chance of violence.

The opportunity was lost. Then followed the gloomy days during which the hearing before the commissioner lasted ; troops held the Court-house and commanded all the avenues.

I will put on record here the famous placards of this period. It is not difficult to see from whose manly pen some of them at least were issued :—

No. I.

KIDNAPPING AGAIN!!

A Man was Stolen last night by the Fugitive Slave Bill Commissioner!

HE WILL HAVE HIS

MOCK TRIAL

On Saturday, May 27, at 9 o'clock, in the Kidnappers' " Court,"
before the Honorable Slave Bill Commissioner,

AT THE COURT HOUSE, IN COURT SQUARE.

SHALL BOSTON STEAL ANOTHER MAN?

Thursday, May 25, 1854.

No. II.

CITIZENS OF BOSTON!

A Free Citizen of Massachusetts—Free by Massachusetts Laws until
his liberty is declared to be forfeited by a Massachusetts Jury—is

NOW IMPRISONED

IN A

MASSACHUSETTS TEMPLE OF JUSTICE!

The Compromises, trampled upon by the Slave Power when in
the path of Slavery, are to be crammed down
the Throat of the North.

THE KIDNAPPERS ARE HERE!

MEN OF BOSTON! SONS OF OTIS, AND HANCOCK, AND THE "BRACE
OF ADAMSES"!

See to it that Massachusetts Laws are not outraged with your consent.
See to it that no Free Citizen of Massachusetts
is dragged into Slavery,

WITHOUT TRIAL BY JURY! '76!

No. III.

Boston, May 27, 1854.

TO THE YEOMANRY OF NEW ENGLAND.

COUNTRYMEN AND BROTHERS,

The Vigilance Committee of Boston inform you that the Mock
Trial of the poor Fugitive Slave has been further postponed to Monday
next, at 11 o'clock A.M.

You are requested, therefore, to come down and lend the moral
weight of your presence and the aid of your counsel to the friends of
justice and humanity in the City.

Come down, then, Sons of the Puritans! for even if the poor victim
is to be carried off by the brute force of arms and delivered over to
Slavery, you should at least be present to witness the sacrifice, and you
should follow him in sad procession with your tears and prayers, and
then go home and take such action as your manhood and your patriotism
may suggest.

Come, then, by the early trains on Monday, and rally in Court
Square! Come with courage and resolution in your hearts; but, this
time, with only such arms as God gave you!

No. IV.

MURDERERS, THIEVES, AND BLACKLEGS

EMPLOYED BY

MARSHAL FREEMAN!!!

MARSHAL FREEMAN has been able to stoop low enough to insult even the
United States Marines, by employing Murderers, Prize-fighters, Thieves,
Three-card-monte men, and Gambling-house Keepers to aid him in the
rendition of Burns.

Let the people understand that United States Marshal Freeman has
not confidence in the courage of his Deputies, nor the valor, powder, and
ball of the United States Marines, to assist him in disgracing Massachusetts, and, therefore, has engaged the services of ———, who fought Jack
Smith, who was arrested, charged with murdering his own mistress!
by throwing her overboard, and who now keeps a brothel in this city;
of ———, and his brother, two three-card-monte robbers; of ———,
known to the police as "Thievy ———," who is "kept" by a prostitute, and escaped from Leverett Street Gaol about two years since,
where he was incarcerated for robbery; of ———, and his brothers,
who are engaged in keeping gambling saloons, and houses of prostitution; and of some fifty other similar characters, all of whom are
known as villains in the criminal records of Massachusetts!!

These are the characters with whom the officers of the United States
Marines are called upon to act. Let the people mark them! They
are in the Court-house. They are petted by Hunker Democrats. They
are supplied with money and rum by the United States, by order of
Marshal Freeman. Such scoundrels, Freemen of Massachusetts, are
employed to trample upon our laws, and insult you, and are supplied
with arms and ammunition to shoot you down if you dare to assert
your just rights.

Will you submit quietly to such insults?

No. V.

NEW DANGER!

It is now rumored that the Slave-holder intends to carry off Burns by
the aid of hired ruffians after the Commissioner shall have set him at
liberty.

CITIZENS, STAND GUARD!

No. VI.

THE MAN IS NOT BOUGHT!

HE IS STILL IN THE SLAVE-PEN, IN THE COURT-HOUSE!

The Kidnapper agreed, both publicly and in writing, to sell him for 1200 dollars. The sum was raised by eminent Boston Citizens and offered him. He then claimed more. The bargain was broken. The Kidnapper breaks his agreement, though the United States Commissioner advised him to keep it.

BE ON YOUR GUARD AGAINST ALL LIES!

WATCH THE SLAVE-PEN!

LET EVERY MAN ATTEND THE TRIAL!

No. VII.

AMERICANS!—FREEMEN!

It has been established out of the mouths of many witnesses, that the poor Prisoner now in the Slave-pen, Court Square, is not the Slave of the Kidnapper Suttle!! Commissioner Loring will doubtless so decide to-day! The spirit of our laws and the hearts within us declare that a Man must not be tried twice for the same offence.

But will the Victim then be set free? Believe it not, until you see it!! The Fugitive Slave Bill was framed with a devilish cunning to meet such cases. It allows that a Man may be tried again. It allows that if one Commissioner refuses to deliver up a Man claimed as a SLAVE to his Pursuer, he may be taken before a Second Commissioner, and a third, until some one is found base enough to do the work.

HALLETT IS AT WORK!

Burns will be seized again, have another Mock Trial, and be forced away. SEE YOU TO IT!! Let there be no armed resistance; but let the whole People turn out, and line the Streets, and look upon the Shame and Disgrace of Boston, and then go away and take measures to elect Men to office who will better guard the honor of the State and Capital!

Per order of the

VIGILANCE COMMITTEE.

Boston, May 31, 1854.

The testimony which was offered in favor of Burns was set aside by the Commissioner, who would not, in the discharge of what he deemed his legal duty, give the prisoner the advantage of a single legal doubt. If he occupied merely a technical position, with which humanity had nothing to do, he might have consistently admitted a technical difficulty. But no, Commissioner Loring did not occupy the passionless official position that was claimed for him. He hastened to discharge the more positive function of " preserving the Union " by ignoring every flaw through which his brother man might creep. Many a distinguished lawyer said, after that day, that the testimony was defective enough to have saved Massachusetts from this crime.

The pro-slavery pressure from within upon the bench was quite as great as the anti-slavery pressure from without. Thus Anthony Burns " had the misfortune to escape from servitude and to be returned to his owner."* The volunteer militia of Massachusetts made a day in State Street more woeful than the day of the Massacre, as they assisted to overawe an immense crowd of indignant men, through whom the slave was escorted in a square of hired ruffians to the wharf. Free bayonets protected ruffians in carrying out the superfluous decision of a slave commissioner! What a day was that, when the merchants of State Street were compelled to stand silent upon the porticoes of their banks and offices, and see the idea of liberty trampled on all the way down that grand historic street !† Those were different days through which we have just lived, when merchants and people of all ranks clustered on those porticoes, filled those windows and balconies, and clung to every shelf of granite, to welcome, with thundering cheers and eyes moistened by patriotic emotion, the successive regiments that bore the flag of civilization and freedom along to Alexandria, over the pavements trodden by the slave's reluctant feet ! It was the North retracing her pro-slavery steps. Not fully seeing whither the thinking bayonets must go, not yet abandoning the flag with deliberate consciousness to a great, just war against slavery itself, but marching that way, with the popular countenance lowering in the direction whence all our ills proceed.

On the Sunday after the attempted rescue, a great crowd of

---

* Letter from Mr. T. B. Curtis, in the *Daily Advertiser*, Feb. 7, 1855.
† State Street was called King Street before the revolution of '76. It was the scene of the Boston Massacre.

earnest people gathered in the Music Hall, to look in the face of the man who had the counsel for the hour. Their hearts reposed upon his brave and magnanimous heart in confidence. He had no pretexts for betraying men. He believed more than all the Supernaturalists in Boston, and believed it more deeply, with life more implicated in the doctrines which exalt and protect human nature. Out of that manly bosom flowed prophecy, scorn, indignation, and encouragement fit for the hour. As he looked over the little desk into that gathering of expectant eyes, he felt more profoundly than ever the truths of this dear country which create her dignity, protect and bless her children, and take her mighty hand to lead into a great future. He stood that day a prophet of freedom, if ever this earth bore a prophet, to frame an indictment of tyranny, and to announce the undying resistance of moral truth to legal exigency. The theme lowered in his speech and in his face. The frank blue eyes caught a steely gleam, as of bayonets levelled to clear the hall, to sweep the great iniquity out by the doors. An undeniable glitter as of steel, seen in that hall more than once, menacing, in the name of the real commonwealth of the people, the Massachusetts of freedom. How little seemed the Fugitive Slave Bill that day! "Take away that bauble!" was the virtual speech, with steel in the eyes of the speaker, now at length become steel in the hands of the doers. Those eyes were never levelled with that threatening expression save to clear the way for human right; never to assault the breast of the people; never in the interest of wrong. Clear, wrathful, patriot eyes, now sunk to sleep, their glances all gone forth into the hearts of many people, their bold looks now marshalled from Washington to New Orleans; how much we need the faith and high purpose out of which they looked on that gloomy Sunday of our sorrow!

FROM THE JOURNAL.

May 29, 1854.—The city is now asleep; but the kidnapper is awake. His victim lies in the same room where Boston retained Mr. Sims. To share the same fate! Well, there is a day of retribution for all this!

All the house is asleep. I have listened at the doors, and heard the low, heavy breathing of them all. How quiet they are! The "higher law" of the Infinite One keeps up the functions of life while we sleep. In Thee we live, and move, and have our being. Thou livest, and movest, and hast Thy being in us; yet far transcendest space, and time, and sense, and soul.

On the 4th of June, two days after the rendition, he preached his sermon of "The New Crime against Humanity." It gave a statement of the movements of Southern domination against the liberties of the country, of the pusillanimity of politicians and clergymen, and of the crime just committed, in which the history of the past legitimately found its climax. Nothing in the old Revolution was ever so stoutly, so intelligently spoken, with more fervid abandonment to a patriotic impulse, or with more reverence for the great God who makes nations through their faith and suffering.

I know well the responsibility of the place I occupy this morning. To-morrow's sun shall carry my words to all America. They will be read on both sides of the Continent. They will cross the ocean. It may astonish the minds of men in Europe to hear of the iniquity committed in the midst of us. Let us be calm and cool, and look the thing fairly in the face.

His words did reach to every quarter, carried by their own power, but also by the event which they denounced, a sullen demon summoned to do unwilling work for truth.

You have not forgotten Webster's speeches at Albany, at Syracuse, at Buffalo, nor his denial of the higher law of God at Capron Springs, in Virginia. "The North Mountain is very high; the Blue Ridge higher still; the Alleghanies higher than either; yet the 'higher law' ranges an eagle's flight above the highest peak of the Alleghanies." What was the answer from the crowd? Laughter! The multitude laughed at the Higher Law. There is no law above the North Mountain; above the Blue Ridge; above the peaks of the Alleghanies; is there? The Fugitive Slave Bill reaches up where there *is no God!*

" Laughter " from North and South to greet the higher law in those days! Weeping for laughter now, because a law of God was laughed at ; and the lips of cannon to enforce at Capron Springs itself the doctrines which were there flouted in the fine October sun ! A truth cannot be turned backward. The more violently it is resisted, the more bloody is its course.

Thus, on the 2nd of June, 1854, Boston sent into bondage her second victim. It ought to have been fifteen days later—the Seventeenth of June. What a spectacle it was ! The day was brilliant; there was not a cloud ; all about Boston there was a ring of happy summer loveliness: the green beauty of June—the grass, the trees, the heaven, the light; and Boston itself was the theatre of incipient civil war !

Why did Commissioner Loring do all this ? He knew the consequences that must follow. He knew what Boston was. We have no monument to Hancock and Adams, but still we keep their graves; and Boston, the dear old mother that bore them, yet in her bosom hides the honored bones of men whom armies could not terrify, nor England bribe. Their spirit only sleeps. Tread roughly—tread roughly on the spot—their spirit rises from the ground! He knew that here were men who never will be silent when wrong is done. He knew Massachusetts; he knew Boston; he knew that the Fugitive Slave Bill had only raked the ashes over fires which were burning still, and that a breath might scatter those ashes to the winds of heaven, and bid the slumbering embers flame.

Listen, O reader, in camps, in cottages, in counting-rooms. The little Lexington belfry rocks again in the morning air.

This circular was issued from his pen on the day that cannon from Bunker's Hill seemed sullenly to emphasize a more glorious past :—

Boston, June 17, 1854.

Dear Sir,—The Vigilance Committee of Boston have directed us to address you on the subject of forming a Vigilance Committee in your town and neighbourhood, for the purpose of aiding persons claimed as Fugitive Slaves.

If you will form such a Committee in your town, we think you may serve the cause of Freedom and Humanity in several ways.

1. You may help such alleged Fugitives to escape from actual danger, by aiding them in their flight to Canada, or some other place of safety, where they will be out of the kidnapper's reach. Thus you may help the individual.

2. You may arouse the sense of justice in the people of your town and neighborhood, and so prepare the way for checking and terminating the wicked institution of Slavery, which is so perilous to the liberties of America. Thus you can aid the Idea of Justice, for each Committee will be a little centre of organized action, where discussion can be carried on, and whence information may be spread abroad.

3. Perhaps you may also, in case of need, furnish pecuniary aid to the alleged Fugitives in other places.

We therefore invite you to organize a Vigilance Committee in your town, and inform us of the names of your Officers whom we may correspond with in case of need. Communications may be addressed to
Yours truly,
THEODORE PARKER,
Chairman of the Executive Committee of the Boston Vigilance Committee.

EXECUTIVE COMMITTEE.

THEODORE PARKER,	WENDELL PHILLIPS,
JOSHUA B. SMITH,	EDMUND JACKSON,
LEWIS HAYDEN,	FRANCIS JACKSON,
SAMUEL G. HOWE,	CHARLES K. WHIPPLE.

FROM HON. CHARLES SUMNER.

Washington, June 7, 1854.

I had just read and admired your great New York effort, as reported in the *Anti-Slavery Standard*, when the *Commonwealth* came this morning with that other fulmination from Boston. Such efforts will deeply plough the public heart. Other ages will bless you, even if we do not all live down the clamor which now besets us.

At last I see daylight. Slavery will be discussed with us *as never before*, and that Fugitive Bill must be nullified. Peaceful legislation by our commonwealth will do it all. At once should be commenced an organization to secure petitions, 1, to Congress; 2, to our own Legislature. Get people committed to the absolute refusal of the whole wickedness.

The curtain will soon lift here. Cuba—Hayti—Mexico. You know the plot. And yet the people sleep.

FROM THE JOURNAL.

June, 1854.—*What I shall do if I am sent to gaol?*

1. Write one sermon a-week, and have it read at Music Hall, and printed the next morning. Who can read it? Write also a prayer, &c. (Prayer, Saturday night).

2. Prepare a volume of sermons from old MSS.

3. Write Memoirs of Life, &c.

4. Vol. I. of "Historical Development of Religion," *i. e.*, the Metaphysics of Religion.

5. Pursue the Russian studies.

The grand jury which was sitting at the time of these events, was not specially summoned to notice them, and therefore, though charged explicitly enough to find a bill against the prominent actors of the night of May 26, separated without doing so. A new grand jury was impanelled in October, but instead of being charged afresh by the judge upon the statute of 1790, in relation to resisting officers serving a process, or upon the statute of 1850, it was referred to the United States Attorney for the instruction contained in the previous charge; and an indictment was found against Mr. Parker, for knowingly and wilfully obstructing, with force and arms, the Marshal of the district, who was attempting to serve and execute the warrant and legal process under which Burns was taken and held; also for making an assault upon said Marshal, who was in the due and lawful discharge of his duties as an officer. Similar indictments were found against Wendell Phillips, who also spoke at the Fanueil Hall meeting, and against Martin Stowell, Rev. T. W.

Higginson, John Morrison, Samuel T. Proudman, and John C. Cluer, who were engaged in the assault.

By laws of the United States, both Grand and Petit Juries may be selected in Courts of the United States by a combination between the U.S. District Attorney and the U.S. Marshal.

TO PROFESSOR EDWARD DESOR.

Nov. 19, 1854.

I shall not be indicted. "Judge Ben," the Honorable Benjamin R. Curtis, with his coadjutors, Ben Hallett and others like him, made the attempt in June, and again in October. But the grand jury found no bill. So Phillips and I escape this time. I should be sorry if a Massachusetts jury should disgrace the State by such meanness; but I should have liked the occasion for a speech. I chalked out the line of defence, and was ready for trial the day the grand jury sat. I think nobody will be punished for the "riot" in June. Now would be a good time for another slave-hunt in Boston. Sumner gave an admirable address before the Mercantile Association last night. He never did a better thing.

FROM THE JOURNAL.

Nov. 29, 1854.—Day before Thanksgiving. This morning, a few minutes after eight, as I sat writing, a rap came on my door. I said, "Come in." A man entered, and stood looking a little awkward. I took him by the hand, bidding him good morning.

"Is this the Rev. Mr. Parker?" he asked.

"So-called," I said; "sit down, if you please."

"I want to speak with you on business," he said. So Miss Stevenson withdrew, and as she shut the door, he said, "Mr. Parker, I have rather a disagreeable business to do. I am come to arrest you."

"Very well—is that all?" said I; "in the United States Circuit Court, I suppose."

"Yes."

"Let me see the warrant?" He presented it. I read it over, about half of it aloud, and a few words to myself—enough to catch the drift of it, and handed it back to him. "Well: what do you want me to do —shall I go down to the Court-house?"

"No. Will you come down to the Marshal's office at ten o'clock?"

"Certainly, where is it?"

"No. 1 in the Court-house."

"First floor?"

"Yes, sir—first floor. I suppose you will have your surety."

"Certainly—four or five of them. I will go and see them."

"One is enough, if he is a real-estate holder."

"Yes; but there are several persons who have asked the privilege of being my bail. For you must not suppose that I did not expect this."

"Very well. I won't stay any longer." I attended him down the stairs. "This is a disagreeable business, Mr. Parker?"

"I make no doubt of it. But I am much obliged to you for the gentlemanly manner in which you have performed your official function."

"Oh—thank you—we don't expect to get into low places."

"Good morning."

"Good morning, sir."

At ten, I went to the office, attended by C. M. Ellis, Esq., as my attorney. Miss Stevenson and L. had previously been to inform the bail of what was going on. Mr. Manley was in the office already. We went to the Supreme Court-room, to wait with Mr. E. till the officer was ready. He soon returned, and we went to the Circuit Court-room, when I recognized in 1500 dollars for my appearance in that Court at 10 A.M. on the first Monday in March (*i. e.* the 85th anniversary of the Boston Massacre.)

Judge Ben Curtis and Judge Peleg Sprague were on the Bench.

His bondsmen were three parishioners, Samuel May, Francis Jackson, and John R. Manley.

Here is a specimen of the letters which came to him from the people at this time. He prized the badly spelled but correct and noble thought :—

Pembroke, December the 21 day, 1854.

DEAR SIR,—I gave notice of A meeting to see if we would form A vigilance committee in this town. The evening was stormy, but theor was A small number of us who came together, and we resolved ourselves into A vigilance committee, and theay chose L. Mclauthlin, Job H. Beal, and Otis P. Josselyn, as the Executive Committee, and theay designated me as thear Chairman, and we shall be reddey to ade the cause of humane liberty when it is in our power so to do. And now, Sir, I must say that I am veary sorry that any man should be arested and brought before A couart for speakeing against making slaves in our State, to send out to Verginner, or any whear elles ; but, sence it is so, I am glad that they have taken such men as yaur Self and Mr. Phillips, our very Captains of the liberty of speech, and men, too, who can defend thear and our rights, and bring up A host of liberty loving men and women to sustain you in your just Cause.

Yours, with respect.

Concord, July 10, 1854.

REV. AND DEAR MR. PARKER,—I received, on the 30th of June last, a circular from you, sir, and the other gentlemen comprising the Executive Committee of the Boston Vigilance Committee. I owe you an appology for not acting sooner up your excellent suggestion; but, the fact is, your circular was received by me at the Post-office, and finding it to be a printed circular, and not looking at the signer, supposed it to be something such as I am receiving almost every day, about some quack medicine, or about some newly invented machine for sale, or some such thing, and did not stop to read it at the time, and put it into my pocket, and forgot to look at it untill about *Independence Day*—*what a farce to call it so! !*

Well, sir, last evening we had a small Anti-Slavery gathering in Concord, and I asked the following questions to those presènt, viz. :— If a slave, who was making his escape, should come to your house, would you aid him by giving him shelter, &c. ? There were present Ralph W. Emerson, Mrs. Mary Brooks, Charles Bowers, John Thoreau, Mary Rice, Nathan B. Stow, Nathan Henry Warren, James Weir, Joshua R. Brown, Stearns Wheeler, Mrs. John Thoreau, Mrs. R. W. Emerson, and William Whiting. We were unanimous in our agreement to aid and assist all in our power to help the fleeing bondman to obtain his God-given rights.

I am, dear sir, your obedient and humble servant,
WILLIAM WHITING.

FROM THE JOURNAL.

Last night of the year.—It is almost twelve : a new year close at hand.

O Thou Spirit who rulest the universe, seeing the end from the beginning, I thank Thee for the opportunities of usefulness which the last year afforded, for all the manifold delights which have clustered round my consciousness. But how little have I done, how little grown ! Inspire me to do more, and become nobler, in purpose, motive, method of my life. Help me to resist new temptations, and do the new duties which the year brings with it. I know not what a day shall bring forth —honor or shame, perhaps a gaol. Help me everywhere to be faithful to Thee. So may I live and serve my brethren more. Yet still may I love my enemies, even as Thou sendest rain on the just and the unjust !

FROM HON. CHARLES SUMNER.

Dec. 12, 1854.

I am glad you have been indicted—pardon me—for the sake of our cause, and for your own fame. Of course you will defend yourself, and answer the whilom speaker at Fanueil Hall face to face.* Don't fail to recount that incident in your speech, where you will naturally review Boston tyranny, not only in courts, but also abroad, at public meetings, and in the world.

I can tell you nothing of history. You know well Campbell's Chancellors and Chief Justices. In reviewing these you will meet the great instances, and will discern the base character of judges—a sad list !

The cases of Scroggs and Jefferies have a barefaced outrageousness

---

* Alludes to Judge Curtis, who at a Union-saving meeting demanded to know how a minister of the Gospel could recommend a juror to break his oath, and clear a fugitive against the law and the facts. Mr. Parker, who was in the gallery, said, "Do you want an answer now ?" The Judge was embarrassed, and the crowd made noise enough to prevent an explanation.

which makes them less applicable than the case of ship-money; the case of Sir Edward Hill, in 1687; the trial of Horne Tooke, in 1796; and at a later day, the trials which killed Lord Ellenborough. Do not fail to master his life and character. Therein you will find more which will be in point than in earlier cases.

Upon the whole, I regard your indictment as a "call" to a new parish, with B. R. Curtis and B. F. Hallett as "deacons," and a pulpit higher than the Strasburg steeple.

TO MR. SUMNER.

Boston, Dec. 15, 1854.

Phillips was arrested to-day, and gave bail with six securities. John Hancock was also once arrested by the British authorities in October, 1768. Great attempts were made to indict Sam Adams, and Edes and Gill, patriotic printers; but no grand jury *then* would find a bill.

Hale gave an admirable lecture on the Trial by Jury last Thursday. It was a happy hit, and every word told on his vast and most responsive audience. It came at the right time.

Thank you for your note which came yesterday. I will work on that hint, and make a sermon which will keep the new "deacons" awake.

In 1845, my friends passed a resolution, "that Theodore Parker should have *a chance to be heard* in Boston." The two brothers-*in-law*, Ben. C. and Ben H. now second the resolution. "A chance to be heard!"

TO MR. ELLIS.

Dec. 19, 1854.

DEAR CHARLES,—I am much obliged to Mr. Hallett for his readiness to accommodate me in the matter referred to; but I did not ask that or any other favor. I simply wish to know the time when the court will proceed to try the matter between it and me. I will accommodate myself to that. I understood from Mr. Phillips that Mr. Hallett said the trials would not take place in March; if so, I need not disappoint some fifteen towns by refusing to lecture there. Excuse me for troubling you.

TO THE SAME.

Boston, Feb. 8, 1855.

These are the points I should make against Commissioner Loring :—

1. He kidnapped a man in Boston who was accused of no offence against any law, divine or human, but who, by the laws of God written in nature, and the constitution and statutes of Massachusetts, and the principles of the Declaration of Independence, was as much entitled to freedom as Mr. Loring himself, or any man in the commonwealth.

2. He was not forced to this, but did it voluntarily. (a). His office did not compel such a wicked service, for Mr. Hallett, in 1850, declined it, and in 1854, Mr. George T. Curtis, who was first applied to for the kidnapping of Mr. Burns, refused the office; in 1851 (in the Sims time) no sheriff or constable of Boston could be found willing to serve the writ of

personal replevin, though a fee of five hundred dollars was allowed, and a bond of indemnity to the extent of three thousand dollars more. (b.) But if the office, in his opinion, required this, then he ought to have resigned his office, either at once or on the passage of the Fugitive Slave Bill, which "required" such a service of him, or, at least, when called on to steal a man. He cannot plead that the office is any extenuation of so heinous an offence as making a citizen of Massachusetts, accused of no fault, a slave of Virginia.

3. He did not do this hastily, but deliberately, after a week for reflection and consultation with his friends and fellow-citizens.

4. He is not now sorry for the offence, but so justifies it on principle that the act is legal and constitutional, and so professes to understand the tenure of his office of commissioner that he would do the same again if called on; and Massachusetts will, again and again, present to the world the spectacle of a commonwealth, democratic and Christian, which keeps in office, as guardian of widows and orphans, a man who is a professional kidnapper. Is she ready to do that?

5. The manner of the kidnapping was as bad as the matter. I will not refer to the mode of arrest, which he is not responsible for, but, (a.) he advised Mr. Phillips, Burns's attorney, "Not to throw obstacles in the way of his being sent back, as he probably will be"! (b.) He confined him in a Court-house of Massachusetts, contrary to the express words of the statute, and the well-known form of law of his own State. (c.) He decided against the evidence in the case, which proved that the man on trial as a slave in Virginia on a certain time, *was actually at work in Boston at that very time.* (d) The evidence he relied on for the identity of Burns, the only thing to be proved, as he declared, was the words alleged to be uttered by Mr. Burns, spoken, if at all, under *duresse*, and subsequently denied by him. (e.) He communicated his decision to parties having an interest adverse to Mr. Burns, twenty-four hours, at least, before it was given in open court.

6. He knows the stealing of a man is wrong. This is not merely matter of inference from his education and position, but from the fact that he declined the fee, ten dollars, his "legal" and "official" recompense for stealing a brother man. This he does, it is supposed, not from general charity towards men-stealers, or from special friendship for Mr. Suttle in this case; but because the money is the price of blood paid for treachery to the Constitution of Massachusetts, and to the natural, essential, and unalienable rights of man.

7. He is the first judicial officer of Massachusetts since 1776 who has kidnapped a man. Had he stolen Mr. Dana or Mr. Ellis, counsel for Mr. Burns, charged with no crime, and delivered them up to the Algerines or Carolinians, he would not more have violated the principles of natural justice and the precepts of the Christian religion. Nay, the offence is worse when committed against a poor man, an unprotected and a friendless man of a despised race, than if committed against rich, educated, and powerful gentlemen, who have material and personal means of defence. Now, the Legislature of Massachusetts is the guardian of the lives and the character of her citizens. If she detains a kidnapper in her high office of Judge of Probate, in her own capital city, she says to the world, "I acknowledge that it is a glory to steal

a man, and so will make the kidnapper also guardian of widows and orphans, giving him a better opportunity to crush those who are ready to perish without his oppression! " Is that the lesson for the guardians of public morals to teach to the youth and maidens of Massachusetts— to teach in the hearing of Fanueil Hall, in sight of Bunker Hill, over the graves of Hancock and Adams ?

8. There are 2038 colored persons in the county of Suffolk ; they must do public business at his office. Is it fair for Massachusetts to force them, in their affliction, to come before a judge who is the official enemy of their race—who kidnaps men of this nation? It adds new terrors to the bitterness of death.

9. If there were no law of God, no conscience in man declaring what is right, no golden rule of religion, bidding "Whatsoever ye would that men should do unto you, do ye even so to them," then it might be enough to plead the law of the United States allows him to steal a man. But as there is a law of God, a conscience, a golden rule, recognized guides of conduct amongst men, Massachusetts cannot detain in such an office a man who on principle will send his innocent brothers into eternal bondage.

The trials commenced upon the 3rd of April, 1855, with the arraignment of Martin Stowell. Hon. John P. Hale, the senior counsel for the defendant, moved that the indictment be quashed. The Court decided to hear the motion, whereupon the jurors were excused for the day, and William L. Burt, the junior counsel, addressed the Court upon some of the specifications of the motion. These were six in number, being substantially (1,) that the warrant was not properly directed and served ; (2,) that the jury in the case was not an impartial jury of the district, as required by law ; (3,) that the acts specified in the indictment did not constitute a crime under the statutes under which the indictment was framed ; (4,) that the indictment did not sufficiently set forth the proceedings wherein the said warrant was based ; (5,) that said indictment and the several counts thereof, was bad on the face of them, for several technical reasons; (6,) and because the warrant issued from and ran into a jurisdiction not authorized by law, &c.

Mr. Ellis, counsel for Mr. Parker, took up the first two reasons for quashing the indictment, and continued on the second day of the trial. Mr. Durant filed the same motion for Mr. Higginson, and pointed out that the warrant itself did not justify the arrest of Anthony Burns, and argued that the Marshal had no right to hold Burns under the warrant, but that his authority ceased with the seizure. Mr. John A. Andrew (now Governor of the State of Massachusetts), counsel for Wendell Phillips, followed, in an argument based upon the sixth objection specified in the motion, and also made the point that the indictment did not sufficiently particularize the offence with which defendant was charged.

On the third day the United States attorney, B. F. Hallett, was ill, and unable to attend ; the Court postponed the case to the tenth of April. On that day Mr. Andrew completed his argument, and Mr. E. W. Merwin, assistant counsel for the prosecution, replied to some of the objections, prefacing the remark that the Government *had no object in the prosecutions* except to maintain the law as a terror to evil-doers, and a protection to those who do well ! The United States attorney, Hallett, then followed in a defence of the indictment, which occupied the fifth day.

On the next day Judge Curtis delivered his opinion, " that the process alleged to have been obstructed was not a legal process in the meaning of the Act of 1790, because there was no averment in the indictment to show that the warrant had been issued by such a Commissioner as the Act of 1850 specifies, and that, as neither of the counts in the indictment describes, by sufficient averments, any offence under the Act of 1790, under which alone the Government claims that the indictment can be supported, it must be quashed."

Whereupon the Court ordered the clerk to enter on the record that the indictment against Martin Stowell is quashed, and the United States attorney, Hallett, then moved the Court to discontinue the cases against the other persons indicted.

C. M. Ellis, Esq., one of the counsel at this trial, says :—

Mr. Parker was at once glad to meet the Government and fight them, and vexed and annoyed at the groundless and disgraceful assault on him. As he said, he would "give them their bellyful." He was untiring alike in doing all he could to urge the trial on and to defy and taunt them to meet him, and in exploring every ground, the grandest and the least, upon which to defeat them.

You know there were indictments against several persons, Wendell Phillips, Higginson, &c. A meeting of the counsel of all was held in my office. We then settled on the plan, which was to make the attack. We were, first, to move to quash for defects on the face of the indictment, as we did, and we parcelled out the branches of this amongst us. After that we proposed to follow up (if, as we expected, the Court would overrule us), by showing the jury that found the indictment was not indifferent, and so on. (You see a note of testimony as to Greenough).

Well, we did *put them on trial* for several days. It was in the old sitting rooms of the old wooden house, then used (and good enough) for such cases, on Bowdoin Square.

The judge showed *himself* out, and the temper of those he stood with. They sneaked off through the smallest place possible, but showed temper; needlessly declared that the jury was well drawn, and slurred at the counsel. You may see Mr. Parker's judgment of it in the leaf of the State Trials he sent me.

He was, I thought, glad of the result. Of course, any defence in such a place, and before such men, must have been very different from the one he wrote, and must have reached the world very dif ferently.

He preferred to be fairly rid of all trouble, to see the " curs sneak off with their tails between their legs," and then to show without (certain) interruption of the judge, or boggle of reporting, what sort of a lash they ought to have had applied to them.

He worked through the summer, and at Dublin (N. H.), on the defence. It is less a defence than an able review of the assaults and defences made in the course of our history by the little garrison manning the fortress of the English Jury. He saw clearly how the central power, in serving slavery, was making inroads on our institutions. Curtis had already declared the jury mere tools, in a way an English judge would have been ashamed of. Mr. Parker then anticipated a long struggle to undermine our institutions one by one,* and he threw himself into the breach upon this one. War has anticipated all of them. But he was right as things were going; that " Defence " and like things, instead of Sumter and Bull Run, would have been the steps of our march to freedom.

FROM MR. ELLIS TO MR. PARKER.

Sept. 8, 1855.

DEAR SIR,—This (more than I thought) is necessary to show the exact case in the briefest form, with nothing collateral, and with no comment.

How far anything else is worth while, either to interest or inform people, now or hereafter, depends on what you have woven into your argument. I suppose you will have most of the things embodied in it. And there they will be preserved best.

Let me, however, hastily note these matters that occur.

1. The leading, active part you and Phillips took (as you had always taken in others) in Burns' trial. *Hinc illæ lachrymæ.*

2. The Court and the Government avoided the only charge for which there was any pretext, viz., " of rescue or attempt to rescue under the Bill of 1850, such as was made in the former cases, in order to avoid the issue, slave or not.

3. No pretence that you did anything save the speech.

4. The wrong of trying a new jury; or the same charge with a second.

5. The illegal construction of the juries, *from a fraction* of the district, and by the Marshal himself, the party concerned.

6. The unsoundness of the charge to the first jury, in law.

* At that very time the Lemmon case was on its way to the Supreme Court from New York ; and from the West the infamous Dred Scott case was taking shape.

7. The wrong of omitting to charge the second, and turning it over to Hallett. It was the judge's duty, not to be delegated. This I count highly improper and very dangerous, not only in the instance, but as a precedent; for, without charge or complaint before a coroner, or presentment, or formal information aliunde, to allow the Government to thus originate the bill, is giving it the power of bending the law to meet the facts in its possession. Tyrants want no more.

8. Greenough, Merwin; singular coincidences of doubtful delicacy, but perhaps nothing.

9. Executive interference.

10. The purpose of the prosecution.

Some of these are slightly legal. One is settled; but no judge is infallible. I believe our views to be the sound ones.

Yours truly,
C. M. ELLIS.

Mr. Parker's defence, a portion of which he had prepared with the purpose of addressing the jury himself, was not disposed of so easily as the indictment. It appeared during the next August, most carefully elaborated, with valuable historical matter upon the development of the jury, the corruptions of the judiciary, and a variety of interesting cases of trial for political offences and liberty of speech. He has written nothing that is so vigorous and effective. The cases from English political and ecclesiastical history can nowhere else be found so dramatically and sympathetically presented. It is a wonder that this "Defence" is so little known. The style of it is better than that of any of his writings, except the last three of the "Sermons of Theism," and some of the "Occasional Discourses." It is sinewy, clear, thoroughly American, and more sustained and flowing than his usual composition. He seldom took the trouble, and never had the time, to regard his style as a matter for anxiety. But here, a favorite historical subject, a most engrossing national question, the right of free speech, and all his own keen personal interest, conspired to make one of the most fascinating books of this epoch. It will be read in fifty years and after more eagerly than at present, and is the book which the future historian of these times will hunt for with eagerness and rejoice in when found.

It contains too frequently repeated allusions to persons known as supporters of the Fugitive Slave Bill, and strenuous advocates for his indictment. The iteration is damaging to the moral effect which he desired to produce. He is not merely unsparing and righteously indignant, but his personal implication led him to call up some points against his opponents too often ; they impede the general movement of the work. This will make the book more valuable to the coming historian of the present generation, who will feel less these faults of taste while he follows his vigorous presentation of the facts. It is the best account extant of judicial and legal tyranny from the reign of James I. to the period of his own indictment.

It is not an objection to his "Defence" that it designates so palpably individuals who were prominent in the service of the bad statute, but that it is so solicitous to do so. That makes his own personality too prominent. But he was right in arraigning men. Of course he hurt their feelings, and the feelings of their relatives. It was right that he should do so, in the interest of all men. It is very extraordinary that persons who complain that his language hurt their feelings, should never once have considered *the feelings of the fugitive and of his family.* They wanted the luxuries of self-respect, consideration, and fidelity to the Constitution, all at the expense of the poor trembling fugitive's necessities of life and freedom.

May there ever be a plain-speaking champion of the weaker side ! If a man in this country undertakes to wring his little luxuries out of the oppressed and suffering, he need not be surprised if some one depicts his arrogant meanness in a stern and unpolite vernacular.

But his sincerity was not all reserved for his opponents. His letters to public men who were his friends, or who were friendly to the ideas which he made paramount, show the same inflexible judgment. He addressed them with a frankness which they could ill sustain, unless they were at heart devoted to the same law of right and the real welfare of the country. The boldness of his requisitions upon friendship, in the name of the righteousness which he was willing to serve to the uttermost, alienated some who could not stand the test. Men like to be flattered for their past service, and entreated to persevere. He was too patriotic, too solemnly penetrated with the dangers of the country, to do either. On this point the dearest friend could never lead him astray. Conscience set aside the susceptible disposition at the first summons of a great political or moral truth ; and he was incapable of making any allowance for the difficulty some men have to be simple-minded. Some noble men, whose services to the commonwealth cannot be too highly rated, sometimes thought that he was intolerant. It was because they were not yet his equals in courage, determination, and straightness. He could dare more, resolve more, and walk more plainly than any of his friends.

It was Dante who used to throw stones at women and children whom he overheard reviling his party ; and, in a heated discussion, he once said, "Such infamous talk is to be answered, not with arguments, but with the knife."

> " Dante, who loved well because he hated,
> Hated wickedness that hinders loving."

Anthony Burns was carried back to the South in vindication of a Republican form of government, and as a symbol in ebony of the constitutional alacrity of the North. No doubt his master, from the time that Anthony held the hands of Parker and Phillips, and felt their love of freedom, considered him a bad piece of property, for he was virtually manumitted when he was remanded. Anthony might take to preaching, for which it seems he had an inborn taste, and the plantation hands would listen, mute as the fishes, but quite as heedful, which his namesake once addressed. So the money which was raised to purchase him in Boston, but which was refused there, by advice of counsel, on great constitutional grounds, became acceptable in Georgia, where a bird in the hand was better than one who might take to the bush, with a whole flock behind him.

Anthony's understanding had not been minutely cultivated at the South, so he passed at first for a rather dull person when he was received into the college at Oberlin, Ohio. The teachers had yet to loosen the clog of stupidity which slavery had fastened to his mind. Their words, in the attempt to discover his capacity for learning something, fell into the calloused marks which bondage made in entering his soul. But it is reported by one who knew him, that, " The change that came over him in a short time was one of the most wonderful things I ever witnessed. When it fairly dawned upon him that he *could* learn to read, his zeal to improve was unbounded. He was at his books the whole time, and his capacity for learning developed more and more. The whole manner of the man was altered ; and the expression of his countenance changed so much that, in less than a year, nobody would have recognized in him the half-stultified wretch, for whose re-enslavement the enlightened City of Boston raised a chivalrous army."

One of the earliest proofs of his new accomplishments was a letter to Mr. Parker; the handwriting may have astonished the illegible scholar, but the love might be expected. Here it is, a little helped in spelling:

Oberlin, Ohio, Jan. 13, 1856.

DEAR MR. PARKER,—SIR,—It is with much pleasure that I am now called upon to take my pen in hand to write you a few lines, which, I truly hope will find you and family at this time enjoying the blessing and happiness of the Lord, and all other brethren and friends. Sir, I suppose that you think that I hath forgotten you and your love and kindness towards me in the time of trouble, but, thanks be to the Lord, I hath not, and shall I, until my latest breath. I still continue to praise thee in the name of the Lord our God.

Dear Mr. Parker, I would have written you a letter long before this, but as you know that my learning or education was very bad, it is for this cause that I did not, but I hope you will not think hard of this; but having made some progress in this my studies, I now avail myself of the opportunity of writing you a few lines, hoping that they will be accepted of by you.

I am here in Oberlin, trying to do the best I can, hoping that, through Christ my Lord, and the assistance of you all, my friends, I shall be able to obtain an education for the purpose of preaching gospel. Oh, that I had that manner and power of speech which you now obtain: methinks that much good might be done in the name of the Lord. When I look at that number of heathen nations where I might, some day, do a great deal of good, it makes me beg for help, when I would not; therefore, for this cause I ask your aid, and the aid of all my friends, in the name of God our Father.

Very respectfully yours,
ANTHONY BURNS.

It seems, then, that his ambition was to fit himself for missionary work among the men of his own race abroad. Mr. Parker inspired him with a more practical conception, as we gather from Anthony's second and last letter of February, 1856.

DEAR MR. PARKER,—It is with much pleasure that I take the opportunity to acknowledge the receipt of your kind letter, which was highly gratifying to me. I was glad to read the words fallen from your mouth; it put me much in mind of the time when I was in the Court-house, in the time of great trouble.

I know that the field is large in the South, where many fear to go, but who knows but that the Lord is a-going to make of me a Moses, in leading His people out of bondage? I believe He hath a greater work for me than many may think, and it is for this cause I beg your prayers. You add that the sooner I get into the field the better, for the harvest is truly ripe, and the laborers, as you say, are few in the South fields.

Please give my best respects to Mr. Phillips, and to all of my friends. The people here want greatly to know who are my friends, but I know of no others greater than you two, therefore I look to you as my friends.

Will you please to pray for me, that I may hold out faithfully to the end?

We doubt if he undertook any Southern expedition to point his sluggish countrymen towards the North Star, or to create among them a legitimate discontent with their condition. But we next find him the pastor of a colored society at St. Catherine's, C.W., to whom he was very devoted. The exposure which he suffered last winter (1861–2) in his unremitting efforts to serve them, and to clear them from debt, planted consumption within him. He freed them from debt, but paid the great one himself not long ago.

CHAPTER XXI.

The Kansas and Nebraska Bill—Capt. John Brown—The Fremont Presidential Campaign —Fac-Simile Letter to Hon. J. P. Hale—Mr. Yeadon—Hon. Charles Sumner— Letters.

DURING the Congressional Session of 1853–54, a Bill to establish a territorial government in Nebraska passed the House of Representatives ; but its passage was unexpectedly resisted in the Senate, principally by members from slave States, on the ground that the Missouri Compromise would have the effect of securing a vast territory for free-labor, to be eventually divided into two or three free States, whose senators and representatives in Congress would fatally preponderate over the interests of slavery. A repeal of the Missouri Compromise was not immediately pressed by the South, but the defeat of the Bill to organize the territory was a preliminary question.

This is the text of the Compromise in the Missouri Bill :—

And be it further enacted, that in all that territory ceded by France to the United States, under the name of Louisiana, which lies north of 36° 30′ north latitude, not included within the limits of the State contemplated by this Act, slavery and involuntary servitude, otherwise than in the punishment of crime, whereof the parties shall have been duly convicted, shall be, and hereby is, prohibited for ever.

Early in 1854, Mr. Douglass, of Illinois, proposed to repeal that clause, by the introduction of the following provision in the Bill for the territorial organization of Nebraska :—

And when admitted as a State or States, the said territory, or any portion of the same, shall be received into the Union, with or without slavery, as their constitutions may prescribe at the time of their admission.

The pretext was that this provision maintained the great principle of popular sovereignty, by which the will of the people of a territory, deliberately expressed by their majority, should decide the character of their local institutions, and not the passage by Congress of a Bill which might eventually be found detrimental to the interests of a State and repugnant to the feelings of its majority. At the same time, the secret motive of this provision which repealed the Missouri Compromise, was betrayed by an amendment to the Territorial Bill, introduced by the Committee on Territories, of which Mr. Douglass was the chairman, to the effect that two territories were to be created out of that part of the national domain called Nebraska, one of which was to preserve the old name, and the other was to be called Kansas. In other words, the South wanted two slave States instead of one. Hence the subsequent title of " Kansas-Nebraska Bill."

Notwithstanding the vigorous opposition of Senators Chase, Sumner, and Seward, and Representatives Wade, Giddings, Gerritt Smith, and others, including one or two from Southern States, the amended Bill passed the Senate on the 4th of March, and the House on the 15th of May.

This abolition of a time-honored compromise stirred all parties at the North with indignation : the old Whig who had hitherto supported every pro-slavery measure of every Administration, in the name of the Constitution, and to preserve the Union, now met his anti-slavery foe of the new Republican party on the same platform. Distinguished men were heard to say, that here at length was a real outrage perpetrated by the South. The violation of the most sacred feelings of the heart by the passage of the Fugitive Slave Bill had not touched them ; the violation of a contract almost converted them to anti-slavery opinions ; so great, in a commercial circle, is the regard for a written promise to do or to pay, so little is the reverence for the unwritten prescription of humanity and equity.

Notwithstanding this inconsistency, a powerful stimulus was given to emigration into the new territories, principally into the more southerly one of Kansas, which promised to become a great agricultural region. For the new converts to a temporary disgust for slavery were monied men, and they helped to frame and feed companies and societies, which sent settlers into the new field, at the same time that the men of Missouri were flocking over the border with their slaves, and Southern bands were organizing to invade the territory and secure it for slavery.

The history of the next few years is that of bloody outrage in Kansas, of intrigue in Congress ; in both places the friends of freedom achieved a noble resistance. The crime against Kansas was met in all the measures behind which the convenient doctrine of popular sovereignty was hiding—the famous Lecompton Bill, for instance, which a temporary pro-slavery majority in the territory, with the aid of executive patronage, succeeded in getting before Congress.

But these details are beyond my limits.

TO PROFESSOR EDWARD DESOR.

Boston, May 24, 1854.

DEAR DESOR,—I thank you for your kind note which yesterday came to hand, and write forthwith, as the steamer goes to-day. The Nebraska Bill passed the House, Monday at 11 P.M., by a vote of 100 nays to 113 yeas. It is a most infamous thing. I had no doubt it would pass from the beginning. It is a Government measure ; not an office-holder in the United States has said a public word against it, not one who holds a Government office, and there are 40,000 such in the nation! I am getting up a convention from all the Free States for the 4th of July, to meet at some central place—Pittsburgh or Buffalo—and organize for efficient action.

I make no doubt that the American Government will take sides with Russia in the coming contest. See why.

1. It is impossible to sustain 2,000,000 Turks, with an empire in a state of decadence, against a population of 11,000,000 Christians who are capable of progress.

2. England and France and Austria do not wish to preserve the Turkish Empire, England wants Candia and Ægypt; France, Tunis and Tripoli ; Austria, Croatia, Bosnia, Servia, Montenegro, &c., as much as Russia wants Moldavia, Wallachia, and Bulgaria. I think each will have what it wants; the quarrel is not about the protection, but the partition of Turkey.

3. In this quarrel the United States hope to seize Cuba and perhaps Hayti. Russia will favor this; (1.) out of hostility to Spain, with whom there appears to be some alienation; (2.) out of hatred to England, whom of course she wishes to molest. And the American Government I think will not openly favor Russia, but secretly, and yet will continue to make money out of both parties.

4. Little is known about the privateers—but I make no doubt there will be plenty of them. There is only one difficulty ; there is no port in Europe for them to take their prizes to.

The North takes little interest in the European struggle, except so far as it raises the price of American produce, and cares not who conquers or who is conquered so long as we can make money by it. Everything is dear, everybody making money; what do we care for besides? The South takes sides with Russia. Alone of all Europe she never found fault with American slavery; she sympathizes with us. This is what the Southern journals have said openly, all winter long. We must have a dreadful chastisement one day. I suppose it will come from our own towns, from civil war.

TO HON. CHARLES SUMNER.

Sunday Night, January, 1855.

DEAR SUMNER,—I have seen only the briefest report of your sayings in Senate, but must needs thank you for it, before I go to bed. Every Session raises you higher and higher. Not that you display more mind than men looked for; but because you stand up in Congress as the man with a conscience which reflects the natural law of God written in the human heart. Here you and Chase stand side by side. Send me the Bill which passed: I want it " summarily."

Yours,

T. P.

TO THE SAME.

Boston, January 14, 1856.

MY DEAR SUMNER,—Many thanks for your two last letters and the various documents. If you could let me have a copy of the "Two Quartos" for Desor, I would send it soon. It is a highly valuable book admirably printed.

I am glad you found —— is in so good humor; he has a large quantity of a low kind of conscientiousness which bears the same relation to morality, that church-going and litany-repeating bears to religion. And as he goes to Peabody's church of the Hunkers, and after him repeats, "Have mercy on us miserable offenders," and calls it "Christianity," so he abstains from voting, now he is judge, and thinks thereby to be fair and just. But the man has no more moral intuitions than an ox. In place of conscience he has attorney logic, powers of deduction. I think him an exceedingly dangerous man to be on the bench of the Supreme Court. If I were the people of the United States I would reconstruct the judicial district, and his should be limited to Nix's Mate in Boston Harbor, or to the Thirteenth Ward of Boston."* "*Fœnum habet in cornu, tu Romane, Caveto!*" We will look after the impeachments. I think we had better limit our efforts to Kane† at first; but yet I would have the petition so general as to cover any case of attack upon the rights of man. We will have one in motion at the Anti-slavery Convention in Boston, week after next; some are already in progress (Wendell Phillips says) in the country.

---

* A ward, namely, on the same footing as the Greek Kalends—nowhere at all.

† Petitions for the impeachment of judges, like Kane of Philadelphia, who ruled to convict men for a violation of the Fugitive Slave Bill.

You see what is done against the Personal Liberty Law * in the General Court. If there is any danger we will have a remonstrance, and Wendell, and various others (T. P. amongst them) will appear before the committee. I fear nothing. For just now there is some indignation against the President's message, and much against the Border ruffians, and I think Massachusetts will not take her tail between her legs at the command of the Pavement (State Street), of Hunkers. But even if this should be done, and the law repealed, it will be no ultimate harm, for it will only have the effect of an ambuscado, and will bring the enemy into a tight place. But I go for victory in every skirmish.

I hope you will not be diverted from your course by anything which the Hunkers say (or do) against the Liberty Law (don't call it Bill—leave that term for the Fugitive Slave Bill). Now is the time for you to strike a great blow. The North is ready, and if you are at all, let it be on the side of going too fast and too far, not the other. It will turn out to your own advantage, as well as the success of the right. For,—

1. The North feels insulted and outraged, though not yet brought into peril—I wish she did feel that as I feel it—and will heartily respond to a trumpet-note from a man who loves liberty. She is tired of the gong which the Whigs and others have been beating as a call to dinner so long.

2. Gardner † is after your place. He has set one eye on the Presidency or Vice-Presidency at least—the other on the *Senatorship*. His chances are not contemptible, especially if all the Know-Nothing lodges continue in full blast as now. If there is only a quantitative difference between him and you, I fear the result. If there be a qualitative difference as between light and darkness—and there really is that unlikeness in your aims and schemes—then I think Gardner goes into private life, and you continue to serve the cause of justice in the Senate of United States. The more decided your course is against slavery, and the further you depart from the Hunkers, the more secure is your position. So it seems to me.

I take *this* ground in my lectures and talks :—

1. Each State must practically interpret the Constitution for itself in making its own laws.

2. The rendition clause must be interpreted to include only such as justly owe service or labor, *i. e.* owe it on contract for a good and sufficient consideration ; and accordingly slaves do not come under that clause at all, for no man can justly owe slave service, &c.

3. Each free State must make a law declaring all persons who enter their borders free, and punish with imprisonment, in State's prison, not less than five nor more than ten years, all who attempt to curtail them ;

---

* Bill introduced into the Massachusetts Legislature to protect her citizens against the operation of the Fugitive Slave Law, by emphasizing the State laws and opinions against slave-catching. It must be understood, that the original clause in the Constitution of the United States, from which the Fugitive Slave Bill purported to derive its authority, simply declared that persons escaping from service were to be given up, but left each State to prescribe the method ; and, of course, implicitly, in the interest of liberty, to make it as difficult as possible. Massachusetts refused the use of her prisons.

† A governor of Massachusetts, elected by Know-Nothing (Anti-Catholic) votes.

must forbid all dealing in men on our soil, all engagement in the American slave-trade.

4. The Const. guarantees to each State a "republican form of Government;" this clause puts slavery in the Southern States as completely in the power of Congress as it puts Papism, Czarism, hereditary nobility, or hereditary monarchy. If South Carolina were to establish a Government, exactly like that of Rome, to-day, Congress would be bound to interfere and establish a republican form of Government. Slavery is as much anti-republican as Papism. Therefore, &c. That is part of my card.

Now a word about the speakership. *

The open war between slavery and freedom is begun in two places,—

1. In Congress. (1.) In the Senate the slave power has taken the committees, and fortified itself in that Sebastopol of despotism. (2.) In the House the fight goes on, the slave power aiming to carry the committees as in the Senate already.

Here we must fight to the bitter end.

2. In Kansas. There the war is not by *ballots* but *bullets*.† Just now the Border ruffians are driven back. It is only for a moment. They will return. But it is sad to think that the only actual victory over slavery attained in our time has been with Sharp's rifles. My dear Sumner, that looks ominous of the means by which we are to resist our enemy. Thank God, I can buy a sword without selling my shirt!

Now, I should as soon think of letting the Border ruffians into Kansas, with their slaves, to organize the slave power in that territory and take possession of the new soil, as I should of letting the Hunkers into the speakership, with their ideas of despotism, to organize the slave power in the committees of that body. I would not yield if I sat till the 4th of March, 1857, in permanent session. ‡

I take it, Kansas cannot this session come in as a free State. It might pass the House, not the Senate; or, if that, not the Cabinet; so it goes over to the next Administration. If that is pro-slavery, see what follows. All the power of the new Cabinet will be directed to put slavery into Kansas; and it may be successful—unless the thermometer stays at 17° below 0 a good while. If slavery goes to Kansas, it goes to all the territories, and then see what a fix we are in.

Now it seems to me possible, with the greatest skill and adroitness, to carry the Presidency for the North. For, there will be—(1,) conscience Whigs;§ (2,) revolting Democrats; (3,) Northern Know-

---

* Alluding to the struggle for the election of Speaker of the House of Representatives, who has great influence in the appointment of committees, &c.

† Alludes to a toast once given at a public dinner by Hon. R. C. Winthrop, a member of the old Whig party,—the substance of which was that ballots and bullets were the only currency of a free people; a sentiment that is not realized in a way that the old Whig party had anticipated. But if the ballots of that party had been consistently and sternly anti-slavery, the bullets might possibly have been dispensed with.

‡ This struggle for the speakership resulted in the election of Mr. (now Major-General) Banks, a Republican.

§ A term which arose during the war with Mexico, when a few Whigs refused to vote for a resolution that war existed by the act of Mexico, simply because war existed by the act of the United States, made upon Mexico by a Pro-slavery Administration, with a view to the future extension of slavery. It was not easy to vote against a war in which the country was already engaged, and thus to refuse supplies for it. A few Whigs did this.

Nothings; (4,). Republicans; (5,) the old anti-slavery organization, Liberty-party men, Garrisonians, &c. All these will want a man who favors the right. On the other side will be—(1,) the straight Whigs;* (2,) the Democrats (I mean the Satanic democracy); they will want a strong slavery man of any stripe.

Can't we find a man thoroughly faithful to humanity, of large powers, who can be elected?

Everything seems to favor us. There is a practical question in Kansas and the territories; the South is arrogant, and the North inclined to be mad. God bless you!

THEODORE PARKER.

FROM THE JOURNAL.

April 2, 1856.—Saw the Kansas party go off, Dr. Charles K. Sanborn at their head, about forty, nearly half of them women and children. There were twenty copies of "Sharp's Rights of the People"† in their hands, of the new and improved edition, and divers Colt's six-shooters also. As the bell rung for the train to move, they were singing, "When I can read my title clear." One of the verses would have some meaning:—

"Should earth against my soul engage,
And hellish darts be hurl'd,
Then I can smile at Satan's rage,
A face a frowning world."

But what a comment were the weapons of that company on the boasted democracy of America! These rifles and pistols were to defend their soil from the American Government, which wishes to plant slavery in Kansas!

Capt. John Brown, of North Elba, a township in the Adirondack Mountains of New York, went to Kansas with his sons, not so much to help develope the embryo State's material as its moral resources, and to do what he could to secure there a preponderance for freedom. At Black Jack and Osawatomie he fired the first shots of the new revolution; they gave a practical voice to the teachings of the Music Hall; for the prayers of the old Presbyterian captain and the anti-supernatural preacher were identical in substance and prophecy, and heard to advantage by the same Father of both, who hates iniquity. They were both Democrats of the New America, whose tread we hear above the graves of these two dear and noble sons; their lives well sepa-

---

* Those, namely, who would vote for anything that the dominant interest conceived to be essential for the preservation of the Union and the "constitutional guarantees." —their motto was, " Our country, right or wrong"—whatever its boundaries might be. The straight Whigs are responsible for a deal of crookedness.
† Sharp's Rifles.

rated religion from theology, their deaths in different ways have made the same essential truths illustrious.

After Capt. Brown left Kansas, he devoted himself to the organization of an attempt to weaken slavery by making raids upon the Border States, whose effect would be, he supposed, to create panic and distrust in the slave-holders, and to excite gradually such a desire for liberty in the blacks that, not content with escaping, they would conspire and form bands in the mountains, centres of disaffection, and ultimately of revolution. What his precise plans were was never known, with any thoroughness of detail, to his friends. They were acquainted with his general object, and thought that the time was good enough, in the failure of political expedients, to try all possible methods of injuring the great enemy of the country and of the rights of man.

Mr. Parker was one of five persons who constituted themselves a committee to aid John Brown in whatsoever attempts he might choose to make to impair the institution of slavery. He had established in Kansas a great reputation for coolness, sagacity, and all manly traits ; he hated the slave-holder and loved his victim. He had uniformly defeated the open or secret efforts of men who had sworn to hunt him down and take his life ; and his success in taking a large body of negroes safe to Canada, out of the very midst of the ruffians in the territory, showed that he possessed ability for the kind of enterprise that he premeditated.

The committee trusted him implicitly, and helped him as far as they could. Mr. Parker never missed a meeting ; he contributed from his own funds and raised money from others. " I have friends," he often said, " who will give me money, without asking any questions, trusting that I will see it properly applied. I can get limited supplies in this way." He believed in John Brown, but not in the success of any particular plan of his. When a member of the committee called upon him to confer as to the possibility of raising a sufficient sum of money to carry on Brown's general work, he said, " I doubt whether things of the kind will succeed. But we shall make a great many failures before we discover the right way of getting at it. This may as well be one of them."

Capt. Brown would not pledge himself to carry out any special plan. He wanted to be left free to make his own plan, at the time and in the direction which might seem to him most promising. Consequently, when the affair at Harper's Ferry took place, the committee knew that it was John Brown's blow, though he had not confided it to them. Neither Mr. Parker nor any other member of the committee endeavored to understand his movements in advance.

Before John Brown's last journey into Kansas, he left a document with Mr. Parker, which history has considerably improved with her annotations and *excursus*. It is written upon a half sheet of paper ; the letters tremble slightly in their downward stroke, as if the fore-finger were conscious that it must not pull a pen like a trigger :—

Old Brown's farewell to the Plymouth Rocks, Bunker Hill Monuments, Charter Oaks, and Uncle Thom's Cabins.

He has left for Kansas; was trying since he came out of the territory to secure an outfit, or, in other words, the *means of arming and thoroughly equiping* his regular minuet men who are mixed up with the people of Kansas; and he leaves the States with a feeling of deepest sadness; that after having exhausted his own small means, and with his family and his brave men suffered hunger, cold, nakedness, and some of them sickness, wounds, imprisonment, cruel treatment, and others death ; that after lying on the ground for months in the most sickly, unwholesome, and uncomfortable places, with sick and wounded, destitute of any shelter, and hunted like wolves ; sustained and cared for in part by Indians ; that after all this, in order to sustain a cause (which every citizen of this "*glorious Republic*" is under equal moral obligation to do; and for the neglect of which he will be held accountable to God) in which every man, woman, and child of the entire human family has a deep and awful interest; that when *no wages are asked or expected,* he cannot secure (amidst all the wealth, luxury, and extravagance of this "Heaven exalted" people) even the necessary supplies of the common soldier.

JOHN BROWN.

Boston, April, A.D. 1857.

Here are letters from John Brown to Mr. Parker. He writes first from Tabor, where the rifles and revolvers were deposited, which were subsequently removed to his hired house in Maryland :—

TO REV. THEODORE PARKER, BOSTON, MASS.

Tabor, Fremont Co., Iowa, Sept. 11, 1857.

MY DEAR SIR,—Please find on other side first number of a series of tracts lately gotten up here. I need not say I did not prepare it, but I would be glad to know what you think of it, and much obliged for any suggestions you see proper to make.

My particular object in writing is to say that I am in immediate want of some 500 or 1000 dollars, for secret service, and no questions asked. I want the friends of freedom to " prove me now herewith." Will you bring this matter before your congregation, or exert your influence in some way, to have it or some part of it raised, and placed in the hands of Geo. L. Stearns, Esq., Boston, subject to my order? I should highly prize a letter from you, directed on the *envelope* to Jonas Jones, Esq., Tabor, Fremont Co., Iowa.

Have no news to send *by letter*.

Very respectfully your friend,

JOHN BROWN.

TO THE SAME.

American House, Boston, March 4, 1858.

MY DEAR SIR,—I shall be most happy to see you at my room (126) in this house, at any and at all hours that may suit your own convenience, or that of friends. Mr. Sanborn asked me to be here by Friday evening or before, and as I was anxious to have all the time I could get, I came on at once. Please call by yourself and with friends as you can. Please inquire for Mr. (not Capt.) Brown, of New York.

Your friend,

JOHN BROWN.

TO THE SAME.

Rochester, N.Y., Feb. 2, 1858.

MY DEAR SIR,—I am again out of Kansas, and am at this time concealing my whereabouts, but for very different reasons, however, than those I had for doing so at Boston last spring. I have nearly perfected arrangements for carrying out an important measure, in which the world has a deep interest, as well as Kansas, and only lack from 500 to 800 dollars to enable me to do so. The same object for which I asked for secret-service money last Fall. It is my only errand here, and I have written some of our mutual friends in regard to it, but none of them understand my views so well as you do; and I cannot explain without their first committing themselves more than I know of their doing. I have heard that Parker Pillsbury, and some others in your quarter, hold out ideas similar to those on which I act, but I have no personal acquaintance with them, and know nothing of their influence or means. Cannot you either by direct or indirect action do something to further me? Do you not know of some parties whom you could induce to give their abolition theories a thorough practical shape? I hope this will prove to be the last time I shall be driven to harass a friend in such a way. Do you think any of my Garrisonian friends either at Boston, Worcester, or in any other place, can be induced to supply a little " straw," if I will absolutely make " bricks" ?

I have written George L. Stearns, Esq., of Medford, and Mr. F. B. Sanborn, of Concord, but I am not informed as to how deeply dyed

Abolitionists those friends are, and must beg of you to consider this communication strictly confidential, unless you know of parties who will feel, and act, and hold their peace. I want to bring the thing about during the next sixty days. Please write, N. Hawkins, care William J. Watkins, Esq., Rochester, New York.

Very respectfully your friend,
JOHN BROWN.

TO THE SAME.

Boston, Mass., March 7, 1858.

MY DEAR SIR,—Since you know that I have an almost countless brood of poor hungry chickens to "scratch for," you will not reproach me for scratching even on the Sabbath. At any rate I trust God will not. I want you to undertake to provide a substitute for an address you saw last season, directed to the officers and soldiers of the United States army. The ideas contained in that address I, of course, like, for I furnished the skeleton. I never had the ability to clothe those ideas in language at all to satisfy myself, and I was by no means satisfied with the style of that address, and do not know as I can give any correct idea of what I want. I will, however, "try." In the first place, it must be short, or it will not be generally read. It must be in the simplest or plainest language; without the least affectation of the scholar about it, and yet be worded with great clearness and power. The anonymous writer must (in the language of the Paddy) be "after others," and not "after himself, at all, at all." If the spirit that "communicated" Franklin's Poor Richard (or some other good spirit) would dictate, I think it would be quite as well employed as the "dear sister spirits" have been for some years past. The address should be appropriate, and particularly adapted to the peculiar circumstances we anticipate, and should look to the actual change of service from that of Satan to the service of God. It should be, in short, a most earnest and powerful appeal to man's sense of right, and to their feelings of humanity. Soldiers are men, and no man can certainly calculate the value and importance of getting a single "nail into old Captain Kidd's chest." It should be provided beforehand, and be ready in advance to distribute, by all persons, male and female, who may be disposed to favor the right.

I also want a similar short address, appropriate to the peculiar circumstances, intended for all persons, old and young, male and female, slave-holding and non-slave-holding, to be sent out broadcast over the entire nation. So by every male and female prisoner on being set at liberty, and to be read by them during confinement. I know that men will listen, and reflect too, under such circumstances. Persons will hear your anti-slavery lectures, or abolition lectures, when they have become virtually slaves themselves. The impressions made on prisoners by kindness and plain dealing, instead of barbarous and cruel treatment, such as they might give, and instead of being slaughtered like vile reptiles, as they might very naturally expect, are not only powerful, but lasting. Females are susceptible of being carried away entirely by the kindness of an intrepid and magnanimous soldier, even when his bare name was a terror but the day previous. Now, dear sir, I have told you about as well as I know how to, what I am anxious at once to secure. Will you write the tracts, or get them written, so that I may commence " colporteur"?

Very respectfully your friend,
JOHN BROWN.

P.S.—If I should never see you again, please drop me a line (enclosed to Stephen Smith, Esq., Lombard Street, Philadelphia) at once, saying what you will encourage me to expect. You are at liberty to make every prudent use of this to stir up any friend. Yours for the right,

J. B.

The attempt at Harper's Ferry was not made till the autumn of 1859, more than a year and a half after the date of this letter. In the meantime Mr. Parker had left the country.

John Brown's final plan was betrayed to the Government by this anonymous letter, which was addressed to the Secretary of War:—

Cincinnati, Aug. 20, 1859.

SIR,—I have lately received information of a movement of so great importance, that I feel it to be my duty to impart it to you without delay. I have discovered the existence of a secret association, having for its object the liberation of the slaves at the South by a general insurrection. The leader of the movement is old John Brown, late of Kansas. He has been in Canada during the winter, drilling the negroes there, and they are only waiting his word to start for the South to assist the slaves. They have one of the leading men, a white man, in an armory in Maryland; where it is situated I have not been able to learn. As soon as everything is ready, those of their number, who are in the Northern States and Canada, are to come in small companies to their rendezvous, which is in the mountains in Virginia. They will pass down through Pennsylvania and Maryland, and enter Virginia at Harper's Ferry. Brown left the North about three or four weeks ago, and will arm the negroes and strike the blow in a few weeks, and so that whatever is done must be done at once. They have a large quantity of arms at their rendezvous, and probably distributing them already. As I am not fully in their confidence this is all the information I can give you. I dare not sign my name to this, but I trust you will not disregard the warning on that account.

But the Secretary took no notice of this warning, either deeming the enterprise preposterous, or desiring that just such an attempt as that might be made, to confirm the disunion feeling of the South; for Southern politicians were meditating the conspiracy in whose interest this very Secretary (John B. Floyd) was at that time removing arms of the United States from Northern to Southern arsenals.

In the night of Sunday, October 16, John Brown took possession of the arsenal at Harper's Ferry. A few details * of his
demeanor subsequent to his surrender, will fitly introduce the
letter which Mr. Parker wrote from Rome, when he heard of the
trial and sentence of his friend.

While the dead and wounded yet lay on the lawn before the engine-
house, Brown was assailed with questions by the bystanders, "which,"
the *Baltimore American* says, "he answered clearly and freely. He
talked calmly to those about him, defending his course, and avowing
that he had only done what was right." The modesty of genuine worth
speaks out in his characteristic answers to two of the questions put to
him.

"Are you Captain Brown, of Kansas ? "

"I am sometimes called so."

"He never assumed the title of Captain," says Redpath,† "even in
Kansas, where titles were as common as proper names."

"Are you Osawatomie Brown ? "

"I tried to do my duty there."

In the words of Redpath, "This sentence was a key to his whole
life. Neither honor nor glory moved him ; the voice of duty was the
only one he heard."

When asked if he expected to kill people, in order to carry his point,
he answered, "I did not wish to do so, but you forced us to it." He
reminded the questioners that he had the town at his mercy ; that he
could have burnt it, and murdered the inhabitants, but did not ; he had
treated the prisoners with courtesy. "His conversation," says the
American, "bore the impression of the conviction that whatever he had
done to free slaves, was right, and that in the warfare in which he was
engaged, he was entitled to be treated with all the respect of a prisoner
of war."

To some of Mason's ‡ questions Brown replied, "I could easily have
saved myself had I exercised my own better judgment rather than
yielded to my feelings. I had the means to make myself secure without any escape, but I allowed myself to be surrounded by being too
tardy. I should have gone away, but I had thirty odd prisoners, whose
wives and daughters were in tears for their safety ; and I felt for them.
Besides, I wanted to allay the fears of those who believed we came here
to burn and kill. For this reason, I allowed the train to cross the
bridge, and gave them full liberty to pass on. I did it only to spare
the feelings of those passengers and their families, and to allay the
apprehensions that you had got here, in your vicinity, a band of men
who had no regard for life and property, nor any feelings of humanity."

When asked his object in coming there, he answered, "We came to

---

* "The Anti-Slavery History of the John Brown Year ; being the Twenty-seventh
Annual Report of the American Anti-Slavery Society."

† Author of a Life of Capt. John Brown.

‡ Senator Mason, of Virginia, the author of the Fugitive Slave Bill, and now (1863)
agent of the Southern Rebellion in London.

free the slaves, and only that." "How do you justify your acts?" "I think I did right, and that others will do right who interfere with you, at any time and at all times. I hold that the golden rule—'Do unto others as you would that others should do unto you'—applies to all who would help others to gain their liberty." To a bystander who put, in substance, the same question, some time after, he replied, "Upon the golden rule—I pity the poor in bondage, that have none to help them; that is why I am here, not to gratify any personal animosity, revenge, or vindictive spirit. It is my sympathy with the oppressed and the wronged, that are as good as you, and as precious in the sight of God." To another question, he said (telling the reporter, "You may report that"), "I want you to understand that I respect the rights of the poorest and weakest of colored people, oppressed by the slave system, just as much as I do those of the most wealthy and powerful. That is the idea that has moved me, and that alone. We expected no reward, except the satisfaction of endeavoring to do for those in distress and greatly oppressed as we would be done by. The cry of distress of the oppressed is my reason, and the only thing that prompted me to come here." "Why did you do it secretly?" "Because I thought that necessary to success; for no other reason." When asked if he had seen Gerritt Smith's letter, which, according to the *New York Herald* of the day before, "speaks of the folly of attempting to strike the shackles off the slaves by the force of moral suasion or legal agitation, and predicts that the next movement made, in the direction of negro emancipation would be an insurrection in the South," he said, "I have not seen the *New York Herald* for some days past; but I presume from your remark about the gist of the letter that I should concur with it. I agree with Mr. Smith that moral suasion is hopeless. I don't think the people of the Slave States will ever consider the subject of slavery in its true light, till some other argument is resorted to than moral suasion." Vallandigham * asked, "Did you expect a general rising of the slaves in case of your success?" "No, sir, nor did I wish it. I expected to gather them up from time to time, and set them free." "Did you expect to hold possession here till then?" "Well, probably, I had quite a different idea. I do not know that I ought to reveal my plans. I am here a prisoner, and wounded, because I foolishly allowed myself to be so. You overrate your strength in supposing I could have been taken if I had not allowed it. I was too tardy after commencing the open attack,—in delaying my movements through Monday night, and up to the time I was attacked by the Government troops. It was all occasioned by my desire to spare the feelings of my prisoners, and their families, and the community at large." The reporter having offered to report anything further he would like to say, he answered, "I have nothing to say, only that I claim to be here in carrying out a measure I believe perfectly justifiable, and not to act the part of an incendiary or ruffian; but to aid those suffering great wrong. I wish to say, furthermore, that you had better, all you people at the South, prepare yourselves

---

* At that time a member of the House of Representatives; at present (1863) the candidate of the Southern Rebellion for the gubernatorial chair of Ohio.

for a settlement of this question, that must come up for settlement, sooner than you are prepared for it. The sooner you are prepared, the better. You may dispose of me very easily. I am nearly disposed of now; but this question is still to be settled—this negro question, I mean: the end of that is not yet. These wounds were inflicted upon me — both sabre cuts on my head, and bayonet stabs in different parts of my body—some minutes after I had ceased fighting, and had consented to surrender, for the benefit of others, not for my own" [this statement was vehemently denied by all around]. "I believe the Major" [meaning Lieut. Stuart, of the United States Cavalry] " would not have been alive but for that; I could have killed him just as easy as a mosquito, when he came in; but I supposed he only came to receive our surrender. There had been loud and long calls of 'Surrender' from us, as loud as men could yell; but in the confusion and excitement, I suppose we were not heard. I do not think the Major, or any one, meant to butcher us after we had surrendered." An officer here stated that the Marines had fired only when fired upon; but Brown insisted that they fired first. He was asked why he did not surrender before the attack. "I did not think it was my duty or interest to do so. We assured the prisoners that we did not wish to harm them, and they should be set at liberty. I exercised my best judgment, not believing the people would wantonly sacrifice their own fellow-citizens, when we offered to let them go, on condition of being allowed to change our position about a quarter of a mile. The prisoners agreed, by vote among themselves, to pass across the bridge with us. We wanted them only as a sort of guarantee of our own safety; that we should not be fired into. We took them, in the first place, as hostages, and to keep them from doing any harm. We did kill some men in defending ourselves: but I saw no one fire except directly in self-defence. Our orders were strict, not to harm any one not in arms against us." " Suppose you had every nigger in the United States, what would you do with them?" With emphasis, " Set them free!" "Your intention was to carry them off and free them?" "Not at all." "Was it your only object to free the negroes?" "Absolutely, our only object." "But you demanded and took Col. Washington's silver and watch." "Yes: we intended freely to appropriate the property of slave-holders to carry out our object. It was that, and only that, and with no desire to enrich ourselves with any plunder whatever."

Vallandigham, in these words, gives the impression made on him by his contact with the unvanquished captive :—" Captain John Brown is as brave and resolute a man as ever headed an insurrection, and, in a good cause and with a sufficient force, would have been a consummate partisan commander. He has coolness, daring, persistency, the Stoic faith and patience, and a firmness of will and purpose unconquerable. He is the farthest possible remove from the ordinary ruffian, fanatic, or madman."

When asked by Colonel Smith, who paid him a visit in company with a son of Governor Wise, " If he desired a clergyman to administer to him the consolations of religion," he answered that " he recognized no slave-holder, lay or clerical, nor any sympathizer with slavery, as a Christian." He gave the same reason afterwards for his refusal to accept the services of some clergymen who called upon him. He said he would as soon be attended to the scaffold by blacklegs or robbers of the worst kind, as by slave-holding ministers, or ministers sympathizing with slavery; and that, if he had his choice, he would rather be followed to the scaffold by barefooted, barelegged, ragged negro children, and their old grey-headed slave mothers, than by clergymen of this character. He would feel, he said, much prouder of such an escort, and wished he could have it. He told clergymen who called upon him, that they, and all slave-holders and sympathizers with slavery, had far more need of prayers themselves than he had, and he accordingly advised them to pray for themselves, and exhibit no concern about him. While making these remarks, he requested that he might not be understood as designing to offer any insult. In a letter to an anti-slavery minister, in Ohio, he said, "There are no ministers of Christ here. These ministers who profess to be Christian and hold slaves or advocate slavery, I cannot abide them. My knees will not bend in prayer with them, while their hands are stained with the blood of souls."

His minister was in a foreign land, also soon to offer himself up a sacrifice and testimony to the convictions of a lifetime.

As he was about leaving the gaol, a black woman with her little child in her arms, stood near his way. He stopped for a moment in his course, stooped over, and, with the tenderness of one whose love is as broad as the brotherhood of man, kissed it affectionately. "That mother," says the *Tribune's* correspondent, in relating the incident, "will be proud of that mark of distinction for her offspring; and some day, when over the ashes of John Brown the temple of Virginian liberty is reared, she may join in the joyful song of praise which, on that soil, will do justice to his memory." The same writer says, "On leaving the gaol, John Brown had on his face an expression of calmness and serenity characteristic of the patriot who is about to die with a living consciousness that he is laying down his life for the good of his fellow-creatures. His face was even joyous, and a forgiving smile rested upon his lips. His was the lightest heart, among friends or foes, in the whole of Charlestown that day, and not a word was spoken that was not an intuitive appreciation of his manly courage. Firmly, and with elastic step, he moved forward. He mounted the waggon which was to convey him to the scaffold, and took his seat with Captain Avis, the gaoler—whose admiration of his prisoner is of the profoundest nature. Mr. Sadler, the undertaker, rode with them. He, too, was one of Brown's staunchest friends in his confinement, and pays a noble tribute to his manly qualities. I was very near the old man, and scrutinized him closely. He seemed to take in the whole scene at a glance, and he straightened himself up proudly, as if to set to the soldiers an example of a soldier's courage. He remarked on the beauty of the country, " the more beautiful " to him, because he had " so long been shut from it." "You are more cheerful than I am, Captain Brown," said Mr. Sadler. " Yes," said the Captain, " I ought to be."

TO FRANCIS JACKSON.

Rome, Nov. 24, 1859.

MY DEAR FRIEND,—I see by a recent telegraph which the steamer of Nov. 2nd brought from Boston, that the Court found Capt. Brown guilty, and passed sentence upon him. It is said Friday, Dec. 2nd, is fixed as the day for hanging him. So, long before this reaches you, my friend will have passed on to the reward of his magnanimous public services, and his pure, upright private life. I am not well enough to be the minister to any congregation, least of all to one like that which, for so many years, helped my soul while it listened to my words. Surely, the 28th Congregational Society in Boston needs a minister, not half dead, but alive all over; and yet, while reading the accounts of the affair at Harper's Ferry, and of the sayings of certain men at Boston, whom you and I know only too well, I could not help wishing I was at home again *to use what poor remnant of power is left to me in defence of the True and the Right.*

America is rich in able men, in skilful writers, in ready and accomplished speakers. But few men dare treat public affairs with reference to the great principles of justice and the American Democracy; nay, few with reference to any remote future, or even with a comprehensive survey of the present. Our public writers ask what effect will this opinion have on the Democratic party, or the Republican party? how will it affect the Presidential election? what will the great State of Pennsylvania, or Ohio, or New York say to it? This is very unfortunate for us all, especially when the people have to deal practically, and that speedily, with a question concerning the very existence of Democratic institutions in America; for it is not to be denied that we must give up DEMOCRACY if we keep SLAVERY, or give up SLAVERY if we keep DEMOCRACY.

I greatly deplore this state of things. Our able men fail to perform their natural function, to give valuable instruction and advice to the people; and at the same time they debase and degrade themselves. The hurrahs and the offices they get are poor compensation for falseness to their own consciences.

In my best estate, I do not pretend to much political wisdom, and still less now while sick; but I wish yet to set down a few thoughts for your private eye, and, it may be, for the ear of the Fraternity. They are, at least, the result of long meditation on the subject; besides, they are not at all new nor peculiar to me, but are a part of the public knowledge of all enlightened men.

1. A MAN HELD AGAINST HIS WILL AS A SLAVE HAS A NATURAL RIGHT TO KILL EVERY ONE WHO SEEKS TO PREVENT HIS ENJOYMENT OF LIBERTY. This has long been recognized as a self-evident proposition, coming so directly from the primitive instincts of human nature, that it neither required proofs nor admitted them.

2. IT MAY BE A NATURAL DUTY OF THE SLAVE TO DEVELOPE THIS NATURAL RIGHT IN A PRACTICAL MANNER, AND ACTUALLY KILL ALL THOSE WHO SEEK TO PREVENT HIS ENJOYMENT OF LIBERTY. For if he continue patiently in bondage—First, he entails the foulest of

curses on his children; and, second, he encourages other men to commit the crime against nature which he allows his own master to commit. It is my duty to preserve my own body from starvation. If I fail thereof through sloth, I not only die, but incur the contempt and loathing of my acquaintances while I live. It is not less my duty to do all that is in my power to preserve my body and soul from slavery; and if I submit to that through cowardice, I not only become a bondman and suffer what thraldom inflicts, but I incur also the contempt and loathing of my acquaintance. Why do freemen scorn and despise a slave? Because they think his condition is a sign of his cowardice, and believe that he ought to prefer death to bondage. The Southerners hold the Africans in great contempt, though mothers of their children. Why? Simply because the Africans are slaves; that is, because the Africans fail to perform the natural duty of securing freedom by killing their oppressors.

3. THE FREEMAN HAS A NATURAL RIGHT TO HELP THE SLAVES RECOVER THEIR LIBERTY, AND IN THAT ENTERPRISE TO DO FOR THEM ALL WHICH THEY HAVE A RIGHT TO DO FOR THEMSELVES.

This statement, I think, requires no argument or illustration.

4. IT MAY BE A NATURAL DUTY FOR THE FREEMAN TO HELP THE SLAVES TO THE ENJOYMENT OF THEIR LIBERTY, AND AS MEANS TO THAT END, TO AID THEM IN KILLING ALL SUCH AS OPPOSE THEIR NATURAL FREEDOM.

If you were attacked by a wolf, I should not only have a *right* to aid you in getting rid of that enemy, but it would be my DUTY to help you in proportion to my power. If it were a MURDERER, and not a wolf, who attacked you, the duty would be still the same. Suppose it is not a murderer who would kill you, but a KIDNAPPER who would enslave, does that make it less my duty to help you out of the hands of your enemy? Suppose he is not a kidnapper who would make you a bondman, but a SLAVEHOLDER who would keep you one, does that remove my obligation to help you?

5. THE PERFORMANCE OF THIS DUTY IS TO BE CONTROLLED BY THE FREEMAN'S POWER AND OPPORTUNITY TO HELP THE SLAVES. (The impossible is never the obligatory). I cannot help the slaves in Dahomey or Bornou, and am not bound to try. I can help those who escape to my own neighborhood, and I ought to do so. My duty is commensurate with my power; and as my power increases my duty enlarges along with it. If I *could* help the bondmen in Virginia to their freedom as easy and effectually as I can aid the runaway at my own door, then I OUGHT to do so.

These five maxims have a direct application to America at this day, and the people of the Free States have a certain dim perception thereof, which, fortunately, is becoming clearer every year.

Thus, the people of Massachusetts *feel* that they ought to protect the fugitive slaves who come into our State. Hence come first, the irregular attempts to secure their liberty, and the declarations of noble men, like Timothy Gilbert, George W. Carnes, and others, that they will do so even at great personal risk; and, secondly, the statute laws made by the Legislature to accomplish that end.

Now, if Massachusetts had the power to do as much for the slaves in Virginia as for the runaways in her own territory, we should soon see those two sets of measures at work in *that* direction also.

I find it is said in the Democratic newspapers that " Capt. Brown had many friends at the North, who sympathized with him in general, and in special approved of this particular scheme of his ; they furnished him with some twelve or twenty thousand dollars, it would seem." I think much more than that is true of us. If he *had* succeeded in running off one or two thousand slaves to Canada, even at the expense of a little violence and bloodshed, *the majority of men in New England would have rejoiced, not only in the end, but also in the means.* The first successful attempt of a considerable number of slaves to secure their freedom by violence will clearly show how deep is the sympathy of the people for them, and how strongly they embrace the five principles I mentioned above. A little success of that sort will serve as *priming* for the popular cannon ; it is already *loaded.*

Of course, I was not astonished to hear that an attempt had been made to free the slaves in a certain part of Virginia, nor should I be astonished if another " insurrection " or " rebellion " took place in the State of ——, or a third in ——, or a fourth in ——. Such things are to be expected ; for they do not depend merely on the private will of men like Capt. Brown and his associates, but on the great general causes which move all human kind to hate Wrong and love Right. Such " insurrections " will continue as long as Slavery lasts, and will increase, both in frequency and in power just as the people become intelligent and moral. Virginia may hang John Brown and all that family, but she cannot hang the HUMAN RACE ; and until that is done noble men will rejoice in the motto of that once magnanimous State— " *Sic semper Tyrannis !* " " Let such be the end of every oppressor."

It is a good Anti-Slavery picture on the Virginia shield—a man standing on a tyrant and chopping his head off with a sword ; only I would paint the sword-holder *black* and the tyrant *white*, to show the *immediate application* of the principle. The American people will have to march to rather severe music, I think, and it is better for them to face it in season. A few years ago it did not seem difficult first to check Slavery, and then to end it without any bloodshed. I think this cannot be done now, nor ever in the future. All the great charters of HUMANITY have been writ in blood. I once hoped that of American Democracy would be engrossed in less costly ink ; but it is plain, now, that our pilgrimage must lead through a Red Sea, wherein many a Pharaoh will go under and perish. Alas! that we are not wise enough to be just, or just enough to be wise, and so gain much at small cost!

Look, now, at a few notorious facts :

I. There are four million slaves in the United States violently withheld from their natural right to life, liberty, and the pursuit of happiness. Now, they are our fellow-countrymen—yours and mine, just as much as any four million *white* men. Of course, you and I owe them the duty which one man owes another of his own nation,—the duty of instruction, advice, and protection of natural rights. If they are starving, we ought to help feed them. The color of their skins, their degraded social condition, their ignorance, abates nothing from their natural claim on us, or from our natural duty toward them.

There are men in all the Northern States who feel the obligation which citizenship imposes on them—the duty to help those slaves. Hence arose the ANTI-SLAVERY SOCIETY, which seeks simply to excite the white people to perform their natural duty to their dark fellow-countrymen. Hence comes CAPT. BROWN's EXPEDITION—an attempt to help his countrymen enjoy their natural right to life, liberty, and the pursuit of happiness.

He sought by violence what the Anti-Slavery Society works for with other weapons. The two agree in the end, and differ only in the means. Men like Capt. Brown will be continually rising up among the white people of the Free States, attempting to do their *natural duty* to their black countrymen—that is, help them to freedom. Some of these efforts will be successful. Thus, last winter Capt. Brown himself escorted eleven of his countrymen from bondage in Missouri to freedom in Canada. He did not snap a gun, I think, although then, as more recently, he had his fighting tools at hand, and would have used them, if necessary. Even now, the Underground Railroad is in constant and beneficent operation. By-and-bye, it will be an Over-ground Railroad from Mason and Dixon's line clear to Canada: the only *tunneling* will be in the Slave States. Northern men applaud the brave conductors of that Locomotive of Liberty.

When Thomas Garrett was introduced to a meeting of political Free-Soilers in Boston, as "the man who had helped 1800 slaves to their natural liberty," even that meeting gave the righteous Quaker *three times three.* All honest Northern hearts beat with admiration of such men; nay, with love for them. Young lads say, "I wish that Heaven would make me such a man." The wish will now and then be father to the fact. You and I have had opportunity enough, in twenty years, to see that this philanthropic patriotism is on the increase at the North, and the special direction it takes is toward the liberation of their countrymen in bondage.

Not many years ago, Boston sent money to help the Greeks in their struggle for *political freedom* (they never quite lost their *personal liberty*), but with the money she sent what was more valuable and far more precious, one of her most valiant and heroic sons, who stayed in Greece to fight the great battle of Humanity. Did your friend, Dr. Samuel G. Howe, lose the esteem of New England men by that act? He won the admiration of Europe, and holds it still.

Nay, still later, the same dear old Boston—Hunkers have never been more than rats and mice in her house, which she suffers for a time, and then drives out twelve hundred of them at once on a certain day of March, 1776,—that same dear old Boston sent the same Dr. Howe to carry aid and comfort to the Poles, then in deadly struggle for their political existence. Was he disgraced because he lay seven-and-forty days in a Prussian gaol in Berlin? Not even in the eyes of the Prussian King, who afterwards sent him a gold medal, whose metal was worth as many dollars as that philanthropist lay days in the despot's gaol. It is said, "Charity should begin at home." The American began a good ways off, but has been working homeward ever since. The Dr. Howe of to-day would and ought to be more ready to help an American to *personal liberty*, than a Pole or a Greek to mere political freedom, and would find more men to furnish aid and comfort to our own countrymen, even if they were black. It would not surprise me if there were other and well-planned attempts in other States to do what Captain Brown heroically, if not successfully, tried in Virginia. Nine out of ten may fail—the tenth will succeed. The victory over Gen. Burgoyne more than made up for all the losses in many a previous defeat; it was the beginning of the end. Slavery will not die a dry death, it may have as many lives as a cat; at last, it will die like a mad dog in a village, with only the enemies of the human kind to lament its fate, and they too cowardly to appear as mourners.

II. But it is not merely white men who will fight for the liberty of Americans ; the negroes will take their defence into their own hands, especially if they can find white men to lead them. No doubt, the African race is greatly inferior to the Caucasian in general intellectual power, and also in that instinct for Liberty which is so strong in the Teutonic family, and just now obvious in the Anglo-Saxons of Britain and America ; besides, the African race have but little desire for vengeance—the lowest form of the love of justice. Here is one example out of many : In Santa Cruz, the old slave laws were the most horrible, I think, I ever read of in modern times, unless those of the Carolinas be an exception. If a slave excited others to run away, for the first offence his right leg was to be cut off; for the second offence, his other leg. This mutilation was not to be done by a surgeon's hand ; the poor wretch was laid down on a log, and his legs chopped off with a plantation axe, and the stumps plunged into boiling pitch to stanch the blood, and to save the *property* from entire destruction ; for the live *Torso* of a slave might serve as a warning. No action of a Court was requisite to inflict this punishment ; any master could thus mutilate his bondman. Even from 1830 to 1846, it was common for owners to beat their offending victims with " tamarind rods " six feet long and an inch in thickness at the bigger end—rods thick set with ugly thorns. When that process was over, the lacerated back was washed with a decoction of the Manchineel, a poison tree, which made the wounds fester, and long remain open.

In 1846, the negroes were in "rebellion," and took possession of the island; they were 25,000, the whites 3000. But the blacks did not hurt the hair of a white man's head; they got their freedom, but they took no revenge! Suppose 25,000 Americans, held in bondage by 3000 Algerines on a little island, should get their masters into their hands, how many of the 3000 would see the next sun go down ?

No doubt, it is through the absence of this desire of natural vengeance, that the Africans have been reduced to bondage, and kept in it.

But *there is a limit even to the negro's forbearance.* San Domingo is not a great way off. The revolution which changed its black inhabitants from tame slaves into wild men, took place after you had ceased to call yourself a boy.

It shows what may be in America, with no white man to help. In the Slave States, there is many a possible San Domingo, which may become actual any day ; and, if not in 1860, then in some other "year of our

Lord." Besides, America offers more than any other country to excite
the slave to love of Liberty, and the effort for it. We are always
talking about "Liberty," boasting that we are "the freest people in the
world," declaring that "a man would die, rather than be a slave." We
continually praise our Fathers "who fought the Revolution." We
build monuments to commemorate even the humblest beginning of that
great national work. Once a year, we stop all ordinary work, and give
up a whole day to the noisiest kind of rejoicing for the War of Independence. How we praise the "champions of Liberty"! How we
point out the "infamy of the British oppressors"! "They would make
our Fathers slaves," say we, "and we slew the oppressor—Sic semper
Tyrannis!"

Do you suppose this will fail to produce its effect on the black man,
one day? The South must either give up keeping "Independence
Day," or else keep it in a little more thorough fashion. Nor is this
all: the Southerners are continually taunting the negroes with their
miserable nature. "You are only half human," say they, "not capable
of freedom." "Hay is good for horses, not for hogs," said the *philosophic*
American who now "represents the great Democracy" at the Court of
Turin. *So, liberty is good for white men, not for negroes.* Have they
souls? I don't know that—*non mi recordo.* "Contempt," says the
proverb, "will cut through the shell of the tortoise." And, one day,
even the sluggish African will wake up under the three-fold stimulus of
the Fourth of July cannon, the whip of the slaveholder, and the sting
of his heartless mockery. Then, if "oppression maketh wise men
mad," what do you think it will do to African slaves, who are familiar
with scenes of violence, and all manner of cruelty? Still more: if the
negroes have not general power of mind, or instinctive love of liberty,
equal to the whites, they are much our superiors in *power of cunning,*
and in *contempt for death*—rather formidable qualities in a servile war.
There already have been several risings of slaves in this century; they
spread fear and consternation. The future will be more terrible. Now,
in case of an insurrection, not only is there, as Jefferson said, "no
attribute of the Almighty" which can take sides with the master, but
there will be many white men who will take part with the slave. Men,
like the Lafayettes of the last century, and the Dr. Howes of this, may
give the insurgent negro as effectual aid as that once rendered to
America and Greece; and the public opinion of an enlightened world
will rank them among its heroes of noblest mark.

If I remember rightly, some of your fathers were in the battle of
Lexington, and that at Bunker Hill. I believe, in the course of the
war which followed, every able-bodied man in your town (Newton) was
in actual service. Now-a-days, their descendants are proud of the fact.
One day, it will be thought not less heroic for a negro to fight for his
personal liberty, than for a white man to fight for political independence,
and against a tax of threepence a pound on tea. Wait a little, and
things will come round.

III. The existence of Slavery endangers all our Democratic institutions. It does this if only tolerated as an exceptional measure—a
matter of present convenience, and still more when proclaimed as an
instantial principle, a rule of political conduct for all time and every

place. Look at this: In 1790, there were (say) 300,000 slaves; soon they make their first doubling, and are 600,000; then their second, 1,200,000; then their third, 2,400,000. They are now in the process of doubling the fourth time, and will soon be 4,800,000; then comes the fifth double, 9,600,000; then the sixth, 19,200,000. Before the year of our Lord nineteen hundred, there will be twenty million slaves!

An Anglo-Saxon with common sense does not like this Africanization of America; he wishes the superior race to multiply rather than the inferior. Besides, it is plain to a one-eyed man that Slavery is an irreconcilable enemy of the progressive development of Democracy; that, if allowed to exist, it must be allowed to spread, to gain political, social, and ecclesiastical power; and all that it gains for the slaveholders is just so much taken from the freemen.

Look at this—there are twenty Southern Representatives who represent nothing but property in man, and yet their vote counts as much in Congress as the twenty Northerners who stand for the will of 1,800,000 freemen. Slavery gives the South the same advantage in the choice of President; consequently the slaveholding South has long controlled the Federal Power of the nation.

Look at the recent acts of the Slave Power! The Fugitive Slave Bill, the Kansas-Nebraska Bill, the Dred Scott decision, the filibustering against Cuba (till found too strong), and now against Mexico and other feeble neighbors, and, to crown all, the actual re-opening of the African slave-trade!

The South has kidnapped men in Boston, and made the Judges of Massachusetts go under her symbolic chain to enter the courts of justice (!). She has burned houses and butchered innocent men in Kansas, and the perpetrators of that wickedness were rewarded by the Federal Government with high office and great pay! Those things are notorious; they have stirred up some little indignation at the North, and freemen begin to think of defending their liberty. Hence came the Free-Soil party, and hence the Republican party—it contemplates no direct benefit to the slave, only the defence of the white man in his national rights, or his conventional privileges. It will grow stronger every year, and also bolder. It must lay down principles as a platform to work its measures on; the principles will be found to require much more than what was at first proposed, and even from this platform Republicans will promptly see that *they cannot defend the natural rights of freemen without destroying that Slavery which takes away the natural rights of a negro.* So, first, the wise and just men of the party will sympathize with such as seek to liberate the slaves, either peacefully or by violence; next, they will declare their opinions in public; and, finally, the whole body of the party will come to the same sympathy and the same opinion. Then, of course, they will encourage men like Captain Brown, give him money and all manner of help, and also encourage the slaves whenever they shall rise to take their liberty, at all hazards. When called to help put down an insurrection of the slaves, they will go readily enough and do the work by removing the cause of insurrection—that is—*by destroying Slavery itself.*

An Anti-Slavery party, under one name or another, will before long control the Federal Government, and will exercise its Constitutional Rights, and perform its Constitutional Duty, and "guarantee a Republican form of Government to every State in the Union." That is a work of time and peaceful legislation. But the short work of violence will be often tried, and each attempt will gain something for the cause of Humanity, even by its dreadful process of blood.

IV. But there is yet another agency that will act against Slavery. There are many mischievous persons who are ready for any wicked work of violence. They abound in the city of New York (a sort of sink where the villainy of both hemispheres settles down, and genders that moral pestilence which steams up along the columns of the *New York Herald* and the *New York Observer*, the great escape-pipes of secular and ecclesiastical wickedness), they commit the great crimes of violence and robbery at home, plunder emigrants, and engage in the slave-trade, or venture on fillibustering expeditions. This class of persons is common in all the South. One of the legitimate products of her "peculiar institution," they are familiar with violence, ready and able for murder. Public opinion sustains such men. Bully Brooks was but one of their representatives in Congress. Now-a-days they are fond of Slavery, defend it, and seek to spread it. But the time must come one day—it may come any time—when the lovers of mischief will do a little fillibustering at home, and rouse up the slaves to rob, burn, and kill. Prudent carpenters sweep up all the shavings in their shops at night, and remove this food of conflagration to a safe place, lest the spark of a candle, the end of a cigar, or a friction-match should swiftly end their wealth, slowly gathered together. The South takes pains to strew her carpenter's shop with shavings, and fill it full thereof. She encourages men to walk abroad with naked candles in their hands and lighted cigars in their mouths; then they scatter friction-matches on the floor, and dance a fillibustering jig thereon. She cries, " Well done! Hurrah for Walker!" " Hurrah for Brooks!" " Hurrah for the barque *Wanderer* and its cargo of slaves! Up with the bowie-knife! Down with justice and humanity!" The South must reap as she sows; where she scatters the wind, the whirlwind will come up. It will be a pretty crop for her to reap. Within a few years the South has BURNED ALIVE eight or ten negroes. Other black men looked on, and learned how to fasten the chain, how to pile the green wood, how to set this Hell-fire of Slavery agoing. The apprentice may be slow to learn, but he has had teaching enough by this time to know the art and mystery of torture; and, depend upon it, the negro will one day apply it to his old tormentors. The Fire of Vengeance may be waked up even in an African's heart, especially when it is fanned by the wickedness of a white man : then it runs from man to man, from town to town. What shall put it out? *The white man's blood!*

Now, Slavery is a wickedness so vast and so old, so rich and so respectable, supported by the State, the Press, the Market, and the Church, that all those agencies are needed to oppose it with—those, and many more which I cannot speak of now. You and I prefer the peaceful method; but I, at least, shall welcome the violent if no other accomplish the end. So will the great mass of thoughtful and good men at the North; else why do we honor the Heroes of the Revolution, and build them monuments all over our blessed New England? I think you gave money for that of Bunker Hill: I once thought it a folly; now I recognize it as a great sermon in stone, which is worth not only all the money it cost to build it, but all the blood it took to lay its corner-stones. Trust me, its lesson will not be in vain—at the North, I mean, for the LOGIC OF SLAVERY will keep the South on its lower course, and drive it on more swiftly than before. "Capt. Brown's expedition was a failure," I hear it said. I am not quite sure of that. True, it kills fifteen men by sword and shot, and four or five men by the gallows. But it shows the weakness of the greatest Slave State in America, the worthlessness of her soldiery, and the utter fear which Slavery genders in the bosoms of the masters. Think of the condition of the City of Washington while Brown was at work!

Brown will die, I think, like a martyr, and also like a saint. His noble demeanor, his unflinching bravery, his gentleness, his calm, religious trust in God, and his words of truth and soberness, cannot fail to make a profound impression on the hearts of Northern men; yes, and on Southern men. For "every human heart is human," &c. I do not think the money wasted, nor the lives thrown away. Many acorns must be sown to have one come up; even then, the plant grows slow; but it is an oak at last. None of the Christian martyrs died in vain; and from Stephen, who was stoned at Jerusalem, to Mary Dyer, whom our fathers hanged on a bough of "the great tree" on Boston Common, I think there have been few spirits more pure and devoted than John Brown's, and none that gave up their breath in a nobler cause. Let the American State hang his body, and the American Church damn his soul; still, the blessing of such as are ready to perish will fall on him, and the universal justice of the Infinitely Perfect God will take him welcome home. The road to heaven is as short from the gallows as from the throne; perhaps, also, as easy.

I suppose you would like to know something about myself. Rome has treated me to bad weather, which tells its story in my health, and certainly does not mend me. But I look for brighter days and happier nights. The sad tidings from America—my friends in peril, in exile, in jail, killed, or to be hung—have filled me with grief, and so I fall back a little, but hope to get forward again. God bless you and yours, and comfort you!

Ever affectionately yours,
THEODORE PARKER.

FROM HON. CHARLES SUMNER.

Senate Chamber, March 26, 1856.

I am glad you are to open on Kansas. Let me suggest to press the admission of Kansas *at once* with her present Constitution. *This is the policy we have adopted,* and it will crowd Douglas and Cass infinitely. This proposition is something practical: and on this we must fight the Presidential election.

Let public meetings and petitions now call, *at once,* for the admission of Kansas as a State. Cannot our Legislature be induced to pass resolutions making this demand?

Seward will make a grand speech. I shall follow as soon as possible and use plain words.

Oh! this enormity is not really understood! The more I think of it the more its wickedness glares.

Ever yours.

FROM THE SAME.

Washington, May 17, 1856.

I have read and admired your speech in the *Post*. It is a whole sheaf of spears against slavery. Alas! alas! the Tyranny over us is complete. Will the people submit? When you read this I shall be saying — in the Senate — they will not! Would that I had your strength. But I shall pronounce the most thorough Philippic ever uttered in a legislative body.

Ever yours.

The following letter alludes to the speech of Mr. Sumner, entitled "The Crime against Kansas," delivered on May 19 and 20, and which the South replied to on the next day by a characteristic argument in the hand of Mr. Brooks.

Burlington, Vt., May 21, 1856.

MY DEAR SUMNER,—God bless you for the brave words you spoke the other day, and have always spoken, of which I hear report in the papers. Send it to me in full as soon as you can.

I have been ill (in head,) and scarce able to do anything for a month, else I should have written you before now. I am a little better just now, but still my head feels like an apple which has been frozen all winter, and is now thawed out. I am in Vermont, lecturing on the condition of the country. Pierce is in open rebellion against the people; he has committed the highest treason against the people, the worst form of *lese majesté*.

I have long wanted to thank you for your services in that matter of the Danish Sound affair. It is quite clear that you are right, that the twofold Executive, Presidential and Senatorial, have no more right to annul a treaty than to annul the Tariff Law, the Law against Piracy, or any other statute. Why did nobody ever think of this before?

There are three wicked things now going on in the United States:

1. Exterminating the Indians in Oregon, &c.

2. Fillibustering against Central America, and "the rest of mankind."

3. Extending Slavery into Kansas and everywhere else. Here, I take it, the Free State men will be immediately put down unless Congress comes to their aid. What can they do—a handful of them, with no arms, no officers, against the border ruffians, 8000 or 10,000 strong, armed by the United States, and officered by the soldiers of our wicked army? Can nothing be done at Washington? Will

N 2

nothing arouse the *People* at the North? Tell me what you think of the Candidates for Republican Nomination. Here is my list of preferences if I could *make* the President :—

    1. Seward.
    2. Chase.
    3. Hale.

But I take it none of these could be elected in the present state of affairs. If we come to actual war, Seward could be chosen, I think: but not now, in the present state of things.

Do tell me how far is Fremont reliable.

          God bless you!

                        Ever yours.

TO HON. J. P. HALE.

                          Boston, May 23, 1856.

My dear Mr. Hale,—Do write and tell me how Sumner is getting on. How much is the noble fellow wounded? Give him my most sympathizing regards and love. I wish I could have taken the blows on my head, and not he, at least half of them. Will the Senate do nothing about it? Think of the scoundrel Brooks let off on bail of 500 dollars! I shall go to the State House as soon as the house meets, to see if I can stir up that body to any action on the matter.

                      Yours truly and heartily,
                             T. P.

Another thorough sermon came of this, which went deep into the indignant heart of the North. For now the cities, as well as the country, were touched, and votes made rapidly in that electric season for Mr. Fremont and for the party of the North. Mr. Parker called his sermon " A New Lesson for the Day." It shows how every measure and outrage is but a logical effect of slavery :—

Be not surprised at this attack on Mr. Sumner; it is no strange thing. It is the result of a long series of acts, each the child of its predecessor, and father of what followed; not exceptional, but instantial, in our history. Look with a little patience after the cause of those outrages at Kansas and at Washington. You will not agree with me to-day; I cannot convince four thousand men, and carry them quite so far all at once. Think of my words when you go home.

The causes of the outrage are then derived from the national and local subservience to the encroachments of Slavery. The brute force in the arm of Preston Brooks sprang no more from wine and Southern hate than it did from Northern apologies and local hate of Mr. Sumner.

Corrupt men at the North, in New England, in Boston, have betrayed the people. They struck at freedom before South Carolina dared lift an arm. The slave-holders know these things, that as often as they have demanded wickedness, Boston has answered the demand; they piece out their small bit of lion's skin with the pelt of many a Northern fox. They are in earnest for slavery: they think New England is not in earnest for freedom. Do you blame them for their inference? A few years ago Mr. Sumner spoke in Boston on the "True Grandeur of Nations," a lofty word before the City Fathers, on the 4th of July, 1845; an argument against war, a plea for peace. As two of our most distinguished citizens came from listening, one said to the other, "Well, if that young man is going to talk in that way, he cannot expect Boston to hold him up." Since then that young man has spoken even nobler words; Boston has not held him up; nay, the controlling part of it has sought to strike him down; counted him one of a "nest of vipers;" done nothing to support, all to overthrow him. Why? Because he was the continual defender of the unalienable rights of man. Slave-holders are not fools; they knew all this. The South never struck a Northern advocate of a tariff, or a defender of the Union. She knew the North would "hold up" the champions of the Union and the tariff. It attacks only the soldiers of freedom, knowing that the controlling power of the North also hates them.

Blame me as much as you please for what I say; ten years hence you will say that I am right. But, ere I go further on, let me do an act of gratitude and justice. In all those dark days behind us, there have been found faithful men who risked their political prospects, the desires of honourable ambition, their social standing, the esteem of their nearest relatives, and were faithful to truth and justice. What treatment have they met with in the parlor, in the forum, in the market, in the church? One day their history must be writ; and some names now hated will appear like those which were the watchwords of the revolution, and are now the heavenly sounds that cheer the young patriot in this night of storms. In such men no city is so rich as this. Daughter of nobleness, she is its mother too. I hope to live long enough to do public honor to their high worth.

Now do you know the seed whence came the bludgeon which struck that handsome and noble head? It was the "ACORN," * in whose shell Boston carried back Thomas Sims in 1851; and on the 19th of April, on the seventy-sixth anniversary of the battle of Lexington, she took him out of that shell and put him in a gaol at Savannah, where he was scourged till a doctor said, "You will kill him if you strike him again!" And the master said, "Let him die." That was the acorn whence grew the bludgeon which struck Charles Sumner.

Mr. Sumner, in carrying out his intention expressed to Mr. Parker, told nothing but the unadorned and modest truth. But how outraged did many exquisite Northern consciences feel because Mr. Sumner said that Mr. Butler, of South Carolina, was

* Name of the brig, owned in Boston, and chartered by the Government to take away Sims.

in love with a harlot—meaning slavery ! There never was a stricter truth declared. This harlot, after maintaining her connection with the North long enough to sap the marrow of its bones, and strike its nerves with the premonitions of paralysis, hastens to betray it when no more pleasure and profit can be derived from the intercourse, and robs the house of its keeper to furnish its precipitate escape. The very deed and spirit of a harlot. It has played the game of harlotry with all its great Northern embracers, using them to feed its extravagances, and dropping them one by one as their fortunes are played out ; grown more and more shameless with every success, wheedling and bullying as its beauty faded, caressing with one hand and pilfering with another, all its veins poisoned by lust and avarice, and breaking out at last into assault and "cursing like a very drab" —what Hogarth shall arise to depict the stages of this harlot's brazen course ?

In the country I expect great good from this wickedness. New England farmers cover the corn they plant with a prayer for God's blessing; this year they will stamp it also with a curse on slavery. The matter will be talked over by the shoemakers, and in every carpenter's and trader's shop. The blacksmith, holding the horse's hoof between his legs, will pause over the inserted nail, and his brow grow darker while the human fire burns within.

There is a war before us worse than Russian. It has already begun: when shall it end ? "Not till slavery has put freedom down," say your masters at the South; "Not till freedom has driven slavery from the continent," let us say and determine.

Having now determined that, the blood we spill sinks fruitfully into the ground.

The original motto of the *Lynchbury Virginian* was "The Rights of the States and the Union of the States," which placed the State Rights in the van and allowed to follow all the Union that might be consistent with that preference. But now the motto is changed by secession to "The Rights of the South and the Union of the South." And the editor justifies the change by saying, among other things, "When the future historian shall connect all the threads of his narrative, and trace to their parent source the bitter streams that are now sweeping over the land, he will find that the poison is exhaled from the 'MAYFLOWER.'"

History has a better memory than that, and though not botanist by profession, can tell mushrooms from toadstools, and will not be likely in the future to trace our political diseases to the wrong plant. Let history " connect all the threads " of her narrative, and trace the bitter stream to its real source.

" In 1620 the pilgrims came to Plymouth, bringing freedom, asking freedom. The *Mayflower*, symbol of earliest spring, has been followed by a whole April and May of civil beauty, whitening and fragrant all round the land. The same year, at Jamestown, a slave-trader from Africa unloaded his freight of bondsmen—whose descendants boast the best blood of Virginia in their veins," a state-right, we presume, " but it is slave-blood, bought, sold, always in the market."

History takes another reminiscence from her immortal urn, and gives it in charge to the armed descendants of the pilgrims, who are marching South with seeds of the *Mayflower* for the Virginia woods.

" In 1607 the Virginia Company had a seal with the device of St. George and the Dragon," and the legend, "*Fas alium superare Draconem*," " It is worth while to kill one dragon more." To do that is the task of the North and of America. " It is kill or be killed ; freedom for all, or slavery for the greater part ; man, or the accidents of man." *Justum est bellum quibus necessarium, et pia arma quibus nulla nisi in armis relinquitur spes.*

How grand a spectacle is the migration hitherward. But there is a migration out, as well as migration in. The route of the American Exodus is not yet open. Its exiles now travel on the Underground Railroad. A box half as large as a coffin is the Mayflower to another pilgrim. Under the British flag they find shelter, and a New Plymouth in Canada.

FROM THE JOURNAL.

Sunday, Sept. 7, 1856.—There is the most ghastly state of things in Kansas. I can think of nothing else. Petitions are on foot for calling an extra Session of the Legislature. If I were the people I would raise a million of dollars at once for this, and send out a committee with power to spend it as they should see fit. Of course, I touched on this Kansas matter in my sermon,* introductory to this new course. How glad I am to be back again. Vacation was just one week (Sunday) more than I wanted.

Sept. 9.—America is now in a state of revolution. There is no

* "Of the Unlikeness of Circumstance and Condition, the Unity of Human Duty, and its Final Reward." The course was practical, industrial, political ; upon the Art of Life : one sermon was upon Franklin.

legal government, but only one which pretends to legality, and has the show and form of law and the substance of power. There are two parties.

1. The Party of Slavery. This has a great majority of the Senate, the Senatorial Executive, the President with his Cabinet, and all his departments, the Presidential Executive, with all the chief people of all the Slave States, all the army, navy, and 40,000 office-holders This party holds possession of the national power, but rules in the *principles* of a party, for the *purposes* of a party, and in the *manner* of a party; for example, Kansas. Not a pro-slavery man has been arrested for any enormity committed there. Now another army of Missouri men attacked and destroyed Osawatomie,* and nothing is done. Men are murdered, and nothing done. But while Lane has committed no offence and nothing is charged on him, fourteen companies of United States solders are ordered out to take him. Jefferson Davis, the famous disunion nullifier, is Secretary of War!!

On the side of this party are the prominent men of the North, Everett, Choate, and the Know-Nothing Party.

2. The Party of Freedom. The battle is in the *centre of the Continent*. And this is the question, Shall slavery or freedom have the heart of America, and then its limbs !

Sept. 14, 1856.—Mr. Yeadon, Editor of the *Charleston Courier*, came to our house by his appointment. He is the person who complimented Mr. Everett at Plymouth, for his speech in defence of slavery, &c. Mr. Garrison, J. Z. Goodrich, Hamilton Willis, and others, came there. Mr. Y. had a long discussion with Garrison about slavery, in which he (Y.) set forth the South Carolina doctrines as usual, and a couple of days later sent me a slip from the *Boston Daily Times*, entitled "Interesting Incident." The incident was the receipt of an affectionate letter from a slave, Joe, to his master at the North, accompanied with a fine daguerreotype portrait of "that image of God carved in ebony." Joe can neither write nor read. So the letter was written for him. Mr. Y. sent me a letter in a feigned hand, signed "A South Carolinian," which was handed to me as I was about to enter the Music-hall. I only read the first paragraph. He told a gentleman that he (Y.) wrote it to induce me to abuse the South !

Joe had the following sentiment manufactured for him, and for a Northern market :—

The servants' (!) crops are also doing splendidly (for you know each servant has his own separate crop, which he finds time to work after he has finished his task, which he generally does pretty early in the day). Old Scrub, a man of fourscore years, will make upwards of forty bushels of rice by himself. Massa Gendroon left here on the 5th of last month for Kansas, in fine spirits, hoping to have a fight with the Abolitionists there, and I bid him good-bye on the cars

* The name of a little settlement of Anti-slavery men in Kansas, whence Capt. Brown derived his *nom de guerre* of Osawatomie, for a successful skirmish with a band of Southerners and Missouri men.

myself, the morning he started. God grant that he may return safe to his family and friends!

Upon the envelope of Mr. Yeadon's letter, Mr. Parker has written: "Within is an anonymous letter from Mr. Yeadon, editor of *Charleston Courier*, S. C., handed to me just before meeting, Sunday, Sept. 14, 1856, while I was waiting in the ante-room. I read the first paragraph—no more. Mr. Y. told Mr. Kendall that he had sent me a letter signed 'A South Carolinian.'"

The author of the letter, to ensure its being read in time to add a perfume to the morning service, wrote underneath the address, "To be read, if possible, before declamation on this morning."

The subject of the sermon for that Sunday was "Religion Considered as the Art of Life." Here are a few sentences from the high-minded editor:—

TO MR. THEODORE PARKER.

SIR,—I would feel it my duty to address you by the title of "Reverend," did I or could I regard you as a Christian minister, preaching the gospel of our Lord and Saviour Jesus Christ; but as I hold you to be anything but a disciple of the meek and lowly Jesus, who came to preach peace on earth and good-will to men—and, indeed, to be one of the most irreverent of men, who would, if he could, the

> " Pulpit-drum ecclesiastic,
> Beat and pound with both fist and stick," *

I cannot conscientiously do more than address you by the ordinary title of respect to unclerical persons.

Thus opened the disciple of the meek and lowly Jesus, whose paper at home was filled with advertisements of women and children for sale, and rewards for men inclining to be free.

Having carefully selected by what handle he shall take up the preacher for the day, he proceeds :—

My purpose is to inform you that a party of Southerners will be present this morning, to see and hear you desecrate the Lord's Day by your usual *quantum* and outpouring of pulpit politics and fanatic declamation and extravagance against slavery and the South. It is, therefore, to be hoped that, stimulated by the provocation of their presence, and for their especial edification, you will pile up the agony

---

* Probably from a States-righted edition of Hudibras.

as high as Mount Olympus, for Mount Zion is, doubtless, too lowly for your purposes and aspirations.

And, pray, why should the religious editor care to mount higher than the auction-block? An agony is piled up there that is more edifying to his views of his Lord and Saviour Jesus Christ.

Are you aware, Sir, that, in your crazy opposition to,.and warfare against, slavery, you are arrogating to yourself a wisdom and a righteousness which not only exceed those of the Scribes and Phari- sees, but which are superior to those of God and patriarch, and of Christ and apostle? God himself *ordained* slavery among the Jews, when he declared, &c.

Then the usual dreary array of scriptural authorities, from Genesis to Onesimus, follows, containing nothing original, unless it be the remark that "Jehovah *himself* returned the first runaway slave to her owner, even the fugitive Hagar to her jealous and persecuting mistress," having, doubtless, conquered his prejudices on the score of humanity, mindful of the promises. Four or five pages of closely-written textual quotations conclude thus :—

Answer these texts, if you can, this day, or for ever hereafter hold your peace.

Yours, as you shall conform yourself to the Gospel model,

A SOUTH CAROLINIAN.

—by construction, leaving the reader in a pleased surmise that the South Carolinian is the Gospel model.

The conversation between Messrs. Yeadon and Garrison and Parker was quite fairly reported by the former in his paper, the *Charleston Courier*, but it is not of sufficient interest to be inserted here.

On the opposite page is a facsimile letter of Mr. Parker to Hon. J. P. Hale, followed by a copy. It is selected for the clearness of its anticipations, which a journey to the West, made by him before the date of this letter, had considerably modified. His letters to Hon. Horace Mann, Prof. Desor, and others, of an earlier date, betray his hopes of the election of Mr. Fremont.

Galesburg 21 Oct. 1856,

my dear Hale,

I'm glad I am not co
rator this year. You win your "Hon"
tty dear this season, Stumping is
Joke. I heard your opponent this
afternoon - Douglass. He   *   *

*   *   *   made one of the most
sophisticated & deceitful speeches I ever
listened to. It was mere brutality in
respect of morals, & sophistry for logic,
in the style & manner of a low blackguard. His enemies said he seldom
never did so ill. But there is a
good deal of rough power in his
ill face. I never saw him before,

I don't know how you think

the election will turn on, but I [...]
for defeat. I _hope_ other men, bet[ter?]
think so. The battle is not t[o?]
by our carrying the Electoral tick[et]
by popular vote. If Buch. gets
Electors:— $1,000,000 I think mig[ht]
be raised to buy the 149th. I thi[nk]
there are 30 men in Boston who [would]
give $5,000 apiece to see it done.
The most important crisis in ou[r]
national History — no presidential [elec]
tion ever turned on such great
questions. It is Despotism or Dem[oc]
racy which the People vote for,
with the true issue now repres[ented]
by the Barons & Nobles. Buch[anan's]
friends would bear this in front [of?]
all: "No unalienable Rights to Li[fe]

...erty & the Pursuit of Happiness." "The
Declaration of Independence a lie."
"a Higher Law" Then might
follow in Historical order. "Slavery in
Kansas." "Slavery in Cuba." "Slavery in
the Territories." "Slavery in all
the Free-States." "Bondage for
Negroes": "Bondage for Poor Whites":
"slavery for Greasy Mechanics" "No
Free Schools": "no Free Press." "no
Free Pulpit." "No Free Speech": no,
&c &c

If Buchanan is President, I think
the Union does not hold it
it's four years — it must end in

civil war, which I have been preparing for these six months past. They are no [Banks?] except for preparing [?]. Last year I bought $1500 worth. This year I shall not order $200 worth. I may want the money for Cannons.

Have you any Plan in case we are defeated? Of course the Principles & Measures of the Administration will remain un= =changed, & the mode of execution will be more intense & [?]. God save the U. S. A.

Yours faithfully,
Theo. Parker

[*Copy.*]

TO HON. J. P. HALE.

Galesburg, Ill., Oct. 21, 1856.

I am glad I am not a senator this year. You win your "Hon." pretty dear this season. Stumping is no joke. I heard your opponent, Douglas, this afternoon. He . . . . made one of the most sophisticated and deceitful speeches I ever listened to. It was mere brutality in respect of morals, and sophistry for logic, in the style and manner of a low blackguard. His enemies said he seldom or never did so ill. But there is a good deal of rough power in his evil face. I never saw him before.

I don't know how you *think* the election will turn out; but I look for defeat. I *hope* otherwise, but still *think* so. The battle is not won by our carrying the electoral tickets by popular vote. If Buchanan gets 148 electors, one million dollars, I think, might be raised to buy the 149th. I think there are thirty men in Boston who would give five thousand dollars apiece to see it done. It is the most important crisis in our national history. No Presidential election ever turned on such great questions. It is despotism or democracy which the people vote for. I wish the true issue was represented by the banners and mottoes. Buchanan's friends would bear this in front of all, "No unalienable rights to life, liberty, and the pursuit of happiness," "The Declaration of Independence a Lie," "No higher law." Then might follow, in historical order, "Slavery in Kansas," "Slavery in Cuba," "Slavery in all the Territories," "Slavery in all the Free States," "Bondage for niggers," "Bondage for poor whites," "Slavery for *greasy mechanics*," "No free schools," "No free press," "No free pulpit," "No free speech," "No free men."

If Buchanan is President, I think the Union does not hold out his four years. It must end in civil war, which I have been preparing for these six months past. I buy no books, except for pressing need. Last year I bought fifteen hundred dollars' worth. This year I shall not order two hundred dollars' worth. I may want the money for cannons.

Have you any plan, in case we are defeated? Of course the principles and measures of the administration will remain unchanged, and the mode of execution will be more intense and rapid.

God save the United States of America!

Yours faithfully,
THEODORE PARKER.

TO HON. HORACE MANN.[*]

Boston, June 27, 1856.

MY DEAR MR. MANN,—Don't think that your labors are obscure or likely to be forgotten in this generation, or for many that are to come. Your works are written all over the commonwealth of Massachusetts, and are in no danger of being forgotten. I know how arduous your position is, also how unpleasant much of the work must be. I fancy you now and then feel a little longing after the well-cultured men and women whom you left behind at the East, and find none to supply in Ohio. But the fresh presence of young people is a compensation.

What a state of things we have now in politics! The beginning of the end! I take it we can elect Fremont; if so, the battle is fought and the worst part of the contest is over. If Buchanan is chosen, see what follows. The principles of the Administration will be the same as now; the measures the same; the mode of applying the principles and executing the measures will be slightly altered—no more. It is plain that another such Administration would ruin the country for men like those of Middlesex County, Massachusetts. I don't think the people will see themselves conquered by 350,000 slaveholders, headed by an old bachelor! If Buchanan is elected, I don't believe the Union holds out three years. I shall go for dissolution.

I wish I could go to the Lakes with you; but a family of most intimate friends will sail for Europe the 23rd of August, to be absent for three years. I want to see them all I can this summer; so we shall all go to Newton Corner, and live near by. Else I should do up my "unpretending luggage," and be off to Lake Superior with you.

I sent you a little sermon for the Sunday after Mr. Brooks struck Sumner, and have another pamphlet in press, containing two speeches made at New York a month ago, which please accept. On the 6th of July I shall preach on "The Prospect before us," and perhaps print.

July 8th, I go to "New York Central University." Such is the "high-phaluting" style and title of a college at Macgrawville, somewhere in New York, and deliver an address on the "Function of the Scholar in a Democracy."

I wish I was where I could see you often, but am glad to know that you are well.

Truly yours,
T. P.

TO PROFESSOR EDWARD DESOR.

Newton Corner, near Boston, 1856.

Mailed Aug. 9th.

—— Now a word about myself. I am busy as can be with all sorts of ecclesiastical, philosophical, and, I am sorry to say, political affairs; have lectured more than 110 times since October, 1855, besides preaching at home, and publishing the various little volumes sent to you, and which, I hope, *reached you at last.* For the future, I shall not lecture much, for I am getting old—forty-six next 24th August, you know!

[*] At this time President of Antioch College, Ohio.

You don't know how bald my head is; my beard is almost white. I am often taken for sixty, or more! The political condition of the country is *bad*, BAD, BAD. But it looks hopeful for the future. I think this is the last Presidential election under the constitution. Yet I do not desire the dissolution until we have freed 4,000,000 slaves, though I should vastly prefer a dissolution to the present state of things. But I do not believe that any permanent union is possible between the North and the South. In ideas, aims, and habits of life, there is more unity between the Neapolitans and the Swiss about the *Vierwaldstätter See*, than between the South and the North. Now, a despotic Government, like Austria, can unite nations as unlike as the Hungarians and Venetians, into one autocracy, for military violence is the stiff iron hoop which holds these different staves together. But in a republic a union must be moral—of principle; or economical—of interest,—at any rate, internal and automatic. None of these conditions seem likely to exist long. Besides, just now there is a fierce hostility between the South and the North : the South hates the North worse than the Lombards hate *i dannati Tedeschi*, worse than the French hated *l'Albion perfide* in 1800-1815. The question is now plainly put in the Presidential election : " Will you have slavery spread over all the land, or will you give freedom an opportunity? There is no other question before us, and this comes in its *naked form*. Buchanan and Fillmore are the two candidates of the slave power—*Fremont* is the one candidate on the other side. The choice lies between Buchanan and Fremont. Fillmore's chance seems good for nothing. Now, I think that Fremont will be chosen on the 4th of November, and then that the South will prepare to break up the union, for, if he succeeds, then slavery is checked, and with it that wicked fillibustering policy which has disgraced the nation, and gladdened the South so long. All this the South knows : the present administration continues in power till March 4th, 1857, and it is quite friendly to the worst designs of the South. So it will allow the slave power to take all the steps preliminary to a dissolution when Fremont comes into office.

But if Fremont is not elected, then I look forward to what is worse than civil war in the other form, viz. a long series of usurpations on the part of the slave power, and of concessions by the North, until we are forced to take the initiative of revolution at the North. That will be the worst form of the case, for then the worst fighting will be among the Northern men—between the friends of freedom and the Hunkers. I expect civil war, and make my calculations accordingly.

You may judge of the strength of my convictions when I tell you that I order no more books from Germany, but send the antiquarian catalogues to the Athenæum unopened! Some pleasant things take place; all the Rabbis of Cambridge go for progress, for humanity, and anti-slavery. Felton is President of the Fremont Club! This will have great influence on the snobs of Boston.

FROM THE JOURNAL.

Nov. 3, 1856.—Sumner comes home to-day. The people receive him in the streets. Old noble Quincy meets him at Roxbury line, and welcomes him as he did Lafayette in 1825. It is worth while to live so long to be so noble as he is. One day he will be my text for a sermon,—if I live, and he does not.

On the next day occurred the Presidential election. The result was foredoomed to slavery; but the Republicans cast a million and a quarter of votes for Col. Fremont, of which Mr. Parker could fairly claim great numbers as his own. They were shapen and tempered at his forge of freedom, where a stal- wart arm had hammered, while a noble passion had fused, many a conscience into those protests. They were ballots; though he was already expecting bullets, as we see:—

FROM THE JOURNAL.

This day is not less critical in our history for the Future than 4th July, '76, was for the Past. At sunrise there were three alternatives:—
1. Freedom may put down slavery peacefully by due course of law.
2. Slavery may put down freedom in the same way.
3. The friends of freedom and its foes may draw swords and fight.
At sunset the people had repudiated the first alternative. Now America may choose between Nos. 2 and 3. *Of course we shall fight.* I have expected civil war for months; now I buy *no more books* for the present. Nay, I think affairs may come to such a pass, that my own property may be confiscated; for who knows that we shall beat at the beginning—and I hung as a traitor! So I invest property accordingly. Wife's will be safe. I don't pay the mortgage till 1862.

TO MISS HUNT, IN EUROPE.

Nov. 17, 1856.

Yesterday was the 80th anniversary of the most terrible defeat of the Americans in the revolutionary war; for Nov. 16, 1776, you remember, Fort Washington fell into the hands of the enemy—2,800 soldiers (the flower of the army), provisions for all winter, ammuni- tion, &c., and more than half the cannons of the nation, if I remember right.

You may guess how the Tories of New York rejoiced in Nov. 17, 1776—how they fired cannons! Well, while I write, the Boston Tories are firing cannons over the defeat of Fremont—fifty-eight at East Boston; fifty-eight more at South Boston—a pretty anniversary, truly, for such a festival!

But they do not know it—" Nemesis is never asleep." I heard the cannons fired for the proclamation of war against Mexico; for the passage of the Fugitive Slave Bill.

If the Curtises had dared, they would have touched off the same guns in honour of the rendition of Thomas Sims and Anthony Burns. Well, American liberty has just had a terrible defeat; apparently worse than the fall of Fort Washington in 1776. But that was no misfortune in the end. Had we gained our independence at less cost, we had valued liberty cheaper even than now.

I don't know but it would have been more fatal if power had fallen into the hands of the Fremonters. I have my doubts of such men as —— and ——. They are not quite solid enough for my taste.

It was they who gave us Gardner for Governor.

At New York and elsewhere, Banks said the election of Fremont would settle the slavery question, and stop agitation for thirty years!

I opened my eyes when I went out West, and saw that the hands of the republicans are not yet quite clean enough to be trusted with power. There has a deal of bad stuff come over to the republican party. I am more than ever of opinion that we must settle this question in the old Anglo-Saxon way—with the *sword*.

There are two constitutions for America—one writ on parchment, and laid up at Washington; the other also on parchment, but on the *head of a drum*. It is to this we must appeal, and before long. I make all my pecuniary arrangements with the expectation of civil war. I buy no books; have not orders out for 50 dollars, and commonly have at least 500 dollars on orders in all parts of the world.

I saw Sumner to-day. He talked an hour or more quite well. He walks with his hand on his loins, but looks well; drinks tea—French wine. Howe says he will get well.

Last Sunday I preached of "The Need of Religious Consciousness, and the Joy thereof; next, of "The Need that this subjective Religious Consciousness should become an Outward Life of noble and various Manhood." Thanksgiving-day — of the "Prospects of Freedom in America." Then will follow one of the "False and True Idea of Education;" then one of "Inheritance"—what we receive of good and ill, and what we bequeath; then of the "Education of Children," of which I know so much! Thanksgiving text—"The harvest is past, the summer is ended"—a sad text for such a day. But Hope is at the bottom of Pandora's box.

Now good bye, for I have little time,   Ever yours,
                                                            T.

Soon after the defeat of Colonel Fremont, the following call was issued for a Convention of the citizens of Massachusetts.

We, the undersigned citizens of Worcester, believing the result of the recent Presidential Election to involve four years more of Pro-Slavery Government, and a rapid increase in the hostility between the two sections of the Union:

Believing this hostility to be the offspring, not of party excitement, but of a fundamental difference in education, habits, and laws:

Believing the existing Union to be a failure, as being a hopeless attempt to unite under one government two antagonistic systems of society, which diverge more widely every year:

And believing it to be the duty of intelligent and conscientious men to meet these facts with wisdom and firmness:

Respectfully invite our fellow-citizens of Massachusetts to meet in Convention at Worcester, on Thursday, January 15, to consider the practicability, probability, and expediency, of a separation between the free and slave states, and to take such other measures as the condition of the times may require.

Thos. W. Higginson, Thos. Earle, Henry H. Chamberlin, Seth Rogers, and others.

MR. PARKER'S REPLY.

Railroad cars from New Haven to Boston, Jan. 18, 1857.

MY DEAR HIGGINSON,—I have no time but car time, and no space but the railroad, so you will excuse me if my letter be writ with a pencil, and dated between nowhere and everywhere.

I cannot attend your Convention to-morrow, as other business takes me elsewhere. Yet I am glad you have called it. For the South has so long cried " Wolf! Wolf!" and frightened every sheepish politician at the North, that it is time somebody should let those creatures have a glimpse of the real animal, and see how the South will like his looks. I once heard of a very honest, sober, and Christian sort of man, who was unequally yoked to one of the most shrewish mates that ever cursed soul or body. She was thriftless, idle, drunken, dirty, lewd, shrill-voiced, with a tongue which went night and day; and was, besides, feeble-bodied, and ugly to look upon. Moreover, she beat the children, starved them, and would not allow them even to attend school, or go to meeting, but brought up the girls in loose ways. Whenever the good man ventured to remonstrate a little, and took the part of one of his own children, the termagant, who came of no good stock herself, but had an "equivocal generation," called him "a beggar," "greasy mechanic," an "Abolitionist," and with ghastly oaths, told him he was "not fit company for a lady of her standing; " and if he found fault with her standing and character, she would leave his bed and board forever, and let his old house fall about his ears for him. She justified her conduct by quoting odd-ends of Scripture. She had "divine authority " for all she was doing. "Wasn't there Jezebel, in the Old Testament, and the strange woman that turned the heart of Solomon, and his head too ? Did not the Book of Proverbs speak of just such a woman as she was ? And was there not another great creature in scarlet, spoken of in the New Testament ? The Book of Revelation was on her side." So the shrew raised her broomstick, and beat the poor hen-pecked husband till he apologized as humbly as any Republican Member of Congress in 1856 or 1857. He did not intend to interfere with her beating his sons or prostituting his girls ; he thought her interpretation of the Bible was right ; there were probably just such women as she in Sodom and Gomorrah ; he begged she "would not leave his house." She "might beat him—he was a non-resistant; but he hoped she would not strike too hard, for it really hurt his feelings."

So it went on till the house became a nuisance to the neighborhood, and the submissive husband was everywhere looked upon as a cowardly sneak. But one day he made up his mind to make a spoon or spoil a horn, and, with his ox-whip in his hand, thus addressed the shrew :—
" Madam, I shall treat you gently, for your wickedness is partly my

fault; but I turn over a new leaf to-day. Either you become a good wife, or else you leave my house, and that forever, with the little bundle of property you brought into it. I shall take the children. Take five minutes to make up your mind. Go, or stay, just as you like."

To the amazement of the man, she fell down at his feet, weeping bitterly, promised all manner of things, and after he had lifted her up, actually began to put the house in order. She treated him with respect, and her children with considerable tenderness, and for many years they lived together with about as much welfare as man and wife commonly enjoy.

I am glad to see any sign of manhood in the North, and I think a fire in the rear of some of our Republican members of Congress will do them no harm. But I do not myself desire a dissolution of the Union just now. Here is the reason. The North is seventeen millions strong; and the South contains eleven millions, whereof four millions are slaves, and four millions are " poor whites." Now, I don't think it quite right for the powerful North to back out of the Union, and leave the four millions "poor whites," and the four millions slaves, to their present condition, with the ghastly consequences which are sure to follow. Men talk a great deal about the compromises of the Constitution, but forget the GUARANTEES of the Constitution. The very article which contains the ambiguous "rendition clause," has also these plain words : "The United States shall guarantee a republican form of Government to every State in the Union." Article IV. sec. 4. (I quote from memory. You can look at the passage.) Now, I would perform that obligation before I dissolved the Union. I don't think it would have been quite fair for strong-minded Moses to stay in Midian keeping his sheep and junketing with his neighbors. No. So the Lord said unto him, Down into Egypt with you ; meet Pharaoh face to face, and bring up all Israel into the land I shall give you. It is not enough to save all your souls alive, but your brethren also, with their wives and little ones. Why, even that hen-pecked husband in the story, had too much stuff to desert his sons and daughters, and run away from their ugly dam. No, sir; the North must do well by those four millions of slaves and those four millions of " poor whites " ; we must bring the mixed multitude even out of the inner house of bondage, peaceably if we can, forcibly if we must.

But if you insist on separation, and will make dissolution the basis of agitation, why, I think much good will come of it. Let me give a hint as to the line of demarkation between the two nations. I would say— Freedom shall take and keep—1. The land east of the Chesapeake Bay. 2. All that is north of the Potomac and the Ohio ; all that is west of the . Mississippi—i.e. all the actual territory with the right of reversion in Mexico, Nicaragua, and the "rest of mankind"; the entire State of Missouri, Arkansas, and Texas, with the part of Louisiana west of the Mississippi.

I think the North will not be content with less than this. Nay, I am not sure that, in case of actual separation, Virginia and Kentucky would not beg us to let the amputating knife go clear down to North Carolina and Tennessee, and cut there ; for I think there is too much freedom yet in the northernmost Slave States to consent to be left to perish with the general rot of the slave limbs.

I used to think this terrible question of freedom or slavery in America would be settled without bloodshed. I believe it now no longer. The South does not seem likely to give way—the termagant has had her will so long. I am sure the North will not much longer bear or forbear. I think we shall not consent to have democracy turned out of the American house, and allow despotism to sit and occupy therein. If the North and the South ever do lock horns and push for it, there is no doubt which goes into the ditch. One weighs seventeen millions, the other eleven millions; but, besides, the Southern animal is exceedingly weak in the whole hind-quarters, four millions in weight; not strong in the fore-quarters, of the same bulk; and stiff only in the neck and head, of which Bully Brooks is a fair sample; while the Northern creature is weak only in the neck and horns, which would become stiff enough in a little time.

Yours for the right, anyhow,
THEODORE PARKER.

Mr. Parker's next important speech was delivered in the hall of the State House, before the Massachusetts Anti-Slavery Convention, January 29, 1858. He proposed to discuss the relation of American slavery to foreign politics, to Russia, France, Germany, and England. Under the latter head, he denied that there had been been any change in the popular feeling of England against slavery.

There may have been a change in the British Government, though I doubt it much; there has been in the London *Times*. In the cotton lords, I take it, there is no alteration of doctrine, only an utterance of what they have long thought. The opinion of the British people, I think, has only changed to a yet greater hatred against Slavery.

Next, he discussed the Dred Scott decision, Walker's Nicaraguan expedition, and the two measures then impending in Congress—the Lecompton constitution and the increase of the army. Passing from these, he laid down the probable programme of the slave power for the future, in its reliance upon a continuance of Northern apathy. He did not fail to notice the municipal and social subservience which had not long ago been manifested on occasion of a visit of the author of the Fugitive Slave Bill to Boston. Then he made a calculation of the amount and character of Northern aid which could be depended on for the next political struggle against the South. But all the distinguished Northern politicians are subject to a peculiar disease, which renders them wholly unreliable for patriotic work, viz. " the Presidential fever."

I will try to describe the specific variety which is endemic in the Northern States, the only place where I have studied the disease. At first the patient is filled with a vague longing after things too high for him. He gazes at them with a fixed stare; the pupils expand. But he cannot see distinctly; crooked ways seem straight—the shortest curve he thinks is a *right* angle; dirty things look clean, and he lays hold of them without perceiving their condition. Some things he sees doubled, especially the number of his friends; others with a semi-vision, and it is always the lower half he sees. All the time he hears a confused noise, like that of men declaring votes, State after State. This noise obscures all other sounds, so that he cannot hear the still, small voice which yet moves the world of men. He can bear no " agitation "; the word " Slavery " disturbs him much; he fears discussion thereof, as a hydrophobiac dreads water. His organ of locality is crazed and erratic in its action; the thermometer may stand at 20 degrees below zero, even lower, if long enough; the Mississippi may be frozen over clear down to Natchez, Hellgate be impassable for ice, and the wind of Labrador blow for months across the Continent to the Gulf of Mexico; still he can't believe there is any North.

The great change in the public sentiment of the North is not underrated in this speech.

Paris, 27 June, 1858.

I have read the first half of your masterly speech, and long for the last.

You have read everything, and probably " Lettres familières écrites d'Italie à quelques amis, en 1739 and 1740, par Charles de Brosses."

* * * * * * *

But my special object was to call your attention to a passage in *Lettre II.*, where a remark is made about the Cardinals, which has its application to our country :—" *Car il n'y a presque point de cardinal qui n'éspère parvenir à son tour (a la papauté), et qui ne soit possédé de la maladie qu'on appelle ici ' la rabbia papalè.'* " So you will find here the prototype of our Presidential Fever.

On my voyage I read your review of Buckle: most able and clear.

Another speech, entitled " The Relation of Slavery to a Republican Form of Government," was delivered before an Anti-Slavery Convention, May 26, of the same year. It is an admirable specimen of a campaigning speech, carefully divided and simply worded, occupied mainly with a grave discussion of the political points which were before the country.

The last occasion on which he made Slavery the subject of his discourse was on the 4th of July, 1858, which was a Sunday. He preached in the Music Hall, upon " The Effect of Slavery on the American People." It is one of his most tranquil and meditative discourses, with scarcely an allusion to the dreadful disgraces of the past, or to the chief actors in the humiliation of Massachusetts and the North.

You and I, American men and women, must end slavery soon, or it ruins our democracy; the sooner the better, and at the smaller cost. And if we are faithful, as our patriot fathers and our pilgrim fathers, then when you and your children shall assemble eighteen years hence (1876) to keep the one-hundredth birthday of the land, there shall not be a slave in all America!

Then what a prospect, what a history is there for the American people, with their industrial democracy! For all men, freedom in the market, freedom in the school, freedom in the Church, freedom in the State! Remove this monstrous evil, what a glorious future shall be ours! The whole mighty Continent will come within the bounds of liberty, and the very islands of the Gulf rejoice.

> And henceforth there shall be no chain,
>   Save underneath the sea;
> The wires shall murmur through the main
>   Sweet songs of liberty!
>
> The conscious stars accord above,
>   The waters wild below;
> And under, through the cable wove,
>   Her fiery errands go.
>
> For He who worketh high and wise,
>   Nor pauses in His plan,
> Will take the sun out of the skies
>   Ere freedom out of man.*

Thus the preacher of a true democracy, and the defender of the American idea, finished his last sermon of liberty, on the last anniversary of her birth which his patriotic heart welcomed in America. It is his last defence of the people, who will yet learn gratitude for his integrity in some future epoch of a peace purchased, as he would have it, only with glory; when, as they fondly recall the causes of their happiness, and linger over the names of men who suffered to save a Republic and to transmit the record of Lexington unblemished to them and to their children, they shall hasten to add another Parker to the list of village boys who wrought their health and faith into America.

He represented and proclaimed a revolution, and devoted all his powers of conscience and understanding to organize the great change by means of timely justice, that he might, if possible, prevent Freedom from stepping to her place through blood. He

---

* From an Ode, by R. W. Emerson, written for a Fourth of July Breakfast and Floral Exhibition, at the Town Hall, Concord, for the benefit of Sleepy Hollow Cemetery.

foresaw and forewarned, but presidential candidates held the ear
of the people during those gloomy seasons, and taught them
there was peace in acquiescence and war in agitation, till acquiescence furnished the opportunity for war. Every concession
was a lease to conspiracy, which occupied the seats of power for
the sole purpose of betraying and humiliating, at some favorable
moment, the very parties who conceded. How timely righteousness would have been, seeking not to be made President, but to
consolidate a great opinion, and peacefully to reclaim the country
before the power which encroached was able to be the power in
possession. To anticipate that bitter end Mr. Parker left his
books, and engaged in agitation.

A few people at the North still amuse themselves with the
paradox that the indignant attacks upon the crimes of Slavery
originated its criminality. The partial resistance made by the
Northern moral sense to its successive encroachments are humor-
ously conceived to have been the cause of its encroaching spirit.
The outcry raised against the evils which are organic in Slavery,
and essential to its productive maintenance, such as ignorance in
the slave and hardness in the master, absence of home and marriages, breeding and the auction-block, cruelty held in check only
by self-interest, is still assumed by an ironical minority of our
fellow-citizens to have retarded the cause of emancipation in the
Border States. They were conscious of these evils, and longing
to be rid of them for ever, but upon being vigorously told of
their existence, preferred to give them a farther trial. The sober
truth is, that the Abolitionists, by fanatically insisting upon the
annexation of Texas, and dragooning Southern politicians into
the support of a measure obnoxious to them, opened fresh
markets to Virginia, and crushed out the beautiful spirit of self-
sacrifice with which that mother of States was just then gravid;
all for the sake ·of an abstract principle ! How many times
during the last thirty years have our Southern brethren been
tyrannically forced to postpone their darling project of extending
some human recognition to the bondmen within their borders, of
securing free-schools and the sanctity of home, and a system of
paid labor, and even a gradual introduction to civic rights, to
these people providentially enslaved in order to be Christianized !
We of the North have much to answer for in selfishly thwarting
these patriarchal instincts !

But people who understand that the policy of slavery was

changed gradually, by pecuniary and political advantage, till at last it developed, from a struggle for bare existence to an ambition to rule and possess this country, so intense and persistent that Northern agitation could not have aggravated it, yet find fault with the methods and spirit of the agitation. They think they would have been sooner converted, or some other people would, if only mild language had been used by anti-slavery men. It is the old story again ; they wish to amend the fact, and to tone down a revolutionary epoch, with its faithful and indignant men, to the amenity of a shallow age, that has nothing worth believing in and no great right at stake. They would fain alter one of the most decided facts in the providential growth of countries and nations. They are the people of an irreproachable taste but feeble intuition ; too feeble to overhear the distant drum whose rolling infects the disposition of the keen-eared men, and becomes their presageful and peremptory speech.

It was made, however, a special charge against Mr. Parker, that he brought up too frequently the persons themselves who had betrayed the American principle from fear, or feebleness, or prejudice—teachers and leaders who ought to have been bold and strong, and partial only for the truth that is above forms and statutes.

It was said of him, " He keeps all his scalps in the desk at the Music Hall. While you are listening to him he suddenly draws one forth, shakes it at the audience, and puts it up again. It was the scalp of a clergyman. You recollect the sin for which he was slain, and grimly recognize and approve. Pretty soon forth comes another, and another ; scalps of marshals, eminent lawyers, democratic office-holders, and South-side clergymen. Your moral sense is rather satisfied to find there on exhibition these trophies of retributive justice ; but it becomes more than satiated to see them shaken aloft a number of Sundays. To see a scalp once is impressive."

It has been said by another critic of the apologetic order, that these repetitions of indictments were made necessary by the character of the audience, which was never the same for a succession of Sundays ; that men from all parts of the country coming to Boston, lingered an hour before his great tribunal, whence the counts of violation of the higher law must be proclaimed to them.

In truth, he was unconscious of any such adaptation to his shifting audience. He did often repeat the famous points he had against individuals. It was the fault of an inflamed and indignant moral sense. It was the impersonal gratification of a wounded conscience. Not a base touch of the animal man, no savageness, as men sometimes imputed, nor malignancy, as his enemies in particular delighted to proclaim, nor vulgar ill-temper, as many amiable women were heard to insist, ever made this custom immoral. He never could forget for a moment the sin of his country, and the crime of those who upheld it. *They* were the real appealers to public vulgarity and coarseness, with their cold and grave propriety : they were violators of the tender laws of the highest propriety, a love for God's oppressed ones.

He had the rights and temper of a prophet, and his sorrows also. The ugly slave-holding fury that was harrying his country-men, pursued him by night and by day; her lashes sank start-ling and rankling into his moral sense ; for in him she found a conscience that could faithfully keep the score of her wickedness. A voice, quivering with indignation, swelling with alarm, con-centrated by a sense of suffering, spoke, reiterated, emphasized, insisted on the injuries which the country's demon was inflicting on the law of God in the soul of man. Apathetic people were repelled by the sight of this internal combat ; amiable people, of average convictions, hurt themselves in stretching up against this stalwart conscience. Indifferent people of every description could not understand that every moment was critical : they resented being drummed into a revolution, when they did not care to urge even a faint objection. Clergymen, spitted by tra-ditional pulpit propriety, and precariously held in place by the cushions, were blown over when this Pentecostal wind smote the house ; as they gathered themselves together and strove to resume a clerical attitude, they naturally exaggerated the force of the blast, because they did not justly appreciate how feebly they stood. But when they undertook to pronounce it a blast from hell, they confirmed the doubt of their spiritual insight which the common people shared. It was not a withering and debilitating sirocco, which lays human nature in the dust, but it was the cool weather coming out of the North, spreading a deep and stainless sky, awful with the rustling spears of the Aurora. Sons of the North woke from their sleep to hail it, and did not shudder at the keen flitting under the blood-red. There was solemn presage and not a ghastly omen in the vivid show.

When he summons the notorious names of history from their base graves to pass before the commissioners under the Fugitive Slave Law; when, calling up each repulsive shade, from Cain to Jefferies, and briefly designating their title to infamy, he dismisses them from the presence of his audience as not abandoned enough yet to take service with the men who felt an obligation to fulfil the requisitions of that law; from what point of view are we to study his language? From no point of view that is claimed by conventional art; from no smooth platform where the rhetoricians gather to carve and whittle platitudes into small ware for the people; from no desk whence the periods of a liturgy roll hollowly in ruts of pews, whose hearts echo the dull refrain; but from the side of the fugitive himself! Close to him, as soon as possible after his arrival, while he is fresh from his freight-box at the station, or haled forth out of a schooner's hold; while the panic is yet unmanning the brawny limbs that professed to own their toil; when he sees in each sharp look an officer, before he is reassured that a single man will take his hand except by fraud to capture him; while it is still uncertain whether he can stay a single night in the City of the Pilgrims, where a law, and learning, and legal duty, and a Southern market are in full conspiracy to seize him, if possible, before the Union falls to pieces; close to the red heart fluttering under that black skin with recollections of atrocities not yet escaped from while a commissioner can be found to serve; close, as Christ stands on the other side of him,—with indignation that a man should be condemned without crime to such misery; with horror that men could dare to approach with evil purpose his holy liberty; with unmeasured hatred of the constitutional pretexts of too subservient men,—there stand to take your artistic and comprehensive view. And if you really have transferred yourself to that woeful position, so that *you have become the man in whose behalf* your imagination is all a-flame with pity, ange , abhorrence; so that *you*, thirsting to be free, must yet wilt with terror at a footstep; so that it is *yourself*, the hunted slave, hoping only for concealment, having braved all perils and agonies for a thousand miles, but not brave enough to stay in the same city with your polished kidnapper,—oh, then the rhetoric of the preacher will be the language of your commonsense!

There stood Theodore Parker through the whole of his career—

close as he could place his noble, gifted soul to the grimy body
of the fugitive. As he looked into that black face, he saw shine
down the starry truths of the bold humanity he preached. He
had a point of view that artists might envy. A part of genius
is its infallible instinct for the place whence men and nature are
seen, not as crowds and masses, but as living symbols of the
Divine intent. And was any country ever yet furnished with
such symbol of the Divine humanity, of all the faith and
fraternity of Jesus, as our own dear country with its fugitives?
Never! Not Greece and Rome, not Judæa itself, furnished such
solicitations to the highest genius of their children!

But sometimes, not content with the stern indictment which
he brought against an imperfect moral sense, he would impute an
additional motive. Here he may be fairly criticized. One man
serves the infamous law with alacrity, having conquered what
little prejudice a prevailing legality of disposition leaves him,
because he wanted to preserve his respectable standing and political availability. If an appointment to an office or a nomination followed, this was the object of the subservience. Another
man was moved by dread of losing his place in State or Church.
Another hastened to save the Union, which was equivalent to
saving his salary. There are two objections to this imputation
of rapacious motives: they can seldom be verified like a fact
which is attested upon oath, and they are not essential to account
for the phenomena. The most subservient man may be one who
hankers for nothing in the gift of the people or the Government.
His subservience is the inevitable result of a conscience all run
to statutes. He is ready, by original or acquired inferiority of
moral sense, to support the most infamous enactment that ever
shocked the undepraved mind under the pretence of law. You
need not suspect that he is influenced by a single after-thought
or selfish consideration. You will expect to find rapacity and
meanness among such men, and it is sometimes notorious; but
you are not obliged to presume it. If a man has consented all
his life to subsist upon such a slender stock of conscience that
the highest thing which he can see, in a critical moment, is a
legal and technical thing, then no amiability of disposition, no
ordinary domestic instincts, no gentlemanly culture, no nice
habits—nothing, neither cleanliness nor conventional godliness,
will restrain him in such a moment from violating the great
creed of Christian humanity. His motive is but the necessity

of his moral state. The men who have most thwarted anti-slavery principles, and have postponed Northern resistance till it has to take the shape of war, have been a huge mob of nice family-men without a spark of moral indignation, except when some custom of trade is infringed, or some great constitutional compromise is violated in the interest which first established it. The technical violation, and not the immoral acquiescence, is the only thing which strikes and alarms this intense legality. See how events condemn this wicked substitution of the lower for the higher law ! Southern ambition has fattened on a Northern constitutional conscience ; and the men who are guilty of this civil war are the men who have consistently countenanced the South in its technical rights. They are still capable of justifying their folly by the astonishing paradox that they strove to avert bloodshed by a course which has led us directly to it.

Mr. Parker early denounced this fatal proclivity, and prophesied in sombre strains its sure results. For doing this, for indignantly attacking the demoralization which trade and law effected, for eagerly pressing on the public conscience the imminent necessity of righteousness and humanity, to save Union, and the country's great idea, and our children's happiness, by saving God's law and letting man's law go, he was honored by a hatred so hearty, that it will dazzle posterity with confirmation of his true renown.

And how will those abortive sacrifices to the Constitution and the Union appear, when the generation which made them is remembered chiefly by them ?

As the legal atrocities of all the world have seemed when the legal exigencies have passed away. History will have to borrow the most incisive pens of the present, to record upon her bronze the immoral technicalities which they arraigned. Mr. Parker's own colors will not be found too deep and glaring for any future painter who may seek in tranquillity to restore the fading picture of our times. The healthiest and highest sense in a man always anticipates the verdict of posterity, as the mountain which never stirs from its firm base lifts remote zones into the air at once, and telegraphs what is far below the horizon.

CHAPTER XXII.

Letters upon Anti-Slavery Politics : to Hon. N. P. Banks—Hon. W. H. Seward—Hon.
S. P. Chase—To and from Hon. Charles Sumner—To and from Hon. Henry Wilson
—To and from Hon. J. P. Hale—To William H. Herndon—To Hon. Horace Mann
—To Gov. Fletcher, Vermont, and others.

THESE are the names of men of high significance for any history of the formation of republican sentiment. They admired
the position which Mr. Parker had achieved, and generously
acknowledged the importance of his influence. With most of
them he was upon friendly terms of giving and receiving
counsel; and they would not be backward to say, that they
have often felt indebted to his enthusiasm, common-sense, and
frankness. They watched his battle with exultation, hastened
to organize and hold every moral advantage which he gained,
and bade him a right hearty God speed.

Most of the letters which are here presented require no explanations. They show clearly enough the method and value of
his thoughts upon political affairs, his high and salutary spirit.

TO GOVERNOR FLETCHER, VERMONT.

Boston, Nov. 27, 1856.

HON. MR. FLETCHER, GOVERNOR OF VERMONT, &C.,—DEAR SIR,—
I have no personal acquaintance with you, but your official position and
conduct make me familiar with your opinions and character, and, after
preaching a Thanksgiving Sermon, "Of the Prospects of Democratic
Institutions in America," I wish to express my profound gratitude to
you, and your State, for the recent appropriation of money in aid of
"the suffering poor in Kansas."

I know the steps which led to the measure: your letters to Judge Conway are before me; I conferred with Mr. Sumner before he wrote his note. I fear General Wilson does not quite understand the significance of this movement—the most important step lately taken by the friends of freedom. A great principle rides behind that measure. The vote of 20,000 dollars is like building one new defence for individual liberty. Hitherto Liberal Governments have been ruined in this manner :—

1. All individuality of classes is made way with, and the men reduced to one homogeneous mass—the people. They do not have intelligence enough to see their unity of interest, and still less sufficient virtue to feel their unity of duty; so they cannot act in concert against a foe who seeks to conquer and command them.

2. Some ambitious man divides them into fictitious parties—one of which so checks the other that he easily masters both, overturns their democratic institutions, and founds a despotism in their place. Old Rome, in Cæsar's time, furnishes an ancient example, and modern France within sixty years has twice afforded a recent instance. After the theocratic oligarchy of Rome had mainly perished, the uniform surface of citizenship, diversified only by the differences of personal character and condition, formed an excellent field for Cæsar to march over, and ascend his autocratic throne. After France in her first revolution had abolished all orders of nobility, all provincial and municipal privileges, there was left an open plain for Napoleon the Great; at once he found little opposition, and conquered the people. And, again, after the war in her late revolution had destroyed the constitutional monarchy, it was not difficult for Napoleon the Little to move on the level surface of democracy, and establish one of the meanest despotisms in the world. There were no great obstacles to impede him, no eminences to surmount.

So it has always been. The nation levels all the eminences; then the country becomes one vast plain, and, behold! there is no defence against the tyrant; and as all level countries are easily traversed by a large army, which is yet checked by a little opposition in a mountainous region, so do all democracies easily fall before a demagogue. The Anglo-Saxon alone has hitherto known how to found and keep a Government with national unity of action for the whole, and a high degree of individual variety of action, personal freedom, for the citizen. This success comes from what seems at first a defect in the ethnological character of this tribe; for while the Anglo-Saxon loves liberty he hates equality—each wanting to be first, and to enjoy a privilege. The Celt, on the contrary, cares little for liberty, but loves equality, and clamors for it, as in France to-day.

The great Anglo-Saxon battle for a Liberal Government took place in England in the seventeenth century (1643–1689); the strife was between the despotic King (the James and Charles) and the people. The King did not find the mass of people the great obstacle to his march; but he was checked, 1, by the privileged classes, the nobles, the clergy, the gentry; and, 2, by the privileged bodies, the great corporations, especially the City of London, whose charter secured its "vested rights." The corporations had unity of interest, which gave them unity of action. So had the privileged class; though the King could buy over individual nobles, priests, and gentlemen, yet he could not make the whole class consent to his despotism—for that would ruin the class itself.

Now, we have got so far on, that in America we have established a democracy with no privileged class, no privileged body, admitting that all persons have an equal right to life, liberty, &c. This is as it should be; it is time to try the experiment of a Liberal Government on the most extended scheme of individual equality of rights. Even if the attempt fail, as I think it will not, it was worth while to try the experiment. But we have not made the continent of people a smooth surface for the cannon of a centralizing tyrant to sweep over—we have roughened it with territorial inequalities; the individual States are to us the same defence that privileged classes and privileged bodies were to our fathers in England in the seventeenth century. These local self-governments are the great barriers against a centralizing despotism—an artificial mountain region where a few men can defend the narrow pass against a great army. The despot must go through this Thermopylæ, where three hundred Spartans can stop an army of Border ruffians.

Franklin, Jefferson, Hancock, and, more than all, Samuel Adams, disliked the Federal Constitution because it limited State rights too much. Seventy years of experience has shown the wisdom of their instinctive democratic distrust. The slave-holders and their vassals at the North have, or fancy they have, a certain unity of interest, and so have always a unity of action. They are the SLAVE POWER. Every ambitious and unscrupulous political adventurer pays court to that slave power, and employs its weapons to fight his own battles, while it employs him to achieve its victories—pays him with office, money, and "honor." The individual States are the great obstacles in the way of this power; these Alpine mountains impede the march of its columns, and enable a few men to defend the liberties of great masses of men who would else have no unity of action.

Hence, the slave power continually attacks the State-rights of the North (and always carries the day); witness the two Fugitive Slave Bills of 1793 and 1850; witness Kane's decision, in 1855, that a slave-holder could take his bondmen to any Northern State, spite of its laws. The Supreme Court is the weapon with which the slave power attacks these bulwarks of freedom and democracy, The people register its most wicked decrees.

Vermont made the earliest Personal Liberty Law, after the Fugitive Slave Bill passed in 1850. She promised to protect all who came within her fortress. Now she sends out a company to erect a little breastwork to strengthen the principal fort. Her conduct is like that of the Corporation of London in the seventeenth century; like that of Connecticut and Massachusetts in the eighteenth, which fell back on their Charters, as fortresses of their inalienable rights.

God bless you and keep you!

Respectfully yours,

T. P.

TO HON. W. H. SEWARD.

May 19, 1854.

DEAR SIR,—It seems to me that the country has now got to such a pass that the people must interfere, and take things out of the hands of the politicians who now control them, or else the American State will be lost. Allow me to show *in extenso* what I mean. Here are two distinct elements in the nation, viz. Freedom and Slavery. The two are hostile in nature, and therefore mutually invasive; both are organized in the institutions of the land. These two are not equilibrious; so the nation is not a figure of equilibrium. It is plain (to me) that these two antagonistic forms cannot long continue in this condition. There are three possible modes of adjusting the balance; all conceivable:—

1. There may be a separation of the two elements. Then each may form a whole, equilibrous, and so without that cause of dissolution in itself, and have a national unity of action, which is indispensable. Or,—

2. Freedom may destroy Slavery; then the whole nation continues as an harmonious whole, with national unity of action, the result of national unity of place. Or,—

3. Slavery may destroy Freedom, and then the nation become an integer—only a unit of despotism. This, of course, involves a complete revolution of all the national ideas and national institutions. It must be an industrial despotism; a strange anomaly. Local self-government must give place to centralization of national power; the State Courts be sucked up by that enormous sponge, the Supreme Court of the United States, and individual liberty be lost in the monstrous mass of democratic tyranny. Then America goes down to utter ruin, covered with worse shame than is heaped on Sodom and Gomorrah. For we also, with horrid indecency, shall have committed the crime against nature, in our Titanic lust of wealth and power.

1. Now I see no likelihood of the first condition being fulfilled. Two classes rule the nation; 1, the mercantile men, who want money, and 2, the political men, who want power. There is a strange unanimity between these two classes. The mercantile men want money as a means of power; the political men want power as a means of money. Well, while the Union affords money to the one and power to the other, both will be agreed, will work together to "save the Union." And as neither of the two has any great political ideas, or reverence for the higher law of God, both will unite in what serves the apparent interest of these two—that will be in favor of Slavery, and of centralized power. Every inroad which the Federal Government makes on the nation will be acceptable to these two classes.

2. Then, considering dissolution as out of the question, is Freedom likely to terminate Slavery? It was thought so by the founders of the Federal institutions, and by the people at large. Few steps were taken in that direction. The Ordnance of 1787, the Abolition of the African Slave-Trade; that is all. For forty-six years not a step!

3. The third condition is the one now most promising to end the matter. See the steps consummated, or only planned. 1, the

Gadsden Treaty; 2, the extension of Slavery into Nebraska; 3, the restoration of slavery to the Free States, either by "decision" of the Supreme Court, or legislation of Congress; 4, acquisition of Cuba, Hayti, &c., as a new arena for Slavery; 5, the re-establishment of the African Slave-Trade; 6, the occupancy of other parts of North America and South America. When all this is done there will be unity of action, unity of idea! *"Auferre, trucidare, rapire falsis nominibus imperium; atque ubi solitudinem faciunt pacem appellant."*

Now this must not be—*it must not be.* The nation must rouse itself. I have been waiting a long time for some event to occur which would blow so loud a horn that it should waken the North, startling the farmer at his plough, and the mechanic in his shop. I believe the time is coming; so I want to have a convention of all the Free States of Buffalo, on Tuesday, the 4th of July next, to consider the state of the Union, and to take measures, 1, to check, 2, to terminate, the enslavement of men in America.

I wish you would advise me in this matter; for I confess I look to *you* with a great deal of confidence in these times of such peril to freedom.

Believe me, respectfully and truly yours,

T. P.

TO GOV. N. P. BANKS, MASSACHUSETTS.

Boston, October 23, 1855.

HON. MR. BANKS,—DEAR SIR,—A political party represents an idea which is advancing or receding in the people; so it is the provisional organization of that idea, preparatory to its ultimate organization in the stable institutions of the people. Just now there are two great ideas in the consciousness of the people, that of Slavery and that of Freedom. One represents the retrograde tendency, the other that of advancing civilization; the first party is well organized, rich, in official position, educated, and far-sighted, but it is cut off from the generous intuitions which will construct the future. The second party, resident in particular spots, exists in the young woods and mills on the rivers of Kansas, hardly more; it is ill-organized, has little political experience, with no official position save in exceptional and quite recent cases, but it is exceedingly powerful through the ideas and the seeds which spring up in the members, and which are so welcome to mankind. All the genius of America is on that side, all the womanly women. It will triumph.

Now you want to enable this party to obtain political power immediately, so that it may triumph forthwith, and, having the government in its hand, at once carry out its ideas, and restrict and destroy the great obstacle in the way of our national development. How shall we do it? that is the question.

Here are two things to consider:—1. What is the maximum of the new ideas which the people will accept in the next presidential election? And, 2. What is the minimum thereof with which you can obtain their confidence, and so their delegated trust?

Look at the last first.

1. Here is the minimum. (1.) A man whose general character and public life is of so noble and humane and faithful a stamp, that it shall be itself a programme of principles, and a guarantee that he will develope them into such measures as the new idea requires. The people believe in the continuity of personal character and personal conduct. They are right. It is easy to find a man who will support the programme with his promise, but unless his general life is a guarantee to that promise I would give nothing for it in him.

(2.) You next want a declaration of ideas, a platform which will sustain your man and your contemplated measures; that platform should contain the principle, the fundamental idea, out of which the action of the new party is to grow. There should be nothing hostile to this principle in the programme, and itself should be stated as clear as the leaders can conceive it, and the people accept and bear it. The amount of this will depend on the characters of these two, the leaders who prepare, and the people who are to accept. I think Mr. Chase has made a fatal error in declaring that Slavery in the States is sacred; it is hostile to the fundamental idea of the movement. Sumner has also erred in his watchword, *Freedom national and Slavery sectional.* I recognize the finality of no *sectional* Slavery even.

3. Now what is the maximum? The Declaration of Independence contains the programme of political principles for the conduct of the whole nation, expressed as clearly as the leaders could make their statement; there was no concealment. Now *my* way of dealing with the nation is this:—I lay down the principle as clearly as I can, demonstrating it ideally by the intuitions of human nature, and experimentally by the facts of human history, and then show what measures follow from it, and what consequences will attend them, as far as *I* can see. I do this because I aim at the general development of the people, and not at the immediate success of any special measure. So I always ask the people to know—(1) the point they start from; (2) the road they go by; (3) the point they aim at. But politicians act often on a different plan, and withhold some of those things from the people. My *maximum of communication* is my own *maximum of attainment.* If I were to lay the platform of the new party, I should fall back on the national declaration of self-evident and unalienable rights, and affirm the universal proposition that man cannot hold property in man. I should expect to fail in the great issue, but to secure such a vote that the fact would modify the opinions, at least the conduct, of the old party which conquered: and besides, by that annunciation of the idea, and the consequent discussion, the whole people would be so educated, that before long there would be an intelligent acceptance thereof by the people, and a desirable victory would be obtained. I think the people would *now* bear and justify this idea—The abolition of Slavery wherever the Federal Government has the power. I doubt that the North will be content with less. On that proposition I think you can unite all the anti-slavery action of the nation, but on nothing less.

You know better than I whether Mr. Fremont reaches to the maximum and minimum as above. But a man like Van Buren or like Gardner will only harm us, and that for a long time.

Truly yours.

TO HON. HENRY WILSON.

Boston, Feb. 15, 1855.

DEAR MR. WILSON,—Ever since your election I have been trying to write you a long letter, but found no minute till now. Let me tell you frankly just how I feel about your election and your future prospects. If I had the power to put whom I would in the Senate, my first choice would have been C. F. Adams or S. C. Phillips—though for either I have not half the personal friendship I feel for you. After them you would have been my man before all others in the State. Besides, there is one reason why I wanted you before even either of them, viz. I wanted to see a shoemaker get right up off his bench and go to the Senate, and that from Massachusetts. I wish you had never been to any but a common school, for I want the nation to see what men we can train up in the public institutions of education which stand open for all.

You have done more than any political man in Massachusetts or New England—in the last ten years perhaps, certainly in the last seven—to liberalize and harmonize the actions of the political parties. We must thank you for much of the organization of the Free-Soil * party; for the revolution of the fogyism of Harvard College; for the election of Charles Sumner, and for the Constitutional Convention, which was worth all the time, and toil, and money which it cost. There is only one thing which made me prefer C. F. A. or S. C. P. to you— here it is. You have been seeking for office with all your might. What makes it appear worse is, you have no mean thing or secretiveness, and so your efforts for office are obvious to all men. Now I don't like this hunting for office in foes; and yet less in my friends. But for this, you would always have been my first choice for the senatorship. As it is—I have seen many men friendly and hostile in all parts of the State, and done what I could to promote your election —for I know the others are out of the question. No man rejoices more in your success. Now let me tell you what I think are the dangers of your position, and also what noble things I expect of you.

1. Your success has been rapid and brilliant. If you do not become a little giddy and conceited, a little overbearing and disposed to swagger, then you resist the temptation which so mars almost all men who have a similar history. Look at almost all the rich men in Boston who started poor or obscure and became famous!

2. You are to live by politics — a costly life with little direct or honest pay, but with manifold opportunities to gain by fraud—private gifts, &c., &c. I think the peril of such a position is very great. See how Webster went to the ground in that way! "A gift perverteth judgment." "Constructive mileage," and such things, are tempting and ruinous.

3. You are popular and successful. You will perhaps look for office above office—for the highest : for nothing American is beyond American hope. Then come the dangers of compromise with your own

---

* The original designation of the Republican party—derived from the question of Freedom and Slavery in the Territories.

sense of right, and of all the evils which follow from that, crouching to the meanness of a party, or the whim of the moment.

It seems to me these are real dangers—and as a real friend I wish to point them out to you at the risk even of hurting your feelings. But it is better that I should tell you, than that you should not heed the peril till too late. Remember, besides, that I am a minister and must be allowed to *preach*.

Now for the noble things which I expect of you. By nature you are a very generous man, sympathizing with mankind in all lofty aspirations—a man of the people—with the popular instincts warm and powerful in you. I look to you as a champion of justice to all men; especially to the feeblest and most oppressed. I know you cannot fail to be faithful to this great question of Slavery. But your connection with the Know-Nothings makes me fear for other forms of justice. The Catholics are also men, the foreigners are men, and the world of America is wide and waste enough for them all. I hope you will never "give up to Know-Nothings what was meant for mankind." What a noble stand Sumner has taken and kept in the Senate! He is one of the few who have grown morally as well as intellectually by his position in Congress. But his example shows that politics do not necessarily debase a man in two years. I hope the office may do as much for you as for your noble and generous colleague.

I hope, my dear Mr. Wilson, you will take this long sermon in the same friendly spirit it has been written in, and believe me now and ever,

Respectfully and truly yours.

TO REV. T. PARKER.

Senate Chamber, Feb. 28, 1855.

REV. THEO. PARKER,—DEAR SIR,—Some days ago I received two sermons from you, for which I am very thankful. I have not yet had time to read them, but I shall do so on my return home. I have read your kind letter, and you may be assured that I sincerely thank you for it. I shall keep it and often read it as the plain and frank views of a true friend. I have not time to write you now in regard to my intentions, but when I return I shall do so. I will say, however, that I shall give no votes here which will infringe upon the rights of any man, black or white, native or foreign.

Yours truly,
HENRY WILSON.

TO HON. HENRY WILSON.

Boston, July 7, 1855.

MY DEAR WILSON,—I cannot let another day pass by without sending you a line —all I have time for—to thank you for the noble service you have done for the cause of Freedom. You stand up most manfully and heroically, and do battle for the right. I do not know how to thank you enough. You do nobly at all places, all times. If the rest of your senatorial term be like this part, we shall see times such as we only wished for but dared not hope as yet. There is a North, a real North, quite visible now.

God bless you for your services, and keep you ready for more! Heartily yours,

T. P.

TO REV. T. PARKER.

Natick, July 23, 1855.

REV. THEODORE PARKER,—DEAR SIR,—On my return from a trip to the West I found your very kind note of July 7, and I need not tell you that I read it with grateful emotions. Your approbation—the approbation of men like yourself, whose lives are devoted to the rights of human nature, cannot but be dear to me. I only regret that I have been able to do so little for the advancement of the cause our hearts love and our judgments approve, that I have not ability to do all that my heart prompts. I hope, however, my dear sir, to do my duty in every position in which I may be placed, if not with the ability which the occasion demands, at least with a stout heart that shrinks not from any danger.

I sometimes read over the letter you were so kind as to send to me when I first took my seat in the Senate. You dealt frankly with me in that letter, and I thank you for it, and I hope to be better and wiser for it. I shall endeavor while in the Senate to act up to my convictions of duty, to do what I feel to be right. If I can so labor as to advance the cause of universal and impartial liberty in the country, I shall be content, whether my action meets the approbation of the politicians or not. I never have, and I never will, sacrifice that cause to secure the interests of any party or body of men on earth. The applause of political friends is grateful to the feelings of every man in public life, especially if he is bitterly assailed by political enemies, but the approbation of his own conscience is far dearer to him.

Last year, after the attempt was made to repeal the prohibition of Slavery in Kansas and Nebraska, the people of the North began to move, and from March to November the friends of freedom won a series of victories. The moment the elections were over in the North, I saw that an effort was to be made by the American organization to arrest the anti-slavery movement. When I arrived at Washington, I was courted and flattered by the politicians. I was even told that I might look to any position if I would aid in forming a national party. I saw that men who had been elected to Congress by the friends of freedom were ready to go into such a movement. I was alarmed. I saw that one of three things must happen—that the anti-slavery men must ignore their principles to make a national party; or they must fight for the supremacy of those principles, and impose them upon the organization, which would drive off the Southern men; or they must break up the party. I came home with the determination to carry the convention if I could; to have it take a moderate but positive anti-slavery position. If not, I determined that it should be broken at the June Council, so that the friends of freedom might have time to rally the people. Since my return in March, I have travelled more than nine thousand miles, written hundreds of letters, and done all I could to bring about what has taken place. But the work is hardly begun. Our anti-slavery friends have a mighty conflict on hand for the next sixteen months. It will demand unwavering resolution, dauntless courage, and ceaseless labor, joined with kindness, moderation, and patience. The next Congress will be the most violent one in our history; it will try our firmness. I hope our friends will meet the issues bravely, and if violence and bloodshed come, let us not falter, but do our duty, even if we fall upon the floors of Congress.

At Philadelphia, for eight days, I met the armed, drunken bullies of the Black Power, without shrinking, and I hope to do so at the next session of Congress, if it shall be necessary. We must let the South understand that threats of dissolving the Union, of civil war, or personal violence, will not deter us from doing our whole duty.

I want to see you some day when you can give me an hour or two, for the purpose of consultation in regard to affairs.

Yours truly,
HENRY WILSON.

FROM MR. SUMNER TO MR. PARKER.

Senate Chamber, Feb. 6, 1852.

*   *   *   *   *   *

Read my speech on Lands.* The Whig press is aroused, but I challenge it. I have the satisfaction of knowing that my argument has been received as original and unanswerable. The attack of the *Advertiser* attests its importance.

I shall always be glad to hear from you, and shall value your counsels.

Ever yours.

TO MR. SUMNER.

Boston, Feb. 9, 1852.

I thank you for your vote on the Office Limitation Bill.† It was eminently just. I like the leading ideas of your speech on the Public Lands also very much. Some of the details of your scheme I am not sure about, because I am not familiar enough with the facts of the case to judge. But the main idea I thank you for with all my heart.

TO THE SAME.

Boston, Feb. 21, 1852.

This is a queer world, and Boston is one of the queerest places in it. Well, here is something that you ought to know, just to remind you of

---

* In favor of appropriating public lands to the building of railroads in the States where they lie.— *Congress Globe*, 1st Session, 32nd Congress. Appendix, p. 134.

† Proposing to limit commissions in the Navy of the United States hereafter to the term of ten years.—*Congress Globe*, Vol. XXIV., Part I. p. 448.

the *religious* character of this goodly and godly city. ——, D.D., &c , &c., said of your Land speech, "it betrays the instinct of the demagogue, and is evidently designed to gain popularity at the West."

He that condemns after that sort enables one to see the motives which animate him.

*   *   *   *   *   *

By the way, here is a good *mot* of Samuel J. May. The wardens of King's Chapel sent him their new edition of the Litany, and May replies : " You have made great improvements in the paper, printing, and binding—all that is beautiful. But I don't see the same progress in the matter of the book, or indication of progress in the prayers. You still confess yourselves "miserable sinners." Now, it is not a good plan to be always *saying* this; if you are so, confess it once, and mend the matter, and be done with it. I don't think, however, that all of you are "miserable sinners." But I think some of you are, *e. g.* the man who voted for the Fugitive Slave Bill, I think, *is* a "miserable sinner."

Yours faithfully,
THEODORE PARKER.

The following note to Dr. S. G. Howe, expresses a temporary dissatisfaction with Mr. Sumner, which was shared by some members of the Free-Soil party, and by many anti-slavery men in 1852, because he seemed to shrink from speaking. At that time an anti-slavery senator was without influence or significance in Washington ; his presence was barely tolerated since he brought credentials of a legal election. And if he undertook to arraign in speech the institution which was governing the country, indifference was changed to contempt and hatred.

Mr. Sumner's scholarly reserve saved him from a premature and incompetent assumption of the great part which he has played ; but he was only studying the ground, and watching for an opportunity.

TO DR. S. G. HOWE.

DEAR CHEV.,*—Do you see what imminent deadly peril poor Sumner is in ? If he does not speak, then he is *dead—dead—dead!* His course is only justifiable by success, and just now the success seems doubtful, and is certainly far more difficult than months ago. Think of the scorn with which ——, and ——, and their crew, will treat him, if he returns without having done his duty ! Think of the indignation of the Free-Soilers !

T. P.

* *Chevalier*, for such a friend, was a fortunate designation.

FROM MR. SUMNER TO MR. PARKER.

Senate Chamber, Aug. 11, 1852.

I must at least acknowledge your letter of friendship and admonition.

I will not argue the question of past delay. To all that can be said on that head there is this explicit answer. With a heart full of devotion to our cause, in the exercise of my best discretion, and on the advice or with the concurrence of friends, I have waited. It may be that this was unwise, but it was honestly and sincerely adopted, with a view to serve the cause. Let this pass.

You cannot desire a speech from me more than I desire to make one. I came to the Senate, on my late motion,* prepared for the work, hoping to be allowed to go on, with the promise of leaders from all sides that I should have a hearing. I was cut off. No chance for courtesy. I must rely upon my rights.

You tell me not to wait for the Civil Appropriation Bill. I know, dear Parker, that it is hardly within the range of possibilities that any other Bill should come forward before this Bill to which my Amendment can be attached. For ten days we have been on the Indian Appropriation Bill. With this the Fugitive Slave Bill is not germane.

The Civil Appropriation Bill will probably pass the House to-day. It will come at once to the Senate—be referred to the Committee on Finance, be reported back by them with amendments. After the consideration of these amendments of the committee, *and not before*, my chance will come. For this I am prepared, with a determination equal to your own. All this delay is to me a source of grief and disappointment. But I know my heart; and I know that sincerely, singly, I have striven for the cause.

You remember the picture in the "Ancient Mariner" of the ship in the terrible calm? In such a calm is my ship at this moment; I cannot move it. But I claim the confidence of friends, for I know that I deserve it.

*   *   *   *   ✿   *

Mason said to me this morning, "I see my friend Theodore Parker

---

* On the 27th of July, Mr. Sumner moved that the Committee on the Judiciary be instructed to consider the expediency of reporting a Bill for the immediate repeal of the Fugitive Slave Bill. But the Whig and Democratic parties at their recent Presidential conventions had declared the finality of the compromises, and, in the spirit of these resolutions, Mr. Sumner was refused an opportunity to discuss his proposition. At a later day he seized an occasion which offered, when, by a timely motion, he was able to secure a hearing. At the beginning of his speech, he thus alluded to the earlier obstructions :—

"And now at last, among these final crowded days of our duties here, but at this earliest opportunity, I am to be heard ; not as a favor but as a right. The graceful usages of this body may be abandoned, but the established privileges of debate cannot be abridged. Parliamentary courtesy may be forgotten, but parliamentary law must prevail. The subject is broadly before the Senate. By the blessing of God it shall be discussed."—*Congress Globe*, 1st Session, 32nd Congress, Appendix, p. 1102. It has been discussed.

is after you. The *Liberator* also calls Butler an *overseer*." * How gross the interpretation by the *Liberator* of the little *sotto voce* between Butler and myself. He stood in front of my desk when he spoke. I had no purpose of discussing the South Carolina laws, and promptly said so. There is a time for all things.

TO THE SAME.

Washington, Saturday Evening.

*.   *   *   *   *   *

In my course I have thought little what people would say, whether Hunkers or Free-Soilers, but how I could most serve the cause. This consciousness sustains me now while I hear reports of distrust, and note the gibes of the press.

Nothing but death, or deadly injustice, overthrowing all rule, can prevent me from speaking. In waiting till I did, I was right.

Ever yours.

TO MR. SUMNER.

West Newton, Sept. 6, 1852.

MY DEAR SUMNER,—You have made a grand speech, well researched, well arranged, well written, and, I doubt not, as well delivered. It was worth while to go to Congress and make such a speech in the Senate. I think you never did anything better as a work of art, never anything more timely. This, so far as you are concerned, will elevate you in the esteem of good men (American as well as European) as a man, an orator, and statesman.

You have now done what I all along said you would do, though I lamented you did not do it long ago.

Now, I look for some brave speeches from you in the State of Massachusetts; not one or two only, but many. Of course you are expected to speak at the convention at Lowell, and the ratification meeting at Boston. But there is a deal to do in Massachusetts this autumn. I thought you did not quite do your duty in 1850-1. If Rantoul and Mann had not been elected, we should have stood in a sad predicament in Congress. If Mann, and some others had relaxed their efforts, the State would have gone very differently, and all its strongholds would have been in the hands of the Hunkers.

Who shall take the place of Rantoul, and (now) of Fowler, who was a brave, good man? It seems to me there was never so much to be done as now.

There is one thing that I think may be brought about. I think we may elect Mann for Governor, and such a Governor no State ever had. I want to talk with you about that and many other things.

While I thank you so heartily for all that you have done, I hope you will remember that you have enlisted for the whole war, and fight new battles, and gain new triumphs to yourself and your cause. I had

* Referring to a remark of Mr. Butler, addressed to Mr. Sumner, which crept into the papers.

not seen a copy of your speech in full till to-day, and did not know when you will be anywhere, or I should have written you before.

Thanks for the documents. I hope to get the President's Message, and the report on Utah by-and-bye. I shall come to see you soon, as you are in town.

Good bye.   T. P.

FROM MR. SUMNER.

Washington, Dec. 17, 1852.

I await the corrected edition of your sermon,* which has produced everywhere a profound impression. The writers for the Washington Union have all read it, and Pryor,† the young Virginian, who has been placed in this establishment as the representative of Mason, Hunter, and Meade, read it through twice, and then announced to his friends that there was but one course for them, viz., "to maintain that Slavery is an unmixed good."

I hope some good friend in Boston will feel able to send a copy of the corrected edition to every member of Congress.

Ever yours.

The next letter alludes to the hostility of the slave-holding majority in the Senate, who controlled the organization through the sympathy of the presiding officer, who is the Vice-President of the United States. He had habitually left the Republican Senators off from the important committees.

TO HON. CHARLES SUMNER.

Boston, Dec. 20, 1852.

I am not at all sorry that Hale and the rest of you are left off from the committees. I am glad of it. It is one of the most foolish measures they could adopt. It is proclaiming this fact to the world :— In the Senate of the United States there is but one party; that it is the party of Slavery; it has two divisions—the *côté droit* and the *côté gauche*, the Democrat and the Whig. If a man is hostile to Slavery, seeks to hinder it from becoming federal, and national, and universal, he is not fit to serve on a committee of the Senate of "the freest and most enlightened nation of the earth"; he is to be cut off as an "*un-healthy member*"! It is always a good thing to drive a man to a declaration of his principles, and to an exhibition of them in act. I love to see a pirate gibbet himself at his own cost.

What Lord Carlisle says of you, on the one side, and what the United States Senate does with you on the other, will look nicely side by side on the pages of some future Bancroft or Hallam.

The Devil is said to be very old, but he must have been a sad child to

* On Mr. Webster.
† Afterwards representative in Congress and General in the Rebel Army.

have got no wiser after such experience. He is still an ass. Justice is the Ass's Bridge at which the poor Devil halts, and cannot budge an inch to get over.

TO MR. SUMNER.

March 5, 1854.

It is Sunday afternoon—yes, evening. I am waiting for a company of philanthropists to come and devise means to help the poor girls in the streets of Boston who are on the way to the brothel. I am sick, too, and have been tormented with rheumatism—on my sofa all the week; but I can't wait longer before thanking you for your brave and noble speech. It was Sumner all over. God bless you! I hope you will always keep the integrity of your own consciousness. We shall be beaten, *beaten*, BEATEN!—I take it, but must fight still.

I will send you a sermon of mine in a day or two.* If the Nebraska Bill passes, I have a scheme on foot which I will tell you of in time. Good bye.

TO SIDNEY HOMER.

April, 24, 1854.

I think we shall not disagree about the matter of Slavery. I feel no ill-will against the slave-holders. I have townsmen there who are slave-holders, nay, *relations*, who have been slave-holders ever since this century came in.† I hate the *institution* only. But we must end it; the two, Slavery and Freedom, cannot exist together in America, more than hawks and hens in the same coop. But so long as we send men like Everett to Congress, why, the South will drive us to the wall, and despise us—not unjustly. When the painted Jezebels of the North, male, not less than female, political, ecclesiastical, ceremonial, literary, will support Slavery, why, the South must despise us!

I have taken the *Richmond Examiner* ‡ for a year and more, to see what the South has to say on Slavery. I read all the Southern books on that theme, even the sermons. I am now writing a little book on the Commercial, &c., Effects of Slavery in the United States, from 1840 to 1850. It will be cyphering—political economy in the main.

---

* "Some Thoughts on the New Assault upon Freedom in America." Feb. 12, 1854.
† An Isaac Parker, seaman, was the witness whom Clarkson found, by accident, after extraordinary exertions to get hold of somebody who could testify to the point of armed boats going up the African river, to kidnap men.—"Hist. Slave Trade, II., 177." Was he too a relative ?
‡ Edited then by John M. Daniel, since Chargé des Affaires at Turin, and now again (1861) editor of the same paper, one of the ablest upon the side of Secession. Mr. Daniel was the only Southern editor, we believe, who published in full Mr. Parker's Discourse on Daniel Webster, not without animadversions from Southern quarters. But he is understood to have thought it worth publishing on account of its prevailing truthfulness, which indeed, many other Southern politicians acknowledged.

The next letter was written on occasion of Mr. Sumner's first attempt to resume his seat in the Senate after the assault made upon him by Mr. Brooks :—

TO MR. SUMNER.

R. R. Cars, Conn. River, February 27, 1857.

MY DEAR SUMNER,—God be thanked you are in your place once more! There has not been an anti-slavery speech made in Congress, unless by Giddings, since you were carried out of it; not one. Now that you bear yourself back again, I hope to hear a blast on that old war-trumpet which shall make the North ring again and the South tremble. How mean the Republicans look now-a-days! Think of Wilson wanting to have "these negro discussions stop." What worse did Webster ever say in his drunkenness and wrath? I wish I could inspire into you a little of my bodily strength just now, for a day or two. Now is the time for a blow, and such a blow! God bless you!

THEODORE PARKER.

TO MR. PARKER.

March 1, 1857.

I have sat in my seat only on one day. After a short time the torment to my system became great, and the cloud began to gather over my brain. I tottered out, and took to my bed. I long to speak, but I cannot. Sorrowfully I resign myself to my condition.

*   *   *   *   *   *

Had I an internal consciousness of strength, I might brave these professional menaces; but my own daily experience, while it satisfies me of my improvement, shows the subtle and complete overthrow of my powers organically, from which I can hope to recover only most slowly, *per intervalla ac spiramenta temporis.*

What I can say must stand adjourned to another day. Nobody can regret this so much as myself, and my unhappiness will be increased if I have not your sympathy in this delay.

I may die; but if I live, a word shall be spoken in the Senate which shall tear Slavery open from its chops to its heel—from its bully chops down to its coward heel!

Till then, patience.

Ever yours.

I fear that you are too harsh upon Wilson, and I fear that you and others will help undermine him by furnishing arguments to the lukewarm and to Hunkers. Bear this in mind, and be gentle.

TO THE SAME.

New York, Brevoort Hotel, March 5, 1858.

Your speech is beautiful, exhaustive, forcible, great ; but why did you have that tail-piece, *desinit in piscem?*

What is doing in Massachusetts? Is everybody asleep? No resolutions *vs.* Lecompton! No persistent daily pushing of the requisition for the discharge of Loring! No inquiry why Massachusetts money and hospitality went to welcome a slave-hunter at Bunker Hill!*

I range daily in the alcoves of Astor, more charming than the gardens of Boccaccio, and each hour a Decameron. Thus I try for comfort in my enforced quietude. But my time is fast coming. I am almost at the end—surely, surely!

TO MR. SUMNER.

March 15, 1858.

Many thanks for your kind letter. It always does me good to see your handwriting even, if nothing more. I know my speech *desinit in piscem*, but I meant it should do so, for the caudal termination is for the slave-holder. By that termination I meant to express my utter contempt for their threat of disunion. I should like to stand in the Senate, and *there* reply to some of their stuff. What a noble opportunity Foster (of Conn.) let slip the other day, when he was catechized on the "Republican Form of Government" of Slave States. I would have given sixpence for the opportunity he had. Men say slavery was consistent with a republican form of government in Athens and Rome. No doubt of it, with the meaning of *republican* at that time. So Abraham's sacrifice of Isaac was "imputed to him for righteousness."

TO REV. W. R. ALGER.

Boston, Newton Corner, July 7, 1857.

My DEAR MR. ALGER,—I shall not go to bed to-night without a line to you. I see by the newspapers which I have just read what the aldermen have done. They don't wish the people to face any kind of music, not even on Independence Day. Let me thank you for the brave, independent, timely, and wise discourse which you gave us on the Fourth.

You will long have the thanks of honest men for your words then spoken, and welcomed by the better and, I judge, the larger, part of the audience. If it is worth while to observe the day at all, except with fireworks, and spectacles, and dinners, *panem ac circenses!* then let the ideas of the Declaration be set forth, and the facts of our condition be compared therewith. In my day there have been four other addresses worthy of the day, one by Sprague, Mann, Sumner, and Whipple. Mann's and Sumner's were works which made a mark.

* Alludes to the municipal deference paid to the author of the Fugitive Slave Bill. See below, a letter to Rev. Mr. Alger.

Now, in a time of extreme peril, you have looked the facts of our condition fairly in the face, and told the people there were two changes to be met: the *despotic Church* of the Irish, the *despotic State* of the slave-holders. A little clique of men, haberdashers in trade and haber-dashers in politics, had just advertised their wares and their principles, on the 17th June, by inviting the author of the Fugitive Slave Bill to come and "call the roll of his slaves at the foot of Bunker's Hill monument." You did right in speaking of the act as "complimentary flunkeyism." I thank you for it. It was a brave, true word.

I know it is not quite pleasant to find such virulent assaults made on you—attacks by the newspapers, attacks by the aldermen. But there is no help for it. You must take hard licks if you would do manly service. I hope you are ready to endure what comes. Hitherto your course has been all prosperous.

If the ministers follow the instinct of their tribe and their individual habit, pray don't be discouraged. There is a To-morrow after To-day, and an Infinite God, to whom belongs truth, justice, and eternity.

Yours faithfully,
THEO. PARKER.

TO HON. CHARLES SUMNER.

Boston, March 28, 1858.

MY DEAR SUMNER,—The session of the General Court is over; it has done good and ill. But, on the whole, so far as Slavery is concerned, it has left us worse than it found us. Banks removed Loring; he could do no less; he dared do no less when the alternative was to remove him directly, or directly refuse to do so.

There was the fixed determination of the people in the State; there were his own words, uttered in private, but intended to affect and con-trol the public vote. He could not avoid removing him when the ques-tion came. But look at this:—

1. He tried to dodge the question by speaking of Loring in a general way with all the other probate judges. He and his party, represented by Duncan of Haverhill, Vose of Springfield, Charles Hale, &c., thought they could play that game. But (1) the Anti-Slavery Convention, and (2) the Democrats, showed the folly of that attempt, and drew the eyes of the people upon the Governor. It was said, "He and his party don't dare do it!" But, finding he must do it,—

2. He deprived the act of all moral significance whatever by the manner he did it in. He might have removed Loring without giving any reasons, and that would have been "*safe*," or by giving the two which were really cogent:—(1.) That Loring held an office in violation of the statute of the State made to meet such cases; and (2) that he had done an inhuman and wicked act, which outraged the sense of the people, and which went to the overthrow of all which it is the business of legislation to uphold and support—that he declared a man to be a piece of property. This had been noble.

Now, Banks did neither the one nor the other; he expressly disclaims all reference to the act of Loring, which had thus outraged the moral sense of the people, and led to the passage of the very law which

removed him, and then recommends the destruction of the Act that
forbids kidnapping in Massachusetts!

The animus of Banks is plain enough; but, depend upon it, he will
"take nothing by that motion." All the Hunkers hate him for removing Loring; they also despise him for the cowardly way in which he
made the removal. Of course they see the hollowness of the act.

Banks' message is poor in substance and shabby in form. It does
him no honor now, and will damage him much hereafter. Nobody can
foresee what the course of events will be between now and next October
and November. But I think he came in with a smaller majority this
last autumn.

Of course he looks for some Federal office in 1860, 1864, or 1868. But
if the anti-slavery tide is not high enough by that time to float a craft
of respectable tonnage, then there is no hope for him at all, and if it
be high enough, then it is a great thing for a man to have his ship
ballasted with anti-slavery Acts, the flag of liberty long flying at his
masthead. Banks don't see this. Does Chase? Does Seward? Why
not? It takes conscience to see the right; intellect won't do it. The
best ears in the world never perceive a rainbow, nor even the sun rise;
but the eyes of any little girl see both.

God bless you and your eyes!

THEODORE PARKER.

TO THE SAME.

Boston, May 6, 1858.

My dear Sumner,—I have not anything special to say, but as you
are most of the time in my thoughts I shall let a little note slip from
under my pen. So the Administration has carried its point in the House
of Representatives. I thought it would be so. Will it be as successful in
Kansas? A territory is normally with the Administration which has
the power for a considerable time. I mean, in the general way, by the
norm of time, not the norm of justice, the Administration controls all
the offices, buys up the able men who are in the market, has lots of
money in its diffusive hands. All Danaës whom this Jupiter Nebulosus
rains gold upon, will bear children like their sire. See how it is in
Oregon; the slave-holder whistles and all the Territory runs at once.
But when Oregon is a State we shall see quite other things. From the
point of view of mere vulgar statecraft, Seward is correct in his vote
to let her in. But from the grand standpoint of Eternal Right,
which is universal expediency for all time in all place, Wilson and
Hale were right. I should have voted as they; so would you also.
There are two courses for the Kansas men to pursue or choose
between:—

1. The pure moral course, *i. e.* to put their new Leavenworth constitution through by their votes, organize under it, and set up their State.
If need be, let them cast their bullets and shoulder their guns, make
ready, and take aim; it won't be necessary to fire. They can't come in
as a State this Congress; but in 1858 we choose a new House of Representatives. The Northern men who voted for Lecompton will go where
their predecessors went after voting for Douglas's Kansas-Nebraska

Bill. The new House of Representatives will make better terms to the Free States than the present House offers to the Slave States. In 1859-60, the outgoing, defeated, and despised Administration of Buchanan won't have the power of bribery, which now enables him to buy up so many Northern men. The Senate will be glad to have Kansas in the Union, and so out of the presidential campaign; and she will come in free and glorious.

2. The pure politic way. Repudiate their own new constitution now, accept the Lecompton constitution with the bribe, come in at once, then repudiate Lecompton, put up the Leavenworth constitution, and be a Free State.

The first is immensely the better way; it is honest, clear, and straight-forward. I have not much confidence in the Northern Free-State men in Kansas. Robinson is a humbug, Pomeroy is ditto, and Jim Lane is Jim Lane; Conway is a noble fellow, about as faithful as Phillips and Garrison. But the *auri sacra fames* misleads the most of them. The Land Fever is more contagious than the Presidential Fever, and equally fatal to the moral powers.

Banks behaves pretty well as Governor, and will be of much service to us. I think how admirably Wilson has borne himself all winter and all the spring.

Yours ever,

T. P.

TO THE HON. HORACE MANN,

Boston, October 19, 1853.

MY DEAR SIR,—I send you the *Anti-Slavery Standard*, only one I have. It may not be the one I borrowed of you. My head has been so ill lately, and I so busy with matters not to be deferred, that I have not been able to do much in reference to the libel matter. There are some of the things which have occurred to me as worth thinking of—the language of Cicero, in the old Roman Republic, against Verres. You will see the passages pointed out in the well-studied article of Smith's Classical Dict., Art. "Verres." There are some nice points of resemblance between that hog and Mr. ——; and also Cicero's oration against Piso (see his article in Smith, Vol. III. p. 372 *et seq.*), and against Antony. The last is not so applicable perhaps; but it shows what license of speech was deemed proper in "the last great man whom Rome never feared." I should not want to make any comparison of —— with Antonius, but with Verres it is proper to compare him.

I am sorry that I am so little read in controversies; but, though I have the reputation, I believe, of washing down my dinner with nice old sulphuric acid, and delighting to spear men with a jest, and to quarrel with all sorts of people, I never read two theological contro-versies through in my life. Things of a truculent sort may be found in Milton—I will look them up—in Horsley's Tracts, in controversy with Priestley; in Whitman's controversy with Stuart. The papers relating to Stuart I have not found as yet. Have you a copy of the *Anti-Jacobin*, in which Canning and the others wrote?

Junius, of course, presents a rich reaping for any one; so do Brougham's speeches; so the *London Quarterly Review*—say in the time when Gifford was the editor. Then the political writings of America, in the time just before the Revolution, and still more before and at the beginning of "the late war."

The trial of John Philip Zenger for libel, at New York, in 1735, is one that offers some nice points. I have not read it since 1836; but it is in the State Trials, and is remarkable for many reasons. I am sorry that I am just now so pressed with work that I have little time at command, but am not less

Truly yours,

THEO. PARKER.

TO HON. J. P. HALE.

Boston, December 19, 1856.

MY DEAR MR. HALE,—Thank you for the good words the telegraph tells of your saying. Send me a *Globe* now and then which contains the words themselves. I am sorry to notice the timidity of the Republican men, not discussing "the relation of master and slave," declaring it is not their intention ever to interfere with Slavery in the States! It is my intention as soon as I can get the power. I will remember the guarantees of the Constitution as well as the compromises! But I write only to ask you to write me what you twice told of the talk with Toombs, when he said the slave-holder would call the roll of his slaves on Bunker Hill.

God bless you!

THEO. PARKER.

FROM HON. J. P. HALE.

Washington, December 23, 1856.

MY DEAR SIR, — As you have requested me to furnish you with an account of the conversation which I had with Mr. Toombs, of Georgia, in relation to the appearance of the slave-holder and his slaves on Bunker Hill, I shall do it. When I first heard the remark, and when I first mentioned it to you, I had no idea of meeting it again, but since it has been made public, and various versions of it have been made, I will give you the conversation as nearly as I can from memory. I do not like to be put in the ungracious attitude of retailing for political purposes, the private conversations I may have had with gentlemen, whether members of the Senate or not. The conversation with Mr. Toombs was not such as to be considered of a confidential character, nor are my relations with Mr. Toombs such as to warrant the assumption of such a conversation between us.

With this preface I will give you, as nearly as I can recollect, the remarks of Mr. Toombs.

He said that the discussions at the North on the subject of Slavery, instead of having weakened or shaken the institution, had had a directly contrary effect on the public mind, both North and South. That the examination of the institution which has been induced by this anti-slavery agitation had had the effect to strengthen the rightfulness and propriety of the institution in the minds of Southerners, and that the same, he had no doubt, was true of the North; and it was in connection with this growth of public opinion at the North favorable to the institution of slavery, that he made the remark that I should see the slave-holder and his slaves on Bunker Hill. This is the substance of the conversation. The precise phraseology, of course, I do not pretend to recollect, but that I have given you the substance I am entirely certain.

With much respect, very truly your friend,

JOHN P. HALE.

TO MR. HALE.

Boston, April 24, 1858.

My dear Hale,—Thank you for writing me so. I have often wanted thus to address you, and sometimes have done it. But I am a little afraid of the "Hon. Gentleman from New Hampshire," the "Hon. Senator." Did not I vote for him once for President?

It is Saturday night now. I have done my sermon, and girded up my loins for to-morrow. Last Sunday I preached on the Infinite Power of God; to-morrow I try the Infinite Wisdom of God, then the Infinite Justice, and at length the Infinite Love. I delight in writing and preaching. No poet has more joy in his song than I in my sermons. I wish I could preach at the House of Representatives. But (1) the House of Representatives would not let me. (2.) I could not come this year. May 31, I go to the Progressive Friends in Chester County, Pennsylvania, and I do not like to be away more than once in a season. I did think of a trip to Washington, and attending the Scientific Association at Baltimore, but I give it up for the Friends.

I am glad you like my revival sermons. They sold 10,000 in ten days, and the demand still continues. They were stereotyped in forty-eight hours after they were preached; but they struck off 5000 copies before they stopped the press to stereotype the matter. I have another I will send you in a day or two, preached two months ago.

I want an Executive Document on the Mexican Boundary, a great quarto volume.

I wish you could magnetize Banks with your great generous honesty; why cannot you? He appointed Parker, the kidnapper's counsel in the Burns case, as his aid. Turned out Loring and appointed the kidnapper's counsel! I do not believe he has ever repented that crime,—I mean Parker! He changed his measures, not his principles I fear. Besides, Banks turns men out of office for mere party motives, and puts worse men in. He is too much of a man to lose. I feel great interest in his welfare and wish somebody would help him. I wonder who are his cronies?

Yours faithfully,

THEODORE PARKER.

What can we do for poor noble Sumner?

TO THE SAME.

Boston, May 12, 1858.

Now a word about Kansas. There are two modes of action for Kansas independence. I. The political course: to accept the Lecompton Constitution, with its bribes; organize under it, but with free State men for its officers. They are in the Union. Next, repudiate that constitution, and make a new one. I find that recommended, but I object to it. 1. It is fraudulent. 2. It can't succeed, as there are seven chances against it to three in its favor (the Government will declare the slavery men elected, &c.). 3. It is false to the friends of Kansas, who have reported her as a virtuous young lady in love with a nice young man, and hostile to the miserable old curmudgeon, her guardian has tried to coax, and then to drive, and finally to bully her into marrying. Now, if both suitors come with her into the meeting-house, and then she chooses the old rich miser, consummates the marriage, gets the settlements fixed as her absolute and exclusive property as *femme sole*, and then runs off with her " nice young man," and squats on the estate conveyed to her by the defrauded husband, I think her reputation is gone, and won't come back " till the kye come home," and her family will be blown upon.

II. The moral course: to accept the new Leavenworth Constitution; organize under it, repudiate the Lecompton and all its works; drill their soldiers, cast their bullets, shoot at targets with " Lecompton" on them, painted either as Old Nick, or Old Buck, and be ready. There will be no fighting, or need of it; only need to be ready to fight, though Kansas will not come into the Union in 1858, or in the winter of 1859. But next autumn a new House of Representatives must be chosen. The Lecompton men of the North will go where the Kansas-Nebraska men went in 1854 and 1856. The defeated and outgoing Administration will not have the means to bribe as in 1857–8. The House will let in Kansas, with yet more generous grants than the Democrats have offered her as bribe for slavery. The Presidential and Senatorial Executive will be glad to get rid of the mischief, and have a clear field for the election battle in the autumn of 1860. So Kansas may be in the Union before Christmas, 1859. She must say " No" to the old lecher who wants to add her to his harem; " Yes" to the young man whom she loves (and he loves her); she will have fortune enough by-and-bye. I meant to have said that in a speech at New York, but rheumatism hindered. I will let it off at Boston in the Anti-Slavery Convention.

Faithfully yours,

THEODORE PARKER.

TO HON. S. P. CHASE.

Boston, March 16, 1854.

MY DEAR SIR,—I thank you heartily for your kind letter of the 12th. It was more welcome for the *admonition* than even for the com-

mendation it contained. I thank you *heartily* for the admonition.*
But, (1), the introduction of my peculiar views in this matter will do
no harm to the special matter in hand. It will only, as I think, prejudice men against *me*, not in favor of the general wickedness, *slavery*,
or the special sin, the enslavement of Nebraska. It is of small consequence to me whether I am unpopular or not. I have nothing to hope
from popular favors, and, thank God, I fear nothing from popular
frowns.

2. I have studied this matter of the Divine origin of the Bible
and the Divine Nature of Jesus of Nazareth all my life. If I understand anything it is that. I say there is no evidence—external or
internal—to show that the Bible or Jesus had anything miraculous in
their origin or nature, or anything divine in the sense that word is
commonly used. The common notion on this matter I regard as an
error—one, too, most *fatal to the development of mankind*. Now, in all
my labors I look to the general development of mankind, as well as to
the removal of every such special sin as *American Slavery*, as *war*,
drunkenness, &c., therefore I introduce my *general principle* along with
my *special measures*. I become personally unpopular, *hated* even; but
the *special measures* go forward obviously; the *general principle* enters
into the public ear, the public mind, and what is true of it will go into
the heart of mankind, and do its work. I think I work prudently—I
know I do not *rashly*, and without consideration.

Here let me say that the thing I value most in a man is *fidelity to his
own nature*, to his mind and conscience, heart and soul. The integrity
of consciousness is to me above all outside agreements or disagree-
ments. So I can esteem a man as much for disagreeing with me as
agreeing.

Allow me also to mention the admiration and esteem I feel for you.
Your whole career, so far as I know it, is most honorable—eminently
manly—religious. Sumner told me your argument in the *Van Zandt*
case was the ablest forensic paper ever prepared in America. My
judgment in such matters is not worth much; but it is the ablest *I*
ever saw; not inferior to the *great* English arguments. I know not
why the *Times* omitted all I also said of you at Fanueil Hall. It was
clumsily said, with no premeditation—the whole speech was *impromptu*.
But this was part of it, that the outer man showed as much intellect as
Webster (his picture was behind me), and his (Mr. Chase's) whole
aspect and history proved that his heart was even better than his
head.

I think you and I take the same view of the Independent
Democratic party. I assent to all in your letters thereon. I often, at
public meetings, have set forth the same opinion. But I confine
myself more to disseminating the *ideas* of political morality, &c., than
to organizing men into political parties. When the idea has hold of
the public mind, I hope to help organize men about the principle for
the sake of some measures thence derived.

I thought of making my statement of the encroachments of the slave
spirit more minute, by enumerating numerous other advances, but I feared

---

* Mr. Chase had deprecated the introduction of Mr. Parker's theological views in
connection with the purely moral points of Anti-slavery.

to weaken the faggot by putting too many sticks in it for the withe to hold. I wish some one would make a special history of the whole thing—like Mr. Newman's "Crimes of the House of Hapsburg."

As soon as I get the census of 1850, I mean to write a book on the "General Influences and Special Effects of Slavery in the United States from 1840 to 1850." If you can send me any *documents*, State or National, or *hints* thereto, I shall be much obliged to you.

Believe me ever, gratefully and truly yours,

THEO. PARKER.

TO THE SAME.

Newton Corner, near Boston, July 25th, 1856.

MY DEAR SIR,—I believe I think more highly of you than you of yourself; for I *do* consider you a great man and a great statesman. I have always expected great things and noble things of you; always shall, and such only. If you are not a great statesman, then who is? and what is the standard to measure men by? I have rejoiced in your many manly and noble deeds—done in times of trial, too—and in the well-deserved honors you have won. I am a minister, and so may easily be supposed to have that sort of *stupid blindness* which so often belongs to the profession. But I am not so stupid as to believe that great offices can be filled, in such times as these, without occasional mistakes and errors, even in great men; and I am glad you wrote me the letter which came a day or two since, for it gives me an opportunity to mention two things which I complained of in the speech at New York, which lay heavy on me.

1. Of the letter in which you accepted the nomination to the Governorship of Ohio.

2. Of the fact that you let the United States kidnappers take off Margaret Garner, after she had broken the laws of your State by killing her own child.

When the letter was first written we all talked it over—I mean your friends in N. E. I spoke with the most suspicious of them; some had been *Whigs*, some *Democrats*, some Know-Nothings. They all thought it was a "backing down;" that it weakened the usual effect of your noble course. Some thought, however, it was made for "buncombe," and that you "could not be elected without it." I have not the papers now at hand—out here in the country—but remember that it seemed to me to foreclose all Federal action against slavery in the Slave States. Now, my notion of the matter is this: the Constitution (I think in section iv. art. 4) provides that the general Government shall guarantee to every State in this *Union a Republican form of Government*. Certainly that is not a Republican form of government where 280,000 white men own 384,000 black men, as in South Carolina. Or if it be, then the Czar or the Pope might claim a Republican form of government for Russia and Rome. Now, if I were the whole people of the North, I should say to South Carolina, "You may establish a Republican form of government for yourself, or we will do it for you; peaceably, if we can, but forcibly, if we must. We shall attend to the

Q 2

guarantees of the constitution, and not allow the majority of the South Carolinians to be bought and sold like cattle." When the anti-slavery spirit is strong enough in the North, we shall do that, if need be. But we may be forced to interfere with slavery in the Slave States by one of two ways: 1, there may be an insurrection, and the only way to put it down may be by *declaring the slaves free*; or, 2, the slaveholders my proceed violently to enslave the poor whites; in which latter case, I take it, the present public opinion in the North would demand the interference of the Federal authorities—notwithstanding the fact that *white* slavery is as constitutional as *black* slavery. Now, it seemed to me that your letter held out a promise that you would not use the Federal authority against slavery, and this would embarrass your future action. I don't object to doing one thing at a time, and insist that each step should be taken in the most cautious and deliberate manner; but would not promise *not to take other steps*. I may easily be wrong, but I thought you did so, if not directly, at least by implication.

2. In the Garner case, I thought the anti-slavery Governor of Ohio would get possession of that noble woman, either by the *hocus pocus* of some legal technicality, which would save appearances, or else by the *red right arm of Ohio*, and I confess I was terribly chagrined that it did not turn out so. If a mechanic had pursued his *fugitive apprentice* to Ohio, and that apprentice had set a barn on fire, or stolen a white hat, I think the apprentice would have been held for trial.

Now, I have made a *clean breast* of the whole matter, which has tormented me a good deal. For I look with anxious eyes on the few men of great ability and noble character, and am much concerned at any mistakes they commit. I know you will honor the motive which leads me to write as I have. I look to you for great services to be done to your country, and shall try all your actions by the justice of the Infinite God.

So, with hearty wishes for your prosperity, believe me

Sincerely your friend,

THEODORE PARKER.

TO THE SAME.

St. Albans, Vt., Feb. 16, 1856.

DEAR SIR,—I write to thank you for your excellent message relating to the Kansas matter, and to ask two favors :—

1. That you would send me a copy of that message, and of your inaugural speech, if in a pamphlet form ; and

2. That you would collect your various speeches, &c., into a volume, as Mr. Seward has done.

I hope you received a copy of my "Defence," which I sent you months ago.

Yours respectfully,

THEO. PARKER.

TO THE SAME.

Boston, March 29, 1858.

MY DEAR SIR,—I had been intending to write you a letter, thanking you for the pamphlet copy of your message, which came to me a few days ago, but I had not time to say all I wished until this day, when your welcome note of 25th inst. came to hand.

I think your last message comes nearer to the ideal of what a Governor's message should be than any one I ever saw. I like much the statistics of the industry, and of the wealth you mention (pp. 4 and 5, *et passim*). Think of it! You have 270,000 landholders—not including town-lots—out of a population of 2,400,000! England has 18,000,000 people, and not more than 30,000 to 35,000 landholders, including the owners of town-lots! There the plough is never in the hands of the owners of the soil; the normal condition of a Briton is that of a tenant, not a freeholder. I hope Ohio will never thus go down.

I am glad to see how rich you are — 849,000,000 dollars to 1,000,000,000 dollars (p. 4), all won out of the earth in fifty or sixty years! Compare that with the Slave States. South Carolina in 1855 was valued at a little less than 169,000,000 dollars, excepting the slaves; that is the value of all the land and things in the State, with its 30,000 square miles of land, and 700,000 people! In 1857 Boston was appraised at 258,000,000 dollars—90,000,000 dollars more than the entire State of South Carolina. What an odds betwixt the results of slave labor and free labor! The property of Massachusetts in 1799 was 97,000,000 dollars; in 1849 it was 597,000,000 dollars; now we guess it at 1,000,000,000 dollars. Yet we have but 7500 square miles of land, one-third of that not being fit for the plough; and our natural products are only trees, stones, and ice—if we except the *cranberries*, which a Southerner thrusts into the mouth of one of our Northern representatives.

I am glad you mention the debt as a bad feature. This is a great blot, and I think your remarks are admirable on it.

But of course the great matter is slavery. If we don't settle the matter right, we go down, just as the other republics have done; and if we do presently annihilate this terrible curse, then, I think, there is such a course open for the American people as the most sanguine poet never dared to dream—an industrial democracy, with the whole continent at our command—the Anglo-Saxon blood in our veins—why, what is too much to expect of such a people? I think slavery is doomed to perish soon. Banks, a not sanguine man, told me a month ago, that he did not know a Southern politician who thought it would last forty years in any Southern State! As you say, the Devil is in great wrath because he knoweth that his *time is short*.

You say well; we want a public opinion, which political men may thence shape into form. But we want one thing more—a man who can wisely and bravely embody what public opinion there is already. Such a man is one of the forces that *make* public opinion; for while the thinkers can only persuade and convince men one by one, and act on thoughtful men, the magistrate, in a high place, moves men by his position and the authority thereof, and moves such as do not think much. In 1860 we shall want a man for the Presidency who has never yielded to the South; we don't want a fanatic, a dreamer, an enthusiast, but we don't want a coward or a trimmer. If such an one had been nominated in 1856, he would have carried the nation, I think. Instead of that we took a Johnny Raw, of whom we knew no evil, but the nation knew of no statesmanlike qualities in him. How could the people trust *him*?

Governor Banks has just now removed Judge Loring. He did not dare to do otherwise. The people demanded the act. But he has damaged himself greatly by the *manner* of the removal. He expressly disclaims *all moral motives for the act*, and then turns round to destroy the personal liberty law, so that he may atone for the removal! He has injured the republican party more than Gardner ever did, and has left us in a worse condition than he found us. He lacked moral courage. God has given us special faculties for special functions; and as the most delicate ear can never see a rainbow, which yet fills the eye of every boy or girl, so the nicest and ablest mind fails to notice the *right*, which is God's idea of expediency, while the humblest man who keeps his conscience clear and active, sees it at once and without much ado. I wonder that able men do not see the immense force of justice in the affairs of men, and the power that a just and fearless statesman is always sure of at length. I should rather *deserve* the Presidency for my great qualities, than have it for twenty years without deserving.

But I did not mean to write a busy man a long letter. May God bless you in your high office and higher talents.

Yours truly,
THEODORE PARKER.

I send you a pamphlet speech.

TO THE SAME.

Boston, August 30, 1858.

MY DEAR MR. CHASE,—It gave me great pleasure to see your face at meeting the last Sunday in February, and I took all possible pains to get near you; but the crowd of friends who wished to bid me good-bye kept me from you. I was forced to go out of town the moment I left the meeting-house, so could not seek you at the hotel. The next morning I took the earliest cars for the West and went to Schenectady, where I had an academical address to deliver before the graduates of Union College. A queer college it is too, where they train up young *politicians*, not young *scholars!* I hoped to find you somewhere on your route, and have a word of talk about the state of the nation, but I must wait another opportunity.

I have just returned from a wagon journey, with a friend, of 700 miles through Massachusetts, New Hampshire, Vermont, and a part of New York, the Adirondac Mountains and the Hudson River region, and the whole length of Connecticut, from New York line to Massachusetts. The weather was delightful, not a bad hour in twenty-one days. We saw such signs of wealth, comfort, temperance, intelligence, and virtue as were exceedingly grateful. I saw but one American with patched trousers, but one American at all drunk, and he had lived at the West, and returned fat and rich to his native village in Vermont, and was making merry over his good fortune. We slept but one night in a great town (Albany), but kept in the little villages, and travelled in the by-roads, resting in little towns. I wish you could pass over the same route to gladden your humane eyes with sights of the welfare which comes from the industrial democracy of the North. You would see the practical superiority of the puritan New-Englander over all the other peoples on the Continent, I think. In parts of Vermont he has been damaged by the Canadian French, who take down the tone of many villages, and even of such towns as St. Albans and Burlington itself. In the border towns of Massachusetts and Connecticut you see the influence of the Dutch, who have *dirtied* the land a little, and given a shiftless look to the people. But elsewhere the sight of the towns and farms, with the schools and meeting-houses, and happy people, was a continual delight. What a change since 1758; but what a yet greater change will another hundred years of peaceful industrial development make. With thanks for your noble services, and hopes for a yet greater future,

Yours faithfully,
THEODORE PARKER.

P.S.—What wonders will 100 years do for Ohio!

TO THE SAME.

Newton Corner (near Boston), July 9, 1858.

MY DEAR SIR,—I sent you a little speech I made the other day at the Anti-Slavery Meeting, which I think quite important, not for any special merit of mine therein, but for the *direction* of it. I hope you will look at the argument.

I send you also a copy of the *Christian Examiner* for July, (it is the Unitarian periodical), which contains an article on the "material condition of the people of Massachusetts." It is not to be known that I wrote it. I want you to see the facts of our condition in this little State, with its 7800 square miles of land, and its niggardly soil and climate. I wish there was a little more *spunk* in the people. If you will let Horace Mann see it after you have done with it I shall be glad, for he still takes a deep interest in the State he has done so much to bless.

I wonder where that collection of your works is which you spoke of two years ago.

I shall send you a Fourth of July sermon in a day or two, which will make the tenth address I have published in six months, which is something for a sick man.

With hearty thanks for your many public services, and hopes for yet more, believe me,

Yours faithfully,
THEODORE PARKER.

TO THE SAME.

Newton Corner (near Boston), July 25, 1858.

MY DEAR SIR,—I was glad to see your face to-day, but grieve that I could not take you by the hand, and have a little talk. But, unluckily, I had to fly out of town as soon as the sermon was over, and you also was gone when I came down from the desk. I go to Schenectady to-morrow, or else I should do myself the favour of seeing you at the Revere House. When you return you will find a letter, and one or two little notions of mine. I hope you will have a good time at Dartmouth. I expect to see Mr. Seward at Union College on Tuesday.

Yours truly,
THEODORE PARKER.

TO THE SAME.

New York, Feb. 4, 1859.

MY DEAR SIR,—I shall not go out of the country—perhaps never to return—without thanking you for the kind letter you sent me a few weeks ago, as well as many kind letters before. Certainly it is unpleasant to be thus stopped in the midst of my work, with my plans but half carried out, and many literary labours only half-done, and yet not to be finished by another hand. Yet I do not complain. If I recover—and the doctors tell me I have one chance in ten! only *nine* chances against me to *one* in my favor!—I shall be thankful for the experience of affection and friendship which my illness has brought from all parts of the land. If I do *not* recover, I shall pass off joyfully, with an entire trust in that Infinite Love which cares more for me than I care for myself.

Let me thank you for the noble services you have rendered your State and your nation, and hope that they will continue to increase and bless mankind.

Faithfully yours,
THEODORE PARKER.

This letter relates to a Convention chosen by the people of Massachusetts, to present a revision of the State Constitution to the popular vote :—

TO MR. ELLIS.

Boston, Nov. 20, 1853.

Another Sunday morning has passed away without my seeing your face. As you have so long been not only a friend to me, but a very dear and near friend—almost a father—I cannot any longer keep from speaking to you with the pen, while I cannot with the mouth. You take such an interest in what goes on at the Music Hall, that I must tell you last Sunday I preached on " The Good among Things Evil, and its

Ultimate Triumph over Them;" that was a continuation of one which you heard on " The Beautiful in Things Homely, the sublime in Things Common, and the Eternal in Things Daily and Transient." To-day I spoke on " Love of God and its Natural Forms of Manifestation." This is only half of the whole, the rest is to follow on Thanksgiving Day, " On the various Forms of Philanthropy which distinguish this Age above all others."

Charles tells me all about you. The rheumatism did not surprise me. I saw how much you felt, and knew it would report itself in some ailment before long. I trust the dry air and fine weather of South Carolina will drive all the ache from your bones, and that Mrs. E. and Katie, and Mary Jane, will banish all aches from your heart. I was quite glad to hear through Charles how well they all were.

You have heard the result of the election. I was surprised at it, for I thought we should carry the New Constitution by a small majority. But I am not very sorry at the result, and the more I think of it the less do I lament.

1. The Convention was faulty in its members. Adams, Mann, Palfrey, Stephen C. Phillips, were left out. They are the four ablest free-soilers in Massachusetts—powerful men, high-minded men, not seekers for office. The free-soilers could not entirely respect a Convention which left out this array of talent and integrity. Then, there was not an anti-slavery man in the Convention. The men who got up the Convention did not want Palfrey or Mann; no attempt was made to elect them; not an anti-slavery man was proposed anywhere. The "leaders" would not think of such men as Phillips or Garrison, or other men who go for abstract right. Now there is a class in Massachusetts, not a large one, but one of a good deal of influence even now, who look up to men of integrity and principle, and trust them.

2. Then the Convention did not trust the people, who were much more radical than their Constitution. The leading men thought the district system was the only right one—but said " The people will not accept it." They thought the judges ought to be elected by the people, but said, " The people are not up to that." So was it with many things. Now there are men in Massachusetts who understand some things. They had not confidence in the Convention when they saw that the Convention was not looking for right, but only for the available. I heard this said many times while the Convention was in session, and told some of the leaders, " If you don't trust the mind and conscience of the people, they will not trust you and your compromise between your own sense of right and their selfishness."

3. Then the Constitution itself was quite faulty. It failed to meet the great difficulty of representation. The Convention shirked the burthen, made a provisional arrangement to last one year, and then left the whole thing to the Legislature and the people. That was only a makeshift. Besides, the Constitution was not consistent as a whole. It lacked unity, and did not rest uniformly on great principles. Thus it went before the people. It had the endorsement of the free-soil party, a party which has been willing to sacrifice its principles ever since 1848. But some of the most eminent men of the party came out and repudiated the New Constitution. Mann had left the State;

S. C. Phillips said not a word for it. Dr. Howe barely tolerated it. It was not so bad as the old one. Palfrey came out against it in a pamphlet, which the free-soilers did not answer, but only abused. Adams spoke against it, spoke well too, in many particulars. Hoar opposed it, so did Josiah Quincy.

The free-soilers had many able men in the field. Dana (who really does not belong with the reformers, and will ere long, I think, slip out of their team,) Sumner, and many smaller men. But H. and B., who are a curse to any party, went bawling all over the State. I should suspect a cause was wrong which such persons defended. Then the *Commonwealth* newspaper was miserably weak. The Whig papers wrote able arguments against the New Constitution. The *Commonwealth* did not meet arguments with arguments, only with sneers, jests, &c. The "Reformers" are defeated, horse, foot, and dragoons. The free-soilers are down flat, at the mercy of Caleb Cushing, whom they made a judge! If this breaks up the coalition, I shall be glad. A free-soiler coalescing with a hunker, who stands on the Baltimore platform,* is what I wish not to see again. But I fear the free-soilers will fall yet lower; we shall see. By-and-bye we shall have better times.

TO HON. GEORGE BANCROFT.

Boston, March 16, 1858.

MY DEAR BANCROFT,—If I don't like your seventh volume it must be not only your fault, for I doubt any man in the United States more carefully reads or more thoroughly admires true history, but a very rare fault besides. For the six goodly volumes only give promise of good to come. Let me thank you heartily for the part you have taken against the Lecompton* wickedness. I only wish it had been a little earlier. A more wicked administration, where can you find it in your modern historical researches?

Here is what I get about the Africans at the battle of Bunker Hill; fighting in it, I mean; my friend William C. Nell, a coloured man of this city, helps me to the facts. He has written a quite valuable book on "The Colored Patriots of the Revolution," Boston, 1855, 1 Vol. 12mo., pp. 396. On p. 21, he mentions the fact that (Peter) Salem, a colored man, shot Major Pitcairn. His authority for it is Col. Swett's "History of Bunker Hill Battle," (3rd ed., Boston, 1827). I suppose you have Col. Swett's pamphlet, but lest it be not at hand I make this extract:—" Among the foremost of the leaders was the gallant Major Pitcairn, who exultingly cried 'The day is ours!' when Salem, a black soldier, and a number of others, shot him through and he fell; " and p. 43, again, " Many Northern blacks were excellent soldiers, but Southern troops could not brook an equality with negroes. Nov. 15, 1775, Washington prohibited their enlistment. Besides Salem, Cuffee Whittemore fought bravely, in the redoubt. He had a ball through his hat on Bunker Hill, fought to the last, and when compelled to

---

* Enunciation of the principles of the Democratic party which has always been the servile instrument of Southern aggression.

† Alludes to the Bill by that name, which was a democratic measure to compel the people of Kansas to become a State upon pro-slavery terms.

retreat, though wounded, the splendid arms of the British officers were prizes too tempting for him to come off empty handed; he seized the sword of one of them slain in the redoubt, and came off with the trophy, which in a few days he unromantically sold. He served faithfully through the war, with many hair-breadth 'scapes from sword and pestilence," pp. 25, 26, of Appendix, note M.

" Gen. Winslow stated a contribution was made in the army for Salem and he was presented to Washington as having slain Pitcairn, who was killed on the British left, according to all authorities," *ibid.*, p. 25, note M.

I requested Mr. Nell to hunt up all the additional information he could get for me touching this matter. He has just reported (3 p.m.) as follows :—

Cornelius Harkell was killed and buried on Bunker Hill; his daughter, Mrs. Harriet Brown, now lives in Revere Street, Boston.

Titus Coburn was in the battle; his widow now lives in Andover, (Mass.), and draws a pension.

Prince Ames was also in the battle; he was from Andover. His widow, Eunice A., Æt. xcii., now lives at Jamaica Plains, and draws a pension.

Barzillai Leu was also in the battle, likewise from Andover. He was a fifer; he has a son of the same name, Barzillai Leu, now living in Boston, and two daughters, Mrs. Farmer and Mrs. Dalton, in S. Russell Street, Mrs. Dalton lives in Charlestown in the summer, on the edge of Bunker Hill.

Cato Howe was in the battle, he was from Plymouth, Mass. His widow died in Belknap Street, in 1856.

In the engravings of the battle when I was a boy, the black man, Peter Salem, appears in the act of shooting Major Pitcairn; but now-a-days a white man is put in his place. Richard Frothingham, in his account of Bunker Hill battle, makes no mention of Peter. He appears, however, on some of the bills of the Monument, Freeman's and Charlestown Banks.

Last 17th of June, when Senator Mason fulfilled Senator Toombs' prophecy, Mr. Everett said :—" It is the monument of the day, of the event of the battle of Bunker Hill, of all the brave men who shared its perils, alike of Prescott, and Putnam, and Warren, the chiefs of the day, and the colored man Salem, who is reported to have shot the gallant Pitcairn as he mounted the parapet."

When you publish your volume I wish you would send Nell a copy. Negroes get few honors.

Yours faithfully,
THEODORE PARKER.

Here is advice to a young friend touching the matter of fugitive slaves :—

TO MISS GROVER.

Boston, Nov. 6, 1857.

MY DEAR MISS GROVER,—I have just conferred with one of the best lawyers in Boston, who thinks there is no danger in the woman's remaining in Lawrence. The Supreme Court of Massachusetts long ago decided (in the *Med* case) that a slave brought to Massachusetts by her master was by that act *free*. It will still adhere to that decision. It seems to me she might quit the service of her claimant, and go *about her business.* I think he would *not dare molest her.* But, perhaps you had better talk with some lawyer in Lawrence. If the young woman is *timid,* and will be in fear of her master, then it will be perfectly safe to send her to the *Quakers.* I don't like to *advise* in this matter. You and she will know better than I which to do. Please let me know what is done finally, and her name, and so oblige,

Yours faithfully,
THEODORE PARKER.

Our Supreme Court will not heed the Dred Scott decision.

TO THE SAME.

Boston, Nov. 20, 1857.

MY DEAR MISS GROVER,—Mr. Stephenson is a very respectable colored man, a clerk in the glass warehouse of one of my friends, in Haverhill Street. He wrote me about the matter you refer to—to learn your name in full. I told him it was *Miss*, not *Mrs.* I am glad the colored people do this, for their sake, and yours.

Truly yours,
THEODORE PARKER.

TO THE SAME.

Boston, Jan. 11, 1858.

DEAR MISS GROVER,—What a world of trouble you have with the black people, whom you would so gladly serve! I sent word to Mr. Stephenson soon as I received your note a month ago, and made inquiries of Mr. Nell, the most "*respectable*" colored man in Boston, and heard no more. He says S. is a good fellow. I don't know what will come of it all. Perhaps you will write an amended version of the Hebrew word, "Put not your trust in *Princes!* "

I hope you will send me a copy of the farewell address. Betty, I suppose, has gone to Tennessee, to become the mother of bondmen and bondwomen till the tenth generation. We must bear as much from *this* untoward generation as Moses from his nation of slaves, who wanted to go back to Egypt, their land of bondage.

I think Plato must have had the advantage of the companion you speak of, and I hope it has been *communicated* to him that he is thought a greater man than ever.

Yours faithfully,
THEODORE PARKER.

TO HON. JOHN APPLETON, BANGOR.

Boston, June 1, 1857.

MY DEAR SIR,—The matter you spoke of the other day is one of such importance that I will set down one or two things which have come to me since you left us.

In Pitiscus, "Lexicon Antiquitatum Romanarum," s. v. "Libertus" is a very valuable essay on the whole matter, full of learning and careful thought. I suppose you will find Pitiscus in the Theological Library at Bangor, if nobody else has it. Pitiscus had the advantage of Rosini's "Corpus Antiquitatum Romanorum," which he had edited. He has some things I think not in Walton.

Rosini, a great authority, says, "*Libertus antiquis temporibus. . . . civis erat, sed publico nullo, nisi Apparitoris, aut Coactoris fungebatur munere. Apparitores autem erant, ut post ostendetur, Præcones, Interpretes, Accensi, Lictores, Viatores, Statores,*" (Amsterdam Ed., 1743, p. 77). He cites (p. 78), a "*Formula manumissionis,*" which Jacobus Cujacius found in an ancient MS., and which, it seems, the master gave in writing to the *Libertus: " Ille civis Romanus esto, ita ut ab hodierna die ingenuus, atque ab omni servitutis vinculo securus permaneat, tanquam si ab ingenuis fuisset parentibus procreatus. Eam denique peragat partem, quamcumque elegerit, ut deinceps nec nobis, nec successoribus nostris, ullum deleat noxiæ conditionis servitium ; sed diebus vitæ suæ sub certa plenissimaque ingenuitate, sicut alii cives Romani, per hunc manumissionis atque ingenuitatis titulum, semper ingenuus et securus existat,*" &c. I don't find the passage in my copy of Jacobus Cujacius (4 vols. fol., 1595), but he has many other good things, s. v. "*Manumissio,*" and "*Libertus.*" He always speaks of a *libertus* as *civis Romanus.* Even the lowest kind of freedmen, *libertus dediticius* is still *civis.* Look here : " *Libertus Dediciorum munere testamentum facere non potest, quia nullius certæ civitatis civis est,*" i. e., he did not belong to any *tribus* or *gens,* I take it. But he was still a *civis* in a passive sense, and so entitled to the benefit of all the laws. His son had all the rights of an *ingenuus.*

For a long time the *libertus* had not a complete *testamentary* right, and the *patronus* had a lien on the property of a deceased *libertus* to a certain extent. But that was the case with a son ; even after his father had manumitted him he still owed certain *munera* to his father during life, and could not alienate his property, though, certainly, the *filius* was as much a *civis* as the *pater* himself. But I suppose you own Cujacius, so I won't worry you with more from him.

It is curious to trace the increase of civil power allowed the different classes of *Cives Romani* from the time when the *Libertus dediticius* was simply a passive citizen, a *non servus,* (as the non-church member was in Massachusetts for a while in the seventeenth century) up to the time when the Emperor Valeus decreed " *Libertorum filios adipisci clarissimam dignitatem non prohibemus.*"

Smith's " Dictionary of Greek and Roman Antiquities " (Lond., 1849) has an article on " *Libertus,*" but it contains some great errors—as that the sons of *libertini* could not have *gentile* rights. Now it appears from Cicero (Leg. II., 22) that " *tanta religio est Sepulchorum, ut extra sacra et gentem inferri fas negent esse* "—none but one of the *gens* could be buried in the tomb of the *gens.* But in the famous tomb of the Scipios—who were certainly very genteel people—there are epitaphs of several *liberti* of that family.

Niebuhr, who was not so much on this as you might look for, says

most of the *clientes* were probably freedmen. ("Hist. Rom.," Lond.,
1851, vol. I., p. 595.)

Yours truly, THEO. PARKER.

TO MR. JAMES ORTON, WILLIAMSTOWN, MASS.

Boston, Feb. 22, 1855.

DEAR SIR,—I have not time to write at length as the theme demands. But it seems to me the American party rests on a very
narrow foundation. I have no blood in my veins which did not come
here between 1620 and 1640, but it is no better than if it had come
between 1820 and 1840. Democracy must rest on humanity, not mere
nationality or on modes of religion. I am as far removed from
Catholicism as any man in America; but I should be ashamed to ask
any religious privilege which I would not grant to any other man in
the country. I would never exclude any man from office on account
of his birth or religious creed; only for his character. Surely I should
prefer a higher law Catholic, to a lower law Protestant; and a noble
man born in Scotland, England, Ireland, to a mean man born on
Plymouth rock.

The new party has done good things :—

(1.) It has rebuked the insolence of the Bishops and Archbishops
of the Catholic Church—who required a severe chastisement.

(2.) It has shown American politicians that they cannot use the
foreign population as before; that was sadly needed in Boston as well
as elsewhere.

(3.) It has checked the administration and beaten them sorely.

(4.) It is knocking the old political parties to pieces with great
rapidity.

All that is good work; but it is not done in the spirit of democracy,
which allows every man his natural rights because he is a man—not a
red-man, or a white-man, or an American man, &c. It is an important
question how long a man ought to be here before he should vote, &c.
Five years may not be long enough, or it may be—I have not made
up my mind about that. But I would welcome the foreigners, they add
to our riches and our national prosperity in general; and it is well that
America should be the asylum of humanity for this century as for the
seventeenth.

Hastily, but truly yours,

THEO. PARKER.

TO W. H. HERNDON, SPRINGFIELD, ILL.

Boston, April 17, 1856.

MY DEAR SIR,—Your letters, the printed matter not less than the
written, rejoice me very much. I honor the noble spirit which breathes
in them all. I did not answer before, for I had no time, and a hundred

letters now lie before me not replied to. When I tell you that I have now lectured eighty-four times since November 1, and preached at home every Sunday but two, when I was in Ohio, and never an old sermon; and have had six meetings a month at my own house, and have written more than a thousand letters, besides a variety of other work belonging to a minister and a scholar, you may judge that I must economize minutes, and often neglect a much valued friend. So please excuse my delay in acknowledging your brave manly words, and believe me,

Faithfully yours,

THEO. PARKER.

TO THE SAME.

Boston, Dec. 31, 1856.

MY DEAR SIR,   *   *   *   *   *

The President is an old man—a man of feeble will, of no ideas— vacillating in his measures, but firm in one principle—to take care of James Buchanan. But he was chosen by the South, at the command of the South; on the platform of the South was he sworn into office. He will, therefore, be forced to yield to the logic of Southern ideas. There is a manifest destiny in that which no will could escape. But he wishes to keep all the party together; so attempts in words to conciliate the North, while in deeds he obeys his sterner masters at the South. Hence his vacillation in regard to Walker and Kansas, to Nicaragua, to the great financial questions.

Now as the Northern institutions and the Southern are founded on ideas exactly opposite and antagonistic, and as the logic thereof impels the people in opposite directions, it is plain that one of three things must happen;—

1. The South may conquer the North.
2. The North may conquer the South.
3. The two may separate without a fight.

I need not say which is likely to happen.

Douglas finds his term is nearly out in the Senate; he knows he will not be re-elected if he continues facing to the South. If he fails of the Senatorship in 1859, he fails of the Presidency in 1860, in 1864. He is ambitious, unprincipled, coarse, vulgar, but strong in the qualities which make a "democratic" leader. He has served the South all along, but the South would not pay him with the nomination in 1856. · He seeks his revenge on its nominee, and on the South itself, while he shall advance his own interest. So he opposes the attempt to force slavery on Kansas. He claims that he does this in consistency with his Kansas and Nebraska Bill, and his doctrine of squatter sovereignty. But he is more inconsistent than it appears at first, for not only did he (1) favor Toombs' Bill; but (2) the Kansas-Nebraska Bill, with its squatter sovereignty, was not a principle of his political philosophy, but only a measure of his political aim to serve the South for his own advancement. So he is now not only obviously inconsistent with his special support of Toombs' Bill, but secretly and personally inconsistent with his whole course of action and uniform adhesion to the South and his perpetual mock at freedom and its supporters.

He is a mad dog, who has grown fat by devouring our sheep; he was trained to that business, this bloodhound of the South.

But as his master has not fed him, as he hoped, he turns round and barks at those whom he once obeyed whenever they whistled for him, and bit whomsoever they told him to seize.

I have no more faith in him now than years ago. But he is biting our enemies. " Dog eat dog," says the Turk ; " Dog eat wolf" say I. No man in the North can do the South such damage. " Seize 'em ! " say I. " Bite 'em ! take hold on 'em, stibboy !! "

Here is his plan of action. He sees the South is determined on putting slavery in Kansas. He sees it can't be done; that if the democratic party insist on the Southern measures, it will be in 1860 where the Whigs were in 1856. In all the Northern States it will be routed and cut to pieces. He won't connect himself with the Southern effort. He won't run for the Presidency in 1860. He has told Walker "I shan't be in your way in 1860." For he foresees the defeat of the democrats at that time, their rally about another platform, under another flag and with different leaders in 1864. He hopes for his own triumph then—his own election.

He anticipated this in 1855–6. Don't you remember " Senator Douglas had a bad sore throat," and could not attend the sessions of the Senate in December, 1855, January, 1856, but in February got better ?

I wait now to see what he will say to the administration treatment of Paulding.

Yours truly,
THEODORE PARKER.

TO THE SAME.

Boston, August 28, 1858.

MY DEAR SIR,—Many thanks for your kind letter and the benevolent things you say about my sermons.

I look with great interest on the contest in your State, and read the speeches, the noble speeches, of Mr. Lincoln* with enthusiasm : one I saw in the *Tribune* of last week will injure Douglas very much. I never recommended the Republicans to adopt Douglas into their family. I said in a speech last January "he is a mad dog;" just now he is barking at the wolf which has torn our sheep. But he himself is more dangerous than the wolf. I think I should not let him into the fold.

---

* These speeches were delivered by Mr. Lincoln, now President of the United States, at the time that a few prominent members of the Republican party hoped, by softening their anti-slavery principles, to avail themselves of the hostility of Mr. Douglas for Mr. Buchanan, and to secure the former for their leader in the impending Presidential campaign. The plan did not succeed.

*   *   Greeley is quite humane, and surrounds himself with some of the best talent in the country. Do you see what the *Richmond Whig* says of Buchanan; that means that the Whig is fattening Edward Everett for the Presidency. Much good may it do him.

I think the Republican party will nominate Seward for the Presidency, and elect him in 1860; then the wedge is entered and will be driven home. Yours truly,

THEODORE PARKER.

TO THE SAME.

Boston, Sept. 9, 1858.

MY DEAR SIR,—Many thanks for your two very interesting and instructive letters. You make the case very clear. I look with intense interest on the contest now raging in Illinois. There is but one great question before the people: Shall we admit Slavery as a principle and found a Despotism, or Freedom as a principle and found a Democracy? This one question comes up in many forms, and men take sides in it. The great mass of the people but poorly see the question; their leaders are often *knaves* and often *fools*. But

Quidquid delirant reges, plectuntur Achivi.

I make no doubt Douglas will be beaten. I thought so in 1854, and looked on him then as a ruined man. What you told me last spring has all come to pass. I am glad Trumbull demonstrated what you name. I thought it could be done. But in the Ottawa meeting, to judge from the *Tribune* report, I thought Douglas had the best of it. He questioned Mr. Lincoln on the great matters of Slavery, and put the most radical questions, which go to the heart of the question, before the people. Mr. Lincoln did not meet the issue. He made a technical evasion; "he had nothing to do with the resolutions in question." Suppose he had not, admit they were forged. Still, they were the vital questions pertinent to the issue, and Lincoln dodged them. That is not the way to fight the battle of freedom.

You say right—that an attempt is making to lower the Republican platform. Depend upon it, this effort will ruin the party. It ruined the Whigs in 1840 to 1848. Daniel Webster stood on higher anti-slavery ground than Abraham Lincoln now.   *   *
*   *   *   *   *   *   *

*   If the Republicans sacrifice their principle for success, then they will not be lifted up, but blown up. I trust Lincoln will conquer.* It is admirable education for the masses, this fight!

Yours truly,

THEODORE PARKER.

I think that these letters will be well enough understood by all who had sufficient interest to follow the political movements of the times in question. For all others, perhaps it is too soon,

---

* Referring to the canvass of Illinois by Messrs. Lincoln and Douglas for the United States' senatorship in the autumn of 1858.

48

it certainly would occupy too much room, and raise too many collateral questions, to attempt to explain and justify all the allusions. On the whole, it may be said, with reference to Mr. Parker's letters, that they show a keener political instinct than the newspapers and speeches of the time betrayed.

TO THE SAME.

Boston, Sept. 23, 1858.

MY DEAR SIR,—Your last letter, just come to hand, is quite important. I shall keep it confidential, but consider the intelligence, and "govern myself accordingly." That "accidental" meeting at Chicago is quite remarkable, and explains many things which seemed queer before.

Last spring you told me much which was new, and foretold what has since happened. I did not understand till now, after reading your last letter, how you could tell what Douglas was after by looking in his eye; now it is clear enough. There is freemasonry in drinking. I long since lost all confidence in ————, both as the representative of a moral principle, and as the adviser of expedient measures. His course in regard to Douglas last winter was inexplicable till now.

We must not lower the Republican platform. Let the Know-Nothings go to their own place; we must adhere to the principle of right! I go for Seward as the ablest and best representative of the Democratic idea, that could now get the nomination. My next choice would be Chase. I put Seward first, because oldest and longest in the field—perhaps, also, the abler.

But if Douglas is defeated, if Trumbull is re-elected in 1860, I think he would be quite as likely to get the nomination.

Massachusetts is likely to send a stronger anti-slavery delegation to Congress than ever before. Some of the Know-Nothings will be discharged (others ought to be). C. F. Adams, J. B. Alley, T. D. Eliot, and George Boutwell, are likely to be members of the next House of Representatives. Governor Banks would, no doubt, lower the Republican platform, if that operation would help him up. But Massachusetts will oppose any such act, so will the people of the North. If we put up a spooney, we shall lose the battle, lose our honor, and be demoralized. Edward Everett is beating every New England bush for voters to elect him. He may beat till the cows come home, and get little from his labor.

What you write about, the letter from the Eastern senator, chagrins me a good deal. But I am sure of this : if the attempt is made by the Republican leaders to lower the platform, then they are beat in 1860, and are ruined as completely as I think Douglas now is. ————, says he would admit new Slave States. I despise such miserable cowardice, all the more in such a man.

Truly yours,

THEODORE PARKER.

TO THE SAME.

Boston, November 13, 1858.

MY DEAR SIR,—I am your debtor for three letters, very instructive ones too. I should not have allowed the account to run on so, had I not been sick. A surgical operation laid me on my bed for nearly three weeks, and, of course, I wrote only with another's hand, and but little even in that wise.

So you "are beaten;" the reasons you give are philosophical and profound, it seems to me. I think you have hit the nail on the head. But I don't agree with you as to Seward. What private reasons you have for your opinion, I cannot say, but his two speeches at Rochester and at Rome don't look like lowering the platform. He never spoke so bold and brave before. He quite outruns his party, and no Republican paper in New England, I fear, has dared to republish them. The Anti-Slavery papers printed one, and perhaps will copy the other.

You are beaten, but I am not sure the Administration do not think it a worse defeat than you do. I think they hated and feared Douglas more than Lincoln. Had Lincoln succeeded, Douglas would be a ruined man. He would have no political position, and so little political power; he would have no original influence in American politics, for he does not deal with principles which a man may spread abroad from the pulpit or by the press, but only with measures that require political place to carry out. He could do the Administration no harm. But now in place for six years more, with his own personal power unimpaired, and his positional power much enhanced, he can do the Democratic party a world of damage.

Here is what I conjecture will take place. There will be a reconstruction of the Democratic platform on Douglas's "principles" (else they lose the nation). This involves (the actual but not expressed) repudiation of Buchanan, and the sacrifice of his Cabinet officers, &c. He will sink as low as Pierce. In 1860 the Convention will nominate a man of the Douglas ideas. Will it be Douglas himself? I doubt it, for he has so many foes in the North and the South, that I think they will not risk him. But if he has heart enough to carry the Convention, then I think the fight will be between him and Seward and that he will be beaten! I look for an Anti-Slavery Administration in 1861—I hope with Seward at its head. But it requires a deal of skill to organize a party to find a harness which all the North can work in; but we shall triumph, *vide* Hammond's speech.

Yours truly,
THEODORE PARKER.

CHAPTER XXIII.

IN the spring of 1856, Mr. Parker volunteered to increase the
amount of labor, which was already so heavy upon him, by supplying the pulpit of an independent society in Watertown. Old
associations and a desire to do something to support a movement
for which his influence was partly responsible, induced him to
make this offer. But it was more than he should have undertaken. For a year he rode from Boston to Watertown, in all
weathers, and preached generally the sermon which he had
delivered in the Music Hall in the forenoon. The only compensation which he desired to receive for this, was the payment of
his livery stable bill. His activity in other directions was not
abated. Lecturing went on as usual ; and his whole life was
controlled and deeply touched by the political and moral questions of the time. It was not possible for the strongest organization to carry so many burdens, and be unfretted by their
weight.

Yet he neglected nothing which he ever undertook to perform.
Every afternoon was devoted to the parochial service of his
immediate parish in Boston ; and he readily answered calls of
this description, which carried him twenty miles and more from
the city. It was on one of these excursions* that he fell upon
some ice in mounting the cars, at a time when he was quite ill,
and sustained a severe shock. He frequently caught heavy colds
upon his lecturing expeditions, but never missed fulfilling his
engagements for any cause whatever, through his own fault or

* Nov. 24 1858. See *post*, pp. 254–55, letter to Miss Cobbe.

remissness ; nor ever, from any cause, failed to keep his appointments more than two or three times through his whole career.

The parochial business of his ministerial office was performed with a deep sense of its delicate and important nature. The number of the visits which he made was very great, but few necessarily to each family or individual. He was a great strengthener and consoler. Whatever trouble he approached, or whatever approached him, was the occasion of an admirable ministry of common-sense, womanly tenderness, and a mighty faith in God. He used to say that the parochial relation taxed him more heavily than all his work, and that the more closely he held it, the more he was convinced that it was work for a genius,—to take a fluttering heart into the hand and calm its fears, to soothe its agonizing throbs, to penetrate the soul's wild weather with serene confidence and the warmth of personal feeling, to make the distracted mind resume or begin its faith in the Infinite Perfection at the very moment when finite imperfection was most palpable ; all this was business for angelic powers. But it was essential to his highest success, and to the affectional cultivation of a true idea of God ; and he never slighted it. If pity, equanimity, devoutness, a manly, brotherly heart contribute much to discharge the pastor's office well, he did not greatly fail. He was simple and childlike to the little ones ; sincere, brotherly, sensible, and genial to the young, and an ever-springing sweet fountain of piety to all. That hand which could crush, as with the weight of many tons, could descend, if needful, with a touch soft as unspoken feeling. He has made his own record where no pen is subtle enough to follow and transcribe.

But how his life ran out by these depleting pipes, which so many truths, so many sorrows, so many studies, so many personal exactions, had attached to his willing nature ! I have not been disposed to mention every illness, and the lapses of time laid waste by incapacity to think or work, and the numerous recoils of an overworked body. Not a season passed without them ; they became more serious every year.

FROM THE JOURNAL.

April 19, 1856.—Last night I was to lecture at New Bedford, and tried to speak, but was so ill that I could not hear or see or speak well. I left the room, and went out with Mr. Robeson, and walked a few minutes. Went to an apothecary's, and drank about a spoonful and a half of sherry wine, which helped me. Spoke, but with great difficulty. Am better to-day, but slenderly and meanly. *I take this as a warning*—not the first.

The letter which follows is a sufficient explanation of the state of his health in 1857.

TO REV. WILLIAM H. FISH.

Newton Corner, July 25, 1857.

MY DEAR FRIEND AND BROTHER,—I thank you for your very kind letter, and the hopes and fears it expresses. I am getting better— slowly, but I hope surely. These are the facts of the case:—I come of a long-lived family. Six Parker fathers, buried in New England, average about seventy-seven years; six Parker mothers go up to near eighty. But my brothers and sisters die early. My parents had eleven children. I am the youngest. All but one lived to attain manly years. All are dead, save my brother, near sixty, and myself. They have the critical period of their life from forty-four to forty-seven. *Five* of them died about that age; only one has surpassed it. I shall be forty-seven the 24th of August next. So I am *in* that critical period. If I live a year, I shall probably go on to seventy, eighty, or ninety.

Here is the cause of the present form of disease. Last February I went to Central New York to lecture. Feb. 9th I was to lecture at Waterford, 10th at Syracuse, 11th at Utica, 12th at Rochester, and then return and reach Boston at midnight of 14th–15th. I should pass every night in my bed except that of the 12th. But, on the contrary, things turned out quite otherwise. The railroad conductor left us in the cars all night at East Albany, in the midst of the inundation. Common New England *prudence* and *energy* would have taken us all over the river. I had no dinner; no supper, except what I had in my wallet [dried fruit and biscuit]; no breakfast the next morning, save a bit of tough beef in an Irish boarding-house. When I awoke on the morning of the 10th, I felt a sharp pain in my right side, not known before. I got to Syracuse that night, 10th, *via* Troy; lectured at Utica the 11th, and at 11 P.M. took the cars for Rochester and rode all night, till 5 or 6 in the next morning, when I got into damp sheets at Rochester, and slept an hour. I was ill all that day, and at night had all the *chills of an incipient fever*. But I lectured, took the cars at 2 or 3 A.M., having waited for them three or four hours in the depôt, and reached Albany in time for the 4 P.M. train, Friday, and got to Boston about 2 A.M. on Saturday, having had no reasonable meal since noon, Thursday. Sunday I preached at Boston and Watertown, as my custom was. The next week I was ill, but lectured *four* times; so the next, and the next, until in March I broke down utterly, and could do no more. Then I had a regular fever, which kept me long in the house; but soon as I could stand on my feet *an hour*, I began to preach. This was a means of cure, and it helped me much *to look into the faces of the people again!*

July 12th, we shut up the Music Hall, and I shall not preach till Sept. 6th. I am devoting all my might to getting well. The pain in the side still continues. I attack it from without by compresses of wet linen, and by homœopathic medicine from within. I have a nice boarding-place, with all manner of agreeable influences about me, and live in the open air all the fine weather. I hope soon to be as well as ever. I am very thankful to the kind people in all parts of the country, who take so generous an interest in me. I have enemies enough, who *hate* me with the intensest bitterness of malice; but I think few men have more friends ; *none warmer and kinder.* But I will not trouble one of the best of them with any more of a dull, egotistic letter in the dog-days.

With love to you and yours,
T. P.

TO THE SAME.

Boston, November 11, 1858.

My very dear Mr. Fish,—I thank you for your kind, sweet letter, which I found so moving that I kept it two days, after tasting its sweetness, before I ventured to read it through; for I am still a little weak, and cannot quite trust the emotional part in such affairs. Have no fear for me now; I have weathered the Cape, and think I may live to the respectable age of my fathers, say eighty or ninety. I think I have conquered the last of my physical enemies. I have submitted to a surgical operation, not painful or dangerous, only exhausting and wearisome ; it laid me on my back some weeks, and has kept me from my pulpit four Sundays; but I shall preach the next time. I can't walk very well as yet; but try it every fair day. I have ridden out four or five times. You must not think so highly of me, my dear friend. Whenever I slip away there will be a plenty of men to take my place and do my work, or a greater in a better way. There is so much prejudice against me, that I sometimes fear I hinder men more than I help them. But yet I have much work to do ; whole continents and islands, which I have begun to clear up, and make into farms and gardens. I want about twenty years more, for serious, solid work; even then I shall be only sixty-eight years old ; twenty years less than Josiah Quincy. But I will not trouble you more; writing, as you see, by another's hand.

Many thanks for your kind memories and wishes. Remember me kindly to your wife. I hope your son will prove worthy of his father and mother.

Believe me, faithfully and gratefully, your friend,

THEODORE PARKER.

TO REV. S. J. MAY.

Boston, Feb. 11, 1858.

Oh! my dear S. J.,—Open thine eyes, look through thy spectacles, and thou shalt once more behold the elegant chirography of thy long-silent friend. A year ago yesterday I was in the good town of Syracuse;

but Archimedes was not there to welcome me. I had passed the night in the inundation at Albany: the pleurisy was in my side, the fever in my blood, and I have been about good for nothing ever since. This has been a stupid winter to me. I have less than half my old joyous power of work, hence I have not written to you these *three months!* I grind out one sermon a week; that is about all I can do. I have lectured seventy-three times—always close at hand—and have done for the season. Last year I lectured eighty times—all the way from the Mississippi to the Penobscot, gave temperance and anti-slavery addresses besides, and preached to two congregations, besides *reading* a deal of hard matter, and writing many things. I am forty-seven by the reckoning of my mother; seventy-four in my own (internal) account. I am an *old man.* Sometimes I think of knocking at Earth's gate with my staff, saying, "Liebe Mutter, let me in!" I don't know what is to come of it. My father died at seventy-seven, a great hale man, sick ten days, perhaps. My grandmother lived to be ninety-three, and, I think, had ne'er a doctor after her eighth baby was born in her thirty-sixth year, or thereabout. But nine of my ten brothers and sisters are already gone forward. None of them saw the forty-ninth birthday. One lives yet, aged sixty. There is a deal of work to do. I enlisted "for the whole war," which is not half over yet.

I am glad you preach only once a day. I think the Society will not return to the old way. Brother Dewey likes it, and other Brothers would try it, *if they dared.* I trust you will be much better, and that soon. It's the Joe-sickness that pulled you down. You took his complaint in your heart, and so broke down. I know how it was. Well, the good boy will go to Europe. How I wish I had a hundred dollars to shoot him in this letter! But alack, and alas! I am poor this time! I can't earn thousands of dollars by lecturing, as hitherto; the factories pay nothing, so I must creep into my shell, which is " 'minished and brought low." I don't like to *be* poor and *act* poor too!

I send your son Joe a letter or two; but I know few persons in Europe at present. I hope he will see the Apthorps, now at Rome. If he goes to Neuchâtel, he must see Desor. All my acquaintances in Germany are now *old* men. He has youth on his side, the dog! which is a capital introduction to nature and " the rest of mankind."

The house is all well and sends "love to dear Mr. May " and his family. Good bye.

T. P.

Here are notes to all the people I can think of. J. won't want to see the theologic men I knew in 1844. Now they are as old as the hills! God bless the boy and his (naughty) father.

In 1857–58, great commercial embarrassments broke up the fierce business habits of the people ; losses, anxieties, and doubts of a financial solution, held the controlling interest of the country in suspense. In this reaction from an over-stimulated state, a revival set in, whose waters covered the flats left bare by retreating prosperity. The prayer-meetings which commenced in that time of great despondency, or which had been in feeble operation before, attracted numbers of people in the cities and towns, who had less to do and more to dread than usual. The law, which was then seen in action, is constant in every age and race, through every apparent variation made by condition and culture. If any widely-acting cause invigorates the popular tone, and lifts it out of depression or indifference, then all hearts rush together to the nearest symbol of their hope, or joy, or hate. From this positive enhancement of life comes a unity, which achieves the best or the worst things of history. And if a common cause impairs the popular tone, a prevailing mood is soon created, part physical and part moral, which also invites the nearest contagion. Every race has oscillated between its shop and its temple. When work goes swimmingly, whether of arms, of arts, or of industrial enter-prises, temples are left open for Te Deums; but when the charac-teristic activity languishes or suffers foreign interference, they resound with threats, misereres, and confessions. In times of greater ignorance the minds of the panic-stricken men are laid waste by superstition, but in an epoch of improving theologies, and when political and moral subjects are more absorbing than doctrinal ones, a milder infection runs through people, if business, the most absorbing subject and pursuit of all in this country, loosens its hold and gives the moody opportunity.

So we had a great revival under natural conditions; but, of course, the theology which invokes a Providence to dissipate a whitlow, upset a boat on Sunday, right another on Monday, and perform in general all that we like or dislike, ascertained that the work was supernatural and special.

Mr. Parker preached a sermon upon the Ecclesiastical and the Philosophical Methods in Religion,* in which he showed what monstrous evils resulted from the Church Theologies; and among them he ranked speculative and practical atheism. It is a clear and healthy discourse, but not remarkably strong with any of his characteristics. There needed not, however, the ex-tensive reporting of his sermon by the daily press, and its diffu-sion in a pamphlet form, to attract the attention of the revivalists towards the great foe of their traditional theology. All his labors entitled him to their notice.

His continually increasing influence must have presented a curious problem to minds which had vehemently denied his

---

* On False and True Theology, Feb. 14, 1858. Published the same year.

insinuation that they believed in a Devil quite as much as in a God. Now, they were in the dilemma of having denied that they believed the Devil was as good as God, and yet of claiming Mr. Parker as a living and triumphant testimony to diabolical ability. From their stand-point the question was embarrassing. At any rate, it became clear to them that something must be done, for he grew more formidable every day. It occurred to them that the real spirit of this "notorious infidel" was misunderstood. How otherwise could he go on so, increasing in favor with man, and doing many undeniably good things? Perhaps the amount of good in this bold, bad man—which came, of course, by nature and not by grace—had created a partiality for him at Court, which was very damaging to the true adherents, and misrepresented, moreover, the Court's general policy. An attempt must therefore be made to disabuse the divine mind of these unfortunate predilections. The proper representations were accordingly made at a prayer meeting, which was held on the afternoon of March 6, at the Park Street Church. Other efforts were doubtless made elsewhere, and on other occasions, but of this we have definite and reliable accounts.

Here is a specimen of some of some of the vigorous insinuations, called praying, which illustrated the spiritual influences of that occasion :—

O Lord, if this man is a subject of grace, convert him, and bring him into the kingdom of Thy dear Son! But if he is beyond the reach of the saving influence of the Gospel, remove him out of the way, and let his influence die with him.

O Lord, send confusion and distraction into his study this afternoon, and prevent his finishing his preparation for his labors to-morrow ; or if he shall attempt to desecrate Thy holy day by attempting to speak to the people, meet him there, Lord, and confound him, so that he shall not be able to speak!

Lord, we know that we cannot argue him down, and the more we say against him, the more will the people flock after him, and the more will they love and revere him ! O Lord, what shall be done for Boston, if Thou dost not take this and some other matters in hand ?

O Lord, if this man will still persist in speaking in public, induce the people to leave him, and to come up and fill this house instead of that!

One brother exhorted the rest to pray that God would "put a hook in this man's jaws, so that he may not be able to speak."

O Lord, meet this infidel on his way, who, like another Saul of Tarsus, is persecuting the Church of God, and cause a light to shine around him, which shall bring him trembling to the earth, and make him an able defender of the faith which he has so long labored to destroy!

One requested his brethren whether, in their places of business or walking in the street, or wherever they might be, to pray for Mr. Parker every day when the clock should strike one.

The latter Christian had probably heard of the destructive effect of a concentric fire opened at the same moment.

What might not be the result if, precisely at one o'clock, arms of all calibre, from the sharp pocket-pistol to the deep-bellowing columbiad, opening from Hanover and Blackstone Street, and Commercial Wharf to Roxbury Neck, poured a converging fire through the Music Hall into the " fortress and defence" beyond?

The gross fetichism of the above prayers is plain to all. They are only bricks from the masonry which builds the popular churches. They are representative prayers, a little more frank than usual; stripped of mastic. Yet people wonder at the charges Mr. Parker used to make, that hatred, low conceptions of God, gross views of prayer, and of the connection between the finite and the infinite, were latent elements of the popular theology, and might at any time appear under sufficient temptation. They are, in fact, *essential* to that theology, wherever it is *consistently* maintained.

When, in the course of a year, Mr. Parker's frame, overtasked by all his deeds of power and of love, had to yield, and he sought in retirement to save a remnant of his time for God's service, it was suspected that the true believers had succeeded in instructing the Chief Ear, and that the favorite had been disgraced. It is hardly credible, even in ecclesiastical America, but will it be believed abroad, that a representative paragraph of pious jubilation actually appeared, attributing Mr. Parker's consumption to the fervent prayers of the elect?

TO MRS. JULIA BRIDGES, WEST NEWTON.

Boston, April 9, 1858.

DEAR MADAM,—I am much obliged to you for the interest you take in my spiritual welfare, and obliged to you for the letter which has just come to hand. I gather from it that you wish me to believe the theological opinions which you entertain and refer to. I don't find that you desire anything more.

I make no doubt the persons who pray for my conversion to the common ecclesiastical theology, and those who pray for my death, are equally sincere and honest. I don't envy them their idea of God when they ask Him to come into my study and confound me, or to

put a hook into my jaws so that I cannot speak. Several persons have
come to "labor with me," or have written me letters to convert me.
They were commonly persons quite ignorant of the very things they
tried to teach me ; they claimed a divine illumination which I saw no
proofs of, in them, in their lives, or their doctrines. But I soon found
it was with them as it is with you; they did not seek to teach me
either piety, which is the love of God, or morality, which is the
keeping of the natural laws He has written in the constitution of man,
but only to induce me to believe their catechism and join their Church.
I see no reason for doing either.

I try to use what talents and opportunities God has given me in the
best way I can. I don't think it is my fault that I regret the absurd
doctrines which I find in the creed of these people who wish to instruct
me on matters of which they are profoundly ignorant.

But the Catholics treated the Protestants in the same way, and the
Jews and the Heathens thus treated the Christians. I find good and
religious men amongst all classes of men, Trinitarians, Unitarians,
Salvationists, and Damnationists, Protestants, Catholics, Jews, Mahome-
dans, Heathen. There is one God for us all, and I have such perfect
love of Him that it long since cast out all fear. Believe me,

Yours truly,

THEODORE PARKER

The supplications offered up in Park Street were answered
appropriately from the Music Hall in the two discourses of April
4 and 11 : one on "A False and True Revival of Religion," the
other on "The Revival of Religion, *which we need.*" They are
an answer to prayer worth considering. They overflow with the
health of unsparing criticism, pure morality, and tender devoutness. They are filled full with the elements which promote a
revival of conscience and piety in the hearts of men, fertile as
the

" —— happy lands that have luxurious names."

Their offence was in their absolute, unvarnished truth-telling
concerning the condition of the Church and the country. Their
picture of the beautiful purification of America, which a true
revival would promote, has the crushing satire of common-sense,
unstintedly spoken, to show what hideous evils are never touched
and cured by the agitation of evangelical sentiment.

Ministers talk of a "revival of religion in answer to prayer"! It
will no more so come than the submarine telegraph from Europe to
America. It is the effectual fervent *work* of a righteous man that
availeth much—his head-work, and hand-work. Gossiping before God,
tattling mere words, asking Him to do my duty—that is not prayer.
I also believe in prayer from the innermost of my heart, else must
I renounce my manhood and the Godhood above and about me.
I also believe in prayer. It is the upspringing of my soul to meet the

Eternal, and thereby I seek to alter and improve myself, not Thee, O Thou Unchangeable, who art perfect from the beginning! Then I mingle my soul with the Infinite Presence. I am ashamed of my wickedness, my cowardice, sloth, fear. New strength comes into me of its own accord, as the sunlight to these flowers which open their little cups. Then I find that he that goeth forth even weeping, bearing this precious aid of prayer, shall, doubtless, come again rejoicing, and bring his sheaves with him.

The technical revival passed away, but Mr. Parker continued manfully his prayer and work against the palpable evils of his country. A French writer has come to the rescue of the revival, and attributes to it the unanimity of sentiment which suddenly awoke in the uncertain North at the bombardment of Fort Sumter ! Orthodox journals do not appear at all eager to accept this alleged efficiency of prayer and conference-meetings, which is gratuitously extended to them. In truth, the genuine revival which has swept through Northern hearts, and is making them more unanimous every day, had been anti-slavery ! And that owes little to the Churches of America, who are carried off by its power, and compelled to serve it after having resisted and blasphemed the spirit. What would not the orthodox Churches give, if history could show them prevailingly faithful, in the days of anti-slavery weakness, to keep alive the protesting conscience, and to feed by prayer and works that great revival of political and moral righteousness which alone shall save this people from its sins ? They cannot claim that crowning testimony to divinity of doctrine.

He always confessed that his over-work had violated natural laws ; whence came a penalty not supernatural.

Aug. 20, 1858.*—The undersigned, members of the Twenty-eighth Congregational Society in Boston, deeply concerned for the health and public usefulness of their beloved friend and pastor, Theodore Parker, earnestly request him, in view of the bronchial affection under which he is laboring, to extend the term of his vacation until such period as, in the judgment of reliable medical advisers, it will be warrantable for him to resume his pastoral functions ; believing that this is a duty which he owes to himself, his family, his friends, and the cause of religion, humanity, and reform ; and trusting that he will not allow the strong desire he will naturally feel to be promptly at his post at the usual time, to override their united wishes and settled convictions on this subject.

---

* This letter followed the counsel of a friend, who was the first to notice Mr. Parker's failing health during a short journey which they made together in August, 1858.

The following letter to Miss Cobbe continues the story of his health :—

TO MISS COBBE.

Boston, Nov. 9, 1858.

My very dear Miss Cobbe,—I sent you a little bit of a sad note some weeks ago; this will be more cheerful and encouraging. I have had a hospital operation performed lately, which laid me on my bed for three or four weeks. I have just recovered, now, and can walk about a little, say half-an-hour at a time, or ride an hour or two, and sit up most of the day. For several Sundays others filled my pulpit; next Sunday I hope to speak for myself, and the half-written sermon lies already before me. I think I have conquered the last of my (corporeal) enemies, and trust a long life of serious work is before me. I have much left to do, much half-done, and yet more projected and prepared for, but not yet adventured on. Twenty years more of healthy solid toil will finish it all, and leave me but sixty-eight, an age not unreasonable for me to desire or expect.

I sent you, at Mrs. Apthorp's request, a little parcel of books by the steamer of last week. They will reach you through Chapman. My friend Mr. Ripley, of New York, has a great admiration for your book, and is trying its fortune with the publishers of that city—more adventurous than any in Boston.

I sent you some little sermons of mine, and an article in the *Examiner* on the Physical Condition of Massachusetts. I trust this will meet you by your birthday, which we shall keep as a festival.

Faithfully yours.

I open this letter, my dear Miss Cobbe, to announce the welcome receipt of yours from Newbridge, announcing your safe return. Sad must it be to depart from such a home! My ancestral home—a common farm, where my fathers lived one hundred and fifty years, is also dear to me; but I can see it in my brother's hands in an hour's ride any day. I wrote to Mrs. Ripley your proposal, but have not her reply. Please remember me to Miss Carpenter, and that delightful company you met at London. Do you know my dear friend, William H. Channing, of Liverpool? I hope you will.

TO THE SAME.

Boston, Dec. 14, 1858.

My very dear Miss Cobbe,—It was exceedingly kind of you to write me the tender and affectionate note which came only last night. I am a deal better than when Mr. Channing saw me on the day of his sailing. I don't wonder he thought it would soon be all over with me. Yet I knew better, even then, feeling an interior spring of life he could not see. I went on improving, until the very day of your letter, Nov. 24, I attended a funeral thirty miles off in the country. The circumstances were so sad and peculiar, that I could not leave the afflicted ones to the poor consolations of a stranger, who did not even believe, much less know, the infinite goodness of God. I met with an accident in getting into the railroad cars, which injured me badly in delicate parts of the body, and I have not walked since—three weeks. But I ride out every day, and, contrary to the advice of all the doctors, I preach every Sunday, which does me *good and not harm.* Otherwise, I live in my library, and have my meals brought up to me. An ugly cough I had is nearly gone; only the lameness continues. The surgeon fears an abscess, which, after all, is, perhaps, the most genial way of ending the mischief. I suffer but little pain except from the lack of tone and vigor that comes of such long confinement. Do not fear; I have the best medical and surgical advice, though I take no medicine but cod-liver oil, which is diet and not drugs. I shall be very cautious, and take special pains to live, for I have a great deal of work begun and not half done, which another cannot finish. Besides, the world is so interesting, and friends so dear, that I find the love of life much more than twenty or thirty years ago.

I hoped to have had a communication from the bookseller, touching your book, but have yet heard nothing. I hope you received one letter from me through Chapman, with some books, from Mrs. Apthorp, &c., and another direct to you at Red Lodge, Bristol, which I meant you should receive on your birthday. I kept that with true festal delight. A venerable friend was eighty-two the same day, and came in to thank me for my letter to him. [Dea. Samuel May.]

Please present my thankful regards to Miss Carpenter, whom I greatly respect and esteem. I hope the good work of humanity prospers in her hands. Accept my hearty thanks for your letters.

TO MR. RIPLEY.

Boston, Nov. 1, 1858.

MY DEAR GEORGE,—My hand trembles, and I must take pains to write, and so write plain, or else not at all. I wrote you my last three weeks ago to-day. While I was putting your name on the envelope, the two surgeons stopped their gigs at my door. This is the first letter I have written since. They did their work faithfully, and I have laid on my back nearly all the time since. I rode out yesterday, and again to-day, and have walked a few steps several times; the evil is all over, I think, and I believe the last of my (corporeal) foes is routed now. I see not why I may not live a hard-working life till I am seventy, eighty, or ninety, as most of my fathers have done in America. I had an ugly cough all summer, which looked ill to one who had lost a mother, and even brothers and sisters, of consumption, not to speak of nieces and other kinfolk. But I think that, too, is mainly over. My standing committee have shut me out of the Music Hall for next Sunday. S. J. May takes my place; but I trust I shall be there the following Sunday.

Many thanks for your friendship, which *never fails.* If we could lie under the great oak-tree at West Roxbury, or ride about the wild little lanes together, I should soon be entirely well; for the vigor of your mind would inspire strength even into my body; but I must do without that, only too thankful to have had it once.

Thank you for the kind and just things you say about Miss Cobbe. My friends, the Hunts and Apthorps, almost worship the maiden. I keep her birthday as one of my domestic holidays, and honor the 4*th of December* with unusual libations.

Furness's new book is   *   *   *   *   full of zeal, piety, and beauty of sentiment! He does not see that only a critic and scholar can deal with such questions as he passes judgment upon.

What he says about Lazarus, &c., is all *bosh!* He knows the Four Gospels are true—knows it subjectively!

But I must write no more. Good bye!

THEODORE.

Don't tell anybody what I say about my health. I don't write such things often.

Thus the year wore away in weakness and increasing disability to perform the ordinary ministerial labors. In preaching he would sometimes steady himself by grasping the desk with both hands. All other pursuits languished, or were entirely abandoned.

FROM THE JOURNAL.

Jan. 1, 1859.—It is Saturday night—eve of the first day of the new year. I have finished my sermon for to-morrow, and I have nothing to do but indulge my feelings for a minute, and gather up my soul. This is the first new year's day that I was ever sick. Now I have been a prisoner almost three months, living in my chamber or my study. I have been out of doors but thrice since Sunday last. The doctor says I mend, and I quote him to my friends. But I have great doubts as to the result. It looks as if this was the last of my new year's days upon earth. I felt so when I gave each gift to-day; yet few men have more to live for than I. It seems as if I had just begun a great work; yet if I must abandon it, I will not complain. Some abler and better man will take my place, and do more successfully what I have entered on. The Twenty-eighth will soon forget me—a few Sundays will satisfy their tears. Some friends may linger long about my grave, and be inly sad for many a day.

The last discourse, preached on January 2, is entitled, " What Religion may do for a Man : a Sermon for the New Year." It has since been published.

About four o'clock on the morning of Sunday, January 9, he was seized with a violent hæmorrhage of the lungs. He wrote in bed, with a pencil, a short letter to his Society, to be read at the meeting for the usual service of the day.

TO THE CONGREGATION AT THE MUSIC HALL.

Sunday Morning, Jan. 9, 1859.

WELL-BELOVED AND LONG-TRIED FRIENDS,—I shall not speak to you to-day ; for this morning, a little after four o'clock, I had a slight attack of bleeding in the lungs or throat. I intended to preach on " The Religion of Jesus and the Christianity of the Church; or the Superiority of Good-will to Man over Theological Fancies."

I hope you will not forget the contribution for the poor, whom we have with us always. I don't know when I shall again look upon your welcome faces, which have so often cheered my spirit when my flesh was weak.

May we do justly, love mercy, and walk humbly with our God, and his blessing will be upon us here and hereafter; for his infinite love is with us for ever and ever!

Faithfully your friend,
THEODORE PARKER.

A profound sensation of grief followed the reading of this note. At a meeting of the parish, which was immediately held, it was voted to continue Mr. Parker's salary for one year, at least, with the understanding that he would seek entire repose from every kind of public duty.

TO JOHN R. MANLEY.*

Boston, Jan. 22, 1859.

MY VERY DEAR MR. MANLEY,—I don't like to trust myself to write you this letter, which I have attempted several times; but I must and will. I don't know how to express my gratitude for the kindness of the Society towards me; it is much more than I deserve, but I will try to merit it for the future. I don't like to be indebted to mankind, but now I am constrained to it; yet, if I get well, I will cancel the obligation; and if I do not, my friends must seek their recompense in their own consciousness, and in the feeble expression of my deep gratitude for their many favors.

The sum which the Society and the fraternity have placed at my disposal, with my own means, will abundantly suffice for a longer time than you refer to. A few months will determine my fate, and I shall know just where I stand—whether I am to recover entirely or partially, or pass quietly away. Trust me, I shall do everything in my power to *recover entirely*, and resume my former functions. If I have any power of mind, any power of prudence and of will, depend upon it, *all shall be devoted to that one end.* My chance of recovery is not more than one in ten. But I do not despair at that state of things; for all the chief things I have done in my life have been accomplished against yet greater odds. Hope will encourage me, but not blind or cheat. I have always walked in difficult places, and am not scared at a new one now.

I had laid out a great, long series of sermons for this winter, on important and attractive themes: all these must wait. I meant to write out and publish the sermon I did *not* preach, and also to

---

* Addressed to him as Chairman of the Standing Committee of the Twenty-eighth Congregational Society.

write a long letter to the Society before I left Boston. But I can't do both. I fear I may not be able to do either until I reach the West Indies. You will all excuse me if I omit both for the present. "A man can but do his best," and it were wicked to injure my chances of recovery by attempting now what can be done safely a few weeks hence. But if I *can* write the *farewell* letter, I will. It will be fourteen years on the 16th February since I first preached to the Society. I knew I was entering on another "thirty years' war," and so wrote it in my journal; but I did not think we should have so many victories in the first half of it. If it turns out that I can serve no more in this warfare, the *cause* will not suffer. Some one quite different from me, but better, will yet for the great principles of religious freedom take my place. Humanity is so rich in ability, that the man of greatest genius for the highest function is never missed by the race of men. There is never a break in the continuous march of mankind. Leaders fall and armies perish, but mankind goes on.

Please show this to the Standing Committee, and with my hearty thanks, my firm resolve to recover, if possible, and my earnest prayer for the success of our common cause,

Faithfully yours,
THEODORE PARKER.

Here follows Mr. Parker's letter to the Society; and succeeding that is one from the Society to him, drawn up before he left Boston, but from prudential motives withheld till after his arrival at Santa Cruz :—

FAREWELL LETTER.*

TO THE MEMBERS OF THE TWENTY-EIGHTH CONGREGATIONAL SOCIETY IN BOSTON.

MUCH-VALUED FRIENDS,—When I first found myself unable to speak to you again, and medical men bade me be silent, and flee off for my life to a more genial clime, I determined, before I went, to make ready and publish my New Year's Sermon, the last I ever preached ; and the one which was to follow it, the last I ever wrote, lying there yet unspoken ; and also to prepare a letter to you, reviewing our past intercourse of now nearly fifteen years.

The phonographer's swift pen made the first work easy, and the last sermon lies printed before you ; the next I soon laid aside, reserving my forces for the last ! But, alas ! the thought, and still more the emotion, requisite for such a letter, under such circumstances, are quite too much for me now. So, with much regret, I find myself compelled by necessity to forego the attempt; nay, rather, I trust, only to *postpone* it for a few weeks.

Now, I can but write this note in parting, to thank you for the patience with which you have heard me so long; for the open-handed generosity which has provided for my unexpected needs; for the continued affection which so many of you have always shown me, and now

---

* First published at the end of the New-year's Sermon.

more tenderly than ever; and yet, above all, for the joy it has given me to see the great ideas and emotions of true religion spring up in your fields with such signs of promise. If my labors were to end to-day, I should still say, "Lord, now lettest thou thy servant depart in peace," for I think few men have seen larger results follow such labors, and so brief. But I shall not think our connection is ended, or likely soon to be : I hope yet to look in your eyes again, and speak to your hearts. So far as my recovery depends on me, be assured, dear friends, I shall leave nothing undone to effect it; and so far as it is beyond human control, certainly you and I can trust the Infinite Parent of us all, without whose beneficent providence not even a sparrow falls to the ground. Living here or in heaven, we are all equally the children of that unbounded Love.

It has given me great pain that I could not be with such of you as have lately suffered bereavements and other affliction, and at least speak words of endearment and sympathy when words of consolation would not suffice.

I know not how long we shall be separated, but, while thankful for our past relations, I shall still fervently pray for your welfare and progress in true religion, both as a society and as individual men and women. I know you will still think only too kindly of

Your minister and friend,

Exeter Place, Jan. 27, 1859.   THEODORE PARKER.

LETTER TO MR. PARKER.

THE MEMBERS OF THE TWENTY-EIGHTH CONGREGATIONAL SOCIETY OF
BOSTON TO THEIR BELOVED MINISTER.

DEAR SIR,—It is many years since you came, at the request of some of us, to preach in this city. A few men and women, acting under the impulse of a deep religious need, which the churches of Boston at that time failed to satisfy, sought to establish a pulpit which should teach a higher idea of religion than yet prevailed, and wherein the largest freedom of thought and speech should be allowed and respected. They asked you to come and stand in such a pulpit, thinking that you would meet their demand, and resolving that you should "have a chance to be heard in Boston,"—a chance which other men were not willing to allow. At their earnest solicitation you came, and the result has shown that they were not mistaken in their choice.

On the formal organization of the Society, when you were installed as its minister, on the 4th of January, 1846, you preached a sermon of "The True Idea of a Christian Church." How well and faithfully you have labored from that time till now to make that idea a fact, and to build up such a church, we all know. From Sunday to Sunday, year after year, with rare exceptions, when other duties or necessities compelled your absence, you have been at your post, and have always discharged the great functions of your office in a manner which has left nothing to be desired on your part; avoiding no responsibility, neglecting no trust, leaving no duty undone, but working with an ability, energy, perseverance, and self-sacrifice, of which it is not, perhaps, becoming in us to speak at length in this place, but which we cannot the less admire and approve. Outside of the pulpit, we have always found you equally faithful to your responsibilities and duties in all the various relations of life.

Nor have your labors and your example been in vain. You have taught us to discern between the traditions of men and the living realities of religion; you have brought home to our consciousness great truths of the intellect, the conscience, the heart, and the soul; you have shown us the infinite perfection of God, and the greatness of human nature, inspired us with a higher reverence for Him, a deeper trust in His universal providence, with a larger faith also in man and his capabilities. You have encouraged us to oppose all manner of wickedness and oppression, to welcome every virtue and humanity, to engage in all good works and noble reforms. From the experience of mankind, of nations, and of individuals, you have drawn great lessons of truth and wisdom for our warning or guidance. Above all, your own noble and manly and Christian life has been to us a perpetual sermon, fuller of wisdom and beauty, more eloquent and instructive even, than the lessons which have fallen from your lips.

In all our intercourse with you, you have ever been to us as a teacher, a friend, and brother, and have never assumed to be our master. You have respected and encouraged in us that free individuality of thought in matters of religion, and all other matters, which you have claimed for yourself; you have never imposed on us your opinions, asking us to accept them because they were yours, but you have always warned us to use a wise discretion, and decide according to our own judgment and conscience, not according to yours. You have not sought to build up a sect, but a free Christian community.

You have, indeed, been a minister to us, and we feel that your ministry has been for our good; that through it we are better prepared to successfully resist those temptations, and to overcome those evils by which we are surrounded in life, to discharge those obligations which devolve upon us as men aiming to be Christians, and to acquit ourselves as we ought.

As we have gathered together from Sunday to Sunday, as we have looked into your face, and your words have touched our sympathies, and stirred within us our deepest and best emotions, as we have come to know you better year by year, and to appreciate more fully the service which you have been doing for us and for other men, and the faithfulness with which you have labored in it, we have felt that ours was indeed a blessed privilege; and we have indulged a hope that our lives might testify to the good influence of your teachings— a hope which we humbly trust has, to some extent at least, been realized. If we have failed to approximate that high ideal of excellence which you have always set before us, the blame is our own, and not yours.

The world has called us hard names, but it is on you that have fallen the hatred, the intolerance, the insults, and the calumnies of men calling themselves Christian. Alas! that they should be so wanting in the first principles of that religion which Christ taught and lived, and which they pretend to honor and uphold. Of those who have opposed us, many have done so through ignorance, misled by the false representations of others; some from conscientious motives; others from selfishness in many forms. Time has already done much to correct this evil with many; it will do more to correct it with others. While the little we may have sacrificed on our part has been as nothing in comparison with all we have gained from our connection with you, as members of this Society, on yours the sacrifice has been great, indeed—not, however, without its recompense to you, also, we hope and trust.

For all that you have been to us, for all that you have done, and borne, and forborne, in our behalf, we thank you kindly, cordially, and affectionately. We feel that we owe you such gratitude as no words of ours can express. If we have not shown it in the past by conforming our lives to that high standard of morality and piety, which you have exemplified in your own, let us, at least, try to do so in the future.

We cannot but feel a just pride in the success of this Church; that in spite of all obstacles, it has strengthened and increased from year to year, and that the circle of its influence has continually widened. Thousands of earnest men and women in this and other lands, who do not gather with us from week to week, look to this Church as their " city of refuge "; their sympathies, their convictions, and their hopes coincide with our own; they are of us, though not with us. Most of them have never listened to your voice, nor looked upon your face, but the noble words which you have uttered are dear to their hearts, and they also bless God for the service which you have done for them.

In all your labors for us and for others, we have only one thing to regret, and that is, that you have not spared yourself, but have sacrificed your health and strength to an extent which, of late, has excited our deepest solitude and apprehension. We thank God that He furnished you with a vigorous constitution, which has stood the test of so many years of incessant and unwearied toil, in so many departments of usefulness, and which has enabled you to accomplish so much as you have already done; but there is a limit to the endurance of even the strongest man, and the frequent warnings which you have received within the past year or two would seem to indicate that Nature will not suffer even the best of her children to transgress the great laws which she has established for their observance, without inflicting the penalty of disobedience, even though they are engaged in the highest and holiest service which man can render unto man. We would not presume to instruct you in this matter; we only repeat what you have yourself often taught us.

A warning now comes of so imperative a nature that it cannot be disregarded.

We need not assure you that the note from you which was read at the Music Hall on Sunday morning last, was listened to by us with the most sincere and heartfelt sorrow—sorrow, however, not unmingled with hope. While we feel the deepest and warmest sympathy for you under the new and serious development of the disease from which you are suffering, we yet trust that it is not too late to arrest its progress, and that, in some more genial clime than ours, relieved from the cares and responsibilities which have borne heavily upon you for so many years, you may regain that soundness of health which shall enable you to resume, at some future day, the great work to which you have devoted your life.

We know with how much reluctance it is that you feel compelled to suspend your labor among us at this time; but there is the less cause for regret on your part, inasmuch as you have, by the services you have already rendered to mankind, far more than earned the right to do so, even if the necessity did not exist.

Whether it is for a longer or a shorter period that you will be separated from us, of course none of us can tell. In any event, God's will be done! and at all times, wherever you may be, you will have our deepest veneration and regard.

Waiting for that happier day when we shall again take you by the hand, and again listen to your welcome voice, we remain,

Your faithful and loving friends,

(In behalf of the Twenty-eighth Congregational Society),

SAMUEL MAY,	JOHN FLINT,
MARY MAY,	WILLIAM DALL,
THOMAS GODDARD,	JOHN R. MANLEY,
FRANCIS JACKSON,	And three hundred others.

Boston, Jan. 11, 1859.

REPLY OF MR. PARKER.

Frederickstad, Santa Cruz, May 9, 1859,

To Samuel May, Mary May, Thomas Goddard, Francis Jackson, John Flint, William Dall, John R. Manley, and the other signers of a Letter to me, dated Boston, Jan. 11, 1859.

DEAR FRIENDS,—Your genial and most welcome letter was handed to me at this place the 6th of March; I had not strength before to bear the excitement it must occasion. It was Sunday morning: and while you were at the Music-Hall, I read it in this little far-off island, with emotions you may imagine easier than I can relate. It brought back the times of trial we have had together, and your many kindnesses to me. I can easily bear to be opposed, and that with the greatest amount of abuse; for habit makes all things familiar. I fear it flatters my pride a little, to be greatly underrated; but to be appreciated so tenderly by your affection, and rated so much above my own deservings, it makes me ashamed that I am no more worthy of your esteem and praise:

" I've heard of hearts unkind, kind deeds
With coldness still returning;
Alas! the gratitude of men
Hath oftener left me mourning!"

Herewith I send you, and all the members of the Society, a long letter, reviewing my life, and especially my connection with you. I began to compose it before I knew of your letter to me, before I left

Boston—indeed, in sleepless nights; but wrote nothing till I was fixed in this place, and then only little by little, as I had strength for the work. I finished it April 19th, and so date it that day. The fair copy sent you is made by my wife and Miss Stevenson, and of course was finished much later. I have had no safe opportunity of sending it direct to you till now, when Miss Thacher, one of our townswomen, returning hence to Boston, kindly offers to take charge of it. If this copy does not reach you, I shall forward another from Europe.

The letter would have been quite different, no doubt, in plan and execution—better, I hope, in thought and language, had I been sound and well; for all a sick man's work seems likely to be infected with his illness. I beg you to forgive its imperfections, and be as gentle in your judgment as fairness will allow.

Though I have been reasonably industrious all my life, when I come to look over what I have actually done, it seems very little in comparison with the opportunities I have had ; only the beginning of what I intended to accomplish. But it is idle to make excuses now, and not profitable to complain.

As that letter is intended for all the members of the Twenty-eighth Congregational Society, I beg you to transmit it to the Standing Committee—I know not their names—who will lay it before them in some suitable manner.

With thanks for the past, and hearty good wishes for your future welfare, believe me,

Faithfully your minister and friend,

THEODORE PARKER.

Frederickstad, Santa Cruz, May 2, 1859.

TO THE STANDING COMMITTEE OF THE TWENTY-EIGHTH CONGREGATIONAL SOCIETY IN BOSTON.

GENTLEMEN AND LADIES,—Here is a letter addressed to the members of your Society. I beg you to lay it before them in such a manner as you may see most fit. Believe me,

Faithfully your minister and friend,

THEODORE PARKER.

This letter, which was published under the title of "Theodore Parker's Experience as a Minister," will be found in the Appendix. Allusions to his object and feelings in writing it occur in a subsequent chapter, in letters to friends. [See Ap. II.]

TO THE LADIES WHO ASSISTED IN SEWING.

Boston, Jan. 31, 1859.

MY DEAR CAROLINE,—Paul wrote to one of his coadjutors to bring the garment that chief apostle to the Gentiles had left behind him. I write to beg you to thank the ladies who have so handsomely made garments for me when about to go among the Gentiles. There seems to have been a whole Dorcas Society making garments ! Please thank them all from me, accepting also your own share of the praise. I shall remember this kindness among those with which "my cup runneth over." I will try to repay you all. God bless you all!

Faithfully yours,

T. P.

TO FRIENDS IN GERMANY.

Jan. 18, 1859.

I am sorry to send such reports of myself as the steamers now carry to you. The worst pains we suffer *vicariously*, through the agony of our friends. My chance of recovery and restoration to my former power is one in eight, Dr. Cabot says; one in ten, I say. The chance of continued life (if such a dawdling existence deserves that name), is greater, and is one in three or four, perhaps. This does not look very promising! But I *will to get well.* I don't say I *will get well.* It would not be quite religious or wise. But I turn all my strength in that direction. I mean to be well, to preach again, &c. If I fall, it will be on that road. You know I shall not complain at either destination, but bear what comes as from the Infinite Perfection.

I shall not write much or often; reserving my strength for myself. But I ask one favor now, viz. that you look over my letters to you, and erase everything which would wound the feelings of any one, should it meet an eye it was not meant for. In the flush and fun of letter-writing, I may have said what might one day give needless pain, should some prying eye hit upon it, and some busy tongue prattle thereof.

* * * * * *

Let me thank you for the many kindnesses received from you all, and for the friendly and beautiful intercourse which has grown up between us. Remember me kindly. Gently forgive what requires that charity, and continue to hold me in your generous regards. Dear Sarah, dear Eliza, God bless you both!—you and *yours* also. Love to mother, Robert, and Hippopotamus. One kiss more for Sarah and Eliza.

Faithfully yours,

T. P.

TO THE SAME.

Jan. 31, 1859.

Thus comes this little mite of a note. We go off in a few days, bound for Santa Cruz, with high hopes and expectations. All hearts are cheerful, and we feel confident of delight. . . . . . .

But I don't think the wind never blows hard in the tropics, or that there are no troubles; but it is a new world we go to, and we all sail for the Blessed Islands. I will not complain if I am left at the Island of the Blessed, though still it is my *will* to pursue the voyage.

Your last letter gave us all great joy. Thank Robert for his to me. The tidings of Willie are *delicious.* But the picture—it filled us all with joy and gladness—he has grown so much; the same type, only developed and enlarged. " What a fine intellectual face ! " they all said, and " I showed him round to the neighbors—neighbors—neighbors." The little good-for-nothing dog! we all feel as much interest in him as if he were born in Exeter Place, almost. I want to ask a favour of Sarah, that she will write to Miss Cobbe, and tell that famous woman that I think her pecuniary matter will be attended to by Charles L. Brace, of Children's Aid Society Rooms, New York. I would, but cannot. Tell her, too, that Saturday night (it is Monday now), I received the first proof-sheet of her book, a handsome 12mo (no woman objects to handsomeness), but, alas! I must return it uncorrected! Tell her the sheets will pass under the eye of a competent proof-reader, and give her my thanks for her sympathy, and also my kind regards.

Last Thursday, in Beacon Street, I met Wm. H. Prescott; to-day, in Tremont Street, I met his coffin. So the living die while the dying live. . . . . . You must believe, dear Sarah, that I *will* to get well.

A consultation of physicians (Drs. Jackson, Flint, Bowditch, and Cabot) was held on Sunday forenoon, January 23. It was found that the fatal disease of his family had already made deep inroads upon his life. Tubercles were formal and progressive ; the bronchia inflamed. His chance of full recovery was pronounced to be as one to ten.

FROM THE JOURNAL.

I must go off to the West Indies, to Europe, and not return. I am ready to die, if need be—nothing to fear. Sorry to leave *work, friends, wife.* . . . . . Still, "*concedo.*" When I see the Inevitable, I fall in love with her. To die will be no evil to me. I should like to finish my work, write up my hints, print my best sermons, finish my book, write my autobiography, with sketches of my acquaintances, put all my papers in order. Yet I am ready. But I *mean* to live, and not die. I laugh at the odds of nine to one. If that is all, I'll conquer. I have fought ninety-nine against one, yes, 999 against one, and conquered. Please God, I will again. *Sursum corda.*

At this heavy moment, when all his glorious earthly labor was about to leave him for ever, it seemed as if his friends, who came with their own love and commiseration, were empowered to speak for the multitudes whom he had blessed, so sudden and deep was the sympathy which set in towards him. And letters came to his sick room with the cordial for which a noble and unselfish heart most languishes. His last days in America were thus soothed and brightened.*

FROM DR. FRANCIS.

Cambridge, Feb. 2, 1859.

DEAR PARKER,—I hear you are to leave your home and your friends this week for the West Indies, and I would not have you leave us without offering, in this way, my most affectionate good-bye and prayer for your health and happiness. It would have given me very great satisfaction to have taken you by the hand, and to have said the parting word ; but I found, on calling at your house at different times, that you could not and ought not run the risk of seeing any company.

---

* Indeed, the letters became so numerous, that he was obliged to publish a card in the *New York Tribune*, expressing, with his gratitude, an inability to reply. The result was a fresh flood of letters from friends who had held back from delicacy ; but to every one of these he replied after reaching Europe.

Your hearty kindness, so long and so abundantly experienced, is a deeply cherished remembrance with me, and I hope I am to enjoy it again, if you shall deem me worthy of it. I have learned much, very much, that is great and good from you; and with all my heart I thank you for it. Your noble life and noble instructions have taught us all the full meaning of that great saying of Plato, ὅπη ἂν ὁ λόγος ὥσπερ πνεῦμα φέρῃ, ταύτῃ ἰτέον,* and how poor do differences of opinion seem in the presence of the Eternal Truth, of which they are but the flickering shadows! No man can have a more supporting sense than yourself of having performed a great and good labor with righteousness of purpose and with singleness of mind, "as under the great Taskmaster's eye." The loving Father, I know, will sustain and lift you up, whatever may betide. To the arms of His love we all commit you, with truest sympathies and with heart-uttered prayers. We remember what a sage of old so finely said, " The memorial of virtue is immortal, because it is known with God and with men: when it is present, men take example at it, and when it is gone they desire it; it weareth a crown and triumpheth for ever, having gotten the victory, striving for undefiled rewards."

May every breeze, dear Parker, be the breath of health and strength to your frame, and may every day's sun shine upon you as a genial, cheering, life-giving power. The dear God, I trust, will return you to us with a restoration of that strength which you have so lavishly expended for others; and if I am then among the living, no one will welcome you back with a more sincere joy.

Farewell! God bless you, and keep you in the arms of His love!

Yours most truly,

CONVERS FRANCIS.

The following was written, and waiting to be sent, before he received, in New York, the letter from Dr. Francis : —

TO DR. FRANCIS.

[Written Jan. 30.]   Feb. 3, 1859.

I am sorry to leave the country on a journey of uncertain duration, and do not like to depart without a word to you. I have much to thank you for. In my earlier life, at Watertown, your devotion to letters, and your diligent study of the best thoughts and the highest themes, offered an example which both stimulated and encouraged me. Then your sermons, always generous and liberal, well-studied and rich in thought, and bearing marks of the learning of the preacher as well as his religion, were a cheer and a solace, while they abounded in instruction. I admired, also, the faithfulness with which you did your duty to all the parish, rich and poor, and your hearty sympathy with all common men in their common pursuits. I have rarely found such things in a minister's life ; for " education " separates the *scholar* from the *people*, and makes them strangers, if not foes.

I thank you, also, for the interest you then took in my studies, for the loan of books, your own and those from the College Library, which I had then no access to. I remember, also, with great delight,

* " Wherever the Logos (or right reason) would bear us on, as a wind, there we must follow."

that in the conversations of the little club,* your learning and your voice were always on the side of progress and freedom of thought. Then, too, you early took a deep, warm interest in the anti-slavery enterprise, when its friends were few, feeble, and despised; and you helped the great cause of human freedom, not merely by word and work, but by the silent and subtle force of example, which sometimes is worth more than all the words and works of a man ; for, while they may fail, I think the other never does.

Let me thank you, too, for the many wise letters you have written me while at home and while abroad. They still live in my memory as a joy which it is pleasant to recall. I leave America, with hopes of returning a sounder and laborious man, to live long and useful years; but you know how fallacious are the hopes of a consumptive man. I do not trust them, but leave the shore as if I should never see it again. I am not sad at this pause or ending of my work. Heaven is as near at forty-eight as at ninety—the age of my uncle, to whom I bade farewell, to-day. I am equal to either fate, though both my wish and my will incline me to the earthly life.

I congratulate you on your sound body and your unfailing health, which are not less your acquisition than your inheritance. Remember me kindly to your wife and family, and believe me,

Faithfully yours,

T. P.

TO REV. C. A. BARTOL.

Jan. 25.

My dear Bartol,—I thank you for your kindness in coming to see me, and for the tenderness of your note. I am not well enough to see any one—it makes my pulses fly. I first met you in 1832 (!) at Mr. Phinney's, at Lexington. It is twenty-seven years since then, and I have never met you since without pleasure. In our long acquaintance—perilous times, too, it has been in—you never did, or said, or looked aught that was unkind toward me. Once I intruded on your kind hospitality, and passed a night at your house, constraining the family to rise at an unchristian hour, for me to travel off to Portland. I have not quite forgiven myself for making so much trouble. You and your wife forgot it long ago. Give her my kind remembrances, and accept for yourself only my thanks for the past and hopes for the future. Faithfully yours,

Theodore Parker.

TO REV. DR. PALFREY.

Boston, Feb. 3, 1859.

My dear Sir,—I write with a pencil, for it is not easy to stoop over a desk and use a pen, but I do not wish to leave the country without a word of thanks to you, though it must needs be a brief one. I thank you for the friendly interest you have taken in me, and I looked with a mournful satisfaction on the card often left at my door, and marked with your welcome and familiar name. Allow me to thank you for kindnesses received in my earlier life, when I was one of your scholars,

---

* Alludes to meetings of the most liberal members of the Unitarian body in and around Boston, for the discussion of transcendental themes. The first meeting was held at the house of Dr. Francis, in Watertown.

and for the instruction I then received. But it is not so much that which I would now thank you for, as it is the noble example of conscientiousness you have set in all public affairs in the latter years of great trial. A finer instance of that great virtue in political life I know not where to seek. It has done me great good to stand by and look on your faithfulness. I now leave the country before you will receive this, and plead the occasion as my excuse for saying to your face, what I have so often said to others. But I must write no more.

Believe me, gratefully and truly yours,
THEODORE PARKER.

My friends have read me part of your admirable "History of New England," when I could not read, and I am both instructed and delighted.

TO REV. MR. FISH.

Boston, Jan. 31, 1859.

MY DEAR MR. FISH,—Many thanks for your very kind letter from Toledo. Really, a man has not lived in vain who finds so many friends when he stands on the brink of the grave. But I hope to return from the *Isles of Blessing*, and do a deal of work before I go to the *Isles of the Blessed.*

I must not write more now. God bless you in your noble labors, and yours with you! Faithfully yours,

THEODORE PARKER.

TO REV. J. T. SARGENT.

Jan. 27.

I shall be off, I think, the end of next week, and I must take you by the hand a minute. I can't talk—the doctors all forbid that. But I wish again to express to you my hearty thanks for the sympathy and kindness I have always received from you. When all the rest of the Boston Association turned against me—except Bartol, who never spoke an unkindly word against me—you were always firmly and fastly my friend, and often did me great service. But the kindness to me personally is less than the religious zeal with which you searched after truth, and defended the right of free thought and free speech. Accept my thanks, my dear Sargent, for this.

I don't like to write much just now—it makes my pulses fly too fast. So believe me, with hearty good wishes for the welfare of you and yours, Faithfully your friend.

TO GEORGE RIPLEY.

Boston, Jan. 10, 1859.

MY DEAR GEORGE,—I lie in my bed and write this, free from all pain—except that of suspense, *incertus quoque fata ferant.* I don't *talk*, and write only this to you. I had an attack of bleeding at the lungs Sunday morning about four o'clock; it lasted half an hour. Of course the finished sermon lies on my desk. The Music Hall will be shut up, I suppose, from this date. I shall go to the West Indies soon as possible, and then to Europe, but hope to be at work again before December. But who knows? The other result I also look in the face. It is a great work I am engaged in, not half done. You and some others love me ; my wife more than herself. I like not to leave these, but I *can* with religious serenity.

Please stop the *Tribune* ; it is paid to January 8, 1859, I think. Stop also the *Cyclopædia*. If I recover I shall want it—if not, not.

Many thanks, my dear George, to you. I never told you the service you rendered me in 1836, and so on. Your words of advice, of profound philosophic thought, and still more, of lofty cheer, did me great good. I count your friendship as one of the brightest spots in my life, which has had a deal of handsome sunshine. God bless you!

THEODORE.

TO REV. INCREASE S. SMITH.

Jan. 25, 1859.

Many thanks for your kind note, and the sympathy of yourself and wife. I also am grateful to you for coming to my help so early in the great fight, when there were almost " none that stood with me." But it will not now do for me to recall those days of my early struggle—it makes my pulses fly too fast. I go, uncertain of the result, but equal to either fate, hoping for the pleasanter, but not afraid of the other— nay, I should also accept that with silent joy, tempered only by sorrow that I could not finish what I began, and by regret to look the last time on my dear ones. But this is enough. Farewell!

TO DR. LAMSON.

Jan.

You and I were neighbors for some years, and I do not like to leave the country on so uncertain an expedition, without a word of gratitude to a valued friend. Especially I have to thank you for encouragement in the hard work of theologic study, which I gathered both from your words and your example.

Hoping you will have a long and happy old age, which I yet may never see, I wish to offer you my thanks for the good of the past.

Astor House, New York, Feb. 5, 1859.

To the Two dear Women who watch over their Mother at No. 2, Florence Street,—This is to say farewell for a time ; but still more to hint my thanks for all the kindness and affection I have received from you both. I have not *now* the power to speak all that I feel in this matter; but you will understand it without many words.

One of you has selected for her lot and labor of life the protection of those innocents whom a worse than Herod would else massacre, and she daily prints the streets with her gospel of beneficence. The other attends to the duties of home, and makes it possible for her sister to shelter the babies of misfortune. So are you both engaged in the same charity, and the same well-spring of love fills the two sister-fountains, one standing in public sunlight, the other in private shade. How have your faces cheered me at meeting on Sunday, and on other days, in your house and mine! What is joy for the moment is joy also for the memory.

Remember me kindly to your mother, to your brother, and his wife, and believe me, Faithfully and affectionately yours.

FROM MR. G. P. DELAPLAINE.

Madison, Wisconsin, Jan. 13, 1859.

REV. THEO. PARKER, BOSTON,—ESTIMABLE FRIEND,—Again the tele-graph startles us with the announcement that a relapse has occurred, and you are once more prostrated by illness, and that you would soon leave the field of your long labors, and seek rest and benefit in a southern clime.

I feel like a child about your departure, and can weep for the bodily sufferings you have to endure. But the Infinite Father is with you, and you are happy. I am glad I am to live so long in this new life, which under your teachings I have so lately commenced, and that you will live so very, very long. I shall see you sometime, and then I will tell you how much I have loved you, how I have cried over your writings, and what sorrow I have felt at the ignorance of men in rela-tion to your doctrine and personal character.

You don't know how much good you have done. The seed is spring-ing up, and bearing fruit all about us. Professors connected with our university, and other educated and intelligent men, come to me for your books, and I am rejoiced to see conversion to the natural religion occurring in several instances. The future is big with hope. When you and I shall have passed away, another generation will revel in the delightful truths which now are only partially understood by men. How happy you must be when you reflect how manly you have been, and how zealously and fearlessly you have advocated the truths you have for so long a time been promulgating!

If you improve in health, pray let me hear from you. I join with the thousands who are hoping for your speedy recovery.

Sincerely and affectionately yours,

GEO. P. DELAPLAINE.

But one more of such letters must suffice. It is from a slave-holder :—

Feb. 28, 1859.—I thank you for the sermon on " What Religion may do for a Man," which I have read, and read again, with profit and de-light, as others of your works.

But in the " Farewell Letter" I observe with lively concern that your health has failed. I earnestly hope that it may be soon restored and that you may be permitted long to witness on earth the good which you have done among men.

But in any event you have, in common with the good and great of all times, the high and rare consolation to know that the light you have shed is imperishable, and will continue to shine after the luminary has been removed.

Among the millions who gratefully participate in that light, without having the honor to know you personally, I would humbly enrol myself, trusting that you will pardon me if I assume an improper liberty in thus expressing my sense of obligation, and the profound respect which I sincerely entertain for your goodness and worth.

CHAPTER XXIV.

SUCH were the faces, sumptuous with reverence and grateful tears, that bent towards the dear house, with unexpected comfort. The door was thronged with these messengers of the heart. With what other psalm could he meet the few tender moments of that last morning, as the time drew near for a farewell to books, to noble labor, farewell to generous enterprises, and to the artless delights of home ?—

> Why art thou cast down, O my soul ? and why art thou
> Disquieted in me ? Hope thou in God,
> For I shall yet praise Him for the help of His countenance.

But as he read, the filial accents trembled, till at length the head fell in tears, and all who were present bowed their heads in uncontrollable but trustful sorrow, and laid them upon the bosom of the Father. Then, with hearty prayers and cheer and help, the steps went forth towards the cypresses of Florence.

He left Boston for New York, in company with his wife, Miss Stevenson, and Mr. George Cabot, on the 3rd of February ; but the *Karnak* did not sail till the 8th. In New York, Dr. and Mrs. Howe joined them for the voyage. His young friend, Rev. O. B. Frothingham, the minister of an Independent society in New York, Mr. Livermore, editor of the *Christian Inquirer*, Count Gurowski, and a few other friends, came with words of encouragement and blessing to bid him farewell on board the ship. A dear friend placed flowers in his state-room, violets for

him and carnations for his wife. He put an Italian violet be·
tween the leaves of his Bible, to mark the text, " I will be with
thee in great waters."

TO MRS. L. D. CABOT, NEWTON.

Astor House, New York, February 6, 1859.

My dear Mother Cabot,—I was sorry to leave Boston without
taking you by the hand once more, and bidding you farewell. I tried
twice to reach your house, but failed to get so far. Last Sunday I was
driven out within three or four miles of you, but was compelled to turn
back. Again, the last day I was in town I determined to renew the
attempt, but the damp and chilly north-east wind made it impossible.
I pray you excuse me for what might seem inattention and neglect. I
was able to see Aunt Fanny, and am very sorry I could not also see
you. But, though at a distance, let me thank you for all the generosity
you have shown me in the twenty-seven years of our acquaintance, and
for every kind and encouraging word you have ever spoken to me.
Little acts of kindness you showed me when I was a student at Cambridge I have ever cherished with warmest gratitude, and now they are
twenty-five or twenty-six years old, I love to recall them to you, who
doubtless forgot them long ago.

We left Boston Thursday morning at eight, and reached the hotel
at six in the evening. All bore the journey well. Lydia is in fine
health and spirits, and as you know she has been the best of all daughters, so to me is she the tenderest and most thoughtful of wives. I
regret exceedingly that, for I know not how long a time, you will lose
her kindly and loving presence, and the little tender attentions she
knows how to pay you so well. But I trust she will return in a year
or so, recruited by her long journey, and renew her offices of filial love.
Perhaps then she will have more time than ever to remain with you, and
comfort you when you need her most.

We shall not sail till Monday—I fear not before Tuesday, and I will
write you by the earliest opportunity after we reach Santa Cruz. I
trust you will continue in health and prosperity, and such happiness as
you can, after I have taken away your daughter.

Believe me, gratefully and affectionately yours,

Theodore Parker.

It is not easy for me to write with a pen, so please excuse the
pencil.

Outside of Sandy Hook they met rough and stormy weather.
His discomfort was very great ; but he managed to use the little
book which he always carried for pencillings.

Feb. 9.—It is just two years ago since I was caught in that inundation
at Albany, and passed the night in the midst of the waters, waking the
next morning with the point of the arrow in my side which now is

letting out my life. What an odds between now and then! I was so able before, and now so good for nothing.

Feb. 10.—Sea-sickness abating a little; lay on the deck ten hours Weather most genial. No cough or *hem* while on deck, but a good deal below, if lying on the right side. The right lung sounds like a tobacco hogshead when rapped.

Feb. 13.—Desor's birthday. Close to Nassau; fleeing from death. All my life-schemes lie prostrate. I stand up to my chin in my grave, yet hoping to scramble out this side. " Give to the winds thy fears."

R. W. E. is preaching for me at Boston. Here the thermometer is 79° in the shade ; the air for forty-eight hours more balmy and voluptuous than I ever knew in New England. We seek out the coolest places to sit in. The sea is smooth, and of a pale blue, such as I never saw before.

The steamer stopped a few hours at Nassau, and he went on shore. The note-book goes ashore with him, and returns to the boat with a long file of little springy sentences, each shouldering a fact.

Quite a pleasure-party of young people have joined us to go to Havana, and return. They came in like butterflies, and soon the ocean had them fast, like a butterfly nipped in a blacksmith's vice.

How impossible it is to conceal character! It is not in the face—in any feature. It appears in the gestures, in all the actions. What advertisements men and women continually make of their innermost secrets !

Feb. 16.—Began letter to Twenty-eighth Congregational Society. It has been feeling and thinking itself out a long time. It is fourteen years this day since I rode to Boston to preach at the Melodeon. I knew I enlisted for a thirty years' war. But now I am wounded, and driven out of the field before half that time is over. Yet I leave much work not done. These three things I must do :—1. Write letter to the parish ; 2. Write out and finish the *last sermon ;* 3. Write my autobiography.

About six o'clock in the afternoon the steamer dropped anchor in the harbor of Havana. Between the beautiful color of the sea and sky, the setting sun hung a great purple cloud. His eye comforted itself after the wearying waters, which were always so disagreeable to him, with the picturesque and warmly-colored scene.

The hotels in the city were so full that they spent the night in the steamboat, and in the morning went to a hotel three miles out of the city. It was found to be so uncomfortable that they returned into the city the next day, and finally succeeded in being well lodged, at Mrs. Almy's. In these journeyings to and fro, a great number of brisk notes were made.

TO MR. MANLEY.

Wolcott House, Havana, February 17, 1859.

MY DEAR MR. MANLEY,—Here we came yesterday, P.M., and passed the night on board the steamer in the damp and chill of the water, which did us all a little harm, making me cough a little more than usual. In general it appears that I am a good deal better than when I left home; all symptoms I think are better, appetite and digestion, excellent spirits, always hopeful and cheery; we all suffered much from sea-sickness, for we struck into a storm as soon as we passed Sandy Hook, which lasted three or four days. But sometimes the weather was delicious, and I lay on the deck eight, ten, twelve, or thirteen hours of the twenty-four. I did not forget 16th February, 1845! Fourteen years after, I slid into the port of Havana. Perhaps some of you thought of the first meeting. I have not recovered to-day from the emotions of yesterday. But I try to keep from *thinking* and *feeling*, and turn all my nervous power to mere *living*. How would it do to ask Rev. Mr. Shackford, of Lynn, to preach for you now and then? He is an *able* man and a good one, as well as a progressive thinker. Last year he asked me to exchange with him. I preached his Ordination Sermon, 19th May, 1841. I think you close the lease of Music Hall, May 22, 1859. What if he should preach you an occasional sermon eighteen years after his ordination?

E. E. Hale offered to do me any kindly things I might need. He would do you a good turn, I think, if asked. I shall always be with you Sunday mornings, and no distance will shut out the Twenty-eighth Congregational Society on *that* day; no, nor on any other for a long time to come. But Dr. Howe comes now and says, "You had better go to bed, *young man !* " So good night.

Feb. 18.—The thermometer stands at 70° in the shade; there is now no sting in the air. But this is not a good climate for a sick man, the nights are damp and chill, and there is a north wind like our north-easters in April, which cuts in to the bones. I long to get out of the place. I think I must ask you one favor more; when I die, I leave the two old guns now in my study to the State of Massachusetts. I fear the house may be burnt down. What *secure* place can they be put in? Would you ask Mr. Warner, Secretary of State, if he could keep them in one of the enormous fire-proof safes in the State House, and so secure them to the Commonwealth, which must one day have them according to my will? I can reclaim them when I return. Please tell Mr. Goddard I meant to have one ride more with him before I went away.

TO THE SAME.

B. (that was the beginning of Boston, which the thought of brought out of the pen.)

Santa Cruz, May 4, 1859.

MY VERY DEAR MR. MANLEY,—I write you this to say (1) that the last letters we had from home were dated April 1st, or a few days before, which came, thirty of them in a lump, about seventeen days ago; (2) that I shall send to Samuel May and Francis Jackson a long letter to the Twenty-eighth Congregational Society, which I ask them (Mr. M. and F. J.) to lay before the standing committee. Of course the standing committee—who are they *now*?—will do what they please with it. It is too long to read before the Society; it would take a common minister *four hours* to preach it, I think, allowing him due time to *cough*, wipe his face, &c. I think it had better be printed after reading before the committee and such as they see fit to invite, and that there should be a preface stating the fact of my illness, &c., and containing my little note of January 9th, which Mr. May read to the congregation; the longer one printed at the end of my New Year's sermon, and the Society's letter to me, which H—— prudently kept till March 6th. It will make quite a sizable pamphlet if printed in·a handsome form; I think it will sell, and so involve no expense to the Society. You will see I have taken some pains with it. L—— and H—— have copied it all out neat; eighty-four pages there are in my MS. Much of it is in H——'s hand, for she cannot read the original (!) which my wife reads to her; it took them eight or ten days to copy it. Please ask the kind Mr. Leighton to give it a diligent proof-reading, remembering that "if it be possible, the printers always get a thing wrong," so they *tell* me. I shall send a list of the persons to whom I wish it sent. We all sail in the *Parana* the middle of May; it is a slow boat, so will not set us down in England before June 3rd or 4th. We shall send many letters by the Misses Thacher. We left Dr. Howe February 22nd, and have not had a line from the faithful companions since. I hope he is well and safe at Boston with his wife, looking after the fools and blind; but he may have been blown up in a Mississippi steamer "seventy times as high as the moon." We have letters from Berlin of March 26th, and from our friends in England whom you do not know of the same date. I have seen one New York paper of last month, April 9th, and no more, so if any one asks me how many States there are in the Union, I say, "There were thirty-two when I left New York, 8th February 1859; they annexed another the following week; there may have been an extra session of Congress, which has admitted Cuba, New Mexico, Old Mexico, Nicaragua, Yucatan, and the rest of mankind." Sickles was on trial at the last dates, and the twelfth juror had just been caught and penned up. Key did much to make murder easy in Washington at the time of Brooks, and the killing of the Irishmen at the hotel. I fear if all his tribe had been thus served as soon as they reached the seat of Government, there would be no quorum of Congress, and so the Union would be dissolved for lack of a Government. I should like to see the Liberator, and to attend an anti-slavery meeting, and hear H. C. Wright call out "Hear, hear!"

Ah, me! who preaches at the Music Hall? What was done at the annual meeting? who is sick? who is *sick no more?* How is poor old Mr. Cass,* Chambers Street Court? If he is alive, send him a box of strawberries from me in their time, and I will pay the price. Ask Caroline Thayer to send me all the news: charming letters she writes —piquant, witty, and *wise*. Give our kind regards to your wife; take

---

* An old grape-pruner of the Twenty-eighth Society.

them to all your family, not forgetting Mary Ann, who opens the door with such a good-natured look to me. Remember me tenderly to all the *saints*, and don't forget,

Faithfully yours,
THEODORE PARKER.

His letters to his physicians always show a cool and minute observation ; at no time was he either insensible to his condition, or incapable of narrowly detailing all his symptoms.

TO DR. CABOT.

Havana, Feb. 17, 1859.

DEAR DR. CABOT,—I know you will like to hear how your patient (and pupil) has got on in his travels.

*   *   *   *   *   *   *

1st. The *general* condition, seems a good deal mended. Appetite excellent, digestion ditto, color of hands and face is *brown Havana*. Strength greater—though it is still an *infinitesimal*—muscular force small ; nervous force no more. I don't lie deep in the sea, and a little gust would tip me over.

2nd. The *trouble* in the *abductor* muscles was exaggerated by the ride to New York, by the little stumble in the Astor House, and still more by the abominable tossings in the storm, perhaps also by scrambling into my berth, and staggering about on deck when I had to move. I walk like a man of ninety.

3rd. The difficulty in the *respiratory organs* is certainly no worse, perhaps better. I cough from 60 to 120 seconds only in 24 hours, but I *hem* one, two, or three hours ; the character of the expectorations is altered a little. There is less *green mucus*, the white matter is less aërated with bubbles than before ; the quantity seldom half as great as in Boston.

1. I feel and hear a *râle muceuse*—it is always in *one spot ;* that forces me to cough, then I raise a little green mucus, and presently the white matter. This happens on the average, since leaving New York, three times in 24 hours, but never while in the free, open, pure air, without a chill.

2. I *hem* without coughing (1) when a little chill comes from a momentary draught of air; (2) when I am hungry, or the digestive organs are out of tune; (3) after any considerable emotion; (4) after talking. I put myself on the smallest allowance of this, and have become more obedient to you since I left Boston.

3. I never *sleep well at sea*—often lie awake till one or two A.M., but sometimes get a nap in the day. Two days were quite exciting, when I got to Nassau and to Havana, and I slept little the following night— only two hours last night—for the air in the cabin in the port of Havana was both close and chilly, but I could find no place to sleep in on shore.

4. I don't like the looks of my eyes ; the pupil is dilated unnaturally, and the whole has that specific look I have noticed in all my relations a little while before this tiger ate them up. I can clasp my left leg with my hands, and have a full half inch to spare !

You, dear Doctor, can put all these things together, and tell what they mean better than I. It is with difficulty I write so long a letter just after landing, so good bye.

THEODORE PARKER.

Cuba I think a bad place for consumptive people, the *air*, when hot or cold, is harsh. I wish I had taken a *sailing* ship from New York to St. Thomas. Took hyposulphites at New York, but not at sea; will resume at St. Croix. Pulse 70-80 at sea, 70-90 now, with the excitement of the land. I think Dr. Flint will like to see this scrawl.

On the 22nd they were at sea again, bound for St. Thomas, which they reached on the 28th, stopping by the way at Nuevitas, the port of Puerto Principe, at Puerta Plata, and at St. John's. He had time to write letters, and get some glimpses of the people, before sailing again, on the 2nd of March. All this time he was very weak, and had in no particular improved.

They reached the town of Frederikstad, West End, Santa Cruz, on the 3rd of March. On the next day his explorations commenced.

Musa sapientum is abundant in all the West Indies. Notice what Bruce says of it, and of the *Ensete;* and inquire if the *musa sapientum* ever occurs in the hieroglyphics (which I doubt), or on the monuments. Ask Dr. Pickering about this. In my little pencil memoranda I put down the names of the plants and trees I find. But, alas! what an odds between travelling for pleasure and knowledge and running away from death!

Yesterday I went to the Protestant burying-ground; the *terminus ad quem* I am travelling, it may be. It is not an attractive-looking place; none that I know of in New England is less so. There the grass comes "creeping, creeping, everywhere"—here only a ragged, coarse, rank sedge comes in tufts to supply its place! The trees look ungenial; the *Bombax ceiba* is the biggest, but uninviting—eaten up by its parasites.

No letters yet. No Congress in session now; and the nation, perhaps, breathes freely. But I should like to know what has been done with the 30,000,000 dollars which the President wanted to help steal Cuba with.*

Most of all, I wish to hear from the Twenty-eighth Congregational Society. In my wakeful hours at the Astor House and at sea, I went the rounds of the parish, and visited all the houses in a visionary way.

He collects all the statistics—number of soldiers, the duties on various articles, exports of sugar, molasses, rum ; notes the climate, the inches of rain, the fruits, the negroes, the birds and fishes, the women and children, the condition of the mules and oxen ; attends marriages, visits a sugar estate, and learns the

* But the appropriation was not made.

process of sugar-making, finds out the clergyman, and what he is doing.

Sunday.—I shall always spend an hour and a half *in my own way* at the time when the Twenty-eighth has its worship.

Read the Society's letter, dated Jan. 11, only two days after my pencil note to them. I think nothing has so moved me as this appreciative and affectionate note. If it overrates me, it is only the exaggeration of love. I could not recover from it all night.

March 10.—How all the work is done here! I saw men and women hoeing in a cane-field; and they were a sight to behold—so slow did they strike. Here there are nine hours of labor; the pay is about twenty cents, and board yourself. All industry is held in contempt. This of course, is the consequence of slavery. Notice the condition of the whole house, floors, &c. None of the servants in it are willing to *wash a floor.* The whites are ashamed to work, so are the negroes; and, of course, both despise such as do work. Six men and one woman were at work repairing the road; one was the overseer, and only gave directions. Some of the others, with great hoes, broke up the earth to be removed, and scraped it into trays, which others took on their heads and carried to the cart. Then all six of the workers took hold, and drew the cart a quarter of a mile, three pulling and three pushing —the overseer attending—and dumped the contents down where they were needed.

March 13, Sunday.—Snow knee-deep at home, I suppose. Not many at meeting, perhaps, in consequence of the storm; and here the fair sky seems eternal.

Here I miss the trees—not one in the precincts of the town—not a place to sit down in the shade—no *grass* to sit on. Bless me, a square rod of Boston Common, with green grass, white clover, and dandelions, would gladden my heart more than all the Palmæ, and Siliquosæ, and Musæ, and Graminaceæ on the Island of the Holy Cross.

March 19.—A most interesting movement is going on here for the elevation of the colored people. Mr. Dubois, the Episcopal minister, takes great pains in this noble work. But the white people do not help the work or much favor it. Mr. Dubois has a Friendly Society of about three hundred colored people, who pay a little sum each week to aid their needy brethren. The most interesting sight in the Island is the street full of colored people on Sunday, going to meeting. Soon as possible they get shoes and new clothing, and keep up their self-respect.

March 20, Sunday.—G. W. Curtis lectures at the Music Hall to-day, where I think I shall not speak again. R. W. E. has been there once, and Solger and Johnson each once. I can't keep the Twenty-eighth out of my head.

He finds some native books, specimens of Creole poetry, from which he makes extracts. And he undertakes to arrange botanically the trees, flowers, and shrubs; but this work came to nothing, for want of time and books.

He was not too weak to indulge in humorous passages with

his friends. His letters, indeed, from the West Indies and Europe, continually show that his disposition, released from the extraordinary labors and cares of his career, returned at a spring to the old geniality. They are full of fun and raillery. They overwhelm everything ridiculous, from the Pope and his flamingo retinue to Italian quacks and fine ladies of fashion, with jovial and knowing criticism. The fun is capital, because it is such excellent sense ; yet sometimes he could be simply merry without being critical.

Here is his revenge upon a delinquent correspondent, from Santa Cruz :—

Dr. Howe left us on board the *Pajaro del Oceano*, Feb. 21, at night, and I had not heard a line from him when I left St. Thomas, May 15, though he had abundant opportunities for sending letters. So by the Misses Thacher I sent to Boston a letter to "The Executor of the late Dr. Samuel G. Howe," and in it suggested this epitaph. The Latin is often sepulchral, as it was intended.

This epitaph is very long, but here are specimens :—

D. O. M.

Hic jacet
Expectans resurrectionem justorum
Omne quod mortale erat
Viri eximii
Samuelis Gridleji Hovve, M.D.
Reliquiæ Græcularum!
Juvenis lusit in universitate Brownensi,
Causa Educationis,
Et Præsidi reverendissimo celeberrimo Messer
Multum displacuit
Sed versatus valde fit
In Linguâ difficilissima Universitat. Brownensis,
Et ejus Artibus, Literis, Philosophiaque:
Inter Proeres pulchros fuit Antinous.
Studuit Artem Medicinæ:
Discipulus multa cadavera deterravit et infrustra secavit
Vi et armis:
Magister multorum Animas Heroum ad Orcum præmature demisit,
Inter Medicos verus Æsculapius.
In terrâ Argivâ,
Et Mavors et Cupido,
Multos Turcos occidit et Arte Medicâ et Gladio.
Quo melius nunquam se sustentabat supra femur militis.
*   *   *   *   *   *
Poetam duxit illustrissimam
Quæ Flores Passionis versu depinxit.

Pro Polonia invictissima bellavit,
Incarceratos visitavit, Cæcos fecit videre;
Mutos dicere, Stultos intelligere (ut ipse;)
Lunaticos in sanam restituit mentem;
Liberavit Servos:
Pyros jucundissimos sibi fecit crescere in hortis;
Inter amicos fidus Achates:
Propter mulieres virginesque et Hercules et Cupido,
Sed pallida Mors æquo pulsat pede
Græculas, Turcos, Heroes,
Et omnium mulieres gentium—
Troas, Tyriasve, Gallicas, Achivas, Romanas, Anglicanas, Americanasque,
Etiam Polos invictissimos, Cæcos, Stultos istos, Lunaticos, Servosque,
Et ipsum!
Vixit annos circiter lxxvii.
Clamant incarcerati, lacrymant cæci,
Mœrunt muti, lugeunt stulti,
Stridunt lunatici.
Atque sedent Servi in Pulvere,
Et Mulieres omnium Gentium conclamant,
Eheu, Eheu, Eheu.

Sunday, April 3.—Went to the Moravian church. The service had one good thing in it; "Bless the sweat of labor and business," if I have got it right. Could not stand the sermon and ran off. The ecclesiastical theology is the greatest humbug in the world.

His Santa Cruz letter to the Twenty-eighth Congregational Society was finished on the 19th of April. Writing afterwards to Mr. Sumner, he says of this letter :—·

Read it as the work of a sick man, writing under many difficulties, amid continual interruptions besides what his own weakness occasioned. The substance is about the same it would have been if written at home. I mean the essential thoughts; but the form and proportion would have been quite different had I set a well hand to work. But it is Parker's apology for himself.

To another friend he writes concerning it :—

It is a sick man's book, and seems poor and inadequate as I read it over now, three months after it was written. I never like to look at my own books when they are fresh from the press. What I heated in my hottest fire, and hammered when it made the shop blaze as the sparkles flew, seems poor and worthless as I look on it all cold, and dull, and inflexible. Yet I wrote this with bloody tears—no work of mine, perhaps, cost me such birth-pangs—for I was too sick to write, and yet must be delivered of my book, and that, too, in such a place!

St. Thomas, May 12, 1859.

MY DEAR DR. CABOT,—We have just arrived here from St. Croix *en route* for England, *via* Southampton; shall take the *Paraña* 15th, 16th, or 17th; the sooner the better. We have stayed a little too long;

but could not avoid it. Everybody said it would be no hotter in May than March, for there was more wind and rain; but they did not come. Not an inch and a quarter of rain in ten weeks! The normal amount of water is about eighty-four inches in this latitude; in the twelve months ending May 1st, 1858, there were forty-two inches; in the last, twelve to twenty-one! The Island is brown as its own sugar. The people are grumbling all the week, and on Sunday praying to the Unchangeable, " that it would please Thee to send us timely and gentle rain "! But it will not come, charm they never so wisely, till they allow the trees to grow on the hill tops.

For the last month the island has been a Dutch oven, a baking kettle. The thermometer stands in the parlor at 86°, from ten till five by day, only goes down to 80° at sunrise—the coolest time! That is the worst weather when clouds hinder the radiation; but for twenty days it has averaged 80° all the time, night and day. I am wet as a frog all the time, day and night, and take off my clothes as you peel an orange! Now for my health. In general health I have mended much since I came to St. Croix, am much stronger, can ride a pacing pony two or three hours, and feel the better for it: can walk two or three miles without much fatigue. My walking five or six hours a-day was one of Dr. Howe's Munchausens! I never walked three hours a-day! He represented me better than I think (of myself). The food is bad; not a decent piece of bread in St. Croix; butter from Denmark, and offensive to eyes, nose and mouth, uneatable; all the meats are insipid. Eggs good till the Cashew nuts became ripe; now the hens eat them and have the yaws, and the eggs are poor. I hate all the dishes except the roast turkey and boiled mutton, which are tolerable. In six weeks I gained three pounds, rising from 145 to 148; but in the last ten days, I have gone down to 144; lost four pounds, sweat it off. I am escaping through my own pores. The cough has ugly features still. I think it is about the same as last January, only a little harder and more agitating to the system; it rasps the throat a little more. The hemming is as before.

* * * * * *

There is no spiritual Hygiene here. The island has three good things: climate (bating the heat), sugar, rum (I mean it is so reported: I hate the stuff). There are 2000 whites, 21,000 colored people. There is only one man on the island who has any science. I have only heard of him; he is a Scotchman. Nobody has any appreciation of science or literature except the few Danes. I found one who knew Kant's great work almost by heart. Not a Creole has ever asked me a question relating to America, except as to the wealth or the food. The women are more insipid than their custard-apples; a man falls back on his own resources and the beautiful nature about him. Here is none of the tropic luxuriance of vegetation, for the whole island is tamed by cultivation, and now chastised with drought. Even the cocoa-trees are dying—an insect, *Aleoydas Cocois*, as far as I can learn, is destroying them as it has at Barbadoes and elsewhere; no progress goes on: only sugar, sugar, rum, rum! I have studied the botany of the island, but with no helps, and shall send home a quantity of seeds, &c. Flowers and plants I shall bring when I return. So I have studied the negroes, and could give quite a lecture on their physiology, phrenology, and psychology, before the Natural History Society. Perhaps I shall, if the medical art gives me my voice again. But the time here would have been unbearable had I not taken other matters in hand. I have written a letter to the Society (Twenty-eighth Congregational) at home. You will have a copy and will scold me for writing it; but I could not help it. If I die it will be a valuable document, and I think it is now before I am dead, and while I have " one chance in eight or ten for recovery." I do not think so highly of that chance now as I did three months ago.

I wrote to Desor to meet me at Antwerp and go to Scandinavia in June; then I will go to him in some part of the summer. We will study the sub-aquatic remains of the Celts in the Swiss Lakes. Steenstrup lectured on them (Sunday, 9th January) at Copenhagen, as I see by the Danish papers. In the winter I want him to go with me to Egypt; what do you say to that? I think I must leave the feminines at Paris or Rome, or elsewhere, and he and I drive off together. I should like to read the Arabian Nights' Entertainments in the original at Cairo, where there are Arabs *in situ*, but still better to study the nature of Egypt on the spot, with so intelligent and good talker as Desor.

Many thanks for your kind and characteristic letter, which came most welcome. I will not trust over much to drugs, "however vaunted." The hypophosphites disturb my stomach, and I gave them up after two (!) bottles.

If I had been at home I should have gone with Wendell Phillips before the Legislature to ask for land for the societies. It brought a tear into my eye to think that I am a good-for-nothing loafer, *fruges consumere* (*desti*) *natus!* But I doubt not you did just as well without me and got the land; but I hope that miserable sectarian mill at Wilbraham got nothing. It is not worth while for Massachusetts to give money to make Methodists of men, or to manufacture any sort of sectarians. I suppose Banks killed the new personal Liberty Bill, but wish it may not prove so, for I hope good things of him.

I could not study the birds much at St. Croix; never shot one, but caught a humming-bird and a yellow-bird in my hands (they flew into the house), and let them go again. I have seen about thirty-five kinds of birds at St. Croix, not forty; the island is so destitute of trees that there is no chance for birds. The pelicans interested me more than any other, but I did not find any one who knew the names of half the birds about him; they sing but little; the laughing-gull frequents the waters, but I saw only one specimen. I found no swallows and no thrushes! Don't they live in such low latitudes? I shall send home some large seeds of some kind of *acacia* (I think it is) which are washed up on the coast from South America or Yucatan. They are called horse-eye, and look a little like their namesake; they are washed up on the coast of Norway also, I think. A large nut called the Guinea cocoa-nut is washed up here on the south-east shore, which the negroes say comes from Africa. I could not find a specimen.

The Creoles here are shamefully uninteresting, except as specimens of the genus Snob. I don't know what the technical name is, so will give a new one, *homo stultissimus.* If I could bring one before the Natural History Society, and get Wm. B. Rogers to explain him in scientific phraseology, it would be refreshing. Such pride based on nothing, such contempt of work and impotence of thought, is amazing. The Danes are rather intelligent; but the Creoles, good Lord deliver us! I should name their women *fœmina insipidissima.* The genus is not worth preserving, and as they all turn out old maids (*faute des hommes*), it is not likely to last long.

Remember me and mine very kindly to yourself and yours. I will get well if I can, and you shall show me off in State Street as your card and advertisement. Heartily yours,

THEODORE PARKER.

TO MR. ELLIS.

St. Croix, April 22, 1859.

Here we have been seven weeks on one of the handsomest little islands in the world—a queer place too; once the thermometer in the night went down to 72°, once in the day (in the shade) it went up to 85°, and stood there from two P.M. till six. But generally the average heat in the house, with all the doors and windows open, is 76° to 79°. The barometer stands always the same, $30\frac{2}{10}$ inches. Judge how dry it is—in March there fell five-tenths of an inch of rain; we have not yet had so much in April. They all complain of drought; indeed, the hills are all brown as Windsor soap, except where the cane crop is still left in the field. There has been no such dry crop since 1837. The whole "thought" of the people is turned to making sugar, rum, and molasses; no culture gets much attention except the cane. You would be quite entertained with the pains they take with that. The island is a mountain in the sea, *i.e.* a cluster of hills quite steep (more so than any in Massachusetts). Their base is rock which comes close to the surface everywhere. The farmers extend their cane-fields to the top of the hills; they plant in rows three feet eight inches apart, and set the canes about two and a half feet apart in the rows. The land is thrown into ridges fourteen or sixteen inches high, which wind round the hills and keep level always. So all the rain runs into the trough between the ridges where the cane is set, and does not wash the ground. That method would be an improvement if applied to our hillsides in New England.

I know the first thing you will ask about is my health. I am much better than when I left home, feel strong, can walk with ease, only hindered by a little lameness in the right leg, which was much worse at home; appetite is excellent; digestion could not be improved; sleep is generally good and abundant, though now and then it fails me, but not more than when I am fully well. Yet still the cough continues, and will not obey me and be gone, charm I never so wisely. I like all the symptoms but that. My face is brown and ruddy, my eyes and teeth look well. I ride on a pony about three times a-week. I would do so twice a-day if it did not worry my leg a little. For nearly a month we had no letters from Boston; last Sunday thirty came in one sending! One of April 1, and a transcript of March 31. Judge of our delight—all containing good news! But I have not heard a word from your household, and I have visions of Mrs. E. with a cough, and Mr. E. with the rheumatism, and getting his feet wet on the sloppy sidewalk in front of the Merchants' Exchange! Jenny has youth on her side and is expected to keep well.

Should not I like to come out after meeting to-morrow and dine with you, and have a piece of nice cheese, and a crisp apple, and a glass of lager-beer! I have a great mind to say I will come, but I fear the horse rail-road car will be full—so I must wait.

What a mess the poor President is in! He can't pass his favorite measures; Congress goes home and leaves him no money to carry on the Post-Office with; his party friends desert him. Still I think the Fillibusters don't dislike him much, and certainly the slave-traders have reason so say, "I know that *my* redeemer liveth!" What a state of things; the slave-trade actually restored!

*   *   *   *   *   *

TO MISS CAROLINE C. THAYER, BOSTON.

Saturday Night, April 23, 1859. (Day before Easter !)
West-End, Santa Cruz.

MY DEAR CAROLINE,—What a nice letter you wrote my wife (who rejoices in the name of *Bear*), which we all rejoiced in last Sunday! We had no letters for a month (Santa Cruz is a dreadful *dry* place for letters) and Sunday morning (Palm Sunday, too), there came *thirty*. Didn't we delight that day ? we read 'em low, and then read 'em loud. You ask what kind of letters we want: take your pen and let her drive—that is the kind of letters. Besides, *I* want all sorts of *parish* news. Tell me all the news—one wants gossip when away from home— just as sick men pick up crumbs of bread when they do not dare eat a mouthful. Snips from the papers will be more welcome than ever. I wish I knew who would preach to-morrow at Music Hall. Ah! I wish it was *I*. But a little cough sticks in my throat, and will stay, I fear,

till I have consulted King Pharaoh, and seen his ◢◣ , and ques-

tioned the *Sphinx :* a dose of mummy may be good for a minister.

But I am not going to write you a letter—only a little note, and send a flower; it comes from a tree called *women's tongues*, which bears a pod that hangs profusely on the tree, and rattles all the time, day and night—I wonder whence the name came ? I would send you one if I could make an envelope long enough. The flower looks quite handsome now and here ; how it will look at Boston I know not. Here are no young men—*white* ones, I mean, and many young women. We had fifteen of them here one night this week, and but *one young man*. I canonically asked the Rev. Dubois, who looks after their present and eternal welfare (and is one of the best of men, working for the blacks also), " Where are the young men who are to marry all these virgins ? " He said, " Oh, we supply the St. Thomas market with that article ; young women go over there, and stay a few months, and if they come home not engaged, we call them " *a protested Bill.*" He is very satirical. Remember me (and us) to all the family.

God bless you!   T. P.

Tell Mr. Ayres that Captain Finney, of the *Anna Hincks*, saw me to-day, and can report the condition of my craft.

TO MRS. APTHORP.

West-End, Frederikstad, March, 1859.
(Written with a pencil out of doors.)

" In the afternoon they came unto a land
In which it seemed always afternoon."

Well, we have got there, this is the place. With nature it seems a perpetual Midsummer's Day, but with man it is "always afternoon." I should think the island was peopled by lotos-eaters. Everything goes lazy. In the morning there is a string of women who go to the spring for water, each with a little pipkin, or pitcher, or jug, or carafe on her head. In six months, time enough is spent to make an aqueduct with a reservoir which would supply the whole town with water. The boys do not run even down-hill, nor the girls romp. To play hoop, jump rope, bat and ball, would be a torture to these dullards. The only game I have seen among the children is top; all the little negroes have a top, and spin it on the hard, smooth street. The cows don't run to pasture, or from it ; even the calves are as sedate as the heaviest oxen, and walk decorously up to their milky supper, and pull as leisurely as if they worked by the day (to pay an old debt), not by the job (and incurring a new one). The ducks lie in the street all day where they can find a shade, and only quack and gabble at night, when the effort is not too heating. Mr. Cockadoodle does not *run* after the hens; he only walks as deliberately as a Dutchman, and it seems as if he ought also to have a pipe in his mouth. The winds blow in a gentle sort, and make no dust, though it has not rained enough to wet a blanket through this never so long. There is a brook outside the little village, but it never runs, it has no current. There are no tides in the sea, only a little slopping against the coral rock.

It is a queer place, this little island of the Holy Cross. But what wealth of vegetation and animation ! The air, the ground, the water, all teems with life ; a fruit drops on the side-walk, and is soon full of insects, which convert the vegetable into animal life. The Saturnian earth soon eats up the bodies of his human children, not sparing their bones. All is strange—the trees, the plants, the flowers, even the birds. Great heavy pelicans are always floating on the sea, or flying a few feet above it. The turkey-buzzard floats in the air like a feather, and seems to move by will not effort, one of the most graceful things I ever saw. The humming-bird, twice as large as ours, lights on a twig, and waits for the flies to come along for his breakfast, though he sometimes acts after his kind, and hovers about the flowers, treading air with his wings, and putting his long beak into the deep-bosomed monopetalous flowers which abound here. Many of the trees and plants are monocotyledonous, and have no network in their leaves, where the fibres all run the same way, like the threads in a skein, and are not woven, but glued together. What gorgeous flowers here are ! Red is the dominant color, which is amongst colors what the cock's crow is amongst singing birds. There is a queer tree growing in the churchyard. It is all branches with no twigs (like a tree-cactus); its boughs are an inch thick at the end. It has not a leaf now, but great red flowers in a cyme, at the end of the boughs. They call it *bois immortelle*, because it pushes out its flowers when its leaves fall off. But it looks repulsive and dangerous, as the *vie immortelle* which the Church preaches—life eternal, but heaven only to one, while it is hell to the nine hundred and ninety-nine. I thought the goddess of vengeance—who never sleeps even at St. Croix—had reared it, and planted it at the church door.

Great quantities of papilionaceous flowers are here, which bear pods. The tamarind is an enormous bean-tree, three feet in diameter, and fifty or sixty feet high. How grand the cocoa-nuts look, and the mountain-palm and the banana; not to speak of the sapodilla (which looks like an apple-tree), and the papao, and the breadfruit! I am never weary of looking at the Flora of this fair-skied island. But I should like a tree to lie down under, and a little grass; we have none here, only some sedgy stuff, solid-stemmed, coarse as flags almost, and growing six feet high, with a top like an old broom. I should like to see a little grass-plot, with white clover and a dandelion. I would fling in a deal of sugar-cane for a New England corn-field. The Tropic harvests are not handsome like the Temperate. The cane lacks color; it is pale as a city girl. There is nothing to equal the beauty of a field of wheat, barley, or rye, or even potatoes in their glory of bloom; a meadow ready for the scythe has no rival in the Southern crops. The cotton plant is not handsomer than a shrub-oak. Coffee I have not seen growing. Orange groves, I think, are a myth; I have seen larger at Rome, under the Pincian in the monastic garden, than I met with at Cuba or here; yet they really do exist. One Cuban, near Matanzas, has 10,000 trees, and they are always handsome, with "their golden lamps in a green night." I must tell a word about the humanities of the place. 21,000 black and colored, 3000 white. White, indeed! there is not a rosy cheek on the island, unless it be lately imported from the North. Here we live in the midst of colored folk; up and down the street, *Prinzens Gade*, far as I can see, there is not a white family.

We live with a Mrs. ——, a widow of 65 years old. She condescends to take boarders at 10 dollars a-week, and takes the greatest pains to feed them well. She belongs to the tip-top aristocracy of the island, and her house is the West-Endest promontory of the West-End of Santa Cruz. Why, her husband was Herr-Master-Collector-General of the Post, when at least 25 ships arrived in a year, and he had an income of 20,000 dollars a-year (she says), and her house cost 45,000 dollars (so she says). I take off a cypher from each sum, and bring it down a little by this reduction descending. They used to live in *Saus und Braus* in his time, that they did. What puncheons of rum, what pipes of wine and brandy did not they have, and what fun, and frolic, and feasting, and dancing, and making love, and marrying and giving in marriage. But alas! "*vergangen ist vergangen, verloren ist verloren.*" The house and all looks now, like the state of things a day or two after Noe entered into the ark, only the ruin is not by water. All the buildings are tumbling down, the garden is never hoed or dug, the fences have fallen, the gates without hinges, the doors lack handles, and the once costly furniture has been battered, and neglected, and maltreated, till you mourn over it all. Old Mr. —— was one of the most intelligent men on the island, and sent his many daughters to Copenhagen for education. One of them, at least, obtained it; a fine, sensible, well cultivated woman of thirty, the Lady Bountiful of the island, with a very tender history of love, which deathnipped in the bud when just ready for bloom. It makes me weep only to think of it.

Here is a better collection of English books than you would be likely to find in a Connecticut river town; but how they, too, are neglected!— The plates gone from the encyclopædias; volumes missing from sets, and the binding off from costly works; books scattered, Vol. I. in this place, II. in a different, III. lost, and IV. under the bed. Mrs. —— talks all the time about herself and her former grandeur, till she sounds as empty as the Heidelberg tun. In the next life I trust we shall be able to hold our *ears* as well as our tongues. I wish I could now.

The town belongs to the negroes and the pigs. A word of each. 1. Of the negros. In the streets you see nobody but negroes and colored people—fine straight backs. All the women are slender. You may walk half an hour and not see a white man. One of these days I will write a word upon the *moral* condition of the Africans here, and their possible future. It is full of hope. But the negro is slow—a loose-jointed sort of animal, a great child. 2. The pig. There are lots of pigs in the streets. Pigs male and pigs female, pigs young and pigs old. Most of them are coal-black, and, like Zaccheus, "little of stature." They are long-nosed and grave-looking animals. I should think they had been through a revival and were preparing for the ministry; a whole Andover, Newton, and Princeton turned into the streets. But they are *slow*, as are all things here. They do not keep their tails flying, like the porkers of New England. A woman, not far off, comes out into the street and now and then calls, "Pik, pik! sough, sough!" (*i.e.* suff, suff,) and her particular pig recognizes the voice and grunts gently, but approvingly, and walks home to his dinner, like an English country gentleman, and not as American members of Congress go to their meals.

I finish this on Sunday, P.M. 27th March. It will go to St. Thomas by packet to-morrow, and the British steamship will convey it to you. What do you think a passage costs from St. Thomas, £38 10s. or £43. for an *outside* cabin! I take the *inside*. You must not let us disturb *your* plans, and put you to *trouble*. We can join you anywhere you know. I want some healthy cheap place for the latter part of the summer, where I can live out of doors and find objects of interest. We mean to see Holland and the Rhine, and Nuremberg, before we go into summer quarters. Lyman will be with us. Dr. Bowditch is to take his daughter to England in the spring. He, too, banks with the Barings, and will go to the chief cities of the Continent. Lyman is a trump. H—— calls him *the lover*, from his attachment to me. Love to all, including the Hippopotamus. Good bye, dear friend that you are.

T.

TO GEORGE RIPLEY.

St. Thomas, May 13.

I have just finished " A Letter to the Twenty-eighth Congregational Society," which I think they will print. I wish I could have had your help in writing it; had I been at home I should have gone to New York to read it to you, for your criticism. It will be harshly criticized. It is a philosophico-biographical exposition of myself and my doings. I shall be charged with the grossest vanity and also pride. I think you will find neither the one nor the other there. It may be the last thing I shall ever write; at any rate I write it with that supposition. I have carefully left out of notice all of my labors and studies which do not bear upon the matter in hand. You will see how much I pass over in silence; whilst others will charge me with lack of reserve. Good heavens! if they knew what I could tell, and should, if I might live to write the Autobiography you spoke of! I give the rationale of Unitarianism, showing its excellence and its fatal defect, and its consequent defalcation. The Unitarians will not like this; I want your judgment on it. I show that I have utterly broken with the ecclesiastical theology of Christendom, and how; and what I offer in its stead.

I don't know that I have published anything more important this long time, though I preached a series of sermons on the "Testimony of the World of Matter to the Existence and Character of God" in 1857-8, which I think the ablest I ever wrote. I wish I could live long enough to print them: each was an hour and a quarter long (hard, abstruse matter) and I did not preach more than two-thirds of the MS.

I have not much instinctive love of life, but just now I should like a year or two more to finish up some things not half done. Still I am ready anytime, and have never had a minute of sadness at the thought of passing to the immortals.

* * * * *

Your friendship has long been very precious to me, and one of the great delights of my life. The volume of sermons I just spoke of I meant to dedicate "To George Ripley, most genial of critics, most faithful of friends." Take the will for the deed. I rather think you must let me slide before long. I doubt that I ever see the State House again. I was ten weeks at Santa Cruz, and no critical feature of my complaint is changed for the better.

To return to the letter to the Society; you will see parts of it were written with tears of blood, but the people won't see it: I don't wish them to. I avoided all that was sentimental or pathetic as far as possible. It is not well conceived nor well expressed, I fear. It is a sick man's letter, written too, when the average temperature was 80°. Commonly I walk in quiet places, often by night, to make my compositions. Boston Common is part of my study at home; so were the woods at West Roxbury; the great oak, you remember—it was part of my library. But here I could not walk for the heat—there is no shade, and the house admitted no privacy. So I wrote under manifold disadvantages.

I think you will be interested in my account of my Orienting myself in metaphysico-theology in the theological school, my fixing in humanity the idea of the Divine, the Just, and the Immortal. In my auto-biography I should (not shall) write it out more fully. I know you will like what I say of the spiritual influences attending my theological development. I mention the leaders of the movement and the agents of the reaction.

* * * * *

God bless you!

T. P.

He left Santa Cruz, and returned to St. Thomas on the 11th of May, to take the steamer for Southampton, which sailed on the 16th.

I leave the tropics with more cough than I brought in. The *critical* symptoms are worse, but others are better.

No plant can live in so dry and poor a soil as hope (*Spes mortalium*). No cactus equals it. Really it lives on itself, —— and —— furnish me examples of this continually. *Moriturus spem habeo nullam.*

May 29.—In no essential symptom is my disease better, in several it is worse—much worse. I have no longer much hope in my bodily power of recuperation; no physical instinct assures me of recovery. I have some faith in the revivifying influence of civilization, which I have been exiled from for four months; some also in this, that my affairs are not ready for my departure—that I have not done my work. But these are feeble arguments against a consumption, with a cough which tells of the destruction of my lungs. I must let myself slide out of this life into the immortal.

May 30.—To be a good traveller one should have all these accomplishments:—

1. He must sail without sea-sickness.
2. He must be able to coax a sleep out of any plank.
3. He must have a stomach that never surrenders.
4. He must take tobacco—especially smoke.
5. He must drink the coffee which he finds everywhere.

My other sickness now gives me the victory over sea-sickness—a great comfort which I am grateful for.

May 31.—A year ago I was at Kennet Square, Pennsylvania, and preached four sermons—lectured at West Chester, &c.

Many ships in sight to day—sounded fifty-five fathoms. We wish for news of the war. Saw a British steamer at 5 A.M., full of troops heading south for the Mediterranean.

How the old scenes come back and people the world anew! I see the faces of my friends whom I saw last year at Kennet Square, whom I may not see again with the mortal bodily eyes. I am troubled still a little by the sea, and by the crowd of passengers who incommode us so at table and elsewhere. When I close my eyes what special shapes are painted on my optic nerves!

Southampton was reached on June 1, and London the same evening, where they lodged at Radley's Hotel.

The note-book goes peering round in every direction. To the Queen's stables, the Court at Westminster Hall, Chief Justice Campbell on the bench, the Thames, to the book-stores, to Mr. Buckle, Mr. Mackay, and other houses, to Guildhall, St. George's Yard, Vulture Inn, Fish Street Hill, Billingsgate, the Tower, the Reform Club, Museum, Speaker's Gallery of the House of Commons by the favor of Mr. Bright, the Museum in Jermyn Street, to Thomas Huxley's Lecture on Fishes, to the College of Surgeons, to a Charity Sermon at St. Paul's. But, he says, " Too feeble to do much."

He also wrote letters and received a good many visitors.

At St. Paul's, yesterday, the wealth, beauty, and famous birth of England sat under the great dome of the Cathedral, while the servants and ignobly born stood without; 8000 children sat alone, and fainted with hunger while they listened to a wretched sermon on human depravity or sung the litanies they had been made to commit to memory.

June 5.—Heard Martineau. Sermon on self-surrender, full of rich religious feeling, and showing the fine culture of the man. But the costume and the printed service-book are a hindrance to progressive thought, and to all freedom.

While he was in London, a young English gentleman called upon him, who had evidently found the satisfaction which his mind and heart required in the writings of Mr. Parker. He did not come to pay his formal thanks ; his whole manner was a demonstration of respect and grateful feeling. On leaving, said he, with much hesitation and modest embarrassment,— " This travelling is a matter of great expense—perhaps, in consequence, you might not be willing always to do something that you would prefer, or to go where motives of pleasure and comfort would otherwise carry you. That ought not to be. Pardon me if I say I know one, deeply indebted to you, who desires to show it, who would be proud to increase the chances for your recovery ; in fact, he stands before you."

How many such unexpected hands of love were stretched out to him during this last year ! The offer was declined, but he accepted the precious love.

TO HON. CHARLES SUMNER.

Radley's Hotel, London, June 7, 1859.

My dear Sumner,—You don't know what delight your letter, which came last night, gave us all. How glad we all are to hear of your improvement in health ! Mr. Seward was here yesterday afternoon, and said he heard indirectly from you every day or two, but did not speak so confidently of your health as I had hoped. To learn from your own mouth of your condition is delightful. Lyman came in the *Ocean Queen* to Cowes, reaching land June 2nd, and London the 3rd. Dear, good soul that he is! he took command of me soon as he arrived, and hoisted his broad pendant, so I sail under his colors. He says we shall all be in Paris in ten days at farthest. I think we shall leave London next Monday. We shall stay but about a week in Paris, then go to Holland, perhaps, and so to Switzerland. Tell me of some decent hotel, that is central and not dear. Yours must be too costly for my taste or pocket. Desor is now at Wiesbaden, gone there this week, for the bath-cure. He asks us to pass a part of the summer with him, and we shall but too joyfully accept the offer.

We'll talk over the Italian affairs, which must be settled sooner than I thought. But I have little hope of any good for Italy. Effete nationalities cannot be rejuvenated, I think. I *guess* the fate of Spain and Asia Minor is before the poor people. The Piedmontese seem the best portion of the race.

Well, it won't be long before we see you. I had a letter from Howe; his visit to the Tropics did him a deal of good.

Yours ever, T. P.

Radley's Hotel, London, June 2, 1859.

To MISS COBBE AND MISS CARPENTER, BOTH MY VERY DEAR FRIENDS, —Let me unite you both in one letter, the first I write on English soil, while the tossings of the sea still keep my head and hand unsteady. Many thanks for your kind letters, which reached me at Santa Cruz, and the two which greeted me yesterday, on board the ship at Southampton. A boat came alongside, and the boatman called out, " Letter for Theodore Parker!" Judge of the trembling joy with which a sick man read your words of kindly greeting! Thanks, many thanks, for your words of welcome!

I know you will wish to know what effect the residence in the West Indies has had. I cannot yet quite say; for the critical symptoms have changed but little, if at all. But I am a deal stronger, with a good appetite, and reasonable strength and spirits, that, if not hilarious as when well, are never sad. Indeed, I am cheerful by temperament, as well as by philosophy, and from principle. In all my illness, and it is now in its third year, I have not had a single sad hour. I have not the average love of life by instinct, and, besides, have such absolute confidence in the INFINITE LOVE, which creates and provides for the world and each individual in it, that I am sure death is always a blessing, a step forward and upward, to the person who dies. My place in the world will soon be filled by wiser and better men, who *may* be guided by any wise word of mine, and certainly will be *warned* by my *errors*. So my departure may be the best thing for the great cause of humanity we all have so much at heart. The burden of sorrow in that case will fall on my intimates, and heaviest of all on my wife; for to her I am all in all! But even such sorrows are blessed in the end they serve.

However, I shall still hope for returning health, and leave no stone unturned to prolong life. I have many things half ready for the press

U 2

which none beside me could print. In special, I have a short volume of sermons on the "Evidence of God found in the World of Matter and of Mind"; they were preached in 1858. I like them better than anything I have done before. Each was about an hour and quarter in the delivery, and what was spoken could be recalled from the notes of the phonographer who daguerreotyped all my words. But I did not preach more than half of what my *brief* contained: the unpreached matter will be lost without me; hard to write it out. Besides, I have volumes more in that state.

Dear friends, do not think me rash to have wasted my strength in this way, for I must preach every week, and I had not time to write out fully all that related to the matter I preached upon. Besides, I must labor in some other way to obtain the means to publish and circulate my new works—for I have been my own Tract Society. Had I lived in England I should have printed more and lectured less: in America I must do as I did.

Your two letters, dear friends, are full of interesting matter, which I am not quite well enough to write on now. I hope to do so when I return from the Continent next year. Yes, at Bristol itself; I wish it were possible now. But we shall stay only a week or ten days in London. Here I found letters, dated Montreux, Switzerland, May 28. My friends are well and happy. I meant to visit Scandinavia with my friend Desor, but hear nothing from him. My American friend Lyman has not arrived, so we are all alone in this great Babel of modern civilization. I have seen nobody but the bankers, Bates and Sturgis (Baring, Brothers, and Co.), old acquaintances, and genial, kindly men. I hope to see Martineau, Newman, and others of the nobler sort, but must be prudent and not talk much with thoughtful men.

When I reached Santa Cruz I went, or rather crawled, for I could hardly walk, to the graveyard, and selected my place of rest if the angel of death should say, "Thus far, O body, but no further!" It seemed odious to lay my bones in ground where the bottom of the grave was dry as the top, and where no grass can grow, but only abominable sedges six or eight feet high. Yet I found a sufficient place under a tamarind and a silk cotton tree (*Bombex ceiba*) though unlovely. But when I trod on English ground I felt that the clods of the valley would be sweet to the crumbling flesh. I would not object to laying my bones where, save six generations, my fathers have left their ashes for eight hundred years. Yet I shall prefer to take home a sound body.

TO MISS COBBE.

Radley's Hotel, June 11, 1859.

My very dear Miss Cobbe,—Your kind note came duly to hand, and the flowers are fresh and blooming still, on the table before me, as I write. I have seen the Martineaus, Newman, Tayler, Ierson, Mr. and Mrs. Shaw, Miss Winkworth, Cholmondeley (whom you don't know —he is a good fellow, and was a while in America), and many others. Mr. Bright and many of his coadjutors I have also seen, and by his courtesy got a place under the gallery and heard the great debate on

Thursday night. But I am losing daily here in the smoke and chill of London. To-morrow we hasten to Paris (Hôtel de Londres, 8, Rue St. Hyacinthe, Rue St. Honoré) where we shall stay a few days, and then take our departure for the Rhine and Switzerland. It is a great luxury to see the Apthorps again and my dear Desor, with whom I shall pass some weeks.

"To be weak is to be miserable." Here I am in the focus of civilization and can do nothing; a little excitement is a little too much, and I must get into a quiet place. It has grieved us all that we could not see you, but if I return next year and in any tolerable condition, I must have that pleasure. I hope I shall often hear from you on the Continent. The Barings will always have my address, and I will besides keep you advised of my whereabouts.

Mrs. P. sends hearty thanks for the flowers, and I have put away the silken thread which bound them among other precious things. Both of the ladies send you their hearty regards. Let me add the best wishes and thanks of

Yours truly,

T. P.

TO ISAAC AND SARAH CLARK, BELMONT, MASSACHUSETTS.

London (Radley's Hotel, Blackfriars),
June 8, 1859.

MY DEAR ISAAC AND SARAH,—My friend, Mr. Lyman, came here to take care of me on the 3rd of June, leaving Boston May 19th; he brought the news that your excellent father had passed on from this world to a better. It did not much surprise me. Yet the last time I heard, he was quite well; had got his petition accepted, and cast the first vote in the new town of Belmont! I am glad he had that satisfaction. But at ninety what are we to expect? When I rode out to see him that last Sunday I spent in Massachusetts, I thought I should not see him again, but yet imagined that *I* should shake off the body before him. I don't know but he was of the same opinion. A tear stood in his eye as I took him by the hand, and said Good bye. Some letters told me the particulars of his passing away—gradually, calmly, quietly; what more could we ask? He came to a great age; he had lived a happy life; his latter years were particularly full of delight; and he died an easy death, and slipped into the other world without knowing it. We must shed some natural tears, but let us not mourn for him. It was only a blessed new birth to him, the mature soul drew near its time and must be born into heaven. He could not have lived many years; they must be years of painful decline of all the senses. Let us not mourn that he has left the earth and gone to the blessed ones of his own family, who have ascended to heaven before him. Let us rather rejoice that he lived so long and happy a life, achieved such an excellent character, and passed so pleasantly from time to eternity. I wish I could have been with you at the time, and could have spoken a word or two about the character I loved and esteemed so much. But that pleasure was denied me.

We went from New York to Havana, stayed there three or four days, then went to St. Thomas, where we stopped two days ; thence to Santa Cruz, and stayed ten weeks. There we lived in a house which had no glass windows, no chimneys, no fire-place. A house in the West Indies is a little piece of out-doors fenced off with a slender partition. I mean it is almost out of doors. So we lived in the open air when within the house. I used to ride on a little pony, who climbed the hills nicely ; and bathe in the sea—that was my only exercise, for it was so hot nobody could walk with any comfort; there were no shady trees. During all the ten weeks we were there it was not cloudy three days ; it did not rain an inch and a quarter ! I saw a grave dug, six feet deep, and the earth at *the bottom* was like ashes, as dry as at the top. I wish I could describe the island to you. It is twenty-three miles long with an average breadth of not more than four or five ; the shores are coral rock, rising generally but two or three feet above the sea itself; though in one place there are cliffs ten or twenty feet high. The sea has no tide, and is commonly still as Fresh-pond, though it flaps a little at the shore. The whole island is but a cluster of hills, the highest about 1500 feet; the steepest part of Wellington Hill is nothing to the abruptness of these miniature mountains. Yet they carry their cultivation to the very top ; the steepest sides are planted with sugar-cane. They throw the land into ridges about three or four feet apart and sixteen or eighteen inches high. These parallels run round the hills nearly level; between them the sugar-cane is planted : the plants are set about a foot apart. Paths making a zigzag lead up to the top of the hill, in which the mules walk to carry up manure and to bring down the crop. For scenes of quiet rural beauty, I have seen nothing equal to some of the best parts of the island. But we are all quite glad at length to get away from it, for it became intolerably hot. There is no relief from the heat; a cool day does not come now and then as with us, and the nights are almost as hot as the days. 11th of May we went back to St. Thomas and stayed till 16th, when, at 3 p.m., we steamed off for England. Here I am as busy as a nail-machine all day and get little rest, there are so many friends. But I refuse all invitations to breakfast, dine, &c., and keep as quiet as I can, doing nothing rash. Please show this to my brother. I shall write him soon, but I avoid letters as much as possible. Believe me, my dear cousins, faithfully and affectionately yours,

THEODORE.

TO DR. HOWE.

Paris, June 15, 1859.

MY DEAR CHEV.,—We left London Sunday morning, June 12, at half-past five, and reached Paris at a quarter-past five p.m., travelling (*viâ* Folkstone and Boulogne) nearly three hundred miles, and that with little fatigue. We had not got fixed in our lodgings before Sumner came to see us. He had been already at the station, but missed us there. He is the finest sight I have yet seen in Europe—he is now so much better than I had hoped. He walks on those great long legs of his at the rate of four or five miles an hour; his counte-

nance is good, good as ever; he walks upright, and sits upright; all
trouble has vanished from his brain; he has still a little difficulty in
the spine, enough to make him feel that he has got a back-bone—we
knew it from other indications. He is the same dear old Sumner as he
used to be before that scoundrel laid him low—winning the admiration
of the Hunkers of Boston and of South Carolina. He is full of information—knowledge of facts, men, and ideas. Monday I rode with
him nearly six hours about Paris—he doing all the talking, for I do
not speak in the streets. He was here again yesterday, and I was at
his room. I never found him more cheerful or more hopeful. It is a
continual feast to see him.

Now you will wish to know a word about myself. I did not like to
write from London, where I had no good to tell. The voyage from
Havana to Santa Cruz wore me down a good deal. W' .n I reached
that place (March 3rd), I could but just crawl about: I went stooping
and feeble. With the help of a cane, I strolled out after breakfast to
see what I could see, and got into the grave-yard, a most hideous-
looking place, where I selected the most unattractive spot, and thought
it likely I should lay my bones there; but I *did not!* I gained color
and weight at Santa Cruz, but lost the latter again; strength increased
all the time. I lost seven pounds' weight in the voyage from St.
Thomas to Southampton, and, of course, have not yet recovered
it. The cough "has increased, and is increasing, and ought to be
diminished." So is it with the expectoration. Yesterday, in company
with my good friend, Dr. Samuel Bigelow, of Paris, I visited Dr. Louis.
Bigelow and Louis both made the examination, and concurred in their
advice, Bigelow explaining to me more minutely than Louis all the
features of the case. Still, I don't know that *my* opinion about myself
is at all changed. But it may be of no value; for the doctors here do
not agree with it, Dr. Bigelow thinking that I may preach again. The
2nd of January, when I turned away from the congregation after the
sermon was over, it flashed into me, "This is the last time, O Parkie!"
—and I turned and looked at the departing multitude as for the last
time. I will do all my *possible* to live; then, if I die, it will not be my
fault.

After the six hours' ride, Mr. Sumner was obliged to go
home and rest; but Mr. Parker went on foot, still exploring
and making calls for some time longer. He was then more
capable of muscular exertion than Mr. Sumner; and to all
appearance, putting the positive disease aside, promised an
earlier return to health.

The note-book was on duty again. The amount of sight-
seeing, visiting, and letter-writing is wonderful to contemplate!

TO DR. CABOT.

Paris, June 16, 1859.

My DEAR CABOT,—I know you will like to hear a word or two from
your docile patient, since leaving St. Croix. We had a good smooth

passage to Southampton (May 16th to June 1st). I took six drops of chloroform in a wine-glass of water, to prevent sea-sickness, and kept horizontal on the deck for the first three or four days. So I escaped the misery of continual vomiting, retching, and straining, which so torment me else at sea. I suffered little this time, but yet lost seven pounds on the voyage. As we got into cooler latitudes, I protected myself abundantly with clothes, &c., keeping on deck twelve or thirteen hours a-day, but in sheltered places ; but yet the cough would increase. After I reached London, the dampness—they called it, " uncommon fine weather it is, for June " !—the clouds and the deadness of the air, full of coal smoke, irritated the cough still more, and of course increased the expectorations. I was very prudent. I accepted no invitations to *breakfast* or *dine*. I once lunched with Martineau. I made no visits, except one or two of necessity, and those but a few minutes in duration. Of course, I could not avoid seeing some hundred persons perhaps, some of them most enlightened and interesting men and women. Many hospitalities were offered me, but I could accept none. "To be weak is to be miserable! " I was out in the evening time, once till half-past eight, once till ten—it is hardly dark at nine, and dawns at half-past two A.M. !—but did myself no harm thereby. Judge of my forbearance. I left the House of Commons at half-past eight (when I had a most distinguished seat), though Sir James Graham and Lord Palmerston were to speak before midnight ; besides, I went into none of the great churches, not even Westminster Abbey! I never went to the theatre, and took special pains not to get fatigued. Professor Rogers happened to be in London for three months, and was exceedingly attentive, kind, affectionate, and *wise*. He insisted on my staying with him, but I did not ; nor even accept his invitations to meet famous *savans*, and talk with them.

Here, at Paris, I sought Dr. Samuel Bigelow, who took me to Louis. I told them my medical and pathological story, and they made a "survey," and reported a little tubercular disease at the top of the right lung, *not extended far, no reason why it should extend or even continue!* He thought little of the cough or the expectoration; thought the greenish-yellowish matter came from the bronchia, not from the decomposition of the tubercles. He has no faith in Dr. Winchester's hypophosphites ; no more in (that abominable) cod-liver oil. He recommended *pillules de Blancard* (iodide of iron, you know), and I have got one hundred of them, to take one at breakfast and at supper for a while ; they look formidable as buckshot, and will kill the consumption, *if they hit it!* Certainly they are big enough. Drs. L. and B. recommend—1. Abstinence from all over-exertion. 2. To keep in the open air as much as possible. 3. To eat abundance of nutritious food, especially *viandes matures.* 4. To drink *vin de Bordeaux,* or *vin de Neuchâtel.* He (Dr. L.) also recommended the baths at Ems and Eaux Bonnes (near the Pyrenees, you know ;) but I found Dr. B. inclined to let me off from them, so I shall go to Montreux (Vaud, Suisse) at once. Dr. L. thinks well of Ægypt, but I fear the discomfort of the land, and the chill of the river (seventy-five days in a boat), and seek some European spot. Do write me (through Mr. Manley) what you think of Rome for a winter residence. I don't refuse Ægypt, though the cost is *enormous*. Now, my dear Cabot, don't think I rode in your gig for nothing. I became a mollusc—an oyster, at the West Indies, and exercised almost exclusively those *nerves of vegetation*, which you discovered. But I had in me a letter to the Twenty-eighth Congregational Society, and I must bring it forth, and when my full time was come, I was in labor four or five hours at a time; but this was *ex necessitate*, not at all *ex voluntate;* besides, it was the only way to get through. I can't "take the leap of Niagara and stop when half-way down." I hope you have seen the thing, by this time; a sick man's baby it must be; the child of sorrows, no doubt; but like others, it must be born! After that, I dropped down into my molluscous condition, and when I saw one of the actual tenants of the mud at London (they grew on *trees* at St. Croix,) I said, "Am I not a clam and a brother?" I never opened my mouth upon oyster or even *shrimp*, except to speak to them respectfully, lest I should commit the crime against nature, and devour my own kind. In Switzerland, I will be as gentle "as a child that is weaned of its mother," and behave myself "like a sucking child."

I shall see Bigelow again, and keep up a correspondence, perhaps, with him; but I want your advice as much as ever, dear, good, hearty friend that you are; please write me through Mr. Manley, who will always know my address. Love from mine to yours. Please hand this to the excellent Dr. Flint, and let him show it to whom he will, as good tidings from

Yours faithfully,
THEODORE PARKER.

On the 19th of June he went to Dijon, on the way to the Lake of Geneva and Montreux. The latter place had been recommended to him for a summer residence.

After dinner the next day he took the tour of Dijon, "the queerest old town I was ever in," and at two in the afternoon was on the way to Geneva. He reached Montreux by boat on the 22nd, landing in a violent thunder-storm, and found lodgings prepared at the Pension Ketterer. Here he met his friends the Hunts and Apthorps.

TO MR. JOSEPH LYMAN.

Montreux, June 22, 1859.

MY DEAR LYMAN,—We reached Dijon about 5 P.M. Sunday, after a most delightful ride through a highly cultivated country. The land is rather sterile by nature, but made abundantly productive by art; the crops were fine; rye, wheat, grass, now and then a little Indian corn, and the beautiful vines of this Côte d'Or. How everything is *utilisée*, every spot of ground, all the water, and the waste of the roads! Nothing is lost; at taverns the guests eat their platters clean.

At Dijon we found a fine hotel (De la Clôche), but prices exorbitant; all tavern-keepers I fear are pirates, and seek to *exploiter* the rest of mankind. It is, I think, the queerest little old town I ever saw. All is mediæval—narrow streets, churches with no approach to the *Renaissance,* of the quaintest fashion. I felt myself carried back to the time of Charles the Bold and Jean Sans Peur, whose tombs are here, with their high-nosed statues lying on the top. We stayed till 2 P.M. next day, then started for Geneva, which we reached at eleven, tired and hungry. I was too weary to do much the next day, but H. and L. visited some of the (few) curiosities of the town. At 3 P.M. we steamed off for Montreux, but met ill weather three-quarters of an hour before reaching it, and at half-past eight landed (in a flat-boat) in a violent thunder-storm. We stayed awhile in a shanty, where Mr. Ketterer was waiting for an English family, and then walked some three-eighths of a mile to his hotel. All was ready for us, fine apartments with a most glorious outlook, good beds, &c. Most of all, there were our blessed friends, all well, and not at all changed since 1856, save only that Willy has grown older, stouter, browner, and more boy-like. What a bright little dog he is! They did not look for us this day, and supposed their ill weather extended to Geneva, and would prevent us from coming there. Our baggage got badly wet, and the industrious —— has been busy all day with unpacking, airing, smoothing-out, and replacing the unwanted articles which fill our trunks and bags.

Do you know what a prospect there is right before my face? The Dent du Midi, 10,000 feet high and twenty miles distant, covered with snow, is as distinctly defined as the steeples of Jamaica Plain appear at your house. Come and see. Apthorp plans many excursions for us. This P.M. (7 now) the weather is delicious, the scenery perfect. Come and make it complete with your presence, and believe me,

Faithfully yours.

—— admired the bronze "counterfeit presentment" of herself as much as I. All send their hearty love. It has rained here every day for a month; now we shall have fair weather.

Greet Sumner, dear, great, noble soul! from me.

T. P.

TO MISS MARY CARPENTER, BRISTOL, ENGLAND.

Montreux (Pension Ketterer), Suisse, June 23, 1859.

MY DEAR MISS CARPENTER,—It grieved me very much to find that I must leave London without seeing you or Miss Cobbe. Really it was too bad, after all your very generous intentions. But when I return to England we will make amends for it, and take our revenge. I need not tell you how much interest I take in your noble work at Bristol. Many things are called CHRISTIANITY, a name dear or hateful as you define it one way or the other; often it means repeating a liturgy and attending church or chapel; sometimes it meant burning men alive; in half of the United States of America it means kidnapping, enslaving men and women! The Christianity which your admirable father loved, taught and lived, was piety and morality, love to God, love to man, the keeping of the natural laws God writes on sense and soul. It is this which I honor and love in you, especially as it takes the form of humanity and loves the unlovely. The greatest heroism of our day spends itself in lanes and alleys, in the haunts of poverty and crime, seeking to bless such as the institutions of the age can only curse. If Jesus of Nazareth were to come back and be the Jesus of London, I think I know what (negative and positive) work he would set about. He would be a new revolution of institutions, applying his universal justice to the causes of ill; but also an angel of mercy, palliating the effects of those causes which could not be at once removed or made well. You are doing this work, the work of humanity: it seems to me you have a genius for it.

Accept my hearty thanks for all your kind intentions, and believe me, faithfully yours,

THEODORE PARKER.

There is lying at the base of Wellington Hill a field, which formerly belonged to the township of Watertown ; it is famous for the great oaks and elms of enormous girth that are still flourishing there, the only specimens of the kind within many a mile. Some chestnut trees, which yet remain in a secluded spot on the confines of Dedham, are the only trees comparable with them for bulk and stateliness. The two largest elms have their feet in moist ground, and a sparkling brook runs between. Over this a plank or fallen branch leads to the great oaks, which flourish on a grassy knoll; it almost encircles a little pond, which in wet weather is quite full. The field is skirted on one side by the road, but the clumps of underwood and barberry bushes scatter many a screen ; and, beyond the knoll of oaks, everything is shut out except the country sights and sound. There are few such spots left in Massachusetts, where trees which shaded the first colonists yet stand. Underneath these oaks the old Watertown settlers used to go for foxes and beavers up towards Waltham Hills.

It was a favorite spot with Mr. Parker ; and not far off, upon Wellington's Hill, the Twenty-eighth Society sometimes held its annual picnic. But in 1859 a letter must serve for the actual bodily presence of the pastor who loved those occasions so well :—

LETTER TO THE TWENTY-EIGHTH CONGREGATIONAL SOCIETY.

Montreux, Switzerland, June 25, 1859.

To all the good people of the Twenty-eighth Congregational Society in Picnic assembled:

Young men and women, and men and women no longer young! Far off in body let me salute you as face to face in spirit; so indeed we are, for I feel as near you as if my eye read your welcome and familiar faces, and saw there what you have been doing the last five months. A year ago, when I told you of the great oak-trees near by, almost as large as John P. Hale in circumference, who stood up before you as the unit of measure, I had a dim presentiment that I should not be with you bodily at your next annual meeting, for I then felt the approach of the evils which have so disturbed me since, and was long in recovering from the slight fatigues of that festal day. But I did not then think that when you should again look at Wellington's Hill, 400 or 500 feet high, the Pic du Midi, 10,000 feet high, sheeted with snow, would seem as near to me.

How little do we know what should happen! That tall mountain,— it passes for nothing in this Alpine family of giants,—looks in at my window all day, and all night long it glitters white in the surrounding darkness: then blushes rosy red, as morning comes up the sky. The snow shifts and varies on its top and sides from day to day, but never wholly disappears, 'tis said. I can throw a walnut from my chamber into the Lake of Geneva, whose blue-green waters are so fair all day. Handsome vineyards are all around me here, yet their crop is not so fair as our own Indian corn, the Pocahontas of the vegetable world, the great American empress of the cereal grasses. The Château Chillon is within fifteen minutes' walk, built on a rock in the Lake, a few yards from the shore, where the water is 500 feet deep, they say. It is very old; there was a castle there used as a prison in 830—and the present structure was put in its present shape in 1248. A romantic little village, full of old houses, with its grey stone church, is perched on the side of mountain, one or two hundred feet above my head.

Most picturesque are the pleasant places where the lines of my present lot have fallen to me! So good comes out of evil! The people here seem contented and happy, and look intelligent and virtuous; they work less than we, save more, and enjoy more. The country is rich, not by nature, but by the toil of many generations. For while, in New England, our last cultivation of the soil is not 240 years old, here you count the triumphs of industry by thousands of years. I think the vine was cultivated here before the time of Julius Cæsar; not to speak of corn and other needful things, which human toil wooed out of this sunny land, perhaps 3000 or 4000 years ago. The soil is poorer than what you stand on, and more stony too; the slopes are steeper than the most abrupt descents about you. But labor conquers all; the steep mountain sides are notched into terraces, whose sides are protected by the stones which once cumbered the ground; the shores are lined with stone to withstand the flapping of the uneasy lake. The soil is rich by art, and bears enormous crops of costly grapes. I love to see the Indian corn scattered here and there among the vines. Nothing is lost, no foot of soil; no ray of sunshine on a wall, but an apricot, a peach, a grape is ripening there. _Use_ has not driven _Beauty_ off—men are not content with the sublime of nature; they must have the handsome artifice of flowers. Pinks, hollyhocks, marigolds, gilliflowers, and the queenly roses blow in all the little gardens. In the homely window of a stone cottage, in the narrow street of Montreux, you will find a fairer show of cactuses, than all tropic St. Croix now furnishes to its proud and lazy inhabitants, equally incapable and regardless of beauty.

Here too all is peace—it is the incidents of peace I have been speaking of; but only eighty miles off, as the crow flies, are the outposts of the Allies; two armies, numbering 300,000 men, are drawing near to kill each other, and before these lines reach you, I suppose they will have reddened the ground with dreadful murder. No doubt the Austrians are the Devil to Italy; their name is legion, and they have possessed it many a sad year, *i dannati Tedeschi*, as the Italians call them! Now Napoleon III., the prince of that class of devils, the very Beelzebub, comes to cast them out. It is good to get rid of the old German devil, even if a new French one turns him off in this rough fashion; it is of a kind that goes not out except by fire and sword. I rejoice therefore in every French victory; it gives Italy some chance for freedom, though I hope little for these effete nations.

You and I may be thankful that our land is not trodden by the hoof of war—not yet, I mean; but the day will come when we also must write our great charter of liberty in blood. No nation in Europe has so difficult a problem to solve as America, none has so great a contradiction in the national consciousness. The spirit of despotism has a lodgment in the United States of America. 350,000 slave-holders keep 4,000,000 in a degrading bondage which Europe only knows in her ancient story, not from present facts. Besides there are 350,000 Hunkers, entrenched behind the colleges, courts, markets, and churches of America, who are armed in this way for the defence of this despotism, and are deadly hostile to all the institutions of democracy.

A great struggle goes on in Europe to-day, in *all* Europe. The actual war is local, confined to a small part of Italy. It may become general before you read this note, and be spread over all the land. For the causes of war are everywhere. It is the great battle of mankind against institutions which once helped but now hinder the progress of humanity—human nature against the limitations of human history. On the one side are the progressive instincts of the race, demanding development, the enjoyment of their natural rights; on the other are the ecclesiastical and political dynasties which now possess the seats of power and the weapons of authority, and say to mankind, "Thus far, but no farther!" We all know how such quarrels must end. Human instincts are a constant force, continually active, never wearing out; while dynasties perish, and are not renewed. The Pope and *his* Christianity will go where the Pontifex went with his heathenism, and one by one the despotism of the Kings will yield to the Constitutional Governments of the people. "Forward," "Upward!" is God's word of command—all thrones, all markets, all churches which stand in the way of men will be trodden under foot of men! The past life of mankind is a struggle with the elements and a battle against its own rulers; but the handsome vineyards of Switzerland and the vast cities of Europe are results of that struggle. The Constitutional Governments of England, old and new, are the triumphs won in that battle! Alas! the fight must continue for years, perhaps, for generations. But peace is sure to come at last. In this great European strife, I find no man dares appeal to America for encouragement. Her 4,000,000 slaves, her attempts to revive the African slave-trade, her courts which lay waste the principles of democracy and justice, her Churches leagued with the stealers of men, are arguments for despotism and against a Republic. No doubt, Austria is the hindmost State of Christian Europe, the most mediæval and despotic; light enters Russia, and is welcome, while Austria repels the dawn of day. But even this despotism has not a slave, while democratic America chains one-seventh of her population, and sets 4,000,000 men for sale. France is the ally of rising Italy; America the helper of Austria, which would hold back the world. Even in your festivities, dear friends, I beg you to remember this, and not be unmindful of what we owe the world.

I trust you will enjoy the day before you and return home the wiser for your delight.

I know you will believe me, faithfully yours,

THEODORE PARKER.

TO MR. MANLEY.

Montreux, Vaud Suisse, June 25, 1859.

MY DEAR MR. MANLEY,—Yesterday's mail brought most welcome letters from you, Mr. May, St. Mathilde, and others. I am glad the letter to the Twenty-eighth came safe to hand; it cost me too much care and toil to have it lost, though I have still the duplicate in my desk. It must be nearly printed by this time, considering the efficiency of the committee who have the matter in charge. The Twenty-eighth, for whom it was meant, will receive it in the spirit of love and kindness, making all due allowance for the short-comings of a sick man; but the outsiders, for whom it was not meant, will, of course, treat it with harshness. My apology for myself will hurt the feelings of many, no doubt. Please see that a copy of it is sent to the excellent Dr. Samuel Cabot, and the "Midsummer Sermon" also. I fear I left his name off of the list I sent Mr. Leighton.

We left London, June 13th, at half-past five a.m., and reached Paris at five; stayed there about a week, and left it at eleven A.M., June 19th, and passed the night at Dijon, one of the queerest old places I ever saw: it was the capital of Burgundy, you know, the residence and burial-place of the famous dukes of that name. Their high-nosed statues still keep the likeness of the family, and show whence come the (ugly) features of the Hapsburgs of Austria and the Bourbons of France, which are traceable to them through the female line. God knows who were the fathers of their families!

From Dijon we went to Geneva next day, and the following came by boat to this charming and most delicious spot, whose name you have read at the head of the letter. Don't you think the Hunts and Apthorps were glad to meet us all, and we to put our arms about their necks? It is almost three years since we saw them sail out of New York Harbour, not thinking we should meet here under such circumstances on the 21st June, 1859.

I visited Dr. Samuel Bigelow (you know his excellent brother, John R. B., and his wife, a charming person); he took me to the famous Dr.

Louis (Baron Louis), and they made an examination, and reported a little tubercular disease at the top of the right lung; not extensive, not necessarily obliged to extend, or sure to continue. Their judgment was eminently favorable, and encouraged my poor wife greatly; she always keeps up a great heart, and is hopeful as the deity who leans on an anchor, never says a discouraging word, and has a smile at each unlucky symptom. There are no artists like these women! Dr. B. is my doctor just now (you must have a relay of doctors, as of horses to put you over the road), and he recommends the hypophosphite of lime (Louis thinks nothing of it), and I take it now, twenty grains a-day, three days in the week. The French chemist who prepares it thinks the American preparations are good for nothing. "No such goods in the market as our goods, sir! Depend upon it, nobody else has got the gen-u-ine article!" That is the cry all the world over. I suppose a money-lender tells his customers (or victims), "My money will go further than any other. In short, sir, my dollars are a leetle sounder than any others in the street!" Since I came here last Tuesday, and it is Saturday now, I have been better than before. I have slept better and coughed less than in any four days since I left St. Croix. That looks well; but the time is a little too short to draw long inferences from. Still, I have never had so good news to write about myself as now! Tell Francis Jackson, that unsurpassably excellent man, that I will not over-work, and I advise him to be as prudent as I am and shall be. I hope he does not go to that cold, raw spot at South Boston this summer! It has handsome flowers, but ugly east winds also on all sides of you. It gives me a touch of the rheumatism only to think of it.

TO JOHN AYRES.

July 31, 1859.

Your last welcome letter, of July 12, was sent me from Montreux by my wife, who is staying there with Hannah, and the Hunts and Apthorps. Mr. Lyman and I are staying a little while on a visit with my friend Desor, whom you may have seen at my house; he is an old and dear friend—now a man of large property, and has a dozen friends staying with him at his mountain farm. It is about 3000 feet above the sea—a most delightful spot. The days are warm and the nights cool. It is Sunday to-day, and you will not jump out of bed for an hour or two yet, for though ten o'clock here, it is only a little after four with you. The letters, the last and the preceding, were quite grateful to me, and seemed like the face of an old friend almost. Many thanks for the wise and prudent interest you took in my affairs, at a most critical period too. I hope F—— keeps his integrity, if he loses his property. I wrote him as soon as I heard of his trouble; he has been an honest man as well as a generous, and I think this little reverse will do him good, and only good; few men can bear long-continued prosperity, especially the sudden and uninterrupted increase of riches. Things are arranged for us better than we can manage them ourselves. I look with great reverence and trust at the *inevitable things in life*. They are often just what we revolt from, but they turn out to be just what we need most of all. Mr. Jackson has written me about the present disposition of my funds, and I feel renewed obligations to you and him and Mr. Manley. Do not take too much interest in an old and sick minister; he will be very thankful for a little. The *New York Herald* of 16th inst., has just been handed me, and I see that Mr. Choate has passed away; a man of great talents, which he greatly abused, often to the worst purposes. He had good qualities, and young men bred in his office both respected and loved the man. I am glad I was not in Boston when he died, for I should have felt bound in duty to preach his funeral sermon, more painful for me to write than it would be for his friends to hear. I should like to preach a sermon on John Augustus, one of the most extraordinary men I ever knew; he created a new department of humanity and loved the unlovely. A murderer or a highway robber does not corrupt society; but a man like Choate, with talent, genius, learning, social position, the most extraordinary power of bewitching men by his speech, *he debauches the people to a terrible extent.* I wonder if any one will write out and preach the dreadful lesson of such a life, and warn the public against being seduced by such men, and young scholars against becoming such? When Robert Rantoul died, the Suffolk Bar took no notice of his death. What a pow-wow they will make over poor Choate! Why? He was one of them, and Rantoul drank from a different spring —at least sometimes.

So you see, there is peace, at least for a time. I took great interest in the war; the prince of devils was casting Satan out of Italy. I like to see the devil's-house of despotism divided against itself, but Beelzebub-Napoleon did not like to cast Satan entirely out; he drives him out of one or two rooms, and leaves him still master of the great hall and all the court-yard. The short of it is, Nap. was afraid. 1. His losses in battle were enormous (he does not dare publish them yet), and he must ask for 100,000 more soldiers if he went on. 2. He feared the spirit of revolution. In a month all Hungary would have been in a revolt; Italy was already in open rebellion. 3. He feared the intervention of the other Powers. Russia would not like a Hungarian revolution in 1859, after she put one down in 1849; if the war was general, and not local, all the great Powers would have a hand in it, at least in settling it. 4. He did not dare offend the Pope and the 40,000 priests at home, who are Roman and not French, and might give him a pretty kettle of fish to fry if they pleased. In a word, he saw that his devil's-house of despotism was divided against itself, and in danger of falling about his head. Now the Emperors are made friends, there seems to be unity of sentiment, of idea, and of aims between them. The Pope is an ugly customer to deal with. If I were Emperor of France, after the Solferino battle I would take him by the scruff of his neck very gently and say to him, "You old cuss you! long enough have you tormented men and made your three millions and a quarter of subjects hate you; that must cease! Keep your infallibility as long as you like, and make the most of that nonsense —decree the immaculate conception of the Mother of God, and his grandmother, and all his aunts, if you like; nay, you may excommunicate all the rest of mankind, the more the merrier, and damn them in the next world; but if you touch the hair of any honest man's head in *this* world—nay, if you wickedly scare a Jewish baby in his cradle—you have got me to settle with, that's all! Your people are to have you for ruler, if they like you; if not, *not!* Now, *pax vobiscum!*"

TO SARAH AND CAROLINE WHITNEY, WEST ROXBURY, MASSACHUSETTS.

Geneva, June 21, 1859.

MY DEAR SARAH AND CAROLINE,—Let me embrace you both in one letter, for I am your debtor, owing each of you a letter, and perhaps more than one. It is now twenty-two years since I was first *ordained* as minister at West Roxbury; this longest day in the year is the anniversary of that event. It is one of the epochs in my life, which I always cherish with fond regard, though the special *ceremony* I thought no more of then than now. Do you remember the council? A great many of them are now dead. John Quincy Adams, and Mr. Lunt, both of the Dr. Wares, Tommy Gray, Dr. Pierce, Dr. Harris, and Mr. Greenwood. It was able men whom I had invited to perform the services—Francis, Ripley, Stetson, Henry Ware, and faithfully they did their duty. One thing happened, a little characteristic of what was afterwards to befall me. After the services were over, they all went down to Tafts for the entertainment. I walked, by some accident in the management; and when I reached the hall everything was eaten up but the sandwiches. I have often thought of it as an omen of much that was to come: so I regarded it then.

I shall never forget the kindness and affection I met with at West Roxbury! When I went to Europe in 1843-4, no day ever passed but I, in imagination, looked in every house in the parish, and fancied what was going on. In the wakeful hours of the night, now-a-days, I do the same, with the present congregation at Boston, but it takes a little longer to visit all the parish now. I often wonder that the people at Spring Street bore with my opinions as gently as they did, for all were not able to take so philosophical views of them as Deacon Farrington. He said, "Mr. Parker makes a distinction between religion and theology; it is a sound distinction. We like his religion; it is exactly what we want: we understand it; and this religion is the principal thing. About the theology we are not quite so clear; much of it is different from what we used to learn. But we were taught many foolish things. Some of his theology we are sure is right; all of it seems like good common-sense; and if some of it does sound a little strange, we are contented to have him preach just what he thinks. For, if he begun by not preaching what he believed, I am afraid he would end by preaching at last what he did not believe at all!" Wise old deacon!— I learned a great many things from him. But I must stop now, and finish elsewhere.

TO THE SAME.

Montreux, Switzerland, June 29, 1859.

What a sweet, kind letter you wrote me, dear Sarah, the day I went off from Boston ! It has dwelt in my memory ever since, like some fragment of a pleasing tune that will keep coming back again and again. How often I think of you all, and of the happy times I have had in your house, both the old one and the new ! I also remember well my first visit to your family, and took much delight in the society of S. and C. all the time I was at Spring Street. I think I shall not forget the past, nor cease to profit by the present and future. There were some very thoughtful persons at West Roxbury, though not one who was what is technically called " an educated man." How we abuse the term " *educated* " !

We are living in one of the handsomest little places in the world. By nature the scenery is grand and sublime ; art has added the delicate beauty of fine culture. Summer and Winter have clasped hands ; the Dent du Midi, 10,000 or 12,000 feet high, and covered with snow, looks in at the window, while the apricots are hanging ripe on the garden walls, and the figs are almost fully grown. Strawberries and cherries abound. Perhaps you will not find the place on the map, but it is at the east end of the Lake of Geneva, between Vevay and the Castle of Chillon. We are not more than a hundred miles in a straight line from the seat of war, where a most ghastly battle was fought last Friday. We have not yet learned the details. I think it will not continue long. The Austrian Emperor went back to Vienna day before yesterday. If he had waited much longer he would have needed a *French passport.* I expect every day to hear the French have taken Venice, and that Padua has risen against the Austrians. Tell the ladies of West Roxbury that I have looked through their eyes for the last four or five months, and no wonder if the world looks fair. We all send love to you all. Give my special regards and thanks to Sally (Henshaw) Whittemore. Think of the Deacon's daughters ! " Weil, I never ! " I hope Captain John's short-horn is well. Give our kind regards to mother, and believe me,

Faithfully yours,

THEODORE PARKER.

TO MRS. E. D. CHENEY, BOSTON.

Montreux (Pension Ketterer), June 28, 1859.

MY DEAR EDNAH,—I have not written you a single line since I fled off from Boston What adds to the mischief, I did not have the coveted opportunity to bid you good bye for I know not how long. Now I have a little breathing spell, being quietly settled down for a few weeks perhaps, and so comes this letter—wholly of friendship and partly of thanks, the latter being something more than the sum of all the parts which the metaphysicians say make up the whole. I have written so much about myself lately—good news, too, since I came to this place, that I am the greatest bore in the world to myself, as bad as Abby Folsom, or even Mr. Mellen, to the Anti-slavery Conventions; no, worse than that, as bad as Mr. A. B. to the Twenty-eighth Congregational. If somebody should announce "The Rev. Theodore Parker," I think I should put on my shoes, after I had taken him coldly by the hand, and tell him, "I am very sorry, sir! but really sir, I have important business which takes me to Vevay, &c. I—I—I beg your pardon, sir, but—but —but—I *must* bid you good morning, sir!" So I should walk off four or five miles in the rain to escape the "devastator of the day;" to such a degree has that gentleman become wearisome to me.

What shall I tell you? There are so many things that I know not which to select, so I will take the people I saw at London. We had not been there forty-eight hours when an old gentleman was announced—a Mr. R. H. Brabant, seventy-nine years old, who had come from Bath to pay me his respects. "You don't know me, sir," said he. "It is only your name that is forgotten," I said; "I remember you very well!" Fifteen years ago he came from Devizes, ninety miles, to see me, and I dined with him at his son-in-law's house (Mr. Hennell, now dead, was the son-in-law). It did me good to see the old gentleman again, full of scholarship and humanity. Mrs. Shaen and Miss Winkworth came to see us, and sat an hour or so; they are sisters, intelligent, cultivated, and thoughtful women, full of literature, ideas, and humanity. You know the Book of Hymns one of these talented sisters has translated from the German. We lunched at the Martineaus' one day—the only time I have taken a meal abroad since I left home: (I wonder if some of my ancestors were not Hibernians, for this is the second Irishism in this letter!) there I saw Mrs. Martineau. She and her husband had called on us before, and her nice daughters, three of them; the married one is with her husband, growing hops in Kent. Pleasant people they all are, in whom the nice artifice of culture has not impaired or concealed the instincts of generous nature. I love such girls. Frank Shaw's daughters are admirable specimens, and Mr. G. W. Curtis has one of them for wife, the better part of that good man. Rev. Mr. Tayler, and several younger men, were at the lunch—interesting and instructed people, all of them. Prof. H. D. Rogers, the kindly, was living at London for the summer. He "goes to Glasgow to teach, and comes to London to learn," so he says. He and his wife came to see us twice—he, besides, every day we were in town. They kindly pressed us to come and live with them all the time we should stay in London—dear, kind souls that they are!

One of the last persons who came to visit us the night before we went away was Ellen Craft! I count that an honor. The last time I saw them before was the day of their flight from Boston. You remember George T. Curtis and his pack (of fellow-creatures) had been barking at them for several weeks—seeking to rend them to pieces. I married William and Ellen in solemn sort in a house on "Nigger Hill," and put a Bible and a sword into his hands, and bade him use both with all his might! I had given him a pistol before. It did me good to meet her again in Blackfriars, London, where the kidnapper would not be held in very high honor. I thought of the time when Hannah and

John Parkman and I rode out to Brookline to bring Ellen into my house, where I might keep her in safety. I took a hatchet along with me for defence; I afterwards had better fighting-tools, and borrowed a pistol of Dr. Bowditch as I returned.* Poor thing! she feels better now than when she lived in my upper chamber, and we did not let the girls go to the street door to let any visitors in. I hope these times will not come again to Boston. Mr. Seward was very polite to me. He is received with great *empressement* by the chief men in London, and is delighted with their kindness; they think, as I do, that they are attending to the next President of the United States. Mr. Bright got us (Lyman and me) a place to attend the House of Commons, and we heard the *great debate* which led to the expulsion of the Derby Ministry. Bright made a fine speech—honest, sincere, manly, and sufficiently eloquent for the House of Commons, which laughs at sentiment. How handsome the English *women* are! Fine large animals, they have good hair, good teeth, good eyes, and a noble complexion (Mrs. Bodichon, who offered us many attentions, is a good type). The children, I think, must be the finest in the world—what a show of them at Hyde Park, at Kensington Gardens, and many other places in London! All our women-kind send their love to you.

TO ISAAC PARKER, ESQ., LEXINGTON, MASS.

Montreux, Switzerland, 28th June, 1859.

My DEAR BROTHER,—I have not written you since I left home; partly abstaining because I had no good news to write which would be satisfactory to you to read; and partly because I did not like to tax myself with any sort of needless labor. Now I think I can give you good tidings of myself.

*   *   *   *   *   *

That is enough about myself, now about things of more interest. You are a farmer, and are naturally interested therefore in the cultivation of the soil. At St. Croix there are 145 estates on the island—from 100 to 400 acres each. About 140 are sugar estates, the rest cattle farms. There are about 23,000 inhabitants—21,000 colored more or less, 2000 pure white. The energies of the people are directed to raising sugar-canes, which they make into sugar, molasses, and rum—the great products of the island. They raise no grain: Indian meal, flour, oats, &c., are all imported. They take little pains with vegetables and fruits; so all are of the most inferior quality except the oranges, which (in winter) are the finest in the world. Apples, peaches, cherries, plums, strawberries, currants, gooseberries, &c., do not grow here. Their melons are miserable, though I think you or I could raise the most delicious water-melons, cantelopes, &c. Plantains and bananas grow with almost no cultivation, and are important articles of food; as fruits they are pretty good, and as vegetables for cooking they are invaluable as the potato is with us. Sweet potatoes, yams, &c., are

---

* The Doctor met him; he was unconcernedly munching an apple, in excellent spirits, perfectly cool, and ready for any contingency.

abundant, and cost little labor.   But all the fruits and vegetables are raised by the negroes on the little patches of land adjoining their cabins, and are their perquisites over and above their regular wages. The village (or city ?) of West-End contains about 800 or 1000 people, who live closely huddled together and raise nothing.   On Wednesdays and Saturdays (especially the latter) there is a market-day.   The negro women fill a little tray with a few potatoes (sweet potatoes, I mean), oranges, bananas, eggs, chickens, &c., put it on their head, and trudge off to town—a mile, two miles, or six or seven miles.   The market is an open place, not paved, without shelter or shade; there the women sit on the ground and spread out their articles for sale.   I never saw one who had goods to the amount of one dollar and fifty cents.

There are some thirty or forty kinds of grass on the island, but none is as good as the wild wood-grass which you find at home, and which the moose would eat, but cows (I think) will not.   Most of their grasses are tall sedgy plants, which do not run and cover the ground, but grow up in bunches, rank and coarse.   There is not a spot of green grass to lie down upon.   The cattle live chiefly by browsing on the bushes and low trees.   All the best hay is brought from the United States or from Europe; so is all the cheese, all the butter, &c.   I wrote Isaac Clarke about the manner of cultivating the cane, the drought of the land, &c., so I will not now repeat it.   The whole island when we left it was brown as Uriah Stearns' Hill, by the pond, in the driest time in August.   It was painful to look at the hills—about the the color of badly burnt coffee.

We reached Southampton June 1st, at 10 A.M., and rode in tho P.M. seventy miles to London.   You never saw such greenness as exists everywhere in England.   It rains almost every day, and so the ground is always moist and the air damp.   The crops in the fields were of wheat, rye, clover, beans (a horse-bean which I never saw cultivated at home), potatoes, cabbages, and all sorts of kitchen vegetables.   They were beginning to make their hay.   I think the average yield there would be two and a half tons to the acre.   New potatoes were in the market, though not so good as the old ones.   Cabbages and cauliflowers were fit for the table and in great abundance; green gooseberries were in all the shops, oranges were cheaper in the market than at St. Thomas, of the finest flavor, too, brought from Spain and Portugal.   England looks like a garden, all is so nicely cultivated; the apple-trees were just getting out of blossom, and the horse-chestnuts were in full bloom; roses abundant; of course there were pinks, gilliflowers, marigolds, &c., &c., everywhere.   Lilacs had passed their bloom, but the prim and the whitethorn were in full feather.

In France we rode about 400 or 500 miles by rail, through the most delicate cultivation, quite superior to that of England.   The crops were clover (white, red, yellow), various other grasses; wheat, rye (the winter rye was ready for the sickle, and the harvest had begun June 12th), potatoes, beans, and in the east part, between Paris and Switzerland, vines and Indian corn.   Of course, potatoes met us everywhere; the strawberries were ripe, the largest I ever saw—many were as large as the yellow peaches which used to grow behind the shop; they were sold from hand-carts all over Paris at about eight or ten cents a quart!

Apricots were abundant, bigger than ours, about eight or nine cents a dozen. I had pears on the 17th of June, about as big as a cent in diameter; cherries were large and cheap—five or six cents a quart—larger than ours, but not so sweet. They have a peculiar melon, which looks like a rough pumpkin-squash; it is about as big as a two-quart measure; I did not taste it, for the price was from one dollar to one dollar fifty cents! but I shall get some of the seeds before I come home. It is a Persian melon, brought to France, I think, in the time of the Crusades. The chief crop in Burgundy—the east part of the middle of France—is the vine. Here the stocks are in rows about two feet apart one way and a little less the other; they allow two, three, or five or six stems to grow up from one stalk, and support them on sticks about three feet high, yet like our bean-poles; they do not grow higher than currant-bushes with us. Between the rows of vines you sometimes find rows of Indian corn—a single stalk in a place.

Here, in Switzerland, the land is very hilly; the hill-sides are notched into steps, the edges protected with a stone wall from three to fifteen feet high, so that the mountain slopes look like stairs. On the level part of the terraces the people raise their vines and their crops. You may judge of the amount of work necessary to notch and terrace the whole country. But here the cultivation is several thousand years old. Apricots and cherries are ripe here. You never saw such economy as prevails here and in France; not a spot of ground is left to be idle. On the banks of the streams there are poplars and willows, which yield an annual harvest for the basket-maker. All the sunny sides of walls are covered with apricots, peaches, pears, or more delicate grape-vines. No little stick of wood is wasted. The chips are picked up in the forests where the wood is cut off; the small brush is made into charcoal, put in bags and sent off to Paris. All the manure of the country roads is carefully gathered up by the peasants, and (on men's backs often, carried to the vineyards. You can know nothing of agricultural economy till you see with your own eyes!

*   *   *   *   *   *

Affectionately, your brother,

T. P.

TO MISS THAYER.

Montreux, Canton de Vaud, Suisse, July 8, 1859.

MY VERY DEAR CAROLINE THAYER,—What a shame that you should have the rheumatic fever, and write a line—which came day before yesterday—with swollen fingers! I hardly dare look at the handsome watch-guard which the paper enfolded lest that should have been *woven*, as well as sent, with a painful hand. First, Mr. Manley's letter frightened us with sad stories; then St. Matilda's of the same date made it appear not so bad. Now we see what it is. Horrible sufferings that fever always brings, I am told. Do tell me what treatment you had, and how it affected you. What brilliant letters you write us, you witch you! full of news and comments upon news! The clippings were invaluable; we brought them from London to this sweet little spot, for we only read in parts in that great noisy Babel where they found us. But that will be the last, for on the Continent the postage is enormous; a letter may weigh a quarter of an ounce, or seven and a half French *grammes*, and be single; half an ounce is double, and so on. Of paper like this with an envelope it takes five sheets to make half an ounce; two go for a single letter.

       *   *   *   *   *   *

I think you would have many things to tell me. Here let me mention several people I wish to be remembered unto, lest I find no room at the end. Very kindly to Mrs. L. B. Meriam; she and her nice good boy will be gone into the country before this reaches you. I hope he keeps in good health; all the family eggs in one basket is a misfortune. To all the Curtises, I don't mean the kidnappers, but Henry C., his wife, and what is thence derived. Nobody has written me a word about Cornie, dear good creature that she is, or her husband, a generous and true man. I heard about Gussie not long ago, though only in general; she is at Conway, I guess. Then there are the Cummingses, Mr. and Mrs., and their dear boy of a Charlie—he is a man now with a moustache: but though he build houses, and write articles in the *North American*, he will always be Charley to me, though I salute him as Mister Cummings. Then there is Mrs. Hager, the smart black-eyed mother, giving her life to the next generation; (what is the number now?) the two Misses Sturgis, and—stop, I should fill up the whole sheet; so instead of the Garrisons and the Jacksons, all the families of them, and the Mays, and Mrs. Bridge, and Mrs. Clarke (Tappan that never should have been), I shall just write, " and the rest of mankind, especially womankind." What is Wendell Phillips doing this summer, and where? Your brother Lowell is busy as ever, and his family as happy and happy-making! That famous boy—he is a bo-hoy now, I take it—" is the finest child that ever was in this world!" So his aunt Caroline says, " because he is a boy " Tell his father I drank the last drop of his Bourbon whiskey—there were two bottles—yesterday. I think it held out like the widow's oil, two bottles in five months and a half.

The doctors at Paris recommended red wine, of which I take daily about half a bottle; it is good claret, and costs (of the grocers) about eight or ten cents a bottle; of the innkeepers two or three times as much, of course. If our people had this we should need no Maine Liquor Law, and the charities of Boston would not have to take care of the miserable relics of drunkenness which now disgrace our civilization. We are all very happy here. The place is beautiful—a little mite of a town stuck on to the side of a mountain; our hotel or boarding-house is just on the edge of the lake, in a charming place. The air is dry as in Exeter Place—thermometer for ten days, from ten to four o'clock, 80° in the shade; nights moderate. Beauty all round us, and our old friends in the house; their boy also " is a famous boy," bright as a mother could wish her only child. All their eggs in one basket, with a frail handle too! Ah, me! what a world it would be if there were not another above it, beyond it, and embracing it all with fond loving arms! I wonder how people contrive to get on in this world who have no faith in the next. I could not live a day; I should so fear some mischief would pounce down on one of my chickabiddies; but I won't preach just now. What a great place that Little Pedlington is which we call Boston! How full it is of great men! To trust the *Transcript*, or the *Courier*, or the *'Tizer*, or the *Post*, it contains enough to save the world if "the rest of mankind" were wicked as Sodom and Gomorrah. No doubt the number is too great to be counted. But it seems to me there is little work for them to do just now, or they would not have condensed all this greatness into a dinner to a successful chess-player. I suppose they had placed the Webster statue, and the Winthrop statue, had wept over Prescott and Humboldt, had seen the ancient and honorable artillery, had heard the great and Thursday lecture, and taken ices at the proper place, and decided that Mr. Agassiz was "the only successor of Von Humboldt"; and even then, after all this, their activity still cried for more work, and they had nothing to do but make it out that Morphy was greater than Prescott or Humboldt, or perhaps even Agassiz, who does not play chess! Great is Little Pedlington, and its great men are greater yet! All here send love, especially Sarah. Get well as fast as you can. My love to all that ever did belong to 111, Harrison Avenue, or ever will.

Yours,   T. P.

FROM THE JOURNAL.

July 1.—Up to this time I have felt so languid that I have done nothing or scarcely anything in the way of my favorite pursuits, contenting myself with enjoying my old friends. Now I will begin something more.

The commencement consisted in gathering various information concerning the neighborhood, and everything about the war which he could lay his hands upon—French soldiers' letters, engravings, maps, and statistics.

In Dijon he purchased De Brosse's "Lettres Familières, écrites en Italie en 1739–40." This he enjoyed reading ; also French publications concerning the resources of Austria, and local histories of Dijon. He made excursions to Chillon, Vevay, &c., and hunted up the books which give historical accounts of the neighborhood; for instance, Vulliemin, "Chillon, Etude Historique," &c. ; Cibrario's "Peter of Savoy" and "Economia Politica del Medio Evo ;" Lichnowski's "Geschichte Hapsb." He amused himself with collecting odd names in the Celtic part of Switzerland, names ending in *ex, ix, az,* but he undertook no composition or study of importance.

MICHELET'S "L'AMOUR."—This book contains much nonsense of a romantic character, and gives a quite incomplete notion of woman. She is an ideal—non-existent and impossible, as he paints her. The husband, ten or twelve years older, is to create the wife ; he lives for himself, she only for him. But the book has also great excellences :—

1. He repudiates the ecclesiastical idea of woman, the type of sin, and substitutes a pure and self-devoted being. 2. He declares the object of marriage is marriage itself. 3. He gives wise counsels founded on knowledge of facts in social life.

Qu'est ce que la Femme? *La Maladie!* He cites this from Hippo-crates. Invert the question, *Qu'est ce que la Maladie?* *C'est la Femme.* And the answer is just about as true.

A French wit said of this book that the title should be " L'Art de Verifier les Dates."

He is the only author that I ever found to quote that highly valuable book of Dr. Lucas, " Hérédite." I am told that Michelet married, late in life, a woman much younger than himself, and generalized from a single fact. 40,000 copies have been sold already, but you don't find the book in sight; it is bought by the women.

July.—I do not think I shall ever preach again, but the habit of thinking sermons has become automatic, and acts like an instinct now; so I put down the subjects on which I shall never write.

Here are some of these subjects :—

1. Of the Lessons which the Old World offers to the New.
2. The Nature and Function of the Will—its use and abuse.
3. The Vice of Jealousy—its origin in the defensive instincts; its natural functions, and its depraved action.
4. Of War—the elements in man it comes from—the part it has played in the development of savage nations—the mischief it produces now—the cause of it in wicked rulers who wish to retard the develop-ment of mankind.
5. The Right of the Oppressed to Slay the Oppressor—rebellion to tyrants.
6. The Means of Religious Development in Theism. I. Show the difficulty now in the period of transition. II. How the human race has got over such difficulties: 1. Judaism *versus* Ægypt and Sabaism; 2. Christianity *versus* Judaism and Heathenism; 3. Protestantism *versus* Romanism. III. The actual helps peculiar to Theism.
7. The Function of the Malevolent Emotions, and the Check on their Abuse.

At a later date these are added :—

The Function of the Disposition to Idleness.
The American Lady; or, Contempt of Useful Work.
The Secondary Value of Labor as a means of Development, 1, of the Individual; 2, of the Nation; 3, of Mankind.

TO MISS COBBE.

Montreux, July 5, 1859.

MY DEAR MISS COBBE,—Here I am in the midst of your friends and mine, and that, too, in one of the finest situations man or woman need wish to live in. You know the place, and so I shall dwell on none of its charms, for, after all, the women part of it interested me far more than its grandeur of lake, mountain, and sky. I have just returned from a mid-day bath in the lake, and am told that you also used to enjoy that natural luxury. I am glad that your good sense leads you to that delicious recreation and enjoyment. In America, many of my young lady friends can swim as well as I can, *i. e.* as we say, "can swim like a duck." I sometimes go out (or lie) and read or sleep under the chestnut-tree, close by, which you frequented a year ago, and which now goes by the name of "Fanny's" tree.* Besides, while I am writing, does not your bear adorn my neckerchief, which it also keeps in place? Many thanks for the handsome little treasure. I waited till yesterday, the day of our national independence, when I ventured to wear it. Now it will be with me continually—"close to my heart and near my eye." I wrote you that your flowers all came safe to hand, fragrant as when you gathered them. A little water soon brought them to their original freshness and beauty. But *flowers* will fade, and so I put a spray of myrtle in my new botany book, which is still in good preservation, and promises to last many a year green, if not fresh.

In London I was too much fatigued and to ill to appear agreeable to my many friends, for the change from the tropical heat of Santa Cruz to the damp and chills of the Thames in the neighborhood of Black-friars was a little severe, not to speak of the excitement which came from escaping out of the barbarism of the West Indies and into the great focus of European civilization. So I was tantalized all the time by the sight of what I could not enjoy; Newman and Martineau, as well as others, I could best see for a few minutes. Mr. Bright got me a good place to see and hear the great debate in Parliament which ended in the dissolution of the Ministry. The Apthorps tell me of your friend, J. Locke, M.P. I wish you would let me hear more of him. There is one John Locke King whom I have been much interested in for his efforts at needful reforms in English institutions, but I suppose he is not the same.

I wonder if you have found the right niche to place your statue in, and if a ragged school be the place for your work; judging from what you wrote Mrs. A—— I should doubt.

"Non omnia possumus omnes."

But you know, while I only guess and inquire. It is a noble place you wish to fill, but there are diversities of gifts even where there is unity of spirit.

What a dreadful state of things in the North of Italy, within 150 miles of us here! Think of 40,000 or 50,000 able-bodied men in the prime of life "killed, wounded, or missing" in one day of battle! I wish the human race might learn to see who the men are that thus misdirect the wrathful instincts of our nature to such wickedness. In these days every war is the result of somebody's wickedness: one day men will see what monsters they have worshipped in the shape of Metternichs and Schwartzenburgs, and the like, and visit them with curses. I should not be sorry to see Austria stripped of her Italian provinces, of her Hungarian provinces, of her Slavic provinces; then if

---

* Note by Miss Cobbe:—"I visited this tree, a magnificent chestnut, June, 1860, and found it dying."

her seven millions of Teutonic people chose to have a despotism, let them, and so small a state will not much endanger the liberty of mankind. I hold Louis Napoleon in loathing, and count him a Beelzebub ; but as he is now casting out other devils and dividing his own house against itself, I rejoice in the success of his terrible armies. Certainly the defeat of Austria is the victory of mankind, even if Napoleon III. be the weapon which does the work. I trust soon to hear that the French fleet has taken Venice, that Padua has followed the example of Ferrara, that Garibaldi contests the passes of the Tyrol, and that Verona falls as Milan, an easy prey. It is well Francis Joseph went home when he did ; had he stayed much longer he would need a French *visé* on his passport before he could get back to Vienna.

I had almost forgotten to tell you that I am much better since reaching this little choice spot. Is it the material influences or the women that have wrought the change ? I don't know ; but feel stronger and cough much less. My spirits are always good, and I trust will be under all circumstances. Indeed if one feels and knows the Infinitely Perfect God, he can bear anything cheerfully. Let me thank you also for the beautiful photograph you so kindly got for me ; I shall give it an honored place at home. My friend Desor will come this week, and by-and-bye we shall go with him to Neuchâtel.

He went to Neuchâtel to see Mr. Desor, on the 12th of July, and spent a day with him in the enjoyment of the neighboring scenery, and returned on the 14th.

July 24.—Note from Desor, asking us to come (and telling how) to his châlet. This is the last day of preaching at the Music Hall for the season.

LES POMMES.

CHAPTER XXV.

Combe-Varin, and Prof. Desor's Châlet, *Les Pommes*—Life there—Herr Küchler—Letters.

IN company with a friend he started on the 26th, and reached Mr. Desor's residence in Combe-Varin the next day.

A fine road leads from Neuchâtel through vineyards and pleasant little hamlets up into the long Jura valley of La Sagne or Des Ponts. It winds at first along the southern slope of the range, and in mounting discloses a lordly panorama of the whole Alpine region, from Rigi and Pilatus, past all the grand summits of the Bernese Oberland, to Mont Blanc, with the blue lakes lying deep between the hills.

The valley of La Sagne ends in one of the deep recesses which are called *Comben* by the people of the Jura. The *Mulden*, or troughs, are the valleys which separate the ranges; the *Clusen* are deep clefts across a range which unite two *Mulden;*

and the *Comben* are longitudinal clefts of a summit, or in the same direction along the side of a range. They are sometimes closed at one end by the hill, and the form is amphitheatrical.

Mr. Desor's châlet, in Combe-Varin, was once a hunting-lodge ; near it he has erected a building for the accommodation of summer guests, the men of science and friends who know the way to this hospitable door. There is a charming view of the La Sagne valley from the comfortable settles of the long house-arbor. A forest of splendid firs covers the hill which rises directly behind the house. A sheltered seat was put up for Mr. Parker in the skirt of this wood. It is on the brink of a deep chasm, at the bottom of which lies the village of Noiraigue. As he sat there he could overlook the pleasant Val de Travers, which is in sight, with eight or ten villages, for more than twenty miles.

It is in the valley next beyond La Sagne, scarce fourteen miles as the crow flies, that the Château de Joux is situated, where Toussaint L'Ouverture pined to death amid the prison damp and cold.

Not far from the châlet stands a tree which was Mr. Parker's favorite during his residence there. It is a double-headed fir, selected, no doubt, because it reminded him of the pine tree at Lexington, which his youthful fancy had devoted, in gentle partnership, to himself and a sister. His name is cut upon the trunk, and underneath it a cross. At the end of the chapter is an engraving of this fir, from a beautiful drawing which was made by Professor Carl Vogt.

In the Preface to the "Album of Combe-Varin," Mayer von Esslingen writes :—"Here and there, where the wood is lighted by clearings, its green carpet is all purpled over for several months with strawberries, whose pleasant red is packed so close that a careful walker can hardly step without shedding the blood of these innocents. The wood of Combe-Varin is guest-free, like the house, and in berrying-time re-echoes with the uproar of the children who come up from the valley with their baskets to feed and gather."

The "Album of Combe-Varin" is a memorial to Theodore Parker and Hans Lorenz Küchler. All of the contributions, except the "Memoir of Küchler," were made by the scientific men who met Mr. Parker at Desor's châlet during the summer of 1859. Desor furnished a paper " Upon the Indication of the Swiss Lakes," in German, and a sketch of Mr. Parker, in French ;

Dr. Moleschott, in German, "A Walk," describing the salutary influence of an ordinary walk upon the heart, the lungs, the nerves, every portion of the body ; Dr. Ch. Martins, in French, " On the Causes of Cold upon High Mountains ; " Jacob Venedey, in German, " H. L. Küchler, a Life-sketch, from the First Half of the Nineteenth Century ; " A. Gressly, in German, " Recollections of a Naturalist from the South of France ; " Dr. Schönbein, the inventor of gun-cotton and the discoverer of ozone, in German, " Upon the Next Phase in the Development of Chemistry ; " Mr. Parker, in English, " A Bumble-bee's Thoughts on the Plan and Purpose of Creation." The volume is furnished with a small map of the environs of Cette, to illustrate Gressly's paper ; an engraving of the five different configurations of Swiss lakes, to accompany Desor's ; a view of Combe-Varin ; a portrait of Küchler ; and one of Mr. Parker, taken from a cast of the cameo for which he sat in Rome in 1860.

Apart from the value of the contributions, this book is interesting as a characteristic of the friendship and toleration which can subsist abroad between scientific men ; of this it is a delicate and noble expression. It could have been projected in no other country, for in no other would intelligent men have enough sentiment for each other to think it worth the while. Here men of science and culture carry on their pursuits for the most part in isolation, if not in jealousy. But abroad, upon the Continent at least, there is an interchange of thought; and men of like tendencies do not resist being drawn together, and are not ashamed to indulge and record their profound sympathies.

At Les Pommes, Professor Desor entertains every summer distinguished naturalists and men of science, who bring the rich contributions of their freshest discoveries and speculations. The guests are left to spend the day in their own pursuits, but meet for dinner and tea at the stroke of the bell, with wits and appetites keenly set by mountain air in the balsamic woods that are more than 3000 feet above the sea. " It would not be easy to find elsewhere a fountain-place so richly springing with instruction and entertainment ; observations made upon worldwide travels, among mountains, and in the various provinces of physical investigation, afford inexhaustible material. Nor does the host lack that gift of calling out, which sets the contributions flowing from all sides. Thus under his mild direction these social hours grow often to a true Decameron, in which communications upon the most interesting discoveries in the domain of science alternate rapidly with the discussion of new, bold problems, or with the narrative of remarkable observations and events. The mild irony, which the ancients hardly knew, the peculiar outgrowth of our modern culture, and which saves our humanity from becoming sentimental, lent its rich flavor to these symposia of Combe-Varin." *

Mr. Parker and his friend were set down by the diligence at Rosière, and thence they had an hour's scramble up the mountain to the house. The pencil is in requisition.

Here only the hardier grains will grow, oats and barley, but no wheat. The snow continues from October to April; the *mercury freezes every winter.* To me it is quite cold to-day, in the wind and out of the sun.

I don't like the condition I find myself in—the lack of wind, of strength, and of warmth. It looks like drawing ever nearer to the end. I have but just life enough to digest my own dinner, and am good for nothing.

But he very soon began to improve, as Professor Desor tells, in his delightful sketch of Mr. Parker, which is published in the " Album of Combe-Varin," and from which a few extracts are here made, showing Mr. Parker's habits and employments during his residence at the châlet.

The summer of 1859, it will be remembered, was excessively hot, so that the solitude of the " Ponts " valley, which is generally distinguished for its great coolness, offered this time most advantageous conditions to an invalid. Here was a social gathering of men of letters, of business, and *savants* of every country. The different elements which all these guests brought with them; the discussions to which their very diverse opinions, in matters of science, philosophy, and religion, and political economy, gave rise; the conferences upon various subjects which were sought and granted; the freedom and good humor which reigned, notwithstanding the occasional warmth of controversy; the exercise which no one could avoid taking, so tempting was the stillness, the freshness of the meadows, or the shade of the great firs; and the excursions to famous spots in the neighborhood,—all this had a happy influence upon Mr. Parker's health. He felt his strength renewed, even to the point of undertaking sustained manual labor.

Like all country-people in America, Mr. Parker had gone chopping in the woods during his youth. The forest around Combe-Varin furnished him an opportunity to exercise anew his wood-cutting skill. His friends tried to dissuade him from it, but in vain. All that we could extort from him was a promise to devote only one hour daily to this exercise, and to attack only the small trees. At the end of some days, however, he announced to us that he felt strong enough to do better, and that he was going to fell a large fir. And he did it, with

* Preface to the Album.

extraordinary dexterity, to the great astonishment of those who stood by, for the Swiss usually cut down their trees with a saw. In half an hour the fir dropped in the direction which had been given to it by the trained axe of Wood-feller Parker.*

These exercises, although violent, seemed to be of the greatest benefit to our friend, Not only had he gained strength by this treatment, but he recovered his spirits and gaiety, and, moreover, increased his weight by six pounds. Such a symptom, with a man whose lungs were diseased, was of a nature to justify the hope, if not of a radical cure, at least of an arrest of the malady. Was it strange that he and his friends gave themselves up to sweet illusions, and felt happy at the prospect which seemed to open before them?

It is evident that the presence of a man like Mr. Parker, under such conditions, in the society of persons devoted to the cultivation of intellectual things, was both a stimulant and a benefit. The greatest liberty for everybody being the rule at Combe-Varin, they never met, except at meals. In the intervals, each one followed his inclination, some to look for flowers, for fruits, for lichens, for fossils, while others went into the woods to read. In the evening, after tea, or during the day, if the weather was unfavorable, they met around the table of the châlet, to discuss some question of general interest. Mr. Parker was of all the most animated, and such was his desire for information that he easily obtained from all the guests communications upon the subjects most familiar to each. Sometimes we had well-meditated dissertations, and the articles which compose this volume, will show, I hope, that they were not devoid of interest and scientific value.

It was natural that one whose mind embraced a wide range of studies, and who was at the same time a master in the art of expressing his ideas, should furnish his contingent to these recreations. We had, indeed, the good fortune to receive many communications from our deceased friend, mostly upon serious subjects, religious, philosophical, such as may be found in his works, or possibly in inedited fragments. Sometimes, also, subjects less grave were the order of the day. Though the society was composed in good part of professors and men of letters, there was no concealment of the imperfection of methods, nor of the whims and weaknesses of the priests of science. Mr. Parker had, more than any other man, a sure eye and a practised judgment when it came to an estimate of the real value of men and things. Simple in his mental habit, as in his physical traits, he specially detested all far-fetched theories, and doctrines framed for occasion and complaisance, and laughed readily at those theologians and natural philosophers who believe that they are called upon at every turn to become the interpreters of the Divine wisdom, power, and goodness. The English, in their Bridgewater Treatises, have made a singular abuse of these untimely appeals to Providence, and have thus compromised the cause which they pretended they were serving. There is no use in trying to bespeak glorifications for God. It is not at all astonishing that the Americans, by habitude or calculation, should have

---

* It was decided to cut the fir, which Mr. Parker had just felled, into planks to make a covered seat, where the guests promised to meet again next summer. But the next year, upon carrying the trunk to the saw, we discovered that it was only sound at the base. The heart was diseased.

carried this farther than the English, in their treatises for popular use, but it seems at least strange that *savants* trained in Europe should fall into the same foible, as appears by a recent work upon the Natural History of the United States. *

Allusion is made to this manner of studying nature in the "History of an Antediluvian Congress of Bumble-bees," which Mr. Parker related to us one evening with a charming humor; he has since kindly prepared it for this Album. It was his last work. †

Thus the six weeks were passed which Mr. Parker was pleased to reckon among the most delightful of his sojourn in Europe, because, in the midst of the pure air of our mountains, surrounded by persons who had all learned to love and to appreciate him, he thought he had recovered health, especially in living with that intellectual life which was indispensable to him, and for which he had languished during his abode in the Antilles. Besides, he met among the guests of Combe-Varin, persons who were very sympathetic with him, particularly Dr. Küchler. Both of them Protestants, the one in his quality of minister of a religious congregation, the other as the preacher to the German-Catholic Church of Heidelberg, they extended a hand to each other across the forms and rites of their respective confessions.

Before proceeding with this narrative, the friends of Mr. Parker may welcome some account of this noble sharer of his last happy summer. The facts are taken from Jacob Venedey's well-written sketch.

Hans Lorenz Küchler was born at Mannheim, of poor

* Mr. Desor alludes to the work of Prof. Agassiz upon the Embryology of the Turtle, which is prefaced by an Essay on Classification. The essay contains passages which refer to the marks of Divine premeditation shown by the laws and facts of the Creation. Many learned men abroad object to this as being non-scientific and transcending the limits of precise knowledge. They claim to confine themselves to the observation of facts, the induction of laws, and the improvement of Methods, and not only refuse to have anything to do with labelling, flattering, and confining Providence, but are shy of the spirit which seeks to connect the second causes immediately with the Infinite Cause. A layman cannot enter into the dispute upon Methods and Classification, but if he loves the attempts to trace the logic of the Infinite Mind, he ought not to shun the opportunity to acknowledge it.

† Upon reading this sprightly essay of Mr. Parker's, I am puzzled to account for the above interpretation of it. It seems levelled at the narrow arguments from design of the Bridgewater school, and at the assumption that any system or method is to be accepted as a finality. But Mr. Parker was eager to follow the Infinite footsteps through the garden of the world. The All-perfect One was to him immanent in every fact, law, and moment. It was his very jealousy for this Divine perfection, out of which men recruit their knowledge from age to age that made him humorous over the attempts to forestall the future by a plan. It is plain that there is some confusion here, for want of a little defining. All religious investigators are not peddlers of a Providence. It is one thing to assume that a scientific formula is a final and exhaustive statement of the Divine intent, and quite another thing to follow that intent, with conscious and religious intelligence, to transmit to the future a tentative survey. And it is one thing to limit investigation to phenomena and their second causes, but quite another thing to deny that they reveal to us the premeditations and continual presence of the infinite mind. Foreign science often tends towards the latter in assuming to be content with the former. But why should European naturalists decline to be led by facts, as Mr. Parker was always led, into a constant recognition of the Mind beneath the facts? Is not Materialism an assumption of a Finality?

parents, Aug. 11, 1808. He was thus but little more than two years the senior of Mr. Parker. His father was a cabinet-maker, and proposed to train his only son and child for the joiner's bench; but his mother read a different career in the broad forehead and clear eyes, and as usual prevailed to have him sent to school. But she privately thought that studying would lead to the priesthood, and Küchler narrowly escaped being a Catholic priest. Bitter was her disappointment, when one day the youthful Hans announced to her that the miracle of the transubstantiation was too much for him, and that celibacy seemed an unnatural condition.

His literary tendencies were a trouble to the father, who was now falling sick and feeble. "The scholar's path is a weary and costly one—where is the money to come from?" The son replied, "My wants shall be few and of the smallest." The father shook his head; but Hans began to give instruction, and helped the family with the penny thus turned. The bitter cares of life confronted him early. But he was healthy, active, laborious, cheerful, and true.

The Greek Revolution was a great excitement to him, and to the young literary circle which met to declaim Körner, Schiller, and the patriotic poets of the time. Küchler, then eighteen years old, dramatized the fall of Missolonghi, and his piece was put upon the stage of the Mannheim theatre, which is so illustrious by Schiller's connection with it.

The father's health was broken, and friends must come forward to help the young man in his career. It was proposed that he should enter a counting-house, but this was resisted by the daughter of the very merchant who made the proposition. For love has sharper eyes than friends and relations; the fair Louise said "No" to the scheme, seeing that in Küchler which soon made her say "Yes" to him. So he went to the University of Heidelberg in 1829.

At first he attempted to study medicine, but the preliminary anatomical studies shocked his feeling, and he turned to jurisprudence. At the time of the Frankfort revolutionary attempt for German unity, in 1833, he was in intimate relations with many who were implicated. Seeing little hope in any movement, he endeavored to restrain his friends. This, however, as his sympathies for nationality and freedom were well known, did not save him from suspicion and denouncement. He was obliged to flee, went to Weissenburg, worked awhile as apprentice to a cabinet-maker, made his way to Paris, in October, became tutor in an English family, and went with them to Switzerland. In 1836, he was teaching a boys' school in Nancy. The faithful Louise obtained permission from the Government for his return; a formal trial hung over him till 1839, ending in a six months' imprisonment, three of which were remitted. He was married in that year, and began the practice of law in Weinheim, a beautiful town on the Bergstrasse, not far from Heidelberg.

In 1844 his wife, to his profound astonishment and grief, insisted upon being divorced from him, in the melancholy and depreciating moods produced by ill-health; bringing forward the pretext that life with her could no longer be happy for him, and that no children could bless him. She eventually carried her point. He went broken-hearted to Heidelberg to pursue his practice of the law, and there became the leader of the German-Catholic movement in that city; he conducted its first service, and its last, when the Government cancelled the permission to have public meetings. He was married again in 1847, the year of revolutions. His judgment was against the chief actors in the German projects, his sympathy was with them. But he soon had the opportunity to show the strength and manliness of his spirit in the consecutive legal defences which he undertook of many of the chief actors in the Baden insurrection. Though he was mainly considerate to clear his clients, he did not fail to utter bold and generous words before the Prussian military commission. Some of the prisoners were acquitted; for others he procured moderate punishments, while some were shot. He was with them in court, in the prison, and at the last fatal hour. His labors and sufferings at this time were of the most shattering kind.

He was pre-eminent in Heidelberg as a man of piety and philanthropy; many good projects were organized and carried through by his good sense, industry, and forgetfulness of self. He was a noble, simple-minded man.

Here Mr. Desor's narrative may be resumed:—

On the edge of the avenue of Combe-Varin there is a fir which now bears the name of Parker. To the shade of this fir the two friends went every day to pass some hours, which they consecrated to the interchange of their ideas and experiences in the matter of religion and the ministerial profession. A natural feeling of respect ordinarily kept the other guests at a distance, but those who in passing chanced to mingle with these intimate conversations, derived from them satisfaction and genuine edification. If they differed in some details, they were all the more in harmony upon the leading questions. Both were opposed to the dogmas of the old theology, which insists that man is naturally perverse. Both Mr. Parker and his friend had faith in humanity; they admitted that man had been created for happiness, and that it can and ought to be attained, without the necessity of expiatory blood, on the sole condition of developing the good elements which are in the heart of all men. They differed somewhat as to the value of the faculties with which our race is endowed, and, consequently, as to the manner of directing them. Mr. Parker was more of a theologian than Mr. Küchler; the religious faculties were for him quite as positive as the intellectual, affectional, or moral faculties. According to him, religion was the fairest prerogative of our being, one which was, therefore, worthy of the greatest solicitude, being fitted to guide man in his approach to the Divinity, while it became, when improperly directed, a formidable instrument in the hands of obscurantists and reactionists. Mr. Küchler appealed, above all, to the affectional faculties, which he considered the most primitive ones, as they are the foundations of society and of the family. Here, then, were some differences of view as to the direction to be lent to education, and upon the part which religion can and ought to fill.

Before Mr. Küchler took leave of Combe-Varin, he obtained from Mr. Parker a promise to come and visit him at Heidelberg, and in the meantime to keep him informed upon all that concerned him, particularly his health. It never occurred to him that he, the robust and healthy man, would be the first to quit the world. When the fatal news arrived the next morning of the death of Küchler, there was a general mourning at Combe-Varin; but no one lamented him more sincerely than his friend Parker.

The relations of Mr. Parker with the other guests of Combe-Varin, without being as intimate as those which he had formed with Mr. Küchler, were not less friendly. It mattered little to him that one was materialist, pantheist, or orthodox, provided one was sincere. He liked and admired that tolerance of our old Europe, which admits all points of view and tempers all contrasts. No doubt the distance was great between him and Moleschott, but each knew and felt that the other was animated with the love of truth. Does not that suffice to create confidence and cement friendship ?

But the autumn was approaching. It was important that Mr. Parker should make choice of a milder climate for the winter. Opinions were divided. Mr. Moleschott recommended Madeira; others inclined to Ægypt, and others to Algiers or the South of France. He, on the contrary, decided for Rome. The scientific, artistic, and, above all, bibliographic treasures of that capital, had an irresistible and fatal attraction for him, and such was the firmness of his will that no consideration could divert him from the project. He departed full of hope, notwithstanding the apprehensions of his friends.

Mr. Parker was not only a philosopher and a theologian; the phenomena of nature had also a great charm for him. In the United

States he made long journeys to join us and participate in our examination of the great coal depots of the Alleghanies. He had studied the aspect of the coasts, and the association of plants and animals on the different strands of the American coast. He liked to collect reports of methods of cultivation, of crops, and of their relations to the soil. He had followed with interest our studies upon the geological structure of the mountain-ranges of the Jura. He experienced a genuine happiness in listening to the brilliant expositions of M. Martins upon meteorology, and particularly his fine composition upon the cold of mountains, which forms the subject of one of the articles in this Album. Later he listened with no less interest to the communications of M. Schönbein upon ozone, and the profound considerations which the learned professor of Basle derived from it for the future of chemistry. And even the minute observations of M. Gressly upon the habits of marine animals captivated him, as much by the new facts which they revealed as by the original observations with which they were seasoned.

But all this did not suffice him. Among the grand natural phenomena which he had not seen were volcanoes and the desert. We were to visit them together, beginning with Vesuvius. I promised him that I would rejoin him at Rome during the winter, to go thence to Naples. This hope appeared to have sustained his courage, in spite of the bad weather which soon commenced, and whose evil effects were not long in making themselves felt.

There are but few connected notes of the excursions which Mr. Parker made in the neighbourhood of Combe-Varin :—

July 28, 1859.—Lac de Doubs.—All of us went to Ponts, thence to Locle, thence to Brenets and the Lac de Doubs. It is singularly beautiful ; a *transversal cut* in the limestone strata (which lie almost, if not quite, level at the upper end, and incline as you go farther down), about four miles long and a quarter wide in the broadest part. Perpendicular rocks, 100 to 120 feet high, form the sides. The Saut de Doubs is at the end, but the water of the lake was some three to five feet lower than the bottom of the river which drains it. The water works through the crevices of the stone and comes out below, where it turns mills. The upper mills, which depend on the water that runs *over* the Saut (fall) have been dry for weeks, if not months.

Moulins Souterrains de Locle.—Locle was once a lake, in the form of a trough, shaped like a boat, only irregular. It was drained some two hundred years ago. Gradually the bottom became dry, the peat was cut out, and men built houses there. Now they use the water which runs down the deep well (made to drain the region) to turn mills. It is used three times in its descent. The last wheel is 120 feet below the surface. All the machinery is iron, and well made. *I* did not go down into the pit, mindful of another whence it is not easy *revocare gradus et superare ad aeras.* Returned at 9.30 P.M., with a little cold in my throat, which made me cough all night.

There is no sand in this valley, or in its neighbourhood. So the people mix sawdust with lime to make mortar. The barley shows the want of silex in the soil, and crinkles down; the straw can't support the head of grain.

Reinwald (one of the guests) says the German military songs are all sad, and refer to the " Soldier's Death "; while those of the French are joyous. *Omnis natura in re minima adest.* It is the national character which speaks there.

How strong is the instinct of hope ! Every man thinks he shall be an exception to the general rule of mankind. In the " Dismal Swamp Lottery " this is the scheme:—

	dols.			dols.
Capital ...	1,000,000	Profit to Company	...	333,000
		Expenses of sale	...	333,000
		Accidental loss ...	...	1,000
		Value of prizes...	...	333,000
				1,000,000

Only one man in three will get his money back, on the average. But each hopes he shall be the lucky one, and the public pays 1,000,000 dollars, when they are sure of getting back only 333,000 dollars.

Aug. 3.—It is six months to-day since I left Boston. Shall I ever see it again ? More than doubtful. Certainly I left it as never again to set eyes on the State House.

In making up his mind where to spend the winter, he deliberately studied the advantages of the various places which were recommended to him. He drew up a list of books in Spanish, English, German, &c., upon Madeira, and began to read them, taking notes of the botany, which seemed chiefly to attract him.

What different counsel in doctors ! Last October, Bowditch wanted me to go to the West Indies, Dr. J. Jackson not.

For hypophosphites—Dr. Flint, of Boston; Dr. Bigelow, of Paris.
Against hypophosphites—Dr. Louis, of Paris.
Indifferent or doubtful—Drs. Bowditch, Cabot, Moleschott.
For cod-liver oil—Cabot (moderate).
Against cod-liver oil—Drs. Louis and Bigelow.

Some think Jongh's is the best preparation of the cod-liver oil. Dr. Moleschott thinks him a humbug and a liar, his oil good for nothing. Bigelow recommends Bordeaux wine ; Moleschott, Malaga before Bordeaux ; Bigelow and Cabot, Jackson and Bowditch, whiskey, brandy, &c. ; Moleschott, pilled barley.

KÜCHLER.—Hans Küchler, an eminent advocate, from Heidelberg, has been staying with us for some time here, and delighted us all with his intelligence and moral purity. Tuesday, Aug. 2, he left us with the Reinwalds, and went to Neuchâtel. They dined with him there the same day; he went on the boat *en route* for home. That very afternoon at Nidau he fell dead of apoplexy.* He was buried there the next day. We did not get the intelligence till Wednesday. At six in the afternoon Desor and the Reinwalds, who had returned, went to Neuchâtel to attend the sad duties of the occasion. Mr. and Mrs. R. go to Heidelberg to console his wife, at least to condole with her. He was the defender of the patriot victims of the Revolution in 1849, one of the chief supports of the German Catholic Church, and often preached in the Assembly at Heidelberg.

I intended, if I lived, to visit him in Heidelberg next spring, and made him my promise to that effect. So the well man goes, and the miserable consumptive invalid still holds on, barking and coughing his useless life away.

August 7.—It is Sunday to-day, and the Music Hall has been shut since July 13. It will never hear my voice again. That is all well enough; I have had my time.

Dr. Charles Martins and his wife have been stopping with M. Desor for a week or ten days. He is a quite learned botanist, and *Physiker* in general, a well-instructed, thoughtful, and liberal man, with a fine talent for talking. M. and Madame Coquet are also here. He is an advocate at Paris, she a Spanish woman and a devout Catholic. Messrs. Martins and Coquet have frequent talks about Catholicism, which they alike hate and despise, as does also Madame M. It interferes with the individual in all forms of hindrance, and is a manifold curse. Probably Catholicism is a greater obstacle to the high development of mankind in Europe now than the classic forms of religion were eighteen hundred years ago. I do not know but Protestantism must be added to the same list; as Arago said, it is "*un peu moins absurd que le Catholicisme*." One rests on its miraculous, divine, infallible Church; the other on its miraculous, divine, infallible Bible: and each is a humbug, though both contain much good.

MOLIÈRE.—Martins says the French *littérateurs* now think Molière the greatest mind and character the nation ever produced in literature. I vainly brought forward Descartes, Montaigne, Voltaire, Pascal, D'Alembert, &c. The chief proofs he brought were—1, his superiority to the ecclesiastical, mediæval, philosophical, and social prejudices of his time; 2, his courageous exposure of the most popular and powerful vices.

Certainly in all these things he was greatly superior to Shakspeare, who seems to negate the highest function of the poet, and hence has so little which can be quoted for the highest purposes of literature.

I will read Molière directly, with his Life, &c. He died of a sudden hæmorrhage of the lungs, and Bossuet, in an occasional sermon, said his death was the Divine vengeance against him, because he had mocked against the Church—as the Church was incarnated in Tartuffe, I take it. Perhaps the *Doctores Medicinæ* thought no better of him than the *Doctores Theologiæ*.

---

* The simple-hearted Germans thought it a pleasant circumstance that when he fell he was lifted into the shop of a cabinet-maker; as it were, dying thus where he began.

TO MRS. APTHORP AND MISS HUNT IN MONTREUX.

Combe-Varin, Switzerland, August 1, 1859.

I shan't try to tell how dear you both are to me, nor how much I have long valued your friendship and affection, nor how much delight it has given me to meet you anew. I get fresh vigor from your society. If I don't speak of such things much, it is because my heart when full of such joy does not overflow into the channel of words. How good your letters have been to me! I do not mean merely for three years, but those which have come gladdening since I left Montreux. How sweet and wise they have been from both of you! Sallie's last was quite a work of art, even without the bears which Willie put in. I did not think the dear " 'Potamus " could do such things so well —it is indeed extraordinary, the conception and the execution too. Cranch, man that he is, could not have done it better. How proud the mother was to go off to the butterfly pasture with her butterfly hunter and catch the little fragments of a rainbow for his development! I also take a vicarious delight in these things, enjoying them through your direct and personal pleasure.

But it is a grand good boy, that little Hippopotamousie, with I know not how noble a future before him! Certainly, if love and wisdom avail aught in the development of inborn talent, it is plain what lies before him, and we all know that these are the mother and father of all unfoldings.

T. P.

TO THE SAME.

Desor's Châlet, August 15, 1859.

Let me metamorphose (that is the profane word) or transfigure (that is the sacred term) myself into a little breath of wind, and come through your keyhole. You will say, perhaps, as the maiden in the classic poem,—

" Veni aura levis ! "

And I make sweet dreams for you, and put a kiss on your sleeping face as soft as the air itself, and not wake you.

I am glad you are so well, and Robert so well, and your mother so well reported of by the Doctor. Blessed are you when all doctors speak well of you! Rejoice and be exceeding glad, for so speak they of your fathers who lived to a great age before you!

Sumner has been at Paris and is now at Havre, at the Bains Frascati, where he actually swims in the sea! He has got a back-bone. We are very happy here—all of us. Good news from home. I think we shall leave for Montreux, Aug. 23. Of course we go to Rome if the Pope does not take to "wearing his hat on one whisker," in which case it will hardly be safe to keep near the old —— !

Can we all pass the winter together ? I would give up home for any safe place with you.

Dear love to all.

T.

TO MR. MANLEY.

Combe-Varin, August 4, 1859.

MY DEAR JOHN R. MANLEY,—Your kind letter of July 12th came here from Montreux, a day or two ago. I am glad you got my last to you and the *Picnic-ians* in due time. I thought it would reach Boston on the night of the 12th or 13th, and that you would look in at the P. O. in the morning. I trust the meeting went off well—without accident. At the last one I had a dim feeling that I should not be there in 1859, and so wrote it down in my book. We have strange premonitions sometimes which we don't heed! I think the beam of life always cracks before it breaks. I have had warnings often enough before now — but could not quite make up my mind to stop till the word came, "No further, my little dear." Mr. Lyman—kindest of men, I call him "Governor"—read me a line from John Ayres' letter to him. It filled me with joy and also with pain. I refer to the money my friends were proposing to raise for me and had already got together. The *joy* was that they should thus value me, where I am now (and perhaps can be hereafter) of no service to them. Of all the Christian graces, Gratitude is the last that sits down to meat—fairest likewise of that handsome sisterhood. The *pain* was, that I could (now, at least) do nothing in return for their good-will—and the recollection that I am now living on their bounty, while once it was my lot to give and not receive. Let me express my warmest thanks to all who thus show their interest in me, and to the rest who feel not less, but may not be able to adopt this form of kindness. My joy will continue with the memory of your kindness. But let me say I do not wish to receive another dollar from my friends; I don't need it. I know what money costs, the sour sweat which earns it, and if I have never been an avaricious man, and perhaps sometimes a generous one, it is not that I didn't know the worth of money. But I don't need this. The voyage to the West Indies and thence to England, the residence in London and Paris, was unavoidably expensive ; now I live at small cost and can continue so to do. The visit to Egypt, which would necessarily cost much money, I have given up as not beneficial to me.

*   *   *   *   *   *

Please, therefore, let the matter stop here—don't give me any more money. If I am not able to preach, I may yet serve the dear old Society in many ways to make up for the money they have already advanced me.

John Augustus is dead. I knew him well—have known him from my boyhood. He married my cousin—a favourite niece of my mother, who I think brought her up; but they were married before I was born. His death is a public loss. I should have preached an occasional sermon on his death had I been at the Music Hall. His life was a great lesson. He was the friend of publicans and sinners to a greater degree than Jesus of Nazareth—if we rely on the records. He had a genius for philanthropy : it showed itself in Lexington, where he lived and carried on the shoemaking business from 1810 till 1829 or 1830. He was an odd man, queer and fantastical, but honest, self-sacrificing, and extraordinarily given to help the helpless and love

the unlovely. I make no doubt he did foolish things in his philanthropy—perhaps wrong things also. But his character was sweet,
and clean, and beautiful. All the members of the United States
Supreme Court might die next month, and the President of the United
States follow suit, and half the Governors of the Union, and unitedly
they would not be so great a loss as poor old John Augustus. The fair
record of his life since 1810 (he was born about 1785, the illegitimate
son of somebody), especially since 1830, would be one of the most extraordinary and instructive pieces of biography ever written. Ministers
preach benevolence and beneficence—he *went* and *did* it. How many
common prostitutes did he pick out of that Slough of Despond! how
many drunkards save from the pit of ruin? how many thieves, and
robbers, and other infamous persons, did he help out of their wickedness? I wish the lives of merchants like Hovey and John L. Emmons;
of deacons like Moses Grant, and shoemakers like John Augustus,
could be written. "The Life and Works" of Calvin Whiting would be
worth two or three lives of King Do-nought, or of Murderous the
Great. Pope Gregory XVI. will have his life written in many
languages, but there will be no history of Hovey, and Emmons, and
Grant, and Augustus, and Whiting, and Saint Matilda, and the other
angels of justice, angels of charity, angels of mercy, whom you and I
know. It makes me a little impatient to remember how much is to be
done to honor the noblest of men, and to recollect that I can do
nothing but *cough*. "But patience to hearts that murmur," &c.—I
won't complain. I am only one little spirt of water running into the
great ocean of humanity; and if I stop here, I shall not be at all
missed there.

The Courts of Boston, I suppose, adjourned when they heard of
Choate's death, as they did all over the United States when Daniel
Webster died (all but the Kidnappers' Court, in Boston; that went on
trying the Shadrach rescuers); but they would take no notice of John
Augustus; yet he had kept hundreds from crime, and bailed thousands
out of gaol; so I hope Judge Russell did adjourn his Court. I am glad
I did not have to preach on Choate; but I fear no minister in Boston
used the occasion to tell the awful moral of the tale. When John
Augustus died, I should have preached of the "Power of Individual
Justice and Philanthropy," and when R. Choate carried up his case
to another tribunal, of the "Abuse of Great Talents and Great Opportunities." Perhaps I should have printed them both in one pamphlet—
the story of the obscure shoemaker and of the great lawyer and
politician! When will men learn to distinguish the chaff from the
wheat? It is only by accident that we got the life of Jesus of Nazareth
written and saved for us, in the poor unsatisfactory style of the first
three Gospels, while the Cæsars had historians enough. But the pleb-
eians are not very democratic as yet, and do not know their prophet
till he has gone up in the chariot of fire, and they miss him from the
path of life.

Kindest remembrances to all yours. Give my salutation to the
Browns, and the Jacksons, and the Garrisons, and the Sparrells. Oh,
dear! when shall I end the list? Good-bye.

Faithfully yours,

T. P.

TO MISS GODDARD AND OTHERS, BOSTON, MASS.

Combe-Varin, Aug. 16, 1859.

To my dear Saint Matilda, and all the other saints that be in the house at No. 2, Florence Street, this goeth (and I hope also cometh), greeting. Most welcome was your letter, which came but a few days ago, and brought us good tidings of your mother. I am glad to hear she has so much freedom from pain, and comes out and enjoys the delicious sunshine in the streets: "walks as far as Decatur Street" sounds quite cheery. That is the way we go. Once the proud mother carried *her* in arms; then trailed her along gently by the hand; next let her run a little, here and there; then the mature woman walks over to Charlestown and back again, nay, much farther, and is not a-weary. Then we reverse the process, and come back again to the original feebleness; and as we were born into this world babies, so babies we go out of it— to be caught by some motherly arms at the next birth as at this. Such is the contrivance of the dear Infinite Perfection, who is Father and Mother to old and young. Once George Combe could work in his study ten or twelve hours a-day; by-and-bye eight or ten; then six or eight, five or six, four or five, three or four, two or three, one or two; then only now and then a little—when the sun broke through the clouds for a few minutes, then was hid. At last it was all over. He had gone to his (unknown) work the other side. A happy life has your mother's been; yet more from the internal tranquillity and trustfulness of her character than from even its outward events. How many bitter drops are poured into the cup of human communion! So is it best. Who could do without his hardships—his misfortunes? Not you, not I, not mortal man. God provides wisely the conditions of human existence. Even for the Carolinian slave there must be a compensation somewhere.

A Mr. Küchler has been staying here with Mr. Desor for a little while —a noble man, one of the distinguished democratic patriots of the nation—not such democrats as they at home, who think there can be no republic without the white man can " wallup his niggur"—who had done large service to the cause of humanity and the progress of mankind. He left us one morning, and died of apoplexy in the afternoon, on his way home to his wife and children at Heidelberg: his body was buried where he died. He was a distinguished lawyer at Heidelberg, and one of the leaders of the Free Church there—a sort of Twenty-eighth Congregational Society—in which he preached in the absence of the minister. As he fell dead in a strange place, his body was carried to the house of one who esteemed him highly, and who was a *boss* cabinetmaker. It was mentioned as a pleasant circumstance, quite grateful to his friends and family, because his father was also a *boss* cabinetmaker, and in his youth he himself had worked in his father's shop. This shows the simplicity of the German character. If N—— A—— should fall dead at Provincetown, and his body be carried to a cabinetmaker's and thence home to burial, no Yankee would think it a pleasing circumstance because N—— A——'s father had been a master in that craft; the American who becomes distinguished or rich, is commonly ashamed of his hard-working relations—not so the Germans. But of course we are the most democratic people in the world—and own 4,000,000 slaves!

You "don't often go to meeting." It is a great misfortune that the Twenty-eighth has no minister who feels some responsibility towards the people, only a lecturer from week to week. A minister with any sort of soul in him, would feel bound to use the various events of the time to convey some sort of lesson—if not of guidance, then, at least, of warning. Now, it is not so; the intellect is the chief faculty addressed, even by Emerson, who never appeals directly to the conscience, still less to the religious faculty in man. Most of the others are, perhaps, less conscientious, certainly less able than he. Besides, I love the custom of public prayers, and have taken more delight in praying with like-hearted people, than ever in preaching to like-minded or otherwise-minded; yet, I think, few men love preaching so well. I wish you might soon find some one permanently to fill my place. It is bad to live from hand to mouth, spiritually or materially.

Love to all the household, especially the dear, venerable mother.

Faithfully yours,
THEODORE PARKER.

Can I tell you how dear you are all to me? I shall not try.

TO MISS THAYER:

Combe-Varin, Aug. 16, 1859.

MY SAINT CAROLINE,—This new pen won't do to write with—that is clear as this muddy ink; so here goes with the old gold one, which has done great service for years. What a train of troubles you have had! A horrible ailment is the rheumatic fever, and the old mode of treating with great doses of colchicum often left another disease, and an incurable—an affection of the heart. Here, and in France, colchicum is used with great caution, and only in small doses. But you had only homœopathic treatment, which, certainly, is as good as none at all, and so have not to recover from the effects of the medicine. I don't find homœopathy has made much mark in Europe, or has the confidence of scientific men. But they bear it this testimony :—1. It is the best in old chronic disorders; 2. It is, also, decidedly the best for young ladies. Besides, in general, the homœopathic doctors attend so well to the dietetic and climatic, and other hygienic remedies, that they often effect cures when others fail. In Paris, homœopathy is the favorite scheme with the poorer people, because they have to pay only the doctor, not also the apothecary, whose business is "organized robbery." (So, indeed, I find it, for at Paris I paid 1 dollar 10 cents for some medicine which the 'potecary here only charges me 16 cents for!) There is a homœopathic hospital at Vienna, which I hear well spoken of for discharging its patients in a good condition; but that may be very unscientific. It seems to me the Paris doctors care little about curing the sick. We have a nice time up here. Do you remember my German friend, Mr. Desor? I made his acquaintance in 1847; it soon became an intimacy: he left Boston in 1852. I always write him on my birthday, he me on his; besides, many other letters come and go. His house is full of visitors, ten or a dozen lodging here at a time; scientific men mostly, with their ladies. "It is a pity you have no wife," I said. "Ugh!" was D.'s answer, "I think I'm better off without; do you think I could have all these women here if I had a wife? Ugh!"

Amongst others, a Doctor Moleschott has been here, a man of great genius, a chemist and professor of physiology at Zurich, the first philosophical anatomist in Germany, as well as practising physician. He made a microscopic examination, and decided that there is no softening of the tubercles, and no laceration of my lungs as yet, and therefore the circumstances are still favorable for the action of medicine and climate. Dr. Cabot, dear good sensible fellow that he is, says I need nutritious food, air, sun, and reasonable exercise, with but moderate medicines. So says Dr. M., so Dr. Bigelow at Paris, so all. Here in fair weather I am out of doors eight or ten hours a-day; the mornings and evenings are too cold and damp. I work in the woods chopping, pruning the trees, &c., of course moderately, and get a kind of exercise which is most delightful to me. I think I have done no imprudent thing since I came to the Continent; but enough about myself.

Here the women work out of doors "from morn till dewy eve," and look as rough as the horses they drive. It is a curious fact that woman deteriorates and rapidly grows old when much exposed to the elements, and constrained to great physical labor. It is against her nature. The same result appears in the Tropics—at Santa Cruz; and the Temperate Zone—at Switzerland: 1. The degeneration of what is specifically feminine; 2. The degeneration of what is generically human. She approximates to the male type of humans, then to that of the inferior animals.

Naturâ duce is an admirable motto in all matters. But our New England women do not work enough in the fields, a good deal of gardening might advantageously be done by their little nimble fingers; the raising of poultry and young cattle would be profitable to the cheeks of our farmers' daughters, as well as their fathers' purses. Just now the New England women in general tend to abhor all manual labor. They must be LADIES (a LADY is a female animal of the human species who won't work, that is the vulgar definition), and so despise the details of housekeeping; they can't make bread, nor cook a dinner, nor cut out and make a shirt for a possible (or impossible) husband, not even for a baby. A deal of mischief comes from this shameful mistake—involuntary celibacy of men who can't afford to keep a lady in the house, and of maidens who would fain marry but not work. We have not seen the end of this mischief, nor shall not in any haste. When a boy I learned to do all kinds of work done in my neighborhood, from the blacksmith's to the clockmaker's, and I thank God I can work with my hands. (I have ground up all Mr. Desor's axes and hatchets, and actually finished a hog's-trough.) If I had a family of daughters and were never so rich, they should all learn thoroughly all the details of good housekeeping, and not only know how each thing should be done, but also how to do it—the process as well as the result.

But I did not mean to draw such a long bow, and preach a ̇ermon to an (invisible) audience 3000 or 400Č ̇miles off. I wish you could have seen some of the specimens of "our family bread" sent ̇me last autumn, after a certain sermon in which I showed how the New England women broke the staff of life over their husband's heads —and the heads along with it. You would have said a woman was worth several ladies. But I need not say this to you, who with all your family, know how to do all sorts of things, and with such admirable skill that Mr. Pierpont said of each, "She hath done what she could!"

What could show the moral degradation of Boston more fully than the funeral honors paid to poor Choate? The town which fired 100 cannons to honor the passage of the Fugitive Slave Bill, which kidnapped Sims and Burns, and whose "respectability" fraternized with the assassins of Charles Sumner, ought logically so to honor the great advocate of rogues and solicitor-general for scoundrels, who called the self-evident truths of our revolutionary fathers only "glittering generalities" and a "noisy abstraction." Such a demonstration is more demoralizing than a bull-fight at Havana. I am glad I was spared the pain of making a *post-mortem* examination of such a man. . . . .

No amount of talent, none of genius, or of good humor, can atone for a life which was a long public treason to that justice which the State and Church are built to preserve. . . . . .

Hearty love to all the household.

Faithfully,

T. P.

P.S.—My wife says, "All Caroline's saints are men!" "I didn't!" she says. Remember me to all the saints and saintesses too.

TO MR. SUMNER.

Combe-Varin, Suisse, Aug. 13, 1859.

What a condition Europe is in just now! Before long there must be a general war—a very dreadful one in its process; very blessed in its results. What a lying scamp Louis Napoleon is! How he lied before the war! "*L'Empire, c'est la paix—toujours la paix.*" (He had better have written it, "*C'est l'épée, toujours l'épée!*" That is *Mr. Punch's* wit.) How he lied to the Italians, "from the Mediterranean to the Adriatic"! How he lied to the Emperor of Austria about the terms which the other Powers would make less favorable! A German says there have been two acts of the Euripidean Trilogy of Louis Napoleon—the *coup d'état* was only a prologue, to put the piece on the stage and notify the audience.

1. Came the Crimean affair, *vide* Sebastopol, &c.
2. Came the Italian affair, *vide* Solferino, &c.

But what will the third be, the finale?

Yet the bulk of the nation seems to like him. How true Cato the elder said of the ancient (and also of the modern) Gauls!—*Pleraque Gallia duas res industriosissime persequitur, rem militaren et argute loqui.*

I render the latter *faire belles phrases.* But his empire must down. He forbids the haberdashers to sell handkerchiefs with Garibaldi's head on them; the journals to mention the name of Cavour, it is said.

How the educated French hate him ! How many despise Guizot, not quite unjustly !

Prince Napoleon had a long private communication the other day with an eminent German *savant* and Republican. He says Louis Napoleon made peace because — (1.) The Italians in Lombardy did not favor him, 1, because they were naturally cowards ; and 2, were disgusted at the conduct of the Turcos, who plundered the peasants. (2.) His army had suffered enormous losses, was badly organized, not well supplied with necessary provisions, was destitute of water ; the artillery had to go three leagues for it, and were as thirsty when they returned as when they went ; it was sickly, and if he had not made peace when he did, he must have retreated the next day. (3.) He found conspiracy at home. "*On y conspire,*" said the Emperor ; "if they can't rule, they will conspire—the Orleanistes, the Republicans, the Evêques." "The Emperor," said Prince Napoleon, "conspired against France, and now fears that *it* will conspire against him !" He has got into a dilemma. If he helps the Legations against the Pope, or leaves them alone to resist that old——, then the Pope is against him and all the 40,000 priests at home, who are more Roman than French. If he helps the Pope against the Legations, then the public opinion of all (enlightened) Europe is against him, and the arms of John Bull. Bull has acted like a great baby—he was scared, and cried like a fool; but there is stuff in the crittur yet, and pride. Louis Napoleon acts foolishly in setting the French papers to stir up hostility against England. He had better let Antwerp fortify, and hold his tongue. I think the peace not worth much. But, alas ! I have little hope of a regeneration of Italy. What confederation can there be between Piedmont and Naples, or Rome ? What is a confederation for freedom good for, presided over by the Pope, the bitterest foe of freedom ? Besides, the federative disposition, which creates the Teutonic confederacies of old times and new, must underlie the new institution, and that is foreign to Italy and all the Romanic peoples ; it is the ethnologic peculiarity of the Teutons, and in the time of Cæsar distinguished them from the Celts. Nothing will keep the Teutonic people out of Italy ; they have had great influence there ever since Dietrich von Bern, and must enter the Peninsula as the Americans go to Mexico. I *wish* differently.

I think Rome will be my winter residence (the Pyramids stick in my crop). I hope the A.'s will go with us, and we shall all live together in some wide, sunny street. I live out of doors eight or ten hours in the day, and have work in the woods, chopping, pruning trees, &c.

We shall go back to Montreux next week. L. has gone to Paris to see the show of soldiers, but returns the 16th or 17th. Juvenal says of Gaul,—

> " Natio comœda, est . . . . . . *
> Si dixeris, ' æstuo,' sudat ! " *

I have the happiest time here. I attend chiefly to botany, geology, zoology, &c., and read.

* Juv. Sat. III., 94–97.

But I have my eyes open on my more special studies. God bless you! If we do not work together hereafter, we have heretofore.

FROM MR. SUMNER.

Bains Frascati, au Havre, August 22, 1859.

How beautifully things move in Tuscany! Who says a people thus composed amidst the grandest trials is not fit for freedom? Who is fit for it, I pray? The Americans with four millions of slaves, and with a leaven of slaveholding tyrants, and foreign immigrants who cannot speak our language? Why these, more than the Italians, full of genius, invention and all knowledge? Against the proletarianism of Italy, I put the slavery of our country, and hold that Italy is full as apt for free institutions as the United States. You doubt. I must borrow a phrase from Charles Fox, addressed to Bonaparte, First Consul, "Clear your head of that nonsense." Of course, I am for freedom everywhere. If I heard of a revolt in the seraglio I should be for it.

Think of old Gino Capponi, blind, led to the urn and voting for the emancipation of his country. Well done, gallant veteran!* It was his ancestor who went forth from Florence to meet Charles VIII. of France, and when the King threatened if his terms were not accepted, " to sound his trumpets," the ambassador of the Republic replied, " If you sound your trumpets, we will ring our bells."

In the next letter Mr. Parker alludes to the resolution offered by Mr. Conway, at a meeting of the Alumni of Cambridge Theological School, July, 1859 ; its passage was opposed for various reasons, and the question finally avoided by an adjournment.

Resolved, That the Association has heard with deep regret of the failure, during the past year, of the health of the Rev. Theodore Parker; and we hereby extend to him our heartfelt sympathy, and express our earnest hope and prayer for his return with renewed strength, and heart unabated, to the post of duty which he has so long filled with ability and zeal."

TO REV. J. F. CLARKE.

Combe-Varin, Canton de Neuchâtel.

MY DEAR JAMES,—What a row you and Conway made at the meeting of Alumni a month ago, or less! You the President of the Unitarian Association! only think of it! I am afraid you are " raised up," " for the disturbance of the Br-rotheren " as Dr. —— would say. Poor men! So they couldn't say, " Well, we're sorry you're sick, and

---

* The venerable Marquis Capponi, who has done so much for historical studies and also for correct sentiment in Italy, was a Member of the Constituent Assembly at Florence, which, in 1859, decreed the independence of Tuscany.

hope you'll get well, and come back to your old place, and go to work!" No: they could not say that—how could they? But this mode of treating the matter will damage those men not a little. "What!" honest men will say, "couldn't you wish your sick brother might get well, and come back, and work against popular wickedness, in low places and high places? Afraid he'd hurt the word o' God, and knock down the Church o' God! Do you think they're so much in danger that a little consumptive minister in Exeter Place could finish one or the other?" . . . I have been in battle for twenty years, treated as no other American ever was, and it is not likely I have escaped without many a wrong deed. You have sometimes told me of my faults. God bless you for it! I took the advice greatly to heart. But a note at Harvard College Chapel won't save a man whose relations all die of consumption soon as that ugly cat puts her claws into their sides. For the ministers' sake, private and public, I should rather they would have passed the resolution which brave, affectionate young Conway presented; for my own sake it is not of the smallest consequence. At twenty-nine it would move me; not at forty-nine.

Here in Europe the Catholic Church is the one great enemy to human progress and welfare. It is the religion of the Romanic people, the Celtic people, the Celto-Romanic, the French, and the Celto-Teutonic communities scattered about in all parts of Germany, and still more in Austria. It is amazing to see how Catholicism penetrates society and controls all individuality. It has greatly demoralized France, which has 40,000 priests, who steal in everywhere and spread their slime over the baby, the child, the maiden, and the man. Protestantism is on the decline in France, for the Government farms the Roman Church; wealth, fashion, all the great institutions are on its side. Once Montpellier was almost Protestant (in the time of Louis XIII.), and contained, say, 40,000 people. Now it is almost wholly Catholic, yet there has been no change of population by migration out or in. It is done by the marriage contract, which transfers the children to Catholic instruction. But it is all hollow. In France Catholicism is official and ecclesiastical, not personal.

The educated, the men of science and letters, have no belief in it; the high merchants, bankers, &c., none; even the great mass of working-men have no belief in Catholicism. They do not confess nor attend meeting; they have no more belief in it than the better class of Athenian common people had in their mythology when Aristophanes wrote his plays, or Lucian his dialogues. Women go to meeting, confess, and accommodate the priests in diverse ways.

When La Place carried his "Mécanique Céleste" to Napoleon for presentation, the Emperor was busy making some sort of *concordat* with the Pope. So, thinking of what he called "religious affairs," meaning theologico-political, he read La Place's preface, and said, "I am surprised you don't mention the name of God." "Sire," said the mathematician, "*je n'ai pas trouvé besoin de cette hypothèse!*" That is the condition of the cultivated Frenchmen. They are not Atheists, they don't touch that question. Somebody said to Arago, "But I am a Protestant!" "That is only to be a little less absurd," was the answer.

Despotism rules everywhere in France—centralized at Paris, diffused from the Channel to the Alps and the Pyrenees! After the armistice of July 11th at Villafranca, the Emperor forbade the newspapers to mention the name of Cavour; it never appears. He ordered the print-sellers to put away the caricatures of Austria; down they went. During the war there were lots of cotton handkerchiefs, some with his head, others with Victor Emmanuel's, yet others with Garibaldi's head on them; after the peace Garibaldi's was forbidden. You cannot find it now; but just before the peace some Italian traders ordered 40,000 each of those handkerchiefs of a Swiss manufacturer, and when peace came countermanded all but the 40,000 of Garibaldi! Napoleon is popular with the army, the priests, the uneducated men; the educated hate him. But there are not 4,000,000 slaves in France, not a kid-napper in Paris! France is rich also; her material interests thrive, alas! not the human interests, high or even low. Remember me kindly to your household. I am staying with Desor in the mountains. His house is full of *savans* and *Gelehrte*.

The unwillingness to appear to recognize Mr. Parker by even a resolution of sympathy, had, of course, its roots in the old controversy, and was shared by many who had learned to admire his anti-slavery faithfulness. They did not see that the very thing which they admired proved the superiority of a moral to a doctrinal or a denominational position.

Here is another mark of this antipathy; but it is also a sign of the growth of his influence among the young preachers, who are nominally called Unitarians. They will certainly become a commanding body, in sympathy with an intelligent people who sit in most of the old Unitarian churches. Let them be little solicitous to preserve a denominational connection. They are fully able to take care of themselves. Let them preach or not in the old pulpits, according to the good-will of the occu-pants. But they have a welcome everywhere, in numerous pews, except in the most strictly sectarian of the city societies.

TO REV. THEODORE PARKER,

Cambridge, April 14, 1857.

DEAR SIR,—The following protest is this day presented to the Faculty of the Divinity School:—

We, members of the senior class, hereby protest against the refusal to sanction our election of Rev. Theodore Parker, as class-preacher, as being a violation of the principle of religious toleration on which this institution was founded, and we respectfully decline to make any election of class-preacher.

(Signed)   " GEORGE F. NOYES.
   " HENRY W. BROWN.
   " GEO. W. BARTLETT."

The matter will probably end here, at present. We have fully deliberated upon the proposition of leaving the school, and have decided that it is unwise. As to having a sermon from you when we graduate, it seems to us that to elect you now would be to violate in spirit the law which we are observing in the letter.

We can talk with you and consider of that in the future.

We have already accomplished our main object, which was to make known the fact that a class of young ministers recognize you as a Christian minister, and worthy to preach their sermon. Whether the sermon be preached or not is comparatively of very little importance.

We have felt for a year past that we had a rare opportunity to help the cause of religious freedom, and to make you some amends for the persecution which you have endured in the cause of truth. We have been faithful to our opportunity, and though not seemingly, have, in reality, been successful in our endeavor.

With the hope that we may be better acquainted than we have yet been, I ask you to accept from my class-mates and myself the warmest regard.

Truly yours,
HENRY W. BROWN.

FROM THE JOURNAL.

SWISS AND GERMAN STUPIDITY.—How many stupid things these Swiss people do! Here is a cross-cut saw which got broken, and it is mended by lapping the two pieces one over the other, and riveting the two together. So a hand-saw had a crack in the edge near the middle, and they mended it by riveting on a patch. This writing-desk I sit at [at Montreux] is so made that a book will slide down the leaf, and I must *chock* it up. They are making a railroad opposite the house; the embankment is fifteen or eighteen feet high, and close to the road; there must be a solid wall of stone six or seven feet thick to support it, for the space is too narrow to allow the natural spread of the gravel. They tipped the dirt, and raised the embankment to the requisite height, and then dug away what was superfluous, dug a ditch four or five feet deep, and laid the foundation of the wall; of course the bank kept sliding down, and the earth must be shovelled over four or five times, and wheeled up the steep bank and put down behind the wall. There were four-wheeled carriages without sideboards, nothing but a frame, to carry the small stones in. So all the stones must be taken out by hand; then they are tossed from one man to another, who tosses them to the place where the masons take them. With abundant water-power, they saw logs by hand; in the country of

z 2

steam-engines they drive piles in the old way; twenty men pulling on a rope and hoisting up the hammer! They have not even a windlass. In a little town in Mecklenburg they have the cholera this year. The population is only 150, of whom 80 died; there were not cabinet-makers enough to make coffins as fast as they were wanted. So the carpenters made them. But the cabinet-makers complained to the authorities that their legal right was invaded. So the carpenters must not make coffins, and the dead had to remain unburied till the small number of cabinet-makers could do the work!

Swiss Newspapers.—I am struck with the excellence of the Swiss newspapers. Take, for instance, such as I see oftenest, the *Bund* (Berne), *Journal de Genève*, *L'Indépendant de Neuchâtel*, *Gazette de Lausanne*. These are small in size, but filled on three pages out of four with quite valuable reading matter, and on the whole are greatly superior to the country papers of America, and the most of the city papers, I fear. The French newspapers, of course, are nothing; they only say what they are commanded (the Government papers), or permitted (the Opposition). The *Times* is hardly more moral than the *New York Herald*; it has lost much of its intellectual talent too.

Aug. 22.—At half-past three P.M. left Desor's hospitable châlet with no little regret. Took the diligence, all four of us, for Yverdon (Ebrodunum; a Latinized name of the Celtic original, I take it). The route is delightful through the Val de Travers.

Next day, reached Geneva about two, and went to the Hotel L'Ecu de Genève, one of the best of these institutions of organized robbery. Surveyed the town again, one of the most thriving in thrifty Switzerland; enormously wealthy, though Basle is before it. Notice the removal of the old walls, and the enlargement of the city, with its consequent increase in population, health, comfort, beauty, wealth; but how it was opposed by the landholders within the walls! Yet it was a scamp who perfected and carried on the good work.

Aug. 24.—My forty-ninth birthday; will it be also the last? Many things look that way. Yet others do not. Still, I count it so, and make no complaint.

Visited the old church of St. Peter where Calvin used to preach; and strolled about the city till ten. At that hour the naturalists had their meeting, eighty or one hundred of them, perhaps, besides strangers. Half-a-dozen Americans among the latter, e. g. T. B. Curtis, Amasa Walker, Dr. Bethune, Mr. Tillinghast.

As it was my birthday I wished to be with my friends, and so at three took the steamer for Montreux, bidding good-bye to Desor, who came to our hotel and on board the boat. At half-past seven we were met at the landing and went to our dear ones again. I found some beautiful little memorials of affection in my room.

Alas! I learned when I came home the death of Horace Mann. I knew nothing of his illness till Howe's letter told me of it. Alas! that I am not at home to say a word in his honor, and to improve the lesson of his grand life for the advantage of the people! Ah, me! "to be weak is to be miserable." Mann has long violated the laws of the body, and falls a victim to his conscientious philanthropy. None of the great Temperance men will hold out long and well. P—— and

G—— will not live out their days. —— stimulates his stomach with red pepper. Brandy even would be better! Wine and beer would be invaluable to all these men.

TO DR. HOWE.

Montreux, Suisse, Aug. 26, 1859.

My dear Chev.,—Yours of August 3rd, with its sad PS. of the 4th, came here on my forty-ninth birthday. I returned at night from a visit of a month to Desor, and my thoughtful wife, who came back the day before, wisely kept the melancholy news from me till the next morning. " *Les Dieux s'en vont!* " How many distinguished men have died of late in 1859, but not a king! " *Les Rois restent!* " I knew nothing of Mann's illness till your letter told me of his death. The last time I saw him—last autumn, I was ill, and he came to see me. He looked almost healthy, with more flesh and more color than I had seen before, and in admirable spirits. Who will do full justice to his great merits as a philanthropist and a statesman? Nobody in America. I have known him since 1836: very well since 1848. I think I understand him as well as I admire, esteem, and love him. But, alas! I am not there to preach his funeral sermon at the Music Hall, to appreciate his great services, to honor his great virtues, to point out his faults, and so let the dead man warn by his failings and instruct by his great merits, and thus continue the lesson of his life, though we can directly see its practical works no more. If you thought of him, in some respects, more highly than I did, I never wished your admiration to be less. If I qualified, I did not diminish it. I think there is but one man in America who has done the nation such great service—that is Garrison; the two were much alike in their philanthropy and hatred of all oppression, in their asceticism and puritanic austerity, in their cleanness of life and readiness to sacrifice their own interests for a general good, in their steadiness of purpose and tenacity of work, and in the severity of their speech and the strength of their personal dislikes. But Garrison had more destructiveness and more courage, and also more moral directness in his modes of executing his plans. Mann did not know that " a straight line is the shortest distance between two points," in morals as in mathematics; Garrison knows no other line in abstract morals or in concrete politics. Mann had benevolence in the heroic degree. I have known none who more deeply and heartily wished for the welfare of mankind; he was also singularly enlightened as to certain modes of carrying out his philanthropy, *e.g.* towards the insane, the poor, the ignorant, and the drunken. But I think his ideas of education were not the most enlightened and comprehensive; that his estimate of woman was unphilosophic and obsolete; and his schemes of penal legislation were quite behind the foremost philanthropy of the day, especially his adhesion to the gallows.

In his intellectual composition he lacked the ideal element to an extraordinary degree, yet his mind was as rich in figures and as vivid as a New England meadow in June. Still, there was little poetry in the man; the useful left no corner for the beautiful. He loved strongly, and idealized the objects of his affection, making them quite other than they were; he also hated terribly, and never, I think, forgave a public or a private foe. His hatred idealized men downwards, and he could see no good in them, or if any, it was deformed by the evil motive he saw (or fancied that he saw), prompting and controlling it all. Like other lawyers and politicians, he judged men ungenerously, and thought their motives mean. He loved few, and liked not many. By nature he had great love of approbation, but in all his life I remember no act in which this mean passion got the better of his conscience, and bent him away from the path of right. His sense of duty was overwhelming. Bred in the worst form of Calvinism, he never quite wiped off the dreadful smooch it makes on the character—nay, he did not extract the dark colors it *bites in* to the spiritual nature of the unlucky child. Hence his low estimate of men, hence his unforgiving disposition. For if he had much justice in the abstract, he had little mercy in the concrete. In his reactionary swing from Dr. Emmon's Calvinism he went about as near Atheism as an intellectual man can go; and, as you say, under such circumstances, "that is pretty near." But his confidence in duty and philanthropy never failed him. He took phrenology for his scheme of metaphysics, and knew no psychology but physiology. This materialism was a great hindrance to him in his educational schemes. It narrowed his views of human nature. He had not great confidence in the moral, and still less in the religious instincts of mankind; so after he had broken with the substance of the popular theology, and rejected its miraculous claims to the uttermost, spurning all "revelation" and all "miracles," he yet clung to the hollow form, and used the language of theology, not as figures of speech, but as symbols of a fact. He did this because he lacked confidence in man's power to walk without that crutch. I know no politician who so hated Calvinism; none who used its language so much, or who, to the public, appeared so much the friend of the ecclesiastic theology of which it is the poison-flower. There was a certain duplicity in the man, at strange variance with the austere purity of his personal life, and the lofty elevation of his purpose. This appears in his work as Secretary of the Board of Education, as Member of Congress, and as President of Antioch College—perhaps more conspicuous in the last office. Had the little narrow, bigoted sect of Christians known his profound convictions, and the moral contempt he felt for their absurd and debasing 'heology, they would never have made him even a teacher in their sc.ool, much less its head. If he had lived he must have felt great embarrassment from this cause, to be met by yet farther duplicity. I like not his taking of bread and wine in the meeting-houses of his sect, nor his having prayers three times a-day at his table. It was an official, not a personal act, and savors of hypocrisy. It was done for example —but it was an instance of falseness to his own convictions. He would not have made a good president of a college, he was too austere; and besides, he could not shut his eyes. Still more, lads at college at once detect all insincerity in their teachers, and judge with terrible justice.

> " Him only pleasure leads and peace attends,
>   Him, only him, the shield of God defends,
>   Whose means are pure and spotless as his ends."

Mann did not know this, or knowing did not heed.
These are his great public works :—

1. He opposed intemperance, I mean drunkenness. The State had no more efficient laborer directly in this great reform. Of course he was an extremist, and went for total abstinence, and ultimately for the entire suppression of all trade in every intoxicating drink, as an article of pleasure or of diet. In 1836 he induced the Legislature to pass a law making it a crime to be drunk in public; the State had had no such law for 150 years, I think. He put the stamp of felony on the hideous vice. As a Temperance lecturer he had great power, for he appealed both to the understanding and the conscience with masterly skill.

2. He worked for the insane. I think no one, or two, or five men in the State did them such wise service as he. But of this you know much more than I.

3. He took up the common schools of Massachusetts in his arms and blessed them. Here was the great work of his life. It was a piece of heroic self-denial to take the secretaryship of the Board of Education. He gave up his profession, and 2500 or 3000 dollars a-year; he abandoned the Presidency of the Senate, and the fairest chance of political honors, for he was one of the most popular and influential men in the Legislature, to work for the public education of the people of Massachusetts fifteen hours a-day, pay his own travelling expenses, and become the butt of all the democratic politicians—Rantoul was the only Democrat in Massachusetts who cared anything for the public schools—of all the lazy schoolmasters that were unfit for their office, and of all the little miserable orthodox ministers who complained of his want of *ng-pái-et-ty* (you know how to *pronounce* that word). How he did work! how he did fight! how he licked the schoolmasters! If one of the little mosquitoes bit him, Mann thought he had never taken quite notice enough of the creature till he had smashed it to pieces with a 48-pound cannon-shot which rung throughout the land. He was the father of Normal Schools. His good work here will live; one hundred years hence three generations will have tasted its blessed influence, the last the deepest of all. His influence went to all New England, and her fair daughter States. It is not often that a man has such an opportunity to serve his kind; in our century I know none who used it better, almost none so well. Massachusetts had but one man fit for the work: he went in at the call of duty; the State is not yet wise enough to honor him for such heroism; it is alike incomprehensible to the Suffolk Bar and the Suffolk Pulpit.

4. He went to Congress at a most trying period. There was a little indirection in his mode of getting there, which I never liked. But when there he proved himself the ablest, the most high-minded and far-sighted, the most moral and statesmanlike man Massachusetts has sent there in the nineteenth century. In point of intellectual ability for the post, only J. Q. Adams was his superior—his long life of politics gave him that superiority; in all other matters I assign the palm to Mann. I did not agree with all his measures, nor accept all his principles, but I honored his integrity and reverenced his power. When Daniel Webster committed the great sin which immediately doubled his popularity in Boston with the Hunkers who had bought

him, and have now given him his post on that stone of shame in the State House Yard, whence Massachusetts will one day cast him down and break it to powder, Horace Mann exposed the wickedness of the deed: none in Congress, I think, did the work so ably. He smote the champion of slavery a blow which sent him reeling home: it was the heaviest Webster ever had. He never recovered from it.

In his public life I find no aims but the noblest of all. Of how many others can you or I say that? He had a great mind, though one of a quite peculiar structure. He was a formidable debater, with, however, the faults that are generic with lawyers. None that I have known could more skilfully expose the weakness of an opponent: of course, he did not always do justice to his opponent; he was combative to an extraordinary degree, and loved the *gaudium certaminis* like an old Goth. His great excellence was moral, not intellectual. He did love his kind; he did hate their oppressors. Philanthropy is the key-note of all his music.

As a lawyer I am told he never took a case that he did not conscientiously think he ought to win. I should be surprised if it was not true. But I don't think he was always quite scrupulous enough as to the means of achieving his end. His policy sometimes bordered on deceit.

As a relative, neighbor, husband, father, his character was admirable, perhaps spotless. Young men loved him—all the doorkeepers at Washington and the other servants of the Capitol; and old men of noble mark looked on him with admiration and esteem. I shall always place him among the noblest men of New England, and thank God I had the privilege of his acquaintance, perhaps of his esteem and friendship; and sometimes the opportunity of doing him some little favor. There are but two men living—Emerson and Garrison—whom I have in public praised so much or ranked so high. How different the three, yet how great their public services to the cause of humanity! None could comprehend the other, though each might admire. When Mann moved out of Massachusetts he left a gap none since has filled. I don't think Ohio was worthy of him, or could appreciate his worth. Yet Boston had little claim on such a soul as his. But, dear old puritanic town, with all its faults the noblest of human cities, it yet gave money for his college! The very men, I think, whose political idols he broke to fragments, and ground to powder, and trod into the mire of the street, gave him dollars for his college!

Oh, Chev. there never was such a city, and though I shall walk in it no more, and my voice never again be heard in its halls or its meeting-houses, perhaps never in its parlors, it still lives in my prayers and my songs of thanksgiving and of praise. Few men have had more delight in it for a dozen years than I; and I murmur not that it is over now and ended. God grant that some nobler man may do better what I attempted!

I sympathize with what you say of the services at the Music Hall. Emerson appeals only to the intellect, the understanding, imagination, reason; never directly to the conscience or the soul—the religious element. I love to read the deep things of the Old Testament and New Testament. They are dear to me, because dear to my fathers and precious to whole nations of men. I love the sweet words of the hymns we used to sing, though often so poorly, and for.my own part, I should as soon renounce the sermon almost as the prayer. It does not influence the dear God who loves me better than I myself, but it does elevate and cheer and comfort me. I think with great pain of the multitude who used to look up to me; in my Sundays I look in upon them as a mass, and in the sleepless hours of night creep round to all their houses, and see how they get on in their joys and sorrows of private life.

But enough of this. Love to all yours, and, I need not say, dear Chevie, to *you*.

T. P.

THE DOUBLE-HEADED FIR, COMBE VARIN.

CHAPTER XXVI.

Letters and Journal at Montreux, and other Places—Letter of Resignation—To the Progressive Friends—To others.

TO GEO. ADAMS, ESQ., BROOKLINE, MASS.

Montreux, Suisse, Sunday, Aug. 28, 1859.

MR. AND MRS. ADAMS,—DEAR FRIENDS,—Many thanks for your kind letters, which came in due time some weeks ago. As man and wife are one, I shall include you both in the same answer. Your words of sympathy were quite welcome and touching. I should have been glad to take you and your children by the hand before I went away; but the time of preparation was so brief, and my strength, both of muscle and nerve, so slight, it was hardly possible for me to bid farewell to any except those I saw every day. Here I hope I am getting better; certainly I have mended in all things save the cough, which still goes on increasing. What effect a Roman winter will have on it I know not, but will continue to hope the best and be ready for the worst.

It is Sunday now—a day. too, of singular beauty, even for this handsome region, where all the days have been fair. It rained last night, and now the air is full of sweetness. The Indian corn, the handsomest of all the bread producing plants, is now about ripe, and sends its sweet fragrance all round on every side; to me it is not only a delicious odor in itself, but it has the charm of association with my early life amid cornfields and other pleasant things of New England country life. As I sit out of doors to write, the lake before me, and mountains covered with snow just opposite, the church bells in the steeple on the mountain side, almost over my head, ring out their pleasant call for meeting. Some six hours hence they will do the same in Brookline and Boston, and all the thousand towns of New England will be musical with the call to meditation, thanksgiving, prayer, and praise.

I am glad you have found a place you like for yourself and family to pass your Sunday mornings in. King is a good fellow, with fine talents, and a brave, humane, and progressive spirit; he will continue to grow for many a year to come, and to do great service, I hope, to mankind. Few ministers have so much talent, or have been so faithful in that trying position, a pulpit. It is unfortunate that we could not at the Music Hall have some one man who would feed the thousands that turn thither so readily; who would feel responsible to the Society, and so use all the events of the day as means of instruction. But that could not be expected; the speaker feels responsible only for the special address he makes on some particular morning, and no more. . . . . I suppose some of our old friends find the services a little cold. Besides, I like the old custom of reading the Bible—the best things in it, I mean; of singing hymns; and especially do I love social prayer, when it is real, living, and deep. But, alas! when I have attended the religious meetings at the churches in New England or Old England, the prayer is almost always the worst part—a prayer without devotion, elevation, or aspiration—one that smites and offends, and makes you feel degraded by listening to it. In nine cases out of ten the minister's prayer is a hateful thing to me, and I always avoid it when I can. But when it is a real, hearty, deep, spontaneous prayer, which comes as the white lily grows in the waters of New England, then I go off cheered, and lifted up, and blessed. Dr. Channing used to say, " It would be a great thing to get rid of the long prayer in our meeting-houses." Oh, if we could get the prayer of pious genius in its place! Several who frequent the Music Hall never come in till that part of the service is ended, and I always respected the spirit of devotion which kept them away from the form of prayer, though I myself so love the spoken word. But I did not mean to preach to you a sermon, though it is Sunday.

I hope you are all happy and well. How Emma and George must have grown by this time! The elder daughters, I don't know what change of name may have happened to them before I return. I hope they will always have a character as beautiful as their faces, and that they will continue to improve in all intellectual and moral excellence. Don't fear that I forget any of my old friends. I make the tour of the Society oftener than before, and look in at all the households once so familiar. Remember me kindly to your excellent neighbors, the Goodings. Theodore will be taller than his namesake before I return. Tell Mr. Gooding I find no such pears as he used to send me last autumn, and that I was sorry not to bid him and his good-bye. With love to all yours, and from all mine, believe me, faithfully,

Your friend,

THEODORE PARKER.

TO MISS COBBE.

Montreux, August 31, 1859.

MY DEAR MISS COBBE,—Your kind note of August 24—my forty-ninth birthday—reminds me how long I have owed you a letter. But I have no great writing faculty in these days, and think it best to make what little nervous power I develope consume itself in building up my shattered body. Besides, I have so many friends in America that I *must* write to, that my strength is sometimes used up before I write my dear ones nearer at hand.

I think we should agree about war. I hate it, I deplore it, but yet see its necessity. All the great charters of humanity have been *writ in blood*, and must continue to be for some centuries. I should let the Italians fight for their liberty till the 28,000,000 were only 14,000,000, and thus resist at that dreadful cost, rather than submit to mean grand-dukes, &c., and meaner Pope, with his Antonellis and the Antonell*as*, who now sway that degraded people. But most wars in these times are got up by the ambition and wickedness of the rulers, who only *exploiter* the people's instinct of defence or of aggression. Such I could visit with the scorn of the human race.

I make no doubt you are right in determining your own course of duty. How seldom can another help us in that! Certainly you and Miss Carpenter are engaged in one of the most grand of all the philanthropics of the age. Dreadfully needed they are, too, in England; indeed, your country, like mine, is full of contradictions, which disgrace us and threaten us with future peril. Mrs. Reid's scheme seems full of promise; but it takes a deal of time to accomplish any great work of human progress. It is with man as with the geological formation of the earth. Enormous periods of time are found indispensable for what we once thought was done in six days. That mythic account (by some dreamer) in Genesis, "Let there be light," has led to much mischief, making men believe that the order of creation was by magic and by sudden violence, not by regular gradual development part after part. That silly myth that tells of the confusion of tongues at Babel, how it misrepresents the actual facts and the gradual development of all the languages of the world, and of the faculties of man, stimulated by the *nature* about him! So the notion of a miraculous revelation of religious truth perverts our efforts and turns us off from the slow, regular attempt to learn the religion God writes in the constitution of the world, and then to express it in nations comfortable, industrious, intelligent, and moral. How many thousand human experiments must go to one human success in the great departments of our progress! When the civilization you and I dream of is attained, men will find it is underlaid by thick strata, full of the organic remains of inferior civilization, each helpful to the high one, which itself is no finality, but only provisional for something more grand and glorious.

I am glad your book is finished. Your charming letter to Mrs. A. told me that and other pleasing facts; and I hope soon to see it. Mr. Sanborn's article has not reached me yet. I am quite shut out from all the English quarterlies, and know little of what takes place in the high world of thought. I am glad you got my little book. I wrote it with tears of blood in that fierce heat of Santa Cruz, and read it with fear and trembling when it reached me a fortnight ago. Please remember it is a *sick man's book*, I mean in its form. The substance, I think, is healthy. It will be more loved and hated than any book of mine; but I hope it may do good, and help guide some benighted voyager, "dim sounding on his perilous way."

When you write to the excellent Mr. Newman, please tell him I am sorry I did not see him the last time he called, for I hoped to have had some conversation with him on matters we touched before. I trust he got my little book. With thanks for your kind remembrances and wishes, believe me,

Faithfully and affectionately yours.

He started, on Sept. 3, for a little tour to Freiburg, Berne, Thun, Interlachen, &c., and returned to Montreux on the 9th.

TO MR. MANLEY.

Freiburg Canton, Freiburg, Suisse, Sept. 3, 1859.

MY DEAR JOHN R. MANLEY,—I shall soon write you a short letter resigning my connection with the dear Twenty-eighth; for I am now only a hindrance, and can never be much of a help. You want a man to be a permanent minister, *responsible to you*. It is clear that I shall preach no more, even if I (partially) recover. Love to all the friends. Step in at the corner of Milk Street sometime, please, and remember me to all the good folks there, and represented there. I don't lose my friendly affection for the dear ones I shall preach to no more. I should have had a sermon on Mann, as well as Choate, had I been there. How contemptible seem the lives of the five or six Presidents when compared with Mann's! The three great concrete evils of America are, 1, drunkenness; 2, ignorance; 3, slavery. Mann warred against all these three with all his good qualities and all of his ill. What a battle he did fight! Choate opposed no one of them; he befriended the worst of them. Yet how is he honored!

    *   *   *   *   *

Lyman leaves us in a few days for Paris, and so we lose another blessing. I am glad James Clarke is to preach for you; he is a faithful man, and never betrays his trust. I am with you every Sunday, and many a day besides. You must accept my resignation; for even after I am mended, I shall not be worth much, and your work demands a stout, well man, with no decay in his lungs. A sick minister is a sort of nuisance. We hope to go to Rome for the winter, and the Apthorps with us, and to have a good time. Tell Mr. Leighton he has done famously with my books—a deal better for the six months than I expected for the twelve. I shall make the sale of the old publish something *new*. He can use it, if he likes, to publish the little Christmas story. I am glad the fraternity do so well as to get W. P. and W. L. G. Massachusetts has not braver men, or better.

What news the papers bring us! A Frenchman said there are 200 religions in America, and but a single gravy. I don't know that any body has since added to the gravy; but it seems Rev. Henry W. Bellows, D.D., has devised a new religion, the 201st—a new Catholic religion, but yet not Roman. It is to be a Church with *authority*, *i. e.* power to command and enforce obedience in the name of God—that is what authority means in the ecclesiastic usage—is to have "mystic rites and symbols"!* What shall we call it?

    *   *   *   *   *

* Alluding to a sermon entitled "The Suspense of Faith," in which a revival of faith was made to depend partly upon a revival of liturgical and ecclesiastical observances.

Absolute ecclesiastical authority without any authoritative person to vest it in! That is certainly as original as a steam-engine would be that had immense power of steam, but was made without any material substance, and got up its force with no fire or water. Talk about a suspense of faith! Faith *in belief!* Have the civilized nations suspended faith *in man,* the actual live man of fact, or in any of his high qualities, and his powers to achieve a noble distinction here and hereafter? Have they suspended faith in *God,* manifesting Himself in nature—all its phenomena so co-ordained to use and beauty by exact law, the constant mode of operation of all material powers ; or manifesting Himself in the consciousness of the individual man and the actions of the race, the regular development of humanity, in which the animal passions are made to serve high spiritual purposes? Have they suspended faith in the noblest forms of *religion*—in love of truth, in justice, morality, philanthropy, in industry, in the performance of every natural duty to the body or the spirit, to man or God! Surely this kind of faith was never so powerful before, and it goes greatening onwards, producing men like Humboldt, like Garrison, like Mann, like Emerson, and their noble fellows of the other sex, Florence Nightingale, Miss Dix, and the rest of them. Out upon such nonsense of words! Man has no faith in HUMBUG! I mean virtuous and intelligent man. What a stupid set of men are the priests of all sects!— always afraid their special form of religion will go to the Devil! I remember —— confessing once, in the ministerial conference, that a man might be completely moral and entirely religious, and yet no *Christian!* " Then what is the use of his being a Christian ? " asked some troublesome body ; and another D.D. answered, " We must never admit that any body can be either religious or moral without being a Christian ; for if we do, we endanger our *holy faith.*" How these creatures talk about the " Christian spirit "! " Oh, he has not got the Christian spirit ! " say they against Garrison and Emerson, &c. &c. Ah, me! the priests of Memphis thought Moses had not the " Egyptian spirit," and they of Jerusalem that Jesus of Nazareth had not the " Pharisaic spirit." One day, the term " Christian spirit " will be made as contemptible as those old words now are, and the ministers will work this change. God bless you and yours!—so say I and mine.

T. P.

TO THE MEMBERS OF THE TWENTY-EIGHTH CONGREGATIONAL SOCIETY IN BOSTON.

Montreux, Sept. 12, 1859.

DEAR AND MUCH-VALUED FRIENDS,—When I wrote you a long letter from Santa Cruz, I did not quite like to say what now seems my duty to write; for I did not wish to destroy the feeble yet fondly-cherished hope that I might one day speak from your pulpit again, and renew my ministry both in your meeting-house and your homes. Though the chances of a certain partial recovery and restoration to some power of work certainly seem greater now than ever before in this present year, yet from the unanimous testimony of skilful and experienced doctors

it appears pretty plain that I shall never be able to address large
audiences, as before; perhaps never again to speak in public at all;
certainly not for years to come. Therefore it seems to me best that
the ecclesiastical and official part of my relation to you as minister
should cease immediately: the personal and friendly part, I trust, will
never end. Accordingly I now resign the great and important trust
you confided to me several years ago.

Since my illness began, you have secured for your pulpit some of the
best talent in America, and also, I think, its greatest genius. The
services of so many able men no doubt give you a greater variety
both of matter and manner of treatment than any one man could
afford, unless indeed he were a quite extraordinary person. But still,
in your public preaching, you have no man who feels such a personal
interest and responsibility towards you as would lead him to study carefully the signs of the times and the various significant events which
continually happen, and report them in sermons for your instruction.
In your private life, chequered all over with hopes and fears, joys and
sorrows—gladdened by the new-born soul, or made sad by some loved
one's departure—you have no one to perform that familiar domestic
duty which is yet a large and highly important part of the minister's
function. I need not say how often my heart yearns towards such of
you as have been in recent affliction, or has bounded to share your new
or accustomed joys.

Of late, two New England men, of extraordinary talents and conspicuous position—which each climbed up to from the humble place
they were born in—have passed off from this mortal scene, the public
taking suggestive notice of the fact; and I lamented that you had no
minister who should feel it his duty to show you and the nation the
comparative value of those two lives, so opposite and hostile in their
chief characteristics, and so differently regarded by the controlling men
of your town—the great unscrupulous advocate, whose chief aim was
by any means to win his client's cause, and the great self-denying philanthropist, whose life was bravely devoted to the highest interests of
his nation and his race, and finally given up with such characteristic
ending as a sacrifice thereto. Besides, another man has lately gone to
his reward from the scene of his philanthropic works in Boston, who
spent his life for the criminal, the drunkard, and the harlot. His function was to cleanse the unclean, to save such as were ready to perish,
and to love the unlovely; thus making the highest words of Jesus of
Nazareth his daily profession of Christianity. Though he held no
public office, sat on no platform of honor in public meetings, nor ever
shared a civic feast, he yet did more service, I think, to Boston than
all her mayors for thirty years. Now, the able and conscientious men
who only speak to you from Sunday to Sunday, will not be likely to
prepare laboriously for you a special sermon on Rufus Choate, or
Horace Mann, or John Augustus, or any public event, even of the
greatest importance; while any large-minded and generous-hearted
man who was your regular minister would feel impelled to use them,
and every signal event of the times, for the furtherance of your highest
interests. I cannot bear to think I stand between you and a service I
may never be able to perform again.

It is not easy nor pleasant to undo even the official ties which now join you and me, so closely knit and holding us so fast and pleasantly together when we have walked in steep and slippery places; but now I feel it were better, for I am only a weight which hinders your upward march. I trust you will soon find some man who will fill my place, not only in your pulpit, but also—perhaps the more difficult task—in your homes and your hearts.

Do not fear that I shall ever be idle; if I recover but partially, I have yet enough to do in which we can still, perhaps, work together as heartily as before, though without any official connection. I know you will not think I shall ever lose the gratitude and affection I have so long felt towards you. For we have wept and prayed together, have been joyful with each other, jointly sharing the deep feelings and lofty ideas of absolute religion, and attending also to its works; and the memory of this will never fade out from your consciousness or mine. Let us be thankful to the dear God for all the good the past has brought us. And now, for the future, also, may ours be the absolute trust in that Infinite Perfection which is Father and Mother to us all—the faith that prevails, the hope that endures, and the love which never fails. So hopes and prays

Your friend,
THEODORE PARKER.

When this letter arrived in Boston, and after it was read to the meeting, addresses were made by Messrs. Hope, Dudley, Sparrell, and Leighton, against accepting the proffered resignation, and the following resolutions passed without a dissenting voice :—

Resolved, That, while we rejoice in the improved health of our minister, and the prospect of his being ultimately restored to his former vigor and usefulness, we sincerely regret that he should deem it best at this time to sever his official connection with us as minister of this society.

Resolved, That, in view of his past services in our behalf, and his success in building up this free Church in the face of obstacles, which have been neither few nor small, we desire that his name shall still be connected with it, and that we may still call him our minister—conscious that such a connection will be for our good, though we miss the guidance of his counsel and the daily blessing of his presence.

Resolved, That we respectfully and affectionately decline to accept his resignation, and that our refusal be accompanied with the assurance of our continued gratitude and veneration.

TO MR. MANLEY.

Sept. 13, 1859.

Within you will find a communication which, perhaps, I ought to have made months ago, nay, in my long letter of April 19; but I could not quite do it then. It is the three events referred to in the letter which give the special occasion for what must one day come. I need not say what pain it gives me to undo even the formal tie which has held us so long, but I shall sleep better now it is done. The condition of my lungs and throat I look upon as a divine command to stop preaching, as much as if—as our fathers used to fancy such things —a voice had spoken out of the clear sky, "Thus far, O Theodore, but no further." I doubt not that it is for the best good of all that it so turns out, and accept it as other similar disappointments for the present, not joyous but grievous—yet destined to work out a far more exceeding, even an eternal weight of Glory. Let us not murmur, but turn,

"To-morrow, to fresh fields and pastures new."

I am still a member of the Twenty-eighth, and nobody will miss me from the pulpit so much as I, myself! To me it has been not only my pride and my delight—my *joy* and my *throne*—as George Herbert would have it, but also my *education*, intellectual, moral, affectional, and religious. I must find something else now, "Before I quite forsake my clay." But I have work enough to do for all the time God spares me, and new work will, no doubt, come to tempt me as before. Besides, I still keep a place in your hearts, and shall, I hope, often look into your homes again.

TO REV. J. T. SARGENT.

Montreux, Sept. 18, 1859.

It is Sunday to-day, and my thought turns homeward with even a stronger flight than on other days of the week, so I shall write a little to one of my dear old friends—"a friend, indeed," also a brother in the same ministry. It is the day when the services at the Music Hall are to begin again, I believe, and James F. Clarke is to stand where I shall stand no more, for I sent my letter of resignation some days ago, as duty and necessity compelled. But my affections will always go with the dear old friends, and on Sundays, when the Music Hall is open, I always come as a silent and unseen minister to look on the congregation, and have "sweet communion together," though we no longer "walk to the house of God in company." It is a tender bond which gets knit by years of spiritual communion—I think, not to be broken in this life. Sunday here, you know, is quite different from what it is in New England, devoted more to gaiety, and to social festivity of a harmless character. But to-day is the annual Fast all over Switzerland, and the land is as still as with us in the most quiet town in New England. I like these Swiss people; they are industrious, thrifty, economical to an extraordinary degree, intelligent and happy. I sometimes think them the happiest people in Europe—perhaps, happier than we in Massachusetts, for they are not so devoured by either a pecuniary or a political ambition.

What a condition we Unitarians are in just now! They put Hunt-ingdon in the place of Dr. Henry Ware, and he turns out to be orthodox, and, as I understand, won't go into the Unitarian pulpit at Brookline, New York, but officiates in the great orthodox Plymouth

Church hard by. Then Brother Bellows comes out with his *"Broad* (?) Church," and, while talking of the "Suspense of Faith," represents the little sect in no very pleasing light. Meantime, the *Examiner*—certainly the ablest journal in America—reports to the denomination the most revolutionary theologic opinions, and that, too, with manifest approbation thereof—witness the half-dozen articles within as many years, by Frothingham, Jun., some of Alger's, that of "Scherb on the Devil," and three on India, China, and Asiatic religions, by an orthodox missionary, now living in Middletown, Connecticut—a noble fellow, too. What is to become of us? To me it is pretty clear the progressive party will continue to go ahead in a circuitous course, for progress is never in a straight line; the regressive party will go back, describing a line with analogous curves.

It is beautiful to see the gradual development of religion in the world, especially among such a people as our own, where the government puts no yoke on men's shoulders. Little by little, men shake off the old traditionary fetters, get rid of their false ideas of man and and God, and come to clear, beautiful forms of religion. Nowhere in the world is this progress so rapid as in America, because in our Northern States the whole mass of the people is educated, and capable of appreciating the best thoughts of the highest minds. Of course, foolish things will be done and foolish words spoken, but on the whole, the good work goes on—not slowly, but surely. I am glad the Catholics have the same rights as the Protestants; if they had not, I should contend for the Catholics as I now do for the negroes. But, I think, after slavery, Catholicism is the most dangerous institution in America, and deplore the growth of its churches. I know the power of an embodied class of men, with unity of sentiment, unity of idea, and unity of aim, and when the aim, the idea, and the sentiment are what we see and know, and the men are governed by such rulers, I think there is danger. Still, it is to be met, not by bigotry and persecution, but by wisdom and philanthropy. I don't believe Catholicism thrives very well ever in a republic, but it loves the soil a despot sticks his bayonet into. Since Louis Napoleon has been on the throne of France the worst class of Catholic priests have come more and more into power. That miserable order, the Capucins, has been revived, and spreads rapidly; more that three hundred new convents have been established since the *coup d'état*; they are filled with more than thirty thousand devotees already! But, in liberally governed Switzerland, Catholicism does not increase, but falls back little by little. No Jesuits are allowed to act in the land. In a few generations we shall overcome the ignorance, stupidity, and superstition of the Irish Catholics in America, at least, in the North; but before that is done, we shall have a deal of trouble. Soon Boston will be a Catholic city, if the custom continues of business men living in the country; and we know what use a few demagogues can make of the Catholic voters. It only requires another capitalist to offer the bishop one thousand five hundred dollars if he will tell his *subjects* to vote against a special person or a special measure. All the Catholics may be expected to be on the side of slavery, fillibustering, and intemperance—I mean all in a body—their Romanism will lead them to support slavery, their

Irishism to encourage fillibustering and drunkenness. But good comes out of evil. I think the Irish Catholics, with their descendants, could not so soon be emancipated in any country as in our dear blessed land. So we need not complain, but only fall to, and do our duty—clean, educate, and emancipate " the gintleman from Carrrk "!

I wonder how it goes on with the poor, and how the Provident Association does its beneficent work? Well and wisely, I hope. I am not quite sorry the Reform School at Westborough is burnt down. The immediate loss to the State is a great one, but the ultimate loss would have been far more, for it was a *school for crime*, and must graduate villains. I wonder men don't see that they can never safely depart from the natural order which God has appointed. Boys are born in *families;* they grow up in *families ;* a few in each household, mixed with girls and with their elders. How unnatural to put five hundred or six hundred boys into one great barn, and keep them there till one-and-twenty, then to expect they would turn out well, and become natural men, after such an unnatural treatment! At the beginning, Dr. Howe, really one of the most enlightened philanthropists I ever met in America or Europe, proposed a central bureau, with a house of temporary deposit for bad boys, and that an agent should place them in families throughout the country. A quarter of the money thus spent would have done a deal of good.

I wonder if you have ever been up to the Industrial School for Girls, at Lancaster. To me that is one of the most interesting institutions in the good old State, and I should like to know how it works. If I were governor of Massachusetts, I think I should not often dine with the " Lancers," or the " Tigers," or the " Ancient and Honorable Artillery," but I should know exactly the condition of every jail and house of correction in the state, and of all the institutions for preventing crime and ignorance. If Horace Mann had been governor, I think he would have done so. But he lost his election through the jealousy of his rivals in the Republican party, I think, and so went out of the State to do good work in another, and die there, killed by excessive toil.

Yesterday I suppose Mr. Everett glorified the Webster statue in the State House. What a pity to put it there! The United States Court Room was the proper place for it, where it might be forever. Now the people will pitch it off its base, and turn it out of the yard one day, to give room, perhaps, for Samuel Adams and John Hancock.

Here, in Europe, my life is dull, and would be intolerable, if it was not introductory to renewed work on earth, or else to another existence in heaven. Here I am necessarily idle, or busy with trifles which seem only a strenuous idleness. Such is the state of my voice that I am constrained to silence, and so fail to profit by the admirable opportunity of intercourse with French, German, and Russian people, who now fill up the house. I do not complain at all of this; but think myself fortunate to be free from pain always, and now also mending.

Remember me to Barnard when you see him. He is doing one of the great Christian works of our time. I never think of it without delight and admiration. Now, dear Sargent, with many thanks for your past friendship, which is still fresh, believe me

Faithfully and truly yours, T. P.

A A 2

TO MR. W. L. GARRISON.

Montreux, Vaud, Suisse, Sept. 20, 1859.

MY DEAR MR. GARRISON,—This is the day when the Crown Prince of Russia, heir-apparent to the throne, becomes of age; and his father has wisely chosen this as the *day of freedom for the serfs* of his vast empire. It is pleasant for an emperor to have the day of his majority that also of the liberation of 22,000,000 of his subjects. It is proper I should write to YOU on this day, who have imperishably connected your name with the cause of freedom in America—a freedom, however, yet to be accomplished for 4,000,000 of our fellow-citizens. So far as I can find out, the emperor was not moved to this great act of enfranchisement either by a moral sentiment of justice and philanthropy, or by an intellectual idea, whose development required such a noble act. But 1, he wished to diminish the power of his nobles, who own all the serfs, and form an aristocracy often hostile to him, and always dangerous; 2, he feared an insurrection of the serfs themselves, who often rise against their owner, burn his houses and butcher his family, and may at any time cause him a great deal of trouble; 3, he wished to increase the revenue, and had the sense to see that a population of free, industrious men is more profitable in the tax-paying line than a horde of slaves. However, the work is far from being done; only a beginning is made as yet. The affair is one of great complication and difficulty. Many of the nobles oppose it, and throw obstacles in the way. Then there are questions of finance, questions of military recruits, questions of mortgage, and questions of pauperism to be settled. Commissioners have been appointed to examine the matter, report the facts, and tell the means for overcoming the difficulties. Some of these Commissioners have already reported; but it will be five or ten years, perhaps twenty, before the business is fully accomplished. So hard a work is it to overcome the wickedness of long centuries. But what helps the matter greatly is this: the master and slave are of the same race and nation, so, when a man is free the stigma is wiped off from him and his children for ever; while with us, alas! the Ethiopian does not change his skin, and hatred of the negro race continues and applies to the free as to the bond; the distinction is ineffaceable. So the American problem of liberation is vastly more difficult than the Russian; for when the legal chain is broke, the work of real emancipation —which is elevation to self-respect, to free individuality of soul and body—is only begun. In St. Croix the brute part of emancipation is accomplished—that is all. It is a great deal; the indispensable first step to all the rest. But it will take three or four generations, I fear, to do the spiritual part of that great work, even there.

It is painful to see how unwillingly the oppressor parts with his power to harm. In Russia—I mean certain parts of the empire in special— drunkenness has been the great curse of the common people; it is so in all northern lands, where the grape does not furnish a moderate stimulant. Some benevolent people got up temperance societies, as with us, and the vice was checked. But the liquor consumed was whisky, made out of potatoes, or out of grain raised by the great landed proprietors, who found a market close at hand in the distilleries, or often owned the distilleries themselves. These proprietors found their profits destroyed by the decrease of drunkenness. So they petition the emperor to put down the temperance societies. They tell him 1, the royal revenue will be impaired, for if men don't *drink* whisky, they won't have to pay the excise tax on it; and, 2, they themselves will be injured by not finding a market for the only produce of their lands! Such is the true spirit of an *oligarchy*—the spirit of *nobles!* I don't find the people—I mean the great mass of men in the common walks of life—doing such things. A few years ago, in a large district in Sweden, the farmers—who owned the land they tilled with their own hands—went and pulled down the distilleries which were turning potatoes and rye into all manner of mischief; others petitioned the government to make a law to enforce temperance. The spirit of oligarchy is the spirit of a clique; that of the people, in large multitudes, is a little different; and as you would trust your property, liberty, life to a jury of twelve common men, with their natural instinct of justice and humanity, rather than to a single judge, however well cultivated, so it is to the great mass of mankind, the universal jury, we must appeal for help in all great works. It was the British people, not the House of Lords or the Church, that set free 800,000 negroes in the West Indies.

I find by the *Invalide Russe*, the great Russian newspaper, that some of the nobles think their order must fall with the emancipation of the serfs, and say "If there are no serfs in Russia, then there can be no nobles!" You would think it was our Southern masters at home who were talking. But here nobody pretends the serfs are of an inferior race, that cannot be civilized, &c. I hope hereafter the Anti-Slavery Society will do honour to the 20th September, 1859, which inaugurated the emancipation of 22,000,000 men. I wish it effected it; but thank God for the beginning.

I see by the European and American papers that the African slave trade is in full career, and some say that 15,000 were imported in the last twelve months. I make no doubt that is a little exaggerated; but the fact seems certain that the slave trade is re-opened. The next step is to *legalize* the trade. That may be done by the Supreme Court of the United States any day, when a case is brought before it; or, as in the Dred Scott decision, when the matter is *non coram judice*, let the judge see fit to volunteer an opinion; or it might be done by the Congress. The Supreme Court is now ready, and perhaps has sent word to the slaveholders of the South that "*Barkis is willin'.*" So I shall not be surprised if the Court thus decides this winter; still less shall I be *sorry;* for the sooner the Court *runs its bill into the ground* the better. We must destroy that Unclean Beast; but it must do more mischief before the people will undertake to get rid of the unclean creature. Congress will not consent to the African slave trade, even if the Supreme Court take the initiative, and by judge-law attempt to control the legislation of the people. The restoration of the African slave trade will turn out a stronger anti-slavery measure than any of the great acts of the slave power since the 7th of March, 1850. A good many politicians, North and South, will be laid out stiff and cold, and stark dead, on that (democratic) plank. Let them be borne to their political burial, and may their last end be like that of John Tyler, who went down into the Old Dominion alone, and has never been since heard from until this day. The slave-breeding States must needs oppose the African slave trade, as New England and Pennsylvania oppose free importation of cloth, hardware, iron, and coal. It is the business of Massachusetts to manufacture cloth, shoes, &c.; she has the apparatus for that work. So Virginia breeds slaves; but if they can be freely imported, her occupation is gone. So she will be hostile to this wickedness. The wheels of humanity, bearing the ark of the world's welfare, often run in deep ruts that are foul with mire.

I have no news to write you from this little place, where only one newspaper comes every day to our house, while *you* sit in the whispering gallery of the world at Boston, and learn things almost before they take place, I suppose, as you read so many journals. Here, of course, the talk is about Italian affairs, and as they seem to depend on the caprice of Louis Napoleon, all the world is anxious to know what he thinks and says about them. Hence the most contradictory rumors get abroad. Spite of the the tyranny of Napoleon—which is directed by the "spirits," so the devotees thereunto declare—France seems quite prosperous in a material way: she is richer than ever before, and rapidly increasing in riches. The mass of the people there seem to care little to increase their liberty. There was no *popular* demand for the freedom of the press; not even for so much as the emperor seems just now disposed to grant. It is a curious fact that while the French have so much military courage, they have so little *civil* or *political* courage. Indeed, they are a people difficult to comprehend.

Believe me, faithfully and truly yours,

THEODORE PARKER.

TO MR. C. M. ELLIS.

Montreux, Sept. 22, 1859.

MY DEAR CHARLES,—Your welcome letter of 22nd ult. came here the 9th inst. Many thanks for it. I was glad to hear directly from your family, and learn that they are well. There has never been a day since I left home that I have not thought of your father and his dear ones. He is one of my oldest friends—none ever had one more friendly and loving. His is the last house I was ever in at home, except my own. I made my last call on him. It was your father who procured for me the invitation to settle at West Roxbury; it was he who induced others (with himself) to ask me to deliver five lectures in Boston in the autumn of 1841; he who finally led me to come to Boston and preach at the Melodeon, and he who has been a friend in need at every turn —thoughtful as a father, kind as a mother. I have not often been taxed with ingratitude. I shall never forget such kindness as his, so long continued and so uniform. Your father's house has been one of my homes at West Roxbury. When I first went there, it was the only place I ever ventured to take tea at without a formal invitation. You know how continual my visits have been there of late years. When the Curtises got me indicted by their packed jury for the "misdemeanor" of a speech, in Fanueil Hall, against kidnapping my own parishioner, and not a newspaper in Boston—the sneaky things!—dared speak out against such abominations, it gave me pleasure to secure the services of your father's son for my defence, and most handsomely were those services rendered and effectually, yet before a Court singularly mean, even in its decision, that the indictment was a bad one.

  *   *   *   *   *   *

How are the ecclesiastical affairs of New England just now? In Ireland an attempt is made to get up a revival; it succeeds as in America—*i. e.*, men, and still more, women are brought into the state of hysteria, and conduct themselves accordingly. But the newspapers of high standing oppose it. In America, even the *New York Tribune* did not dare do so, still less *Tizers* and *Couriers*. But here, either the conductors of the press are men of more character than with us, and so, on their own account, dare oppose public opinion when it is wrong; or else in the more numerous. classes of society there is a greater variety of opinion, and so the editor feels safe in developing his own individuality. Certainly the London *Times*, though as unscrupulous as the *New York Herald*, or *New York Observer* even, is yet as individual as the House of Commons itself. In England, there is an enormous body of rude men, almost wholly uneducated, superstitious and gross in their passions and manners, who, for generations to come, must be the food of revivalists and hell-fire preachers, like Spurgeon. In a certain state of society a revival is as natural as the plague or the cholera in a certain state of the air in a close-pent town. But as Europe has out-grown the plague—which once made frightful havoc in London—so one day will she and America get rid of the revival, which still commits such outrages in New York and Boston.

I wonder how the Unitarian Autumnal Convention comes on, and what they discuss, and how they do it. No sect had ever a finer opportunity to advance the religious development of a people. But they let it slide, and now they must slide with it. In 1838, the Unitarians were the controlling party of Boston; the railroads were just getting opened, and it was plain the population, the Protestant population, of the town would soon double. Young men, with no fortune but their character, would come in from the country and settle and grow rich; the Unitarians ought to have welcomed such to their churches; have provided helps for them, and secured them to the Unitarian fold. Common policy would suggest that course—not less than a refined humanity. But they did no such thing; they loved *pecunia pecuniata* not *pecunia pecunians*. They were aristocratic and exclusive in their tastes, not democratic and inclusive. So they shoved off those young country fellows, and now rejoice in their very respectable but very little congregations. The South of Boston is not in the Unitarian churches; a church of old men goes to its grave: one of young men goes to its work. The Unitarian ministers are old, not in years, but in feebleness. They graduate old—not in wisdom, but in lack of hope, in distrust of men, in fear; their School of the Prophets is an institution for the senilification of youth.

Besides, they neglected their theological duty, which clearly was to lead further on the progress of religious thought. The sect looks now like an old-fashioned Puritan meeting-house, with its tall, handsome, aspiring steeple blown off, and a little dirty thimble-shaped cupola, ten feet high, put in its place. The progressive spirit of the age, and the high philanthropy of the age, have gone elsewhere.

The great destinies of humanity are not confided to the hands of a single sect. Theological progress in America goes without leaders; its movement is democratic of the people, not oligarchic of a few scholars. The most advanced ideas are not urged in the rich and well-educated congregations, where the pews are costly, and the hands are white; it is in the great (or little) congregations of most young men and women that you must look for the instinct of progress, and the power which one day will build new churches, and fill them with pious emotion, which also will turn into great moral life. So the stone that the (anointed) builders rejected, becomes the head of the corner! So was it, so is it, so will it ever be. The great burthens of the Lord are laid on shoulders which seem quite inadequate for the work. Yet the shoulders bear up the ark, and carry it over many a red desert, and over many a Jordan all swollen with the drainage of mountains.

Remember me kindly to your wife and all the children, to your sisters also, and their dear ones, and, above all, to your father and mother, to whom I owe so much of both gratitude and love. Remember me kindly to John A. Andrew, a right noble man, whom I hope to see Chief Justice of Massachusetts one day. He has the instinct of justice in the heroic degree, and that in a judge is worth more than the capacious understanding of —— or ——.

Now accept my own best wishes for yourself, and believe me, faithfully yours.

FROM THE JOURNAL.

Sept. 25, 1859.—Sunday is always rather a sober day with me, for I think of those few sheep in the wilderness of Boston, who are probably getting scattered because they have no shepherd. Especially is the hour of their service a sad one—not exactly sad, but anxious, and I must give up the observance of it, I feel much like the mother whom the German legends tell of, that died in child-bed, and for nine weeks, every night, left her grave and came to the cradle side of the baby and wept. There is a tender little poem on that theme. I put it into English once. I leave my grave and weep at the hour of Sunday service of the Twenty-eighth. Yet I shall see them no more. The presage of the New Year's sermon turns out correct: "It is the last time, O Parkie!"

Here are some verses of Mr. Parker's unfinished translation of the German poem :—

> When a wife in child-bed dies,
>   She is restless in the tomb,
> And from slumber will arise,
>   Through weeping for her home.

At the hour of midnight dead,
From her coffin, love-beguiled,
Seeks with still and gentle tread
The cradle of her child.

Looks therein with faithful eye,
Listens to its baby-breath;
Smoothes the covering tenderly
With hand now cold in death.

Seeing it will nothing need,
Frees the mother from her weight,
And she flies away with speed
Through the churchyard gate.

TO THE REV. A. A. LIVERMORE.

Montreux, Sept. 26, 1859.

My dear Livermore,—I wonder how the world of American theology goes on: now and then I hear a little from it, never much. Some one sent me Mr. Bellows' Sermon in the *Tribune* on the Suspense of Faith; but it had so many words in it—great long ones, too—that I could not make much else out of the thing. Yet B. is a good fellow.

How our theological culture (or often only show of culture) stultifies the man! Look at the Catholic devotees in Europe, and then at the various Protestant ones. My preaching days are all ended now. Even if I live some years it must be with my mouth shut. It is now commonly painful to talk with my friends in the usual low tone of voice. Public speaking is for ever out of the question. I wonder if you have seen my letter to the Twenty-eighth Congregational Society. It makes a little volume. I asked the publisher to send you a copy. Of course it contains much you never can like, perhaps not even tolerate; but it holds the chief doctrines I have come to; and I came to them honestly and with sore toil, often. I never found fault with men for faithfully adhering to their opinions, however diverse from mine; never doubted that deepest piety and noblest morality exist in men who hold such doctrines in utter abhorrence. I have known Catholics and Jews deeply religious in the highest sense of the word, not to speak of all manner of Protestant sects. I say to all:—

"Si quid novisti rectius istis,
Candidus imperte;
Si non his utere mecum."

I have had to fight a battle, Livermore, and a terrible one, too; and I often stood (almost) alone. Of course I aimed so as to hit, and drew the bow so the arrows might go clear through, and leave a clean hole whence they passed; for it was no holiday with me, and I did not play a child's game. But I have shot no shaft in self-defence, till compelled to do it in the United States' Court; and have had no personal quarrel with man or maid. I opposed doctrines which I deemed false, and measures I thought injurious; when public persons did wicked things—kidnapped my parishioners—*e.g*, I called them by name and exposed their wicked works. Nine-tenths of my preaching has been positive; building up, not pulling down, except by implication. I have broken up wild land and ploughed also anew the old, which was foul with weeds. No doubt I have sometimes crushed down a tender, useful herb; but whenever I saw such before the coulter, I lifted my plough out of the ground and spared a whole square yard of baneful weeds for the one sweet flower they girt about with their poison; nay, after the share had passed, I felt the furrow with my hands, to reserve some little herb of grace which might have been turned over in the general stirring of the ground. No man in America since Adams and Jefferson has been so abused in public and private. But I confess to you, Livermore, I have never felt a resentful feeling against anyone which lasted from sundown till sunrise, except in two cases—atrocious cases they were, too. For a year I felt emotions I did not like towards one man; he took pains to insult me whenever we met, so I avoided him. But during that time I never spoke an ill word of him. At length I saw him in the street one day, went over and took his cold, unwilling hand, and asked tenderly after his little ones. At length he caved in; and though he has since changed neither character nor conduct, I feel different towards him, and free to criticise his acts. The other man did not trouble me a month.

This letter is too egotistic to be shown to anyone; but you and I were young together once, and so I take the liberty of an old friend with you. I don't wish others to see what I have writ. Many thanks for your kind letter last winter, and your two friendly visits to me at New York, and kindly words of farewell. Love to your wife and from mine.

Yours faithfully,
T. P.

FROM THE PROGRESSIVE FRIENDS.

To our well-beloved Friend and Fellow-Laborer in the cause of Truth and Righteousness, Theodore Parker, the Pennsylvania Yearly Meeting of Progressive Friends sendeth greeting.

As we are about to close our Seventh Annual Convocation, our hearts turn with loving tenderness to thee. We remember with gratitude how thy presence cheered us in former years, and how the words of truth that fell from thy lips were as sunlight and dew upon our hearts, enlightening our minds and quickening us to more earnest labor in the cause of humanity. We cannot deny ourselves the pleasure of sending to thee across the ocean a message of sympathy and affection; of heartfelt regret for the illness which has compelled thee to suspend thy public labors, and of hope for thy speedy and complete recovery. The earnest prayer of our hearts is, that the voice which has so often blessed us may not be long silent, but be again lifted up with new power in behalf of truth and righteousness.

Signed by direction and on behalf of the Meeting, 1st of sixth month, 1859.

JOSEPH A. DUGDALE, ⎫
ELIZABETH JACKSON, ⎬ *Clerks.*
OLIVER JOHNSON, ⎭

MR. PARKER'S REPLY.

Montreux, Switzerland, 25th of ninth month, 1859.

To the Progressive Friends in Pennsylvania—Dear Friends,— Your kindly letter of the first of sixth month, signed by your clerks, Joseph A. Dugdale, Elizabeth Jackson, and Oliver Johnson—persons well known and highly esteemed—reached me but yesterday, for it was long delayed in Paris. Let me now, from a full heart, thank you for your generous expression of such sympathy and regard. In these times, when a difference of theological opinions so often hinders all feeling of human brotherhood, your words come to me full of sweetness and encouragement. How pleasant it is to find religion without bigotry; devotion to God with no hatred of his children!

Once I intended and promised to speak also to each of the other congregations of Progressive Friends ; but now I think you will never again hear my voice in your yearly meetings ; for even if I somewhat recover my health, it seems I must hereafter address men only with the pen, and no longer also with the living word. Yet I trust I shall never fail, with what powers I have, to help forward the cause of truth and righteousness, so dear to you all.

I kept sacred the anniversary of your last meeting with devout gratitude for the opportunity I twice had of preaching before you what to me is far more dear than this earthly, mortal life, for the friendly reception my words found amongst you, and the cheering talk I had with many of you in private. The faces of the men and women I value so much came up before me and peopled the solitude of the ocean. I was, when sailing through, comparing their human loveliness with the else mere material beauty of the sea. This year I could not gather with you at the yearly meeting; yet was I present in spirit, and joined in your spoken or silent prayer for the truth which shall make all men free, and for the love that shall add its most precious blessings to all human kind.

Long may the spirit of truth and love, the spirit of religion, live in your hearts, shedding its gladness and its beauty on your daily lives, while it keeps your feet in the paths of righteousness, and strengthens your hands for every duty which God demands of you. Believe me faithfully

Your friend,
THEODORE PARKER.

TO MR. LYMAN.

Montreux, September 26, 1859.

I have not much to write to you, O most excellent Governor, but must now and then remind you that there is a large province here, in No. 10, Pension Ketterer, that requires a great deal of ruling, and which now lies wholly ungoverned and disorderly. There is no knowing (at Paris) how I behave (at Montreux). Sometimes I cough, and there is no governor to tell me, " Here is the chloroform mixture which *you are* TO TAKE ! " And when I propose some such thing like walking up to the *auberge*, to say, " It won't do ; besides, I have been there and got the wine : *le voici !* "

Baron Von Roenne, you know, is here, and he recommends a certain medicine for my throat. I must take a new pen for the name : *Struveischerobersalzbrunnenartificielmineralwasser.* *

I think, if that does not cure my throat, it will lock my jaws. Apthorp will seek for it at Vevay this blessed afternoon, and perhaps bring it home in the *Dampfschleppschifffahrtsgesellschaftgelegenheitswagen,†* and if so I shall take the *zahnbrecherische Materiel* ‡ to-morrow morning in *warmen Milch.* The said Struve lives at Dresden, and brews all sorts of *Mineralwasser* better than Nature herself produces them, and cheaper a great deal. That beats all Natur' !

Fields (Ticknor and Fields) is at Vevay ; left Boston in June. I was *stivering* along the road from Montreux, eating grapes, and heard somebody call out, " Can you tell me the way to Boston Meetin' House ? " and, behold ! there was Fields, with a great handsome beard (not equal to the Governor's, though !) and an umbrella. He had seen in the *New York Times* that I was at Montreux, and walked over to see the *crittur.* He is well and happy ; his wife with him. He wants to stay all winter, but doubts the possibility.

I have a great mind to run down to Paris and see you before you flit for Boston, but the better part of valor is discretion. Brandy only helps the cough for three or four hours at a time, producing no permanent good, I fear. Begin with February 1st, 1858, and divide the time into periods of three months up to August 1st ; there has been a continuous though irregular increase of that malady in each period, except from February 1st, 1859, to May 1st, when perhaps it ebbed, though it went up again to its former level by May 17th, when I sailed for England. This don't look very well for the next nine months, or for ultimate recovery. But I steadily gain in weight, and last Saturday went up to 158½ lbs. I have not weighed so much for twenty-nine years ! I shall overtake *you* before long, and the province will be bigger than the Governor ! ! !

---

* If Mr. Parker has the letters right, it means "Struve's chief salt-springs artificial mineral-water."
† Steamboat-Express Company's accommodation-coach.
‡ Jaw-breaking stuff.

FROM THE JOURNAL.

Sept. 27.—Towards night a little cloud gathers over Villeneuve, as I look at it from the hill below the Pension and Post-Office. It is about twice as high as the steeple top. Next comes another little cloud, and so on. They extend in regular strata when the wind does not blow much. But there is always a thin space between the strata, in which there is no cloud. Sometimes there are seven or eight strata.

Went to Vevay on market day. A large young ox, fit for a wagon, costs 80 to 100 dollars; hay, 4 francs per 100 *livres*—say 80 cents for a cwt.; cheese, 45 to 80 centimes [9 to 16 cents] a *livre;* grapes, 30 centimes [6 cents]; cauliflowers, 1 to 2 francs [19 to 38 cents] a piece; small cabbages, 15 centimes [8 cents] a piece. Tubs, baskets, &c., about a third cheaper than with us. Hardware is cheaper. Bacon sides, 40 to 45 centimes a *livre.* Potatoes about 60 to 70 centimes a bushel. All *fruit* dearer than with us—at least this year, which is bad for fruit. The country people seem honest, virtuous-looking people, but have not the quick intelligence of Yankees.

He had decided to go to Rome from Marseilles, but before setting out upon that journey he went to Mr. Desor's residence at Neuchâtel to spend the vintage season, starting on October 6, and reaching there the same evening. Professor Schönbein was there, and scientific discussions alternated with the wine-making, and the little note-book gathered up all the facts.

On the 12th he left for Marseilles, by the way of Geneva and Lyons, and sailed on the 17th. On the 19th he was at Rome, in the Hôtel de l'Angleterre, and looking about for winter lodgings.

TO MISS CAROLINE THAYER.

Montreux, October 2, 1859.

MY DEAR CAROLINE,—It is Sunday, 4 P.M., and while I know not how many are listening to R. W. E., I sit out of doors on a shawl, with my back against an English walnut tree (the nuts are all gathered; they were not many nor good this year), and my feet in the sun, and write you this. The (miserable) Italians talk of their *dolce far niente.* I find it a piece of wretchedness, which I try to be patient in bearing and suffering. However, it is not like having the rheumatism at the same time; and if I must be idle, I thank the Divine Providence that I need not endure other pains at the same time.

You wished I could have seen the Aurora, did you? So you did, and sent it in your letter. I can believe you are electrified with not only wisdom, but wit also. What a dangerous thing this same wit is thought to be! I find some one in the newspaper—I think you sent me a slip of it—charges me with it. Did you ever hear the like? He complains that I bring my " unhallowed wit into the pulpit." As he speaks only of the unhallowed, I suppose he does not object to the wit itself after it has been through that process ; but he thinks it awful as it is. Hallowed, &c., is used chiefly in the Bible, and not often there. I don't know exactly what it means, but suppose it is something very good—that it improves the thing hallowed, *i. e.* developes it after its kind, and so enhances its function. If that be what it means, then he had better not have my wit at all. For if he, the said plaintiff, has run with the footmen, and they wearied him, then how will he contend with HORSES, *i. e.* with wit mounted on a hallowing. If the little stream of my wit, when unhallowed, is too much of a sprinkle for his ecclesiastical meadow, and himself therein hay-making, then what will he do in the swelling of a whole Jordan of hallowed wit?

*   *   *   *   *   *

Had a muster at Camp Massachusetts, Concord, did you? Well, if I had been Governor of Massachusetts, her Chief Executive Officer, and Commander-in-Chief of the Forces raised and to be raised, I think I should not have suffered all that gambling and rowdying, and think I should have pitched something out of that "barn;" not the "girls"—I would have sent them home, if homes the poor creatures had—but the sordid wretches who brought them there, exploitering the woman's wretchedness. These I should have pitched into their proper place.

We have also had a deal of mustering here in Switzerland—camps in many places; for they had their full training all over the country last month. The cars and steamboats were full of the citizen soldiers. I never saw finer looking bodies of young men anywhere. No noise, no rowdyism, no drunkenness; all was decorous and orderly. Democratic Massachusetts has something yet to learn from the older Democracy of Switzerland.

Saint Matilda writes me that Miss (Doctress) Hunt has taken to preaching, and been "*handsomely* received in eighteen universities and meeting-houses in Maine." I am glad of it, and hope such a reception will do her good, and that she will go into the nineteenth much improved. I like handsome receptions for all strong-minded women, and am glad the Universalists have the good sense to see what is appropriate, and to renounce the doctrine of eternal damnation even in this world. I hope all women lecturers will hereafter have a handsome reception everywhere. Do ask Mr. Slack to get the fraternity to do their possible this winter.

I saw an admirable piece of poetry from the pen of brave old John Pierpont, entitled, "Not on the Battle-field." He never wrote, I think, an unpoetic verse ; but I should like to know if, at his age, he has fire enough yet left to sing such a song as that.

I wish I could have been present at the wedding, and done my possible to make two lovers happy. But, alas, that also is over, as well as my preaching days! Give my heartiest congratulations to the young people, and all the good wishes your auntly feelings will suggest. Of course you think the child Nattie would reconcile the father to any thing! That is because he is a boy. I remember you rejoiced at his birth. Lydia says, " Caroline thinks the smallest streamlet of boyhood is worth more than a whole Dead Sea of girls!" You know that nurses always treat boys better than girls; even in that little red pulpy lump of new-born humanity they recognize their future lord and master, and so open their treasury and bring out the gold, the frankincense and the myrrh of their instinctive homage! How true it was to nature when the Methodist minister in his pulpit told of the noble deed of some young man who saved a family from drowning, though at the peril of his own life, and then said, " God be thanked for young men!" How true it was to nature that several women cried out, "Amen! Glory to God!" " *Si natura furcâ expelles tamen usque recurrit!*"

Do tell me how E. A. Crowninshield came to die. He was doing well when I left home; riding on horseback, and getting fat. But why do they sell his books? Such a library should be given to the city, or the Historical Society. His books, almost all of them, lie off my track; they are also costly editions—a rich man's collection more than a scholar's. Besides, what have I to do with buying more books? "Thou fool, this night," &c. I will ask your kindness to look after only one work; No. 691, a Mexican MS. I will give ten dollars for it. He did not give three dollars, buying it at Guild's sale, several years ago, while some booby was talking to me, and I foolishly listened to him and not the auctioneer. It may go for much more, or it may for much less. I will give only ten dollars, but don't expect to get it. Please keep all this secret—to yourself—till the proper time. Many thanks for sending me the catalogue. Choate's library must be a fine one; if well I should pick a deal out of it, but now I shall let it slide. There is a time for buying books and a time to refrain from buying books. The latter is mine.

We shall start for Rome about the 13th or 20th. If Rome don't agree with me, I shall pull up stakes and push off for Malta, or some other place. But it is hard running away from death—go where you will he is there before you. Rome promises me more than any other place. In Egypt I should have nothing but the climate and the monuments (I have seen Sphinxes enough already, and don't like the tribe, though one in stone may be better than those of flesh and blood), and one cannot live on weather and stone alone. I have lots of out-door work to do in the fine weather, and reading for the foul. I can't talk (fortunate I am not a woman, you will say), and silence diminishes my comfort greatly. But I can read and write. I shall keep out of galleries and churches.

Tell Wendell Phillips if he bring all malefactors to his anvil, he must hammer Governor Banks, for assisting in breaking the laws at Concord. He says he is "fighting with wild beasts." He will have his hands full before he gets through with them; then there are the *tame* beasts to deal with!

Yours ever,
T. P.

TO ISAAC PARKER, LEXINGTON.

Lyons, Oct. 11, 1859.

The vintage is the most interesting part of the year to the Swiss; the most joyous also. The vines were just getting into blossom when I reached Montreux; so I have seen all the vine process from end to end. I think I told you how the plant is trained up to little stakes; now let me say a word or two on the gathering of the grapes. When they are fully ripe, men and women go to that work, each having a little tub with two handles, which would hold three half-pecks, and a crooked little knife, with which he cuts off the clusters. He throws the grapes into his tub, and when that is full, empties it into a large, tall tub, called a *brante*. A man then takes a long stick, with a punch at the end, and punches them till most of them are crushed to pieces. He then empties them (carrying the *brante* on his back), into a huge tub in a cellar that will hold thirty or forty hogsheads. There they remain twenty-four hours, if white grapes, or five or six days, if red. Here they ferment a little, and become warm; then a bare-footed man rolls up his trousers to the knees, gets in, and shovels out the contents, which are carried in tubs to the press. The press is in the cellar—is a platform of timber, six or twelve inches thick, resting on huge beams. The old-fashioned presses have posts at the end, and an enormous beam (thirty by thirty-six inches sometimes) of oak, and a wooden screw, twelve inches in diameter.* This is turned with a long lever, and, to give it the last squeeze, a rope is fastened to the end of the lever and put round a capstan. After the grape *cheese* has been pressed about twelve hours, they run up the screw and cut the pumice (called *mac*) into long strips, eighteen inches wide and four feet long (the size of the press), and leave them a foot apart; then put on the followers and give it another squeeze for twelve hours more; so it becomes pretty dry. Then it is taken off and sent to the distiller, who puts it in water for fourteen or twenty days, till it ferments, and he then makes a sort of brandy out of it. The juice of the grape as it runs from the press is caught in a tub, and then put into enormous casks, that will hold from twenty-five to a hundred hogsheads; then it ferments; then, next March, it will be drawn off into other casks and left a few months or a year, when it is put into hogsheads for sale, or into bottles. There is a great difference in the quality of the wine of different years. This year it is uncommonly excellent, and brings 50 per cent. more than the common price. The whole process, you see, is a good deal like an old-fashioned way of making cider; not a bit cleaner, only the grapes are not rotten, as the apples often were (and still are, no doubt); no *straw* is needed, and no *water* is added (!) . . . So much for the wine.

The Swiss kitchen-gardens are much like the one you and I have taken so much pains with, containing cabbages, beets, carrots, parsley, summer savoy, thyme, sage, hoarhound, white turnips and French

---

* The new presses have a great iron screw *fastened under the press;* the nut is turned with levers; the saw goes through the cheese.

turnips, celery, lettuce, onions, several kinds of marigold, sunflowers, pinks, roses, creepers, daffodils, &c. Parsnips I have not seen in Europe. I shall try and get some seeds of vegetables we don't raise at home. I send you an ear of the best Indian corn—it grew 3000 or 4000 feet above the sea, and was ripe by the middle of September; also some chestnuts—plant them in some nice place (I think they will ripen at Lexington); also some stones of red-fleshed peaches of great size. Love to yourself and your family from all of us. Remember me (and L.) to the distant children and grandchildren, also to Bowers Simonds and the other neighbors. Wife and Miss S. are well. L. weighs 146½ pounds! I do well in all but the cough, which continues still. Good-bye. Affectionately your

BROTHER THEODORE.

Love to the Clarkes.

TO HON. CHARLES SUMNER.

Desor's, Neuchâtel, Oct. 11, 1859.

Your letter of Sunday, my dear Sumner, came yesterday. So you go home. Well, you go to new work and new honor. *My* career is ended. I have resigned my ministry, and stand unrelated to the world. Yours opens afresh, and new work and new triumphs are before you. I don't complain of my lot (it gives me never a melancholy minute: the world don't need me—I have done all my possible, and must henceforth be still or die), and I thank God for you and yours. America needs *you*, never more than now. " Your voice will in New England create new soldiers." I think we shall see a triumph of the Republican party next year—it will be a step to the triumph of Republican principles one day, but not in 1860, I fear.

Banks seems to let himself slide out of popular favor in Massachusetts; but he has, in an eminent degree, the qualities which make an American politician, and will continue in public life for many years, I take it.

I hope you will take care of your health now you have got it back again. I wish you did not return till November, for I fear the excitement which must attend your going back to Boston. I would not have your friends kill you.

Some day (perhaps) I shall look over your engravings with you in Boston, and get the advantage of your criticisms. At any rate, I rejoice with you in your treasures of art. I also have many *incunabula,* though but few Elzevirs.

Italy has a world of peril before her; and spite of all the nobleness shown by the Piedmontese, Tuscans, &c., I have little hope and much fear for her future. I think she will dwindle from age to age, and die out at length ; but I am now to see with my own eyes. Don't fear for me at Rome, for (1) I have been there before, in 1843-4, and know the place ; (2) I am forty-nine years old, and know enough to keep out of dangers. The excitement will not be excessive. I mean to live out of doors all the fine weather, to study the geology, botany, architecture, and antiquities of the place, often making excursions into the Contorni, for I want to see the people. I shall keep out of galleries, especially out of catacombs, even out of churches. Yet St. Peter's is always warm, and safe too. I shall find books for rainy days and winter nights. I shall get summer apartments, and be sure of them, and also of fire. I mean to do lots of Italian reading, though it is rather thin and poor, I think. In January, Desor, the kind and wise man, will come to Rome, and we (he and I) shall go to Naples and the South of Italy for a month. So I think I have a pretty good programme for the winter. Then, in the spring, we will come north to South and Central Germany, and go up to Scandinavia, perhaps, and get home in August or the beginning of September, if I do not leave my bones somewhere here before that time. Now, good-bye, and God bless you!

Yours ever,

T. P.

CHAPTER XXVII.

Arrival at Rome—Letters to Joseph Lyman, J. R. Manley, Dr. Howe, Miss Cobbe, Hon. Gerritt Smith—Journal.

AT Rome, on the 23rd, they took possession of rooms, which he describes in the next letter, at No. 16, Via delle Quattro Fontane. He very soon began to explore the topography of Rome and the contents of the book-stores, and surrounded himself with books and maps to study the ancient and mediæval history of the city. These pursuits were too enticing, the scenes and associations too absorbing ; every monument, church, procession, fête-day, stimulated his favorite ideas. He was too eager to make the most of his wintering in the great city, and his body was taxed too much for the soul.

TO MR. LYMAN.

Hôtel de l'Angleterre, Rome, October 21, 1859.

Here we are, O Governor, in "the Eternal City," and on the look-out for winter lodgings. The first letter must be to you, and I trust it will reach you in your quiet home. "Again he bringeth them to their desired haven," said a sea-captain, "is one of the most blessed words in the Bible, Old Testament, or New Testament." At Marseilles, up to half-past 7 o'clock P.M. Monday, there was no letter from you, and none possible till half-past 9 o'clock next day. I found none at Rome, but others from Boston up to 28th ult. So I suppose you have steamed off for America. We had a delightful time in the *Pausilippe* from Marseilles to Civita Vecchia—weather perfect, sea smooth, ship excellent. We reached Civita Vecchia between 7 and 8 o'clock Wednesday, and after many little delays at Custom-house, &c., got to the hotel at Rome about 4 o'clock P.M. ; stowed away the ladies as well as we could, and A. and myself set off to hunt up apartments. . . . So far had I got, O Governor, when something put an end to writing. It is now Saturday, Oct. 22nd, and we have found an *appartamento* at No. 16, Via delle Quattro Fontane, *quattro piano*—that means fourth story —120 stairs from the ground; but the four flights are all easy, 30 steps in each, the *risers* being less the higher you go up. We have four rooms, all finely furnished with all manner of needful conveniences. So it seems *now* at least. We pay 48 scudi (48 dollars, and a little more) a month for them. The price is high, but I found no rooms which pleased me so much. (1.) The situation is lofty, the best in Rome, with a fine view of the whole city from the various windows, so the air is good, dry, free from all damp. (2.) We have abundance of sunlight; the street runs a little south of due east and west. The sun comes into our east windows at rising, and into the south windows about half-past nine o'clock in the shortest days, and stays till it goes down. So you see we have the sun all the time he is worth looking at. (3.) The rooms and furniture are of a high grade with respect to neatness and comfort. (4.) The A.'s and H.'s are under the same roof with us, in the third story, so if I should become very sick, there is help close at hand; and company for my wife at any rate. All the (material) elements look auspicious.

  *   *   *   *   *   *

Considering that I am an *invalide misérable* (was not that the title you used to put after my name in the hotel books?) and *must* have sunlight at all costs, I think I am not very extravagant.

  *   *   *   *   *   *

The weather is rainy, and is likely to continue so for some weeks, I fancy, for it is the rainy season (Oct. 15 to Nov. 10 or 15), and it has been a very dry, cold summer and autumn; hence more rain than usual is looked for. I should be glad to escape the damp, my worst enemy, but could not. The rain had begun in Switzerland, and doubtless will continue a month. How can a body run away from the rain when "it raineth everywhere"? I hope something from the climate of Rome, and quite as much from the entertainment it will offer, in a cheap, healthy, and not exciting fashion. I shall keep out of churches, and not go into any catacomb, until my friends lay me in one. I am running away from an American catacomb, and don't incline to a Roman. Theatres I shall leave to the rest of mankind, but shall live out of doors as much as possible in fine weather; and we keep housed when it is so wet as to make me cough. I find one thing cheap in Rome, viz. Italian books, and especially the binding thereof; but book-buying is behind me, and I shall only indulge in what is indispensable for my well-being here this season. No English seem likely to come here this winter; they seem thoroughly frightened. But Americans will be pretty plenty, judging from rumor. I shall not write many letters, I fear; partly because I don't like stooping over a desk to write, and partly for the cost of postage.

So far had I written, O Governor, when again something stopped the pen; now it is Tuesday, 25th, and we are fixed in our new home. And a fine situation it is, on almost the highest ground in Rome, with the whole city before us; under our feet, a magnificent prospect in each direction. The Pope's Quirinal Palace is close to us; his gardens lie between. The Pincian is on the other side, with its fine gardens and magnificent trees. Story lives in the Palazzo Barberini, just behind us. St. Peter's is in full sight. From the top of the Pincian, a street, wide and handsome, runs pretty straight to the Porta della Croce and Porta Maggiore, for it forks so as to reach both; this is called in different parts Via Sistina, Via Felice, Via delle Quattro Fontane, Via di San Eusebio, and Via di Croce. (I believe the Porta Croce does not exist, or is walled up.)

The rooms are fourteen or fifteen feet high; the windows seven or eight feet wide, and proportionally high. Nos. 1, 2, 3 and 4, are carpeted; the furniture is good *for Italy*. Of course, New England comfort and New England cleanliness are not to be expected. Our dinner is sent us from a *trattoria*, and costs one dollar for us all, and leaves us a bit of cold meat, &c., for breakfast. We shall have hot water from the landlord, who also attends to the service of the chambers, and make our own breakfast. All kinds of wine, including Malaga, are abundant, and not dear. Brandy, and gin, and whiskey, are common in the shops. So you see I need not go dry (and I don't mean to). We have laid in our little stock of groceries; the tea you bought in Paris will work after its kind, and a little you gave me also of the *flowers of tea* is still left and fragrant as ever. The A.'s are moving in to-day, one story below us. I thought it important that we should all be under the same roof; first, because my wife wants their company in the evening, and they hers; second, I may get sick and end my days here, in which case it would be highly important to have such friendly help at hand by night and day. But don't fear for *me*. I have no intention of leaving my bones in this Roman earth, which is twice cursed, politically and ecclesiastically.

I have for years been looking for a certain book by Nieuwendt (a Dutchman) on the Existence of God, and have often got scent of it. I wanted to read it before publishing my own sermons (1857) on that theme. To-day I found it in a stall, and bought it (a large handsome quarto) for 50 cents! If I were a heathen, I should look on this as an auspicious omen (*quod felix, faustum fortunatum sit*), that I should live to finish my book.* If so, I will ask no more; yet, if not, will still give God thanks for a life singularly rich in blessed experiences and sweet and long enduring friendships, among which let me number yours as one of the dearest. By this time I suppose you are "half-seas over." Good luck to you!

> " Sic te diva potens Cypri,
> Sic fratres Helenæ, lucida sidera,
> Ventorumque regat pater,
> Obstrictis aliis præter *Brittanicarum*
> Navis quæ tibi creditum
> Debes *Lymanium*, finibus *Americis*,
> Reddas incolumem, precor,
> Et serves animum dimidium meæ.†

What is Paris with its civilization to the *Placens uxor?*

* On the Development of Religion.
† Hor. Car., Lib. I. 3. Ad Virgilium.

Please tell Mr. Manley to present my letter of resignation to the parish; it must be done—sooner the better. Love to you and yours from me and mine.

TO MR. MANLEY.

October 25 : at night.

All looks quite prosperous and promising just now ; I think really I shall be better off in Rome than in Egypt. Why should I go to Egyptian darkness, " which might be felt "! That of Boston is thick enough and palpable ; surely you don't want me to go among the "plagues of Egypt"! I fear they are worse now than of old, for the plague of fleas is added to the plague of lice, not to speak of bakksheesh. I have seen so many strong-minded women in my life, that I think I shall let the Sphinx slide. I can do without her. Rome will not be very exciting, not more so than Newton Corner to me, but yet instructive. I can find enough to occupy my mind (and body) without thinking about myself. I shall be very careful, for I know that I am on a bad shore, and can only get off by availing myself of every little flaw of wind. Depend upon it I shall use all the little helps in my power, as well as the great ones. After all, if it turns out as we do *not* wish, it is only another step upward and onward. I should like to take it at eighty or ninety, but will not find fault if told to " move on " at fifty or forty-nine and a half even. I mended a great deal in Switzerland, and left it much better than I went in. Half of my improvement there I must thank Professor Desor for. I stayed more than five weeks with him, and got such a bodily vigor from him as will last me a long time. I am doing well now, here in Rome, though the weather has been rainy all the time since we came (19th inst.) ; to-day it has cleared up, and looks like fine weather, but I expect a fortnight of wet. It is the time for rain now.

I hope you will give my letter of resignation to the Twenty-eighth at once, if you have not already. A sick minister is a curse hanging on to the necks of his friends. It will torment me greatly to be in that condition, and retard my recovery. I know the kindness of your manly heart, and that of many more men, and women too. But let me not " crowd the mourners." The 1000 dollars already got, I suppose, " must go where it is sent " ; but I trust the Society will do no more for me in that way. I live so economically that I need no more in Europe ; that I am sure of, and when I come home I have enough for reasonable comfort. So do let me not hinder the Society I would so gladly help. Lyman will tell you all about me, dear, good soul that he is. No sister could be more tender and affectionate. He thinks I ought to resign ; so they all think here. Don't let your love for me blind your just eyes.

Wednesday Morning, half-past 7.   Oct. 26.

I have, my dear Mr. Manley, a little more paper left, and wish to add a word or two more. The weather seems fixed and settled, thermometer at seven o'clock, in the shade, 58°. The windows dripped this morning with congealed moisture. I have felt no such cold since last February except as we came near the coast of England in May. I don't know how the first frost will affect my cough, but hope for the best. Enough about myself. I scattered the copies of my letter (which reached me at Montreux) among my friends, and hear pleasant tidings from them. Some of the ministers in Switzerland are not quite so unwilling to pray for my restoration as poor Mr. —— and Mr. Broadchurch. I think I told you that Mr. Küchler, a noble fellow, stayed at Desor's, and died of apoplexy the day he left us. I wrote his wife a consoling letter, and she wrote back to Desor, how much comfort she found in my sermon " Of Immortal Life," which long ago was translated into German. It gave me great pleasure to find that I could cheer and comfort a widow in her loneliness in Germany, though I can no longer stand in a pulpit in Boston. My life has been singularly rich in work; few men at eighty have had so much of the highest kind of delight, and I certainly do not complain that at fifty I must come down to a lower platform, and content myself with an inferior kind of happiness. God be thanked for the past, and for the present also!

Tell me how Hepworth preached. I hope much good from this brave young man. What did Mr. Noyes accomplish in his sermon? I don't see who is to fill your pulpit, that can also fill the house, except Emerson and Phillips; but doubtless the right person is waiting somewhere. Certainly you have genius for the office you have held in the Twenty-eighth, and without you, it seems as if it must have come to nought long since. I think it will be more difficult to fill your place than mine. Remember me kindly to your household, the Sparrells, and all the Saints. Please stop at Mrs. Vinton's sometime when you go by, and remember me to her—also to Mr. Thaxter, the optician, near the Old South. Do you ever see Samuel Downer? I shall write him by-and-bye : he is a noble fellow. Now, good-bye and God bless you!

Faithfully yours,

T. P.

The Midsummer Sermon gave me as much pleasure to read as to preach almost. Really I liked it in print, as I do not often anything of mine. Did it sell at all? There are some errors of the press, that I will send a list of to Mr. Leighton. Everett's Webster oration. . . . But what he tells about the *red line* on Oswald's map shows how foolish it was in Webster to make such a treaty. I mentioned the fact in the last edition of my sermon on Webster (Additional Sermons, &c.), though I knew it well enough before. Everett adds some important details, which glorify himself, but damage Webster's reputation as a diplomatist.

TO MR. G. RIPLEY.

Rome, Oct. 29, 1859.

MY DEAR GEORGE,—Here I am at Rome, once more living in my " own hired house," that is, in a suite of rooms 120 steps from the ground-floor, and enjoying the prospect of all Rome. I am in the ancient Regio Alta Semita on the Esquiline Hill : the Pope's Palace of the Esquiline is just before me : his gardens come close to my house.

St. Peter's, also, is before me in full view, and the Etruscan Hills beyond it. "Rome was not built in a day." You would assent to this if you were to walk about in it, and see how old and how various the things in it appear to be. It was a queer place to build a city in: the soil about it is not fertile in corn, wine, oil, or even figs, and never was; the *flavem Tiberim* has an ugly trick of overflowing its banks (it does not fall more than a foot in a mile between Rome and the sea) and filling up the low swampy tracts beween the hills, and making the place unhealthy; the water was not good nor abundant; (here and there was a little spring, like that where Numa consulted the nymph Egeria.) The Romans even now know little of the art of making wells. The place had none of the natural advantages which mark out the situation of New York, Philadelphia, Baltimore, Cincinnati, Boston, &c. It is a queer place now: 175,000 inhabitants; 4900 priests, and 1900 nuns. Lots of churches, where the priests are " propitiating God," *soli cum solo*, for the people don't come in to see how the work is done. What a heathenish place it is! Hardly was it more so in the times of Augustus Cæsar. The Roman religion is addressed only to the senses, and must, ere long, go the same road as the Egyptian religion, and its successors. Protestantism will in due time follow, it being a little less absurd than Catholicism. Thus the tree of religion drops its leaves continually after they have done their work, and itself grows greater and greater by the help of each one of them. I wonder ministers don't see that Christianity is one leaf in this immense tree, and must fall when its work is done. But they don't and won't. But the men of science and philosophy throughout Europe have utterly broken with the first principles of what is historically called Christianity, *i. e.* the supernatural revelation, the incarnation of God in a virgin's womb, the atonement, the eternal damnation of mankind (all except a few miserable creatures), the devilish character of the Deity. These are the essentials of the "revealed religion" of the Christianity of the Church, and they will go to their own place. *Nihil saltatim, omne gradatim* is the rule of the world. How slow all things go on! The solidarity of earth and man extends even to their history—the same enormous periods are necessary in one as the other.

Et quæ fuit tibi Romam causa videndi ?

you will ask me. I have my fears of Ægypt, where the doctors sent me; it is a dull place; objects of interest few and far between. I have some pictures of the Pyramids, which, it is said, look very much like the originals.

*   *   *   *   *   *

Here I am booked for six months—if I live so long—having paid my board for that time. I have a deal of work to do, as follows :— (1,) to study the geology of Rome; (2,) its flora and fauna; (3,) its archæology: (4,) its architecture. I have begun already, though I have been here but a few days. This work will keep me out of doors all the pleasant weather, and turn my mind off from myself, one of the most disagreeable subjects of contemplation. I can't attend much to the fine arts, painting and sculpture, which require a man to be in doors. And, by the way, the fine arts do not interest me so much as the coarse arts which feed, clothe, house, and comfort a people. I should rather be such a great man as Franklin than a Michael Angelo; nay, if I had a son, I should rather see him a great mechanic, who organized use, like the late George Stephenson in England, than a great painter like Rubens, who only copied beauty. In short, I take more interest in a cattle-show than in a picture-show, and feel more sympathy with the Pope's bull than his *bullum.* Men talk to me about the "absence of art" in America (you remember the stuff which Margaret Fuller used to twaddle forth on that theme, and what transcendental nonsense got delivered from gawky girls and long-haired young men); I tell them we have cattle-shows, and mechanics' fairs, and ploughs and harrows, and saw-mills; sowing machines, and reaping machines; thrashing machines, planing machines, &c. There is not a saw-mill in Rome; I doubt if there is in the Pontifical States. All the timber is sawed by hand. Mr. Topsawyer stands on the log, Mr. Pitsawyer stands underneath; all the stone they veneer their houses with, is sawed by hand! At the revival of letters the Italian people turned to the arts of beauty, the Teutonic people to science and the arts of use. What an odds between the Italians in 1450 and the English! What a different odds to-day! I love beauty—beauty in nature, in art, in the dear face of man and woman; but when a nation runs after beauty to the neglect of use—alas! for that people. The assembly of Roman cardinals, in full costume, all of those "educated men," all riding to council in great red coaches, and with their big-calved servants, is a grand sight; while the Senate of Massachusetts, shoemakers, farmers, storekeepers, lawyers, knowing small Latin and less Greek, walking through the crooked streets of Boston as they go to council, has a rough look. But which has the spirit of legislation?

It is a curious fact in history, that the Germans set up the great printing presses in Italy in the fifteenth century in all the chief towns; to-day the best book-store in Rome, even for Italian books, is kept by a German. It is he who sells Cardinal Maï's publications, even his "Codex Vat." The history of Rome is writ by Gibbon, Niebuhr, Arnold, Mommsen, not by Italians. It is a German who tells the Italians what language was spoken here before "Romulus and Remus had been suckled." Even the Latin classics, Lucretius, Ennius, Virgilius, Horatius, Cicero, Quinctilian, must be edited by Germans, not Italians. I think no good edition of any Latin author has been published in Italy for a hundred years. Livy is best edited by a German, so is Pliny. Orelli, who made the famous edition of Cicero, is a Swiss; though the name sounds Italian, it is not so at all. Rome is the head-quarters of priests; they have little to do, yet they don't edit even the fathers of their Latin Church. *Fruges consumere nati;* they are as useless as a ghost—I wish as harmless. The best thing I hear of them is that they don't keep their unnatural vows! Yet they are a fine-looking body of men: they alone of all Rome look clean.

The Italian women are generally handsome. In America, as in France, Germany, and Switzerland, the homely women are in the majority, and of course have things their own way; here they are in a small minority. The Lord be praised for all his mercies!

Do you want to know something about the undersigned? Well, I can walk four, five, six, or seven hours a-day without fatigue; have a good appetite, good digestion, good spirits. I weighed yesterday 200 pounds; alas! they were only Roman pounds, and make but 150 by the New England steelyards. I have been above that, and am sinking down a little just now. Running from Death is poor business—he gets there before you. I may recover and dawdle a few more years on earth, and finish some of my many books; I may not. Either way I am content. Few men have had a life so rich as mine in work and the results of work; perhaps none will leave it with a more perfect trust in the infinite perfection of the Cause of all.

Do you know the stories I tell about you, what new myths? I hope I shall get home to tell them at Brace's, or somewhere else, you being present! It would astonish you to know what a great man you are! I trust you attend meeting every Sunday, and listen devoutly to the Rev. S——. Dr. Pierce said of him, "If he ain't a v-e-r-r-y great man, he's v-e-r-r-y greatly mistaken." I trust you believe in him "and all his works."

Remember me to the virtuous Republicans—both genders of them —to Hildreth and Dana—to Brace if you see him, and believe me,

Yours faithfully,

T. P.

TO MR. MANLEY.

Rome, St. Guy Fawkes' Day (5th Nov.), 1859.

My dear John Manley,—Yesterday I went into the Church of St. Carlo (Carlo *Borromaeo*, you know), and saw the Pope, a kind-looking, fat-headed old man. There were some sixty Cardinals (in full toggery), and lots of Bishops, Archbishops, and Senators in the church. Eight men toted the old Pope round in the great chair, while he held up his right hand to bless the people. Mass was said by some high functionary, and the Pope sat in a great chair, where many of the dignitaries came up to kiss his hand—he holding it under his robe—so it was only the old clothes they kissed. I think that would not quite content a youthful lover. The Pope rode in a splendid state coach, drawn by six horses (I had the honor of talking with his coachman), followed by one or two other empty state coaches, to give additional dignity to His Holiness. Cardinals and others had elegant carriages, several to one person sometimes—with three footmen to each. Antonelli's coach is a quite plain one. But the significant part of the thing is this: there were 2000 French soldiers in the street, and a battalion of Italian horse; and besides, in the church the Pope's Swiss Guard and about 200 Italian soldiers—all fully armed, with bayonets fixed. This was to make it safe for "the Father of the People" to come and bless "his children"! That is a comment on the Roman Question! I walked about in the street, after I had seen enough of the tomfoolery in the church, looked at the carriages, talked with the soldiers, &c.; and then went to other business. Afterwards I saw the whole boodle of them go off. It really was a grand show. The Roman religion is nothing but a show; the Pope is a puppet, his life a ceremony; only his taking snuff is real, and he does that "after the worst kind," as the Yankees say; I mean, to the fullest extent. Get converted to Romanism at Rome! One must be a fool to think of it. I should as soon go over to the worship of "Osiris, Orus, Apis, Isis," after looking at the mummies of Thebes, as accept Romanism after seeing Rome.

I could never quite take in the consciousness of men, who in Berlin or Boston became Atheists, or thought they became such. Here, I can understand the cause, process, and result; and am not at all surprised to be told there are more Atheists in Rome than in any other city. Alas! how ungrateful the world is! there is no church here consecrated to Guy Fawkes! It is a great omission. I fear none of the Roman girls and boys are reminded of his great services. You and I know better:—

"Don't you remember the Fifth of November?
The gunpowder treason and plot?
For I see no reason, why gunpowder treason
Should ever be forgot!"

So I write you this on his day. I think his name ought to be added to the list of worthies whom the (New England) kidnappers address in their prayers. "St. Guy Fawkes, pray for us!" would sound well at the opening of the court, of which (so W. P. says) Ben Hallett represents the religion!

It is now Thursday, November 10th, and I have just got your welcome favor of the 18th–19th, ult., with its three enclosures: thanks for them all. I suppose the Twenty-eighth did right in declining my resignation. If they had been I, they would have resigned as I did, for I feared I might embarrass them in their action. But let it be as they will, only they must pay me no more money. I was always economical and thrifty, never avaricious; now I live at the world's cost, I am bound to live as cheap as I can. I would help if I could. God forbid that I should hinder my best friends! I shall take all possible pains to get well, and here there is much to help me, and all of life or strength I have, or hope to have, is at the service of the Twenty-eighth. I neither can nor wish to do better than to help them. I have no ambition but to "help the cause along."

I read J. F. C.'s sermon and paper in the *Unitarian Quarterly*. He is a dear good soul, and I thank him heartily for all the kind things he says about me. He cannot get rid of his old theology, nor I of my *new*. But his does not hinder him in any good word or work.

*　　*　　*　　*　　*

Hepworth is a fine fellow, I have great hope of him He is strong and good, with his face set in the right direction. Do not you see that the Unitarians are making a revolution forwards? Think of the character of the *Examiner*, of our "excellent quarterly journal," as Father Briggs used to call it, of the *Register*; think of Hedge as President of the Association, ... and J. F. C. as its Secretary, to manipulate all the churches! Clarke's Christ is not a *dead* Christ, but the actual live one who thunders in Matthew xxv., and has also the blessed beatitudes. The signs of the Unitarian times are decidedly hopeful.

*   *   *   *   *

A. D. Mayo is a fine fellow. I know him well. His quality is admirable; he wants bulk—that is all. His metal is nice and fine, and he is faithful entirely, I think.

How famously the Fraternity goes on. The extracts from R. Leighton's poem made me think highly of it; he has true poetry in him, and has proved it before. I am glad the Fraternity will print it. What a brilliant affair was Wendell's oration! but too full of detraction. It must have been delicious to hear it. What a genius he has for "fighting with wild beasts"! Sam Johnson's sermon came in the same *Liberator*. Johnson has genius, but not practical sense to make a leader. He is nice and fine, an admirable scholar, and as unselfish as it is possible for man to be. But it takes a deal of stuff to make a great minister.

*   *   *   *   *

I took cold on arrival at Rome—who could help it with such a rain? —had a bad cough, sleepless nights, and other disagreeable symptoms, and obviously was sliding downhill; now things are mending again, the cough is abating, appetite good again, and sleep reasonable for a man who does nothing. The weather has been fine for two or three days past; like our best in the beginning of September; to-day they call it *winter*, and say there will be few days cooler this winter. At half-past eight A.M., the thermometer was 58°, now, at five P.M., in the wind where the sun has not shown since twelve, I can't coax it below 67°. For about a fortnight in January, the water freezes in the mountains a little. Oranges ripen in the open air, and are fit for the table about January or February; and even the aloes (*Agave Mexicana*) and palm-trees grow here freely. You may judge the temperature by the vegetation. The air is just now damper than I like, but Dr. Appleton has been here seven or eight years with his wife, a consumptive woman, you know; and he says Rome is just the place for me! He has just returned from Naples, and already has kindly done me many favors, and offers more. Story came here years ago for the consumption, and is now alive and hearty, full of kindly offices and noble sculpture. All these, and many more speak well of Rome as a winter residence for a consumptive man; of course, I don't know how it may turn out, but have done the best I could in the choice of winter quarters, and shall do my best in trying to get well. Please tell Mr. Leighton, I think he does just right, about the tract and the Christmas story. I meant the latter should be for 1856, not 1859. Remember me kindly to the fraternity, and all the *saints*. I rejoice in your wife's continued health and beautiful cheerfulness, which her husband so helps. Miss Cushman, the Westons, Miss Hosmer, and Miss Stebbins, all are here and all friendly.

Good bye !

T. P.

Rome, Forefather's Day, 1859.

My dear John Manley,—I put the above date at the head of this letter, but I shall not finish it till Saturday, for we have only one mail a-week which connects with America. Your envelope of November 16th did not reach me till December 16th, though Mr. Jackson's of 22nd November came on the 10th instant: the *Traveller* of November 29th, the *Atlas* and *Bee* of 28th, came to-day with quite different reports of Wheelock's sermon at the Music Hall, on the 27th. Both make it out a brave discourse. How good it is! I enclose a letter to him which you may read if you have a mind to, and then please enclose it to him. We all read it with great delight. It is a dear good country, that New England! and a dear good old place is Boston too—that nest of kidnappers!

*   *   *   *   *   *

But good old Boston has the habit of thinking things over a second time, and a third time, and is pretty sure to settle down right at the last. Think of Rev. Manning and Rev. Neale on the same platform with Emerson and Phillips, to thank God for John Brown, and raise money for his family! Why, the spirit of "'76" has got back to the Old South! I know, of course, what must have been said by the ——'s and ——'s.

*   *   *   *   *   *

Long before this all the John Brown affair is over; the actors in that great drama hanged, and their bones buried. But the end is not yet. What a Session of Congress we are to have; what a presidential election! I hope that Seward will be the candidate, and the Republicans will not make fools of themselves any longer. But I fear for their half-way men, who have no principle, and want office instead. Seward seems to me the ablest statesman in America; and as honest as any man likely to be nominated. Certainly, his course as a whole has been highly honorable to him, consistent, and progressively hostile to Slavery. In 1850 he showed there was a law higher than the Fugitive Slave Bill in the Constitution; and in 1858 declared there was an "irrepressible conflict" between Freedom and Slavery. His party were ashamed of both these self-evident truths when he uttered them, and his enemies mocked (you heard the Curtis-Hallett troop in Fanueil Hall scoff at the higher law); but the sober thoughtful men of the North welcomed both of his brave words, and I hope will duly honor each.

Rome is an ugly old place; the weather for nine or ten weeks beats anything I ever knew in New England for badness. There are few foreigners in Rome, only 4000 names on the police books, up to December 1st, while there were 10,000 last year. In the present month more have gone away than have come hither. Strangers are afraid of tumults and revolution. No doubt the people hate Papal Government badly enough; but I think 10,000 soldiers will keep the cowardly city quiet.

It is funny to read the speeches of the gentlemen at Cork, sympathizing with His Holiness the Pope. Of course they have not a word of sympathy for the people whom the Pope has *sot* on these many centuries. The Irishman is always a Paddy. He loves tyrants in Europe; in America is ever on the side of rum, ignorance, and Slavery; a wretched race of people for us to import and breed from in America. But in Ireland they send the Pope not a single copper penny of help, only *blarney*, which he has enough of at home, poor old chough! One of the Irish speakers said the Pope " did not need any matar-rial help, for he had already the intercession of the Saints—all of them—and the pr-romis made to St. Pater " ! Much good may they do him ! I should like to see him scare up a cent on the London Exchange on that security. The " pr-romis to Pater " would be excellent collateral with the Rothschilds and the Barings !

The Roman robbers made a false move here, a little while ago; they began at the wrong end, and robbed Antonelli's brother and one of the high French functionaries. The consequence was the police waited upon one of the *boss* thieves and told him the property must come back or " there would be the Pope to pay." So the money was restored, but 300 or 400 miserable creatures have been haled off to prison, where it is easier to get in than out. There is much distress on account of the absence of strangers, and the evil falls on cab-drivers, keepers of public-houses, on men who rent apartments (some of the latter are honest!) and servants in general. One other class suffers—the beggars; (I never saw an Italian give a *baiocco* to one of them)!

I told you, I think, that Miss Cushman was quite kind and attentive to me and mine ; and that Dr. Appleton took me under his special care, and watches over me very tenderly. The Brownings—poetess and poet both, and little boy besides—are here. I like them much, and hope a good deal of pleasure from their society. The Storys I see often ; full of kindness and hospitality, as also of fun and wit. I am greatly indebted to him and her. Rev. C. T. Thayer and wife are here for the winter ; kind and friendly, both of them, as they always were. I was much surprised when he walked into my room the other day. All the Americans that I have seen sympathize with Capt. Brown and his movement ! Of course this would not include the minister Stockton—a New Jersey Democrat. He gives a dinner-party to-night, but I don't attend such places, for I am not here to dine out, but to get well (if I can), as I neglect nothing that looks that way.

                                                                    T. P.

TO THE MISSES GODDARD.

                                        Rome, Saturday, November 26, 1859.

My dear Rebecca and Matilda,—So the long-suffering mother went to keep her thanksgiving in the kingdom of heaven ! Well, it was a blessed relief from the pain and torment of the much-enduring flesh. Strange that a frame so slight should hold out so long in such a storm ! But so it was; and as you say, it was doubtless all right. So we must trust. It is all over now, the voyage ended, the soul secure in its new harbor. How curious it is! Such are not lost to us, but gone before!

> " The saints on earth and those above
>   But one communion make;
> All join in God, the causal love,
>   And of His life partake."

Their memory sweetens the earth, while their actual presence is in their own heaven, unapproached and unapproachable, save to immortal feet. When I left home I knew too well that I should never see her again; it was highly doubtful that I should set my eyes on her children. But I hoped for her a quiet discharge from the warfare of life, and did not dream that so gentle a bird must take flight in such a dreadful winter. I am glad you will not hide your faces in hideous black; I hate the mourning of dress. It is to sorrow what flogging in school is to correction. Still let such wear it as like; it is *fashionable*, and the genius of fashion which so rules the living may appropriately sit on the coffin and beat it with his heels.

I am glad you have cares enough to take up your thoughts, and divert them from over much dwelling on the past. Work is the salvation of mankind—to the afflicted soul not less than to the body, which should eat bread won by the sweat of its brow. But I wish you could take a little run off to some other place for a few weeks, with your brother and his wife, all the remaining family of you, say to Washington or Charleston. Change of place is often a great relief to sense and soul! Sometimes we are the worst companions for ourselves, and should get into other society. I have seen from your letters how much the watching, the anxiety, and the sympathy have worn upon you, for the actual self always writes its condition between the lines, and we tell what we would not.

*   *   *   *   *   *

I don't think it quite just to impute Captain Brown's conduct to a desire to take vengeance for the murder of his sons; if that were the motive, he would have sought a cheap and easy revenge on the actual transgressors in Missouri; but, if I am rightly informed, he has cherished this scheme of liberating the slaves in Virginia for more than thirty years, and laid his plans when he was a land-surveyor in that very neighborhood where his gallows (I suppose) has since grown. This is in accordance with his whole character and life.

I am much grieved to find Caroline is yet so ill; but trust better days are before her. Remember me tenderly to Mrs. Flint and Mrs. Whiting; as well as the great-hearted doctor. You know how much our sympathies have all along been with you. Now, good-bye.

Faithfully,

THEODORE PARKER.

TO MISS L. OSGOOD, MEDFORD, MASSACHUSETTS.

Rome, December 2, 1859.

MY DEAR MISS OSGOOD.—A few days ago I learned that your much-esteemed and noble-minded sister had passed upwards into her glory onward. Yesterday, while I was on the point of writing to you,

I received your letter of the 8th instant, announcing the same event, so sad to you, to her so joyous and triumphant. I thank you most heartily, my dear Miss Osgood, for writing me so tender and beautiful a letter. Your sister lived as she ought, and died as she had lived. Your account of it shows how characteristic it all was; no complaining, no fearing, no increase of religious action—because all along it had been normal and sufficient. I am glad you "respected her silence," and did no violence to her free spiritual individuality in the last hours more than in the long life which preceded. Your sister was a noble woman; this appeared not only in her intellectual power and its consequent attainments, but also still more in the use she made of all her gifts! Spite of her two-and-seventy years, she was yet one of the youngest women that I knew, so much was she alive, so open-minded for new truth, and so open-hearted to all forms of duty; either the stern of reproving, or the tender of embracing and loving. Old things did not lose their hold on her, if good, though her eye went forth to "fresh fields and pastures new," and new things, if good, were still as welcome at threescore and ten, as if the earthly life had been before her and not chiefly behind. She sympathized with all the best movements of this generation whose fathers she had seen grow up. I have never known such an example before, and look upon it now with continual delight and gratitude. Spite of bodily feebleness, she seemed to be what the Greeks called ἀγήραος; a quality they attributed only to the gods. It was in her character that she should have what Socrates prayed for, Θανατὸς εὔελπις, a death full of good hope; it was also fortunate it should be a εὐθανάσια, a death without pain. She filled up her season with good deeds, rejoiced in them, and developed her character into beautiful proportion; now she has gone to keep her thanksgiving day in the commonwealth of heaven, whose glory eye hath not seen, nor ear heard, nor the heart of man conceived of yet.

I am glad you find the enduring consolation which human nature craves, in the great religion which that same human nature affords. If we are sure of God, we are not long left in doubt of any other good thing. This world must be so made, that all things shall work together for good, though we know not how. I need not say what sweetness of peace and what depth of joy have come to me from the consciousness of such religion; but now, when I go stooping and feeble, when my career of usefulness seems ended, and I can serve no more, but only stand and wait, I find additional comfort in the testimony of many persons on both the Continents, who tell me that I have helped them to a consciousness of the deep things in their own souls, and so have helped make them nobler men, at least more faithful to their conscience, and more hopeful to human kind. I do not complain that I cannot now be useful. I thank God that I could; and am content with whatever lies before me—life or death, health or sickness.

We are well situated here, on the Quirinal Mountain; all Rome lies before us; St. Peter's is a mile and a half off, but clearly visible, from its floor to its cross on the top. What a world of ancient art and modern art; and underneath them both what a history! The tale of Rome is a tragedy, the profoundest, the saddest ever enacted, and that, too with the world for its stage. As I sit at my window by day, or lie sleepless on my bed at night, it is wonderful the scenes that come up before me, in that great drama of Rome. I have been reading Mommsen's History (to the time only of Cæsar's Dictatorship as yet), and much more on the great theme. It is all the more interesting to me when I daily visit the spots where the deeds were done, and see the monuments often of the acts themselves. But still, spite of all this, my heart turns home, and I consider the American drama getting acted now.

How young we are! Yet we have a more difficult problem to settle than the oldest European State is now vexed with—a democracy with 4,000,000 slaves, mocking at the first principles of all human society, the four great Northern cities all on the side of despotism! I take it Congress assembles for fresh scenes of violence. Nobody knows whose head will be broken next—Seward's, Wilson's, Sumner's, Hale's. I do not wonder at Captain Brown's attempt at Harper's Ferry: it is only the beginning; the end is not yet. But such is my confidence in democratic institutions that I do not fear the result. There is a glorious future for America, but the other side of the *Red Sea!*

All mine send most friendly sympathy. You know you have that of

Yours faithfully and affectionately,

THEODORE PARKER.

TO REV. J. F. CLARKE.

Rome, Nov. 9, 1859.

A queer place is this old Rome—a city off of the track of the human race, and not allowing any cross-cuts to be made to it or near it. Really, the capital of Christendom is the stronghold of the Devil—ὅπου ὁ Σατανᾶς κατοικεῖ. But sometimes the people give the Government a good shot—through the hands of Pasquin. Thus, for example, when the Pope's emissary went to the Conference at Zurich, there appeared this neat little satire on Pasquin's statue. Pasquin asks the emissary—

" Can you speak German ? "

" No."

" French ? "

" No."

" English ? "

" No."

" Italian ? "

" No."

" What can you speak ? "

" Only Latin."

" What can you say in that ? '

" *Sicut erat in principio, nunc est, et semper erit in æternum !* "

Again, Homario says to Pasquin, about the time when King Bomba was on his last legs. " What have you seen? "

" A man with a *grave tumore.*"

" Had he anything else ? "

" Yes—take off the *t;* that leaves *Umore!* " (Always used in a bad sense, unless qualified by an adjective.)

" What will become of him ? "

" Take off the next letter, *u—More!*" (He's going to die!)

C C

" But when ? "

" Take off the next letter, *m—Ore !* " (Right away.)

" But who is this unfortunate man ? "

" Take off the next letter, *o—Re !*" (The King.)

" But what will become of him when he dies; will he go to heaven or hell ? "

" Take off the next letter, *r—E !* " (Alas for him!)

Here's one more. A traveller comes home, and Pasquin calls him.

" Where have you been ? "

" By land, and sea, and air."

" What did you see at sea ? "

" *Grande battimenti* " (great ships)

" And what by land ? "

" *Molte armate* " (great armies).

" And what in the air ? "

" *Per aria molti preti* " (many priests blown up sky-high).

But, alas! these poor wretches seem to think they have done enough when they have touched off a squib. Better our fathers, " Trust in God, but keep your *powder* dry ! "

A mediæval Latin (Gaudissidium Malaterra) said well of Rome :—

> " Fons quondam totius laudis, nunc es fraudis fovea;
> Moribus es depravata, exhausta nobilibus,
> Pravis studiis inservis, nec est pudor frontibus :
> Surge Petre, Summe Pastor ! Finem pone talibus!"

But enough of old Rome—and the new. Think of it : St. Peter's Church cost 46,800,000 scudi, when a scudi was worth at least 1 dollar 75 cents. It takes 30,000 dollars a-year to keep this great toy in order now.

O James, life is poor to me at Rome, amid all the wonders of antiquity and the marvels of art. At home, how rich it was through my power of work ! But I can still thank God for my affliction, not knowing how it will end. Remember me to your family, and also to the Russells. God bless you for the past, and in the present and future! Faithfully yours.

FROM THE JOURNAL.

Nov. 1.—All Saint's Day. A great festa, bells ringing all night, cannons firing, with all the noisy demonstrations which attend the 4th of July. We went to St. Agatha, and saw the sixty or eighty young Belgians, who are in process of being metamorphosed into priests. I was struck with the inferiority of their heads; amongst them all, not one superior head—hardly one up to the average. That is a good sign that only the least noble part of men go into the priesthood. In Rome, it is not so. What is called Christianity is in the same process of decay as the Roman religion in the time of Cicero; *i.e.* all the thoughtful men reject its essential doctrines; this is so both among Catholics and Protestants.

Nov. 4.—Great tomfoolery in the Church of San Carlo in Corso. The Pope was there, some sixty cardinals, other high functionaries the Roman Senate, &c. There were showy dresses and gaudy coaches. Notice, above all, the thousands of soldiers that were necessary to preserve the life of the Pope when he goes to attend mass in San Carlo! About 2000 French soldiers, a battalion of Italian foot, another of horse, and the Swiss Guard!

Received the *Unitarian Quarterly*, containing a notice of T. P.'s. letter. What a change in the tone of Unitarian periodicals in a few years!

Nov. 16.—The insurrection of Capt. Brown excites much attention in America, as well it may. But it is the beginning of the birth-pains of liberty. There is a logic in the history of freedom.

> " *Its* purposes will ripen fast,
> Unfolding every hour;
> The bud may have a bitter taste,
> But sweet will be the flower."

Nov. 29.—Went to Miss Hosmer's studio. N.B. the Zenobia she is now making, also the Minerva in plaster.

Went to Terry's studio. N.B. the Parting of Tobit on his Journey (the Spotted Dog); the scene from Shakspeare's "Tempest;" also the beautiful portrait of Mrs. Crawford's boy, and the handsome woman in the Albanese costume. I think Terry has a deal of talent and thought so in 1844.

TO MISS COBBE.

Nov., 1859.

I wonder if you have seen Cardinal Maï's publication of the "Codex Vaticanus." He puts into the New Testament many passages which are not at all to be found in his Codex, and yet has the candor to confess the fact in the margin! But since his death his assistant has printed a cheap edition of the New Testament part of the work, just as the Codex actually is—thus confessing the fault of the former work.

I am glad you saw my friend Samuel Joseph May. He is a fine specimen of the ministerial profession—one of the wisest and noblest men I ever knew in my life. There is no fault in the man except excess of generosity. He is interested in all the progressive humanities of the age—not least in the elevation of woman. You may believe all he says of everybody except myself; I think he loves me a little too well to see me quite as I am. Alas! it is not merely passional love which blinds the eyes of women to men, and *vice versá*, but the purely affectional does the same. I am glad you heard him preach. His face is a grand benediction. He is minister of Syracuse, New York, a town of 40,000 population, and has, in fourteen or fifteen years, reconstructed the town—I mean its morals. He organized its charities and its schools, lyceums, &c. I call him the Archimedes of Syracuse. He finds his ποῦ στῶ there, and will move the earth—if he have time.

I am reading "Adam Bede," a quite extraordinary book; but I wonder that any one should have doubted that a woman wrote it. Strange is it that we tell the universal part of our history in all we write, and that a nice eye often reads even our private experience between the lines.

We shall keep your birthday with due honor on the 4th of next month. And now, my dear friend, may God bless you, and fit you for great and good works!

The expedition of John Brown to Harper's Ferry, the capture of himself and some of his men, his trial and conviction, took place in the autumn of this year. Mr. Parker's letter to Francis Jackson, dated Nov. 24, is in Chap. XXI.

FROM THE JOURNAL.

Dec. 2, " Santa Bibiana's Day."* Day appointed to hang Capt. Brown.—It is now 6 p.m., and I suppose it is all over with my friends at Charlestown, Va., and that six corpses lie there, ghastly, stiff, dead. How the heart of the slave-holders rejoices! But there is a day after to-day. John Brown did not fear the gallows; he had contemplated it, no doubt, as a possible finger-post to indicate the way to heaven. It is as good as a cross. It is a pity they could not have had two thieves to hang with Brown. There have been anti-slavery meetings to-day, at Boston, Worcester, Salem, New Bedford, Providence, &c. The telegraph has spread the news of Brown's death, I suppose, over half the Union by this time. It is a great dark day in America. Thunder and lightnings will come out of it.

TO PROFESSOR DESOR.

Rome (Poste Restante), Dec. 7, 1859.

I am rejoiced to hear such good tidings of the Küchlers. I will set about my papers immediately, and will do nothing else till both are finished. Shall I send them to you by mail, or wait till you come here en route for Naples? My wife shall copy them out in a good, fair hand. I have not felt in spirits to write anything of late: affairs at home have filled me with anxiety. You have not, perhaps, heard that Captain Brown, with fifteen or twenty men, made an attempt to free the slaves of Virginia, at Harper's Ferry. His two sons were shot, and most of his men. He and five or six men were taken prisoners, and have had such a " trial " as slave-holders give such men; are convicted, and hung before now. Brown was a friend of mine—his two sons have been at my house. Other friends of mine have been forced to fly from their country. Attempts are made to implicate many prominent men at the North, and there will be a deal of trouble. I should not be surprised to see Dr. Howe in Rome this winter, for there seems to be some evidence against him which makes the slave-holders suspect him. So he may have to flee off for his life, or to avoid exposing other men. The South talk very big, and utter threats against all the leading men of the North—Seward, Hale, Wilson, Sumner, &c. Congress came together yesterday, and there will be a stupid message from the President, and a stormy session all winter. I look for more broken heads before summer. We are coming upon a great crisis in American history, and a civil war seems at no great distance. The slave-holders will be driven, by the logic of their principles, to demand what the

* Bibiana, Virgin and Martyr at Rome, in the year 363, towards the end of the reign of Julian the Apostate. She was tied to a pillar and scourged to death with loaded whips. A chapel was afterwards constructed, in the times of Christian freedom, over the place where she was secretly buried; and a church now stands there, rebuilt in 1628.

free men of the North will not consent to: then comes the split—not without blood! All national constitutions are writ on the parchment of a drum-head, and published with the roar of cannon!

I have no hope for the people of Italy, specially none for the Romans. These are a miserable people, out of whom all *virtus* seems to have perished utterly. I am told the Pope is in sad want of money: "*Es fehlt ihm jetzt an Ablassgelt!*" He gets nothing from Romagna, and as he owes more than 70,000,000 dollars, he can't borrow, except at great and ruinous interest. The sooner he and the like of him go to the Devil the better. He has just published an *edictum* against crinolines, and forbids women accoutred therein to enter the churches. We all send our heartiest love to you, the Apthorps included. Remember me to the good Marie. Yours,

THEODORE PARKER.

My little book, "Experience," &c., which you have, has been republished in London, and here a Swede is translating it into his own melodious Northern tongue. I don't know whether or not he will find anybody to publish it in Sweden, for I see a Bill has been introduced to their Popular (!) Assembly to make the priests censors of the press, with unconditional power.

TO MR. LYMAN

Rome, December 10, 1859.

Oh, best of governors, your letter of 18th ult., came swiftly to hand and relieved my anxiety (which was getting to be strong), lest you were sick, or some ailment had befallen your family. But the letter puts me at ease. Here I am rather rich in newspapers, so all the details of the Harper's Ferry affair are soon made known to us. See how the slave-holders hold their "bloody assizes" in Virginia! Well, the worse they behave the better for us and ours. This is the ἀρχη τῶν ὀδινῶν—the beginning of birth-pains; the end is far enough away. How often I have wished I was in my old place, and at my old desk! But I too should have had to straighten a rope or else to flee off, no doubt, for it is not likely I could have kept out of harm's way in Boston. I sent a little letter to Francis Jackson, touching the matter which he will show you, perhaps. Wendell said some brave things, but, also some rash ones, which I am sorry for, but *the whole was noble.* B—— is faithful to his clerical instinct of cunning, not his personal of humanity; I read his sermon with a sad heart, and F——'s with pain. Noble brave Garrison is true to himself as always, and says, "I am a non-resistant, and could not pull a trigger to free four million men, but Captain Brown in his fighting is faithful to his conscience, as I to mine, and acted as nobly as Cromwell, and Fayette and Washington; yes, more nobly, for his act was pure philanthropy. All honor to the fighting saint—now he is also a martyr!" That is the short of what the *Liberator* says.

The "Twenty-eighth" did not accept my resignation, but made some handsome resolutions. Perhaps it is better so. Yet sure I am that my preaching days are all over and left behind me, even if my writing and breathing time continue, which I think will not last long.

I do all I can to live, but make all my calculations for a (not remote) termination of my work here. I buy no books, except such as are indispensable to keep me from eating my own head off.

Miss Cushman is here, and very kind to me; the Storys most hospitable people as well as entertaining; we all dined there on Thanksgiving day. Dr. Appleton (of Boston) has helped me to many things. I have seen Mrs. Crawford, and of course all the American artists, painters, and sculptors, The Brownings came a few days ago, and I have seen them both. I like her much! He, too, seems a good fellow, full of life; intense Italians are they both.

He was very busy at this time making topographical explorations, to identify the famous spots.

Weather cold and chilly. Walked and examined the walls from Porta Pia to Porta Maggiore.

At the Forum, to identify the places. Not all settled yet, spite of Bunsen and Canino.

Robert Browning came in the afternoon. Visited the Forum again. Cosmos and Damien * —Santa Maria in Cosmedin—Temple of Janus, and that of Ceres; the Mausoleum of Augustus.

Went to an auction of books at 47 Piazza del Jesu. A fine copy of Baronius, Lucca edition, thirty-eight folios, sold for only ninety-nine dollars! Were I not a worthless corpse I had given one dollar more.

Dec. 10.—Went to the Storys in the afternoon to see a juggler please the children.

On December 12, after visiting nearly a dozen sites and ruins—a great day's work—he made the following entry :—

To-night this happened. Since the fever in February and March, 1857, I have felt there was an adhesion of the pleura of the right side, and I never breathe without a feeling of constraint there, or pulling. After a long and violent coughing I felt the adhesion give way. The right lung moved as freely as the left. This marks a crisis—of healing or of finishing.

But on the next day the same restless visiting and exploring went on, in the churches and the Quirinal gardens ; the latter were damp and chilly. The day after, he complained of a bad cold, but went about in the Trastevere quarter, the Island in the Tiber, and tried to find the remains of Pompey's theatre. His cough greatly weakened him at this time.

Dec. 17.—Writing a little story for Desor. It goes hard and seems likely to be the last thing I write for the press. Küchler went, and I shall soon follow. The cough is worse than ever before. It is plain where I am going.

The little story was written for the Album, and is there printed, with the title, " A Bumble-bee's Thoughts on the Plan

* These are churches : the surname, "in Cosmedin," comes from a square in Constantinople.

and Purpose of Creation." It was the last thing from his pen written with the intent to publish.

One or two extracts will show its clear and lively style :—

Look at the relation between us and the world of matter. It seems to exist only for our use. Here I will mention but a single fact, and from that you can easily judge of all, for it is a crucial fact, a guide-board instance that indicates the road which nature travels on. The red-clover grows abundantly all over the world; in its deep cup there lies hid the most delicious honey, the nectar of the world! But that cup is so deep no other insect can reach the sweet treasure at the bottom; even the common honey-bee, who stands next below us in the scale of being, must pass it by—longed for but not touched! Yet our proboscis is so constructed that with ease we suck this exquisite provision which nature furnishes solely for us!

Now, Gentlemen, it is plain that WE are the crown of the universe; we stand on the top of the world; all things are for us. I say it with calm deliberation and also with most emphatic certainty: *The Bumble-bee is the Purpose of the Universe!* (Tremendous applause.) Yes, Gentlemen, the Plan of the Universe intends the Bumble-bee as its end and final cause. Without him the world would be as unmeaning as a flower with no honey in its breast. As I look over the long line of causes and effects which compose the universe; as I thence dissolve away the material part thereof and look at the idea, the meaning and ultimate purpose, I see all things point to the Bumble-bee as the perfection of finite being—I had almost said of all being. He alone is the principal, the finality ; all else is but provisional. He alone is his own excuse for being; his existence is the reason why he is here; but all other things are only that he may be; their excuse for existence is only this—that they prepare for him, provide for him, and shelter him. Some things do this directly, some in a circuitous manner; but though they serve other purposes, yet their end is to serve him. For him is the world of matter and its four elements, with their manifold forces, static and dynamic too; for him its curious combinations, which make up the world of organization and vegetation; all is but material basis for him.

What a difference between US and the highest Infusoria. The two seem hardly to belong to the same world. How much vaster the odds between us and the inorganic matter, the primeval atoms of the world! Yet even from that to us there has been no leap; the continuity of being is never broken. Step by step went on the mighty work. It seemed, indeed, to have no meaning; there was only a chaos of organization and decomposition, attraction and repulsion, growth and decay, life and death, progress and regress. But at length the end is reached, the idea shines through the more material fact. One evening the sun went down on a world without meaning; the next morning it rose, and, behold! there were Bumble-bees. The Chaos of transient night has become the Kosmos of eternal day! (Immense sensation—prolonged applause.) Shall I say the Bumble-bee was created ? No, gentlemen, that were to adduce a mere theory. That he came as the resultant of all the forces there or heretofore active in the universe ? No more is this to be allowed in such an assembly. The Bumble-bee is mind—mind in himself, for himself, of himself, by himself! So he exists of his own accord; his being is his will; he exists because he wills to be. Perhaps I might say that all things anterior to him were but an efflux from him. For with a being so vast as the Bumble-bee's, the effect may well precede the cause, and the non-existent Bumble-bee project out of himself all actual existence!

Do not think me presumptuous in standing forth as the representative of Bumble-beedom in this matter. I have peculiar advantages. I have attained great and almost unexampled age. I have buzzed four summers; I have dozed as many winters through; the number of my years equals that of my legs and antennæ on one side; and still my eye is not dim nor my natural vigor abated. This fact gives me an advantage over all our short-lived race. My time has been devoted to science, " all summer in the field, all winter in my cell;" this has been my motto all my life. I have travelled wide, and seen the entire world. Starting from this, my ancestral spot, I made expeditions east, west, north, and south. I travelled four entire days in each direction, and stopped only at the limits of the world. I have been up to the top of the highest fir tree (*abies pectinata*). Yes, have flown over it, and touched the sky. I have been deeper down in the earth than any Bumble-bee; ten times my own length—it makes me shudder to think of it—and then I touched the bottom of the monstrous world! I have lived in familiarity with all the philosophers now on earth, and have gathered all that time has left of the great thinkers before me. I am well acquainted with the summits of Bumble-bee consciousness, in times past and present. If any Bumble-bee may criticise, surely I am that one! And if I am judge of anything, it is of the universe itself; for I have studied it all my life. If I know anything, or can know anything, it is the all of things, the world of matter and the world of mind!

FROM THE JOURNAL.

Dec. 22.—Wrote several letters. It is Forefather's Day, and will bring up many reflections at home. As I get weaker and weaker—and the decline is obvious from week to week—I feel less inclination to read. It gets a little irksome to write, and I sit still, idle-handed, idle-minded. It is now pretty clear that I do not go out of Rome again. The cough at night exhausts me much, and the next morning I feel languid. By-and-bye the bleeding will come back—there are little specks of blood now—and these things will hasten to their conclusion. I don't like the thought of a grave in Rome, for the soil is really oppressed with a two-fold curse; but I shall find the clods of the valley sweet to my flesh even there. I had hoped to live long enough to save from waste some few things half-done, and to finish one or two more which none else can, but must let them slide. If I were at home I could work a little."

Dec. 25. Christmas Day.—A deal of noise and show in the town. Went to some churches—to Santa Maria Maggiore. Noticed the little chapel in the Borghese Chapel, where there is a curious sculpture of the Baby-God and his mother and putative father; the cattle in the back-ground looking on.

Went to Ara Coeli. Noticed the funny show of the Baby and the Heavenly Host, and God the Father in the clouds.

Really the city is as polytheistic as in the days of the Cæsars.

L. and I, and all the Apthorps and Hunts dine together to-day. I sit at all entertainments as the coffin in the Egyptian feasts.

N.B. What I wrote in my journal last Christmas or New Year's Day. Surely this will be the last; but, really, I die slow.

Dec. 27.—Porta St. Lorenzo. Went to that old church out of the walls. It is a great Festa to-day. Spots of snow on the road-side in the shade at noon. None yet on Soracte, I think.

TO JOHN AYRES.

Rome, Immaculate Conception Day.

Here we all are in old Rome. Bad weather we had of it for a long time; really it rained forty days and forty nights, though not without ceasing. I thought an umbrella was almost as necessary as a hat and shoes. Now it is better—fair by day and night—the thermometer about 24° to 28° at sunrise. Roses bloom in all the gardens, and violets under the hedges, while the Ilexes are ripening their slender acorns, and the orange-trees are fuller of fruit than I left or found them at St. Croix. We have seen many things here peculiar to Rome. The Pope showed himself at the Church of San Carlo one day, surrounded by about 2500 soldiers, and was borne about in a chair on men's shoulders, while he "blessed the people." I hear the Pope's *hired man* ringing the bells in the night. He begins about three or four o'clock, and keeps it up till sunrise. He must be much overworked and up early in the morning. The Pope's *Tom-cat* comes under my windows in the dark, and gets on the cross in the neighbourhood, and behaves no better than his brothers in Boston. The Pope's bull, I take it, is kept in the stall as a "dangerous beast," and only let out on certain great occasions. But the *Pope's Gal*—I have not seen her yet. I am told she is arrayed in purple and scarlet color, and decked with gold and precious stones, and pearls, &c., and when she rides out, it is on a beast with seven heads and ten horns; indeed, you may read an account of her and her cattle in the Book of Revelations (chap. xiv.); when she appears in public I will tell you. A few days ago a funny thing took place in the church of San Andrea delle Frutte. A man caught his feet in the wide-spread crinoline of a lady kneeling on the pavement, and fell his whole length to the ground. The congregation clapped their hands and laughed aloud; it made a great scandal, so the Pope issued an edict, forbidding women to enter the church except with their heads veiled, and their bodies clad in modest raiment. For, he says, they come to church, now-a-days, in such guise that they are a sight to behold—"a spectacle to men," referring to the fact that naughty young men come into the churches to see the maidens and matrons show their legs as they kneel or stoop! I don't know what effect it will have in Rome, but if all the ministers in Boston, and the standing committees of the societies there agreed to say, "We will have no crinolines in our meeting houses," the women would say, "What do we care? Then you don't have us, that's all; we can't exhibit on the common, or in the streets, all the week; go to thunder with your old meetin' us." But the Pope tells the poor creatures they shall go to church, and they shan't wear their favourite garments there. It is hard —I don't know what will happen, but fear this successor of St. Peter will encounter troubles not mentioned by St. Paul, in his melancholy catalogue; and to the perils of waters and false brethren will have to add, perils of women and perils of crinolines. The Sultan has undertaken the same desperate business of meddling with the women's clothes;—it may cost him his life—" Touch not, handle not," were good counsel to them both. I think the Pope had better stick to his own apocalyptic *Gal,* and rig her up in scarlet colors, and let the rest of womankind alone.

Yesterday, a new building was dedicated for the *education of priests who are to convert America to the true faith*—don't you think they will have their hands full before they are done with this business? The American Minister, Hon. Mr. Stockton, was present at the ceremony. A queer dead people these Romans are. I have no hope for their political regeneration! They have a bad reputation for treachery and lying, which I fear is but too well deserved. Last spring there was a revolution in North Italy, as you know. Well: the Romans also got a little uneasy, and the Government thought it must do something to keep them quiet. So it gave them a holiday and had a procession of costly carriages in the Corso, and rich men hung handsome-colored cloths out at their windows, and the people became contented and quiet. What if Governor Gage had given the people of Massachusetts a holiday in 1775, and had fireworks on Boston Common just after the battle of Lexington; or if President Buchanan should order a parade of marines at the Navy-yard, in Charlestown, to quiet the agitation about the Harper's Ferry affair! Much good is to come of that experiment of our friend Brown. Ten years ago it would have been too early; now it is just in time! I find brave words have been spoken about him and his, by Phillips, Emerson, and Clarke, but I hear of no others. * * * * *

  * * * * * *
  * * * * * *
  * * * * * *
  * * * * * *
  * * * * * *

  * * Clarke's sermon of Brown was his best, I think, wise in matter and condensed in form of expression. X—— would make a powerful preacher if he did not drown his thought in a Dead Sea of words. What a pity! you don't want a drove of oxen to drag a cart-load of potatoes on a smooth road. I wish ministers and lecturers would be a little more generous of thought and more stingy of words; they and we should be better off and like each other more.

What a state of things in Virginia!—a hay-stack takes fire in Charlestown, and they send 1000 or 2000 soldiers, with two batteries of cannon, to put down the insurrection, and when they get to the spot there is nothing but the white ashes of the hay, and the stack-pole burnt and blackened. "There is no danger from the slaves," "not the least," "none at all;" how Buchanan must have bleated in his message, and what a stormy time we are to have this winter! Whose head will get broke next? I know not. I trust Sumner is in his place before now, and about his noble work. These things are only the beginning of sorrows; but they are birth-sorrows for freedom, not the pains of death.

Poor Mr. Everett! I wonder if he "buckled on his knapsack and shouldered his musket." I fear he said, "my habits are very unmilitary," and stayed at home. Doctor Howe, I learn, has gone to Canada; I may meet him here before spring. Really I think the 28th may be thankful their minister fell into a consumption a year ago, for I believe they would rather lose him by a cough than a halter. It is not quite likely I should have kept entirely free from Brown if I had been at home and in full activity; how bravely he acts, how nobly he speaks, even the slaveholders feel the influence of his magnetic character. "We sow in tears," &c.

I see there is likely to be another Mexican war; of course I don't know the merits of the case; but take it for granted they do not lie on the American side of the border; but it is clear that all Mexico must fall into our hands. I wish it would not come quite so soon. I doubt that it ever becomes slave territory; the inhabitants there sympathize with the negro.

To-day came S——'s anonymous pamphlet, "The Crisis of Unitarianism," and it has many good things in it, well expressed too; but it betrays rather a peevish spirit. S—— is a good fellow, full of generous instincts, with a natural fondness for the true and the right, the beautiful, and the good; he has made sacrifices in time of trouble, and stood upright when many found their account in stooping or lying flat. I shall always think of him with gratitude and not without admiration.

  * * * * * *

I wrote him a long letter from Montreux, which he must have received before I got his pamphlet. He says my letter from St. Croix is a little morbid; so it is, so it must be: do you know the odds between a sick man and a sound? Here it is. Mr. Saw-and-grind has a grist mill turned by a great wide mill-pond, that has four or five reserve ponds all full of water; it runs over the flush boards and jumps and laughs as it goes rollicking down the stream. Mr. S. has some little machinery for his own sport, and amuses the neighbors with showing it off now and then; he saws at one end of his mill; he grinds at the other; he has a great up-and-down saw and cylinder saws likewise, not to speak of his gang of saws which cut twelve boards at one time. Besides this are saws for laths, for shingles, and clapboards; nay, he makes boxes out of the boards in this room; he has mill-stones for maize, for rye, and for wheat; he cracks corn for the cattle, he grinds and bolts it for men. All this goes on when his pond is full—all at once—but then comes a dry time—all his reserve ponds are exhausted, no water runs over the dam, the flush boards are all dry as hay; then he stops play-wheels; by-and-bye gives up all sawing: as the water gets lower, the wheels move slow. He does not bolt meal to flour, nor crack corn for the cattle, he only *grinds* for men; next, he only grinds an hour or two a day for his neighbors or friends, or for poor folks; then only an hour a week for his own *family*, the water is so low. At length the mill stops, the great wheel is dry as a bone, presently the water in the flume does not come near the bottom of the gate, there is but little in the pond: the cows drink there no more, the water lilies are dried up, the fish are all dead. Finally all the water is gone, you can walk right through the mill-pond over the black and parched earth; the mill is dead; don't expect the poor miller to grind or saw then, still less to amuse his friends with play. God be thanked the water is not lost; all this mill-power is but exhaled to heaven. Love to your family, neighbors, and all.

THEODORE PARKER.

TO DR. FLINT.

Rome, December 31, 1859.

MY DEAR DR. FLINT,—I have not written you a line since I left Boston, though there has not been a day but you and yours have been in my thoughts; indeed one of my occupations in the pauses of sleep is to make visits to all my friends in Boston and its neighborhood, and as it is day there while it is already night here, I find them always up and glad to see me. Now I think I shall worry you with a few words.

Well: the Harper's Ferry affair is over—I mean Captain Brown has been hanged, and his associates and the troops have gone home again to boast of their exploits—the military achievements of the chivalry of Virginia! It ought to have taken place in South Carolina, and then the valiant General Quattelbum would have been out with his soldiers, of whom "one can chase a thousand, and two ten thousand put to flight!" The effect is not over, nor ever will be. Brown's little spark was not put out till it had kindled a fire which will burn down much more than far-sighted men look for. The Northern sky is full of lightning, long treasured up; Brown was one bright clear flash into the Southern ground; the thunder rattles all over the Union now, there will be other strokes by-and-bye.

*   *   *   *   *   *   *

I find great complaints made against the courts of Virginia. Certainly the proceedings were hasty and irregular, the general conduct shameless and atrocious; the judge held his "bloody assizes" with small regard to the rights of the accused, or the customary forms of law. He did not give Captain Brown time to confer with his counsel; he had *not* a fair trial. So far so bad. But what did Massachusetts do a few years ago? She arrested Thomas Sims for a thief, and then tried him as a runaway slave! He had committed no crime. Yet he was sent into slavery for life! The courts of Massachusetts were asked to give him the benefit of those statutes made to prevent such injustice, or of the common law older than the State itself, and they refused; they would do nothing, when the matter was tried in Woodbury's court, and it was left for him to decide whether Sims could have the *benefit* of the *Habeas Corpus*, as well as the shadow of its form. While he was giving his final judgment, a prominent lawyer of Boston, handed him a note to help the judicial mind to still more legal iniquity, and he used its hints; and when the decision of the judge was given that Sims should have no protection from the supreme court of the United States, any more than from the courts of Massachusetts, but he must be delivered over to the commissioner, and so be made a slave of, the respectability of Boston clapped their hands. The slave-holders who crowded the court-house at Virginia, did not applaud when John Brown was found guilty! It seems the first disgrace of Boston was not enough; for not six years ago, her judge of probate, guardian of widows and orphans, took the city by a *coup de droit*, a law-lick, captured a Baptist minister, and run him off to slavery! The court assigned counsel to Captain Brown; but in the case of Anthony Burns, the "court" told his counsel, "You had better throw no obstacle in the way of his being sent back to slavery, as he *probably will be!*" Really the Virginia jury decided according to Virginia law, and the evidence before them, when they found Brown guilty; but when Judge Loring found Burns guilty, it was in utter disregard of the facts of the case abundantly testified to in the court. Judge Parker, in Virginia, gave his charge in open court; the verdict of the jury also was first delivered in public; but Judge Loring gave his decision (that Burns was a slave) to the slave-hunter in private, more than twelve hours before it was made in open court. Brown was condemned by a jury of twelve men, but Massachusetts let Sims and Burns be dragged off to slavery on the mere word of a kidnapper who was to receive five dollars if he freed the man, or ten dollars if he enslaved him! There was law enough in Massachusetts to save both of these poor victims of oppression, every advocate knew it; but the judges of the supreme court of Massachusetts broke down all that law with one puff of their breath.

* * * * * *

Loring was kicked out of his offices, and so out of the State, but he was far from being the great offender! The Court-house of Boston was turned into a barracoon, the enemies of Massachusetts Democracy kept their prisoners in it for more than a week, and defended themselves with sword and gun. Massachusetts did not dare dislodge them, though she had abundant law on her side. They put a Southern chain round the Court-house, all round it, and her suppliant Judges stooped and crouched down, and lay low and crawled under that chain to go to the seats they had long dishonored! No Virginia minister has said a word against Slavery; they all defend it as democratic, biblical, Christian and divine; some of them went to Brown even in his cell to convert *him* to that opinion. But in Boston the two great heads of Unitarianism . . . .
Did Virginia even in those days show any sympathy with freedom, with real Democracy, or befriend any of its measures? Not once. But when the Fugitive Slave Bill passed Congress, the respectability of Boston fired 100 jubilant cannon. When the first kidnapper came, that same respectability had a great Union Meeting in Fanueil Hall, where it resolved that Boston should be prostituted to the slave-hunter: he might come when he would, her door was always open, and she ready and willing!

* * * * * *

I think Massachusetts is the foremost State in the world—spite of the two hundred thousand Paddies and children of Paddies, whose poverty, ignorance, nastiness, superstition and crime lower the general average. She is in advance of every other 1,200,000 people in industry, intelligence, and virtue. Boston too is the noblest of cities, and the seed of religious fire never is quenched out from her venerable hearth ; it is the home of great ideas, sure one day to be great facts. But after all this she can't say to Virginia "let me pull out the mote out of thine eye." So I was glad the Legislature, though in love with its own extra-session, was modest enough to refuse to adjourn on the day her sister hanged one of the noblest of New England's patriots. Let us work, and pray, trust in God, and keep our powder dry ; but not say to Virginia, "Massachusetts is faithful." She is *not* faithful—one day she will be. It was a good while from the Boston massacre to the evacuation of Boston.

We sometimes do a little injustice to our own State and the slow way we have of doing great things. In the South there is no respect for personal freedom ; hence the slavery of the negroes ; hence the enormous tyranny of public opinion over the minority ; hence men like Mr. Helper, Mr. Underwood, and many more, are driven out of the country because they favour democratic institutions. Neither Washington nor Jefferson would be suffered to live in Virginia to-day. There is as little respect in the South for general law, either local or Federal. Hence the continual interruptions of the regular course of judicial proceedings to get at the end more swiftly. I refer to the *lynchings* that are so common. Hence, too, the violations of positive law—not to serve the higher law of justice, which all statutes in general are supposed to aim at, but to carry out the purposes of selfish passion or selfish calculation. Hence came the importation of slaves from Africa, the fillibustering against Cuba, &c., and the threat to dissolve the Union. These things being so, philanthropic Northerners—impatient of process, but greedy of result—praise the " courage " and " determination " of the South in adhering to her idea. It is quite foolish—at least, short-sighted. Look here ! In the North, especially in New England, there is a profound respect for personal freedom, represented by INDIVIDUAL LIBERTY. Hence any man is free till he commits a crime, and is punished for it by law made beforehand and made known. Hence industry is free, opinion free, the press free, and the tongue ! The atheist is free to attack all religion, the bigot to denounce the wrath of God against all who doubt the bigot's stupid creed. On the 4th of July, at Salem, twenty or thirty years ago, R. H. D. delivered the address before the town of Salem, and attempted to show that democracy was a mistake, we ought to have a limited monarchy, &c. (this is after the best of my recollection). His right to deliver his opinion in a 4th of July oration was held sacred. Webster, Choate, and shoals of the " democratic " small-fry, have opposed the most valued institutions and ideas of New England ; ministers preached the most ghastly doctrines, which would make democracy impossible. Nobody questions their right ; their worst enemies would defend their right to speak and print, and would never seek to abridge it : so profound is this respect for personal freedom of body and of spirit. But along with this, there is also a profound respect for social unity, represented by GENERAL LAW. Hence we obey laws we know to be unjust ;

obey them at first or allow them to be enforced, simply because they are laws; but, at the same time, go to work to rid ourselves of them in a regular legal way. (I know there are two exceptions to this, in the disobedience of the Usury Laws and the Maine Liquor Law; but these exceptions, when understood, don't detract much from what I said above.) The resistance Massachusetts makes to the Fugitive Slave Bill is an example of this. If Wendell Phillips could have got a scrap of law as big as a dollar, and a constable's pole to put in front, he could have had hundreds of men to follow and take Sims or Burns out of jail. But as that could not be done, these two victims went back to slavery. At this time we have thrown a few threads of law round the fugitive, and on them I think the people would lay hold, and rescue any runaway in these times.

But the New Englanders must do their work in regular manner and form—by due course of law. If a man commits a great crime—a fraud, for example—and there is no statute that will reach him, we never think of lynching the wretch; we make a law for the future and let the past go. Now this love of law gives us an immense advantage over the South in the long run, though they often get the start of us in carrying a special measure. No doubt we sometimes go too far, and allow the final purpose of law, which is the preservation of individual liberty, to be defeated. But in a democratic community, when the appeal to the people is so direct and comes so soon, even this failing leans to virtue's side. Soon as we get a little individual liberty, we hedge it round with general law. Hence the progress of Democracy in New England is continuous and certain. So we have social unity of action represented by law, and individual variety of action represented by liberty, and that to a degree no people ever had before.

In this particular affair Massachusetts has done admirably—never so well before. It is curious to see how even Boston makes progress in her hate against slavery. It is not thirty years since a mob of "respectable gentlemen" broke up a meeting of women, who came together to debate on slavery. Leverett Street Gaol was the only safe place for Garrison! When the Fugitive Slave Bill passed, the family of kidnappers fired one hundred cannons. Sims was taken off by them without much trouble, though at the darkest hours of the night. But in the Burns time, what a row there was! (If Captain Brown had been in Boston, there would have been a rescue. We had only miserable scholars for leaders—lawyers, ministers, doctors—not men with *fists*.) How the Kansas Bill and the Dred Scott decision thinned the ranks of the Hunkers! And now see how Massachusetts sympathises with John Brown—think of towns tolling their meeting-house bells for an hour on the day Virginia hung that milk-brother of Washington and Jefferson! Such things have not been done since the times of the Stamp Act. Think of the old South on the platform, with Emerson and Phillips. Think of such a sermon as Wheelock's, at the Music Hall. God bless the dear old State! God bless the dear old town! Massachusetts can't call Virginia hard names; she will do much better, will overpower her sister by the great truths which will become great institutions, and surpass her in respect for liberty and respect for law, which will mean reverence for the eternal right.

Kindest love from me and mine to your excellent wife, to Mrs. Whiting, the admirable woman much tried and not found wanting, and also to the babies, and last not least to their kind and wise father.

Affectionately and thankfully,

THEODORE PARKER.

FROM THE JOURNAL.

Dec. 31.—Cloudy and foggy in the morning; fair and showery at noon! Rode out of the Porta St. Giovanni for two hours. I have had a bad cold lately, with a shocking cough. A little blood comes now and then. Wrote letters. *Here endeth the last year.*

And the last of the little note-books that he lived to finish was laid away by the industrious hand.

CEMETERY AT FLORENCE.

CHAPTER XXVIII.

1860—Progress of the Disease—Letters to Mrs. Cheney, John Ayres, Joseph Lyman, Dr. Howe, Hon. Gerritt Smith, and others—The Last Days—May 10.

HE now became more and more absorbed every day with watching the progressive steps of his disease.   This he had been in the habit of doing from the beginning, with a coolness as if the patient and the observer were two different persons.   But as soon as his power of working began to fail so decisively that he found the will incompetent to whip the body to its tasks, a disappointment and restlessness began to disturb the great tranquillity which he had maintained.   Labors of love and study had always been his refuge from physical and mental ills.   But here at last came a weakness, rushing in upon his life by all the avenues of his various gifts at once ; the rugged understanding, the indomitable will, the ardent philanthropy, were now only so many sluices to let in mortality.   Such a strong life could not feel itself thus daily demoralized, till all the glorious past activity seemed reduced to the frivolous and annoying duty of observing its own decay, without betraying the fever of the unnatural conflict.   The substantial fabric, built against all weathers, for prolonged uses, to outwear and survive an ordinary lapse of time, was violently pulled to pieces and levelled with the ground just as maturity had knit its parts and was spreading its hardy color over all.   A less pious and childlike spirit in such a powerful nature would have resented this vandalism of a hostile fate.   But the sweet dependent prayers of a whole life had been confirming the advantage gained by its earliest struggle, when began a trust in the Infinite Goodness.   These prayers burned purely upon this altar of a nervous body bent with premature decay. Pitying friends and observers could see how hard it was for this stalwart man to yield to dissolution ; for his roots were still deep in the open country, that dear soil of Lexington, invigorated by the sun and rain—yes, and with blood ! He could not quietly shrivel up or fall apart ; the big branches went reluctantly to the ground.

Now, it was quite evident—the clearness of his mind, the calmness of his inward expectation, the effusions of his love, were the evidence—that he had never in his most vigorous and scornful days stated too strongly the difference between religion and theology. As the body, almost petulantly, dropped away, the members of his faith in that Infinite Perfection, Infinite Goodness, Infinite Presence and Influence, which he had preached and obeyed, were one by one uncovered. Sometimes to those who stood the closest to him, especially at the last, it seemed as if he were impatiently trying to get off those lendings, to show, not by words and set allusions, but by a likeness in love, the Father and the Mother to whom he had always prayed.

But all that remains to show to others are a few more letters, which preserve to the last his tender friendships and the clearness of his mind.

TO MRS. CHENEY, BOSTON.

Rome, Dec. 31, 1859.

A happy new year to my dear Ednah, and little Daisy, and the rest of the family in Somerset Street, in Bowdoin Street, or wherever else ! I have long since written you letters in fancy ; but as it is not so easy to do it in fact, leaning over a table, I think you have not received one of them this long time. When I was here in 1844, I often saw Mr. Cheney, though he was quite ill, even then. Now I am the sick one, and he is at rest, where the body ceases from troubling the soul that museth in many things. Here are many American artists—Terry (whom Mr. Cheney knew very well, I think), Paige, Wilds, Story, not to speak of the sisters in the arts, Miss Stebbins, Hattie Hosmer, and Miss Landor. Story has a fine genius ; he has now finished a Judith, which is quite remarkable. All the other Judiths I have seen are revolting. The artist takes her when the deed is done, and she is there in cold blood, with the gory head in her hand. You forget the motive of the deed, and the provocation which caused it, in your horror at the ghastly head and the cruel-looking sword. You go off with a shudder, and dream dreadful dreams of some great, black-eyed, bony woman coming to chop you to pieces. But Story sculptures the heroine before her thought has become a deed. It is only a purpose, a will; she prays to Jehovah of Hosts to give courage to her womanly heart and strength to her maidenly arm to strike the blow. So she stands there, the sword half behind her, loosely held in the left hand, while her uplifted right hand and devout face, turned heavenward, tell the prayer she puts up. It is a Jewish woman, large, determined, and handsome. You would look at it often, and always with pleasure. He has likewise a Hero, holding up a torch and looking into the darkness for poor Leander. I like it very much, but don't comprehend it yet so well as the Judith.

So far I wrote yesterday, when fatigue, occasioned by many interruptions, overcame me, and the hour of closing the mail drew near, and so the envelope must go to America with no word to *you*. It is now Jan. 1, 1860, and while you are still asleep and hid by 3000 or 4000 miles of distance, I wish you and yours a happy new year! How lightly we often say these words of common courtesy!

Mr. Story is at work on the statue of President Quincy, for the alumni of Harvard College, and, I doubt not, will make a fine thing out of it. The price offered (7500 dollars), is quite too small, even if the work were to be delivered in Rome, while, I believe, he is to deliver it in Cambridge. The block of marble, delivered at his studio, will cost 1000 dollars, and may have such a flaw in it that he must pay an additional 1000 dollars for another. Quincy is a grand figure for a statue, and will look well in his academic robes, put into stone. I am glad Story has the work, even if he loses money by it. But Powers had 12,000 dollars for his Webster, though delivered at Munich.

Rome is a good place for a well man who is also a scholar; but for an unscholarly Yankee I should think it would be the most unsatisfactory spot in Europe. The past is all; there is no present but misery, and no future but decay and destruction. It is a fossil city—the Pope is a fossil ruler, *pre-mediæval*. It is as impossible that a pope should be a progressive king, and rule in the spirit of the great idea of the nineteenth century, as that a sinner should be virtuous or a thief just. There is a contradiction in the adjunct.

The Romans are a handsome people. Homely women are in the minority here. Well, as every woman has an inalienable right to be handsome, I rejoice that this demand of her nature gets its supply. The men are handsome; so are the boys, the finest-looking young fellows I have ever seen. Then they are so graceful. I have never seen a lubberly boy in all Rome; there are no *gawkies*, even in the country. They are not awkward, but use their limbs well; they stand well, and walk well. I think the men are handsomer on the whole than the women—I mean such as you see in the streets, and indeed, a stranger sees no others. This may come from the fact that the women of the common people are more overworked than the men, and so do not attain their natural development so well. Woman needs finer material conditions than man. The most noticeable industry of Rome is devoted to the fine arts—none of the coarse arts of usefulness prevail much here. But it is a curious fact that in ancient and modern times hardly any *native* of Rome has acquired any considerable distinction in sculpture, painting, architecture, or music—the most sensuous

D D 2

of all. It is rare that a Roman born has been distinguished in any department of letters.

Of course, the architecture of a city strikes a visitor first. He knows the outside look of the parts of the hive before he gets familiar with the character or the habits of the workers or the drones who live in it. Of course, the most illustrious buildings are the churches. "Heathen" Rome and "Christian" are alike in many things. The latter has the most gods, however. But in this they differ: the heathen city did not go much into the business of building temples for the gods—what she had was quite small, and generally no great things in point of cost or beauty, I think; while the buildings for the use of men—baths, basilicas, theatres, and the like, and public palaces for kings, were of great size and beauty, as well as surprising in point of numbers. But the Christian city runs to churches for the use of the gods, *i. e.* for Christ, the Virgin Mary, and the little saints who crowd the almanac with their names and the town with their churches. It is amazing to see how church-mad the Romans have been in times past; or, if not the Romans, at least, their masters, the popes, bishops, cardinals, &c. Generally these buildings are homely structures on the outside, made of dingy brick, or of a ragged sort of stone (travertine), which soon tarnishes in this dampest of all moist cities, and looks homely forever. In the inside you are struck with the enormous wealth which the buildings cost (St. Peter's took up over 58,000,000 dollars, and is by no means finished, only stuccoed, when marble was both meant and required), with the extraordinary beauty of the material, and the admirable workmanship expended on all the details, from the mosaic pavement, of many-colored and precious marbles, up to the ceiling of the nave, which is made of wood curiously carved and lavishly gilt. The size also fills you with admiration in some of the greater basilicas, which cover from one to three acres of ground. St. Peter's, I think, covers about six acres. But there is not one of these churches which lifts you up with wonder, with admiration, and with awe. Here is the inferiority of this Roman architecture compared with the Teutonic, which appears in many forms, and is known by many names, Gothic being the chief and most common. The Roman basilica—even St. Peter's—denotes "Rest in the attained"—no more; and disposes to quiet and slumber. "*Dormi dulce,*" it seems to say. But the great Teutonic meeting-houses for the people—as you find them in Germany, in the Teutonic parts of France, Burgundy, Normandy, Frankia; in Switzerland, Holland, Belgium, and England—indicate a longing after the ideal and an aspiration to attain it. They dispose to meditation, thought, and heroic life; for they seem to say, "*Surge et labora dum Dies vocatur.*" Both styles have grown out of the heart of the people, and a great crop of literature, corresponding to the temples and political and social institutions, from the same dissimilar roots.

The priests, the (French) soldiers, and the beggars, are the most active people here, after those devoted to the hard necessities of life. The first are quite worthy of study. There are 37,000 in the Roman States, in a population of 3,250,000. Here, in Rome, the secular clergy, with the regulars of the superior monastic orders, to judge from their looks and bearing, have come from the superior classes of the people, and bear about the same relation to Rome that the graduates of Harvard College do to Massachusetts, both in respect to birth and education. They are well-dressed, neat, and clean, always decorous; such is the virtue of the clerical class in all lands—except the Spanish-American provinces, it may be — intelligent-looking, and kindly to strangers. (Indeed, all Italians are good-mannered and gentlemanly). But in their faces there is a curious contradiction of feelings portrayed, viz. a strong self-esteem; a pride of station, of class and function; and a sense of humility, of abasement, of original sin, of being the offscouring of the world. One is natural, the other conventional; one comes from the great stream of sacerdotal power which sweeps throughout the land, the other is a reflection from the little eddies formed by its banks, and the slight roughnesses which "dusk and shiver" on its surface, as a puff of wind blows this way or that. It is quite curious to trace these two conflicting expressions in the sacerdotal face of Rome. They appear also in Papal literature. The Pope is the most arrogant sovereign in Europe—the infallible. Others represent armies, and threaten you with the gallows; he represents God, and menaces the rest of mankind with eternal hell! But alone of all sovereigns, he calls himself *Servus Servorum*, dates his haughtiest mandates from "our little hovel of the Vatican," and seals it with "*sigillo piscatoris*" (the seal of a common fisherman)!

But here is the end of my paper. Much love to all your family, ascending and descending. How I should like to sit down to tea with them all once more! Only I can't talk; voice all gone. Don't forget to include Gussie Curtis, and ask her to extend the salutation to her family, both in Charlestown and Brookline, where that dear, good Cornie has gone. Remember me specially to St. Mary (Shannon), of Newton Corner. My wife sends the kindest of good wishes to you and yours. (I would put in a daisy, if it would not make the letter overweight). Miss S. and the Hunts add theirs.

Faithfully yours,
THEOD. PARKER.

TO MISS COBBE.

Rome, Jan. 1, 1860.

MY VERY DEAR MISS COBBE,—Your kind letter, with its Yule and new year's greeting, came but a day or two ago, and was most welcome. Thanks for the friendly wishes, and the friendly spirit which warms the ground they grow out of. We have the mistletoe here in Rome, at least in its neighborhood, though different from that in England and Normandy; and the holly is perhaps even finer than in England itself; so we have the material means for a Yule celebration. Alas, only such! "How can we sing the songs of Zion in a strange land?" And Rome is utterly foreign to me and mine. I abhor its form of religion, which is only ceremony. I despise its theology, and find little to respect in its lying, treacherous, and unreliable inhabitants. It is a city of the dead. It has a threefold past, but no future. The Pope says, "If the heathen rage, and the people imagine a vain thing, and the kings of the earth set themselves, and the rulers take counsel together against the Lord and against His Anointed," he, the Pope, will do as his sainted predecessors have done, will go to the Catacombs of St. Calixtus, and live there in the protection of the Lord! It is Mr. Mantalini's threat when his wife chid him for his naughtiness—"I will throw mĕself into the Tems. I will drown, I will! I will be a most demnition body!"

What you say of the triumph of liberal ideas gladdens me much. I know it *must* come, only I always expect such results to come slowly; for I have learned, by long experience, that humanity does not advance by *leaps*, but by steps. England is a slow, solemn country; but no nation is more sure. How much she has done in the last 300 years for the deliverance of mankind from the thraldom of the Middle Ages! Your country and mine are two nations, but I thank God we are only one people, with the same literature, language, ideas, and blood; it is good blood, too.

Kind-hearted Miss Carpenter tells me of the box of clothing for Captain Brown's family. I rejoice at it. Brown was a singularly noble man. I have known him for four or five years, and count his friendship one of the honors of my life. We have had nothing done in such heroic sort for a long time before. The excitement he has caused has had no parallel. A storm now rages in all parts of the Union, which will not blow over in any haste. Congress is fighting already. There can be no unity of action between North and South till Slavery is at an end, and that must pass away with violence; perhaps soon! Who knows?

I wish it was this winter, not a former one, that you could spend here! Would not we have a good time? But I should be the *passive* party, for I cannot talk without pain, nor indeed can I stoop over a table to write more than four or five minutes at a time, without serious inconvenience. But I could see you and hear you. We have much pleasure in the society of the Apthorps, &c., all living under the same roof, and though the weather is almost as bad as that of London, still the winter slides off pleasantly. But it is so different from my former experience, sixteen years ago, when the days were not long enough to use up my superfluous energy. To be weak *is* to be miserable. I pass a life of strenuous idleness—a life that has no future.

Your countrymen, Mr. and Mrs. Browning, are here, and very pleasant people they are, too; I rejoice in them. I have seen also Mr. Arthur Russell, brother of your minister here—an intelligent and agreeable person.

Here there is such a dearth of periodicals, quarterlies, &c., that I do not know what takes place in the wide world of literature and science. Of course, nothing takes place in Rome; a city which has no interest in science or letters.

Please remember me kindly to Miss Carpenter. I hope her generous labors will be always blessed with high results. And accept my hearty good wishes for the new year, while you believe me

Yours affectionately.

TO MR. MANLEY.

Chief City of Ecclesiastical Humbug, Jan. 6, 1860.

I think I have no Roman news to write. Of course, you know all the public acts of the Pope and his gang, from the extracts of European newspapers at home; but here is one little item which shows how things are managed here. You remember the ferocious attack made on Mr. Perkins and his family last summer, at Perugia. Mr. Stockton, the American minister, visited Cardinal Antonelli, the Pope behind the Pope, and demanded satisfaction and money. A. put him off with evasions and foolish arguments, and so the interview ended in nothing. But the next day a priest visited Mr. S. and talked over the matter freely; he was a great friend to America, thought the conduct of the soldiers at P. was atrocious, &c. S. was a little cautious, but told his opinions freely. Then the priest asked, "If A. does not comply with your request, what shall you do?" and S. replied, "There is only one thing for me, *i.e.* to demand my passports immediately and go home; there the affair will make so much noise that I shall probably be the next President!" The priest went off, and the next day came a letter from A., telling S. that his terms should be forthwith acceded to! So much for spunk and a sharp look-out. Of course the priest was a spy of the Cardinal, sent to find out how the matter lay on the minister's mind.

    *   *   *   *   *   *

Of course, I have read the speeches at Fanueil Hall, and the list of signers to the call.* It was a most characteristic meeting. ——— could no more comprehend John Brown and his heroism, than a New Zealand cannibal could understand Florence Nightingale or Matilda Goddard. He has no moral organs by which to judge of such a phenomenon. Cushing attributes fine powers and culture to Garrison, R. W. E., and W. P.; as if *intellect* alone explained the rise of the Anti-Slavery Party! Why, there is *mind* enough among the Hunkers! But the Anti-Slavery men appealed to the *conscience* of the people, and their *instincts of humanity*, and are now getting their answer.

    *   *   *   *   *

But that meeting will do as much good as the Union Meeting in 1850. The property and standing of Boston would have condemned the patriots of Middlesex County on the 20th of April, 1775, and the heroes of Bunker Hill on the 18th of June that year. Hancock, Adams, &c., were but the Garrisons, and R. W. E.'s and W. P.'s of that day. But no American has died in this century whose chance of earthly immortality is worth half so much as John Brown's. The ex-Governors of Massachusetts are half forgotten before they are wholly dead; rhetoricians and sophists are remembered while they are talking; but a man who crowns a noble life with such a glorious act as John Brown's at Harper's Ferry is not forgotten in haste; the red martyr must be a precious man. A happy New Year to you all; kindest love to you and yours. Please send my wife's letter to Emmeline Jackson, and my love to all the Jacksons; *they* are kindred to John Brown!

Good bye! T. P.

* To save the Union again, imperilled by John Brown.

The following letter from Mr. Apthorp to Mr. Lyman describes the condition of Mr. Parker at the opening of the new year :—

Rome, January 16, 1860.

My dear Lyman,—You will easily believe me when I say that I have very many times felt impelled to write to you since we parted, and there is only one reason why I have refrained from doing so, and this is the difficulty of giving you *such* an account of Mr. Parker as I wished and constantly hoped from day to day I should be able to give on the change of the weather, which we were all expecting. To be sure, I thought it encouraging that our friend did not go astern faster under such extremely unfavorable circumstances; yet I could not conceal from myself that there was and is a constant diminution of vitality, notwithstanding the very slight symptomatic changes, and the positive improvement of the weather, at intervals, lasting six and eight days at a time. His cough has been at times much diminished, his sleep much improved, his strength considerably increased, and his spirits better; but, even at such times, he has sensibly lost flesh. This fact he magnifies, as he does all unfavorable appearances, being, in this respect, no exception to ordinary invalids. My theory of treatment for him has always been *rest* for his weak and over-used lungs; and when I accompany him every other day and oftener on his walks, I scarcely talk at all, for in this way alone can I prevent his talking. He, however, sees a variety of persons, and so loves to talk that it is quite impossible to prevent him. Of course, in my opinion, he suffers injury in consequence. . . . .
. . . . I do not *know* that the self-forgetfulness enforced in this way may not offset the damage suffered by the lungs; but my opinion is, that the despondency could not work such positive injury. We often express wonder that physicians know so little of the effects of remedies and of climate on disease; yet the materials for determining these subtle facts in a given case are very partial and imperfect, and very inferior to those enjoyed by a careful nurse or attendant on the sick man. I have watched Mr. Parker with the closest scrutiny now for four months, and I cannot say with any confidence that weather has or has not worked any positive change on him in any one instance. He has had increased activity of prominent symptoms on a change from damp to dry, and one set of theorists here say, " That might have been expected ; it is always so with consumptive persons." But also he has had the same changes on a variation from dry to damp, and another set says—"All right, the damp always acts so on the lungs." You will wish I might make some *résumé* after the study of all the phenomena, and yet I feel my incapacity to do more than to give you my impressions, and compare his present condition with what it was or seemed to me when you left him in Montreux. He is, I think, ten or twelve pounds lighter, more nervous and desponding, looks thinner in the face, complexion paler, eyes much *feebler*-looking, having lost a great deal of their fire and expression. His power of walking is greater than it was then, and his breathing certainly not more diffi-

cult, as far as can be ascertained by the ear, when he goes uphill or upstairs. His cough (which has varied at times) is now about the same as it was then, not worse in any respect; his appetite sharp and regular. He has his own theories (or caprice) about his drinks—a point upon which I think he errs, drinking too great a variety—Marsala, Sicily port, Monongahela whisky, and occasionally trying other things. These and all liquors he takes, as you know, in very moderate quantities; yet I fear that the variety is prejudicial. For a month past he has been apprehending a hæmorrhage, which he said would occur on the anniversary of the first attack, January 9th. "You will see that I am not mistaken in this," he several times said to me. It is now the 16th, and, as good luck would have it, he was rather unusually well on that and the few neighboring days. He now says the 20th must pass before he is safe from an attack, and I think his spirits may rise if he passes that point in safety. The life he leads is very uniform, and may be described as follows:—He rises at nine, breakfasts at half-past nine or ten. At eleven to half-past eleven, we start out, go "down town" to Piazza di Spagna, thence to the post-office (about a mile), and then wander about the streets at a rather moderate pace; mercury averaging during these hours, say 48° Fahrenheit. At one or half-past one he always gets hungry, goes into a *café*, and calls for some light lunch, say fried ham (little zephyr bits), a roll, and a glass of water. Then we resume our trudge, and I always get him indoors by three, as the streets of Rome are considered unhealthy after that hour. A part (say from a half to a whole hour) of this time is always devoted to looking over old musty books, either at the stalls in the street or at the old book-stores. His eyes are everywhere; nothing escapes them; he runs them over the fruit-stalls, selects any new kind of nut or other fruit, asks what it is and where it grew, and tastes it; every placard on the walls, be it bull of Pope, *Invito Sacro*, or (and especially) " *Vendita di una Libreria*." Occasionally we pass *through* a church, where his comments are characteristic, commonly summed up with an expressive "H–m!" which you are familiar with. He looks even upon painting rather with the moral than the æsthetic eye, and with difficulty discovers the beauty of the mediæval and pre-mediæval paintings athwart their ghastly subjects. This proves not the blindness of the æsthetic eye, but the transparency of all those media which intercept or dim the moral vision of the ordinary man. His reasoning powers were never clearer or sharper. We were together, a week or two since, on a visit to Mrs. Browning. Mr. Browning was present, and the conversation turned on Guerronnière's pamphlet,* which had just then appeared. Mrs. Browning had not seen it, only heard generally its contents, or rather purport. Mr. Parker had seen a translation of it in the *Times*, and proceeded, in his unique way, to state its grounds, its argument, and then to draw his own inferences as to its real meaning, object, and probable effect. Mr. Browning stood up with his back to the fire, Mrs. Browning sat with her face turned half round towards him, and I sat so that I could at once see the faces of all three. It was very interesting to observe

* Le Pape et le Congrès.

how spell-bound they were; and Mrs. B. said to me, some days after, "What a masterly statement! What a wonderful man!" But to return to my diary, or, rather, Mr. Parker's. Arrived at home he takes to the sofa, generally, more tired than I approve, and sometimes get a nap. Dinner comes at five, and very often with evening a visitor comes in—either the Count Frölich, of Sweden; Dr. Appleton, an old parishioner, with wife; or George Bemis, of the Suffolk Bar. Every night at eight he comes down one story to our room, with cap and shawl, and sits, never over an hour, except the Storys be present, when he sometimes extends his visit to ten o'clock, Mrs. Parker generally with him.

We are served from a German *trattoria*, which is far superior to the best Italian that we have known, and get simple, good, and quite American fare, roast and boiled. Provisions are unprecedentedly cheap this winter, owing to the diminished demand, and we reap the comforts of this exceptional state of things. My programme *seems* to have filled up the day; but you know the man, and will not be surprised that a vast amount of reading and writing is dovetailed into it. His shelves show a long range of learned works on Rome and Italy, and his diary* is swelling under his indefatigable pen. Social correspondence is by no means neglected, and the well man shrinks abashed before his indomitable industry and his power of work.

Here the course of life is resumed with Mr. Parker's letters to various friends. First comes a careful archæological survey of Rome.

TO MR. CHARLES ELLIS.

Rome, Jan. 29, 1860.

MY DEAR MR. ELLIS.—It is a great while since I have written you, but I know you will not think that I ever cease to remember that you are one of my oldest and best friends, as well as one of the best beloved. But it is not now quite so easy to write as when I could sit half a day with a pen in my hand and not be weary; and besides, here, where we have but one room with a fire in it, there are continual interruptions which make writing impossible.

But I wonder if you would not like a word or two about this famous old city and its neighborhood? I think so, and accordingly will set down the result of my observations upon it in regular order.

I. The Rome of Nature. An irregular range of mountains, broken and interrupted here and there, sweeps round and encloses a sort of amphitheatre of level or undulating land, bounded on one side by the sea, which this range of mountains approaches at both ends. This amphitheatre contains Rome and the Campagna, or field about

---

* The Diary for these months contains only scraps from newspapers and pamphlets, epitaphs, concetti, brief characterizations of books read. The last page is an Italian quotation from Novæ's "Elementi della Storia de Sommi Pontifici," Roma, 1785, relating to the fable of Pope Joan.

Rome. It is irregular in shape, perhaps thirty or forty miles across in each direction. This territory has two rivers, the Tiber and the Anio, a branch of the Tiber, which receives it 'about twenty miles from the sea. There are several smaller streams which run *directly* to the sea, but are short and small. The land slopes gradually from the mountains to the sea, but is broken into gentle swells, or into low but steep-sided hills. The mountains are of volcanic origin, except here and there, where you find an isolated calcareous summit, like Soracte, standing alone; but a ridge of hills, lower than the mountains, and twenty or thirty miles long on the north-east side of this amphitheatre, is also of limestone. All the plain, with its small hills, is also volcanic. Along the shore you find rolled pebbles of various character—granitic, volcanic, calcareous. The natural plants are pines, cypresses, oaks—three kinds, one of them evergreen—chestnuts, alders, maples, ashes, poplars, willows, &c., all different from our own. Perhaps the fig, the walnut, and the vine are also natives; other fruit-trees have been introduced by man. The plants of the grass kind are numerous; there is great profusion of flowers. The soil is rich by nature, and the climate such that the cattle keep the field all the year; the sheep have lambs in the early spring, and again late in the summer; the woods and fields are always green; the ground never freezes, and if snow falls, it lies but a few hours, and seldom extends half an inch in depth. It never freezes in the day-time, even if the weather is cloudy; the rain falls about forty inches a-year (we have forty-seven at Boston and only twenty-seven at London) yet it seems to me it rains almost every day since I have been here. The land slopes from the mountains to the sea about one foot in a mile, or a little more; so the soil requires artificial drainage to make it healthy and serviceable for farms and gardens. Originally, I suppose, the whole surface was covered with a great, thick, rich forest, but that has long ago disappeared; still, the edge of the sea is fringed with a deep wood, and the sides of the mountains are covered with trees. Once there were many volcanoes in this ridge of mountains, but they have long been silent, and now the craters are lakes of pure clear water, still retaining their circular shape and great depth. Indeed, all the lakes hereabouts are volcanic cups, once filled with fire, now full of water.

II. Rome of the Pre-Romans. The city of Rome was founded 754 B.C., but before that time this territory was pretty thickly settled, and the land apparently cultivated well; large towns were scattered about, one of three hundred thousand or four hundred thousand inhabitants a few miles off; many small towns must have been in the neighborhood. But now no relics remain of those ancient peoples, save here and there the ruins of a city all covered up and hid so completely that, for one thousand years, nobody knew where it once had been. But Greek and Roman writers keep the traditions of those peoples, and preserve a few fragments of their language; nay, a little farther off we find, now and then, a monumental inscription. Here is one curious fact—all over Central and Northern Europe we find monuments of the time when the inhabitants were savage, or just advancing out of primitive wildness. Their tools of *bone*, of *stone*, of *copper*, and of *iron* mark the successive steps of their progress; but, in this neighborhood, no such marks of ancient savagery have ever been found; and, so far as I know, all Italy has not a *stone tomahawk* to exhibit, or an *arrowhead of flint.* I can't account for the fact.

III. Rome of the Roman Kings. About fifteeen miles from the sea, on the right bank of the Tiber, and two miles below its junction with the Anio, there is a cluster of hills, ten or fifteen of them, close to the river; some of them were originally one hundred and twenty or two hundred feet high above the level of the river, which is twenty feet above the sea. Towards the water the sides were steep; there were little ponds or swamps, between the hills; the valleys were always damp. This is the first rising ground between the sea and the mountains. There the city was built, small at first, and at length spreading out to the size of Paris, twelve or thirteen miles in circumference. The first government was by kings and an oligarchic senate. The kingdom lasted from 754 to 510, and has left a few monuments. (1.) A subterraneous canal for draining the lowest parts of the city. It is made of stone, arched; is about six hundred feet long and twelve feet high; it is thirteen or fourteen feet wide at one end, and ten or eleven at the other, where it enters the river. You will see the skill of the engineer who thus made it keep itself clear. (2.) A gaol with thick walls and a deep dungeon. (3.) Fragments of the city wall, partly of stone, partly of earth, in which cabbages, lettuces, and other kitchen vegetables are cultivated now. Such are the chief remains of a kingdom, which ceased 2370 years ago—a Sewer, a Prison, and a Wall.

IV. Rome of the Roman Consuls. (570 to 29 B.C.) This has left us as visible monuments—(1) the foundations of a few small temples now covered up with other buildings, or with ruins; (2) the foundation of part of the present Capitol; (3) some bridges now in ruins, or else built over anew; (4) the remains of some aqueducts, long since fallen to decay; (5) fragments of the foundation of a theatre, all covered up with modern structures; (6) a few tombs, some of them celebrated for beauty or costliness; and (7) several great public highways built with wonderful solidity. The Roman Republic has left few visible remains.

V. Rome of the Emperors. (29 B.C. to 476 A.C.) This has left us (1) great highways; (2) great aqueducts; (3) bridges, now built over anew; (4) a long line of walls of brick or stone; (5) the ruins of a few temples, small, as the Roman temples always were; (6) the ruins of enormous baths; (7) the Colosseum, a magnificent ruin; (8) palaces and villas, all ruins now; (9) two enormous triumphal columns; (10) several triumphal arches, three of them pretty complete; (11) old temples converted into churches—the finest of these is the Pantheon, the fairest relic of the ancient architecture in Italy, perhaps in the world; (12) obelisks brought from Egypt and set up in Rome; (13) funeral monuments in great number—the most remarkable are the mausoleums of Augustus and Hadrian, and the pyramid of Caius Cestius; (14) statues, bas-reliefs, and bronzes in great numbers, some of them brought from conquered countries. Most of these works date from the earlier portion of the Empire: after the year 300, scarce anything was added to the wealth and beauty of Rome, except what is next to be named.

VI. Rome of the Popes. (Say 200 A.C. to 1860.) This period laps on that of the Empire one hundred and seventy-six years; the beginning (200 A.C.) is arbitrary, but I think the power of the Popes did not show itself before that time. This may be distributed into three periods— 1. The Dark Ages, say till 800, the time of Charlemagne. 2. The Middle Ages, from 800 to 1450. 3. Modern Times, 1450 till now.

(1.) Papal Rome in the Dark Ages. (i.) We have funeral monuments of the Christians ; (ii.) the Catacombs, with their strange and curious contents; (iii.) churches—but not one of them in its present form dates back to 300. Perhaps the St. Agnes is the oldest of all, built in 324, and not much altered since. The great churches of this period were the old St. Peter's, St. Paul's-beyond-the-Wall, St. John of Lateran ; but all these are swept away and rebuilt. Four famous churches are still standing of this time, made out of old heathen temples ; all the others were made out of the materials of former buildings, destroyed that these might be built. See how the number of churches increased. From 400 to 500 there were thirty-six new churches built; from 500 to 600, four ; from 600 to 700, seventeen ; from 700 to 800, twelve—all, I think, built out of the ruins of Pagan temples, for the Christians were the first destroyers of Imperial Rome. (iv.) Statues, bas-reliefs, and mosaics in great abundance have come from this period, all indi- cating decay of everything except " *ng-piety* " (you know how to pro- nounce that word).

(2.) Papal Rome in the Middle Ages. Here come (i.) churches, though in no great number—from 800 to 900, fourteen ; 900 to 1000, ten ; 1000 to 1100, three; 1100 to 1200, eighteen ; 1200 to 1300, sixteen ; 1300 to 1400, only one. These were times of trouble, of war, of continual disturbance. For three hundred or four hundred years in the time of the Empire, Rome contained a population of one million five hundred thousand ; but in 1377, it had dwindled down to seventeen thousand ! (ii.) Towers and other fortified buildings. These were very numerous, belonging to the feudal system, and the time of war. These were built by ruining the old structures ; but most of them have passed away. Indeed, most of the churches of this period are either demolished or else reconstructed, more or less. (iii.) Funeral monu- ments of this age are scattered about in many churches, or collected in museums. (iv.) There are sculptures, and mosaics, and, perhaps, frescoes of this age.

(3.) Papal Rome in Modern Times. All the present city dates from this period, and is not older than the year 1450. (i.) Here come the churches. Even St. Peter's is since 1500. From 1500 to 1600, sixty churches and convents were built ; from 1600 to 1700, fifty-five ; from 1700 to 1800, twenty-three. (ii.) Palaces and public buildings—all these are modern ; of the eighty palaces mentioned in guide-books, not one is before 1480. From 1500 to 1600, there were built thirty-four ; 1600 to 1700, twenty-two ; 1700 to 1800, six. (iii.) Houses and shops of the common people—all these are modern. The whole town dates since 1500. Really, it is surprising to see what wealth of church and palace has been created in three hundred and fifty years. St. Peter's Church cost about fifty million dollars ! With us at home, what we call churches are meeting-houses, for the accommodation of men and women who hope to get some instruction therein; here they are "for the glory of God," or oftener of some miserable beast of a saint. Accordingly, you often go into a church which has cost one million dollars, and find service going on, but attended only by the gang of priests whose business it is to do that work. The people are not there ; so, many churches are built where there are no people, and never will be. St. Paul's-out-of-the-Walls dates back to the fourth century, if not earlier; it has often been destroyed and rebuilt—it is in process of reconstruction now. It will cost more than all the meeting-houses of Boston.

TO MRS. C. ELLIS.

Rome, Feb. 3, 1860.

My dear Mrs. Ellis,—I had made ready the foregoing letter to your excellent husband ,when the *Transcript* told me that he had passed to a sphere where letters are not needed to communicate between soul and soul. Yesterday, there came a letter from Francis Jackson, of 13th ult., giving me more particulars of his departure. I need not tell you or your children how much I sympathize with you in your loss; it is but too well known. But, my dear sorrowing friends, he has lost nothing, but has made an unspeakable gain. Not long ago poor Katie went before him, lamenting that she must go alone. Now he is with her. Nay, she went to make ready a place in heaven for her father, who so tenderly prepared a place for her on earth. Let us not complain. Tenderly loved by those who knew him best, widely respected by many whom he worked with in the various duties of the day, at a considerable age, he has gone home. He has shaken off a worn-out and broken body, continually racked with torturing pains, and risen up a freed and unfettered spirit. I think the suddenness of his departure was not the least of many mercies. He was saved that long lingering which torments so many of us, and makes the road to the grave so rough and difficult; he had none of the "hope deferred which maketh the heart sick." Mr. Jackson wrote me that he was taken ill of the paralysis Sunday, "and died at the going down of the sun." I think it fortunate for him, for you, for us all, that he was spared that long agony which wearies out the days of many, who perish at last of that disease. I know how difficult it is for wife and children to think so at first; after a while our eyes open, and we discover a mercy where at first we saw only a terror.

I need not say how highly I esteemed your husband, or how I loved him, nor what reason I had for both. He was one of my oldest friends, one of the faithfulest, one of the nearest and dearest. I have known him twenty-two years, and that, too, with increasing esteem and affection. He was a large-minded man, observant and thoughtful. He had his own way of looking at things, original and independent. I have not known many men with such fine large natural powers ; they were admirably well-disciplined also. How tender and loving he was at home I need not say ; but his charity went out abroad, and did service to men whom he never saw ; they were lifted up and comforted, though they saw not the arm that he put round them. His sympathies were so ready, and his mind so active, that, spite of his white hairs and suffering body, he still continued young. He welcomed all new thought when almost seventy years old as readily as a man of twenty-five. This keeping a young heart is quite rare, and always beautiful. I need not say how much I valued his counsel. It was he that induced me to deliver my first course of lectures in Boston in 1841. I said, " I am too young to engage in such a work ; " and he answered earnestly, " We don't ask you to be older now, but to do what you can till you become so." I went and did what I could then. I am old enough now ! Again, in 1846, I was in doubt about coming to Boston to preach in the Melodeon. I distrusted my own talents. I feared that only a few would accept the doctrines I had to offer, for *I* saw clearly where those doctrines would lead, and the failure would make matters worse than before. It was mainly through his persuasion that I gave up my self-distrust and fear, lest others could not accept what I was yet so anxious to offer them. His friendship never failed, and I never asked him in vain to help another—he often went further in such matters than I wished. It is just a year to-day since I left home, expecting not to see him again. Yours was the last house I went to in America. In my sickness I made but four visits ; one to see my uncle, aged ninety-one ; one to see Mrs. Goddard, seventy-eight; another to see my wife's aunt, almost eighty ; and the last to bid good-bye at your house. I could not visit my wife's mother, aged seventy-five. Of the four I took by the hand only one is left on earth. Perhaps they have already greeted each other in the great commonwealth of heaven, where they have entered into the joy of their Lord, and tasted the fulness of his blessing ! Accept the tenderest sympathy for you and yours of, affectionately and faithfully your friend,

T. P.

TO DR. CABOT.

Rome, Feb. 3, 1860.

My dear Dr. Cabot,—It is a year to-day since I last saw you, when, armed with your seven-league boots, you came and so kindly and affectionately helped me off. In many respects I am now a deal better than then, when local troubles had brought me down pretty low. I have had a great variety of climates and situations in twelve months. Snow was a foot deep on the by-ways of New York when I left the city, Feb. 8, 1859. In an hour after starting our steamboat struck into a horrible storm, which was three days thick. How sea-sick we were—what troubles we went through ! The little, long, thin, deep, sharp propeller, with no side wheels, turned in the water as quick as an eel—a most uncomfortable ship. But when, on the fourth day, we got into smooth water, with just wind enough to keep the boat steady, and the sub-tropical sun shone out of a cloudless sky; when the shallow water had that exquisitely beautiful amethystine color, the Island of Nassau showed us its green hills, its cocoa-nut trees full of fruit, its lemon and orange trees, and its various palms, its sugar-canes and its enormous oleanders, fifteen or twenty feet high. I felt as I fancy the souls do that are released from a miserable body, and enter at once upon the eternal paradise! I never experienced such sensations—I can never forget them. At St. Croix, on my arrival, I was terribly weak. I could but just walk round the house and garden, and could only write by holding my left hand to steady the other—writing with a hand and a fist. But the momentum of a long active life, and the habit of intellectual industry, put me upon tasks above my strength.

*   *   *   *   *   *

I did best at Combe-Varin with Desor. There I had highly intellectual companions, the best of food, the choicest of wine, and work in the woods. We lived in a cup or trough on the top of the mountains. When the sun was up high, the weather was delicious, but when the shadows of the mountains began to grow long and reach across the valley, the radiation of heat in that clear, thin atmosphere was strangely rapid; and as the air grew cool I began to cough, and went in-doors and lighted my peat fire, and read the newest works of German science. I did well there . . . . .

You must not think I slighted your advice in taking Rome and not Egypt for the winter (sometime I will tell you more of the reasons than I care to write). It is a most fitful climate. I have been here near four months, and have seen no particle of dust till yesterday. It has rained almost all the time; yet, out of the 120 days, there have been but eight when I have not walked out an hour or two. Now and then, as yesterday and the day before, the weather is perfectly beautiful; it rains to-day, and we had a rainbow at 7 o'clock A.M. I always know the night before what the weather will be next day in general. Rome is the dampest city I was ever in. The walls and roofs are green and yellow with fuci and lichens of various kinds; but the soft, moist air feels as grateful to sore lungs as the steam of the sugar-houses did at St. Croix—it seems healing and wholesome. The *tramontana* wind, a westerly current, is cold and arid. That makes me cough at once; but if it should continue a few days—it is never violent, or more than fifteen miles the hour—I think it would cease to trouble me. On the whole, Rome has done better for me than I expected or hoped: it was a *pis aller* at the best, my coming here. I have held my own more than I hoped. At first I got too much fatigued by long walks—four to six hours a-day. Then I was sleepless, and sweat at night; but Story told me the cause (*expertus discet*), and I avoided it, and mended. I have been very careful about exposure. I have not been in a palace, a library (!), or a gallery of painting or sculpture since I came here, and do not see the inside of a church much oftener than Falstaff saw his own knee. Do commend me for my prudence. When I first came, I got the requisite books descriptive of Rome, that I might have some indoor work, and need not eat my own head off in the long evenings. So I have read a good deal on Roman history, antiquities, topography, art, &c., &c. I can't talk, nor visit, nor go to the theatre, but have yet found not a little sort of amusement. I look after the book-auctions; there have been ten already. I go in the warm part of the day and look over the books for sale in the evening, and so learn what is the staple reading of the clergy, for all these are the libraries of deceased ministers. Miserable stuff these collections are, in general, the dryest of dead books—mummified literature .Yet now and then I find works of great value and rarity sold for a trifle. A sick man must not buy big books for himself; but if the College Library had let me have 400 or 500 dollars to spend here, I could have saved them 400 or 500 dollars more. Now and then I get a little thing for myself, at a small cost. So I get amusement and occupation, and cheat myself into the belief that I am doing something, and am going to live and work again. And in this, "the pleasure is as great in being cheated as to cheat." But I will tell you no more about myself, except that I expect Desor here every week: he is to go to Naples, &c., with me for a month! Do you know the Canton of Neuchâtel made him a citizen a few weeks ago! This is the first time the honor has been conferred on any one since 1848.

Now a word about Roman affairs. The people of this melancholy city live to laugh; and if they cannot make a revolution, they will have their funny caricatures. You may judge that Pio IX. is not particularly well beloved in Rome just now, especially as the "fear of change perplexing kings" keeps strangers out of the city, which lives chiefly upon them. The old fellow does not behave well now-a-days. He lost his temper the other morning at a breakfast in the American College, and made a foolish speech. He got red in the face, and pounded the table with his fists. He said the ideas of the nineteenth century were deadly hostile to the divine authority of the Roman Church; spoke of Garibaldi, though without naming him, as an assassin (*sicario*), and referred obliquely, but clearly and obviously, to Louis Napoleon as an incendiary (*incenditore*); but he said, " I am not afraid. I will pray to God, and He will change the elements!" (" *Ma io non ho paura, preghero all, Iddio ed egli' cambiero gli elementi.*") The poor old thing forgetting that the God whom the nineteenth century knows, made the elements to suit his purposes at first, and works by developing, not changing them! He is an obstinate, conscientious, good man; but full of ideas that are *pre-mediæval*. He is a logical Pope, and can no more escape from being reactionary and a despot than the Devil can help promoting *sin*, to talk in the mythological way of ministers at home. But he will live to see the ideas of the nineteenth century shake his Pontifical State to pieces, I think and trust. When his temporal power is limited to this city, with 176,000 antiquated, good-natured people, his spiritual power will be worth little, except with the Paddies in Ireland.

The Roman Academy (*Pontificia Accademia Romana di Archeologio*) will hold a meeting next Thursday, and the President, Professor Cav. Salvatore Betti, will treat this question, " Whether Julius Cæsar and Augustus ever thought of removing their Seat of Empire to Old Troy ? " It would be a fit subject for some of the *Betties* of the American Academy at Boston to discuss. Do propose it; you are a member. I intend to leave Rome about April 20-23 for Florence, and thence go slowly to Germany, over the Simplon, if the weather will allow, or if not, then by Venice and the Tyrol. Desor wants me to come and pass the summer amid his pine-woods, and get to America about September 1st. I don't know what to do; tell me. Is it better to come to Boston about

July 1st, and have to go into the country for two months, or about September 1st, and live in my own house in town?

With love from mine to yours, believe me, gratefully and obediently,

Your faithful patient,

THEODORE PARKER.

TO MISS COBBE.

Roma, 1860.

MY VERY DEAR MISS COBBE,—I attended to your kind note, which came last week, as fast as I could, but have not been able to answer it till now. I have no photograph of myself with me, nor do I like those taken in America. The lithograph which you have from Mrs. Hunt is not much esteemed by my critical friends at home, more than by myself; for while the lower part of the face, they say, is good, the upper part is not much like me. As soon as I could make arrangements, I sat to a photographer here in Rome three times, but only took cold; while he, who, *I* think, is only a bungler in taking faces, made most hideous things which I would not keep in the bottom of a trunk. Miss Hunt has a daguerreotype, taken seven or eight years ago, which is fine in some points, it is said; and if my bungler can get a picture of that I will send it, but that has no beard, while I now have an ample covering to my face.

My friends or foes could not have been further out of the way than in saying what you mention as to my opinion about divorce. I have preached on almost all matters of great public concern in America except this divorce question, on which I have never given any opinion in public, and never but twice, as I remember, touched it at all. Once, in a course of lectures on the New Testament, commenting on Jesus's opinion on marriage and divorce, I gave a history of both in the Jewish and the Christian Churches. Again, in a lecture on " The Savage, the Hebrew, the Classic, the Christian, and the Philosophic Idea of Woman," I spoke of marriage and divorce in heathen nations, of course briefly, and in a manner purely objective and historical. I have not touched this great matter for two reasons: (1) I don't feel quite competent to deal with it, and perhaps never shall, even if I live; and (2) things are going on very well without my interference, perhaps better without it. All the progressive States of America are changing their laws of divorce, and in New England they have altered much in fifty or even in twenty years. The instinct and reflection of the people demand a change. In the new Western States the alterations are very great and rapid. In private, I do *not* share the opinions attributed to me, and have painfully spent much time in attempting to reconcile married people who at first sought a divorce. Yet, out of many trials, I remember but *one* where the attempt was at all successful. I have small sympathy with men and women who would either make or break a marriage lightly; but I do not think material adultery is the only breach of marriage. I think I once petitioned the Massachusetts Legislature to make habitual drunkenness a ground for divorce, if the aggrieved party desired it. But proper notions of marriage, and so of divorce, can only come as the result of a slow but thorough revolution in the idea of woman. At present all is chaotic in the relation between her and man; hence the ghastly evils of involuntary celibacy, of unnatural marriage, and of that dreadful and many-formed vice which disgraces our civilization. But we shall gradually outgrow this feudalism of woman, and Kosmos will come where Chaos was. I have few things more at heart than the elevation of woman, and have written much on that theme which may never yet see the light.

I am quite delighted that my little book finds favor in England. I see there are two editions of it; one, which Chapman sent me, for a shilling. I know the idea of Theism must prevail, and shake down at length the Roman Catholic Church and the Teutonic Protestant Church, both representing the idea of an *imperfect Deity*, who makes only special revelations of Himself by miracle. How many minds are now at work in that direction! I trust you will soon find a working place suited to your genius and your culture. I think I could aid you in getting your books before the American public. But you have left the matter in good hands.

T. P.

TO MR. MANLEY.

Feb. 8, 1860.

Mr. Ellis was one of the oldest and most dear friends that I left behind me in America. We have been intimate many years. He had towards me something of the affection of a father, and liked me, not merely for what I was to the world at large, but for what he felt me to be to him. His personal kindness and tenderness has added joy to me for now many a year. I have known few men so well born as he, with so good endowments of body and mind. He was not what is pedantically called an "educated man," but I have found not many with faculties so well developed and disciplined as his. How stupid is the New England notion of what makes an educated man! A little Latin, a little Greek, a little of speculative mathematics and knowledge of a few books—but the understanding, the imagination, the reason, may lie a howling wilderness, and the conscience be as unproductive and lifeless as the Dead Sea. Talk with Rev. Dr. Choker; you say he is an "educated man," though he has not mind and conscience enough to know that it is a *Devil*, not a *God*, who would create men to damn them eternally. Talk with Capt. Goodwin, and you say "he is not educated," though he has all his intellectual and moral faculties in the most healthful activity; can build a ship, and sail her round the world, selling one cargo well and profitably, and buying another; can amputate a leg, and make a wooden one to take its place; and manage the affairs of any town in Plymouth County!

In my sense of the word Mr. Ellis was a man educated well—his moral faculties were also expanded with good proportions; his instincts of humanity became quicker and more generous as he grew older. He was one of the most thoughtful and thinking heads at the Music Hall;

how manly and earnest he looked! I made my last American visit in his house, thinking we should not meet again in this world. His life has seemed very uncertain for years, so much rheumatism, with such an affection of the heart; perhaps he did not know so much of the latter as I did. To his family his loss is a great one; their habitation is left unto them desolate. He has lost nothing—but shaken off a dull, painful, worn-out body, and gone home. There are not many I shall miss so much if I return home, as I trust I shall. When I heard of his departure, I had a letter written for him descriptive of Rome.

What a ghastly affair was that at Lawrence *—nearly as many killed and wounded as the Americans lost at Bunker Hill. Those battles of industry also have their victims. I see they had a day of religious observance at Lawrence on the occasion, and am glad of it. It is natural for us in our sorrow as in our joy, to flee to the Infinite for consolation and hope. But, alas! how few ministers there are who can see and tell the causes of this disaster in human ignorance and cupidity; its function, to tell us of the error we commit, and warn us against repeating it; and its consequences, full of beneficence and man's triumph over the elements. These hundreds of innocent people died, not one of them forgotten before God: they slept in heaven instead of a factory boarding-house, and woke next morning, not to the sharp ring of the mill-bell, but to the gladsome call, " Come, ye beloved, enter into the joy of your Lord! "

But their death is not in vain on earth; they fell as the New England soldiers fell in our defeats at Bunker Hill, and White Plains, and many another fatal battle-field : but all helps to the great victory which is to come. Harsh words are said against the mill-owners, builders, &c.; they did the best they knew, risking their money and reputation on the factory; they certainly constructed ill. This winter, Massachusetts will make laws to prevent such catastrophes for the future, perhaps have a Board of Commissioners of Construction in every county, to look after such great buildings; and for the next fifty years no factory will be built to fall down. The walls of this house I now live in, are thicker on the fifth story than the Pemberton Mills in the first, and *solid* too. Americans are careless, and must suffer until they learn prudence. Conform to natural law, and it shall be well with thee! That is the language of all " accidents."

I hope to stand next winter well in Boston. Spring is beginning here (we have had birds and flowers all winter), and the new grass looks sweet and beautiful. Love from mine to all yours, and to many, many more, from, yours faithfully and thankfully,

T. P.

TO MISS COBBE.

What a hopeful state the European world is now in! Never has it been so interesting since the French Revolution of 1789. It is pleasant to Americans to find England on the side of progress and humanity in this great battle of the nations. From 1770 till 1833 she went the

---

* The sudden falling of a great mill, many stories high, with great loss of life.

other way, and with all her might opposed the great movement which first made an industrial democracy of America, and next destroyed the feudal system in Europe, and at length will shake down all despotic thrones, with "fear of change perplexing kings."

What is commonly called Christianity, *i.e.*, the absurd scheme of theology and church organization which now obtains in all Catholic and Protestant lands, can never again engage the minds of enlightened men; once it could, and Europe blossomed with a new literature and a new art. The "Divina Commedia," the "Paradise Lost," with the cathedrals in all the countries, those are flowers in verse or flowers in stone that show mighty vegetative power lay in the air and the ground. But future ages will see no such growth. It is a better age you and I live in, and a grander and more natural religion will bloom into fairer poetry than past times ever won from their mythologic tales. What a different Paradise will the future Dantes and Miltons be inspired to see and paint before the longing eyes of men for them to transfigure into human life!

Heartily and faithfully yours,
T. P.

TO HON. GERRIT SMITH.

Rome, February 16, 1860.

My dear Mr Smith,—It is with great pain that I have heard of the illness which the recent distressing events have brought on your much-enduring frame, which was so shattered by illness before. When I saw you last I did not think my next letter would be from such a place or for such a purpose. But such is the uncertainty of all mortal things. Some of the rumors relate that you will perhaps come to Europe for health. If this be so, I trust I shall have the good fortune to meet you somewhere. We have many Americans at Rome—two or three hundred, it is said—of whom about forty are from Boston, not to mention the permanent inhabitants. So, you see, one need not lack companionship. Besides, here are many more from Massachusetts and New England.

I feel great anxiety about the immediate future of America; the remote future I have no doubts about. We must see much darker hours before it is daylight—darker, and also bloody I think, for nations don't settle their difficulties without passion, and so without what comes of passion. The slave-holders are in great wrath. I am waiting for the Supreme Court of the United States (in the Lemmon case) to decide, as it must, that a master may take his slaves in transit through a Free State, and keep them in it a reasonable time, subject not only to his own caprice, but defiant of the laws of that State. Certainly, the slave-holders must have eminent domain over the Free States, and Bondage must exercise right of way in New York and New England. Next year, or the year after, it must decide for the African Slave-Trade! "There is one general grievance," said Oliver Cromwell, in the House of Commons, "and that is the Law!"

But I did not mean to worry you with a long letter, so with heartiest sympathy for your sufferings, and profound respect for your character and service, believe me,

Faithfully and truly yours,
T. P.

TO MR. MANLEY.

February 23.

I have the American news up to February 1st, and wish I felt as sure of the action of Congress for the next four months as for the last two. Really it is a great thing to have two months of the session gone and no harm done ! I think I know what the Supreme Court will decide in the Lemmon case, and if the Democratic party triumph next autumn, what it will decide in the African Slave-Trade case in 1861 or 1862. It lies in the logic of Slavery to extend itself over all the nation, and to annihilate all democratic institutions. The conflict between it and freedom is irrepressible. The Republicans are very mean, that they refuse to stand by Seward, when he, with a statesman's prudence, asserted what was a notorious fact. But the Republicans represent only a transitional party, and are perhaps good enough to be beaten a few times more. This is clear; the Anti-Slavery spirit is now so fairly awake in the North, that it cannot be put down; neither the misconduct of a man nor a party can much retard its progress, or hinder its ultimate success.

Mr. Gladstone, you will see, has published his budget before the House of Commons in England. One of the most important movements of the age is there going forward, the establishment of a most liberal commercial intercourse between the two foremost and most powerful nations of Europe. It is curious to read the comments of the British press on Mr. G.'s statement. They publish it in full, as he made it in the House of Commons, and then say it is a great subject, full of many complications, requiring much time and thought for us to master it. By-and-bye, we shall give our opinion. Now, how differently would a similar paper be taken by the American Press, which I think the most contemptible in the world ! But, fortunately, there is this odds in the influence of the British and American journals : in England, thoughtful and serious men go to the editorials for instruction and advice ; in America, nobody does so except the rank and file of the old Democratic party, whose sole maxim of politics is, Do as you are bid ! Things refuse to be mismanaged for ever, and some great abuses correct themselves; nobody listens to a common scold. There is no fair criticism in America on works of science and literature. ——'s book was about as destitute of all merit as any book I remember to have seen of late years. It had not a good scene, nor a good paragraph, a good sentence, or even a good line or phrase, which was original; but he received more commendation from the great "critical journals of commerce" than Emerson in all his life, for all his works up to that time. Agassiz has had admiration and flattery enough to make an ordinary professor sick, but no criticism, since he came amongst us.

When he expounded his scheme of classification to the naturalists of Switzerland and Geneva, last August, they gave him needed criticism, and he smarted terribly under their examination. In America, anybody (or nobody) feels competent to pass judgment on all works of thought, of literature, science, and art; no matter how ignorant he may be. So all American editors, with the rarest exceptions, are ready on two legs to pronounce judgment on a book like Buckle's, or Darwin's, or J. S. Mill's. All they need is pen and ink; all else, like reading and writing, comes by nature. "Can you read and write, Patrick?" said a gentleman to a Paddy. "No doubt of it, yir honnerr—I niver thried!" was the answer. Jonathan Cocksure, editor of the *National Conservative, Spread Eagle,* and *Universal Democrat* "thries" his hand at criticizing a work of statesmanship, of physics, or metaphysics, and finds the types *compose* as readily on that theme as any other, and finds he has become a great "American critic," while Patrick is still bothered with his A B C.

*   *   *   *   *   *

I am one of the most careful of men, and have not only come up to the ideal oyster that Dr. Cabot used to propose as my standard, but have gone over the other side. Yet I find a little amusement. There have been ten or fifteen book auctions. I don't dare stay at the sale (in a little, damp, cold, brick-floored shop) from four to five P.M, but have my bid. So I always have the fun of the hunt, and sometimes actually bag a little game. The cost is but a trifle, which my severe economy has saved many times over in twelve months; and if I die my wife will not be the poorer, while the books are worth to Boston much more than they cost me, and if I live they are special tools which I want for a particular purpose. I would go to the theatre with Rev. N. L. Frothingham, D.D., and Rev. Harriet Beecher Stowe, D.D., if I could. They rejoice in this beautiful entertainment, and it is a shame they have been kept from it so long.

Faithfully yours,

THEODORE PARKER.

TO PROFESSOR DESOR.

Rome, February 24, 1860.

. . . . Here in Rome I am out of the way of all books, except Lives of the Saints, &c., &c. But yet I learn of Mr. Darwin's work on "Principles of Selection in Natural History." It is one of the most important works the British have lately contributed to science. He does not believe in Agassiz's foolish notion of an interposition of God when a new form of lizard makes its appearance on the earth. Indeed, a God who only works by fits and starts is no God at all. Science wants a God that is a constant force and a constant intelligence, immanent in every particle f matter. The old theological idea of God is as worthless for science as it is for religion. I should like to live long enongh to finish and print a course of sermons I preached in 1858, on "The Testimony of Matter and Mind to the Existence and

Character of God." *   It certainly is the most important thing I have done in my life ; but is left not fit for publication.   If I don't do that work some one else will ;· a little later, but perhaps better.   But I must end my scrawling letter.   My wife and Miss S. send all manner of good wishes to you and yours.   Remember me kindly to the *qute Marie*.   Let Spitz have her *culbute*, and may the great strong *Hengst*† carry you safely and happily on many a journey!   Let me see you here soon ; for *you* are the medicine I need most of all, and may do me just the good thing I need to set me on my legs again.

Faithfully and affectionately yours,

THEODORE PARKER.

TO GEORGE JACKSON, ESQ., BOSTON.

Rome, March 1, 1860.

MY DEAR MR. JACKSON,—Mr. Manley's last note of February 7th informed me that your wife's soul calmly, and with no pain, took flight for heaven a little while before.   I know that ties knit so tenderly as that between you and her, and which had joined the two so beautifully and so long, cannot be broken, however gently, without a terrible shock to the survivor.   But the good woman had reached a good old age, and seen her children and children's children about her growing up or grown, and then one night so serenely passed forward and ceased to be mortal !   I need not speak of her character, least of all to *you* and yours ; but in the manner of her departure there is something quite cheering and consoling.   Who would not wish for such a smooth sail out of this little sea and into the great wide haven we are all bound to ?   It seems to me, your wife and Mr. Charles Ellis were highly-favored mortals, they had so quick and smooth a passage ; while others are months, and even years, in getting across.   Most men dread *dying*, but not *death*.   I can't think our present deaths are natural, or to continue always.   If something were not wrong in our mode of life, we should all slide out of the world as gently as old Mr. Bradlee or as your own wife ; but we must bear the misfortunes which others entail upon us.   If it were *fate* it could not be borne ; but when we look on it as Providence, the work of an Infinite Father and Mother, who looks eternally before and eternally looks after, and rules all things from love as motive and for blessedness as end, we can take almost anything with a smile.

I can't help the belief that we shall be joined to our dear ones in the next life, and this conviction sweetens many an hour else filled with bitterness.   I don't know that we can pay any one a higher compliment than that of hoping to meet him in the kingdom of heaven.   Our affections

---

* The sermons alluded to were preached in 1858.   They are five in number :—
>   No. 880. The Progress of True Theological Ideas.   Part I.—Historical.
>   „   881. The Same.   Part II.—Conjectural.
>   „   885. The Progress of God in the World of Matter.
>   „   889. The Evidence of God in the Relations between the World of Matter and of Mind.   Part I.
>   „   890. The Same.   Part II.

† *Spitz* was a terrier dog, and *Hengst* was one of the horses,—*culbute* was Spitz's habitual summerset.

are so infinite in their desires, and yet the time to gratify them is so short, and interrupted so on earth—partly by our cares, and in part by our defects of temper and other follies—that it seems as if there must be another world where the little plant of love should become a great strong tree. It is a beautiful arrangement of the world, that we commonly forget the failings and wrong-doings of those near to us soon after they are gone, while their excellences come out like the stars at night, and show us a whole heaven of beauty we had not been conscious of before. It is in this way, doubtless, that your wife will live in your memory and your children's memory for many a year, and grow more lovely as she is transfigured by the idealizing effect of the most elevated feelings of our nature. How fortunate you have been in the long continuance of your marriage—nearly forty-six years, if I remember right —while the average length of wedded life in our State of Massachusetts is hardly *ten!* Happy in its length, happy in its character, and happy in its close—so noiseless and without pain to the departing one. The whole seems beautiful. The ancients used to pray for what they called *Euthanasia*—a beautiful dying—and it was not so foolish as most prayers of old time, or new. Your wife had the blessing, I suppose, without asking for it. I hope your daughters are well, and resigned and cheerful; such a state of feeling makes life so easy and delightful.

> " If on our daily course our mind
> We set to hallow all we find,
> New treasures still, of costly price,
> God will provide for sacrifice:
> Old friends, old scenes will lovelier be,
> As more of heaven in each we see.
> Some softening gleam of love and prayer
> Will dawn on every cross and care."

I have taken great pleasure in your daughters' society in days past, and can only regret that my life has been so shamefully busy that I had no more time for that and similar entertainments. But I did not choose my cares; they were forced upon me against my will. I should have selected a little easier lot; but it is all over now, and too late to repent.

Remember me kindly to your brothers—Francis I often hear from; good, kind soul that he is—and their families, and believe me, with tenderest sympathy, faithfully your friend,

THEODORE PARKER.

TO MISS C. THAYER.

March 2, 1860.

*　　*　　*　　*　　*　　*

I see some one has written a paper on Thomas Paine, in the *Atlantic*, which excites the wrath of the men who were not worthy to stoop down and untie the latchet of his shoes, or to black his shoes, or even to bring them home to him from the shoe-blacks. Yet Paine was no man for my fancying—in the latter years of his life he was filthy in his personal habits; there seems to me a tinge of lowness about him. But it must not be denied that he seems to have had less than the average amount of personal selfishness or vanity; his instincts were human and elevated, and his life mainly devoted to the great purposes of humanity. His political writings fell into my hands in my early boyhood, and I still think they were of immense service to the country. His theological works I know less of, chiefly from his enemies; they are not always in good taste, nor does he always understand the Scriptures of Old Testament and New Testament he comments upon. But I think he did more to promote piety and morality amongst men, than a hundred ministers of that age in America. He did it by showing that religion was not responsible for the absurd doctrines taught in its name. For this reason honest but bigoted ministers opposed him. They had a right to; but they misrepresented his doctrines.

      *   *   *   *   *

I am glad the brave old John Pierpont is to preach at the Music Hall. I think he did greatly wrong in expunging all anti-slavery matter from his school books; but it was under great temptation; and who is there, in a public life of more than fifty years, that has made but a single error? He is a noble old man, and never, so far as I know, gave a mean counsel in his public teaching! I wish he was rich and not poor. I often asked him to preach for me in the Melodeon, but he always refused.

How fortunate Mrs. George Jackson was in her swift death! these *long dyings* are terrible and unnatural. Dr. Frothingham is here, and very kind to me, coming to read me his new poems in the evenings. Christopher Thayer had returned from Naples, and is kind and attentive. But no stranger has done me such service as Dr. Appleton; there is no end to his attention and kindness. Now love from me and mine "all round to the neighbors, neighbors, neighbors!" and believe me, faithfully yours,

THEODORE PARKER.

TO ISAAC PARKER, LEXINGTON, MASS.

Rome, March 16, 1860.

MY DEAR BROTHER,—I don't know what will interest you most in a city where all things would be equally strange; but as you are a farmer, I shall take it for granted that what relates to your own business will also prove most welcome in a letter. Well, Rome is surrounded by an immense desert, extending to the sea on the one side, to the mountains on the other, and reaching out forty or fifty miles between the sea and the mountains. This desert bears little but wild grass, which is fed upon by great flocks of sheep (whose wool is better than their mutton), swine, cows, and buffaloes. Some part of it is cultivated with wheat— once in three years they get a crop; the land lies fallow the rest of the time. The oxen are small, but well-made, cream-colored or grey, with long horns; they are very docile and serviceable; the yoke rests on the

neck just back of the horns; they draw by a broad strap across the
forehead, though some have the yoke where we put it, and use very
clumsy bows. All oxen have a sort of ring in the nose, which can be
removed at pleasure. Milk is poor and thin, the butter white and
meagre; it is not the climate for butter and cheese, though the beef is
as good as at home.

In the winter the farmer drives his hogs into the forests, where they
thrive on the acorns of an evergreen oak—one of the fairest trees in
this handsome land; by day they go at large; at night the owner blows
a conch shell, and they come home and are shut up in pens. The
hogs are black, small (would weigh about 200 lbs.), but well-made. Nobody lives in this desert, save here and there on a little knoll of land,
but once the whole broad expanse, from the mountains to the sea, was
full of towns and villas, fields and gardens.

The chief articles of culture by the farmer are the fruits—grapes,
apples, pears, oranges, pomegranates, peaches, apricots, quinces, filberts,
chestnuts, and wall fruits, and many vegetables not known to Americans. Potatoes are never good on the Continent of Europe. Lettuce
is far better than with us, so are the cauliflowers, which are as easily
cultivated here as cabbages at Lexington, and sold cheap. Apples are
poor—very poor, close-grained, tough, and indigestible; they bring from
two to twenty cents a pound (!) and are as cheap now as last October.
About two-thirds of the space within the city walls is uninhabited; a
considerable part of it is occupied with kitchen gardens, which are cultivated with great skill. Take a great one which I visited the other day,
as big as Boston Common. It has a ridge of land running through it,
twenty or forty feet high; the chief thing cultivated is the grape vine.
The vines are set in rows, and trained to stakes like bean poles, only
not so high. But as the vines occupy the land with their shade only
from May till October, there is room also for a winter crop; so to
facilitate that, the ground on the south side of the ridge is thrown into
furrows, running east and west, shaped, thus :—

The sloping side is towards the south, and is planted with lettuce,
which requires all the sun it can get in the winter; that towards the north
is set out with a sort of French turnip, which grows all winter with less
light and heat. That is what I call making a nice use of the winter sun.

All country produce is brought to town in carts. I have never seen
a waggon in Rome. The wheels are about as big as those of our ox-
carts, the felloes as deep, but the hubs and spokes more slender; the
axletree is about a foot shorter than ours. The body of the cart
varies according to the load—hay, faggots, bags of charcoal, wine, &c.
The cart is not painted, and is washed about as often as you put water
on your chaise, and is commonly nearly as dirty; for the country
roads here are very poor. It is drawn generally by three horses or
mules, yoked abreast, though sometimes by a single pair of long-
horned oxen. The driver sits on the left-hand side of the front-end of
his cart, and, as the weather is variable, he has a sort of tent over his
head attached to a cart-stake, which he can remove at pleasure; it is
made of untanned cow-hide. Indeed, in the winter he wears leggings,

which come up to the hips, made of untanned skin of the goat, sheep, or ox, and which look funny. The horses and mules wear bridles, without blinders or bits ; instead of the latter, they have a rough chain or ragged bit of iron, which goes round the creature's nose, by which he is guided. Horses, mules, and asses are shamefully ill-treated by the farming people, over-worked, under-fed, and beaten with dreadful blows. The little carts which ply about the city have axles about three and a half feet long, while the body is not more than two feet wide. The driver always sits in the cart.

The chief diet of the Romans is vegetables. They have many about as nutritious as asparagus. Cabbages they make much use of. The people look weak and ill-fed ; they do not live long. Country people have a warm meal but once a week, on Sunday. Then there is a soup of vegetables, some boiled beans, and a bit of meat. The rest of the time their food is bread, with a raw onion, a bit of salt, and dried hog's-flesh, and a little wine. The bread is poor stuff ; but, on the whole, better than what one gets in the country towns of New England ; for here it is only sour and indigestible, not also poisoned with soda and saleratus. Pumpkin-seeds are a common article of food. Do you know that pumpkins, fed to cows, seeds and all, make them dry up, but without the seeds they increase the quantity of milk ? The seeds are a powerful diuretic. I have no good news to write about my health. We all send love to all—I, not forgetting the neighbors.

Faithfully your brother,

THEODORE PARKER.

TO MISS MARY T. DREW, BOSTON.

Rome, Mar. 17, 1860.

MY DEAR MARY,—This sheet is ruled as whopper-jawed as some women cut their bread; but I hope you will excuse it. I wonder what will interest you most in Rome ; something that belongs to housekeeping, no doubt. Here all the washing is done in cold water, at great public stone fountains. The kitchens here would astonish you. I think five bushels of charcoal would last a decent family a year, to do all their cooking with. They have no pot so large as our tea-kettle at home; half a dozen copper stew-pans make up the *battery*, as they call a set of kitchen tools. The people live chiefly on vegetables, like our greens, and look ill-fed and hungry. I have seen only one *fat* man in Rome, and he came in the day before, and went off the next day.

I have lost fifteen to twenty pounds of flesh in the five months that I have been here, and am by no means gaining now. Good nutritious food, in our sense of the word, is not to be had in Rome for love or money. The weather has not been cold this winter; there has seldom been any ice in the fountains or streets. But the weather has been cloudy, rainy, windy, changeable, and disagreeable. I have many times wished myself in my quiet study, where, if I could not improve, I could at least do something, and so be of some little use to mankind. Here I get no better, and can do nothing. It grieved me a great deal to hear that you fell and sprained your wrist so badly. You have a whole siege of troubles; but I am glad to believe the worst of it is all over now. Mr. Manley and Miss Thayer keep me informed about you. Please ask George, when he writes, to tell me if the box ever arrived from St. Thomas, and what condition the contents were in. There was a glass jar, with a great flower in spirits of wine, meant for John L. Russell, of Salem; did he ever get it?

I hope you do not allow yourself to lack such help as a doctor can give you; it is not much, after all, but it is something. Remember me kindly to all your friends. My wife and Miss S. send their kindest wishes to you; I need not say that I add mine. I know how much you took Mrs. Follen's death to heart; but she was fortunate to die so easy and so quick. Remember me to George and his companion, and believe me,

Truly your friend,
THEODORE PARKER.

TO DR. HOWE.

Rome, March 23, 1860.

What you say about the lady learning her accomplishments, &c., is wholly true, I think; in ninety-nine cases out of a hundred, what are called accomplishments are handsome *wens*, grown on the person, not *limbs* developed naturally out of it. If a real poet, philosopher, painter, statesman, were sent where he could not exercise his developed talents, it were cruel; but to send him where his wife cannot spread her crinoline or wear her diamonds, and gossip nonsense with similar "ornamental females," yet where her real *womanly* qualities would be called out and developed in daily life, that is no misfortune, but a blessing. How much humbug there is about what we call *education!* I thank God I am "an uneducated man," but I should be very sorry not to be both a developed and an instructed one in command of my most valuable faculties.

I like not the look of things in the Republican party. Seward's speech came to-day, but from L.'s comment I expect not much satisfaction : more from Abraham Lincoln, at the Cooper Institute.

Once governors, senators, representatives, &c., were the leaders of the rank and file, whom they instructed, directed, and commanded. The people looked up to Sam Adams and John Adams for counsel and direction. Now these functionaries are *servants*, to obey the rank and file ; they give little counsel, are seldom (any one of them) in advance thereof; but as they have not wholly lost the traditionary notion of old time, they refuse to obey the better portion of their constituency ; " It will offend the slave-holders ; it will injure the party," &c., &c. Who looks for instruction or advice to governor, or senator, or representative? So is it with ministers. When they were superior to the parish in talent, culture, progressive virtue, the parish looked up to the pulpit. Who but a fool ever quotes his minister as authority now-a-days?

The following letter to Dr. Howe commences with some allusions to the Harper's Ferry affair ; the Senate Bill was to clothe a committee with power to send for and arrest persons for examination, to obtain knowledge concerning the supposed originators of the movement. :—

I think the Senate Bill for raising the committee, &c., was well enough in *its principle—i.e.* if I understand it. However, it should have provided for the security of the men (and women) it may summon. The testimony of men like you and others ought to be taken in Massachusetts, where you are safe and not liable to be kidnapped ; for —— and —— limit their operations to *colored* people. Of course, the Republicans lack spunk. When the patriots from 1765 to 1775 were so brave and hearty, how happens it that their analogons in 1845–1860 lack all manner of heroism ? *In these times they are looking for office*, and put the Anti-Slavery horse they ride on through only such paces as will bring themselves into honor and power. But this horse will fling some of them, for it is a very " cantankerous critter when he gits his dander up and is a little riled."

I feel anxious to know how Seward will speak in the Senate, and would have given a penny for an hour more of talk with him before he left Europe. American politics engross so much of my attention, that I have written little on Italian or European affairs. Indeed, Boston is a better place for that than Rome, as you well know; yet I began a letter on that theme a week ago. I know not when it will get itself ended, for I cannot now sit down at 9 A.M. and have an hour's sermon ready at 2 P.M. Oh, Chev.," to be weak is to be miserable," and this slow way of dying, though painless, is yet tormenting, with its perpetual delusions and *mirages of power*, which prove nothing but idle dreams.

Is there to be a statue to Horace Mann in the yard of the State-house ? If so, who is to make it ? Story is at work on that of Josiah Quincy ; and a grand thing it will be, too ; very grand, I think. It seems to me he has a great deal of talent, and I wish the Mann statue might be wrought out by his hands, for he has alike the head to understand him, and the heart to admire and esteem. Besides, Story is a capital, good fellow, full of all manner of generous ideas and kindly feelings.

Several Bostonians are here, and I see most of them ; but, alas! I cannot talk, except with considerable pain. Dr. A. gave me a very sensible counsel,—

" Semper auditor tantum, nunquam ne *repone ;* "

and I keep it as well as I can.

Our political affairs look very ill, but all the more hopeful for that reason : they must be much worse before they can be at all better. I had two admirable and profound letters from Lyman on American politics lately. Nobody that I know looks so deeply into these matters, or sees so clearly, unless it be ——, who has the advantage of talking with many persons of diverse modes of thinking. The " irrepressible conflict" comes on; and when the North, in the multiplicity of its interests, looks at the one great and fundamental matter which concerns the existence of freedom, and shows its teeth, then the slave-holders will yield to the superior force that is brought against them, and the —— and the ——. will sneak over to the Anti-Slavery side, and bellow louder than real lovers of freedom.* Still I think we shall see bloodshed before we get through.

TO MR. LYMAN.

I like much what you said about the mode of improving the laws and political institutions of the United States. I have often thought of that scheme; of asking the judges to tell what defects they found in the law, or what redundances. Judge Jackson was one of the committee that revised the statutes in 1837, and as a judge of large experience, had valuable things to suggest; and as he sat in the gallery of the House of Representatives during the discussion of his work, he could explain the working of laws as he had found them. It then seemed to me it would be well to ask all the judges each year to tell how the mill worked in their hands, and what alteration they would like. But your other suggestion is new to me—viz. that a statute should declare that no decision of a court should foreclose the question for the future. It is highly important to limit that old rule *stare decisis*, which perpetuates the ill while it helps to preserve accidental good also. I wish we had some journal devoted to political science, which should give us an article on each session of every legislature in America, and tell what good and ill there was in its new work: it might attend also to the legislation of other countries. But I suppose there is not intellectual or moral talent in our people for such a work—to produce or to appreciate it. So we must stumble along in the dark. Did you ever read M. Comte's "Traité sur la Législation"? It is a very thoughtful book; I have studied it a good deal. He aims to examine and appreciate the causes under which mankind advances, remains stationary, or retrogrades, and is divided into so many books. It is a rare book in America I hear; but I have the Bruxelles reprint of it, a large octavo in green paper, on the shelf at the right hand of the north fire-place in my study. I think on the third shelf from the floor; if not there, it is in the neighborhood.

TO MISS COBBE.

Mar. 27.

MY DEAR MISS COBBE,—I am writing this with your new and commodious pen, the first words I have written with it—for I wished to consecrate it by writing to you. It is very nice and convenient. I never saw but one before yours came. Rome has not used me well this winter, and I shall leave it but with one regret, viz. that I came here at all. I have lost three pounds a-month since I left Switzerland, and

* The fanatics for legality and for the "Union as it is" are just beginning to fulfil this little prophecy (1861).

have gained nothing but a great cough ; and I am as weak as I am emaciated. Indeed, I felt perfectly *démoralisé*, and long to get out of the place, where I remain now only to fulfil a little engagement. In less than ten days I shall be *en route* for Florence, I hope. I promised to do what I could for the photograph : nothing came of it. Indeed, I am only fit to sit as a model for St. Jerome taking his last communion, and should make a better one than Domenichino had for his famous picture here. But I have sat for a cameo,* and my friends think the work successful. When it is completed I will send a photograph of that to Mr. Shaen, at London, and perhaps it will be better either than nothing or one from the original in its present condition. Hoping soon to see you face to face, believe me, &c.

TO MR. RIPLEY.

Shrove-Tuesday, A.S., 1860.

My dear George,—I have not written you this long time, partly because it costs money to send a letter—and in these degenerate days, when I earn nothing and never shall, I must be careful of my pennies as never before—and partly also because it is not good for my rotten lungs to stoop over a table like this. But just now I find a young man going to New York direct (and directly, too), who offers to take what I write, and I cannot well resist the temptation. So here comes a little note.

Old Rome is a modern city ; her 80 palaces, and almost all of her 300 or 360 churches, are since 1450. In running my eye over the 274 (I think that is the number) of Popes, I am struck with many able men, and some great ones—some utterly wicked and heartless, but not very many. Gregory I. and VII., Innocent III., Sixtus V., Julius II., and Paul IV., were all men of power, great power, though the two last were about as unprincipled and wicked wretches as you could find in the American Congress or the chairs of New York editors. It is curious to see how a logical necessity controls those poor wretches. The Papacy is too strong for the individual who bears it, and crushes him down. Some Protestants think there can be a reform Pope. It were as idle to expect an Anti-Slavery President elected by the Democratic party. William Lloyd Garrison himself, in that post, could not behave other than James Buchanan does. You can't have a progressive Pope more than a virtuous Devil ; it is *contradictio in adjecto*. Of course, I hope no good from the Papacy, and wish none for it. But it is in an ugly fix just now. Commonly, the Carnival here is celebrated with great splendor. All the Roman gentility, respectability, &c., are in the streets with their fine carriages ; but this year they knew that to keep Carnival in the Corso (the theatre of this tomfoolery) was to rejoice with the Pope ; so they left it to the foreigners, and themselves went out to the Porta Pia, a place in nowise related to the Carnival, and drove about to their hearts' content. But at Milan, I learn, the patriots turn out

* Which was done by Saulini, but not with such result as to warrant presenting it in volumes which contain engravings from Story's noble bust, from Cheney's crayon, and from the earlier photograph.

with great glee to express joy at the hopes of Italy. Really, the Piedmontese and the rest of them have done admirably ; and while Louis Napoleon has played his cards with a master's hand, and shuffled them skilfully besides, the luck of the game is on his side.

* * * * * *

But oh, George, let me thank you for putting my letter to Francis Jackson (concerning John Brown*), in the *Tribune*, into all three editions. I know I must be indebted *to you* for that favor : it is not public opinion yet ; it will be by-and-bye, and as I have nought to hope or fear, I can afford to wait in this as with other matters. I have cast my grain in the waters many times, and have lived long enough to see the waters gone and the open fields getting ripe. What care I who has the name of " seedsman ?" if I see men and women thrive on corn I sowed for them in sweat and tears? I never asked name or gratitude, only chance to do my duty.

Oh, George, the life I am here slowly dragging to an end—tortuous, but painless—is very, very imperfect, and fails of much I meant to hit and might have reached, nay, should, had there been ten or twenty years more left for me ! But, on the whole, it has not been a mean life, measured by the common run of men ; never a selfish one. Above all things else, I have sought to teach the true idea of man, of God, of religion, with its truths, its duties, and its joys. I never fought for myself, nor against a private foe ; but have gone into the battle of the nineteenth century, and followed the flag of humanity. Now I am ready to die, though conscious that I leave half my work undone, and much grain lies in my fields, waiting only for him that gathereth sheaves. I would rather lay my bones with my fathers and mothers at Lexington, and think I may ; but will not complain if earth or sea shall cover them up elsewhere. It is idle to run from death !

* * * * *

Believe me faithfully, and with manifold gratitude, your friend,

T. P.

TO JOHN AYRES.

Rome, April 7, 1860.

Not much of a letter will you get from me this time ; for Mr. Sawandgrind's pond is pretty low, and he does no more grinding, only now and then mumbles something, which he makes believe he grinds. Still, if his pond go down, his spirits keep up, though he expects no more rain this summer.

I hope the dear girls do well at Yellow Springs. What a shame that New England has no Girls' College, where a real, good, thorough education can be given to young women on some terms ! Quack seminaries we have in abundance, where they take in the raw material " with two towels and a spoon, and finish off young ladies," and send the tawdry things out into the world, almost utterly ignorant of all things necessary for comfort in life.

I trust I shall soon get away from Rome ; I only stay now to finish

* See Vol. II., p. 170.

a little engagement I have with a friend, who is making my bust; but my friend Desor will come this week, perhaps to-morrow, and he will take charge of me, and carry me whither he will. I do not know but I shall go with him to Neuchâtel a little later in the season, and perhaps find me a quiet resting-place. I feel much anxiety for our friend Stephenson, but hope you will write better tidings of him and his. Remember me most kindly to all the good people at West Newton. I often look back with great pleasure on the jovial times we have had together, not without gratitude to the Ultimate Source of all joy. I hope Joseph H. Allen still continues to instruct and elevate the people there; few ministers do either—few can; but yet, perhaps, many try. What a poor tool they work with! Of all the humbugs now before the world, none is so impudent and gross as this which, in all the sects (with, perhaps, two exceptions) passes for Christianity. How would Jesus of Nazareth protest against it, if now here, and only what he was in the A.D. 25 or 30!

H—— must shoot an arrow at his former associates; and they who honored him for his ill qualities before, when directed against their foes, abuse him now when he turns them against the Unitarians. Had he taken as long a step forward as now backward, how would all the land ring with condemnation! It is an old world—even New England is, and it takes a long time to mend it; but with truth, and right, and love on a man's side, and earthly eternity before his brave words, he needs not despair of triumph at the last.

The trees are in blossom, and at Frascati, March 31, I found the fields covered with all manner of handsome flowers, such as we never see in America. I wish I could eat one of your Baldwin apples, or a russet. Remember me to the Popes, to Patience, whom I have not heard of this long time, and to your excellent wife, and all the "little ones."

T. P.

TO MR. LYMAN.

April 4.

Yesterday, with Dr. Appleton, we all went out to Frascati, about twelve miles off, and then to Tusculum—I on a jackăss; the others walked. The day was fine, the expedition successful in all respects, and we had as good a time as a party can with a sick man in it. Cicero had a splendid place out there, but he got less inspiration from it than R. W. E. from a plain wooden house in Concord. Cicero was a great man, with all his many weaknesses. I always feel a mingling of pity and veneration for "the last great man whom Rome never feared." I have studied the philosophy of Roman history somewhat more minutely than before, and think I have got the hang of the people and their institutions. They were gross, material, warlike, but energetic and full of will. They invented nothing. What Virgil makes Anchises say,*

" Excudent alii spirantia mollius aera,
    Credo equidem; vivos ducent de marmore vultus;

* Æneid, VI., 846-852.

Orabunt causas melius, cœlique meatus
Describent radio et surgentia sidera dicent:
Tu regere imperio populos, Romane, memento;
Hæ tibi erunt artes "—

I wish what follows were as true :—

" Pacisque imponere morem,
Parcere subjectis, et debellare superbos."—

This they never did. It is instructive to see how all their politics followed as the logical necessity of their first principles. It is just so in the United States to-day. When the Federal Government undertook to capture fugitive slaves by its own arm in 1793, it acknowledged the right of man to own property in man, as much as in land and things; and as it did not offer to recover other runaway property, it actually declared this peculiarly worthy of executive protection. From this first principle all subsequent slave legislation has proceeded with inevitable logic, and much more will.

In January I began to write you a long, elaborate letter on the great problem of American politics—to establish an Industrial Democracy in America; and its three questions, immediate, proximate, and ultimate, *i.e.* 1. Shall the party which claims that man can be the property of man continue to wield the Federal power? 2. Shall that doctrine be allowed to exist and be a force in Federal affairs? 3. Shall it be allowed to develope itself in any individual State? But I shall never be well enough to do it. Seward's speech* is able, statesmanlike, widelooking; but it shows two things—1. He is satisfied that the Republican party has fallen back since 1858. 2. That he will accommodate himself to that low standard to gain votes for the Presidency.

* * * * * *

Who is so fit a man as thou, O Governor, to edit the *Remains of T. P.?* Will you look over my papers some time and do it? It is the last favor!

Good-bye, and God bless you !

T. P.

TO THE SAME.
Rome, April 14.

At last, O, Governor, I can write you good news. Desor has come! He was never better; so big, with such a chest, and arms, and legs! Why, it made me feel strong (for a minute) only to look at him. He dined with us Tuesday and Wednesday, but it wears on me a little too much even to have him all day; and then I go tired to bed and get up not fresh in the morning. So for *his* sake and mine (for I only talk in a whisper) he dined at his own hotel for the last two days.

He will tell you, I suppose, how he finds me, and perhaps will give a more faithful report than I can. We intend to leave Rome on Saturday, April 21, in a *vettura*, with Dr. Appleton and his wife, and Desor. We shall have a whole carriage, with one spare seat, to ourselves; shall go by Perugia, and be about six days in overcoming a hundred and fifty miles. It looks quite feasible. Then we *intend* to

* In the Senate, February, 1860.

follow the spring into Switzerland. But who knows what a day will bring forth?

The hygienic result of my residence in Rome is a large negative quantity; the æsthetic is equal to zero. But Story has made a fine bust of me; to-morrow it will be put into plaster. My wife and Miss Stevenson think the likeness perfect, and they are perhaps the best judges. I shall send home a cast, and you can judge of that. It may reach there before my wife does, in which case, perhaps Manley will set it on his shelf, and my special friends look upon it.

Rejoice with me that I seem so near the end of residence at Rome! How near I am I know not; but I think I can see through now, and have the fatal one hundred and twenty stairs to mount only seven times more! I can comprehend the treadmill now.

I mean to write you a word or two on the looks of America across the sea, but perhaps had better use my time and weakness in putting some few things of my early history together, which one day you will kindly use. I meant to write a full little history of my little life till twenty-one; but as I never could write in *foul, dark weather*, so was it irksome to think of it in such health as I have long had, and I have got only ten or twenty pages of introductory matter, touching the circumstances and men about me at birth. But my early story no man can tell save me, and I shall use up my time on that, from my first year to the twenty-first. But I may bring little to pass. I will try and not write more sad things, if you will excuse these.

This is believed to be the last letter he ever wrote with pen and ink.

The fragment of an Autobiography, committed to Mr. Lyman, forms the second chapter of Vol. I.

Mr. Desor records his impressions upon joining Mr. Parker:—

What he had gained in strength and condition at Combe-Varin, he soon lost at Rome. The miseries of the Papal *régime*, together with the damp climate and some annoyances, had affected his state to a singular degree, so that when, after delays independent of my volition, I was able to rejoin him, I found him changed as if ten years older. He was no longer the Parker of Combe-Varin; he was an old man. Surrounded by the tenderest care, on the part of his wife and his friends; treated with fraternal solicitude by his physician, Dr. Appleton, who was also his friend and confidant; he alone, of all, had not lost his courage. Neither had he entirely renounced the prospect of profiting by his sojourn in Italy to study its flora and geological structure. To this end he had, according to custom, surrounded himself with all the accessible manuals and documents upon the subject. It was impossible to be better prepared in understanding and memory; unfortunately, the body no longer had corresponding strength. After having made a few excursions by carriage into the interior, it was evident to every one that the projected tour was impossible, and he was not slow also to recognize it. In the meantime we were still waiting for the fair weather, which had long been due. The month of April, generally so fine at Rome, was cold and rainy. To thwarted hopes, succeeded uneasiness and a morbid desire to quit Rome and its frightful climate as soon as possible, in order to reach Florence. His condition was so much worse that we became anxious as to the issue of the journey. He, on the contrary, would not hear a word about postponing it. One day when I found him reclining on his bed alone, I thought it my duty to apprise him of my apprehensions concerning the journey. " Should you fail upon the route, to die in a tavern!" He smiled and asked me to sit down near him; he took my hand and said, " Listen to me, my friend. You know that I have some command over myself, and that I have sometimes put my will to the test. Well : I will not die here; I will not leave my bones in this detested soil; I will go to Florence, and I will get there—that I promise you." Then resuming, with a less emphatic tone, he added, " Let me once get upon my couch at Madame Molini's, in Florence, there may happen what will. I don't promise beyond that." It would have been imprudent and cruel to oppose this decided wish. We started the next day for Florence, by the way of Perugia, but not until Dr. Sarjent, the physician who was called in consultation, had approved our plan.

The journey from Rome to Florence by *vetturino* lasted five days, during which our patient displayed admirable fortitude. He was too feeble to visit with us the celebrated sites and places which occurred along our route. Whenever we reached a hotel, his first and almost only want was to rest. But he insisted that we, his travelling companions, should visit everything accessible, and be careful to lose nothing out of regard for him. When we returned, he loved to hear in detail our impressions, and made us tell our observations upon the nature and accidents of the soil, the peculiarities of the flora, the aspects of the country and its inhabitants. He shared our indignation every time that we were victimized by some of the numerous stratagems which the police of His Holiness are so adroit in exploiting to the detriment of travellers. That only increased his impatience to get out of this country, doubly cursed, as he said, by political and ecclesiastical tyranny. So he enjoined us with warmth to apprise him when we crossed the frontier, and not to hesitate to wake him if he was asleep. This we did. After having left the last station of the Papal police, when I bade him notice at a distance by the side of the road a post, newly painted red, white, and green,* he roused as if electrified, and his eyes threw upon me one of those piercing and eloquent glances which only come from a heart profoundly moved. One who has done so much for liberty loves to meet it on his way. At that point, we crossed into the Kingdom of Italy, and he knew that if he died, his bones would at least repose in a land henceforth free.

Having arrived at Florence, it happened as he had foreseen and predicted. Overcome by the fatigues of the journey, he had but one desire, to rest. He reached his bed, never more to quit it.

Miss Cobbe, who had never seen him, but whose life had been spiritually saved and strengthened by his published words, was

---

* Then the Sardinian colors, and now the colors of the Kingdom of Italy; and the post was newly painted because the territory had been just annexed.

in Florence at this time, anxiously waiting to see him. They had long corresponded, and were to meet thus at last.

He lies quite quietly on his bed, with his back to the light—his eyes are always trembling. I do not think he sees anything, except vaguely. They say he must have made a great effort to be as collected as he was with me yesterday; to-day, it was nearly all wandering, about what he would do in America, how he would lie still in his house, and be very comfortable and happy.

He received me yesterday when I went to his bedside very tenderly, saying, " After all our wishes to meet, how strange it should be thus at last! You are not to think or say you have seen me—this is only the *memory* of me. Those who love me most can only wish me a speedy passage to the other world. Of course I am not *afraid* to die " (he said this with what I could have supposed his old fire), "but there was so much to do." I said, " You have given your life to God—to his truth and his work, as truly as any old martyr of them all." "I do not know," he replied; "I had great powers committed to me ; I have but half used them." I gave him a nosegay of tea-roses and lilies of the valley, and there came over his face the most beautiful smile I ever saw on a human countenance. I wonder how any one can have spoken of his face as plain or Socratic. To me it seems the noblest, most loveable face in the world. He said afterwards, " Do not speak of what you feel for me. It makes me too unhappy to leave you." Then, suddenly, with wonderful effort and power, he began discussing Italian literature—then the flowers of America. I saw he had talked enough and tried to go away.

It seems my visit did him no harm. He spoke of me afterwards very tenderly, Mrs. Parker said, and told her she must see me every day. He could not see me often ; it was a great pleasure; but it made his heart swell too high. He had a good night, and this morning again wished to see me. Alas ! he wandered in mind nearly all the time, only his face lighted up as before at the sight of the lilies of the valley. (He had said he liked them best.) He asked what day it was. I said, " It is Sunday—a blessed day ! " " True, it *is* a blessed day," said he, suddenly, seriously, " when one has got over the superstition of it ! " He then seemed to fall off into vague, but not painful dreams, and to doze, so I just kissed his hand gently, and left him without speaking. My impression is, that the end will not be for some days, perhaps a week, but that his thoughts will never do more than show some faint rays of light again.

It was to this friend that he said later, in a wandering mood, taking her hand eagerly, " I have something to tell you—there are two Theodore Parkers now. One is dying here in Italy, the other I have planted in America. He will live there, and finish my work." Then giving her a beautiful bronze inkstand which he had set apart for her, he said, " God bless you !" with the greatest solemnity and tenderness.

Another friend gathers a few recollections of these failing hours :—

When he was in a dreamy, half-conscious state, he sometimes thought that he was on board a steamer, and on his way home to America ; and sometimes, perhaps more frequently, he thought himself at home, and would ask his wife to go round to the houses of his friends upon kind errands and with affectionate messages, to Miss Goddard, Miss Thayer, and others. During nearly the whole time he seemed conscious of his dying state (always when he appeared to be intelligent, and often when his mind was dreamy and wandering), and he then gave tender messages to his wife and friends. At times he seemed to think that Miss Cobbe was Mrs. Russell, and once, holding some flowers in his hand, he said,

" Dear Sally Russell gave me these ! "

He longed for rest and quiet, as a sick man might, when worn and fatigued with the constant movement of a ship at sea, and he would speculate thus :

" When we get home and settled in the country, how peaceful, quiet, and happy we will be ! "

Once he thought he was arriving in the railway cars on the Boston and Worcester Railway, at the " Newton Corner " station, with his wife, on their way to visit her mother ; and he mentioned the particular room which they would occupy.

He sent a most kind and tender last message to Miss Mary Shannon, especially confiding his wife to her affectionate friendship after he should have departed from this world. Whenever he required any assistance to move him, he required it from those about him in the most careful manner, generally requesting his wife or Miss Stevenson, consulting always their ease and comfort as much as possible, and to the last, though at times quite decided and positive as to what should be done for him, considerate of the strength and convenience of those who were attending him, and tenderly grateful for all the services rendered by them.

To his wife, watching with him one of his last nights, he said,—

" Lay down your head on the pillow, ' Bearsie,' and sleep ; for you have not slept for a very long time."

The old simplicity, the old friends and pleasures, penetrated all his wanderings ; their fidelity was a better kind of meaning. Once he tried a letter, the last :—

Florence, May 3.

My dear John Ayres,—So I shall still call you—will you come over to-morrow and see us, just after your dinner-time ? Bring me a last year's apple if you can, or any new melon.

Yours truly,

T. P.

You get into my house not far from good Mr. Cummings's grocery.

And vaguely talking, still friends and their tokens are remembered well enough.

"Mr. Gooding's pears—thank him! Couldn't forget the autumn pears."

"Love to Aunt Mary (Shannon); that is all I can send her."

"Tell the Miss Thayers I would like to see them, that I went away in February, 1859, and came back in July, 1860. I should like to touch them, and tread on Boston Common."

He was in great trouble one day about his library, and declared that everything was in confusion. As it happened, this strong impression of his was at the very time when good Mary Drew was busying herself in the study, with housewifely intentions.

When he would talk with his wife, who gently checked him, he would say, "Oh, it don't hurt me to talk bear-talk." When the fever fits came over him, he would sometimes try to dress; "When is that vessel going—will it not go soon?"

Thus a few days were passed in great weakness, but without the least suffering. The mind made no effort, all the faculties and senses were sunk in dreaminess, as the body gradually parted with its little residue of life. On the 10th of May he lay motionless, with innocent look, as of a child just falling into slumber—a simple look; but it baffled the dear friends, who could not see how the great soul went that day to another ministry.

The semblance of sleep did not fade from the face. The cheeks were flushed, the white full beard lay over the thin lips, and the head fell a little to one side beneath a garland of the roses of Florence, which had been brought to his pillow.

On Sunday, the 13th of May, at four in the afternoon, the hour corresponding to that in which he used to stand at the desk of the Music Hall, an old friend, the Rev. Mr. Cunningham, held the fitting funeral service over the body of this pure and righteous man. He read the Beatitudes. It was a feast-day in Florence, and the streets were filled with the gay people; banners were hung out of the windows, under which the friends passed to the place where he was to sleep. At first they felt hurt; but a sudden impulse effaced the idea of any incongruity, and they whispered to each other, "It *is* a festival—the Feast of an

Ascension ! " and they called to mind the closing words of his last sermon, " Friend, come up higher."

There is no gloom in the place where his worn-out body rests. A few cypresses are there, " Nature's spires, pointing up into the infinite cloudless heaven above."

Let me borrow the description of the place, written by one who sought it in love and veneration :—

The little Protestant cemetery lies just outside the Pinti Gate, the city wall itself forming one side of the enclosure. You enter by a high gateway into an outer court, and through a second gate into the cemetery. The ground rises slightly, is covered with daisied turf, and planted with tall cypresses and flowering shrubs. There are many monuments, mostly of white marble, in simple and good taste, and the whole place, carefully kept, is as cheerful a spot as one would choose for the burial-place. Through the trees and above the wall you get pleasant glimpses of the neighbouring hills. After a little search we found Mr. Parker's grave, near the centre of the grounds, and at the foot of a cypress tree, close to the cross-path. It is enclosed in a border of grey marble, and at the head is a plain stone of the same material, with only this inscription :—

THEODORE   PARKER,

BORN AT LEXINGTON, MASS.,

UNITED   STATES   OF   AMERICA,

AUG. 24, 1810,

DIED AT FLORENCE, MAY 10, 1860.

Within the stone border is an edging of periwinkle, and in the centre a few plants of violet. There is also a small foot-stone, and at the side was a small pine-tree in a pot.

A week ago we went again to the cemetery, to fulfil a purpose we had cherished, of planting some ivy upon the grave. We had gathered two plants in a wild spot of the pleasant Boboli garden, in the morning. It was the loveliest of spring days; the sky of tenderest blue, without a cloud, and full of glowing light. The sunshine lay warmly on the grey, ivied wall, upon the dark cypresses; and every daisy in the sod was wide open with delight. As we set our ivies in the earth, the birds sang rapturously over our heads. Then we carefully trimmed the bordering, and afterwards cut from the turf two roots of daisies, and set them between the violets upon the grave. The tree in the pot was an American pine, which the gardener would plant at the head of the grave.

Upon the ledge behind the little farmhouse at Lexington, there are also pines, beneath which he breathed his childish prayers. The earliest symbol of Massachusetts flourishes well at the places where this American life rose and where it set. Plant, O countrymen, the healing life into your hearts; build political and spiritual freedom from this native tree!

THE GRAVE.

APPENDIX.

No. I.

COPY OF THE WILL OF THEODORE PARKER.

[The portions of the Will which went into effect are printed in large type, those which did not go into effect, *in small italics*, and the conditions which made them inoperative, IN SMALL CAPITALS.]

I, Theodore Parker, of Boston, in the County of Suffolk and Commonwealth of Massachusetts, Minister of the Twenty-eighth Congregational Society in said Boston, do make this my last Will and Testament: I give, bequeath, and devise all the Real and Personal Property of which I shall die seized and possessed, or to which I shall be entitled or have any claim at my death, in manner following, to wit:—

First. To the proper authorities of the Commonwealth of Massachusetts, I give the two fire-arms, formerly the property of my honored grandfather, Captain John Parker, late of Lexington, in the county of Middlesex; to wit, the large musket, or King's arm, which was by him captured from the British on the morning of the 19th of April, 1775, in the Battle of Lexington, and which is the first fire-arm taken from the enemy in the War for Independence; and also the smaller musket which was used by him in that battle while fighting "in the sacred cause of God and his country"; and I desire that these relics of the Revolution may be placed in the Senate Chamber of this Commonwealth, and there sacredly kept *in perpetuam rei memoriam.*

Second. To my much-valued friend, Wendell Phillips, of Boston, I give the folio copy of the "English State Trials" in 11 volumes, with many portraits interleaved, which is now in my library; but if the said Wendell be deceased at the administration of my estate, then the second article of my Will is to be wholly inoperative and void.

Third. To my much-valued friend, Charles Sumner, of Boston, I give the copy of the "Parliamentary History of England" in 36 volumes, which is now in my library; but if at the administration of my estate the said Charles be deceased, then this third article of my Will is to be wholly inoperative and void.

Fourth. To Miss Hannah E. Stevenson, of Boston, my much-valued friend, now, and for a long time, an inmate of my household, I give the old copy of Schrevelius' Greek Lexicon, which I purchased with much toil in my boyhood, and also the common Bible which lies on my desk, and the little taper-holder which I have long used; and I request her, with the consent of my wife, Lydia D. Parker, to select such book or books from my library as she may desire; but if at the administration of my estate the said Hannah be deceased, then this fourth article of my Will is to be wholly inoperative and void.

Fifth. To my friend Miss Caroline C. Thayer, of Boston, I give the copy of the " Biographical Dictionary' in 15 volumes, with many portraits interleaved; but if at the administration of my estate the said Caroline be deceased, then this fifth article of my Will is to be wholly inoperative and void.

Sixth. To my friend Miss Sarah N. Hunt, now, or late, residing temporarily at Dresden, in the Kingdom of Saxony, I give the hymn-book which lies on my desk, and the small copy of George Herbert's poems; but if at the administration of my estate the said Sarah be deceased, then this sixth article of my Will is to be wholly inoperative and void.

Seventh. To my brother Isaac Parker, of Lexington aforesaid, I forgive and remit all that he now owes me as the principal and interest of several notes of hand given me by him for value received.

Eighth. To the proper authorities of the City of Boston aforesaid, I give all my books which are not otherwise disposed of in the preceding or following articles of this Will, that they may be put in the Public Library of the City for the use and benefit of such as have access thereto, and be read on such terms as the Directors of the said Library shall think just; and I desire that, so far as consistent with public utility, the said books be kept in alcoves or on shelves by themselves, and I desire that the said books shall in no case be sold or given away by the said Directors, or any other persons, or exchanged for other books; but in case the authorities aforesaid decline to accept the books on these conditions, then, on the same conditions, they are to be given to the Library of Harvard College, in Cambridge. However, this eighth article of my Will is to be wholly inoperative and void unless it receive the consent of my wife aforesaid, if living at my decease, as will more fully appear from the following article :—

Ninth. To my well-beloved wife, Lydia D. Parker aforesaid, I give all my manuscripts, journals, sermons, lectures, and letters, and also any and all books she may wish to retain from my library, *even if she desires the whole*, the same to be at her free and absolute disposal, and she is to have six months to determine what she will keep and retain.

Furthermore, to her, the said Lydia, I do give, bequeath, and devise all the residue of my estate, as well real as personal, not bequeathed in the preceding Articles of this Will; to wit, all the property of which I shall be seized and possessed at my death, or which I shall then be entitled to, or to which I shall have any claim ; the same to be her absolute property, and so entirely subject to her disposal, to have and to hold to her and to her heirs forever.

But if the said Lydia shall not be alive at my death, or if we shall both decease at the same moment, then this ninth Article of my Will is to be wholly inoperative and void.

TENTH. IF AT MY DEATH MY WIFE THE AFORESAID LYDIA BE NO LONGER LIVING, OR IF WE DECEASE AT THE SAME MOMENT, THEN I DISTRIBUTE THE REMAINDER OF MY ESTATE NOT DISPOSED OF IN ARTICLES ONE, TWO, THREE, FOUR, FIVE, SIX, SEVEN, AND EIGHT OF THIS WILL AS FOLLOWS :—

I. If my wife, the said Lydia, shall decease at the same moment with myself, and leave a Will disposing of property not distributed by me in the above-named Articles of this Will, One, Two, Three, Four, Five, Six, Seven, and Eight, then her Will is to be sacredly observed, notwithstanding the following provisions of this Will : but if there be no such Will of hers, then,—

II. To Miss Hannah E. Stevenson, Miss Sarah H. Hunt, and Miss Caroline C. Thayer, aforesaid, I restore the various keepsakes and gifts received from them, if they be living. And to the said Hannah, if living at the administration of my estate, I give the large inkstand, which for many years has stood on my desk, and also the sum of One thousand dollars: but if she is not living, then this provision is to be null and void.

III. To George Colburn Cabot, formerly my ward, and now a member of my household, I give the sum of Two thousand dollars; but if he be not living at the administration of my estate, and leave no issue, then this provision is to be null and void.

IV. To Mary Drew, who has long lived in my family, I give Five hundred dollars; but if she be not living at my death, then this clause also is to be null and void.

V. To the Executors of this Will, hereinafter named, I make this request: that they will make arrangements with any bookseller for the publication of such portions of my manuscripts, sermons, &c., as they shall see fit, suitably indemnifying themselves for their labor, but not making my estate chargeable with any cost in consequence of such publication.

VI. To the proper authorities of the City of Boston, I give all my books not otherwise disposed of in this Will, as I have already provided in the eighth Article thereof, and also all my manuscripts, journals, sermons, lectures, letters, &c., &c., on the conditions named in said eighth Article ; and if these be not accepted by the said authorities, then on the same terms I bequeath the said books and manuscripts to the Library of Harvard College aforesaid. But this disposition of the said manuscripts is not to conflict with the right of the Executors mentioned in the preceding section of this tenth Article of my Will.

VII. I direct that all the residue of my estate be divided into two equal parts, which I thus distribute and dispose of :—

A. To the grandchildren of my late esteemed father, John Parker, of Lexington, I give the one equal part, that is to the children of the late John Parker, of Brighton, Hannah Parker Greene, Lydia Parker Herrick, and Hiram Stearns Parker, and also to the children of Isaac Parker, of Lexington, who is now living ; providing that if any grandchild be deceased leaving issue, that issue shall receive the parent's part, and also providing that during the life of the said Isaac and of his wife, Martha M. Parker, the income of their children's portion shall be annually paid to him or her.

B. I direct the Executors of my Will to bestow the other equal part on such charitable and philanthropic institutions, or expend it for such charitable and philanthropic purposes, as they in their judgment shall think most worthy and deserving thereof, and I desire them to make their final decision and the disposition of this portion of my estate within two years of my decease.

Explanatory Article. As part of the library furniture, I desire that my study—table, or desk, and also the great table of oak and mahogany, once the property of John Parker, of Lexington, my grandfather's grandfather, which is now in my study, shall be considered as an appurtenance of the library above-mentioned, and follow the disposition made of that, in Article Eight of this Will.

I appoint John R. Manley, Esq., of Boston; Frederic W. G. May, Esq., of Boston; and Franklin B. Sanborn, Esq., of Concord, Mass.; to be the Executors of this my last Will and Testament. I hereby revoke all former Wills made by me.

In witness whereof, I have hereunto set my hand and seal, this twenty-fifth day of May, A.D. eighteen hundred and fifty-seven.

Signed, sealed, published, and declared by the said Theodore as and for his last Will and Testament, in the presence of us who, in his presence and in the presence of each other, and at his request, have hereunto put our hands, at Boston, on the day aforesaid as witnesses,

FREDERICK CABOT.
MARY E. CABOT.   THEODORE PARKER.   L. S.
WM. F. CABOT.

I, Theodore Parker, of Boston, do make this Codicil to my last Will and Testament, whereto this is appended, signed by me on or about the twenty-fifth day of May, in the year eighteen hundred and fifty-seven.

First. If my wife Lydia Cabot be living at the time of my decease, I request her to give some books from my library to each of the following persons if they be then living; namely, to Mrs. Eliza H. Apthorp; to Miss Eliza M. Thayer, and each of her two sisters, Mrs. Nichols and Mrs. Balch; to Misses Rebecca and Matilda Goddard; to Misses Sarah and Caroline Whitney; and also to Franklin B. Sanborn the copy of Heyne's edition of Homer, now in my library.

SECOND. IF I SHOULD SURVIVE MY SAID WIFE, OR IF WE DECEASE AT THE SAME MOMENT, THEN—

I. I confirm and decree all the bequests made by her, in the memorandum annexed to her Will, published and declared on or about the 31st day of January, in the year eighteen hundred and fifty-nine, and direct my executors to comply with her wishes therein set forth.

II. I return each of the little gifts I have received from numerous friends to the giver, if then living.

III. I confirm the bequests made in the first section of this Codicil, and direct my Executors to do what I there requested of my wife.

IV. To each of my Executors I give one of my gold pencil-cases.

V. I thus bestow little gifts and keepsakes:—

1. To Sarah S. Russell, wife of George R. Russell, of West Roxbury, I give the silver cup marked with my name, and also the large silver pencil-case; but if she be not living at my decease this is void.

2. To Miss Hannah E. Stevenson, of Boston, I give the two portraits by Cheney of my wife and myself; but at her death they are to revert to George C. Cabot, of

Boston; and at his demise to the Public Library of the City of Boston, to be kept in the Library, and near each other.

3. *To Franklin B. Sanborn, of Concord aforesaid, if living at my death, I give my gold watch.*

4. *To George C. Cabot, aforesaid, I give all the pictures, portraits, miniatures, engravings and daguerreotypes, and also the various ornaments about the house, that he may keep them as his own, or distribute a part of them among my friends; but if he be not living at my decease, this clause is void.*

I hereby revoke all parts of my Will which are inconsistent with the provisions of this Codicil.

In witness whereof, I have hereunto set my hand and seal this thirty-first day of January, in the year eighteen hundred and fifty-nine.

Signed, sealed, published, and declared by the said Theodore, as and for a Codicil to his last Will and Testament, in the presence of us who, in his presence and in the presence of each other, and at his request, have hereunto put our hands and seals, at Boston, on the day aforesaid, as witnesses,

FRANCIS CABOT.
JOHN H. CABOT.   THEODORE PARKER. L. S.
WM. F. CABOT.

No. II.

THE LETTER FROM SANTA CRUZ, CALLED "THEODORE PARKER'S EXPERIENCE AS A MINISTER."

LETTER TO THE MEMBERS OF THE TWENTY-EIGHTH CONGREGATIONAL
SOCIETY OF BOSTON.

MY DEAR AND VALUED FRIENDS,—After it became needful that I should be silent, and flee off from my home, I determined, at least, before I went, to write you a letter, touching our long connection, and my efforts in your service, and so bid you farewell. But the experienced doctors and other wise friends forbid the undertaking, and directed me to wait for a more favorable time, when the work might be more leisurely and better done, with less risk also to my life; promising indeed a time when it would not diminish the chances of recovery. In the twenty-four days which came between the sudden, decisive attack, and my departure from Boston, there was little time for even a sound, well man to settle and arrange his worldly affairs, to straighten out complicated matters, and return thanks to the many that have befriended him in the difficult emergencies of life—for surely I left home as one not to set eyes on New England again. Since then there has been no time till now when I have had strength to endure the intellectual labor, and still more the emotional agitation, which must attend such a review of my past life. Consumption having long since slain almost all my near kinsfolk, horsed on the North-wind, rode at me also, seeking my life. Swiftly I fled hither, hoping in this little quiet and fair-skied Island of the Holy Cross to hide me from his monstrous sight, to pull his arrows from my flesh, and heal my wounded side. It is yet too soon to conjecture how or when my exile shall end; but at home, wise, friendly, and hopeful doctors told me I had "but one chance in ten" for complete recovery, though more for a partial restoration to some small show of health, I suppose, and power of moderate work. But if the danger be as they say, I do not despair nor lose heart at such odds, having often in my life contended against much greater, and come off triumphant, though the chances against me were a hundred or a thousand to one. Besides, this is now the third time that I remember friends and doctors despairing of my life. Still, I know that I am no longer young, and that I stand up to my shoulders in my grave, whose uncertain sides at any moment may cave in and bury me with their resistless weight. Yet I hope to climb out this side, and live and work again amid laborious New England men; for, though the flesh be weak and the spirit resigned to either fate, yet still the will to live, though reverent and submissive, is exceeding strong, more vehement than ever before, as I have still much to do—some things to begin upon, and many more lying now half done, that I alone can finish—and I should not like to suffer the little I have done to perish now for lack of a few years' work.

I know well both the despondency of sick men that makes the night seem darker than it is, and also the pleasing illusion which flits before consumptive patients; and while this Will-o'-the-wisp comes flickering from their kindred's grave, they think it is the breaking of a new and more auspicious day. So indeed it is, the Day-spring from on high, revealing the white, tall porches of Eternity. Let you and me be neither cheated by delusive hopes, nor weakened by unmanly fears, but, looking the facts fairly in the face, let us meet the inevitable with calmness and pious joy, singing the wealthy psalm of life :—

> " Give to the winds thy fears;
>   Hope and be undismay'd !
> God hears thy sighs and count thy fears—
>   God shall lift up thy head !
>
> Though comprehended not,
>   Yet Earth and Heaven tell
> He sits a Father on the throne :
>   God guideth all things well !"

But while my strength is but weakness, and my time for this letter so uncertain, I will waste neither in a lengthened introduction, knowing " it were a foolish thing to make a long prologue, and be short in the story itself."

In this letter I must needs speak much of myself, and tell some things which seem to belong only to my private history; for without a knowledge of them, my public conduct might appear other than it really is. Yet I would gladly defer them to a more fitting place, in some brief autobiography to be published after my death; but I am not certain of time to prepare that, so shall here, in small compass, briefly sketch out some small personal particulars which might elsewhere be presented in their full proportions, and with appropriate light and shade. As this letter is confidential and addressed to YOU, I could wish it might be read only to the members of the Twenty-eighth Congregational Society, or printed solely for their affection, not also published for the eye of the world; but that were impossible, for what is offered to the hearts of so many, thereby becomes accessible to the eyes and ears of all who wish to see and hear; so what I write private to you, becomes public also for mankind, whether I will or not.

In my early boyhood I *felt* I was to be a minister, and looked forward with eager longings for the work to which I still think my nature itself an "effectual call," certainly a deep one, and a continuous. Few men have ever been more fortunate than I in having pains judiciously taken with their intellectual culture.

My early education was not costly, as men count expense by dollars; it was exceeding precious, as they might reckon outlay by the fitness of the process to secure a development of natural powers. By father and mother, yes, even by brothers and sisters, great and unceasing care was taken to secure power of observation, that the senses might grasp their natural objects; of voluntary attention, fixed, continuous, and exact, which, despite of appearances, sees the fact just as it is, no more, no less; of memory, that holds all things firm as gravitation, and yet, like that, keeps them unmixed, not confusing the most delicate outline, and reproduces them at will, complete in the whole, and perfect in each part; much stress was also laid on judgment and inventive imagination. It was a great game they set me to play; it was also an advantage that the counters cost little money, but were common things, picked up daily on a farm, in a kitchen, or a mechanic's thoughtful shop. But still more, pains were taken with my moral and religious culture. In my earliest boyhood I was taught to respect the instinctive promptings of conscience, regarding it as the "voice of God in the soul of man," which must always be obeyed; to speak the truth without evasion or concealment; to love justice and conform to it; to reverence merit in all men, and that regardless of their rank or reputation; and, above all things, I was taught to love and trust the dear God. He was not presented to me as a great King, with force for his chief quality, but rather as a Father, eminent for perfect justice, and complete and perfect love, alike the parent of Jew and Gentile, Christian and non-Christian, dealing with all, not according to the accident of their name and situation, but to the real use each should make of his talents and opportunities, however little or great. I was taught self-reliance, intellectual, moral, and of many another form; to investigate all things with my own eyes; carefully to form opinions for myself, and while I believed them reasonable and just, to hold and defend them with modest firmness. Inquiry was encouraged in all directions.

Of course, I took in many of the absurd theological opinions of the time; but I think few New Englanders born of religious families in the first ten years of this century, were formally taught so little superstition. I have met none with whom more judicious attempts were made to produce a natural unfolding of the religious and moral faculties; I do not speak of results, only of aim and process. I have often been praised for virtues which really belonged to my father and mother, and if they were also mine, they must have come so easy under such training, that I should feel entitled to but small merit for possessing them. They made a careful distinction between a man's character and his creed, and in my hearing never spoke a bigoted or irreverent word.

As my relatives and neighbors were all hard-working people, living in one of the most laborious communities in the world, I did not fail to learn the great lesson of personal industry, and to acquire power of work—to begin early, to continue long, with strong and rapid stroke. The discipline and habit of bodily toil were quite easily transferred to thought, and I learned early to apply my mind with exact, active, and long-continued attention, which outward things did not disturb; so while working skilfully with my hands, I could yet think on what I would.

Good books by great masters fell into even my boyish hands; the best English authors of prose and verse, the Bible, the Greek and Roman classics—which I at first read mainly in translations, but soon became familiar with in their original beauty—these were my literary helps. What was read at all, was also studied, and not laid aside till well understood. If my books in boyhood were not many, they were much, and also great.

I had an original fondness for scientific and metaphysical thought, which found happy encouragement in my early days: my father's strong, discriminating, and comprehensive mind also inclining that way, offered me an excellent help. Nature was all about me; my attention was wisely directed to both use and beauty, and I early became familiar with the flora of New England, and attentive also to the habits of beast and bird, insect, reptile, fish. A few scientific works on natural history gave me their stimulus and their help.

After my general preliminary education was pretty well advanced, the hour came when I must decide on my profession for life. All about me there were ministers who had sufficient talents; now and then one admirably endowed with learning; devout and humane men, also, with no stain on their personal character. But I did not see much in the clerical profession to attract me thither; the notorious dulness of the Sunday services, their mechanical character, the poverty and insignificance of the sermons, the unnaturalness and uncertainty of the doctrines preached on the authority of a "divine and infallible revelation," the lifelessness of the public prayers, and the consequent heedlessness of the congregation, all tended to turn a young man off from becoming a minister. Beside, it did not appear that the New England clergy were leaders in the intellectual, moral, or religious progress of the people; if they tried to seem so, it was only the appearance which was kept up. "Do you think our minister would dare tell his audience of their actual faults?"—so a rough blacksmith once asked me in my youth. "Certainly I do!" was the boyish answer. "Humph!" rejoined the smith, "I should like to have him begin, then!" The genius of Emerson soon moved from the clerical constellation and stood forth alone, a fixed and solitary star. Dr. Channing was the only man in the New England pulpit who to me seemed great. All my friends advised me against the ministry—it was "a narrow place, affording no opportunity to do much!" I thought it a wide place.

The legal profession seemed to have many attractions. There were eminent men in its ranks, rising to public honors, judicial or political; they seemed to have more freedom and individuality than the ministers. For some time I hesitated, inclined that way, and made preliminary studies in the law. But at length the perils of that profession seemed greater than I cared to rush upon. Mistaking sound for sense, I thought the lawyer's moral tone was lower than the minister's, and dared not put myself under that temptation I prayed God not to lead me into. I could not make up my mind to defend a cause I knew to be wrong, using all my efforts to lead judge or jury to a decision I thought unjust. A powerful and successful practitioner told me "none could be a lawyer without doing so," and quoted the well-known words of Lord Brougham. I saw men of large talents yielding to this temptation, and counting as great success what to me even then seemed only great ruin. I could not decide to set up a law-mill beside the public road, to put my hand on the winch, and by turning one way, rob innocent men of their property, liberty, life; or, by reversing the motion, withdraw the guilty from just punishment, pecuniary or corporeal. Though I hesitated some time, soon as I got clearness of sight, I returned to my first love, for that seemed free from guile. I then asked myself these three questions :—

1. "Can you seek for what is eternally true, and not be blinded by the opinions of any sect, or of the Christian Church; and can you tell the truth you learn, even when it is unpopular and hated?" I answered, "I CAN!" Rash youth is ever confident.

2. "Can you seek the eternal right, and not be blinded by the statutes and customs of men, ecclesiastical, political, and social; and can you declare that eternal right you discover, applying it to the actual life of man, individual and associated, though it bring you into painful relations of men?" Again I swiftly answered, "I CAN."

3. "Can you represent in your life that truth of the intellect and that right of the conscience, and so not disgrace with your character what you preach with your lips?" I doubted of this more than the others; the temptation to personal wickedness seemed stronger than to professional deceit — at least it was then better known; but I answered, "I CAN TRY, AND WILL!"

Alas! I little knew all that was involved in these three questions, and their prompt, youthful answers. I understand it better now.

So I determined to become a Minister, hoping to help mankind in the most important of all human concerns, the development of man's highest powers.

Zealously I entered on my theological education, with many ill-defined doubts, and some distinct denials, of the chief doctrines of the ecclesiastical theology of Christendom.

1. In my early childhood, after a severe and silent struggle, I made way with the ghastly doctrine of Eternal Damnation and a wrathful

God; this is the Goliath of that theology. From my seventh year I have had no *fear* of God, only an ever-greatening love and trust.

2. The doctrine of the Trinity, the "great mystery of Revelation," had long since gone the same road. For a year, though born and bred among Unitarians, I had attended the preachings of Dr. Lyman Beecher, the most powerful orthodox minister in New England, then in the full blaze of his talents and reputation, and stirred also with polemic zeal against "Unitarians, Universalists, Papists, and Infidels." I went through one of his "protracted meetings," listening to the fiery words of excited men, and hearing the most frightful doctrines set forth in sermon, song, and prayer. I greatly respected the talents, the zeal, and the enterprize of that able man, who certainly taught me much, but I came away with no confidence in his theology; the better I understood it, the more self-contradictory, unnatural, and hateful did it seem. A year of his preaching about finished all my respect for the Calvinistic scheme of theology.

3. I had found no evidence which to me could authorize a belief in the supernatural birth of Jesus of Nazareth. The two-fold Biblical testimony was all; that was contradictory and good for nothing; we had not the affidavit of the mother, the only competent human witness, nor even the declaration of the son; there was no circumstantial evidence to confirm the statement in the Gospels of a most improbable event.

4. Many miracles related in the Old and New Testament seemed incredible to me; some were clearly impossible, others ridiculous, and a few were wicked; such, of course, I rejected at once, while I still arbitrarily admitted others. The general question of miracles was one which gave me much uneasiness, for I had not learned carefully to examine evidence for alleged historical events, and had, besides, no clear conception of what is involved in the notion that God ever violates the else constant mode of operation of the universe. Of course I had not then that philosophical idea of God which makes a theological miracle as impossible as a round triangle, or any other self-evident contradiction.

5. I had no belief in the plenary, infallible, verbal inspiration of the whole Bible, and strong doubts as to the miraculous inspiration of any part of it. Some things were the opposite of divine; I could not put my finger on any great moral or religious truth taught by revelation in the New Testament, which had not previously been set forth by men for whom no miraculous help was ever claimed. But, on the whole matter of Inspiration, I lacked clear and definite ideas, and found neither friend nor book to help me.

In due time I entered the Theological School at Cambridge, then under the charge of the Unitarians, or "Liberal Christians." I found excellent opportunities for study : there were able and earnest professors, who laid no yoke on any neck, but left each man free to think for himself, and come to such conclusions as he must. Telling what they thought they knew, they never pretended they had learned all that may be known, or winnowed out all error from their creed. They were honest guides, with no more sophistry than is perhaps almost universal in that calling, and did not pretend to be masters. There, too, was a large library containing much valuable ancient lore, though, alas! almost none of the new theologic thought of the German masters. Besides, there was leisure, and unbounded freedom of research; and I could work as many hours in the study as a mechanic in his shop, or a farmer in his field. The pulpits of Boston were within an easy walk, and Dr. Channing drew near the zenith of his power.

Here, under these influences, I pursued the usual routine of theological reading, but yet, of course, had my own private studies, suited to my special wants. It is now easy to tell what I then attempted without always being conscious of my aim, and what results I gradually reached before I settled in the ministry.

I. I studied the Bible with much care. First, I wished to learn, What is the Bible—what books and words compose it? this is the question of criticism; next, What does the Bible mean—what sentiments and ideas do its words contain? this is the question of interpretation. I read the Bible critically, in its original tongues, the most important parts of it also in the early versions, and sought for the meaning early attributed to its words, and so studied the works of Jewish Rabbis on the Old Testament, and of the early Christian Fathers on both New and Old; besides, I studied carefully the latest critics and interpreters, especially the German.

I soon found that the Bible is a collection of quite heterogeneous books, most of them anonymous, or bearing names of doubtful authors, collected none knows how, or when, or by whom; united more by caprice than any philosophic or historic method, so that it is not easy to see why one ancient book is kept in the Canon and another kept out. I found no unity of doctrine in the several parts; the Old Testament "reveals" one form of religion, and the New Testament one directly its opposite; and in the New Testament itself, I found each writer had his own individuality, which appears not only in the style, the form of thought, but quite as much in the doctrines, the substance of thought, where no two are well agreed.

Connected with this Biblical study, came the question of inspiration and of miracles. I still inconsistently believed, or half believed, in the direct miraculous interposition of God, from time to time, to set things right which else went wrong, though I found no historic or philosophic reason for limiting it to the affairs of Jews and Christians, or the early ages of the Church. The whole matter of miracles was still a puzzle to me, and for a long time a source of anxiety; for I had not studied the principles of historic evidence, nor learned to identify and scrutinize the witnesses. But the problem of inspiration got sooner solved. I believed in the immanence of God in man, as well as matter, His activity in both; hence, that all men are inspired in proportion to their actual powers, and their normal use thereof; that truth is the test of intellectual inspiration, justice of moral, and so on. I did not find the Bible inspired, except in this general way, and in proportion to the truth and justice therein. It seemed to me that no part of the Old Testament or New could be called the "Word of God," save in the sense that all truth is God's word.

II. I studied the historical development of religion and theology amongst Jews and Christians, and saw the gradual formation of the great ecclesiastical doctrines which so domineered over the world. As I found the Bible was the work of men, so I also found that the Christian Church was no more divine than the British State, a Dutchman's shop, or an Austrian's farm. The miraculous infallible Bible, and the miraculous, infallible Church, disappeared when they they were closely looked at; and I found the fact of history quite different from the pretension of theology.

III. I studied the historical development of religion and theology amongst the nations not Jewish or Christian, and attended as well as I then could to the four other great religious sects—the Brahmanic, the Buddhistic, the Classic, and the Mohammedan. As far as possible at that time, I studied the sacred books of mankind in their original tongues, and with the help of the most faithful interpreters. Here the Greek and Roman poets and philosophers came in for their place, there being no sacred books of the classic nations. I attended pretty carefully to the religion of savages and barbarians, and was thereby helped to the solution of many a difficult problem. I found no tribe of men destitute of religion who had attained power of articulate speech.

IV. I studied assiduously the metaphysics and psychology of religion. Religious consciousness was universal in human history. Was it then natural to man, inseparable from his essence, and so from his development? In my own consciousness I found it automatic and indispensable; was it really so likewise in the human race? The authority of Bibles and Churches was no answer to that question. I tried to make an analysis of humanity, and see if by psychologic science I could detect the special element which produced religious consciousness in me, and religious phenomena in mankind—seeking a cause adequate to the facts of experience and observation. The common books of philosophy seemed quite insufficient; the sensational system, so ably presented by Locke in his masterly Essay, developed into various forms by Hobbes, Berkeley, Hume, Paley, and the French Materialists, and modified, but not much amended, by Reid and Stewart, gave little help; it could not legitimate my own religious instincts, nor explain the religious history of mankind, or even of the British people, to whom that philosophy is still so manifold a hindrance. Ecclesiastical writers, though able as Clarke and Butler, and learned also as Cudworth and Barrow, could not solve the difficulty; for the principle of authority, though more or less concealed, yet lay there, and, like buried iron, disturbed the free action of their magnetic genius, affecting its dip and inclination. The brilliant mosaic, which Cousin set before the world, was of great service, but not satisfactory. I found most help in the works of Immanuel Kant, one of the profoundest thinkers in the world, though one of the worst writers, even of Germany; if he did not always furnish conclusions I could rest in, he yet gave me the true method, and put me on the right road.

I found certain great primal intuitions of human nature, which depend on no logical process of demonstration, but are rather facts of consciousness given by the instinctive action of human nature itself I will mention only the three most important which pertain to religion.

1. The instinctive intuition of the divine, the consciousness that there is a God.

2. The instinctive intuition of the just and right, a consciousness that there is a moral law, independent of our will, which we ought to keep.

3. The instinctive intuition of the immortal, a consciousness that the essential element of man, the principle of individuality, never dies.

Here, then, was the foundation of religion, laid in human nature itself, which neither the atheist nor the more pernicious bigot, with their sophisms of denial or affirmation, could move, or even shake. I had gone through the great spiritual trial of my life, telling no one of its hopes or fears; and I thought it a triumph that I had psychologically established these three things to my own satisfaction, and devised a scheme which to the scholar's mind, I thought, could legitimate what was spontaneously given to all, by the great primal instincts of mankind.

Then I proceeded to develop the contents of these instinctive intuitions of the divine, the just, and the immortal, and see what God actually is, what morality is, and what eternal life has to offer. In each case I pursued two methods—the inductive and deductive.

First, from the history of mankind—savage, barbarous, civilised, enlightened—I gathered the most significant facts I could find relating to men's opinions about God, Morality, Heaven, and Hell, and thence made such generalisations as the facts would warrant, which, however, were seldom satisfactory; for they did not represent facts of the universe, the actual God, justice, and eternal life, but only what men had thought or felt thereof; yet this comparative and inductive theology was of great value to me.

Next, from the primitive facts of consciousness, given by the power of instinctive intuition, I endeavoured to deduce the true notion of God, of justice, and futurity. Here I could draw from human nature, and not be hindered by the limitations of human history; but I know now better than it was possible then, how difficult is this work, and how often the inquirer mistakes his own subjective imagination for a fact of the universe. It is for others to decide whether I have sometimes mistaken a little grain of brilliant dust in my telescope for a fixed star in heaven.

To learn what I could about the spiritual faculties of man, I not only studied the sacred books of various nations, the poets and the philosophers who professedly treat thereof, but also such as deal with sleep-walking, dreams, visions, prophecies, second-sight, oracles, ecstacies, witchcraft, magic wonders, the appearance of devils, ghosts, and the like. Besides, I studied other works which lie out from the regular highway of theology, the spurious books attributed to famous Jews or Christians, Pseudepigraphy of the Old Testament, and the Apocrypha of the New, with the strange fantasies of the Neoplatonists and Gnostics. I did not neglect the writings of the Mystics, though at that time I could only make a beginning with the more famous or most tenderly religious; I was much attracted to this class of men, who developed the element of piety, regardless of the theologic ritualism of the church, the philosophic discipline of the schools, or the practical morality of common life. By this process, I not only learned much of the abnormal action of the human spirit, and saw how often a mere fancy passes for fact, and a dreamer's subjective whim bestrides some great harbour of the world for a thousand years, obstructing all tall ships, until an earthquake throws it down; but I also gleaned up many a precious flower which bloomed unseen in those waste places of literature, and was unknown to the authorised floras of the school or church.

I left the Theological School with reluctance, conscious of knowing so little of what I must presently teach, and wishing more years for research and thought. Of course my first sermons were only imitations; and even if the thought might, perhaps, be original, the form was old, the stereotype of the pulpit. I preached with fear and trembling, and wondered that old and mature persons, rich in the experience of life, should listen to a young man, who might, indeed have read and thought, but yet had had no time to live much and know things by heart. I took all possible pains with the matter of the discourse, and always appealed to the religious instinct in mankind. At the beginning I resolved to preach the natural laws of man as they are writ in his constitution, no less and no more. After preaching a few months in various places, and feeling my way into the consciousness of men, I determined to preach nothing as religion which I had not experienced inwardly, and made my own, knowing it by heart. Thus, not only the intellectual, but also the religious part of my sermons would rest on facts that I was sure of, and not on the words of another. I was indebted to another young candidate for the hint. I hope I have not been faithless to the early vow. A study of the English State Trials, and a careful analysis of the arguments of the great speeches therein, helped me to clearness of arrangement, and distinctness in the use of terms. Here and in the Greek and Latin orations I got the best part of my rhetorical culture.

On the longest day of 1837, I was ordained Minister of the Unitarian Church and Congregation at West Roxbury, a little village near Boston, one of the smallest societies in New England, where I found men and women whose friendship is still dear and instructive. I had thought freely, and freely preached what I thought; none had ever questioned my right. At the Theological School, the professors were then teachers to instruct, not also inquisitors to torture and to damn; satisfied of the religious chartacer of the pupils, they left each to develop his own free spiritual individuality, responsible only to his own conscience and his God. It was then the boast of the little Unitarian party, that it respected individuality, freedom of thought, and freedom of speech, and had neither Inquisitors nor Pope. Great diversity of opinion prevailed amongst Unitarians, ministers and laymen, but the unity of religion was more thought of than the variety of theology. At ordinations, for some years, their councils had ceased to inquire into the special opinions of the candidate, leaving him and the society electing to settle the matter. The first principle of congregationalism certainly requires this course. As a sect, the Unitarians had but one distinctive doctrine—the unity of God without the Trinity of Persons. Christendom said, " Jesus of Nazareth is Jehovah of Hosts!" The Unitarians answered, " He is not!" At my ordination, none of the council offered to catechise me, or wished to interfere with what belonged to me and the congregation, and they probably thought of my piety and morality more than of the special theology which even then rode therewith in the same panniers. The able and earnest ministers who preached the sermon, delivered the charge, and gave me the right hand of fellowship, all recommended study, investigation, originality, freedom of thought and openness of speech, as well as humanity, and a life of personal religiousness. One, in his ordaining prayer, his hand on my head, put up the petition, " that no fondness for literature or science, and no favorite studies may ever lead this young man from learning the true religion, and preaching it for the salvation of mankind!" Most heartily did I say " Amen!" to this supplication.

For the first year or two the congregation did not exceed seventy persons, including the children. I soon became well acquainted with all in the little parish, where I found some men of rare enlightenment, some truly generous and noble souls. I knew the characters of all, and the thoughts of such as had them. I took great pains with the composition of my sermons ; they were never out of my mind. I had an intense delight in writing and preaching; but I was a learner quite as much as a teacher, and was feeling my way forward and upward with one hand, while I tried to lead men with the other. I preached natural laws, nothing on the authority of any church, any tradition, any sect, though I sought illustration and confirmation from all these sources. For historical things, I told the historical evidence ; for spiritual things, I found ready proof in the primal instincts of the soul, and confirmation in the life of religious men. The simple life of the farmers, mechanics, and milk-men, about me, of its own accord, turned into a sort of poetry, and re-appeared in the sermons, as the green woods, not far off, looked in at the windows of the meeting-house. I think I preached only what I had experienced in my own inward consciousness, which widened and grew richer as I came into practical contact with living men, turned time into life, and mere thought became character.

But I had much leisure for my private humanitarian and philosophic studies. One of the professors in the Theological School had advised against my settling " in so small a place," and warned me against " the seductions of an easy chair," telling me I must become a " minister at large for all mankind," and do with the pen what I could not with the voice. I devoted my spare time to hard study. To work ten or fifteen hours a-day in my literary labours, was not only a habit, but a pleasure ; with zeal and delight I applied myself anew to the great theological problems of the age.

Many circumstances favored both studious pursuits and the formation of an independent character. The years of my preliminary theological study, and of my early ministry, fell in the most interesting period of New England's spiritual history, when a great revolution went on—so silent that few men knew it was taking place, and none then understood its whither or its whence.

The Unitarians, after a long and bitter controversy, in which they were often shamelessly ill-treated by the "orthodox," had conquered, and secured their ecclesiastical right to deny the Trinity, "the Achilles of dogmas;" they had won the respect of the New England public; had absorbed most of the religious talent of Massachusetts, founded many churches, and possessed and liberally administered the oldest and richest college in America. Not yet petrified into a sect, they rejoiced in the large liberty of "the children of God," and owning neither racks nor dungeons, did not covet any of those things that were their neighbor's. With less education and literary skill, the Universalists had fought manfully against Eternal Damnation—the foulest doctrine which defiles the pages of man's theologic history—secured their ecclesiastical position, wiping malignant statutes from the law books, and, though in a poor and vulgar way, were popularising the great truth that God's chief attribute is LOVE, which is extended to all men. Alone of all Christian sects, they professedly taught the immortality of man in such a form that it is no curse to the race to find it true! But, though departing from those doctrines which are essential to the Christian ecclesiastic scheme, neither Universalist nor Unitarian had broken with the authority of Revelation, the word of the Bible, but still professed a willingness to believe both Trinity and Damnation, could they be found in the miraculous and infallible Scripture.

Mr. Garrison, with his friends, inheriting what was best in the Puritan founders of New England, fired with the zeal of the Hebrew prophets and Christian martyrs, while they were animated with a spirit of humanity rarely found in any of the three, was beginning his noble work, but in a style so humble that, after much search, the police of Boston discovered there was nothing dangerous in it, for "his only visible auxiliary was a negro boy." Dr. Channing was in the full maturity of his powers, and after long preaching the dignity of man as an abstraction, and piety as a purely inward life, with rare and winsome eloquence, and ever progressive humanity, began to apply his sublime doctrines to actual life in the individual, the state, and the church. In the name of Christianity, the great American Unitarian called for the reform of the drunkard, the elevation of the poor, the instruction of the ignorant, and, above all, for the libération of the American slave. A remarkable man, his instinct of progress grew stronger the more he travelled, and the further he went, for he surrounded himself with young life. Horace Mann, with his coadjutors, began a great movement, to improve the public education of the people. Pierpont, single-handed, was fighting a grand and twofold battle—against drunkenness in the street, and for righteousness in the pulpit—against fearful ecclesiastic odds maintaining a minister's right and duty to oppose actual wickedness, however popular and destructive. The brilliant genius of Emerson rose in the winter nights, and hung over Boston, drawing the eyes of ingenuous young people to look up to that great, new star, a beauty and a mystery, which charmed for the moment, while it gave also perennial inspiration, as it led them forward along new paths, and towards new hopes. America has seen no such sight before; it is not less a blessed wonder now.

Besides, the Phrenologists, so ably represented by Spurzheim and Combe, were weakening the power of the old supernaturalism, leading men to study the constitution of man more wisely than before, and laying the foundation on which many a beneficent structure was soon to rise. The writings of Wordsworth were becoming familiar to the thoughtful lovers of nature and of man, and drawing men to natural piety. Carlyle's works got reprinted at Boston, diffusing a strong, and then also, a healthy influence on old and young. The writings of Coleridge were reprinted in America, all of them "aids to reflection," and brilliant with the scattered sparks of genius; they incited many to think, more especially young Trinitarian ministers; and, spite of the lack of both historic and philosophic accuracy, and the utter absence of all proportion in his writings; spite of his haste, his vanity, prejudice, sophistry, confusion, and opium—he yet did great service in New England, helping to emancipate enthralled minds. The works of Cousin, more systematic, and more profound as a whole, and far more catholic and comprehensive, continental, not insular, in his range, also became familiar to the Americans—reviews and translations going where the eloquent original was not heard—and helped to free the young mind from the gross sensationalism of the academic philosophy on one side, and the grosser supernaturalism of the ecclesiastic theology on the other.

The German language, hitherto the priceless treasure of a few, was becoming well known, and many were thereby made acquainted with the most original, deep, bold, comprehensive, and wealthy literature in the world, full of theologic and philosophic thought. Thus, a great storehouse was opened to such as were earnestly in quest of truth. Young Mr. Strauss, in whom genius for criticism was united with extraordinary learning and rare facility of philosophic speech, wrote his "Life of Jesus," where he rigidly scrutinised the genuineness of the Gospels and the authenticity of their contents, and with scientific calmness, brought every statement to his steady scales, weighing it, not always, justly, as I think, but impartially always, with philosophic coolness and deliberation. The most formidable assailant of the ecclesiastical theology of Christendom, he roused a host of foes, whose writings—mainly ill-tempered, insolent, and sophistical—it was yet profitable for a young man to read.

The value of Christian miracles, not the question of fact, was discussed at Boston, as never before in America. Prophecy had been thought the Jachin, and miracles the Boaz, whereon alone Christianity could rest; but, said some, if both be shaken down, the Lord's house will not fall. The claims of ecclesiastical tradition came up to be settled anew; and young men, walking solitary through the moonlight, asked, "Which is to be permanent master—a single accident in human history, nay, perchance only the whim of some anonymous dreamer, or the substance of human nature, greatening with continual development, and

"Not without access of unexpected strength?"

The question was also its answer.

The rights of labor were discussed with deep philanthropic feeling, and sometimes with profound thought, metaphysic and economic both. The works of Charles Fourier—a strange, fantastic, visionary man, no doubt, but gifted also with amazing insight of the truths of social science—shed some light in these dark places of speculation. Mr. Ripley, a born Democrat, in the high sense of that abused word, and one of the best cultured and most enlightened men in America, made an attempt at Brook Farm, in West Roxbury, so to organise society that the results of labour should remain in the workman's hand, and not slip thence to the trader's till; that there should be "no exploitation of man by man," but toil and thought, hard work and high culture, should be united in the same person.

The natural rights of woman began to be inquired into, and publicly discussed; while in private, great pains were taken in the chief towns of New England, to furnish a thorough and comprehensive education to such young maidens as were born with two talents, mind and money.

Of course a strong reaction followed. At the Cambridge Divinity School, Professor Henry Ware, Jun., told the young men, if there appeared to them any contradiction between the reason of man and the letter of the Bible, they "must follow the written Word," "for you can never be so certain of the correctness of what takes place in your own mind, as of what is written in the Bible." In an ordination sermon, he told the young minister not to preach himself, but Christ; and not to appeal to human nature for proof of doctrines, but to the authority of revelation. Other Unitarian ministers declared, "There are limits to free inquiry;" and preached, "Reason must be put down, or she will soon ask terrible questions;" protested against the union of philosophy and religion, and assumed to "prohibit the banns" of marriage between the two. Mr. Norton—then a great name at Cambridge, a scholar of rare but contracted merit, a careful and exact writer, born for controversy, really learned and able in his special department, the interpretations of the New Testament—opened his mouth and spoke: the mass of men must accept the doctrines of religion solely on the authority of the learned, as they do the doctrines of mathematical astronomy; the miracles of Jesus—he made merry at those of the Old Testament—are the only evidence of the truth of Christianity; in the popular religion of the Greeks and Romans, there was no conception of God; the new philosophic attempts to explain the fact of religious consciousness were "the latest form of infidelity;" the great philosophical and theological thinkers of Germany were "all atheists;" "Schleiermacher was an atheist," as was also Spinoza, his master, before him; and Cousin, who was only "that Frenchman," was no better; the study of philosophy, and the neglect of "Biblical criticism," were leading mankind to ruin—everywhere was instability and insecurity!

Of course, this reaction was supported by the ministers in the great churches of commerce, and by the old literary periodicals, which never knew a star was risen till men wondered at it in the zenith; the Unitarian journals gradually went over to the opponents of freedom and progress, with lofty scorn rejecting their former principles, and repeating the conduct they had once complained of; Cambridge and Princeton seemed to be interchanging cards. From such hands Cousin and Emerson could not receive needed criticism, but only vulgar abuse. Dr. Channing could "not draw a long breath in Boston," where he found the successors of Paul trembling before the successors of Felix. Even Trinitarian Moses Stuart seemed scarcely safe in his hard-bottomed Hopkinsian chair, at Andover. The Trinitarian ministers and city schoolmasters galled Horace Mann with continual assaults on his measures for educating the people. Unitarian ministers struck hands with wealthy liquor dealers to drive Mr. Pierpont from his pulpit, where he valiantly preached " temperance, righteousness, and judgment to come," appealing to " a day after to-day." Prominent anti-slavery men were dropped out of all wealthy society in Boston, their former friends not knowing them in the streets; Mr. Garrison was mobbed by men in handsome coats, and found defence from their fury only in a jail; an assembly of women, consulting for the liberation of their darker sisters, was driven with hootings into the street. The Attorney-General of Massachusetts brought an indictment for blasphemy against a country minister, one of the most learned Biblical scholars in America, for publicly proving that none of the " Messianic prophecies " of the Old Testament was ever fulfilled by Jesus of Nazareth, who accordingly was not the expected Christ of the Jews. Abner Kneeland, editor of a newspaper, in which he boasted of the name "Infidel," was clapped in jail for writing against the ecclesiastical notion of God, the last man ever punished for blasphemy in the State. At the beck of a Virginian slave-holder, the Governor of Massachusetts suggested to the Legislature the expediency of abridging the old New England liberty of speech.

The movement party established a new quarterly, the *Dial*, wherein their wisdom and their folly rode together on the same saddle, to the amazement of lookers-on. The short-lived journal had a narrow circulation, but its most significant papers were scattered wide by newspapers which copied them. A *Quarterly Review* was also established by Mr. Brownson, then a Unitarian minister and " sceptical democrat" of the most extravagant class, but now a Catholic, a powerful advocate of material and spiritual despotism, and perhaps the ablest writer in America against the rights of man and the welfare of his race. In this he diffused important philosophic ideas, displayed and disciplined his own extraordinary talents for philosophic thought and popular writing, and directed them towards Democracy, Transcendentalism, "New Views," and the " Progress of the Species."

I count it a piece of good fortune that I was a young man when these things were taking place, when great questions were discussed, and the public had not yet taken sides.

After I became a Minister I laid out an extensive plan of study, a continuation of previous work. I intended to write a " History of the Progressive Development of Religion among the leading Races of Mankind," and attended at once to certain preliminaries. I studied the Bible more carefully and comprehensively than before, both the criticism and interpretation ; and, in six or seven years, prepared an " Introduction to the Canonical Scriptures of the Old Testament," translated from the German of Dr. Wette, the ablest writer in the world on that theme; the book as published was partly his and partly mine. This work led me to a careful study of the Christian Fathers of the first five centuries, and of most of the great works written about the Bible and Christianity. I intended to prepare a similar work on the New Testament, and the Apocrypha of both Old and New. I studied the philosophers, theologians, and Biblical critics of Germany, the only land where theology was then studied as a science, and developed with scientific freedom. I was much helped by the large learning, and nice analysis of these great thinkers, who have done as much for the history of the Christian movement as Niebuhr for that of the Roman State. But as I studied the profound works of Catholic and Protestant, the regressive and the progressive men, and got instruction from all, I did not feel inclined to accept any one as my master, thinking it lawful to ride on their horses without being myself either saddled or bridled.

The critical study of the Bible only enhanced my reverence for the great and good things I found in the Old Testament and New. They were not the less valuable because they were not the work of "miraculous and infallible inspiration," and because I found them mixed with some of the worst doctrines ever taught by men; it was no strange thing to find pearls surrounded by sand, and roses beset with thorns. I liked the Bible better when I could consciously take its contradictory books each for what it is, and felt nothing commanding me to accept it for what it is not; and could freely use it as a help, not slavishly serve it as a master, or worship it as an idol. I took no doctrine for true, simply because it was in the Bible; what therein seemed false or wrong, I rejected as freely as if I had found it in the sacred books of the Buddhists or Mormons.

I had not preached long before I found, as never before, that practically, the ecclesiastical worship of the Bible hindered the religious welfare and progress of the Christians more than any other cause.

With doctors, the traditionary drug was once a fetish, which they reverenced and administered without much inquiring whether it would kill or cure. But now, fortunately, they are divided into so many sects, each terribly criticising the other, the spirit of philosophic scepticism and inquiry by experiment has so entered the profession, that many have broken with that authority, and ask freely, "How can the sick man recover?" The worship of the traditionary drug is getting ended.

With lawyers, the law of the land, custom, or promulgated statue, is also a fetish. They do not ask, "Is the statute right?—will its application promote justice?" which is the common interest of all men; but only, "Is it law?" To this judge and advocate must prostitute their conscience; hence the personal ruin which so often is mistaken for personal success.

With Protestant ministers, the Bible is a fetish; it is so with Catholic priests likewise, only to them the Roman Church is the master fetish, the "big thunder," while the Bible is but an inferior and subservient idol. For ultimate authority, the minister does not appeal to God, manifesting Himself in the world of matter and the world of man, but only to the Bible; to that he prostitutes his mind and conscience, heart and soul; on the authority of an anonymous Hebrew book, he will justify the slaughter of innocent men, women, and children, by the thousand; and, on that of an anonymous Greek book, he will believe, or at least command others to believe, that man is born totally depraved, and God will perpetually slaughter men in hell by the million, though they had committed no fault, except that of not believing an absurd doctrine they had never heard of. Ministers take the Bible in the lump as divine; all between the lids of the book is equally the "Word of God," infallible and miraculous; he that believeth it shall be saved, and he that believeth not shall be damned; no amount of piety and morality can make up for not believing this. No doctor is ever so subordinate to his drug, no lawyer lies so prone before statute and custom, as the mass of ministers before the Bible, the great fetish of Protestant Christendom. The Ephesians did not so worship their great goddess Diana and the meteoric stone which fell down from Jupiter. "We can believe anything," say they, "which has a 'Thus saith the Lord' before or after it." The Bible is not only master of the soul, it is also a talisman to keep men from harm; bodily contact with it, through hand or eye, is a part of religion; so it lies in railroad stations, in the parlors and sleeping chambers of taverns, and the cabin of ships, only to be seen and touched not read. The pious mother puts it in the trunk of her prodigal son, about to travel, and while she knows he is wasting her substance upon harlots and in riotous living, she contents herself with the thought that "he has got his Bible with him, and promised to read a chapter every day!" So the Catholic mother uses an image of the "Virgin Mother of God," and the Rocky Mountain savage a bundle of grass: it is a fetish.

But with this general worship of the Bible there is yet a cunning use of it; as the lawyers twist a statute to wring out a meaning they know it does not contain, but themselves put in, or warp a decision till it fits their purpose, so, with equal sophistry, and perhaps self-deceit, do the Ministers twist the Bible to support their special doctrine: no book has been explained with such sophistry. Thus, some make the Apostle Paul a Unitarian, and find neither Divinity nor the pre-existence ascribed to Jesus in the fourth Gospel; while others discover the full-blown Trinity in the first verse of the first chapter of the first book in the Bible; nay, yet others can find no devil, no wrathful God, and no eternal damnation, even in the New Testament. But all these ministers agree that the Bible is the "Word of God," "His only Word," miraculous and infallible, and that belief in it is indispensable to Christianity, and continually preach this to the people.

I had not long been a minister, before I found this worship of the Bible as a fetish hindering me at each progressive step. If I wished to teach the nobleness of man, the Old Testament and New were there with dreadful condemnations of human nature; did I speak of God's love for all men, the Bible was full of ghastly things—chosen people, hell, devil, damnation—to prove that he loved only a few, and them not overmuch; did I encourage free individuality of soul, such as the great Bible-men themselves had, asking all to be Christians as Jesus was a Christ, there were texts of bondage, commanding a belief in this or that absurdity. There was no virtue, but the Scriptures could furnish an argument against it. I could not deny the existence of ghosts and witches, devils and demons, haunting the earth, but Revelation could be quoted against me. Nay, if I declared the constancy of nature's laws, and sought therein great argument for the constancy of God, all the miracles came and held their mythologic finger up. Even slavery was " of God," for the " divine statutes " in the Old Testament admitted the principle that man might own a man as well as a garden or an ox, and provided for the measure. Moses and the Prophets were on its side, and neither Paul of Tarsus nor Jesus of Nazareth uttered a direct word against it. The best thing in the Bible is the free genius for religion, which is itself inspiration, and not only learns particular truths through its direct normal intercourse with God, but creates new men in its own likeness, to lead every Israel out of his Egypt, and conduct all men to the Land of Promise : whoso worships the Bible, loses this.

I set myself seriously to consider how I could best oppose this monstrous evil ; it required great caution. I feared lest I should weaken men's natural trust in God, and their respect for true religion, by rudely showing them that they worshipped an idol, and were misled into gross superstition. This fear did not come from my nature, but from ecclesiastical tradition, and the vice of a New England theologic culture. It has been the maxim of almost every sect in Christendom that the mass of men, in religious matters, must be ruled with authority, that is, by outward force ; this principle belongs to the idea of a supernatural revelation ; the people cannot determine for themselves what is true, moral, religious ; their opinions must be made for them by supernatural authority, not by them through the normal use of their higher faculties ! Hence the Catholic priest appeals to the supernatural Church to prove the infallibility of the Pope, the actual presence of the body and blood of Jesus in the sacramental bread and wine ; hence the Protestant appeals to the supernatural Bible, to prove that Jesus was born with no human father, the total depravity of all men, the wrath of God, the existence of a devil, and the eternal torments of hell. Besides, the man of superior education is commonly separated from sympathizing with the people, and that by the very culture they have paid for with their toil, and which ought to unite the two ; he has little confidence in their instinct or reflection.

I had some of these unnatural doubts and fears ; but my chief anxiety came less from distrust of mankind, than from diffidence in my own power to tell the truth so clear and well that I should do no harm. However, when I saw the evil which came from this superstition, I could not be silent. In conversation and preaching, I explained little details—this was poetry in the Bible, and not matter of fact : that was only the dress of the doctrine, not truth itself ; the authors of Scripture were mistaken here and there ; they believed in a devil, which was a popular fancy of their times ; a particular prophecy has never been fulfilled.

But the whole matter must be treated more philosophically, and set on its true foundation. So, designing to save men's reverence for the grand truths of the Bible, while I should wean them away from worshipping it, I soon laboriously wrote two sermons on the contradictions in the Scripture—treating of historic contradictions, where one part is at variance with another, or with actual facts, authenticated by other witnesses; of scientific contradictions, passages at open variance with the facts of the material universe; and of moral and religious contradictions, passages which were hostile to the highest intuitions and reflections of human nature. I made the discourses as perfect as I then could at that early stage of my life: very imperfect and incomplete I should, doubtless, find them now. I then inquired about the expediency of preaching them immediately. I had not yet enough practical experience of men to authorize me to depart from the ecclesiastical distrust of the people; I consulted older and enlightened ministers. They all said "No: preach no such thing! You will only do harm." One of the most learned and liberal ministers of New England advised me never to oppose the popular religion! "But, if it be wrong to hinder the religious welfare of the people— what then?" Why, let it alone; all the old philosophers did so; Socrates sacrificed a cock to Æsculapius! He that spits on the wind spits in his own face; you will ruin yourself, and do nobody any good!

Silenced, but not convinced, I kept my unpreached sermons, read books on kindred matters, and sought to make my work more complete as a whole, and more perfect in all its parts. At length I consulted a very wise and thoughtful layman, old, with large social experience, and much esteemed for sound sense, one who knew the difficulties of the case, and would not let his young children read the Old Testament, lest it should injure their religious character. I told him my conviction and my doubts, asking his advice. He also thought silence wiser than speech, yet said there were many thoughtful men who felt troubled by the offensive things in the Bible, and would be grateful to any one who could show that religion was independent thereof. But, he added, "If you try it, you will be misunderstood." Take the society at ——, perhaps one of the most intelligent in the city; you will preach your sermons, a few will understand and thank you. But the great vulgar, who hear imperfectly and remember imperfectly, and at the best understand but little, they will say, " He finds faults in the Bible! What does it all mean; what have we got left?" And the little vulgar, who hear and remember still more imperfectly, and understand even less, they will exclaim, " Why the man is an Infidel! He tells us there are faults in the Bible. He is pulling down religion!" Then it will get into the newspapers, and all the ministers in the land will be down upon you! No good will be done, but much harm. You had better let it all alone!

I kept my sermons more than a year, doubting whether the little congregation would be able to choose between truth and error when both were set before them, and fearing lest I should weaken their faith in pure religion, when I showed it was not responsible for the contradictions in the Hebrew and Greek Scriptures! But at length I could wait no longer; and to ease my own conscience, I preached the two sermons, yet not venturing to look the audience in the face and see the immediate result. In the course of the week, men and women of the commonest education, but of earnest character and profound religious feeling, took pains to tell me of the great comfort I had given them by showing, what they had long felt, that the Bible is one thing and religion another; that the two had no necessary connection: that the faults of the Old Testament or the New need not hinder any man from religious development; and that he never need try to believe a statement in the Bible which was at variance with his reason and his conscience. They thanked me for the attempt to apply common-sense to religion and the Bible. The most thoughtful and religious seemed the most instructed. I could not learn that any one felt less reverence for God, or less love for piety and morality. It was plain I had removed a stone of stumbling from the public path. The scales of ecclesiastical tradition fell from my eyes; by this crucial experiment, this guide-board instance, I learned that the mass of men need not be led blind-fold by clerical authority, but had competent power of self-direction, and while they needed the scholar as their help, had no need of a self-appointed master. It was clear that a teacher of religion and theology should tell the world all he knew thereunto appertaining, as all teachers of mathematics or of chemistry are expected to do in their profession.

I had once felt very happy, when I could legitimate these three great primal instinctive intuitions, of the divine, the just, and the immortal; I now felt equally joyous at finding I might safely appeal to the same instincts in the mass of New England men, and build religion on that imperishable foundation.

I continued my humble studies, philosophical and theological; and as fast as I found a new truth, I preached it to gladden other hearts in my own parish, and elsewhere, when I spoke in the pulpits of my friends. The neighbouring ministers became familiar with my opinions and my practice, but seldom uttered a reproach. At length, on the 19th of May, 1841, at the ordination of Mr. Shackford, a thoughtful and promising young man, at South Boston, I preached a "Discourse of the Transient and Permanent in Christianity." The Trinitarian ministers who were present joined in a public protest; a great outcry was raised against the sermon and its author. Theological and commercial newspapers rang with animadversions against its wickedness. "Unbeliever," "Infidel," "Atheist," were the titles bestowed on me by my brothers in the Christian ministry; a venerable minister, who heard the report in an adjoining county, printed his letter in one of the most widely circulated journals of New England, calling on the Attorney-General to prosecute, the grand jury to indict, and the judge to sentence me to three years' confinement in the State Prison for blasphemy!

I printed the sermon, but no bookseller in Boston would put his name to the title-page—Unitarian ministers had been busy with their advice. The Swedenborgian printers volunteered the protection of their name; the little pamphlet was thus published, sold, and vehemently denounced. Most of my clerical friends fell off; some would not speak to me in the street, and refused to take me by the hand; in their public meetings they left the sofas or benches when I sat down, and withdrew from me as Jews from contact with a leper. In a few months most of my former ministerial coadjutors forsook me, and there were only six who would allow me to enter their pulpits. But yet one Unitarian minister, Rev. John L. Russell, though a stranger till then, presently after came and offered me his help in my time of need! The controlling men of the denomination determined, "This young man must be silenced!" The Unitarian periodicals were shut against me and my friends—the public must not read what I wrote. Attempts were secretly made to alienate my little congregation, and expel me from my obscure station at West Roxbury. But I had not gone to war without counting the cost. I well knew beforehand what awaited me, and had determined to fight the battle through, and never thought of yielding or being silenced. I told my opponents the only man who could "put me down" was myself, and I trusted I should do nothing to bring about that result. If thrust out of my own pulpit, I made up my mind to lecture from city to city, from town to town, from village to village, nay, if need were from house to house, well assured that I should not thus go over the hamlets of New England till something was come. But the little society came generously to my support and defence, giving me the heartiest sympathy, and offered me all the indulgence in their power. Some ministers and generous-minded laymen stood up on my side, and preached or wrote in defence of free thought and free speech, even in the pulpit. Friendly persons, both men and women, wrote me letters to cheer and encourage, also to warn—this against fear, that against excess and violence; some of them never gave me their names, and I only have this late opportunity to thank them for their anonymous kindness. Of course scurrilous and abusive letters did not fail to appear.

Five or six men in Boston thought this treatment was not quite fair; they wished to judge neither a man nor his doctrines unheard, but to know at length what I had to say; so they asked me to deliver a course of five lectures in your city, on religious matters. I consented, and in the autumn of 1841 delivered five lectures on "Matters pertaining to Religion;" they were reported in some of the newspapers, most ably and fully in the *New York Tribune*, not then the famous and powerful sheet it has since become. I delivered the lectures several times that winter in New England towns, and published them in a volume the next spring. I thought no bookseller would put his name to the title-page; but when the work was ready for the public eye, my friend, the late Mr. James Brown, perhaps the most eminent man in the American book trade, volunteered to take charge of it, and the book appeared with the advantage of issuing from one of the most respectable publishing-houses in the United States. Years afterwards he told me that two "rich and highly respectable gentlemen of Boston" begged him to have nothing to do with it; "we wish," said they, "to render it impossible for him to publish his work!" But the bookseller wanted fair-play.

The next autumn I delivered in Boston six "Sermons for the Times," treating of theology, of religion, and of its application to life. These also were repeated in several other places. But, weary with anxiety and excess of work, both public and private, my health began to be seriously impaired; and in September, 1843, I fled off to Europe, to spend a year in recovery, observation, and thought. I ·had there an opportunity to study nations I had previously known only by their literature, and by other men's words; to see the effect which despotic, monarchic, and aristocratic institutions have on multitudes of men, who, from generation to generation, had lived under them; to study the effect of those forms of religion which are enforced by the inquisitor or the constable; and in many forms, to see the difference between freedom and bondage. In their architecture, painting, and sculpture, the European cities afforded me a new world of art, while the heterogeneous crowds which throng the streets of those vast ancient capitals, so rich in their historic monuments, presented human life in forms I had not known before. It is only in the low parts of London, Paris and Naples, that an American learns what the ancients meant by the "People," the "Populace," and sees what barbarism may exist in the midst of wealth, culture, refinement, and manly virtue. There I could learn what warning and what guidance the Old World had to offer to the New. Visiting some of the seats of learning, which, in Europe, are also sometimes the citadel of new thought and homes of genius, I had an opportunity of conversing with eminent men, and comparing their schemes for improving mankind with my own. Still more, I had an entire year, free from all practical duties, for revising my own philosophy and theology, and laying out plans for future work. My involuntary year of rest and inaction turned out, perhaps, the most profitable in my life, up to that time, in the acquisition of knowledge, and in preparing for much that was to follow.

Coming home the next September, with more physical strength than ever before, I found a hearty welcome from the many friends who crowded the little meeting-house to welcome my return—as before to bid me God-speed—and resumed my usual labours, public and private. In my absence, my theological foes had contented themselves with declaring that my doctrines had taken no root in America, and my personal friends were turning off from the error of their ways; but the sound of my voice roused my opponents to new activity, and ere long the pulpits and newspapers rang with the accustomed warfare. But even in Boston there were earnest ministers who lifted up their voices in behalf of freedom of thought in the study, and free speech in the pulpit. I shall never cease to be grateful to Mr. Pierpont, Mr. Sargent, and James Freeman Clarke, "friends in need, and friends in deed." They defended the principle of religious freedom, though they did not share the opinions it led me to, nor always approve of the manner in which I set them forth. It was zeal for the true and the right, not special personal friendship for me, which moved them to this manly course. In the most important orthodox Quarterly in America, a young Trinitarian minister, Rev. Mr. Porter, reviewed my

"Discourse of Religion," not doing injustice to author or work, while he stoutly opposed both. A few other friendly words were also spoken; but what were these among so many!

Under these circumstances you formed your society. A few earnest men thought the great principle of religious freedom was in danger; for, indeed, it was ecclesiastically repudiated, and that, too, with scorn and hissing by the Unitarians—the "liberal Christians!" the "party of progress"—not less than by the orthodox. Some of you came together, privately first, and then in public, to look matters in the face, and consider what ought to be done. A young man proposed this resolution: "*Resolved*, That the Rev. Theodore Parker shall have a chance to be heard in Boston." That motion prevailed, and measures were soon taken to make the resolution an event. But, so low was our reputation, that, though payment was offered in advance, of all the unoccupied halls in Boston, only one could be hired for our purpose; but that was the largest and most central. So, one rainy Sunday, the streets full of snow, on the 16th of February, 1845, for the first time I stood before you to preach and pray: we were strangers then! I spoke of the "Indispensableness of True Religion for Man's Welfare in his Individual and his Social Life." I came to build up piety and morality; to pull down only what cumbered the ground. I was then in my thirty-fifth year, and had some knowledge of the historical development of religion in the Christian world. I knew that I came to a "thirty years' war," and I had enlisted for the whole, should life hold out so long. I knew well what we had to expect at first; for we were committing the sin which all the great world-sects have held unpardonable — attempting to correct the errors of theory and the vices of practice in the Church. No offence could ecclesiastically be greater; the Inquisition was built to punish such; to that end blazed the faggots at Smithfield, and the cross was set up on Calvary. Truth has her cradle near Golgotha. You knew my spirit and tendency better than my special opinions, which you then gave a " chance to be heard in Boston." But I knew that I had thoroughly broken with the ecclesiastical authority of Christendom; its God was not my God, nor its Scriptures my Word of God, nor its Christ my Saviour; for I preferred the Jesus of historic fact to the Christ of theologic fancy. Its narrow, partial, and unnatural heaven I did not wish to enter on the terms proposed, nor did I fear, since earliest youth, its mythic, roomy hell, wherein the triune God, with his pack of devils to aid, tore the human race in pieces for ever and ever. I came to preach "another Gospel," sentiments, ideas, actions, quite unlike what belonged to the theology of the Christian Church. Though severely in earnest, I came to educate men into true religion as well as I could, I knew I should be accounted the worst of men, ranked among triflers, mockers, infidels, and atheists. But I did not know all the public had to offer me of good or ill; nay, I did not know what was latent in myself, nor foresee all the doctrines which then were hid in my own first principles, what embryo fruit and flowers lay sheathed in the obvious bud. But at the beginning I warned you that if you came, Sunday after Sunday, you would soon think very much as I did on the great matters you asked me to teach—because I had drawn my doctrine from the same human nature which was in you, and that would recognise and own its child.

Let me arrange, under three heads, some of the most important doctrines I have aimed to set forth.

I. THE INFINITE PERFECTION OF GOD.—This doctrine is the cornerstone of all my theological and religious teaching—the foundation, perhaps, of all that is peculiar in my system. It is not known to the Old Testament or the New; it has never been accepted by any sect in the Christian world; for, though it be equally claimed by all, from the Catholic to the Mormon, none has ever consistently developed it, even in theory, but all continually limit God in power, in wisdom, and still more eminently in justice and in love. The idea of God's imperfection has been carried out with dreadful logic in the " Christian Scheme." Thus it is commonly taught, in all the great theologies, that, at the crucifixion of Jesus, " the Creator of the universe was put to death, and his own creatures were his executioners." Besides, in the ecclesiastic conception of Deity, there is a fourth person to the God-head—namely, the Devil, an outlying member, unacknowledged, indeed, the complex of all evil, but as much a part of the Deity as either Son or Holy Ghost, and far more powerful than all the rest, who seem but jackals to provide for this "roaring lion," which devours what the others but create, die for, inspire, and fill. I know this statement is ghastly—the theologic notion it sets forth, to me, seems far more so. While the Christians accept the Bible as the "Word of God," direct, miraculous, infallible, containing a complete and perfect "revelation" of His nature, His character, and conduct, it is quite impossible for them to accept, or even tolerate, the infinite perfection of God. The imperfect and cruel character attributed to God, rejoicing in his hell and its legions of devils, is the fundamental vice of the ecclesiastical theology, which so many accept as their "religion," and name the hideous thing " Christianity!" They cannot escape the consequence of their first principle; their gate must turn on its own hinge.

I have taught that God contains all possible and conceivable perfection:—the perfection of being, self-subsistence, conditioned only by itself; the perfection of power, all-mightiness; of mind, all-knowingness; of conscience, all-righteousness; of affection, all-lovingness; and the perfection of that innermost element, which in finite man is personality, all-holiness, faithfulness to Himself.

The infinitely perfect God is immanent in the world of matter, and in the world of spirit, the two hemispheres which to us make up the universe; each particle thereof is inseparable from Him, while He yet transcends both, is limited by neither, but in Himself is complete and perfect.

I have not taught that the special qualities I find in the Deity are all that are actually there; higher and more must doubtless appear to beings of larger powers than man's. My definition distinguishes God from all other beings; it does not limit him to the details of my conception. I only tell what I know, not what others may know, which lies beyond my present consciousness.

He is a perfect Creator, making all from a perfect motive, for a perfect purpose, of perfect substance, and as a perfect means ; none other are conceivable with a perfect God. The motive must be love, the purpose welfare, the means the constitution of the universe itself, as a whole and in parts—for each great or little thing coming from Him must be perfectly adapted to secure the purpose it was intended for, and achieve the end it was meant to serve, and represent the causal motive which brought it forth. So there must be a complete solidarity between God and the two-fold universe which He creates. The perfect Creator is thus also a perfect providence; indeed, creation and providence are not objective accidents of Deity, nor subjective caprices, but the development of the perfect motive to its perfect purpose, love becoming a universe of perfect welfare.

I have called God Father, but also Mother, not by this figure implying that the Divine Being has the limitations of the female figure—as some ministers deceitfully allege of late, who might have been supposed to know better than thus to pervert plain speech—but to express more sensibility, the quality of tender and unselfish love, which mankind associates with Mother than aught else beside.

II. THE ADEQUACY OF MAN FOR ALL HIS FUNCTIONS.—From the infinite perfection of God their follows unavoidably the relative perfection of all that He creates. So, the nature of man, tending to a progressive development of all his manifold powers, must be the best possible nature, most fit for the perfect accomplishment of the perfect purpose, and the attainment of the perfect end, which God designs for the race and the individual. It is not difficult in this general way to show the relative perfection of human nature, deducing this from the infinite perfection of God; but I think it impossible to prove it by the inductive process of reasoning from concrete facts of external observation, of which we know not yet the entire sum, nor any one, perhaps, completely. Yet I have travelled also this inductive road, as far as it reaches, and tried to show the constitution of man's body, with its adaptation to the surrounding world of matter, and the constitution of his spirit, with its intellectual, moral, affectional, and religious powers, and its harmonious relation with the world of matter, which affords them a playground, a school, and a workshop. So I have continually taught that man has in himself all the faculties he needs to accomplish his high destination, and in the world of matter finds, one by one, all the material helps he requires.

We all see the unity of life in the individual; his gradual growth from merely sentient and passive babyhood, up to thoughtful, self-directing manhood. I have tried to show there was a similar unity of life in the human race, pointing out the analogous progressive development of mankind, from the state of ignorance, poverty, and utter nakedness of soul and sense, the necessary primitive conditions of the race, up to the present civilization of the leading nations. The primitive is a wild man, who gradually grows up to civilization. To me, the notorious facts of human history, the condition of language, art, industry, and the foot-prints of man left all over the torrid and temperate lands, admit of no other interpretation. Of course it must have required many a thousand years for Divine Providence to bring this child from his mute, naked, ignorant poverty, up to the many-voiced, many-coloured civilization of these times; and, as in the strata of mountain and plain, on the shores of the sea, and under "the bottom of the monstrous world," the geologist finds proof of time immense, wherein this material Cosmos assumed its present form, so in ruins of cities, in the weapons of iron, bronze, or stone, found in Scandinavian swamps, on the sub-aquatic enclosures of the Swiss lakes, in the remains of Egyptian industry, which the holy Nile, "mother of blessings"—now spiritual to us, as once material to those whose flesh she fed—has covered with many folds of earth and kept for us; and still more in the history of art, science, war, industry, and the structure of language itself, a slow-growing plant, do I find proof of time immense, wherein man, this spiritual Cosmos, has been assuming his present condition, individual domestic, social, and national, and accumulating that wealth of things and thoughts which is the mark of civilization. I have tried to show by history the progressive development of industry and wealth, of mind and knowledge, of conscience and justice, of the affections and philanthropy, of the soul and true religion; the many forms of the family, the community, state and church, I look on as so many "experiments in living," all useful, each, perhaps, in its time and place, as indispensable as the various geological changes. But this progressive development does not end with us; we have seen only the beginning; the future triumphs of the race must be vastly greater than all accomplished yet. In the primal instincts and automatic desires of man, I have found a prophecy that what he wants is possible, and shall one day be actual. It is a glorious future on earth which I have set before your eyes and hopes, thereby stimulating both your patience to bear now what is inevitable, and your thought and toil to secure a future triumph to be had on no other terms. What good is not with us is before, to be attained by toil and thought, and religious life.

III. ABSOLUTE OR NATURAL RELIGION.—In its complete and perfect form, this is the normal development, use, disipline, and enjoyment of every part of the body, and every faculty of the spirit; the direction of all natural powers to their natural purposes. I have taught that there were three parts which make up the sum of true religion; the emotional part, of right feelings, where religion at first begins in the automatic, primal instinct; the intellectual part, of true ideas, which either directly represent the primitive, instinctive feeling of whoso holds them, or else produce a kindred, secondary, and derivative feeling in whoso receives them; and the practical part, of just actions, which correspond to the feelings and the ideas, and make the mere thought or emotion into a concrete deed. So, the true religion which comes from the nature of man, consists of normal feelings towards God and man, of correct thoughts about God, man, and the relation between them, and of actions corresponding to the natural conscience when developed in harmony with the entire constitution of man.

But this religion which begins in the instinctive feelings, and thence advances to reflective ideas, assumes its ultimate form in the character of men, and so appears in their actions, individual, domestic, social, national, ecclesiastical, and general—human; it builds manifold institutions like itself, wherein it rears up men in its own image. All the six great historic forms of religion—the Brahmanic, Hebrew, Classic, Buddhistic, Christian, Mohammedan—profess to have come miraculously from God, not normally from man; and, spite of the excellence which they contain, and the vast service the humblest of them has done, yet each must ere long prove a hindrance to human welfare, for it claims to be a finality, and makes the whole of human nature wait upon an accident of human history—and that accident the whim of some single man. The absolute religion which belongs to man's nature, and is gradually unfolded thence, like the high achievements of art, science, literature, and politics, is only distinctly conceived of in an advanced stage of man's growth; to make its idea a fact, is the highest triumph of the human race. This is the idea of humanity, dimly seen but clearly felt, which has flitted before the pious eyes of men in all lands and many an age, and been prayed for as the "Kingdom of Heaven." The religious history of the race is the record of man's continual but unconscious efforts to attain this "desire of all nations;" poetic stories of the "golden age," or of man in the garden of Eden, are but this natural wish looking back and fondly dreaming that "the former days were better than these." But while all the other forms of religion must ultimately fail before this, fading as it flowers, each one of them has yet been a help towards it, probably indispensable to the development of mankind. For each has grown out of the condition of some people, as naturally as the wild primitive flora of Santa Cruz has come from the state of this island—its geologic structure and chemical composition, its tropic heat, and its special situation amid the great currents of water and of air; as naturally as the dependent fauna of the place comes from its flora. Thus in the religions of mankind, as in the various governments, nay, as in the different geologic periods, there is diversity of form, but unity of aim; destruction is only to create; earthquakes, which submerge the sunken continents whose former mountains are but islands now, and revolutions, in which the Hebrew and Classic religious went under, their poetic summits only visible, have analogous functions to perform—handmaids of creation both.

For these three great doctrines—of God, of Man, of Religion—I have depended on no Church and no Scripture; yet have I found things to serve me in all Scriptures and every Church. I have sought my authority in the nature of man—in facts of consciousness within me, and facts of observation in the human world without. To me the material world and the outward history of man do not supply a sufficient revelation of God, nor warrant me to speak of infinite perfection. It is only from the nature of man, from facts of intuition, that I can gather this greatest of all truths, as I find it in my consciousness reflected back from Deity itself.

I know well what may be said of the "feebleness of all the human faculties," their "unfaithfulness and unfitness for their work;" that the mind is not adequate for man's intellectual function, nor the conscience for the moral, nor the affections for the philanthropic, nor the soul for the religious, nor even the body for the corporeal, but that each requires miraculous help from a God who is only outside of humanity! There is a denial which boldly rejects the immortality of man and the existence of Deity, with many another doctrine, dear and precious to mankind; but the most dangerous scepticism is that, which, professing allegiance to all these, and crossing itself at the name of Jesus, is yet so false to the great primeval instincts of man, that it declares he cannot be certain of anything he learns by the normal exercise of any faculty! I have carefully studied this school of doubt, modern, not less than old, as it appears in history. In it there are honest inquirers after truth, but misled by some accident, and also sophists, who live by their sleight of mind, as jugglers by their dexterity of hand. But the chief members of this body are the mockers, who, in a world they make empty, find the most fitting echo to their hideous laugh; and churchmen of all denominations, who are so anxious to support their ecclesiastic theology, that they think it is not safe on its throne till they have annihilated the claim of reason, conscience, the affections, and the soul to any voice in determining the greatest concerns of man—thinking there is no place for the Christian Church or the Bible till they have nullified the faculties which created both, and rendered Bible-makers and Church-founders impossible. But it is rather a poor compliment these ecclesiastic sceptics pay their Deity, to say He so makes and manages the world that we cannot trust the sights we see, the sounds we hear, the thoughts we think, or the moral, affectional, religious emotions we feel; that we are certain neither of the intuitions of instinct, nor the demonstrations of reason, but yet by some anonymous testimony, can be made sure that Balaam's she-ass spoke certain Hebrew words, and one undivided third-part of God was "born of the Virgin Mary, suffered under Pontius Pilate, was crucified, descended into hell, and the third day rose again," to take away the wrath which the other two undivided third-parts of God felt against all mankind!

It is not for me to say there is no limit to the possible attainments of man's religious or other faculties. I will not dogmatise where I do not know. But history shows that the Hercules' Pillars of one age are sailed through in the next, and a wide ocean entered on, which in due time is found rich with islands of its own, and washing a vast continent not dreamed of by such as slept within their temples of old, while it sent to their very coasts its curious joints of unwonted cane, its seeds of many an unknown tree, and even elaborate boats, wherein lay the starved bodies of strange-featured men, with golden jewels in their ears. No doubt there are limits to human industry, for finite man is bounded on every side; but, I take it, the Hottentot, the Gaboon Negro, and the wild man of New Guinea, antecedently, would think it impossible that mankind should build the Pyramids of Egypt for royal ostentation, for defence throw up the fortresses of Europe and the wall of China, or for economic use lay down the roads of earth, of water, iron, wood, or stone, which now so swiftly help to develop the material resources and educate the spiritual powers of Europe and America. Still less would they conceive it possible for men to make all the farms, the mills, the shops, the houses, and the ships of civilised mankind. But the philosopher sees it is possible for toil and thought soon to double, and then multiply manifold the industrial attainments of Britain or New England.

No doubt there may be a limit to mathematic thought, though to me that would seem boundless, and every scientific step therein to be certain; but the barefooted negro who goads his oxen under my window, and can only count his two thumbs, is no limit to Archimedes, Descartes, Newton, and La Place, no more are these men of vast genius a limit to the mathematic possibility of humankind. They who invented letters, arithmetic symbols, gunpowder, the compass, the printing press, the telescope, the steam-engine, and the telegraph, only ploughed in corners of the field of human possibility, and showed its bounds were not where they had been supposed. A thousand years ago, the world had not a man, I think, who could even dream of such a welfare as New England now enjoys! Who shall tell industrious, mathematic, progressive mankind, "Stop there; you have reached the utmost bound of human possibility; beyond it economy is waste, and science folly, and progress downfall!" No more is the atheistic mocker or the ecclesiastic bigot commissioned to stop the human race with his cry, "Cease there, mankind, thy religious search! for, thousand-million-headed as thou art, thou canst know nought directly of thy God, thy duty, or thyself! Pause, and accept my authenticated word; stop, and despair!"

I know too well the atheistic philosopher's bitter mock, and the haughty scorn of theologic despisers of mankind, who, diverse in all besides, yet agree in their contempt for human nature, glory in the errors of genius, or the grosser follies of mankind, and seek out of the ruins of humanity to build up, the one his palace, and the other his church. But I also know that mankind heeds neither the atheistic philosopher nor the theologic despiser of his kind; but, faithful to the great primeval instincts of the soul, believing, creating, and rejoicing, goes on its upward way, nor doubts of man or God, of sense or intellect.

These three great doctrines I have preached positively, as abstract truth, representing facts of the universe; that might be peaceful work. But they must take a concrete form, and be applied to the actual life of the individual family, community, state, and church; this would have a less peaceful look; for I must examine actual institutions, and criticise their aim, their mode of operation, and their result. The great obvious social forces in America may be thus summed up:—

1. There is the organised trading power—having its home in the great towns, which seeks gain with small regard to that large justice which represents alike the mutual interests and duties of all men, and to that humanity which interposes the affectional instinct when conscience is asleep. This power seems to control all things, amenable only to the all-mighty dollar.

2. The organised political power, the parties in office, or seeking to become so. This makes the statutes, but is commonly controlled by the trading power, and has all of its faults often intensified; yet it seems amenable to the instincts of the people, who, on great occasions, sometimes interfere and change the traders' rule.

3. The organised ecclesiastical power, the various sects which, though quite unlike, yet all mainly agree in their fundamental principle of

vicariousness—an alleged revelation, instead of actual human faculties, salvation from God's wrath and eternal ruin, by the atoning blood of crucified God. This is more able than either of the others; and though often despised, in a few years can control them both. In this generation no American politician dares affront it.

4. The organised literary power, the endowed colleges, the periodical press, with its triple multitude of journals—commercial, political, theological—and sectarian tracts. This has no original ideas, but diffuses the opinion of the other powers whom it represents, whose will it serves, and whose kaleidoscope it is.

I must examine these four great social forces, and show what was good in them, and what was ill; ascertain what natural religion demanded of each, and what was the true function of trade, government, a church, and a literature. When I came to a distinct consciousness of my own first principle, and my consequent relation to what was about me, spite of the good they contained, I found myself greatly at variance with all the four. They had one principle and I another; of course, our aim and direction were commonly different and often opposite. Soon I found that I was not welcome to the American market, state, church, nor press. It could not be otherwise; yet I confess I had not anticipated so thorough a separation betwixt me and these forces which control society, but had laid out work I could not execute alone, nor perhaps without the aid of all the four.

It is not now, my friends, worth while for me to enter on the details of these plans which have come to nothing, and which I shall probably never work out; but I ought at least to name some of the most important things I hoped to do. When I first came to Boston I intended to do something for the perishing and dangerous classes in our great towns. The amount of poverty and consequent immorality in Boston is terrible to think of, while you remember the warning of other nations, and look to the day after to-day! Yet it seemed to me the money given by public and private charity—two fountains that never fail in Puritanic Boston—was more than sufficient to relieve it all, and gradually remove the deep-seated and unseen cause which, in the hurry of business and of money, is not attended to. There is a hole in the dim-lit public bridge, where many fall through and perish! Our mercy pulls a few out of the water; it does not stop the hole, nor light the bridge, nor warn men of the peril. We need the great charity that palliates effects of wrong, and the greater justice which removes the cause.

Then there was drunkenness, which is the greatest concrete curse of the labouring Protestant population of the North, working most hideous and wide extended desolation. It is as fatal as starvation to the Irish Catholic. None of the four great social forces is its foe. There, too, was prostitution; men and women mutually polluted and polluting, blackening the face of society with dreadful woe. Besides, in our great towns I found thousands, especially the poorer Irish, oppression driving them to us, who, save the discipline of occasional work, got no education here except what the streets taught them in childhood, or the Popish priest and the American demagogue—their two worst foes—noisily offered in their adult years; it seemed to me not difficult for the vast charity of Boston to furnish instruction and guidance to this class of the American people, both in their childhood and their later youth. That admirable institution, the Warren Street Chapel—well-nigh the most Christian public thing in Boston—and the Children's Aid Society at New York, with its kindred, abundantly show how much can be done, and at how little cost.

Still more, I learned early in life that the criminal is often the victim of society, rather than its foe, and that our penal law belongs to the dark ages of brute force, and aims only to protect society by vengeance on the felon, not also to elevate mankind by refining him. In my boyhood I knew a man, the last result of generations of ancestral crime, who spent more than twenty years in our State Prison, and died there, under sentence for life, whose entire illegal thefts did not amount to twenty dollars! and another, not better born, who lawfully stole houses and farms, lived a "gentleman," and at death left a considerable estate, and the name of Land-shark. While a theological student I taught a class in the Sunday School of the State Prison, often saw my fellow-townsman, became well acquainted with several convicts, learned the mode of treatment, and heard the sermons and ghastly prayers which were let fly at the heads of the poor, unprotected wretches; I saw the "orthodox preachers and other helps," who who gave them "spiritual instruction," and learned the utter insufficiency of our penal law to mend the felon or prevent his growth in wickedness. When I became your minister I hoped to do something for this class of men, whose crimes are sometimes but a part of their congenital misfortune or social infamy, and who are bereft of the sympathy of mankind, and unconstitutionally beset with sectarian ministers, whose function is to torment them before their time.

For all these, the poor, the drunken, and the ignorant, for the prostitute, and the criminal, I meant to do something, under the guidance, perhaps, or certainly with the help, of the controling men of the town or state; but, alas! I was then fourteen years younger than now, and did not quite understand all the consequences of my relation to these great social forces, or how much I had offended the religion of the state, the press, the market, and the church, The cry, "Destroyer," "Fanatic," "Infidel," "Atheist," "Enemy of Mankind," was so widely sounded forth that I soon found I could do little in these great philanthropies, where the evil lay at our own door. Many as you are for a religious society, you were too few and too poor to undertake what should be done; and outside of your ranks I could look for little help, even by words and counsel. Besides, I soon found my very name was enough to ruin any new good enterprise. I knew there were three periods in each great movement of mankind—that of sentiment, ideas, and action: I fondly hoped the last had come; but when I found I had reckoned without the host, I turned my attention to the two former, and sought to arouse the sentiment of justice and mercy, and to diffuse the ideas which belonged to this five-fold reformation. Hence I took pains to state the facts of poverty, drunkenness, ignorance, prostitution, crime; to show their cause, their effect, and their mode of cure, leaving it for others to do the practical work. So, if I wanted a measure tarried in the Legislature of the town or state, or by some private benevolent society, I did my work by stealth. I sometimes saw my scheme prosper, and read my words in the public reports, while the whole enterprise had been ruined at once if my face or name had appeared in connection with it. I have often found it wise to withhold my name from petitions I have myself set agoing and found successful; I have got up conventions, or mass meetings, whose "managers" asked me not to show my face thereat.

This chronic and progressive unpopularity led to another change of my plans, not abating my activity, but turning it in another direction. To accomplish my work, I must spread my ideas as widely as possible, without resorting to that indecency of advertising so common in America. There was but one considerable publishing-house in the land that would continue to issue my works—this only at my own cost and risk. As it had only a pecuniary interest therein, and that so slight, in its enormous business, my books did not have the usual opportunity of getting known and circulated. They were seldom offered for sale, except in one book-store in Boston; for other States, I must often be my own bookseller. None of the Quarterlies or Monthlies was friendly to me; most of the newspapers were hostile; the *New York Tribune* and *Evening Post* were almost the only exceptions. So my books had but a small circulation at home in comparison with their diffusion in England and Germany, where, also, they received not only hostile, but most kindly notice, and sometimes from a famous pen. But another opportunity for diffusing my thought offered itself in the Lyceum or public lecture. Opposed by these four great social forces at home, I was surprised to find myself becoming popular in the lecture-hall. After a few trials I "got the *hang* of the new school-house," and set myself to serious work therein.

For a dozen years or more, I have done my share of lecturing in public, having many invitations more than I could accept. The task was always disagreeable, contrary to my natural disposition and my scholarly habits. But I saw the nation had reached an important crisis in its destination, and, though ignorant of the fact, yet stood hesitating between two principles. The one was slavery, which I knew leads at once to military despotism—political, ecclesiastical, social—and ends at last in utter and hopeless ruin; for no people fallen on that road has ever risen again; it is the path so many other Republics have taken and finished their course, as Athens and the Ionian towns have done, as Rome and the Commonwealths of the Middle Ages. The other was freedom, which leads at once to industrial democracy—respect for labor, government over all, by all, for the sake of all, rule after the eternal right as it is writ in the constitution of the universe—securing welfare and progress. I saw that these four social forces were advising, driving, coaxing, wheedling, the people to take the road to ruin; that our "great men," in which "America is so rich beyond all other nations of the earth," went strutting along that path to show how safe it is, crying out "Democracy," "Constitution," "Washington," "Gospel," "Christianity," "Dollars," and the like, while the instincts of the people, the traditions of our history, and the rising genius of men and women well-born in these times of peril, with still, small voice, whispered something of self-evident truths and inalienable rights.

I knew the power of a great Idea; and spite of the market, the State, the Church, the press, I thought a few earnest men in the lecture halls of the North, might yet incline the people's mind and heart to justice and the eternal law of God—the only safe rule of conduct for nations, as for you and me—and so make the American experiment a triumph and a joy for all humankind. Nay, I thought I could myself be of some service in that work; for the nation was yet so young, and the instinct of popular liberty so strong, it seemed to me a little added weight would turn the scale to freedom. So I appointed myself a home missionary for lectures.

Then, too, I found I could say what I pleased in the lecture-room, so long as I did not professedly put my thought into a theologic or political shape; while I kept the form of literature or philosophy, I could discourse of what I thought most important, and men would listen one hour, two hours, nay, three hours: and the more significant the subject was, the more freely, profoundly, and fairly it was treated, the more would the people come, the more eagerly listen and enthusiastically accept. So I spared no labour in preparation or delivery, but took it for granted the humblest audience, in the least intelligent town or city, was quite worthy of my best efforts, and could understand my facts and metaphysic reasonings. I did not fear the people would be offended, though I hurt their feelings never so sore.

Besides, the work was well paid for in the large towns, while the small ones did all they could afford—giving the lecturer for a night more than the schoolmaster for a month. The money thus acquired, enabled me to do four desirable things, which it is not needful to speak of here.

Since 1848, I have lectured eighty or a hundred times each year— in every Northern State east of the Mississippi, once also in a Slave State, and on slavery itself. I have taken most exciting and important subjects, of the greatest concern to the American people, and treated them independent of sect or party, street or press, and with what learning and talent I could command. I put the matter in quite various forms—for each audience is made up many. For eight or ten years, on an average, I have spoken to sixty or a hundred thousand persons in each year, besides addressing you on Sundays, in the great hall you throw open to all comers.

Thus I have had a wide field of operation, where I might rouse the sentiment of justice and mercy, diffuse such ideas as I thought needful for the welfare and progress of the people, and prepare for such action as the occasion might one day require. As I was supposed to stand nearly alone, and did not pretend to represent any one but myself, nobody felt responsible for me; so all could judge me, if not fairly, at least with no party or sectarian prejudice in my favor; and as I felt responsible only to myself and my God, I could speak freely: this was a two-fold advantage. I hope I have not spoken in vain. I thought that by each lecture I could make a new, deep, and lasting impression of some one great truth on five thoughtful men, out of each thousand who heard me. Don't think me extravagant; it is only *one-half of one per cent!* If I spoke but thus efficiently to sixty thousand in a winter, there would be three hundred so impressed, and in ten years it would

480 APPENDIX.

be three thousand! Such a result would satisfy me for my work and my loss of scholarly time in this home mission for lectures. Besides, the newspapers of the large towns spread wide the more salient facts and striking generalizations of the lecture, and I addressed the eyes of an audience I could not count nor see.

Still more, in the railroad cars and steamboats I travelled by, and the public or private houses I stopped at when the lecture was over, strangers came to see me; they were generally marked men—intellectual, moral, philanthropic, at any rate, inquiring and attentive. We sometimes talked on great matters; I made many acquaintances, gained much miscellaneous information about men and things, the state of public opinion, and, perhaps, imparted something in return. So I studied while I taught.

Nor was this all. I had been ecclesiastically reported to the people as a "disturber of the public peace," "an infidel," "an atheist," "an enemy to mankind." When I was to lecture in a little town, the minister, even the Unitarian, commonly stayed at home. Many, in public or private, warned their followers "against listening to that bad man. Don't look him in the face!" Others stoutly preached against me. So, in the bar-room "I was the song of the drunkard," and the minister's text in the pulpit. But, when a few hundreds, in a mountain town of New England, or in some settlement on a prairie of the West, or, when many hundreds, in a wide city, did look me in the face, and listen for an hour or two while I spoke, right on, of matters familiar to their patriotic hopes, their business, and their bosoms, as their faces glowed in the excitement of what they heard, I saw the clerical prejudice was stealing out of their mind, and I left them other than I found them. Nay, it has often happened that a man has told me, by letter or by word of mouth, " I was warned against you, but I *would go and see for myself;* and when I came home I said, 'After all, this is a man, and not a devil; at least, he seems human. Who knows but he may be honest, even in his theological notions? Perhaps he is *right* in his religion. Priests have been a little mistaken sometimes before now, and said hard words against rather good sort of men, if we can trust the Bible. I am glad I heard him.'"

Judging from the results, now pretty obvious to whoso looks, and by the many affectionate letters sent me from all parts of the North, I think I did not overrate the number of thoughtful men who possibly might be deeply and originally influenced by what I said in the lectures. Three thousand may seem a large number; I think it is not excessive. In the last dozen years, I think scarcely any American, not holding a political office, has touched the minds of so many men, by freely speaking on matters of the greatest importance, for this day and for ages to come. I am sure I have uttered great truths, and such are never spoken in vain; I know the effect a few great thoughts had on me in my youth, and judge others by what I experienced myself. Those ministers were in the right, who, years ago, said, " Keep that man out of the lecture-room; don't let it him be seen in public. Every word he speaks, on any subject, is a blow against our religion!" They meant, against their theology.

Such are the causes which brought me into the lecture-room. I did not neglect serving YOU, while I seemed only to instruct other men; for every friend I made in Pennsylvania or Wisconsin became an auxiliary in that great cause, so dear to you and me. Nay, I did not abandon my scholarly work while travelling and lecturing. The motion of the railroad cars gave a pleasing and not harmful stimulus to thought, and so helped me to work out my difficult problems of many kinds. I always took a sack of books along with me, generally such as required little eyesight and much thought, and so was sure of good company; while travelling I could read and write all day long; but I would not advise others to do much of either; few bodies can endure the long-continued strain on eye and nerve. So, I lost little time, while I fancied I was doing a great and needful work.

When I first came before you to preach, carefully looking before and after, I was determined on my purpose, and had a pretty distinct conception of the mode of operation. It was not my design to found a sect, and merely build up a new ecclesiastical institution, but to produce a healthy development of the highest faculties of men, to furnish them the greatest possible amount of most needed instruction, and help them each to free spiritual individuality. The Church, the State, the community, were not ends, a finality of purpose, but means to bring forth and bring up individual men. To accomplish this purpose I aimed distinctly at two things: first, to produce the greatest possible healthy development of the religious faculty, acting in harmonious connection with the intellectual, moral, and affectional; and second, to lead you to help others in the same work. Let me say a word in detail of each part of my design.

I. According both to my experience and observation, the religious element is the strongest in the spiritual constitution of man, easily controlling all the rest for his good or ill. I wished to educate this faculty under the influence of the true idea of God, of man, and of their mutual relation. I was not content with producing morality alone—the normal action of the conscience and will, the voluntative keeping of the natural law of right: I saw the need also of piety—religious feeling toward the divine, that instinctive, purely internal love of God, which, I think, is not dependent on conscience. I was led to this aim partly by my own disposition, which, I confess, naturally inclined me to spontaneous pious feeling, my only youthful luxury, more than to voluntary moral action; partly by my early culture, which had given me much experience of religious emotions; and partly, also, by my wide and familiar acquaintance with the mystical writers, the voluptuaries of the soul, who dwelt in the world of pious feeling, heedless of life's practical duties, and caring little for science, literature, justice, or the dear charities of common life.

I count it a great good fortune that I was bred among religious Unitarians, and thereby escaped so much superstition. But I felt early that the "liberal" ministers did not do justice to simple religious feeling; to me their preaching seemed to relate too much to outward things, not enough to the inward pious life; their prayers felt cold; but certainly they preached the importance and the religious value of morality as no sect, I think, had done before. Good works, the test of true religion, noble character, the proof of salvation, if not spoken, were yet implied in their sermons, spite of their inconsistent and traditionary talk about "Atonement," "Redeemer," "Salvation by Christ," and their frequent resort to other pieces of damaged phraseology. The effect of this predominant morality was soon apparent. In Massachusetts, the head-quarters of the Unitarians, not only did they gather most of the eminent intellect into their ranks, the original talent and genius of the most intellectual of the States, but also a very large proportion of its moral talent and moral genius, most of the eminent conscience and philanthropy. Leaving out of sight pecuniary gifts for theological and denominational purposes, which come from peculiar and well-known motives, where the Trinitarians are professedly superior, I think it will be found that all the great moral and philanthropic movements in the State—social, ecclesiastical, and political—from 1800 to 1840, have been chiefly begun and conducted by the Unitarians. Even in the Anti-Slavery enterprise, the most profound, unrespectable, and unpopular of them all, you are surprised to see how many Unitarians—even ministers, a timid race—have permanently taken an active and influential part. The Unitarians certainly once had this moral superiority, before the free, young, and growing party became a sect, hide-bound, bridled with its creed, harnessed to an old, lumbering, and crazy chariot, urged with sharp goads by near-sighted drivers, along the dusty and broken pavement of tradition, noisy and shouting, but going nowhere.

But yet, while they had this great practical excellence, so obvious once, I thought they lacked the deep, internal feeling of piety, which alone could make it lasting; certainly they had not that most joyous of all delights. This fact seemed clear in their sermons, their prayers, and even in the hymns they made, borrowed, or "adapted." Most powerfully preaching to the understanding, the conscience, and the will, the cry was ever, "Duty, duty! work, work!" They failed to address with equal power the soul, and did not also shout "Joy, joy! delight, delight!" "Rejoice in God always, and again I say unto you, rejoice!" Their vessels were full of water; it was all laboriously pumped up from deep wells; it did not gush out, leaping from the great spring, that is indeed on the surface of the sloping ground, feeding the little streams that run among the hills, and both quenching the wild asses' thirst, and watering also the meadows newly mown, but which yet comes from the rock of ages, and is pressed out by the cloud-compelling mountains that rest thereon—yes, by the gravitation of the earth itself.

The defect of the Unitarians was a profound one. Not actually, nor consciously, but by the logic of their conduct, they had broke with the old ecclesiastic supernaturalism, that with its whip of fear yet compelled a certain direct, though perverted, action of the simple religious element in the Trinitarians: ceasing to fear "the great and dreadful God" of the Old Testament, they had not quite learned to love the all-beautiful and altogether lovely of the universe. But in general they had no theory which justified a more emotional experience of religion. Their philosophy, with many excellences, was sure of no great spiritual truth. To their metaphysics eternal life was only probable: the great argument for it came not from the substance of human nature, only from an accident in the personal history of a single man;

its proof was not *intuitive*, from the primal instincts of mankind; nor *deductive*, from the nature of God; nor yet *inductive* from the general phenomena of the two-fold universe; it was only *inferential*, from the "resurrection of Christ"—an exceptional fact, without parallel in the story of the race, and that resting on no evidence! Nay, in their chief periodical, when it represented only the opinions of the leaders of the sect, one of their most popular and powerful writers declared the existence of a God was not a certainty of metaphysical demonstration, not even a fact of consciousness. So this great truth, fundamental to all forms of religion, has neither an objective, necessary, and ontological root in the metaphysics of the universe, nor yet a mere subjective, contingent, and psychological root in the consciousness of John and Jane, but, like the existence of "phlogiston" and "the celestial æther" of the interstellar spaces, it is a matter of conjecture, of inference from observed facts purely external and contingent; or, like the existence of the "Devil," is wholly dependent on the "miraculous and infallible revelation." Surely, a party with no better philosophy, and yet rejecting instinct for guide, breaking with the supernatural tradition at the Trinity, its most important link, could not produce a deep and continuous action of the religious element in the mass of its members, when left individually free; nor when organized into a sect, with the discipline of a close corporation, could it continue to advance, or even to hold its own, and live long on its "Statement of Reasons for Not Believing the Trinity." Exceptional men—like Henry Ware, Jun., who leaned strongly towards the old supernaturalism, or like Dr. Channing, whose deeper reflection or reading supplied him with a more spiritual philosophy—might escape the misfortune of their party; but the majority must follow the logic of their principle. The leaders of the sect, their distinctive creed only a denial, always trembling before the orthodox, rejected the ablest, original talent born among them; nay, sometimes scornfully repudiated original genius, each offering a more spiritual philosophy, which they mocked at as "transcendental," and turned off to the noisy road of other sects, not grateful to feet trained in paths more natural. After denying the Trinity, and the Deity of Christ, they did not dare affirm the humanity of Jesus, the naturalness of religion to man, the actual or possible universality of inspiration, and declare that man is not amenable to ecclesiastic authority, either the oral Roman tradition, or the written Hebrew and Greek Scriptures; but naturally communing with God, through many faculties, by many elements, has in himself the divine well of water, springing up full of everlasting life, and sparkling with eternal truth, and so enjoys continuous revelation.

Alas! after many a venturous and profitable cruise, while in sight of port, the winds all fair, the little Unitarian bark, o'ermastered by its doubts and fears, reverses its course, and sails into dark, stormy seas, where no such craft can live. Some of the fragments of the wreck will be borne by oceanic currents where they will be used by the party of progress to help to build more sea-worthy ships; whilst others, when water-logged, will be picked up by the great orthodox fleet, to be kiln-dried in a revival, and then serve as moist, poor fuel for its culinary fires. It is a dismal fault in a religious party, this lack of piety, and dismally have the Unitarians answered it; yet let their great merits and services be not forgot.

I found this lack of the emotional part of religion affected many of the reformers. Some men called by that name, were indeed mere selfish tongues, their only business to find fault and make a noise; such are entitled to no more regard than any other common and notorious scolds. But, in general, the leading reformers are men of large intellect, of profound morality, earnest, affectional men, full of philanthropy, and living lives worthy of the best ages of humanity. But as a general thing, it seemed to me they had not a proportionate development of the religious feelings, and so had neither the most powerful solace for their many griefs, nor the profoundest joy which is needful to hold them up mid all they see and suffer from. They, too, commonly shared this sensational philosophy, and broke with the ecclesiastic supernaturalism which once helped to supply its defects.

Gradually coming to understand this state of things, quite early in my ministry I tried to remedy it; of course I did the work at first feebly and poorly. I preached piety, unselfish love towards God, as well as morality, the keeping of his natural law, and philanthropy, the helping of his human children. And I was greatly delighted to find that my discourses of piety were as acceptable as my sermons of justice and charity, touching the souls of earnest men. Nay, the more spiritual of the ministers asked me to preach such matters in their pulpits, which I did gladly.

You have broken with the traditions of the various churches whence you have come out, and turned your attention to many of the evils of the day; when I became your minister, I feared lest, in a general disgust at ecclesiastical proceedings, you should abandon this very innermost of all true religion; so I have taken special pains to show that well-proportioned piety is the ground of all manly excellence, and though it may exist, and often does, without the man's knowing it, yet, in its highest form, he is conscious of it. On this theme I have preached many sermons, which were very dear to me, though perhaps none of them has yet been published. But coming amongst you with some ministerial experience, and much study of the effect of doctrines and ecclesiastical modes of procedure, I endeavored to guard against the vices which so often attend the culture of this sentimental part of religion, and to prevent the fatal degeneracy that often attends it. When the religious element is actively excited under the control of the false theological ideas now so prevailing, it often takes one or both of these two misdirections :—

1. It tends to an unnatural mysticism, which dries up all the noble emotions that else would produce a great useful character. The delicate and refined woman developes the sentiment of religion in her consciousness; surrounded by wealth, and seduced by its charms, she reads the more unpractical parts of the Bible, especially the Johannic writings, the Song of Solomon, and the more sentimental portions of the Psalms; studies Thomas à Kempis, Guyon, Fénélon, William Law, Keble; pores over the mystic meditations of St. Augustine and Bernard; she kneels before her costly *Prie-Dieu*, or other sufficient altar, pours out her prayers, falls into an ecstasy of devout feeling, and,

elegantly dishevelled like a Magdalen, weeps most delicious tears. Then rising thence, she folds her idle, unreligious hands, and, with voluptuous scorn, turns off from the homely duties of common life; while, not only the poor, the sick, the ignorant, the drunken, the enslaved, and the abandoned, are left uncared-for, but her own household is neglected, her husband, her very children go unblessed. She lives a life of intense religious emotion in private, but of intense selfishness at home, and profligate worldliness abroad. Her pious feeling is only moonshine; nay, it is a Will-o'-the-wisp, a wandering fire, which

"Leads to bewilder, and dazzles to blind."

She is a voluptuary of the soul, often likewise in the senses; her prayers are worth no more than so much novel-reading; she might as well applaud Don Giovanni with her laugh at the opera, as St. John with her tears at church. This woman's religion is internal glitter, which gives nor light nor heat. "Like a fly in the heart of an apple, she dwells in perpetual sweetness," but also in perpetual sloth, a selfish wanton of the soul. In his *Parc aux Cerfs*, Louis XV. trained his maiden victims to this form of devotion!

2. It leads to ecclesiastical ritualism. This is the more common form in New England, especially in hard men and women. They join a church, and crowd the ecclesiastical meetings. Bodily presence there is thought a virtue; they keep the Sunday severely idle; their ecclesiastical decorum is awful as a winter's night at the North Pole of cold; with terrible punctuality they attend to the ordinance of bread and wine, looking grim and senseless as the death's head on the tombstones close by. Their babies are sprinkled with water, or themselves plunged all over in it; they have morning prayers and evening prayers, grace before meat, and after meat, grace; nay, they give money for the theological purposes of their sect, and religiously hate men not of their household of faith. Their pious feeling has spent itself in secreting this abnormal shell of ritualism, which now cumbers them worse than Saul's great armour on the stripling shepherd lad. What can such Pachyderms of the church accomplish that is good, with such an elephantiasis to swell, and bark, and tetter every limb? Their religious feeling runs to shell, and has no other influence. They sell rum, and trade in slaves or coolies. They are remorseless creditors, unscrupulous debtors; they devour widows' houses. Vain are the cries of humanity in such ears, stuffed with condensed wind. Their lives are little, dirty, and mean.

Mindful of these two vices, which are both diseases of the misdirected soul, and early aware that devoutness is by no means the highest expression of love for God, I have attempted not only to produce a normal development of religious feeling, but to give it the normal direction to the homely duties of common life, in the kitchen, the parlor, nursery, school-room, in the field, market, office, shop, or ship, or street, or wherever the lines of our lot have fallen to us; and to the "primal virtues," that shine aloft as stars which mariners catch glimpses of 'mid ocean's rack, and learn their course, and steer straight in to their desired haven; and also, to the "charities that soothe, and heal, and bless," and which are scattered at mankind's feet like flowers, each one a beauty the bee sucks honey from, and a seed to sow the world with wholesome loveliness; for it is plain to me that the common duties of natural life are both the best school for the development of piety, and the best field for its exercise when grown to manly size.

II. Partly for your education in true religion, and partly to promote the welfare of your brother man, I have preached much on the great social duties of your time and place, recommending not only "palliative charity," but still more "remedial justice." So I have not only preached on the private individual virtues, which are, and ought to be, the most constant theme of all pulpits, but likewise, on the public social virtues, that are also indispensable to the general welfare. This work brought me into direct relation with the chief social evils of our day. In treating these matters I have proceeded with much caution, beginning my attack a great way off. First of all, I endeavoured to establish philosophically the moral principle I should appeal to, and show its origin in the constitution of man, to lay down the natural law so plain that all might acknowledge and accept it; next I attempted to show what welfare had followed in human history from keeping this law, and what misery from violating it; then I applied this moral principle of nature and the actual experience of history to the special public vice I wished to whelm over. Such a process may seem slow; I think it is the only one sure of permanent good effects. In this manner I have treated several prominent evils.

1. I have preached against intemperance, showing the monstrous evil of drunkenness, the material and moral ruin it works so widely. My first offence in preaching came when I first spoke on the misery occasioned by this ghastly vice. The victims of it sat before me, and were in great wrath; they never forgave me. Yet, I have not accepted the opinion of the leading temperance men, that the use of intoxicating drinks is in itself a moral or a physical evil. I found they had not only a medical, but also a dietetic use to serve, and in all stages of development above the savage, man resorts to some sort of stimulus as food for the nervous system: for a practice so nearly universal, I suppose there must be a cause in man's natural relation to the world of matter. Accordingly, I do not like the present legal mode of treating the vice, thinking it rests on a false principle which will not long work well; yet public opinion, now setting strong against this beastly vice, required the experiment, which could never be tried under better auspices than now. But I have gladly joined with all men to help to put down this frightful vice, which more than any other concrete cause hinders the welfare and progress of the working people of the North. It was the first public social evil I ever attacked. I have not ceased to warn old and young against this monstrous and ugly sin, and to call on the appointed magistrates to use all their official power to end so fatal a mischief. In a great trading town, of course, such calls are vain; the interest of the few is against the virtue of the people.

2. I have preached against covetousness—the abnormal desire of accumulating property. In the Northern States our civilization is based on respect for industry in both forms, toil and thought. Property is the product of the two: it is human power over nature, to

make the material forces of the world supply the wants of man; its amount is always the test of civilization. Our political and social institutions do not favor the accumulation of wealth in a few men or a few families; no permanent entails are allowed; it follows the natural laws of distribution amongst all the owner's children, or according to his personal caprice; in a few generations a great estate is widely scattered abroad. But as we have no hereditary honors, office, or even title, and as wealth is all the parent can bequeath his child, it becomes not only a material power, but also a social distinction—the only one transmissible from sire to son. So wealth, and not birth from famous ancestors, is the thing most coveted; the stamp of the all-mighty dollar is the mark of social distinction; science may be accounted folly, and genius madness, in the paved or the furrowed town, but money is power in each. American "aristocracy" rests on this moveable basis; it is plutocracy: every poor white boy may hope to trundle its wheels on to his little patch of ground, for the millionaire is not born, but self-made. Hence comes an intense desire of riches; a great amount of practical talent goes out in quest thereof. Beside its intrinsic character, respect for money is in America what loyalty to the crown and deference to feudal superiors is in England: "the ox knoweth his owner, and the ass his master's crib," and the Americans the millionnaire, the highest product of plutocracy.

Now, on the whole, I do not find this desire of property excessive in the people of the North. I would greaten rather than lessen it, for it is the motive of our general enterprise, the proximate cause of much of our welfare and success. No nation was ever too well fed, housed, clad, adorned, and comforted in general; poverty, subordination to material want, is still the great concrete barrier to civilization; "the nations of the world *must*" think chiefly of what they shall eat and drink, and wherewithal be clothed. In this generation, the productive industry of New England seems vulgar to careless eyes, and excessive to severe ones; but it is yet laying the material and indispensable foundation for a spiritual civilization in some future age, more grand, I think, than mankind has hitherto rejoiced in. For not only will the people's property be greater in proportion to their number—their power to feed, clothe, house, adorn, and comfort themselves—but it will be more widely distributed, consequently directed with more wisdom and humanity, and so bring forth and develope both more and higher talents. I have advised all men to shun poverty; to seek a generous competence for themselves and their dependents, and that too by honest work, earning all they take. I see that a great fortune, thus acquired, may now be a nobler honor than all the red laurels of Nelson or Wellington, as well as a power of use and beauty for time to come. I honor the manly, self-denying enterprise which starts with no heritage but itself, and honestly earns a great estate. The man who makes a school-book like Colburn's "First Lessons in Arithmetic," or invents a labor-saving contrivance like the sewing-machine, or the reaping and thrashing machines, or who by trade developes the resources of the country, deserves a pay proportionate to his service. A Boston merchant died in 1847, who had so helped to turn the rivers of New England into spinners and weavers, that I think he earned millions of dollars more than he received. If a man fully pay in efficient, productive toil and thought, he is entitled to all he gets, one dollar or many million dollars; he earns his riches, gives equivalent for equivalent—for all honest traffic is but actual barter, mutual exchange of my work and your work—and if his estate be but what he has thus actually and honestly paid for with a service given, equivalent to the service received, what he can virtuously keep or humanely apply and expend, then it will never be too large.

But covetousness—the lust after property already created; the dishonest desire to get wealth without paying for it with proportionate service by toil and thought; the wish to hoard it as the chief object in life, holding for no generous use; to expend it in personal luxury, making man a delicate swine to eat and drink beyond the needs of generous nature, a butterfly to glitter in the public sun, or before the private stars of fashion, a sloth, to lie idle and deform the ground; or to exhibit it for ostentation, fostering an unwieldy self-esteem or more disgraceful vanity—this is a vice I have warned men against continually; I began early. It is a popular and most respectable offence, often counted a virtue. It assumes many forms, now terrible and then ridiculous. I have dealt with it accordingly, now exposing its injustice or its folly, now satirising its vulgar indecency; now showing that the ill-bred children of men grossly rich come to a fate no better than the sons and daughters of the grossly poor; that voluntary beggars in ruffles and voluntary beggars in rags, are alike supported at the public cost, pay nothing for what they take, and so should be objects of contempt in a world where he is greatest who does the most and best.

I have often spoken of the tyranny of the rich over the thriving and the poor—our country, state, and town, all furnishing grievous examples of the fact. "As the lion eateth up the wild ass in the wilderness, so the rich eateth up the poor," is as true now in New England as two thousand years ago in Egypt. But when I have seen a man with large talents for business helping others while he helped himself, enriching his workmen, promoting their education, their virtue, and self-respect, I have taken special delight in honoring such an act of practical humanity. Happily we need not go out of Boston to find examples of this rare philanthropy.

3. As I was a schoolmaster at seventeen, though more from necessity than early fitness, I fear, and chairman of a town school committee at twenty-two, I have naturally felt much interest in the education of the people, and have often preached thereon. But I have seen the great defect of our culture, both in public and private schools; our education is almost entirely intellectual, not also moral, affectional, and religious. The Sunday-schools by no means remedy this evil, or attempt to mend it; they smartly exercise the devotional feelings, accustom their pupils to a certain ritualism, which is destined only to serve ecclesiastical and not humane purposes; they teach some moral precepts of great value, but their chief function is to communicate theological doctrine, based on the alleged supernatural revelation, and confirmed by miracles, which often confound the intellect, and befool the conscience. They do not even attempt any development of the

higher faculties to an original activity at all commensurate with the vigorous action of the understanding. In the public schools there are sometimes devotional exercises, good in themselves, but little pains is directly taken to educate or even instruct the deeper faculties of our nature. The evil seems to increase, for of late years many of the reading-books of our public and private schools seem to have been compiled by men with only the desire of gain for their motive, who have rejected those pieces of prose or poetry which appeal to what is deepest in human nature, rouse indignation against successful wrong, and fill the child with generous sentiments and great ideas. Sunday-school books seem yet worse, so loaded with the superstitions of the sects. The heroism of this age finds no voice nor language in our schools.

But this lack of morality in our schemes of culture appears most eminent in the superior education, in colleges, and other costly seminaries for maids and men. The higher you go up in the scale of institutions, the less proportionate pains is taken with the development of conscience, the affections, and the soul; in the dame school for infants, something is done to make the child " a good boy," or " a good girl," but almost nothing in the richest and most respectable colleges. They are commonly seats of an unprogressive and immoral conservatism, where the studious youth may learn many an important discipline— mathematical, philological, scientific, literary, metaphysical, and theo-logic—but is pretty sure to miss all effective instruction in the great art and science of personal or public humanity. Hence our colleges are institutions not only to teach the mind, but also for the general *hunkerization* of young men; and a professor is there sometimes un-scrupulously appointed whose nature and character make it notorious that his chief function must necessarily be to poison the waters of life, which young men, from generation to generation, will be compelled to bow down at, and drink! In the last forty years, I think no New England college, collective faculty, or pupils, has shown sympathy with any of the great forward movements of mankind, which are indicated by some national outbreak, like the French Revolutions of 1830 or 1848!

From this fatal defect of our scheme of culture, it comes to pass that the class which has the superior education — ministers, professors, lawyers, doctors, and the like—is not only never a leader in any of the great humane movements of the age, where justice, philanthropy, or piety is the motive, but it continually retards all efforts to reform evil institutions, or otherwise directly increase the present welfare or the future progress of mankind. The scholars' culture has palsied their natural instincts of humanity, and gives them instead, neither the personal convictions of free, moral reflection, nor the traditional commands of church authority, but only the maxims of vulgar thrift, " get the most, and give the least; buy cheap, and sell dear! " Exceptional men, like Channing, Pierpont, Emerson, Ripley, Mann, Rantoul, Phillips, Sumner, and a few others, only confirm the general rule, that the educated is also a selfish class, morally not in advance of the mass of men. No thoughtful, innocent man, arraigned for treason, would like to put himself on the college, and be tried by a jury of twelve scholars; it were to trust in the prejudice and technic sophistry of a class, not to "put himself on the country," and be judged by the moral instincts of the people.

Knowing these facts—and I found them out pretty early—I have told them often in public, and shown the need of a thorough reform in our educational institutions. Still more have I preached on the necessity that YOU should do in private for your children what no school in this age is likely to attempt—secure such a great development of the moral, affectional, and religious powers, as shall preserve all the high instincts of nature, while it enriches every faculty by the information given. I need not now speak of what I had long since intended to do amongst you in this matter, when the opportunity should offer; for, alas! when it came, my power to serve you quickly went.

4. I have preached much on the condition of woman. I know the great, ineffaceable difference between the spiritual constitution of her and man, and the consequent difference in their individual, domestic, and social functions. But, examining the matter both philosophically and historically, it seems clear that woman is man's equal, individually and socially entitled to the same rights. There is no conscious hostility or rivalry between the two, such as is often pretended; man naturally inclines to be a little more than just to her, she a little more than fair to him; a man would find most favor with a jury of women, as boys with nurses. But, certainly, her condition is sadly unfortunate; for, whether treated as a doll or drudge, she is practically regarded as man's inferior, intended by nature to be subordinate to him, subservient to his purposes; not a free spiritual individuality like him, but a dependent parasite or a commanded servant. This idea appears in all civilized legislation; and in the "revealed religion" of Jews and Christians, as well as in that of Brahmins and Mohammedans. Even in New England, no public provision is made to secure superior education for girls as for boys. Woman has no place in the superior industry—shut out from the legal, clerical, and medical professions, and the higher departments of trade, limited to domestic duties, and other callings which pay but little; when she does a man's service she has but half of his reward; no political rights are awarded to her; she is always taxed, but never represented. If married, her husband has legally an unnatural control over her property and her person, and, in case of separation, ovet her children. A young man with superior talents, born to no other heritage, can acquire wealth, or, unaided, obtain the best education this age makes possible to any one: but with a woman it is not so; if poor, she can only be enriched by marriage; hence mercantile wedlock is far more pardonable in her; no talents, no genius can secure a poor man's daughter her natural share in the high culture of the age. The condition of woman follows unavoidably from the popular idea, which she also shares often in the heroic degree, that she is by nature inferior to man: prostitution and its half-known evils come from this as naturally as crime and drunkenness from squalid want—as plants from seeds.

I have preached the equivalency of man and woman—that each in some particulars is inferior to the other, but, on the whole, mankind and womankind, though so diverse, are yet equal in their natural faculties ; and have set forth the evils which come to both from her present inferior position, her exclusion from the high places of social or political trust. But I have thought she will generally prefer domestic to public functions, and have found no philosophic or historic argument for thinking she will ever incline much to the rough works of man, or take any considerable part in Republican politics ; in a court like that of Louis XV., or Napoleon III., it might be different; but I have demanded that she should decide that question for herself, choose her own place of action, have her vote in all political matters, and be eligible to any office.

In special, I have urged on you the duty of attending to the education of young women, not only in accomplishments—which are so often laborious in the process, only to be ridiculous in the display, and idle in their results—but in the grave discipline of study, and for the practical duties of life. A woman voluntarily ignorant of household affairs and the management of a family, should be an object of pity or of contempt; while the women of New England incline to despise the indispensable labor of housekeeping, and can neither make wearable garments, nor eatable bread, I have sometimes doubted whether the men of New England, irritated, with their sour fare, would think them quite fit to make laws for the State, or even for the Union. I have also called your attention to those most unfortunate outcasts, the friendless young girls in the streets of your own city, the most abandoned of the perishing class, who will soon become the most harmful of the dangerous class— for prostitution is always two-fold, male as well as female damnation.

It is delightful to see the change now taking place in the popular idea of woman, and the legislation of the Northern States. This reform at once will directly affect half the population, and soon also the other half. I am not alarmed at the evils which obviously attend this change —the growing dislike of maternal duties, the increase of divorces, the false theories of marriage, and the unhappy conduct which thence results ; all these are transient things, and will soon be gone—the noise and dust of the wagon that brings the harvest home.

5. The American people are making one of the most important experiments ever attempted on earth, endeavoring to establish an industrial democracy, with the principle that all men are equal in their natural rights, which can be alienated only by the personal misconduct of their possessor; the great body of the people is the source of all political power, the maker of all laws, the ultimate arbiter of all measures; while the special magistrates, high and low, are but appointed agents, acting under the power of attorney the people intrusts them with. This experiment was perhaps never tried before, certainly not on so large a scale, and with so fair an opportunity for success; but wise men have always foretold its utter failure, and pointed to the past as confirming this prophecy. Certainly, we have human history against us, but I think human nature is on our side, and find no reason to doubt the triumph of the American idea. So I have taken a deep interest in politics, important not merely as representing the national house-keeping, but also the public morality, and so tending to help or hinder the people's success. Never failing to vote, I have yet kept

myself out of the harness of every party; responsible to none and for none, I have been free to blame or praise the principles and the purposes of all, their measures and their men. Addressing such multitudes, most of them younger than I, in times like the last fourteen years, when such important interests came up for public adjudication, and when the great principles of all national morality have been solemnly denied by famous officials, men also of great personal power, who declared that human governments were amenable to no natural law of God, but subject only to the caprice of magistrate or elector—I have felt a profound sense of my responsibility to YOU as a teacher of religion. So I have preached many political sermons, examining the special measures proposed, exposing the principle they rested on, and the consequences they must produce, and applying the lessons of experience, the laws of human nature, the great doctrines of absolute religion, to the special conduct of the American people. No doubt, I have often wounded the feelings of many of YOU. Pardon me, my friends! if I live long I doubt not I shall do so again and again. YOU never made me your minister to flatter, or merely to please, but to instruct and serve.

Treating of politics, I must speak of the conspicuous men engaged therein, when they come to die, for such are the idols of their respective parties. In America there are few objects of conventional respect —no permanent classes who are born to be reverenced; and as men love to look up and do homage to what seems superior, a man of vulgar greatness, who has more of the sort of talent all have much of, is sure to become an idol if he will but serve the passions of his worshippers: so with us, a great man of that stamp has a more irresponsible power than elsewhere among civilized men; for he takes the place of king, noble, and priest, and controls the public virtue more. The natural function of a great man is to help the little ones: by this test I have endeavored to try such as I must needs speak of. Not responsible for their vice or virtue, I have sought to represent them exactly as I found them, and that, too, without regard to the opinion of men, who only looked up and worshipped, not asking what. If I were an assayer of metals I should feel bound to declare the character of the specimens brought before me, whether lead or silver; shall I be less faithful in my survey of a great man, "more precious than the fine gold of Ophir"? I am no flatterer, nor public liar-general; when such a one is wanted he is easily found, and may be had cheap; and I cannot treat great men like great babies. So, when I preached on Mr. Adams, who had done the cause of freedom such great service, on General Taylor, and Mr. Webster, I aimed to paint them exactly as they were, that their virtues might teach us, and their vices warn. Still further to promote the higher education of the people, and correct an idolatry as fatal as it is stupid, as dangerous to the public as it is immediately profitable to wily rhetoricians, I have prepared lectures on four great famous Americans—Franklin, Washington, Adams, and Jefferson. The last, however, was not delivered when my present illness laid me low. I wished to daguerreotype these great, noble men, and place true pictures before the people.

Perhaps no part of my public labors has been condemned with more noise and violence than this attempt at historic truth. Certainly I did depart from the panegyrical custom of political and clerical eulogizers of the famous or the wealthy dead; but I have confidence enough in the people of the Northern States to believe they will prefer plain truth to the most rhetorical lies.

I have not quite disdained to turn your eyes to little, mean men, when set in high office, that you might get instruction from their folly or wickedness. So, when the chief magistrate of the city was notoriously the comrade of drunkards, and of the most infamous of humankind, and that of the State was celebrated chiefly for public and private lying, and both abused their office, to promote their own little purposes of mischief or of gain, debauching the public virtue, as well as wasting the people's money—I did not fail to advertise the fact, that YOU at least might learn by the lesson which cost the public so dear.

6. I have preached against war, showing its enormous cost in money and men, and the havoc it makes of public and private virtue. A national occasion was not wanting; for, obedient to the whip of the Slave-power, which hag-rides the nation still, the American Government —not the people, nor even Congress—plunged us into a wicked contest with Mexico, she clearly in the right, we notoriously in the wrong. I have often spoken against war, and tried to discourage that "excessive lust for land," that aggressive and invasive spirit, which is characteristic of both the American and British people. It is clear that the strongest races will ultimately supplant the feebler, and take their place, as the strong grasses outroot the weak from the farmer's meadow. I complain not of this just natural law, which indeed pervades the universe; but the work need not be done by violence, nor any form of wrong. So I have preached against the *fillibustering* of America, and the not less wicked *diplomatizing* and *soldiering* by which our parent across the sea accomplishes the same thing, though with even more harshness and cruelty.

Yet I have not preached the doctrine of the non-resistants, who never allow an individual to repel wrong by material violence; nor that of the ultra-peace men, who deny a nation's right to stave off an invader's wickedness with the people's bloody hand. The wrathful emotions are also an integral part of humanity, and with both nations and individuals have an indispensable function to perform, that of self-defence, which, in the present state of civilization, must sometimes be with violence, even with shedding aggressive blood. It is against needless and wicked wars—the vast majority are such—that I have preached; against the abuse ambitious rulers make of the soldier's trained art to kill, and of the wrathful, defensive instincts of the multitude. In this age, I think the people do not make war against the peaceful people of another land; nay, in New England, the most democratic country, we have too much neglected the military art, I fear— a mistake we may bitterly regret in that strife between the Southern habit of despotism, and the Northern principle of democracy, which any day may take the form of civil war, and one day must. For America will not always attempt to carry a pitcher of poison on her left shoulder, and one of pure water on her right; one or the other must soon go to the ground.

7. I have spoken against Slavery more than any concrete wrong,

because it is the greatest of all, " the sum of all villanies," and the most popular, the wanton darling of the Government. I became acquainted with it in my early childhood, and learned to hate it even then, when, though I might not comprehend the injustice of the principle, I could yet feel the cruelty of the fact. I began to preach against it early, but used the greatest circumspection, for I knew the vulgar prejudice in favor of all successful tyranny, and wished my few hearers thoroughly to accept the principle of justice, and apply it to this as to all wrongs. But even in the little meeting-house at West Roxbury, though some of the audience required no teaching in this matter, the very mention of American Slavery as wicked at first offended all my hearers who had any connection with the " Democratic " party. Some said they could see no odds between claiming freedom for a negro slave, and " stealing one of our oxen," the right to own cattle including the right to own men; they thought Slavery could ride behind them on the same pillion with " Democracy," according to the custom of their masters. But, as little by little I developed the principle of true democracy, showing its root in that love of your neighbor as yourself, which Jesus both taught and lived, and of that eternal justice which comes even to savage bosoms, and showed how repugnant Slavery is to both— gradually all the more reflective and humane drew over to the side of freedom; and they who at first turned their faces to the floor of their pews when I announced Slavery as the theme for that day's sermon, ere many years turned on me eyes flashing with indignation against wrong, when I told the tale of our national wickedness; they have since given me the heartiest sympathy in my humble efforts to moralise the opinions and practice of the people.

My Friends,—Since I have been your minister, I have preached much on this dreadful sin of the nation, which now threatens to be also its ruin; for, while in my youth Slavery was admitted to be an evil, commercially profitable, but morally wrong, an exceptional measure, which only the necessity of habit might excuse, but which nothing could justify, of late years it is declared a " moral good," " the least objectionable form of labor," fit for Northern whites not less than African negroes, one of those guide-board instances which indicate the highway of national welfare. For some years Slavery has been the actual first principle of each Federal Administration; to this all interests must bend, all customs and statutes conform, and the nation's two great documents, containing our programme of political principles and of political purposes, must be repudiated and practically annulled; the Supreme Court has become only the jesuitical propaganda of Slavery.

For some years, while busied with theological matters, and with laying the metaphysic foundation of my own scheme, I took no public part in the Anti-Slavery movements outside of my own little village. But when I became your minister and had a wider field to till, when the ambition of the Slave-power became more insolent by what it fed upon, and the North still tamer and more servile under the bridle and the whip of such as were horsed thereon, a different duty seemed quite clear to me. I have seldom entered your pulpit without remembering that you and I lived in a land whose church members are not more numerous than its slaves; as many " communing with God " by bread and wine, so many communing with man by chains and whips; and that not only the State, press, and market, but also the Church takes a "South-side view of slavery," as indeed she does of each other wickedness presently popular, and "of good report"! Since 1845, I have preached against all the great invasive measures of the Slave-power, exposing their motive, the first principle they refer to, and show-ing that they are utterly hostile to that democracy which is justice; and all tend to establish a despotism, which at first may be industrial and many-headed, as now in Louisiana, but next must be single-headed and military, as already in France, and finally must lead to national ruin, as in so many countries of the Old World.

In due time the Fugitive Slave Bill came up from seed which wicked men had sown and harrowed into the Northern soil; Boston fired her hundred cannons with delight, and they awoke the ministers, sitting drowsy in their churches of commerce, mid all the pavements of the North, who thought an angel had spoke to them. Then I preached against Slavery as never before, and defied the impudent statute, whereto you happily said *Amen* by the first clapping of hands which for years had welcomed a sermon in Boston; how could you help the natural indecorum? When, roused by these jubilant guns, one minister, so generous and self-devoted, too, in many a noble work, called on his parishioners to enforce that wicked act, which meant to kidnap mine, and declared that if a fugitive sought shelter with him he would drive him away from his own door; when another uttered words more notorious, and yet more flagrant with avaricious inhumanity, which I care not now to repeat again; and when the cry, "No higher law!" went down from the market, and, intoned by the doctorial leaders of the sects, rang through so many commercial churches throughout the Northern land, I did not dare refuse to proclaim the monstrous fact as one of the unavoidable effects of Slavery, whose evil seed must bear fruit after its kind, and to gibbet the wrong before the eyes of the people, to whom I appealed for common justice and common humanity. When two men, holding mean offices under the Federal Government, one of them not fit by nature to do a cruel deed, actually stole and kid-napped two innocent inhabitants out from your city of Franklin, and Hancock, and Adams, and attempted, with their unclean, ravenous jaws, to seize yet others, and rend the manhood out of them, I preached against these jackals of Slavery and their unhuman work; and have now only to lament that my powers of thought and speech were no more adequate fitly to expose the dark infamy of that foul deed, against which I asked alike the people's justice and their wrath; I knew I should not ask in vain. And when a drunken bully from South Caro-lina, in Congress, fitly representing the first principle, if not the first persons of his State—where none can serve in even the Lower House of Assembly "unless he be seized in his own right of ten negro slaves" —made his assault, not less cowardly than brutal, on our noble Senator, wounding him with worse than death, and while the United States Attorney sought "to make murder safe and easy in the capital," not dreaming it would one day, unpunished, reach his own heart, I spoke of that matter, and showed it was the cowards of Massachusetts who drew the blow on her faithful champion, and that no "anodyne" could make them less than glad that it was struck!

But why speak more of those sad days? Others may come with sterner face, not black but red! However, a blessed change in public opinion now goes calmly on in Massachusetts, in New England, and all the North, spite of the sophistry and cunning of ambitious men smit with the Presidential fever. The death of a dozen leading Anti-Slavery men to-day would not much retard it, for the ground is full of such!

8. But I have preached against the errors of the ecclesiastic theology more than upon any other form of wrong, for they are the most fatal mischiefs in the land. The theological notion of God, man, and the relation between them, seems to me the greatest speculative error mankind has fallen into. Its gloomy consequences appear:—Christendom takes the Bible for God's word, His last word; nothing new or different can ever be expected from the source of all truth, all justice, and all love; the sun of righteousness will give no added light or heat on the cold darkness of the human world. From portions of this "infallible revelation," the Roman Church logically derives its despotic and hideous claim to bind and loose on earth, to honor dead men with sainthood, or to rack and burn with all the engines mechanic fancy can invent, or priestly cruelty apply; and hereafter to bless eternally, or else for ever damn. Hence, both Protestant and Catholic logically derive their imperfect, wrathful Deity, who creates men to torment them in an endless hell, "paved with the skulls of infants not a span long," whereinto the vast majority of men are, by the million, trodden down for everlasting agony, at which the elect continually rejoice. Hence, they derive their Devil, absolutely evil, that ugly wolf whom God lets loose into his fold of lambs ; hence, their total depravity, and many another dreadful doctrine which now the best of men blind their brothers' eyes withal, and teach their children to distrust the Infinite Perfection which is nature's God, dear Father and Mother to all that is. Hence, clerical sceptics learn to deny the validity of their own superior faculties, and spin out the cobwebs of sophistry, wherewith they surround the field of religion, and catch therein unwary men. Hence, the Jews, the Mohammedans, the Mormons, draw their idea of woman, and their right to substitute such gross conjunctions for the natural marriage of one to one. There the slave-holder finds the chief argument for his ownership of men, and in Africa or New England, kidnaps the weak, his mouth drooling with texts from "the authentic word of God"; nay, there the rhetorician finds reason for shooting an innocent man who but righteously seeks that freedom which nature declares the common birthright of mankind. It has grieved me tenderly to see all Christendom make the Bible its fetish, and so lose the priceless value of that free religious spirit which, communing at first hand with God, wrote its grand pages, or poured out its magnificent beatitudes.

Christendom contains the most intellectual nations of the earth, all of them belonging to the dominant Caucasian race, and most of them occupying regions very friendly to the development of the highest faculties of man. Theirs, too, is the superior machinery of civilization, political, ecclesiastical, domestic, social. Nowhere on earth does the clerical mass so connect itself with the innermost of man. Christendom is the bold leader in all intellectual affairs—arts of peace and war, science, literature, skill to organise and administer mankind. But yet the Christian has no moral superiority over the Jews, the Mohammedans, the Brahmins, the Buddhists, at all commensurate with this intellectual power. In the sum of private and public virtues, the Turk is before the Christian Greek. For fifteen hundred years the Jews, a nation scattered and peeled, and exposed to most degrading influences, in true religion have been above the Christians! In temperance, chastity, honesty, justice, mercy, are the leading nations of Christendom before the South-Asiatics, the Chinese, the islanders of Japan? Perhaps so—but have these " Christians " a moral superiority over those " heathens " equal to their mental superiority? It is notorious they have not. Why is this so, when these Christians worship a man whose religion was love to God and love to men, and who would admit to heaven only for righteousness, and send to hell only for lack of it? Because they worship him, reject the natural goodness he relied upon, and trust in the " blood of Christ which maketh free from all sin." It is this false theology, with its vicarious atonement, salvation without morality or piety, only by belief in absurd doctrines, which has bewitched the leading nations of the earth into such practical mischief. A false idea has controlled the strongest spiritual faculty, leading men to trust in "imputed righteousness," and undervalue personal virtue. Self-denying missionaries visit many a far-off land "to bring the heathens to Christ." Small good comes of it; but did they teach industry, thrift, letters, honesty, temperance, justice, mercy, with rational ideas of God and man, what a conversion there would be of the Gentiles! Two-and-thirty thousand Christian ministers are there in the United States, all " consecrated to Christ;" many of them are able men, earnest and devoted, but, their eyes hood-winked and their hands chained by their theology, what do they bring to pass? They scarce lessen any vice of the State, the press, or the market. They are to " save souls from the wrath of God."

I have preached against the fundamental errors of this well-compacted theological scheme, showing the consequences which follow thence, and seldom entered your pulpit without remembering Slavery, the great sin of America, and these theological errors, the sacramental mistake of Christendom. But I have never forgotten the great truths this theology contains, invaluable to the intellect, the conscience, the heart and soul. I have tried to preserve them all, with each good institution which the Church, floating over the ruins of an elder world, has borne across that deluge, and set down for us where the dove of peace has found rest for the sole of her foot, and gathered her olive-branch to show that those devouring waters are dried up from the face of the earth. To me the name of Christianity is most exceeding dear, significant of so great a man and of such natural emotions, ideas, and actions, as are of priceless value to mankind. I know well the errors, also, of the doubters and deniers, who in all ages have waged war against the superstitious theology of their times, and pulled down what they could not replace with better. I have not sat in the seat of the scornful; and while I warned men against the snare of the priest, I would not suffer them to fall into the mocker's pit. I have taken exquisite delight in the grand words of the Bible, putting it before all other sacred literature of the whole ancient world; to me it is more dear when I regard them not as the miracles of God, but as the work of earnest men, who did their uttermost with holy heart. I love to read the great truths of religion set forth in the magnificent poetry of psalmist and prophet, and the humane lessons of the Hebrew peasant, who summed up the prophets and the law in one word of LOVE and set forth man's daily duties in such true and simple speech! As a master, the Bible were a tyrant; as a help, I have not time to tell its worth; nor has a sick man speech for that, nor need I now, for my public and private teachings sufficiently abound in such attempts. But yet, to me the great men of the Bible are worth more than all their words; he that was greater than the temple, whose soul burst out its walls, is also greater than the Testament, but yet no master over you and me, however humble men!

In theological matters, my preaching has been positive, much more than negative, controversial only to create; I have tried to set forth the truths of natural religion, gathered from the world of matter and of spirit: I rely on these great ideas as the chief means for exciting the religious feelings, and promoting religious deeds; I have destroyed only what seemed pernicious, and that I might build a better structure in its place.

Of late years a new form of Atheism—the ideal, once thought impossible—has sprung up; perhaps Germany is its birth-place, though France and England seem equally its home. It has its representatives in America. Besides, the Pantheists tell us of their God, who is but the sum-total of the existing universe of matter and of mind, immanent in each, but transcending neither, imprisoned in the two; blind, planless, purposeless, without consciousness, or will, or love; dependent upon the shifting phenomena of finite matter and of mind, finite itself; a continual becoming this or that, not absolute being, self-subsistent and eternally the same perfection: their God is only law, the constant mode of operation of objective and unconscious force; yet is it better than the churchman's God, who is caprice alone, subjective, arbitrary, inconstant, and with more hate than love. I have attempted to deal with the problem of the Pantheist and the Atheist, treating both as any other theological opponents: I have not insulted them with harsh names, nor found occasion to impute dishonorable motives to such as deny what is dearer than life to me; nor attempted to silence them with texts from sacred books; nor to entangle them in ecclesiastic or metaphysic sophistries: nor to scare with panic terrors, easily excited in an Atheistic or a Christian's heart. I have simply referred them to the primal instincts of human nature, and their spontaneous intuition of the divine, the just, and the immortal; then, to what science gathered from the world of matter, and the objective history of man in his progressive development of individual and of social power. I have shown the causes which lead to honest bigotry within the Christian Church, and to honest Atheism without; I hope I have done injustice neither to this nor that. But it was a significant fact I could not fail to make public, that, while the chief doctors of commercial divinity in the great

American trading towns, and their subservient colleges, denied the higher law, and with their Bibles laid humanity flat before the kidnappers in Cincinnati, Philadelphia, New York, and Boston, the so-called Atheists and Pantheists over all the Northern land revered the instinctive justice of the soul, and said, "Thou shalt not steal, nor lie. Thou shalt do no wrong; 'tis nature's self forbids !"

Preaching such doctrines in a place so public, and applying them to life, I am not surprised at the hostility I have met with from the various sects. In no country would it have been less, or tempered more sweetly ; no, nor in any age ; for certainly I have departed from the fundamental principle of the Catholics and the Protestants, denied the fact of a miraculous revelation given exclusively to Jews and Christians, denied the claim to supernatural authority, and utterly broke with that vicariousness which puts an alleged revelation in place of common sense, and the blood of a crucified Jew instead of excellence of character. In the least historic of the New Testament Gospels it is related that Jesus miraculously removed the congenital blindness of an adult man, and because he made known the fact that his eyes were thus opened, and told the cause, the Pharisees cast him out of their synagogue. What this mythic story relates as an exceptional measure of the Pharisees, seems to have founded a universal principle of the Christian Church, which cannot bear the presence of a man who, divinely sent, has washed in the pool of Siloam, and returned seeing and telling why.

I knew at the beginning what I must expect: that at first men younger than I, who had not learned over much, would taunt me with my youth ; that others, not scholarly, would charge me with lack of learning competent for my task ; and cautious old men, who did not find it convenient to deny my facts, or answer my arguments, would cry out, " This young man must be put down ! " and set their venerable popular feet in that direction. Of course I have made many mistakes, and could not expect a theologic opponent, and still less a personal enemy, to point them out with much delicacy, or attempt to spare my feelings ; theological warfare is not gentler than political or military ; even small revolutions are not mixed with rose-water. The amount of honest misunderstanding, of wilful misrepresenting, of lying, and of malignant abuse, has not astonished me ; after the first few months it did not grieve me ; human nature has a wide margin of oscillation, and accommodates itself to both Torrid and Frigid Zones. But I have sometimes been a little surprised at the boldness of some of my critics, whose mistakes proved their courage extended beyond their information. An acquaintance with the historic development of mankind, a knowledge of Greek and Hebrew, familiarity with the metaphysic thought of the human race, is certainly no moral merit ; but in theologic discussions it is a convenience which some of my opponents have not always paid quite sufficient respect to, though they were not thereby hindered from passing swift judgment. Criticism is the easiest of all arts, or the most difficult of all.

It did not surprise me that other ministers, Unitarian and Trinitarian, should refuse to serve with me on the committee of a college or a school, to attend the same funeral or wedding, to sit on the same bench at a public meeting, to remain in the same public apartment, and trade at the same book-store, to return my salutation in the street, or reply to my letters; that they should invent and spread abroad falsehoods intended to ruin me; but I confess I have sometimes been astonished that such men " could not see any sign of honesty, of love of truth, of philanthropy, or religion," in my writings or my life, but must set down all to "vanity and love of the praises of men." But "it is fit to be instructed, even by an enemy." Let you and me learn from ours to hate those theological doctrines which can so blind the eyes and harden the hearts of earnest, self-denying men; let us not imitate the sophistry and bigotry we may have suffered from, and certainly have been exposed to.

I have found most friendly recognition where I did not expect it. Men with adverse theological opinions have testified to the honest piety they thought they found in my writings, and joined with me in various practical works of humanity, leaving me to settle the abstract questions of divinity with the Divine Himself. Indeed, I never found it necessary to agree with a man's theology before I could ride in his omnibus or buy his quills. No two Unitarian ministers, I think, differ more in their theology than Rev. James Freeman Clarke and I, but for twenty years there has been the warmest friendship between us; that noble man and I have gone hand in hand to many of the most important philanthropics of the age; and I think he will not be offended by this public recognition of our affectional intimacy. I could say similar things of other men, whom I have not named, but might thereby scare their timid reputation from its nest, and addle their hopes of future usefulness.

Besides, I have found kindly and generous critics in America, and still more in England and Germany, who did me perhaps more than justice, while they honestly pointed out what they must regard as my faults. Though I have been written and spoken against more than any American not connected with political parties, yet, on the whole, I do not complain of the treatment I have received; all I asked was a hearing: that has been abundantly granted. You opened wide the doors, my opponents rang the bell all Saturday night, and Sunday morning the audience was there. I think no other country would allow me such liberty of speech; I fear not even England, which has yet so generously welcomed every free thought.

Of late years the hatred against me seems to have abated somewhat; old enemies relaxed their brows a little, and took back, or else denied, their former calumnies; nay, had kind words and kind deeds for me and mine. " Let bygones be bygones," is a good old rule.

> "The fondest, the fairest, the truest that met,
> Have still found the need to forgive and forget."

I think few men in America have found sympathy in trouble from a greater variety of persons than I, in my present disappointment and illness, from men and women of all manner of ecclesiastical connections. I could not always thank them by private letters, but I need not say how grateful their kindly words have been, for—I may as well confess it—after all, I am not much of a fighter; my affections are developed far better than my intellect. It may be news to the public; to YOU it is but too well known.

Yet, let it not surprise you that in some quarters this theologic odium continues still, and shows itself in "revival meetings" by public prayers that God would go to my study, and confound me there, so that I could not write my sermon; or meet me in your pulpit, and put a hook in my jaws so that I could not speak; or else remove me out of the world. Such petitions, finding abundant biblical example, are not surprising when they came from such places, on such occasions, and from men whose mind and conscience are darkened by the dreadful theology that still haunts many such places. But other instances must find a different explanation. Less than two years ago, the senior class in the Cambridge Divinity School, consisting, I think, of but four pupils, invited me to deliver the customary address before them and the public, the Sunday before their graduation. The theological faculty, consisting of three Unitarian Doctors of Divinity, interposed their veto and forbid me from speaking; such a prohibition, I think, had never been made before. These doctors were not ignorant men, or bigoted; they attend no "revival meetings," but, speaking intellectually, they belong among the most enlightened scholars in America; none of them "was ever accused of believing too much;" yet they saw fit to offer me the greatest ecclesiastical, academical, and personal insult in their professional power, in the most public manner, and that, too, at a time when I was just recovering from severe illnesss, and fluttering 'twixt life and death—the scrutinizing physician telling me the chances were equally divided between the two; I could only stand in the pulpit to preach by holding on to the desk with one hand while I lifted the other up. Others might have expected such treatment from these men; I confess, my friends, that I did not.

Since my present illness began, some of my theological foes have, publicly to the world, and privately to me, expressed their delight that I am not likely to trouble them much longer; in my present feebleness they read the answer to their prayers for my removal. It was the Psalmist's petition, "Let not mine enemies triumph over me!" But I shall utter none such. If I fall and die, let "mine enemies" rejoice as much as they will at the consequent thought that there is one feeble voice the less, rebuking the vice of the press, the State, the market, and the Church, to speak a word of truth, freedom, justice, and natural religion; let them be glad there is one weak arm the less reaching out help to the poor, the drunken, the ignorant, the harlot, the felon, and the slave; let them thank God for the premature decrepitude of my voice, the silence of my study, where worms perchance devour my books, more dear even than costly; let them find "answer to our prayers" in the sorrow of my personal friends—there are now many such—in the keen distress of my intimates, and the agony of my wife; I complain nothing thereat. Every tree must bear after its own kind, not another, and their "religion" must yield such fruits. Let them triumph in these results, and thank their God that He has "interposed," and thus granted their petition; it is small satisfaction compared with what they hope for in the next life, where, as their theology teaches, the joy of the elect in heaven will be enhanced by looking down into hell, and beholding the agony of their former neighbors and friends, husband or wife, nay, their own children also, and remembering that such suffering is endless, "and the smoke of their torment ascendeth up for ever and ever." Let them triumph in this; but let them expect no other or greater result to follow from my death. For to the success of the great truths I have taught, it is now but of the smallest consequence whether I preach in Boston and all the lyceums of the North, or my body crumbles in some quiet, nameless grave. They are not MY truths! I am no great man whom the world hinges on; nor can I settle the fate of a single doctrine by my authority. Humanity is rich in personalities, and a man no larger than I will not long be missed in the wide field of theology and religion. For immediately carrying a special measure, and for helping this or that, a single man is sometimes of great value; the death of the general is the loss of the battle, perhaps the undoing of a State; but after a great truth of humanity is once set a-going, it is in the charge of mankind, through whom it first came from God; it cannot perish by any man's death. Neither State, nor press, nor market, nor Church, can ever put it down; it will drown the water men pour on it, and quench their hostile fire. Cannot the Bible teach its worshippers that a grave is no dungeon to shut up Truth in; and that Death, who slays alike the priest and the prophet, bows his head before her, and passes harmless by? To stone Stephen did not save the church of the Pharisees. A live man may harm his own cause; a dead one cannot defile his clean immortal doctrines with unworthy hands.

In these tropic waters, not far off, in time of strife, on a dark night, but towards morning, an English ship-of-war once drew near what seemed a hostile vessel under sail. She hailed the stranger, who answered not; then hailed again—no answer; then fired a shot across the saucy bows, but still there was no reply; next fired at her, amidships, but got not a word in return. Finally, the man-of-war cleared for action, began battle in earnest, serving the guns with British vigor, but found no return, save the rattle of shot rebounding and falling back into the heedless sea. Daylight presently came with tropic suddenness, and the captain found he spent his powder in battering a great rock in the ocean! So, many a man has fought long against a truth which he fancied was but a floating whim, bound to yield to his caprice; but, at last, the dawning light has shown him it was no passing ship, of timber and cordage and canvas, driven by the wind and tossed by the undulations of the sea, but a SAIL-ROCK, resting on the foundations of the world, and amenable neither to the men-of-war that sailed in the wind, nor yet to the undulation of the sea whereon they came and went. It is one thing to rejoice at the sickness and death of a short-lived heretic, but it is another and a little different, to alter the constitution of the universe, and put down a fact of spontaneous human consciousness, which also, is a truth of God.

When I first came amongst you, and lived in a trading town where a great variety of occupations lay spread out before me all the time, and preached to such crowds of men as offered a wide diversity of nature, character, and conduct, I found not only an opportunity to work, but also to learn and grow. You say I have taught you much; I hope it is so, but you have been a large part of your own schooling; for I have also learned much from you: the audience has always furnished a large part of the sermon and the prayer. I have received much direct instruction, and that in matters of deep concern, from some of you, by hearing your words and looking at your lives; the indirect help to my power of thought and speech, I fear you would hardly credit should I attempt to tell. It is enough to say now, that amongst you I have found men and women, often in quite humble stations, who have added new elements of both strength and beauty to my notion of what constitutes a " glorious human creature," in particular excellences their actual surpassing my ideal. I have been a learner quite as much as a teacher; indeed, out of nearly a thousand sermons I have written, I think there are not five-and-twenty which are not also steps in my own development, studies I have learned by, quite as much as lessons you have been taught with.

To me, human life in all its forms, individual and aggregate, is a perpetual wonder; the flora of the earth and sea is full of beauty and of mystery which science seeks to understand; the fauna of land and ocean is not less wonderful; the world which holds them both, and the great universe that folds it on every side, are still more wonderful, complex, and attractive, to the contemplating mind. But the universe of human life, with its peculiar worlds of outer sense and inner soul, the particular faunas and floras which therein find a home, are still more complex, wonderful, and attractive; and the laws which control it seem to me more amazing than the mathematic principles that explain the celestial mechanics of the outward world. The Kosmos of matter seems little compared to this Kosmos of immortal and progressive man; it is my continual study, discipline, and delight. Oh, that some young genius would devise the " novum organum" of humanity, determine the " principia" thereof, and with deeper than mathematic science, write out the formulas of the human universe, the celestial mechanics of mankind !

In your busy, bustling town, with its queerly-mingled, heterogeneous population, and its great diversity of work, I soon learned to see the unity of human life under all this variety of circumstances and outward condition. It is easy for a simple-hearted man, standing on a central truth, to reduce them all to one common denomination of humanity, and ascertain the relative value of individuals in this comparative morality. The huckster, with a basket, where apples, pea-nuts, candy, and other miscellaneous small stores, are huddled together, is a small merchant; the merchant, with his warehouse, his factory, or bank, his ships on many a sea, is a great huckster; both buy to sell, and sell to gain; the odds is quantative, not in kind, but in bulk. The cunning lawyer, selling his legal knowledge and forensic skill to promote a client's gainful wickedness; the tricksy harlot, letting out her person to a stranger's unholy lust; the deceitful minister, prostituting his voice and ecclesiastical position to make some popular sin appear decent and Christian, " accordant with the revealed word of God "—all stand in the same column of my religious notation. In the street I see them all pass by, each walking in a vain show, in different directions, but all consilient to the same end !

So, the ambitious vanities of life all seem of nearly the same value when laid side by side on this table of exchange. The poetess, proud of her superiority over other "silly women" in the "vision and the faculty divine," or in but the small "accomplishment of verse"; the orator, glorying in his wondrous art, longer than other men to hold the uplooking multitude with his thread of speech, and thereby pour his thought or will into the narrow vials of so many minds; and the scavenger, who boasts that he "can sweep round a lamp-post better than any man in the gang"—all seem alike to an eye that looks beneath and above the rippling tide of phenomenal actions, learning its whither and its whence, and knowing the unseen causes which control this many-billowed sea of life. The diamonds of many-skirted Empress Eugénie at Versailles, and the Attleborough jewellery of the bare-footed charwoman Bridget, at Cove Place, are symbols of the same significance, and probably of the same value, to their respective occupants. The man not winged with talent, whom a political party cranes up to some official eminence he could not reach by the most assiduous crawling ; and the dawdling woman, who can make neither bread to eat nor clothes to wear, nor yet order any household even of only two, whom an idle hand, and a pinkish cheek, and a lolling tongue, have fastened to another, but bearded, fool—these seem wonderfully alike to me; and I say to both, "May God Almighty have mercy on your souls!" So, the effort after nobleness of character is ever the same, clad in whatever dress; the black washerwoman, on Negro Hill, as, with a frowzy broom, a mop, and a tub or two, she keeps the wolf away from her unfathered babies, all fugitives from slavery, and thence looks up to that dear God whom she so feels within her heart a very present help in her hour of need, which is her every hour—to me seems as grand as Paul preaching on Mars Hill to the Athenian senators; nay, not less glorious than Jesus of Nazareth on his mountain, uttering blessed beatitudes to those thousands who paused in their pilgrimage towards Jerusalem, to look and listen to one greater than the temple, and destined to control men's hearts when that city, compactly built, has not stone left on stone. The thoughtful eye, like the artistic hand, invests with the same magnificence the Hebrew preachers and the negro washerwoman, borrowing the outward purple from the glory within. It is the same great problem of duty which is to be wrought out by all—huckster, merchant, lawyer, harlot, minister, poetess, orator, Eugénie, and Bridget, unworthy officer, and idle, helpless wife, Dinah on Negro Hill, Paul at the Areopagus, and Jesus on Mount Tabor; and it is not of such future consequence to us as men fancy, whether the tools of our work be a basket or a warehouse, a mop or a cross; for the divine justice asks the same question of each, "What hast thou done with *thy* gifts and opportunities?" Feeling the democracy of mankind, and preaching it in many a form, I have learned to estimate the worth of men by the quality of their character, and the amount of their service rendered to mankind. So of each I ask but two questions, "What are you? What do you do?" The voluntary beggar in rags, and the voluntary beggar in ruffles, alike answer, "Nought!"

In my preaching I have used plain, simple words, sometimes making what I could not find ready, and counted nothing unclean, because merely common. In philosophic terms, and in all which describes the inner consciousness, our Saxon speech is rather poor, and so I have been compelled to gather from the Greek or Roman stock forms of expressions which do not grow on our homely and familiar tree, and hence, perhaps, have sometimes scared you with "words of learned length." But I have always preferred to use, when fit, the every-day words in which men think and talk, scold, make love, and pray, so that generous-hearted philosophy, clad in a common dress, might more easily become familiar to plain-clad men. It is with customary tools that we work easiest and best, especially when use has made the handles smooth.

Illustrations I have drawn from most familiar things which are before all men's eyes, in the fields, the streets, the shop, the kitchen, parlor, nursery, or school; and from the literature best known to all —the Bible, the newspapers, the transient speech of eminent men, the talk of common people in the streets, from popular stories, school-books, and nursery rhymes. Some of you have censured me for this freedom and homeliness, alike in illustration and in forms of speech, desiring "more elegant and sonorous language," "illustrations derived from elevated and conspicuous objects," "from dignified personalities." A good man, who was a farmer in fair weather and a shoemaker in foul, could not bear to have a plough or a lap-stone mentioned in my ser-mon—to me picturesque and poetic objects, as well as familiar—but wanted "kings and knights," which I also quickly pleased him with. But for this I must not only plead the necessity of my nature, de-lighting in common things, trees, grass, oxen, and stars, moonlight on the water, the falling rain, the ducks and hens at this moment noisy under my window, the gambols and prattle of children, and the com-mon work of blacksmiths, wheelwrights, painters, hucksters, and traders of all sorts; but I have also on my side the example of all the great masters of speech—save only the French, who disdain all com-mon things, as their aristocratic but elegant literature was bred in a court, though rudely cradled elsewhere, nay, born of rough loins— of poets like Homer, Dante, Shakspere, Goethe, of Hebrew David, and of Roman Horace: of philosophers like Socrates and Locke; of preachers like Luther, Latimer, Barrow, Butler, and South; nay, elegant Jeremy Taylor, "the Shakspere of divines," owes half his beauty to these weeds of nature, which are choicest flowers when set in his artistic garden. But one need not go beyond Jesus of Nazareth and the first three gospels to learn great lessons in the art of speech; for in him you not only reverence the genius for religion, which intui-tively sees divine truth and human duty, but wonder also at the power of speech that tells its tale as deliverly as the blackbird sings or the water runs down-hill. Besides, to me common life is full of poetry and pictoral loveliness; spontaneously portrayed, its events will fill my mind as one by one the stars come out upon the evening sky, like them each one "a beauty and a mystery." It is therefore a necessity of my nature that the sermon should publicly reflect to you what pri-vately hangs over it with me, and the waters rained out of my sky when cloudy, should give back its ordinary stars when clear. Yet, for the same reason, I have also fetched illustrations from paths of literature and science, less familiar, perhaps, to most of you, when they, better than aught else, would clear a troubled thought; so in my rosary of familiar beads, I have sometimes strung a pearl or two which science brought from oceanic depths, or fixed thereon the costly gems where ancient or modern art has wrought devices dearer than the precious stone itself.

Using plain words and familiar illustrations, and preaching also on the greatest themes, I have not feared to treat philosophic matters with the rigor of science, and never thought I should scare you with statistic facts, which are the ultimate expression of a great principle doing its work by a constant mode of operation, nor by psychologic analysis, or metaphysical demonstration. Ministers told me I was "preaching over the heads of the people"; I only feared to preach below their feet, or else aside from their ears. Thus handling great themes before attentive men, I have also dared to treat them long, for I read the time not on the dial, but the audience. I trust you will pardon the offence which I perhaps shall not repeat.

MY FRIENDS,—I said that in my early life I feared the temptations that beset the lawyer's path, and, trembling at the moral ruin, which seemed so imminent, turned to the high ecclesiastic road. Alas! the peril is only different, not less. The lawyer is drawn to one kind of wickedness, the minister to another: their sophistry and cunning are about equal, only in the one case it is practised in the name of "law," and for an obvious "worldly end," and in the other in the name of "Gospel," and professedly to secure "salvation." Learning to distinguish sound from significance, I have not found the moral tone of ministers higher than that of lawyers, their motives purer, their behavior more honest, or their humanity more prompt and wide, only their alms are greater in proportion to their purse. In choosing the clerical, not the legal profession, I think I encountered quite as much peculiar peril as I shunned. The Gospel-mill of the minister is managed with as much injustice as the law-mill of the other profession.

It is not for me to say I have succeeded in keeping any portion of my youthful vow. Yet one thing I am sure of; I never appealed to a mean motive nor used an argument I did not think both just and true, I have employed no conscious sophistry, nor ever disguised my ignorance.

Together we have tried some things, which did not prosper, and so came to an end.

We attempted Sunday afternoon meetings, for free discussion of what pertains to religion. I hoped much good from that experiment; yet it was made not only a vanity, but also a vexation of spirit, by a few outsiders, who talked much, while they had little or nothing to say; there could be no wisdom where their voices were heard.

Next, we tried lectures on the Bible, Sunday afternoons, which continued during the wintry half of several years. I gave six general lectures on the origin and history of the Old and New Testaments, and then turned to the criticism and interpretation of the several books of the latter. With Tischendorf's edition of the original text in my hand, I translated the three Synoptic Gospels, the four undoubted

Epistles of Paul, the Acts, and the "Johannic" writings—Revelation, Gospel, Epistles—explaining each book, verse, and word, as well as I could. I intended to treat all the other canonical and apocryphal books of the New and Old Testaments in the same way. But either the matter was too learned, or the manner too dull, for it did not succeed well, bringing a class of but a few scores of persons. This experiment was abandoned when we removed to the Music Hall, and had no place for an afternoon meeting.

I have long meditated other things, which might, perhaps, be helpful to select classes of young men and women; but as they are now not likely to be more than thoughts, I will not name them here.

Last year you organized your fraternity : the movement was spontaneous on your part, not originating in any hint of mine. Though I had long wanted such an association, so various in its purposes, and so liberal in its plan, I did not venture to propose it, preferring it should come without my prompting in 1858, rather than merely by it ten years before. A minister as sure of the confidence of his hearers as I am of yours, is often a little inclined to be invasive, and thrust his personality on that of his congregation, making his will take the place of their common sense; hence many trees of clerical planting fail, because they originate only with the minister, and root but into him. I hope great good from this fraternity, and have laid out much work for myself to do with its help. To mention but one thing, I intended this season to deliver before it ten easy lectures on the first three centuries of the Christian era, and show how the Christianity of the Christians, alas! not the more humane and natural religion of Jesus, developed itself in ideas—the doctrines of the Biblical and Patristic books; in institutions —the special churches, each a republic at first, with individual variety of action, but gradually degenerating into a despotic monarchy, with only ecclesiastical unity of action; and finally, after compromising with the Hebrew and classic schemes, how it became the organized religion of the civilized world, a new force in it both for good and evil, the most powerful organization on earth. In my sleepless nights last autumn, I sketched out the plan and arranged the chief details ; but it must now pass away, like other less systematic visions of a sick man in his sleep.

When a young man, it was pa , of my original plan to leave the practical work of continual preaching, a little before I should be fifty years old, and devote the residue of my life to publishing works which I hoped might be of permanent value, separating the two periods by a year or two of travel in the American tropics and the Mediterranean countries of the Old World ; so I thought I might be most useful to mankind, for I did not anticipate or desire long life, and did not originally rate very high my ability to affect the mass of men by direct word of mouth, and made no pretensions to that most popular of intellectual attainments, that eloquence which, like other beauty, is at once a pleasure and a power, delighting whom it compels. But, when I found the scholarly class more unfriendly than the multitude, I began to think I had chosen the wrong audience to address ; that it was the people, not the scholars, who were to lead in philosophic thought; and when you gave me a chance to be heard in Boston, and

I preached on from year to year, great crowds of men, who were not readers but workers in the week, coming and continuing to listen to the longest of sermons, wherein great subjects were treated without respect to popular prejudice, ecclesiastical, political, or social, and that, too, without sparing the severest attention of the hearers; when I found these multitudes seemed to comprehend the abstractest reasoning, and truths most universal, and appeared to be instructed, set free, and even elevated to higher hopes both here and hereafter, and to noble character; when, with all my directness of homely speech, I found myself welcome in most of the lecture halls between the Mississippi and the Penobscot, and even beyond them, having thence two or three hundred invitations a-year; when the national crisis became nearer and more threatening, and I saw my sentiments and ideas visibly passing into the opinion and the literature of the people, and thence coming out in the legislation of New England and the other Northern States— I thought it not quite time to withdraw, and my early purposes were a little shaken. I intended to continue some ten years more in severe practical work, till about sixty, then retire, not to lie down in the grave like a camel under his load at night, but hoping to enjoy a long, quiet autumn of twenty years or so, when I might accomplish my philosophic and literary works, and mow up as provender for future time what I had first raised as green grass, and then mowed down to make into sound hay, but have now left, alas! either strewn where it grew or but loosely raked together, not yet carted into safe barns for the long winter, or even stacked up and sheltered against immediate spoiling by a sudden rain in harvest.

Besides, I felt quickened for practical work by the great exigencies of the nation, the importance of the fight already going on between despotism on one side with its fugitive slave bills, New England kidnappers and sophists, in bar or pulpit, and democracy on the other, with its self-evident truths, inalienable rights, and vast industrial and educational developments—a battle not yet understood, but destined to grow hot and red ere long—and by the confidence I have always felt in the ultimate triumph of the right and true, the beautiful and good. Moreover, I was encouraged in my course by the soundness and vigor of my bodily frame, not stout, perhaps, and strong, but capable of much and long-continued work of the most various kinds, not tiring soon, nor easily made ill, but quick recovering from both fatigue and sickness; and by the long average life of six generations of American fathers and mothers. But I have now learned by experience that it is not wise to cherish wide personal hopes in a narrow life, or seek to make an apple-tree larger than the orchard.

For some years, I have been warned that I was not only spending the full income of life, but encroaching a little on the capital stock. But what wise man even is always wise? The duties were so urgent, the call for help so imploring, the labor at once so delightful in its process and so prophetic of good results, and I felt such confidence in my bodily power and ancestral longevity, that I did not sufficiently heed the gentle admonition; till, last year, in March, nature at once gave way, and I was compelled to yield to a necessity above my will. I need not tell the fluctuations in my health since then; rather, my friends, let me again thank YOU for the prompt and generous sympathy you gave then and ever since.

Immediately after my present illness, I left your pulpit empty for a day. YOU wrote me a letter signed by many a dear familiar name, and but for the haste, I know it had been enriched with the signatures of all; it was dated at Boston, January 11th. Your affection wrote the lines, and a kindred wisdom kept them from me till I was able to bear this unexpected testimonial of your sympathy and love. On Sunday, the 6th of March, while you were listening to—alas! I know not whom you looked to then—my eyes filled with tears as I first read your words of delicate appreciation and esteem. My friends, I wish I were worthy of such reverence and love; that my service were equal to your gratitude. I have had more than sufficient reward for my labors with you; not only have I seen a good work and a great prosper in my hands as you held them up, but in public, and still more in private, you have given me the sweetest, best of outward consolations—the grateful sympathy of earnest, thoughtful, and religious men. If my public life has been a battle, wherein my head grows bald, my beard turns grey, and my arm becomes feeble, before their time, it has been also a triumph, whose crown is not woven of the red-flowered laurels of war, but of the olive, the lily, the violet, and the white rose of peace. I have no delight in controversy; when assailed, I have never returned the assault; and though continually fired upon for many years from the bar-room and the pulpit, and many other "coigne of vantage" betwixt the two, I never in return shot back an arrow, in private or public, until in the United States Court I was arraigned for the "misdemeanour" of making a speech in Fanueil Hall against that kidnapping in Boston, perpetrated by the public guardian of widows and orphans; then I prepared my *Defence*, which had been abler were I more a lawyer, though less a minister.

To compose sermons, and preach them to multitudes of men of one sort but many conditions, thereto setting forth the great truths of absolute religion, and applying them to the various events of this wondrous human life, trying to make the constitution of the universe the common law of men, illustrating my thought with all that I can gather from the world of matter, its use and beauty both, and from the world of man, from human labors, sorrows, joys, and everlasting hopes —this has been my great delight. Your pulpit has been my joy and my throne. Though press and State, market and meeting-house, have been hostile to us, YOU have yet given me the largest Protestant audience in America, save that which orthodox Mr. Beecher, who breaks with no theologic tradition of the New England Church, inspires with his deep emotional nature, so devout and so humane, and charms with his poetic eloquence, that is akin to both the sweet-briar and the rose, and all the beauty which springs up wild amid New England hills, and to the loveliness of common life; I have given you my sermons in return, at once my labor and delight. My life is in them, and all my character, its good and ill; thereby you know me better than I, perhaps, myself—for a man's words and his face when excited in sermon and in prayer tell all he is, the reflection of what he has done. Sermons are never out of my mind; and when sickness brings on me the consciousness that I have nought to do, its most painful part, still, by long habit all things will take this form; and the gorgeous vegetation of the tropics, their fiery skies so brilliant all the day, and star-lit too with such exceeding beauty all the night; the glittering fishes in the market, as many-colored as a gardener's show, these Josephs of the sea; the silent pelicans, flying forth at morning and back again at night; the strange, fantastic trees, the dry pods rattling their historic bones all day, while the new bloom comes fragrant out beside, a noiseless prophecy; the ducks rejoicing in the long-expected rain; a negro on an ambling pad; the slender-legged, half-naked negro children in the street, playing their languid games, or oftener screaming 'neath their mother's blows, amid black swine, hens, and uncounted dogs; the never-ceasing clack of women's tongues, more shrewd than female in their shrill violence; the unceasing, multifarious kindness of our hostess; and, overtowering all, the self-sufficient, West Indian Creole pride, alike contemptuous of toil, and ignorant and impotent of thought—all these common things turn into poetry as I look on or am compelled to hear, and then transfigure into sermons, which come also spontaneously by night and give themselves to me, and even in my sleep say they are meant for you. Shall they ever be more than the walking of

> "A sick man in his sleep,
> Three paces and then faltering" ?

The doctors cannot tell; I also know not, but hope and strive to live a little longer, that I may work much more. Oh, that the truths of absolute religion, which human nature demands, and offers, too, from the infinitely perfect God who dwells therein, while He transcends the universe,—oh, that these were an idea enlightening all men's minds, a feeling in their hearts, and action in their outward life! Oh, that America's two-and-thirty thousand ministers, Hebrew, Christian, Mormon, knew these truths, and to mankind preached piety and morality, and that theology which is the science of God and his two-fold universe, and forgot their mythologic and misguiding dreams! Then what a new world were ours! Sure I would gladly live to work for this.

I may recover entirely, and stand before you full of brown health, equal to the manifold labors of that position, live to the long period of some of my fathers, and at last die naturally of old age. This to me seems most desirable, though certainly not most probable.

Or, I may so far recover, that I shall falter on a score of years or so, one eye on my work, the other on my body, which refuses to do it, and so urge my weak and balky horse along a miry, broken road. If this be so, then, in some still, little rural nook, in sight of town, but not too nigh, I may finish some of the many things I have begun, and left for the afternoon or evening of my days; and yet, also, from time to time, meet you again, and, with words of lofty cheer, look on the inspiring face of a great congregation. With this I should be well content; once it was the ideal of my hope.

In either of these cases, I see how the time of this illness, and the discipline alike of disappointment and recovery, would furnish me new power. Several times in my life has it happened that I have met with what seemed worse than death, and, in my short-sighted folly, I said, " Oh, that I had wings like a dove ! for then would I fly away and be at rest !" Yet my griefs all turned into blessings ; the joyous seed I planted came up discipline, and I wished to tear it from the ground; but it flowered fair, and bore a sweeter, sounder fruit than I expected from what I set in earth. As I look over my life, I find no disappointment and no sorrow I could afford to lose ; the cloudy morning has turned out the fairer day ; the wounds of my enemies have done me good. So wondrous is this human life, not ruled by fate, but Providence, which is Wisdom married unto Love, each infinite ! What has been, may be. If I recover wholly, or but in part, I see new sources of power besides these waters of affliction I have stooped at ; I shall not think I have gone through "the Valley of Baca" in vain, nor begrudge the time that I have lingered there, seeming idle ; rainy days also help to seed the ground. One thing I am sure of : I have learned the wealth and power of the grateful, generous feelings of men, as I knew them not before, nor hoped on earth to find so rich. High as I have thought of human nature, I had not quite done justice to the present growth of these beautiful faculties. Here and now, as so oft before, I have found more treasure than I dreamed lay hidden where I looked.

But if neither of these hopes becomes a fact, if the silver cord part soon above the fountain, and the golden bowl be broke, let not us complain ; a new bowl and a stronger cord, shall serve the well of life for you. Though quite aware how probable this seems, believe me, I have not yet had a single hour of sadness ; trust me, I shall not. True, it is not pleasant to leave the plough broken in the furrow just begun, while the seed-corn smiles in the open sack, impatient to be sown, and the whole field promises such liberal return. To say farewell to the thousands I have been wont to preach to and pray with, now joyous, and tearful now—it has its bitterness to one not eighty-four but forty-eight. To undo the natural ties more intimately knit of long-continued friendship and of love—this is the bitter part. But if it be my lot, let not you nor me complain. Death comes to none except to bring a blessing ; it is no misfortune to lay aside these well-loved weeds of earth, and be immortal. To you, as a congregation, my loss may be easily supplied ; and to me it is an added consolation to know that, however long and tenderly remembered, I should not long be missed ; some other will come in my place, perhaps, without my defects, possessed of nobler gifts, and certainly not hindered by the ecclesiastical and social hostility which needs must oppose a man who has lived and wrought as I. It will not always be unpopular justly to seek the welfare of all men. Let us rejoice that others may easily reap golden corn where we have but scared the wild beasts away, or hewn down the savage woods, burning them with dangerous fire, and make the rich, rough ground smooth for culture. It was with grimmer fight, with sourer sweat, and blacker smoke, and redder fire that the fields were cleared where you and I now win a sweet and easy bread.

What more shall I say to sweeten words of farewell, which must have a bitter taste? If I have taught you any great religious truths or roused therewith emotions that are good, apply them to your life, however humble or however high and wide; convert them into deeds, that your superior religion may appear in your superior industry, your justice, and your charity, coming out in your housekeeping and all manner of work. So when your

> " Course
> Is run, some faithful eulogist may say,
> He sought not praise, and praise did overlook
> His unobtrusive merit; but his life,
> Sweet to himself, was exercised in good,
> That shall survive his name and memory."

Let no fondness for me, now heightened by my illness and my absence too, blind your eyes to errors which may be in my doctrine, which must be in my life; I am content to serve by warning where I cannot guide by example. Mortal, or entered on immortal life, still let me be your minister, to serve, never your master, to hinder and command. Do not stop where I could go no further, for, after so long teaching, I feel that I have just begun to learn, begun my work. "No man can feed us always;" welcome, then, each wiser guide who points you out a better way. On earth I shall not cease to be thankful for your patience, which has borne with me so much and long; for your sympathy, nearest when needed most, and the examples of noble Christian life, which I have found in some of you,

> " To whom is given
> The joy that mixes man with heaven :
> Who, rowing hard against the stream,
> See distant gates of Eden gleam,
> And never dream it is a dream;
> But here by secret transport led,
> Even in the charnels of the dead,
> The murmur of the fountain-head :
> Who will accomplish high desire,
> Bear and forbear, and never tire—
> Like Stephen an unquenchèd fire,
> As, looking upward, full of grace,
> He pray'd, and from a happy place
> God's glory smote him on the face ! "

Here they add to my joy; perhaps their remembrance will add to my delight in heaven.

May you be faithful to your own souls; train up your sons and daughters to lofty character, most fit for humble duty; and to far cathedral heights of excellence, build up the being that you are, with feelings, thoughts, and actions, that become "a glorious human creature," by greatly doing the common work of life, heedful of all the charities, which are twice blest, both by their gifts and their forgiveness too. And the Infinite Perfection, the Cause and Providence of all that is, the Absolute Love, transcending the time and space it fills, OUR

FATHER and OUR MOTHER too, will bless you each beyond your prayer forever and forever. Bodily absent, though present still with you by the immortal part, so hopes and prays

Your minister and friend,

THEODORE PARKER.

Fredericksted, West-End, Santa Cruz,
April 19, 1859.

No. III.

LETTER TO DR. BOWDITCH.

Boston, October 12, 1858.

MY DEAR BOWDITCH,—A long time ago I promised to write you the result of some of my observations on Consumption; hitherto I have actually had no time, for what strength I have had for the last sixteen months has been greedily consumed as fast as it was produced hour by hour; but yesterday two of your (surgical) brethren, Drs. Cabot and Hodges, made a nice little operation for me, which will lay me on my back for a week or two, so in this moment of forced idleness I will try and keep my promise which has been neglected so long a time.

I will begin with the (consumptive) history of a single family which I will call the P's.

I. P. came to this country in 1634, and died 1690, aged eighty-one, leaving many sons and daughters. He had no consumption.

II. P. his son, died aged eighty-six, leaving also many sons and daughters, and no consumption.

III. P. the son of the preceding, born 1664, at the family seat, in 1709 moved to another new settlement and built him a great house, which was thus situated: on the south-east slope of a large range of hills, screened from the north and west winds, but open to the south and south-east; all the hills were heavily timbered, chiefly with oak, hickory, and pine. To the north-east, at the distance of some miles, hills of small elevation; these also, thickly covered with woods, shut out the sharp cold wind from that quarter.*

The ground about the house, above it and below, was then wet, springy, and spongy, in consequence of the great woods on the hills; the culture and drainage have since remedied that evil.

But about fifty rods from the house, and perhaps sixty feet below it, there began a great fresh meadow of spongy peat, from two to fifteen feet in depth. This meadow, with its ramifications and spongy adjuncts, reaching up the hill-sides in various places and filling the wooded ravines, would contain, say, perhaps, two or three hundred acres. It was always wet all the year through; its neighborhood damp

---

* These woods have since been cut down, and the east and north-east wind now come in with all their terrors.

and chilly, especially towards evening; fogs could often be seen gathering there towards night of a clear day.

P. died at the age of eighty-two, with no sign of consumption in him, or his family, or their paternal or maternal ancestors.

IV. P., son of the preceding was born before his father removed to L.; but attended him in that removal, and died at the age of ——, leaving many sons and daughters, still with no signs of consumption.

He inherited his father's house, and his children were born in or near it.

V. P., son of the preceding, and born in his grandfather's house, married into a very long-lived family. His widow lived to ninety-three. He died of epidemic dysentery (needlessly, such being the medical ignorance of the times) at the age of forty-six.

VI. P., son of the preceding, and in the same house, married a Miss S., who was descended from a similar family, which had lived for a hundred or a hundred and fifty years in a similar situation, a mile and a half off, where the house stood on the north-west side of a hill, and near a similar range of wet, spongy meadow, though less in depth and extent. Hitherto consumption had appeared in neither the P.'s nor the S.'s.

P. had eleven children, and himself died a hale old man at seventy-seven; but his wife had passed away from him by consumption at about the age of sixty. Of his children, eight died of consumption, two of them between sixteen and nineteen; the rest were married, and attained various ages from twenty-five to forty-nine. Only two of his children are now living; one sixty, with no signs of pulmonary disease; the other forty-eight, I hope equally free from the family taint.

Two of the grandchildren of P. have also died of consumption. One son of P. moved from the family homestead, and settled on the piece of wet, spongy land, exposed to the bleakest west, north, and north-east wind.

He had six children, all of whom died of consumption between twenty and twenty-four. The parents soon followed, dying of a broken heart.

Early branches of the P. family, who were settled in dry and sound localities, remain to this day, I think, free from that malady.

Another large family, settled in the neighborhood of the same great meadow for, perhaps, the same length of time, has been consumptive for two generations, though many of them have removed to better situations, or were even born therein.

The S. family in the generation I spoke of consisted of ten sons and two daughters.

Both daughters died of consumption, but I think none of the sons, though the daughters of the sons, and several of their male children who grew up *temperate* did. One of the daughters married P.; the other one married a strong, hearty man of enormous stature, with no tendency to any specific disease. She had four sons, one intemperate, who is now fifty-five years old and well; three temperate, all settled in healthy place, and at wholesome business, and all died of consumption between twenty and twenty-five.

Hence I draw carefully these inferences—

1st. That the healthiest of families, living in such a situation as I have described, generation after generation, acquire the consumptive disposition, and so die thereof.

2nd. That it sometimes requires several generations to attain this result.

3rd. That members of the family born with this consumptive disposition often perish thereby, though they live and are even born in healthy localities.

4th. Intemperate habits (where the man drinks a pure, though coarse and fiery, liquor, like New England rum) tend to check the consumptive tendency, though the drunkard who himself escapes its consequences, may transmit the fatal seed to his children.

In addition to what I have already mentioned, here are two striking cases :—

(1.) I know a consumptive family living in a situation like that I have mentioned, for, perhaps, the same length of time, who had four sons. Two of them were often drunk, and always intemperate, one of them as long as I can remember ; both consumptive in early life, but now both hearty men from sixty to seventy. The two others were temperate, one drinking moderately, the other but occasionally. They both died of consumption, the oldest not over forty-five.

(2.) Another consumptive family in such a situation as has been already described, had many sons and several daughters. The daughters were all temperate, married, settled elsewhere, had children, died of consumption, bequeathing it also to their posterity. But five of the sons whom I knew were drunkards, some of the extremest description; they all had the consumptive build, and in early life showed signs of the disease, but none of them died of it; some of them are still burning in rum. There was one brother temperate, a farmer, living in the healthiest situation. But I was told he died some years ago of consumption.

You can make any use you please of this paper, which I think accurate in all its details, but I beg you by no means to let any one know who is the author of it.

It is an ill wind which blows nobody good. For if I had been in my chair and not on my bed you would not have read this paper quite so easily, but would have painfully deciphered it from the sad hand of

Yours faithfully,

THEODORE PARKER.

PS.—Please accept the queer old volume of " Plantini Imagines Humani Corporis, 1566."

I hope you will find valuable information in your (doctorial) predecessor's MS. prescriptions of remedies.

No. IV.

TO JOSEPH LYMAN.

Montreux, Sept. 15, 1859.

* * * * * * *

I mean to live, but may die any time, and so wish to provide a little for that latter contingency; and, as you are going home, I will give you a hint. Should I die, and the 28th take any notice of the fact, I should wish this arrangement of services to be conducted by J. F. Clarke and Wendell Phillips:

I. A Voluntary by the Choir—perhaps a Chant of Ps. cxxxix. v. 1–4, 7–12, 17, 18, 23, 24.
II. Scriptures. Micah vi. 8. Matt. xxii. 37–40. John iv. 23, 24. 1 John, Ep. iii. 18–20; iv. 7, 12, 16, 18. Ps. xxiii. 1, 4, 6; xxvii. 10, 13. Matt. xxv. 34–40, and v. 3–12.
III. A brief Funeral Prayer.
IV. Hymn, "While Thee I seek," &c.
V. Remarks by Wendell Phillips.
VI. Hymn, "Nearer, my God, to Thee."

I shall tell my executors that I want no monument, but a little plain old-fashioned grave-stone of blue slate—it won't cost five dollars—without any *paint* on it, with only my name and the date of birth and death.

In a subsequent direction given to his friend only a few weeks before his death, and dated Rome, April 4, 1860, he desired to have the Hymn sung that was written by Professor Norton,—

> My God, I thank Thee, may no thought
> Ere deem Thy chastisements severe;

Adding that the Professor had no love for him, but that the lines were religious and beautiful.

These directions were observed, though some additions were made, at the funeral services which took place at the Music Hall, upon receipt of the news that he had passed away.

No. V.

The following letters from Hon. S. P. Chase, Secretary of the Treasury, U.S., should have been placed in their appropriate connection with the letters received by him from Mr. Parker, that all the allusions might be made intelligible; but they came too late for insertion.

FROM HON. S. P. CHASE TO MR. PARKER.

Washington, Feb. 13, 1854.

My DEAR SIR,—Thanks for your kind letter. It does me good. Praise from the sincere who are also of the noble and true co-workers for humanity is very grateful.

I shall be very glad to see you afterward. There is hope that we may yet floor the rascals.

By the way, your discourse on "Webster" reached me, but was forthwith abstracted by somebody, to whom I hope it did good. Can you lend me another copy?

Seward and Sumner will quit themselves like men, and I have got a battery of small guns to fire.

Yours cordially,
S. P. CHASE.

Washington, March 12, 1854.

My DEAR SIR,—Your Sermon on the Nebraska question reached me this morning, and I have read it with the greatest interest. It is a noble discourse, going to the root of more matters than one. Its lofty sentiments inspire me with fresh determination to maintain the right, while my hope feeds on the anticipation that from many hearts must come the responsive echoes of such an utterance.

Shall I not say to you frankly, however, how much I regret that on the great question of the Divine origin of the Bible and the Divine nature of Christ your views are so little in harmony with those of almost all who labor with you in the great cause of human enfranchisement and progress; and that I could not help wishing that in this sermon your distinctive opinions had not been brought forward?

* * * * *

Some of your expressions grate harshly on my ears.

Far from me, however, is the wish to trammel your conscientious utterance of your own convictions; and I know you will trust my assurance that in my heart of hearts I honor you for your bold and manful defence of justice, truth, and right against oppression, falsehood, and wrong.

Yours faithfully,
S. P. CHASE.

Washington, April 5, 1854.

My dear Sir,—Your kind letter gave me a great deal of pleasure. Most earnestly do I wish that I were able to do the work which your more than kind estimate would judge me qualified for. But my consciousness tells me that you overrate me greatly. I am only fit to do common work that lies right before me from day to day, and, in truth, I have no aspiration to do any other. I never could fancy myself a great man, or ever realize that I occupied a great position; and I suppose both these ideas necessary to great achievement, especially political achievement.

I wish we thought more alike on some things; but it is not for me to argue with you. Let me rather rejoice that on the great questions of practical duty concerning the progress and elevation of our race we are so much at one.

There is reason to hope that the Nebraska iniquity sleeps the sleep that knows no waking, and that the speeches now being delivered concerning it in the House may be classed as obituary notices. If it be dead, or rather when assured that it is dead, I shall rejoice that the first stone cast at the monster went from my sling. Let not the people, however, be over-confident. They should still pour in their memorials, and especially the resolutions of their public meetings. The New Hampshire and Connecticut elections are *memorials* which some politicians will be likely to hold in lasting remembrance.

With many thanks to you, dear Sir, for your well-timed blow at the great iniquity, and for your every other service to the noble cause of freedom and progress,

I remain,
Most cordially your friend,
S. P. Chase.

Columbus, June 23, 1856.

My dear Sir,—I have been reading your "New Lesson for the Day," sent me, I suppose, by your kindness, and feel moved to write you and thank you for this, and renew my thanks for your former utterances in behalf of human liberty. The time is sharp and *thorny*, but we will pluck freedom out of it. I know not how it is, but I have never felt in the least inclined to despair of the Republic; and now I feel sure that out of the storm and danger of the present will emerge the peace and safety of liberty guarded by law. Sumner's grievous wrong will do more to open men's eyes to the true character of the men that slavery makes than ten thousand speeches, however eloquent in utterance or perfect in argument. And the vilenesses perpetrated in Kansas will expose the thorough recklessness in selection of means with which the slave power seeks its ends. The people wake up slowly, but they will awake, and then woe to tyrants and their abettors wheresoever!

Sincerely yours,
S. P. Chase.

Columbus, July 17, 1856.

MY DEAR SIR,—You have laid me under additional obligations to you by sending me " The Great Battle." It is a fit characterisation of the struggle in which you have dealt so many and so manful blows on the right side.

But I have somewhat to complain of in your first speech. You say, on the supposition that the slaves were white: " Do you believe Governor Chase would have said, ' No slavery outside of Slave States, but inside of Slave States just as much enslavement of Anglo-Saxon men as you please?' "

My first objection to this is the apparent assertion that I have said, " Inside of Slave States, just as much enslavement as you please! " I never said that; for I never thought it. There is no spot on earth in which I would sanction slavery. Indeed, I do not suppose you think there is; but your sentence is so constructed as to convey an idea which was not in your mind. My other objection to it is its intimation that my constitutional views on the slavery question are determined by considerations of the color or origin of the enslaved. God forbid! If every slave in the South were bleached to-morrow, if every drop of African blood could be, by miracle, converted into purest Anglo-Saxon, the constitutional power of the General Government on slavery in the States would be no whit enlarged. If the National Government has not the power to abolish the slavery of the black man in the Slave States, it certainly would have no power to abolish the slavery of the white man. Indeed, not a few white men, to all practical intents and purposes, and some probably of pure Circassian blood, are now slaves in the United States.

I adopt your motto very cheerfully and heartily : " No slavery anywhere in America! " No slavery anywhere on earth! The latter is, you say, the " topmost " idea. The first, then, is *not* topmost. My sentence, " No slavery outside of Slave States," also, is *not topmost*. But it is, to an ambitious man, anxious to get to the top, quite as important. It is *fundamental*. It is the first in the series. The General Government has power to prohibit slavery everywhere outside of Slave States. A great majority of the people now accept this idea. Comparatively few adopt the suggestion that Congress can legislate abolition within Slave States. That proposition, most who have studied our institutions regard as including the doctrine of consolidation and subversion of State Sovereignties, and other consequences dangerous to the rights of the people and tending to bring in despotism. I say, then, take the conceded proposition, and make it practical. Make it a living active reality! Then you have taken a great step. Slavery is *denationalized*. The faith and practice of the National Government is on the side of freedom. Then, encouraged by national example, by the sympathies, cheering words and liberal aid of good men and patriots, let the men of the Slave States organize for the enfranchisement of their own communities. By-and-by, and not far off, you will come to the second idea, " No slavery in America! " Then, let the moral influence and wise action of the nation, wholly enfranchised, be made active on the side of universal freedom. And, by-and-by, the third grand thought becomes a divine reality : " No slavery anywhere on earth," which day may God and men of a divine spirit speed !

I write in great haste, but you get my ideas. I don't pretend to be a very wise or expert statesman, or anything of that sort; but a roughly-trained practical man, who wishes to *do* something for truth, justice, and human progress, and who would prefer that what little he does or says should be so spoken of, that nothing in his example of word or deed shall even seem to contribute to the upholding of wrong.

Very cordially your friend,
S. P. CHASE.

Columbus, March 25, 1858.

It was a great gratification to hear from you. It would be a greater to see you. You *hang*, surrounded by others of like faith and freedom, in my dining-room; and you *lie*, in somewhat worse company, on my table in the Executive Chamber; for Buchanan and Gardner are there too, not to be saved even by the salt of your introductory association. But I would rather see you neither hanging nor lying, but living, speaking, moving! Why can't you come West ? Other lights than the Star of Empire should take their way westward.

As to getting rid of slavery, it will be accomplished when the mind of the nation is penetrated by such thoughts as your writings inspire. There must be a new birth and a new baptism of the American nation in the faith of man's manhood before it will be thoroughly accomplished.

I work in the political field. It is mine, because God seems to have better fitted me for it than for any other. It seems to me I can do some good in it. But, after all, what is our political work but the growth into substantial form of the great ideas which higher thinkers put forth, and the preparation for larger like growths ? I want to see the National Government divorced from slavery, and its influence put on the side of freedom. This seems to me a possible, practical work. Once accomplished, the doom of slavery is sealed. Its final extinction is certain, the regeneration of the nation inevitable, and a future—how grand and inspiring !—assured. What hope for the nation—for man, then !

But I have no time for much writing to-day. I am grateful for all you can do of personal kindness, and reciprocate fully every sentiment of friendly regard, and remain,

Cordially yours,
S. P. CHASE.

Newport, R.I., August 16, 1858.

MY DEAR SIR,—To fail to see you was to lose one of the principal gratifications I promised myself in New England. After you closed your sermon, I paused awhile, thinking to wait for you ; but the situation, amid a retreating crowd, was an awkward one, and I retired, confidently expecting to call in the evening. Governor Banks came in and dispelled this idea, by saying that he had just met you going into the country. So there was an end. I went back to Boston not long

—say two weeks—after, and you were absent still. Your note, which I received at Concord, had previously apprised me of you elsewhere; and so this time I was not disappointed.

My visit to New England was a very pleasant one. Much has gratified me. Cordial welcomes, earnest sympathies, noble men, noble women too, glorious scenery, grand industries, have spoken eloquently to eyes, ears, and heart. My inmost sentiments say, God bless and guard New England! I shall go back to my own great adopted State with new aspirations, not for place, I hope, but for achievement. How much I should like to do! How little I can do!

Take, my dear Sir, these words of farewell; assure yourself of my sincere gratitude for all your appreciation of what I have poorly attempted, rather than fitly done, and of my earnest purpose to deserve by effort, if not by accomplishment, something of the good-will which has been so liberally manifested towards me.

I shall be ever very glad to hear from you.

Sincerely your friend,
S. P. CHASE.

Columbus, January 13, 1859.

MY DEAR SIR,—I read in a Boston paper to-day your note to your congregation with deep sorrow. Most earnestly do I hope your illness is but temporary. The report of the paper that your physicians have ordered you to the West Indies has prompted this hurried note, that the assurance of my truest sympathy and earnest prayers for your restoration speedily to your people, and to all of us who labour for human advancement, may reach you before you sail, if possible.

Most truly yours,
S. P. CHASE.

No. VI.

These letters of acknowledgment should have been appended to the letters to Robert White, Vol. I., pp. 383–394; but they did not arrive in time. Such a warm confession of indebtedness to the influence of Mr. Parker is a welcome contribution to his Life :—

FROM J. CORLIES WHITE TO MRS. PARKER.

New York, January 4, 1862.

DEAR MADAM,—We all rejoiced to hear that you intend to publish a memoir of your lamented husband, whose memory is cherished in the very heart of hearts of all our family.

My father loved and honored Mr. Parker above his other friends, and we all felt deeply the kindly influence that gradually loosened the ties which bound him to a cold and heartless superstition, and gave us back the Father we had lost. Although my father never formally dissolved his connection with the Society of Shakers, yet from the time his acquaintance with Mr. Parker commenced until his death he became more and more estranged from Shakerism; and we have the satisfaction of knowing that, in his last days, the barrier which an alien faith had raised between him and his family had been entirely broken down.

We well knew, too, through whose agency this result was brought about, and you can readily believe that the kind sentiments you express for the family of your husband's friend are cordially reciprocated by us.

New York, January 20, 1862.

MY DEAR MADAM,—Merely as a matter of form, I have consulted my family as to the use you should make of my father's name and letters in the Memoir, and find there is no objection on their part, more than on my own, to your making such use of either as you may see fit in its preparation. Do not, my dear Madam, hesitate to make any use of them that may serve to illustrate your husband's correspondence. Perchance it may help to light others on their way, as it did my father—others enveloped in the same cloud of error.

With much respect, I remain, your friend,

JOHN CORLIES WHITE.

INDEX.